'eve•ning class corso *m* serale
'eve•ning dress *for woman* vestito *m* da sera; *for man* abito *m* scuro
eve•ning 'pa•per giornale *m* della sera

Compounds

◆ **lay into** *v/t (attack)* aggredire
◆ **lay on** *v/t (provide)* offrire

Phrasal verbs entered as headwords

mim•ic ['mɪmɪk] **1** *n* imitatore *m*, -trice *f* **2** *v/t* (*pret & pp* ***-ked***) imitare
critica *f* (*pl* -che) criticism

Grammatical information

privato 1 *agg* private; ***in privato*** in private **2** *m* private citizen

Entries divided into grammatical categories

recitare ⟨1l & b⟩ **1** *v/t* recite; TEA play (the part of); *preghiera* say **2** *v/i* act

Information on Italian conjugations

rospo *m* toad; *fig* F ***ingoiare il rospo*** lump it F
nerd [nɜːd] P fesso *m*, -a *f* P; *in style* tamarro *m* P

Register labels

lampadina *f* light bulb; ***lampadina tascabile*** torch, *Am* flashlight
sub•way ['sʌbweɪ] *Br (passageway)* sottopassaggio *m*; *Am* metropolitana *f*

American and British variants

A B C D E F G H I J K L M N O P Q R S T U V W XY Z

Italian
Concise Dictionary

Italian – English
Inglese – Italiano

Berlitz Publishing
New York · Munich · Singapore

Edited by the Langenscheidt editorial staff

Based on a dictionary compiled by LEXUS

Activity section by Heather Bonikowski

Book in cover photo: © Punchstock/Medioimages

Berlitz Publishing
193 Morris Avenue
Springfield, NJ 07081
USA

Printed in Germany
ISBN-13: 978-981-268-017-4
ISBN-10: 981-268-017-9

1. 2. 3. 4. 5. 11 10 09 08 07

Preface

This new dictionary of English and Italian is a tool with more than 45,000 references for learners of the Italian language at beginner's or intermediate level.

Thousands of colloquial and idiomatic expressions have been included. The user-friendly layout with all headwords in blue allows the user to have quick access to all the words, expressions and their translations.

Clarity of presentation has been a major objective. Is the *mouse* you need for your computer, for example, the same in Italian as the *mouse* you don't want in the house? This dictionary is rich in sense distinctions like this - and in translation options tied to specific, identified senses.

Vocabulary needs grammar to back it up. In this dictionary you will find extra grammar information on Italian conjugation and on irregular verb forms.

The additional activity section provides the user with an opportunity to develop language skills with a selection of engaging word puzzles. The games are designed specifically to improve vocabulary, spelling, grammar and comprehension in an enjoyable style.

Designed for a wide variety of uses, this dictionary will be of great value to those who wish to learn Italian and have fun at the same time.

Contents

How to use the dictionary

To get the most out of your dictionary you should understand how and where to find the information you need. Whether you are yourself writing text in a foreign language or wanting to understand text that has been written in a foreign language, the following pages should help.

1. How and where do I find a word?

1.1 The word list for each language is arranged in alphabetical order and also gives irregular forms of verbs and nouns in their correct alphabetical order. Sometimes you might want to look up terms made up of two separate words, for example **falling star**, or hyphenated words, for example **absent-minded**. These words are treated as though they were a single word and their alphabetical ordering reflects this.
The only exception to this strict alphabetical ordering is made for English *phrasal verbs* - words like **go off**, **go out**, **go up**. These are positioned in an alphabetical block directly after their main verb (in this case **go**).

1.2 Italian feminine headwords of the form **-trice** are shown as follows:

> **albergatore** *m*, **-trice** *f* hotel keeper

Here **-trice** means **albergatrice**.

1.3 Pronunciation for English headwords is given in square brackets. You can look up the spelling of a word in your dictionary in the same way as you would in a spelling dictionary. American spelling variants are marked *Am.* If just a single letter is omitted in the American spelling, this is put between round brackets:

> **colo(u)r — hono(u)r — travel(l)er**

2. How do I split a word?

Italians find English hyphenation very difficult. All you have to do with this dictionary is look for the bold dots between syllables. These dots show you where you can split a word at the end of a line but you should avoid having just one letter before or after the hyphen as in **a·mend** or **thirst·y**. In such cases it is better to take the entire word over to the next line.

3. Long dashes

In the Italian-English part of the dictionary, when a headword is repeated in a phrase or compound with an altered form, a long dash is used:

> **impronta** *f* impression, mark; ***-e*** *pl* ***digitali*** fingerprints

Here **-e digitali** means **impronte digitali**.

4. What do the different typefaces mean?

4.1 All Italian and English headwords and the Arabic numerals differentiating between parts of speech appear in **bold**:

> **incisivo 1** *agg* incisive **2** *m dente* incisor
> **itch** [ɪtʃ] **1** *n* prurito *m* **2** *v/i* prudere

4.2 *Italics* are used for:

a) abbreviated grammatical labels: *adj*, *adv*, *v/i*, *v/t* etc

b) gender labels: *m*, *f*, *mpl* etc

c) all the indicating words which are the signposts pointing to the correct translation for your needs, eg:

> **mix·ture** [mɪkstʃə(r)] miscuglio *m*; *medicine* sciroppo *m*
> **pro·fuse·ly** [prə'fju:slɪ] *adv thank* con grande effusione; *bleed* copiosamente
> **rugoso** rough; *pelle* wrinkled; *albero* gnarled
> **terra** *f* earth; (*regione*, *proprietà*, *terreno agricolo*) land; (*superficie del suolo*) ground; (*pavimento*) floor

4.3 All phrases (examples and idioms) are given in ***secondary bold italics***:

> **sym·pa·thet·ic** [sɪmpəθetɪk] *adj* ... ***be sympathetic towards an idea*** simpatizzare per un- 'idea
> **premio** *m* (*pl* -mi) ... ***premio Nobel per la pace*** Nobel peace prize

4.4 The normal typeface is used for the translations. It is also used for Italian plural forms.

4.5 If a translation is given in italics, and not in the normal typeface, this means that the translation is more of an *explanation* in the other language and that an explanation has to be given because there just is no real equivalent:

> **'Mid·lands** *npl regione f nell'Inghilterra centrale*
> **ragioneria** *f* book-keeping; EDU *high school specializing in business studies*

5. Stress

To indicate where to put the **stress** in English words, the stress marker appears before the syllable on which the main stress falls:

> **on·ion** [njən] cipolla *f*
> **rec·ord**[1] ['rekɔːd] *n* MUS disco *m* ...
> **record**[2] [rɪːkɔːd] *v/t electronically* registrare ...

Stress is shown either in the pronunciation or, if there is no pronunciation given, in the actual headword or compound itself.

> **'rec·ord hold·er** primatista *m/f*

6. What do the various symbols and abbreviations tell you?

6.1 A solid blue diamond is used to indicate a phrasal verb:

> ◆ **auction off** *v/t* vendere all'asta

6.2 A white diamond is used to divide up longer entries into more easily digested chunks of related bits of text:

> **a** *prp* ◇ *stato in luogo*: ***a Roma*** in Rome; ***a casa*** at home ◇ *moto a luogo*: ***andare a Roma*** go to Rome; ***andare a casa*** go home ◇ *tempo* ...

6.3 The abbreviation F tells you that the word or phrase is used colloquially rather than in formal contexts. The abbreviation V warns you that a word or phrase is vulgar or taboo. Be careful how you use these words. Words or phrases labelled P are slang.

These abbreviations, F, V and P are used both for headwords/phrases and for the translations of headwords/phrases. They come after the headword and before any phrase or indicated sense to be translated. They are given after the translation, but only if the translation has the same register as the headword/example. If there is no such label given, then the word or phrase is neutral.

6.4 A colon before an English or Italian phrase means that usage is restricted to this specific example (at least as far as this dictionary's translation is concerned):

> **tru·ant** ['truːənt]: ***play truant*** marinare la scuola
> **tuck** [tk] ... **2** *v/t*: ***tuck sth into sth*** infilare qc in qc
> **'shoe·string** *n*: ***do sth on a shoestring*** fare qc con pochi soldi

7. Does the dictionary deal with grammar too?

7.1 All English headwords are given a part of speech label:

> **tooth·less** ['tu:θlɪs] *adj* sdentato
> **top·ple** ['tɒpl] **1** *v/i* crollare **2** *v/t government* far cadere

But if a headword can only be used as a noun (in ordinary English) then no part of speech is given:

> **tooth·paste** dentifricio *m*

7.2 Italian headwords are not given parts of speech in cases where the grammar of the translation matches the grammar of the Italian:

> **esclusivo** exclusive
> **piuttosto** rather

But:

> **planetario** (*pl* -ri) **1** *agg* planetary **2** *m* planetarium

And Italian gender markers are given, as well as Italian plural forms:

> **pinacoteca** *f* (*pl* -che) art gallery
> **farmacista** *m/f* (*mpl* -i) chemist, *Am* pharmacist

7.3 If an English translation of an Italian adjective can only be used in front of a noun, and not after it, this is marked with *attr*:

> **fiabesco** (*pl* -chi) fairytale *attr*

7.4 If the Italian, unlike the English, doesn't change form if used in the plural, this is marked with *inv*:

> **fine settimana** *m inv* weekend

7.5 If the English, in spite of appearances, is not a plural form, this is marked with *nsg*:

> **mea·sles** [mizlz] *nsg* morbillo *m*

7.6 Irregular English plurals are identified:

> **the·sis** ['θi:sɪs] (*pl* ***theses*** ['θi:si:z]) tesi *f inv*
> **thief** [θi:f] (*pl* ***thieves*** [θi:vz]) ladro *m*, -a *f*
> **trout** [traʊt] (*pl* ***trout***) trota *f*

7.7 Words like **physics** or **media studies** have not been given a label to say if they are singular or plural for the simple reason that they can be either, depending on how they are used.

7.8 Irregular and semi-irregular verb forms are identified:

> **sim·pli·fy** ['sɪmplɪfaɪ] *v/t* (*pret & pp* ***-ied***) semplificare **sing** [sɪŋ] *v/t & v/i* (*pret* ***sang***, *pp* ***sung***) cantare

7.9 Cross-references are given to tables of Italian conjugations:

finire ⟨4d⟩ **fischiare** ⟨1k⟩

7.10 Grammatical information is provided on the prepositions you'll need in order to create complete sentences:

ear·mark ['ɪəmɑːk] *v/t* riservare; ***earmark sth for sth*** riservare qc a qc
tremare ⟨1b⟩ tremble, shake (***di***, ***per*** with)

Abbreviations

see	→	vedi
registered trademark	®	marchio registrato
abbreviation	*abbr*	abbreviazione
adjective	*adj*	aggettivo
adverb	*adv*	avverbio
adjective	*agg*	aggettivo
agriculture	AGR	agricoltura
mountaineering	ALP	alpinismo
American English	*Am*	inglese americano
anatomy	ANAT	anatomia
architecture	ARCHI	architettura
article	*art*	articolo
astronomy	AST	astronomia
astrology	ASTR	astrologia
attributive usage	*attr*	uso attributivo
motoring	AUTO	automobilismo
civil aviation	AVIA	aviazione
adverb	*avv*	avverbio
biology	BIO	biologia
botany	BOT	botanica
British English	*Br*	inglese britannico
chemistry	CHEM	chimica
chemistry	CHIM	chimica
commerce, business	COM	commercio
computers, IT term	COMPUT	informatica
conditional	*cond*	condizionale
conjunction	*cong*	congiunzione
subjunctive	*congiunt*	congiuntivo
conjunction	*conj*	congiunzione
law	DIR	diritto
et cetera	*ecc*	eccetera
education	EDU	educazione
for example	*eg*	per esempio
electricity, electronics	EL	elettricità, elettronica
electricity, electronics	ELEC	elettricità, elettronica
especially	*esp*	specialmente
et cetera	*etc*	eccetera
euphemistic	*euph*	eufemismo
familiar, colloquial	F	familiare
feminine	*f*	femminile
feminine noun and adjective	*f/agg*	sostantivo femminile e aggettivo
feminine plural	*fpl*	femminile plurale
railway	FERR	ferrovia
figurative	*fig*	figurato
philosophy	FIL	filosofia
financial	FIN	finanze
physics	FIS	fisica
physiology	FISIOL	fisiologia
formal usage	*fml*	uso formale
photography	FOT	fotografia
future	*fut*	futuro
cooking	GASTR	gastronomia
generally	*gen*	generalmente
geography	GEOG	geografia
geologia	GEOL	geology
gerund	*ger*	gerundio
grammatical	GRAM	grammatica
humorous	*hum*	uso spiritoso
imperative	*imper*	imperativo
imperfect	*imperf*	imperfetto
indicative	*ind*	indicativo
IT term	INFOR	informatica
interjection	*int*	interiezione
invariable	*inv*	invariabile
ironic	*iron*	ironico
law	LAW	diritto
masculine	*m*	maschile
masculine noun and adjective	*m/agg*	sostantivo maschile e aggettivo
masculine and feminine	*m/f*	maschile e femminile
masculine plural	*mpl*	maschile plurale
nautical	MAR	marineria, navigazione
mathematics	MAT	matematica
mathematics	MATH	matematica
medicine	MED	medicina
metallurgy	METAL	metallurgia
meteorology	METEO	meteorologia
military	MIL	militare
mineralogy	MIN	mineralogia
motoring	MOT	automobilismo
music	MUS	musica
noun	*n*	sostantivo
nautical	NAUT	marineria, navigazione
negative	*neg*	in senso negativo
plural noun	*npl*	sostantivo plurale
singular noun	*nsg*	sostantivo singolare
optics	OPT	ottica
oneself	O.S.	sé, se stesso
optics	OTT	ottica
popular, slang	P	popolare
painting	PAINT	pittura
pejorative	*pej*	spregiativo
photography	PHOT	fotografia
physics	PHYS	fisica
painting	PITT	pittura
plural	*pl*	plurale
politics	POL	politica
past participle	*pp*	participio passato

present participle	*p pr*	participio presente
present	*pr*	presente
past historic	*p.r.*	passato remoto
present subjunctive	*pr congiunt*	presente congiuntivo
preposition	*prep*	preposizione
preterite	*pret*	preterito
present indicative	*pr ind*	presente indicativo
pronoun	*pron*	pronome
preposition	*prp*	preposizione
psychology	PSI	psicologia
psychology	PSYCH	psicologia
something	qc	qualcosa
someone	qu	qualcuno
radio	RAD	radio
railway	RAIL	ferrovia
religion	REL	religione
skiing	SCI	sci
singular	sg	singolare
someone	s.o.	qualcuno
sports	SP	sport
humorous	*spir*	uso spiritoso
pejorative	*spreg*	spregativo
something	sth	qualcosa
theatre	TEA	teatro
technology	TEC	tecnica
technology	TECH	tecnica
telecommunications	TELEC	telecomunicazione
theatre	THEA	teatro
typography, typesetting	TIP	tipografia
television	TV	televisione
vulgar	V	volgare
auxiliary verb	*v/aus*	verbo ausiliario
auxiliary verb	*v/aux*	verbo ausiliario
intransitive verb	*v/i*	verbo intransitivo
reflexive verb	*v/r*	verbo riflessivo
transitive verb	*v/t*	verbo transitivo
zoology	ZO	zoologia

Italian Spelling and Pronunciation

1. The Italian Alphabet

The twenty-one letters of the Italian alphabet are listed below with their names and with their sounds given as approximate English equivalents.

LETTER	NAME	APPROXIMATE SOUND
a	a	Like *a* in English *father*, eg **facile**, **padre**.
b	bi	Like *b* in English *boat*, eg **bello**, **abate**.
c	ci	When followed by **e** or **i**, like c*h* in English *cherry*, eg **cento**, **cinque**; if the **i** is unstressed and followed by another vowel, its sounds is not heard, eg **ciaria**, **cieco**. When followed by **a**, **o**, **u**, or a consonant like *c* in English *cook*, eg **casa**, **come**, **cura**, **credere**. **Ch**, which is used before **e** and **i**, has likewise the sound of *c* in English *cook*, eg **chiesa**, **perchè**.
d	di	Like *d* in English *dance*, eg **dare**, **madre**.
e	e	Has two sounds. One like *a* in English *make*, eg **ferro**; and one like *e* in English *met*, eg **festa**.
f	effe	Like *f* in English *fool*, eg **farina**, **efelide**.
g	gi	When followed by **e** or **i**, like *g* in English *general*, eg **gelato**, **ginnasta**; if the **i** is unstressed and followed by another vowel, its sound is not heard, eg **giallo**, **giorno**. When followed by **a**, **o**, **u** or a consonant, like *g* in English *go*, eg **gamba**, **goccia**, **gusto**, **grado**. **Gh**, which is used before **e** and **i**, has likewise the sound of *g* in English *go*, eg **ghisa**. When the combination **gli** (a) is a form of the definite article or the personal pronoun, (b) is final in a word, or (c) comes between two cowels, ist has the sound of Castilian *ll*, which is somewhat like *lli* in English *million*, eg (a) **gli uomini**, **gli ho parlato ieri**, (b) **battagli**, (c) **figlio**, **migliore**. When it is (a) initial (except in the world **gli**, above), (b) preceded by a consonant, or (c) followed by a consonant, it is pronounced like *gli* in English *negligence*, eg (a) **glioma**, (b) **ganglio**, (c) **negligenza**. The combination **gl** followed by **a**, **e**, **o**, or **u** is pronounced like *gl* in Eglish *globe*, eg **glabro**, **gleba**, **globo**, **gluteo**, **inglese**. **Gn** has the sound of Castilian ñ, which is somewhat like

		ni in English *onion*, eg **signore**, **gnocco**.
h	acca	Always silent, eg **ha**, **hanno**. See **ch** under **c** above and **gh** under **g** above.
i	i	Like *i* in English *machine*, eg **piccolo**, **sigla**. When unstressed and followed by another vowel, like *y* in English *yes*, eg **piatto**, **piede**, **fiore**, **fiume**. For **i** in *ci*, see **c** above, in **gi**, see **g** above, ad in **sci**, see **s** below.
l	elle	Like *l* in English *lamb*, eg **labbro**, **lacrima**.
m	emme	Like *m* in English *money*, **eg mano**, **come**.
n	enne	Like *n* in English *net*, eg **nome**, **cane**.
o	o	Has two sounds. One like *o* in English *note*, eg **sole**; and one like *o* in English hot, eg **donna**.
p	pi	Like *p* in English *pot*, eg **passo**, **carpa**.
q	cu	This letter is always followed by the letter **u** and the combination has the sound of *qu* in English *quart*, eg **quanto**, **questo**.
r	erre	Like *r* in English *rubber*, with a slight trill, eg **roba**, **carta**.
s	esse	Has two sounds. When initial and followed by a vowel, when preceded by a consonant and followed by a vowel, and when followed by **c** [k] **f**, **p**, **q**, or **t**, like s in English *see*, eg **sale**, **falso**, **scappare**, **spazi**, **stoffa**. When standing between two vowels and when followed by **b**, **d**, **g** [g], **l**, **m**, **n**, **r** or **v**, like *z* in English *zero*, eg **paese**, **sbaglio**, **svenire**. However, **s** standing between two vowels in some words and initial *s* followed by **b**, **d**, **g** [g], **l**, **m**, **n**, **r**, or **v** in some foreign borrowings are pronounced like *s* in *see*, eg **casa**, **tesa**, **smoking**, **slam**. When initial **s** stands between two vowels in a compound, its pronuniciation remains that of initial s, eg **autoservizio**. **Sc**, when followed by **e** or **i** has the sound of *sh* in English *shall*, eg **scelta**, **scimmia**; if the **i** is unstressed and followed by another vowel, its sound is not heard, eg **sciame**, **sciopero**. **Sch** has the sound of *sc* in English *scope*, eg **scherzo**, **schiavo**. An **s** coming between two vowels is generally pronounced like *z* in English zero in the north of Italy.

t	ti	Like *t* in English *table*, eg **terra**, **pasto**.
u	u	Like *u* in English *rule*, eg **luna**, **mulo**. When followed by a vowel, like *w* in English *was*, eg **quanto**, **querra**, **nuovo**.
v	vu	Like *v* in English *vain*, eg **vita**, **uva**.
z	zeta	Has two sounds. One like *ts* in English *nuts*, eg **grazia**, **zucchero**; and one like *dz* in English *adze*, eg **zero**, **mezzo**.

The following five letters are found in borrowings from other languages.

LETTER	NAME	EXAMPLES
j	i lunga	**jazz**
k	cappa	**ko**
w	vu doppia	**whisky**
x	ics	**xenofobo**, **xilofono**
y	ìpsilon	**yacht**, **yoghurt**

Consonants written double are longer than consonants written single, that is, it takes a longer time to pronounce them, eg **camino** *chimney*, and **cammino** *road*, **capello** *hair* and **cappello** *hat*. Special attention is called to the following double consonants: **cc** followed by **e** or **i** has the sound of *ch ch* in English *beach chair*, that is a lengthended *ch*, eg **accento**; **cch** has the sound of *kk* in English *book-keeper*, eg **becchino**; **cq** has the sound of *kk* in English *book-keeper*, eg **acqua**; **gg** followed by **e** or **i** has the sound of *ge j* in English *carriage joiner*, eg **peggio**; **ggh** has the sound of *g g* in English *tag game*, eg **agghindare**.

2. Stress and Accent Marks

Whenever stress is shown as part of regular spelling, it is shown on **a**, **i**, and **u** by the grave accent mark, eg **libertà**, **giovedì**, **gioventù**, on close **e** and **o** by the acute accent mark, eg **perché**, and on open **e** and **o** by the grave accent mark, eg **caffè**, **parlò**.

Guidelines on Stress

(a) In words of two syllables, the stress falls on the syllable next to the last, eg **casa**, **muro**, **terra**. If the syllable next to the last contains a diphthong, that is, a combination of a strong vowel (**a**, **e**, or **o**) and a weak vowel (**i** or **u**), the strong vowel is stressed, regardless of which vowel comes first, eg **daino**, **eroico**, **neutro**, **fiato**, **duale**, **siepe**, **fiore**, **buono**.

(b) In words of more than two syllables, the stress may fall on the syllable next to the last, eg **andata**, **canzone**, **pastore** or on a preceding syllable, eg **missile**, **gondola**, **mandorla**. In these positions also the stressed syllable may contain a diphthong, eg **incauto**, **idraulico**, **fiocina**.

(c) If a weak vowel in juxtaposition with a strong vowel is stressed, the two vowels constitute two separate syllables, eg **abba·ino**, **ero·ina**, **pa·ura**, **miriade**, **via**.

(d) Two strong vowels in juxtaposition constitute two separate syllables, eg **pa·ese**, **aureola**, **idea**, **oceano**.

(e) Two weak vowels in juxtaposition generally consitute a diphthong in which the first vowel is stressed in some words, eg **fluido** and the second vowel in others, eg **piuma**.

(f) If a word ends in a diphthong, the diphthong is stressed, eg **marinai**, **parlai**, **eroi**.

English Pronunciation

Vowels

[ɑː]	*father* [ˈfɑːðə(r)]
[æ]	*man* [mæn]
[e]	*get* [get]
[ə]	*about* [əˈbaʊt]
[ɜː]	*absurd* [əbˈsɜːd]
[ɪ]	*stick* [stɪk]
[iː]	*need* [niːd]
[ɒ]	*hot* [hɒt]
[ɔː]	*law* [lɔː]
[ʌ]	*mother* [ˈmʌðə(r)]
[ʊ]	*book* [bʊk]
[uː]	*fruit* [fruːt]

Diphthongs

[aɪ]	*time* [taɪm]
[aʊ]	*cloud* [klaʊd]
[eɪ]	*name* [neɪm]
[eə]	*hair* [heə(r)]
[ɪə]	*here* [hɪə(r)]
[ɔɪ]	*point* [pɔɪnt]
[əʊ]	*oath* [əʊθ]
[ʊə]	*tour* [tʊə(r)]

Consonants

[b]	*bag* [bæg]
[d]	*dear* [dɪə(r)]
[f]	*fall* [fɔːl]
[g]	*give* [gɪv]
[h]	*hole* [həʊl]
[j]	*yes* [jes]
[k]	*come* [kʌm]
[l]	*land* [lænd]
[m]	*mean* [miːn]
[n]	*night* [naɪt]
[p]	*pot* [pɒt]
[r]	*right* [raɪt]
[(r)]	pronounced only at the end of a word followed by a word starting with a vowel: *where* [weə(r)]
[s]	*sun* [sʌn]
[t]	*take* [teɪk]
[v]	*vain* [veɪn]
[w]	*wait* [weɪt]
[z]	*rose* [rəʊz]
[ŋ]	*bring* [brɪŋ]
[ʃ]	*she* [ʃiː]
[ʧ]	*chair* [ʧeə(r)]
[dʒ]	*join* [dʒɔɪn]
[ʒ]	*leisure* [ˈleʒə(r)]
[θ]	*think* [θɪŋk]
[ð]	*the* [ðə]
[ˈ]	means that the following syllable is stressed: *ability* [əˈbɪlətɪ]

Part 1

Italian-English Dictionary

A

A *abbr* (= ***autostrada***) M (= motorway)
a *prp* ◇ *stato in luogo*: ***a Roma*** in Rome; ***a casa*** at home
◇ *moto a luogo*: ***andare a Roma*** go to Rome; ***andare a casa*** go home
◇ *tempo*: ***alle quattro*** at four o'clock; ***a Natale*** at Christmas; ***a maggio*** in May; ***a vent'anni*** at the age of twenty; ***a giorni*** any day now; ***a domani!*** see you tomorrow!
◇ *modo*: ***a piedi*** on foot; ***alla moda*** in fashion; ***al burro*** GASTR in butter
◇ *mezzo*: ***ricamato a mano*** embroidered by hand, hand-embroidered; ***fatto a macchina*** machine-made
◇ *con valore distributivo*: ***a due a due*** two at a time; ***a poco a poco*** little by little
◇ *prezzo, misura*: ***a che prezzo*** at what price; ***al metro*** by the metre; ***100 km all'ora*** 100 km an hour
AAS *abbr* (= ***Azienda Autonoma di Soggiorno***) tourist board
ab. *abbr* (= ***abitanti***) inhabitants
abate *m* abbot
abbacchiato downhearted
abbacchio *m* (*pl* -cchi) GASTR young lamb
abbagliante **1** *agg* dazzling **2** *m gen pl* ***-i*** AUTO full beam
abbagliare ⟨1g⟩ dazzle
abbaglio *m* (*pl* -gli): ***prendere un abbaglio*** make a blunder
abbaiare ⟨1i⟩ bark
abbandonare ⟨1a⟩ abandon
abbandono *m* abandon; (*rinuncia*) abandonment; ***stato di abbandono*** state of disrepair
abbassamento *m* lowering
abbassare ⟨1a⟩ *prezzo* lower; *radio* turn down; ***abbassare la voce*** lower one's voice
abbassarsi (*chinarsi*) bend down; *prezzo* come down; *fig* ***abbassarsi a*** stoop to
abbasso *int*: ***abbasso la scuola!*** down with school!
abbastanza enough; (*alquanto*) quite; ***ho mangiato abbastanza*** I've had enough to eat; ***sono abbastanza soddisfatto*** I'm quite satisfied
abbattere ⟨3a⟩ knock down; *casa* demolish; *albero* cut down; *aereo* shoot down; *fig* dishearten
abbattersi fall; *fig* become disheartened
abbattimento *m* knocking down; *casa* demolition; *albero* cutting down; *aereo* shooting down; *fig* despondency
abbattuto disheartened
abbazia *f* abbey
abbellire ⟨4d⟩ embellish
abbeverare ⟨1m⟩ water
abbi, abbia → ***avere***
abbicci *m inv* abc; *fig* basics *pl*
abbigliamento *m* clothing; ***abbigliamento sportivo*** sportswear; ***industria*** *f* ***dell'abbigliamento*** clothing industry
abbinare ⟨1a⟩ match; (*combinare*) combine
abboccare ⟨1d⟩ *di pesce* bite; TEC join; *fig* swallow the bait
abboccato *vino* medium sweet
abbonamento *m a giornale*, TEA subscription; *a treno, bus* season-ticket; ***abbonamento annuale*** yearly subscription; yearly ticket; ***abbonamento mensile*** monthly subscription; monthly ticket
abbonare ⟨1c & o⟩ take out a subscription for; (*condonare*) deduct
abbonarsi subscribe
abbonato *m* subscriber; TELEC ***elenco*** *m* ***degli -i*** telephone directory
abbondante abundant; *porzione* generous; *vestito* loose; *nevicata* heavy
abbondanza *f* abundance
abbordabile *persona* approachable; *prezzo* reasonable
abbordare ⟨1a⟩ **1** *v/t persona* approach; F *persona dell'altro sesso* chat up F; *argomento* tackle **2** *v/t* MAR board
abbottonare ⟨1a⟩ button up
abbozzare ⟨1c⟩ sketch; ***abbozzare un sorriso*** smile faintly
abbozzo *m* sketch
abbracciare ⟨1f⟩ embrace, hug; *fig* take up
abbracciarsi embrace, hug
abbraccio *m* (*pl* -cci) embrace, hug; ***un abbraccio*** *a fine lettera* love
abbreviare ⟨1k & b⟩ abbreviate
abbreviazione *f* abbreviation
abbronzante *m* sun-tan lotion; ***lettino*** *m* ***abbronzante*** sunbed
abbronzare ⟨1a⟩ *pelle* tan
abbronzarsi get a tan
abbronzato tanned
abbronzatura *f* tan
abbrustolire ⟨4d⟩ roast
abbuffarsi ⟨1a⟩ stuff o.s. (***di*** with)
abbuono *m* FIN discount

abdicare ⟨1l & d⟩ abdicate

abdicazione *f* abdication

abete *m* fir

abile good (***in*** at); fit (***a*** for)

abilità *f inv* ability

abilitazione *f* qualification

abisso *m* abyss

abitabile habitable; ***cucina*** *f* ***abitabile*** dining kitchen

abitacolo *m* AUTO passenger compartment

abitante *m/f* inhabitant

abitare ⟨1l⟩ **1** *v/t* live in **2** *v/i* live

abitato **1** *agg* inhabited **2** *m* built-up area

abitazione *f* house

abiti *mpl* clothes

abito *m* dress; *da uomo* suit; ***abito da sera*** evening dress

abituale usual

abituare ⟨1l⟩ accustom (***a*** to)

abituarsi: ***abituarsi a*** get used to

abitudinario (*pl* -ri) **1** *agg* of fixed habits **2** *m* creature of habit

abitudine *f* habit

abolire ⟨4d⟩ abolish

abolizione *f* abolition

abominevole abominable

aborigeno **1** *agg* aboriginal **2** *m* aboriginal

abortire ⟨4d⟩ MED miscarry; *volontariamente* have an abortion; *fig* fail

abortista *m/f* pro-choice campaigner

aborto *m* MED miscarriage; *provocato* abortion

abrogare ⟨1e & c or 1l⟩ repeal

abrogazione *f* repeal

abusare ⟨1a⟩: ***abusare di*** abuse; (*appropriarsi*) take advantage of; ***abusare nel bere*** drink to excess

abusivo illegal

abuso *m* abuse; ***abuso sessuale*** sexual abuse

a.C. *abbr* (= ***avanti Cristo***) BC (= before Christ)

acacia *f* (*pl* -cie) acacia

acca *f*: ***non capire un'acca*** not understand a thing

accademia *f* academy; ***accademia di belle arti*** art college

accademico (*pl* -ci) academic

accadere ⟨2c⟩ happen

accaduto *m*: ***raccontami l'accaduto*** tell me what happened

accaldarsi ⟨1a⟩ get overheated

accaldato overheated

accalorarsi ⟨1a⟩ *fig* get excited

accampamento *m* camp

accampare ⟨1a⟩ **1** *v/t*: ***accampare scuse*** come up with excuses **2** *v/i e* **accamparsi** camp

accanimento *m* (*tenacia*) tenacity; (*furia*) rage

accanirsi ⟨4d⟩ (*ostinarsi*) persist; ***accanirsi contro qu*** rage against s.o.

accanito *odio* fierce; *tifoso* dedicated; *fumatore* inveterate; ***lavoratore*** *m* ***accanito*** hard worker

accanto **1** *prp* ***accanto a*** next to **2** *avv* near, nearby; *abitare* next door

accantonare ⟨1a⟩ put aside

accappatoio *m* (*pl* -oi) bathrobe; *da mare* beachrobe

accarezzare ⟨1a⟩ caress; *speranza* cherish; *animale* stroke

accasciarsi ⟨1f⟩ flop down

accatastare ⟨1a⟩ pile up

accattonaggio *m* begging

accattone *m* beggar

accavallare ⟨1a⟩ cross

accavallarsi *fig* overlap

accecare ⟨1b & d⟩ **1** *v/t* blind **2** *v/i* be blinding

accedere ⟨3a⟩: ***accedere a*** enter

accelerare ⟨1b & m⟩ speed up; AUTO accelerate

accelerato **1** *agg* fast; *treno* slow **2** *m* slow train

acceleratore *m* AUTO accelerator

accelerazione *f* acceleration

accendere ⟨3c⟩ light; RAD, TV turn on

accendersi light up; *apparecchio* come on

accendino *m*, **accendisigari** *m inv* lighter

accennare ⟨1a⟩ indicate; *con parole* mention; ***accennare a fare qc*** show signs of doing sth

accenno *m* (*cenno*) gesture; (*indizio*) sign; (*allusione*) hint

accensione *f* ignition; AUTO ***accensione elettronica*** electronic ignition

accento *m* accent

accentuare ⟨1b & m⟩ accentuate

accertare ⟨1b⟩ check

accertarsi: ***accertarsi di qc*** check sth

acceso *colore* bright; *motore* running; *TV*, *luce* on

accessibile accessible; *prezzo* reasonable

accesso *m* access; *fig e* MED fit; ***divieto d' accesso*** no entry

accessori *mpl* accessories

accessoriato AUTO complete with accessories

accessorio secondary

accetta *f* ax(e)

accettabile acceptable

accettare ⟨1b⟩ accept

accettazione *f* acceptance; (*di albergo*) reception; ***accettazione bagagli*** check-in

accetto: ***bene / male accetto*** welcome / not welcome
acchiappare ⟨1a⟩ catch
acciaio *m* (*pl* -ai) steel; ***acciaio inossidabile*** stainless steel
accidentale accidental
accidentato *terreno* rough
accidenti *int* F damn! F; *di sorpresa* wow!
accigliato frowning
accingersi ⟨3d⟩: ***accingersi a fare qc*** be about to do sth
acciottolato *m* cobbles *pl*
acciuffare ⟨1a⟩ grab
acciuga *f* (*pl* -ghe) anchovy
acclamare ⟨1a⟩applaud
acclimatarsi ⟨1m⟩ get acclimatized
accludere ⟨3q⟩ enclose
accluso enclosed; ***qui accluso*** enclosed
accogliente welcoming
accogliere ⟨3ss⟩ welcome; *richiesta* grant
accollare ⟨1c⟩ shoulder
accollarsi take on
accollato *abito* high-necked
accoltellare ⟨1b⟩ knife
accolto *pp* → ***accogliere***
accomodamento *m* arrangement; (*accordo*) agreement
accomodante accommodating
accomodare ⟨1c & m⟩ (*riparare*) mend; *lite* resolve; (*sistemare*) arrange
accomodarsi make o.s. at home; ***si accomodi!*** come in!; (*sedersi*) have a seat!
accompagnamento *m* accompaniment; ***lettera*** *f* ***di accompagnamento*** covering letter
accompagnare ⟨1a⟩ accompany
accompagnatore *m*, **-trice** *f* escort; MUS accompanist
acconciatura *f* hairdo
acconsentire ⟨4b⟩ consent (***a*** to)
accontentare ⟨1b⟩ satisfy
accontentarsi be happy (***di*** with)
acconto *m* deposit
accoppiare ⟨1k & c⟩ couple; *animali* mate
accoppiarsi pair off
accorciare ⟨1f⟩ shorten
accorciarsi get shorter
accordare ⟨1c⟩ grant; MUS tune; (*armonizzare*) harmonize
accordarsi agree; *di colori* match
accordo *m* agreement; (*armonia*) harmony; MUS chord; ***essere d'accordo*** agree; ***mettersi d'accordo*** reach an agreement; ***d'accordo!*** OK!
accorgersi ⟨3d⟩: ***accorgersi di*** notice
accorrere ⟨3o⟩ hurry; ***accorrere in aiuto di qu*** rush to help s.o.
accortezza *f* forethought
accorto 1 *pp* → ***accorgersi* 2** *agg* shrewd
accostare ⟨1c⟩ approach; *porta* leave ajar
accostarsi get close
accreditare ⟨1b & m⟩ confirm; FIN credit
accredito *m* credit
accrescere ⟨3n⟩ increase
accrescersi grow bigger
accudire ⟨4d⟩ **1** *v/t* look after **2** *v/i*: ***accudire a qc*** attend to sth
accumulare ⟨1m⟩ accumulate
accumulatore *m* battery
accumulazione *f* accumulation
accuratezza *f* care
accurato careful
accusa *f* accusation; DIR charge; ***Pubblica Accusa*** public prosecutor
accusare ⟨1a⟩ accuse; DIR charge; ***accusare ricevuta*** acknowledge receipt
accusato *m*, **-a** *f* accused
accusatore *m* prosecutor
acerbo unripe
acero *m* maple
aceto *m* vinegar; ***aceto balsamico*** balsamic vinegar; ***mettere sott'aceto*** pickle
acetone *m* nail varnish remover
ACI *abbr* (= ***Automobile Club d'Italia***) Automobile Club of Italy
acidità *f* acidity; ***acidità di stomaco*** heartburn
acido 1 *agg* acid; *fig* sour; ***piogge*** *fpl* ***acide*** acid rain *sg* **2** *m* acid
ACLI *abbr* (= ***Associazione Cristiana dei Lavoratori Italiani***) Italian trade union association
acne f acne
acqua *f* water; ***acqua corrente*** running water; ***acqua minerale*** mineral water; ***acqua potabile*** drinking water; ***acqua di rubinetto*** tap water; ***acqua ossigenata*** hydrogen peroxide; ***una teoria che fa acqua*** a theory that doesn't hold water; ***acqua in bocca!*** keep it under your hat!; ***ha l'acqua alla gola*** (*non ha tempo*) he's pushed for time; **-e** *pl* waters; **-e** *pl* ***territoriali*** territorial waters; ***in cattive -e*** in deep water
acquaforte *f* etching
acquaio *m* (*pl* -ai) sink
acquaragia *f* turpentine
acquario *m* (*pl* -ri) aquarium; ASTR **Acquario** Aquarius
acquatico (*pl* -ci) aquatic; ***sci*** *m* ***acquatico*** water skiing; *oggetto* waterski; ***uccello*** *m* ***acquatico*** waterfowl
acquavite *f* brandy
acquazzone *m* downpour
acquedotto *m* aqueduct
acqueo: ***vapore*** *m* ***acqueo*** water vapo(u)r

acquerello *m* water-colo(u)r
acquirente *m/f* purchaser
acquisizione *f* acquisition
acquistare ⟨1a⟩ **1** *v/t* buy; *fig* gain **2** *v/i* improve (***in*** in)
acquisto *m* purchase; ***potere** m **d'acquisto*** purchasing power; ***acquisto a rate*** hire purchase, *Am* installment plan
acquolina *f*: ***mi viene l'acquolina in bocca*** my mouth's watering
acre sour; *voce* harsh
acrilico (*pl* -ci) acrylic
acrobata *m/f* acrobat
acustica *f* acoustics
acustico (*pl* -ci) acoustic
acuto 1 *agg* intense; *nota*, *dolore* sharp; *suono*, *voce* shrill; MED acute **2** *m* MUS high note
ad *prp* → ***a*** (*before vowels*)
adagiare ⟨1f⟩ *persona* lay down
adagiarsi lie down
adagio 1 *avv* slowly; *con cautela* cautiously **2** *m* (*pl* -gi) MUS adagio
adattamento *m* adaptation; (*rielaborazione*) reworking
adattare ⟨1a⟩ adapt
adattarsi (*adeguarsi*) adapt (***a*** to); (*addirsi*) be suitable (***a*** for); ***questo colore non ti si adatta*** the colour doesn't suit you
adattatore *m* adaptor
adatto right (***a*** for)
addebitare ⟨1m⟩: FIN ***addebitare qc a qu*** debit s.o. with sth; *fig* ascribe sth to s.o.
addebito *m* FIN debit; ***nota** f **di addebito*** debit note
addensarsi ⟨1b⟩ thicken
addestramento *m* training
addestrare ⟨1b⟩ train
addetto 1 *agg* assigned (***a*** to) **2** *m*, **-a** *f* person responsible; ***addetto alle pubbliche relazioni*** public relations officer; *fig* ***addetto ai lavori*** expert; ***addetto culturale*** cultural attaché; ***vietato l'ingresso ai non -i*** authorized personnel only
addio 1 *int* goodbye **2** *m* goodbye, farewell
addirittura (*assolutamente*) absolutely; (*perfino*) even
additivo *m* additive
addizionare ⟨1a⟩ add
addizione *f* addition
addobbare ⟨1c⟩ decorate
addobbo *m* decoration
addolcire ⟨4d⟩ sweeten; *fig* soften
addolorare ⟨1a⟩ grieve
addome *m* abdomen
addomesticare ⟨1b, d & n⟩ tame
addominale abdominal
addormentare ⟨1b⟩ get (off) to sleep
addormentarsi fall asleep
addormentato asleep; (*assonnato*) sleepy
addossare ⟨1c⟩ (*appoggiare*) lean (***a*** on); *fig colpa* put, lay (***a*** on)
addossarsi lean (***a*** on); *fig* shoulder
addosso 1 *prp* on; *vicino* next to **2** *avv*: ***avere addosso*** *vestiti* have on; ***avere addosso qu*** have s.o. breathing down one's neck
addurre ⟨3e⟩ produce
adeguare ⟨1a⟩ adjust
adeguarsi conform; ***adeguarsi alle circostanze*** adjust to circumstances
adeguato adequate
adempiere ⟨4d & g⟩: ***adempiere a*** *dovere* carry out, do
aderente 1 *agg vestito* tight **2** *m/f* follower
aderire ⟨4d⟩: ***aderire a*** adhere to; *partito* support; *richiesta* agree to
adesione *f* adhesion; (*consenso*) agreement
adesivo 1 *agg* adhesive **2** *m* sticker
adesso now; ***da adesso in poi*** from now on; ***fino adesso*** up to now; ***per adesso*** for the moment
adiacente adjacent; ***adiacente a*** next to, adjacent to
adibire ⟨4d⟩ use
adirarsi ⟨1a⟩ get angry
adirato angry
adolescente *m/f* adolescent, teenager
adolescenza *f* adolescence, teens *pl* F
adoperare ⟨1m & c⟩ use
adorare ⟨1a⟩ adore
adorazione *f* adoration
adornare ⟨1a⟩ adorn
adottare ⟨1c⟩ adopt
adottivo *genitori* adoptive; *figlio* adopted
adozione *f* adoption
adrenalina *f* adrenalin
adriatico (*pl* -ci) **1** *agg* Adriatic; ***mare** m **Adriatico*** Adriatic Sea **2** *m*: **Adriatico** Adriatic
adulare ⟨1a⟩ flatter
adulazione *f* flattery
adulterare ⟨1m⟩ adulterate
adulterio *m* (*pl* -ri) adultery
adulto 1 *agg* adult **2** *m*, **-a** *f* adult
adunare ⟨1a⟩ assemble
aerare ⟨1l⟩ air
aerazione *f* airing
aereo 1 *agg* air *attr*; *fotografia*, *radici* aerial; ***base** f **-a*** air base; ***compagnia** f **-a*** airline; ***ponte** m **aereo*** airlift; ***posta** f **-a*** airmail **2** *m* plane; ***aereo di linea*** airliner
aerobica *f* aerobics *sg*
aerobus *m inv plane that makes short-*

haul flights
aerodinamico aerodynamic
aeronautica *f* aeronautics; ***aeronautica militare*** Air Force
aeroplano *m* plane, aeroplane, *Am* airplane
aeroporto *m* airport
aerosol *m inv contenitore* aerosol
aerospaziale aerospace *attr*
aerostato *m* aerostat, lighter-than-air aircraft
aerostazione *f* air terminal
afa *f* closeness, mugginess
affabile affable
affaccendarsi ⟨1b⟩ busy o.s. (***in*** with)
affaccendato busy
affacciarsi ⟨1f⟩ appear
affamato starving
affannato breathless
affanno *m* breathlessness; *fig* anxiety
affare *m* matter, business; FIN transaction; ***-i*** *pl* business *sg*; ***non sono -i tuoi*** it's none of your business; ***uomo*** *m* ***d'-i*** businessman; ***ministro*** *m* ***degli Affari Esteri*** *Foreign Secretary*; ***giro*** *m* ***d'-i*** turnover
affarista *m/f* (*mpl* -i) wheeler-dealer
affascinante fascinating
affascinare ⟨1m⟩ fascinate
affaticare ⟨1d⟩ tire
affaticarsi tire o.s. out
affatto completely; ***non è affatto vero!*** there's not the slightest bit of truth in it!
affermare ⟨1a⟩ state
affermarsi become established
affermazione *f* assertion; (*successo*) achievement
afferrare ⟨1b⟩ seize, grab F; (*comprendere*) grasp
afferrarsi cling (***a*** to), hold on (***a*** to)
affettare[1] ⟨1a⟩ (*tagliare*) slice
affettare[2] ⟨1b⟩ *ammirazione ecc* affect
affettato[1] *m* sliced meat
affettato[2] *agg* affected
affettatrice *f* slicer
affetto *m* affection
affettuoso affectionate
affezionarsi ⟨1a⟩: ***affezionarsi a qu*** become fond of s.o.
affezionato: ***affezionato a qu*** fond of s.o.
affiancare ⟨1d⟩ place side by side; *fig* support
affibbiare ⟨1k⟩: ***affibbiare qc a qu*** saddle s.o. with sth
affidabilità *f* dependability
affidamento *m* trust; ***fare affidamento su*** rely on
affidare ⟨1a⟩ entrust
affidarsi: ***affidarsi a*** rely on
affiggere ⟨3mm⟩ *avviso* put up
affilare ⟨1a⟩ sharpen; *fig* make thinner
affilato sharp; *naso* thin
affiliare ⟨1g⟩ *a una società* affiliate
affiliato 1 *m*, ***-a*** *f* member **2** *agg*: ***società*** *f* ***-a*** affiliate
affiliazione *f* affiliation
affinché so that
affine similar
affinità *f inv* affinity
affiorare ⟨1a⟩ *dall'acqua* emerge; *fig* (*mostrarsi*) appear
affissione *f* bill-posting
affisso 1 *pp* → ***affiggere*** **2** *m* bill
affittacamere *m/f* landlord; *donna* landlady
affittare ⟨1a⟩ *locali, terre* let; (*prendere in affitto*) rent; ***affittasi*** to let
affitto *m* rent; ***dare in affitto*** let; ***prendere in affitto*** rent
affliggere ⟨3cc⟩ distress; *di malattia* trouble, plague
afflitto distressed
affluente *m* tributary
affluenza *f fig* influx
affluire ⟨4d⟩ flow; *di persone* pour in
afflusso *m* influx
affogare ⟨1c & e⟩ *v/t & v/i* drown
affollamento *m* crowd
affollare ⟨1c⟩, **affollarsi** crowd
affollato crowded
affondare ⟨1a⟩ *v/t & v/i* sink
affrancare ⟨1d⟩ free; *posta* frank
affrancatura *f* franking; *tassa di spedizione* postage
affresco *m* (*pl* -chi) fresco
affrettare ⟨1a⟩ speed up
affrettarsi hurry
affrontare ⟨1a⟩ face, confront; *spese* meet
affronto *m* insult
affumicare ⟨1d & m⟩ *stanza* fill with smoke; *alimenti* smoke
affumicato smoked
affusolato tapering
afoso sultry
Africa *f* Africa
africano 1 *agg* African **2** *m*, **-a** *f* African
afrodisiaco *m/agg* aphrodisiac
agave *f* agave
agenda *f* diary
agente *m/f* agent; ***agente di cambio*** stockbroker; ***agente immobiliare*** estate agent, *Am* realtor; ***agente inquinante*** pollutant; ***agente di pubblica sicurezza*** police officer; ***agente di vendita*** sales representative; ***agente di viaggio*** travel agent
agenzia *f* agency; ***agenzia di cambio*** bureau de change; ***agenzia immobiliare*** estate agency, *Am* real estate office;

agenzia pubblicitaria advertising agency; ***agenzia di viaggi*** travel agency
agevolare ⟨1m⟩ make easier
agevolato FIN on easy terms
agevolazione *f* FIN special term
agevole easy
agganciare ⟨1f⟩ hook; *cintura*, *collana* fasten
aggeggio *m* (*pl* -ggi) gadget
aggettivo *m* adjective
agghiacciante spine-chilling
aggiornamento *m* updating; (*rinvio*) postponement; ***corso*** *m* ***d'aggiornamento*** refresher course
aggiornare ⟨1a⟩ (*mettere al corrente*) update; (*rinviare*) postpone
aggiornarsi keep up to date
aggirare ⟨1a⟩ surround; *fig ostacolo* get round
aggirarsi hang about; FIN be in the region of
aggiudicare ⟨1d & m⟩ award; *all'asta* knock down
aggiungere ⟨3d⟩ add
aggiunta *f* addition
aggiustare ⟨1a⟩ (*riparare*) repair; (*sistemare*) settle
agglomerato *m*: ***agglomerato urbano*** built-up area
aggrapparsi ⟨1a⟩ cling, hold on (***a*** to)
aggravante 1 *agg* aggravating **2** *f* aggravation
aggravare ⟨1a⟩ *punizione* increase; (*peggiorare*) make worse
aggravarsi worsen, deteriorate
aggravio *m* (*pl* -vi): ***aggravio fiscale*** tax increase
aggraziato graceful
aggredire ⟨4d⟩ attack
aggressione *f* aggression; (*attacco*) attack; POL ***patto*** *m* ***di non aggressione*** non-aggression pact
aggressività *f* aggressiveness
aggressivo aggressive
aggressore *m* attacker; POL aggressor
agguato *m* ambush; ***tendere un agguato a qu*** ambush s.o., set an ambush for s.o.
agguerrito hardened
agiatezza *f* comfort
agiato comfortable, well-off; (*comodo*) comfortable
agibile fit for human habitation
agile agile
agilità *f* agility; *fig* liveliness
agio *m* (*pl* -gi) ease; ***vivere negli agi*** live in comfort; ***sentirsi a proprio agio*** feel at ease
agire ⟨4d⟩ act; *comportarsi* behave, act; *di medicina* take effect; DIR take action (***contro*** against)
agitare ⟨1l⟩ shake; *fazzoletto* wave; *fig* (*turbare*) upset, agitate; ***agitare prima dell'uso*** shake before use
agitato agitated; *mare* rough
agitazione *f* agitation
agli *prp* ***a*** and *art* ***gli***
aglio *m* (*pl* -gli) garlic
agnello *m* lamb
agnolotti *mpl type of ravioli*
ago *m* (*pl* -ghi) needle
agonia *f* agony
agonismo *m* competitiveness
agonistico (*pl* -ci) competitive
agopuntura *f* acupuncture
agorafobia *f* agoraphobia
agosto *m* August; ***in agosto*** in August
agraria *f* agriculture
agrario (*pl* -ri) agricultural; *riforma* agrarian
agricolo agricultural
agricoltore *m* farmer
agricoltura *f* agriculture
agrifoglio *m* holly
agriturismo *m* farm holidays *pl*
agro sour
agrodolce bittersweet; GASTR sweet and sour
agronomo *m*, **-a** *f* agricultural economist
agrumi *mpl* citrus fruit *sg*
aguzzare ⟨1a⟩ sharpen; ***aguzzare la vista*** keep one's eyes peeled
aguzzo pointed
ah! oh!
ahi! ouch!
ai *prp* ***a*** and *art* ***i***
Aids *m o f* Aids
airbag *m inv* airbag
A.I.R.E. *abbr* (= ***Anagrafe degli Italiani Residenti all'Estero***) register of Italian citizens resident overseas
airone *m* heron
aiuola *f* flower bed
aiutante *m/f* assistant
aiutare ⟨1a⟩ help
aiuto *m* help, assistance; *persona* assistant; ***aiuto allo sviluppo*** development aid *or* assistance; ***chiedere aiuto a qu*** ask s.o. for help
aizzare ⟨1a⟩ incite
al *prp* ***a*** and *art* ***il***
ala *f* (*pl* -i) wing
alabastro *m* alabaster
alano *m* Great Dane
alba *f* dawn; ***all'alba*** at dawn
Albania *f* Albania
albanese *agg*, *m/f* Albanian
albeggiare ⟨1f⟩ dawn
alberato tree-lined

albergare ⟨1b & e⟩ put up
albergatore *m*, **-trice** *f* hotel keeper
alberghiero hotel *attr*
albergo *m* (*pl* -ghi) hotel; ***guida*** *f* ***degli -ghi*** hotel guide
albero *m* tree; MAR mast; AVIA, AUTO shaft; ***albero genealogico*** family tree; ***albero motore*** drive shaft; ***albero di Natale*** Christmas tree
albicocca *f* (*pl* -cche) apricot
albicocco *m* (*pl* -cchi) apricot (tree)
albo *m* notice board; (*registro*) register; ***radiare dall'albo*** strike off
album *m inv* album
albume *m* albumen
alcalino alkaline
alcol *m* alcohol
alcolico (*pl* -ci) **1** *agg* alcoholic; ***gradazione*** *f* ***-a*** alcohol content **2** *m* alcoholic drink
alcolismo *m* alcoholism
alcolizzato *m*, **-a** *f* alcoholic
alcoltest *m inv* Breathalyzer®
alcuno **1** *agg* any; ***non alcuno*** no, not any **2** *pron* any; ***-i*** *pl* some, a few
aldilà *m*: ***l'aldilà*** the next world, the hereafter
aletta *f* fin
alfabetico (*pl* -ci) alphabetical
alfabeto *m* alphabet
alfanumerico (*pl* -ci) INFOR alphanumeric
alfiere *m scacchi* bishop
alfine eventually
alga *f* (*pl* -ghe) seaweed
algebra *f* algebra
Algeria *f* Algeria
algerino **1** *agg* Algerian **2** *m*, **-a** *f* Algerian
aliante *m* glider
alice *f* anchovy
alienare ⟨1b⟩ DIR transfer; *persone* alienate
alienarsi become lienated
alienato **1** *agg* alienated **2** *m*, **-a** *f* madman; *donna* madwoman
alienazione *f* alienation; ***alienazione mentale*** madness
alimentare ⟨1a⟩ **1** *v/t* feed **2** *agg* food *attr*; ***generi*** *mpl* ***-i*** foodstuffs
alimentazione *f* feeding
alimento *m* food; ***alimento base*** basic food(stuff); ***-i*** *pl* DIR alimony *sg*
aliquota *f* share; ***aliquota d'imposta*** rate of taxation
aliscafo *m* hydrofoil
alito *m* breath
all. *abbr* (= ***allegato***) enc(l). (= enclosed
all', alla *prp* ***a*** and *art* ***l', la***
allacciamento *m* TEC connection
allacciare ⟨1f⟩ fasten; TEC connect
allagamento *m* flooding
allagare ⟨1e⟩ flood
allargare ⟨1e⟩ widen; *vestito* let out; *braccia* open
allargarsi widen
allarmare ⟨1a⟩ alarm
allarmarsi become alarmed
allarme *m* alarm; ***dare l'allarme*** raise the alarm; ***allarme smog*** smog alert
allattare ⟨1a⟩ *bambino* feed
alle *prp* ***a*** and *art* ***le***
alleanza *f* alliance
allearsi ⟨1b⟩ ally o.s.
alleato **1** *agg* allied **2** *m*, **-a** *f* ally
allegare ⟨1e⟩ *documento* enclose, inclose
allegato *m* enclosure; INFOR attachment; ***qui allegato*** enclosed
alleggerire ⟨4d⟩ lighten; *fig dolore* ease
allegria *f* cheerfulness
allegro **1** *agg* cheerful; *colore* bright **2** *m* MUS allegro
allenamento *m* training
allenare ⟨1b⟩, **allenarsi** train (***per*** for; ***a*** in)
allenatore *m*, **-trice** *f* trainer
allentare ⟨1b⟩ **1** *v/t* loosen; *fig disciplina, sorveglianza* relax **2** *v/i e* **allentarsi** loosen
allergia *f* allergy
allergico (*pl* -ci) allergic (***a*** to)
allestimento *m* preparation; MAR fitting out; TEA ***allestimento scenico*** sets *pl*, scenery
allestire ⟨4d⟩ prepare; MAR fit out; TEA stage
allevamento *m* BOT, ZO breeding
allevare ⟨1b⟩ BOT, ZO breed; *bambini* bring up, raise
allevatore *m*, **-trice** *f* breeder
alleviare ⟨1b & k⟩ alleviate
allievo *m*, **-a** *f* pupil, student
alligatore *m* alligator
allineamento *m* alignment
allineare ⟨1m⟩ line up; FIN adjust; TIP align
allinearsi line up; *fig* ***allinearsi con qu*** align o.s. with s.o.
allo *prp* ***a*** and *art* ***lo***
allodola *f* skylark
alloggiare ⟨1f & c⟩ **1** *v/t* put up; MIL billet **2** *v/i* stay, put up
alloggio *m* (*pl* -ggi) accommodation; ***dare alloggio a qu*** put s.o. up; ***vitto e alloggio*** bed and board
allontanare ⟨1a⟩ take away; *fig pericolo, sospetto* avert
allontanarsi go away; *fig* grow apart
allora **1** *avv* then **2** *cong* then; ***d'allora in poi*** from then on; ***fin d'allora*** since then

alloro *m* laurel; GASTR bay
alluce *m* big toe
allucinante F incredible, mind-blowing F
allucinazione *f* hallucination
alludere ⟨3q⟩ allude (***a*** to)
alluminio *m* aluminium, *Am* aluminum
allungamento *m* lengthening
allungare ⟨1e⟩ lengthen; (*diluire*) dilute; *mano* stretch out, put out
allungarsi *di giorni* get longer; *di persona* stretch out, lie down
allusione *f* allusion
alluvione *f* flood
almeno at least
alogena *f* halogen
Alpi *fpl* Alps
alpinismo *m* mountaineering
alpinista *m/f* mountain climber
alpino Alpine
alquanto 1 *agg* some **2** *avv* a little, somewhat
alt *int* stop
altalena *f* swing
altare *m* altar
alterare ⟨1l⟩ alter
alterarsi (*guastarsi*) go bad *or* off; (*irritarsi*) get angry
alterazione *f* alteration
alterco *m* (*pl* -chi) altercation
alternare ⟨1b⟩, **alternarsi** alternate
alternativa *f* alternative
alternativo alternative
alternato: ***corrente*** *f* ***-a*** alternating current
alterno: ***a giorni*** *pl* ***-i*** on alternate days
altezza *f* height; *titolo* Highness
alticcio (*pl* -cci) tipsy
altitudine *f* GEOG altitude
alto 1 *agg* high; *persona* tall; ***a voce -a*** in a loud voice; *leggere* aloud; ***in alto*** at the top; *moto* up; ***a notte -a*** in the middle of the night **2** *m* top
altoatesino 1 *agg* South Tyrolean **2** *m*, **-a** *f* person from South Tyrol
altoforno *m* blast furnace
altoparlante *m* loudspeaker
altopiano *m* (*pl* altipiani) plateau
altrettanto *agg*, *pron* as much; **-i** *pl* as many
altrimenti (*in modo diverso*) differently; (*in caso contrario*) otherwise
altro 1 *agg* other; ***un altro*** another; ***l'altr'anno*** last year; ***l'altro giorno*** the other day; ***l'altro ieri*** the day before yesterday **2** *pron* other; ***l'un l'altro*** one another; ***gli altri*** other people; ***tra l'altro*** what's more, moreover; ***desidera altro?*** anything else?; ***tutt'altro che*** anything but
altronde: ***d'altronde*** on the other hand
altrove elsewhere
altruismo *m* altruism
altura *f* hill
alunno *m*, **-a** *f* pupil, student
alzacristallo *m inv* AUTO window winder
alzare ⟨1a⟩ raise, lift; *prezzi* increase, raise; (*costruire*) build, erect; ***alzare le spalle*** shrug (one's shoulders)
alzarsi stand up, rise; *da letto* get up; *di sole* come up, rise
amabile lovable; (*gentile*) pleasant, kind; *vino* sweet
amabilità *f* pleasantness
amaca *f* (*pl* -che) hammock
amalgamare ⟨1m⟩ amalgamate
amante *m/f* lover; ***amante della musica*** music lover
amare ⟨1a⟩ love; *amico* be fond of
amareggiare ⟨1f⟩ embitter
amareggiato embittered
amarena *f* sour black cherry
amarezza *f* bitterness
amaro 1 *agg* bitter **2** *m liquore* bitters *pl*
ambasciata *f* embassy
ambasciatore *m*, **-trice** *f* ambassador
ambedue both
ambientale environmental
ambientalista 1 *agg* environmental **2** *m/f* environmentalist
ambientarsi ⟨1b⟩ become acclimatized
ambiente *m* BIO environment; ***ambiente di lavoro*** work environment; ***protezione*** *f* ***dell'ambiente*** environmental protection
ambiguità *f inv* ambiguity
ambiguo ambiguous
ambito *m* sphere
ambizione *f* ambition
ambizioso ambitious
ambo 1 *agg* both; ***in -i casi*** in both cases **2** *m* (*lotteria*) double
ambulante 1 *agg* travel(l)ing **2** *m/f* pedlar
ambulanza *f* ambulance
ambulatorio *m* MED (*pl* -ri) outpatients
America *f* America
americano 1 *agg* American **2** *m*, **-a** *f* American **3** *m* American English
ametista *f* amethyst
amianto *m* asbestos
amichevole friendly
amicizia *f* friendship
amico (*pl* -ci) **1** *agg* friendly **2** *m*, **-a** *f* (*pl* -che) friend; ***amico intimo*** close friend
amido *m* starch
ammaccare ⟨1d⟩ dent; *frutta* bruise
ammaccatura *f* dent; *su frutta* bruise
ammaestrare ⟨1b⟩ teach; *animali* train
ammalarsi ⟨1a⟩ fall ill
ammalato 1 *agg* ill **2** *m*, **-a** *f* ill person

ammanco *m* (*pl* -chi) deficit
ammanettare ⟨1a⟩ handcuff, put handcuffs on
ammarare ⟨1a⟩ *di aereo* put down in the water; *di navetta spaziale* splash down
ammassare ⟨1a⟩, **ammassarsi** mass
ammasso *m* pile; GEOL mass
ammazzare ⟨1a⟩ kill; *animali* slaughter
ammazzarsi (*suicidarsi*) kill o.s.
ammenda *f* (*multa*) fine; ***fare ammenda di*** make amends for
ammesso *pp* → ***ammettere***
ammettere ⟨3ee⟩ admit; (*supporre*) suppose; (*riconoscere*) acknowledge; ***ammesso che …*** supposing (that) …
amministrare ⟨1a⟩ administer; *azienda* manage, run
amministrativo administrative
amministratore *m*, **-trice** *f* administrator; *di azienda* manager; ***amministratore delegato*** managing director
amministrazione *f* administration; ***amministrazione comunale*** local council; ***pubblica amministrazione*** public administration; ***spese*** *fpl* ***d'amministrazione*** administrative costs
ammiraglia *f* flagship
ammiraglio *m* (*pl* -gli) admiral
ammirare ⟨1a⟩ admire
ammiratore *m*, **-trice** *f* admirer
ammirazione *f* admiration
ammirevole admirable
ammissibile admissible
ammobiliare ⟨1g⟩ furnish
ammobiliato furnished
ammodo **1** *agg inv* respectable **2** *avv* properly
ammollo: ***in ammollo*** soaking
ammonimento *m* reprimand, admonishment; (*consiglio*) warning
ammonire ⟨4d⟩ reprimand, admonish; (*avvertire*) warn; DIR caution
ammonizione *f* reprimand, admonishment; SP warning; DIR caution
ammontare **1** *v/i* ⟨1a⟩: ***ammontare a*** amount to **2** *m* amount; ***per un ammontare di …*** in the amount of …
ammorbidire ⟨4d⟩ soften
ammortamento *m* FIN amortization
ammortizzare ⟨1a⟩ FIN amortize
ammortizzatore *m* AUTO shock absorber
ammucchiare ⟨1g⟩ pile up
ammucchiarsi pile up, accumulate
ammuffire ⟨4d⟩ go mo(u)ldy; *fig* mo(u)lder away
ammutolire ⟨4d⟩ be struck dumb
amnesia *f* amnesia
amnistia *f* amnesty
amo *m* hook; *fig* bait
amore *m* love; ***per l'amore di qu*** for love of s.o.; ***per l'amor di Dio*** for goodness' sake, for the love of God; ***fare l'amore con qu*** make love to s.o.
amoreggiare ⟨1f⟩ flirt
amorevole loving
amoroso loving, affectionate; *sguardo* amorous; *lettera*, *poesia* love *attr*
amperaggio *m* (*pl* -gi) amperage
ampiezza *f di stanza* spaciousness; *di gonna* fullness; *fig di cultura* breadth; *fig* ***ampiezza di vedute*** broadmindedness
ampio (*pl* -pi) *stanza* spacious, large; *abito* roomy; *gonna* full
ampliamento *m* broadening, widening; *di edificio* extension
ampliare ⟨1l⟩ broaden, widen; *edificio* extend
amplificare ⟨1m & d⟩ TEC *suono* amplify
amplificatore *m* amplifier
ampolla *f* cruet
amputare ⟨1l⟩ amputate
amputazione *f* amputation
amuleto *m* amulet
anabbagliante dipped
anabolizzante *m* anabolic steroid
anacronistico (*pl* -ci) anachronistic
anagrafe *f ufficio* registry office
analcolico (*pl* -ci) **1** *agg* non-alcoholic **2** *m* non-alcoholic drink
anale anal
analfabeta *m/f* (*mpl* -i) illiterate person, person who cannot read or write
analfabetismo *m* illiteracy
analgesico (*pl* -ci) *m/agg* analgesic
analisi *f inv* analysis; ***analisi del sangue*** blood test
analista *m/f* (*mpl* -i) analyst; ***analista programmatore*** systems analyst
analizzare ⟨1a⟩ analyse, *Am* analyze
analogia *f* analogy
analogo (*pl* -ghi) analogous
ananas *m inv* pineapple
anarchia *f* anarchy
anarchico (*pl* -ci) **1** *agg* anarchic **2** *m*, **-a** *f* anarchist
ANAS *abbr* (= ***Azienda Nazionale Autonoma della Strada***) Italian Roads Department
anatomia *f* anatomy
anatomico (*pl* -ci) anatomical
anatra *f* duck
anca *f* (pl -che) hip
anche too, also, as well; (*perfino*) even; ***anche se*** even if
ancora[1] *avv* still; *di nuovo* again; *di più* (some) more; ***non ancora*** not yet; ***ancora una volta*** once more, one more time; ***dammene ancora un po'*** give me a bit

more
ancora[2] *f* anchor; ***gettare l'ancora*** drop anchor
ancoraggio *m* (*pl* -ggi) anchoring; *luogo* anchorage
ancorare ⟨1l⟩ anchor
ancorarsi anchor; *fig* ***ancorarsi a*** cling to
andamento *m di vendite* performance
andare ⟨1p⟩ **1** *v/i* go; (*funzionare*) work; ***andare via*** (*partire*) leave; *di macchia* come out; ***andare bene*** suit; *taglia* fit; ***andare a cavallo*** ride; ***andare a passeggio*** walk; ***andare a male*** go off; ***andare a finire*** turn out; ***andare in bicicletta*** cycle; ***come va?*** how are you?, how are things?; ***non mi va*** *di vestito* it doesn't fit me; ***non mi va di venire*** I don't feel like coming **2** *m*: ***coll'andare del tempo*** with the passage of time; ***a lungo andare*** in the long run
andarsene go away
andata *f* outward journey; ***c'era più traffico all'andata*** there was more traffic on the way there; ***biglietto*** *m* ***di andata*** single (ticket), *Am* oneway ticket; ***biglietto*** *m* ***di andata e ritorno*** return (ticket), *Am* roundtrip ticket
andatura *f* walk; SP pace
andirivieni *m inv* toing and froing
androne *m* hallway
aneddoto *m* anecdote
anello *m* ring; ***anello di fidanzamento*** engagement ring
anemia *f* an(a)emia
anemico (*pl* -ci) an(a)emic
anemone *m* anemone
anestesia *f* an(a)esthesia; *sostanza* an(a)esthetic
anestesista *m/f* (*mpl* -i) an(a)esthetist
anestetico *m* (*pl* -ci) an(a)esthetic
anfetamina *f* amphetamine
anfibio (*pl* -bi) **1** *agg* amphibious **2** *m* ZO amphibian; MIL amphibious vehicle
anfiteatro *m* amphitheatre, *Am* -theater
anfora *f* amphora
angelo *m* angel; ***angelo custode*** guardian angel
anglicano 1 *agg* Anglican **2** *m*, **-a** *f* Anglican
anglista *m/f* student of English
anglosassone Anglo-Saxon
angolare angular
angolo *m* corner; MAT angle; ***angolo cottura*** kitchenette; MAT ***angolo retto*** right angle; SP ***calcio*** *m* ***d'angolo*** corner kick;
angoloso angular
angoscia *f* (*pl* -sce) anguish
angoscioso *pieno d'angoscia* anguished; *che da angoscia* distressing, heart-rending
anguilla *f* eel
anguria *f* water melon
angusto narrow
anice *m* GASTR aniseed
anidride *f*: ***anidride carbonica*** carbon dioxide
anima *f* soul; ***non c'è anima viva*** there isn't a soul to be seen; F ***rompere l'anima a qu*** get on s.o.'s nerves F
animale 1 *agg* animal *attr* **2** *m* animal; ***animale domestico*** pet
animare ⟨1l⟩ give life to; *conversazione* liven up; (*promuovere*) promote
animato *strada* busy; *conversazione*, *persona* animated
animatore *m*, **-trice** *f di gruppo* leader
animazione *f* animation; INFOR ***animazione al computer*** computer animation
animo *m* nature; (*coraggio*) heart; ***farsi animo*** be brave; ***perdersi d'animo*** lose heart
anisetta *f aniseed-flavoured liqueur*
anitra *f* duck
annacquare ⟨1a⟩ water down
annaffiare ⟨1k⟩ water
annafiatoio *m* (*pl* -oi) watering can
annali *mpl* annals
annata *f* vintage; (*anno*) year; *importo* annual amount
annegare ⟨1e⟩ **1** *v/t* drown **2** *v/i e* ***annegarsi*** drown
annerire ⟨4d⟩ **1** *v/t* blacken **2** *v/i e* ***annerirsi*** turn black, blacken
annessione *f* POL annexation
annesso 1 *pp* → ***annettere*** **2** *agg* annexed; (*allegato*) enclosed, attached **3** *m edificio* annex(e)
annettere ⟨3m⟩ POL annex; ARCHI add; (*allegare*) enclose, attach
annidarsi ⟨1a⟩ nest
anniversario *m* (*pl* -ri) anniversary
anno *m* year; ***buon anno!*** Happy New Year!; ***anno finanziario*** financial year; ***anno scolastico*** school year; ***quanti -i hai?*** how old are you?; ***ho 33 -i*** I'm 33 (years old)
annodare ⟨1c⟩ tie (together); *cravatta* tie, knot
annoiare ⟨1i⟩ bore; (*dare fastidio a*) annoy
annoiarsi get bored
annoiato bored
annotare ⟨1c⟩ make a note of; *testo* annotate
annotazione *f* note; *in testo* annotation
annuale annual, yearly; *di un anno* year--long
annuario *m* (*pl* -ri) yearbook

annuire ⟨4d⟩ (*assentire*) assent (***a*** to)
annullamento *m* cancellation; *di matrimonio* annulment
annullare ⟨1a⟩ cancel; *matrimonio* annul; *gol* disallow; (*vanificare*) cancel out
annunciare ⟨1f⟩ announce
annunciatore *m*, **-trice** *f* RAD, TV announcer
Annunciazione *f* REL Annunciation
annuncio *m* (*pl* -ci) announcement; *in giornale* advertisement; ***-i*** *pl* ***economici*** classified ads, classifieds; ***annuncio pubblicitario*** ad(vert), advertisement
annunziare ⟨1a⟩ → ***annunciare***
annuo annual, yearly
annusare ⟨1a⟩ sniff; *fig* smell
annuvolarsi ⟨1a⟩ cloud over
anomalo anomalous
anonimo anonymous; ***società*** *f* ***-a*** limited company
anoressia *f* anorexia
anoressico anorexic
anormale abnormal
ANSA *abbr* (= ***Agenzia Nazionale Stampa Associata***) Italian Press Agency
ansa *f* handle; *di un fiume* bend
ansia *f* anxiety; ***con ansia*** anxiously
ansimare ⟨1l⟩ wheeze
ansioso anxious
antagonismo *m* antagonism
antagonista *m/f* (*mpl* -i) antagonist
antartico (*pl* -ci) Antarctic *attr*
antecedente 1 *agg* preceding **2** *m* precedent
antefatto *m* prior event
anteguerra *m* pre-war years *pl*
antenato *m*, **-a** *f* ancestor
antenna *f* RAD, TV aerial; ZO antenna; ***antenna parabolica*** satellite dish
anteporre ⟨3ll⟩ put before
anteposto *pp* → ***anteporre***
anteprima *f* preview
anteriore front; *precedente* previous
anti ... anti ...
antiatomico (*pl* -ci) anti-nuclear; ***rifugio*** *m* ***antiatomico*** fallout shelter
antibiotico (*pl* -ci) *m/agg* antibiotic
anticamente in ancient times
anticamera *f* ante-room; ***fare anticamera*** be kept waiting
antichità *f inv* antiquity; ***negozio*** *m* ***d'antichità*** antique shop
anticiclone *m* anticyclone
anticipare ⟨1m⟩ anticipate; *denaro* pay in advance; *partenza, riunione ecc* bring forward
anticipo *m* advance; (*caparra*) deposit; ***in anticipo*** ahead of time, early
antico (*pl* -chi) **1** *agg* ancient; *mobile* antique **2** ***gli -chi*** *pl* the ancients
anticoncezionale *m/agg* contraceptive
anticonformista *m/f* (*mpl* -i) nonconformist
anticongelante *m* anti-freeze
anticorpo *m* antibody
anticostituzionale unconstitutional
antidoto *m* antidote
antifurto 1 *adj* antitheft **2** *m* anti-theft device
antigas *inv* gas *attr*
antincendio *inv* fire *attr*
antinebbia *m inv* foglamp
antiorario: ***in senso antiorario*** anticlockwise, *Am* counterclockwise
antipasto *m* starter
antipatia *f* antipathy
antipatico (*pl* -ci) disagreeable
antiquariato *m* antique business, antiques; ***negozio*** *m* ***di antiquariato*** antique shop
antiquario *m* (*pl* -ri), **-a** *f* antique dealer
antiquato antiquated
antiriflesso *inv* anti-glare
antiruggine *m* rust inhibitor
antirumore: ***protezione*** *f* ***antirumore*** soundproofing
antisemitismo *m* anti-Semitism
antisettico (*pl* -ci) *m/agg* antiseptic
antisismico (*pl* -ci) earthquake-proof
antitesi *f* FIL antithesis
antiurto shockproof
antologia *f* anthology
antracite *f* anthracite
antropologia *f* anthropology
anulare *m* ring finger
anzi in fact; (*o meglio*) (or) better still
anzianità *f* old age; ***anzianità di servizio*** seniority
anziano 1 *agg* elderly; *per servizio* (most) senior **2** *m*, **-a** *f* old man; *donna* old woman; ***gli -i*** the elderly
anziché rather than
anzitutto first of all
aorta *f* aorta
apatia *f* apathy
apatico (*pl* -ci) apathetic
ape *f* bee
aperitivo *m* aperitif
aperto 1 *pp* → ***aprire*** **2** *agg* open; ***di mentalità aperta*** broad-minded; ***all' aperto*** *piscina* open-air; ***mangiare all'aperto*** eat outside *or* in the open air
apertura *f* opening; PHOT aperture; ***apertura di credito*** loan agreement; ***apertura alare*** wingspan
apice *m* apex; *fig* height
apicoltore *m*, **-trice** *f* bee-keeper
apicoltura *f* bee-keeping

apnea *f* SP free diving
apolide **1** *agg* stateless **2** *m* stateless person
apolitico (*pl* -ci) apolitical
apoplessia *f* apoplexy
apoplettico (*pl* -ci) apoplectic
apostolico (*pl* -ci) apostolic
apostolo *m* apostle
apostrofare ⟨1m & c⟩ reprimand; GRAM add an apostrophe to
apostrofo *m* apostrophe
appagare ⟨1e⟩ satisfy
appaiare ⟨1i⟩ match
appallottolare ⟨1c & n⟩ roll up into a ball
appalto *m* (*contratto*) contract; ***dare in appalto*** contract out; ***prendere in appalto*** win the contract for; ***gara** f **di appalto*** call for tenders
appannare ⟨1a⟩ mist up
appannarsi *di vetro* mist up; *di vista* grow dim
apparato *m* TEC, *fig* apparatus; ***apparato digerente*** digestive system
apparecchiare ⟨1g⟩ *tavola* set, lay; (*preparare*) prepare
apparecchiatura *f* equipment
apparecchio *m* (*pl* -cchi) TEC device; AVIA F plane; *per denti* brace; ***apparecchio fotografico*** camera; F ***portare l'apparecchio*** wear a hearing aid
apparente apparent
apparenza *f* appearance; ***salvare le -e*** save face
apparire ⟨4e⟩ appear
appariscente striking, eyecatching
apparizione *f* apparition
appartamento *m* flat, *Am* apartment
appartarsi ⟨1a⟩ withdraw
appartenere ⟨2q⟩ belong
appassionare ⟨1a⟩ excite; (*commuovere*) move
appassionarsi become excited (***a*** by)
appassionato passionate
appassire ⟨4d⟩ wither
appellarsi ⟨1b⟩ appeal (***a*** to; ***contro*** against)
appello *m* appeal; ***fare appello a qu*** appeal to s.o.; DIR ***ricorrere in appello*** lodge an appeal
appena **1** *avv* just **2** *cong* as soon as
appendere ⟨3c⟩ hang
appendiabiti *m* hatstand
appendice *f* appendix
appendicite *f* appendicitis
Appennini *mpl* Apennines
appesantire ⟨4d⟩ make heavier
appesi, **appeso** *pp* → ***appendere***
appetito *m* appetite; ***stuzzicare l'appetito*** whet one's appetite; ***buon appetito!*** enjoy your meal!
appetitoso appetizing
appianare ⟨1a⟩ level; *lite* smooth over
appiattire ⟨4d⟩ flatten
appiccicare ⟨1m & d⟩ stick
appiccicarsi stick
appiccicoso sticky; *fig* clingy
appigliarsi ⟨1g⟩ grab hold (***a*** of)
appiglio *m* (*pl* -gli) *per mani* fingerhold; *per piedi* toehold; *fig* excuse
applaudire ⟨4a or d⟩ *v/t & v/i* applaud
applauso *m* applause
applicare ⟨1l & d⟩ *etichetta* attach; *regolamento* apply
applicarsi: ***applicarsi a qc*** apply o.s. to sth
applicazione *f* application
appoggiare ⟨1f & c⟩ lean (***a*** against); (*posare*) put; *fig* support, back
appoggiarsi: *appoggiarsi a* lean on; *fig* rely on, lean on
appoggiatesta *m inv* headrest
appoggio *m* (*pl* -ggi) support
apporre ⟨3ll⟩ put; ***apporre la firma su qc*** put one's signature to sth
apportare ⟨1c⟩ bring; *fig* (*causare*) cause
apposito appropriate
apposta deliberately, on purpose; *specialmente* specifically
apprendere ⟨3c⟩ learn; *notizia* hear
apprendista *m/f* (*mpl* -i) apprentice
apprendistato *m* apprenticeship
apprensione *f* apprehension
apprensivo apprehensive
appreso *pp* → ***apprendere***
appresso **1** *prp* close, near; (*dietro*) behind; ***appresso a qu*** near s.o., close to s.o. **2** *avv* near, close by; ***portarsi qc appresso*** bring sth (with one)
apprezzare ⟨1b⟩ appreciate
approccio *m* (*pl* -cci) approach
approdare ⟨1c⟩ land; *di barca* moor, tie up; *fig* ***non approdare a nulla*** come to nothing
approdo *m* landing; *luogo* landing stage
approfittare ⟨1a⟩: ***approfittare di qc*** take advantage of sth
approfondire ⟨4d⟩ deepen; *fig* study in depth
appropriarsi ⟨1m & c⟩: ***appropriarsi di qc*** appropriate sth
appropriato appropriate
approvare ⟨1c⟩ approve of; *legge* approve
approvazione *f* approval
approvvigionamento *m* supply
appuntamento *m* appointment
appuntare ⟨1a⟩ pin; *avviso* pin up
appuntito pointed; *matita* sharp
appunto **1** *m* note; ***prendere -i*** take notes

2 *avv*: **(*per l'*)*appunto*** exactly
apribottiglie *m inv* bottle opener
aprile *m* April
aprire ⟨4f⟩ open; *rubinetto* turn on
aprirsi open; ***aprirsi con qu*** confide in s.o., open up to s.o.
apriscatole *m inv* can-opener, *Br* tin-opener
aquila *f* eagle
aquilone *m* kite
arabesco *m* (*pl* -chi) arabesque; *spir* scrawl, scribble
Arabia Saudita *f* Saudi (Arabia)
arabo 1 *agg* Arab **2** *m*, **-a** *f* Arab **3** *m* Arabic
arachide *f* peanut
aragosta *f* lobster
arancia *f* (*pl* -ce) orange
aranciata *f* orangeade
arancio 1 *agg inv* orange **2** *m* (*pl* -ci) *albero* orange tree; *colore* orange
arancione *m/agg* orange
arare ⟨1a⟩ plough, *Am* plow
aratro *m* plough, *Am* plow
arazzo *m* tapestry
arbitraggio *m* (*pl* -ggi) arbitration; SP refereeing
arbitrare ⟨1l⟩ arbitrate in; SP referee
arbitrario (*pl* -ri) arbitrary
arbitro *m* arbiter; SP referee
arbusto *m* shrub
arca *f* (*pl* -che) (*cassa*) chest; REL ***l'arca di Noè*** Noah's Ark
arcaico (*pl* -ci) archaic
arcangelo *m* archangel
arcata *f* ANAT, ARCHI arch
archeologia *f* arch(a)eology
archeologo *m* (*pl* -gi), **-a** *f* arch(a)eologist
archetto *m* MUS bow
architetto *m* architect
architettonico (*pl* -ci) architectural
archiviare ⟨1k⟩ file
archivio *m* (*pl* -vi) archives, records
arcipelago *m* (*pl* -ghi) archipelago
arcivescovo *m* archbishop
arco *m* (pl -chi) bow; ARCHI arch; ***arco di tempo*** space of time; ***orchestra*** *f* ***d'-chi*** string orchestra
arcobaleno *m* rainbow
ardente *fig* ardent
ardere ⟨3uu⟩ *v/t* & *v/i* burn
area *f* surface; *zona* area; ***area fabbricabile*** site that may be built on; SP ***area di rigore*** penalty area; ***area di servizio*** service area
arena *f* arena
arenarsi ⟨1a⟩ run aground; *fig* come to a halt
areo ... → ***aereo*** ...
argano *m* winch
argentato silver-plated
argenteria *f* silver(ware)
Argentina *f* Argentina
argentino 1 *agg* Argentinian **2** *m*, **-a** *f* Argentinian
argento *m* silver; ***argento vivo*** quicksilver; FERR ***carta*** *f* ***d'argento*** *travel pass for people over a certain age*; ***nozze*** *fpl* ***d'argento*** silver wedding *sg*
argilla *f* clay
argilloso clayey
arginare ⟨1l⟩ embank
argine *m* embankment
argomento *m* argument; (*contenuto*) subject; ***cambiare argomento*** change the subject
arguto witty; (*perspicace*) shrewd
arguzia *f* wit; *espressione* witticism, witty remark; (*perspicacia*) shrewdness
aria *f* **1** air; ***aria condizionata*** air conditioning; ***all'aria aperta*** outside, in the fresh air; ***corrente*** *f* ***d'aria*** draught; ***mandare all'aria qc*** ruin sth **2** (*aspetto*) appearance; (*espressione*) air; ***aver l'aria stanca*** look tired; ***ha l'aria di non capire*** he looks as if he doesn't understand; ***darsi delle -e*** give o.s. airs **3** MUS tune; *di opera* aria
aridità *f* dryness
arido dry, arid
arieggiare ⟨1f⟩ *stanza* air
ariete *m* ZO ram; ASTR **Ariete** Aries
aringa *f* (*pl* -ghe) herring
arista *f* GASTR chine of pork
aristocratico (*pl* -ci) **1** *agg* aristocratic **2** *m*, **-a** *f* aristocrat
aristocrazia *f* aristocracy
aritmetica *f* arithmetic
arma *f* (*pl* -i) weapon; ***arma da fuoco*** firearm; ***-i*** *pl* ***convenzionali*** conventional weapons; ***-i*** *pl* ***nucleari*** nuclear weapons; ***-i*** *pl* ***atomiche, biologiche e chimiche*** atomic, biological and chemical weapons; ***chiamare alle -i*** call up; *fig* ***essere alle prime -i*** be a beginner, be just starting out
armadio *m* (*pl* -di) cupboard; ***armadio a muro*** fitted cupboard
armamentario *m* (*pl* -ri) *gen spir* paraphernalia
armamento *m* armament; ***industria*** *f* ***degli -i*** armaments industry
armare ⟨1a⟩ arm; ARCHI reinforce
armarsi arm o.s. (***di*** with)
armata *f* army; MAR fleet
armato armed
armatore *m* shipowner
armatura *f* armo(u)r; (*struttura*) frame-

work
armistizio *m* (*pl* -zi) armistice
armonia *f* harmony
armonica *f* (*pl* -che) harmonica; ***armonica a bocca*** mouth organ
armonico (*pl* -ci) harmonic
armonioso harmonious
armonizzare ⟨1a⟩ *v/t & v/i* harmonize
arnese *m* tool
arnia *f* beehive
aroma *m* (*pl* -i) aroma
aromatico (*pl* -ci) aromatic
aromatizzare ⟨1a⟩ flavo(u)r
aromaterapia *f* aromatherapy
arpa *f* harp
arpione *m pesca* harpoon
arrabattarsi ⟨1a⟩ do everything one can
arrabbiarsi ⟨1k⟩ get angry
arrabbiato angry; (*idrofobo*) rabid
arrampicarsi ⟨1m & d⟩ climb
arrampicata *f* climb
arrampicatore *m*, **-trice** *f* climber; ***arrampicatore sociale*** social climber
arrangiamento *m* arrangement
arrangiare ⟨1f⟩ arrange
arrangiarsi (*accordarsi*) agree (***su*** on); (*destreggiarsi*) manage
arrecare ⟨1b & d⟩ bring; *fig* cause
arredamento *m* décor; *mobili* furniture; *arte* interior design
arredare ⟨1b⟩ furnish
arredatore *m*, **-trice** *f* interior designer
arrendersi ⟨3c⟩ surrender; *fig* give up
arrendevole soft, yielding
arrestare ⟨1b⟩ stop, halt; DIR arrest
arrestarsi stop
arresto *m* coming to a stop; DIR arrest
arretrato 1 *agg* in arrears; *paese* underdeveloped; ***numero*** *m* ***arretrato*** *di giornale* back number **2** ***-i*** *mpl* arrears
arricchire ⟨4d⟩ *fig* enrich
arricchirsi get rich
arricciare ⟨1f⟩ *capelli* curl; ***arricciare il naso*** turn up one's nose
arringa *f* (*pl* -ghe) DIR closing speech for the defence
arrivare ⟨1a⟩ arrive; ***arrivare a*** reach; ***arrivare primo*** arrive first; ***arrivare puntuale*** arrive on time; ***arrivare a fare qc*** manage to do sth; F ***non ci arriva*** he doesn't get it F, he doesn't understand
arrivederci, **arrivederla** goodbye
arrivista *m/f* (*mpl* -i) social climber
arrivo *m* arrival; SP finishing line; ***-i internazionali*** international arrivals
arrogante arrogant
arroganza *f* arrogance
arrossire ⟨4d⟩ blush
arrostire ⟨4d⟩ *carne* roast; *ai ferri* grill
arrosto *m* roast; ***arrosto d'agnello*** roast lamb
arrotolare ⟨1m & c⟩ roll up
arrotondare ⟨1a⟩ round off; *stipendio* supplement
arroventato red-hot
arruffare ⟨1a⟩ *capelli* ruffle
arruffato ruffled
arrugginire ⟨4d⟩ **1** *v/t* rust **2** *v/i* e **arrugginirsi** rust; *fig* become rusty
arruolamento *m* enlistment
arruolare ⟨1o⟩ enlist
arruolarsi enlist, join up
arsenale *m* arsenal; MAR dockyard
arso 1 *pp* → ***ardere*** **2** *agg* burnt; (*secco*) dried-up
arsura *f* blazing heat
arte *f* art; (*abilità*) gift; ***le -i*** *pl* ***figurative*** the figurative arts; ***-i*** *pl* ***grafiche*** graphic arts; ***storia*** *f* ***dell'arte*** history of art; ***un discorso fatto ad arte*** a masterly speech
artefatto *voce* disguised
artefice *m/f fig* author, architect
arteria *f* artery; ***arteria stradale*** arterial road
arterioso arterial
artico (*pl* -ci) Arctic *attr*
articolare 1 *agg* articular **2** *v/t* ⟨1m⟩ articulate; (*suddividere*) divide
articolazione *f* ANAT articulation
articolo *m* item, article; GRAM ***articolo determinativo*** definite article; GRAM ***articolo indeterminativo*** indefinite article; ***-i*** *pl* ***di consumo*** consumer goods; ***articolo di fondo*** leading article; ***articolo di prima necessità*** basic
artificiale artificial
artificio *m* (*pl* -ci) artifice; ***fuochi*** *mpl* ***d'artificio*** fireworks
artificioso *maniere* artificial
artigianale handmade, handcrafted
artigianato *m* craftsmanship
artigiano *m*, **-a** *f* craftsman; *donna* craftswoman
artiglieria *f* artillery
artiglio *m* (*pl* -gli) claw
artista *m/f* (*mpl* -i) artist
artistico (*pl* -ci) artistic
arto *m* limb
artrite *f* arthritis
artrosi *f* rheumatism
ascella *f* armpit
ascendente 1 *agg* ascending; *strada* sloping upwards; *movimento* upwards **2** *m* ASTR ascendant; *fig* influence
ascensione *f di montagna* ascent; REL Ascension
ascensore *m* lift, *Am* elevator
ascesa *f* ascent

ascesso *m* abscess
asceta *m* (*pl* -i) ascetic
ascia *f* (*pl* -sce) ax(e)
asciugacapelli *m* hairdryer
asciugamano *m* towel; ***asciugamano da bagno*** bath towel
asciugare ⟨1e⟩ dry
asciugarsi dry o.s.; ***asciugarsi i capelli*** dry one's hair
asciugatrice *f* tumble dryer
asciutto 1 *agg* dry; ***rimanere a bocca -a*** end up with nothing **2** *m*: *fig* ***trovarsi all'asciutto*** be stony broke
ascoltare ⟨1a⟩ listen to
ascoltatore *m*, **-trice** *f* listener
ascolto *m* listening; ***dare / prestare ascolto*** listen (***a*** to); ***indice*** *m* ***di ascolto*** ratings *pl*
asettico (*pl* -ci) aseptic
asfaltare ⟨1a⟩ asphalt
asfalto *m* asphalt
asfissia *f* asphyxia
asfissiare ⟨1k⟩ asphyxiate
Asia *f* Asia
asiatico (*pl* -ci) **1** *agg* Asian **2** *m*, **-a** *f* Asian
asilo *m* shelter; ***richiesta*** *f* ***di asilo politico*** request for political asylum; ***asilo infantile*** nursery school; ***asilo nido*** day nursery
asimmetrico (*pl* -ci) asymmetrical
asino *m* ass (*anche fig*)
asma *f* asthma
asmatico (*pl* -ci) asthmatic
asociale antisocial
asola *f* buttonhole
asparago *m* (*pl* -gi) spear of asparagus; ***-gi*** asparagus *sg*
aspettare ⟨1b⟩ wait for; ***aspettare un bambino*** be expecting a baby; ***farsi aspettare*** keep people waiting
aspettarsi expect; ***dovevo aspettarmelo*** I should have expected it
aspettativa *f* expectation; *da lavoro* unpaid leave
aspetto[1] *m* look, appearance; *di problema* aspect; ***sotto quest'aspetto*** from that point of view
aspetto[2] *m*: ***sala*** *f* ***d'aspetto*** waiting room
aspirante 1 *agg* TEC suction *attr* **2** *m/f* applicant
aspirapolvere *m* vacuum cleaner
aspirare ⟨1a⟩ **1** *v/t* inhale; TEC suck up **2** *v/i*: ***aspirare a qc*** aspire to sth
aspirina *f* aspirin
asportare ⟨1c⟩ take away
aspro sour; (*duro*) harsh; *litigio* bitter
assaggiare ⟨1f⟩ taste, sample
assaggio *m* (*pl* -ggi) taste, sample
assai 1 *agg* a lot of **2** *avv con verbo* a lot; *con aggettivo* very; (*abbastanza*) enough
assalire ⟨4m⟩ attack
assaltare ⟨1a⟩ → ***assalire***
assalto *m* attack; *fig* ***prendere d'assalto*** storm
assassinare ⟨1a⟩ murder; POL assassinate
assassinio *m* murder; POL assassination
assassino 1 *agg* murderous **2** *m*, **-a** *f* murderer; POL assassin
asse[1] *f* board; ***asse da stiro*** ironing board
asse[2] *m* TEC axle; MAT axis
assecondare ⟨1a⟩ support; (*esaudire*) satisfy
assediare ⟨1k⟩ besiege
assedio *m* (*pl* -di) siege
assegnare ⟨1a⟩ *premio* award; (*destinare*) assign
assegno *m* cheque, *Am* check; ***assegno in bianco*** blank cheque (*Am* check); ***assegno sbarrato*** crossed cheque (*Am* check); ***assegno turistico*** traveller's cheque, *Am* traveler's check; ***contro assegno*** cash on delivery; ***-i familiari*** child benefit; ***emettere un assegno*** issue *or* write a cheque (*Am* check)
assemblea *f* meeting; ***assemblea generale*** annual general meeting
assennato sensible
assentarsi ⟨1b⟩ go away, leave
assente absent, away; *fig* absent-minded
assenza *f* absence; ***assenza di qc*** lack of sth
assessore *m* council(l)or; ***assessore comunale*** local councillor
assetato thirsty
assetto *m* order; MAR trim
assicurare ⟨1a⟩ insure; (*legare*) secure; *lettera, pacco* register
assicurarsi make sure, ensure
assicurata *f* registered letter
assicurato 1 *agg* insured; *lettera, pacco* registered **2** *m*, **-a** *f* person with insurance
assicurazione *f* insurance; ***assicurazione dei bagagli*** luggage insurance; ***assicurazione di responsabilità civile*** liability insurance; ***assicurazione sulla vita*** life insurance; ***assicurazione casco*** comprehensive insurance
assideramento *m* exposure
assiduo (*diligente*) assiduous; (*regolare*) regular
assieme together
assillante nagging
assillare ⟨1a⟩ pester
assillo *m fig persona* pest, nuisance; (*pre-*

occupazione) nagging thought
assimilare ⟨1m⟩ assimilate
assimilazione *f* assimilation
assise *fpl*: ***Corte** f **d'assise*** *Crown Court*
assistente *m/f* assistant; ***assistente sociale*** social worker; ***assistente di volo*** flight attendant
assistenza *f* assistance; ***assistenza medica*** medical care; ***assistenza sociale*** social work; ***assistenza tecnica*** after-sales service
assistere ⟨3f⟩ **1** *v/t* assist, help; (*curare*) nurse **2** *v/i* (*essere presente*) be present (***a*** at), attend (***a*** sth)
asso *m* ace; *fig* ***piantare in asso*** leave in the lurch
associare ⟨1f⟩ take into partnership; *fig* ***associare qu a qc*** associate s.o. with sth
associarsi enter into partnership (***a*** with); (*unirsi*) join forces; (*iscriversi*) subscribe (***a*** to); (*prendere parte*) join (***a*** sth)
associazione *f* association; ***associazione per la difesa dei consumatori*** consumer association
assoggettare ⟨1b⟩ subject
assolato sunny
assolo *m inv* MUS solo
assolto *pp* → ***assolvere***
assolutamente absolutely
assoluto absolute
assoluzione *f* DIR acquittal; REL absolution
assolvere ⟨3g⟩ DIR acquit; *da un obbligo* release; *compito* carry out, perform; REL absolve, give absolution to
assomigliare ⟨1g⟩: ***assomigliare a qu*** be like s.o., resemble s.o.
assomigliarsi be like *or* resemble each other
assonnato sleepy
assorbente **1** *agg* absorbent **2** *m*: ***assorbente igienico*** sanitary towel
assorbire ⟨4c or 4d⟩ absorb
assordante deafening
assordare ⟨1a⟩ **1** *v/t* deafen **2** *v/i* go deaf
assortimento *m* assortment
assortito assorted; ***essere ben assortito con*** go well with
assorto engrossed
assuefare ⟨3aa⟩ accustom (***a*** to)
assuefarsi become accustomed (***a*** to)
assuefatto *pp* → ***assuefare***
assuefazione *f* resistance, tolerance; *agli alcolici, alla droga* addiction
assumere ⟨3h⟩ *impiegato* take on, hire; *incarico* take on
assunzione *f di impiegato* employment, hiring; REL **Assunzione** Assumption
assurdità *f* absurdity
assurdo absurd
asta *f* pole; FIN auction; ***mettere all'asta*** sell at auction, put up for auction
astemio (*pl* -mi) **1** *agg* abstemious **2** *m*, **-a** *f* abstemious person
astenersi ⟨2q⟩: ***astenersi da*** abstain from
astensione *f* abstention; ***astensione dal voto*** abstention
asterisco *m* (*pl* -chi) asterisk
astigmatico (*pl* -ci) astigmatic
astigmatismo *m* astigmatism
astinenza *f* abstinence
astio *m* (*pl* -ti) ranco(u)r
astratto abstract
astringente *m/agg* MED astringent
astro *m* star
astrologia *f* astrology
astrologo *m* (*pl* -gi), **-a** *f* astrologer
astronauta *m/f* (*mpl* -i) astronaut
astronave *f* spaceship
astronomia *f* astronomy
astronomico (*pl* -ci) astronomical
astronomo *m*, **-a** *f* astronomer
astuccio *m* (*pl* -cci) case
astuto astute
ateismo *m* atheism
ateneo *m* university
ateo *m*, **-a** *f* atheist
atlante *m* atlas
atlantico (*pl* -ci) Atlantic; ***Oceano** m **Atlantico*** Atlantic Ocean
atleta *m/f* (*mpl* -i) athlete
atletica *f* athletics; ***atletica leggera*** track and field (events)
atletico (*pl* -ci) athletic
atmosfera *f* atmosphere
atmosferico (*pl* -ci) atmospheric
atomico (*pl* -ci) atomic
atomo *m* atom
atrio *m* (*pl* -ri) foyer; ***atrio della stazione*** station concourse
atroce appalling
atrocità *f* atrocity
attaccabrighe *m o f inv* F troublemaker
attaccamento *m* attachment
attaccante *m* SP forward
attaccapanni *m inv* clothes hook; *a stelo* clothes hanger
attaccare ⟨1d⟩ **1** *v/t* attach; (*incollare*) stick; (*appendere*) hang; (*assalire*) attack; (*iniziare*) begin, start **2** *v/i* stick; F ***attaccare a fare qc*** start doing sth
attaccarsi stick; (*aggrapparsi*) hold on (***a*** to)
attacco *m* (*pl* -cchi) attack; (*punto di unione*) junction; EL socket; SCI binding; MED fit; (*inizio*) beginning
attardarsi ⟨1a⟩ linger

atteggiamento *m* attitude
atteggiarsi ⟨1f⟩: ***atteggiarsi a*** pose as
attendere ⟨3c⟩ **1** *v/t* wait for **2** *v/i*: ***attendere a*** attend to
attendibile reliable
attenersi ⟨2q⟩ stick (***a*** to)
attentare ⟨1b⟩: ***attentare a*** attack; ***attentare a la vita di qu*** make an attempt on s.o.'s life
attentato *m* attempted assassination
attento 1 *agg* attentive; ***stare attento a*** be careful of **2** *int* ***attento!*** look out!, (be) careful!
attenuante *f* extenuating circumstance
attenuare ⟨1m & b⟩ reduce; *colpo* cushion
attenuarsi lessen, decrease
attenzione *f* attention; ***attenzione!*** look out!, (be) careful!; ***far attenzione a qc*** mind *or* watch sth
atterraggio *m* (*pl* -ggi) landing; ***atterraggio di fortuna*** emergency landing
atterrare ⟨1b⟩ **1** *v/t avversario* knock down, knock to the ground; *edificio* demolish, knock down **2** *v/i* land
attesa *f* waiting; (*tempo d'attesa*) wait; (*aspettativa*) expectation
atteso *pp* → ***attendere***
attestare ⟨1b⟩ certify
attestato *m* certificate; ***attestato di frequenza*** good attendance certificate
attico *m* (*pl* -ci) attic
attiguo adjacent (***a*** to)
attimo *m* moment
attinente relevant (***a*** to)
attirare ⟨1a⟩ attract
attitudine *f* attitude; ***avere attitudine per qc*** have an aptitude for sth
attivare ⟨1a⟩ activate
attività *f* activity; *pl* FIN assets; ***che attività svolgi?*** what do you do (for a living)?; ***avere un'attività in proprio*** have one's own business
attivo 1 *agg* active; FIN ***bilancio*** *m* ***attivo*** credit balance **2** *m* FIN assets *pl*; GRAM active voice
atto *m* act; (*gesto*) gesture; *documento* deed; ***atto di fede*** act of faith; ***all'atto pratico*** when it comes to the crunch; ***mettere in atto*** carry out; ***prendere atto di*** note; DIR ***mettere agli -i*** enter in the court records
attorcigliare ⟨1g⟩, **attorcigliarsi** twist
attore *m*, **-trice** *f* actor; *donna* actress
attorno: ***attorno a qc*** round sth; ***qui attorno*** around here
attraccare ⟨1d⟩ MAR berth, dock
attracco *m* (*pl* -cchi) MAR berth
attraente attractive
attrarre ⟨3xx⟩ attract
attrattiva *f* attraction
attratto *pp* → ***attrarre***
attraversare ⟨1b⟩ *strada, confine* cross; ***attraversare un momento difficile*** be going through a bad time
attraverso across
attrazione *f* attraction
attrezzare ⟨1a⟩ equip
attrezzarsi get o.s. kitted out
attrezzato equipped
attrezzatura *f* equipment, gear F
attrezzo *m* piece of equipment; ***-i*** *pl* ***da ginnastica*** apparatus
attribuire ⟨4d⟩ attribute
attributo *m* attribute
attrice *f* → ***attore***
attrito *m* friction
attuale current
attualità *f* news; ***d'attualità*** topical
attualizzare ⟨1a⟩ update
attuare ⟨1l⟩ put into effect
attuazione *f* putting into effect
audace bold
audacia *f* boldness
audioleso 1 *agg* hearing-impaired **2** *m*, **-a** *f* person with hearing difficulties, person who is hearing-impaired
audiovisivo audiovisual
audizione *f* audition
augurare ⟨1l⟩ wish; ***augurare a qu buon viaggio*** wish s.o. a good trip
augurio *m* (*pl* -ri) wish; ***fare gli -ri di Buon Natale a qu*** wish s.o. a Merry Christmas; ***tanti -ri!*** all the best!
aula *f di scuola* class room; *di università* lecture theatre *or* room
aumentare ⟨1a⟩ **1** *v/t* increase; *prezzi* increase, raise, put up **2** *v/i* increase; *di prezzi* increase, rise, go up
aumento *m* increase, rise; ***aumento salariale*** pay rise; ***aumento dei prezzi*** increase *or* rise in prices
aureo golden
aureola *f* halo
auricolare *m* earphone
aurora *f* dawn; ***aurora boreale*** northern lights *pl*
ausiliare 1 *agg* auxiliary **2** *m* GRAM auxiliary
ausiliario (*pl* -ri) auxiliary
austerità *f* austerity
australe southern
Australia *f* Australia
australiano 1 *agg* Australian **2** *m*, **-a** *f* Australian
Austria *f* Austria
austriaco (*mpl* -ci) **1** *agg* Austrian **2** *m*, **-a** *f* Austrian

autenticare ⟨1m, d & b⟩ authenticate
autenticità *f* authenticity
autentico (*pl* -ci) authentic
autista *m/f* (*mpl* -i) driver
auto *f inv* → ***automobile***
auto ... auto ..., self- ...
autoadesivo 1 *agg* self-adhesive **2** *m* sticker
autoambulanza *f* ambulance
autobiografia *f* autobiography
autobomba *f* car bomb
autobus *m* bus; ***autobus di linea*** city bus
autocaravan *f* camper van
autocarro *m* truck, *Br* lorry
autocisterna *f* tanker
autocontrollo *m* self-control
autocritica *f* self-criticism
autodidatta *m/f* (*mpl* -i) self-taught person
autodifesa *f* self-defence, *Am* -defense
autodromo *m* motor racing circuit
autofinanziamento *m* self-financing
autogol *m inv* own goal
autografo *m* autograph
autogrill *m inv* motorway café
autolavaggio *m* (*pl* -ggi) car-wash
automa *m* (*pl* -i) robot
automatico (*pl* -ci) **1** *agg* automatic **2** *m bottone* press stud fastener
automezzo *m* motor vehicle
automobile *f* car; ***automobile da corsa*** racing car; ***automobile da noleggio*** hire car
automobilismo *m* driving; SP motor racing
automobilista *m/f* (*mpl* -i) driver
autonoleggio *m* (*pl* -ggi) car rental; (*azienda*) car-rental firm
autonomia *f* autonomy; TEC battery life
autonomo autonomous
autoradio *f inv* car radio
autore *m*, **-trice** *f* author; DIR perpetrator
autorevole authoritative
autorimessa *f* garage
autorità *f inv* authority; ***autorità portuale*** port authorities *pl*
autoritario (*pl* -ri) authoritarian
autorizzare ⟨1a⟩ authorize
autorizzazione *f* authorization
autoscatto *m* automatic shutter release
autoscuola *f* driving school
autosilo *m inv* multistorey car park, *Am* parking garage
autosoccorso *m* self-help
autostop *m*: ***fare l'autostop*** hitchhike
autostoppista *m/f* (*mpl* -i) hitchhiker
autostrada *f* motorway, *Am* highway; ***autostrada informatica*** information highway
autotreno *m* articulated lorry, *Am* semi
autovettura *f* motor vehicle
autrice *f* → ***autore***
autunno *m* autumn, *Am* fall
avambraccio *m* (*pl* -cci) forearm
avanguardia *f* avant-garde; ***all'avanguardia*** avant-garde *attr*; *azienda* leading-edge; ***essere all'avanguardia in*** lead the way in
avanti 1 *avv* in front, ahead; ***d'ora in avanti*** from now on; ***andare avanti*** *di orologio* be fast; ***mandare avanti*** be the head of; ***essere avanti nel programma*** be ahead of schedule **2** *int* ***avanti!*** come in! **3** *m* SP forward
avanzare ⟨1a⟩ **1** *v/i* advance; *fig* make progress; (*rimanere*) be left over **2** *v/t* put forward
avanzo *m* remainder; FIN surplus; ***gli -i*** *pl* the leftovers
avaria *f* failure
avariato damaged; *cibi* spoiled
avarizia *f* avarice
avaro 1 *agg* miserly **2** *m*, **-a** *f* miser
avena *f* oats *pl*
avere ⟨2b⟩ **1** *v/t* have; ***avere 20 anni*** be 20 (years old); ***avere fame / sonno*** be hungry / sleepy; ***avere caldo / freddo*** be hot / cold; ***avere qualcosa da fare*** have something to do; ***avercela con qu*** have it in for s.o.; ***che hai?*** what's up with you? **2** *v/aus* have; ***hai visto Tony?*** have you seen Tony?; ***hai vistoTony ieri?*** did you see Tony yesterday? **3** *m* FIN credit; ***dare e avere*** debits and credits; ***-i*** *mpl* wealth *sg*
avi *mpl* ancestors
aviatore *m* flyer
aviazione *f* aviation; MIL Air Force
avidità *f* avidness
avido avid
aviogetto *m* jet
AVIS *abbr* (= ***Associazione Volontari Italiani del Sangue***) Italian blood donors' association
avocado *m* avocado
avorio *m* ivory
avvalersi ⟨2r⟩: ***avvalersi di qc*** avail o.s. of sth
avvallamento *m* depression
avvantaggiare ⟨1f⟩ favo(u)r
avvantaggiarsi: ***avvantaggiarsi di qc*** take advantage of sth
avvedersi ⟨2s⟩: ***avvedersi di qc*** notice sth
avveduto astute
avvelenamento *m* poisoning
avvelenare ⟨1a⟩ poison
avvelenarsi poison o.s.

avvenimento *m* event
avvenire ⟨4p⟩ **1** *v/i* (*accadere*) happen **2** *m* future
Avvento *m* Advent
avventore *m* regular customer
avventura *f* adventure
avventurarsi ⟨1a⟩ venture
avventuriero *m*, **-a** *f* adventurer; *donna* adventuress
avventuroso adventurous
avvenuto *pp* → ***avvenire***
avverarsi ⟨1a⟩ come true
avverbio *m* (*pl* -bi) adverb
avversario (*pl* -ri) **1** *agg* opposing **2** *m*, **-a** *f* opponent
avversione *f* aversion (***per*** to)
avvertenza *f* (*ammonimento*) warning; (*premessa*) foreword; ***avere l'avvertenza di*** be careful to; ***-e*** *pl* (*istruzioni per l'uso*) instructions
avvertimento *m* warning
avvertire ⟨4b⟩ warn; (*percepire*) catch
avviamento *m* introduction; TEC, AUTO start-up
avviare ⟨1h⟩ start
avviarsi set out, head off
avviato established
avvicendare ⟨1b⟩ alternate
avvicendarsi alternate
avvicinamento *m* approach
avvicinare ⟨1a⟩ approach; ***avvicinare qc a qc*** move sth closer to sth
avvicinarsi approach, near (***a*** sth)
avvilire ⟨4d⟩ depress; *mortificare* humiliate
avvilirsi demean o.s.; *scoraggiarsi* become depressed
avvilito *scoraggiato* depressed
avvio *m*: ***dare l'avvio a qc*** get sth under way
avvisare ⟨1a⟩ (*informare*) inform, advise; (*mettere in guardia*) warn
avviso *m* notice; ***a mio avviso*** in my opinion; ***mettere qu sull'avviso*** warn s.o.
avvitare ⟨1a⟩ screw in; *fissare* screw
avvocato *m* lawyer
avvolgere ⟨3d⟩ wrap
avvolgibile *m* roller blind
avvolto *pp* → ***avvolgere***
avvoltoio *m* (*pl* -oi) vulture
azienda *f* business; ***azienda a conduzione familiare*** family business; ***azienda autonoma di soggiorno*** tourist information office
aziendale company *attr*
azionare ⟨1a⟩ activate; *allarme* set off
azionario share; ***capitale*** *m* ***azionario*** share capital
azione *f* action; (*effetto*) influence; FIN share; FIN ***azione ordinaria*** ordinary share; ***emettere -i*** issue shares
azionista *m/f* (*mpl* -i) shareholder; ***maggiore azionista*** majority shareholder
azoto *m* nitrogen
azzannare ⟨1a⟩ bite into
azzardarsi ⟨1a⟩ dare
azzardato foolhardy
azzardo *m* hazard; ***gioco*** *m* ***d'azzardo*** game of chance
azzerare ⟨1b⟩ TEC reset
azzuffarsi ⟨1a⟩ come to blows
azzurro **1** *agg* blue **2** *m colore* blue; SP ***gli -i*** *pl* the Italians, the Italian national team

B

babbo *m* F dad F, *Am* pop F; ***Babbo Natale*** Father Christmas, Santa (Claus)
babbuino *m* baboon
babordo *m* MAR port (side)
baby-sitter *m/f inv* baby-sitter
bacato wormeaten
bacca *f* (*pl* -cche) berry
baccalà *m inv* dried salt cod
baccano *m* din
bacchetta *f* rod; MUS *del direttore d'orchestra* baton; *per suonare il tamburo* (drum) stick; ***bacchetta magica*** magic wand
bacheca *f* (*pl* -che) notice board; *di museo* showcase
baciare ⟨1f⟩ kiss
baciarsi kiss (each other)
bacillo *m* bacillus
bacinella *f* basin; FOT tray
bacino *m* basin; ANAT pelvis; MAR port
bacio *m* (*pl* -ci) kiss
baco *m* (*pl* -chi) worm; ***baco da seta*** silkworm
bada *f*: ***tenere a bada qu*** keep s.o. at bay
badare ⟨1a⟩: ***badare a*** look after; (*fare attenzione a*) look out for, mind; ***badare ai fatti propri*** mind one's own business; ***non badare a spese*** spare no expense
baffo *m*: ***-i** pl* m(o)ustache; *di animali* whiskers
bagagliaio *m* (*pl* -ai) FERR luggage van, *Am* baggage car; AUTO boot, *Am* trunk
bagaglio *m* (*pl* -gli) luggage, *Am* baggage; ***deposito** m **-i*** left luggage (office), *Am* baggage checkroom; ***fare i -i*** pack; ***spedire come bagaglio appresso*** send as accompanied luggage
bagliore *m* glare; *di speranza* glimmer
bagnante *m/f* bather
bagnare ⟨1a⟩ wet; (*immergere*) dip; (*inzuppare*) soak; (*annaffiare*) water; *di fiume* flow through
bagnarsi get wet; *in mare ecc* swim, bathe
bagnato wet; ***bagnato di sudore*** dripping with sweat; ***bagnato fradicio*** soaked, wet through
bagnino *m*, ***-a** f* lifeguard
bagno *m* bath; *stanza* bathroom; *gabinetto* toilet; ***bagno di fango*** mud bath; ***fare il bagno*** have a bath; ***mettere a bagno*** soak; *nel mare ecc* (have a) swim; ***bagno degli uomini*** gents, *Am* men's room; ***bagno per donne*** ladies' (room)
bagnomaria *m inv* double boiler, bain marie
baia *f* bay
baio *m* (*pl* bai): ***cavallo** m **baio*** bay
baita *f* mountain chalet
balaustra *f* balustrade
balbettare ⟨1a⟩ stammer; *bambino* babble, prattle
balbettio *m* stammering; *di bambino* babble, prattle
balbuzie *f* stutter
balbuziente *m/f* stutterer
balcanico (*pl* -ci) Balkan; ***paesi** mpl **-ci*** Balkans
balconata *f* TEA dress circle, *Am* balcony
balcone *m* balcony
baldoria *f* revelry; ***fare baldoria*** have a riotous time
balena *f* whale
balenare ⟨1a⟩: *fig* ***gli è balenata un'idea*** an idea flashed through his mind
baleno *m* lightning; ***in un baleno*** in a flash
balestra *f* AUTO leaf spring
balia[1] *f*: ***in balia di*** at the mercy of
balia[2] *f*: ***balia asciutta*** nanny
balla *f* bale; *fig* F (*frottola*) fib F
ballare ⟨1a⟩ *v/t & v/i* dance
ballata *f* MUS ballad
ballerina *f* dancer; *di balletto* ballet dancer; *di rivista* chorus girl; (*scarpa*) ballet shoe; ZO wagtail
ballerino *m* dancer; *di balletto* ballet dancer
balletto *m* ballet
ballo *m* dance; (*il ballare*) dancing; (*festa*) ball; ***corpo** m **di ballo*** corps de ballet; ***essere in ballo*** *persona* be involved; *essere in gioco* be at stake; ***abbiamo in ballo un lavoro importante*** we've got a big job on at the moment; ***tirare in ballo qc*** bring sth up
balneare *località, centro* seaside *attr*; ***stagione** f **balneare*** swimming season; ***stabilimento** m **balneare*** lido; ***stazione** f **balneare*** seaside resort
balocco *m* (*pl* -cchi) toy
balordo 1 *agg ragionamento* shaky; *idea* stupid; *tempo, consiglio* unreliable **2** *m* (*teppista*) lout
balsamico (*pl* -ci) *aceto* balsamic; *aria* balmy
balsamo *m per i capelli* hair conditioner; *fig* balm, solace
baltico (*pl* -ci) Baltic
balzare ⟨1a⟩ jump, leap; ***balzare in piedi***

jump *or* leap to one's feet; *fig* ***un errore che balza subito agli occhi*** a mistake that suddenly jumps out at you
balzo *m* jump, leap; *fig* ***cogliere la palla al balzo*** jump at the chance
bambagia *f* cotton wool, *Am* absorbent cotton
bambinaia *f* nanny
bambino *m*, **-a** *f* child; *in fasce* baby; ***bambino in provetta*** test-tube baby
bambola *f* doll
bambolotto *m* baby boy doll
bambù *m* bamboo; ***canna*** *f* ***di bambù*** bamboo cane
banale banal
banalità *f inv* banality
banana *f* banana
banano *m* banana tree
banca *f* (*pl* -che) bank; INFOR ***banca dati*** data bank; ***banca degli organi*** organ bank
bancarella *f* stall
bancario (*pl* -ri) **1** *agg istituto, segreto* banking *attr*; *deposito, estratto conto* bank *attr* **2** *m*, **-a** *f* bank employee
bancarotta *f* bankruptcy
banchetto *m* banquet
banchiere *m* banker
banchina *f* FERR platform; MAR quay; *di strada* verge; *di autostrada* hard shoulder; ***banchina spartitraffico*** central reservation, *Am* median strip
banchisa *f* ice floe
banco *m* (*pl* -chi) FIN bank; *di magistrati, di lavoro* bench; *di scuola* desk; *di bar* bar; *di chiesa* pew; *di negozio* counter; ***banco corallino*** coral reef; ***banco di sabbia*** sandbank; ***banco del lotto*** *place that sells State lottery tickets*; ***vendere qc sotto banco*** sell sth under the counter
bancogiro *m* giro
bancone *m* (work)bench
bancomat® *m inv* (*distributore*) cash-point, *Am* ATM; (*carta*) cash card
banconota *f* banknote, *Am* bill
banda *f* band; *di delinquenti* gang; INFOR ***banda perforata*** punched tape
banderuola *f* weathercock (*anche fig*)
bandiera *f* flag
bandire ⟨4d⟩ proclaim; *concorso* announce; (*esiliare*) banish; *fig* (*abolire*) dispense with
bandito *m* bandit
banditore *m all'asta* auctioneer
bando *m* proclamation; (*esilio*) banishment
bar *m inv* bar
bara *f* coffin
baracca *f* (*pl* -cche) hut; *spreg* hovel; F ***mandare avanti la baracca*** keep one's head above water
baraccopoli *f inv* shanty town
barare ⟨1a⟩ cheat
baratro *m* abyss
barattare ⟨1a⟩ barter
baratto *m* barter
barattolo *m* tin, *Am* can; *di vetro* jar
barba *f* beard; ***farsi la barba*** shave; *fig* ***che barba!*** what a nuisance!, what a pain! F
barbabietola *f* beetroot, *Am* red beet; ***barbabietola da zucchero*** sugar beet
barbarico (*pl* -ci) barbaric
barbarie *f* barbarity
barbaro **1** *agg* barbarous **2** *m* barbarian
barbecue *m inv* barbecue
barbiere *m* barber
barboncino *m* (miniature) poodle
barbone[1] *m* (*cane*) poodle
barbone[2] *m*, **-a** *f* (*vagabondo*) tramp
barca *f* (*pl* -che) boat; ***barca a remi*** rowing boat, *Am* rowboat; ***barca a vela*** sailing boat, *Am* sailboat
barcaiolo *m* boatman
barcollare ⟨1c⟩ stagger
barcone *m* barge
barella *f* stretcher
baricentro *m* centre of gravity
barile *m* barrel
barista *m/f* (*mpl* -i) barman, *Am* bartender; *donna* barmaid; *proprietario* bar owner
baritono *m* baritone
baro *m* cardsharp
barocco (*pl* -cchi) *m/agg* Baroque
barometro *m* barometer
barone *m*, **-essa** *f* baron; *donna* baroness; *fig* ***barone dell'industria*** tycoon
barra *f* bar; MAR tiller; ***barra spaziatrice*** space bar
barricare ⟨1l & d⟩ barricade
barricata *f* barricade
barriera *f* barrier (*anche fig*); ***barriera doganale*** tariff barrier
baruffa *f* (*litigio*) squabble; (*zuffa*) brawl; ***far baruffa*** squabble; (*venirse alle mani*) brawl
barzelletta *f* joke
basare ⟨1a⟩ base
basarsi be based (***su*** on)
basco (*pl* -chi) **1** *agg* Basque **2** *m*, **-a** *f* Basque **3** *m* (*berretto*) beret
base *f* base; *fig* basis; ***in base a*** on the basis of
basette *fpl* sideburns
basilare basic
basilica *f* (*pl* -che) basilica
basilico *m* basil

bassezza *f* lowness; *fig* (*viltà, azione meschina*) vileness
basso 1 *agg* low; *di statura* short; MUS bass; *fig* despicable; ***a -a voce*** in a low voice, quietly; ***a capo basso*** with bowed head; ***a occhi -i*** looking downwards, with lowered eyes; ***fare man -a di qc*** steal sth **2** *avv*: ***in basso*** *stato* down below; ***più in basso*** further down; ***da basso*** *in una casa* downstairs **3** *m* MUS bass
bassopiano *m* (*pl* bassipiani) GEOG lowland
bassorilievo *m* (*pl* bassorilievi) bas-relief
bassotto *m* dachshund
basta → ***bastare***
bastardo *m*, **-a** *f cane* mongrel; *fig* bastard
bastare ⟨1a⟩ be enough; (*durare*) last; ***basta!*** that's enough!; ***adesso basta!*** enough is enough!; ***basta che*** (*purché*) as long as
bastimento *m* ship
bastonare ⟨1a⟩ beat
bastone *m* stick; *di pane* baguette, French stick; *fig* ***il bastone e la carota*** the carrot and stick (approach); ***bastone da passeggio*** walking stick
battaglia *f* battle (*anche fig*)
battagliero combative
battello *m* boat
battente *m di porta* wing; *di finestra* shutter
battere ⟨3a⟩ **1** *v/i* (*bussare, dare colpi*) knock **2** *v/t* beat; *record* break; ***senza battere ciglio*** without batting an eyelid; ***battere le mani*** clap (one's hands); ***battere i piedi*** stamp one's feet; ***batteva i denti dal freddo*** his teeth were chattering with cold; ***battere a macchina*** type; ***battere bandiera*** fly a flag
battersela run off
battersi fight
batteria *f* battery; MUS drums *pl*
batteri *mpl* bacteria
batterista *m/f* (*pl* -i) drummer
battesimo *m* christening, baptism
battezzare ⟨1a⟩ christen, baptize
battibaleno *m*: ***in un battibaleno*** in a flash
battibecco *m* (*pl* -cchi) argument
batticuore *m* palpitations *pl*; *fig* ***con un gran batticuore*** with great anxiety
battimano *m* applause
battipanni *m inv* carpet beater
battistero *m* baptistry
battistrada *m inv* AUTO tread
battito *m del polso* pulse; *delle ali* flap (of its wings); *della pioggia* beating; ***battito cardiaco*** heartbeat
battuta *f* beat; *in dattilografia* keystroke; MUS bar; TEA cue; *nel tennis* service; ***fare una battuta di caccia*** go hunting; ***battuta di spirito*** wisecrack; ***non perdere una battuta*** not miss a word
baule *m* trunk; AUTO boot, *Am* trunk
bavaglino *m* bib
bavaglio *m* (*pl* -gli) gag
bavero *m* collar
bazar *m inv* bazaar
bazzecola *f* trifle
bazzicare ⟨1l & d⟩ **1** *v/t un posto* haunt; *persone* associate with **2** *v/i* hang about
Bce *abbr* (= ***Banca centrale europea***) Central European Bank
beatificare ⟨1n & d⟩ beatify
beatitudine *f* bliss
beato happy; REL blessed; ***beato te!*** lucky you!
beauty-case *m inv* toilet bag
bebè *m inv* baby
beccaccia *f* (*pl* -cce) woodcock
beccare ⟨1d⟩ peck; F *fig* (*cogliere sul fatto*) nab F; F *fig malattia* catch, pick up F
beccarsi *fig bisticciare* squabble; F *malattia* catch, pick up F
beccheggiare ⟨1f⟩ MAR pitch
becchino *m* grave digger
becco *m* (*pl* -cchi) beak; *di teiera ecc* spout; CHIM ***becco Bunsen*** Bunsen burner; F ***chiudi il becco!*** shut up! F, shut it! F; ***non avere il becco di un quattrino*** be broke
befana *f kind old witch who brings presents to children on Twelfth Night*; REL Twelfth Night; *fig* old witch
beffa *f* hoax; ***farsi -e di qu*** make a fool of s.o.
beffardo scornful
beffare ⟨1b⟩ mock
beffarsi: ***beffarsi di*** mock
bega *f* (*pl* -ghe) (*litigio*) fight, argument; (*problema*) can of worms
begli → ***bello***
begonia *f* begonia
belare ⟨1b⟩ bleat
Bei *abbr* (= ***Banca europea per gli investimenti***) EIB (= European Investment Bank)
bei → ***bello***
belga (*mpl* -gi) *agg, m/f* Belgian
Belgio *m* Belgium
belladonna *f* BOT deadly nightshade
bellezza *f* beauty; ***istituto*** *m* ***di bellezza*** beauty salon; ***prodotti*** *mpl* ***di bellezza*** cosmetics
bellico (*pl* -ci) (*di guerra*) war *attr*; (*del tempo di guerra*) wartime *attr*
bellicoso bellicose
bello 1 *agg* beautiful; *uomo* handsome;

tempo fine, nice, beautiful; ***questa è -a!*** that's a good one!; ***a -a posta*** on purpose; ***hai un bel dire*** in spite of what you say; ***nel bel mezzo*** right in the middle; ***farsi bello*** get dressed up; ***scamparla bello*** have a narrow escape **2** *m* beauty; ***sul più bello*** at the worst possible moment
belva *f* wild beast
belvedere *m inv* viewpoint
bemolle *m inv* MUS flat
benché though, although
benda *f* bandage; *per occhi* blindfold
bendare ⟨1b⟩ MED bandage
bene 1 *avv* well; ***bene!*** good!; ***per bene*** properly; ***stare bene*** *di salute* be well; *di vestito* suit; ***ben ti sta!*** serves you right!; ***va bene!*** OK!; ***andare bene a qu*** *di abito* fit s.o.; *di orario, appuntamento* suit s.o.; ***di bene in meglio*** better and better; ***sentirsi bene*** feel well **2** *m* good; ***fare bene alla salute*** be good for you; ***per il tuo bene*** for your own good; ***voler bene a qu*** love s.o.; (*amare*) love s.o.; ***-i*** *pl* assets, property *sg*; ***-i*** *pl* ***di consumo*** consumer goods; ***-i*** *pl* ***culturali*** cultural heritage *sg*; ***-i*** *pl* ***immobili*** real estate *sg*; ***-i*** *pl* ***pubblici*** public property *sg*
benedetto 1 *pp* → ***benedire*** **2** *agg* blessed; REL ***acqua*** *f* ***-a*** holy water
benedire ⟨3t⟩ bless
benedizione *f* blessing
beneducato well-mannered
benefattore *m*, **-trice** *f* benefactor
beneficenza *f* charity; ***spettacolo*** *m* ***di beneficenza*** benefit (performance)
beneficio *m* (*pl* -ci) benefit; ***a beneficio di*** for the benefit of
benefico (*pl* -ci) beneficial; *organizzazione, istituto* charitable; *spettacolo* charity *attr*
benemerito worthy
benessere *m* well-being; (*agiatezza*) affluence
benestante 1 *agg* well-off **2** *m/f* person with money
benestare *m* consent
benevolenza *f* benevolence
benevolo benevolent
benigno MED benign
beninteso of course; ***beninteso che*** provided that
benone splendid
benpensante *m/f* moderate; *spreg* conformist
benservito *m*: ***dare il benservito a qu*** thank s.o. for their services
bensì but rather
bentornato welcome back
benvenuto 1 *agg* welcome **2** *m* welcome; ***dare il benvenuto a qu*** welcome s.o.
benvisto well thought of
benvolere: ***farsi benvolere da qu*** win s.o. over
benvoluto well-liked
benzina *f* petrol, *Am* gas; ***serbatoio*** *m* ***della benzina*** petrol (*Am* gas) tank; ***benzina normale*** 4-star, *Am* premium; ***benzina senza piombo*** unleaded petrol (*Am* gas); ***fare benzina*** get petrol (*Am* gas)
benzinaio *m* (*mpl* -ai), **-a** *f* petrol *or Am* gas station attendant
bere 1 *v/t* ⟨3i⟩ drink; *fig* swallow; *fig* ***darla a bere a qu*** take s.o. in **2** *m bevanda* drink; *atto* drinking
berlina *f* AUTO saloon
berlinese 1 *agg* Berlin **2** *m/f* Berliner
Berlino *m* Berlin
bermuda *mpl* Bermuda shorts
bernoccolo *m* bump; *fig* flair; ***aver il bernoccolo di qc*** have a flair for sth
berretto *m* cap
berrò → ***bere***
bersaglio *m* (*pl* -gli) target; *fig di scherzi* butt
besciamella *f* béchamel
bestemmia *f* swear-word
bestemmiare ⟨1k⟩ **1** *v/i* swear (***contro*** at) **2** *v/t* curse
bestia *f* animal; *persona brutale* beast; *persona sciocca* blockhead; *fig* ***andare in bestia*** fly into a rage
bestiale bestial; F (*molto intenso*) terrible
bestiame *m* livestock
bettola *f spreg* dive
betulla *f* birch
bevanda *f* drink
beve → ***bere***
bevibile drinkable
bevitore *m*, **-trice** *f* drinker
bevuta *f* drink; *azione* drinking
biada *f* fodder
biancheria *f* linen; ***biancheria intima*** underwear
bianco (*pl* -chi) **1** *agg* white; *foglio* blank; ***dare carta -a a qu*** give s.o. a free hand, give s.o. carte blanche; ***notte*** *f* ***-a*** sleepless night; ***sciopero*** *m* ***bianco*** work-to-rule **2** *m* white; ***bianco d'uovo*** egg white; ***lasciare in bianco*** leave blank; ***di punto in bianco*** point-blank; GASTR ***riso*** *m* ***in bianco*** rice with butter and cheese; ***mangiare in bianco*** avoid rich food; ***in bianco e nero*** *film* black and white; ***in bianco*** *assegno* blank
biancospino *m* hawthorn
biasimare ⟨1l⟩ blame

biasimevole blameworthy
biasimo *m* blame
bibbia *f* bible
biberon *m inv* baby's bottle
bibita *f* soft drink
bibliografia *f* bibliography
bibliografico (*pl* -ci) bibliographical
biblioteca *f* (*pl* -che) library; *mobile* book-case
bibliotecario *m* (*pl* -ri), **-a** *f* librarian
bicamerale POL two-chamber
bicameralismo *m* two-chamber system
bicamere *m inv* two-room flat (*Am* apartment)
bicarbonato *m*: ***bicarbonato* (*di sodio*)** bicarbonate of soda
bicchiere *m* glass; ***un bicchiere di birra*** a glass of beer; ***bicchiere da birra*** beer-glass; ***bicchiere di carta*** paper cup
bicentenario *m* bicentenary
bici *f inv* F bike F
bicicletta *f* bike, bicycle; ***andare in bicicletta*** cycle, ride a bicycle; ***bicicletta pieghevole*** folding bike; ***bicicletta da corsa*** racing bike; ***gita*** *f* ***in bicicletta*** bike ride
bidè *m inv* bidet
bidone *m* drum; *della spazzatura* (dust)-bin, *Am* garbage can; F (*imbroglio*) swindle F
biella *f* TEC connecting rod
biennale **1** *agg che si fa ogni due anni* biennial; *che dura due anni* two-year **2** ***Biennale*** *f* (***di Venezia***) Venice Arts Festival
biennio *m* (*pl* -nni) period of two years
bietola *f* beet
bifase two-phase
bifora *f* ARCHI mullioned window
biforcarsi ⟨1d⟩ fork
biforcazione *f* fork
bigamia *f* bigamy
bigamo *m*, **-a** *f* bigamist
bigiotteria *f* costume jewellery, *Am* costume jewelry; (*negozio*) jewel(l)er's
bigliettaio *m* (*pl* -ai), **-a** *f* booking office clerk; *sul treno*, *tram* conductor
biglietteria *f* ticket office, booking office; *di cinema*, *teatro* box office
biglietto *m* ticket; ***biglietto aereo*** airline *or* plane ticket; ***biglietto d'andata e ritorno*** return ticket, *Am* roundtrip ticket; ***biglietto d'auguri*** (greetings) card; ***biglietto da visita*** business card; ***biglietto di banca*** banknote, *Am* bill; ***biglietto della lotteria*** lottery ticket; ***un biglietto da 10 dollari*** a ten-dollar bill; ***fare il biglietto*** buy the ticket
bigodino *m* roller
bigotto **1** *agg* bigoted **2** *m*, **-a** *f* bigot
bikini *m inv* bikini
bilancia *f* (*pl* -ce) scales; FIN balance; ASTR ***Bilancia*** Libra; ***bilancia commerciale*** balance of trade; ***bilancia dei pagamenti*** balance of payments
bilanciare ⟨1f⟩ balance; (*pareggiare*) equal, be equal to; *fig* weigh up; FIN ***bilanciare un conto*** balance an account
bilanciarsi balance
bilancio *m* (*pl* -ci) balance; (*rendiconto*) balance sheet; ***bilancio annuale*** annual accounts; ***bilancio consuntivo*** closing balance; ***bilancio dello Stato*** national budget; ***bilancio preventivo*** budget; ***fare il bilancio*** draw up a balance sheet; *fig* take stock; ***relazione*** *f* ***annuale di bilancio*** annual report
bilaterale bilateral
bile *f* bile; *fig* rage
biliardo *m* billiards *sg*
bilico *m*: ***essere in bilico*** be precariously balanced; *fig* be undecided
bilingue bilingual
bilione *m* (*mille miliardi*) million million, *Am* trillion; (*miliardo*) billion
bilocale *m* two-room flat (*Am* apartment)
bimbo *m*, **-a** *f* child
bimensile every two weeks, *Br* fortnightly
bimestrale *ogni due mesi* bimonthly; *che dura due mesi* two-month (long)
bimotore **1** *agg* twin-engine **2** *m* twin-engine plane
binario **1** *agg* binary **2** *m* (*pl* -ri) track; (*marciapiede*) platform
binocolo *m* binoculars *pl*
biochimica *f* biochemistry
biodegradabile biodegradable
biodinamica *f* biodynamics
biografia *f* biography
biografico (*pl* -ci) biographical
biografo *m*, **-a** *f* biographer
biologia *f* biology
biologico (*pl* -ci) biological; (*verde*) organic; ***da culture -che*** organic
biologo *m* (*pl* -gi), **-a** *f* biologist
biondo blonde
bioritmo *m* biorhythm
biossido *m* dioxide
biotopo *m* biotope
biplano *m* biplane
bipolare bipolar
biposto *m/agg* two-seater
birbante *m* rascal
birichino **1** *agg* naughty **2** *m*, **-a** *f* little devil
birillo *m* skittle
biro® *f inv* biro, ballpoint (pen)
birra *f* beer; ***birra chiara*** lager; ***birra scu-***

ra brown ale; ***birra in lattina*** canned beer; ***birra alla spina*** draught (beer); ***lievito*** *m* ***di birra*** brewer's yeast; ***a tutta birra*** flat out
birreria *f pub that sells only beer*; *fabbrica* brewery
bis *m inv*, *int* encore
bisbetico (*pl* -ci) bad-tempered
bisbigliare ⟨1g⟩ whisper
bisbiglio *m* whisper
bisca *f* (*pl* -che) gambling den
biscia *f* (*pl* -sce) grass snake
biscotto *m* biscuit, *Am* cookie
bisessuale bisexual
bisestile: ***anno*** *m* ***bisestile*** leap year
bisettimanale every two weeks, *Br* fortnightly
bisnonno *m*, **-a** *f* great-grandfather; *donna* great-grandmother
bisognare ⟨1a⟩: ***bisogna farlo*** it must be done, it needs to be done; ***non bisogna farlo*** it doesn't have to be done, there's no need to do it
bisogno *m* need; (*mancanza*) lack; (*fabbisogno*) requirements; ***in caso di bisogno*** if necessary, if need be; ***avere bisogno di qc*** need sth; ***non ce n'è bisogno*** there is no need
bisognoso needy
bisonte *m* ZO bison
bistecca *f* (*pl* -cche) steak; ***bistecca ai ferri*** grilled *or Am* broiled steak; ***bistecca alla fiorentina*** charcoal grilled steak
bisticciare ⟨1f⟩ quarrel
bisticcio *m* (*pl* -cci) quarrel
bisturi *m inv* MED scalpel
bit *m inv* INFOR bit
bitter *m inv* aperitif
bivaccare ⟨1d⟩ bivouac
bivacco *m* (*pl* -cchi) bivouac
bivio *m* (*pl* -vi) junction; *fig* crossroads
bizantino Byzantine
bizzarro bizarre
bizzeffe: ***a bizzeffe*** galore
blando mild, gentle
blatta *f* cockroach
blindare ⟨1a⟩ armo(u)r-plate
blindato armo(u)red
blitz *m inv* blitz
bloccare ⟨1c & d⟩ block; MIL blockade; (*isolare*) cut off; *prezzi*, *conto* freeze
bloccarsi *di ascensore*, *persona* get stuck; *di freni*, *porta* jam
bloccaruota *m* AUTO wheel clamp, *Am* Denver boot; ***mettere il bloccaruota a*** clamp
bloccasterzo *m* AUTO steering lock
blocchetto *m per appunti* notebook
blocco *m* (*pl* -cchi) block; *di carta* pad; MIL blockade; ***blocco stradale*** road block; ***blocco dei fitti*** rent control; ***comprare in blocco*** buy in bulk; ***blocco dei prezzi*** price-freeze; ***blocco delle esportazioni*** export ban, embargo
bloc-notes *m inv* writing pad
blu blue
blusa *f* blouse
boa[1] *m inv* ZO boa constrictor
boa[2] *f* MAR buoy
boato *m* rumble
bob *m inv* SP bobsleigh, bobsled
bobbista *m/f* (*pl* -i) bobsledder
bobina *f* spool; *di film* reel; AUTO ***bobina d'accensione*** ignition coil
bocca *f* (*pl* -cche) mouth; (*apertura*) opening; ***igiene*** *f* ***della bocca*** oral hygiene; ***in bocca al lupo!*** good luck!; ***vuoi essere sulla bocca di tutti?*** do you want to be the talk of the town?; ***lasciare la bocca amara*** leave a bad taste; ***rimanere a bocca aperta*** be dumbfounded; *fig* ***rimanere a bocca asciutta*** come away empty-handed
boccaccia *f* (*pl* -cce) (*smorfia*) grimace
boccaglio *m* (*pl* -gli) *di maschera per il nuoto* mouthpiece
boccale *m* jug; *da birra* tankard
boccetta *f* small bottle
boccheggiare ⟨1f⟩ gasp
bocchino *m per sigarette* cigarette holder; MUS, *di pipa* mouthpiece
boccia *f* (*pl* -cce) (*palla*) bowl; ***gioco*** *m* ***delle -cce*** bowls
bocciare ⟨1c & f⟩ (*respingere*) reject, vote down; EDU fail; *boccia* hit, strike
bocciatura *f* failure
bocciolo *m* bud
bocconcino *m* morsel
boccone *m* mouthful; ***boccone amaro*** bitter pill
bocconi face down
body *m inv* body
boia *m inv* executioner; F ***fa un freddo boia*** it's bloody freezing F
boicottaggio *m* boycott
boicottare ⟨1c⟩ boycott
bolgia *f fig* bedlam
bolide *m* AST meteor; ***come un bolide*** like greased lightning
bolla[1] *f* bubble; MED blister
bolla[2] *f documento* note, docket; ***bolla di consegna*** delivery note
bollare ⟨1a⟩ stamp; *fig* brand
bollente boiling hot
bolletta *f* bill; ***bolletta della luce*** electricity bill; ***bolletta di consegna*** delivery note; F ***essere in bolletta*** be hard up F
bollettino *m*: ***bollettino meteorologico***

weather forecast
bollire ⟨4c⟩ *v/t & v/i* boil
bollito 1 *agg* boiled **2** *m* boiled meat
bollitore *m* kettle
bollo *m* stamp; ***bollo (di circolazione)*** road tax (disk); ***marca*** *f* ***da bollo*** revenue stamp
bomba *f* bomb; ***a prova di bomba*** bombproof; ***bomba a mano*** hand grenade; ***bomba a orologeria*** time bomb; ***bomba atomica*** atomic bomb
bombardamento *m* shelling, bombardment; (*attacco aereo*) air raid; *fig* bombardment
bombardare ⟨1a⟩ bomb; *fig* bombard
bombardiere *m* bomber
bombola *f* cylinder; ***bombola (di gas)*** gas bottle, gas cylinder
bomboniera *f* wedding keep-sake
bonaccia *f* MAR calm
bonaccione *m*, **-a** *f* kind-hearted person
bonario (*pl* -ri) kind-hearted
bonifica *f* (*pl* -che) reclamation
bonificare ⟨1m & d⟩ FIN (*scontare*) allow, discount; (*accreditare*) credit; AGR reclaim; (*prosciugare*) drain
bonifico *m* FIN (*sconto*) allowance, rebate; (*trasferimento*) (money) transfer
bontà *f inv* goodness; (*gentilezza*) kindness
bonus-malus *m inv assicurazione* no-claims bonus system
bora *f* bora (*a cold north wind*)
borbottare ⟨1a⟩ mumble
bordello *m* brothel; *fig* F bedlam F; (*disordine*) mess
bordo *m* (*orlo*) edge; MAR, AVIA, AUTO ***a bordo*** on board; ***salire a bordo*** board, go on board
boreale northern; ***aurora*** *f* ***boreale*** northern lights *pl*
borgata *f* village; (*rione popolare*) suburb
borghese 1 *agg* middle-class; ***in borghese*** in civilian clothes; ***poliziotto*** *m* ***in borghese*** plainclothes policeman **2** *m/f* middle-class person; ***piccolo borghese*** petty bourgeois, lower middle-class person
borghesia *f* middle classes *pl*
borgo *m* (*pl* -ghi) village
boria *f* conceit
borico (*pl* -ci): ***acido*** *m* ***borico*** boric acid
borotalco *m* talcum powder, talc
borraccia *f* (*pl* -cce) flask
borsa *f* bag; (*borsetta*) handbag, *Am* purse; *per documenti* briefcase; FIN Stock Exchange; ***borsa della spesa*** shopping bag; ***borsa termica*** cool bag; ***borsa di studio*** scholarship; ***borsa merci*** Commodities Exchange; ***borsa nera*** black market; ***borsa valori*** Stock Exchange; ***bollettino*** *m* (o ***listino*** *m*) ***di borsa*** share index; ***metter mano alla borsa*** put one's hand in one's pocket
borsaiolo *m*, **-a** *f* pickpocket
borseggio *m* (*pl* -ggi) pickpocketing
borsellino *m* purse, *Am* coin purse
borsetta *f* handbag, *Am* purse
borsista *m/f* (*mpl* -i) *speculatore* speculator; *studente* scholarship holder
boscaglia *f* brush, scrub
boscaiolo *m* woodcutter
bosco *m* (*pl* -schi) wood
boscoso wooded
bossolo *m di proiettili* (shell) case
BOT, bot *abbr* (= ***Buono Ordinario del Tesoro***) treasury bond
botanica *f* botany
botanico (*pl* -ci) **1** *agg* botanical **2** *m*, **-a** *f* botanist
botola *f* trapdoor
botta *f* blow; (*rumore*) bang; ***fare a -e*** come to blows
botte *f* barrel; ARCHI ***volta*** *f* ***a botte*** barrel vault
bottega *f* (*pl* -ghe) shop; (*laboratorio*) workshop
bottegaio *m* (*pl* -ai), **-a** *f* shopkeeper
botteghino *m* box office; (*del lotto*) *sales outlet for lottery tickets*
bottiglia *f* bottle
bottiglieria *f* wine merchant's
bottino *m* loot
botto *m* (*rumore*) bang; ***di botto*** all of a sudden
bottone *m* button; ***bottone automatico*** press-stud, *Am* snap fastener; ***attaccare un bottone a qu*** sew a button on for s.o.; *fig* buttonhole s.o.
bovino 1 *agg* bovine **2** *m*: ***-i*** *pl* cattle
box *m inv per auto* lock-up garage; *per bambini* playpen; *per cavalli* loose box
boxe *f* boxing
bozza *f* draft; TIP proof
bozzetto *m* sketch
bozzolo *m* cocoon
braccetto *m*: ***a braccetto*** arm in arm
bracciale *m* bracelet; (*fascia*) armband; *di orologio* watch strap
braccialetto *m* bracelet
bracciante *m/f* day labo(u)rer
bracciata *f nel nuoto* stroke
braccio *m* (*pl* le braccia *e* i bracci) arm; ***braccio di mare*** sound; ***a -a aperte*** with open arms; ***portare in braccio qu*** carry s.o.; *fig* ***essere il braccio destro di qu*** be s.o.'s right-hand man; ***incrociare le -a*** fold one's arms; *fig* go on strike

bracciolo *m* arm(rest)
bracco *m* (*pl* -cchi) hound
bracconiere *m* poacher
brace *f* embers *pl*; ***alla brace*** char-grilled, *Am* -broiled
braciola *f* GASTR chop
branca *f* (*pl* -che) branch (*anche fig*)
branchia *f* gill
branco *m* (*pl* -chi) ZO *di cani, lupi* pack; *di pecore, uccelli* flock; *fig spreg* gang
brancolare ⟨1l⟩ grope
branda *f* camp-bed
brandello *m* shred, scrap; ***a -i*** in shreds *or* tatters
brano *m di testo, musica* passage
brasato *m* GASTR *di manzo* braised beef
Brasile *m* Brazil
brasiliano **1** *agg* Brazilian **2** *m*, **-a** *f* Brazilian
bravata *f* boasting; *azione* bravado
bravo good; (*abile*) clever, good; ***bravo!*** well done!
bravura *f* skill
break *m inv* break
breccia *f* (*pl* -cce) breach
bretella *f* (*raccordo*) slip road, *Am* ramp; ***-e*** *pl* braces, *Am* suspenders
breve short; ***in breve*** briefly, in short
brevettare ⟨1a⟩ patent
brevetto *m* patent; *di pilota* licence, *Am* license; ***ufficio*** *m* ***dei -i*** patent office
brevità *f* shortness
brezza *f* breeze
bricco *m* (*pl* -cchi) jug, *Am* pitcher
briciola *f* crumb
briciolo *m fig* grain, scrap
bricolage *m* do-it-yourself
briga *f* (*pl* -ghe): ***darsi la briga di fare qc*** take the trouble to do sth; ***attaccar briga con qu*** pick a quarrel with s.o.
brigadiere *m* MIL sergeant
brigante *m* bandit
brigata *f* party, group; MIL brigade
briglia *f* rein; *fig* ***a briglia sciolta*** at breakneck speed
brillante **1** *agg* sparkling; *colore* bright; *fig* brilliant **2** *m* diamond
brillare ⟨1a⟩ **1** *v/i* shine **2** *v/t mina* blow up
brillo tipsy
brina *f* hoar-frost
brindare ⟨1a⟩ drink a toast (***a*** to), toast (***a*** sth); ***brindare alla salute di qu*** drink to *or* toast s.o.
brindisi *m inv* toast
brio *m* liveliness; MUS brio
brioche *f inv* brioche
brioso lively
britannico (*pl* -ci) **1** *agg* British **2** *m*, **-a** *f* Briton
brivido *m di freddo, spavento* shiver; *di emozione* thrill
brizzolato *capelli* greying, *Am* graying
brocca *f* (*pl* -cche) jug, *Am* pitcher
broccato *m* brocade
broccoli *mpl* broccoli *sg*
brodo *m* (clear) soup; *di pollo, di manzo, di verdura* stock; ***minestra*** *f* ***in brodo*** soup; ***brodo ristretto*** consommé
brodoso watery, thin
bronchiale bronchial
bronchite *f* bronchitis
broncio *m*: ***avere*** (*o* ***tenere***) ***il broncio*** sulk; ***mi ha tenuto il broncio per tre giorni*** he sulked for three days
bronco *m* (*pl* -chi) ANAT bronchus
broncopolmonite *f* bronchopneumonia
brontolare ⟨1l⟩ grumble; *di stomaco* rumble
brontolio *m* grumble; *di stomaco* rumble
brontolone **1** *agg* grumbling **2** *m*, **-a** *f* grumbler
bronzo *m* bronze
bruciapelo: ***a bruciapelo*** point-blank
bruciare ⟨1f⟩ **1** *v/t* burn; (*incendiare*) set fire to; ***bruciare le tappe*** forge ahead **2** *v/i* burn; *fig di occhi* sting
bruciarsi burn o.s.
bruciato burnt; *dal sole* scorched, parched
bruciatura *f* burn
bruciore *m* burning sensation; ***bruciore di stomaco*** heartburn
bruco *m* (*pl* -chi) grub; (*verme*) worm
brufolo *m* spot
brughiera *f* heath, moor
brulicare ⟨1l & d⟩ swarm
brulichio *m* swarming
brullo bare
bruno brown; *capelli* dark
brusco (*pl* -schi) sharp; *persona, modi* brusque, abrupt; (*improvviso*) sudden
brutale brutal
brutalità *f inv* brutality
bruto **1** *agg*: ***forza*** *f* ***-a*** brute force **2** *m* brute
brutta *f*: (***copia*** *f*) ***brutta*** rough copy
bruttezza *f* ugliness
brutto ugly; (*cattivo*) bad; *tempo, tipo, situazione, affare* nasty; ***una -a notizia*** bad news
Bruxelles *f* Brussels
buca *f* (*pl* -che) hole; (*avvallamento*) hollow; *del biliardo* pocket; ***buca delle lettere*** letter-box, *Am* mailbox
bucaneve *m inv* snowdrop
bucare ⟨1d⟩ make a hole in; (*pungere*) prick; *biglietto* punch; ***bucare una gomma*** have a puncture, *Am* have a flat

(tire); *fig* ***avere le mani bucate*** be a spendthrift
bucarsi prick o.s.; *con droga* shoot up
bucato *m* washing, laundry; ***fare il bucato*** do the washing
buccia *f* (*pl* -cce) peel
bucherellare ⟨1b⟩ make holes in; ***bucherellato dai tarli*** riddled with woodworm
buco *m* (*pl* -chi) hole; ***buco dell' ozono*** hole in the ozone layer; ***buco nero*** black hole
budello *m* (*pl* le budella) gut; (*vicolo*) alley
budget *m inv* budget
budino *m* pudding
bue *m* (*pl* buoi) ox, *pl* oxen; *carne* beef
bufalo *m* buffalo
bufera *f* storm; ***bufera di neve*** snowstorm
buffet *m inv* buffet; *mobile* sideboard
buffo funny
buffone *m*, **-a** *f* buffoon, fool; *di corte* fool, jester
bugia[1] *f* candle holder
bugia[2] *f* (*menzogna*) lie; ***dire -e*** tell lies, lie
bugiardo 1 *agg* lying **2** *m*, **-a** *f* liar
bugigattolo *m* cubby-hole
buio 1 *agg* dark **2** *m* darkness; ***al buio*** in the dark; ***buio pesto*** pitch dark
bulbo *m* BOT bulb
Bulgaria *f* Bulgaria
bulgaro 1 *agg* Bulgarian **2** *m*, **-a** *f* Bulgarian
bulletta *f* tack
bullone *m* bolt
buoi → ***bue***
buon → ***buono***
buonafede *f*: ***in buonafede*** in good faith
buonanotte *int*, *f* good night; ***dare la buonanotte*** say good night
buonasera *int*, *f* good evening; ***dare la buonasera*** say good evening
buongiorno *int*, *m* good morning, hello; ***dare il buongiorno*** say good morning *or* hello
buongustaio *m* (pl -ai), **-a** *f* gourmet
buongusto *m* good taste; ***di buongusto*** in good taste
buono 1 *agg* good; (*valido*) good, valid; *momento*, *occasione* right; ***alla -a*** informal, casual; ***-a fortuna*** good luck; ***a buon mercato*** cheap; ***di buon'ora*** early; ***di buon grado*** willingly; ***avere buon naso*** have a good sense of smell; ***buono a nulla*** good-for-nothing **2** *m* good; FIN bond; (*tagliando*) coupon, voucher; ***buono del tesoro*** Treasury bond; ***buono pasto*** *o* ***mensa*** luncheon voucher; ***buono regalo*** gift voucher; ***buono sconto*** money-off coupon
buonsenso *m* common sense
buonuscita *f* (*liquidazione*) golden handshake
burattino *m* puppet
burbero gruff, surly
burla *f* practical joke, trick
burlarsi ⟨1a⟩: ***burlarsi di qu*** make fun of s.o.
burlone *m*, **-a** *f* joker
burocrate *m* bureaucrat
burocratico (*pl* -ci) bureaucratic
burocrazia *f* bureaucracy
burrasca *f* (*pl* -sche) storm
burrascoso stormy
burro *m* butter; GASTR ***al burro*** in butter; ***tenero come il burro*** soft as butter
burrone *m* ravine
bussare ⟨1a⟩ knock; ***bussare alla porta*** knock at the door
bussola *f* compass; ***bussola magnetica*** magnetic compass; ***perdere la bussola*** lose one's bearings
busta *f per lettera* envelope; *per documenti* folder; (*astuccio*) case; ***busta paga*** pay packet
bustarella *f* bribe
bustina *f*: ***bustina di tè*** tea bag
busto *m* ANAT torso; *scultura* bust; (*corsetto*) girdle
buttafuori *m inv* TEA call-boy; *di locale notturno* bouncer
buttare ⟨1a⟩ **1** *v/i* BOT shoot, sprout **2** *v/t* throw; ***buttare via*** throw away; *fig* waste; ***buttare giù*** knock down; *lettera* scribble down; *boccone* gulp down; F ***buttare la pasta*** put the pasta on
buttarsi throw o.s.; *fig* have a go (***in*** at); ***buttarsi giù*** (*saltare*) jump; *fig* lose heart, get discouraged
by-pass *m inv* by-pass
byte *m inv* INFOR byte

C

ca. *abbr* (= ***circa***) ca (= circa)
c.a. *abbr* (= ***corrente alternata***) AC (= alternating current)
cabaret *m inv* cabaret
cabina *f di nave*, *aereo* cabin; *di ascensore*, *funivia* cage; ***cabina balneare*** beach hut; ***cabina di guida*** driver's cab; ***cabina elettorale*** polling booth; ***cabina telefonica*** phone box, *Am* pay phone
cabinato *m* cabin cruiser
cabriolè, **cabriolet** *m inv* convertible
cacao *m* cocoa
caccia (*pl* -cce) **1** *f* hunting; ***andare a caccia*** go hunting (***di*** sth); ***dare la caccia a qu*** chase after s.o. **2** *m* MIL *aereo* fighter; *nave* destroyer
cacciagione *f* GASTR game
cacciare ⟨1f⟩ hunt; (*scacciare*) drive out; (*ficcare*) shove; ***cacciare*** (***via***) chase away
cacciarsi: ***dove ti eri cacciato?*** where did you get to?
cacciatora *f*: GASTR ***alla cacciatora*** stewed
cacciatore *m*, **-trice** *f* hunter; ***cacciatore di frodo*** poacher
cacciavite *m inv* screwdriver
cachemire *m inv* cashmere
cachet *m inv* MED capsule
cacio *m* cheese
cactus *m inv* cactus
cadavere *m* corpse
cadente: ***stella*** *f* ***cadente*** shooting star
cadere ⟨2c⟩ fall; *di edificio* fall down; *di capelli*, *denti* fall out; *di aereo* crash; ***cadere dalle nuvole*** be thunderstruck; ***lasciar cadere*** drop; ***lasciarsi cadere su una poltrona*** collapse into an armchair
caduta *f* fall; ***caduta massi*** falling rocks; ***caduta di tensione*** drop in voltage
caffè *m inv* coffee; *locale* café; ***caffè corretto*** *espresso with a shot of alcohol*; ***caffè macchiato*** *espresso with a splash of milk*
caffeina *f* caffeine; ***senza caffeina*** caffeine free
caffellatte *m inv hot milk with a small amount of coffee*
caffettiera *f* (*bricco*) coffee pot; (*macchinetta*) coffee maker
cafone *m* boor
cagionevole delicate, sickly
cagliare ⟨1g⟩ curdle
cagna *f* bitch
calabrese *agg*, *m/f* Calabrian
calabrone *m* hornet
calamari *mpl* squid
calamita *f* magnet
calamità *f inv* calamity; ***calamità naturale*** natural disaster
calante: ***luna*** *f* ***calante*** waning moon
calare ⟨1a⟩ **1** *v/t* lower; *prezzi* reduce, lower **2** *v/i di vento* drop; *di prezzi* fall, come down; *di sipario* fall; *di sole* set, go down; ***calare di peso*** lose weight; ***è calato del 20%*** it's down 20%
calca *f* throng
calcagno *m* (*pl* i calcagni *o* le calcagna) heel
calcare[1] ⟨1d⟩ (*pigiare*) press down; *con i piedi* tread; *parole* emphasize; ***calcare la mano*** exaggerate; ***calcare le scene*** become an actor, take up acting
calcare[2] *m* limestone
calcareo chalky
calce[1] *f* lime
calce[2] *m fig*: ***in calce*** below
calcestruzzo *m* concrete
calciare ⟨1f⟩ kick
calciatore *m* footballer, soccer player
calcina *f* (*malta*) mortar
calcinaccio *m* (*pl* -cci) (*intonaco*) bit of plaster; *di muro* bit of rubble
calcio *m* (*pl* -ci) kick; *attività* football, soccer; MIL butt; CHIM calcium; ***giocare al calcio*** play football *or* soccer; ***campionato*** *m* ***di calcio*** football *or* soccer championship; ***calcio di rigore*** penalty kick
calco *m* (*pl* -chi) mo(u)ld
calcolare ⟨1l⟩ calculate; (*valutare*) weigh up
calcolatore *m* calculator; *fig* calculating person; *elettronico* computer
calcolatrice *f* calculator; ***calcolatrice tascabile*** pocket calculator; ***calcolatrice da tavolo*** desktop calculator
calcolo *m* calculation; MED stone; ***calcolo preventivo*** estimate
caldaia *f* boiler
caldarrosta *f* roast chestnut
caldo **1** *agg* warm; (*molto caldo*) hot; ***non mi fa né caldo né freddo*** it's all the same to me **2** *m* warmth; *molto caldo* heat; ***ho caldo*** I'm warm; I'm hot
calendario *m* (*pl* -ri) calendar; ***calendario delle manifestazioni*** calendar of events

C

calibrare ⟨11⟩ calibrate
calibro *m* calibre, *Am* caliber; TEC callipers
calice *m* goblet; REL chalice
calle *f a Venezia* lane
calligrafia *f* calligraphy
callo *m* corn; ***fare il callo a qc*** become hardened to sth
calma *f* calm; ***prendersela con calma*** take it easy
calmante *m* sedative
calmare ⟨1a⟩ calm; *dolore* soothe
calmarsi *di dolore* ease (off)
calmo calm
calo *m di peso* loss; *dei prezzi* drop, fall
calore *m* warmth; *intenso* heat
caloria *f* calorie
caloroso *fig* warm
calpestare ⟨1a⟩ walk on; *fig* trample over
calunnia *f* slander
calunniare ⟨1k⟩ slander
calura *f* heat
calvario *m* REL Calvary; *fig* ordeal
calvizie *f* baldness
calvo bald
calza *f da donna* stocking; *da uomo* sock; ***calza elastica*** support stocking; ***fare la calza*** knit
calzamaglia *f* tights *pl*, *Am* pantyhose; *da ginnastica* leotard
calzare 1 *v/t scarpe* put on; (*indossare*) wear **2** *v/i fig* fit
calzascarpe *m* shoehorn
calzatoio *m* (*pl* -oi) shoehorn
calzature *fpl* footwear *sg*
calzaturificio *m* (*pl* -ci) shoe factory
calzettone *m* knee sock
calzino *m* sock
calzolaio *m* (*pl* -ai) shoemaker
calzoleria *f* shoe shop
calzoncini *mpl* shorts; ***calzoncini da bagno*** (swimming) trunks
calzone *m* GASTR *folded-over pizza*
calzoni *mpl* trousers, *Am* pants
camaleonte *m* chameleon
cambiale *f* bill (of exchange); ***cambiale in bianco*** blank bill; ***girare una cambiale*** endorse a bill; ***pagare una cambiale*** hono(u)r a bill; ***cambiale a vista*** sight bill; ***cambiale a scadenza fissa*** fixed-term bill
cambiamento *m* change; ***cambiamento climatico*** climate change
cambiare ⟨1k⟩ **1** *v/t* change; (*scambiare*) exchange; AUTO ***cambiare la marcia*** change gear; ***cambiare casa*** move (house); ***cambiare idea*** change one's mind **2** *v/i e* **cambiarsi** change
cambiavalute *m* o *f inv* currency dealer, money-broker
cambio *m* (*pl* -bi) change; FIN, (*scambio*) exchange; AUTO, TEC gear; ***cambio automatico*** automatic gearshift; ***cambio dell'olio*** oil change; ***cambio d'indirizzo*** change of address; ***in cambio*** in exchange (***di*** for); ***dare il cambio a qu*** relieve s.o.; ***fare cambio con qu*** swap *or* exchange with s.o.
camelia *f* camellia
camera *f* room; ***camera da letto*** bedroom; ***camera singola*** single room; ***camera matrimoniale*** double room; ***camera a due letti*** twin room; ***camera d'albergo*** hotel room; ***camera blindata*** strong room; ***Camera dei Deputati*** *House of Commons*; FOT ***camera oscura*** darkroom; ***camera d'aria*** inner tube; ***camera dell'industria e del commercio*** chamber of commerce
cameraman *m inv* cameraman
camerata *f stanza* dormitory; *in ospedale* ward
cameriera *f* waitress; (*domestica*) maid
cameriere *m* waiter; (*domestico*) manservant
camerino *m* dressing room
camice *m di medico* white coat; *di chirurgo* gown
camicetta *f* blouse
camicia *f* (*pl* -cie) shirt; ***camicia sportiva*** sports shirt; ***camicia da notte*** nightdress
caminetto *m* fireplace
camino *m* chimney; (*focolare*) fireplace
camion *m inv* truck, *Br* lorry
camioncino *m* van
camionista *m* (*pl* -i) truck driver, *Br* lorry driver
cammello *m* camel; *stoffa* camel hair
camminare ⟨1a⟩ walk; (*funzionare*) work, go
camminata *f* walk
cammino *m*: ***un'ora di cammino*** an hour's walk; ***mettersi in cammino*** set out
camomilla *f* camomile; (*infuso*) camomile tea
camoscio *m* (*pl* -sci) chamois; ***scarpe*** *fpl* ***di camoscio*** suede shoes
campagna *f* country; *fig*, POL campaign; ***vivere in campagna*** live in the country; ***campagna pubblicitaria*** advertising campaign; ***campagna elettorale*** election campaign
campana *f* bell
campanello *m* bell; *della porta* doorbell; ***campanello d'allarme*** alarm bell
campanile *m* bell tower
campanula *f* campanula

campare ⟨1a⟩ live; ***campare alla giornata*** live for the moment
campeggiare ⟨1f⟩ camp
campeggiatore *m* camper
campeggio *m* camping; *posto* camp site
camper *m inv* camper van
campestre rural
camping *m* camp site
campionario *m* (*pl* -ri) samples
campionato *m* championship; ***campionato mondiale*** world championship
campione *m* sample; (*esemplare*) specimen; *di stoffa* swatch; SP champion
campo *m* field; ***campo giochi*** playground; ***campo di golf*** golf course; ***campo di calcio*** football *or* soccer pitch; ***campo di concentramento*** concentration camp; ***campo da tennis*** tennis court; ***campo di ricerche*** area of research; ***campo sportivo*** sports ground; ***campo profughi*** refugee camp
camposanto *m* (*pl* camposanti) cemetery
camuffare ⟨1a⟩ disguise
Canada *m* Canada
canadese 1 *agg* Canadian **2** *m/f* Canadian **3** *f half-litre* (*Am -liter*) *bottle of beer*
canale *m* channel; *artificiale* canal
canalizzazione *f* channelling; (*conduttura*) pipe
canapa *f* hemp
canarino *m* canary
cancellare ⟨1b⟩ cross out; *con gomma* rub out, erase; INFOR delete; *debito* write off, cancel; *appuntamento* cancel
cancellata *f* railings *pl*
cancelleria *f*: ***articoli*** *mpl* ***di cancelleria*** stationery
cancelliere *m* chancellor; DIR clerk of the court
cancello *m* gate
cancerogeno carcinogenic
cancrena *f* gangrene
cancro *m* MED cancer; ASTR, GEOG ***Cancro*** Cancer
candeggiante *m* stain remover
candeggina *f* bleach
candela *f* candle; ***candela d'accensione*** spark plug
candelabro *m* candelabra
candeliere *m* candlestick
candidarsi ⟨1l⟩ stand (for election)
candidato *m*, **-a** *f* candidate
candidatura *f* candidacy, candidature
candido pure white; (*sincero*) frank; (*innocente*) innocent, pure; (*ingenuo*) naive
canditi *mpl* candied fruit
cane *m* dog; *di arma da fuoco* hammer, cock; ***cane da guardia*** guard dog; ***freddo cane*** freezing cold; ***non c'era un cane*** there wasn't a soul about; F ***fatto da -i*** botched F
canestro *m* basket
canguro *m* kangaroo
canile *m* (*casotto*) kennel; *luogo* kennels
canino 1 *agg* dog *attr* **2** *m* (*dente*) canine (tooth)
canna *f* reed; (*bastone*) stick; P joint P; ***canna fumaria*** flue; ***canna da pesca*** fishing rod; ***canna da zucchero*** sugar cane
cannella *f* GASTR cinnamon
cannelloni *mpl* cannelloni *sg*
cannibale *m* cannibal
cannocchiale *m* telescope
cannonata *f fig*: ***è una cannonata*** it's terrific
cannone *m* MIL gun, cannon; (*asso*) ace
cannuccia *f* (*pl* -cce) straw
canoa *f* canoe
canone *m* FIN rental (fee); RAD, TV licence (fee); (*norma*) standard
canottaggio *m a pagaie* canoeing; *a remi* rowing; ***circolo*** *m* ***di canottaggio*** rowing club
canottiera *f* vest
canotto *m* rowing boat, *Am* rowboat; ***canotto pneumatico*** rubber dinghy; ***canotto di salvataggio*** lifeboat
cantante *m/f* singer
cantare ⟨1a⟩ sing
cantautore *m*, **-trice** *f* singer-songwriter
cantiere *m* building *or* construction site; MAR shipyard
cantina *f* cellar; *locale* wineshop
canto[1] *m* (*canzone*) song; (*il cantare*) singing; ***canto popolare*** folk song; ***canto del cigno*** swan song
canto[2] *m*: ***dal canto mio*** for my part; ***d'altro canto*** on the other hand
cantonata *f* (*grosso sbaglio*) blunder
cantone *m* POL canton; ***Lago*** *m* ***dei Quattro Cantoni*** Lake Lucerne
canzonare ⟨1a⟩ tease
canzone *f* song; ***la solita canzone*** the same old story
canzoniere *m* songbook
caos *m* chaos
caotico (*pl* -ci) chaotic
C.A.P. *abbr* (= ***Codice di Avviamento Postale***) postcode, *Am* zip code
capace (*abile*) capable; (*ampio*) large, capacious; ***capace di fare qc*** capable of doing sth
capacità *f inv* ability; (*capienza*) capacity; FIN ***capacità di acquisto*** purchasing power; INFOR ***capacità di memoria*** memory
capanna *f* hut

C

capannone *m* shed; AVIA hangar
caparra *f* FIN deposit
capello *m* hair; ***-i*** *pl* hair *sg*; GASTR ***-i d'angelo*** *very thin noodles*; ***ne ho fin sopra i -i!*** I've had it up to here!; ***per un capello*** by the skin of one's teeth
capezzolo *m* nipple
capiente large, capacious
capienza *f* capacity
capigliatura *f* hair
capillare MED capillary
capire ⟨4d⟩ understand; ***capisco*** I see; ***si capisce!*** naturally!, of course!; ***far capire qc a qu*** make s.o. understand sth, get s.o. to see sth; ***farsi capire*** make o.s. understood
capitale 1 *agg* capital; *fig* major **2** *f città* capital **3** *m* FIN capital; ***capitale d'esercizio*** working capital; ***capitale disponibile*** available capital; ***capitale fisso*** fixed capital; ***capitale iniziale*** start-up capital; ***fuga*** *f* ***di -i*** flight of capital; ***capitale proprio*** equity capital; ***capitale sociale*** share capital
capitalismo *m* capitalism
capitalista *agg*, *m/f* (*mpl* -i) capitalist
capitaneria *f*: ***capitaneria di porto*** port authorities *pl*
capitano *m* captain
capitare ⟨1l⟩ *di avvenimento* happen; *di persona* find o.s.; ***se mi capita l'occasione di venire*** if I get a chance to come; ***capitare in cattive mani*** fall into the wrong hands; ***mangio dove capita*** I don't always eat in the same place; ***capitare a proposito*** come along at the right time; ***sono cose che capitano*** these things happen
capitello *m* ARCHI capital
capitolo *m* chapter; ***avere voce in capitolo*** have a say in the matter
capitombolo *m* tumble, fall
capo *m* ANAT head; *persona* head, chief, boss F; GEOG cape; ***capo del governo*** head of government; ***capo dello Stato*** head of state; ***capo di vestiario*** item of clothing; ***da capo*** from the beginning; ***ti seguirò in capo al mondo*** I'll follow you to the ends of the earth; ***per sommi -i*** briefly; ***andare a capo*** start a new paragraph; ***non venire a capo di nulla*** be unable to come to any kind of conclusion; ***questa storia non ha né capo né coda*** this story just doesn't make sense
capobanda *m/f di delinquenti* ringleader
capodanno *m* New Year's Day
capofamiglia *m/f* head of the family
capofitto: ***a capofitto*** headlong
capogiro *m* dizzy spell
capogruppo *m/f* group leader; POL leader
capolavoro *m* masterpiece
capolinea *m* terminus
capolista *f* SP leaders *pl*
capoluogo *m* (*pl* capoluoghi) principal town
capomastro *m* (*pl* capomastri) master builder
caporeparto *m/f* (*mpl* capireparto, *fpl* caporeparto) *di fabbrica* foreman; *donna* forewoman; *di ufficio* superintendent
caposala *m/f* (*mpl* capisala, *fpl* caposala) *in ospedale* ward sister; *uomo* charge nurse
caposaldo *m* (*pl* capisaldi) stronghold
caposezione *m/f* (*mpl* capisezione, *fpl* caposezione) section chief
capostazione *m/f* (*mpl* capistazione, *fpl* capostazione) station master
capostipite *m/f* founder
capotavola: ***a capotavola*** at the head of the table
capote *f inv* AUTO hood, (soft) top
capotreno *m/f* (*mpl* capitreno, *fpl* capotreno) guard
capoufficio *m/f* (*mpl* capiufficio, *fpl* capoufficio) supervisor
capoverso *m* (*pl* capoversi) paragraph; TIP indent(ation)
capovolgere ⟨3d⟩ turn upside down; *piani* upset; *situazione* reverse
capovolgersi turn upside down; *di barca* capsize
capovolgimento *m* complete change
capovolto *pp* → ***capovolgere***
cappa *f* (*mantello*) cloak; *di cucina* hood; ***cappa del camino*** cowl
cappella *f* chapel
cappellano *m* chaplain
cappelletti *mpl pasta, shaped like little hats, with meat, cheese and egg filling*
cappello *m* hat; ***cappello di paglia*** straw hat; ***senza cappello*** hatless; ***mettersi il cappello*** put one's hat on
cappero *m* caper
cappio *m* noose
cappone *m* capon; ***far venire la pelle di cappone a qu*** give s.o. the creeps
cappotto *m* coat
cappuccino *m bevanda* cappuccino
cappuccio *m* (*pl* -cci) hood; *di penna* top, cap
capra *f* (nanny)goat; (*cavalletto*) trestle
capretto *m* kid
capriccio *m* (*pl* -cci) whim; *di bambini* tantrum; ***fare i -i*** have tantrums
capriccioso capricious; *bambino* naughty; *tempo* changeable

Capricorno ASTR, GEOG Capricorn
capriola *f* somersault
capriolo *m* roe deer; GASTR venison
capro *m* billy goat; ***capro espiatorio*** scapegoat
capsula *f* capsule; *di dente* crown; ***capsula spaziale*** space capsule
captare ⟨1a⟩ RAD pick up
carabina *f* carbine
carabiniere *m* police officer
caraffa *f* carafe
caramella *f* sweet
caramello *m* caramel
carato *m* carat
carattere *m* character; (*caratteristica*) characteristic; (*lettera*) character, letter; **-i** *pl* TIP typeface; INFOR font
caratteristica *f* characteristic
caratteristico (*pl* -ci) characteristic
caratterizzare ⟨1a⟩ characterize
caravan *m inv* caravan
caravanning *m inv* caravanning
carboidrato *m* carbohydrate
carbone *m* coal
carbonella *f* charcoal
carburante *m* fuel
carburatore *m* carburet(t)or
carcassa *f di animale* carcass; TEC (*intelaiatura*) frame; MAR, F wreck
carcerato *m*, **-a** *f* prisoner
carcerazione *f* imprisonment; ***carcerazione preventiva*** preventive detention
carcere *m* (*pl* le -ri) jail, prison
carceriere *m*, **-a** *f* jailer, gaoler
carciofo *m* artichoke
cardellino *m* goldfinch
cardiaco (*pl* -ci) cardiac, heart
cardinale 1 *agg* cardinal; ***punto** m **cardinale*** cardinal point **2** *m* REL cardinal
cardine *m* hinge
cardiologia *f* cardiology
cardiologo *m* (*pl* -gi), **-a** *f* (*pl* -ghe) heart specialist, cardiologist
cardo *m* thistle
carena *f* MAR keel
carenza *f* lack (***di*** of)
carestia *f* shortage
carezza *f* caress
carezzare ⟨1a⟩ caress
cargo *m aereo* air freighter; *nave* cargo ship
cariato: ***dente** m **cariato*** decayed tooth
carica *f* (*pl* -che) (*incarico*) office; *fig* (*slancio*, *energia*) drive; TEC load; MIL (*attacco*) charge; SP tackle; ***in carica*** in office; ***durata** f **della carica*** term of office; ***tornare alla carica*** insist
caricare ⟨1d & 1⟩ load; MIL charge; *orologio* wind up
caricarsi overload o.s. (***di*** with); PSI psych o.s. up; ***caricarsi di debiti*** get heavily into debt
caricatura *f* caricature
caricaturista *m/f* (*mpl* -i) caricaturist
carico (*pl* -chi) **1** *agg* loaded; EL charged; *caffè* strong; *colore* deep; *orologio* wound up **2** *m* load; FIN charge, expense; MAR cargo; DIR ***a carico di*** (*contro*) against; ***essere a carico di qu*** be dependent on s.o.; ***carico utile*** payload; ***lettera** f* (o ***polizza** f*) ***di carico*** bill of lading; ***carico di lavoro*** workload
carie *f inv* tooth decay
carino (*grazioso*) pretty; (*gentile*) nice
carisma *m* charisma
carità *f* charity; ***per carità!*** for goodness sake!, for pity's sake!
carnagione *f* complexion
carnale carnal; ***fratello** m **carnale*** blood brother
carne *f* flesh; GASTR meat; ***carne di maiale / manzo*** pork / beef; ***carne tritata*** mince
carneficina *f* slaughter
carnevale *m* carnival
carnivoro *m* carnivore
carnoso fleshy
caro 1 *agg* dear; (*costoso*) dear, expensive; ***mi è molto caro*** I am very fond of him / it; ***a caro prezzo*** dearly **2** *avv* a lot; ***costare caro*** be very expensive; *fig* have a high price **3** *m* dear; **-i** *pl* loved ones, family
carogna *f* carrion; F swine
carosello *m* merry-go-round
carota *f* carrot
carotide *f* carotid artery
carovana *f* caravan
carovita *m* high cost of living; ***indennità** f **di carovita*** cost of living allowance
carpa *f* carp
carpentiere *m* carpenter
carpire ⟨4d⟩: ***carpire qc a qu*** get sth out of s.o.
carponi on all fours
carrabile → ***carraio***
carraio: ***passo** m **carraio*** driveway
carreggiata *f* roadway; ***rimettersi in carreggiata*** *fig* catch up
carrello *m* trolley; AVIA undercarriage; ***carrello elevatore*** fork-lift truck; ***carrello portabagagli*** baggage trolley, *Am* baggage cart
carretto *m* cart
carriera *f* career; ***fare carriera*** come a long way; ***di gran carriera*** at top speed
carriola *f* wheelbarrow
carro *m* cart; AST Bear; FERR ***carro bestia-***

C

me cattle truck; FERR ***carro merci*** goods wagon, *Am* freight car; ***carro armato*** tank; ***carro attrezzi*** breakdown van, tow truck, *Am* wrecker; ***carro funebre*** hearse
carrozza *f* FERR carriage; ***carrozza con cuccette*** sleeper; ***carrozza ristorante*** restaurant car
carrozzella *f per bambini* pram; *per invalidi* wheelchair
carrozzeria *f* bodywork, coachwork
carrozziere *m* AUTO (*progettista*) (car) esigner; (*costruttore*) coachbuilder; *chi fa riparazioni* panel beater
carrozzina *f* pram
carta *f* paper; GASTR (*menù*) menu; GEOG ***carta geografica*** map; ***carta assegni*** cheque (guarantee) card; ***carta da bollo*** official stamped paper; ***carta da gioco*** (playing) card; ***carta da lettere*** note paper; ***carta da macero*** waste paper (for pulping); ***carta da parati*** wallpaper; ***carta d'argento*** *card that entitles people over a certain age to reduced fares*; ***carta di credito*** credit card; ***carta d'identità*** identity card; AVIA ***carta d'imbarco*** boarding pass; ***carta igienica*** toilet paper; ***carta stagnola*** silver paper; GASTR tinfoil; ***carta stradale*** road map; ***carta telefonica*** phone card; ***carta velina*** tissue paper; AUTO ***carta verde*** green card; ***carta vetrata*** sandpaper
cartacarbone *f* carbon paper
cartamodello *m* (*pl* cartamodelli) pattern
cartamoneta *f inv* paper money
cartapecora *f* parchment, vellum
cartapesta *f* papier-mâché
cartastraccia *f* waste paper
carteggio *m* (*pl* -ggi) correspondence
cartella *f* (*borsa*) briefcase; *di alunno* schoolbag, satchel; *copertina per documenti* folder, file; *foglio dattiloscritto* page; ***cartella clinica*** medical record
cartellino *m* (*etichetta*) label; *con prezzo* price tag; (*scheda*) card; SP ***cartellino giallo / rosso*** yellow / red card; ***cartellino orario*** clocking-in card
cartello *m* sign; *nelle dimostrazioni* placard; FIN cartel; ***cartello stradale*** road sign
cartellone *m pubblicitario* hoarding, *Am* billboard; TEA bill
cartiera *f* paper mill
cartilagine *f* cartilage
cartina *f* GEOG map; (*bustina*) packet; *per sigarette* cigarette paper
cartoccio *m* (*pl* -cci) paper bag; *a cono* paper cone; GASTR ***al cartoccio*** baked in tinfoil, en papillote
cartografia *f* cartography
cartoleria *f* stationer's
cartolina *f* postcard; ***cartolina illustrata*** picture postcard; ***cartolina postale*** postcard
cartoncino *m* (thin) cardboard; (*biglietto*) card
cartone *m* cardboard; ***-i*** *pl* ***animati*** cartoons
cartuccia *f* (*pl* -cce) cartridge
casa *f edificio* house; (*abitazione*) home; FIN company; ***casa di cura*** nursing home; ***casa editrice*** publishing house; ***casa dello studente*** hall of residence; ***casa a schiera*** terraced house; ***casa unifamiliare*** single-family dwelling; ***casa per le vacanze*** holiday home; ***case popolari*** council houses; ***seconda casa*** second home; ***essere di casa*** be like one of the family; ***dove stai di casa?*** where do you live?; ***cambiar casa*** move (house); ***fatto in casa*** home-made; ***andare a casa*** go home; ***essere a casa*** be at home; SP ***giocare in / fuori casa*** play at home / away
casalinga *f* (*pl* -ghe) housewife
casalingo (*pl* -ghi) domestic; (*fatto in casa*) home-made; *persona* home-loving; ***cucina*** *f* ***-a*** home cooking; ***-ghi*** *mpl* household goods
cascare ⟨1d⟩ fall (down); *fig* ***cascarci*** fall for it
cascata *f* waterfall
cascina *f* (*casa colonica*) farmhouse; (*caseificio*) dairy farm
casco *m* (*pl* -chi) helmet; *dal parrucchiere* hair dryer; ***-chi*** *pl* ***blu*** UN forces, blue berets F
caseggiato *m* (*edificio*) block of flats, *Am* apartment block
caseificio *m* (*pl* -ci) dairy
casella *f di schedario* pigeon hole; (*quadratino*) square; ***casella postale*** post office box
casellario *m* (*pl* -ri) pigeon holes; ***casellario giudiziario*** criminal records (office)
casello *m autostradale* toll booth
casereccio (*pl* -cci) homemade
caserma *f* barracks
casino P *m* brothel; (*rumore*) din, racket; (*disordine*) mess; ***casino di caccia*** hunting lodge
casinò *m inv* casino
caso *m* case; (*destino*) chance; (*occasione*) opportunity; ***caso d'emergenza*** emergency; ***per caso*** by chance; ***a caso*** at random; (***in***) ***caso che*** in case; ***in caso contrario*** should that not be the case; ***in***

ogni caso in any case, anyway; ***in nessun caso*** under no circumstances; ***nel peggiore dei -i*** if the worst comes to the worst
casolare *m* farmhouse
caspita! goodness (gracious)!, good heavens!
cassa *f* case; *di legno* crate; *di negozio* till; *sportello* cash desk, cashpoint; (*banca*) bank; ***cassa acustica*** speaker; ***cassa comune*** kitty; ***cassa continua*** night safe; ***cassa da morto*** coffin; ***cassa di risparmio*** savings bank; ***cassa integrazione*** *form of income support*; ***cassa malattia*** *department administering health insurance scheme*; ***cassa toracica*** ribcage; ***orario*** *m* ***di cassa*** opening hours
cassaforte *f* (*pl* casseforti) safe
cassapanca *f* (*pl* cassapanche) chest
casseruola *f* (sauce)pan
cassetta *f* box; *per frutta, verdura* crate; (*musicassetta*) cassette; ***cassetta delle lettere*** (*buca*) post box, *Am* mailbox; (*casella*) letterbox, *Am* mailbox; ***cassetta del pronto soccorso*** first-aid kit; ***cassetta di sicurezza*** strong box; ***successo*** *m* ***di cassetta*** box office hit; ***pane*** *m* ***a cassetta*** sliced loaf
cassetto *m* drawer; AUTO ***cassetto portaoggetti*** glove compartment
cassettone *m* chest of drawers; ***soffitto*** *m* ***a -i*** panelled ceiling
cassiere *m*, **-a** *f* cashier; *di banca* teller; *di supermercato* checkout assistant
cassonetto *m* dustbin
casta *f* caste
castagna *f* chestnut
castagno *m* chestnut (tree)
castano *capelli* chestnut; *occhi* brown
castello *m* castle; TEC (*impalcatura*) scaffolding; ***letti*** *mpl* ***a castello*** bunk beds
castigare ⟨1e⟩ punish
castigo *m* (*pl* -ghi) punishment
castità *f* chastity
castoro *m* beaver
castrare ⟨1a⟩ castrate; *gatto* neuter; *femmina di animale* spay
casual 1 *agg* casual **2** *m* casual clothes, casual wear
casuale chance, casual
casualità *f* chance nature
cataclisma *m* (*pl* -i) disaster
catacomba *f* catacomb
catalizzatore *m* catalyst; AUTO catalytic converter; ***catalizzatore a tre vie*** three-way catalytic converter
catalogare ⟨1m & e⟩ catalog(ue)
catalogo *m* (*pl* -ghi) catalog(ue); ***catalogo di vendita per corrispondenza*** mail order catalog(ue)
catapecchia *f* shack
catapultare ⟨1a⟩ catapult
catarifrangente *m* reflector; *lungo la strada* reflector, *Br* cat's eye
catarro *m* catarrh
catasta *f* pile, heap
catasto *m* land register
catastrofe *f* catastrophe
catastrofico (*pl* -ci) catastrophic
categoria *f* category; *di albergo* class; ***categoria a rischio*** at risk category
categorico (*pl* -ci) categoric(al)
catena *f* chain; ***-e*** *pl* ***da neve*** snow chains; ***reazione*** *f* ***a catena*** chain reaction; ***catena di montaggio*** assembly line; ***catena montuosa*** mountain range, chain of mountains
catenaccio *m* (*pl* -cci) bolt; SP defensive tactics
cateratta *f* (*chiusa*) sluice(gate); (*cascata*) falls; MED cataract
catino *m* basin
catrame *m* tar
cattedra *f* *scrivania* desk; *incarico di insegnamento* teaching post; ***cattedra universitaria*** university chair
cattedrale *f* cathedral
cattiveria *f* wickedness; *di bambini* naughtiness; *azione* nasty thing to do; *parole crudeli* nasty thing to say
cattività *f* captivity
cattivo bad; *bambino* naughty, bad; ***con le buone o con le -e*** by hook or by crook
cattolicesimo *m* (Roman) Catholicism
cattolico (*pl* -ci) **1** *agg* (Roman) Catholic **2** *m*, **-a** *f* (Roman) Catholic
cattura *f* capture; (*arresto*) arrest
catturare ⟨1a⟩ capture; (*arrestare*) arrest
caucciù *m* rubber
causa *f* cause; (*motivo*) reason; DIR lawsuit; ***fare causa*** sue (***a qu*** s.o.); ***a causa di*** because of; ***per causa tua*** because of you
causale *f* cause, reason
causare ⟨1a⟩ cause
cautela *f* caution; (*precauzione*) precaution
cauto cautious
cauzione *f* (*deposito*) security; *per la libertà provvisoria* bail
Cav. *abbr* (= **Cavaliere**) *Italian title awarded for services to the country*
cava *f* quarry
cavalcare ⟨1d⟩ ride
cavalcata *f* ride
cavalcavia *m inv* flyover
cavalcioni: ***a cavalcioni*** astride

C

cavaliere *m* rider; *accompagnatore* escort; *al ballo* partner
cavalla *f* mare
cavallerizzo *m*, **-a** *f* horseman; *donna* horsewoman
cavalletta *f* grasshopper
cavalletto *m* trestle; FOT tripod; *da pittore* easel
cavallo *m* horse; *scacchi* knight; *dei pantaloni* crotch; ***cavallo da corsa*** race horse; AUTO ***cavallo vapore*** horsepower; ***andare a cavallo*** go riding; ***vivere a cavallo di due secoli*** straddle two centuries
cavallone *m* breaker
cavalluccio *m* (*pl* -cci): ***cavalluccio marino*** sea horse
cavare ⟨1a⟩ take out; *dente* take out, extract; ***cavarsela*** manage, get by
cavarsi: ***cavarsi da un impiccio*** get out of trouble
cavatappi *m inv* corkscrew
caverna *f* cave
cavernoso: ***una voce -a*** a deep voice
cavia *f* guinea pig (*anche fig*)
caviale *m* caviar
caviglia *f* (*pl* -glie) ANAT ankle
cavillo *m* quibble
cavità *f inv* cavity
cavo 1 *agg* hollow **2** *m* cable; ***cavo d'accensione*** plug lead; ***cavo di avviamento*** jump leads; ***cavo di ormeggio*** mooring rope; ***cavo da rimorchio*** tow rope; ***cavo in fibra ottica*** optic fibre cable; ***televisione f via cavo*** cable TV
cavolfiore *m* cauliflower
cavolo *m* cabbage; ***cavolo di Bruxelles*** Brussels sprout; ***cavolo rapa*** kohlrabi; ***cavolo verzotto*** Savoy cabbage
cazzo *m* P dick P, prick P
CC *abbr* (= ***Carabinieri***) Italian police force
cc *abbr* (= ***centimetri cubici***) cc (= cubic centimetres)
c.c. *abbr* (= ***corrente continua***) DC (= direct current)
c/c *abbr* (= ***conto corrente***) current account, *Am* checking account
CD *m inv* CD; ***lettore*** *m* ***CD*** CD player
CD-Rom *m inv* CD-Rom; ***drive*** *m* ***per CD-Rom*** CD-Rom drive
ce → ***ci*** (before ***lo, la, li, le, ne***)
c'è there is
cecchino *m* sniper
cece *m* chickpea
cecità *f* blindness
ceco 1 *agg* Czech **2** *m*, **-a** *f* Czech
cecoslovacco (*pl* -cchi) **1** *agg* Czechoslovakian **2** *m*, **-a** *f* Czechoslovakian

cedere ⟨3a⟩ **1** *v/t* (*dare*) hand over, give up; (*vendere*) sell, dispose of; ***cedere il posto*** give up one's seat **2** *v/i* give in, surrender (***a*** to); *muro*, *terreno* collapse, give way; ***non cedere!*** don't give in!
cedevole soft
cedibile transferable, assignable
cedola *f* coupon; ***cedola di consegna*** delivery note
cedro *m del Libano* cedar
CEE, Cee *abbr* (= ***Comunità Economica Europea***) EEC (= European Economic Community)
cefalo *m* ZO mullet
ceffone *m* slap
celebrare ⟨1l & b⟩ celebrate
celebrazione *f* celebration
celebre famous
celebrità *f inv* fame; (*persona*) celebrity
celere fast, speedy, swift; ***posta*** *f* ***celere*** swiftair®, *Am* Fedex®
celeste sky blue; (*divino*) heavenly (*anche fig*)
celibato *m* celibacy
celibe 1 *agg* single, unmarried **2** *m* bachelor
cella *f* cell
cellula *f* cell; ***cellula fotoelettrica*** photoelectric cell; ***cellula solare*** solar cell
cellulare 1 *agg* cell *attr*; ***telefono*** *m* ***cellulare*** mobile phone, *Am* cell(ular) phone **2** *m* prison van; (*telefono*) mobile
cellulite *f* cellulite
cellulosa *f* cellulose
celtico (*pl* -ci) Celtic
cemento *m* cement; ***cemento armato*** reinforced concrete
cena *f* supper, evening meal; *importante, con ospiti* dinner; ***cena in piedi*** buffet
cenacolo *m* PITT Last Supper
cenare ⟨1a⟩ have supper; *formalmente* dine
cencio *m* (*pl* -ci) rag, piece of cloth; (*per spolverare*) duster; ***bianco come un cencio*** white as a sheet
cenere *f* ash; ***le Ceneri*** *fpl* Ash Wednesday
cenno *m* sign; *della mano* wave; *del capo* nod; *con gli occhi* wink; (*breve notizia*) mention; (*allusione*) hint; ***far cenno a qu*** *con la mano* wave to s.o.; *con il capo* nod to s.o.; *con gli occhi* wink at s.o.; ***far cenno di voler andare*** signal that one wants to leave; ***far cenno di sì*** nod (one's head); ***far cenno di no*** shake one's head
cenone *m* feast, banquet; ***cenone di San Silvestro*** *special celebratory meal on New Year's Eve*
censimento *m* census

censura *f* censorship
censurare ⟨1a⟩ censor
centenario (*pl* -ri) **1** *agg* hundred-year-old **2** *m* (*persona*) centenarian; (*anniversario*) centenary
centesimo 1 *agg* hundredth **2** *m*: ***centesimo di dollaro*** cent; ***badare al centesimo*** count every penny
centigrado *m* centigrade
centimetro *m* centimetre, *Am* -meter; ***centimetro cubo*** cubic centimetre (*Am* -meter); ***centimetro quadrato*** square centimetre (*Am* -meter)
centinaio *m* (*pl* le centinaia) hundred; ***un centinaio di*** about a hundred, a hundred or so
cento hundred; ***per cento*** per cent; ***cento per cento*** one hundred per cent; ***cento di questi giorni*** many happy returns
centrale 1 *agg* central **2** *f* station, plant; ***centrale atomica*** *o* ***nucleare*** nuclear power station
centralinista *m/f* switchboard operator
centralino *m* switchboard
centralizzare ⟨1a⟩ centralize
centrare ⟨1b⟩ TEC centre, *Am* center; ***centrare il bersaglio*** hit a bull's eye
centrifuga 1 *agg* centrifugal **2** *f* spin-dryer; TEC centrifuge
centrifugare ⟨1e & m⟩ spin-dry; TEC centrifuge
centro *m* centre, *Am* center; *di bersaglio* bull's eye; ***centro commerciale*** shopping centre; ***centro della città*** town *or* city centre, *Am* downtown; ***centro residenziale*** residential area; ***centro storico*** old (part of) town; ***fare centro*** hit the bull's eye; *fig* hit the nail on the head
ceppo *m*: ***ceppo bloccarruota*** wheel clamp; ***mettere il ceppo a*** clamp
cera[1] *f* wax; *per lucidare* polish; ***cera da scarpe*** shoe polish
cera[2] *f* look; ***avere una brutta cera*** look awful
ceralacca *f* sealing wax
ceramica *f* (*pl* -che) *arte* ceramics *sg*; *oggetto* piece of pottery
cerata *f* oilskins *pl*
cerca *f*: ***in cerca di …*** in search of …
cercare ⟨1d⟩ **1** *v/t* look for **2** *v/i*: ***cercare di fare*** try to do
cerchia *f* circle
cerchio *m* (*pl* -chi) circle
cerchione *m* TEC rim
cereale 1 *agg* grain *attr* **2** ***-i*** *mpl* grain, cereals
cerealicoltura *f* grain farming
cerebrale: ***commozione*** *f* ***cerebrale*** concussion
cerimonia *f* ceremony; REL service; **-e** *pl* (*convenevoli*) pleasantries; ***fare -e*** stand on ceremony; ***senza tante -e*** (*bruscamente*) unceremoniously
cerimoniale *m/agg* ceremonial
cerimonioso ceremonious
cerino *m* (wax) match
cernia *f* grouper
cerniera *f* hinge; ***cerniera lampo*** zip (fastener), *Am* zipper
cernita *f* selection, choice
cero *m* (large) candle
cerotto *m* (sticking) plaster
certezza *f* certainty
certificare ⟨1m & d⟩ certify
certificato *m* certificate; ***certificato medico*** medical certificate; ***certificato di garanzia*** guarantee; ***certificato di nascita*** birth certificate; ***certificato di sana e robusta costituzione*** certificate of good health
certo 1 *agg* (*sicuro*) certain, sure (***di*** of; ***che*** that); ***un certo signor Federici*** a (certain) Mr Federici; ***ci vuole un certo coraggio*** it takes (some) courage; ***di una -a età*** of a certain age; ***-i*** some; ***-e cose non si dicono*** there are some things you just don't say; ***un certo non so che*** a certain something, a certain je ne sais quoi **2** *avv* (*certamente*) certainly; (*naturalmente*) of course; ***certo che …*** surely … **3** *pron*: ***-i, -e*** some, some people
certosa *f* Carthusian monastery
cervello *m* (*pl* i cervelli, le cervella) brain; GASTR brains; ***farsi saltare le -a*** blow one's brains out; ***lambiccarsi il cervello*** rack one's brains
cervo *m* deer; *carne* venison; ***cervo volante*** stag beetle
cesareo: ***taglio*** *m* ***cesareo*** C(a)esarean (section), C section
cesellare ⟨1b⟩ chisel
cesello *m* chisel
cesoie *fpl* shears
cespuglio *m* (*pl* -gli) bush, shrub
cessare ⟨1b⟩ stop, cease
cessate il fuoco *m* ceasefire
cessazione *f di contratto* termination; ***cessazione di esercizio*** closure, going out of business
cessione *f* transfer, handover
cesso *m* P bog P
cesta *f* basket
cestinare ⟨1a⟩ throw away, bin F
cestino *m* little basket; *per la carta* wastepaper basket
cesto *m* basket
cetaceo *m* cetacean
ceto *m* (social) class; ***ceto medio*** middle

class
cetra *f* zither
cetriolino *m* gherkin
cetriolo *m* cucumber
cf., cfr. *abbr* (= ***confronta***) cf (= compare)
cg *abbr* (= ***centigrammo***) cg (= centigram)
CGIL *abbr* (= ***Confederazione Generale Italiana del Lavoro***) Italian trade union organization
chalet *m inv* chalet
charter *m inv* charter
che 1 *agg* what; ***a che cosa serve?*** what is that for?; ***che brutta giornata!*** what a filthy day! **2** *pron persona*: soggetto who; *persona*: *oggetto* who, that, *fml* whom; *cosa* that, which; ***che?*** what?; ***ciò che*** what; ***non c'e di che*** don't mention it, you're welcome **3** *cong dopo il comparativo* than; ***sono tre anni che non la vedo*** I haven't seen her for three years
check-in *m inv* AVIA check-in; ***fare il check-in*** check in
chemioterapia *f* chemotherapy, chemo F
chetichella: ***alla chetichella*** stealthily
chi who; ***di chi è il libro?*** whose book is this? ***a chi ha venduto la casa?*** who did he sell the house to?; ***c'è chi dice che*** some people say that; ***chi ... chi*** some ... others
chiacchiera *f* chat; (*maldicenza*) gossip; (*notizia infondata*) rumo(u)r; ***far due -e con qu*** have a chat with s.o.
chiacchierare ⟨1l⟩ chat, chatter; *spreg* gossip
chiacchierata *f* chat
chiacchierone 1 *agg* talkative, chatty; (*pettegolo*) gossipy **2** *m*, **-a** *f* chatterbox; (*pettegolo*) gossip
chiamare ⟨1a⟩ call; TELEC (tele)phone, ring; ***andare a chiamare qu*** go and get s.o., fetch s.o.; ***mandare a chiamare qu*** send for s.o.; (*convocare*) call in; TELEC ***chiamare in teleselezione*** call direct, dial direct
chiamarsi be called; ***come ti chiami?*** what's your name?; ***mi chiamo ...*** my name is ...
chiamata *f* call; TELEC (tele)phone call; ***chiamata a carico del destinatario*** reverse charge call, *Am* collect call; ***chiamata interurbana*** long-distance call
chiara *f* egg white
chiarezza *f* clarity
chiarimento *m* clarification
chiarire ⟨4d⟩ clarify
chiarirsi become clear
chiaro 1 *agg* clear; *colore* light, pale; (*luminoso*) bright; ***chiaro e tondo*** definite **2** *m* light; ***chiaro di luna*** moonlight; ***mettere in chiaro*** (*appurare*) throw light on; (*spiegare*) clarify **3** *avv* plainly; (*con franchezza*) frankly
chiaroscuro *m* PITT chiaroscuro
chiaroveggente *m/f* clairvoyant
chiasso *m* din, racket; ***fare chiasso*** make a din *or* racket; *fig* cause a sensation
chiassoso noisy
chiatta *f* barge; ***ponte*** *m* ***di -e*** pontoon bridge
chiave 1 *agg inv* key **2** *f* key; MUS clef; ***chiave d'accensione*** ignition key; ***chiave della macchina*** car key; ***chiave inglese*** spanner, *Am* monkey wrench; ***sotto chiave*** under lock and key
chiavistello *m* bolt
chiazza *f* (*macchia*) stain; *sulla pelle*, *di colore* patch
chic *inv* chic, stylish, elegant
chicco *m* (*pl* -chi) grain; (*di caffè*) bean; ***chicco d'uva*** grape
chiedere ⟨3k⟩ *per sapere* ask (***di*** about); *per avere* ask for; (*esigere*) demand, require; ***chiedere qc a qu*** ask s.o. sth; ***chiedere di qu*** (*chiedere notizie di*) ask about s.o.; *per parlargli* ask for s.o.; ***chiedere un piacere a qu*** ask s.o. a favo(u)r, ask a favo(u)r of s.o.; ***chiedere scusa a qu*** apologize to s.o.
chiedersi wonder (***se*** whether)
chiesa *f* church
chiesto *pp* → ***chiedere***
chiglia *f* MAR keel
chilo *m* kilo; ***mezzo chilo*** half a kilo
chilogrammo *m* kilogram
chilometraggio *m* AUTO *mileage*
chilometrico *indennità* per kilometre
chilometro *m* kilometre, *Am* -meter; ***-i*** *pl* ***all'ora*** kilometres (*Am* -meters) per hour
chilowatt *m inv* kilowatt
chimica *f* chemistry
chimico (*pl* -ci) **1** *agg* chemical; ***sostanze*** *fpl* ***-che*** chemicals **2** *m*, **-a** *f* chemist
chinare ⟨1a⟩ *testa* bend; *occhi* lower
chinarsi stoop, bend down
chincaglierie *fpl* knick-knacks, ornaments
chinino *m* quinine
chioccia *f fig* mother hen
chiocciola *f* snail; ***scala*** *f* ***a chiocciola*** spiral staircase
chiodato: SP ***scarpe*** *fpl* ***-e*** spikes
chiodo *m* nail; ***chiodo di garofano*** clove; *fig* ***chiodo fisso*** obsession, idée fixe; ***roba da -i!*** it's unbelievable!
chioma *f* mane; *di cometa* tail
chiosco *m* (*pl* -chi) kiosk
chiostro *m* cloister

C

chip *m inv* chip
chiromante *m/f* palmist
chiropratico *m*, **-a** *f* chiropractor
chirurgia *f* surgery
chirurgico (*pl* -ci) surgical
chirurgo *m* (*pl* -ghi) surgeon
chissà who knows; (*forse*) maybe
chitarra *f* guitar
chitarrista *m/f* (*mpl* -i) guitarist
chiudere ⟨3b⟩ close, shut; *a chiave* lock; *strada* close off; *gas*, *luce* turn off; *fabbrica*, *negozio per sempre* close down, shut down; *fig* ***chiudere un occhio*** turn a blind eye; FIN ***chiudere in pareggio*** break even; ***chiudere in perdita / in attivo*** show a loss/a profit
chiudersi *di porta*, *ombrello* close, shut; *di ferita* heal up; ***chiudersi in se stesso*** withdraw into o.s.
chiunque anyone; *relativo* whoever
chiusa *f di fiume* lock; *di discorso* conclusion
chiuso 1 *pp* → ***chiudere*** **2** *agg* closed, shut; *a chiave* locked; (*nuvoloso*) cloudy, overcast; *persona* reserved
chiusura *f* closing, shutting; AUTO ***chiusura centralizzata*** central locking; ***chiusura lampo*** zip (fastener), *Am* zipper; ***ora*** *f* ***di chiusura*** closing time
choc *m inv* shock
ci 1 *pron* us; ***non ci ha parlato*** he didn't speak to us; ***ci siamo divertiti molto*** we had a great time; ***ci vogliamo bene*** we love each other; ***ci penso*** I'm thinking about it **2** *avv* here; (*lì*) there; ***ci sei?*** are you there?; ***c'è …*** there is …; ***ci sono …*** there are …; ***ci vuole tempo*** it takes time
C.ia *abbr* (= ***compagnia***) Co. (= company)
ciabatta *f* slipper
cialda *f* wafer
ciambella *f* GASTR *type of cake, baked in a ring-shaped mo(u)ld*; (*salvagente*) lifebelt
cianfrusaglia *f* knick-knack
ciao! *nell'incontrarsi* hi!; *nel congedarsi* 'bye!, cheerio!
ciarlatano *m* charlatan
ciarpame *m* junk
ciascuno 1 *agg* each; (*ogni*) every **2** *pron* everyone
cibarsi ⟨1a⟩ feed on, eat (***di*** sth)
cibernetica *f* cybernetics
cibo *m* food; ***-i*** *pl* foodstuffs, foods; ***cibo pronto*** fast food
cicala *f* (*insetto*) cicada
cicalino *m* buzzer, bleeper
cicatrice *f* scar
cicatrizzare ⟨1a⟩, **cicatrizzarsi** heal
cicca *f* (*pl* -che) (*mozzicone*) stub, butt; (*gomma da masticare*) (chewing) gum
ciccia *f* (*grasso*) flab
ciccione *m*, **-a** *f* fatty
cicciottello chubby
cicerone *m* guide
ciclabile: ***pista*** *f* ***ciclabile*** bike *or* cycle path
ciclamino *m* cyclamen
ciclico cyclical
ciclismo *m* cycling, bike riding
ciclista *m/f* (*mpl* -i) cyclist
ciclistico bike *attr*, cycle *attr*
ciclo *m* cycle
ciclomotore *m* moped
ciclone *m* cyclone
cicloturismo *m* cycling holidays
cicogna *f* stork
cicoria *f* chicory
cieco (*pl* -chi) **1** *agg* blind; ***vicolo*** *m* ***cieco*** dead end, blind alley **2** *m*, **-a** *f* blind man; *donna* blind woman
cielo *m* sky; REL heaven; ***grazie al cielo*** thank heaven(s)
cifra *f* figure; (*monogramma*) monogram; (*somma*) amount, sum; (*codice*) cipher, code; ***cifra d'affari*** turnover; ***numero*** *m* ***di sei -e*** six digit number
cifrato (*messaggio*) in cipher, in code
ciglio *m* (*pl* le ciglia) ANAT eyelash; (*pl* i cigli) (*bordo*) edge
cigno *m* swan
cigolare ⟨1l⟩ squeak
cigolio *m* squeak
Cile *m* Chile
cilecca: ***far cilecca*** *di arma da fuoco* misfire
cileno 1 *agg* Chilean **2** *m*, **-a** *f* Chilean
ciliegia *f* (*pl* -ge) cherry
ciliegio *m* (*pl* -gi) cherry (tree)
cilindrata *f* TEC cubic capacity; ***automobile*** *f* ***di media cilindrata*** middle of the range car
cilindrico (*pl* -ci) cylindrical
cilindro *m* cylinder; *cappello* top hat
cima *f* top; ***in cima all'armadio*** on top of the wardrobe; ***da cima a fondo*** from top to bottom; *fig* from beginning to end; ***non è una cima*** he's no Einstein
cimentarsi ⟨1l⟩: ***cimentarsi in*** embark on
cimice *f* bug; *dei letti* bed bug; (*puntina da disegno*) drawing-pin
ciminiera *f* smokestack
cimitero *m* cemetery
Cina *f* China
cinciallegra *f* great tit
cincilla, cincillà *f* chinchilla
cin cin! F cheers!

C

cineamatore *m* video enthusiast
cineforum *m inv film followed by a discussion*; *club* film club
cinema *m inv* cinema, *Am luogo* movie theater; ***cinema d'essai*** experimental cinema; *luogo* art cinema, art house
cinematografia *f* cinematography; *industria* film *or* movie industry
cinematografico (*pl* -ci) film *attr*, movie *attr*
cinepresa *f* cine camera
cinese *agg*, *m/f* Chinese
cineteca *f* film library
cinetico (*pl* -ci) kinetic
cingere ⟨3d⟩ (*circondare*) surround
cinghia *f* strap; (*cintura*) belt; ***tirare la cinghia*** tighten one's belt
cinghiale *m* wild boar; ***pelle f di cinghiale*** pigskin
cinguettare ⟨1a⟩ twitter
cinguettio *m* twittering
cinico (*pl* -ci) **1** *agg* cynical **2** *m* **-a** *f* cynic
cinismo *m* cynicism
cinquanta fifty
cinquantenario *m* fiftieth anniversary
cinquantenne *m/f* 50-year-old
cinquantesimo *m/agg* fiftieth
cinquantina *f*: ***una cinquantina di*** about 50
cinque five
cinquecento **1** *agg* five hundred **2** *m*: ***il Cinquecento*** the sixteenth century
cinquemila five thousand
cintare ⟨1a⟩ enclose
cinto *pp* → ***cingere***
cintura *f* belt; (*vita*) waist; ***cintura di salvataggio*** lifebelt; ***cintura di sicurezza*** seat-belt
cinturino *m* strap
ciò (*questo*) this; (*quello*) that; ***ciò che*** what; ***con tutto ciò*** even so, in spite of all that; ***ciò nonostante*** nevertheless
ciocca *f* (*pl* -cche) *di capelli* lock
cioccolata *f* chocolate
cioccolatino *m* chocolate
cioccolato *m* chocolate
cioè that is, i. e.
ciondolare ⟨1l⟩ dangle; *fig* hang about
ciondolo *m* pendant
ciotola *f* bowl
ciottolo *m* pebble
cipolla *f* onion; *di pianta* bulb
cipollina *f* small onion; ***erba f cipollina*** chives *pl*
cipresso *m* cypress (tree)
cipria *f* (face) powder
circa **1** *avv* (round) about **2** *prp* about
circo *m* (*pl* -chi) circus
circolare **1** *v/i* ⟨1l⟩ circulate; *di persone* move along; ***le auto non possono circolare*** it's impossible to drive **2** *agg* circular **3** *f lettera* circular
circolazione *f* traffic; MED circulation; DIR ***libera circolazione*** freedom of movement; ***circolazione del sangue*** circulation of the blood; ***mettere in circolazione*** *voci* spread; ***ritirare dalla circolazione*** withdraw from circulation
circolo *m* circle; (*club*) club; ***circolo vizioso*** vicious circle
circondare ⟨1a⟩ surround
circonferenza *f* circumference
circonvallazione *f* ring road
circoscrivere ⟨3tt⟩ circumscribe
circoscrizione *f* area, district; ***circoscrizione elettorale*** constituency
circostante surrounding
circostanza *f* circumstance; (*occasione*) occasion
circuito *m* SP (*percorso*) track; EL circuit; EL ***corto circuito*** short circuit
CISL *abbr* (= ***Confederazione Italiana Sindacati Lavoratori***) Italian trade union organization
cisterna *f* cistern; (*serbatoio*) tank; ***nave f cisterna*** tanker
cisti *f* ANAT cyst
cistifellea *f* gall bladder
cistite *f* cystitis
CIT *abbr* (= ***Compagnia Italiana del Turismo***) Italian Tourist Board
citare ⟨1a⟩ quote; *come esempio* cite, quote; DIR *testimone* summons; *in giudizio* sue
citazione *f* quotation, quote; DIR summons
citofono *m* entry phone; *in uffici* intercom
città *f* town; *grande* city; ***città dormitorio*** dormitory town; ***città giardino*** garden city; ***città universitaria*** university town (*in the provinces*); ***la città vecchia*** the old (part of) town; ***Città del Vaticano*** Vatican City; ***la città eterna*** the Eternal City
cittadina *f* (small) town
cittadinanza *f* citizenship; (*popolazione*) citizens; ***cittadinanza onoraria*** freedom of the city
cittadino **1** *agg* town *attr*, city *attr* **2** *m*, **-a** *f* citizen; (*abitante di città*) city dweller
ciuccio *m* F (*succhiotto*) dummy, *Am* pacifier
ciuffo *m* tuft
civetta *f* ZO (little) owl; *fig* ***far la civetta*** flirt
civico (*pl* -ci) (*della città*) municipal, town *attr*; *delle persone* civic; ***numero m civi-***

co (street) number
civile 1 *agg* civil; *civilizzato* civilized; (*non militare*) civilian; ***guerra*** *f* ***civile*** civil war; ***matrimonio*** *m* ***civile*** civil marriage; ***stato*** *m* ***civile*** marital status **2** *m* civilian
civiltà *f inv* civilization; (*cortesia*) civility
clacson *m inv* horn
clamoroso *fig* sensational
clandestino 1 *agg* clandestine; (*illegale*) illegal **2** *m*, **-a** *f* stowaway
clarinetto *m* clarinet
classe *f* class; (*aula*) classroom; ***classe operaia*** working class; ***classe turistica*** tourist class; ***di classe*** classy
classicismo *m* classicism
classico (*pl* -ci) **1** *agg* classical; (*tipico*) classic **2** *m* classic
classifica *f* classification; (*elenco*) list; *sportiva* league standings, league table; *musicale* charts
classificare ⟨1m & d⟩ classify
classificatore *m* (*cartella*) folder; *mobile* filing cabinet, *Am* file cabinet
classismo *m* class consciousness
clausola *f* clause; (*riserva*) proviso
claustrofobia *f* claustrophobia
clavicola *f* collar-bone, clavicle
clemente merciful; *tempo* mild
clemenza *f* clemency; *di tempo* mildness
cleptomane *m/f* kleptomaniac
clericale clerical
clero *m* clergy
clessidra *f* hourglass
clic *m inv* click; ***mediante clic*** by clicking
cliccare ⟨1d⟩ INFOR click (***su*** on)
cliché *m inv fig* cliché
cliente *m/f* customer; *di professionista* client; *di albergo* guest; MED patient; ***cliente abituale*** regular
clientela *f* customers *pl*, clientele; *di professionista* clients *pl*; *di medico* patients *pl*; ***clientela abituale*** patrons *pl*, regular customers *pl*
clima *m* (*pl* -i) climate
climatico (*pl* -ci) climate *attr*, climatic; ***stazione*** *f* ***climatica*** health resort
clinica *f* (*pl* -che) (*ospedale*) clinic; (*casa di cura*) nursing home; ***clinica medica*** clinical medicine
clinico (*pl* -ci) **1** *agg* clinical **2** *m* clinician
clip *m inv* clip
clonare ⟨1a⟩ BIO clone
cloro *m* chlorine
clorofilla *f* chlorophyl(l)
cloroformio *m* chloroform
club *m inv* club
cm *abbr* (= ***centimetro***) cm (= centimetre)
c.m. *abbr* (= ***corrente mese***) of this month, inst.
CNR *abbr* (= ***Consiglio Nazionale delle Ricerche***) Italian National Research Council
coabitare ⟨1m⟩ share a flat (*Am* an apartment), be flatmates (*Am* roommates)
coagularsi ⟨1m⟩ *di sangue* coagulate, clot; *di latte* curdle
coalizione *f* coalition; ***governo*** *m* ***di coalizione*** coalition government
coalizzarsi ⟨1a⟩ join forces; POL form a coalition
cobra *m inv* cobra
cocaina *f* cocaine
cocainomane 1 *agg* addicted to cocaine **2** *m/f* cocaine addict
coccinella *f* ladybird, *Am* ladybug
coccio *m* (*pl* -cci) earthenware; *frammento* fragment (of pottery), shard
cocciuto stubborn, obstinate
cocco 1 *m* (*pl* -cchi) (*albero*) coconut palm *or* tree; ***noce*** *f* ***di cocco*** coconut **2** *m*, **-a** *f* (*persona prediletta*) darling
coccodrillo *m* crocodile
coccolare ⟨1l & c⟩ F cuddle; (*viziare*) spoil
cocente scorching; *fig* scathing
cocktail *m inv bevanda* cocktail; *festa* cocktail party
cocomero *m* water melon
coda *f* tail; (*fila*) queue, *Am* line; *di veicolo*, *treno* rear; MUS coda; ***coda di paglia*** guilty conscience; ***coda dell'occhio*** corner of the eye; ***piano*** *m* ***a coda*** grand piano; ***fare la coda*** queue (up), *Am* stand in line
codardo 1 *agg* cowardly **2** *m*, **-a** *f* coward
codazzo *m* swarm
codesto 1 *agg* that **2** *pron* that one
codice *m* code; ***codice a barre*** bar code; ***codice civile*** civil code; ***codice di avviamento postale*** post code, *Am* zip code; ***codice fiscale*** tax code; ***codice stradale*** Highway Code
codificare ⟨1m & d⟩ *dati* encode; DIR codify
codino *m* pigtail, plait
coefficiente *m* coefficient
coerente coherent; *fig* consistent
coerenza *f* coherence; *fig* consistency
coesione *f* cohesion
coesistenza *f* coexistence
coetaneo 1 *agg* the same age (***di*** as) **2** *m*, **-a** *f* contemporary, person of the same age
cofanetto *m* casket
cofano *m* AUTO bonnet, *Am* hood
cogestione *f* joint management; ***coge-***

stione aziendale worker participation
cogliere ⟨3ss⟩ pick; (*raccogliere*) gather; (*afferrare*) seize; *occasione* take, seize, jump at; (*capire*) grasp; ***cogliere di sorpresa*** catch unawares, take by surprise; ***cogliere sul fatto*** catch in the act, catch red-handed
cognac *m inv* cognac
cognato *m*, **-a** *f* brother-in-law; *donna* sister-in-law
cognizione *f* knowledge; FIL cognition; ***parla con cognizione di causa*** he knows what he's talking about
cognome *m* surname; ***nome*** *m* ***e cognome*** full name
coi *prp* ***con*** and *art* ***i***
coincidenza *f* coincidence; FERR connection; ***perdere la coincidenza*** miss one's connection
coincidere ⟨3q⟩ coincide
coinquilino *m*, **-a** *f in condominio* fellow tenant; *in appartamento* flatmate, *Am* roommate
coinvolgere ⟨3d⟩ involve (***in*** in)
coinvolto *pp* → ***coinvolgere***
col *prp* ***con*** and *art* ***il***
colabrodo *m inv* strainer
colapasta *m inv* colander
colare ⟨1a⟩ **1** *v/t* strain; *pasta* drain **2** *v/i* drip; (*perdere*) leak; *di naso* run; *di cera* melt; ***colare a fondo*** *o* ***a pico*** sink, go down
colata *f di metallo* casting; *di lava* flow
colazione *f prima* breakfast; *di mezzogiorno* lunch; ***colazione al sacco*** picnic; ***far colazione*** have breakfast, breakfast
colei *pron f* the one; ***colei che*** the one that
colera *m* cholera
colesterolo *m* cholesterol
colica *f* (*pl* -che) colic
colino *m* strainer
colla *f* glue; *di farina* paste
collaborare ⟨1m⟩ co-operate, collaborate; *con giornale* contribute
collaboratore *m*, **-trice** *f* collaborator; *di giornale* contributor; ***collaboratore*** *m* ***esterno*** freelance(r); ***-trice*** *f* ***domestica*** home help
collaborazione *f* co-operation, collaboration
collana *f* necklace; *di libri* series
collant *m inv* tights *pl*, *Am* pantyhose
collare *m* collar
collasso *m* collapse; ***collasso cardiaco*** heart failure
collaudare ⟨1a⟩ test; *fig* put to the test
collaudo *m* test
colle *m* hill; (*valico*) pass
collega *m/f* (*mpl* -ghi) colleague, co-worker
collegamento *m* connection; MIL liaison; RAD, TV link; ***collegamento aereo / ferroviario*** connecting flight / train
collegare ⟨1a⟩ connect, link
collegarsi RAD, TV link up
collegiale 1 *agg* collective **2** *m/f* boarder
collegio *m* (*pl* -gi) boarding school; ***collegio elettorale*** constituency
collera *f* anger; ***andare in collera*** get angry; ***essere in collera con qu*** be angry with s.o.
collerico (*pl* -ci) irascible
colletta *f* collection
collettività *f* community
collettivo *m/agg* collective
colletto *m* collar
collezionare ⟨1a⟩ collect
collezione *f* collection; ***fare collezione di qc*** collect sth, make a collection of sth
collezionista *m/f* collector; ***collezionista di francobolli*** stamp collector
collina *f* hill
collinoso hilly
collirio *m* eyewash
collisione *f* collision; ***entrare in collisione*** collide
collo *m* neck; (*bagaglio*) piece *or* item of luggage; (*pacco*) package; ***collo del piede*** instep
collocamento *m* placing; (*impiego*) employment; ***agenzia*** *f* ***di collocamento*** employment agency; ***ufficio*** *m* ***di collocamento*** Jobcentre
collocare ⟨1l & d⟩ place, put; ***collocare a riposo*** retire
collocazione *f* place, job
colloquiale colloquial
colloquio *m* (*pl* -qui) talk, conversation; *ufficiale* interview; (*esame*) oral (exam)
colluttazione *f* scuffle
colmare ⟨1a⟩ fill (***di*** with); *fig di gentilezze* overwhelm (***di*** with); ***colmare un vuoto*** bridge a gap
colmo 1 *agg* full (***di*** of) **2** *m* summit, top; *fig* (*culmine*) height; ***è il colmo!*** that's the last straw!
colomba *f* ZO, *fig* dove
colombo *m* pigeon
colon *m* colon
Colonia *f*: ***acqua*** *f* ***di Colonia*** eau de Cologne
colonia *f* colony; *per bambini* holiday camp; ***colonia marina*** seaside holiday camp
coloniale colonial
colonico (*pl* -ci): ***casa*** *f* ***-a*** farmhouse
colonizzare ⟨1a⟩ colonize

colonna *f* column; *di veicoli* line; *fig* mainstay; ***colonna sonora*** sound track; ***colonna vertebrale*** spinal column
colonnato *m* colonnade
colonnello *m* colonel
colonnina *f della benzina* petrol (*Am* gas) pump
colorante *m* dye; ***senza -i*** with no artificial colo(u)rings
colorare ⟨1a⟩ colo(u)r; *disegno* colo(u)r in
colorato colo(u)red
colorazione *f* colo(u)ring
colore *m* colo(u)r; *carte* suit; *poker* flush; ***gente*** *f* ***di colore*** colo(u)red people; ***scatola*** *f* ***dei -i*** paint box; ***colore a olio*** oil (paint); ***a -i*** *film*, *televisione* colo(u)r *attr*; ***farne di tutti i -i*** get up to all sorts of mischief
colorito 1 *agg volto* rosy-cheeked; *fig* (*vivace*) colo(u)rful **2** *m* complexion
coloro *pron pl* the ones; ***coloro che*** those who
colossale colossal
colosso *m* colossus
colpa *f* fault; REL sin; ***dare a qu la colpa di qc*** blame s.o. for sth; ***non è colpa sua*** it's not her fault; ***per colpa tua*** because of you; ***senso*** *m* ***di colpa*** sense of guilt; ***sentirsi in colpa*** feel guilty
colpevole 1 *agg* guilty **2** *m/f* culprit, guilty party
colpire ⟨4d⟩ hit, strike; *fig* impress, leave an impression on; ***colpire nel segno*** hit the nail on the head
colpo *m* blow; (*fig*) blow, shock; *di pistola* shot; MED stroke; ***colpo apoplettico*** apoplectic fit; ***colpo di calore*** heat stroke; ***colpo di sole*** sunstroke; ***colpo di stato*** coup d'état; ***colpo di telefono*** phone call; ***colpo di testa*** whim; ***fare colpo*** make an impact; ***sul colpo, di colpo*** suddenly
coltellata *f ferita* stab wound
coltello *m* knife
coltivare ⟨1a⟩ AGR, *fig* cultivate
coltivatore *m* farmer
coltivazione *f* cultivation; *di prodotti agricoli e piante* growing; *campi coltivati* crops
colto[1] *agg* cultured, learned
colto[2] *pp* → ***cogliere***
coltura *f* growing; *piante* crop
colui *pron m* the one; ***colui che*** the one that
coma *m* coma
comandamento *m* commandment
comandante *m* commander; AVIA, MAR captain
comandare ⟨1a⟩ **1** *v/t* (*ordinare*) order, command; *esercito* command; *nave* captain, be captain of; FIN *merci* order; TEC control; ***comandare a distanza*** operate by remote control **2** *v/i* be in charge
comando *m* order, command; TEC control; ***comando a distanza*** remote control
combaciare ⟨1f⟩ fit together; *fig* correspond
combattente *m* soldier, serviceman
combattere ⟨3a⟩ *v/t* & *v/i* fight
combattimento *m* fight; SP match, fight
combinare ⟨1a⟩ combine; (*organizzare*) arrange; ***combinare un guaio*** make a mess; ***oggi ho combinato poco*** I got very little done today
combinarsi go well together
combinazione *f* combination; (*coincidenza*) coincidence; ***per combinazione*** by chance
combustibile 1 *agg* combustible **2** *m* fuel
combustione *f* combustion
come 1 *avv* as; (*in modo simile o uguale*) like; *interrogativo*, *esclamativo* how; (*prego?*) pardon?; ***fa' come ti ho detto*** do as I told you; ***lavora come insegnante*** he works as a teacher; ***come me*** like me; ***un cappello come il mio*** a hat like mine; ***come sta?*** how are you?, how are things?; ***com'è bello!*** how nice it is!; ***come mai?*** how come?, why?; ***oggi come oggi*** nowadays; ***come se*** as if **2** *cong* (*come se*) as if, as though; (*appena*, *quando*) as (soon as); ***come se niente fosse*** as if nothing had happened
cometa *f* comet
comfort *m inv* comfort; ***dotato di tutti i comfort moderni*** with all mod cons
comicità *f* funniness
comico (*pl* -ci) **1** *agg* funny, comical; *genere* comic **2** *m*, **-a** *f* comedian; *donna* comedienne
comignolo *m* chimney pot
cominciare ⟨1f⟩ start, begin (***a*** to); ***a cominciare da oggi*** (starting) from today; ***tanto per cominciare*** to begin *or* start with
comitato *m* committee; ***comitato direttivo*** steering committee
comitiva *f* group, party
comizio *m* meeting
Comm. *abbr* (= ***Commendatore***) *Italian title awarded for services to the country*
commando *m* commando
commedia *f* comedy; *fig* play-acting
commediografo *m*, **-a** *f* playwright
commemorare ⟨1m & b⟩ commemorate
commemorazione *f* commemoration

commentare ⟨1a⟩ comment on
commentatore *m*, **-trice** *f* commentator
commento *m* comment
commerciale commercial; *relazioni*, *trattative* trade *attr*; *lettera* business *attr*
commercialista *m/f* accountant
commercializzare ⟨1a⟩ market
commerciante *m/f* merchant; (*negoziante*) shopkeeper
commerciare ⟨1b & f⟩ deal (***in*** in)
commercio *m* (*pl* -ci) trade, business; *internazionale* trade; *di droga* traffic; ***commercio all'ingrosso*** wholesale trade; ***commercio al minuto*** retail trade; ***camera*** *f* ***di commercio*** chamber of commerce; ***essere in commercio*** be available; ***mettere in commercio qc*** put sth on the market
commessa *f* (*ordinazione*) order
commesso *m*, **-a** *f* shop assistant, *Am* sales clerk; (*impiegato*) clerk; ***commesso viaggiatore*** travel(l)ing salesman
commestibile 1 *agg* edible **2** ***-i*** *mpl* foodstuffs
commettere ⟨3ee⟩ commit; *errore* make
commiserare ⟨1m⟩ feel sorry for
commissariato *m*: ***commissariato*** (***di pubblica sicurezza***) police station
commissario *m* (*pl* -ri) *di polizia* (police) superintendent; *membro di commissione* commissioner
commissionare ⟨1a⟩ FIN commission
commissione *f* commission; (*incarico*) errand; ***Commissione europea*** European Commission; ***-i*** *pl* shopping *sg*; ***fatto su commissione*** made to order
commosso 1 *pp* → ***commuovere*** **2** *agg fig* moved, touched
commovente moving, touching
commozione *f* emotion; ***commozione cerebrale*** concussion
commuovere ⟨3ff⟩ move, touch
commuoversi be moved *or* touched
comò *m inv* chest of drawers
comodino *m* bedside table
comodità *f inv* comfort; (*vantaggio*) convenience
comodo 1 *agg* comfortable; *vestito* loose, comfortable; (*facilmente raggiungibile*) easy to get to; (*utile*) useful, handy; F *persona* laid back F; ***stia comodo!*** don't get up! **2** *m* comfort; ***con comodo*** at one's convenience; ***far comodo*** *di denaro* come in useful, be handy; ***le fa comodo così*** she finds it easier that way; ***fare il propio comodo*** do as one pleases
compagnia *f* company; (*gruppo*) group; REL order; ***compagnia aerea*** airline; ***compagnia di assicurazioni*** insurance company; ***far compagnia a qu*** keep s.o. company
compagno *m*, **-a** *f* companion; (*convivente*), FIN partner; POL comrade; ***compagno di scuola*** schoolfriend, schoolmate; ***compagno di squadra*** team mate; ***compagno di viaggio*** travelling companion
comparativo *m/agg* comparative
comparire ⟨4e⟩ appear; (*essere pubblicato*) come out, appear; (*far figura*) stand out
comparizione *f*: DIR ***mandato*** *m* ***di comparizione*** summons
comparsa *f* appearance; TEA person with a walk-on part; *in film* extra
comparso *pp* → ***comparire***
compartimento *m* compartment
compassione *f* compassion, pity; ***provare compassione per qu*** feel sorry for s.o.
compasso *m* (pair of) compasses
compatibile compatible
compatire ⟨4d⟩: ***compatire qu*** feel sorry for s.o.
compatriota *m/f* (*mpl* -i) compatriot
compatto compact; *folla* dense; *fig* united
compensare ⟨1b⟩ (*controbilanciare*) compensate for, make up for; (*ricompensare*) reward; (*risarcire*) pay compensation to
compenso *m* (*ricompensa*, *risarcimento*) compensation; (*retribuzione*) fee; ***in compenso*** (*d'altra parte*) on the other hand; ***dietro compenso*** for a fee
compera *f* purchase; ***fare le -e*** go shopping
competente competent; (*responsabile*) appropriate
competenza *f* (*esperienza*) competence; ***essere di competenza di qu*** be s.o.'s responsibility
competere ⟨3a⟩ (*gareggiare*) compete
competitività *f* competitiveness
competitivo competitive
competizione *f* competition
compiacente too eager to please
compiacenza *f* overeagerness to please
compiacere ⟨2k⟩ please
compiacersi (*provare piacere*) be pleased (***di*** with); ***mi compiaccio con te*** congratulations
compiaciuto *pp* → ***compiacere***
compiangere ⟨3d⟩ pity; *per lutto* mourn
compianto *pp* → ***compiangere***
compiere ⟨4g⟩ (*finire*) complete, finish; (*eseguire*) carry out; ***compiere gli anni*** have one's birthday

compiersi (*avverarsi*) happen
compilare ⟨1a⟩ compile; *modulo* complete, fill in
compilatore *m* INFOR compiler
compilazione *f* compilation
compimento *m* completion
compito[1] *agg* polite
compito[2] *m* task; EDU ***i -i*** *pl* homework *sg*
compiuto *lavoro*, *opera* completed, finished; ***ha 10 anni -i*** he's 10
compleanno *m* birthday; ***buon compleanno!*** happy birthday!
complementare complementary
complemento *m* complement; GRAM object
complessato full of complexes
complessivo all-in
complesso 1 *agg* complex, complicated **2** *m* complex; MUS group; *di circostanze* set, combination; ***in*** *o* ***nel complesso*** on the whole
completamento *m* completion
completare ⟨1b⟩ complete
completo 1 *agg* complete; (*pieno*) full; TEA sold out **2** *m* set; (*vestito*) suit; ***al completo*** (*pieno*) full (up); TEA sold out
complicare ⟨1l & d⟩ complicate
complicarsi get complicated
complicato complicated, complex
complicazione *f* complication
complice *m/f* DIR accomplice
complimentarsi ⟨1d⟩: ***complimentarsi con qu*** congratulate s.o. (***per*** on)
complimento *m* compliment; ***fare un complimento a qu*** pay s.o. a compliment; ***-i!*** congratulations!; ***non fare -i!*** help yourself!
componente 1 *m* component **2** *m/f* (*persona*) member
componibile modular; *cucina* fitted
componimento *m* composition; DIR settlement
comporre ⟨3ll⟩ (*mettere in ordine*) arrange; MUS compose; TELEC ***comporre un numero*** dial a number
comporsi: ***comporsi di*** consist of, be made up of
comportamento *m* behavio(u)r
comportare ⟨1c⟩ involve
comportarsi behave
compositore *m*, **-trice** *f* composer
composizione *f* composition; *di fiori* arrangement; DIR settlement
composta *f* stewed fruit; (*terricciato*) compost
composto 1 *pp* → ***comporre*** **2** *agg* compound; *abiti*, *capelli* tidy, neat; ***composto da*** made up of; ***stai composto*** keep still; *seduto* sit properly **3** *m* compound
comprare ⟨1a⟩ buy, purchase; (*corrompere*) bribe, buy off
compratore *m*, **-trice** *f* buyer, purchaser
compravendita *f* buying and selling
comprendere ⟨3c⟩ (*includere*) comprise, include; (*capire*) understand
comprensibile understandable
comprensione *f* understanding
comprensivo (*tollerante*) understanding; ***comprensivo di*** inclusive of
compreso 1 *pp* → ***comprendere*** **2** *agg* inclusive; (*capito*) understood; ***tutto compreso*** all in; ***compreso te*** including you
compressa *f* (*pastiglia*) tablet; *di garza* compress
compresso *pp* → ***comprimere***
comprimere ⟨3r⟩ press; (*reprimere*) repress; FIS compress
compromesso 1 *pp* → ***compromettere*** **2** *m* compromise; DIR ***compromesso di vendita*** agreement to sell
compromettere ⟨3ee⟩ compromise
compromettersi compromise o.s.
computer *m inv* computer; ***assistito dal computer*** computer-assisted; ***computer portatile*** portable (computer), laptop
computerizzare ⟨1a⟩ computerize
computisteria *f* book-keeping, accountancy
comunale *del comune* municipal, town *attr*; ***consiglio*** *m* ***comunale*** town council; ***palazzo*** *m* ***comunale*** town hall
comune 1 *agg* common; *amico* mutual; (*ordinario*) ordinary, common; ***in comune*** in common; ***non comune*** unusual, uncommon; ***fuori del comune*** out of the ordinary **2** *m* municipality; ***palazzo*** *m* ***del comune*** town hall
comunemente commonly
comunicare ⟨1m & d⟩ **1** *v/t notizia* pass on, communicate; *contagio* pass on; REL give Communion to **2** *v/i* (*esprimersi*) communicate; *di persone* keep in touch, communicate
comunicato *m* announcement, communiqué; ***comunicato stampa*** press release
comunicazione *f* communication; (*annuncio*) announcement; TELEC (*collegamento*) connection; ***dare comunicazione di qc a qu*** tell s.o. about sth; TELEC ***la comunicazione si è interrotta*** I've been cut off; TELEC ***comunicazione internazionale*** international call
comunione *f* REL communion; *di idee* sharing
comunismo *m* Communism
comunista *m/f* (*mpl* -i) Communist
comunità *f* community; ***Comunità euro-***

C

pea European Community
comunitario community *attr*; *dell'UE* Community *attr*
comunque 1 *cong* however, no matter how; ***comunque vadano le cose*** whatever happens **2** *avv* (*in ogni modo*) in any case, anyhow; (*in qualche modo*) somehow; (*tuttavia*) however
con with; (*mezzo*) by; ***con questo tempo*** in this weather; ***con tutto ciò*** for all that; ***avere con sé*** have with *or* on one
conato *m*: ***conato di vomito*** retching
concedere ⟨3l⟩ grant; *premio* award; ***ti concedo che*** I admit that
concedersi: ***concedersi qc*** treat o.s. to sth
concentramento *m* concentration
concentrare ⟨1b⟩, **concentrarsi** concentrate
concentrazione *f* concentration
concentrico (*pl* -ci) concentric
concepibile conceivable
concepimento *m* conception
concepire ⟨4d⟩ conceive; (*ideare*) devise, conceive
concernere ⟨3a⟩ concern; ***per quanto mi concerne*** as far as I'm concerned
concerto *m* concert; *composizione* concerto
concessionario *m* (*pl* -ri) agent; ***concessionario esclusivo*** sole agent
concessione *f* concession
concesso *pp* → ***concedere***
concetto *m* concept; (*giudizio*) opinion
concezione *f* conception; *fig* idea (***di*** for)
conchiglia *f* shell
conciare ⟨1f⟩ *pelle* tan; (*sistemare*) arrange; ***come ti sei conciato!*** what a state *or* mess you're in!; ***conciare qu per le feste*** tan s.o.'s hide, give s.o. a good hiding
conciliare ⟨1k⟩ reconcile; *multa* pay, settle; ***conciliare il sonno*** be conducive to sleep
conciliazione *f* reconciliation; DIR settlement
concimare ⟨1a⟩ *pianta* feed
concime *m* manure; ***concime chimico*** chemical fertilizer
conciso concise
concitato excited
concittadino *m*, **-a** *f* fellow citizen
concludere ⟨3q⟩ conclude; (*portare a termine*) achieve, carry off; ***concludere un affare*** clinch a deal; ***non ho concluso nulla*** I got nowhere
concludersi end, close
conclusione *f* conclusion; ***in conclusione*** in short
conclusivo conclusive
concluso *pp* → ***concludere***
concordanza *f* agreement
concordare ⟨1c⟩ **1** *v/t* agree (on); GRAM make agree **2** *v/i* (*essere d'accordo*) agree; (*coincidere*) tally
concordato 1 *agg* agreed on **2** *m* agreement; REL concordat; DIR settlement
concorde *agg* in agreement; (*unanime*) unanimous; (*simultaneo*) simultaneous
concordia *f* harmony
concorrente 1 *agg* (*rivale*) competing, rival **2** *m/f in una gara, gioco* competitor, contestant; FIN competitor
concorrenza *f* competition
concorrenziale competitive
concorrere ⟨3o⟩ (*contribuire*) concur; (*competere*) compete (***a*** for); *di strade* converge; ***concorrere per un posto*** compete for a position
concorso 1 *pp* → ***concorrere* 2** *m* (*competizione*) competition, contest; ***bandire un concorso*** announce a competition
concreto concrete; (*pratico*) practical
condanna *f* DIR sentence
condannare ⟨1a⟩ condemn (***a*** to); DIR sentence (***a*** to)
condensare ⟨1b⟩, **condensarsi** condense
condensazione *f* condensation
condimento *m* seasoning; *di insalata* dressing
condire ⟨4d⟩ season; *insalata* dress; *fig* spice up
condito seasoned
condividere ⟨3q⟩ share
condiviso *pp* → ***condividere***
condizionale 1 *m/agg* conditional **2** *f* suspended sentence
condizionamento *m* PSI conditioning; ***condizionamento dell'aria*** air conditioning
condizionare ⟨1a⟩ PSI condition
condizionato: ***con aria -a*** with air conditioning, air-conditioned
condizionatore *m* air conditioner
condizione *f* condition; ***-i** pl* ***di lavoro*** working conditions; ***a condizione che*** on condition that
condoglianze *fpl* condolences; ***fare le condoglianze a qu*** express one's condolences to s.o.
condominio *m* (*comproprietà*) joint ownership; *edificio* block of flats, *Am* condo
condomino *m* owner-occupier, *Am* condo owner
condonare ⟨1a⟩ remit
condono *m* remission; ***condono fiscale*** conditional amnesty for tax evaders

condotta *f* (*comportamento*) behavio(u)r, conduct; (*canale*) piping
condotto 1 *pp* → ***condurre*** **2** *m* pipe; ANAT duct
conducente *m/f* driver; ***conducente di autobus*** bus driver
condurre ⟨3e⟩ lead; (*accompagnare*) take; *veicolo* drive; *azienda* run; *acque, gas* carry, take
conduttore *m*, **-trice** *f* RAD, TV presenter; FERR (*controllore*) conductor
conduttura *f* (*condotto*) pipe
confederazione *f* confederation
conferenza *f* conference; ***conferenza al vertice*** summit (conference); ***conferenza stampa*** press conference
conferimento *m* conferring
conferire ⟨4d⟩ **1** *v/t* (*dare*) confer; *premio* award **2** *v/i*: ***conferire con qu*** confer with s.o.
conferma *f* confirmation
confermare ⟨1a⟩ confirm
confessare ⟨1b⟩, **confessarsi** confess
confessione *f* confession
confessore *m* confessor
confetto *m* GASTR sugared almond; MED pill
confettura *f* jam
confezionare ⟨1a⟩ *merce* wrap, package; *abiti* make
confezione *f* wrapping, packaging; *di abiti* making; ***confezione regalo*** gift wrap; ***-i*** *pl* (*abiti*) garments
conficcare ⟨1d⟩ hammer, drive
confidare ⟨1a⟩ **1** *v/t* confide **2** *v/i*: ***confidare in*** trust in, rely on
confidarsi: ***confidarsi con*** confide in
confidenza *f* (*familiarità*) familiarity; (*fiducia*) confidence, trust; ***avere confidenza con qu*** be familiar with s.o.; ***prendere confidenza con qc*** familiarize o.s. with sth
confidenziale (*riservato*) confidential; ***strettamente confidenziale*** strictly confidential
configurare ⟨1a⟩ configure
configurazione *f* configuration
confinante neighbo(u)ring
confinare ⟨1a⟩ border (***con*** sth); *fig* confine
confine *m* border; *fra terreni*, *fig* boundary
confisca *f* (*pl* -che) seizure
confiscare ⟨1d⟩ confiscate
conflitto *m* conflict
confluire ⟨4d⟩ merge
confondere ⟨3bb⟩ confuse, mix up; (*imbarazzare*) embarrass
confondersi get mixed up
conformare ⟨1a⟩ (*rendere adatto*) adapt
conformarsi: ***conformarsi a*** conform to; (*adattarsi*) adapt to
conforme (*simile*) similar; ***conforme a*** in accordance with; ***copia*** *f* ***conforme*** (certified) true copy
conformismo *m* conformity
conformista *m/f* (*mpl* -i) conformist
conformità *f* conformity; ***in conformità a*** in accordance with
confortare ⟨1c⟩ comfort
confortevole comfortable
conforto *m* comfort
confrontare ⟨1a⟩ compare
confronto *m* confrontation; (*comparazione*) comparison; ***a confronto di, in confronto a*** compared with; ***maleducato nei -i di qu*** rude to s.o.
confusione *f* confusion; (*disordine*) muddle, mess; (*baccano*) noise, racket; (*imbarazzo*) embarrassment
confuso 1 *pp* → ***confondere*** **2** *agg* (*non chiaro*) confused, muddled; (*imbarazzato*) embarrassed
congedare ⟨1b⟩ dismiss; MIL discharge
congedarsi take leave (***da*** of)
congedo *m* (*permesso*) leave; MIL *assoluto* discharge
congelare ⟨1b⟩ **1** *v/t* freeze **2** *v/i e* **congelarsi** freeze
congelato frozen
congelatore *m* freezer
congenito congenital
congestionare ⟨1a⟩ congest
congestionato congested; *volto* flushed
congestione *f* congestion
congettura *f* conjecture
congiungere ⟨3d⟩ join
congiungersi join (up)
congiuntivite *f* conjunctivitis
congiuntivo *m* GRAM subjunctive
congiunto 1 *pp* → ***congiungere*** **2** *m*, **-a** *f* relative, relation
congiuntura *f* ANAT joint; ***congiuntura economica*** economic situation
congiunzione *f* GRAM conjunction
congiura *f* conspiracy, plot
congratularsi ⟨1m⟩: ***congratularsi con qu*** congratulate s.o. (***per*** on)
congratulazioni *fpl*: ***fare le propie congratulazioni a qu*** congratulate s.o.; ***-i!*** congratulations!
congressista *m/f* (*mpl* -i) convention participant
congresso *m* convention
conguaglio *m* (*pl* -gli) balance
CONI *abbr* (= ***Comitato Olimpico Nazionale Italiano***) Italian Olympic Committee

C

coniare ⟨1k & c⟩ mint; *fig* coin
conifere *fpl* conifers
coniglio *m* (*pl* -gli) rabbit
coniugare ⟨1l, c & e⟩ conjugate
coniugato married
coniugazione *f* conjugation
coniuge *m/f* spouse; ***-i*** *pl* husband and wife; ***i -i Rossi*** Mr and Mrs Rossi
connazionale *m/f* compatriot
connessione *f* connection
connotati *mpl* features
cono *m* cone; ***cono gelato*** ice-cream cone
conoscente *m/f* acquaintance
conoscenza *f* knowledge; *persona* acquaintance; (*sensi*) consciousness; ***per conoscenza*** cc; ***fare la conoscenza di qu*** make s.o.'s acquaintance, meet s.o.; ***perdere conoscenza*** lose consciousness, faint
conoscere ⟨3n⟩ know; (*fare la conoscenza di*) meet; ***conoscere qu di vista*** know s.o. by sight
conoscitore *m*, **-trice** *f* connoisseur
conosciuto well-known, famous
conquista *f* conquest
conquistare ⟨1a⟩ conquer; *fig* win
consacrare ⟨1a⟩ consecrate; *sacerdote* ordain; (*dedicare*) dedicate
consacrarsi devote o.s. (***a*** to)
consacrazione *f* consecration; *di sacerdote* ordination
consanguineo *m*, **-a** *f* blood relative
consapevole: ***consapevole di*** conscious of, aware of
consapevolezza *f* consciousness, awareness
conscio conscious, aware
consecutivo (*di seguito*) consecutive; ***tre giorni -i*** three consecutive days, three days in a row
consegna *f di lavoro, documento* handing in; *di prigionero, ostaggio* handover; ***consegna a domicilio*** home delivery; ***consegna bagagli*** left luggage, *Am* baggage checkroom
consegnare ⟨1a⟩ *lavoro, documento* hand in; *prigionero, ostaggio* hand over; *merci, posta* deliver
conseguente consequent
conseguenza *f* consequence; ***di conseguenza*** consequently; ***in conseguenza di qc*** as a result of sth
conseguire ⟨4a⟩ **1** *v/t* achieve; *laurea* obtain **2** *v/i* follow
consenso *m* (*permesso*) consent, permission
consentire ⟨4b⟩ **1** *v/i* (*accondiscendere*) consent **2** *v/t* allow
conserva *f* preserve; ***conserva di pomodoro*** tomato purée; ***conserva di frutta*** jam
conservante *m* preservative
conservare ⟨1b⟩ keep; GASTR preserve
conservarsi keep; *in salute* keep well
conservatore *m*, **-trice** *f* conservative
conservatorio *m* (*pl* -ri) music school, conservatoire
conservazione *f* preservation
considerare ⟨1m⟩ consider
considerazione *f* consideration; (*osservazione*) remark, comment; ***prendere in considerazione*** take into consideration
considerevole considerable
consigliare ⟨1g⟩ advise; (*raccomandare*) recommend
consigliarsi ask for advice
consigliere *m* adviser; ***consigliere municipale*** town council(l)or
consiglio *m* (*pl* -gli) piece of advice; (*organo amministrativo*) council; ***consiglio d'amministrazione*** board (of directors); ***Consiglio d'Europa*** Council of Europe; ***consiglio dei ministri*** Cabinet
consistente substantial; (*denso*) thick
consistenza *f* (*densità*) consistency, thickness; *di materiale* texture; *di argomento* basis
consistere ⟨3f⟩ consist (***in, di*** of)
consocio *m* (*pl* -ci), **-a** *f* associate
consolare[1] ⟨1c⟩ console, comfort
consolare[2] *agg* consular
consolarsi console o.s.
consolato *m* consulate; ***consolato generale*** consulate general
consolazione *f* consolation
console[1] *m diplomatico* consul; ***console generale*** consul general
console[2] *f mobile* console
consolidare ⟨1m & c⟩ consolidate
consolidarsi stabilize
consonante *f* consonant
consorte *m/f* spouse; ***principe*** *m* ***consorte*** prince consort
consorzio *m* (*pl* -zi) *di imprese* consortium
constatare ⟨1l⟩ ascertain, determine; (*notare*) note
constatazione *f* statement
consueto usual
consuetudine *f* habit, custom; (*usanza*) custom, tradition
consulente *m/f* consultant; ***consulente legale*** legal adviser; ***consulente tributario*** tax consultant
consulenza *f* consultancy; ***consulenza aziendale*** management consultancy
consultare ⟨1a⟩ consult

C

consultarsi: ***consultarsi con qu*** consult s.o.
consultazione *f* consultation; ***opera** f **di consultazione*** reference book
consultorio *m* family planning clinic
consumare ⟨1a⟩ *acqua, gas* use, consume; (*logorare*) wear out; (*mangiare*) eat, consume; (*bere*) drink
consumarsi wear out
consumatore *m*, **-trice** *f* consumer
consumazione *f* food; (*bevanda*) drink
consumismo *m* consumerism
consumo *m* consumption; (*usura*) wear; ***beni** mpl **di consumo*** consumer goods
consuntivo *m* FIN closing balance
contabile *m/f* book keeper
contabilità *f* FIN *disciplina* accounting; *ufficio* accounts department; ***tenere la contabilità*** keep the books
contachilometri *m inv* mileometer, clock F
contadino 1 *agg* rural, country *attr* **2** *m*, **-a** *f* peasant
contagiare ⟨1f⟩ infect
contagio *m* (*pl* -gi) infection; *per contatto diretto* contagion; (*epidemia*) outbreak
contagioso infectious
contagiri *m inv* rev(olution) counter
contagocce *m inv* dropper
container *m inv* container
contaminare ⟨1m⟩ contaminate, pollute
contaminazione *f* contamination, pollution
contante *m* cash; ***in -i*** cash
contare ⟨1a⟩ **1** *v/t* count **2** *v/i* count; ***contare di fare qc*** plan on doing sth
contascatti *m inv time meter on phone*
contatore *m* meter
contatto *m* contact
conte *m* count
contegno *m* behavio(u)r; (*atteggiamento*) restraint
contemplare ⟨1b⟩ contemplate; DIR provide for
contemplazione *f* contemplation
contemporaneamente at the same time
contemporaneo 1 *agg* contemporary (***di*** with); *movimenti* simultaneous **2** *m*, **-a** *f* contemporary
contendere ⟨3c⟩ **1** *v/t*: ***contendere qc a qu*** compete with s.o. for sth **2** *v/i* (*competere*) contend
contendersi contend for, compete for
contenere ⟨2q⟩ contain, hold; (*reprimere*) repress; (*limitare*) limit
contenersi contain o.s.
contenitore *m* container
contentare ⟨1b⟩ please
contentarsi be content (***di*** with);
contentezza *f* happiness
contento pleased (***di*** with); (*lieto*) glad, happy
contenuto *m* contents *pl*
contesa *f* dispute
conteso *pp* → ***contendere***
contessa *f* countess
contestare ⟨1b⟩ protest; DIR serve
contestatore *m*, **-trice** *f* protester
contestazione *f* protest
contesto *m* context
contiene → ***contenere***
contiguo adjacent (***a*** to)
continentale continental
continente *m* continent
continuare ⟨1m⟩ **1** *v/t* continue **2** *v/i* continue, carry on (***a fare*** doing)
continuazione *f* continuation; *di film* sequel; ***in continuazione*** over and over again; (*ininterrottamente*) non stop
continuità *f* continuity
continuo (*ininterrotto*) continuous; (*molto frequente*) continual; ***di continuo*** (*ininterrottamente*) continuously; (*molto spesso*) continually; EL ***corrente** f **-a*** direct current
conto *m* (*calcolo*) calculation; FIN account; *in ristorante* bill, *Am* check; ***conto corrente*** current account, *Am* checking account; ***conto corrente postale*** Post Office account; ***conto profitti e perdite*** profit and loss account; ***conto vincolato*** term deposit; ***rendere conto di qc*** account for sth; ***rendersi conto di qc*** realize sth; ***fare conto su qu*** count on s.o.; ***tenere conto di qc*** take sth into account; ***conto alla rovescia*** countdown; ***per conto mio*** (*secondo me*) in my opinion; (*da solo*) on my own; ***sapere qc sul conto di qu*** know sth about s.o.; ***in fin dei -i*** when all's said and done, after all
contorcere ⟨3d⟩ twist
contorcersi: ***contorcersi dal dolore / dalle risate*** roll about in pain / laughing
contorno *m* outline, contour; GASTR accompaniment
contorto twisted
contrabbandare ⟨1a⟩ smuggle
contrabbandiere *m* smuggler
contrabbando *m* contraband
contrabbasso *m* MUS double bass
contraccambiare ⟨1k⟩ return
contraccambio *m* (*pl* -bi) return
contraccettivo *m* contraceptive
contraccezione *f* contraception
contraccolpo *m* rebound; *di arma da fuoco* recoil
contraddire ⟨3t⟩ contradict

contraddizione *f* contradiction
contraffare ⟨3aa⟩ (*falsificare*) forge; (*imitare*) imitate
contraffatto forged; *voce* imitated
contraffazione *f* (*imitazione*) imitation; (*falsificazione*) forgery
contralto *m* MUS (contr)alto
contrappeso *m* counterbalance
contrapporre ⟨3ll⟩ set against
contrapporsi (*contrastare*) clash; ***contrapporsi a*** oppose
contrapposizione *f* opposition; ***mettere in contrapposizione*** contrast
contrapposto *pp* → ***contrapporre***
contrariamente: ***contrariamente a*** contrary to
contrariare ⟨1k⟩ *piani* thwart, oppose; *persona* irritate, annoy
contrariato irritated, annoyed
contrarietà *fpl inv* difficulties, problems
contrario (*pl* -ri) **1** *agg* contrary; *direzione* opposite; *vento* adverse; ***essere contrario*** be against (***a*** sth) **2** *m* contrary, opposite; ***al contrario*** on the contrary
contrarre ⟨3xx⟩ contract
contrarsi contract
contrassegnare ⟨1a⟩ mark
contrassegno *m* mark; FIN (***in***) ***contrassegno*** cash on delivery
contrastante contrasting
contrastare ⟨1a⟩ **1** *v/t* contrast; (*ostacolare*) hinder **2** *v/i* contrast (***con*** with)
contrasto *m* contrast; (*litigio*, *discordia*) disagreement, dispute
contrattacco *m* (*pl* -cchi) counter-attack
contrattare ⟨1a⟩ negotiate; *persona* hire
contrattempo *m* hitch
contratto[1] *pp* → ***contrarre***
contratto[2] *m* contract; ***contratto d'affitto*** lease
contrattuale contractual
contravvenire ⟨4p⟩ contravene
contravvenzione *f* contravention; (*multa*) fine
contrazione *f* contraction; (*riduzione*) reduction
contribuente *m/f* taxpayer
contribuire ⟨4d⟩ contribute
contributo *m* contribution; ***-i*** *pl* ***sociali*** social security (*Am* welfare) contributions
contro against
controbattere ⟨3a⟩ (*replicare*) answer back; (*confutare*) rebut
controcorrente **1** *agg* non-conformist **2** *avv* against the current; *in fiume* upstream
controffensiva counter-offensive
controfigura *f in film* stand in
controfirmare ⟨1a⟩ countersign
controindicazione *f* MED contraindication
controllare ⟨1c⟩ control; (*verificare*) check
controllo *m* control; (*verifica*) check; MED check-up; ***controllo alla frontiera*** customs inspection; ***controllo dei biglietti*** ticket inspection; ***controllo*** (***dei***) ***passaporti*** passport control; ***controllo della qualità*** quality control
controllore *m* controller; *di bus*, *treno* ticket inspector; ***controllore di volo*** air-traffic controller
controluce *f*: ***in controluce*** against the light
contromano: ***andare a contromano*** be going the wrong way
contromarca *f* (*pl* -che) token
contromisura *f* countermeasure
controproducente counterproductive
controproposta *f* counter-proposal
contrordine *m* counterorder
controsenso *m* contradiction in terms; (*assurdità*) nonsense
controversia *f* controversy, dispute; DIR litigation
controverso controversial
controvoglia unwillingly
contusione *f* bruise
contuso bruised
convalescente **1** *agg* convalescent **2** *m/f* person who is convalescent
convalescenza *f* convalescence; ***essere in convalescenza*** be convalescing
convalidare ⟨1m⟩ validate
convegno *m* convention; *luogo* meeting place
convenevoli *mpl* pleasantries
conveniente (*vantaggioso*) good; (*opportuno*) appropriate
convenienza *f di prezzo*, *offerta* good value; *di gesto* appropriateness; ***fare qc per convenienza*** do sth out of self-interest
convenire ⟨4p⟩ **1** *v/i* gather, meet; (*concordare*) agree; (*essere opportuno*) be advisable, be better **2** *v/t* (*stabilire*) stipulate
convento *m di monache* convent; *di monaci* monastery
convenuto *pp* → ***convenire***
convenzionale conventional
convenzione *f* convention; (*accordo*) agreement, convention
convergere ⟨3uu⟩ converge
conversare ⟨1b⟩ talk, make conversation
conversazione *f* conversation
conversione *f* conversion; AUTO U-turn
convertibile convertible
convertibilità *f* convertibility

convertire ⟨4b or d⟩ convert
convertirsi be converted
convincere ⟨3d⟩ convince
convinto *pp* → ***convincere***
convinzione *f* conviction
convivente *m/f* common-law husband; *donna* common-law wife
convivenza *f* living together, cohabitation
convivere ⟨3zz⟩ live together
convocare ⟨1l, c & d⟩ call, convene
convocazione *f* calling, convening
convoglio *m* (*pl* -gli) MIL, MAR convoy; FERR train
cooperare ⟨1m & c⟩ co-operate (***a*** in); (*contribuire*) contribute (***a*** to)
cooperativa *f*: (***società*** *f*) ***cooperativa*** co-operative; ***cooperativa di consumo*** cooperative (store)
cooperativo cooperative
cooperazione *f* cooperation
coordinamento *m* co-ordination
coordinare ⟨1m⟩ co-ordinate
coordinata *f* MAT co-ordinate
coordinatore *m*, **-trice** *f* co-ordinator
coordinazione *f* co-ordination
coperchio *m* (*pl* -chi) lid, top
coperta *f* blanket; MAR deck; ***coperta imbottita*** quilt
copertina *f* cover
coperto 1 *pp* → ***coprire* 2** *agg* covered (***di*** with); *cielo* overcast, cloudy **3** *m* cover, shelter; *piatti e posate* place; *prezzo* cover charge; ***essere al coperto*** be under cover, be sheltered
copertone *m* AUTO tyre, *Am* tire
copertura *f* cover; ***copertura delle spese*** covering one's costs
copia *f* copy; FOT print, copy; ***in duplice copia*** in duplicate
copiare ⟨1k & c⟩ copy
copione *m per attore* script
copioso copious, abundant
copisteria *f* copy centre (*Am* center)
coppa *f* cup; (*calice*) glass; ***coppa*** (***di***) ***gelato*** dish of ice-cream; AUTO ***coppa dell'olio*** oil sump
coppetta *f di gelato* tub
coppia *f* couple, pair; ***gara*** *f* ***a -e*** doubles
copricapo *m inv* head covering
copricostume *m inv* beachrobe
coprifuoco *m* curfew
copriletto *m inv* bedspread, coverlet
coprire ⟨4f & c⟩ cover; *errore*, *suono* cover up
coprirsi (*vestirsi*) put something on; (*rannuvolarsi*) become overcast
coproduzione *f* co-production, joint production
coraggio *m* courage; (*sfacciataggine*) nerve; ***farsi coraggio*** be brave
coraggioso brave, courageous
corallo *m* coral
Corano *m* Koran
corazza *f* MIL armo(u)r; ZO shell
corazzata *f* battleship
corazzato MIL armo(u)red; *fig* hardened (***contro*** to)
corda *f* cord; (*fune*) rope; (*cordicella*) string; MUS string; ***corda vocale*** vocal cord; ***essere giù di corda*** feel down *or* depressed; ***tenere qu sulla corda*** keep s.o. in suspense *or* on tenterhooks; ***tagliare la corda*** cut and run
cordame *m* MAR rigging
cordata *f* ALP rope, roped party
cordiale 1 *agg* cordial; ***-i saluti*** *mpl* kind regards **2** *m* cordial
cordialità *f* cordiality
cordoglio *m* (*dolore*) grief, sorrow; (*condoglianze*) condolences *pl*
cordone *m* cord; *di marciapiedi* kerb, *Am* curb; (*sbarramento*) cordon; ***cordone ombelicale*** umbilical cord
coreografia *f* choreography
coreografo *m*, **-a** *f* choreographer
coriandolo *m* BOT coriander; ***-i*** *mpl* confetti
coricare ⟨1l, c & d⟩ (*adagiare*) lay down; (*mettere a letto*) put to bed
coricarsi lie down
cornacchia *f* crow
cornamusa *f* bagpipes *pl*
cornea *f* cornea
cornetta *f* MUS cornet
cornetto *m* (*brioche*) croissant; (*gelato*) cone, cornet
cornice *f* frame
cornicione *m* ARCHI cornice
corno *m* (*pl gen* le corna) horn; *ramificate* antlers; ***corno da scarpe*** shoehorn; *fig* F ***fare le -a a qu*** cheat on s.o. F; ***facciamo le -a!*** touch wood!; F ***non m'importa un corno*** I don't give a damn F
cornuto F cheated, betrayed
coro *m* chorus; *cantori* choir; ***in coro*** (*insieme*) all together
corona *f* crown; (*rosario*) rosary; ***corona di fiori*** wreath
coronaria *f* ANAT coronary artery
coronario: ***vasi*** *mpl* ***-i*** coronary arteries
corpetto *m da donna* bodice
corpo *m* body; MIL corps; ***corpo celeste*** heavenly body; ***corpo diplomatico*** diplomatic corps; ***corpo di ballo*** dancers *pl*; (***a***) ***corpo a corpo*** hand-to-hand
corporatura *f* build
corporazione *f* corporation

C

corpulento stout, corpulent
Corpus Domini *m* Corpus Christi
corredo *m* equipment; *da sposa* trousseau; *da neonato* layette
correggere ⟨3cc⟩ correct
correggersi correct o.s.
correlazione *f* correlation
corrente **1** *agg* current; *acqua* running; *lingua* fluent; ***di uso corrente*** in common use **2** *m*: ***essere al corrente*** know (***di*** sth); ***tenersi qu al corrente*** keep s.o. up to date, keep s.o. informed **3** *f* current; *fig di opinione* trend; *fazione* faction; ***corrente continua*** direct current; ***corrente d'aria*** draught
correre ⟨3o⟩ **1** *v/t* run; ***correre il pericolo*** run the risk **2** *v/i* run; (*affrettarsi*) hurry; *di veicolo* speed; *di tempo* fly; ***correre in aiuto di qu*** rush to help s.o.; ***correre dietro a qu*** run after s.o.; ***lascia correre!*** let it go!, leave it!; ***corre voce*** it is rumo(u)red
correttezza *f* correctness; (*onestà*) honesty
corretto **1** *pp* → ***correggere*** **2** *agg* correct; ***caffè*** *m* ***corretto*** coffee laced with alcohol
correzione *f* TIP correction
corrida *f* bullfight
corridoio *m* (*pl* -oi) corridor; *in aereo, teatro* aisle
corridore *m in auto* racing driver; *a piedi* runner
corriera *f* coach, bus
corriere *m* courier; ***corriere della droga*** drugs courier, mule P
corrispondente **1** *agg* corresponding **2** *m/f* correspondent; ***corrispondente estero*** foreign correspondent
corrispondenza *f* correspondence; (*posta*) post; ***vendita*** *f* ***per corrispondenza*** mail order (shopping)
corrispondere ⟨3hh⟩ **1** *v/t* (*pagare*) pay; (*ricambiare*) reciprocate **2** *v/i* correspond; (*coincidere*) coincide; (*equivalere*) be equivalent
corrisposto **1** *pp* → ***corrispondere*** **2** *agg* reciprocated
corrodere ⟨3b⟩, **corrodersi** corrode, rust
corrompere ⟨3rr⟩ corrupt; *con denaro* bribe
corrosione *f* corrosion
corrosivo corrosive
corroso *pp* → ***corrodere***
corrotto **1** *pp* → ***corrompere*** **2** *agg* corrupt
corrugare ⟨1e⟩ wrinkle; ***corrugare la fronte*** frown
corruzione *f* corruption; *con denaro* bribery
corsa *f* run; *attività* running; *di autobus* trip, journey; (*gara*) race; ***corsa agli armamenti*** arms race; ***corsa a ostacoli*** *ippica* steeplechase; *atletica* hurdles; ***di corsa*** at a run; *in fretta* in a rush; ***vettura*** *f* ***da corsa*** racing car; ***fare una corsa*** rush, dash; **-e** *pl* races
corsia *f* aisle; *di ospedale* ward; AUTO lane; ***corsia di emergenza*** emergency lane; ***corsia di sorpasso*** overtaking lane; ***a tre -e*** three-lane
Corsica *f* Corsica
corsivo *m* italics *pl*
corso[1] **1** *agg* Corsican **2** *m*, **-a** *f* Corsican
corso[2] **1** *pp* → ***correre*** **2** *m* course; (*strada*) main street; FIN *di moneta* circulation; *di titoli* rate; ***corso d'acqua*** watercourse; ***corso di lingue*** language course; ***corso dei cambi*** exchange rate, rate of exchange; ***corso di chiusura*** closing rate; FIN ***fuori corso*** out of circulation; TIP ***in corso di stampa*** being printed; ***lavori*** *mpl* ***in corso*** work in progress; ***si sposeranno nel corso dell'anno*** they'll get married this year
corte *f* court; ***Corte di giustizia europea*** European Court of Justice
corteccia *f* (*pl* -cce) bark
corteggiare ⟨1f⟩ court
corteo *m* procession
cortese polite, courteous
cortesia *f* politeness, courtesy; ***per cortesia!*** please!
cortile *m* courtyard
cortina *f* curtain
corto short; ***tagliar corto*** cut it short; ***essere a corto di quattrini*** be short of money
cortocircuito *m* short (circuit)
cortometraggio *m* short
corvo *m* rook; ***corvo imperiale*** raven
cosa *f* thing; (***che***) ***cosa*** what; ***qualche cosa*** something; ***dimmi una cosa*** tell me something; ***una cosa da nulla*** a trifle; ***un'altra cosa*** another thing; **-e** *pl* ***da vedere*** sights; ***fra le altre -e*** among other things; ***tante belle -e!*** all the best!
coscia *f* (*pl* -sce) thigh; GASTR leg
cosciente conscious
coscienza *f* conscience; (*consapevolezza*) consciousness; ***agire secondo coscienza*** listen to one's conscience; ***senza coscienza*** unscrupulous
coscienzioso conscientious
così so; (*in questo modo*) like this; ***così così*** so-so; ***e così via*** and so on; ***per così dire*** so to speak; ***proprio così!*** exactly!; ***basta così!*** that's enough!

cosicché and so
cosiddetto so called
cosiffatto such
cosmesi *f* cosmetics *pl*
cosmetico (*pl* -ci) **1** *agg* cosmetic **2** *m* cosmetic
cosmico (*pl* -ci) cosmic
cosmo *m* cosmos
cosmonauta *m/f* (*pl* -ti) cosmonaut
cosmopolita cosmopolitan
coso *m* F what-d'you-call-it F
cospargere ⟨3uu⟩ sprinkle; (*coprire*) cover (***di*** with)
cosparso *pp* → ***cospargere***
cospirare ⟨1a⟩ conspire
cospiratore *m*, **-trice** *f* conspirator
cospirazione *f* conspiracy
costa *f* coast, coastline; (*pendio*) hillside; ANAT rib; *di libro* spine
costante **1** *agg* constant, steady; MAT constant **2** *f* MAT constant
costanza *f* perseverance
costare ⟨1c⟩ cost; ***costare caro*** be expensive, cost a lot; *fig* cost dearly; ***quanto costa?*** how much is it?
costata *f* rib steak; ***costata di agnello*** lamb chop
costeggiare ⟨1f⟩ skirt, hug
costellazione f constellation
costiero coastal
costituire ⟨4d⟩ constitute; *società* form, create
costituirsi give o.s. up
costituzionale constitutional
costituzione *f* constitution
costo *m* cost; ***costo della vita*** cost of living; ***prezzo*** *m* ***di costo*** cost price; ***-i*** *pl* ***di produzione*** production costs; ***a costo di perdere*** even if it means losing; ***ad ogni costo*** at all costs
costola *f* rib; *di libro* spine
costoletta *f* GASTR cutlet
costoro *pron pl* they; *complemento* them
costoso expensive, costly
costretto *pp* → ***costringere***
costringere ⟨3d⟩ force, compel
costrizione *f* constraint
costruire ⟨4d⟩ build, construct
costruttivo *fig* constructive
costruttore *m*, **-trice** *f* builder; (*fabbricante*) manufacturer
costruzione *f* building, construction; GRAM construction
costui *pron m* he; *complemento* him
costume *m* (*usanza*) custom; (*condotta*) morals *pl*; (*indumento*) costume; ***costume da bagno*** swimming costume, swimsuit; *da uomo* (swimming) trunks; ***costume nazionale*** national costume
cotechino *m kind of pork sausage*
cotenna *f* pigskin; *della pancetta* rind
cotogna *f* quince
cotoletta *f* cutlet; ***cotoletta alla milanese*** *breaded cutlet fried in butter*
cotone *m* cotton; MED ***cotone idrofilo*** cotton wool, *Am* absorbent cotton
cotta *f* F crush
cottimo *m*: ***lavorare a cottimo*** do piecework
cotto **1** *pp* → ***cuocere*** **2** *agg* done, cooked; F *fig* head over heels in love (***di*** with)
cottura *f* cooking
coupon *m inv* coupon
covare ⟨1a⟩ **1** *v/t* sit on, hatch; *fig malattia* sicken for, come down with; *rancore* harbo(u)r **2** *v/i* sit on eggs
covo *m* den; (*nido*) nest; *fig* hideout
covone *m* sheaf
cozza *f* mussel
cozzare ⟨1c⟩: ***cozzare contro*** crash into; *fig* clash with
C.P. *abbr* (= ***Casella Postale***) PO Box (= Post Office Box)
crac *m inv fig* crash
crampo *m* cramp
cranio *m* (*pl* -ni) skull
crash *m* INFOR: ***andare in crash*** crash
cratere *m* crater
cravatta *f* tie; ***cravatta a farfalla*** bow-tie
crawl *m* SP crawl, freestyle
creare ⟨1b⟩ create; *fig* (*causare*) cause
creatività *f* creativity
creativo **1** *agg* creative **2** *m* copywriter
creato **1** *pp* → ***creare*** **2** *m* creation
creatore **1** *agg* creative **2** *m* Creator **3** *m*, **-trice** *f* creator
creatura *f* creature
creazione *f* creation
credente *m/f* believer
credenza[1] *f* belief
credenza[2] *f mobile* dresser
credenziali *fpl* credentials
credere ⟨3a⟩ **1** *v/t* believe; (*pensare*) believe, think; ***lo credo bene!*** I should think so too!; ***credersi*** believe *or* think o.s. to be **2** *v/i* believe; ***credere a qu*** believe s.o.; ***credere in qu*** believe in s.o.; ***credo in Dio*** I believe in God; ***non ci credo*** I don't believe it; ***non credevo ai miei occhi*** I couldn't believe my eyes
credibile credible
credibilità *f* credibility
credito *m* credit; *fig* trust; (*attendibilità*) reliability; ***comprare a credito*** buy on credit; ***dare credito a qc*** believe sth; ***fare credito a qu*** give s.o. credit
creditore *m*, **-trice** *f* creditor

credo *m inv* credo
crema *f* cream; *di latte e uova* custard; ***crema da barba*** shaving foam; ***crema idratante*** moisturizer, moisturizing cream; ***crema solare*** suntan lotion
cremare ⟨1b⟩ cremate
cremazione *f* cremation
cren *m* horseradish
crepa *f* crack
crepaccio *m* (*pl* -cci) cleft; *di ghiacciaio* crevasse
crepare ⟨1b⟩ (*spaccarsi*) crack; F (*morire*) kick the bucket F; ***crepare dalle risa*** split one's sides laughing
crêpe *f inv* pancake
crepitare ⟨1l & b⟩ crackle
crepuscolo *m* twilight
crescendo *m* MUS crescendo
crescente growing; *luna* waxing
crescere ⟨3n⟩ **1** *v/t* bring up, raise **2** *v/i* grow; (*aumentare*) grow, increase
crescione *m* watercress
crescita *f* growth; (*aumento*) growth, increase; ***crescita economica*** economic growth
cresima *f* confirmation
cresimare ⟨1l & b⟩ confirm
crespo *capelli* frizzy
cresta *f* crest; *di montagna* peak
creta *f* clay
cretino F **1** *agg* stupid, idiotic **2** *m*, **-a** *f* idiot
CRI *abbr* (= ***Croce Rossa Italiana***) Italian Red Cross
cric *m inv* AUTO jack
criminale 1 *agg* criminal **2** *m/f* criminal; ***criminale di guerra*** war criminal
criminalità *f* crime
criminalizzare ⟨1a⟩ criminalize
crimine *m* crime
criniera *f* mane
cripta *f* crypt
crisantemo *m* chrysanthemum
crisi *f* crisis; MED fit; ***crisi energetica*** energy crisis; ***crisi degli alloggi*** housing shortage
cristallizzare, cristallizzarsi ⟨1a⟩ crystallize
cristallo *m* crystal; ***bicchiere** m **di cristallo*** crystal glass
cristianesimo *m* Christianity
cristianità *f* (*i cristiani*) Christendom
cristiano 1 *agg* Christian **2** *m*, **-a** *f* Christian
Cristo *m* Christ
criterio *m* (*pl* -ri) criterion; (*buon senso*) common sense
critica *f* (*pl* -che) criticism
criticare ⟨1l & d⟩ criticize
critico (*pl* -ci) **1** *agg* critical **2** *m*, **-a** *f* critic
croato 1 *agg* Croatian **2** *m*, **-a** *f* Croat, Croatian
Croazia *f* Croatia
croccante 1 *agg* crisp, crunchy **2** *m* GASTR nut brittle
crocchetta *f* GASTR potato croquette
croce *f* cross; ***Croce Rossa*** Red Cross; ***farsi il segno della croce*** cross o.s.; ***a occhio e croce*** at a rough guess
crocevia *m* crossroads *inv*
crociata *f* crusade
crociera *f* cruise; ARCHI crossing; ***velocità** f **di crociera*** cruising speed
crocifiggere ⟨3mm⟩ crucify
crocifissione *f* crucifixion
crocifisso 1 *pp* → ***crocifiggere*** **2** *m* crucifix
croco *m* BOT crocus
crollare ⟨1c⟩ collapse
crollo *m* collapse
cromare ⟨1c⟩ chrome, chromium-plate
cromatico (*pl* -ci) MUS chromatic
cromo *m* chrome
cronaca *f* (*pl* -che) chronicle; *di partita* commentary; ***fatto di cronaca*** news item; ***cronaca nera*** crime news; ***essere al centro della cronaca*** be front-page news
cronico (*pl* -ci) chronic
cronista *m/f* (*mpl* -i) reporter; *di partita* commentator
cronologia *f* chronology
cronologico (*pl* -ci) chronological
cronometrare ⟨1a⟩ time
cronometro *m* chronometer; SP stopwatch
crosta *f* crust; MED scab; *di formaggio* rind
crostacei *mpl* shellfish
crostata *f* GASTR tart
crostino *m* GASTR crouton
cruciale crucial
cruciverba *m inv* crossword (puzzle)
crudele cruel
crudeltà *f* cruelty
crudo raw
crumiro *m*, **-a** *f* scab
crusca *f* bran
cruscotto *m* dashboard; *scomparto* glove compartment
c.s. *abbr* (= ***come sopra***) as above
CSI *abbr* (= ***Comunità di Stati Indipendenti***) CIS (= Commonwealth of Independent States)
c.to *abbr* (= ***conto***) acct (= account)
Cuba *f* Cuba
cubano 1 *agg* Cuban **2** *m*, **-a** *f* Cuban
cubetto *m* (small) cube; ***cubetto di***

ghiaccio ice cube
cubico (*pl* -ci) cubic
cubo 1 *agg* cubic **2** *m* cube
cuccagna *f*: (***paese*** *m* ***della***) ***cuccagna*** land of plenty
cuccetta *f* FERR couchette; MAR berth
cucchiaiata *f* spoonful
cucchiaino *m* teaspoon
cucchiaio *m* (*pl* -ai) spoon; ***cucchiaio da tavola*** tablespoon
cuccia *f* (*pl* -cce) dog's basket; *esterna* kennel
cucciolo *m* cub; *di cane* puppy
cucina *f* kitchen; *cibi* food; ***cucina casalinga*** home cooking; ***cucina a gas*** gas cooker *or* stove; ***libro di cucina*** cook book
cucinare ⟨1a⟩ cook
cucinino *m* kitchenette
cucire ⟨4a⟩ sew; ***macchina*** *f* ***da cucire*** sewing-machine
cucito 1 *agg* sewn **2** *m* sewing
cucitura *f* seam
cuculo *m* cuckoo
cuffia *f da piscina* swimming cap; RAD, TV headphones *pl*; ***cuffia da bagno*** shower cap
cugino *m*, **-a** *f* cousin
cui *persona* who, whom *fml*; *cose* which; ***la casa in cui abitano*** the house they live in, the house in which they live, the house where they live; ***il cui nome*** whose name; ***per cui*** so
culinario cookery *attr*, culinary; ***arte*** *f* ***-a*** culinary art, cookery
culla *f* cradle
cullare ⟨1a⟩ rock
culminante: ***punto*** *m* ***culminante*** climax
culminare ⟨1l⟩ culminate
culmine *m* peak
culo V *m* arse V, *Am* ass V
culto *m* cult; *religione* religion
cultura *f* culture; ***cultura di massa*** mass culture; ***cultura generale*** general knowledge
culturale cultural
culturismo *m* body-building
cumulativo cumulative; ***biglietto*** *m* ***cumulativo*** group ticket
cumulo *m* heap, pile
cuneo *m* wedge
cunetta *f fondo stradale* bump
cuocere ⟨3p⟩ cook; *pane* bake
cuoco *m* (*pl* -chi), **-a** *f* cook
cuoio *m* leather; ***cuoio capelluto*** scalp; F ***tirare le -a*** kick the bucket F
cuore *m* heart; *carte* ***-i*** *pl* hearts; ***di cuore*** wholeheartedly; ***senza cuore*** heartless; *fig* ***nel cuore di*** in the heart of; ***nel cuore della notte*** in the middle of the night; ***stare a cuore a qu*** be very important to s.o.
cupo gloomy; *suono* deep
cupola *f* dome
cura *f* care; MED treatment; ***cura dimagrante*** diet; ***avere cura di qc*** take care of sth; ***casa*** *f* ***di cura*** nursing home
curabile curable
curare ⟨1a⟩ take care of; MED treat
curarsi look after o.s.; ***non curarti di loro*** don't care about them
curato *m* parish priest
curatore *m*, **-trice** *f fiduciario* trustee; *di testo* editor; ***curatore fallimentare*** official receiver
curia *f* curia
curiosare ⟨1a⟩ have a look around; *spreg* pry (***in*** into)
curiosità *f inv* curiosity
curioso curious
cursore *m* INFOR cursor
curva *f* curve
curvare ⟨1a⟩ curve; *schiena* bend
curvarsi bend
curvatura *f* curve
curvo curved; *persona* bent
cuscinetto *m* TEC bearing; ***cuscinetto a sfere*** ball bearing; POL ***stato*** *m* ***cuscinetto*** buffer state
cuscino *m* cushion; (*guanciale*) pillow
custode *m/f* caretaker; ***angelo*** *m* ***custode*** guardian angel
custodia *f* care; DIR custody; (*astuccio*) case
custodire ⟨4d⟩ (*conservare*) keep
cute *f* skin
CV *abbr* (= ***Cavallo Vapore***) HP (= horsepower); (= ***curriculum vitae***) CV (= curriculum vitae)
cyclette *f* exercise bike

D

da *prp stato in luogo* at; *moto da luogo* from; *moto a luogo* to; *tempo* since; *con verbo passivo* by; ***viene da Roma*** he comes from Rome; ***sono da mio fratello*** I'm at my brother's (place); ***ero da loro*** I was at their place; ***passo da Firenze*** I'm going via Florence; ***vado dal medico*** I'm going to the doctor's; ***da ieri*** since yesterday; ***da oggi in poi*** from now on, starting from today; ***da bambino*** as a child; ***l'ho fatto da me*** I did it myself; ***qualcosa da mangiare*** something to eat; ***francobollo da 1000 lire*** 1000 lire stamp; ***la donna -i capelli grigi*** the woman with grey hair
dà → ***dare***
daccapo → ***capo***
dado *m* dice; GASTR stock cube; TEC nut
dagli *prp* **da** and *art* ***gli***
dai[1] *prp* **da** and *art* ***i***
dai[2] → ***dare***
daino *m* deer; (*pelle*) buckskin
dal *prp* **da** and *art* ***il***
dalia *f* dahlia
dall', dalla, dalle, dallo *prp* **da** and *art* ***l', la, le, lo***
daltonico *agg* (*pl* -ci) colo(u)r-blind
dama *f* lady; *gioco* draughts, *Am* checkers
damasco *m* (*pl* -chi) damask
damigiana *f* demijohn
danaro *m* → ***denaro***
danese 1 *m/agg* Danish **2** *m/f* Dane
Danimarca *f* Denmark
danneggiare ⟨1f⟩ (*rovinare*) damage; (*nuocere*) harm
danno *m* damage; (*a persona*) harm; ***risarcire i -i a qu*** compensate s.o. for the damage; ***-i*** *pl* ***all'ambiente*** environmental damage, damage to the environment
dannoso harmful
danza *f* dance; ***danza classica*** ballet
danzare ⟨1a⟩ *v/t & v/i* dance
dappertutto everywhere
dappoco *agg inv* (*inetto*) worthless; (*irrilevante*) minor, unimportant
dapprima at first
dare ⟨1r⟩ **1** *v/t* give; ***dare qc a qu*** give s.o. sth, give sth to s.o.; ***dare uno sguardo a qc*** have a look at sth; ***dammi del tu*** call me 'tu'; ***mi dia del lei*** address me as 'lei'; ***dare peso a qc*** give weight to sth; SP ***dare il via*** give the off; *fig* ***dare il via a qc*** get sth under way **2** *v/i di finestra* overlook (***su*** sth); *di porta* lead into (***su*** sth); *fig* ***dare nell'occhio*** attract attention, be noticed **3** *m* FIN debit; ***dare e avere*** debit and credit
darsi *v/r* give each other; (*dedicarsi*) devote o.s. (***a*** to); ***darsi al commercio*** go into business; ***darsela a gambe*** take to one's heels; ***può darsi*** perhaps
darsena *f* dock
data *f* date; ***data di nascita*** date of birth; ***data di scadenza*** expiry date; ***senza indicazione di data*** undated
datare ⟨1a⟩ **1** *v/t* date; *lettera* date, put the date on **2** *v/i*: ***a datare da oggi*** from today
dato 1 *pp* → ***dare*** **2** *agg* (*certo*) given, particular; (*dedito*) addicted (***a*** to); ***in -i casi*** in certain cases; ***dato che*** given that **3** *m* piece of data; ***-i*** *pl* data; INFOR ***elaborazione*** *f* ***dei dato*** data processing; ***supporto*** *m* ***dato*** data medium
datore *m*, **-trice** *f*: ***datore di lavoro*** employer
dattero *m* date; (*albero*) date palm
dattilografare ⟨1n⟩ type
dattilografia *f* typing
dattilografo *m*, **-a** *f* typist
davanti 1 *prp*: ***davanti a*** in front of **2** *avv* in front; (*dirimpetto*) opposite; ***se mi stai davanti*** if you stand in front of me **3** *agg inv* front **4** *m* front
davanzale *m* window sill
davanzo more than enough
davvero really
dazio *m* (*pl* -zi) duty; (*posto*) customs; ***dazio d'importazione*** import duty; ***dazio d'esportazione*** export duty; ***esente da dazio*** duty-free
d.C. *abbr* (= ***dopo Cristo***) AD (= anno domini)
dea *f* goddess
debito 1 *agg* due, proper **2** *m* debt; (*dovere*) duty; FIN ***debito pubblico*** national debt; ***avere un debito con qu*** be in debt to s.o.; *fig* ***sentirsi in debito verso qu*** feel indebted to s.o.
debitore *m*, **-trice** *f* debtor; ***essere debitore di qc a qu*** owe s.o. sth, owe sth to s.o.
debole 1 *agg* weak; (*voce*) weak, faint; (*luce*) dim **2** *m* weakness; ***avere un debole per qu*** have a soft spot for s.o.
debolezza *f* weakness
debuttante *m/f* beginner; *artista* perform-

er at the start of his / her career
debuttare ⟨1a⟩ make one's début
debutto *m* début
decadente decadent
decadenza *f* decadence
decaffeinato decaffeinated, decaff F
decalcomania *f* transfer, *Am* decal
decano *m* dean
decappottabile *f/agg* AUTO convertible
decathlon *m* decathlon
decedere ⟨3l⟩: ***è deceduto ieri*** he died yesterday
decelerare ⟨1b & m⟩ *v/t & v/i* slow down
decennio *m* (*pl* -ni) decade
decente *agg* decent
decentramento *m* decentralization
decentrare ⟨1b⟩ decentralize
decesso *m* death
decidere ⟨3q⟩ **1** *v/t questione* settle; *data* decide on, settle on; ***decidere di fare qc*** decide to do sth **2** *v/i* decide
decidersi decide (***a*** to), make up one's mind (***a*** to)
decifrare ⟨1a⟩ decipher
decimale *m/agg* decimal
decimetro *m* decimetre, *Am* -meter
decimo *m/agg* tenth
decina *f* MATH ten; ***una decina*** about ten
decisione *f* decision; (*risolutezza*) decisiveness; ***prendere una decisione*** make a decision; ***decisione della maggioranza*** majority decision
decisivo decisive
deciso 1 *pp* → ***decidere* 2** *agg* (*definito*) definite; (*risoluto*) determined; (*netto*) clear; (*spiccato*) marked
declassare ⟨1a⟩ *oggetto* downgrade; *persona* demote
declinare ⟨1a⟩ **1** *v/t* decline; ***declinare ogni responsabilità*** disclaim all responsibility **2** *v/i* (*tramontare*) set; (*diminuire*) decline
declinazione *f* GRAM declension
declino *m fig* decline
decodificatore *m* decoder
decollare ⟨1c⟩ take off
decollo *m* take-off
decomporre ⟨3ll⟩ **1** *v/i* (*putrefarsi*) decompose **2** *v/t* CHIM break down
decomposizione *f* decomposition; CHIM breaking down
decompressione *f* decompression
decongestionare ⟨1a⟩ *strada*, MED relieve congestion in; ***decongestionare il traffico*** relieve traffic congestion
decorare ⟨1b⟩ decorate
decoratore *m*, **-trice** *f* decorator
decorazione *f* decoration
decoro *m* decorum
decoroso decorous
decorrenza *f*: ***con immediata decorrenza*** with immediate effect
decorrere ⟨3o⟩ *v/i* pass; ***a decorrere da oggi*** with effect from today
decorso 1 *pp* → ***decorrere* 2** *m di malattia* course
decrepito decrepit
decrescere ⟨3n⟩ decrease, fall
decreto *m* decree; ***decreto-legge*** *m decree passed in exceptional circumstances that has the force of law*
dedica *f* (*pl* -che) dedication
dedicare ⟨1b & d⟩ dedicate
dedicarsi dedicate o.s.
dedito dedicated (***a*** to); *a un vizio* addicted (***a*** to)
dedizione *f* dedication
dedurre ⟨3e⟩ deduce; FIN deduct; (*derivare*) derive
deduttivo deductive
deduzione *f* deduction
defalcare ⟨1d⟩ deduct
defalco *m* (*pl* -chi) deduction
defezione *f* defection
deficiente 1 *agg* (*mancante*) deficient, lacking (***di*** in) **2** *m/f* backward person; *insulto* idiot, moron
deficienza *f* (*scarsezza*) deficiency, lack (***di*** of)
deficit *m inv* deficit; ***deficit del bilancio pubblico*** budget deficit, public spending deficit
definire ⟨4d⟩ define; (*risolvere*) settle
definitivo definitive
definizione *f* definition; DIR settlement
deflettore *m* AUTO quarterlight
deflusso *m* ebb
deformare ⟨1a⟩ deform; *legno* warp; *metallo* buckle; *fig* distort
deformarsi *di legno* warp; *di metallo* buckle; *di scarpe* lose their shape
deformazione *f* deformation; *di legno* warping; *di metallo* buckling; *fisica* deformity; *fig*, OTT distortion
deforme deformed
defunto 1 *agg* dead; *fig* defunct **2** *m*, **-a** *f* DIR: ***il defunto*** the deceased
degenerare ⟨1m & b⟩ degenerate (***in*** into)
degente *m/f* patient
degenza *f* stay (in bed / hospital)
degli *prp* ***di*** and *art* ***gli***
degnare ⟨1a⟩ **1** *v/t*: ***degnare qu di una parola*** deign to speak to s.o. **2** *v/i e* **degnarsi**: ***degnarsi di*** deign to, condescend to
degno worthy; ***degno di nota*** noteworthy; ***degno di un re*** fit for a king

D

degradante degrading, demeaning
degradare ⟨1a⟩ degrade; *da un rango* demote
degradarsi demean o.s., lower o.s.; CHIM degrade; *di ambiente, edifici* deteriorate
degradazione *f* degradation
degrado *m* deterioration; ***degrado ambientale*** damage to the environment
degustazione *f* tasting; ***degustazione del vino*** wine tasting
dei[1] *prp* ***di*** and *art* ***i***
dei[2] (*pl* di ***dio***): ***gli dei*** *mpl* the Gods
del *prp* ***di*** and *art* ***il***
delatore *m*, **-trice** *f* informer
delega *f* (*pl* -ghe) delegation; (*procura*) proxy
delegare ⟨1l & b & e⟩ delegate
delegato 1 *agg*: ***amministratore*** *m* ***delegato*** managing director **2** *m*, **-a** *f* delegate; ***delegato sindacale*** (trade) union delegate
delegazione *f* delegation
delfino *m* dolphin
deliberare ⟨1m⟩ **1** *v/t* decide **2** *v/i* DIR deliberate (***su*** on)
delicatezza *f* delicacy; (*discrezione*) tact, delicacy; (*debolezza*) frailty, delicacy
delicato delicate; (*persona*) frail, delicate; (*colore*) soft
delimitare ⟨1m⟩ define
delineare ⟨1m⟩ outline
delinquente *m/f* criminal; *fig* scoundrel; ***delinquente minorile*** juvenile delinquent
delinquenza *f* crime; ***delinquenza minorile*** juvenile delinquency; ***delinquenza organizzata*** organized crime
delirare ⟨1a⟩ be in raptures, rave; MED be delirious
delirio *m* (*pl* -ri) delirium; *fig* frenzy
delitto *m* crime; ***corpo*** *m* ***del delitto*** corpus delicti
delizia *f* delight
delizioso delightful; *cibo* delicious
dell', della, delle, dello *prp* ***di*** and *art* ***l', la, le, lo***
delta *m* delta
deltaplanista *m/f* (*mpl* -ti) hang-glider
deltaplano *m* hang-glider; *attività* hang-gliding
deludere ⟨3q⟩ disappoint
delusione *f* disappointment
deluso disappointed
demagogo *m* (*pl* -ghi) demagog(ue)
demanio *m* State property
demente *m/f* MED person with dementia; F lunatic F
demenza *f* MED dementia; F lunacy F, madness F
democratico (*pl* -ci) **1** *agg* democratic **2** *m*, **-a** *f* democrat
democrazia *f* democracy
democristiano *m/agg* Christian Democrat
demografia *f* demography
demogafico demographic
demolire ⟨4d⟩ demolish (*anche fig*); *macchine* crush
demolizione *f* demolition; *di macchine* crushing
demone *m* spirit
demonio *m* (*pl* -ni) devil
demoralizzarsi ⟨1a⟩ become demoralized, lose heart
demotivato demotivated
denaro *m* money; ***denaro contante*** cash
denatalità *f* decline in the birth rate
denaturato CHIM: ***alcol*** *m* ***denaturato*** methlyated spirits *pl*
denominare ⟨1m & c⟩ name, call
denominazione *f* name; ***denominazione di origine controllata*** *term signifying that a wine is of a certain origin and quality*
denotare ⟨1l & b or c⟩ denote, be indicative of
densità *f* density; *della nebbia* thickness, density; ***densità della popolazione*** population density
denso dense; *fumo, nebbia* thick, dense
dentario (*pl* -ri) dental
dentata *f* bite; *segno* toothmark
dente *m* tooth; ***dente del giudizio*** wisdom tooth; ***dente di leone*** dandelion; ***mal*** *m* ***di -i*** toothache; *fig* ***stringere i -i*** grit one's teeth; ***parlare fra i -i*** mumble; GASTR ***al dente*** al dente, *still slightly firm*
dentice *m fish native to the Mediterranean*
dentiera *f* dentures
dentifricio *m* (*pl* -ci) toothpaste
dentista *m/f* (*mpl* -ti) dentist
dentro 1 *prp* in, inside; (*entro*) within; ***dentro di sé*** inwardly **2** *avv* in, inside; (*nell' intimo*) inwardly; ***qui / lì dentro*** in here / there; F ***metter dentro*** put inside *or* away F
denuclearizzato nuclear-free, denuclearized
denuncia *f* (*pl* -ce) denunciation; *alla polizia, alla società di assicurazione* complaint, report; *di nascita, morte* registration; ***denuncia dei redditi*** income tax return
denunciare ⟨1f⟩ denounce; *alla polizia, alla società di assicurazione* report; *nascita* register
denunzia → ***denuncia***
denutrito undernourished

deodorante *m* deodorant
depilare ⟨1a⟩ *con pinzette* pluck; *con rasoio* shave; *con ceretta* wax
depilatorio (*pl* -ri) **1** *agg* depilatory **2** *m* hair-remover, depilatory
dépliant *m inv* leaflet; (*opuscolo*) brochure
deplorare ⟨1c⟩ deplore
deplorevole deplorable
deporre ⟨3ll⟩ **1** *v/t* put down; *uova* lay; *re, presidente* depose; ***deporre il falso*** commit perjury **2** *v/i* DIR testify, give evidence (***a favore di*** for, ***a carico di*** against)
deportare ⟨1c⟩ deport
depositare ⟨1m & c⟩ deposit; (*posare*) put down, deposit; (*registrare*) register
depositato: ***marchio*** *m* ***depositato*** registered trademark
deposito *m* deposit; (*magazzino*) warehouse; MIL, *rimessa* depot; FERR ***deposito bagagli*** left-luggage office, *Am* baggage checkroom; ***deposito di munizioni*** ammunition dump; FIN ***deposito vincolato*** term deposit
deposizione *f* deposition; *da un'alta carica* removal; *di regnante*; overthrow
deposto *pp* → ***deporre***
depravato *m*, **-a** *f* depraved person
depressione *f* depression; ***depressione atmosferica*** atmospheric depression; ***zona*** *f* ***di depressione atmosferica*** area of low pressure, low
depresso **1** *pp* → ***deprimere*** **2** *agg* depressed
deprezzamento *m* depreciation
deprezzare ⟨1b⟩ lower the value of
deprezzarsi depreciate
deprimente depressing
deprimere ⟨3r⟩ depress
deprimersi get depressed
depurare ⟨1a⟩ purify
depuratore *m* purifier
depurazione *f* purification; ***impianto*** *m* ***di depurazione*** purification plant
deputato *m*, **-a** *f* Member of Parliament, *Am* Representative
deragliare ⟨1g⟩ FERR go off *or* leave the rails; ***far deragliare*** derail
deridere ⟨3g⟩ deride
derisione *f* derision
deriso *pp* → ***deridere***
deriva *f* MAR drift; ***andare alla deriva*** drift
derivare ⟨1a⟩ **1** *v/t* derive **2** *v/i*: ***derivare da*** come from, derive from
derivazione *f* derivation; (*discendenza*) origin; EL shunt; TELEC extension
dermatologia *f* dermatology
dermatologo *m* (*pl* -gi), **-a** *f* dermatologist
derrate *fpl* food
derubare ⟨1a⟩ rob
descritto *pp* → ***descrivere***
descrivere ⟨3tt⟩ describe
descrizione *f* description
deserto **1** *agg* deserted; ***isola*** *f* ***-a*** desert island **2** *m* desert
desiderare ⟨1m⟩ (*volere*) want, wish; *intensamente* long for, crave; *sessualmente* desire; ***desidera?*** can I help you?; ***farsi desiderare*** play hard to get; (*tardare*) keep people waiting; ***lascia a desiderare*** it leaves a lot to be desired
desiderio *m* (*pl* -ri) wish (***di*** for); *intenso* longing (***di*** for); *sessuale* desire (***di*** for)
design *m inv* design
designare ⟨1a⟩ (*nominare*) appoint, name; (*fissare*) fix, set
designer *m/f inv* designer
desistere ⟨3f⟩: ***desistere da*** desist from
desolante distressing
desolato desolate; ***sono desolato!*** I am so sorry
desolazione *f* desolation; (*dolore*) distress
dessert *m inv* dessert
destare ⟨1a⟩ *fig* (a)rouse, awaken
destarsi *fig* be aroused, be awakened
destinare ⟨1a⟩ destine; (*assegnare*) assign; *con il pensiero* mean, intend; *data* fix, set; (*indirizzare*) address (***a*** to)
destinatario *m* (*pl* -ri), **-a** *f di lettera* addressee
destinazione *f*: (***luogo*** *m* ***di***) ***destinazione*** destination
destino *m* destiny
destra *f* right; (*mano*) right hand; ***a destra*** *stato* on the right, to the right; *moto* to the right
destreggiarsi ⟨1f⟩ manœuvre, *Am* maneuver
destrezza *f* skill, dexterity
destro right; (*abile*) skil(l)ful, dexterous
destrorso **1** *agg persona* right-handed; TEC clockwise **2** *m*, **-a** *f* right-hander, right-handed person
detenere ⟨2q⟩ hold; *in prigione* detain, hold
detenuto *m*, **-a** *f* prisoner
detenzione *f imprigionamento* detention; ***detenzione abusiva di armi*** possession of illegal weapons
detergente *m* detergent; *per cosmesi* cleanser
deteriorabile perishable
deteriorarsi ⟨1a⟩ deteriorate
determinare ⟨1m & b⟩ determine, establish; (*causare*) cause, lead to
determinato certain; (*specifico*) particu-

D

lar, specific; (*risoluto*) determined
determinazione *f* determination
detersivo *m* detergent; *per piatti* washing-up liquid, *Am* dishwashing liquid; *per biancheria* detergent, *Br* washing powder
detestare ⟨1b⟩ hate, detest
detonare ⟨1c⟩ detonate
detrarre ⟨3xx⟩ deduct (***da*** from)
detratto *pp* → ***detrarre***
detrazione *f* deduction
detrito *m* debris; GEOL detritus
detta *f*: ***a detta di*** according to
dettaglio *m* (*pl* -gli) detail; FIN ***commercio*** *m* ***al dettaglio*** retail trade
dettare ⟨1a⟩ dictate; ***dettare legge*** lay down the law
dettato *m* dictation
dettatura *f* dictation; ***scrivere sotto dettatura*** take dictation
detto 1 *pp* → ***dire***; ***detto fatto*** no sooner said than done; ***come non detto*** let's forget it **2** *agg* said; (*soprannominato*) known as **3** *m* saying
devastare ⟨1a⟩ devastate
devastazione *f* devastation
deve, devi → ***dovere***
deviare ⟨1h⟩ **1** *v/t traffico, sospetti* divert **2** *v/i* deviate
deviazione *f* deviation; *di traffico* diversion
devo → ***dovere***
devolvere ⟨3g⟩ POL devolve
devoluto *pp* → ***devolvere***
devoluzione *f* POL devolution
devoto 1 *agg* devoted; REL devout **2** *m*, **-a** *f* devotee; REL ***i -i*** the devout
devozione *f* devotion; REL devoutness
di 1 *prp* of; *con il comparativo* than; ***di ferro*** (made of) iron; ***io sono di Roma*** I'm from Rome; ***l'auto di mio padre*** my father's car; ***una tazza di caffè*** a cup of coffee; ***di giorno*** by day; ***parlare di politica*** talk about politics; ***d'estate*** in the summer; ***di questo passo*** at this rate; ***di chi è questo libro?*** whose is this book?, who does this book belong to?; ***più bello di*** prettier than **2** *art* some; *interrogativo* any, some; *neg* any; ***del vino*** some wine
di' → ***dire***
dia → ***dare***
diabete *m* diabetes
diabetico (*pl* -ci) **1** *agg* diabetic **2** *m*, **-a** *f* diabetic
diadema *m* diadem
diaframma *m* (*pl* -i) diaphragm
diagnosi *f inv* diagnosis
diagnosticare ⟨1n, c & d⟩ diagnose
diagonale 1 *agg* diagonal **2** *f* diagonal (line)
diagramma *m* (*pl* -i) diagram
dialetto *m* dialect
dialisi *f inv* dialysis
dialogo *m* (*pl* -ghi) dialog(ue)
diamante *m* diamond
diametro *m* diameter
diapason *m inv* tuning fork
diapositiva *f* FOT slide
diario *m* (*pl* -ri) diary
diarrea *f* diarrh(o)ea
diavolo *m* devil; ***un buon diavolo*** a good fellow; ***mandare qu al diavolo*** tell s.o. to get lost
dibattere ⟨3a⟩ debate, discuss
dibattersi struggle; *fig* struggle (***in*** with)
dibattito *m* debate
dicembre *m* December
diceria *f* rumo(u)r
dichiarare ⟨1a⟩ state; *ufficialmente* declare; *nei giochi di carte* bid; ***ha qualcosa da dichiarare?*** anything to declare?
dichiararsi declare o.s.
dichiarazione *f* declaration; ***dichiarazione dei redditi*** income tax statement; ***dichiarazione doganale*** customs declaration
diciannove nineteen
diciannovesimo *m/agg* nineteenth
diciassette seventeen
diciassettesimo *m/agg* seventeenth
diciottenne *m/f* eighteen-year-old
diciotto eighteen
diciottesimo *m/agg* eighteenth
didattica *f* didactics
dieci ten; ***alle / verso le dieci*** at / about ten (o'clock)
diesel *m* diesel
dieta *f* diet; ***essere a dieta*** be on a diet
dietetica *f* dietetics
dietetico (*pl* -ci) diet *attr*
dietista *m/f* dietitian, dietician
dietro 1 *prp* behind; ***dietro l'angolo*** round the corner; ***dietro di me*** behind me; ***uno dietro l'altro*** *nello spazio* one behind the other; *nel tempo* one after the other; ***dietro ricevuta*** on receipt **2** *avv* behind; *in auto* in the back; ***di dietro*** *stanza, porta* back; *zampe* hind; AUTO rear **3** *m inv* back
difatti *cong* in fact
difendere ⟨3c⟩ defend; (*proteggere*) protect
difensiva *f* defensive; ***stare sulla difensiva*** be on the defensive
difensivo defensive
difensore *m* defender; ***difensore d'ufficio*** legal aid lawyer, *Am* public defender
difesa *f* defence, *Am* defense; ***difesa dei***

consumatori consumer protection; ***legittima difesa*** self-defence (*Am* -defense)
difeso *pp* → ***difendere***
difetto *m* (*imperfezione*) defect; *morale* fault, flaw; (*mancanza*) lack; ***far difetto*** be lacking
difettoso defective
diffamare ⟨1a⟩ slander; *scrivendo* libel
diffamazione *f* defamation of character
differente different (***da*** from, *Am* than)
differenza *f* difference; ***differenza di prezzo*** difference in price; ***a differenza di*** unlike
differenziare ⟨1f⟩ differentiate
differenziarsi differ (***da*** from)
differire ⟨4d⟩ postpone
difficile difficult; (*improbabile*) unlikely
difficoltà *f inv* difficulty; ***senza difficoltà*** easily, without any difficulty
diffida *f* DIR injunction
diffidare ⟨1a⟩ **1** *v/t* DIR issue an injunction against; ***diffidare qu dal fare qc*** warn s.o. not to do sth **2** *v/i*: ***diffidare di qu*** distrust s.o., mistrust s.o.
diffidente distrustful, mistrustful
diffidenza *f* distrust, mistrust
diffondere ⟨3bb⟩ diffuse; *fig* spread
diffondersi *fig* spread; (*dilungarsi*) enlarge
diffusione *f di luce, calore* diffusion; *di giornale* circulation
diffuso 1 *pp* → ***diffondere*** **2** *agg* widespread; (*luce*) diffuse
difterite *f* diphtheria
diga *f* (*pl* -ghe) *fluviale* dam; *litoranea* dyke; *portuale* breakwater
digerire ⟨4d⟩ digest; F (*tollerare*) stomach F
digestione *f* digestion
digestivo 1 *agg* digestive **2** *m after-dinner drink*, digestif
digitale digital; ***impronta*** *f* ***digitale*** fingerprint
digitare ⟨1l⟩ INFOR key
digiunare ⟨1a⟩ fast
digiuno 1 *agg* fasting; *fig privo* lacking (***di*** in); ***essere digiuno di notizie*** have no news, not have any news **2** *m* fast; ***a digiuno*** on an empty stomach
dignità *f* dignity
dignitoso dignified
digrignare ⟨1a⟩ gnash
dilagare ⟨1e⟩ flood; *fig* spread rapidly
dilaniare ⟨1k⟩ tear apart
dilapidare ⟨1m⟩ squander
dilatare ⟨1a⟩ FIS expand; *occhi* open wide
dilatarsi *di materiali, metalli* expand; *di pupilla* dilate
dilatazione *f* expansion; *di pupilla* dilation
dilazionare ⟨1a⟩ defer, delay
dilazione *f* extension
dileguarsi ⟨1a⟩ vanish, disappear
dilemma *m* (*pl* -i) dilemma
dilettante *m/f* amateur; *spreg* dilettante
dilettare ⟨1b⟩ delight
dilettarsi: ***dilettarsi di qc*** dabble in sth, do sth as a hobby; ***dilettarsi a fare qc*** take delight in doing sth
diletto[1] **1** *agg* beloved **2** *m*, **-a** *f* beloved
diletto[2] *m* (*piacere*) delight; ***fare qc per diletto*** do sth for pleasure
diligente diligent; (*accurato*) accurate
diligenza *f* diligence
diluire ⟨4d⟩ dilute
dilungarsi ⟨1e⟩ *fig* dwell (***su*** on)
diluviare ⟨1k⟩ pour down
diluvio *m* downpour; *fig* deluge; ***diluvio universale*** Flood
dimagrante: ***cura*** *f* ***dimagrante*** diet
dimagrire ⟨4d⟩ lose weight
dimenare ⟨1a⟩ wave; *coda* wag
dimenarsi throw o.s. about
dimensione *f* dimension; (*grandezza*) size; (*misure*) dimensions
dimenticanza *f* forgetfulness, absent-mindedness; (*svista*) oversight
dimenticare ⟨1m & d⟩ forget
dimenticarsi forget (***di*** sth; ***di fare qc*** to do sth)
dimestichezza *f* familiarity
dimettere ⟨3ee⟩ dismiss (***da*** from); *da ospedali* discharge, release (***da*** from); *da carceri* release (***da*** from)
dimettersi resign (***da*** from)
dimezzare ⟨1b⟩ halve; (*dividere*) halve, divide in two
diminuire ⟨4d⟩ **1** *v/t* reduce, diminish; *prezzi* reduce, lower **2** *v/i* decrease, diminish; *di prezzi, valore* fall, go down; *di vento, rumore* die down
diminuzione *f* decrease; *di prezzi, valore* fall, drop (***di*** in)
dimissioni *fpl* resignation *sg*; ***dare le dimissioni*** resign, hand in one's resignation
dimora *f* residence; ***senza fissa dimora*** of no fixed abode
dimostrare ⟨1a⟩ demonstrate; (*interesse*) show; (*provare*) prove, show
dimostrarsi prove to be
dimostrazione *f* demonstration; (*prova*) proof
dinamica *f* dynamics
dinamico (*pl* -ci) dynamic
dinamismo *m* dynamism
dinamite *f* dynamite

D

D

dinamo *f inv* dynamo
dinanzi *prp*: ***dinanzi a*** *al cospetto di* before
dinastia *f* dynasty
dingo *m inv* dingo
dinosauro *m* dinosaur
dintorno 1 *avv* around **2** *m*: ***-i*** *pl* neighbo(u)rhood
dio *m* (*pl* gli dei) *idolo* god; ***Dio*** God; ***grazie a Dio!*** thank God!, thank goodness!; ***per l'amor di Dio*** for God's *or* goodness sake
diocesi *f inv* diocese
diossina *f* dioxin
dipartimento *m* department
dipendente 1 *agg* dependent **2** *m/f* employee
dipendenza *f* dependence; (*edificio*) annex(e); ***essere alle dipendenza di*** work for
dipendere ⟨3c⟩: ***dipendere da*** (*essere subordinato a*) depend on; (*essere mantenuto da*) be dependent on; (*essere causato da*) derive from, be due to; ***dipende*** it depends; ***questo dipende da te*** it's up to you
dipeso *pp* → ***dipendere***
dipingere ⟨3d⟩ paint; *fig* describe, depict
dipinto 1 *pp* → ***dipingere* 2** *m* painting, picture
diploma *m* (*pl* -i) diploma, certificate; ***diploma di laurea*** degree (certificate)
diplomarsi ⟨1c⟩ obtain a diploma
diplomatico (*pl* -ci) **1** *agg* diplomatic **2** *m* diplomat
diplomato 1 *agg* qualified **2** *m*, **-a** *f* holder of a diploma
diplomazia *f* diplomacy
diporto *m*: ***imbarcazione*** *f* ***da diporto*** pleasure boat
diradare ⟨1a⟩ thin out
diradarsi thin out; *di nebbia* clear, lift
dire ⟨3t⟩ **1** *v/t* say; (*raccontare*) tell; ***dire qc a qu*** tell s.o. sth; ***vale a dire*** that is, in other words; ***a dire il vero*** to tell the truth; ***come si dice … in inglese?*** what's the English for … ?; ***voler dire*** mean **2** *v/i* ***dire bene di qu*** speak highly of s.o.; ***dico sul serio*** I'm serious **3** *m*: ***per sentito dire*** by hearsay; ***hai un bel dire*** say what you like
direttissima *f* ALP shortest *or* most direct route; DIR ***processo*** *m* ***per direttissima*** summary proceedings *pl*
direttiva *f* directive
direttivo 1 *agg di direzione di società* managerial; *comitato*, *consiglio*, POL executive *attr* **2** *m di società* board (of directors); POL leadership
diretto 1 *pp* → ***dirigere* 2** *agg* (*immediato*) direct; ***diretto a*** aimed at; *lettera* addressed to; ***essere diretto a casa*** be heading for home; RAD, TV ***in*** (***ripresa***) ***-a*** live **3** *m* direct train; SP straight
direttore *m*, **-trice** *f* manager; *più in alto nella gerarchia* director; MUS conductor; EDU headmaster, headmistress *f*, *Am* principal; *di giornale*, *rivista* editor (in chief); ***direttore generale*** chief executive officer; ***direttore delle vendite*** sales manager; ***direttore d'orchestra*** conductor; ***direttore tecnico*** technical manager; SP coach and team manager
direzione *f* direction; *di società* management; *di partito* leadership; *ufficio* office; *sede generale* head office; ***in direzione di Roma*** in the direction of Rome
dirigente 1 *agg classe*, *partito* ruling; *personale* managerial **2** *m/f* executive; POL leader
dirigere ⟨3u⟩ direct; *azienda* run, manage; *orchestra* conduct
dirigersi head (***a, verso*** for, towards)
dirigibile *m* airship, dirigible
dirimpetto opposite, across the way; ***dirimpetto a*** facing, in front of
diritto 1 *agg* straight **2** *avv* straight **3** *m* right; DIR law; ***-i*** *pl* (*il compenso*) fees; ***-i d'autore*** copyright; ***diritto commerciale*** commercial law; ***diritto costituzionale*** constitutional law; ***diritto internazionale*** international law; ***diritto di precedenza*** right of way; ***diritto di voto*** right to vote; ***-i*** *pl* ***umani*** human rights; ***parità*** *f* ***di -i*** equal rights; ***aver diritto a*** be entitled to; ***di diritto*** by rights
dirittura *f* straight line; SP straight; *fig* rectitude; ***in dirittura d'arrivo*** in the home straight
diroccato ramshackle
dirottamento *m* hijack(ing)
dirottare ⟨1c⟩ *traffico* divert; *aereo* reroute; *con intenzioni criminali* hijack
dirottatore *m*, **-trice** *f* hijacker
dirotto: ***piove a dirotto*** it's pouring
dirupo *m* precipice
disabile 1 *agg* disabled **2** *m/f* disabled person
disabitato uninhabited
disabituare ⟨1n⟩: ***disabituare qu a qc*** get s.o. out of the habit of sth
disaccordo *m* disagreement
disadattato 1 *agg* maladjusted **2** *m/f* (social) misfit
disadatto unsuitable (***a*** for); *persona* unsuited (***a un lavoro*** to a job)
disadorno bare, unadorned
disagiato uncomfortable; *vita* hard

disagio *m* (*pl* -gi) (*difficoltà*) hardship; (*scomodità*) discomfort; (*imbarazzo*) embarrassment; ***essere a disagio*** be ill at ease
disambientato out of place
disapprovare ⟨1c⟩ disapprove of
disapprovazione *f* disapproval
disappunto *m* disappointment
disarmare ⟨1a⟩ disarm
disarmato unarmed; *fig* defenceless
disarmo *m* POL disarmament
disastro *m* disaster
disastroso disastrous
disattento inattentive
disattenzione *f* inattention, lack of attention; *errore* careless mistake
disavanzo *m* deficit; ***disavanzo della bilancia commerciale*** trade deficit; ***disavanzo commerciale con l'estero*** foreign trade deficit
disavventura *f* misadventure
disboscamento *m* deforestation
disboscare ⟨1d⟩ deforest
disbrigo *m* (*pl* -ghi) dispatch
discapito *m*: ***a discapito di qu*** to the detriment *or* disadvantage of s.o.
discarica *f* (*pl* -che) dumping; (*luogo*) dump
discendente 1 *agg inv* descending **2** *m/f* descendant
discendenza *f* descent; (*discendenti*) descendants
discendere ⟨3c⟩ descend; (*trarre origine*) be a descendant (***da*** of), be descended (***da*** from); *da veicoli, da cavallo* alight (***da*** from)
discepolo *m* disciple
discesa *f* descent; (*pendio*) slope; *di bus* exit; SCI ***discesa libera*** downhill (race); ***strada** f **in discesa*** street that slopes downwards
dischetto *m* INFOR diskette, floppy F
disciogliere ⟨3ss⟩ dissolve; *neve* melt
disciolto *pp* → ***disciogliere***
disciplina *f* discipline
disciplinare 1 *agg* disciplinary **2** *v/t* ⟨1a⟩ discipline
disciplinato disciplined
disco *m* (*pl* -chi) disc, *Am* disk; SP discus; MUS record; INFOR disk; INFOR ***disco rigido*** hard disk; AUTO ***disco orario*** parking disc; ***disco volante*** flying saucer
discobolo *m* discus thrower
discografia *f elenco* recordings, discography; *attività* record industry
discolo 1 *agg* wild, unruly **2** *m* troublemaker
discolpare ⟨1a⟩ clear
discontinuo intermittent; (*disuguale*) erratic
discorde not in agreement, clashing
discordia *f* discord; (*differenza di opinioni*) disagreement; (*litigio*) argument
discorrere ⟨3o⟩ talk (***di*** about)
discorso 1 *pp* → ***discorrere* 2** *m pubblico, ufficiale* speech; (*conversazione*) conversation, talk; ***che -i!*** what rubbish!
discoteca *f* (*pl* -che) *locale* disco; *raccolta* record library
discrepanza *f* discrepancy
discreto (*riservato*) discreet; (*abbastanza buono*) fairly good; (*moderato*) moderate, fair
discrezione *f* discretion; ***a discrezione di*** at the discretion of
discriminare ⟨1m⟩ **1** *v/i* discriminate **2** *v/t stranieri, donne* discriminate against
discriminazione *f* discrimination
discussione *f* discussion; (*litigio*) argument
discusso *pp* → ***discutere***
discutere ⟨3v⟩ **1** *v/t proposta, caso* discuss, talk about; *questione* debate; (*mettere in dubbio*) question; (*contestare*) dispute **2** *v/i* talk; (*litigare*) argue; (*negoziare*) negotiate
discutibile debatable
disdegnare ⟨1a⟩ disdain
disdetta *f* DIR notice; *fig* bad luck
disdetto *pp* → ***disdire***
disdire ⟨3t⟩ *impegno* cancel; *contratto* terminate
disegnare ⟨1a⟩ draw; (*progettare*) design
disegnatore *m*, **-trice** *f* draughtsman, *Am* draftsman; *donna* draughtswoman, *Am* draftswoman; (*progettista*) designer
disegno *m* drawing; (*progetto*) design; ***disegno di legge*** bill
diserbante *m* weed-killer, herbicide
diserbare ⟨1a⟩ weed
diseredare ⟨1b⟩ disinherit
diseredato underprivileged, disadvantaged
disertare ⟨1b⟩ **1** *v/t* desert; ***disertare una riunione*** not attend a meeting **2** *v/i* desert
disertore *m* deserter
diserzione *f* desertion
disfare ⟨3aa⟩ undo; *letto* strip; (*distruggere*) destroy; ***disfare la valigia*** unpack
disfarsi *di neve, ghiaccio* melt; ***disfarsi di*** get rid of
disfatta *f* defeat
disfatto *pp* → ***disfare***
disfunzione *f* MED disorder
disgelo *m* thaw
disgrazia *f* misfortune; (*incidente*) accident; (*sfavore*) disgrace; ***per disgrazia***

D

unfortunately
disgraziato 1 *agg* (*sfortunato*) unlucky, unfortunate **2** *m*, **-a** *f* poor soul; F (*farabutto*) bastard F
disgregare ⟨1b⟩ break up
disgregarsi break up, disintegrate
disguido *m* hiccup, hitch
disgustare ⟨1a⟩ disgust
disgustarsi be disgusted (***di*** by)
disgusto *m* disgust
disgustoso disgusting
disidratato dehydrated
disilludere ⟨3b⟩ disillusion
disillusione *f* disillusionment
disilluso disillusioned
disimparare ⟨1a⟩ forget
disinfettante *m* disinfectant
disinfettare ⟨1b⟩ disinfect
disinfezione *f* disinfection
disingannare ⟨1a⟩ disillusion
disinibito uninhibited
disinnescare ⟨1d⟩ *bomba* defuse
disinnestare ⟨1a⟩ AUTO *marcia* disengage
disinquinare ⟨1a⟩ clean up
disinserire ⟨4d⟩ disconnect
disinteressarsi take no interest (***di*** in)
disinteressato disinterested
disinteresse *m* lack of interest; (*generosità*) unselfishness
disintossicare ⟨1m, c & d⟩ detoxify
disintossicazione *f* treatment for drug / alcohol addiction, *Am* detox F
disinvolto confident
disinvoltura *f* confidence
dislessia *f* dyslexia
dislessico dyslexic
dislivello *m* difference in height; *fig* difference
disobbedire → ***disubbidire***
disoccupato 1 *agg* unemployed, jobless **2** *m*, **-a** *f* person who is unemployed, person without a job; ***i -i*** the unemployed, the jobless
disoccupazione *f* unemployment; ***disoccupazione giovanile*** unemployment among the young, youth unemployment
disonestà *f* dishonesty
disonesto dishonest
disonorare ⟨1a⟩ bring dishono(u)r on
disonore *m* dishono(u)r
disopra 1 *avv* above; ***al disopra di*** above **2** *agg* upper **3** *m* top
disordinato untidy, messy
disordine *m* untidiness, mess; ***in disordine*** untidy, in a mess; ***-i*** *pl* riots, public disorder *sg*
disorganizzazione *f* disorganization, lack of organization
disorientare ⟨1b⟩ disorient(ate)
disorientamento *m* disorientation
disorientato disorient(at)ed
disotto 1 *avv* below; ***al disotto di*** beneath **2** *agg* lower **3** *m* underside
dispari odd
disparità *f* disparity
disparte: ***in disparte*** aside, to one side
dispendio *m* waste
dispendioso expensive
dispensa *f* *stanza* larder; *mobile* cupboard; *pubblicazione* instal(l)ment; DIR exemption; ***dispensa universitaria*** duplicated lecture notes
dispensare ⟨1b⟩ dispense; (*esonerare*) exonerate
disperare ⟨1b⟩ despair (***di*** of); ***far disperare qu*** drive s.o. to despair
disperarsi despair
disperato desperate
disperazione *f* despair, desperation
disperdere ⟨3uu⟩ disperse; *energie*, *sostanze* squander; ***non disperdere nell'ambiente*** please dispose of carefully
disperdersi disperse
dispersione *f* dispersal; CHIM, FIS dispersion; *fig di energie* waste
disperso 1 *pp* → ***disperdere*** **2** *agg* scattered; (*sperduto*) lost, missing
dispetto *m* spite; ***per dispetto*** out of spite; ***a dispetto di qc*** in spite of sth; ***fare -i a qu*** annoy *or* tease s.o.
dispettoso mischievous
dispiacere 1 *v/i* ⟨2k⟩ (*causare dolore*) upset (***a*** s.o.); (*non piacere*) displease (***a*** s.o.); ***mi dispiace*** I'm sorry; ***le dispiace se apro la finestra?*** do you mind if I open the window? **2** *m* (*rammarico*) regret, sorrow; (*dolore*) grief, sadness; (*delusione*) disappointment; ***-i*** (*preoccupazioni*) worries, troubles
display *m* display
disponibile available; (*cortese*) helpful, obliging
disponibilità *f* availability; (*cortesia*) helpfulness
disporre ⟨3ll⟩ **1** *v/t* arrange; (*stabilire*) order **2** *v/i* (*decidere*) make arrangements; ***abbiamo già disposto diversamente*** we've made other arrangements; ***disporre di qc*** have sth (at one's disposal)
dispositivo *m* TEC device
disposizione *f* arrangement; (*norma*) provision; (*attitudine*) aptitude (***a*** for); ***stare / mettere a disposizione di qu*** be / put at s.o.'s disposal
disposto 1 *pp* → ***disporre*** **2** *agg*: ***disposto a*** ready to, willing to; ***essere ben disposto verso qu*** be well disposed to s.o.
dispotico (*pl* -ci) despotic

disprezzare ⟨1b⟩ despise

disprezzo *m* contempt

disputa *f* dispute, argument

disputare ⟨1l⟩ **1** *v/i* argue **2** *v/t* SP take part in; ***disputarsi qc*** compete for sth

dissanguare ⟨1a⟩ *fig* bleed dry, bleed white

disseminare ⟨1m⟩ scatter, disseminate; *fig* spread

dissenso *m* dissent; (*dissapore*) argument, disagreement

dissenteria *f* dysentery

dissentire ⟨4b⟩ disagree (***da*** with)

disseppellire ⟨4d⟩ exhume

dissertazione *f* dissertation

disservizio *m* (*pl* -zi) poor service; (*inefficienza*) inefficiency; (*cattiva gestione*) mismanagement

dissestare ⟨1b⟩ FIN destabilize

dissestato *strada* uneven; *finanze* precarious

dissesto *m* ruin, failure; ***dissesto ecologico*** environmental meltdown

dissetante thirst-quenching

dissetare ⟨1a⟩: ***dissetare qu*** quench s.o.'s thirst

dissetarsi quench one's thirst

dissidente *m/f* dissident

dissimulare ⟨1m⟩ conceal, hide

dissimulazione *f* concealment

dissipare ⟨1l⟩ dissolve; (*sperperare*) squander

dissociare ⟨1f⟩ dissociate

dissociarsi dissociate o.s. (***da*** from)

dissodare ⟨1c⟩ till

dissoluto dissolute

dissolvere ⟨3g⟩ dissolve; *dubbi*, *nebbia* dispel

dissolversi dissolve; (*svanire*) vanish

dissonante dissonant; *fig* discordant

dissonanza *f* MUS dissonance; *fig* clash

dissuadere ⟨2i⟩: ***dissuadere qu da fare qc*** dissuade s.o. from doing sth

dissuaso *pp* → ***dissuadere***

distaccare ⟨1d⟩ detach; SP leave behind

distaccarsi *da persone* detach o.s. (***da*** from)

distacco *m* (*pl* -cchi) detachment (*anche fig*); (*separazione*) separation; SP lead

distante distant, remote, far-off; ***distante da*** far from

distanza *f* distance (*anche fig*); ***comando*** *m* ***a distanza*** remote control

distanziare ⟨1g⟩ **1** *v/t* space out; SP leave behind; (*superare*) overtake

distare ⟨1a⟩: ***l'albergo dista 100 metri dalla stazione*** the hotel is 100 metres from the station; ***quanto dista da qui?*** how far is it from here?

distendere ⟨3c⟩ (*adagiare*) lay; *gambe*, *braccia* stretch out; *muscoli* relax; *bucato* hang out; *nervi* calm

distendersi lie down; (*rilassarsi*) relax

distensione *f* relaxation; POL détente

distensivo relaxing

distesa *f* expanse

disteso **1** *pp* → ***distendere*** **2** *agg* stretched out; (*rilassato*) relaxed

distillare ⟨1a⟩ distil, *Am* distill

distilleria *f* distillery

distinguere ⟨3d⟩ distinguish

distintivo **1** *agg* distinctive **2** *m* badge

distinto **1** *pp* → ***distinguere*** **2** *agg* (*diverso*) different, distinct; (*chiaro*) distinct; *fig* distinguished; ***-i saluti*** yours faithfully

distinzione *f* distinction

distorsione *f* distortion; MED sprain

distrarre ⟨3xx⟩ distract; (*divertire*) entertain

distrarsi (*non essere attento*) get distracted; (*svagarsi*) take one's mind off things

distratto **1** *pp* → ***distrarre*** **2** *agg* absent-minded

distrazione *f* absent-mindedness; (*errore*) inattention; (*svago*) amusement; *che distrae da un'attività* distraction

distretto *m* district

distribuire ⟨4d⟩ distribute; *premi* award, present

distributore *m* distributor; ***distributore*** (***di benzina***) (petrol, *Am* gas) pump; ***distributore automatico*** vending machine; ***distributore automatico di biglietti*** ticket machine

distribuzione *f* distribution; *posta* delivery

distruggere ⟨3cc⟩ destroy

distruttivo destructive

distrutto *pp* → ***distruggere***

distruzione *f* destruction

disturbare ⟨1a⟩ disturb; (*dare fastidio a*) bother; (*sconvolgere*) upset

disturbarsi: ***non si disturbi*** please don't bother

disturbi *mpl* RAD interference *sg*

disturbo *m* trouble, bother; MED ***-i*** *pl* ***di circolazione*** circulation problems

disubbidiente disobedient

disubbdienza *f* disobedience

disubbidire ⟨4d⟩: ***disubbidire a*** disobey

disuguaglianza *f* disparity, difference

disuguale different; *terreno* uneven; *fig* inconsistent, erratic

disumano inhuman

disuso *m*: ***in disuso*** in disuse, disused

ditale *m* thimble

dito *m* (*pl* le dita) finger; *del piede* toe; ***un***

D

dito di vino a drop of wine
ditta *f* company, firm; ***ditta fornitrice*** supplier; ***ditta di vendite per corrispondenza*** mail-order company
dittafono® *m* dictaphone®
dittatore *m* dictator
dittatura *f* dictatorship
diurno daytime *attr*; ***albergo** m* ***diurno*** *place where travellers can have a shower / shave*
diva *f* diva
divagare ⟨1e⟩ digress
divampare ⟨1a⟩ *di rivolta*, *incendio* break out; *di passione* blaze
divano *m* sofa; ***divano letto*** sofa bed
divaricare ⟨1m & d⟩ open (wide)
divario *m* (*pl* -ri) difference
divenire ⟨4p⟩ become
diventare ⟨1b⟩ become; *rosso*, *bianco* turn, go; ***diventare grande*** grow up
diverbio *m* (*pl* -bi) argument
divergente diverging, divergent
divergenza *f* divergence; *di opinioni* difference
divergere ⟨3uu & 3a⟩ diverge
diversamente differently; (*altrimenti*) otherwise
diversificare ⟨1n & d⟩ **1** *v/t* diversify **2** *v/i e* **diversificarsi** differ
diversità *f* difference; (*varietà*) diversity
diversivo *m* diversion, distraction
diverso 1 *agg* (*differente*) different (***da*** from, *Am* than); ***-i*** *pl* several; ***da -i giorni*** for the past few days **2** *mpl* ***-i*** several people
divertente amusing
divertimento *m* amusement; ***buon divertimento!*** have a good time!, enjoy yourself / yourselves!
divertire ⟨4b⟩ amuse
divertirsi enjoy o.s., have a good time
dividendo *m* dividend
dividere ⟨3q⟩ divide; (*condividere*) share
dividersi *di coppia* separate; (*scindersi*) be split, be divided (***in*** into)
divieto *m* ban; ***divieto d'importazione*** import ban; AUTO ***divieto di segnalazioni acustiche*** please do not use your horn; ***divieto di sosta*** no parking
divincolarsi ⟨1m⟩ twist, wriggle
divinità *f inv* divinity
divino divine
divisa *f* uniform; FIN currency
divisione *f* division; ***divisione del lavoro*** division of labo(u)r
divisorio (*pl* -ri) **1** *agg* dividing; ***parete** f* ***-a*** partition wall, stud wall **2** *m* partition
divo *m* star
divorare ⟨1c⟩ devour
divorziare ⟨1c & g⟩ get a divorce
divorziato divorced
divorzio *m* (*pl* -zi) divorce
divulgare ⟨1e⟩ divulge, reveal; (*rendere accessibile*) popularize
divulgazione *f* divulging; *scientifica ecc* popularization
dizionario *m* (*pl* -ri) dictionary
DNA *abbr* (= ***acido deossiribonucleico***) DNA (= deoxyribonucleic acid)
do¹ → ***dare***
do² *m inv* MUS C; *nel solfeggio della scala* doh
dobbiamo → ***dovere***
D.O.C., **doc** *abbr* (= ***Denominazione d'Origine Controllata***) *term signifying that a wine is of a certain origin and quality*
doccia *f* (*pl* -cce) shower; ***fare la doccia*** take a shower
docente 1 *agg* teaching; ***personale** m* ***docente*** teaching staff **2** *m/f* teacher
docile docile
documentare ⟨1a⟩ document
documentarsi collect information
documentario *m* documentary
documentazione *f* documentation
documento *m* document; ***-i*** *pl* papers; ***-i dell'autoveicolo*** car documents
dodici twelve
dogana *f* customs; (*dazio*) (customs) duty
doganale customs *attr*; ***barriera** f* ***doganale*** tariff barrier; ***controllo** m* ***doganale*** customs check; ***dichiarazione** f* ***doganale*** customs declaration; ***formalità** fpl* ***-i*** customs formalities
doganiere *m* customs officer
doglie *fpl*: ***avere le -e*** be in labo(u)r
dogma *m* (*pl* -i) dogma
dolce 1 *agg* sweet; *carattere*, *voce*, *pendio* gentle; *acqua* fresh; *clima* mild; *ricordo* pleasant; *suono* soft **2** *m* (*portata*) dessert, sweet; *di sapore* sweetness; (*torta*) cake; ***-i*** *pl* sweet things
dolcezza *f* sweetness; *di carattere*, *voce* gentleness; *di clima* mildness; *di ricordo* pleasantness; *di suono* softness
dolciastro sweetish; *fig* syrupy, sugary
dolcificante *m* sweetener
dolciumi *mpl* sweets, *Am* candy *sg*
dolente painful, sore
dolere ⟨2e⟩ hurt, be painful; ***mi duole la schiena*** my back hurts, I have a sore back
dolersi be sorry (***di*** for); (*lagnarsi*) complain (***di*** about)
dollaro *m* dollar
dolo *m* malice
Dolomiti *fpl* Dolomites

dolorante sore, painful
dolore *m* pain
doloroso painful
doloso malicious
domanda *f* question; (*richiesta*) request; FIN demand; ***fare una domanda a qu*** ask s.o. a question; ***domanda e offerta*** supply and demand
domandare ⟨1a⟩ **1** *v/t per sapere*: *nome, ora, opinione ecc* ask; *per ottenere*: *informazioni, aiuto ecc* ask for; ***domandare un favore a qu*** ask s.o. a favour; ***domandare scusa*** apologize **2** *v/i*: ***domandare a qu*** ask s.o.; ***domandare di qu*** *per sapere come sta* ask after s.o.; *per parlargli* ask for s.o.
domandarsi wonder, ask o.s.
domani 1 *avv* tomorrow; ***domani mattina*** tomorrow morning; ***domani sera*** tomorrow evening; ***a domani!*** see you tomorrow! **2** *m* tomorrow
domare ⟨1a⟩ tame; *fig* control
domattina tomorrow morning
domenica *f* (*pl* -che) Sunday; ***la domenica, di domenica*** on Sundays
domestico (*pl* -ci) **1** *agg* domestic; ***animale*** *m* ***domestico*** pet **2** *m*, **-a** *f* servant; *donna* maid
domiciliato: ***domiciliato a*** domiciled at
domicilio *m* domicile; (*casa*) home
dominante dominant; *idee* prevailing; *classe* ruling
dominare ⟨1l & c⟩ **1** *v/t* dominate; *materia* master; *passioni* master, overcome **2** *v/i* rule (***su*** over), be master (***su*** of); *fig di confusione* reign
dominazione *f* domination
dominio *m* (*pl* -ni) (*controllo*) control, power; *fig* (*campo*) domain, field
domino *m* mask, domino
donare ⟨1a⟩ donate, give; *sangue* give
donatore *m*, **-trice** *f* donor; ***donatore di sangue*** blood donor
donazione *f* donation
dondolare ⟨1l⟩ **1** *v/t culla* rock; *testa* nod **2** *v/i* sway; (*oscillare*) swing
dondolarsi *su altalena* swing; *su sedia* rock; *fig* hang around
dondolio *m* (gentle) rocking
dondolo *m*: ***cavallo*** *m* ***a dondolo*** rocking horse; ***sedia*** *f* ***a dondolo*** rocking chair
donna *f* woman; *carte da gioco* queen; ***donna di servizio*** home help; ***scarpe*** *fpl* ***da donna*** women's *or* ladies' shoes
donnola *f* weasel
dono *m* gift
dopo 1 *prp* after; ***dopo di te*** after you; ***dopo mangiato*** after eating, after meals; ***subito dopo il bar*** just past the bar **2** *avv* (*in seguito*) afterward(s), after; (*poi*) then; (*più tardi*) later; ***il giorno dopo*** the day after, the next day **3** *conj*: ***dopo che*** after
dopobarba *m inv* aftershave
dopodomani the day after tomorrow
dopoguerra *m inv* post-war period
dopopranzo *m* afternoon
doposci *m inv* après-ski; ***doposci*** *pl stivali* après-ski boots
dopotutto after all
doppiaggio *m di film* dubbing
doppiare ⟨1k⟩ *film* dub; SP lap; MAR round
doppiatore *m*, **-trice** *f* dubber
doppio (*pl* -pi) **1** *agg* double **2** *m* double; SP doubles
doppine *m* duplicate
doppipetto *m* double-breasted jacket
dorare ⟨1c⟩ gild; GASTR brown
dorato 1 *pp* → ***dorare*** **2** *agg* gilded; *sabbia, riflessi* golden; GASTR browned
dorico (*pl* -ci) ARCHI Doric
dormicchiare ⟨1k⟩ doze
dormiglione *m*, **-a** *f* late riser
dormire ⟨4c⟩ sleep
dormita *f* (good) night's sleep
dormitorio *m* (*pl* -ri) dormitory
dormiveglia *m*: ***essere nel dormiveglia*** be only half awake
dorso *m* back; (*di libro*) spine; SP backstroke
dosaggio *m* (*pl* -gi) proportion; *di medicina* dosage
dosare ⟨1c⟩ measure out; *fig* be sparing with; *parole* weigh
dose *f* quantity, amount; MED dose; ***una buona dose di coraggio*** a lot of courage
dosso *m di strada* hump; ***togliersi gli abiti di dosso*** get undressed, take one's clothes off
dotare ⟨1c⟩ provide, supply (***di*** with); *fig* provide, endow (***di*** with)
dotato gifted; ***dotato di*** equipped with
dotazione *f* equipment; *finanziaria* endowment; ***dato in dotazione a qu*** issued to s.o.
dote *f* dowry; *fig* gift
dott. *abbr* (= ***dottore***) Dr (= doctor)
dotto 1 *agg* learned **2** *m* scholar
dottorato *m* doctorate; ***dottorato di ricerca*** doctorate in scientific research
dottore *m* doctor (***in*** of)
dottoressa *f* (woman) doctor
dottrina *f* doctrine
dott.ssa *abbr* (= ***dottoressa***) Dr (= doctor)
dove where; ***dove sei?*** where are you?; ***di dove sei?*** where are you from?; ***fin dove?*** how far?; ***per dove si passa?*** which

way do you go?; ***mettilo dove vuoi*** put it wherever you like

dovere ⟨2f⟩ **1** *v/i* have to, must; ***devo averlo*** I must have it, I have to have it; ***non devo dimenticare*** I mustn't forget; ***deve arrivare oggi*** she is supposed to arrive today; ***come si deve*** (*bene*) properly; *persona* very decent; ***doveva succedere*** it was bound to happen; ***dovresti avvertirlo*** you ought to *or* should let him know **2** *v/t* owe **3** *m* duty; ***per dovere*** out of duty

dovunque **1** *avv* (*dappertutto*) everywhere; (*in qualsiasi luogo*) anywhere **2** *conj* wherever

dovuto **1** *pp* → **dovere** **2** *agg* due; ***dovuto a*** because of, due to

dozzina *f* dozen; ***una dozzina di uova*** a dozen eggs; ***se ne vendono a dozzina*** they are sold by the dozen

dragare ⟨1e⟩ dredge

drago *m* (*pl* -ghi) dragon

dragoncello *m* tarragon

dramma *m* (*pl* -i) drama

drammatico (*pl* -ci) dramatic

drammatizzare ⟨1a⟩ dramatize

drammaturgia *f* theatre, *Am* theater

drammaturgo *m* (*pl* -ghi) playwright

drastico (*pl* -ci) drastic

drenaggio *m* drainage

drenare ⟨1a⟩ drain

dribblare ⟨1a⟩ SP dribble

dritto **1** *agg* straight **2** *avv* straight (ahead) **3** *m di indumento*, *tessuto* right side **4** *m*, **-a** *f* F crafty devil F

drive *m inv* INFOR drive

drizzare ⟨1a⟩ (*raddrizzare*) straighten; (*erigere*) put up, erect; ***drizzare le orecchie*** prick up one's ears

drizzarsi: ***drizzarsi in piedi*** rise to one's feet

droga *f* (*pl* -ghe) drug; ***-ghe*** *pl* ***pesanti / leggere*** hard / soft drugs

drogare ⟨1c & e⟩ drug

drogarsi SP take drugs

drogato *m*, **-a** *f* drug addict

drogheria *f* grocer's

dubbio (*pl* -bbi) **1** *agg* doubtful; (*equivoco*) dubious **2** *m* doubt; ***essere in dubbio fra*** hesitate between; ***mettere qc in dubbio*** doubt sth; ***senza dubbio*** undoubtedly, without a doubt

dubbioso doubtful

dubitare ⟨1l⟩ doubt (***di*** sth); ***dubito che venga*** I doubt whether he'll come

duca *m* (*pl* -chi) duke

ducato *m* (*territorio*) duchy

duchessa *f* duchess

due two; ***a due a due*** in twos, two by two; ***tutt'e due*** both of them; ***vorrei dire due parole*** I'd like to say a word or two

duecento **1** *agg* two hundred **2** *m*: ***il Duecento*** the thirteenth century

duello *m* duel

duemila two thousand

duepezzi *m inv* bikini; (*vestito*) two-piece (suit)

duetto *m* duet; (*persone*) duo, couple

duna *f* (sand) dune

dunque **1** *conj* so; (*allora*) well (then) **2** *m*: ***venire al dunque*** come to the crunch

duomo *m* cathedral

duplex *m inv* party line

duplicato *m* duplicate

duplice double; ***in duplice copia*** in duplicate

durante *prp* during; ***vita natural durante*** for ever and ever

durare ⟨1a⟩ last; (*conservarsi*) keep, last

durata *f* duration, length; *di prodotto* life; ***per tutta la durata di*** throughout; ***durata di volo*** flight time

duraturo lasting

durevole lasting

durezza *f* hardness; *di carne* toughness; (*asprezza*) harshness

duro **1** *agg* hard; *carne*, *persona* tough; *inverno*, *voce* harsh; *congegno*, *meccanismo* stiff; *pane* stale; (*ostinato*) stubborn; F (*stupido*) thick F; ***duro d'orecchi*** hard of hearing; ***tieni duro!*** don't give up!, hang in there! **2** *m* tough guy

durone *m* callous

duttile ductile; *fig* malleable

E

E *abbr* (= ***est***) E (= east)
e and
è → ***essere***
ebanista *m/f* (*mpl* -i) cabinet maker
ebano *m* ebony
ebbe, **ebbi** → ***avere***
ebbene well
ebbrezza *f* drunkenness; *fig* thrill
ebraico (*pl* -ci) **1** *agg* Hebrew; *religione* Jewish **2** *m* Hebrew
ebreo 1 *m*, **-a** *f* Jew; ***gli -i*** the Jews **2** *agg* Jewish
ecc. *abbr* (= ***eccetera***) etc (= et cetera)
eccedente excess
eccedenza *f* excess; (*il di più*) surplus; ***peso*** *m* ***in eccedenza*** excess weight
eccedere ⟨3a⟩ **1** *v/t* exceed, go beyond **2** *v/i* go too far; ***eccedere nel bere*** drink too much
eccellente excellent
eccentrico (*pl* -ci) eccentric
eccessivo excessive
eccesso *m* excess; ***eccesso di personale*** overmanning; ***eccesso di velocità*** speeding
eccetera et cetera
eccetto except
eccettuare ⟨1m & b⟩ except
eccezionale exceptional; ***in via eccezionale*** as an exception
eccezionalmente exceptionally
eccezione *f* exception
ecchimosi *f inv* bruise
eccitante 1 *agg* exciting **2** *m* stimulant
eccitare ⟨1l & b⟩ excite
eccitarsi get excited
eccitazione *f* excitement
ecclesiastico (*pl* -ci) **1** *agg* ecclesiastical **2** *m* priest
ecco (*qui*) here; (*là*) there; ***ecco come*** this is how; ***ecco fatto*** that's that; ***ecco tutto*** that's all; ***eccomi*** here I am; ***eccoli*** here they are; ***eccoti il libro*** here is your book
eclissare ⟨1a⟩ eclipse
eclissarsi *fig* slip away
eclisse *f*, **eclissi** *f inv* eclipse; ***eclisse solare*** solar eclipse; ***eclisse lunare*** lunar eclipse
eco *m/f* (*pl* gli echi) echo
ecografia *f* scan
ecologia *f* ecology
ecologico (*pl* -ci) ecological
ecologista 1 *m/f* ecologist **2** *agg* ecological
ecologo *m* (*pl* -gi), **-a** *f* ecologist
economia *f* economy; *scienza* economics *sg*; ***fare economia*** economize (***di*** on); ***economia di mercato*** market economy; ***università Economia e Commercio*** business school; **-*e*** *pl* savings
economico (*pl* -ci) economic; (*poco costoso*) economical; ***classe*** *f* ***economico*** economy class
economista *m/f* (*mpl* -i) economist
economizzare ⟨1a⟩ **1** *v/t* save **2** *v/i* economize (***su*** on)
economo 1 *agg* thrifty **2** *m*, **-a** *f* bursar
ecosistema *m* ecosystem
eczema *m* (*pl* -i) eczema
ed and
edera *f* ivy
edicola *f* newspaper kiosk
edificare ⟨1m & d⟩ build; *fig* edify
edificio *m* (*pl* -ci) building; *fig* structure
edile construction *attr*, building *attr*
edilizia *f* construction, building; (*urbanistica*) town planning
editare ⟨1a⟩ INFOR edit
editore 1 *agg* publishing **2** *m*, **-trice** *f* publisher; (*curatore*) editor
editoria *f* publishing
editoriale 1 *agg* publishing **2** *m* editorial
edizione *f* edition; ***edizione straordinaria*** *di telegiornale* special news bulletin; *di giornale* extra (edition); ***la quarta edizione del congresso XY*** the fourth XY conference
educare ⟨1l, b & d⟩ educate; (*allevare*) bring up; *gusto*, *orecchio*, *mente* train
educativo education *attr*; (*istruttivo*) educational
educato: (***ben***) ***educato*** well brought-up, polite
educazione *f* education; *dei figli* upbringing; (*buone maniere*) (good) manners; ***educazione fisica*** physical education
effervescente *bibita* fizzy, effervescent; *aspirina* soluble; *personalità* bubbly, effervescent
effettivamente (*in effetti*) in fact; *per rafforzare un'affermazione* really, actually
effettivo 1 *agg* (*reale*) real, actual; (*efficace*) effective; *personale* permanent; MIL regular **2** *m* FIN sum total
effetto *m* (*conseguenza*) effect; (*impressione*) impression; FIN (*cambiale*) bill (of exchange); ***effetto serra*** greenhouse

effect; ***fare effetto*** (*funzionare*) work; (*impressionare*) make an impression; ***fare l'effetto di essere ...*** give the impression of being ...; ***-i*** *pl* ***collaterali*** side effects; ***-i*** *pl* ***personali*** personal effects *or* belongings; ***a tutti gli -i*** to all intents and purposes; ***in -i*** in fact

E

effettuare ⟨1m & b⟩ carry out; *pagamento* make
effettuarsi take place; ***il servizio non si effettua la domenica*** there is no Sunday service
efficace effective
efficacia *f* effectiveness
efficiente efficient; (*funzionante*) in working order
efficienza *f* efficiency
Egitto *m* Egypt
egiziano 1 *agg* Egyptian **2** *m*, **-a** *f* Egyptian
egizio ancient Egyptian
egli *pron m* he
egocentrico egocentric
egoismo *m* selfishness, egoism
egoista 1 *agg* selfish **2** *m/f* (*mpl* -i) selfish person, egoist
egr. *abbr* (= ***egregio***) *form of address used in correspondence*
egregio (*pl* -gi) distinguished; *nelle lettere* ***egregio signore*** Dear Sir
eguale → ***uguale***
eh? eh?, what?
ehi! oi!
E.I. *abbr* (= ***Esercito Italiano***) Italian army
elaborare ⟨1m⟩ elaborate; *dati* process; *piano* draw up, work out
elaborato elaborate
elaboratore *m*: ***elaboratore elettronico*** computer
elaborazione *f* elaboration; ***elaborazione elettronica dei dati*** electronic data processing; ***elaborazione dei testi*** word processing
elasticità *f* elasticity; (*agilità*) agility, suppleness; *fig* flexibility; *della mente* quickness
elastico (*pl* -ci) **1** *agg* elastic; *norme*, *orari* flexible **2** *m* rubber band
elefante *m* elephant
elegante elegant
eleganza *f* elegance
eleggere ⟨3cc⟩ elect
elementare elementary; ***scuola*** *f* ***elementare*** primary school, *Am* elementary school
elemento *m* element; (*componente*) component; ***-i*** *pl* (*rudimenti*) rudiments; (*fatti*) data
elemosina *f* charity; ***chiedere l'elemosina*** beg
elemosinare ⟨1n & c⟩ *v/t* & *v/i* beg
elencare ⟨1b & d⟩ list
elenco *m* (*pl* -chi) list; ***elenco telefonico*** phone book F, telephone directory
eletto 1 *pp* → ***eleggere*** **2** *agg* chosen
elettorale electoral; ***campagna*** *f* ***elettorale*** election campaign
elettorato *m* electorate
elettore *m*, **-trice** *f* voter
elettrauto *m inv auto electrics garage*; *persona* car electrician
elettricista *m/f* (*pl* -i) electrician
elettricità *f* electricity
elettrico (*pl* -ci) electric; ***centrale*** *f* ***-a*** power station
elettrocardiogramma *m* (*pl* -i) electrocardiogram
elettrodo *m* electrode
elettrodomestico *m* (*pl* -ci) household appliance
elettrolisi *f* electrolysis
elettromagnetico electromagnetic
elettromotore *m* electric motor
elettromotrice *f* FERR electric locomotive
elettrone *m* electron
elettronica *f* electronics
elettronico electronic
elettroshock electroshock
elettrotecnica *f* electrical engineering
elettrotecnico (*pl* -ci) **1** *agg* electrical **2** *m* electrical engineer
elevare ⟨1b⟩ raise; *costruzioni* erect; (*promuovere*) promote; *fig migliorare* better
elevato high; *fig* elevated, lofty
elevazione *f* elevation
elezione *f* election
eliambulanza *f* air ambulance
elica *f* (*pl* -che) MAR propeller, screw; AVIA propeller
elicottero *m* helicopter
eliminare ⟨1m⟩ eliminate
eliminatoria *f* SP heat
eliminazione *f* elimination
elio *m* helium
eliporto *m* heliport
élite *f* elite, élite
ella *pron f* she
ellenico (*pl* -ci) Hellenic
ellenismo *m* Hellenism
ellepì *m inv* LP
elmetto *m* helmet
elmo *m* helmet
elogiare ⟨1f & c⟩ praise
elogio *m* (*pl* -gi) praise
eloquente eloquent
eloquenza *f* eloquence

eludere ⟨3q⟩ elude; *sorveglianza, domanda* evade
elusivo elusive
elvetico (*pl* -ci) Swiss
emanare ⟨1a⟩ **1** *v/t* give off; *legge* pass **2** *v/i* emanate, come (***da*** from)
emanazione *f di calore, raggi* emanation; *di legge* passing
emancipare ⟨1m⟩ emancipate
emanciparsi become emancipated
emancipazione *f* emancipation
emarginare ⟨1m⟩ marginalize
emarginato *m*, **-a** *f* person on the fringes of society
ematoma *m* (*pl* -i) h(a)ematoma
embargo *m* (*pl* -ghi) embargo
emblema *m* (*pl* -i) emblem
embolia *f* embolism
embrione *m* embryo
emergenza *f* emergency; ***freno*** *m* ***d'emergenza*** emergency brake; ***in caso di emergenza*** in an emergency
emergere ⟨3uu⟩ emerge; (*distinguersi*) stand out
emersione *f* emersion
emerso *pp* → ***emergere***
emesso *pp* → ***emettere***
emettere ⟨3ee⟩ *luce* give out, emit; *grido, verdetto* give; *calore* give off; FIN issue; TEC emit
emicrania *f* migraine
emigrante *m/f* emigrant
emigrare ⟨1a⟩ emigrate
emigrato *m*, **-a** *f* person who has emigrated
emigrazione *f* emigration
emisfero *m* hemisphere
emissario *m* (*pl* -ri) GEOG outlet; (*agente segreto*) emissary
emissione *f* emission; *di denaro, francobolli* issue; RAD broadcast; ***banca*** *f* ***di emissione*** bank of issue, issuing bank; ***data*** *f* ***di emissione*** date of issue; ***-i*** *pl* ***inquinanti*** toxic emissions
emittente **1** *agg* issuing; (*trasmittente*) broadcasting **2** *f* RAD transmitter; TV channel; ***emittente privata*** commercial channel
emoglobina *f* h(a)emoglobin
emorragia *f* h(a)emorrhage
emorroidi *fpl* h(a)emorroids
emostatico *m* h(a)emostat
emotivo emotional; (*sensibile*) sensitive
emozionante exciting, thrilling
emozionato excited; (*agitato*) nervous; (*commosso*) moved; (*turbato*) upset
emozionare ⟨1a⟩ (*appassionare*) excite; (*commuovere*) move; (*turbare*) upset
emozionarsi get excited; (*commuoversi*) be moved
emozione *f* emotion; (*agitazione*) excitement
empirico (*pl* -ci) empirical
emporio *m* (*pl* -ri) *negozio* department store
emulsione *f* emulsion
enciclopedia *f* encyclop(a)edia
enciclopedico (*pl* -ci) encyclop(a)edic
endovenoso intravenous
ENEL *abbr* (= ***Ente Nazionale per l'Energia Elettrica***) Italian electricity board
energetico *fabbisogno, consumo ecc* energy *attr*; *alimento* energy-giving
energia *f* energy; ***energia eolica*** wind power; ***energia nucleare*** nuclear energy; ***energia solare*** solar power
energico (*pl* -ci) strong, energetic
enfasi *f* emphasis
enfatizzare ⟨1a⟩ emphasize
ENI *abbr* (= ***Ente Nationale Idrocarburi***) state-owned oil company
enigma *m* (*pl* -i) enigma
enigmatico (*pl* -ci) enigmatic
ENIT *abbr* (= ***Ente Nazionale Italiano per il Turismo***) Italian tourist board
ennesimo MAT nth; F ***per l'-a volta*** for the hundredth time F
enorme enormous
enoteca *f* (*pl* -che) (*negozio*) wine merchant's (*specializing in fine wines*)
ente *m* organization; FIL being; ***ente per il turismo*** tourist board; ***gli enti locali*** the local authorities
entrambi both
entrare ⟨1a⟩ (*andare dentro*) go in, enter; (*venire dentro*) come in, enter; ***la chiave non entra*** the key won't go in, the key doesn't fit; *fig* ***questo non c'entra*** that has nothing to do with it; ***entrare in una stanza*** enter a room, go into / come into a room; ***entrare in carica*** take up one's duties; ***non entro più nei pantaloni*** I can't get into my trousers any more
entrata *f* entrance; *in parcheggio* entrance, way in; *in un paese* entry; INFOR input; FIN ***-e*** *pl* (*reddito*) income; (*guadagno*) earnings; ***entrata libera*** admission free
entro within
entroterra *m inv* hinterland
entusiasmare ⟨1a⟩ arouse enthusiasm in
entusiasmo *m* enthusiasm
entusiasta enthusiastic
entusiastico (*pl* -ci) enthusiastic
enumerare ⟨1m⟩ enumerate
enumerazione *f* enumeration
enzima *m* (*pl* -i) enzyme
epatite *f* hepatitis; ***epatite virale*** viral

E

hepatitis
epica *f* epic
epicentro *m* epicentre, *Am* -center; *fig* centre
epidemia *f* epidemic; ***epidemia di influenza*** flu epidemic
epidermide *f* skin; MED epidermis
Epifania *f* Epiphany
epilessia *f* epilepsy
epilettico (*pl* -ci) **1** *agg* epileptic **2** *m*, **-a** *f* epileptic
episodio *m* (*pl* -di) episode
epistolare: ***stile*** *m* ***epistolare*** style of letter-writing
epoca *f* (*pl* -che) age; (*periodo*) period, time; ***auto*** *f* ***d'epoca*** vintage car; ***mobili*** *mpl* ***d'epoca*** period furniture
epurare ⟨1a⟩ *fig* purge
eppure (and) yet
E.P.T. *abbr* (= ***Ente Provinciale per il Turismo***) provincial tourist board
equatore *m* equator
equatoriale equatorial
equazione *f* equation
equilatero equilateral
equilibrare ⟨1a⟩ balance
equilibrato balanced; *fig* well-balanced
equilibrio *m* (*pl* -ri) balance; *fig* common sense
equino horse *attr*; ***carne*** *f* ***-a*** horsemeat
equinozio *m* (*pl* -zi) equinox
equipaggiamento *m* equipment
equipaggiare ⟨1f⟩ equip; MAR, AVIA *con personale* man, crew
equipaggio *m* (*pl* -ggi) crew
equiparare ⟨1m⟩ make equal
equipazione *f* equalization; ***equipazione di diritti*** equal rights
équipe *f inv* team; ***lavoro*** *m* ***di équipe*** team work
equitazione *f* horse riding
equivalente *m*/*agg* equivalent
equivalenza *f* equivalence
equivoco (*pl* -ci) **1** *agg* ambiguous; (*sospetto*) suspicious; F (*losco*) shady F **2** *m* misunderstanding
era *f* (*epoca*) age, era; GEOL era; ***era atomica*** atomic age; ***era glaciale*** Ice Age
era, **erano** → ***essere***
erba *f* grass; GASTR ***-e*** *pl* herbs; ***-e aromatiche*** herbs; ***alle -e*** with herbs; *fig* ***in erba*** budding
erbaccia *f* (*pl* -cce) weed
erborista *m*/*f* (*pl* -i) herbalist
erboristeria *f* herbalist's
erboso grassy
erede *m*/*f* heir; *donna* heiress
eredità *f* inheritance; BIO heredity
ereditare ⟨1m & b⟩ inherit
ereditarietà *f* heredity
ereditario (*pl* -ri) hereditary
ereditiera *f* heiress
eremita *m* (*pl* -i) hermit
eresia *f* heresy
eretico **1** *agg* heretical **2** *m* (*pl* -ci), **-a** *f* heretic
eretto **1** *pp* → ***erigere*** **2** *agg* erect
erezione *f* building; FISIOL erection
ergastolano *m*, **-a** *f* person serving a life sentence, lifer F
ergastolo *m* life sentence
ergonomico (*pl* -ci) ergonomic
erica *f* heather
erigere ⟨3u⟩ erect; *fig* (*fondare*) establish, found
erigersi *fig* set o.s. up (***a*** as)
eritema *m* (*pl* -i) *cutaneo* rash; ***eritema solare*** sunburn
ermafrodito *m* hermaphrodite
ermellino *m* ermine
ermetico (*pl* -ci) (*a tenuta d'aria*) airtight; *fig* obscure
ernia *f* MED hernia; ***ernia del disco*** slipped disc
ero → ***essere***
eroe *m* hero
erogare ⟨1l, b & e⟩ *denaro* allocate; *gas, acqua* supply
erogazione *f di denaro* allocation; *di gas ecc* supply
eroico (*pl* -ci) heroic
eroina *f droga* heroin; *donna eroica* heroine
eroinomane *m*/*f* heroin addict
erosione *f* GEOL erosion
erotico (*pl* -ci) erotic
erotismo *m* eroticism
errare ⟨1b⟩ wander, roam; (*sbagliare*) be mistaken
errata corrige *m inv* correction
erroneamente mistakenly
errore *m* mistake, error; ***errore di battitura*** typographical error, typo F; ***errore di calcolo*** mistake in the addition; ***errore di ortografia*** spelling mistake; ***errore di stampa*** misprint; ***errore giudiziario*** miscarriage of justice; ***per errore*** by mistake
erta *f*: ***stare all'erta*** be on the alert
erudito **1** *agg* erudite, learned **2** *m*, **-a** *f* erudite person
erudizione *f* erudition, learning
eruttare ⟨1a⟩ *di vulcano* erupt
eruzione *f* eruption; MED rash
es. *abbr* (= ***esempio***) eg (= for example)
esagerare ⟨1m⟩ **1** *v/t* exaggerate **2** *v/i* exaggerate; (*eccedere*) go too far (***in*** in)
esagerato **1** *agg* exaggerated; *zelo* exces-

sive; *prezzo* exorbitant **2** *m*, **-a** *f*: ***sei il solito esagerato!*** you're exaggerating as usual!
esagerazione *f* exaggeration
esagonale hexagonal, six-sided
esagono *m* hexagon
esalare ⟨1a⟩ **1** *v/t odori* give off; ***esalare il respiro*** exhale **2** *v/i* come, emanate (***da*** from)
esaltare ⟨1a⟩ exalt; (*entusiasmare*) elate
esaltarsi become elated
esaltato 1 *agg* elated; (*fanatico*) fanatical **2** *m* fanatic
esaltazione *f* exaltation; (*eccitazione*) elation
esame *m* exam(ination); MED (*test*) test; (*visita*) examination; ***esame d'idoneità*** aptitude test; ***esame di guida*** driving test; ***prendere in esame*** examine
esaminare ⟨1m⟩ examine (*anche* MED)
esaminatore *m*, **-trice** *f* examiner
esasperante exasperating
esasperare ⟨1m⟩ (*inasprire*) exacerbate; (*irritare*) exasperate
esasperarsi become exasperated
esasperato exasperated
esasperazione *f* exasperation
esattezza *f* accuracy; ***con esattezza*** exactly; ***per l'esattezza*** to be precise
esatto 1 *pp* → ***esigere*** **2** *agg* exact; *risposta* correct, right; *in punto* exactly; ***esatto!*** that's right!
esattoria *f* tax office
esaudire ⟨4d⟩ grant; *speranze* fulfil
esauriente exhaustive
esaurimento *m* exhaustion; FIN ***svendita f fino a esaurimento della merce*** clearance sale; MED ***esaurimento nervoso*** nervous breakdown
esaurire ⟨4d⟩ exhaust; *merci* run out of
esaurito (*esausto*) exhausted; FIN sold out; *pubblicazioni* out of print; TEA ***fa il tutto esaurito*** it is playing to a full house
esausto exhausted
esca *f* (*pl* -che) bait (*anche fig*)
esce → ***uscire***
eschimese *agg*, *m/f* Inuit, Eskimo
esclamare ⟨1a⟩ exclaim
esclamazione *f* exclamation
escludere ⟨3q⟩ exclude; *possibilità*, *ipotesi* rule out
esclusione *f* exclusion
esclusiva *f* exclusive right, sole right; FIN ***esclusiva di vendita*** sole agency
esclusivo exclusive
escluso 1 *pp* → ***escludere*** **2** *agg* excluded; (*impossibile*) out of the question, impossible **3** *m*, **-a** *f* person on the fringes of society
esco → ***uscire***
escogitare ⟨1m & c⟩ contrive
escoriazione *f* graze
escrementi *mpl* excrement *sg*
escursione *f* trip, excursion; *a piedi* hike; ***escursione di un giorno*** day trip
escursionismo *m* touring; *a piedi* hiking, walking
escursionista *m/f* tourist; *a piedi* hiker, walker
esecutivo *m/agg* executive
esecutore *m*, **-trice** *f* DIR executor; MUS performer; ***esecutore testamentario*** executor
esecuzione *f* (*realizzazione*) carrying out; MUS performance; DIR execution; ***esecuzione capitale*** execution
eseguire ⟨4b or 4d⟩ carry out; MUS perform
esempio *m* (*pl* -pi) example; ***per esempio, ad esempio*** for example; ***prendere esempio da qu*** follow s.o.'s example
esemplare 1 *agg* exemplary **2** *m* specimen; (*copia*) copy
esentare ⟨1b⟩ exempt (***da*** from)
esente exempt; ***esente da tasse*** tax free
esequie *fpl* funeral (service) *sg*
esercente *m/f* shopkeeper
esercitare ⟨1m & b⟩ exercise; (*addestrare*) train; *professione* practise
esercitarsi practise
esercitazione *f* exercise
esercito *m* army
esercizio *m* (*pl* -zi) exercise; (*pratica*) practice; *di impianti* operation, use; (*anno finanziario*) financial year, *Am* fiscal year; FIN *azienda* business; *negozio* shop; ***esercizio pubblico*** commercial premises
esibire ⟨4d⟩ *documenti* produce; *mettere in mostra* display
esibirsi *in uno spettacolo* perform; *fig* show off
esibizione *f* exhibition; (*ostentazione*) showing off; (*spettacolo*) performance
esibizionista *m/f* show-off; PSI exhibitionist
esigente exacting, demanding
esigenza *f* demand; (*bisogno*) need
esigere ⟨3w⟩ demand; (*riscuotere*) exact
esile slender; (*voce*) faint
esiliare ⟨1k⟩ exile
esilio *m* (*pl* -li) exile
esistente existing
esistenza *f* existence
esistere ⟨3f⟩ exist
esitare ⟨1l & b⟩ hesitate
esitazione *f* hesitation

E

esito *m* result, outcome; FIN sales, turnover
eskimo *m inv giacca* parka
esodo *m* exodus; *di capitali* flight
esofago *m* (*pl* -ghi) œsophagus, *Am* esophagus
esonerare ⟨1m & c⟩ exempt (***da*** from)
esonero *m* exemption
esorbitante exorbitant
esordiente *m/f* beginner
esordio *m* (*pl* -di) introduction, preamble; (*inizio*) beginning; TEA début
esordire ⟨4d⟩ begin; TEA make one's début
esortare ⟨1c⟩ (*incitare*) urge; (*pregare*) beg
esortazione *f* urging
esoterico (*pl* -ci) esoteric
esoterismo *m* esotericism
esotico (*pl* -ci) exotic
espandere ⟨3uu⟩ expand
espandersi expand; (*diffondersi*) spread
espansione *f* expansion
espansività *f fig* warmth, friendliness
espansivo FIS, TEC expansive; *fig* warm, friendly
espatriare ⟨1m & k⟩ leave one's country
espatrio *m* (*pl* -i) expatriation
espediente *m* expedient; ***vivere di -i*** live by one's wits
espellere ⟨3y⟩ expel
esperienza *f* experience; ***per esperienza*** from experience
esperimento *m* experiment
esperto *m/agg* expert
espiare ⟨1h⟩ atone for
espirare ⟨1a⟩ breathe out, exhale
espirazione *f* exhalation
esplicito explicit
esplodere ⟨3q⟩ **1** *v/t colpo* fire **2** *v/i* explode
esplorare ⟨1c⟩ explore
esploratore *m*, **-trice** *f* explorer; ***giovane*** *m* ***esploratore*** boy scout
esplorazione *f* exploration
esplosione *f* explosion; *fig* ***esplosione demografica*** population explosion
esplosivo *m/agg* explosive
esploso *pp* → ***esplodere***
esponente *m/f* exponent
esporre ⟨3ll⟩ expose (*anche* PHOT); *avviso* put up; *in una mostra* exhibit, show; (*riferire*) present; *ragioni*, *caso* state; *teoria* explain
esporsi expose o.s. (***a*** to); (*compromettersi*) compromise o.s.
esportare ⟨1c⟩ export
esportatore 1 *agg* exporting; ***paese*** *m* ***esportatore*** exporting country, exporter **2** *m*, **-trice** *f* exporter
esportazione *f* export
esposimetro *m* FOT exposure meter
espositore *m*, **-trice** *f* exhibitor
esposizione *f* (*mostra*) exhibition; (*narrazione*) presentation; FOT exposure
esposto 1 *pp* → ***esporre*** **2** *agg in mostra* on show; ***esposto a*** exposed to; *critiche* open to; ***esposto a sud*** south facing **3** *m* statement; (*petizione*) petition
espressione *f* expression
espressivo expressive
espresso 1 *pp* → ***esprimere*** **2** *agg* express **3** *m posta* express letter; FERR express; (***caffè*** *m*) ***espresso*** espresso; ***macchina*** *f* ***espresso*** espresso machine; ***per espresso*** express
esprimere ⟨3r⟩ express
esprimersi express o.s.
espropriare ⟨1m & c⟩ expropriate
espropriazione *f* expropriation
esproprio *m* expropriation
espulsione *f* expulsion
espulso *pp* → ***c***
essa *pron f persona* she; *cosa*, *animale* it
essenza *f* essence
essenziale 1 *agg* essential **2** *m*: ***l'essenziale è*** the main thing is
essere ⟨3z⟩ **1** *v/i* be; ***essere di*** (*provenire di*) be *or* come from; ***essere di qu*** (*appartenere a*) belong to s.o.; ***lei è di Roma*** she is *or* comes from Rome; ***è di mio padre*** it is my father's, it belongs to my father; ***c'è*** there is; ***ci sono*** there are; ***sono io*** it's me; ***cosa c'è?*** what's the matter?, what's wrong?; ***non c'è di che!*** don't mention it!; ***chi è?*** who is it?; ***ci siamo!*** here we are!; ***sono le tre*** it's three o'clock; ***siamo in quattro*** there are four of us; ***se fossi in te*** if I were you; ***sarà!*** if you say so! **2** *v/aus*: ***siamo arrivati alle due*** we arrived at two o'clock; ***non siamo ancora arrivati*** we haven't arrived yet; ***è stato investito*** he has been run over **3** *m* being; ***essere umano*** human being
esso *pron m persona* he; *cosa*, *animale* it
est *m* east; ***a est di*** east of
estasi *f* ecstasy
estate *f* summer; ***estate di San Martino*** Indian summer; ***in estate, d'estate*** in (the) summer
estendere ⟨3c⟩ extend
estendersi *di territorio* extend; (*allungarsi*) stretch; *fig* (*diffondersi*) spread
estensione *f* extension; (*vastità*) expanse; MUS range
estenuante exhausting
esteriore *m/agg* exterior, outside

esteriorità *f* appearance
esterno 1 *agg* external; ***per uso esterno*** for external use only **2** *m* outside; *in film* location shot; ***all'esterno*** on the outside
estero 1 *agg* foreign; ***ministro*** *m* ***degli Affari -i*** Foreign Secretary, *Am* Secretary of State **2** *m* foreign countries; ***all'estero*** abroad
esteso 1 *pp* → ***estendere*** **2** *agg* extensive; (*diffuso*) widespread; ***per esteso*** in full
estetica *f* (a)esthetics
estetista *f* beautician
estinguere ⟨3d⟩ extinguish, put out; *debito* pay off; *sete* quench
estinguersi die out
estinto 1 *pp* → ***estinguere*** **2** *agg* extinct; *debito* paid off **3** *m*, **-a** *f* deceased
estintore *m* fire extinguisher
estinzione *f* extinction; FIN redemption, paying off
estirpare ⟨1a⟩ uproot; *dente* extract; *fig* eradicate
estivo summer *attr*
estorcere ⟨3d⟩ *denaro* extort
estorsione *f* extortion
estorto *pp* → ***estorcere***
estradare ⟨1a⟩ extradite
estradizione *f* extradition
estraneo 1 *adj* outside (***a*** sth); ***corpo*** *m* ***estraneo*** foreign body **2** *m*, **-a** *f* stranger; *persona non autorizzata* unauthorized person
estrarre ⟨3xx⟩ extract; *pistola* draw out; ***estrarre a sorte*** draw
estratto 1 *pp* → ***estrarre*** **2** *m* extract; *documento* abstract; FIN ***estratto conto*** statement (of account)
estrazione *f* extraction
estremista *m/f* (*pl* -i) extremist
estremità *f inv* extremity; *di corda* end; (*punta*) tip; (*punto superiore*) top
estremo 1 *agg* extreme; (*più lontano*) farthest; (*ultimo nel tempo*) last, final; ***l'-a sinistra*** the far *or* extreme left; ***l'Estremo Oriente*** the Far East **2** *m* (*estremità*) extreme; ***gli -i*** *di un documento* the main points
estro *m* (*ispirazione artistica*) inspiration
estromettere ⟨3ee⟩ expel, *Am* expell
estroverso extrovert(ed)
estuario *m* (*pl* -ri) estuary
esuberante (*vivace*) exuberant
esuberanza *f* exuberance
esule *m/f* exile
esultare ⟨1a⟩ rejoice
età *f inv* age; ***all'età di*** at the age of; ***età della pietra*** Stone Age; ***raggiungere la maggiore età*** come of age; ***limiti*** *mpl* ***d'età*** age limit; ***avere la stessa età*** be the same age
etere *m* ether
eternità *f* eternity
eterno eternal; (*interminabile*) endless, never-ending; *questione, problema* age-old; ***in eterno*** for ever and ever
eterogeneo heterogen(e)ous
eterosessuale heterosexual
etica *f* ethics
etichetta *f* label; *cerimoniale* etiquette
etico ethical
etimologia *f* etymology
etiope *agg*, *m/f* Ethiopian
Etiopia *f* Ethiopia
etiopico *m/agg* Ethiopian
etnico (*pl* -ci) ethnic
etrusco (*pl* -chi) **1** *agg* Etruscan **2** *m*, **-a** *f* Etruscan
ettaro *m* hectare
etto *m* hundred grams
ettogrammo *m* (*pl* -i) hundred grams *pl*, hectogram
ettolitro *m* hectolitre, *Am* -liter
eucalipto *m* eucalyptus
eucaristia *f* REL Eucharist
euforia *f* euphoria
euforico (*pl* -ci) euphoric
euro *m inv* euro
eurocheque *m inv* Eurocheque
eurodeputato *m*, **-a** *f* Euro MP
eurodollaro *m* Eurodollar
euromercato *m* euromarket
Europa *f* Europe
europeo 1 *agg* European **2** *m*, **-a** *f* European
eurovisione *f* Eurovision
evacuare ⟨1m⟩ evacuate
evacuazione *f* evacuation
evadere ⟨3q⟩ **1** *v/t* evade; (*sbrigare*) deal with; ***evadere le tasse*** evade taxes **2** *v/i* escape (***da*** from)
evaporare ⟨1m⟩ evaporate
evaporazione *f* evaporation
evasione *f* escape; *fig* escapism; ***evasione fiscale*** *f* tax evasion
evasivo evasive
evaso 1 *pp* → ***evadere*** **2** *m*, **-a** *f* fugitive
evasore *m*: ***evasore fiscale*** tax evader
evenienza *f* eventuality
evento *m* event
eventuale possible
eventualità *f inv* eventuality; ***nell'eventualità che*** in the event that; ***per ogni eventualità*** for every eventuality
eventualmente if necessary
evidente evident
evidenza *f* evidence; ***mettere in evidenza*** emphasize, highlight
evidenziatore *m* highlighter

evitare ⟨1l & b⟩ avoid; ***evitare il fastidio a qu*** spare s.o. the trouble
evoluto 1 *pp* → ***evolvere* 2** *agg* developed; (*progredito*) progressive, advanced; *senza pregiudizi* open minded, broad-minded
evoluzione *f* evolution
evolvere ⟨3s⟩ **1** *v/t* develop **2** *v/i e* **evolversi** evolve, develop
evviva hurray

ex ... (*nelle parole composte*) ex-, former
expertise *f inv* expertise
extra 1 *agg inv* extra; ***di qualità extra*** top quality **2** *m inv* extra
extracomunitario 1 *agg* non-EC, non-EU **2** *m*, **-a** *f* non-EC *or* non-EU citizen
extraconiugale extramarital
extraeuropeo non-European
extraterrestre *agg*, *m/f* extra-terrestrial

fa 1 → ***fare*** **2** *avv*: ***5 anni fa*** 5 years ago **3** *m* MUS F; *nel solfeggio della scala* fa(h)
fabbisogno *m* needs *pl*, requirements *pl*
fabbrica *f* (*pl* -che) factory, *Am* plant
fabbricante *m/f* manufacturer
fabbricare ⟨1l & d⟩ manufacture; ARCHI build; *fig* fabricate
fabbricato *m* building
fabbricazione *f* manufacturing; ARCHI building
fabbro *m*: ***fabbro*** (***ferraio***) blacksmith
faccenda *f* matter
faccende *fpl* housework *sg*
facchino *m* porter
faccia *f* (*pl* -cce) face; (*risvolto*, *aspetto*) facet; (*lato*) side; ***faccia tosta*** cheek; ***faccia a faccia*** face to face; ***di faccia a*** opposite, in front of; ***in faccia*** in the face; ***gliel'ha detto in faccia*** he told him to his face
facciata *f* ARCHI front, façade; *di foglio* side; *fig* (*esteriorità*) appearance
faccio → ***fare***
facile easy; *di carattere* easy-going; (*incline*) prone (***a*** to); ***è facile a dirsi!*** easier said than done!; ***è facile che venga*** he is likely to come; ***non è mica una cosa facile*** it isn't that easy
facilità *f* ease; (*attitudine*) aptitude, facility; ***con facilità*** easily; INFOR ***facilità d'uso*** user-friendliness
facilitare ⟨1m⟩ facilitate
facilitazione *f* facility; ***-i*** *pl* ***di prezzo*** easy terms
facilmente easily
facoltà *f inv* faculty; (*potere*) power; ***avere la facoltà di scelta*** have a choice, be able to choose
facoltativo optional
facoltoso wealthy
facsimile *m* facsimile
faggio *m* (*pl* -ggi) beech (tree)
fagiano *m* pheasant
fagiolini *mpl* green beans
fagiolo *m* bean
fagotto *m* bundle; MUS bassoon; *fig* ***far fagotto*** pack up and leave
fai → ***fare***
fai da te *m inv* do-it-yourself, DIY
falce *f* scythe
falciare ⟨1f⟩ cut (with a scythe); *fig* mow down
falciatrice *f* lawn-mower
falco *m* (*pl* -chi) hawk
falda *f* layer; GEOL stratum; *di cappello* brim; (*pendio*) slope; (*piede di monte*) foot; ***falda acquifera*** water table
falegname *m* carpenter
falegnameria *f* carpentry
falena *f* moth
falla *f* MAR leak; ***tappare una falla*** stop *or* plug a leak (*anche fig*)
fallimento *m* failure; FIN bankruptcy
fallire ⟨4d⟩ **1** *v/t* miss **2** *v/i* fail; FIN go bankrupt
fallito 1 *agg* unsuccessful, failed; FIN bankrupt **2** *m* failure; FIN bankruptcy
fallo *m* fault; (*errore*) error, mistake; SP foul; ***mettere il piede in fallo*** lose one's footing; ***cogliere in fallo qu*** catch s.o. out; (*in flagrante*) catch s.o red-handed
falò *m inv* bonfire
falsare ⟨1a⟩ *verità*, *fatti* distort
falsario *m* (*pl* -ri) forger
falsificare ⟨1m & d⟩ forge
falsificazione *f* forgery
falsità *f* falsity, falseness; (*menzogna*) lie; (*ipocrisia*) insincerity
falso 1 *agg* false; (*sbagliato*) incorrect, wrong; *oro*, *gioielli* imitation, fake F; (*falsificato*) forged, fake F **2** *m* (*falsità*) falsehood; *oggetto falsificato* forgery, fake F; DIR forgery
fama *f* fame; (*reputazione*) reputation; ***di fama mondiale*** world-famous
fame *f* hunger; ***aver fame*** be hungry
famiglia *f* family; ***famiglia numerosa*** large family
familiare 1 *agg* family *attr*; (*conosciuto*) familiar; (*semplice*) informal **2** *m/f* relative, relation
familiarità *f* familiarity
familiarizzare ⟨1a⟩ familiarize
familiarizzarsi familiarize o.s.
famoso famous
fanale *m* AUTO, MAR, AVIA, FERR light; (*lampione*) street lamp
fanalino *m* AUTO: ***fanalino di coda*** tail-light; *fig* ***essere il fanalino di coda*** bring up the rear
fanatico (*pl* -ci) **1** *agg* fanatical **2** *m*, ***-a*** *f* fanatic
fanciullo *m*, ***-a*** *f lit* (young) boy; *ragazza* (young) girl
fandonia *f* lie
fango *m* (*pl* -ghi) mud; MED ***-ghi*** *pl* mud-baths
fangoso muddy

fannullone *m*, **-a** *f* lazy good-for-nothing
fantascienza *f* science fiction
fantasia *f* fantasy; (*immaginazione*) imagination; (*capriccio*) fancy; MUS fantasia
fantasma *m* (*pl* -i) ghost
fantasticare ⟨1m & d⟩ day-dream (***di*** about)
fantastico (*pl* -ci) fantastic
fante *m carte da gioco* jack
fanteria *f* MIL infantry
fantoccio *m* (*pl* -cci) puppet (*anche fig*)
farabutto *m* nasty piece of work
faraona *f*: (***gallina*** *f*) ***faraona*** guinea fowl
farcire ⟨4d⟩ GASTR stuff; *torta* fill
farcito stuffed; *dolce* filled
fard *m inv* blusher
fardello *m* bundle; *fig* burden
fare ⟨3aa⟩ **1** *v/t* do; *vestito*, *dolce*, *errore* make; *biglietto*, *benzina* buy, get; ***fare*** **(*dello*)** ***sport*** play sport; ***fare il pieno*** fill up; ***fare un bagno*** have a bath; ***fare il conto*** *al ristorante* prepare the bill; ***fare il medico/l'insegnante*** be a doctor / teacher; ***non fa niente*** it doesn't matter; ***fare vedere qc a qu*** show sth to s.o.; ***farcela*** manage; ***non c'e la faccio più*** I can't take any more; ***2 più 2 fa 4*** 2 and 2 make(s) 4; ***quanto fa?*** how much is it?; ***far fare qc a qu*** get s.o. to do sth **2** *v/i*: ***questo non fa per me*** this isn't for me; ***faccia pure!*** go ahead!, carry on!; ***qui fa bello / brutto*** the weather here is nice / awful; ***fa freddo / caldo*** it's cold / warm
farsi (*diventare*) grow; F (*drogarsi*) shoot up F; ***farsi grande*** grow tall; ***si sta facendo tardi*** it's getting late; ***farsi avanti*** step forward; ***farsi la barba*** shave; ***farsi male*** hurt o.s.
farfalla *f* butterfly
farina *f* flour
farinaceo 1 *agg* starchy **2 *-cei*** *mpl* starchy foodstuffs
faringe *f* pharynx
faringite *f inflammation of the pharynx*
farmaceutico (*pl* -ci) pharmaceutical
farmacia *f* pharmacy; *negozio* chemist's, *Am* drugstore
farmacista *m/f* (*mpl* -i) chemist, *Am* pharmacist
farmaco *m* (*pl* -ci) drug
faro *m* MAR lighthouse; AVIA beacon; AUTO headlight; ***-i*** *pl* ***fendinebbia*** fog lamps *or* lights
farsa *f* farce
fascia *f* (*pl* -sce) band; MED bandage; ***fascia elastica*** crepe bandage; ***fascia oraria*** (time) slot
fasciare ⟨1f⟩ MED bandage
fasciatura *f* (*fascia*) bandage; *azione* bandaging
fascicolo *m* (*opuscolo*) booklet, brochure; (*incartamento*) file, dossier
fascino *m* fascination, charm
fascio *m* (*pl* -sci) bundle; *di fiori* bunch; *di luce* beam
fascismo *m* Fascism
fascista *agg*, *m/f* (*mpl* -i) Fascist
fase *f* phase; AUTO stroke; *fig* ***essere fuori fase*** be out of sorts; ***fase di lavorazione*** production stage
fastidio *m* (*pl* -di) bother, trouble; ***dare fastidio a qu*** bother s.o.; ***le dà fastidio se … ?*** do you mind if … ?; ***un sacco di -i*** a lot of bother
fastidioso (*irritante*) irritating, annoying; (*irritabile*) irritable
fasto *m* pomp
fastoso sumptuous
fata *f* fairy
fatale fatal; ***era fatale che non si sarebbero mai più rivisti*** they were fated never to meet again
fatalità *f inv* (*il fato*) fate; (*disavventura*) misfortune
fatato magic, enchanted
fatica *f* (*pl* -che) (*sforzo*) effort; (*stanchezza*) fatigue; ***a fatica*** with a great deal of effort; ***faccio fatica a crederci*** I find it hard to believe
faticare ⟨1d⟩ toil; ***faticare a*** find it difficult to
faticoso tiring; (*difficile*) laborious
fatt. *abbr* (= ***fattura***) inv (= invoice)
fattibile feasible
fatto 1 *pp* → ***fare*** **2** *agg* done; AGR ripe; ***fatto a mano*** hand-made; ***fatto di legno*** made of wood; ***fatto in casa*** home-made; ***fatto per qu / qc*** (tailor-)made for s.o./sth **3** *m* fact; (*avvenimento*) event; (*faccenda*) affair, business; ***il fatto è che …*** the fact is that …; ***cogliere sul fatto*** catch red-handed; ***di fatto*** *agg* real; *avv* in fact, actually; ***passare a vie di fatto*** come to blows; ***in fatto di*** as regards
fattore *m* (*elemento*) factor; AGR farm manager; ***fattore di protezione antisolare*** sun protection factor
fattoria *f* farm; (*casa*) farmhouse
fattorino *m* messenger; *per consegne* delivery man; *posta* postman, *Am* mailman
fattura *f* (*lavorazione*) workmanship; *di abiti* cut; FIN invoice; ***rilasciare una fattura a qu*** invoice s.o.
fatturare ⟨1a⟩ FIN invoice
fatturato *m* FIN (*giro d'affari*) turnover
fauna *f* fauna
fava *f* broad bean

favola *f* (*fiaba*) fairy tale; (*storia*) story; *morale* fable; (*meraviglia*) dream; ***una vacanza da favola*** a dream holiday
favoloso fabulous
favore *m* favo(u)r; ***prezzo** m **di favore*** special deal; ***a favore di qu*** in favo(u)r of s.o.; ***per favore!*** please!; ***fare un favore a qu*** do s.o. a favo(u)r
favorevole favo(u)rable
favorire ⟨4d⟩ **1** *v/t* favo(u)r; (*promuovere*) promote **2** *v/i*: ***vuol favorire?*** would you care to join me / us?; ***favorisca i documenti!*** your papers, please!; ***favorisca nello studio*** would you go into the study please
favorito *m/agg* favo(u)rite
fax *m inv* fax; ***mandare un fax a qc*** send s.o. a fax, fax s.o.
faxare ⟨1a⟩ fax
fazione *f* faction
fazzolettino *m*: ***fazzolettino di carta*** tissue
fazzoletto *m* handkerchief; *per la testa* headscarf
f.co *abbr* (= ***franco***) free
febbraio *m* February
febbre *f* fever; ***ha la febbre*** he has a *or* is running a temperature; ***febbre da fieno*** hay fever
febbrifugo *m* (*pl* -ghi) MED *drug that reduces the temperature*
febbrile feverish
fecondare ⟨1a⟩ fertilize
fecondazione *f* fertilization; ***fecondazione artificiale*** artificial insemination
fecondità *f* fertility
fecondo fertile
fede *f* faith; (*fedeltà*) loyalty; *anello* wedding ring; ***aver fede in qc*** have faith in s.o.; ***tener fede a una promessa*** keep a promise
fedele 1 *agg* faithful; (*esatto, conforme all'originale*) true **2** *m* REL believer; ***i -i*** *pl* the faithful
fedeltà *f* faithfulness; MUS ***alta fedeltà*** hi-fi, high fidelity
federa *f* pillowcase
federale federal
federazione *f* federation
fegato *m* liver; *fig* courage, guts *pl* F
felce *f* fern
felice happy; (*fortunato*) lucky
felicità *f* happiness
felicitarsi ⟨1m⟩: ***felicitarsi con qu per qc*** congratulate s.o. on sth
felicitazioni *fpl* congratulations
felino feline
felpa *f* sweatshirt
feltro *m* felt
femmina *f* (*figlia*) girl, daughter; ZO, TEC female
femminile 1 *agg* feminine; (*da donna*) women's **2** *m* GRAM feminine
femminilità *f* feminity
femminismo *m* feminism
femminista *m/f* (*mpl* -i) feminist
femore *m* femur
fendinebbia *m inv* fog lamp *or* light
fenicottero *m* flamingo
fenomeno *m* phenomenon
feriale: ***giorno** m **feriale*** weekday
ferie *fpl* holiday *sg*, *Am* vacation *sg*; ***andare in ferie*** go on holiday (*Am* vacation)
ferimento *m* wounding
ferire ⟨4d⟩ wound; *in incidente* injure; *fig* hurt
ferirsi injure o.s.
ferita *f* wound; *in incidente* injury
ferito 1 *agg* wounded; *in incidente* injured; *fig sentimenti* hurt; *orgoglio* injured **2** *m* casualty
fermacarte *m inv* paperweight
fermacravatta *m* tiepin
fermaglio *m* (*pl* -gli) clasp; *per capelli* hair slide; (*gioiello*) brooch
fermare ⟨1a⟩ stop; DIR detain
fermarsi stop; (*restare*) stay, remain
fermata *f* stop; ***fermata dell' autobus*** bus stop; ***fermata facoltativa** o **fermata a richiesta*** request stop
fermentare ⟨1a⟩ ferment
fermentazione *f* fermentation
fermento *m* yeast; *fig* ferment
fermezza *f* firmness
fermo 1 *agg* still, motionless; *veicolo* stationary; (*saldo*) firm; *mano* steady; ***star fermo*** (*non muoversi*) keep still; ***l'orologio è fermo*** the watch has stopped **2** *int* ***fermo!*** (*alt!*) stop!; (*immobile!*) keep still! **3** *m* DIR detention
fermoposta *m* poste restante
feroce fierce, ferocious; *animale* wild; (*insopportabile*) dreadful
ferocia *f* ferocity
ferragosto *m August 15 public holiday*; *periodo* August holidays
ferramenta *f* hardware; *negozio* hardware store, ironmonger's *Br*
ferrato FERR: ***strada** f **-a*** railway line, *Am* railroad; *fig* ***essere ferrato in qc*** be well up in sth
ferro *m* iron; (*arnese*) tool; *fig* ***di ferro*** *memoria, salute* excellent; *stomaco* cast-iron; ***ferro da calza*** knitting needle; ***ferro da stiro a vapore*** steam iron; ***ferro di cavallo*** horseshoe; ***ferro battuto*** wrought iron; GASTR ***ai -i*** grilled, *Am* broiled

ferrovia *f* railway, *Am* railroad; ***ferrovia metropolitana*** *o* ***sotterranea*** underground, *Am* subway
ferrovecchio *m* (*pl* -cchi) scrap merchant
ferroviario (*pl* -ri) rail(way) *attr*, *Am* railroad *attr*
ferroviere *m* rail (*Am* railroad) worker
fertile fertile
fertilità *f* fertility
fertilizzante *m* fertilizer
fesso *m* F idiot F; ***far fesso qu*** con s.o F
fessura *f* (*spaccatura*) crack; (*fenditura*) slit, slot
festa *f* feast; *di santo* feast day; (*ricevimento*) party; (*compleanno*) birthday; (*onomastico*) name day; ***festa della mamma / del papà*** Mother's/Father's Day; ***festa nazionale*** national holiday; ***buone -e!*** *a Natale* Merry Christmas and a happy New Year!
festeggiamenti *mpl* celebrations
festeggiare ⟨1f⟩ celebrate; *persona* have a celebration for
festival *m inv* festival
festività *f inv* festival; ***festività*** *pl* celebrations, festivities
festivo festive; ***giorno*** *m* ***festivo*** holiday
festoso happy, cheerful
feto *m* f(o)etus
fetta *f* slice; ***a -e*** sliced
feudale feudal
fiaba *f* fairy tale
fiabesco (*pl* -chi) fairytale *attr*
fiacca *f* weariness; (*svogliatezza*) laziness; ***battere la fiacca*** slack, be a shirker
fiacco (*pl* -cchi) (*debole*) weak; (*svogliato*) lazy; FIN *mercato* sluggish
fiaccola *f* torch
fiala *f* phial
fiamma *f* flame; MAR pennant; GASTR ***alla fiamma*** flambé
fiammante: ***rosso*** *m* ***fiammante*** fiery red; ***nuovo fiammante*** brand new
fiammifero *m* match
fiancheggiare ⟨1f⟩ border; *fig* support
fianco *m* (*pl* -chi) side; ANAT hip; ***fianco a fianco*** side by side; ***di fianco a qu*** beside s.o.; ***al tuo fianco*** by your side
fiasco *m* (*pl* -chi) flask; *fig* fiasco
fiato *m* breath; ***senza fiato*** breathless; MUS ***strumento*** *m* ***a fiato*** wind instrument; ***tutto d'un fiato*** in one go; ***riprendere fiato*** catch one's breath
fibbia *f* buckle
fibra *f* fibre, *Am* fiber; ***di forte fibra*** robust, sturdy; ***fibra morale*** moral fibre (*Am* fiber); ***fibra sintetica*** synthetic; ***fibra di vetro*** fibreglass, *Am* fiberglass
fibroso fibrous
ficcanaso *m/f* F nosy parker F
ficcare ⟨1d⟩ thrust; F (*mettere*) shove F
ficcarsi get; ***ficcarsi nei guai*** get into hot water; ***ficcarsi qc in testa*** get sth into one's head; ***dove s'è ficcato?*** where can it / he have got to?
fico *m* (*pl* -chi) *frutto* fig; *albero* fig (tree); ***fico d'India*** prickly pear
fidanzamento *m* engagement
fidanzarsi ⟨1a⟩ get engaged
fidanzata *f* fiancée
fidanzato *m* fiancé; ***i -i*** *pl* the engaged couple
fidarsi: ***fidarsi di qu / qc*** trust s.o./sth, rely on s.o./sth; ***non mi fido di chiederlo a mio padre*** I don't dare ask my father
fidato trustworthy
fideiussione *f* DIR guarantee
fido 1 *agg* trusted, trusty **2** *m* FIN credit
fiducia *f* confidence; ***avere fiducia in qu*** have faith in s.o.; ***di fiducia*** *persona* reliable, trustworthy; *incarico* responsible
fiduciaria *f* ***fiduciaria*** FIN trust company
fiduciario (*pl* -ri) **1** *agg* DIR *atto*, *società* trust *attr* **2** *m* trustee
fiducioso trusting
fienile *m* barn
fieno *m* hay
fiera[1] *f animale* wild beast
fiera[2] *f mostra* fair
fierezza *f* pride
fiero proud
fifa F *f* nerves, jitters F; ***aver fifa*** have the jitters, be jittery
figlia *f* daughter
figliastra *f* stepdaughter
figliastro *m* stepson
figlio *m* (*pl* -gli) son; ***avere -gli*** *pl* have children; ***essere figlio unico*** be an only child
figlioccia *f* (*pl* -cce) goddaughter
figlioccio *m* (*pl* -cci) godson
figura *f* figure; (*illustrazione*) illustration; (*apparenza*) appearance; ***far brutta figura*** make a bad impression
figurare ⟨1a⟩ **1** *v/t fig* imagine; ***figurati!*** just imagine!, just think!; ***si figuri!*** not at all!, of course not! **2** *v/i* (*apparire*) appear; (*far figura*) make a good impression
figurato (*illustrato*) illustrated; *linguaggio*, *espressione* figurative
figurina *f da raccolta* collector card, trading card
figurino *m* fashion sketch
fila *f* line, row; (*coda*) queue, *Am* line; ***di fila*** in succession; ***tre giorni di fila*** three days running, three days in succession; ***in fila indiana*** in single file; ***fare la fila***

queue, *Am* wait in line
filamento *m* filament
filare⟨1a⟩ **1** *v/t* spin **2** *v/i di ragno* spin; *di ragionamento* make sense; *di formaggio* go stringy; *di veicolo* travel; F (*andarsene*) take off F; ***fila!*** go away!, shoo!; ***filare diritto*** (*comportarsi bene*) behave (o.s.) **3** *m di alberi* row
filarmonico (*pl* -ci) philharmonic
filastrocca *f* (*pl* -cche) *m* nursery rhyme
filatelia *f* philately
filato 1 *agg* (*logico*) logical; ***andare di filato a casa*** go straight home; ***per 10 ore filate*** for ten hours straight **2** *m* yarn; *per cucire* thread
file *m inv* INFOR file
filetto *m* GASTR fillet; TEC thread
filiale *f* branch; (*società affiliata*) affiliate
filigrana *f su carta* watermark; *in oreficeria* filigree
film *m inv* film, movie; ***film giallo*** thriller; ***film in bianco e nero*** black and white film
filmare ⟨1a⟩ film
filmato *m* short (film)
filo *m* (*pl anche* le -a) thread; *metallico* wire; *di lama* edge; *d'erba* blade; *fig* ***un filo di vergogna / rispetto*** an ounce of shame / respect; *fig* ***filo conduttore*** lead; ***filo interdentale*** (dental) floss; ***filo spinato*** barbed wire; ***filo di voce*** whisper; ***per filo e per segno*** in detail; ***dare del filo da torcere a qu*** make things difficult for s.o.
filobus *m inv* trolley(bus)
filodrammatica *f* amateur dramatic society
filologia *f* philology
filologo *m* (*pl* -gi) philologist
filone *m* MIN vein; *pane* French stick; *fig* tradition
filosofia *f* philosophy
filosofico (*pl* -ci) philosophic(al)
filosofo *m* philosopher
filovia *f* trolley(bus)
filtrare⟨1a⟩ **1** *v/t* strain, filter **2** *v/i fig* filter out
filtro *m* filter; ***filtro dell'olio*** oil filter; ***filtro di carta*** filter paper
fin → ***fine***, ***fino***
finale 1 *agg* final **2** *m* end **3** *f* SP final
finalista *m/f* finalist
finalmente (*alla fine*) at last; (*per ultimo*) finally
finanza *f* finance; ***-e*** *pl* finances; ***ministro*** *m* ***delle -e*** Minister of Finance
finanziamento *m* funding
finanziare ⟨1g⟩ fund, finance
finanziario (*pl* -ri) financial
finanziere *m* financier; (*guardia di finanza*) *Customs and Excise officer*; *lungo le coste* coastguard
finché until; (*per tutto il tempo che*) as long as
fine 1 *agg* fine; (*sottile*) thin; *udito, vista* sharp, keen; (*raffinato*) refined **2** *m* aim; ***al fine di ...*** in order to ...; ***secondo fine*** ulterior motive **3** *f* end; ***alla fine*** in the end; ***alla fin fine, in fin dei conti*** after all, when all's said and done; ***senza fine*** endless
fine settimana *m inv* weekend
finestra *f* window
finestrino *m* window; AUTO ***finestrino posteriore*** rear window
finezza *f* fineness; (*sottigliezza*) thinness; (*raffinatezza*) refinement
fingere⟨3d⟩ **1** *v/t*: ***fingere sorpresa / dolore*** pretend to be surprised / to be in pain **2** *v/i*: ***fingere di*** pretend to
fingersi pretend to be
finire⟨4d⟩ **1** *v/t* finish, end; ***finiscila!*** stop it! **2** *v/i* end, finish (***in*** in); ***andrà a finire male*** *cosa* this will all end in tears; *persona* he / she will come to no good
finito finished; (*venduto*) sold out; ***è finita*** it's over; ***farla finita con qc*** put an end to sth
finlandese 1 *m/agg* Finnish **2** *m/f* Finn
Finlandia *f* Finland
fino[1] *agg* fine; (*acuto*) sharp; *oro* pure
fino[2] *prp tempo* till, until; *luogo* as far as; ***fino a domani*** until tomorrow; ***fino a che*** (*per tutto il tempo che*) as long as; (*fino al momento in cui*) until; ***fin da ieri*** since yesterday
fino[3] *avv* even; ***fin troppo*** more than enough
finocchio *m* (*pl* -cchi) fennel
finora so far
finta *f* pretence, *Am* pretense, sham; SP feint; ***far finta di*** pretend to
fintantoché until
finto 1 *pp* → ***fingere* 2** *agg* false; (*artificiale*) artificial; (*simulato*) feigned
finzione *f* pretence, *Am* pretense, sham
fiocco *m* (*pl* -cchi) bow; ***fiocco di neve*** snowflake; ***-cchi*** *pl* ***d'avena*** oat flakes, rolled oats; *fig* ***coi -cchi*** first-rate
fioco (*pl* -chi) weak; *luce* dim
fionda *f* catapult
fioraio *m* (*pl* -ai), ***-a*** *f* florist
fiordaliso *m* cornflower
fiordo *m* fiord
fiore *m* flower; *fig* ***il*** (***fior***) ***fiore*** the cream; *nelle carte* ***-i*** *pl* clubs; ***disegno*** *m* ***a -i*** floral design; ***a fior d'acqua*** on the surface of the water; ***essere in fiore*** be in flower

F

fiorente flourishing
fiorentino **1** *agg* Florentine **2** *m*, **-a** *f* Florentine; GASTR ***alla -a*** with spinach; *bistecca* charcoal grilled **3** *f* GASTR T-bone steak
fioretto *m* SP foil
fiorire ⟨4d⟩ flower; *fig* flourish
fioritura *f* flowering (*anche fig*)
Firenze *f* Florence
firma *f* signature; (*il firmare*) signing; FIN ***avere la firma*** be an authorized signatory
firmamento *m* firmament
firmare ⟨1a⟩ sign
firmatario *m* (*pl* -ri) signatory
firmato *abito*, *borsa* designer *attr*
fisarmonica *f* (*pl* -che) accordion
fiscale tax, fiscal; *fig spreg* rigid, unbending
fiscalità *f* taxation; (*pignoleria*) rigidity, lack of flexibility
fischiare ⟨1k⟩ **1** *v/t* whistle; ***fischiare qu*** boo s.o. **2** *v/i di vento* whistle
fischio *m* (*pl* -chi) whistle; SP ***fischio finale*** final whistle
fisco *m* tax authorities *pl*, Inland Revenue, *Am* Internal Revenue; ***il fisco*** the taxman
fisica *f* physics; ***fisica nucleare*** nuclear physics
fisico (*pl* -ci) **1** *agg* physical **2** *m* physicist; ANAT physique
fisiologia *f* physiology
fisionomia *f* face; *fig di popolo*, *città* appearance; (*carattere*) character
fisioterapia *f* physiotherapy
fisioterapista *m/f* (*mpl* -i) physiotherapist
fissare ⟨1a⟩ (*fermare*) fix; (*guardare intensamente*) stare at; (*stabilire*) arrange; (*prenotare*) book
fissarsi (*stabilirsi*) settle; (*ostinarsi*) set one's mind (***di*** on); (*avere un'idea fissa*) become obsessed (***di*** with); ***fissarsi in mente*** memorize
fissatore *m* (*per capelli*) hair-spray; FOT fixer
fissazione *f* (*mania*) fixation (***di*** about)
fisso **1** *agg* fixed; *stipendio*, *cliente* regular; *lavoro* permanent **2** *avv* fixedly
fitta *f* sharp pain
fitto[1] **1** *agg* (*denso*) thick; ***fitto di*** full of **2** *avv nevicare*, *piovere* hard
fitto[2] *m* rent
fiume *m* river; *fig* flood, torrent; ***letto** m **del fiume*** river bed
fiutare ⟨1a⟩ smell; *cocaina* snort; ***fiutare un imbroglio*** smell a rat
fiuto *m* sense of smell; *fig* nose
flacone *m* bottle
flagrante flagrant; ***cogliere qu in flagrante*** catch s.o. red-handed
flanella *f* flannel
flash *m inv* FOT flash; *stampa* newsflash
flatulenza *f* flatulence
flauto *m* flute
flemma *f* calm
flemmatico (*pl* -ci) phlegmatic
flessibile flexible
flessione *f* bending; GRAM inflection; (*diminuzione*) dip, (slight) drop
flipper *m inv* pinball machine; ***giocare a flipper*** play pinball
flirt *m inv* flirtation
flirtare ⟨1a⟩ flirt
F.lli *abbr* (= ***fratelli***) Bros (= brothers)
floppy disk *m inv* floppy (disk)
flora *f* flora
floreale floral
floricultura *f* flower-growing industry
florido flourishing
floscio (*pl* -sci) limp; *muscoli* flabby
flotta *f* fleet
fluido *m/agg* fluid
fluorescente fluorescent
fluoro *m* fluorine
flusso *m* flow; ***flusso e riflusso*** ebb and flow
fluttuare ⟨1l⟩ FIN, *fig* fluctuate
fluttuazione *f* fluctuation; ***fluttuazione dei prezzi*** price fluctuation
fluviale river *attr*
f.m. *abbr* (= ***fine mese***) end of the month
FMI *abbr* (= ***Fondo Monetario Internazionale***) IMF (= International Monetary Fund)
f.to *abbr* (= ***firmato***) sgd (= signed)
foca *f* (*pl* -che) seal
focaccia *f* (*pl* -cce) focaccia; (*dolce*) *sweet type of bread*; ***rendere pan per focaccia*** give tit for tat
focalizzare ⟨1a⟩ focus on
foce *f* mouth
focolaio *m* (*pl* -ai) *fig* hotbed
focolare *m* hearth; TEC furnace
focoso fiery
fodera *f interna* lining; *esterna* cover
foderare ⟨1l & c⟩ *all'interno* line; *all'esterno* cover
fodero *m* sheath
foggia *f* (*pl* -gge) *f di abito*, *acconciatura* style
foglia *f* leaf
fogliame *m* foliage
foglio *m* (*pl* -gli) sheet; INFOR ***foglio elettronico*** spreadsheet; ***foglio rosa*** *provisional driving licence*; ***foglio di via obbligatorio*** expulsion order
fogna *f* sewer
fognatura *f* sewers *pl*, sewage pipes *pl*

folata *f* gust
folclore *m* folklore
folcloristico (*pl* -ci) folk *attr*
folgorare ⟨1l⟩ *di fulmine, idea* strike; *di corrente elettrica* electrocute; ***folgorare qu con lo sguardo*** glare at s.o.
folgorato struck
folklore *m* → ***folclore***
folla *f* crowd; *fig* host
folle[1] *agg* mad
folle[2] AUTO: ***in folle*** in neutral
follia *f* madness
folto thick
fondale *m* MAR sea bed; TEA backcloth, backdrop
fondamentale fundamental
fondamento *m* foundation; ***le -a*** *fpl* the foundations; ***senza fondamento*** unfounded
fondare ⟨1a⟩ found
fondarsi be based (***su*** on)
fondato founded
fondatore *m*, **-trice** *f* founder
fondazione *f* foundation
fondere ⟨3bb⟩ **1** *v/t* (*liquefare*) melt; METAL smelt; *colori* blend **2** *v/i* melt
fondersi melt; FIN merge
fonderia *f* foundry
fondiario (*pl* -ri) land *attr*
fondo 1 *agg* deep **2** *m* bottom; (*sfondo*) background; *terreno* property; FIN fund; SP long-distance; SCI cross-country, langlauf; ***-i*** *pl denaro* funds; ***a fondo*** (*profondamente*) in depth; *fig* ***in fondo*** basically; ***in fondo alla strada / al corridoio*** at the end *or* bottom of the road / of the corridor; ***essere in fondo al treno*** be at the rear of the train; FIN ***fondo d'ammortamento*** depreciation fund; ***andare a fondo*** (*affondare*) sink; (*approfondire*) get to the bottom (***di*** of); ***-i*** *pl* ***di magazzino*** old *or* unsold stock *sg*
fondotinta *m inv* foundation
fonduta *f* cheese fondue
fonetica *f* phonetics
fontana *f* fountain
fonte *m/f* spring; *fig* source; ***fonte energetica*** source of energy; ***da fonte attendibile*** from a reliable source
footing *m* jogging
foraggio *m* (*pl* -ggi) forage
forare ⟨1a⟩ *di proiettile* pierce; *con il trapano* drill; *biglietto* punch; *pneumatico* puncture
foratura *f di pneumatico* puncture
forbici *fpl* scissors; ***un paio di forbici*** a pair of scissors
forca *f* (*forcone*) pitchfork
forcella *f* TEC fork
forchetta *f* fork; ***essere una buona forchetta*** have a big appetite
forcina *f* hairpin
forcipe *m* forceps *pl*
forcone *m* pitchfork
foresta *f* forest
forestale forest *attr*
foresteria *f* guest accommodation
forestiero 1 *agg* foreign **2** *m*, **-a** *f* foreigner
forfait *m inv* lump sum; SP withdrawal; ***a forfait*** on a lump-sum basis
forfettario flat-rate, all in; ***prezzo*** *m* ***forfettario*** lump sum
forfora *f* dandruff
forma *f* form; (*sagoma*) shape; TEC (*stampo*) mo(u)ld; ***essere in forma*** be in good form
formaggiera *f dish for grated cheese*
formaggino *m* processed cheese
formaggio *m* (*pl* -ggi) cheese
formale formal
formalità *f inv* formality
formare ⟨1a⟩ shape; TELEC ***formare il numero*** dial the number
formarsi form; (*svilupparsi*) develop; *di un'idea* take shape
formato *m* size; *di libro* format
formattare ⟨1a⟩ INFOR format
formazione *f* formation; *fig addestramento* training; SP line-up; ***formazione professionale*** vocational training
formica[1] *f* (*pl* -che) ZO ant
formica[2®] Formica®
formicaio *m* (*pl* -ai) anthill
formicolare ⟨1m⟩ *di mano, gamba* tingle; *fig* ***formicolare di*** teem with
formicolio *m sensazione* pins and needles *pl*
formidabile (*straordinario*) incredible; (*poderoso*) powerful
formula *f* formula
formulare ⟨1l⟩ *teoria, ipotesi* formulate; (*esprimere*) express
fornaio *m* (*pl* -ai) baker; *negozio* bakery
fornello *m* stove
fornire ⟨4d⟩ supply (***qc a qu*** s.o. with sth)
fornirsi get (***di*** sth), get hold (***di*** of)
fornitore *m* supplier
fornitura *f* supply
forno *m* oven; (*panetteria*) bakery; ***forno a microonde*** microwave (oven); GASTR ***al forno*** *carne, patate* roast; *mele, pasta* baked
foro[1] *m* (*buco*) hole
foro[2] *m romano* forum; DIR (*tribunale*) (law) court
forse perhaps, maybe; ***mettere in forse*** cast doubt on
forte 1 *agg* strong; *suono* loud; *pioggia*

F

heavy; *taglia* large; *somma* considerable, substantial; *dolore* severe **2** *avv* (*con forza*) hard; (*ad alta voce*) loudly; (*velocemente*) fast **3** *m* (*fortezza*) fort; ***questo è il suo forte*** it's his strong point

fortezza *f* MIL fortress; ***fortezza d'animo*** strength of character

fortificare ⟨1m & d⟩ *rendere più forte* strengthen; MIL fortify

fortino *m* MIL blockhouse

fortuito chance

fortuna *f* fortune; ***avere fortuna*** be successful; (*essere fortunato*) be lucky; ***buona fortuna!*** good luck!; ***fare fortuna*** make a fortune; ***per fortuna*** luckily; ***di fortuna*** makeshift; ***atterraggio*** *m* ***di fortuna*** emergency landing

fortunatamente fortunately

fortunato lucky, fortunate

foruncolo *m* pimple

forza *f* strength; (*potenza*) power; *muscolare* force; ***forza di gravità*** force of gravity; ***per cause di forza maggiore*** because of circumstances beyond my / our control; ***a viva forza*** by force; ***a forza di ...*** by dint of ...; ***per forza*** against my / our will; ***per forza!*** (*naturalmente*) of course!; ***forza!*** come on!; ***-e*** *pl* (***armate***) MIL armed forces

forzare ⟨1c⟩ force

foschia *f* haze

fosco (*pl* -schi) dark

fosfato *m* phosphate

fosforescente phosphorescent

fosforo *m* phosphorus

fossa *f* pit, hole; (*tomba*) grave; ***fossa comune*** mass grave

fossato *m* ditch; *di fortezza* moat

fossetta *f* dimple

fossile 1 *agg* fossil *attr* **2** *m* fossil

fosso *m* ditch

foto *f inv* photo, snap

fotocellula *f* photocell

fotocopia *f* photocopy

fotocopiare ⟨1k & c⟩ photocopy

fotocopiatrice *f* photocopier

fotogenico (*pl* -ci) photogenic

fotografare ⟨1m & c⟩ photograph

fotografia *f arte* photography; (*foto*) photograph; ***fotografia formato tessera*** passport-size photograph; ***fotografia aerea*** aerial photograph; ***fotografia a colori*** colo(u)r photograph

fotografico (*pl* -ci) photographic; ***macchina*** *f* ***-a*** camera; ***articoli*** *mpl* ***-ci*** photographic equipment

fotografo *m* photographer

fotomontaggio *m* (*pl* -gi) photomontage

fotoreporter *m/f inv* photo journalist

fotoromanzo *m* story told in pictures

fra *prp* ◇ between; ***fra Roma e Londra*** between Rome and London
◇ among; ***fra questi ragazzi*** out of all these boys; ***fra di noi*** between you and me; ***fra l'altro*** what's more
◇ in; ***fra breve*** in a very short time, soon; ***fra tre giorni*** in three days
◇ ***fra sé e sé*** to himself / herself

frac *m inv* tails

fracassare ⟨1a⟩ smash

fracasso *m di persone* din; *di oggetti che cadono* crash

fradicio (*pl* -ci) rotten; (*bagnato*) soaked, soaking wet; ***ubriaco fradicio*** blind drunk F, blotto F

fragile fragile; *persona* frail, delicate

fragola *f* strawberry

fragore *m* roar; *di tuono* rumble

fraintendere ⟨3c⟩ misunderstand

frammentario (*pl* -ri) fragmentary

frammento *m* fragment

frana *f* landslide

franare ⟨1a⟩ collapse

francamente frankly

francese 1 *m/agg* French **2** *m/f* Frenchman; *donna* Frenchwoman; ***i -i*** *pl* the French

franchezza *f* frankness

franchigia *f* FIN exemption; *posta* freepost; ***franchigia doganale*** exemption from customs duties

Francia *f* France

franco (*pl* -chi) **1** *agg* frank; FIN free; ***farla -a*** get away with it; ***franco domicilio*** free delivery, carriage paid **2** *m* FIN franc

francobollo *m* stamp; ***due -i da ... lire*** two ... lire stamps

frangente *m* (*onda*) breaker; (*situazione*) (difficult) situation

frangia *f* (*pl* -ge) fringe

frantumare ⟨1a⟩ shatter

frantumi *mpl* splinters; ***in frantumi*** in smithereens; ***mandare in frantumi*** smash to smithereens

frappé *m inv* milkshake

frase *f* phrase; ***frase fatta*** cliché

frassino *m* ash (tree)

frastagliato: ***costa*** *f* ***-a*** jagged coastline

frastuono *m* racket

frate *m* REL friar, monk

fratellastro *m* step-brother; *con legami di consanguineità* half-brother

fratello *m* brother; ***-i*** *pl fratello e sorella* brother and sister

fraterno brotherly, fraternal

frattaglie *fpl* GASTR offal *sg*; *di pollo* giblets

frattanto meanwhile, in the meantime

frattempo *m*: ***nel frattempo*** meanwhile, in the meantime
frattura *f* fracture
fratturare ⟨1a⟩ fracture
fratturarsi: ***fratturarsi una gamba*** break one's leg
frazionare ⟨1a⟩ (*dividere in parti*) break up, split up
frazionarsi split (***in*** into)
frazione *f* fraction; POL small group; (*borgata*) hamlet; ***frazione decimale*** decimal fraction; ***una frazione di secondo*** a split second
freccia *f* (*pl* -cce) arrow; AUTO ***freccia*** (***di direzione***) indicator
freddezza *f* coldness
freddo 1 *agg* cold; *fig* ***a sangue freddo*** in cold blood **2** *m* cold; ***ho freddo*** I'm cold; ***fa freddo*** it's cold
freddoloso: ***essere freddoloso*** feel the cold
freddura *f* pun, play on words
freezer *m inv* freezer
fregare ⟨1e⟩ rub; F (*imbrogliare*) swindle F; F (*battere*) beat, wipe the floor with F; F *a un esame* fail; F (*rubare*) pinch F, lift F; P ***me ne frego di quello che pensano*** I don't give a damn what they think F
fregata *f* MAR frigate
fregatura *f* F (*imbroglio*) rip-off F; (*ostacolo, contrarietà*) pain F
fregio *m* ARCHI frieze
fremere ⟨3a⟩ (*tremare*) tremble, quiver
frenare ⟨1a⟩ AUTO brake; *folla, lacrime, risate* hold back; *entusiasmo, impulso* restrain
frenarsi (*dominarsi*) restrain o.s.
frenata *f* braking; ***fare una frenata*** brake; ***segni*** *mpl* ***di frenata*** tyre marks
freno *m* AUTO brake; *del cavallo* bit; ***freno d'allarme*** emergency brake; ***freno a mano*** handbrake, *Am* parking brake; ***freno a pedale*** foot-brake; ***porre freno a qc*** curb sth; *fig* ***senza freno*** without restraint; ***tenere a freno la lingua*** curb one's tongue
frequentare ⟨1b⟩ *luoghi* frequent; *scuola, corso* attend; *persona* associate with
frequentato popular; *strada* busy
frequente frequent; ***di frequente*** frequently
frequenza *f* frequency; *scolastica* attendance; ***un'alta frequenza di spettatori*** a large audience; ***con frequenza*** frequently
freschezza *f* freshness; *di temperatura* coolness
fresco (*pl* -chi) **1** *agg* fresh; *temperatura* cool; *fig* F ***stai fresco !*** you're for it! F, you've had it! F **2** *m* coolness; ***prendere il fresco*** take the air; ***fa fresco*** it's cool; ***mettere in fresco*** put in a cool place; *fig* F ***al fresco*** inside F
frescura *f* cool(ness)
fretta *f* hurry; ***aver fretta*** be in a hurry; ***non c'è fretta*** there's no hurry, there's no rush; ***in tutta fretta, in fretta e furia*** in great haste
frettoloso *saluto, sorriso* hurried; *lavoro* rushed; *persona* in a hurry
fricassea *f* GASTR fricassee
friggere ⟨3cc⟩ **1** *v/t* fry **2** *v/i* sizzle
friggitoria *f shop that sells deep fried fish etc*
friggitrice *f* deep fryer
frigido MED frigid
frigo *m* fridge
frigorifero 1 *agg* cold *attr*; *camion, nave, vagone* refrigerated **2** *m* refrigerator
fringuello *m* chaffinch
frittata *f* GASTR omelette, *Am* omelet; *fig* ***ormai la frittata è fatta*** the damage is done
frittella *f* fritter; *fig* (*macchia*) grease stain
fritto 1 *pp* → ***friggere* 2** *agg* fried **3** *m* fried food; ***fritto misto*** assortment of deep-fried food
frittura *f metodo* frying; ***frittura di pesce*** fried fish
frivolo frivolous
frizionare ⟨1a⟩ rub
frizione *f* friction; AUTO clutch
frizzante *bevanda* fizzy, sparkling; *aria* crisp; *fig parola, motto* biting, sharp
frodare ⟨1c⟩ defraud (***di*** of); ***frodare il fisco*** evade *or* dodge Ftax
frode *f* fraud
frontale frontal; ***scontro*** *m* ***frontale*** head-on collision
fronte 1 *f* forehead; ***di fronte a*** (*dirimpetto*) opposite, facing; *in presenza di* before; *a confronto di* compared to *or* with; ***la casa, vista dal di fronte*** the house, seen from the front **2** *m* front; ***fronte caldo*** warm front; ***far fronte agli impegni*** face up to one's responsibilities; ***far fronte alle spese*** make ends meet
fronteggiare ⟨1f⟩ (*stare di fronte a*) face; (*far fronte a*) face, confront
frontespizio *m* (*pl* -zi) title page; ARCHI frontispiece
frontiera *f* border, frontier; ***guardia*** *f* ***di frontiera*** border guard; ***valico*** *m* ***di frontiera*** border crossing
frontone *m* ARCHI pediment
fronzolo *m* frill
frottola *f* F fib F
frugale frugal

F

F

frugare ⟨1e⟩ **1** *v/i* (*rovistare*) rummage **2** *v/t* (*cercare con cura*) search, rummage through
fruire ⟨4d⟩: ***fruire di qc*** benefit from sth
frullare ⟨1a⟩ GASTR blend, liquidize; *uova* whisk
frullato *m* milk-shake
frullatore *m* liquidizer, blender
frullino *m* whisk
frumento *m* wheat
frusciare ⟨1f⟩ rustle
fruscio *m* rustle
frusta *f* whip; GASTR whisk
frustare ⟨1a⟩ whip
frustino *m* riding crop
frustrare ⟨1a⟩ frustrate
frustrazione *f* frustration
frutta *f* fruit; ***frutta candita*** candied fruit; ***frutta fresca*** fresh fruit; ***frutta secca*** nuts
fruttare ⟨1a⟩ **1** *v/t* yield **2** *v/i* fruit
frutteto *m* orchard
fruttifero fruitful; FIN interest-bearing
fruttivendolo *m*, **-a** *f* greengrocer
frutto *m* fruit; ***-i** pl **di mare*** seafood *sg*
fruttuoso profitable
FS *abbr* (= ***Ferrovie dello Stato***) Italian State railways
fu → ***essere***
fucilare ⟨1a⟩ shoot
fucilata *f* shot
fucile *m* rifle
fucina *f* forge
fuga *f* (*pl* -ghe) escape; MUS fugue; ***fuga di gas*** gas leak; FIN ***fuga di capitali*** flight of capital
fuggevole fleeting
fuggiasco *m* (*pl* -schi) fugitive
fuggifuggi *m inv* stampede
fuggire ⟨4a⟩ flee
fuggitivo *m* fugitive
fulcro *m* fulcrum
fuliggine *f* soot
fuligginoso sooty
fulminante *sguardo* withering; *malattia* which strikes suddenly
fulminare ⟨1l⟩ *di sguardo* look daggers at, glare at; ***rimanere fulminato*** *da fulmine* be struck by lightning; *da elettricità* be electrocuted; *fig* be thunderstruck
fulminarsi *di lampadina* blow
fulmine *m* lightning
fulmineo fast, rapid
fumaiolo *m* MAR funnel; FERR chimney; *di casa* chimney pot
fumare ⟨1a⟩ smoke
fumatore *m*, **-trice** *f* smoker; FERR ***scompartimento*** *m* ***per -i/non -i*** smoking / non-smoking compartment
fumetto *m* comic strip; ***-i** pl **per ragazzi*** comics
fumo *m* smoke; (*vapore*) steam; *fig* ***andare in fumo*** (*fallire*) go up in smoke; (*svanire*) come to nothing; ***mandare in fumo*** shatter
fumoso smoky; *fig* (*oscuro*) muddled
fune *f* rope; (*cavo*) cable; ***tiro** m **alla fune*** tug-of-war
funebre funeral *attr*; *fig* gloomy, funereal; ***carro** m **funebre*** hearse
funerale *m* funeral
fungere ⟨3d⟩ act (***da*** as)
fungo *m* (*pl* -ghi) mushroom; MED fungus; ***fungo velenoso*** poisonous mushroom; ***fungo prataiolo*** field mushroom
funicolare *f* funicular railway
funivia *f* cableway
funzionamento *m* operation, functioning
funzionare ⟨1a⟩ operate, function; ***non funzionare*** be out of order; *di orologio* have stopped
funzionario *m* (*pl* -ri) official, civil servant
funzione *f* function; (*carica*) office; REL service, ceremony; ***mettere in funzione*** put into operation; ***in funzione di ...*** depending on; ***variare in funzione di ...*** vary with ...
fuoco *m* (*pl* -chi) fire; FIS, FOT focus; ***dar fuoco a qc*** set fire to sth; ***-chi d'artificio*** fireworks; MIL ***far fuoco*** (open) fire; FOT ***mettere a fuoco*** focus
fuorché except
fuori **1** *prp stato* outside, out of; *moto* out of, away from; ***fuori di casa*** outside the house; ***fuori città*** out of town; ***fuori luogo*** out of place; ***fuori mano*** out of the way; ***fuori di sé*** beside o.s.; ***fuori uso*** out of use **2** *avv* outside; *all'aperto* out of doors; SP out; ***di fuori*** outside; ***fuori!*** out!
fuoribordo *m inv* motorboat; *motore* outboard motor
fuoriclasse *agg*, *m/f inv* champion
fuorigioco *m inv* offside; ***essere nel fuorigioco*** be offside
fuoriserie **1** *agg* made to order, custom made **2** *f inv* AUTO custom-built model
fuoristrada *m inv* off-road vehicle
fuoriuscita *f di gas* leakage, escape
fuoriuscito *m* exile
fuorviare ⟨1h⟩ **1** *v/i* go astray **2** *v/t* lead astray
furbizia *f* cunning
furbo cunning, crafty
furfante *m* rascal, rogue
furgoncino *m* (small) van
furgone *m* van

furia *f* fury, rage; ***a furia di …*** by dint of …
furibondo furious, livid
furioso furious; *vento*, *lotta* violent
furore *m* fury, rage; ***far furore*** be all the rage
furtivo furtive
furto *m* theft; ***furto con scasso*** burglary
fusa *fpl*: ***fare le fusa*** purr
fuscello *m* twig
fuseaux *mpl* leggings
fusibile *m* EL fuse
fusione *f* fusion; FIN merger; ***fusione nucleare*** nuclear fusion
fuso[1] *pp* → ***c***; METAL molten; *burro* melted
fuso[2] *m* spindle; ***fuso orario*** time zone
fusto *m* (*tronco*) trunk; (*stelo*) stem, stalk; *di metallo* drum; *di legno* barrel
futile futile
futilità *f* futility
futuristico futuristic
futuro *m*/*agg* future; ***in futuro*** in future; ***in un lontano / prossimo futuro*** in the distant / near future

G

g *abbr* (= ***grammo***) g (= gram)
gabbia *f* cage; ***gabbia di mattia*** *fig* madhouse; ***gabbia toracica*** rib cage
gabbiano *m* (sea)gull
gabinetto *m* toilet; POL cabinet; ***gabinetto medico / dentistico*** doctor's/dentist's surgery; POL ***gabinetto ombra*** shadow cabinet
gaffe *f* blunder, gaffe
gaelico *m* Gaelic
gala *f* (*ricevimento*) gala; ***serata*** *f* ***di gala*** gala evening
galante gallant
galanteria *f* gallantry
galantuomo (*pl* -uomini) *m* gentleman
galassia *f* galaxy
galateo *m libro* book of etiquette; *comportamento* etiquette, (good) manners
galera *f* (*prigione*) jail, prison
galla *f* BOT gall; ***a galla*** afloat; ***venire a galla*** (come to the) surface; *fig* come to light; ***tenersi a galla*** stay *or* keep afloat
galleggiante 1 *agg* floating **2** *m* (*boa*) buoy
galleggiare ⟨1f⟩ float
galleria *f* gallery; *passaggio con negozi* (shopping) arcade; FERR, MIN tunnel; TEA circle
Galles *m* Wales
gallese 1 *m/agg* Welsh **2** *m/f* Welshman; *donna* Welshwoman
gallina *f* hen
gallo *m* cock; SP ***peso*** *m* ***gallo*** bantam weight
gallone *m* MIL stripe; *unità di misura* gallon
galoppare ⟨1c⟩ gallop
galoppo *m* gallop; ***al galoppo*** at a gallop
gamba *f* leg; *fig* ***in gamba*** (*capace*) smart, bright; (*in buona salute*) healthy, (fighting) fit; *persona anziana* spry, sprightly; ***darsela a -e*** take to one's heels
gamberetto *m* shrimp
gambero *m* prawn
gambo *m di fiore, bicchiere* stem; *di pianta, fungo* stalk
gamma *f* range; MUS scale
gancio *m* (*pl* -ci) hook; ***gancio di traino*** tow-hook
gara *f* competition; *di velocità* race; ***gara automobilistica*** car race; ***gara eliminatoria*** heat; ***fare a gara*** compete
garage *m inv* garage; ***garage sotteraneo*** underground car park (*Am* parking garage)
garagista *m* (*pl* -i) (*custode*) garage attendant; (*meccanico*) mechanic
garante *m* guarantor.
garantire ⟨4d⟩ **1** *v/t* guarantee; (*assicurare*) ensure **2** *v/i* (*farsi garante*) stand guarantor (***per*** for)
garantito guaranteed
garanzia *f* guarantee; ***essere in garanzia*** be under guarantee
garbato courteous, polite
garbo *m* courtesy, politeness; (*modi gentili*) good manners *pl*; (*tatto*) tact
gardenia *f* gardenia
gareggiare ⟨1f⟩ compete
gargarismo *m* gargle; (*collutorio*) mouthwash; ***fare i -i*** gargle
garofano *m* carnation; GASTR ***chiodi*** *mpl* ***di garofano*** cloves
garza *f* gauze
garzone *m* boy
gas *m inv* gas; ***a gas*** gas *attr*; AUTO ***dare gas*** accelerate; ***gas asfissiante*** poison gas; ***gas lacrimogeno*** tear gas; ***gas naturale*** natural gas; ***gas di scarico*** exhaust (fumes)
gasato 1 *agg bibita* fizzy; (*eccitato*) excited **2** *m*, **-a** *f* bighead
gasolio *m per riscaldamento* oil; AUTO diesel fuel
gastrico (*pl* -ci) gastric; ***succhi*** *mpl* ***-ci*** digestive juices
gastrite *f* gastritis
gastronomia *f* gastronomy
gastronomico (*pl* -ci) gastronomic
gatta *f* (female) cat
gattino *m* kitten
gatto *m* cat; *maschio* (tom) cat; ***c'erano quattro -i*** there was hardly anybody there
gavetta *f* MIL mess tin; ***fare la gavetta*** come up through the ranks
gay *m/agg* gay
gazza *f* magpie
gazzella *f* gazelle
gazzetta *f* gazette; ***gazzetta ufficiale*** official journal, gazette
gazzosa *f* fizzy drink
GB *abbr* (= ***Gran Bretagna***) GB (= Great Britain)
G.d.F. *abbr* (= ***Guardia di Finanza***) Customs and Excise
gel *m inv* gel

gelare ⟨1b⟩ **1** *v/t* freeze **2** *v/i e* **gelarsi** freeze; ***mi si è gelato il sangue*** my blood ran cold
gelata *f* frost
gelateria *f* ice-cream parlo(u)r
gelatina *f* gelatine; ***gelatina di frutta*** fruit jelly
gelato 1 *agg* frozen **2** *m* ice cream; ***gelato alla vaniglia*** vanilla ice cream; ***gelato di fragola*** strawberry ice cream
gelido freezing
gelo *m* (*brina*) frost; *fig* chill
gelosia *f* jealousy
geloso jealous (***di*** of)
gelso *m* mulberry (tree)
gelsomino *m* jasmine
gemellaggio *m* twinning
gemello 1 *agg* twin **2** *m di camicia* cuff link **3** *m*, **-a** *f* twin; ASTR ***Gemelli*** *pl* Gemini
gemere ⟨3a⟩ groan
gemito *m* groan
gemma *f* (*pietra preziosa*) gem, jewel; BOT bud; *fig* gem
gene *m* BIO gene
genealogia *f* genealogy
genealogico (*pl* -ci) genealogical; ***albero*** *m* ***genealogico*** family tree
generale 1 *agg* general; ***in generale*** in general; TEA ***prova*** *f* ***generale*** dress rehearsal **2** *m* MIL general
generalità *f inv* general nature; ***le generalità*** *pl* personal details
generalizzare ⟨1a⟩ generalize
generalmente generally
generare ⟨1l & b⟩ (*dar vita a*) give birth to; (*causare*) generate, create; *sospetti* arouse; *elettricità*, *calore* generate
generatore *m* EL generator
generazione *f* generation
genere *m* (*tipo*, *specie*) kind; BIO genus; GRAM gender; ***in genere*** generally; ***unico nel suo genere*** unique; ***-i*** *pl* ***alimentari*** foodstuffs; ***-i*** *pl* ***di consumo*** consumer goods; ***genere umano*** mankind, humanity
generico (*pl* -ci) generic; ***medico*** *m* ***generico*** GP, general practitioner
genero *m* son-in-law
generosità *f* generosity
generoso generous (***con*** to)
genesi *f* genesis
genetico (*pl* -ci) genetic; ***ingegneria*** *f* ***-a*** genetic engineering
gengiva *f* gum
geniale ingenious; *idea* brilliant
genialità *f* genius; (*ingegnosità*) ingeniousness
genio *m* (*pl* -ni) genius; (*inclinazione*) talent; ***andare a genio*** be to one's liking; ***lampo*** *m* ***di genio*** brainwave
genitali *mpl* genitals
genitori *mpl* parents
gennaio *m* January
genocidio *m* genocide
Genova *f* Genoa
genovese *m/agg* Genoese
gentaglia *f* scum
gente *f* people *pl*; ***quanta gente !*** what a crowd!; *iron* ***gente bene*** upper-crust
gentile kind; *nelle lettere* ***gentile signora*** Dear Madam
gentilezza *f* kindness
gentiluomo (*pl* -uomini) *m* gentleman
genuino genuine; *prodotto alimentare* traditionally made; *risata* spontaneous
genziana *f* gentian
geografia *f* geography; ***geografia economica*** economic geography
geografico (*pl* -ci) geographic; ***carta*** *f* ***-a*** map
geologia *f* geology
geologico (*pl* -ci) geological
geologo *m* (*pl* -gi), **-a** *f* geologist
geometra *m/f* surveyor
geometria *f* geometry
geometrico (*pl* -ci) geometric(al)
geranio *m* (*pl* -ni) geranium
gerarchia *f* hierarchy
gerarchico (*pl* -ci) hierarchical; ***per via -a*** through the proper channels
gerente *m/f* manager
gergo *m* (*pl* -ghi) slang; *di una professione* jargon
geriatrico (*pl* -ci) geriatric; ***istituto*** *m* ***geriatrico*** old people's home
Germania *f* Germany
germe *m* germ; *fig* (*principio*) seeds *pl*; ***in germe*** in embryo
germinare ⟨1l & b⟩ germinate
germogliare ⟨1g & c⟩ sprout
germoglio *m* (*pl* -gli) shoot
geroglifico *m* (*pl* -ci) hieroglyph
gerundio *m* (*pl* -di) gerund
gesso *m* MIN gypsum; MED, *scultura* plaster cast; *per scrivere* chalk
gesticolare ⟨1m⟩ gesticulate
gestione *f* management
gestire ⟨4d⟩ manage
gesto *m con il braccio*, *la mano* gesture; *con la testa* nod
gestore *m* manager
Gesù *m* Jesus; ***Gesù bambino*** baby Jesus
gettare ⟨1b⟩ throw; *fondamenta* lay; *grido* give, let out; ***gettare fuori*** throw out; ***gettare via*** throw away
gettarsi throw o.s.; *di fiume* flow, empty (***in*** into)

getto *m* jet; ***di getto*** in one go; ***a getto continuo*** continuously
gettone *m* token; *per giochi* counter; *per giochi d'azzardo* chip; ***gettone*** (***telefonico***) (telephone) token; ***gettone di presenza*** (*indennità*) attendance fee; ***telefono*** *m* ***a gettone*** *telephone that takes tokens*
ghetto *m* ghetto
ghiacciaio *m* (*pl* -ai) glacier
ghiacciare ⟨1f⟩ *v/t & v/i* freeze
ghiacciato *lago*, *stagno* frozen; *bibita* ice-cold; ***tè*** *m* ***ghiacciato*** iced tea
ghiaccio *m* (*pl* -cci) ice; *sulla strada* black ice
ghiacciolo *m* icicle; (*gelato*) ice lolly
ghiaia *f* gravel
ghianda *f* acorn
ghiandola *f* gland
ghigliottina *f* guillotine
ghignare ⟨1a⟩ sneer
ghigno *m* sneer
ghiotto *persona* greedy; *fig: di notizie ecc* avid (***di*** for); (*appetitoso*) appetizing
ghiottoneria *f difetto* gluttony; *cibo* delicacy
ghirigoro *m* doodle
ghirlanda *f* garland
ghiro *m* dormouse; ***dormire come un ghiro*** sleep like a log
ghisa *f* cast iron
già already; (*ex*) formerly; ***già!*** of course!
giacca *f* (*pl* -cche) jacket; *di abito maschile* jacket; ***giacca a vento*** windproof jacket, windcheater; ***giacca di pelle*** leather jacket
giacché since
giacenza *f* (*pl* -ze) (*merce per la vendita*) stock; (*merce invenduta*) unsold goods *pl*; *periodo* stock time; ***giacenza di cassa*** cash in *or* on hand; ***-e*** *pl* ***di magazzino*** stock in hand
giacere ⟨2k⟩ lie
giacimento *m* MIN deposit
giacinto *m* hyacinth
giada *f* jade
giaggiolo *m* iris
giaguaro *m* jaguar
giallo 1 *agg* yellow; ***libro*** *m* ***giallo, film*** *m* ***giallo*** thriller **2** *m* yellow; (*libro*, *film*) thriller
Giappone *m* Japan
giapponese *agg*, *m/f* Japanese
giardinaggio *m* gardening
giardiniera *f donna* gardener; *mobile* plant stand; GASTR (mixed) pickles
giardiniere *m* gardener
giardino *m* garden; ***giardino botanico*** botanical gardens *pl*; ***giardino d'infanzia*** kindergarten; ***giardino pubblico*** park
giarrettiera *f* garter
giavellotto *m* javelin
gigante 1 *agg* gigantic, giant *attr* **2** *m* giant
gigantesco (*pl* -chi) gigantic
giglio *m* (*pl* -gli) lily
gilè *m inv* waistcoat, *Am* vest
gin *m inv* gin
ginecologo *m* (*pl* -gi), **-a** *f* gyn(a)ecologist
ginepro *m* juniper
ginestra *f* broom
gingillarsi ⟨1a⟩ fiddle; (*perder tempo*) fool around
gingillo *m* plaything; (*ninnolo*) knick-knack
ginnastica *f* exercises *pl*; *disciplina sportiva* gymnastics; *in palestra* P.E., physical education; ***ginnastica presciistica*** warm-up exercises (for skiers); ***una ginnastica mentale*** a mental exercise
ginocchio *m* (*pl* -cchi *e* le -cchia) knee; ***stare in ginocchio*** be on one's knees, be kneeling
giocare ⟨1o⟩ **1** *v/i* play; *d'azzardo*, *in Borsa* gamble; (*scommettere*) bet; ***giocare a*** *tennis*, *flipper* play; ***giocare d'astuzia*** use cunning **2** *v/t* play; (*ingannare*) trick
giocarsi (*perdere al gioco*) gamble away; (*beffarsi*) make fun; *carriera* destroy, throw away
giocatore *m*, **-trice** *f* player; *d'azzardo* gambler
giocattolo *m* toy
gioco *m* (*pl* -chi) game; ***il gioco*** gambling; ***gioco d'azzardo*** game of chance; ***gioco da bambini*** child's play; ***gioco di prestigio*** conjuring trick; ***gioco elettronico*** computer game; ***Giochi Olimpici*** Olympic Games; ***l'ho detto per gioco !*** I was joking!
giocoliere *m* juggler
gioia *f* joy; (*gioiello*) jewel; *fig* ***darsi alla pazza gioia*** go wild (with excitement)
gioielleria *f* jeweller's (shop), *Am* jewelry store
gioielliere *m*, **-a** *f* jeweller, *Am* jeweler
gioiello *m* jewel
gioire ⟨4d⟩ rejoice (***di*** in)
giornalaio *m* (*pl* -ai), **-a** *f* newsagent
giornale *m* (news)paper; (*rivista*) magazine; (*registro*) journal; ***giornale radio*** news (bulletin); ***giornale scandalistico*** *testata* tabloid; *stampa in genere* gutter press
giornaliero 1 *agg* daily; ***abbonamento*** *m* ***giornaliero*** day pass; ***spese*** *fpl* ***-e*** day-to-day expenses **2** *m* day labo(u)rer
giornalino *m per ragazzi* comic; ***giornali-***

no aziendale inhouse newspaper, staff magazine
giornalismo *m* journalism
giornalista *m/f* (*mpl* -sti) journalist, reporter
giornalistico (*pl* -ci) *attività, esperienza* journalistic; *agenzia, servizio* news *attr*
giornalmente daily
giornata *f* day; ***giornata (lavorativa) di 8 ore*** 8-hour day; ***lo finiremo in giornata*** we'll finish it today *or* by the end of the day; ***vivere alla giornata*** live from day to day
giorno *m* day; ***giorno di arrivo / partenza*** arrival / departure date; ***giorno di paga*** payday; ***giorno feriale*** weekday, working day; ***giorno festivo*** (public) holiday; ***illuminato a giorno*** floodlit; ***l'altro giorno*** the other day; ***ogni giorno*** every day; ***a -i*** (*fra pochi giorni*) in a few days (time); ***al giorno*** a day; ***al giorno d'oggi*** nowadays; ***in pieno giorno*** in broad daylight; ***di giorno*** by day
giostra *f* merry-go-round, *Am* carousel
giovane 1 *agg* young; (*giovanile*) youthful **2** *m/f* young man, youth; *ragazza* young woman, girl; ***i -i*** pl young people
giovanile youthful
giovanotto *m* young man, youth
giovare 〈1a〉 (*essere utile*) be useful (***a*** to); (*far bene*) be good (***a*** for)
giovarsi: ***giovarsi di*** make use of; *consigli* take
Giove *m* Jupiter
giovedì *m inv* Thursday; ***di giovedì*** on Thursdays
gioventù *f* youth; (*i giovani*) young people *pl*
gioviale jovial, jolly
giovinezza *f* youth
giradischi *m* record player
giraffa *f* giraffe
giramondo *m/f* rolling stone, wanderer
girandola *f* (*fuoco d'artificio*) Catherine wheel; (*giocattolo*) windmill; (*banderuola*) weather vane
girare 〈1a〉 **1** *v/t* turn; *ostacolo* get round; *posto, città, negozi* go round; *mondo, paese* travel round; *film* shoot; (*mescolare*) mix; FIN endorse **2** *v/i* turn; *rapidamente* spin; (*andare in giro*) wander *or* roam around; *con un veicolo* drive around; ***mi gira la testa*** I feel dizzy, my head is spinning
girarrosto *m* GASTR spit
girasole *m* sunflower
girata *f* turn; (*passeggiata a piedi*) walk, stroll; *in macchina* drive; FIN endorsement; ***girata in bianco*** blank endorsement
giravolta *f* turn; AUTO spin; *fig* U-turn
girevole revolving
girino *m* tadpole
giro *m* turn; (*circolo*) circle; (*percorso abituale*) round; (*deviazione*) detour; (*passeggiata a piedi*) walk, stroll; *in macchina* drive; *in bicicletta* ride; *di pista* lap; *di motore* rev(olution); (*viaggio*) tour; ***giro d'affari*** turnover; ***giro di capitali*** circulation of capital; ***giro turistico della città*** city sightseeing tour; ***fare il giro dei negozi*** go round the shops; ***nel giro di una settimana*** within a week; ***senza tanti -i di parole*** without beating about the bush so much; ***giro di prova*** test drive; ***essere in giro*** (*da qualche parte*) be around (somewhere); (*fuori*) be out; ***mettere in giro*** spread; *fig* ***prendere in giro qu*** pull s.o.'s leg; ***a giro di posta*** by return of post
girocollo *m inv*: ***maglione*** *m* ***a girocollo*** crewneck (sweater)
gironzolare 〈1m〉 hang around; ***gironzolare per negozi*** wander about the shops
girovagare 〈1m, c & e〉 wander about
girovago (*pl* -ghi) **1** *agg gente* nomadic **2** *m* wanderer; (*ambulante*) itinerant
gita *f* trip, excursion; ***andare in gita*** go on a trip *or* excursion; ***gita domenicale*** Sunday outing; ***gita in bicicletta*** bike ride
gitano *m*, **-a** *f* gypsy
gitante *m/f* (day) tripper
giù down; (*sotto*) below; (*da basso*) downstairs; ***andar giù*** go down; *fig* ***non mi va giù*** it sticks in my throat; *fig* ***essere giù*** be down *or* depressed; *di salute* be run down; ***mandar giù*** swallow (*anche fig*); ***un po' più in giù*** a bit lower down; ***su e giù*** up and down; ***da Roma in giù*** south of Rome
giubbotto *m* sports jacket; ***giubbotto di salvataggio*** life jacket
giudicare 〈1l & d〉 **1** *v/t* judge; (*considerare*) consider, judge; ***giudicare male qu*** misjudge s.o.; ***lo hanno giudicato colpevole*** he has been found guilty. **2** *v/i* judge
giudice *m* judge; ***giudice istruttore*** examining magistrate; ***giudice di gara*** referee
giudiziario (*pl* -ri) judicial; ***vendita*** *f* ***-a*** sale by order of the court
giudizio *m* (*pl* -zi) judg(e)ment; (*senno*) wisdom; DIR (*causa*) trial; (*sentenza*) verdict; ***a mio giudizio*** in my opinion; ***giudizio civile*** civil action, lawsuit; ***mettere giudizio*** turn over a new leaf

giudizioso sensible
giugno *m* June
giunco *m* (*pl* -chi) reed
giungere ⟨3d⟩ **1** *v/t*: ***giungere le mani*** clasp one's hands **2** *v/i* arrive (***a*** in, at), reach (***a*** sth); ***giungere a Roma / alla stazione*** arrive in Rome / at the station, reach Rome / the station; *fig* ***giungere in porto*** reach one's goal; ***questa mi giunge nuova*** it's news to me
giungla *f* jungle
giunta *f* addition; POL junta; ***giunta comunale*** town council; ***per giunta*** in addition, moreover
giunto *pp* → ***giungere***
giuntura *f* ANAT joint
giuramento *m* oath; ***falso giuramento*** perjury; ***fare un giuramento*** swear an oath; ***prestare giuramento*** take the oath
giurare ⟨1a⟩ swear
giurato **1** *agg* sworn **2** *m* member of the jury
giuria *f* jury
giuridico (*pl* -ci) legal
giurisdizione *f* jurisdiction
giurisprudenza *f* jurisprudence
giurista *m/f* (*mpl* -sti) jurist
giustezza *f* accuracy; *di argomentazione* soundness; TIP justification
giustificare ⟨1m & d⟩ justify
giustificazione *f* justification
giustizia *f* justice; ***fare giustizia sommaria*** administer summary justice
giusto **1** *agg* just, fair; (*adatto*) right, appropriate; (*esatto*) correct, right, exact **2** *avv* correctly; *mirare* accurately; (*proprio, per l'appunto*) just; ***giusto!*** that's right! **3** *m* (*uomo giusto*) just man; ***pretendo solo il giusto*** I just want what is rightfully mine
glaciale glacial, icy
gladiolo *m* gladiolus
glassa *f* GASTR icing
gli **1** *art mpl* the; ***avere gli occhi azzurri*** have blue eyes **2** *pron* (*a lui*) (to) him; (*a esso*) (to) it; (*a loro*) (to) them; ***dagli i libri*** give him / them the books, give the books to him / them
glicemia *f* glyc(a)emia
glicerina *f* glycerine
glicine *m* wisteria
glie: ***gliela, glielo, glieli, gliele, gliene*** = *pron* **gli** *or* **le** *with pron* **la, lo, li, le, ne**
globale global
globo *m* globe; ***globo oculare*** eyeball; ***globo terrestre*** globe
globulo *m* globule; MED corpuscle; ***globulo rosso / bianco*** red / white blood cell
gloria *f* glory
glorificare ⟨1m & d⟩ glorify
glorioso glorious
glossa *f* gloss
glossario *m* (*pl* -ri) glossary
glucosio *m* glucose
gnocchi *mpl* (*di patate*) gnocchi (*small potato dumplings*)
gnorri *m* F: ***fare lo gnorri*** act dumb F
goal *m inv* SP goal
gobba *f* hump
gobbo **1** *agg* hunchbacked **2** *m* hunchback
goccia *f* (*pl* -cce) drop; ***a goccia a goccia*** little by little
gocciolare ⟨1l⟩ drip
gocciolio *m* (*pl* -ii) drip
godere ⟨2a⟩ **1** *v/t* enjoy; ***godersela*** enjoy o.s. **2** *v/i* (*rallegrarsi*) be delighted (***di*** at)
godimento *m* enjoyment
goffo awkward, clumsy
gol *m inv* SP goal
gola *f* throat; (*ingordigia*) greed(iness), gluttony; GEOG gorge; ***mal*** *m* ***di gola*** sore throat; ***far gola a*** tempt
golf *m inv* golf; (*cardigan*) cardigan; (*maglione*) sweater; ***giocatore*** *m* ***di golf*** golf player, golfer
golfista *m/f* golfer
golfo *m* gulf
golosità *f* (*ghiottoneria*) greed(iness), gluttony; (*leccornia*) delicacy
goloso greedy; ***essere goloso di dolci*** have a sweet tooth
golpe *m inv* coup
gomito *m* elbow; ***curva*** *f* ***a gomito*** sharp bend; *fig* ***alzare il gomito*** hit the bottle
gomitolo *m* ball (of wool)
gomma *f* rubber; *per cancellare* eraser; (*pneumatico*) tyre, *Am* tire; ***gomma da masticare*** (chewing) gum; AUTO ***gomma di scorta*** spare tyre (*Am* tire); ***avere una gomma a terra*** have a flat tyre (*Am* tire)
gommapiuma *f* foam rubber
gommato *carta* gummed; *tessuto* rubberized
gommista *m* (*pl* -i) tyre (*Am* tire) specialist
gommone *m* rubber dinghy
gondola *f* gondola
gondoliere *m* gondolier
gonfiare ⟨1k⟩ **1** *v/t con aria* inflate; *le guance* puff out; *fig* (*esagerare*) exaggerate, magnify **2** *v/i e* **gonfiarsi** swell up; *fig* puff up
gonfio (*pl* -fi) swollen; *pneumatico* inflated; *stomaco* bloated; *fig* puffed up (***di***

with); *fig* ***a -e vele*** splendidly
gonfiore *m* swelling
gonna *f* skirt; ***gonna a pieghe*** pleated skirt; ***gonna pantalone*** culottes *pl*
gorgo *m* (*pl* -ghi) whirlpool
gorgogliare ⟨1g⟩ *di stomaco* rumble; *dell'acqua* gurgle
gorilla *m inv* gorilla; F (*guardia del corpo*) bodyguard, gorilla F
gotico (*pl* -ci) *m/agg* Gothic
gotta *f* MED gout
governante 1 *f* housekeeper **2** *m* ruler
governare ⟨1b⟩ POL govern, rule; MAR steer
governativo government *attr*; *scuola* state *attr*
governatore *m* governor
governo *m* government; MAR steering; ***governo di coalizione*** coalition government; ***governo di minoranza*** minority government
gozzo *m* MED goitre, *Am* goiter
gozzovigliare ⟨1g⟩ make merry
gracchiare ⟨1k⟩ *di corvo* caw; *di rane* croak; *di persona* squawk
gracidare ⟨1l⟩ croak
gracile (*debole*) delicate
gradasso *m* boaster
gradazione *f* gradation; (*sfumatura*) shade; ***gradazione alcolica*** alcohol(ic) content
gradevole pleasant, agreeable
gradimento *m* liking
gradinata *f* flight of steps; *stadio* stand; *a teatro* gallery, balcony
gradino *m* step
gradire ⟨4d⟩ like; (*desiderare*) wish; ***gradirei sapere*** I would like to know; ***gradisce un po' di vino?*** would you like some wine?
gradito pleasant; (*bene accetto*) welcome
grado[1] *m* degree; *in una gerarchia*, MIL rank; ***30 -i all'ombra*** 30 degrees in the shade; ***in grado di lavorare*** capable of working, fit for work; ***essere in grado di*** be in a position to; ***per -i*** by degrees
grado[2] *m*: ***di buon grado*** willingly
graduale gradual
graduare ⟨1l⟩ graduate
graduatoria *f* list
graduazione *f* graduation
graffa *f* TIP brace
graffiare ⟨1k⟩ scratch
graffio *m* (*pl* -ffi) scratch
graffiti *mpl* graffiti
grafia *f* (hand)writing
grafica *f* graphics *pl*
grafico (*pl* -ci) **1** *agg* graphic **2** *m* (*diagramma*) graph; (*disegnatore*) graphic artist
grafite *f* graphite
grafologia *f* handwriting analysis
grammatica *f* grammar
grammaticale grammatical
grammo *m* gram(me)
gran → ***grande***
grana 1 *f* grain; F (*seccatura*) trouble; F *soldi* dough F, cash; F ***piantare una grana*** stir up trouble; F ***pieni di grana*** rolling in money F **2** *m inv cheese similar to Parmesan*
granaio *m* (*pl* -ai) barn
granata *f* MIL grenade; BOT pomegranate
Gran Bretagna *f* Great Britain
granchio *m* (*pl* -chi) crab; *fig* blunder; *fig* ***prendere un granchio*** make a blunder
grandangolare *m* FOT wide-angle lens
grande big, large; (*alto*) big, tall; (*largo*) wide; *fig* (*intenso, notevole*) great; (*adulto*) grown-up, big; (*vecchio*) old; FERR ***grande velocità*** high speed; ***non è un gran che*** it's nothing special
grandezza *f* (*dimensione*) size; (*larghezza*) width; (*ampiezza*) breadth; (*altezza*) height; *fig* (*eccellenza*) greatness; (*grandiosità*) grandeur
grandinare ⟨1l⟩ hail
grandinata *f* hailstorm
grandine *f* hail
grandioso grand
granduca *m* (*pl* -chi) grand duke
granducato *m* grand duchy
granduchessa *f* grand duchess
granello *m* grain; ***granello di pepe*** peppercorn; ***granello di polvere*** speck of dust; ***granello di sabbia*** grain of sand
granita *f type of ice made of frozen crystals of coffee or fruit syrup*
granito *m* granite
grano *m* (*chicco*) grain; (*frumento*) wheat; *fig* grain, ounce
granturco *m* maize, corn
grappa *f* grappa, *brandy made from the remains of the grapes used in wine-making*
grappolo *m* bunch
grassetto *m* TIP bold (type)
grasso 1 *agg* fat; (*unto*) greasy; *cibo* fatty **2** *m* fat; *di bue, pecora* suet; ***macchia f di grasso*** grease stain; ***grasso lubrificante*** grease; ***privo di -i*** fat-free
grassoccio (*pl* -cci) plump
grata *f* grating
gratella *f*, **graticola** *f* GASTR grill
gratifica *f* bonus
gratin *m*: ***al gratin*** au gratin
gratinato → ***al gratin***
gratis free (of charge)

G

gratitudine *f* gratitude
grato grateful; (*gradito*) welcome; ***vi sarei grato se …*** I would be grateful if …, I would appreciate it if …
grattacapo *m* problem, headache F
grattacielo *m* skyscraper
grattare ⟨1a⟩ scratch; (*raschiare*) scrape; (*grattugiare*) grate; F swipe F, pinch F
grattugia *f* (*pl* -ge) grater
grattugiare ⟨1f⟩ grate; ***pane*** *m* ***grattugiato*** breadcrumbs *pl*
gratuito free (of charge); (*infondato*) gratuitous
gravare ⟨1a⟩ **1** *v/t* burden **2** *v/i* weigh (***su*** on)
grave (*pesante*) heavy; (*serio*) serious; (*difficile*) hard
gravidanza *f* pregnancy
gravità *f* seriousness, gravity; FIS (***forza*** *f* ***di***) ***gravità*** (force of) gravity
gravoso onerous
grazia *f* grace; (*gentilezza*) favo(u)r; REL grace; DIR pardon; ***in grazia di*** thanks to; ***con grazia*** gracefully; ***colpo*** *m* ***di grazia*** coup de grâce
graziare ⟨1g⟩ pardon
grazie *int* thank you, thanks; ***tante grazie*** thank you so much; ***grazie a*** thanks to; ***grazie a Dio!*** thank goodness!
grazioso charming; (*carino*) pretty
Grecia *f* Greece
greco (*pl* -ci) **1** *agg* Greek **2** *m*, **-a** *f* Greek
gregge *m* (*pl* le -ggi) flock
greggio (*pl* -ggi) **1** *agg* (*non lavorato*) raw, crude **2** *m* crude (petroleum)
grembiule *m* apron
grembo *m* lap; (*materno*) womb; *fig* bosom
gremito crowded
gretto (*avaro*) mean; (*di mente ristretta*) narrow-minded
gridare ⟨1a⟩ **1** *v/t* shout, yell; ***gridare aiuto*** shout for help **2** *v/i* shout, yell; (*strillare*) scream
grido *m* (*pl gen* le -da) shout, cry
grigio (*pl* -gi) grey, *Am* gray; *fig* (*triste*) sad; (*scialbo*) dull, dreary
grigiore *m* greyness, *Am* grayness; *fig* (*monotonia*) dullness, dreariness
griglia *f* (*grata*) grating; GASTR grill; ***alla griglia*** grilled
grilletto *m* trigger
grillo *m* cricket; *fig* (*capriccio*) fancy, whim
grimaldello *m device for picking locks*
grinfie *fpl fig* clutches
grinta *f* grit; *fig* determination
grinza *f di stoffa* crease
grinzoso *viso* wrinkled; (*spiegazzato*) creased
grissino *m* bread stick
grondaia *f* gutter
grondare ⟨1a⟩ **1** *v/i* (*colare*) pour; (*gocciolare*) drip; ***grondare di sudore*** be dripping with sweat **2** *v/t* drip with
groppa *f* back
groppo *m*: ***avere un groppo alla gola*** have a lump in one's throat
grossezza *f* (*dimensione*) size; (*spessore*) thickness; (*l'essere grosso*) largeness
grossista *m/f* (*mpl* -i) wholesaler
grosso 1 *agg* big, large; (*spesso*) thick; *mare* rough; *sale*, *ghiaia* coarse; F ***pezzo*** *m* ***grosso*** big shot F; ***questa è -a!*** this is too much!; ***sbagliarsi di grosso*** make a big mistake; ***farla -a*** make a fine mess **2** *m* bulk
grossolano coarse; *errore* serious
grossomodo roughly
grotta *f* cave; *artificiale* grotto
grottesco (*pl* -chi) grotesque
groviglio *m* (*pl* -gli) tangle; *fig* muddle
gru *f inv* crane
gruccia *f* (*pl* -cce) crutch; *per vestiti* hanger
grumo *m* clot; *di farina* lump
gruppo *m* group; ***gruppo sanguigno*** blood group; ***gruppo di lavoro*** working group; ***a -i*** in groups
guadagnare ⟨1a⟩ earn; (*ottenere*) gain
guadagno *m* gain; (*profitto*) profit; (*entrate*) earnings *pl*; ***margine*** *m* ***di guadagno*** profit margin
guaina *f* sheath; (*busto*) corset, girdle
guaio *m* (*pl* -ai) trouble; (*danno*) damage; ***-ai a te se lo fai!*** woe betide you if you do!; ***essere nei -ai*** be in trouble
guancia *f* (*pl* -ce) cheek
guanciale *m* pillow
guanto *m* glove
guantone *m*: ***guantone da boxe*** boxing glove
guardaboschi *m inv* forest ranger
guardacaccia *m inv* gamekeeper
guardacoste *m inv* MAR coastguard
guardalinee *m inv* SP assistant referee, linesman
guardamacchine *m* car park (*Am* parking lot) attendant
guardare ⟨1a⟩ **1** *v/t* look at; (*osservare, stare a vedere*) watch; (*custodire*) watch, look after; (*esaminare*) check **2** *v/i* look; (*controllare*) check; *di finestra* overlook (***su*** sth); *di porta* lead (***su*** to); ***guardare a sud*** face south
guardarsi look at o.s.; ***guardarsi da*** beware of; (*astenersi*) refrain from
guardaroba *m inv* cloakroom, *Am* check-

room; *armadio* wardrobe

guardarobiere *m*, **-a** *f* cloakroom attendant

guardia *f* guard; ***guardia forestale*** forest ranger; ***guardia di finanza*** *Customs and Excise officer*; ***guardia di pubblica sicurezza*** policeman; ***guardia del corpo*** bodyguard; ***guardia medica, medico*** *m* ***di guardia*** doctor on duty; ***fare la guardia*** keep guard *or* watch; ***stare in guardia*** be on one's guard

guardiano *m*, **-a** *f* (*custode*) warden; (*portiere*) caretaker; (*guardia*) guard; *di parco* keeper, ***-a notturno*** night watchman

guardone *m* voyeur

guardrail *m inv* guardrail

guarigione *f* recovery; ***in via di guarigione*** on the mend

guarire ⟨4d⟩ **1** *v/t* cure **2** *v/i* recover; *di ferita* heal

guarnire ⟨4d⟩ decorate; *abiti* trim; GASTR garnish

guarnizione *f* (*abbellimento*) trimming; GASTR garnish; *di rubinetto* washer; AUTO ***guarnizione del freno*** brake lining

guastafeste *m/f inv* spoilsport

guastare ⟨1a⟩ spoil, ruin; *meccanismo* break

guastarsi break down; *di tempo* change for the worse; *di cibi* go bad, spoil

guasto **1** *agg* broken; *telefono, ascensore* out of order; AUTO broken down; *cibi* bad, off F; *dente* rotten, decayed **2** *m* fault, failure; AUTO breakdown

guerra *f* war; ***guerra civile*** civil war; ***guerra lampo*** blitz; ***guerra fredda*** Cold War

guerrafondaio *m* (*pl* -ai) war-monger

guerriglia *f* guerrilla warfare

guerrigliero *m*, **-a** *f* guerrilla

gufo *m* owl

guida *f* guidance; (*persona, libro*) guide; AUTO driving; ***guida alpina*** mountain guide; ***guida telefonica*** phone book; ***guida turistica*** tourist guide; AUTO ***guida a destra/a sinistra*** right-hand / left-hand drive

guidare ⟨1a⟩ guide; AUTO drive

guidatore *m*, **-trice** *f* driver

guinzaglio *m* (*pl* -gli) lead, leash

guizzare ⟨1a⟩ dart

guscio *m* (*pl* -sci) shell

gustare ⟨1a⟩ taste; *fig* enjoy

gusto *m* taste; (*sapore*) flavo(u)r; *fig* (*piacere*) pleasure; ***buon / cattivo gusto*** good / bad taste; ***senza gusto*** tasteless

gustoso tasty; *fig* delightful

H

h *abbr* (= ***ora***) h (= hour)
ha *abbr* (= ***ettaro***) ha (= hectare)
ha, hai, hanno → ***avere***
habitat *m inv* BIO habitat
habitué *m/f inv* regular customer
hacker *m/f* INFOR *inv* hacker
hall *f inv* foyer
hamburger *m inv* hamburger
handicap *m inv* handicap
handicappato **1** *agg* disabled, handicapped **2** *m*, **-a** *f* disabled *or* handicapped person
hard disk *m inv* INFOR hard disk
hardware *m inv* INFOR hardware
harem *m inv* harem
hashish *m* hashish
henné *m inv* henna
herpes *m inv* herpes
hg *abbr* (= ***ettogrammo***) hg (= hectogram)
hinterland *m inv* hinterland
hit parade *f inv* hit parade
hl *abbr* (= ***ettolitro***) hl (= hectolitre)
hm *abbr* (= ***ettometro***) hm (= hectometre)
ho → ***avere***
hobby *m inv* hobby
hockey *m inv* hockey; ***hockey su ghiaccio*** ice hockey
holding *f inv* holding
hostess *f inv* hostess; ***hostess di terra*** (*guida*) member of ground staff
hotel *m inv* hotel
hot dog *m inv* hot dog

I

i *art mpl* the
iberico (*pl* -ci) Iberian
iceberg *m inv* iceberg
icona *f* icon
iconografia *f* iconography
Iddio *m* God
idea *f* idea; (*opinione*) opinion; ***idea fissa*** obsession, idée fixe; ***cambiare idea*** change one's mind; ***non avere la minima idea di qc*** not have the slightest idea about sth; ***scambio*** *m* ***di -e*** exchange of views; ***neanche per idea!*** of course not!
ideale *m/agg* ideal
idealizzare ⟨1a⟩ idealize
ideare ⟨1b⟩ *scherzo, scusa* think up; *metodo, oggetto nuovo* invent; *piano, progetto* devise
ideatore *m*, **-trice** *f* originator; *di metodo, oggetto nuovo* inventor
idem ditto
identico (*pl* -ci) identical
identificare ⟨1n & d⟩ identify
identificazione *f* identification
identikit® *m inv* Identikit
identità *f inv* identity
ideologia *f* ideology
ideologico (*pl* -ci) ideological
idioma *m* (*pl* -i) idiom
idiomatico (*pl* -ci) idiomatic
idiota **1** *agg* idiotic, stupid **2** *m/f* (*mpl* -i) idiot, fool
idiozia *f* stupidity, idiocy; (*assurdità*) nonsense; ***un'idiozia*** a stupid *or* idiotic thing to do / say
idolo *m* idol
idoneità *f* suitability; *qualifica* qualification
idoneo suitable (***a*** for)
idrante *m* hydrant
idratante *della pelle* moisturizing
idratare ⟨1a⟩ *la pelle* moisturize
idraulico **1** *agg* hydraulic; ***impianto*** *m* ***idraulico*** plumbing **2** *m* (*pl* -ci) plumber
idrico water *attr*
idromassaggio *m* Jacuzzi®, whirlpool bath
idroelettrico hydroelectric
idrofilo: ***cotone*** *m* ***idrofilo*** cotton wool, *Am* absorbent cotton
idrofobo zo rabid; (*furioso*) foaming at the mouth
idrogeno *m* hydrogen
idroplano *m* hydroplane
iena *f* hyena
ieri yesterday; ***ieri l'altro, l'altro ieri*** the day before yesterday; ***ieri mattina*** yesterday morning
igiene *f* hygiene; ***igiene del corpo*** personal hygiene; ***ufficio*** *m* ***d'igiene*** public health office
igienico (*pl* -ci) hygienic; ***carta*** *f* ***-a*** toilet paper
ignaro unaware (***di*** of)
ignorante (*non informato*) ignorant; (*incolto*) uneducated; (*maleducato*) rude
ignoranza *f* ignorance
ignorare ⟨1a⟩ (*non considerare*) ignore; (*non sapere*) not know; ***lo ignoro*** I don't know
ignoto unknown
il *art m sg* the; ***il signor Conte*** Mr Conte; ***il martedì*** on Tuesdays; ***3000 lire il chilo*** 3000 lire a kilo; ***mi piace il caffè*** I like coffee
illecito illicit
illegale illegal
illegalità *f* illegality
illeggibile illegible
illegittimo illegitimate
illeso unhurt
illimitato unlimited
ill.mo *abbr* (= ***illustrissimo***) *formal style of address in correspondence*
illogico (*pl* -ci) illogical
illudere ⟨3q⟩ deceive
illudersi delude o.s.
illuminare ⟨1m⟩ light up; *fig* enlighten
illuminazione *f* lighting; *fig* flash of inspiration; ***illuminazione stradale*** street lighting
illusione *f* illusion
illuso **1** *pp* → ***illudere*** **2** *m/f* (*sognatore*) dreamer
illusorio (*pl* -ri) illusory
illustrare ⟨1a⟩ illustrate
illustratore *m*, **-trice** *f* illustrator
illustrazione *f* illustration
illustre illustrious
imballaggio *m* (*pl* -ggi) *operazione* packing; (*involucro*) package
imballare ⟨1a⟩ pack; AUTO ***imballare il motore*** race the engine
imballo *m* → ***imballaggio***
imbalsamare ⟨1a⟩ embalm; *animale* stuff
imbambolato *occhi, sguardo* blank; *dal sonno* bleary-eyed; ***non star lí fermo imbambolato!*** don't stand there gawping!
imbarazzante embarrassing

imbarazzare ⟨1a⟩ embarrass

imbarazzato embarrassed

imbarazzo *m* embarassment; (*disturbo*) trouble; ***non avere che l'imbarazzo della scelta*** be spoilt for choice; ***imbarazzo di stomaco*** upset stomach; ***mettere in imbarazzo qu*** embarrass s.o.

imbarcadero *m* landing stage

imbarcare ⟨1d⟩ embark; *carico* load

imbarcarsi go on board, embark; ***imbarcarsi in un'impresa*** embark on an undertaking

imbarcazione *f* boat; ***imbarcazione da diporto*** pleasure boat

imbarco *m* (*pl* -chi) *di passeggeri* boarding, embarkation; *di carico* loading; (*banchina*) landing stage

imbattersi ⟨3a⟩: ***imbattersi in qu*** bump into s.o.

imbattibile unbeatable

imbecille 1 *agg* idiotic, stupid **2** *m/f* imbecile, fool

imbiancare ⟨1d⟩ **1** *v/t* whiten; *con pitture* paint; *tessuti* bleach **2** *v/i e* **imbiancarsi** go white

imbianchino *m* (house) painter

imboccare ⟨1d⟩ *persona* feed; *fig* prompt; ***imboccare una strada*** turn into a road

imboccatura *f* (*apertura*) opening; (*ingresso*) entrance; MUS mouthpiece

imbocco *m* entrance

imboscata *f* ambush

imbottigliamento *m* bottling; AUTO traffic jam

imbottigliare ⟨1g⟩ bottle; *di veicoli* hold up; ***sono rimasto imbottigliato nel traffico*** I was stuck in a traffic jam

imbottire ⟨4d⟩ stuff; *giacca* pad; *fig* (*riempire*) cram, stuff

imbottito stuffed; *panino* filled

imbottitura *f* stuffing; *di giacca* padding

imbranato clumsy

imbrattare ⟨1a⟩ soil; (*macchiare*) stain

imbrattatele *m/f inv* dauber

imbrogliare ⟨1g & c⟩ **1** *v/t* (*raggirare*) take in; (*truffare*) cheat, swindle; *fig* confuse **2** *v/i* cheat

imbroglio *m* (*pl* -gli) (*truffa*) trick; *fig* (*pasticcio*) mess

imbroglione *m*, **-a** *f* cheat, swindler

imbronciato sulky

imbrunire ⟨4d⟩ get dark

imbruttire ⟨4d⟩ **1** *v/t* make ugly **2** *v/i* become ugly

imbucare ⟨1d⟩ *posta* post, *Am* mail

imburrare ⟨1a⟩ butter

imbuto *m* funnel

imitare ⟨1a or 1l⟩ imitate

imitazione *f* imitation

immagazzinare ⟨1a⟩ store

immaginare ⟨1m⟩ imagine; (*supporre*) suppose; ***s'immagini!*** not at all!

immaginario (*pl* -ri) imaginary

immaginazione *f* imagination

immagine *f* image

immancabile *cortesia, sorriso* unfailing; *persona* ever present; *macchina fotografica* inevitable

immangiabile inedible

immatricolare ⟨1n⟩ register

immatricolarsi enrol, *Am* enroll; *all'università* matriculate, enrol

immatricolazione *f* registration; *all'università* matriculation, enrol(l)ment

immaturità *f* immaturity

immaturo *persona* immature; (*precoce*) premature; *frutto* unripe

immedesimarsi ⟨1n⟩ identify (***in*** with)

immediatamente immediately

immediato immediate; (*pronto*) prompt

immenso immense

immergere ⟨3uu⟩ immerse, dip; (*lasciare immerso*) soak

immergersi plunge; *di subacqueo, sottomarino* dive; *fig* immerse o.s. (***in*** in)

immeritato undeserved

immersione *f* immersion; *di subacqueo, sottomarino* dive

immerso 1 *pp* → ***immergere*** **2** *agg* immersed

immettere ⟨3ee⟩ introduce (***in*** into); INFOR *dati* enter; (*portare*) lead (***in*** into)

immettersi: ***immettersi in*** get into

immigrante *m/f* immigrant

immigrare ⟨1a⟩ immigrate

immigrato *m*, **-a** *f* immigrant

immigrazione *f* immigration; (*immigrati*) immigrants *pl*; FIN inflow

imminente imminent; *pericolo* impending; *pubblicazione* forthcoming

imminenza *f* imminence

immischiare ⟨1k⟩ involve

immischiarsi meddle (***in*** with), interfere (***in*** in)

immissione *f* introduction; *di manodopera* intake; INFOR *di dati* entry

immobile 1 *agg* motionless, still **2** *mpl*: **-i** real estate *sg*

immobiliare: ***agente*** *m/f* ***immobiliare*** estate agent, *Am* realtor; ***società*** *f* ***immobiliare*** *di compravendita* property company; *di costruzione* construction company

immobilismo *m* inactivity; POL opposition to progress

immobilità *f* immobility; POL, FIN inactivity

immobilizzare ⟨1a⟩ immobilize; FIN *capitali* tie up
immondizia *f* (*gen pl*) rubbish, refuse, *Am* trash
immorale immoral
immoralità *f* immorality
immortale immortal
immortalità *f* immortality
immune MED immune (***a*** to); (*esente*) free (***da*** from)
immunità *f* immunity
immunitario: ***sistema*** *m* ***immunitario*** immune system
immunizzare ⟨1a⟩ immunize
immunodeficienza *f* immunodeficiency
immutabile *decisione, legge* unchangeable; *principi, tradizioni* unchanging
immutato unchanged
impacchettare ⟨1a⟩ (*confezionare*) wrap (up); (*mettere in pacchetti*) package
impacciare ⟨1f⟩ *movimenti* hamper; *persona* hinder
impacciato (*imbarazzato*) embarrassed; (*goffo*) awkward, clumsy
impaccio *m* (*pl* -cci) (*ostacolo*) hindrance; (*situazione difficile*) awkward situation; (*imbarazzo*) awkwardness
impacco *m* (*pl* -cchi) MED compress
impadronirsi ⟨4d⟩: ***impadronirsi di qc*** take possession of sth, seize sth; *fig* master sth
impagabile priceless
impaginare ⟨1m⟩ TIP paginate
impaginazione *f* pagination
impalcatura *f temporanea* scaffolding; *fig* framework, structure
impallidire ⟨4d⟩ *di persona* turn pale
impanare ⟨1a⟩ GASTR coat with breadcrumbs
impanato in breadcrumbs, breaded
impantanarsi ⟨1a⟩ get bogged down
impaperarsi ⟨1m⟩ falter
imparare ⟨1a⟩ learn (***a*** to)
imparentarsi ⟨1b⟩: ***imparentarsi con qu*** become related to s.o.
impari unequal; MAT odd
impartire ⟨4d⟩ give
imparziale impartial
imparzialità *f* impartiality
impassibile impassive
impastare ⟨1a⟩ mix; *pane* knead
impasto *m* GASTR dough; (*mescolanza*) mixture
impatto *m* impact
impaurire ⟨4d⟩ frighten
impaurirsi become frightened
impaziente impatient
impazienza *f* impatience
impazzata: ***all'impazzata*** *correre* at breakneck speed; *colpire* wildly
impazzire ⟨4d⟩ go mad *or* crazy; ***far impazzire qu*** drive s.o. mad *or* crazy
impeccabile impeccable
impedimento *m* hindrance; (*ostacolo*) obstacle; DIR impediment; ***essere d'impedimento*** be a hindrance
impedire ⟨4d⟩ prevent; (*ostruire*) block, obstruct; (*impacciare*) hinder; ***impedire a qu di fare qc*** prevent s.o. *or* keep s.o. from doing sth
impegnare ⟨1a⟩ (*dare come pegno*) pawn; (*riservare*) reserve, book; *spazio, corsia* occupy, take up; SP *avversario* keep under pressure; (*costringere*) oblige; ***impegnare qu*** *di lavoro* keep s.o. busy *or* occupied; ***impegnare qu per contratto*** bind s.o. by contract
impegnarsi (*prendersi l'impegno*) commit o.s., undertake (***a*** to); (*concentrarsi*) apply o.s. (***in*** to); ***mi sono impegnata a farlo*** I've committed myself to doing it, I've undertaken to do it
impegnativo (*che richiede impegno*) demanding; *pranzo, serata, abito* formal; (*vincolante*) binding
impegnato (*occupato*) busy; *fig* (politically) committed; ***sono già impegnato*** I've made other arrangements, I'm doing something else
impegno *m* commitment; (*appuntamento*) engagement; (*zelo*) zeal, care; COM ***senza impegno*** with no commitment
impensabile unthinkable
impensato unexpected
imperante (*dominante*) prevailing
imperare ⟨1b⟩ rule (***su*** over)
imperativo *m/agg* imperative
imperatore *m*, **-trice** *f* emperor; *donna* empress
impercettibile imperceptible
imperdonabile unforgivable
imperfetto *m/agg* imperfect
imperfezione *f* imperfection
impermeabile 1 *agg* waterproof **2** *m* raincoat
impermeabilità *f* impermeability
impermeabilizzare ⟨1a⟩ waterproof
impero *m* empire; (*potere*) rule
impersonale impersonal
impersonare ⟨1a⟩ personify; (*interpretare*) play (the part of)
impertinente impertinent
impertinenza *f* impertinence
imperturbabile imperturbable
imperturbabilità *f* imperturbability
imperversare ⟨1b⟩ rage; *fig di moda* be all the rage
impeto *m* impetus, force; (*accesso*) out-

burst; (*slancio*) passion, heat; ***parlare con impeto*** speak forcefully

impetuoso impetuous

impiantare ⟨1a⟩ *azienda*, *ufficio* set up; *congegno*, *apparecchiatura* install; MED implant

impianto *m operazione* installation; (*apparecchiature*) plant; (*sistema*) system; MED implant; ***impianto elettrico*** wiring; ***impianto di risalita*** ski lift; ***impianto di riscaldamento*** heating system; ***impianto stereo*** stereo (system); ***-i*** *pl* ***sanitari*** bathroom fixtures and fittings

impiastro *m* poultice; *fig* pain in the neck

impiccare ⟨1d⟩ hang

impiccarsi hang o.s.

impicciare ⟨1f⟩ be in the way

impicciarsi: ***impicciarsi di*** *o* ***in qc*** interfere *or* meddle in sth

impiccio *m* (*pl* -cci) (*ostacolo*) hindrance; (*seccatura*) bother; ***essere d'impiccio*** be in the way; ***essere in un impiccio*** be in trouble

impiegare ⟨1b & e⟩ (*usare*) use; *tempo*, *soldi* spend; (*metterci*) take; (*assumere*) employ; ***ho impiegato un'ora*** it took me an hour

impiegato *m*, **-a** *f* employee; ***impiegato di banca*** bank clerk; ***impiegato di ruolo*** permanent employee

impiego *m* (*pl* -ghi) (*uso*) use; (*occupazione*) employment; (*posto*) job; FIN investment; ***domanda*** *f* ***d'impiego*** job application; ***offerta*** *f* ***d'impiego*** job offer

impietosire ⟨4d⟩ move to pity

impietosirsi be moved to pity

impigliare ⟨1g⟩ entangle

impigliarsi get entangled

impigrire ⟨4d⟩ **1** *v/t* make lazy **2** *v/i e* **impigrirsi** get lazy

implacabile implacable

implicare ⟨1l & d⟩ (*coinvolgere*) implicate; (*comportare*) imply

implicito implicit

implorare ⟨1c⟩ implore

impolverato dusty, covered with *or* in dust

imponente imposing, impressive

imponibile **1** *agg* taxable **2** *m* taxable income

impopolare unpopular

impopolarità *f* unpopularity

imporre ⟨3ll⟩ impose; *prezzo* fix

imporsi (*farsi valere*) assert o.s.; (*avere successo*) be successful, become established; (*essere necessario*) be necessary

importante important

importanza *f* importance; ***darsi importanza*** give o.s. airs; ***senza importanza*** not important, unimportant

importare ⟨1c⟩ **1** *v/t* FIN, INFOR import **2** *v/i* matter, be important; (*essere necessario*) be necessary; ***e a te che te ne importa?*** what's it to you?; ***non importa*** it doesn't matter; ***non gliene importa niente*** he couldn't care less

importatore *m*, **-trice** *f* importer

importazione *f* import; ***importazione clandestina*** smuggling; ***permesso*** *m* ***d'importazione*** import permit

importo *m* amount

importunare ⟨1a⟩ (*assillare*) pester; (*disturbare*) bother

importuno troublesome; *domanda*, *osservazione* ill-timed

imposizione *f* imposition; (*tassazione*) taxation; (*tassa*) tax

impossessarsi ⟨1b⟩: ***impossessarsi di*** seize

impossibile impossible

impossibilità *f* impossibility

imposta[1] *f* tax; ***imposta di consumo*** excise duty; ***imposta diretta / indiretta*** direct / indirect tax; ***imposta sul reddito*** income tax; ***imposta sul valore aggiunto*** value added tax; ***imposta sul fatturato*** sales tax; ***ufficio*** *m* ***delle -e*** tax office

imposta[2] *f di finestra* shutter

impostare ⟨1c⟩ *lavoro* plan; *problema* set out; *lettera* post, *Am* mail

imposto *pp* → ***imporre***

impostore *m* impostor

impotente powerless; (*inefficace*) ineffectual; MED impotent

impotenza *f* powerlessness; MED impotence

impraticabile *strada* impassable

impratichirsi ⟨4d⟩ get practice (***in*** in)

imprecare ⟨1d & b⟩ curse, swear (***contro*** at)

imprecazione *f* curse

imprecisato *numero*, *quantità* indeterminate; *motivi*, *circostanze* not clear

imprecisione *f* inaccuracy

impreciso inaccurate

impregnare ⟨1a⟩ impregnate; (*imbevere*) soak

impregnarsi become impregnated (***di*** with)

imprenditore *m*, **-trice** *f* entrepreneur

imprenditoriale entrepreneurial

impreparato unprepared

impresa *f* (*iniziativa*) enterprise, undertaking; (*azienda*) business, firm; ***impresa familiare*** family business; ***piccola impresa*** small business; ***impresa di servizi pubblici*** utility company

impresario *m* (*pl* -ri) contractor; TEA im-

presario
impressionabile impressionable; FOT sensitive
impressionante impressive; (*spaventoso*) frightening; (*sconvolgente*) upsetting, shocking
impressionare ⟨1a⟩ (*turbare*) upset, shock; (*spaventare*) frighten; (*colpire*) impress; FOT expose
impressionato FOT exposed; ***impressionato favorevolmente*** (favourably) impressed
impressione *f* impression; (*turbamento*) shock; (*paura*) fright; TIP printing
impresso *pp* → ***imprimere***
imprevedibile unforeseeable; *persona* unpredictable
imprevisto 1 *agg* unexpected **2** *m* unforeseen event; ***salvo imprevisti*** all being well
imprigionare ⟨1a⟩ imprison
imprimere ⟨3r⟩ impress; *fig nella mente* fix firmly, imprint; *movimento* impart; TIP print
improbabile unlikely, improbable
improbabilità *f* unlikelihood, improbability
improduttivo unproductive
impronta *f* impression, mark; (*orma*) footprint; (*traccia*) track; *fig* mark; ***-e*** *pl* ***digitali*** fingerprints
improprio (*pl* -ri) improper
improvvisamente suddenly
improvvisare ⟨1a⟩ improvize
improvvisarsi take on the role of
improvvisata *f* surprise
improvvisato improvized, impromptu
improvviso sudden; (*inaspettato*) unexpected; ***all'improvviso*** suddenly; (*inaspettatamente*) unexpectedly
imprudente careless; (*non saggio*) imprudent, rash
imprudenza *f* carelessness; (*mancanza di saggezza*) imprudence, rashness
impugnare ⟨1a⟩ grasp; DIR contest
impugnatura *f* grip; (*manico*) handle
impulsivo impulsive
impulso *m* impulse
impunità *f* impunity
impunito unpunished
impuntarsi (*ostinarsi*) dig one's heels in
imputato *m*, **-a** *f* accused
imputazione *f* charge
imputridire rot
in *prp* in; *moto a luogo* to; ***in casa*** at home; ***è in Scozia*** he is in Scotland; ***va in Inghilterra*** he is going to England; ***in italiano*** in Italian; ***in campagna*** in the country; ***essere in viaggio*** be travelling; ***viaggiare in macchina*** travel by car; ***nel 1999*** in 1999; ***una giacca in pelle*** a leather jacket; ***in vacanza*** on holiday; ***se fossi in te*** if I were you, if I were in your place
inabile unfit (***a*** for); (*disabile*) disabled
inabitabile uninhabitable
inabitato uninhabited
inaccessibile inaccessible, out of reach; *fig persona* unapproachable; *prezzi* exorbitant
inaccettabile unacceptable
inacidire ⟨4d⟩, **inacidirsi** turn sour
inadatto unsuitable (***a*** for), unsuited (***a*** to)
inadeguato inadequate
inafferrabile elusive; (*incomprensibile*) incomprehensible
inalare ⟨1a⟩ inhale
inalatore *m* inhaler, puffer F
inalazione *f* inhalation
inalterabile *sentimento* unchangeable; *colore* fast; *metallo* non-tarnish
inalterato unchanged
inamidare ⟨1m⟩ starch
inammissibile inadmissible
inanimato inanimate; (*senza vita*) lifeless
inappellabile final, irrevocable
inappetenza *f* lack of appetite
inarcare ⟨1d⟩ *schiena* arch; *sopracciglia* raise
inaridire ⟨4d⟩ **1** *v/t* parch **2** *v/i* dry up
inaspettato unexpected
inasprimento *m* (*intensificazione*) worsening; *di carattere* embitterment
inasprire ⟨4d⟩ exacerbate, make worse; *carattere* embitter
inasprirsi get worse; *di persona* become embittered
inattaccabile unassailable
inattendibile unreliable
inatteso unexpected
inattività *f* inactivity
inattivo *persona, capitale* idle; *vulcano* dormant
inattuabile (*non fattibile*) impracticable; (*non realistico*) unrealistic
inaugurare ⟨1m⟩ *mostra* (officially) open, inaugurate; *lapide, monumento* unveil; F *oggetto nuovo* christen F
inaugurazione *f di mostra* (official) opening, inauguration; *di lapide* unveiling; F *di oggetto nuovo* christening F
inavvertenza *f* inadvertence
inavvertito unnoticed
incagliarsi ⟨1g⟩ MAR run aground
incalcolabile incalculable
incalzante *pericolo* imminent; *richieste* pressing

incalzare ⟨1a⟩ pursue; *fig con richieste* ply
incamminarsi ⟨1m⟩ set out
incandescente incandescent; *fig* heated
incantare ⟨1a⟩ enchant
incantarsi (*restare affascinato*) be spellbound; (*sognare a occhi aperti*) be in a daze; TEC jam
incantato *per effetto di magia* enchanted; (*trasognato*) in a daze; (*affascinato*) spellbound
incantesimo *m* spell
incantevole delightful, charming
incanto[1] *m* (*incantesimo*) spell; ***come per incanto*** as if by magic
incanto[2] *m* COM auction; ***mettere all'incanto*** sell at auction, put up for auction
incapace 1 *agg* incapable (***di*** of); (*incompetente*) incompetent **2** *m/f* incompetent person
incapacità *f* (*inabilità*) inability; (*incompetenza*) incompetence
incappare ⟨1a⟩: ***incappare in*** *nebbia, difficoltà* run into
incapricciarsi ⟨1f⟩: ***incapricciarsi di qu*** take a liking to s.o.
incarcerare ⟨1m⟩ imprison
incaricare ⟨1m & d⟩ (*dare istruzioni a*) instruct; ***incaricare qu di fare qc*** tell *or* instruct s.o. to do sth
incaricarsi: ***incaricarsi di qc*** (*occuparsi di*) see to sth, deal with sth
incaricato *m*, **-a** *f* (*responsabile*) person in charge; (*funzionario*) official, representative
incarico *m* (*pl* -chi) (*compito*) task, assignment; (*nomina*) appointment; ***per incarico di*** on behalf of
incarnare ⟨1a⟩ embody
incarnazione *f* incarnation
incartamento *m* file, dossier
incartare ⟨1a⟩ wrap (up) (in paper)
incarto *m* wrapping; (*incartamento*) file, dossier
incassare ⟨1a⟩ COM (*riscuotere*) cash; *fig colpi, insulti ecc* take
incasso *m* (*riscossione*) collection; (*somma incassata*) takings *pl*
incastonare ⟨1a⟩ set
incastonatura *f* setting
incastrare ⟨1a⟩ fit in; F *fig* (*far apparire colpevole*) frame F; (*mettere in una posizione difficile*) corner F
incastro *m* joint
incatenare ⟨1a⟩ chain
incavato hollow; *occhi* deep-set
incendiare ⟨1b & k⟩ set fire to
incendiario *m* (*pl m* -ri), **-a** *f* arsonist, firebug F
incendio *m* (*pl* -di) fire; ***incendio doloso*** arson
incenerimento *m* incineration
incenerire ⟨4d⟩ reduce to ashes
inceneritore *m* incinerator
incenso *m* incense
incensurato irreproachable; DIR ***essere incensurato*** have a clean record
incentivare ⟨1a⟩ (*incrementare*) boost
incentivo *m* incentive
incerata *f* oilcloth
incertezza *f* uncertainty
incerto 1 *agg* uncertain **2** *m* uncertainty
incessante incessant
incetta *f*: ***fare incetta di qc*** stockpile sth
inchiesta *f* investigation; FIN ***inchiesta di mercato*** market survey; ***commissione** f* ***d'inchiesta*** committee *or* board of inquiry
inchinare ⟨1a⟩ bow
inchinarsi bow
inchino *m* bow; *di donna* curtsy
inchiodare ⟨1c⟩ **1** *v/t* nail; *coperchio* nail down; *fig* ***essere inchiodato in un luogo*** be stuck in a place **2** *v/i* AUTO jam on the brakes
inchiostro *m* ink; ***inchiostro di china*** Indian ink
inciampare ⟨1a⟩ trip (***in*** over); ***inciampare in qu*** run into s.o.
incidentale (*casuale*) accidental; (*secondario*) incidental
incidente *m* (*episodio*) incident; ***incidente aereo*** plane crash; ***incidente stradale*** road accident
incidere[1] ⟨3q⟩ *v/i* affect (***su*** sth)
incidere[2] ⟨3q⟩ *v/t* engrave; (*tagliare*) cut; (*registrare*) record
incidersi *fig* (*restare impresso*) be engraved (***in*** on)
incinta pregnant
incirca: ***all'incirca*** more or less
incisione *f* engraving; (*acquaforte*) etching; (*taglio*) cut; MED incision; (*registrazione*) recording
incisivo 1 *agg* incisive **2** *m* (*dente*) incisor
incitare ⟨1l⟩ incite
incivile uncivilized; (*villano*) rude, impolite
inclinare ⟨1a⟩ **1** *v/t* tilt **2** *v/i*: ***inclinare a*** (*tendere a*) be inclined to
inclinato tilted
inclinazione *f* inclination
incline inclined (***a*** to)
includere ⟨3q⟩ include; (*allegare*) enclose, inclose; ***incluso il servizio*** service included
inclusivo inclusive
incluso 1 *pp* → ***includere*** **2** *agg* included;

(*compreso*) inclusive; (*allegato*) enclosed
incoerente (*incongruente*) inconsistent
incoerenza *f* inconsistency
incognita *f* unknown quantity
incognito *m*: ***in incognito*** incognito
incollare ⟨1c⟩ stick; *con colla liquida* glue
incollarsi stick (***a*** to)
incolonnare ⟨1a⟩ *numeri ecc* put in a column; *persone* line up
incolore colo(u)rless
incolpare ⟨1a⟩ blame
incolparsi: ***incolparsi a vicenda*** blame each other
incolto uneducated; (*trascurato*) unkempt; AGR uncultivated
incolume unharmed
incolumità *f* safety
incombente *pericolo* impending
incombenza *f* task
incominciare ⟨1f⟩ start, begin (***a*** to)
incomodare ⟨1m & c⟩ inconvenience
incomodarsi put o.s. out; ***non si incomodi!*** don't put yourself out!, please don't go to any trouble!
incomodo 1 *agg* (*inopportuno*) inconvenient; (*scomodo*) uncomfortable **2** *m* inconvenience
incompatibile incompatible; (*intollerabile*) unacceptable
incompatibilità *f* incompatibility
incompetente incompetent; ***sono incompetente in materia*** I'm no expert
incompetenza *f* incompetence
incompiuto unfinished
incompleto incomplete
incomprensibile incomprehensible, impossible to understand
incomprensione *f* lack of understanding; (*malinteso*) misunderstanding
incompreso misunderstood
inconcepibile inconceivable
inconciliabile irreconcilable
inconcludente inconclusive; *persona* ineffectual
incondizionato unconditional
inconfondibile unmistakable
inconfutabile indisputable
inconsapevole (*ignaro*) unaware
inconsapevolezza *f* lack of awareness
inconscio *m/agg* unconscious
inconsistente insubstantial; *fig* (*infondato*) unfounded; (*vago*) vague
inconsistenza *f* flimsiness
inconsolabile inconsolable
inconsueto unusual
incontentabile hard to please, very demanding; (*perfezionista*) perfectionist
incontestato undisputed
incontrare ⟨1a⟩ **1** *v/t* meet; *difficoltà* come up against, encounter **2** *v/i e* **incontrarsi** meet (***con*** s.o.)
incontrario: ***all'incontrario*** the other way round; (*nel modo sbagliato*) the wrong way round
incontrastato undisputed
incontro 1 *m* meeting; ***incontro di calcio*** football match; POL ***incontro al vertice*** summit (meeting) **2** *prp*: ***incontro a*** towards; ***andare incontro a qu*** go and meet s.o.; *fig* meet s.o. halfway
inconveniente *m* (*svantaggio*) drawback; (*ostacolo*) hitch
incoraggiamento *m* encouragement
incoraggiante encouraging
incoraggiare ⟨1f⟩ encourage
incorniciare ⟨1f⟩ frame
incoronare ⟨1a⟩ crown
incoronazione *f* coronation
incorporare ⟨1m & c⟩ incorporate
incorreggibile incorrigible
incorrere ⟨3o⟩: ***incorrere in*** *sanzioni* incur; *errore* make
incorruttibile incorruptible
incosciente unconscious; (*irresponsabile*) reckless
incoscienza *f* unconsciousness; (*insensatezza*) recklessness
incostante changeable; *negli affetti* fickle
incostanza *f* changeableness; *negli affetti* fickleness
incostituzionale unconstitutional
incostituzionalità *f* unconstitutionality
incredibile incredible
incredulo incredulous, disbelieving
incrementare ⟨1a⟩ increase
incremento *m* increase, growth; ***incremento demografico*** population growth
increspare ⟨1a⟩ *acque* ripple; *capelli* frizz; *tessuto* gather
incriminare ⟨1m⟩ indict
incrociare ⟨1f⟩ **1** *v/t* cross **2** *v/i* MAR, AVIA cruise
incrocio *m* (*pl* -ci) (*intersezione*) crossing; (*crocevia*) crossroads; *di razze animali* cross(-breed)
incrollabile indestructible; *fig* unshakeable
incubatrice *f* incubator
incubazione *f* incubation
incubo *m* nightmare
incudine *f* anvil
incurabile incurable
incurante heedless (***di*** of)
incuria *f* negligence
incuriosire ⟨4d⟩: ***incuriosire qu*** make s.o. curious, arouse s.o.'s curiosity
incuriosirsi become curious
incursione *f* raid; ***incursione aerea*** air

I

raid
incurvare ⟨1a⟩ bend
incustodito unattended, unguarded; *passaggio a livello* unmanned
indaco *m/agg* indigo
indaffarato busy
indagare ⟨1e⟩ **1** *v/t cause*, *fenomeni* investigate **2** *v/i* investigate (***su, intorno a*** sth)
indagine *f* (*ricerca*, *studio*) research; *della polizia* investigation; ***indagine di mercato*** market survey; ***indagine demoscopica*** (public) opinion poll
indebitare ⟨1m⟩, **indebitarsi** get into debt
indebitato in debt
indebolimento *m* weakening
indebolire ⟨4d⟩ *v/t & v/i* weaken
indecente indecent
indecenza *f* (*vergogna*) disgrace, outrage; (*mancanza di pudore*) indecency
indecisione *f* indecision; *abituale* indecisiveness
indeciso undecided; *abitualmente* indecisive
indefinito indefinite
indegno unworthy
indelebile indelible; *colore* fast
indenne *persona* uninjured; *cosa* undamaged
indennità *f inv* (*gratifica*) allowance, benefit; (*risarcimento*) compensation; ***indennità di trasferta*** travel allowance; ***indennità parlamentare*** MP's allowance
indennizzare ⟨1a⟩ compensate (***per*** for)
indennizzo *m* (*compenso*) compensation
indescrivibile indescribable
indesiderato unwanted
indeterminato *tempo* unspecified, indefinite; *quantità* indeterminate
India *f* India
indiano 1 *agg* Indian; ***in fila -a*** in single file **2** *m*, **-a** *f* Indian
indicare ⟨1l & d⟩ show, indicate; *col dito* point at *or* to; (*consigliare*) suggest, recommend; (*significare*) mean
indicativo *m* GRAM indicative
indicato (*consigliabile*) advisable; (*adatto*) suitable
indicatore 1 *agg* indicative; ***cartello*** *m* ***indicatore*** road sign **2** *m* indicator; (*strumento*) gauge, indicator; ***indicatore del livello di carburante*** fuel gauge; AUTO ***indicatore di direzione*** indicator
indicazione *f* indication; (*direttiva*) direction; (*informazione*) piece of information; MED ***-i*** *pl* directions (for use); ***-i*** *pl* ***stradali*** road signs
indice *m* index; ANAT index finger, forefinger; TV ***indice di ascolto*** ratings *pl*
indicibile indescribable, inexpressible
indietreggiare ⟨1f⟩ draw back; *camminando all'indietro* step back; MIL retreat
indietro behind; *tornare*, *girarsi* back; ***essere indietro*** *con il lavoro* be behind; *mentalmente* be backward; *nei pagamenti* be in arrears; *di orologio* be slow; ***dare indietro*** (*restituire*) give back; ***tirarsi indietro*** draw back; *fig* back out; ***all'indietro*** backwards; AUTO ***fare marcia indietro*** reverse; *fig* back-pedal
indifeso undefended; (*inerme*) defenceless, helpless
indifferente indifferent; ***lasciare qu indifferente*** leave s.o. cold, cut no ice with s.o.; ***non indifferente*** appreciable, considerable; ***per me è indifferente*** it's all the same to me
indifferenza *f* indifference
indigeno 1 *agg* native, indigenous **2** *m*, **-a** *f* native
indigestione *f* indigestion
indigesto indigestible
indignare ⟨1a⟩: ***indignare qu*** make s.o. indignant, arouse s.o.'s indignation
indignarsi get indignant (***per*** about)
indignazione *f* indignation
indimenticabile unforgettable
indipendente independent (***da*** of); ***indipendente dalla mia volontà*** outside my control
indipendentemente independently; ***indipendentemente dall'età*** regardless of age, whatever the age
indipendenza *f* independence
indire ⟨3t⟩ *conferenza*, *elezioni*, *sciopero* call; *concorso* announce
indiretto indirect
indirizzare ⟨1a⟩ direct; *lettera* address; (*spedire*) send
indirizzario *m* address book; *per spedizione* mailing list
indirizzo *m* address; (*direzione*) direction
indisciplina *f* lack of discipline, indiscipline
indisciplinato undisciplined
indiscreto indiscreet
indiscrezione *f* indiscretion
indiscriminato indiscriminate
indiscusso unquestioned
indiscutibile unquestionable
indispensabile 1 *agg* indispensable, essential **2** *m* essentials *pl*
indispettire ⟨4d⟩ irritate
indispettirsi get irritated
indispettito irritated
indisporre ⟨3ll⟩ irritate
indisposizione *f* indisposition
indisposto (*ammalato*) indisposed

indistinto indistinct, faint
indistruttibile indestructible
indivia *f* endive
individuale individual
individualismo *m* individualism
individualista *m/f* (*mpl* -i) individualist
individualità *f* individuality
individuo *m* individual
indivisibile indivisible
indiviso undivided
indizio *m* (*pl* -zi) clue; (*segno*) sign; (*sintomo*) symptom; DIR **-i** *pl* circumstantial evidence *sg*
indole *f* nature
indolente indolent
indolenza *f* indolence
indolore painless
indomani *m*: ***l'indomani*** the next day
indossare ⟨1c⟩ (*mettersi*) put on; (*portare*) wear
indossatore *m*, **-trice** *f* model
indotto *pp* → ***indurre***
indovinare ⟨1a⟩ guess; *futuro* predict
indovinato (*ben riuscito*) successful; (*ben scelto*) well chosen
indovinello *m* riddle
indovino *m*, **-a** *f* fortune-teller
indubbiamente undoubtedly
indugiare ⟨1f⟩ **1** *v/t partenza* delay **2** *v/i* (*tardare*) delay; (*esitare*) hesitate; (*attardarsi*) linger
indugiarsi linger
indugio *m* (*pl* -gi) delay; ***senza indugio*** without delay
indulgente indulgent; *giudice, sentenza* lenient
indulgenza *f* indulgence; *di giudice, sentenza* leniency
indumento *m* garment, item of clothing; ***gli -i*** *pl* clothes
indurire ⟨4d⟩ **1** *v/t* harden; *fig cuore* harden; *corpo* toughen (up) **2** *v/i e* **indurirsi** go hard, harden
indurito hardened
indurre ⟨3e⟩ induce
industria *f* industry; (*operosità*) industriousness; ***industria automobilistica*** car industry; ***industria dei servizi*** service industry, services; ***industria pesante*** heavy industry
industriale **1** *agg* industrial **2** *m* industrialist
industrializzare ⟨1a⟩ industrialize
industrializzazione *f* industrialization
ineccepibile irreproachable; *ragionamento* faultless
inedito unpublished; *fig* novel
inefficace ineffective
inefficacia *f* ineffectiveness
inefficiente inefficient
inefficienza *f* inefficiency
ineguagliabile (*senza rivali*) unrivalled; (*senza confronto*) incomparable, beyond compare
ineguaglianza *f* inequality
ineguale (*non uguale*) unequal; (*discontinuo*) uneven
inequivocabile unequivocal
inerte (*inoperoso*) idle; (*immobile*) inert, motionless; (*senza vita*) lifeless; FIS inert
inerzia *f* inertia; (*inattività*) inactivity; ***forza*** *f* ***d'inerzia*** force of inertia
inesattezza *f* inaccuracy
inesatto inaccurate
inesauribile inexhaustible
inesorabile inexorable
inesperienza *f* inexperience, lack of experience
inesperto inexperienced
inesplicabile inexplicable
inesplorato unexplored
inesploso unexploded
inesprimibile (*indicibile*) indescribable
inestimabile inestimable; *bene* invaluable
inetto inept
inevaso pending
inevitabile inevitable
inezia *f* trifle
infallibile infallible
infame **1** *agg* (*turpe*) infamous, foul; *spir* horrible, terrible **2** *m/f* P (*delatore*) grass P
infantile *letteratura, giochi* children's; *malattie* childhood; (*immaturo*) childish, infantile
infanzia *f* childhood; (*primi mesi*) infancy (*anche fig*); (*bambini*) children
infarinare ⟨1a⟩ (dust with) flour
infarinatura *f fig* smattering
infarto *m cardiaco* heart attack
infastidire ⟨4d⟩ annoy, irritate
infaticabile tireless
infatti in fact
infatuarsi ⟨1m⟩: ***infatuarsi di qu*** become infatuated with s.o.
infedele **1** *agg* unfaithful; *traduzione* inaccurate **2** *m/f* REL infidel
infedeltà *f inv* unfaithfulness
infelice unhappy; (*inopportuno*) unfortunate; (*malriuscito*) bad
infelicità *f* unhappiness
inferiore **1** *agg* lower; *fig* inferior (***a*** to); ***di qualità inferiore*** of inferior quality; ***essere inferiore a qu*** be inferior to s.o., be s.o.'s inferior; ***inferiore alla media*** below average **2** *m/f* inferior; (*subalterno*) subordinate

inferiorità *f* inferiority; ***complesso** m **d'inferiorità*** inferiority complex

infermeria *f* infirmary

infermiere *m*, **-a** *f* nurse

infermità *f inv* illness

infermo 1 *agg* (*ammalato*) ill; (*invalido*) invalid **2** *m*, **-a** *f* invalid

infernale infernal

inferno *m* hell

inferriata *f* grating; (*cancellata*) railings *pl*

infertilità *f* infertility

infestare ⟨1b⟩ infest

infettare ⟨1b⟩ infect

infettarsi become infected

infettivo infectious

infetto infected

infezione *f* infection

infiammabile flammable

infiammare ⟨1a⟩ *fig*, MED inflame

infiammarsi become inflamed

infiammazione *f* inflammation; ***infiammazione alla gola*** inflammation of the throat

infierire ⟨4d⟩ *di maltempo*, *malattie* rage; ***infierire su*** o ***contro*** savagely attack

infilare ⟨1a⟩ *fili*, *corde*, *ago* thread; (*inserire*) insert, put in; (*indossare*) put on; *strada* take; ***infilare le mani in tasca*** put one's hands in one's pockets; ***infilare la porta*** *uscendo / entrando* slip out / in

infilarsi *indumento* slip on; (*conficcarsi*) stick; (*introdursi*) slip (***in*** into); (*stiparsi*) squeeze (***in*** into)

infiltrare ⟨1a⟩ infiltrate

infiltrarsi seep; *fig* infiltrate

infiltrazione *f* infiltration; *di liquidi* seepage

infilzare ⟨1a⟩ pierce; *perle* thread; *fig* string together

infimo lowest

infine (*alla fine*) finally, eventually; (*insomma*) in short

infinità *f* infinity; ***ho un'infinità di cose da fare*** I've got no end of things to do

infinito 1 *agg* infinite **2** *m* infinity; GRAM infinitive; ***ripetere all'infinito*** say over and over again

infischiarsi ⟨1k⟩ F: ***infischiarsi di*** not give a hoot about F; ***me ne infischio*** I couldn't care less F

infittire *v/t* & *v/i* ⟨4d⟩ thicken

inflazione *f* inflation; ***tasso** m **d'inflazione*** (rate of) inflation

inflessibile inflexible

inflessibilità *f* inflexibility

inflessione *f* inflection

infliggere ⟨3cc⟩ inflict

inflitto *pp* → ***infliggere***

influente influential

influenza *f* influence; MED flu, influenza

influenzabile easily influenced, impressionable

influenzare ⟨1b⟩ influence

influire ⟨4d⟩: ***influire su*** influence, have an effect on

influsso *m* influence

infondato unfounded, without foundation

infondere ⟨3bb⟩ *fig* instil

inforcare ⟨1d⟩ *occhiali* put on; *bicicletta* get on, mount

informale informal

informare ⟨1a⟩ inform (***di*** of)

informarsi find out (***di, su*** about)

informatica *f scienza* information technology, computer science

informatico (*pl* -ci) **1** *agg* computer *attr* **2** *m*, **-a** *f* computer scientist

informato informed

informatore *m*, **-trice** *f* informant; *della polizia* informer

informazione *f* piece of information; ***ufficio** m **-i*** information office

informe shapeless

informicolirsi ⟨4d⟩ have pins and needles

infortunio *m* (*pl* -ni) accident; ***infortunio sul lavoro*** accident at work, industrial accident; ***assicurazione** f **contro gli -i*** accident insurance

infossato *occhi* deep-set, sunken

infrangere ⟨3d⟩ break

infrangibile unbreakable; ***vetro** m **infrangibile*** shatterproof glass

infranto *pp* → ***infrangere***

infrarosso infrared

infrasettimanale midweek

infrastruttura *f* infrastructure

infrazione *f* offence, *Am* offense; ***infrazione al codice stradale*** traffic offence (*Am* offense)

infreddatura *f* cold

infruttuoso fruitless

infuocare *fig* inflame

infuocato (*caldissimo*) scorching, blistering; *discorso*, *tramonto* fiery

infuori: ***all'infuori*** outwards; ***all'infuori di*** except

infuriare ⟨1k⟩ **1** *v/t* infuriate, enrage **2** *v/i* rage

infuriarsi fly into a rage

infuriato furious

infusione *f*, **infuso** *m* infusion; (*tisana*) herbal tea

ingaggiare ⟨1f⟩ (*reclutare*) recruit; *attore*, *cantante lirico* engage; SP sign (up); (*iniziare*) start, begin

ingaggio *m* (*pl* -ggi) (*reclutamento*) recruitment; SP signing; (*somma*) fee

ingannare ⟨1a⟩ deceive; ***ingannare il tempo*** kill time
ingannarsi deceive o.s.
inganno *m* deception, deceit
ingarbugliare ⟨1g⟩ tangle; *fig* confuse, muddle
ingarbugliarsi get entangled; *fig* get confused
ingegnarsi ⟨1a⟩ do one's utmost (***a, per*** to)
ingegnere *m* engineer
ingegneria *f* engineering; ***ingegneria genetica*** genetic engineering; ***ingegneria meccanica*** mechanical engineering
ingegno *m* (*mente*) mind; (*intelligenza*) brains *pl*; (*genio*) genius; (*inventiva*) ingenuity
ingegnoso ingenious
ingelosire ⟨4d⟩ **1** *v/t* make jealous **2** *v/i* be jealous
ingente enormous
ingenuità *f* ingenuousness
ingenuo ingenuous
ingerenza *f* interference
ingerire ⟨4d⟩ swallow
ingerirsi interfere
ingessare ⟨1b⟩ put in plaster
ingessatura *f* plaster
Inghilterra *f* England
inghiottire ⟨4d⟩ swallow
ingiallire ⟨4d⟩ *v/t & v/i* yellow, turn yellow
ingiallito yellowed
inginocchiarsi ⟨1k⟩ kneel (down)
ingiù: ***all'ingiù*** down(wards)
ingiungere ⟨3d⟩: ***ingiungere a qu di fare qc*** order s.o. to do sth
ingiunzione *f* injunction; ***ingiunzione di pagamento*** final demand
ingiuria *f* insult
ingiuriare ⟨1k⟩ insult
ingiustificato unjustified
ingiustizia *f* injustice
ingiusto unjust, unfair
inglese **1** *m/agg* English **2** *m/f* Englishman; *donna* Englishwoman *f*
ingoiare ⟨1i⟩ swallow
ingolfare ⟨1a⟩, **ingolfarsi** flood
ingombrante cumbersome, bulky
ingombrare ⟨1a⟩ *passaggio* block (up); *stanza, mente* clutter (up)
ingombro **1** *agg passaggio* blocked; *stanza, mente* cluttered (up) **2** *m* hindrance, obstacle; ***essere d'ingombro*** be in the way
ingordo greedy
ingorgare ⟨1e⟩ block
ingorgarsi get blocked
ingorgo *m* (*pl* -ghi) blockage; ***ingorgo stradale*** traffic jam
ingovernabile ungovernable
ingozzare ⟨1a⟩ *cibo* devour, gobble up; *persona* stuff (***di*** with)
ingozzarsi stuff o.s (***di*** with)
ingranaggio *m* (*pl* -ggi) gear; *fig* machine;
ingranare ⟨1a⟩ engage; *fig* F ***le cose cominciano a ingranare*** things are beginning to work out
ingrandimento *m* enlargement; *di azienda, città* expansion, growth
ingrandire ⟨4d⟩ enlarge; *azienda, città* expand, develop; (*esagerare*) exaggerate
ingrandirsi grow
ingrassare ⟨1a⟩ **1** *v/t animali* fatten (up); (*lubrificare*) grease **2** *v/i* get fat, put on weight; *di birra, burro ecc* be fattening
ingratitudine *f* ingratitude
ingrato ungrateful; *lavoro, compito* thankless
ingrediente *m* ingredient
ingresso *m* entrance; (*atrio*) hall; (*accesso*) admittance; INFOR input; ***ingresso libero*** admission free; ***vietato l'ingresso*** no entry, no admittance
ingrossare ⟨1c⟩ **1** *v/t* make bigger; (*gonfiare, accrescere*) swell **2** *v/i e* **ingrossarsi** get bigger; (*gonfiarsi*) swell
ingrossato swollen
ingrosso: ***all'ingrosso*** (*all'incirca*) roughly, about; COM wholesale; ***commercio*** *m* ***all'ingrosso*** wholesale (trade)
ingualcibile crease-resistant
inguaribile incurable
inguinale groin *attr*; ***ernia*** *f* ***inguinale*** hernia
inguine *m* ANAT groin
ingurgitare ⟨1m⟩ gulp down
inibire ⟨4d⟩ prohibit, forbid; PSI inhibit
inibito inhibited
inibizione *f* PSI inhibition
iniettare ⟨1b⟩ inject; ***iniettare qc a qu*** inject s.o. with sth; ***occhi*** *mpl* ***iniettati di sangue*** bloodshot eyes
iniettarsi: ***iniettarsi qc*** inject o.s. with sth
iniezione *f* injection; ***motore*** *m* ***a iniezione*** fuel-injection engine
inimicarsi ⟨1d⟩ fall out (***con*** with)
inimicizia *f* enmity
inimitabile inimitable
inimmaginabile unimaginable
ininterrotto continuous
iniziale **1** *agg* initial; ***stipendio*** *m* ***iniziale*** starting salary **2** *f* initial
inizializzare ⟨1a⟩ INFOR initialize
iniziare ⟨1g⟩ **1** *v/t* begin, start; *ostilità, dibattito* open; *fig* initiate **2** *v/i* begin, start; *di ostilità, dibattito* open; ***iniziare a fare qc*** begin *or* start doing sth, begin *or* start

to do sth
iniziativa *f* initiative; ***iniziativa privata*** private enterprise; ***di mia iniziativa*** on my own initiative; ***spirito*** *m* ***d'iniziativa*** initiative
inizio *m* (*pl* -zi) start, beginning; ***avere inizio*** start, begin; ***dare inizio a qc*** start sth
in loco on the premises
innaffiare ⟨1k⟩ water
innaffiatoio *m* (*pl* -oi) watering can
innalzare ⟨1a⟩ raise; (*erigere*) erect
innalzarsi rise
innamorarsi ⟨1a⟩ fall in love (***di*** with)
innamorato 1 *agg* in love (***di*** with) **2** *m*, **-a** *f* boyfriend; *donna* girlfriend
innanzi 1 *prp* before; ***innanzi a*** in front of; ***innanzi tutto*** first of all; (*soprattutto*) above all **2** *avv stato in luogo* in front; (*avanti*) forward; (*prima*) before; ***d'ora innanzi*** from now on
innato innate, inborn
innaturale unnatural
innervosire ⟨4d⟩: ***innervosire qu*** make s.o. nervous; (*irritare*) get on s.o.'s nerves
innervosirsi get nervous; (*irritarsi*) get irritated
innestare ⟨1b⟩ BOT, MED graft; EL *spina* insert; AUTO *marcia* engage
innesto *m* BOT, MED graft; AUTO clutch; EL connection
inno *m* hymn; ***inno nazionale*** national anthem
innocente innocent
innocenza *f* innocence
innocuo innocuous, harmless
innovativo innovative
innovazione *f* innovation
innumerevole innumerable
inodore odo(u)rless
inoffensivo harmless, inoffensive
inoltrare ⟨1a⟩ forward
inoltrarsi advance, penetrate (***in*** into)
inoltrato late
inoltre besides
inondare ⟨1a⟩ flood
inondazione *f* flood
inoperoso idle
inopportuno (*inadatto*) inappropriate; (*intempestivo*) untimely; *persona* tactless
inorridire ⟨4d⟩ **1** *v/t* horrify **2** *v/i* be horrified
inorridito horrified
inospitale inhospitable, unwelcoming
inosservato unobserved, unnoticed; (*non rispettato*) disregarded; ***passare inosservato*** go unnoticed
inossidabile stainless
inquadrare ⟨1a⟩ *dipinto*, *fotografia* frame; *fig* put into context
inquadrarsi be part of
inquadratura *f* frame
inqualificabile *fig* unspeakable
inquietante *che preoccupa* worrying; *che turba* disturbing
inquietare ⟨1b⟩ (*preoccupare*) worry; (*turbare*) disturb; ***fare inquietare qu*** make s.o. cross
inquietarsi (*preoccuparsi*) get worried; (*impazientirsi*) get cross
inquieto restless; (*preoccupato*) worried, anxious; (*adirato*) angry
inquietudine *f* anxiety
inquilino *m*, **-a** *f* tenant
inquinamento *m* pollution; *da sostanze radioattive* contamination; ***inquinamento acustico*** noise pollution; ***inquinamento atmosferico*** air pollution; ***inquinamento dell'ambiente*** pollution
inquinante 1 *agg* polluting; ***non inquinante*** environmentally friendly; ***sostanza*** *f* ***inquinante*** pollutant **2** *m* pollutant
inquinare ⟨1a⟩ pollute; *fig* (*corrompere*) corrupt; DIR *prove* tamper with
insabbiamento *m di porto* silting up; *fig* shelving
insabbiare ⟨1k⟩ *fig* shelve
insabbiarsi *di porto* get silted up; *fig* grind to a halt
insaccare ⟨1d⟩ put in bags
insaccati *mpl* sausages
insalata *f* salad; ***insalata mista*** mixed salad; ***insalata verde*** green salad
insalatiera *f* salad bowl
insanabile (*incurabile*) incurable; *fig* (*irrimediabile*) irreparable
insanguinato bloodstained
insaponare ⟨1a⟩ soap
insapore tasteless
insaporire ⟨4d⟩ flavo(u)r
insaputa: ***all'insaputa di qu*** unknown to s.o.
insaziabile insatiable
inscatolare ⟨1m⟩ tin, can
inscenare ⟨1a⟩ stage
inscindibile inseparable
insegna *f* sign; (*bandiera*) flag; (*stemma*) symbol; (*decorazione*) decoration
insegnamento *m* teaching
insegnante 1 *agg* teaching; ***corpo*** *m* ***insegnante*** staff **2** *m/f* teacher
insegnare ⟨1a⟩ teach; ***insegnare qc a qu*** teach s.o. sth
inseguimento *m* chase, pursuit
inseguire ⟨4b⟩ chase, pursue
inseminazione *f* insemination; ***inseminazione artificiale*** artificial insemination
insenatura *f* inlet

insensato 1 *agg* senseless, idiotic **2** *m*, **-a** *f* fool, idiot
insensibile insensitive (***a*** to); *parte del corpo* numb
insensibilità *f* insensitivity; *di parte del corpo* numbness
inseparabile inseparable
inserire ⟨4d⟩ insert; (*collegare*: *in elettrotecnica*) connect; *annuncio* put in, place
inserirsi fit in; *in una conversazione* join in
inserto *m* (*pubblicazione*) supplement; (*insieme di documenti*) file
inservibile unusable
inserviente *m/f* attendant
inserzione *f* insertion; *sul giornale* ad (-vert), advertisement
insetticida *m* (*pl* -i) insecticide
insettifugo *m* (*pl* -ghi) insect repellent
insetto *m* insect
insicurezza *f* insecurity, lack of security
insicuro insecure
insidia *f* (*tranello*) snare; (*inganno*) trick
insidioso insidious
insieme 1 *avv* together; (*contemporaneamente*) at the same time **2** *prp*: ***insieme a, insieme con*** together with **3** *m* whole; *di abiti* outfit; ***nell'insieme*** on the whole
insignificante insignificant
insinuare ⟨1m⟩ insert; *fig dubbio, sospetto* sow the seeds of; ***insinuare che*** insinuate that
insinuarsi penetrate; *fig* ***insinuarsi in*** creep into
insinuazione *f* insinuation
insipido insipid
insistente insistent
insistenza *f* insistence
insistere ⟨3f⟩ insist; (*perseverare*) persevere; ***insistere a fare qc*** insist on doing sth
insoddisfacente unsatisfactory
insoddisfatto unsatisfied; (*scontento*) dissatisfied
insoddisfazione *f* dissatisfaction
insofferente intolerant
insofferenza *f* intolerance
insolazione *f* sunstroke
insolente insolent
insolenza *f* insolence; *espressione* insolent remark
insolito unusual
insolubile insoluble
insoluto unsolved; *debito* unpaid, outstanding
insolvente insolvent
insolvenza *f* insolvency
insolvibile insolvent
insomma (*in breve*) briefly, in short; ***insomma!*** well, really!
insonne sleepless
insonnia *f* insomnia
insonnolito sleepy
insonorizzazione *f* soundproofing
insopportabile unbearable, intolerable
insorgere ⟨3d⟩ rise (up) (***contro*** against); *di difficoltà* come up, crop up
insormontabile insurmountable
insorto 1 *pp* → ***insorgere*** **2** *m* rebel
insospettabile above suspicion; (*impensato*) unsuspected
insospettato unsuspected
insospettire ⟨4d⟩ **1** *v/t*: ***insospettire qu*** make s.o. suspicious, arouse s.o.'s suspicion **2** *v/i e* **insospettirsi** become suspicious
insostenibile untenable; (*insopportabile*) unbearable
insostituibile irreplaceable
insperato unhoped for; (*inatteso*) unexpected
inspiegabile inexplicable
inspirare ⟨1a⟩ breathe in, inhale
instabile unstable; *tempo* changeable
instabilità *f* instability; *del tempo* changeability
installare ⟨1a⟩ install
installazione *f* installation
instancabile tireless, untiring
insù: ***all'insù*** upwards
insubordinato insubordinate
insubordinazione *f* insubordination
insuccesso *m* failure
insufficiente insufficient; (*inadeguato*) inadequate
insufficienza *f* (*scarsità*) insufficiency; (*inadeguatezza*) inadequacy; ***insufficienza cardiaca*** cardiac insufficiency
insulare *popolazione, flora ecc* island *attr*
insulina *f* insulin
insulso *fig* (*privo di vivacità*) dull; (*vacuo*) inane; (*sciocco*) silly
insultare ⟨1a⟩ insult
insulto *m* insult
insuperabile insuperable; (*ineguagliabile*) incomparable
insuperato unsurpassed
insurrezione *f* insurrection
intaccare ⟨1d⟩ (*corrodere*) corrode; *fig* (*danneggiare*) damage; *scorte, capitale* make inroads into
intagliare ⟨1g⟩ carve
intaglio *m* carving
intanto (*nel frattempo*) meanwhile; (*per ora*) for the time being; (*invece*) yet; ***intanto che*** while
intarsio *m* (*pl* -si) inlay
intasamento *m* blockage; ***intasamento***

del traffico traffic jam

intasare ⟨1a⟩ block

intasarsi get blocked

intasato blocked

intascare ⟨1d⟩ pocket

intatto intact

integrale 1 *agg* whole; MAT integral; *edizione* unabridged; ***pane*** *m* ***integrale*** wholemeal bread **2** *m* MAT integral

integrare ⟨1l⟩ integrate; (*aumentare*) supplement

integrarsi integrate

integrazione *f* integration; ***cassa*** *f* ***integrazione*** *form of income support*

integrità *f* integrity

intelaiatura *f* framework

intelletto *m* intellect

intellettuale *agg*, *m/f* intellectual

intelligente intelligent

intelligenza *f* intelligence; ***intelligenza artificiale*** artifical intelligence, AI

intendere ⟨3c⟩ (*comprendere*) understand; (*udire*) hear; (*voler dire*) mean; (*avere intenzione*) intend; (*pretendere*) want; ***s'intende!*** naturally!, of course!

intendersi (*capirsi*) understand each other; (*accordarsi*) agree; ***intendersi di qc*** know a lot about sth; ***intendersela*** have an affair (***con*** with)

intenditore *m*, **-trice** *f* connoisseur, expert

intensificare ⟨1n & d⟩ intensify

intensificarsi intensify

intensità *f* intensity; EL strength

intensivo intensive

intenso intense

intento 1 *agg* engrossed (***a*** in), intent (***a*** on) **2** *m* aim, purpose

intenzionale intentional, deliberate

intenzione *f* intention; ***avere l'intenzione di fare qc*** intend to do sth; ***con intenzione*** intentionally; ***senza intenzione*** unintentionally

interamente entirely, wholly

interagire ⟨4d⟩ interact

interattivo interactive

interazione *f* interaction

intercalare 1 *v/t* insert **2** *m* stock phrase

intercambiabile interchangeable

intercapedine *f* cavity

intercedere ⟨3a⟩ intercede (***presso*** with; ***per*** on behalf of)

intercettare ⟨1b⟩ intercept

intercettazione *f* interception; ***-i*** *pl* ***telefoniche*** phone tapping *sg*

intercontinentale intercontinental

intercorrere ⟨3o⟩ *di tempo* elapse; (*esserci*) exist, be

interdentale: ***filo*** *m* ***interdentale*** (dental) floss

interdetto 1 *pp* → ***interdire*** **2** *agg* (*sbalordito*) astonished; (*sconcertato*) puzzled **3** *m*, **-a** *f* F idiot F

interdire ⟨3t⟩ forbid; ***interdire a qu di fare qc*** forbid s.o. to do sth; DIR ***interdire qu*** deprive s.o. of his / her civil rights

interdizione *f* ban

interessamento *m* interest; (*intervento*) intervention

interessante interesting; ***in stato interessante*** pregnant

interessare ⟨1b⟩ **1** *v/t* interest; (*riguardare*) concern **2** *v/i* matter

interessarsi be interested, take an interest (***a, di*** in); (*occuparsi*) take care (***di*** of)

interessato 1 *agg* interested (***a*** in); (*implicato*) involved (***a*** in); *spreg parere*, *opinione* biased; *persona* self-interested **2** *m*, **-a** *f* person concerned

interesse *m* interest; (*tornaconto*) benefit; ***tasso*** *m* ***d'interesse*** interest rate; ***interesse composto*** compound interest; ***per interesse*** out of self-interest; ***senza interesse*** of no interest; FIN ***senza -i*** interest-free

interfaccia *f* (pl -cce) INFOR interface

interferenza *f* interference

interferire ⟨4d⟩ interfere

interfono *m* intercom

interiezione *f* interjection

interiora *fpl* entrails

interiore *m/agg* interior

interlocutore *m*, **-trice** *f*: ***la sua -trice*** the woman he was in conversation with

interludio *m* interlude

intermediario *m* (*pl* -ri), **-a** *f* intermediary

intermedio (*pl* -di) intermediate; *bilancio*, *relazione* interim

intermezzo *m* intermezzo

interminabile interminable

intermittente intermittent

internamento *m* internment; *in manicomio* committal

internare ⟨1b⟩ intern; *in manicomio* commit

internazionale international

internet *m* Internet; ***navigare nell'internet*** surf the Net

internista *m/f* (*pl* -i) internist

interno 1 *agg* internal, inside *attr*; GEOG inland; POL, FIN domestic; *fig* inner; ***alunno*** *m* ***interno*** boarder **2** *m* (*parte interna*) inside, interior; GEOG interior; TELEC extension; ***via Dante n. 6 interno 9*** 6 via Dante, Flat 9; ***ministero*** *m* ***dell'Interno*** *o* ***degli Interni*** Home Office, *Am* Department of the Interior; ***all'interno*** inside; SP ***interno destro / sinistro*** inside right / left

intero whole, entire; (*completo*) complete; ***latte*** *m* ***intero*** whole milk; MAT ***numero*** *m* ***intero*** integer; ***un anno intero*** a whole *or* full year; ***l'-a somma*** the full amount
interpellare ⟨1b⟩ consult
interporre ⟨3ll⟩ *autorità*, *influenza* bring to bear
interporsi intervene
interpretare ⟨1m & b⟩ interpret; *personnagio* play; MUS play, perform
interpretazione *f* interpretation; TEA, MUS, *film* performance
interprete *m*/*f* interpreter; *attore*, *musicista* performer; ***interprete simultaneo*** (***-a***) interpreter; ***fare da interprete*** interpret, act as interpreter
interpunzione *f* punctuation
interrogare ⟨1m, b & e⟩ question; EDU test
interrogativo 1 *agg* GRAM interrogative; *occhiata* questioning; ***punto*** *m* ***interrogativo*** question mark **2** *m* (*domanda*) question; (*dubbio*) doubt
interrogatorio *m* (*pl* -ri) questioning
interrogazione *f* questioning; *domanda* question; EDU oral test
interrompere ⟨3rr⟩ interrupt; (*sospendere*) break off, stop; *comunicazioni*, *forniture* cut off
interrotto *pp* → ***interrompere***
interruttore *m* EL switch
interruzione *f* interruption
intersecare ⟨1m, b & d⟩ intersect
intersezione *f* intersection
interurbana *f* long-distance (phone) call
interurbano intercity; ***comunicazione*** *f* ***-a*** long-distance (phone) call
intervallo *m* interval; *di scuola*, *lavoro* break
intervenire ⟨4p⟩ intervene; (*partecipare*) take part, participate (***a*** in); MED operate
intervento *m* intervention; (*partecipazione*) participation; MED operation; ***pronto intervento*** emergency services
intervista *f* interview
intervistare ⟨1a⟩ interview
intervistatore *m*, **-trice** *f* interviewer
intesa *f* (*accordo*) understanding; (*patto*) agreement; SP team work
inteso 1 *pp* → ***intendere*** **2** *agg* (*capito*) understood; (*destinato*) intended, meant (***a*** to); ***siamo -i?*** agreed?; ***ben inteso*** needless to say, of course
intestare ⟨1b⟩ *assegno* make out (***a*** to); *proprietà* register (***a*** in the name of); ***carta*** *f* ***intestata*** letterhead, letterheaded notepaper
intestatario *m* (*pl* -ri), **-a** *f di assegno* payee; *di proprietà* registered owner
intestazione *f* heading; *su carta da lettere* letterhead
intestinale intestinal
intestino *m* intestine, gut
intimare ⟨1l or 1a⟩ order
intimazione *f* order
intimidazione *f* intimidation
intimidire ⟨4d⟩ intimidate
intimità *f* privacy; *di un rapporto* intimacy
intimo 1 *agg* intimate; (*segreto*) private; (*accogliente*) cosy, *Am* cozy; *amico* close, intimate **2** *m persona* close friend, intimate; (*abbigliamento*) underwear
intimorire ⟨4d⟩ frighten
intingere ⟨3d⟩ dip
intingolo *m* sauce
intitolare ⟨1m⟩ (*dare il titolo a*) call, entitle; (*dedicare*) dedicate (***a*** to)
intitolarsi be called
intollerabile intolerable
intollerante intolerant
intolleranza *f* intolerance
intonacare ⟨1m, c & d⟩ plaster
intonaco *m* (*pl* -chi) plaster
intonare ⟨1c⟩ *strumento* tune; *colori* co-ordinate
intonarsi (*armonizzare*) go well (***a, con*** with)
intonato MUS in tune; ***colori*** *pl* ***-i*** colours that go well together
intontire ⟨4d⟩ daze
intontito dazed
intoppo *m* (*ostacolo*) hindrance; (*contrattempo*) snag
intorno 1 *prp*: ***intorno a*** around; (*circa*) (round) about, around; (*riguardo a*) about **2** *avv* around; ***tutt'intorno*** all around; ***guardarsi intorno*** look around
intossicare ⟨1m, c & d⟩ poison
intossicazione *f* poisoning; ***intossicazione alimentare*** food poisoning
intralciare ⟨1f⟩ hinder, hamper
intralcio *m* (*pl* -ci) hindrance
intramuscolare MED intramuscular
intransigente intransigent
intransitivo intransitive
intraprendente enterprising
intraprendenza *f* enterprise
intraprendere ⟨3c⟩ undertake
intrattabile intractable; *prezzo* fixed, non-negotiable
intrattenere ⟨2q⟩ entertain; ***intrattenere buoni rapporti con qu*** be on good terms with s.o.
intrattenersi dwell (***su*** on)
intravedere ⟨2s⟩ glimpse, catch a glimpse of; *fig* (*presagire*) anticipate, see
intravisto *pp* → ***intravedere***

I

intrecciare ⟨1f⟩ plait, braid; (*intessere*) weave
intrecciarsi intertwine
intreccio *m* (*pl* -cci) *fig* (*trama*) plot
intricato tangled; *disegno* intricate; *fig* complicated
intrigante scheming; (*affascinante*) intriguing
intrigo *m* (*pl* -ghi) plot
intrinseco (*pl* -ci) intrinsic
introdurre ⟨3e⟩ introduce; (*inserire*) insert
introdursi get in
introduzione *f* introduction
introito *m* income; (*incasso*) takings *pl*
intromettersi ⟨3ee⟩ interfere; (*interporsi*) intervene
intromissione *f* interference; (*intervento*) intervention
introvabile impossible to find
introverso 1 *agg* introverted **2** *m*, **-a** *f* introvert
intrufolarsi ⟨1m⟩ sneak in
intruglio *m* (*pl* -gli) concoction
intrusione *f* intrusion
intruso *m*, **-a** *f* intruder
intuire ⟨4d⟩ know instinctively
intuito *m* intuition
intuizione *f* intuition
inumano inhuman
inumidire ⟨4d⟩ dampen, moisten
inumidirsi get damp
inutile useless; (*superfluo*) unnecessary, pointless
inutilità *f* uselessness
inutilizzabile unusable
inutilizzato unused
inutilmente pointlessly, needlessly
invadente 1 *agg* nosy **2** *m/f* busybody
invadenza *f* nosiness
invadere ⟨3q⟩ invade; (*occupare*) occupy; (*inondare*) flood
invaghirsi ⟨4d⟩: ***invaghirsi di*** take a fancy to
invalidare ⟨1m⟩ invalidate
invalidità *f* disability
invalido 1 *agg* disabled; DIR invalid **2** *m*, **-a** *f* disabled person
invano in vain
invariabile invariable
invariabilità *f* unchanging nature
invariato unchanged
invasione *f* invasion (***di*** of)
invasore *m* invader
invecchiare ⟨1k⟩ **1** *v/t* age **2** *v/i* age, get older; *di vini, cibi* mature; *fig* (*cadere in disuso*) date
invece instead; (*ma*) but; ***invece di fare*** instead of doing
inveire ⟨4d⟩: ***inveire contro*** inveigh against
invenduto unsold
inventare ⟨1b⟩ invent
inventario *m* (*pl* -ri) inventory
inventore *m*, **-trice** *f* inventor
invenzione *f* invention
invernale winter *attr*; ***sport*** *mpl* ***-i*** winter sports
inverno *m* winter; ***d'inverno*** in winter
inverosimile improbable, unlikely
inversione *f* (*scambio*) reversal; AUTO ***inversione di marcia*** U-turn
inverso 1 *agg* reverse **2** *m* opposite
invertire ⟨4b or 4d⟩ reverse; (*capovolgere*) turn upside down; CHIM, EL invert; ***invertire la marcia*** turn round; ***invertire le parti*** exchange roles
investigare ⟨1m, b & e⟩ investigate
investigatore *m*, **-trice** *f* investigator
investigazione *f* investigation
investimento *m* investment; *di veicolo* crash; *di pedone* running over; ***investimento di capitali*** capital investment
investire ⟨4d or 4b⟩ *pedone* run over; *veicolo* smash into, collide with; FIN, *fig* invest
inviare ⟨1h⟩ send
inviato *m*, **-a** *f* envoy; *di giornale* correspondent
invidia *f* envy
invidiare ⟨1k⟩ envy
invidioso envious
invincibile invincible
invio *m* (*pl* -vii) dispatch; INFO ***tasto*** *m* ***d'invio*** enter key
inviolabile inviolable
invisibile invisible
invitante *profumo* enticing; *offerta* tempting
invitare ⟨1a⟩ invite
invitato *m*, **-a** *f* guest
invito *m* invitation; ***invito a presentarsi*** summons *sg*
invocare ⟨1c & d⟩ invoke; (*implorare*) plead for, beg for
invocazione *f* invocation; (*richiesta*) plea
invogliare ⟨1g & c⟩ induce
involontario (*pl* -ri) involuntary
involtini *mpl* GASTR *rolled stuffed slices of meat*
involto *m* bundle; (*pacco*) parcel
involucro *m* wrapping
inzaccherare ⟨1m⟩ spatter with mud
inzuppare ⟨1a⟩ soak; (*intingere*) dip
inzuppato soaked
io 1 *pron* I; ***io stesso*** myself; ***sono io!*** it's me! **2** *m inv* ego
iodio *m* iodine
ionico (*pl* -ci) ARCHI Ionic

iosa: ***a iosa*** in abundance, aplenty
iperalimentazione *f* overfeeding
iperattivo hyperactive
iperbole *f figura retorica* hyperbole; MAT hyperbola
ipermercato *m* hypermarket
ipersensibile hypersensitive
ipertensione *f* high blood pressure
ipnosi *f* hypnosis
ipnotizzare ⟨1a⟩ hypnotize
ipocalorico (*pl* -ci) low in calories
ipocrisia *f* hypocrisy
ipocrita 1 *agg* hypocritical **2** *m/f* (*mpl* -i) hypocrite
ipoteca *f* (*pl* -che) mortgage; ***accendere un'ipoteca*** take out a mortgage
ipotecare ⟨1b & d⟩ mortgage
ipotesi *f* hypothesis
ipotetico (*pl* -ci) hypothetical
ipotizzare ⟨1a⟩ hypothesize
ippica *f* (horse) riding
ippocastano *m* horse chestnut
ippodromo *m* race-course
ippopotamo *m* hippo(potamus)
ira *f* anger; ***avere uno scatto d'ira*** fly into a rage
iracheno 1 *agg* Iraqi **2** *m*, **-a** *f* Iraqi
Iran *m* Iran
iraniano 1 *agg* Iranian **2** *m*, **-a** *f* Iranian
Iraq *m* Iraq
irascibile irritable, irascible
iride *f* (*arcobaleno*) rainbow; ANAT, BOT iris
Irlanda *f* Ireland
irlandese 1 *agg* Irish **2** *m* Irish Gaelic **3** *m/f* Irishman; *donna* Irishwoman
ironia *f* irony
ironico (*pl* -ci) ironic(al)
ironizzare ⟨1a⟩ be ironic
IRPEF *abbr* (= ***Imposta sul Reddito delle Persone Fisiche***) income tax
irradiare ⟨1k⟩ *v/t & v/i* radiate
irradiazione *f* radiation
irraggiungibile unattainable
irragionevole unreasonable
irrazionale irrational
irreale unreal
irrealizzabile unattainable
irrefrenabile uncontrollable
irregolare irregular
irregolarità *f inv* irregularity
irreparabile irreparable
irreperibile impossible to find
irreprensibile irreproachable
irreprimibile irrepressible
irrequietezza *f* restlessness
irrequieto restless
irresistibile irresistible
irresponsabile irresponsible
irresponsabilità *f* irresponsibility
irrestringibile non-shrink; *parzialmente* shrink-resistant
irrevocabile irrevocable
irriconoscibile unrecognizable
irrigare ⟨1e⟩ irrigate
irrigazione *f* irrigation
irrigidire ⟨4d⟩ stiffen; *fig disciplina* tighten
irrigidirsi stiffen
irrigidito stiff
irrilevante irrelevant
irrimediabile irremediable
irrinunciabile *diritto* inalienable
irripetibile unrepeatable
irrisorio (*pl* -ri) derisive; *quantità, somma di denaro* derisory; *prezzo* ridiculously low
irritabile irritable
irritabilità *f* irritability
irritante irritating
irritare ⟨1l or 1a⟩ irritate
irritarsi become irritated
irrobustire ⟨4d⟩ strengthen, build up
irrompere ⟨3rr⟩ burst (***in*** into)
irruzione *f*: ***fare irruzione in*** burst into; *di polizia* raid
iscritto 1 *pp* → ***iscrivere*** **2** *m*, **-a** *f* member; *a gare, concorsi* entrant; EDU pupil, student **3** *m*: ***per iscritto*** in writing
iscrivere ⟨3tt⟩ register; *a gare, concorsi* enter (***a*** for, in); EDU enrol(l) (***a*** at)
iscriversi *in un elenco* register; ***iscriversi a*** *partito, associazione* join; *gara* enter; EDU enrol(l) at
iscrizione *f* inscription
islamico (pl -ci) Islamic
Islanda *f* Iceland
islandese 1 *m/agg* Icelandic **2** *m/f* Icelander
isola *f* island; ***isola pedonale*** pedestrian precinct; ***isola spartitraffico*** traffic island
isolamento *m* isolation; TEC insulation; ***isolamento acustico*** soundproofing
isolano *m*, **-a** *f* islander
isolante 1 *agg* insulating **2** *m* insulator
isolare ⟨1l⟩ isolate; TECH insulate
isolarsi isolate o.s., cut o.s. off
isolato 1 *agg* isolated; TECH insulated **2** *m* outsider; *di case* block
ispettore *m*, **-trice** *f* inspector
ispezionare ⟨1a⟩ inspect
ispezione *f* inspection
ispirare ⟨1a⟩ inspire
ispirarsi *di artista* get inspiration (***a*** from)
ispirazione *f* inspiration; (*impulso*) impulse; (*idea*) idea
Israele *m* Israel
israeliano *m*, **-a** *f* Israeli
issare ⟨1a⟩ hoist

I

istallare ⟨1a⟩ → ***installare***
istantanea *f* snap
istantaneo instantaneous
istante *m* instant; ***all'istante*** instantly
istanza *f* (*esigenza*) need; (*domanda*) application; DIR petition
ISTAT *abbr* (= ***Istituto Centrale di Statistica***) central statistics office
isterico (*pl* -ci) hysterical
istigare ⟨1l & e⟩ instigate
istintivo instinctive
istinto *m* instinct
istituire ⟨4d⟩ establish
istituto *m* institute; *assistenziale* institution, home; ***istituto di bellezza*** beauty salon; ***istituto di credito*** bank
istituzione *f* institution
istmo *m* isthmus
istrice *m* porcupine
istruire ⟨4d⟩ educate, teach; (*dare istruzioni a, addestrare*) instruct
istruirsi educate o.s.
istruito educated
istruttivo instructive
istruttore *m*, **-trice** *f* instructor
istruzione *f* education; (*direttiva*) instruction; ***-i** pl **per l'uso*** instructions (for use)
Italia *f* Italy
italiano 1 *m/agg* Italian; ***parla italiano?*** do you speak Italian? **2** *m*, **-a** *f* Italian
itinerario *m* (*pl* -ri) route, itinerary
ittico (*pl* -ci) fish
iugoslavo → ***yugoslavo***
iuta *f* jute
IVA *abbr* (= ***Imposta sul Valore Aggiunto***) VAT (= value-added tax)

J

jazz *m* jazz
jazzista *m/f* (*mpl* -i) jazz musician
jeans *mpl* jeans
jeep *f inv* jeep
jet *m inv* jet
jet-lag *m inv* jet lag
jet-set *m inv* jet set
jockey *m inv* jockey
jogging *m* jogging; ***fare jogging*** jog, go for a jog
joint-venture *f inv* joint venture
jolly *m inv* joker
joule *m inv* joule
joy-stick *m inv* joystick
judo *m* judo
juke-box *m inv* jukebox
jumbo *m* jumbo
junior *m/agg* (*pl* juniores) junior

K

karatè *m* karate
kg *abbr* (= ***chilogrammo***) kg (= kilogram)
killer *m inv* killer
kit *m inv* kit
kitsch *agg inv*, *m* kitsch
kiwi *m inv* BOT kiwi (fruit)
km *abbr* (= ***chilometro***) km (= kilometre)
km/h *abbr* (= ***chilometri all'ora***) km/h (= kilometres per hour)
kmq *abbr* (= ***chilometri quadrati***) km^2 (= square kilometres)
knock-out knock-out
k.o.: ***mettere qu k.o.*** knock s.o. out; *fig* trounce s.o.
kolossal *m inv* epic
krapfen *m inv* GASTR doughnut
kümmel *m* kümmel
kV *abbr* (= ***chilovolt***) kV (= kilovolt)
kW *abbr* (= ***chilowatt***) kW (= kilowatt)
kWh *abbr* (= ***chilowattora***) kWh (= kilowatt hour)

L

L *abbr* (= ***lira***) L (= lire)
l *abbr* (= ***litro***) l (= litre)
l' = ***lo, la***
la[1] *art fsg* the; ***la signora Rossi*** Mrs Rossi; ***la domenica*** on Sundays; ***mi piace la birra*** I like beer
la[2] *pron* **1** *sg* (*persona*) her; (*cosa, animale*) it; ***la prenderò*** I'll take it **2** *anche* **La** *sg* you
la[3] *m* MUS A; *nel solfeggio della scala* la(h)
là there; ***di là*** that way; (*in quel luogo*) in there; ***di là di*** on the other side of; ***più in là*** further on; *nel tempo* later on
labbro *m* (*pl* le -a) lip
labile (*passeggero*) fleeting, short-lived
labirinto *m* labyrinth
laboratorio *m* (*pl* -ri) lab, laboratory; (*officina*) workshop
laboriosità *f* laboriousness; *di persona* industriousness
laborioso laborious; *persona* hard-working, industrious
laburista **1** *agg* Labo(u)r **2** *m/f* Labo(u)r Party member; *elettore* Labo(u)r supporter
lacca *f* (*pl* -cche) lacquer; *per capelli* hair spray, lacquer
laccare ⟨1d⟩ lacquer
laccio *m* (*pl* -cci) tie, (draw)string; ***-cci*** *pl* ***delle scarpe*** shoe laces
lacerante *dolore, grido* piercing
lacero tattered, in tatters
lacrima *f* tear
lacrimare ⟨1l⟩ water
lacrimevole heart-rending; ***film*** *m* ***lacrimevole*** tear-jerker
lacrimogeno: ***gas*** *m* ***lacrimogeno*** tear gas
lacuna *f* gap
lacunoso incomplete
ladino **1** *agg* South Tyrolean **2** *m*, ***-a*** *f* South Tyrolean
ladro *m*, ***-a*** *f* thief
laggiù down there; *distante* over there
laghetto *m* pond
lagna *f* (*lamentela*) whining; *persona* whiner; (*cosa noiosa*) bore
lagnanza *f* complaint
lagnarsi ⟨1a⟩ complain (***di*** about)
lago *m* (*pl* -ghi) lake; ***lago artificiale*** reservoir; ***lago di Garda*** Lake Garda
laguna *f* lagoon
laico (*pl* -ci) **1** *agg scuola, stato* secular **2** *m*, ***-a*** *f* member of the laity
lama *f* blade; ***lama di coltello*** knife blade
lamentare ⟨1a⟩ lament, deplore
lamentarsi complain (***di*** about)
lamentela *f* complaint
lamento *m* whimper
lamentoso whining
lametta *f*: ***lametta*** (***da barba***) razor blade
lamiera *f* metal sheet; ***lamiera ondulata*** corrugated iron
lamina *f* foil; ***lamina d'oro*** gold leaf
lampada *f* lamp; ***lampada alogena*** halogen lamp; ***lampada a stelo*** floor lamp, *Br* standard lamp; ***lampada al neon*** neon light
lampadario *m* (*pl* -ri) chandelier
lampadina *f* light bulb; ***lampadina tascabile*** torch, *Am* flashlight
lampante blindingly obvious
lampeggiare ⟨1f⟩ flash
lampeggiatore *m* AUTO indicator; FOT flashlight
lampione *m* streetlight
lampo *m* lightning; ***in un lampo*** in a flash
lampone *m* raspberry
lana *f* wool; ***pura lana vergine*** pure new wool
lancetta *f* needle, indicator; *di orologio* hand
lancia *f* (*pl* -ce) spear; MAR launch; ***lancia di salvataggio*** lifeboat
lanciare ⟨1f⟩ throw; *prodotto* launch; ***lanciare un'occhiata*** glance, take a quick look; ***lanciare un urlo*** give a shout, shout
lanciarsi rush; ***lanciarsi contro*** throw o.s at, attack; F ***lanciarsi in un'impresa*** embark on a venture; F ***mi lancio*** I'll go for it F, I'll take the plunge F
lancinante *dolore* piercing
lancio *m* (*pl* -ci) throwing; *di prodotto* launch; ***lancio del disco*** discus; ***lancio del giavellotto*** javelin; ***lancio del peso*** putting the shot
languire ⟨4a or 4d⟩ languish
languore *m* lang(u)or; ***ho un languore allo stomaco*** I'm feeling peckish
lanificio *m* (*pl* -ci) wool mill
lanterna *f* lantern; (*faro*) lighthouse
lapide *f* gravestone; *su monumento* plaque
lapis *m inv* pencil
lardo *m* lard
larghezza *f* width, breadth; ***larghezza di vedute*** broad-mindedness

largo (*pl* -ghi) **1** *agg* wide, broad; *indumento* loose, big; (*abbondante*) large, generous; ***largo di manica*** generous **2** *m* width; (*piazza*) square; ***andare al largo*** head for the open sea; ***al largo di*** off the coast of; ***farsi largo*** elbow one's way through; ***stare alla -a da*** steer clear of, keep away from
larice *m* larch
laringe *f* larynx
laringite *f* laryngitis
larva *f* ZO larva
lasagne *fpl* lasagne *sg*
lasciapassare *m inv* pass
lasciare ⟨1f⟩ leave; (*abbandonare*) give up; (*concedere*) let; (*smettere di tenere*) let go; ***lascia andare!, lascia perdere!*** forget it!
lasciarsi separate, leave each other; ***lasciarsi andare*** let o.s. go
lascito *m* legacy
lascivo lascivious
laser *m inv*, *agg inv* laser
lassativo *m/agg* laxative
lasso *m*: ***lasso di tempo*** period of time
lassù up there
lastra *f di pietra* slab; *di metallo*, *ghiaccio*, *vetro* sheet; MED X-ray
lastrico *m* (*pl* -chi *o* -ci): *fig* ***ridursi sul lastrico*** lose everything
latente latent
laterale lateral
laterizio *m* (*mpl* -zi) bricks and tiles *pl*
latino 1 *agg* Latin; ***latino-americano*** Latin-American **2** *m* Latin; ***latino-americano, -a*** Latin-American
latitante *m/f* fugitive
latitudine *f* latitude
lato *m* side; ***a lato di, di lato a*** beside; ***d'altro lato*** on the other hand
latrare ⟨1a⟩ bark
latrato *m* barking
latrina *f* latrine
latta *f* can, tin; ***latta di benzina*** petrol can, *Am* gas can
lattaio *m* (*pl* -ai), **-a** *f* milkman; *donna* milkwoman
lattante *m* infant, small baby
latte *m* milk; ***latte a lunga conservazione*** long-life milk; ***latte intero*** whole milk; ***latte materno*** mother's milk; ***latte scremato*** skim(med) milk
latteo milk *attr*; ***Via*** *f* ***Lattea*** Milky Way
latteria *f* dairy
lattice *m* latex
latticinio *m* (*pl* -ni) dairy product
lattina *f* can, tin
lattuga *f* (*pl* -ghe) lettuce
laurea *f* degree
laurearsi ⟨1l⟩ graduate
laureato *m*, **-a** *f* graduate
lava *f* lava
lavabile washable; ***lavabile in lavatrice*** machine-washable
lavabo *m* basin
lavacristallo *m* AUTO windscreen (*Am* windshield) washer
lavaggio *m* (*pl* -ggi) washing; ***lavaggio a secco*** dry-cleaning; ***lavaggio del cervello*** brainwashing
lavagna *f* blackboard; GEOL slate; ***lavagna luminosa*** overhead projector
lavanda *f* BOT lavender
lavanderia *f* laundry; ***lavanderia a gettone*** laundrette
lavandino *m* basin; *nella cucina* sink
lavapiatti *m/f inv* dishwasher
lavare ⟨1a⟩ wash; ***lavare i panni*** do the washing
lavarsi wash; ***lavarsi le mani*** wash one's hands; ***lavarsi i denti*** brush *or* clean one's teeth
lavastoviglie *f inv* dishwasher
lavatoio *m* (*pl m* -oi) laundry; *di casa* laundry (room), utility room
lavatrice *f* washing machine
lavello *m* basin; *nella cucina* sink
lavina *f* avalanche
lavorare ⟨1a⟩ **1** *v/i* work **2** *v/t materia prima* process; *legno* carve; *terra* work
lavorativo: ***giorno*** *m* ***lavorativo*** working day
lavorato *legno* carved
lavoratore *m*, **-trice** *f* worker; ***lavoratore autonomo*** self-employed person; ***lavoratore dipendente*** employee
lavorazione *f di materia prima* processing; *di legno* carving
lavoro *m* work; (*impiego*) job; ***lavoro di gruppo*** teamwork; ***lavoro malfatto*** botched job; ***lavoro nero*** moonlighting; ***-i*** *pl* ***occasionali*** *o* ***saltuari*** odd jobs; ***per lavoro*** on business; ***condizioni*** *fpl* ***di lavoro*** working conditions; ***permesso*** *m* ***di lavoro*** work permit; ***posto*** *m* ***di lavoro*** place of work, workplace; ***-i in corso*** roadworks, work in progress; ***senza lavoro*** unemployed
le[1] *art fpl* the
le[2] *pron fsg* to her; *fpl* them; *anche* ***Le*** you
leader *m/f inv* leader
leale loyal
lealtà *f* loyalty
lebbra *f* leprosy
lebbroso *m*, **-a** *f* leper
lecca-lecca *m inv* lollipop
leccare ⟨1d⟩ lick; F ***leccare qu*** suck up to s.o. F, lick s.o.'s boots F

L

leccio *m* (*pl* -cci) holm oak
leccornia *f* appetizing dish, delicacy
lecito legal, permissible; ***se mi è lecito*** if I may
lega *f* (*pl* -ghe) league; METAL alloy
legale **1** *agg* legal **2** *m/f* lawyer
legalità *f* legality
legalizzare ⟨1a⟩ legalize
legame *m* tie, relationship; (*nesso*) link, connection
legamento *m* ANAT ligament
legare ⟨1e⟩ tie; *persona* tie up; (*collegare*) link; *fig di lavoro* tie down
legarsi *fig* tie o.s. down
legazione *f* legation
legge *f* law; ***studiare legge*** study *or* read law; ***a norma di legge*** up to standard; ***a norma di legge …*** complies with …; ***fuori legge*** illegal, unlawful
leggenda *f* legend; *di carta geografica ecc* key
leggendario (*pl* -ri) legendary
leggere ⟨3cc⟩ read; ***leggere le labbra*** lip-read; ***leggere nel pensiero a qu*** read s.o.'s mind
leggerezza *f* lightness; *fig* casualness; ***con leggerezza*** thoughtlessly, unthinkingly
leggero light; (*lieve, di poca importanza*) slight; (*superficiale*) thoughtless; *caffè* weak; ***alla -a*** lightly, lightheartedly
leggibile legible
leggio *m* (*pl* -ii) lectern; MUS music stand
legislativo legislative
legislatore *m* legislator
legislatura *f periodo* term of parliament
legislazione *f* legislation
legittimare ⟨1m⟩ approve
legittimazione *f* approval
legittimo legitimate
legna *f* (fire)wood; ***far legna*** collect firewood
legname *m* timber; ***legname da costruzione*** lumber
legno *m* (*pl* i -i) wood; ***di legno*** wooden
legumi *mpl* peas and beans; *secchi* pulses
lei *pron fsg soggetto* she; *oggetto, con preposizione* her; ***lei stessa*** herself; *anche* ***Lei*** you; ***dare del lei a qu*** address s.o. as 'lei'
lembo *m di gonna* hem, bottom; *di terra* stip
lente *f* lens; ***-i*** *pl* glasses, spectacles, specs F; ***-i*** *pl* (***a contatto***) contact lenses, contacts F; ***lente d'ingrandimento*** magnifying glass
lentezza *f* slowness
lenticchia *f* lentil
lentiggine *f* freckle
lento slow; (*allentato*) slack; *abito* loose
lenza *f* fishing rod
lenzuolo *m* (*pl* i -i *e* le -a) sheet
leone *m* lion; ASTR ***Leone*** Leo
leonessa *f* lioness
leopardo *m* leopard
lepre *f* hare
lercio filthy
lesbica *f* lesbian
lesionare damage
lesione *f* MED injury
lessare ⟨1a⟩ boil
lessico *m* (*pl* -ci) vocabulary; (*dizionario*) glossary
lesso **1** *agg* boiled **2** *m* boiled beef
letale lethal
letame *m* manure, dung
letargo *m* (*pl* -ghi) lethargy
lettera *f* letter; ***alla lettera*** to the letter; ***lettera assicurata*** registered letter; ***lettera commerciale*** business letter; ***lettera di accompagnamento*** covering letter; FIN ***lettera di cambio*** bill of exchange; ***lettera espresso*** (letter sent) express delivery; ***lettera raccomandata*** recorded delivery letter
letterale literal
letterario (*pl* -ri) literary
letterato *m*, **-a** *f* man / woman of letters
letteratura *f* literature
lettino *m* cot; *dal medico* bed; *dallo psicologo* couch; ***lettino solare*** sunbed
letto[1] *m* bed; ***letto a una piazza*** single bed; ***letto matrimoniale*** double bed; ***andare a letto*** go to bed; ***essere a letto*** be in bed
letto[2] *pp* → ***leggere***
lettore *m*, **-trice** *f* reader; *all' università* lecturer in a foreign language; INFOR disk drive; ***lettore compact disc*** CD player; ***lettore ottico*** optical character reader
lettura *f* reading
leucemia *f* leuk(a)emia
leva *f* lever; MIL call-up, *Am* draft; AUTO ***leva del cambio*** gear lever
levante *m* east
levare ⟨1b⟩ (*alzare*) raise, lift; (*togliere*) take, (re)move; (*rimuovere*) take out, remove; *macchia* remove, get out; *dente* take out, extract; ***levare l'ancora*** weigh anchor
levarsi get up, rise; *di sole* rise, come up; *indumento* take off; ***levarsi il vizio di fare qc*** get out of the habit of doing sth; ***levatelo dalla testa!*** you can get that idea out of your head!
levata *f di posta* collection
levatrice *f* midwife
levigare ⟨1l, b & e⟩ smooth down
levigato smooth

L

lezione *f* lesson; *all'università* lecture; *fig* ***dare una lezione a qu*** teach s.o. a lesson
li *pron mpl* them
lì there; ***lì per lì*** there and then; ***giù di lì*** thereabouts; ***di lì a pochi giorni*** a few days later
libanese *agg*, *m/f* Lebanese
Libano *m* (the) Lebanon
libbra *f* pound
libellula *f* dragon-fly
liberale 1 *agg* generous; POL liberal **2** *m/f* liberal
liberalità *f* generosity
liberalizzare ⟨1a⟩ liberalize
liberalizzazione *f* liberalization
liberamente freely
liberare ⟨1l⟩ release, free; (*sgomberare*) empty; *stanza* vacate
liberarsi: ***liberarsi di*** get rid of
liberazione *f* release; *di nazione* liberation
libero free; *camera d'albergo* vacant, free
libertà *f inv* freedom, liberty; ***mettersi in libertà*** change into more comfortable clothes; ***libertà di stampa*** freedom of the press; ***prendersi la libertà di fare qc*** take the liberty of doing sth; ***libertà provvisoria*** bail
Libia *f* Libya
libico (*pl* -ci) **1** *agg* Libyan **2** *m*, **-a** *f* Libyan
libraio *m* (*pl* -ai) bookseller
librario (*pl* -ri) book *attr*
libreria *f* bookstore, *Br* -shop; (*biblioteca*) book collection, library; *mobile* bookcase
libretto *m* booklet; MUS libretto; ***libretto di assegni*** cheque book, *Am* check book; AUTO ***libretto di circolazione*** registration document; ***libretto di risparmio*** bank book
libro *m* book; ***libro di testo*** textbook; ***libro illustrato*** picture book
licenza *f* FIN licence, *Am* license, permit; MIL leave; EDU school leaving certificate; ***licenza di costruzione*** building *or* construction permit; ***licenza di esercizio*** trading licence (*Am* license)
licenziamento *m* dismissal; *per motivi economici* dismissal, *Br* redundancy
licenziare ⟨1g⟩ dismiss; *per motivi economici* dismiss, lay off, *Br* make redundant; ***licenziare alle stampe*** pass for press
licenziarsi resign
liceo *m* high school; ***liceo classico*** (***scientifico***) *high school that specializes in arts* (*science*) *subjects*
lido *m* beach
lieto happy; ***lieto di conoscerla*** nice *or* pleased to meet you
lieve light; (*di poca gravità*) slight, minor; *sorriso*, *rumore* faint
lievitare ⟨1l & b⟩ rise; *fig* rise, be on the increase
lievito *m* yeast; ***lievito in polvere*** baking powder
lilla *m/agg* lilac
lillà *m* lilac (tree)
lima *f* file
limare ⟨1a⟩ file
limetta *f* emery board; *di metallo* nail file
limitare ⟨1l⟩ limit, restrict (***a*** to); (*contenere*) limit, contain
limitato limited; FIN ***società f a responsabilità -a*** limited company; ***è limitato*** *di persona* he's got his limitations
limitazione *f* limitation; ***limitazione delle nascite*** birth control; ***senza -i*** without restriction
limite *m* limit; (*confine*) boundary; ***limite di età*** age limit; ***limite di velocità*** speed limit; ***al limite*** at most, at the outside; ***nei -i del possibile*** to the best of one's ability
limitrofo bordering, neighbo(u)ring
limonata *f* lemonade
limone *m* lemon; (*albero*) lemon tree
limpidezza *f* cleanness
limpido clear; *acqua* crystal-clear, limpid
lince *f* lynx
linciare ⟨1f⟩ lynch
linea *f* line; ***linea dell'autobus*** bus route; ***mantenere la linea*** keep one's figure; TELEC ***restare in linea*** stay on the line, not hang up
lineamenti *mpl* (*fisionomia*) features
lineare linear
lineetta *f* dash
linfonodo *m* lymph node
lingotto *m* ingot
lingua *f* tongue; (*linguaggio*) language; ***lingua madre*** mother tongue; ***lingua parlata*** colloquial language; ***lingua straniera*** foreign language; ***lingua nazionale*** official language
linguaggio *m* (*pl* -ggi) language; ***linguaggio tecnico*** technical language, jargon; INFOR ***linguaggio di programmazione*** programming language
linguistica *f* linguistics
lino *m* BOT flax; *tessuto* linen
liofilizzato freeze-dried
liquidare ⟨1l⟩ (*pagare*) pay; *merci* clear; *azienda* liquidate; *fig questione* settle; *problema* dispose of; *persona* F liquidate F, dispose of F
liquidazione *f* liquidation; ***liquidazione totale*** clearance sale

liquidità *f* liquid assets *pl*, liquidity
liquido *m/agg* liquid
liquirizia *f* liquorice
liquore *m* liqueur
lira *f* lira
lirica *f* (*pl* -che) lyric poem; MUS ***la lirica*** opera
lirico (*pl* -ci) lyric; *cantante* opera *attr*; ***teatro** m **lirico*** opera house
lisca *f* (*pl* -che) fishbone
lisciare ⟨1f⟩ smooth (down); (*accarezzare*) stroke; *capelli* straighten
liscio (*pl* -sci) smooth; *bevanda* straight, neat; *fig* ***passarla -a*** get away with it
liso worn
lista *f* (*elenco*) list; (*striscia*) strip; ***lista d'attesa*** waiting list; ***in lista d'attesa*** on the waiting list, wait-listed; AVIA on standby; ***lista dei vini*** wine list
listino *m*: ***listino di borsa*** share index; ***listino prezzi*** price list
Lit. *abbr* (= ***lire italiane***) L (= lire)
lite *f* quarrel, argument; JUR lawsuit; ***lite coniugale*** marital dispute
litigare ⟨1l & e⟩ quarrel, argue
litigio *m* (*pl* -gi) quarrel, argument
litigioso argumentative, quarrelsome
litografia *f* lithography
litografo *m* lithograph
litorale 1 *agg* coastal **2** *m* coast
litoranea *f* coast road
litoraneo coast *attr*, coastal
litro *m* litre, *Am* liter
Lituania *f* Lithuania
lituano 1 *agg* Lithuanian **2** *m*, **-a** *f* Lithuanian
liturgia *f* liturgy
liturgico (*pl* -ci) liturgical
liutaio *m* (*pl* -ai) lute maker
liuto *m* lute
livella *f* level
livellamento *m* levelling
livellare ⟨1b⟩ level
livello *m* level; AUTO ***livello dell'olio*** oil level; *fig* ***ad altissimo livello*** first-class, first-rate; ***sopra il livello del mare*** above sea level; ***livello di vita*** standard of living
livido 1 *agg* livid; *braccio*, *viso* black and blue; *occhio* black; *per il freddo* blue **2** *m* bruise
lo 1 *art m/sg* the **2** *pron m/sg* him; *cosa*, *animale* it; ***non lo so*** I don't know
lobo *m* lobe
locale 1 *agg* local; MED ***anestesia** f **locale*** local an(a)esthetic **2** *m* room; *luogo pubblico* place; FERR local train
località *f inv* town; ***località balneare*** seaside resort; ***località turistica*** tourist resort
localizzare ⟨1a⟩ locate; (*delimitare*) localize
locandina *f* TEA bill
locatario *m* (*pl* -ri), **-a** *f* tenant
locatore *m*, **-trice** *f* landlord; *donna* landlady
locazione *f* rental
locomotiva *f* locomotive
locomozione *f* locomotion; ***mezzo** m **di locomozione*** means of transport
locuzione *f* fixed expression
lodare ⟨1c⟩ praise
lode *f* praise
lodevole praiseworthy, laudable
loggia *f* (*pl* -gge) loggia
loggione *m* TEA gallery
logica *f* logic
logico (*pl* -ci) logical
logorare ⟨1l⟩ wear out
logorio *m* wear and tear
logoro *indumento* worn (out), threadbare
lombaggine *f* lumbago
Lombardia *f* Lombardy
lombardo 1 *agg* of Lombardy **2** *m*, **-a** *f* native of Lombardy
lombata *f* loin
lombo *m* loin
lombrico *m* (*pl* -chi) earthworm
Londra *f* London
longevo longlived
longitudine *f* GEOG longitude
lontananza *f* distance; *tra persone* separation
lontano 1 *agg* far; *nel tempo* far-off; *passato*, *futuro*, *parente* distant; ***alla -a*** *conoscere* vaguely, slightly; ***siamo cugini alla -a*** we're distant cousins **2** *avv* far (away); ***da lontano*** from a distance; ***abita molto lontano?*** do you live very far away?
lontra *f* otter
loquace talkative
lordo dirty; *peso*, *reddito ecc* gross
loro 1 *pron soggetto* they; *oggetto* them; *forma di cortesia*, *anche* **Loro** you **2** *possessivo* their; *forma di cortesia*, *anche* **Loro** your; ***il loro amico*** their / your friend; ***i loro genitori*** their / your parents **3** *pron*: ***il loro*** theirs; *forma di cortesia*, *anche* **Loro** yours
lotta *f* struggle; SP wrestling; *fig* fight
lottare ⟨1c⟩ wrestle, struggle (***con*** with); *fig* fight (***contro*** against; ***per*** for)
lottatore *m* wrestler
lotteria *f* lottery; ***biglietto** m **della lotteria*** lottery ticket
lotto *m* lottery; *di terreno* plot
lozione *f* lotion; ***lozione dopobarba*** aftershave

L.st. *abbr* (= ***lira sterlina***) £ (= pound)
lubrificante *m* lubricant; AUTO lubricating oil
lubrificare ⟨1m & d⟩ lubricate
lucchetto *m* padlock
luccicare ⟨1l & d⟩ sparkle
luccio *m* (*pl* -cci) pike
lucciola *f* glowworm
luce *f* light; ***luce al neon*** neon light; ***dare alla luce un figlio*** give birth to a son; *fig* ***far luce su qc*** shed light on sth; AUTO ***-i*** *pl* ***di posizione*** side lights; ***-i*** *pl* ***posteriori*** rear lights
lucente shining, gleaming
lucentezza *f* shininess
lucertola *f* lizard
lucidare ⟨1l⟩ polish; *disegno* trace
lucidatrice *f* floor polisher
lucido 1 *agg superficie, scarpe* shiny; FOT glossy; *persona* lucid **2** *m* polish; *disegno* transparency; ***lucido da scarpe*** shoe polish
lucrativo lucrative
lucro *m*: ***a scopo di lucro*** profit-making; ***senza fini di lucro*** non-profit-making
luglio *m* July
lugubre sombre, *Am* somber, lugubrious
lui *pron msg soggetto* he; *oggetto* him; ***a lui*** to him; ***lui stesso*** himself
lumaca *f* (*pl* -che) slug
lume *m* (*lampada*) lamp; *luce* light; *fig* ***perdere il lume della ragione*** lose one's mind
luminosità *f* luminosity; FOT speed
luminoso luminous; *stanza* bright, full of light; ***sorgente*** *f* ***-a*** light source
luna *f* moon; *fig* ***avere la luna storta*** be in a mood; ***luna crescente / calante*** crescent / waning moon; ***luna piena*** full moon; ***luna di miele*** honeymoon
luna-park *m inv* amusement park, *Br* funfair
lunario *m*: ***sbarcare il lunario*** make ends meet
lunatico (*pl* -ci) moody
lunedì *m inv* Monday; ***il*** *o* ***di lunedì*** on Mondays
lunetta *f* ARCHI lunette
lunghezza *f* length
lungo (*pl* -ghi) **1** *agg* long; *caffè* weak; ***non essere lungo!*** don't be long!, don't take forever!; ***a lungo*** at length, for a long time; *fig* ***alla -a*** in the long run; ***andare per le -ghe*** drag on; ***di gran -a*** by far **2** *prp* along; (*durante*) throughout
lungolago *m* (*pl* -ghi) lakeside, lakeshore
lungomare *m inv* sea front
lunotto *m* AUTO rear window
luogo *m* (*pl* -ghi) place; ***luogo di nascita*** birthplace, place of birth; ***avere luogo*** take place, be held; ***fuori luogo*** out of place; ***in primo luogo*** in the first place; ***in qualche luogo*** somewhere, someplace; ***in nessun luogo*** nowhere
lupo *m* wolf
lurido filthy
lusinga *f* (*pl* -ghe) flattery
lusingare ⟨1e⟩ flatter
lusinghiero flattering
lussazione *f* dislocation
lusso *m* luxury; ***albergo*** *m* ***di lusso*** luxury hotel
lussuoso luxurious
lustrare ⟨1a⟩ polish
lustro *m* shine, lustre, *Am* luster; *fig* prestige; (*periodo*) five-year period
lutto *m* mourning

M

m *abbr* (= ***metro***) m (= metre)
ma but; (*eppure*) and yet; ***ma cosa dici?*** what are you talking about?; ***ma va!*** nonsense!; ***ma no!*** not at all!, of course not!
maccheroni *mpl* macaroni *sg*
macchia *f* spot; *di sporco* stain; (*bosco*) scrub; ***allargarsi a macchia d'olio*** spread like wildfire
macchiare ⟨1k⟩ stain, mark
macchiato stained; ***caffè*** *m* ***macchiato*** *espresso with a splash of milk*
macchina *f* machine; (*auto*) car; *fig* machinery; ***macchina fotografica*** camera; ***macchina da cucire*** sewing machine; ***macchina da presa*** cine camera; ***macchina da scrivere*** typewriter; ***macchina sportiva*** sports car; ***macchina a noleggio*** hire car, rental car; ***fatto a macchina*** machine made
macchinario *m* (*pl* -ri) machinery
macchinista *m* (*pl* -i) FERR train driver
macedonia *f*: ***macedonia*** (***di frutta***) fruit salad
macellaio *m* (*pl* -ai), **-a** *f* butcher
macellare ⟨1b⟩ butcher
macelleria *f* butcher's
macerie *fpl* rubble *sg*
macigno *m* boulder
macinacaffè *m inv* coffee mill, coffee grinder
macinapepe *m inv* pepper mill, pepper grinder
macinare ⟨1l⟩ grind
macinino *m* mill; *spir* old banger
macrobiotica *f* health food; ***negozio*** *m* ***di macrobiotica*** health food shop
macrobiotico (*mpl* -ci) macrobiotic
macroscopico (*pl* -ci) *fig* huge, enormous; *errore* monumental, colossal
Madonna *f* Madonna, Our Lady; PITT ***Madonna con bambino*** Madonna and Child
madonnaro *m pavement artist specializing in sacred images*
madre *f* mother
madrelingua 1 *f* mother tongue **2** *m/f* native speaker
madrepatria *f* native land, mother country
madreperla *f* mother-of-pearl
madrevite *f* nut
madrina *f* godmother
maestà *f* majesty
maestoso majestic
maestrale *m* north-west wind
maestranze *fpl* workers
maestria *f* mastery
maestro 1 *agg* (*principale*) main; MAR ***albero*** *m* ***maestro*** main mast; ***muro*** *m* ***maestro*** loadbearing wall **2** *m* master; MUS, PITT maestro, master; ***colpo*** *m* ***da maestro*** masterstroke **3** *m*, **-a** *f* teacher; ***maestro di nuoto*** swimming teacher *or* instructor; ***maestro di sci*** ski instructor
mafia *f* Mafia
maga *f* witch
magari 1 *avv* maybe, perhaps **2** *int* ***magari!*** if only! **3** *cong* ***magari venisse*** if only he would come
magazzinaggio *m* storage
magazzino *m* warehouse; *di negozio* stock room; (*emporio*) factory shop; ***grandi -i*** *pl* department stores
maggio *m* May
maggiolino *m* June bug, May beetle
maggiorana *f* marjoram
maggioranza *f* majority; ***maggioranza azionaria*** majority shareholding
maggiorare ⟨1a⟩ increase
maggiore 1 *agg* bigger; (*più vecchio*) older; MUS major; ***il maggiore*** the biggest; *figlio* the oldest; *artista* the greatest; *azionista* the major, the largest; ***la maggior parte del tempo / di noi*** most of the time / of us, the majority of the time / of us; ***andare per la maggiore*** be a crowd pleaser **2** *m* MIL major
maggiorenne adult *attr*
maggioritario (*pl* -ri) majority; ***sistema*** *m* ***maggioritario*** first-past-the-post system
magia *f* magic
magico (*pl* -ci) magic(al)
magistrale (*eccellente*) masterful; ***istituto*** *m* ***magistrale*** teacher training college
magistrato DIR *m* magistrate
maglia *f* top; (*maglione*) sweater; SP shirt, jersey; *ai ferri* stitch; ***lavorare a maglia*** knit; SP ***maglia gialla*** yellow jersey
maglieria *f* knitwear
maglietta *f* tee-shirt
maglione *m* sweater
magnanimo magnanimous
magnesia *f* magnesia
magnesio *m* magnesium
magnete *m* magnet
magnetico (*pl* -ci) magnetic
magnifico (*pl* -ci) magnificent

magnolia *f* magnolia
mago *m* **1** (*pl* -ghi) wizard **2** (*pl* -gi) ***i re -gi*** the Three Wise Men, the Magi
magro thin; *cibo* low in fat; *fig consolazione* small; *guadagno* meagre, *Am* meager
mai never; (*qualche volta*) ever; ***mai più*** never again; ***più che mai*** more than ever; ***non accetterò mai e poi mai*** I will never agree, never; ***chi ha mai detto che …*** who said that …; ***come mai?*** how come?; ***se mai*** if ever; ***meglio tardi che mai*** better late than never; ***dove / perché mai?*** where / why on earth?
maiale *m* pig; (***carne*** *f* ***di***) ***maiale*** pork
maiolica *f* (*pl* -che) majolica
maionese *f* mayonnaise
mais *m* maize
maiuscola *f* capital (letter)
maiuscolo capital
mal → ***male***
malandato *vestito*, *divano*, *macchina* dilapidated; *persona* poorly, not very well
malanno *m* misfortune; (*malattia*) illness
malapena: ***a malapena*** hardly, barely
malaria *f* malaria
malaticcio (*pl* -cci) sickly
malato 1 *agg* ill; ***essere malato di cuore*** have heart problems; ***malato di mente*** mentally ill **2** *m*, **-a** *f* ill person
malattia *f* illness; ***essere / mettersi in malattia*** be / go on sick leave; ***malattia infettiva*** infectious disease; ***-e*** *pl* ***della pelle*** skin diseases; ***-e*** *pl* ***veneree*** sexually transmitted diseases
malavita *f* underworld
malavoglia *f* unwillingness, reluctance; ***di malavoglia*** unwillingly, grudgingly, reluctantly
malconcio (*pl* -ci) *vestito*, *divano*, *macchina* dilapidated, the worse for wear; *persona* poorly, not very well
malcontento 1 *agg* discontented, dissatisfied **2** *m* discontent
malcostume *m* immorality
maldestro awkward, clumsy
male 1 *m* evil; ***che c'è di male?*** where's the harm in it?; ***andare a male*** go off, go bad; ***aversela*** *o* ***prendersela a male*** take it the wrong way; MED ***mal di gola*** sore throat; ***mal di testa / di denti*** headache / toothache; ***mal di mare*** seasickness; ***far male a qu*** hurt s.o.; ***mi fa male il braccio*** my arm hurts; ***il cioccolato mi fa male*** chocolate doesn't agree with me; ***fare male alla salute*** be bad for you; ***farsi male*** hurt o.s. **2** *avv* badly; ***capire male*** misunderstand; ***di male in peggio*** from bad to worse; ***meno male!*** thank goodness!; ***stare male*** (*essere malato*) be ill; (*essere giù*) be depressed; ***il giallo mi sta male*** yellow doesn't suit me, I don't suit yellow; ***il divano sta male qui*** the couch doesn't look right here; ***sta male …*** it's not done to …; ***mi ha risposto male*** he gave me a rude answer
maledetto 1 *pp* → ***maledire*** **2** *agg* dratted, damn(ed)
maledire ⟨3t⟩ curse
maledizione *f* curse; ***maledizione!*** damn!
maleducato bad-mannered, uncouth
malessere *m* indisposition; *fig* malaise
malfamato disreputable
malfatto *cosa* badly made
malfattore *m* criminal
malformazione *f* MED, BIO malformation
malgoverno *m* POL misgovernment
malgrado 1 *prp* in spite of, despite **2** *avv* ***mio / tuo malgrado*** against my / your will **3** *cong* although
maligno malicious, spiteful; MED malignant
malinconia *f* melancholy
malinconico (*pl* -ci) melancholic
malincuore: ***a malincuore*** reluctantly, unwilling
malintenzionato 1 *agg* shady, suspicious **2** *m*, **-a** *f* shady character
malinteso *m* misunderstanding
malizia *f* (*cattiveria*) malice, spite; (*astuzia*) trick; ***con malizia*** maliciously, spitefully
malizioso malicious, spiteful; *sorriso* mischievous
malloppo *m* (*refurtiva*) loot
malmenare ⟨1a⟩ mistreat
malmesso *vestito*, *divano*, *macchina* the worse for wear; ***sono un po' malmesso*** I'm a bit hard up
malnutrito under-nourished
malnutrizione *f* malnutrition
malore *m*: ***è stato colto da un malore*** he was suddenly taken ill
malsano unhealthy
malsicuro unsafe
malta *f* mortar
maltempo *m* bad weather
malto *m* malt
maltrattare ⟨1a⟩ mistreat, ill-treat
malumore *m* bad mood; ***essere di malumore*** be in a bad mood
malvagio (*pl* -gi) evil, wicked
malvisto unpopular
malvivente *m* lout
malvolentieri unwillingly, reluctantly
mamma *f* mother, mum; ***mamma mia!*** goodness!
mammella *f* breast

mammifero *m* mammal
mammografia *f* mammography
manager *m/f* manager
manageriale managerial, management *attr*
mancanza *f* lack (***di*** of); (*errore*) oversight; ***mancanza di abitazioni*** housing shortage; ***mancanza di corrente*** power failure; ***mancanza di personale*** lack of staff, staff shortage; ***per mancanza di tempo*** for lack of time
mancare ⟨1d⟩ **1** *v/i* be missing; (*venire meno*) fail; (*morire*) pass away; ***a qu manca qc*** s.o. lacks sth; ***mi mancano le forze*** I don't have the strength; ***mi manca la casa*** I miss home; ***mi mancano 5000 lire*** I'm 5000 lire short; ***manca la benzina nella macchina*** the car needs filling up; ***mancano tre mesi a Natale*** it's three months to Christmas; ***sentirsi mancare*** feel faint; ***non mancherò*** I'll do that, I'll be sure to do it; ***c'è mancato poco che cadesse*** he almost fell; ***ci mancherebbe altro!*** no way!, you must be joking!; ***mancare di qc*** (*non avere*) lack sth, be lacking in sth; ***mancare di fare qc*** fail *or* omit to do sth; ***mancare di parola*** break one's promise **2** *v/t* miss
mancato *occasione* missed, lost; *tentativo* unsuccessful; ***è un poeta mancato*** he should have been a poet; ***mancato pagamento*** non-payment
manchevole faulty, defective
mancia *f* (*pl* -ce) tip
manciata *f* handful
mancino 1 *agg* left-handed; *fig* ***colpo*** *m* ***mancino*** blow beneath the belt, dirty trick **2** *m*, **-a** *f* left-hander
mandante *m/f* DIR client; F *person who hires a contract killer*
mandare ⟨1a⟩ send; ***mandare qu a prendere qc*** send s.o. for sth; ***mandare a monte*** ruin, send up in smoke F; *fig* ***mandare giù*** digest, take in
mandarino *m* BOT mandarin (orange)
mandato *m* POL mandate; DIR warrant; ***mandato bancario*** banker's order; ***mandato di pagamento*** payment order; ***mandato d'arresto*** arrest warrant
mandibola *f* jaw
mandolino *m* mandolin
mandorla *f* almond
mandorlo *m* almond tree
mandria *f* herd
maneggevole easy to handle, manageable
maneggiare ⟨1f⟩ handle (*anche fig*)
maneggio *m* (*pl* -ggi) handling; *per cavalli* riding school
manesco (*pl* -chi) a bit too ready with one's fists
manette *fpl* handcuffs
manganello *m* truncheon
mangereccio (*pl* -ci) edible
mangiabile edible
mangiacassette *m inv*, **mangianastri** *m inv* cassette player
mangiare 1 *v/t* ⟨1f⟩ eat; *fig* squander; ***mangiarsi le parole*** mumble; ***mangiarsi un'occasione*** throw away *or* waste an opportunity **2** *m* food
mangime *m* fodder
mangiucchiare ⟨1g⟩ snack, eat between meals
mango *m* (*pl* -ghi) mango
mania *f* mania
manica *f* (*pl* -che) sleeve; ***senza -che*** sleeveless; ***è un altro paio di -che!*** that's another kettle of fish
manicaretto *m* delicacy
manichino *m* dummy
manico *m* (*pl* -chi o -ci) handle; *di violino* neck
manicomio *m* (*pl* -mi) mental home
manicotto *m* TEC sleeve
manicure *f inv* manicure; (*persona*) manicurist
maniera *f* (*modo*) way, manner; (*stile*) manner; ***-e*** *pl* manners
manifattura *f* manufacture; (*stabilimento*) factory
manifestante *m/f* demonstrator
manifestare ⟨1b⟩ **1** *v/t* (*esprimere*) express; (*mostrare*) show, demonstrate **2** *v/i* demonstrate
manifestarsi appear, show up; *di malattia* manifest itself
manifestazione *f* expression; *il mostrare* show, demonstration; ***manifestazione di protesta*** demonstration, demo F; ***manifestazione sportiva*** sporting event
manifesto 1 *agg* obvious **2** *m* poster
maniglia *f* handle; *di autobus, metro* strap
manipolare ⟨1m⟩ manipulate; *vino* adulterate
manipolazione *f* manipulation; *di vino* adulteration
mano *f* (*pl* -i) hand; ***a portata di mano*** within reach; ***fuori mano*** out of the way, not easy to get at; *fig* ***alla mano*** approachable; ***di seconda mano*** second-hand; ***dare una mano a qu*** give s.o. a hand; ***mettere mano a qc*** start sth; ***lavo le pentole che sporco a mano a mano*** I wash the dirty pots as I go along; ***tenersi per mano*** hold hands; ***man mano che*** as (and when); ***ha le -i bucate*** money just

M

slips through his fingers; ***-i in alto!*** hands up!
manodopera *f* labo(u)r
manomettere ⟨3ee⟩ tamper with
manopola *f* knob
manoscritto *m* manuscript
manovale *m* hod carrier
manovella *f* starting handle; TEC crank
manovra *f* manoeuvre, *Am* maneuver
manovrare ⟨1c⟩ **1** *v/t* TEC operate; FERR shunt; *fig* manipulate **2** *v/i* manoeuvre, *Am* maneuver
mansarda *f* (*locale*) attic
mansueto docile
mantello *m* (*cappa*) cloak; *di animale* coat; (*strato*) covering, layer
mantenere ⟨2q⟩ keep; *famiglia* keep, maintain; *in buono stato* maintain; ***mantenersi in forma*** keep in shape
mantenimento *m* maintenance; *di famiglia* keep
manto *m* cloak; *di animale* coat; *fig* ***manto di neve*** mantle of snow
manuale 1 *agg* manual **2** *m* manual, handbook
manubrio *m* (*pl* -ri) handlebars *pl*
manutenzione *f* maintenance
manzo *m* steer, bullock; *carne* beef
mappa *f* map
mappamondo *m* globe
maratona *f* marathon
maratoneta *m/f* (*mpl* -i) marathon runner
marca *f* (*pl* -che) brand, make; (*etichetta*) label; ***marca da bollo*** revenue stamp
marcare ⟨1d⟩ mark; *goal* score
marcato *accento*, *lineamenti* strong
marchiare ⟨1k⟩ brand (*anche fig*)
marchio *m* (*pl* -chi) FIN brand; ***marchio depositato*** registered trademark
marcia *f* (*pl* -ce) march; SP walk; TEC AUTO gear; ***marcia indietro*** reverse; ***mettersi in marcia*** set off
marciapiede *m* pavement, *Am* sidewalk; FERR platform
marciare ⟨1f⟩ march
marcio (*pl* -ci) bad, rotten; (*corrotto*) corrupt, rotten to the core; ***avere torto marcio*** be totally wrong
marcire ⟨4d⟩ go bad, rot; *fig* rot
marco *m* (*pl* -chi) mark
mare *m* sea; ***in alto mare*** on the high seas
marea *f* tide; *fig* ***una marea di*** loads of; ***alta marea*** high tide; ***bassa marea*** low tide; ***marea nera*** oil slick
mareggiata *f* storm
maremoto *m* tidal wave
margarina *f* margarine
margherita *f* marguerite
margheritina *f* daisy
margine *m* margin; (*orlo*) edge, brink; ***margine di guadagno*** profit margin; ***vivere ai -i della società*** live on the fringes of society
marina *f* coast(line); MAR navy; PITT seascape
marinaio *m* (*pl* -ai) sailor
marinare ⟨1a⟩ GASTR marinate; F ***marinare la scuola*** play truant, *Br* bunk off school F
marinato GASTR marinated
marino sea, marine
marionetta *f* puppet, marionette
marito *m* husband
marittimo maritime
marmellata *f* jam; ***marmellata di arance*** marmalade
marmitta *f* AUTO silencer, *Am* muffler; ***marmitta catalitica*** catalytic converter
marmo *m* marble
marmotta *f* marmot; ***dormire come una marmotta*** sleep like a log
marocchino 1 *agg* Moroccan **2** *m*, **-a** *f* Moroccan
Marocco *m* Morocco
marrone 1 *agg* (chestnut) brown **2** *m colore* (chestnut) brown; (*castagno*) chestnut
marsala *m* Marsala, *type of dessert wine*
marsina *f* tails
Marte *m* Mars
martedì *m inv* Tuesday; ***martedì grasso*** Shrove Tuesday, *Br* Pancake Day F
martello *m* hammer; ***martello pneumatico*** pneumatic drill
martire *m/f* martyr
martirio *m* (*pl* -ri) martyrdom
martora *f* marten
marxismo *m* Marxism
marxista *m/f* (*mpl* -i) Marxist
marzapane *m* marzipan
marziano *m* Martian
marzo *m* March
mascalzone *m* rogue, rascal
mascara *m inv* mascara
mascarpone *m* mascarpone
mascella *f* jaw
maschera *f* mask; *in cinema*, *teatro* usher; *donna* usherette; ***maschera antigas*** gas mask; ***maschera subacquea*** face mask; ***ballo m in maschera*** masked ball
mascherare ⟨1l⟩ mask; *fig* camouflage, conceal
mascherarsi put on a mask; (*travestirsi*) dress up (***da*** as)
maschile *spogliatoio*, *abito* men's; *caratteristica* male; GRAM masculine
maschilista (*pl* -i) **1** *m* male chauvinist, sexist **2** *agg* chauvinistic, sexist

maschio (*pl* -chi) **1** *agg* male; ***hanno tre figli -i*** they have three sons *or* boys **2** *m* (*ragazzo*) boy; (*uomo*) man; zo male
mascolino masculine
mascotte *f inv* mascot
massa *f* mass; EL earth; F ***una massa di cosa da fare*** masses of things to do F
massacrare ⟨1a⟩ massacre
massacro *m* massacre
massaggiare ⟨1f⟩ massage
massaggiatore *m*, **-trice** *f* masseur; *donna* masseuse
massaggio *m* (*pl* -ggi) massage
massaia *f* housewife
massiccio (*pl* -cci) **1** *agg* massive; *oro, noce ecc* solid **2** *m* massif
massima *f* saying, maxim; (*temperatura*) maximum; ***di massima*** *progetto* preliminary; ***in linea di massima*** generally speaking, on the whole
massimale *m* maximum
massimo **1** *agg* greatest, maximum **2** *m* maximum; ***al massimo*** at most
mass media *mpl* mass media
masso *m* rock
masterizzare *v/t* INFOR burn
materizzatore *m* INFOR writer
masticare ⟨1l & d⟩ chew
mastice *m* mastic; (*stucco*) putty
mastino *m* mastiff
mastodontico (*pl* -ci) gigantic, enormous
masturbare ⟨1a⟩, *gen* **masturbarsi** masturbate
masturbazione *f* masturbation
matassa *f* skein
matematica *f* mathematics, maths F, *Am* math F
matematico (*pl* -ci) **1** *agg* mathematical **2** *m*, **-a** *f* mathematician
materassino *m* airbed, lilo®
materasso *m* mattress
materia *f* matter; (*materiale*) material; (*disciplina*) subject; ***materia facoltativa*** optional subject; ***materia obbligatoria*** compulsory subject; ***materia prima*** raw material; ***materia sintetica*** synthetic (material)
materiale **1** *agg* material; (*rozzo*) coarse, rough **2** *m* material; TEC equipment
materialista (*mpl* -i) **1** *agg* materialistic **2** *m/f* materialist
maternità *f inv* motherhood; *in ospedale* maternity
materno maternal; ***scuola*** *f* ***-a*** nursery school
matita *f* pencil; ***matita colorata*** colo(u)red pencil; ***matita per gli occhi*** eye pencil; ***matita per sopracciglia*** eyebrow pencil
matrice *f* matrix
matricola *f* register; *all'università* first-year student
matrigna *f* stepmother
matrimoniale matrimonial
matrimonio *m* (*pl* -ni) marriage; *rito* wedding
mattina *f* morning; ***di mattina*** in the morning; ***questa mattina*** this morning; ***domani mattina*** tomorrow morning
mattinata *f* morning; TEA matinee
mattiniero: ***essere mattiniero*** be an early bird
mattino *m* morning; ***di buon mattino*** early in the morning
matto **1** *agg* mad, crazy, insane (***per*** about); ***avere una voglia -a di qc*** be dying for sth; ***essere matto da legare*** be insane, be mad as a hatter **2** *m*, **-a** *f* madman, lunatic; *donna* madwoman, lunatic; ***mi piace da -i andare al cinema*** I'm mad about the cinema
mattone *m* brick; *fig* ***che mattone!*** what a turgid piece of writing!
mattonella *f* tile
mattutino morning *attr*
maturare ⟨1a⟩ *interessi* accrue; ***maturare una decisione*** reach a decision
maturità *f* maturity; (*diploma*) *A level*
maturo *frutto* ripe; *persona* mature; ***i tempi sono -i*** the time is ripe
mausoleo *m* mausoleum
mazza *f* club; (*martello*) sledgehammer; *da baseball* bat; ***mazza da golf*** golf club
mazzo *m* bunch, bundle; ***mazzo di fiori*** bunch of flowers, bouquet; ***mazzo di chiavi*** bunch of keys; ***mazzo di carte*** pack *or* deck of cards
mc *abbr* (= ***metro cubo***) m^3 (= cubic metre)
me (= ***mi*** before ***lo, la, li, le, ne***) me; ***dammelo*** give me it, give it to me; ***come me*** like me; ***fai come me*** do what I do; ***per me*** for me; ***secondo me*** in my opinion
meccanica *f* mechanics; *di orologio* mechanism; ***la meccanica di un incidente*** how an accident happened; ***meccanica di precisione*** precision engineering
meccanicamente mechanically
meccanico (*pl* -ci) **1** *agg* mechanical **2** *m* mechanic
meccanismo *m* mechanism
mecenate *m/f* sponsor
mèche *f inv* streak
medaglia *f* medal
medesimo (very) same; ***il medesimo*** the (very) same; ***la -a*** the (very) same
media *f* average; ***in media*** on average; ***su-***

M

periore (***inferiore***) ***alla media*** above (below) average; ***media oraria*** average speed
mediano 1 *agg* central, middle **2** *m* SP half-back
mediante by (means of)
mediatore *m*, **-trice** *f* mediator
mediazione *f* mediation
medicamento *m* medicine
medicare ⟨1l, b & d⟩ *persona* treat; *ferita* clean, disinfect
medicazione *f* treatment; (*bende*) dressing
medicina *f* medicine; ***medicina interna*** internal medicine; ***medicina legale*** forensic medicine; ***medicina sportiva*** sports medicine
medicinale 1 *agg* medicinal **2** *m* medicine
medico (*pl* -ci) **1** *agg* medical; ***visita*** *f* ***-a*** medical examination, physical F **2** *m* doctor; ***medico generico*** general practitioner, *Br* GP; ***medico di famiglia*** family doctor; ***medico di guardia*** duty doctor
medievale medi(a)eval
medio (*pl* -di) **1** *agg età, classe ecc* middle *attr*; *guadagno, statura, rendimento* average **2** *m* middle finger
mediocre mediocre
mediocrità *f* mediocrity
medioevo *m* Middle Ages
meditare ⟨1l & b⟩ **1** *v/t* think about; (*progettare*) plan **2** *v/i* meditate; (*riflettere*) think; ***meditare su qc*** think about sth
meditazione *f* meditation; (*riflessione*) consideration, reflection
mediterraneo 1 *agg* Mediterranean **2** *m* ***Mediterraneo*** Mediterranean (Sea)
medium *m/f inv* medium
medusa *f* ZO jellyfish
megalomania *m* megalomania
meglio 1 *avv* better; ***meglio!, tanto meglio!*** so much the better!, good!; ***alla meglio*** to the best of one's ability; ***di bene in meglio*** better and better **2** *agg* better; *superlativo* best **3** *m* best; ***fare del proprio meglio*** do one's best **4** *f* ***avere la meglio su*** get the better of
mela *f* apple
melagrana *f* pomegranate
melanzana *f* aubergine, *Am* eggplant
melma *f* mud
melo *m* apple (tree)
melodia *f* melody
melodico (*pl* -ci) melodic
melodramma *m* (*pl* -i) melodrama
melodrammatico melodramatic
melograno *m* pomegranate tree
melone *m* melon
membrana *f* membrane; ***membrana del timpano*** eardrum
membro *m* (*pl* le membra) ANAT limb; *persona* (*pl* i -i) member
memorabile memorable
memorandum *m inv* memo(randum); (*promemoria*) memo
memoria *f* memory; INFOR storage capacity; ***a memoria*** by heart; ***in memoria di*** in memory of; ***memoria centrale*** main memory; ***questo nome non ti richiama alla memoria niente*** doesn't that name remind you of anything?; ***-e*** *pl* memoirs
memorizzare ⟨1a⟩ memorize; INFOR save
menare ⟨1a⟩ lead; F (*picchiare*) hit
mendicante *m/f* beggar
mendicare ⟨1l, d or 1d⟩ **1** *v/t* beg (for); *aiuto, lavoro ecc* beg for, plead for **2** *v/i* beg
menefreghismo *m* couldn't-care-less attitude
meninge *f*: F ***spremersi le -i*** rack one's brains F
meningite *f* meningitis
meno 1 *avv* less; *superlativo* least; MATH minus; ***il meno possibile*** as little as possible; ***di meno*** at least; ***a meno che*** unless; ***per lo meno*** at least; ***sono le sei meno un quarto*** it's a quarter to six; ***sempre meno*** less and less; ***fare a meno di qc*** do without sth; ***venir meno a qcno*** *forze* desert s.o.; ***venir meno alla parola data*** not keep one's word **2** *prp* except
menomato damaged; (*handicappato*) disabled
menomazioni *fpl* damage *sg*
mensa *f di fabbrica* canteen; MIL mess; ***mensa universitaria*** refectory
mensile 1 *agg* monthly; ***tessera*** *f* ***mensile*** *per treno, autobus* monthly season ticket **2** *m* (*periodico*) monthly
mensilità *f inv* salary
mensola *f* bracket
menta *f* mint; ***menta piperita*** peppermint
mentale mental
mentalità *f inv* mentality
mentalmente mentally
mente *f* mind; ***malato di mente*** mentally ill; ***avere in mente di fare qc*** be planning to do sth, be thinking about doing sth; ***tenere a mente qc*** bear sth in mind; ***non mi viene in mente il nome di ...*** I can't remember the name of ...; ***mi è uscito di mente*** it slipped my mind
mentire ⟨4d or b⟩ lie
mento *m* chin
mentre while
menù *m inv* menu *anche* INFOR
menzionare ⟨1a⟩ mention
menzogna *f* lie

meraviglia *f* wonder; ***a meraviglia*** marvel(l)ously, wonderfully
meravigliare ⟨1g⟩ astonish
meravigliarsi: ***meravigliarsi di*** be astonished by; ***mi meraviglio di te*** you astonish me
meravigliato astonished
meraviglioso marvel(l)ous, wonderful
mercante *m* merchant
mercanteggiare ⟨1f⟩ bargain, haggle
mercantile 1 *agg nave* cargo *attr*; *porto* commercial **2** *m* cargo ship
mercanzia *f* merchandise
mercato *m* market; ***mercato coperto*** covered market, indoor market; ***mercato estero*** foreign market; ***mercato mondiale*** world market; ***mercato interno*** domestic market; ***mercato unico europeo*** single European market; ***mercato nero*** black market; ***mercato delle pulci*** flea market; ***a buon mercato*** cheap, inexpensive
merce *f* goods; ***merce di contrabbando*** contraband
merceria *f* (*pl* -ie) haberdashery
mercoledì *m inv* Wednesday; ***mercoledì delle Ceneri*** Ash Wednesday
mercurio *m* mercury; AST **Mercurio** Mercury
merda P shit P
merenda *f* snack
meridiana *f* sundial
meridiano 1 *agg* midday *attr* **2** *m* meridian
meridionale 1 *agg* southern; ***Italia*** *f* ***meridionale*** southern Italy **2** *m/f* southerner
meridione *m* south; ***il Meridione*** southern Italy
meringa *f* (*pl* -ghe) meringue
meritare ⟨1l & b⟩ **1** *v/t* deserve; ***non merita un prezzo così alto*** it's not worth that much **2** *v/i*: ***un libro che merita*** a worthwhile book; ***non ti arrabbiare, non merita*** don't get angry, it's/he's not worth it
meritevole worthy (***di*** of)
merito *m* merit; ***in merito a*** as regards; ***per merito suo*** thanks to him
merletto *m* lace
merlo *m* ZO blackbird; ARCHI ***-i*** *pl* battlements
merluzzo *m* cod
meschino mean, petty; (*infelice*) wretched
mescolanza *f* mixture
mescolare ⟨1l⟩ mix; *insalata* toss; *caffè* stir
mescolarsi mix, blend
mese *m* month; ***una volta al mese*** once a month; ***ai primi del mese*** on the first of every month
messa[1]: ***messa in piega*** set; ***messa in scena*** production; AUTO ***messa in marcia*** starting; ***messa in moto*** start-up; FOT ***messa a fuoco*** focussing; ***messa a punto*** *di meccanismo* adjustment; *di motore* (fine-)tuning; *di testo* finalization
messa[2] *f* REL mass; ***messa solenne*** high mass
messaggero *m* messenger
messaggio *m* (*pl* -ggi) message
messale *m* missal
messicano 1 *agg* Mexican **2** *m*, **-a** *f* Mexican
Messico *m* Mexico
messinscena *f* production; *fig* act
messo *pp* → ***mettere***
mestiere *m* trade; (*professione*) profession; ***essere del mestiere*** be a professional *or* an expert
mestolo *m* ladle
mestruazione *f* menstruation
meta *f* destination; SP try; *fig* goal, aim
metà *f inv* half; *punto centrale* middle, centre; ***siamo a metà del viaggio*** we're half-way there; ***a metà prezzo*** half price; ***a metà strada*** halfway; ***fare a metà*** go halves (***di*** on)
metabolico metabolic
metabolismo *m* metabolism
metadone *m* methadone
metafora *f* metaphor
metaforico (*pl* -ci) metaphorical
metallico (*pl* -ci) metallic
metallizzato metallic
metallo *m* metal; ***metallo prezioso*** precious metal
metallurgia *f* metallurgy
metamorfosi *f inv* metamorphosis
metano *m* methane
metanodotto *m* gas pipeline
meteora *f* meteor
meteorite *m o f* meteorite
meteorologico (*pl* -ci) meteorological, weather *attr*; ***bollettino*** *m* ***meteorologico*** weather forecast; ***servizio*** *m* ***meteorologico*** weather service
meticoloso meticulous
metodico (*pl* -ci) methodical
metodo *m* method
metrica *f* metrics
metrico (*pl* -ci) metric
metro[1] *m* metre, *Am* meter; ***metro quadrato*** square metre (*Am* meter); ***metro cubo*** cubic metre (*Am* meter)
metrò[2] *m inv* (*metropolitana*) underground, *Am* subway
metronotte *m inv* night watchman

metropoli *f inv* metropolis
metropolitana *f* underground, *Am* subway
mettere ⟨3ee⟩ put; *vestito* put on; ***mettere a punto*** *meccanismo* adjust; *motore* (fine-)tune; ***mettere in moto*** start (up); ***mettere in ordine*** tidy up; ***mettere al sicuro*** put away safely; ***mettere su casa*** set up house; ***mettiamo che*** let's assume that
mettersi *abito, cappello ecc* put on; ***mettersi a letto*** go to bed, take to one's bed; ***mettersi a sedere*** sit down; AVIA, AUTO ***mettersi la cintura*** fasten one's seat belt; ***mettersi a fare qc*** start to do sth; ***mettersi in cammino*** set out, get going
mezzaluna *f* (*pl* mezzelune) half moon, crescent; GASTR *two-handled chopper*
mezzanino *m* mezzanine
mezzanotte *f* midnight
mezzo 1 *agg* half; ***uno e mezzo*** one and a half; ***mezz'ora*** half-hour; ***le sei e mezzo*** half-past six; ***mezzo chilo*** a half kilo; ***a -a strada*** halfway; ***di -a età*** middle-aged **2** *avv* half **3** *m* (*parte centrale*) middle; (*metà*) half; (*strumento*) means *sg*; (*veicolo*) means *sg* of transport; ***prendere un mezzo pubblico*** use public transport; ***-i*** *pl* ***di comunicazione di massa*** mass media; ***-i*** *pl* ***di pagamento*** means of payment; ***per mezzo di*** by means of; ***a mezzo posta*** by post,; ***in mezzo a*** *due persone, due libri* between; ***in mezzo a quei documenti*** in the middle of *or* among those papers; ***in mezzo alla stanza*** in the middle of the room; ***nel mezzo di*** in the middle of; ***giusto mezzo*** happy medium
mezzobusto *m* (*pl* mezzibusti) half-length photograph / portrait
mezzofondo *m* middle distance
mezzogiorno *m* midday; GEOG ***Mezzogiorno*** south (of Italy), southern Italy
mezzoservizio *m*: ***lavorare a mezzoservizio*** work part-time
mg *abbr* (= ***milligrammo***) mg (= milligram)
mi[1] *m* MUS E; *nel solfeggio della scala* me, mi
mi[2] *pron* me; *riflessivo* myself; ***eccomi*** here I am
miagolare ⟨1l⟩ miaow, mew
miagolio *m* miaowing, mewing
mica: ***non ho mica finito*** I'm nowhere near finished; ***non è mica vero*** there's not the slightest bit of truth in it; ***mica male*** not bad at all
miccia *f* fuse
micidiale *veleno, clima* deadly; *fatica, sforza* exhausting, killing
micio F *m* (*pl* -ci) (pussy) cat
micosi *f inv* mycosis
microbiologia *f* microbiology
microbo *m* microbe
microcamera *f* miniature camera
microchirurgia *f* microsurgery
microclima *m* microclimate
microcomputer *m inv* microcomputer
microcosmo *m* microcosm
microfilm *m inv* microfilm
microfono *m* microphone, mike F
microonda *f* microwave; ***forno*** *m* ***a -e*** microwave (oven)
microprocessore *m* microprocessor
microrganismo *m* microorganism
microscopico (*pl* -ci) microscopic
microscopio *m* (*pl* -pi) microscope
midollo *m* marrow; ***midollo osseo*** bone marrow; ***midollo spinale*** spinal cord
miei *mpl* di ***mio*** my
miele *m* honey
mietere ⟨3a⟩ harvest
migliaio *m* (*pl* -aia *f*) thousand; ***un migliaio*** a *or* one thousand; *fig* ***un migliaio di persone*** thousands of people; ***a migliaia*** in their thousands
miglio[1] *m* (*pl* -glia *f*) *misura* mile; ***miglio marino*** nautical mile
miglio[2] *m grano* millet
miglioramento *m* improvement
migliorare ⟨1a⟩ **1** *v/t* improve **2** *v/i e* **migliorarsi** improve, get better
migliore better; ***il migliore*** the best
mignolo *m* (*o* ***dito mignolo***) little finger; *del piede* little toe
migrare ⟨1a⟩ migrate
migrazione *f* migration
-mila thousand; ***due-mila*** two thousand
milanese 1 *agg* of Milan **2** *m/f* inhabitant of Milan
Milano *f* Milan
miliardario *m* (*pl* -ri), **-a** *f* billionaire, multimillionaire
miliardo *m* billion
milionario *m* (*pl* -ri), **-a** *f* millionaire; *donna* millionairess
milione *m* million
militare ⟨1l⟩ fight, militate (***contro*** against; ***per*** for); ***militare in un partito*** be a member of a party **2** *agg* military **3** *m* soldier; ***fare il militare*** do one's military service
militarismo *m* militarism
militarista *m/f* (*mpl* -i) militarist
militarizzare ⟨1a⟩ hand over to the military; *partito* structure like the army
milite *m* soldier; ***il milite ignoto*** the Unknown Soldier

militesente exempt from military service
milizia *f* militia
mille (*pl* mila) a thousand
millefoglie *m inv* vanilla slice
millennio *m* (*pl* -nni) millennium
millepiedi *m inv* millipede
millesimo *m/agg* thousandth
milligrammo *m* milligram(me)
millimetro *m* millimetre, *Am* -meter
milza *f* spleen
mimetizzare ⟨1a⟩ MIL camouflage
mimetizzarsi camouflage o.s.; *fig* ***mimetizzarsi tra la folla*** get lost in the crowd
mimica *f* mime
mimo *m* mime
mimosa *f* mimosa
min. *abbr* (= ***minuto***) min (= minute)
mina *f* mine; *di matita* lead
minaccia *f* (*pl* -cce) threat
minacciare ⟨1f⟩ threaten
minaccioso threatening
minare ⟨1a⟩ mine; *fig* undermine
minato: ***campo*** *m* ***minato*** minefield
minareto *m* minaret
minatore *m* miner
minatorio (*pl* -ri) threatening
minerale *m/agg* mineral
minestra *f* soup; ***minestra di fagioli*** bean soup; ***minestra di verdura*** vegetable soup
minestrina *f* clear soup, broth
minestrone *m* minestrone, *thick vegetable soup*
miniatura *f* miniature
miniera *f* mine (*anche fig*)
minigolf *m inv* miniature golf
minigonna *f* mini(skirt)
minimizzare ⟨1a⟩ minimize
minimo **1** *agg* least, slightest; *prezzo, offerta* lowest; *salario, temperatura* minimum **2** *m* minimum; ***come minimo, dovresti ...*** you should at least ...
ministero *m* ministry; (*gabinetto*) government, ministry; ***pubblico ministero*** *state prosecutor*
ministro *m* minister; ***ministro degli Esteri*** Foreign Secretary, *Am* Secretary of State; ***ministro degli Interni*** Home Secretary, *Am* Secretary of the Interior; ***primo ministro*** Prime Minister; ***consiglio*** *m* ***dei -i*** Cabinet
minoranza *f* minority
minorato **1** *agg* severely handicapped **2** *m*, **-a** *f* severely handicapped person
minore **1** *agg* minor; *di età* younger; *distanza* shorter; *più piccolo* smaller; **2** *m/f*: ***vietato ai -i di 18 anni*** no admittance to those under 18 years of age; *film* X-rated
minorenne **1** *agg* under-age **2** *m/f* minor
minuscola *f* small letter, lower case letter
minuscolo tiny, miniscule
minuto **1** *agg persona* tiny; *oggetto* minute; *descrizione, indagine* detailed; ***commercio*** *m* ***al minuto*** retail trade **2** *m* minute; ***60 pulsazioni al minuto*** 60 beats a minute; ***ho i -i contati*** I don't have a minute to spare
minuzioso *descrizione* detailed; *ricerca* meticulous
mio (*pl* miei) **1** *agg* my; ***un mio amico*** a friend of mine, one of my friends; ***i miei amici*** my friends **2** *pron*: ***il mio*** mine; ***questo libro è mio*** this book is mine, this is my book; ***i miei*** my parents
miope short-sighted
miopia *f* short-sightedness, myopia
mira *f* aim; (*obiettivo*) target; ***prendere la mira*** take aim; ***prendere di mira*** aim at; *fig* ***prendere di mira qu*** have it in for s.o.
miracolo *m* miracle; ***per miracolo*** by a miracle, miraculously
miraggio *m* (*pl* -ggi) mirage
mirare ⟨1a⟩ aim (***a*** at)
mirino *m* MIL sight; FOT viewfinder
mirtillo *m* bilberry
mirto *m* myrtle
miscela *f* mixture; *di caffè, tabacco* blend
miscelatore *m* GASTR mixer; *rubinetto* mixer tap
mischia *f* (*rissa*) scuffle; SP, (*folla*) scrum
mischiare ⟨1k⟩ mix; *carte* shuffle
mischiarsi mix
miscuglio *m* (*pl* -gli) mixture
miserabile wretched, miserable
miserevole pitiful
miseria *f* (*povertà*) poverty; (*infelicità*) misery; ***costare una miseria*** cost next to nothing; F ***porca miseria!*** damn and blast! F
misericordia *f* mercy; ***avere misericordia di qu*** have pity on s.o.
misero wretched
misfatto *m* misdeed
missaggio *m* (*pl* -ggi) → ***mixaggio***
missare → ***mixare***
missile *m* missile; ***missile a lunga gittata*** long-range missile
missionario *m* (*pl* -ri), **-a** *f* missionary
missione *f* mission
misterioso mysterious
mistero *m* mystery
mistico (*pl* -ci) mystic(al)
misto **1** *agg* mixed **2** *m* mixture; ***misto lana*** wool mix
misura *f* measurement; (*taglia*) size; (*provvedimento*), *fig* measure; MUS

bar; ***-e*** *pl* ***preventive*** preventive measures; ***unità*** *f* ***di misura*** unit of measurement; ***con misura*** in moderation; ***su misura*** made to measure
misurabile measurable, which can be measured
misurare ⟨1a⟩ measure; *vestito* try on; ***misurare le spese*** limit one's spending
misurarsi *in una gara* compete; ***misurarsi con*** compete with
misurato restrained
misurino *m* measuring spoon
mite *persona, inverno* mild; *condanna* light
mitigare ⟨1l & e⟩ lessen; *dolore* ease, lessen
mito *m* myth
mitologia *f* mythology
mitologico (*pl* -ci) mythological
mitra *m inv*, **mitragliatrice** *f* machine gun
mitt. *abbr* (= ***mittente***) from
mittente *m/f* sender
mixaggio *m* mixing
mixare ⟨1k⟩ mix
ml *abbr* (= ***millilitro***) ml (= millilitre)
M.M. *abbr* (= ***Marina Militare***) Italian navy
mm *abbr* (= ***millimetro***) mm (= millimetre)
mobile 1 *agg* mobile; *ripiano, pannello* removeable; ***squadra*** *f* ***mobile*** flying squad **2** *m* piece of furniture; ***-i*** *pl* furniture
mobilia *f* furnishings
mobilificio *m* furniture-making factory
mobilio *m* → ***mobilia***
mobilità *f* mobility
mobilitare ⟨1m⟩ mobilize
moca *m* mocha
mocassino *m* moccasin
moda *f* fashion; ***alla moda*** fashionable, in fashion; *vestirsi* fashionably; ***di moda*** fashionable, in fashion; ***fuori moda*** out of fashion, unfashionable
modalità *f inv* method
modella *f* model
modellare ⟨1b⟩ model
modello 1 *agg* model **2** *m* model; (*indossatore*) male model; *di vestito* style; (*formulario*) form
modem *m inv* INFOR modem
moderare ⟨1l & c⟩ moderate
moderato moderate
moderatore *m*, **-trice** *f* moderator
moderazione *f* moderation
modernizzare ⟨1a⟩ modernize
moderno modern
modestia *f* modesty
modesto modest; *prezzo* very reasonable
modico (*pl* -ci) reasonable
modifica *f* (*pl* -che) modification
modificare ⟨1m & d⟩ modify
modo *m* (*maniera*) way, manner; (*mezzo*) way; MUS mode; GRAM mood; ***modo di dire*** expression; ***modo di vedere*** way of looking at things; ***per modo di dire*** so to speak; ***se hai modo di passare da me*** if you could drop by; ***a modo mio*** in my own way; ***ad ogni modo*** anyway, anyhow; ***di modo che*** so that; ***in che modo?*** how?; ***in special modo*** especially
modulo *m* form; (*elemento*) module; ***modulo di domanda*** application form; ***modulo d'iscrizione*** registration form; ***modulo di versamento*** *banca* pay-in slip
mogano *m* mahogany
moglie *f* (*pl* -gli) wife
mola *f* grindstone; *di mulino* millstone
molare 1 *v/t* ⟨1c⟩ grind **2** *m* molar
mole *f* (*grandezza*) size
molecola *f* molecule
molestare ⟨1b⟩ bother, trouble; *sessualmente* sexually harass
molestia *f* bother, nuisance; ***molestia sessuale*** sexual harassment
molesto annoying
molla *f* spring; *fig* spur; ***-e*** *pl* tongs
mollare ⟨1c⟩ *corda* release, let go; F *schiaffo, ceffone* give; F *fidanzato* dump; ***mollare la presa*** let go
molle soft; (*bagnato*) wet
molleggiare ⟨1f⟩ be springy
molleggio *m* springs
molletta *f* hairgrip; *da bucato* clothes peg *or* pin
mollica *f* (*pl* -che) crumb
mollusco *m* (*pl* -chi) mollusc, *Am* mollusk
molo *m* pier
molotov *f inv* Molotov cocktail
molteplice multifaceted
moltiplicare ⟨1m & d⟩ **1** *v/t* multiply (***per*** by) **2** *v/i e* **moltiplicarsi** multiply
moltitudine *f* multitude, host
molto 1 *agg* a lot of; *con nomi plurali* a lot of, many **2** *avv* a lot; *con aggettivi* very; ***molto meglio*** much better, a lot better; ***da molto***for a long time; ***fra non molto*** before long
momentaneo momentary, temporary
momento *m* moment; ***dal momento che*** from the moment that; *causale* since; ***a -i*** sometimes, at moments; ***per il momento*** for the moment; ***del momento*** short-lived; ***sul momento*** at the time
monaca *f* (*pl* -che) nun
monaco *m* (*pl* -ci) monk

M

monarca *m* (*pl* -chi) monarch
monarchia *f* monarchy
monarchico (*pl* -ci) **1** *agg* monarchical **2** *m*, **-a** *f* monarchist
monastero *m* monastery; *di monache* convent
mondano society; (*terreno*) worldly; ***fare vita -a*** go out
mondare ⟨1a⟩ *frutta* peel
mondiale 1 *agg* world *attr*; *economia* world *attr*, global; *fenomeno, scala* worldwide; ***di fama mondiale*** world-famous **2** *m*: ***i -i*** *di calcio* the World Cup
mondo *m* world; ***giro*** *m* ***del mondo*** world tour, tour round the world; ***l'altro mondo*** the next world; ***il più bello del mondo*** the most beautiful in the world; ***divertirsi un mondo*** enjoy o.s. enormously *or* a lot
monello *m*, **-a** *f* imp, little devil
moneta *f* coin; (*valuta*) currency; (*denaro*) money; (*spiccioli*) change; ***moneta d'oro*** gold coin
monetario (*pl* -ri) monetary; ***Fondo*** *m* ***monetario internazionale*** International Monetary Fund
mongolfiera *m* hot-air balloon
monito *m* reprimand
monografia *f* monograph
monogramma *m* (*pl* -i) monogram
monolocale *m* bedsit
monologo *m* (*pl* -ghi) monolog(ue)
monopattino *m* child's scooter
monopolio *m* (*pl* -li) monopoly
monopolizzare ⟨1a⟩ monopolize
monoposto *m* single-seater
monotonia *f* monotony
monotono monotonous
monouso disposable, throwaway
montacarichi *m inv* hoist
montaggio *m* (*pl* -ggi) TECH assembly; *di film* editing
montagna *f* mountain; *fig* **-e** *pl* ***russe*** rollercoaster *sg*
montagnoso mountainous
montanaro *m*, **-a** *f person who lives in the mountains*
montare ⟨1a⟩ **1** *v/t* go up, climb; *cavallo* get onto, mount; TEC assemble; *film* edit; GASTR whip; ***montare la guardia*** mount guard **2** *v/i* go up; *venire* come up; ***montare in*** *macchina* get into; ***montare su*** *scala* climb; *pullman* get on
montarsi: ***montarsi la testa*** get a swollen head, get bigheaded
montatura *f di occhiali* frame; *di gioiello* mount; *fig* set-up F, frame-up F
monte *m* mountain; *fig* mountain, pile; ***a monte*** upstream; *fig* ***mandare a monte*** ruin, mess up F
montone *m* ram; *pelle, giacca* sheepskin
montuoso mountainous
monumento *m* monument
moquette *f inv* fitted carpet
mora *f* BOT *del gelso* mulberry; *del rovo* blackberry
morale 1 *agg* moral **2** *f* morals *pl*; *di favola ecc* moral **3** *m* morale; ***essere giù di morale*** be feeling a bit down; ***tirare su il morale a qu*** cheer s.o. up, lift s.o.'s spirits
moralista *m/f* (*mpl* -i) moralist
morbidezza *f* softness
morbido soft
morbillo *m* measles *sg*
morbo *m* disease
morboso *fig* unhealthy, unnatural; *curiosità* morbid
mordace *fig* biting, mordant
mordere ⟨3uu⟩ bite
morena *f* moraine
morfina *f* morphine
moribondo dying
morire ⟨4k⟩ die; *fig* ***morire di paura*** be scared to death; F ***muoio dalla voglia di una birra*** I could murder a pint F, I'm dying for a beer F
mormorare ⟨1l⟩ murmur; (*bisbigliare, lamentarsi*) mutter
mormorio *m* murmuring; (*brontolio*) muttering
morsetto *m* TEC clamp; EL terminal
morsicare ⟨1l, c & d⟩ bite
morso 1 *pp* → ***mordere*** **2** *m* bite; *di cibo* bit, mouthful; *per cavallo* bit; ***i -i*** *pl* ***della fame*** the pangs of hunger
mortale *ferita, malattia* fatal; *offesa, nemico* deadly; *uomo* mortal
mortalità *f* mortality
morte *f* death
mortificare ⟨1m & d⟩ mortify
mortificazione *f* mortification
morto 1 *pp* → ***morire*** **2** *agg* dead; ***stanco morto*** dead tired **3** *m*, **-a** *f* dead man; *donna* dead woman; ***i -i*** *pl* the dead
mortorio *m*: F ***essere un mortorio*** be deadly dull *or* boring
mortuario (*pl* -ri) death; ***camera*** *f* ***-a*** chapel
mosaico *m* (*pl* -ci) mosaic
mosca *f* (*pl* -che) fly; ***peso*** *m* ***mosca*** flyweight; ***mosca cieca*** blindman's buff; ***restare con un pugno di -e*** come away empty-handed
moscatello *m* muscatel
moscato 1 *agg* muscat; ***noce*** *f* ***-a*** nutmeg **2** *m* muscatel
moscerino *m* gnat, midge

M

moschea *f* mosque
moscio (*pl* -sci) thin, flimsy; *fig* limp, washed out
moscone *m* zo bluebottle; (*imbarcazione*) pedalo
mossa *f* movement; *fig e di judo, karate* move
mosso 1 *pp* → **muovere 2** *agg mare* rough
mostarda *f* mustard
mosto *m* must, *unfermented grape juice*
mostra *f* show; (*esposizione*) exhibition; *fig* **mettere in mostra** show off
mostrare ⟨1a⟩ show; (*indicare*) point out
mostrarsi appear
mostro *m* monster
mostruoso monstrous
motel *m inv* motel
motivare ⟨1a⟩ cause; *personale* motivate; (*spiegare*) explain, give reasons for
motivazione *f* (*spiegazione*) explanation; (*stimolo*) motivation
motivo *m* reason; MUS theme, motif; *su tessuto* pattern; **per quale motivo?** for what reason?, why?
moto[1] *m* movement; **fare moto** get some exercise; **mettere in moto** *motore* start (up); *fig* set in motion
moto[2] *f* (motor)bike
motocicletta *f* motorcycle
motociclista *m/f* (*mpl* -i) motorcyclist
motociclo *m* motorcycling
motore *m* engine; **motore Diesel** diesel engine; **motore a due tempi** two-stroke engine; **motore a quattro tempi** four-stroke engine; **motore a combustione** internal combustion engine; INFOR **motore di ricerca** search engine; **motore fuoribordo** outboard (motor *or* engine); **veicolo** *m* **a motore** motor vehicle; **accendere il motore** start (up) the engine, turn the key in the ignition; **fermare il motore** turn off the engine
motorino *m* moped; **motorino d'avviamento** starter
motorizzato motorized; F **sei motorizzato** have you got wheels? F
motoscafo *m* motorboat
motoscooter *m inv* (motor) scooter
motrice *f* FERR railcar
motteggio *m* (*pl* -ggi) joke
motto *m* motto
mouse *m inv* INFOR mouse
movente *m* motive
movimento *m* movement; (*vita*) life, bustle
mozione *m* motion; **mozione di fiducia** vote of confidence
mozzarella *f* mozzarella, *buffalo-milk cheese*
mozzicone *m* cigarette end, (cigarette) stub
mozzo *m* TEC hub
mq *abbr* (= **metro quadrato**) sq m (= square metre)
mucca *f* (*pl* -cche) cow
mucchio *m* (*pl* -cchi) pile, heap
muco *m* (*pl* -chi) mucus
mucosa *f* mucous membrane
muffa *f* mo(u)ld; **sapere di muffa** taste mo(u)ldy; **fare la muffa** go mo(u)ldy
mughetto *m* lily-of-the-valley
mugolare ⟨1l⟩ *di cane* whine; (*gemere*) moan, whine
mugolio *m* whining
mugugnare ⟨1a⟩ grumble
mulattiera *f* mule track
mulatto *m*, **-a** *f* mulatto
mulinello *m su canna da pesca* reel; *vortice d'acqua* eddy
mulino *m* mill; **mulino a vento** windmill
mulo *m* mule
multa *f* fine
multare ⟨1a⟩ fine
multicolore multicolo(u)red
multiculturale multicultural
multimediale multimedia
multinazionale *f/agg* multinational
multiplo multiple
multiuso multipurpose
mungere ⟨3d⟩ milk
municipale municipal; **consiglio** *m* **municipale** town council
municipio *m* (*pl* -pi) town council, municipality; *edificio* town hall
munire ⟨4d⟩: **munire di** supply with, provide with
munizioni *fpl* ammunition
muovere ⟨3ff⟩ **1** *v/t* move **2** *v/i partire* move off (**da** from); **muovere incontro a qu** move towards s.o.
muoversi move; F (*sbrigarsi*) get a move on F
muraglia *f* wall
murale 1 *agg* wall *attr* **2** *m* PITT mural
murare ⟨1a⟩ (*chiudere*) wall up
muratore *m* bricklayer
muratura *f* brickwork
murena *f* moray (eel)
muro *m* (*pl anche* le mura) wall; **muro del suono** sound barrier; *fig* **mi ha messo con le spalle al muro** he'd got my back against the wall; **le -a** *fpl* (city) walls
muschio *m* (*pl* -chi) BOT moss
muscolare muscular; **strappo** *m* **muscolare** strained muscle
muscolatura *f* muscles *pl*
muscolo *m* muscle

muscoloso muscular
museo *m* museum; ***museo etnologico*** folk museum; ***museo d'arte*** museum
museruola *f* muzzle
musica *f* music; ***musica da camera*** chamber music; ***musica leggera*** light music, easy-listening music
musicale musical; ***strumento*** *m* ***musicale*** musical instrument
musicassetta *f* (music) tape
musicista *m/f* (*mpl* -i) musician
muso *m di animale* muzzle; ***tenere il muso a qu*** be in a huff with s.o.
musone *m* sulker
musulmano 1 *agg* Muslim, Moslem **2** *m*, **-a** *f* Muslim, Moslem
muta *f di cani* pack; SP wetsuit
mutabile changeable
mutamento *m* change
mutande *fpl di donna* knickers; *di uomo* (under)pants
mutandine *fpl* knickers;***mutandine*** (***da bagno***) (swimming) trunks
mutare ⟨1a⟩ *v/t & v/i* change
mutevole → ***mutabile***
mutilare ⟨1l⟩ mutilate
mutilato *m* disabled ex-serviceman
mutilazione *f* mutilation
muto 1 *agg* dumb; (*silenzioso*) silent, dumb; ***essere muto dallo stupore*** be struck dumb with astonishment; ***film*** *m* ***muto*** silent movie **2** *m*, **-a** *f* mute
mutua *f fund that pays out sickness benefit*; ***medico*** *m* ***della mutua*** doctor recognized by the mutua
mutuato *m*, **-a** *f person entitled to sickness benefit*
mutuo 1 *agg* mutual **2** *m* mortgage

M

N

N *abbr* (= ***nord***) N (= north)
n. *abbr* (= ***numero***) No. (= number)
nacchere *fpl* castanets
nafta *f* naphtha
nano 1 *agg* dwarf **2** *m*, **-a** *f* dwarf
napoletano 1 *agg* Neapolitan **2** *m*, **-a** *f* Neapolitan
Napoli *f* Naples
nappa *f* tassel; (*pelle*) nappa (*type of soft leather*)
narciso *m* BOT narcissus
narcosi *f inv* narcosis
narcotico *m* (*pl* -ci) narcotic
narcotizzare ⟨1a⟩ drug
narice *f* nostril
narrare ⟨1a⟩ tell, narrate
narratore, -trice *f* narrator
nascere ⟨3gg⟩ be born; BOT come up; *fig* develop, grow up; *di sole* rise, come up; ***sono nato a Roma*** I was born in Rome; ***le è nata una figlia*** she's had a little girl
nascita *f* birth; ***fin dalla nascita*** from birth
nascondere ⟨3hh⟩ hide, conceal
nascondersi hide
nascondiglio *m* (*pl* -gli) hiding place
nascosto 1 *pp* → ***nascondere* 2** *avv*: ***di nascosto*** in secret; ***di nascosto a qu*** unbeknownst to s.o.
nasello *m* (*pesce*) hake
naso *m* nose
nastro *m* tape; *per capelli, di decorazione* ribbon; ***nastro adesivo*** adhesive tape, Sellotape®, *Am* Scotch tape®; ***nastro isolante*** insulating tape, *Am* friction tape; ***nastro magnetico*** magnetic tape
Natale *m* Christmas; ***vigilia*** *f* ***di Natale*** Christmas Eve; ***buon Natale!*** Merry Christmas!
natale *agg* of one's birth
natalità *f* birth rate, number of births
natalizio (*pl* -zi) Christmas
natante 1 *agg* floating **2** *m* boat
nativo 1 *agg* native **2** *m*, **-a** *f* native
NATO *abbr* (= ***Organizzazione del Trattato nord-atlantico***) NATO (= North Atlantic Treaty Organization
nato → ***nascere***
natura *f* nature; PITT ***natura morta*** still life; ***contro natura*** unnatural; ***essere paziente per natura*** be patient by nature, be naturally patient; ***secondo natura*** in harmony with nature
naturale natural; ***scienze*** *fpl* ***-i*** natural sciences
naturalezza *f* naturalness; ***con naturalezza*** naturally
naturalizzare ⟨1a⟩: ***è naturalizzato americano*** he's a naturalized American
naturalmente naturally, of course; *comportarsi* naturally
naufragare ⟨1l & e⟩ *di nave* be wrecked; *di persona* be shipwrecked; *fig* be ruined, come to grief
naufragio *m* (*pl* -gi) shipwreck; *fig* ruin; ***fare naufragio*** *di nave* be wrecked; *di persona* be shipwrecked
naufrago *m* (*pl* -ghi), **-a** *f* survivor of a shipwreck
nausea *f* nausea; ***avere la nausea*** feel sick, *Am* feel nauseous; ***dare la nausea a qu*** make s.o. feel sick, nauseate s.o. (*anche fig*)
nauseare ⟨1l⟩ nauseate (*anche fig*)
nautica *f* seamanship
nautico (*pl* -ci) nautical
navale naval; ***cantiere*** *m* ***navale*** shipyard
navata *f* ARCHI: ***navata centrale*** nave; ***navata laterale*** aisle
nave *f* ship; ***nave da carico*** cargo ship *or* vessel; ***nave passeggeri*** passenger ship; ***nave traghetto*** ferry
navetta 1 *agg inv*: ***bus*** *m* ***navetta*** shuttle bus **2** *f* shuttle; ***navetta spaziale*** space shuttle
navicella *f di astronave* nose cone
navigabile navigable
navigare ⟨1l & e⟩ sail; INFOR navigate
navigatore *m* navigator
navigazione *f* navigation
nazionale 1 *agg* national **2** *f* national team; ***la nazionale italiana*** the Italian team
nazionalismo *m* nationalism
nazionalista *m/f* (*mpl* -i) nationalist
nazionalistico (*pl* -ci) nationalistic
nazionalità *f inv* nationality
nazionalizzare ⟨1a⟩ nationalize
nazione *f* nation
N. B. *abbr* (= ***nota bene***) NB (= nota bene)
N.d.A. *abbr* (= ***nota dell'autore***) author's note
N.d.E. *abbr* (= ***nota dell'editore***) publisher's note
N.d.T. *abbr* (= ***nota del traduttore***) translator's note
NE *abbr* (= ***nord-est***) NE (= northeast)

ne 1 *pron* (*di lui*) about him; (*di lei*) about her; (*di loro*) about them; (*di ciò*) about it; ***ne sono contento*** I'm happy about it; ***ne ho abbastanza*** I have enough **2** *avv* from there; ***ne vengo adesso*** I've just come back from there
né: ***né ... né*** neither ... nor; ***non l'ho trovato né a casa né in ufficio*** I couldn't find him either at home or in the office
neanche neither; ***io non vado – neanch'io*** I'm not going – neither am I *or* me neither F; ***non l'ho neanche visto*** I didn't even see him; ***neanche per sogno!*** in your dreams!
nebbia *f* fog
nebbioso foggy
nebulosa *f* AST nebula
nebuloso *fig* vague, hazy
necessaire *m inv*: ***necessaire (da viaggio)*** beauty case
necessario (*pl* -ri) **1** *agg* necessary **2** *m*: ***il necessario per vivere*** the basic necessities *pl*
necessità *f inv* need; ***ho necessità di parlarti*** I need to talk to you; ***articolo*** *m* ***di prima necessità*** essential; ***in caso di necessità*** if necessary, if need be; ***fare qc senza necessità*** do sth needlessly; ***per necessità*** out of necessity
nefrite *f* MED nephritis
negare ⟨1e⟩ deny; (*rifiutare*) refuse
negativa *f* negative
negativo *m/agg* negative
negato: ***essere negato per qc*** be hopeless at sth
negazione *f* denial; GRAM negative
negli *prp* ***in*** and *art* ***gli***
negligente careless, negligent
negligenza *f* carelessness, negligence
negoziante *m/f* shopkeeper
negoziare ⟨1g & c⟩ **1** *v/t* negotiate **2** *v/i* negotiate, bargain; FIN ***negoziare in*** trade in, deal in
negoziato *m* negotiation; ***-i*** *pl* ***di pace*** peace negotiations
negoziazione *f* negotiation
negozio *m* (*pl* -zi) shop; (*affare*) deal; ***negozio di generi alimentari*** food shop; ***negozio specializzato*** specialist shop
negro 1 *agg* black **2** *m*, **-a** *f* black (man / woman)
nei, nel, nell', nella, nelle, nello *prp* ***in*** and *art* ***i, il, l', la, le, lo***
nemico (*pl* -ci) **1** *agg* enemy *attr* **2** *m*, **-a** *f* enemy
nemmeno neither; ***nemmeno io*** me neither; ***nemmeno per idea!*** don't even think about it!
neo *m* mole; *fig* flaw
neonato *m*, **-a** *f* infant, newborn baby
neppure not even; ***non ci vado – neppure io*** I'm not going – neither am I *or* me neither F
nero 1 *agg* black; *fig giornata, periodo* black; *umore* awful, filthy F **2** *m* black; *di seppia* ink **3** *m*, **-a** *f* black (man / woman)
nerofumo *m* lampblack
nervo *m* nerve; ***dare sui*** (*o* ***ai***) ***-i a qu*** get on s.o.'s nerves
nervosismo *m* nervousness
nervoso 1 *agg* nervous; (*irritabile*) edgy; (*asciutto*) sinewy; ***esaurimento*** *m* ***nervoso*** nervous breakdown **2** *m* F: ***il nervoso*** irritation; ***mi viene il nervoso*** I'm beginning to get really irritated, this is getting on my nerves
nespola *f* medlar
nespolo *m* medlar (tree)
nessuno 1 *agg* no; ***non chiamare in nessun caso*** don't call in any circumstances; ***c'è -a notizia?*** is there any news? **2** *pron* nobody, no one; ***hai visto nessuno?*** did you see anyone *or* anybody?
nettezza *f* cleanliness; ***nettezza urbana*** cleansing department
netto clean; (*chiaro*) clear; *reddito, peso* net; ***interrompere qu di netto*** break in on s.o.
netturbino *m*, **-a** *f* dustman
neurologia *f* neurology
neurologico neurological
neurologo *m* (*pl* -gi), **-a** *f* neurologist
neutrale neutral
neutralità *f* neutrality
neutralizzare ⟨1a⟩ neutralize
neutro neutral; GRAM neuter
neve *f* snow
nevicare ⟨1l & d⟩ snow
nevicata *f* snowfall
nevoso snowy
nevralgia *f* neuralgia
nevralgico (*pl* -ci) neuralgic; ***punto*** *m* ***nevralgico*** specially painful point; *fig* weak point
nevrosi *f* neurosis
nevrotico (*pl* -ci) **1** *agg* neurotic; F short-tempered, quick to fly off the handle F **2** *m*, **-a** *f* neurotic
nicchia *f* niche
nichel *m* nickel
nicotina *f* nicotine
nido *m* nest
niente 1 *pron m* nothing **2** *avv* nothing; ***non ho niente*** I don't have anything, I have nothing; ***lo fai tu? – niente affatto!*** are you going to do it? – no, I am not!; ***tu hai detto che ... – niente affatto!*** you

said that … - no, I did not!; ***non ho per niente fame*** I'm not at all hungry; ***non ho capito per niente*** I didn't understand a thing
niente(di)meno no less; ***niente(di)meno!*** that's incredible! you don't say!
ninfea *f* water-lily
nipote *m/f di zio* nephew; *donna, ragazza* niece *f*; *di nonno* grandson; *donna, ragazza* granddaughter *f*
nitidezza *f* clarity, clearness; FOT sharpness
nitido clear; FOT sharp
nitrire ⟨4d⟩ neigh
NO *abbr* (= ***nord-ovest***) NW (= northwest)
no no; ***no e poi no*** absolutely not!, no and that's final!; ***come no!*** of course!, naturally!; ***se no*** otherwise; ***dire di no*** say no; ***credo di no*** I don't think so
nobile 1 *agg* noble **2** *m/f* aristocrat
nobiltà *f* nobility
nocca *f* (*pl* -cche) knuckle
nocciola *f* hazelnut; ***color*** *m* ***nocciola*** hazel
nocciolina *f*: ***nocciolina*** (***americana***) peanut, ground-nut, monkey-nut
nocciolo[1] *m* (*albero*) hazel (tree)
nocciolo[2] *m di frutto* stone; *di questione* heart, kernel
noce 1 *m* walnut (tree); (*legno*) walnut **2** *f* walnut; ***noce di cocco*** coconut; ***noce moscata*** nutmeg
nocepesca *f* nectarine
nocivo harmful
nodo *m* knot; *fig* crux; FERR junction; ***avere un nodo in gola*** have a lump in one's throat
noi *pron soggetto* we; *con prp* us; ***a noi*** to us; ***con noi*** with us; ***senza di noi*** without us
noia *f* boredom; ***-e*** *pl* trouble *sg*; ***dar noia a qu*** annoy s.o.; ***venire a noia a qu*** start to bore s.o.
noioso boring; (*molesto*) annoying
noleggiare ⟨1f⟩ hire; MAR, AVIA charter
noleggio *m* hire; MAR, AVIA charter; ***noleggio*** (***di***) ***biciclette*** bike hire
nolo *m* hire; ***prendere a nolo*** hire; ***dare a nolo*** hire out
nome *m* name; GRAM noun; ***nome di battesimo*** Christian name; ***nome e cognome*** full name; ***conoscere qu di nome*** know s.o. by name; ***in nome di*** in the name of
nomignolo *m* nickname
nomina *f* appointment
nominare ⟨1l & c⟩ (*menzionare*) mention; *a un incarico* appoint (***a*** to)
non not; ***non ho fratelli*** I don't have any brothers, I have no brothers; ***non ancora*** not yet; ***non che io non voglia*** not that I don't want to; ***non cedibile*** not transferable, non-transferable
nonché let alone; (*e anche*) as well as
noncurante nonchalant, casual; ***noncurante di*** mindless of, heedless of
noncuranza *f* nonchalance, casualness
nondimeno nevertheless
nonno *m*, **-a** *f* grandfather; *donna* grandmother; ***-i*** *pl* grandparents
nonnulla *m inv* trifle
nono *m/agg* ninth
nonostante despite; ***ciò nonostante*** however
nonsenso *m* nonsense
non stop *agg inv* nonstop
nontiscordardimé *m inv* forget-me-not
non vedente *m/f* blind person
nord *m* north; ***mare*** *m* ***del nord*** North Sea; ***a***(***l***) ***nord di*** (to the) north of
nordest *m* north-east
nordico (*pl* -ci) northern; *lingue* Nordic
nordovest *m* north-west
norma *f* (*precetto*) rule, precept; TEC standard; ***-e per l'uso*** instructions (for use); ***a norma di legge*** up to standard; ***a norma di legge …*** complies with …
normale normal
normalità *f* normality
normalizzare ⟨1a⟩ normalize; (*uniformare*) standardize
norvegese *agg, m/f* Norwegian
Norvegia *f* Norway
nostalgia *f* nostalgia; ***avere nostalgia di casa*** feel homesick; ***avere nostalgia di qu*** miss s.o.
nostrale local, home *attr*
nostrano local, home *attr*
nostro 1 *agg* our; ***i -i genitori*** *pl* our parents; ***un nostro amico*** a friend of ours **2** *pron*: ***il nostro*** ours
nota *f* note; FIN bill; ***degno di nota*** noteworthy; ***nota spese*** expense account; ***prendere nota di qc*** make a note of sth; *situazione, comportamento* take note of sth
notaio *m* (*pl* -ai) notary (public)
notare ⟨1c⟩ (*osservare*) notice; (*annotare*) make a note of, note down; *con segni* mark; ***è da notare che*** please note that; ***ti faccio notare che*** I'll have you know that
notariato *m* notaryship
notarile notarial
notevole *degno di nota* notable, noteworthy; *grande* considerable, substantial
notificare ⟨1m & d⟩ serve (***a*** on)

N

notizia *f* piece *or* bit *or* item of news; ***avere -e di qu*** have news of s.o., hear from s.o.; ***-e*** *pl* ***sportive*** sports news; ***le ultime -e*** *pl* the latest news
notiziario *m* (*pl* -ri) RAD, TV news
noto well-known; ***rendere noto*** announce
notorietà *f* fame; *spreg* notoriety
notorio (*pl* -ri) well-known; *spreg* notorious
nottambulo *m*, **-a** *f* night owl
nottata *f* night; ***fare la nottata*** stay up all night
notte *f* night; ***di notte*** at night; ***buona notte!*** good night!; ***nel cuore della notte*** in the middle of the night
notturno night(-time) *attr*; *animale* nocturnal; ***ore*** *fpl* ***-e*** hours of darkness
novanta ninety
novantesimo *m/agg* ninetieth
nove nine
novecento 1 *agg* nine hundred **2** *m*: ***il Novecento*** the twentieth century
novella *f* short story
novembre *m* November
novità *f* *inv* novelty; (*notizia*) piece *or* item of news; ***essere una novità sul mercato*** be new on the market
novizio (*pl* -zi) **1** *agg* novice **2** *m*, **-a** *f* beginner, novice; REL novice
nozione *f* notion, idea; ***-i*** *pl* ***di base*** rudiments
nozionistico (*pl* -ci) superficial
nozze *fpl* wedding *sg*; ***nozze d'argento*** silver wedding (anniversary); ***sposarsi in seconde nozze*** get married for the second time, remarry
ns. *abbr* (= ***nostro***) our(s), *used in correspondence*
NU *abbr* (= ***Nazioni Unite***) UN (= United Nations); (= ***nettezza urbana***) cleansing department
nube *f* cloud
nubifragio *m* (*pl* -gi) cloudburst
nubile *donna* single, unmarried
nuca *f* (*pl* -che) nape of the neck
nucleare nuclear
nucleo *m* FIS nucleus (*anche fig*); ***nucleo urbano*** urban centre
nudismo *m* naturism, nudism
nudista *m/f* (*mpl* -i) naturist, nudist
nudità *f* nudity, nakedness
nudo 1 *agg* nude, naked; (*spoglio*) bare; ***a occhio nudo*** to the naked eye **2** *m* PITT nude
nulla 1 *avv* nothing; ***è solo una cosa da nulla*** it's nothing; ***per nulla*** for nothing; ***non per nulla*** not for nothing **2** *m* nothing; ***non ti ho portato un bel nulla*** I haven't brought you anything at all
nullaosta *m*: *fig* ***ottenere il nullaosta*** get the green light *or* go-ahead
nullo invalid; *gol* disallowed; *voto* spoiled; ***dichiarare nullo*** declare null and void
numerale *m* numeral
numerare ⟨1l⟩ number
numerato numbered
numerico (*pl* -ci) numerical
numero *m* number; *arabo, romano* numeral; *di scarpa* size; ***numero di casa*** home (tele)phone number; ***numero di targa*** registration number, *Am* license number; ***numero di telefono*** phone number; ***numero di volo*** flight number; TELEC ***sbagliare numero*** dial the wrong number; ***numero verde*** 0800 number, *Am* toll-free number; ***numero legale*** quorum; EDU ***numero chiuso*** restricted enrol(l)ment; ***sono venuti in gran numero*** lots of them came; F ***dare i -i*** talk nonsense
numeroso numerous; *famiglia, classe* large
nuocere ⟨3ii⟩: ***nuocere a*** harm; ***il fumo nuoce alla salute*** smoking is bad for you
nuora *f* daughter-in-law
nuotare ⟨1c⟩ swim
nuotata *f* swim
nuotatore *m*, **-trice** *f* swimmer
nuoto *m* swimming; ***attraversare la Manica a nuoto*** swim across the Channel; ***nuoto sincronizzato*** synchronized swimming
nuovamente again
nuovo 1 *agg* new; ***di nuovo*** again; ***essere nuovo in una città*** be new to a town; ***nuovo fiammante*** brand new **2** *m*: ***che c'è di nuovo?*** what's new?
nutriente nourishing
nutrimento *m* food
nutrire ⟨4d or 4a⟩ feed
nutrirsi: ***nutrirsi di*** live on
nutritivo nutritious
nutrizione *f* nutrition
nuvola *f* cloud; *fig* ***cadere dalle -e*** be taken aback
nuvoloso cloudy
nylon *m* nylon

O *abbr* (= ***ovest***) W (= west)
o *cong* or; ***o … o*** either … or
oasi *f inv* oasis
obbedire → ***ubbidire***
obbligare ⟨1l, c & e⟩: ***obbligare qu a fare qc*** oblige *or* compel s.o. to do sth
obbligarsi commit o.s. (***a fare*** to doing), undertake (***a fare*** to do)
obbligatorio (*pl* -ri) obligatory, compulsory
obbligazione *f* obligation; FIN bond
obbligo *m* (*pl* -ghi) obligation; ***d'obbligo*** obligatory
obesità *f* obesity
obeso obese
obiettare ⟨1b⟩ object, say (***a*** to)
obiettivo 1 *agg* objective **2** *m* aim, objective; FOT lens
obiettore *m*: ***obiettore di coscienza*** conscientious objector
obiezione *f* objection; ***fare obiezione di coscienza*** be a conscientious objector
obliquo oblique
obliterare ⟨1m⟩ *biglietto* punch
oblò *m inv* MAR porthole
oca *f* (*pl* -che) *f* goose; *fig* silly woman
occasionale casual; ***i rapporti*** *mpl* ***-i*** casual sex
occasionalmente occasionally
occasione *f* (*opportunità*) opportunity, chance; (*evento*) occasion; (*affare*) bargain; ***automobile*** *f* ***d'occasione*** second-hand *or* used car; ***cogliere l'occasione*** seize the opportunity, jump at the chance F; ***all'occasione*** if necessary; ***in occasione di*** on the occasion of
occhiaie *fpl* bags under the eyes
occhiali *mpl* glasses, specs *Br* F; ***occhiali da sole*** sunglasses
occhiata *f* look, glance; ***dare un'occhiata a*** have a look at, glance at; (*sorvegliare*) keep an eye on
occhiello *m* buttonhole
occhio *m* (*pl* -cchi) eye; ***a occhio nudo*** to the naked eye; ***a occhio e croce*** roughly; ***dare nell'occhio*** attract attention, be noticed; ***a quattr' -i*** in private
occidentale western; ***Europa*** *f* ***occidentale*** Western Europe
occidente *m* west; ***a occidente di*** (to the) west of
occorrente 1 *agg* necessary **2** *m* necessary materials *pl*
occorrenza *f*: ***all'occorrenza*** if necessary, if need be
occorrere ⟨3o⟩ be necessary; (*accadere*) occur; ***mi occorre*** I need; ***Le occorre altro?*** (do you need) anything else?; ***occorre programmare le cose*** we / you need to plan things; ***non occorre!*** there's no need!
occupare ⟨1l & c⟩ *spazio* take up, occupy; *tempo* occupy, fill; *posto* have, hold; *persona* keep busy; *di esercizio* occupy
occuparsi take care (***di*** of), deal (***di*** with); ***occupati degli affari tuoi!*** mind your own business!; ***occuparsi di qu*** look after s.o., take care of s.o.
occupato TELEC engaged, *Am* busy; *posto, appartamento* taken; *gabinetto* engaged; *persona* busy; *città, nazione* occupied
occupazione *f di città, paese* occupation; (*attività*) pastime; (*impiego*) job
oceano *m* ocean; ***Oceano Atlantico*** Atlantic Ocean; ***Oceano Pacifico*** Pacific Ocean
OCSE *abbr* (= ***Organizzazione per la Cooperazione e lo Sviluppo Economico***) OECD (= Organization for Economic Co-operation and Development)
oculista *m/f* (*pl* -i) ophthalmologist
od = ***o*** (*before a vowel*)
odiare ⟨1k⟩ hate, detest
odierno modern-day *attr*, of today, today's
odio *m* hatred
odioso hateful, odious
odontotecnico *m*, **-a** *f* dental technician
odorare ⟨1a⟩ **1** *v/t* smell **2** *v/i* smell (***di*** of)
odorato *m* sense of smell
odore *m* smell, odo(u)r; ***-i*** *pl* GASTR herbs
odoroso fragrant, sweet-smelling
offendere ⟨3c⟩ offend
offendersi take offence, *Am* offense
offensiva *f* offensive
offensivo offensive
offerente *m* bidder; ***maggior offerente*** highest bidder
offerta *f* offer; FIN supply; REL offering; (*dono*) donation; *in asta* bid; ***offerta d'impiego*** job offer; ***offerta pubblica di acquisto*** takeover bid; ***offerta speciale*** special offer
offesa *f* offence, *Am* offense
offeso *pp* → ***offendere***
officina *f* workshop; *per macchine* garage
offrire ⟨4f & c⟩ offer; ***ti offro da bere*** I'll

buy *or* stand F you a drink; ***posso offrirti qualcosa?*** can I get you anything?
oggettivo objective
oggetto *m* object; ***-i** pl **di valore*** valuables
oggi today; ***d'oggi*** of today, today's; ***da oggi a domani*** overnight; ***da oggi in poi*** from now on; ***oggi stesso*** today, this very day; ***oggi come oggi*** at the moment; ***oggi pomeriggio*** this afternoon
oggigiorno nowadays
ogni every; ***ogni tanto*** every so often; ***ogni sei giorni*** every six days; ***ad ogni modo*** anyway
Ognissanti *m inv* All Saints Day
ognuno everyone, everybody
Olanda *f* Holland
olandese **1** *agg m* Dutch **2** *m/f* Dutchman; *donna* Dutchwoman
oleandro *m* oleander
oleoso oily
olfatto *m* sense of smell
oliare ⟨1k⟩ oil
oliera *f type of cruet for oil and vinegar bottles*
Olimpiadi *fpl* Olympic Games, Olympics; ***Olimpiadi invernali*** Winter Olympics
olimpionico (*pl* -ci) **1** *agg* Olympic *attr* **2** *m*, **-a** *f* Olympic contestant
olio *m* (*pl* -li) oil; ***olio dei freni*** brake fluid; ***olio lubrificante*** lubricating oil, lube; ***olio per il cambio*** gearbox oil; ***olio extra-vergine d'oliva*** extra-virgin olive oil; ***olio solare*** suntan oil
oliva *f* olive
olivo *m* olive (tree)
olmo *m* elm (tree)
OLP *abbr* (= ***Organizzazione per la Liberazione della Palestina***) PLO (= Palestine Liberation Organization)
oltraggiare ⟨1f⟩ offend, outrage
oltraggio *m* (*pl* -ggi) offence, *Am* offense, outrage
oltre **1** *prp in spazio*, *tempo* after, past; (*più di*) over; ***vai oltre il semaforo*** go past the traffic lights; ***aspetto da oltre un'ora*** I've been waiting for more than *or* over an hour; ***oltre a*** apart from **2** *avv nello spazio* further; *nel tempo* longer
oltremare overseas
omaggio *m* (*pl* -ggi) homage; (*dono*) gift; ***copia (in) omaggio*** free *or* complimentary copy; ***omaggio pubblicitario*** (free) gift; ***essere in omaggio con*** come free with
ombelico *m* (*pl* -chi) navel
ombra *f* shadow; *zona non illuminata* shade; *fig* ***un'ombra di tristezza*** a touch of sadness; ***all'ombra*** in the shade
ombrello *m* umbrella
ombrellone *m* parasol; *sulla spiagggia* beach umbrella
ombretto *m* eye shadow
ombroso shady; *fig persona* touchy
omelette *f inv* omelette, *Am* omelet
omeopatia *f* homeopathy
omeopatico (*pl* -ci) **1** *agg* homeopathic **2** *m*, **-a** *f* homeopath
omero *m* humerus
omesso *pp* → ***omettere***
omettere ⟨3ee⟩ omit, leave out
omicida (*mpl* -di) **1** *agg* murderous **2** *m/f* murderer
omicidio *m* (*pl* -di) murder; ***omicidio colposo*** manslaughter; ***tentato omicidio*** attempted murder
omogeneizzato homogenized
omogeneo homogenous
omologare ⟨1m, c & e⟩ approve
omonimo **1** *agg* of the same name **2** *m* homonym **3** *m*, **-a** *f* namesake
omosessuale *agg*, *m/f* homosexual
omosessualità *f* homosexuality
OMS *abbr* (= ***Organizzazione Mondiale della Sanità***) WHO (= World Health Organization)
on. *abbr* (= ***onorevole***) Hon (= honourable)
oncologia *f* oncology
oncologo *m*, **-a** *f* oncologist
onda *f* wave; ***-e** pl **corte*** short wave; ***-e** pl **lunghe*** long wave; ***-e** pl **medie*** medium wave; RAD ***andare in onda*** go on the air
ondata *f* wave; ***ondata di caldo*** heat wave; ***ondata di freddo*** cold spell
ondeggiare ⟨1f⟩ *di barca* rock; *di bandiera* flutter
ondulato *capelli* wavy; *superficie* uneven; *cartone*, *lamiera* corrugated
onestà *f* honesty
onesto honest; *prezzo*, *critica* fair
onice *m* onyx
onnipotente omnipotent
onnipotenza *f* omnipotence
onnipresente ubiquitous
onnisciente omniscient
onniscienza *f* omniscience
onnivoro **1** *agg* omnivorous **2** *m*, **-a** *f* omnivore
onomastico *m* (*pl* -ci) name day
onorare ⟨1a⟩ be a credit to; ***onorare qu di qc*** hono(u)r s.o. with sth
onorario (*pl* -ri) **1** *agg* honorary **2** *m* fee
onorato respected, hono(u)red
onore *m* hono(u)r; ***in onore di*** in hono(u)r of
onorevole **1** *agg* hono(u)rable **2** ***Onorevole*** *m/f* Member of Parliament

onorificenza *f* hono(u)r
ONU *abbr* (= ***Organizzazione delle Nazioni Unite***) UN (= United Nations)
OPA *abbr* (= ***Offerta Pubblica di Acquisto*** (***di azioni di società***)) takeover bid
opacità *f di vetro* opaqueness; *di colore, foto* darkness
opaco (*pl* -chi) *vetro* opaque; *calze, rossetto* dark
opera *f* work; MUS opera; ***opera d'arte*** work of art; ***opera buona*** good deed; ***mettersi all'opera*** set to work
operaio (*pl* -ai) **1** *agg* working **2** *m*, **-a** *f* worker; ***operaio specializzato*** skilled worker
operare ⟨1l & c⟩ **1** *v/t cambiamento* make; *miracoli* work; MED operate on **2** *v/i* act
operativo operational; *ricerca* applied; *ordine* operative; ***piano*** *m* ***operativo*** plan of operations
operatore *m*, **-trice** *f* operator; *televisivo, cinematografico* cameraman; ***operatore di Borsa*** market trader; ***operatore sociale*** social worker; ***operatore turistico*** tour operator
operazione *f* operation; ***operazione finanziaria*** transaction
operetta *f* operetta
operoso hard-working, industrious
opinione *f* opinion; ***secondo la tua opinione*** in your opinion
oppio *m* opium
opporre ⟨3ll⟩ put forward, offer; *scuse, resistenza* offer
opporsi be opposed
opportunista *m/f* opportunist
opportunità *f inv* opportunity; *di decisione* timeliness; ***pari opportunità*** *pl* equal opportunities
opportuno suitable, appropriate; ***al momento opportuno*** at a suitable time, at the opportune moment
opposizione *f* opposition; POL ***all'opposizione*** in opposition
opposto 1 *pp* → ***opporre*** **2** *agg* opposite **3** *m* POL opposition
oppressione *f* oppression
oppressore *m* oppressor
opprimente oppressive
opprimere ⟨3r⟩ oppress
oppure or (else)
optare ⟨1c⟩: ***optare per*** choose, opt for
opuscolo *m* brochure
opzione *f* option
ora [1] *f* time; *unità di misura* hour; ***che ora è?, che -e sono?*** what time is it?, what's the time?; ***ora legale*** daylight saving time; ***ora locale*** local time; ***-e*** *pl* ***straordinarie*** overtime *sg*; ***ora di punta*** rush hour; TELEC peak time; ***di buon'ora*** early
ora [2] **1** *avv* now; ***sono rientrato or ora*** I've only just got back; ***per ora*** for the moment, for the time being; ***ora come ora*** at the moment; ***d'ora in poi*** from now on **2** *cong* now
orafo *m*, **-a** *f* goldsmith
orale 1 *agg* oral **2** *m* oral (exam)
orario (*pl* -ri) **1** *agg tariffa*, hourly; *velocità* per hour; RAD ***segnale orario*** time signal; ***in senso orario*** clockwise **2** *m di treno, bus, aeroplano* timetable, *Am* schedule; *di negozio* hours of business; *al lavoro* hours of work; ***orario di apertura / chiusura*** opening / closing time; ***orario di sportello*** banking hours; ***orario flessibile*** flexitime; ***in orario*** on time
orata *f* gilthead bream
oratore *m*, **-trice** *f* speaker
oratorio 1 *agg* (*pl* -ri) as an orator **2** *m* oratory
orbita *f*; AST orbit; ANAT eye-socket; ***in orbita*** in orbit
orchestra *f* orchestra; (*luogo*) (orchestra) pit
orchestrale 1 *agg* orchestral **2** *m/f* member of an orchestra
orchestrare ⟨1b⟩ orchestrate (*anche fig*)
orchestrazione *f* orchestration
orchidea *f* orchid
ordigno *m* device; ***ordigno esplosivo*** explosive device
ordinale *m/agg* ordinal
ordinamento *m* rules and regulations; ***ordinamento sociale*** rules governing society
ordinare ⟨1l⟩ order; *stanza* tidy up; MED prescribe; REL ordain
ordinario (*pl* -ri) ordinary; *mediocre* pretty average
ordinato tidy
ordinazione *f* order; REL ordination
ordine *m* order; ***mettere in ordine*** tidy up; ***ordine alfabetico*** alphabetical order; ***ordine di pagamento*** payment order; ***di prim'ordine*** first-rate, first-class; ***ordine del giorno*** agenda; ***l'ordine dei medici*** *the medical association*; ***ordine permanente*** FIN standing order
orecchino *m* earring
orecchio *m* (*pl* -cchi) ear; MUS ***a orecchio*** by ear
orecchioni *mpl* mumps *sg*
orefice *m/f* goldsmith
oreficeria *f* goldsmithing; (*gioielleria*) jewel(l)er's
orfano 1 *agg* orphan **2** *m*, **-a** *f* orphan
orfanotrofio *m* orphanage
organico (*pl* -ci) organic

organismo *m* organism; *fig* body
organista *m/f* (*mpl* -i) organist
organizzare ⟨1a⟩ organize
organizzazione *f* organization
organo *m* organ
orgasmo *m* orgasm
orgoglio *m* pride
orgoglioso proud
orientabile adjustable, swivelling
orientale 1 *agg* eastern; (*dell'Oriente*) Oriental; ***Europa*** *f* ***orientale*** Eastern Europe **2** *m/f* Oriental
orientamento *m*: ***senso*** *m* ***d'orientamento*** sense of direction; ***orientamento professionale*** professional advice
orientare ⟨1b⟩ *antenna*, *schermo* turn; ***orientare qu verso una carriera*** guide *or* steer s.o. towards a career
orientarsi get one's bearings
oriente *m* east; ***l'Oriente*** the Orient; ***Medio Oriente*** Middle East; ***Estremo Oriente*** Far East; ***ad oriente di*** (to the) east of
origano *m* oregano
originale *m/agg* original
originalità *f* originality
originalmente originally
originario (*pl* -ri) original; ***essere originario di*** come from, be a native of; *popolo* originate in
origine *f* origin; ***in origine*** originally
origliare ⟨1g⟩ eavesdrop
orizzontale horizontal
orizzonte *m* horizon
orlare ⟨1a⟩ hem
orlo *m* edge; *di vestito* hem
orma *f* footprint; *fig* ***seguire le -e di qu*** follow in s.o.'s footsteps
ormai by now
ormonale hormonal
ormone *m* hormone
ornamentale ornamental
ornamento *m* ornament
ornare ⟨1a⟩ decorate
ornitologia *f* ornithology
ornitologico ornithological
ornitologo *m*, **-a** *f* ornithologist
oro *m* gold; ***d'oro*** (made of) gold
orologeria *f* clock- and watch-making; *negozio* watchmaker's
orologiaio *m* (*pl* -ai) (clock- and) watch--maker
orologio *m* (*pl* -gi) clock; *portatile* watch; ***orologio a cucù*** cuckoo clock; ***orologio da polso*** wristwatch; ***orologio da tasca*** pocket watch; ***orologio subacqueo*** waterproof watch
oroscopo *m* horoscope
orrendo horrendous
orribile horrible
orrore *m* horror (***di*** of); ***avere qc in orrore*** hate sth
Orsa *f*: ***Orsa maggiore / minore*** Ursa Major / Minor, the Great / Little Bear
orsacchiotto *m* bear cub; (*giocattolo*) teddy (bear)
orso *m* bear; *fig* hermit; ***orso bianco*** polar bear
ortaggio *m* (*pl* -ggi) vegetable
ortica *f* (*pl* -che) nettle
orticaria *f* nettle rash
orticoltura *f* horticulture
orto *m* vegetable garden, kitchen garden; ***orto botanico*** botanical gardens
ortodossia *f* orthodoxy
ortodosso orthodox
ortografia *f* spelling
ortolano *m*, **-a** *f* market gardener
ortopedia *f* orthop(a)edics
ortopedico (*pl* -ci) **1** *agg* orthop(a)edic **2** *m*, **-a** *f* orthop(a)edist
orzaiolo *m* stye
orzata *f drink made from crushed almonds, sugar and water*
orzo *m* barley; ***orzo perlato*** pearl barley
osare ⟨1c⟩ dare
oscenità *f inv* obscenity
osceno obscene
oscillare ⟨1a⟩ *di corda* sway, swing; *di barca* rock; FIS oscillate; *fig di persona* waver, hesitate; *di prezzi* fluctuate
oscillazione *f di barca* rocking; ***oscillazione dei prezzi*** price fluctuations *pl*
oscurare ⟨1a⟩ obscure; *luce* block out
oscurità *f* darkness; *fig* obscurity; ***nell'oscurità*** in the dark
oscuro 1 *agg* dark; (*sconosciuto*) obscure **2** *m* dark; ***essere all'oscuro di qc*** be in the dark about sth
ospedale *m* hospital
ospitale hospitable
ospitalità *f* hospitality
ospitare ⟨1l & c⟩ put up; SP be at home to
ospite *m/f* guest; *chi ospita* host; *donna* hostess
ospizio *m* (*pl* -zi) old folk's home
ossatura *f* bone structure; *fig*, ARCHI structure
osseo bone *attr*
osservare ⟨1b⟩ (*guardare*) look at, observe; (*notare*) see, notice, observe; (*far notare*) point out, remark; (*seguire*) abide by, obey; ***osservare una dieta*** keep to a diet, follow a diet; ***le faccio osservare che*** I'll have you know that
osservatore *m*, **-trice** *f* observer, watcher
osservatorio *m* (*pl* -ri) AST observatory; ***osservatorio meteorologico*** *f* weather

station
osservazione *f* observation; (*affermazione*) remark, observation
ossessione *f* obsession (***di*** with); ***avere l'ossessione di*** be obsessed with
ossessivo obsessive
ossia or rather
ossidabile liable to tarnish
ossidare ⟨1l & c⟩ tarnish
ossidazione *f* tarnish
ossigeno *m* oxygen; ***tenda*** *f* ***ossigeno*** oxygen tent
osso *m* (ANAT *pl* le ossa) bone; ***di osso*** bone *attr*, made of bone; ***osso sacro*** sacrum; ***in carne e -a*** in the flesh
ossobuco *m* (*pl* ossibuchi) marrowbone; GASTR ossobuco, *stew made with knuckle of veal*
ostacolare ⟨1m⟩ hinder
ostacolo *m* obstacle; *nell'atletica* hurdle; *nell'equitazione* fence, jump; *fig* stumbling block, obstacle
ostaggio *m* (*pl* -ggi) hostage; ***prendere qu in ostaggio*** take s.o. hostage
ostello *m*: ***ostello della gioventù*** youth hostel
osteoporosi *f* osteoporosis
osteria *f* inn
ostetrica *f* obstetrician; (*levatrice*) midwife
ostetricia *f* obstetrics
ostetrico (*pl* -ci) **1** *agg* obstetric(al) **2** *m* obstetrician
ostia *f* Host
ostile hostile
ostilità *f inv* hostility
ostinarsi ⟨1a⟩ dig one's heels in; ***ostinarsi a fare qc*** persist in doing sth
ostinato obstinate
ostinazione *f* obstinacy
ostrica *f* (*pl* -che) oyster
ostruire ⟨4d⟩ block, obstruct
ostruito blocked
ostruzione *f* (*ostacolo*) obstruction, blockage
otite *f* ear infection
otorinolaringoiatra *m/f* (*pl* -i) ear, nose and throat specialist, ENT specialist
ottagonale octagonal
ottagono octagon
ottano *m* octane; ***numero*** *m* ***di -i*** octane rating *or* number
ottanta eighty
ottantesimo *m/agg* eightieth
ottava *f* MUS octave
ottavo *m/agg* eighth
ottenere ⟨2q⟩ get, obtain
ottengo → ***ottenere***
ottenibile obtainable
ottica *f* optics; *fig* viewpoint, point of view
ottico (*pl* -ci) **1** *agg* optical **2** *m* optician
ottimale optimum
ottimismo *m* optimism
ottimista *m/f* (*mpl* -i) optimist
ottimistico (*pl* -ci) optimistic
ottimizzare ⟨1a⟩ optimize
ottimo excellent, extremely good
otto 1 *agg* eight; ***oggi a otto*** a week today **2** *m* eight; ***otto volante*** big dipper
ottobre *m* October
ottocento 1 *agg* eight hundred **2** *m*: ***il Ottocento*** the nineteenth century
ottone *m* brass; MUS ***-i*** *pl* brass (instruments)
otturare ⟨1a⟩ block; *dente* fill
otturatore *m* FOT shutter
otturazione *f* blocking; *di dente* filling
ottuso obtuse
ovaia *f* ANAT ovary
ovale *m/agg* oval
ovazione *f* ovation
overdose *f inv* overdose
ovest *m* west
ovile *m* sheep pen; *fig* fold
ovini *mpl* sheep
ovunque everywhere
ovvero or rather; (*cioè*) that is
ovvio (*pl* -vvi) obvious
oziare ⟨1g⟩ laze around, be idle
ozio *m* (*pl* -zi) laziness, idleness
ozioso lazy, idle
ozono *m* ozone; ***buco*** *m* ***nell'ozono*** hole in the ozone layer; ***strato*** *m* ***d' ozono*** ozone layer

P

p. *abbr* (= ***pagina***) p (= page)
pacato calm, unhurried
pacchetto *m* package, small parcel; *di sigarette, biscotti* packet; ***pacchetto azionario*** block of shares; ***pacchetto turistico*** package holiday
pacchiano vulgar, in bad taste
pacco *m* (*pl* -cchi) parcel, package; ***pacco bomba*** parcel bomb; ***pacco postale*** parcel
pace *f* peace; ***lasciare in pace qu*** leave s.o. alone *or* in peace
pacifico (*pl* -ci) **1** *agg* peaceful **2** *m*: ***il Pacifico*** the Pacific
pacifismo *m* pacifism
pacifista *m/f* (*mpl* -i) pacifist
padano *agg* of the Po; ***pianura*** *f* **-a** Po Valley
padella *f di cucina* frying pan
padiglione *m* pavilion; ***padiglione auricolare*** auricle
Padova *f* Padua
padovano **1** *agg* Paduan **2** *m*, **-a** native of Padua
padre *m* father
padrino *m* godfather
padronanza *f* (*controllo*) control; (*conoscenza*) mastery; ***padronanza di sé*** self-control
padrone *m*, **-a** *f* boss; (*proprietario*) owner; *di cane* master; *donna* mistress; ***padrone di casa*** man / lady of the house; *per inquilino* landlord; *donna* landlady
paesaggio *m* (*pl* -ggi) scenery; PITT, GEOG landscape
paesaggista *m/f* PITT landscape painter *or* artist
paesano **1** *agg* country *attr* **2** *m*, **-a** *f* person from the country; *spreg* country bumpkin
paese *m* country; (*villaggio*) village; (*territorio*) region, area; ***i Paesi Bassi*** *pl* the Netherlands; ***paese d'origine*** country of origin; ***-i*** *pl* ***in via di sviluppo*** developing countries; ***paese membro*** member state
paga *f* (*pl* -ghe) pay
pagabile payable; ***pagabile a vista*** payable at sight
pagamento *m* payment; ***pagamento anticipato*** payment in advance; ***pagamento alla consegna*** cash on delivery; ***pagamento in contanti*** payment in cash, cash payment; ***pagamento a rate*** payment in insta(l)lments; ***altre sono a pagamento*** others you have to pay for
pagare ⟨1e⟩ **1** *v/t acquisto* pay for; *conto, fattura, debito* pay; ***ti pago qualcosa da bere*** I'll buy you *or* stand you a drink; ***gliela faccio pagare*** he'll pay for this **2** *v/i* pay; ***pagare anticipatamente*** pay in advance; ***pagare in contanti*** pay (in) cash; ***pagare a rate*** pay in instal(l)ments
pagella *f* report, *Am* report card
paghetta *f* pocket money
pagina *f* page; ***a pagina 10*** on page 10; ***-e gialle*** Yellow Pages; ***pagina elettronica*** screen page; ***pagina Web*** Web site
paglia *f* straw
paio *m* (*pl* le paia): ***un paio di*** *scarpe, guanti ecc* a pair of; ***un paio di volte*** a couple of times
pala *f* shovel; *di elica, turbina, remo* blade; ***pala d'altare*** altarpiece
palasport *m inv* indoor sports arena
palato *m* palate
palazzina *f* luxury home
palazzo *m* palace; (*edificio*) building; *con appartamenti* block of flats, *Am* apartment block; ***palazzo comunale*** town hall; ***palazzo di giustizia*** courthouse; ***palazzo dello sport*** indoor sports arena
palco *m* (*pl* -chi) dais; TEA stage
palcoscenico *m* (*pl* -ci) stage
palese obvious
Palestina *f* Palestine
palestinese *agg*, *m/f* Palestinian
palestra *f* gym
paletta *f* shovel; *per la spiaggia* spade; FERR signal(l)ing paddle
paletto *m* tent peg
palla *f* ball; ***palla di neve*** snowball; *fig* ***cogliere la palla al balzo*** jump at the chance
pallacanestro *f* basketball
pallanuoto *f* water polo
pallavolo *f* volley ball
palliativo *m* palliative
pallido pale
pallina *f di vetro* marble; ***pallina da golf*** golf ball; ***pallina da tennis*** tennis ball
pallino *m nel biliardo* cue ball; *nelle bocce* jack; *munizione* pellet; *fig* ***avere il pallino della pesca*** be mad about fishing, be fishing mad; ***a -i*** *pl* with spots, spotted
palloncino *m* balloon
pallone *m* ball; *calcio* football, soccer; AVIA balloon; ***pallone sonda*** weather

balloon
pallore *m* paleness, pallor
pallottola *f* pellet; *di pistola* bullet
palma *f* palm
palmo *m* hand's breadth; ANAT palm; ***a palmo a palmo*** gradually, bit by bit, inch by inch
palo *m* pole; *nel calcio* (goal)post
palombaro *m* diver
palpabile *fig* palpable
palpare ⟨1a⟩ feel; MED palpate
palpebra *f* eyelid
palpitare ⟨1l⟩ *del cuore* pound
palpitazione *f* palpitation
palpito *m del cuore* beat
paltò *m inv* overcoat, heavy coat
palude *f* marsh
paludoso marshy
palustre marshy; *pianta* marsh
panacea *f* panacea
panca *f* (*pl* -che) bench; *in chiesa* pew
pancarré *m* sliced loaf
pancetta *f* pancetta, *cured belly of pork*
panchetto *m* footstool
panchina *f* bench
pancia *f* (*pl* -ce) *m* stomach, belly F; *di animale* belly; ***mal m di pancia*** stomach-ache, belly-ache F; ***mettere su pancia*** develop a paunch
panciotto *m* waistcoat, *Am* vest
panciuto big-bellied
pancreas *m inv* pancreas
pane *m* bread; ***pane bianco*** white bread; ***pane nero*** (o ***di segala***) black *or* rye bread; ***pane integrale*** wholewheat bread
panetteria *f* bakery
panettiere *m/f* baker
panettone *m* panettone, *cake made with candied fruit*
panfilo *m* yacht; ***panfilo a motore*** motor yacht
pangrattato *m* breadcrumbs *pl*
panico (*pl* -ci) *m* panic
paniere *m* basket
panificio *m* (*pl* -ci) bakery
panino *m* roll; ***panino imbottito*** filled roll
paninoteca *f* sandwich shop
panna *f* cream; ***panna montata*** whipped cream
panne *f*: ***essere in panne*** have broken down, have had a breakdown
pannello *m* panel; ***pannello solare*** solar panel
panno *m pezzo di stoffa* cloth; ***-i*** *pl* clothes; ***se fossi nei tuoi -i*** if I were in your shoes
pannocchia *f* cob
pannolino *m* nappy; *per donne* sanitary towel
panorama *m* (*pl* -i) panorama; *fig* overview
panoramica *f* FOT panorama, panoramic view; *fig* overview
pantaloncini *mpl* shorts
pantaloni *mpl* trousers, *Am* pants
pantera *f* ZO panther
pantofola *f* slipper
pantomima *f* pantomime
paonazzo purple
papà *m inv* daddy, dad
papa *m* Pope
papale papal
paparazzo *m*: ***i paparazzoi*** *pl* the paparazzi
papavero *m* poppy
papera *f fig* (*errore*) slip of the tongue
papero *m*, **-a** *f* gosling
papillon *m inv* bow tie
papiro *m* papyrus
pappa *f* food
pappagallo *m* parrot
paprica *f* paprika
par. *abbr* (= ***paragrafo***) para (= paragraph)
parabrezza *m inv* windscreen, *Am* windshield
paracadutare ⟨1a⟩ parachute in
paracadute *m inv* parachute
paracadutista *m/f* (*mpl* -i) parachutist
paracarro *m* post
paradiso *m* heaven, paradise; ***paradiso terrestre*** heaven on earth, Eden
paradossale paradoxical
paradosso *m* paradox
parafango *m* (*pl* -ghi) mudguard, *Am* fender
parafulmine *m* lightning rod
paraggi *mpl* neighbo(u)rhood *sg*; ***nei paraggi di*** (somewhere) near
paragonabile comparable
paragonare ⟨1a⟩ compare
paragone *m* comparison; ***a paragone di*** compared with, in *or* by comparison with; ***senza paragone*** incomparable
paragrafo *m* paragraph
paralisi *f* paralysis
paralitico *m*, **-a** *f* (*mpl* -ci) paralyzed person
paralizzare ⟨1a⟩ paralyze
parallela *f* parallel line; ***-e*** *pl* parallel bars
parallelo *m/agg* parallel
paraluce *m inv* FOT lens hood
paralume *m* lampshade
parametro *m* parameter
paranoia *f* paranoia
paranoico (*pl* -ci) **1** *agg* paranoid **2** *m*, **-a** *f*

person with paranoia
paranormale *m/agg* paranormal
paraocchi *mpl* blinkers (*anche fig*)
parapendio *m* SP paragliding
parapetto *m* parapet; MAR rail
paraplegico **1** *agg* paraplegic **2** *m*, **-a** *f* paraplegic
parare ⟨1a⟩ **1** *v/t ornare* decorate; *proteggere* shelter; *occhi* shield; *scansare* parry **2** *v/i* save
parasole *m* parasol; FOT lens hood
parassita *m/f* (*mpl* -i) parasite
parata *f* parade
paraurti *m inv* bumper
parcheggiare ⟨1f⟩ *v/t & v/i* park
parcheggio *m* parking; *luogo* car park, *Am* parking lot; ***parcheggio sotteraneo*** underground car park; ***divieto di parcheggio*** no parking
parchimetro *m* parking meter
parco[1] (*pl* -chi) *agg*: ***essere parco nel mangiare*** eat sparingly
parco[2] *m* (*pl* -chi) park; ***parco dei divertimenti*** amusement park; ***parco naturale*** nature reserve; ***parco nazionale*** national park; ***parco macchine*** fleet (of vehicles)
parecchio **1** *agg* a lot of **2** *pron* ***parecchi*** *mpl*, ***parecchie*** *fpl* quite a few **3** *avv* quite a lot
pareggiare ⟨1f⟩ **1** *v/t* even up; (*uguagliare*) match, equal; *conto* balance **2** *v/i* SP draw
pareggio *m* (*pl* -ggi) SP draw
parente *m/f* relative
parentela *f* relationship; *parenti* relatives, relations
parentesi *f* bracket; (***detto***) ***fra parentesi*** by the by; *fig* ***aprire una parentesi*** digress slightly
parere **1** *v/i* ⟨2h⟩ seem, appear; ***pare che*** it seems that, it would appear that; ***che te ne pare?*** what do you think (of it)?; ***non ti pare?*** don't you think?; ***a quanto pare*** by all accounts; ***non mi pare vero!*** I can't believe it! **2** *m* opinion; ***a mio parere*** in my opinion, to my way of thinking
parete *f* wall; ***parete divisoria*** partition wall
pari **1** *agg* equal; *numero* even; ***essere di pari altezza*** be the same height; ***al pari di*** like; ***alla pari*** the same; SP ***finire alla pari*** end in a draw; ***senza pari*** unrivalled, unequalled **2** *m* (social) equal, peer; ***da pari a pari*** as an equal
Parigi Paris
parigino (of) Paris, Parisian
parità *f* equality, parity; ***parità di diritti*** equal rights; ***a parità di condizioni*** all things being equal
parka *m inv* parka
parlamentare **1** *agg* Parliamentary **2** *v/i* ⟨1a⟩ negotiate **3** *m/f* (*pl* -ri) Member of Parliament, MP
parlamento *m* Parliament; ***Parlamento europeo*** European Parliament
parlare ⟨1a⟩ talk, speak (***a qu*** to s.o.; ***di qc*** about sth); ***parlare del più e del meno*** make small talk; ***parla inglese?*** do you speak English?
parmigiano *m* (*formaggio*) Parmesan
parodia *f* parody
parola *f* word; (*facoltà*) speech; ***parola d'ordine*** password; **-e** *pl* ***crociate*** crossword (puzzle) *sg*; ***essere di parola*** keep one's word; ***chiedere la parola*** ask for the floor; ***parola per parola*** word for word
parolaccia *f* swear word
parquet *m* parquet floor
parrocchia *f* parish
parrochiale parish *attr*
parroco *m* (*pl* -ci) parish priest
parrucca *f* (*pl* -cche) wig
parrucchiere *m*, **-a** *f* hairdresser; ***parrucchiere per signora*** ladies' hairdresser
parte *f* part; (*porzione*) portion; (*lato*) side; DIR party; ***parte civile*** plaintiff; ***far parte di una società*** belong to a society, be a member of a society; ***prendere parte a*** take part in; ***a parte*** separate; ***scherzi a parte*** joking apart; ***mettere da parte qc*** put sth aside; ***dall'altra parte della strada*** on the other side of the street; ***da nessuna parte*** nowhere; ***da tutte le -i*** everywhere; ***da parte mia*** for my part, as far as I'm concerned; *regalo ecc* from me; ***in parte*** in part, partly; ***in gran parte*** largely
partecipante *m/f* participant
partecipare ⟨1m⟩ **1** *v/t* announce **2** *v/i*: ***partecipare a*** *gara* take part in; *dolore, gioia* share
partecipazione *f* (*intervento*) participation; (*annunzio*) announcement; FIN holding; ***partecipazione agli utili*** profit-sharing
parteggiare ⟨1f⟩: ***parteggiare per*** support
partenza *f* departure; SP start; INFOR ***partenza a freddo*** cold start; ***essere di partenza*** be just about to leave, be on the point of leaving; *fig* ***punto*** *m* ***di partenza*** starting point, point of departure
participio *m* (*pl* -pi) participle
particolare **1** *agg* particular; *segretario* private; ***in particolare*** in particular **2** *m* particular, detail

particolareggiato detailed
particolarità *f inv* special nature
partigiano *m*, **-a** *f* partisan
partire ⟨4a⟩ leave; AUTO, SP start; ***partire per*** leave for; ***partire per l'estero*** go abroad
partita *f* SP match; *di carte* game; *di merce* shipment; ***partita IVA*** VAT registration number; ***partita amichevole*** friendly (match); ***partita di calcio*** football match
partito *m* POL party; ***partito d'opposizione*** opposition (party); ***prendere partito*** make up one's mind; ***essere ridotto a mal partito*** be in a bad way
partitura *f* score
partner *m/f inv* partner
parto *m* birth; ***parto cesareo*** C(a)esarean (section)
partorire ⟨4d⟩ give birth to
part time 1 *agg* part-time **2** *avv* part time
parziale partial; *fig* biased
pascolo *m* pasture
Pasqua *f* Easter
pasquale Easter *attr*
Pasquetta *f* Easter Monday
passaggio *m* (*pl* -ggi) passage; *in macchina* lift, *Am* ride; *atto* passing; SP pass; ***essere di passaggio*** be passing through; ***passaggio pedonale*** pedestrian crossing, *Br* zebra crossing; ***passaggio a livello*** level crossing, *Am* grade crossing; ***dare un passaggio a qu*** give s.o. a lift (*Am* ride)
passante *m/f* passer-by
passaporto *m* passport; ***controllo*** *m* ***dei -i*** passport control
passare ⟨1a⟩ **1** *v/i* (*trasferirsi*) go (***in*** into); SP pass; *di legge* be passed, pass; *di tempo* go by *or* past, pass; ***passare attraverso delle difficoltà*** have a difficult time; ***passare da / per Milano*** go through Milan; ***passare dal panettiere*** drop by the baker's; ***mi è passato di mente*** it slipped my mind; ***passare di moda*** go out of fashion; ***passare inosservato*** go unnoticed; ***passare per imbecille*** be taken for a fool **2** *v/t confine* cross; (*sorpassare*) overstep; (*porgere*) pass; (*trascorrere*) spend; TELEC ***ti passo Claudio*** here's Claudio
passata *f* quick wipe; GASTR ***passata*** (***di pomodoro***) passata, *sieved tomato pulp*
passatempo *m* pastime, hobby
passato 1 *pp* → ***passare*** **2** *agg* past; *alimento* pureed; ***l'anno passato*** last year **3** *m* past; GASTR puree
passatoia *f* runner
passaverdura *m inv* food mill
passeggero 1 *agg* passing, short-lived **2** *m*, **-a** *f* passenger
passeggiare ⟨1f⟩ stroll, walk
passeggiata *f* stroll, walk; (*percorso*) walk
passeggino *m* pushchair
passeggio *m* (*pl* -ggi): ***andare a passeggio*** go for a walk
passe-partout *m inv* (*chiave*) master key
passerella *f* (foot)bridge; MAR gangway; AVIA ramp; *per sfilate* catwalk
passero *m* sparrow
passionale passionate; *delitto* of passion
passione *f* passion; REL Passion
passivo 1 *agg* passive; ***fumo*** *m* ***passivo*** second-hand smoke **2** *m* GRAM passive; FIN liabilities *pl*
passo *m* step; (*impronta*) footprint; *di libro* passage; GEOG pass; ***a passo di lumaca*** at a snail's pace; ***passo falso*** false move; AUTO ***avanzare a passo d'uomo*** crawl; ***passo carrabile*** driveway; ***fare due -i*** go for a walk *or* a stroll; *fig* ***fare il primo passo*** take the first step
pasta *f* paste; (*pastasciutta*) pasta; (*impasto*) dough; (*dolce*) pastry; ***pasta dentifricia*** toothpaste; ***pasta frolla*** shortcrust pastry; ***pasta sfoglia*** puff pastry
pastasciutta *f* pasta
pastella *f* batter
pastello *m* pastel
pasticca *f* (*pl* -cche) pastille
pasticceria *f* pastries *pl*, cakes *pl*; *negozio* cake shop
pasticciere *m*, **-a** *f* confectioner
pasticcino *m* pastry
pasticcio *m* (*pl* -cci) GASTR pie; *fig* mess; ***pasticcio di fegato d'oca*** pâté de foie gras; ***essere nei -i*** be in a mess
pastiglia *f* MED tablet, pill
pastina *f small pasta shapes for soup*
pasto *m* meal
pastorale 1 *m* bishop's staff, crozier **2** *f* REL pastoral letter
pastore 1 *m*, **-a** *f* shepherd **2** *m* REL: ***pastore*** (***evangelico***) pastor
pastorizzato pasteurized
patata *f* potato; ***-e*** *pl* ***fritte*** (French) fries, *Br* chips; ***-e*** *pl* ***lesse*** boiled potatoes; ***-e*** *pl* ***arrosto*** roast potatoes
patatine *fpl* crisps, *Am* chips; (*fritte*) French fries, *Br* chips
patente *f*: ***patente*** (***di guida***) driving licence, *Am* driver's license
paternalismo *m* paternalism
paternità *f* paternity
paterno paternal, fatherly
patetico (*pl* -ci) pathetic
patire ⟨4d⟩ **1** *v/i* suffer (***di*** from) **2** *v/t* suffer (from)

patito 1 *agg* of suffering **2** *m*, **-a** *f* fan; ***patito del jazz*** jazz fan
patologia *f* pathology
patologico pathological
patria *f* homeland
patrigno *m* stepfather
patrimonio *m* (*pl* -ni) estate; ***patrimonio artistico*** artistic heritage; ***patrimonio ereditario*** genetic inheritance; *fig* ***un patrimonio*** a fortune
patriota *m/f* (*mpl* -i) patriot
patriottico patriotic
patriottismo *m* patriotism
patrocinio *m* support, patronage
patrono *m*, **-a** *f* REL patron saint
patteggiare ⟨1f⟩ negotiate
pattinaggio *m* (*pl* -ggi) skating; ***pattinaggio artistico*** figure skating; ***pattinaggio su ghiaccio*** ice skating; ***pattinaggio a rotelle*** roller skating
pattinare ⟨1l⟩ skate; AUTO skid
pattinatore *m*, **-trice** *f* skater
pattino *m* SP skate; ***pattino a rotelle*** roller skate; ***pattino in linea*** roller blade
patto *m* pact; ***a patto che*** on condition that; ***venire a -i*** come to terms
pattuglia *f* patrol
pattumiera *f* dustbin
paura *f* fear; ***avere paura di*** be frightened of; ***mettere*** (*o* ***fare***) ***paura a qu*** frighten s.o.
pauroso fearful; *che fa paura* frightening
pausa *f* pause; *durante il lavoro* break
pavimento *m* floor
pavone *m* peacock
pazientare ⟨1b⟩ be patient
paziente *agg*, *m/f* patient
pazienza *f* patience
pazzesco (*pl* -chi) crazy
pazzia *f* madness
pazzo 1 *agg* mad, crazy; ***è pazzo da legare*** he's off his head; ***andare pazzo per*** be mad *or* crazy about **2** *m*, **-a** *f* madman; *donna* madwoman
p.c. *abbr* (= ***per conoscenza***) cc (= carbon copy)
p.e. *abbr* (= ***per esempio***) eg (= for example)
pecca *f* (*pl* -cche) fault
peccare ⟨1b & d⟩ sin; ***peccare di*** be guilty of
peccato *m* sin; (***che***) ***peccato !*** what a pity!
pecora *f* sheep
pecorino *m/agg*: (***formaggio*** *m*) ***pecorino*** pecorino (*ewe's milk cheese*)
peculiarità *f inv* special feature, peculiarity
pedaggio *m* (*pl* -ggi) toll
pedalare ⟨1a⟩ pedal
pedale *m* pedal; ***pedale dell'acceleratore*** accelerator
pedalò *m inv* pedalo
pedana *f* footrest; SP springboard
pedante pedantic
pedata *f* kick; (*impronta*) footprint
pediatra *m/f* (*mpl* -i) p(a)ediatrician
pediatria *f* p(a)ediatrics
pedicure 1 *m/f* chiropodist, *Am* podiatrist **2** *m inv* pedicure
pedina *f* draughtsman; *fig* cog in the wheel
pedinare ⟨1a⟩ shadow, follow
pedofilia *f* p(a)edophilia
pedofilo *m*, **-a** *f* p(a)edophile
pedonale pedestrian; ***zona*** *f* ***pedonale*** pedestrian precinct; ***strisce*** *fpl* ***-i*** pedestrian crossing *sg*
pedone *m* pedestrian
peggio 1 *avv* worse **2** *m*: ***il peggio è che*** the worst of it is that; ***avere la peggio*** get the worst of it; ***di male in peggio*** from bad to worse
peggioramento *m* deterioration, worsening
peggiorare ⟨1a⟩ **1** *v/t* make worse, worsen **2** *v/i* get worse, worsen
peggiore worse; *superlativo* worst; ***il peggiore*** the worst; ***nel peggiore dei casi*** if the worst comes to the worst
pegno *m d'amore*, *respetto ecc* token; ***dare qc in pegno*** pawn sth
pelare ⟨1a⟩ peel; *pollo* pluck; *fig* F fleece F
pellame *m* skin, pelt
pelle *f* skin; ***pelle scamosciata*** suede; ***avere la pelle d'oca*** have gooseflesh; *fig* ***essere pelle e ossa*** be nothing but skin and bones
pellegrinaggio *m* (*pl* -ggi) pilgrimage
pellegrino *m*, **-a** *f* pilgrim
pelletteria *f* leatherwork; **-e** *pl* leather goods
pellicano *m* pelican
pellicceria *f* furrier's
pelliccia *f* (*pl* -cce) fur; *cappotto* fur coat
pellicola *f* film; ***pellicola a colori*** colo(u)r film; ***pellicola trasparente*** cling film
pelo *m* hair, coat; (*pelliccia*) coat; ***a pelo dell'acqua*** on the surface of the water; *fig* ***per un pelo*** by the skin of one's teeth
peluria *f* down
pena *f* (*sofferenza*) pain, suffering; (*punizione*) punishment; ***pena di morte*** death penalty; ***stare in pena per qu*** worry about s.o.; ***vale la pena soffrire tanto?*** is it worth suffering so much?; ***non ne vale la pena*** it's not worth it; ***mi fa pena***

P

I feel sorry for him / her; ***a mala pena*** hardly
penale **1** *agg* criminal; *codice* penal **2** *f* penalty
penalista *m/f* (*mpl* -i) criminal lawyer
penalità *f inv* penalty
penalizzare ⟨1a⟩ penalize
pendenza *f* slope
pendere ⟨3a⟩ hang; (*essere inclinato*) slope; *fig* ***pendere dalle labbra di qu*** hang on s.o.'s every word
pendio *m* slope
pendolare *m/f* commuter
pendolo *m* pendulum
pene *m* penis
penetrante *dolore*, *freddo* piercing; *fig sguardo* piercing, penetrating; *analisi* penetrating
penetrare ⟨1l & b⟩ **1** *v/t* penetrate **2** *v/i*: ***penetrare in*** enter
penicillina *f* penicillin
peninsulare peninsular
penisola *f* peninsula; ***penisola iberica*** Iberian peninsula
penitenza *f* REL penance; *in gioco* forfeit
penitenziario *m* (*pl* -ri) prison
penna *f* pen; *di uccello* feather; ***penna biro®*** ballpoint (pen), biro; ***penna stilografica*** fountain pen; ***penna a feltro*** felt-tip (pen)
pennarello *m* felt-tip (pen)
pennello *m* brush
penombra *f* half-light
penoso painful
pensare ⟨1b⟩ think; ***pensare a*** think about *or* of; ***pensare a fare qc*** (*ricordarsi di*) remember to do sth; ***pensare di fare qc*** think of doing sth; ***che ne pensa?*** what do you think?; ***cosa stai pensando?*** what are you thinking about?; ***ci penso io*** I'll take care of it; ***senza pensare*** without thinking
pensiero *m* thought; (*preoccupazione*) worry; ***stare in pensiero*** be worried *or* anxious (***per*** about); ***un piccolo pensiero*** (*regalo*) a little something
pensieroso pensive
pensile hanging
pensilina *f* shelter
pensionamento *m* retirement
pensionato *m*, **-a** *f* pensioner, retired person; (*alloggio*) boarding house
pensione *f* pension; (*albergo*) boarding house; ***pensione completa*** full board; ***mezza pensione*** half board; ***andare in pensione*** retire
pensoso pensive, thoughtful
pentagono *m* pentagon
Pentecoste *f* Whitsun
pentimento *m* remorse
pentirsi ⟨4b or 4d⟩ *di peccato* repent; ***pentirsi di aver fatto qc*** be sorry for doing sth
pentola *f* pot, pan; ***pentola a pressione*** pressure cooker
penultimo last but one, penultimate
penuria *f* shortage (***di*** of); ***penuria di alloggi*** housing shortage
penzolare ⟨1l⟩ dangle
penzoloni dangling
peonia *f* peony
pepare ⟨1a⟩ pepper
pepato peppered
pepe *m* pepper
peperone *m* pepper
per **1** *prp* for; *mezzo* by; ***per qualche giorno*** for a few days; ***per questa ragione*** for that reason; ***per tutta la notte*** throughout the night; ***per iscritto*** in writing; ***per esempio*** for example; ***dieci per cento*** ten per cent; ***uno per uno*** one by one **2** *cong*: ***per fare qc*** (in order) to do sth; ***stare per*** be about to
pera *f* pear
peraltro however
perbene **1** *agg* respectable **2** *avv* properly
percento **1** *m* percentage **2** *avv* per cent
percentuale *f/agg* percentage
percepire ⟨4d⟩ perceive; (*riscuotere*) cash
percezione *f* perception
perché because; (*affinché*) so that; ***perché?*** why?
perciò so, therefore
percorrere ⟨3o⟩ *distanza* cover; *strada*, *fiume* travel along
percorso **1** *pp* → ***percorrere*** **2** *m* (*tragitto*) route
percossa *f* blow
percosso → ***percuotere***
percuotere ⟨3ff⟩ strike
percussione *f* percussion; MUS ***-i*** *pl* percussion
perdere ⟨3b & 3uu⟩ **1** *v/t* lose; *treno*, *occasione* miss; ***perdere tempo*** waste time; ***perdere di vista*** lose sight of; *fig* lose touch with **2** *v/i* lose; *di rubinetto*, *tubo* leak; ***a perdere*** disposable
perdersi get lost; ***perdersi d'animo*** lose heart
perdita *f* loss; *di gas*, *di acqua* leak; ***essere in perdita*** be making a loss; ***perdita di tempo*** waste of time; ***si estendeva a perdita d'occhio*** it stretched as far as the eye could see
perditempo **1** *m/f inv* idler **2** *m inv* waste of time
perdonare ⟨1a⟩ forgive
perdono *m* forgiveness; ***ti chiedo perdo-***

no please forgive me
perenne eternal, never-ending; BOT perennial
perfettamente perfectly
perfetto 1 *agg* perfect **2** *m* GRAM perfect (tense)
perfezionamento *m* adjustment, further improvement; ***corso*** *m* ***di perfezionamento*** further training
perfezionare ⟨1a⟩ perfect, further improve
perfezione *f* perfection; ***a perfezione*** to perfection, perfectly
perfezionista *m/f* perfectionist
perfido treacherous
perfino even
perforare ⟨1c⟩ drill through
perforazione *f* perforation
pergola *f* pergola
pergolato *m* pergola
pericolante on the verge of collapse
pericolo *m* danger; (*rischio*) risk; ***fuori pericolo*** out of danger; ***mettere in pericolo*** endanger, put at risk
pericoloso dangerous
periferia *f* periphery; *di città* outskirts
periferico (*pl* -ci) peripheral; *quartiere* outlying; INFOR ***unità*** *f* ***-a*** peripheral
perifrasi *f inv* circumlocution
periodico (*pl* -ci) **1** *agg* periodic **2** *m* periodical; ***periodico mensile*** monthly
periodo *m* period; ***periodo di transizione*** transition period
peripezia *f* misadventure
perito 1 *agg* expert **2** *m*, **-a** *f* expert
peritonite *f* peritonitis
perizia *f* skill, expertise; *esame* examination (by an expert)
perla *f* pearl; ***perla coltivata*** cultured pearl; ***collana*** *f* ***di -e*** pearl necklace
perlina *f* bead
perlomeno at least
perlopiù usually
perlustrare ⟨1a⟩ patrol
permaloso easily offended, touchy
permanente 1 *agg* permanent **2** *f* perm
permanenza *f* permanence; *in un luogo* stay
permesso 1 *pp* → ***permettere*** **2** *m* permission; (*breve licenza*) permit; MIL leave; ***permesso d'atterraggio*** permission to land; ***permesso di lavoro*** work permit; ***permesso di soggiorno*** residence permit; **(è)** ***permesso?*** may I?; ***con permesso*** excuse me
permettere ⟨3ee⟩ allow, permit
permettersi afford
pernacchia *f* F raspberry F
pernice *f* partridge
perno *m* pivot
pernottamento *m* night, overnight stay
pernottare ⟨1c⟩ spend the night, stay overnight
pero *m* pear (tree)
però but
perpendicolare *f/agg* perpendicular
perpetuo perpetual
perplesso perplexed
perquisire ⟨4d⟩ search
perquisizione *f* search; ***perquisizione personale*** body search; ***mandato*** *m* ***di perquisizione*** search warrant
persecuzione *f* persecution; ***mania*** *f* ***di persecuzione*** persecution complex
perseguitare ⟨1m⟩ persecute
perseguitato *m*: ***perseguitato politico*** person being persecuted for their political views
perseverante persevering
perseveranza *f* perseverance
perseverare ⟨1m & b⟩ persevere
persiana *f* shutter
persiano Persian
persino → ***perfino***
persistente persistent
persistenza *f* persistence
persistere ⟨3f⟩ persist
perso *pp* → ***perdere***
persona *f* person; ***a*** (*o* ***per***) ***persona*** a head, each; ***in persona, di persona*** in person, personally
personaggio *m* (*pl* -ggi) character; (*celebrità*) personality
personale 1 *agg* personal **2** *m* staff, personnel; AVIA ***personale di terra*** ground staff *or* crew; ***riduzione*** *f* ***del personale*** cuts in staff, personnel cutbacks
personalità *f inv* personality
personalmente personally
personificare ⟨1n & d⟩ personify
perspicace shrewd
perspicacia *f* shrewdness
persuadere ⟨2i⟩ convince; ***persuadere qu a fare qc*** persuade s.o. to do sth
persuasione *f* persuasion
persuasivo persuasive
persuaso *pp* → ***persuadere***
pertanto and so, therefore
pertinente relevant, pertinent
pertinenza *f* relevance, pertinence
perturbazione *f* disturbance; ***perturbazione atmosferica*** atmospheric disturbance
peruviano 1 *agg* Peruvian **2** *m*, **-a** *f* Peruvian
pervenire ⟨4p⟩ arrive; ***far pervenire*** send
perverso perverse
pervertito *m*, **-a** *f* pervert

P

p.es. *abbr* (= ***per esempio***) eg (= for example)
pesante heavy; *fig libro, film* boring
pesantezza *f* heaviness; ***pesantezza di stomaco*** indigestion
pesapersone *f inv* scales; *in negozio ecc* weighing machine
pesare ⟨1a⟩ **1** *v/t* weigh; *ingredienti* weigh out **2** *v/i* weigh
pesca[1] *f* (*pl* -che) (*frutto*) peach
pesca[2] *f* fishing; ***pesca con la lenza*** angling
pescare ⟨1d⟩ fish for; (*prendere*) catch; *fig* dig up; *ladro, svaligiatore ecc* catch (red-handed)
pescatore *m* fisherman
pesce *m* fish; ***pesce spada*** swordfish; ***pesce d'aprile*** April Fool; ASTR ***Pesci*** *pl* Pisces
pescecane *m* (*pl* pescicani) shark
peschereccio *m* (*pl* -cci) fishing boat
pescheria *f* fishmonger's
pescivendolo *m*, **-a** *f* fishmonger
pesco *m* (*pl* -chi) peach (tree)
pescoso with abundant supplies of fish
peso *m* weight; ***peso netto*** net weight; ***di nessun peso*** of no importance, unimportant; ***a peso*** by weight; *fig* ***non voglio essere un peso per te*** I don't want to be a burden to you
pessimismo *m* pessimism
pessimista **1** *agg* pessimistic **2** *m/f* (*mpl* -i) pessimist
pessimistico (*pl* -ci) pessimistic
pessimo very bad, terrible
pestaggio *m* (*pl* -ggi) F going-over F
pestare ⟨1a⟩ *carne, prezzemolo* pound; *con piede* step on; (*picchiare*) beat up
peste *f* plague; *persona* pest
pesticida *m* (*pl* -i) pesticide
pesto *m* pesto, *paste of basil, olive oil and pine nuts*
petalo *m* petal
petardo *m* banger
petizione *f* petition
peto *m* F fart F
petroliera *f* (oil) tanker
petrolifero oil *attr*
petrolio *m* oil, petroleum, ***petrolio greggio*** crude
pettegolare ⟨1m⟩ gossip
pettegolezzo *m* piece *or* item of gossip
pettegolo **1** *agg* gossipy **2** *m*, **-a** *f* gossip
pettinare ⟨1l & b⟩ comb
pettinarsi comb one's hair
pettinatura *f* hairstyle, hairdo
pettine *m* comb
pettirosso *m* robin
petto *m* chest; (*seno*) breast; ***petto di pollo*** chicken breast; ***a doppio petto*** double-breasted
pezza *f* cloth; (*toppa*) patch
pezzo *m* piece; *di motore* part; ***da / per un pezzo*** for a long time; ***due -i*** bikini; ***pezzo di ricambio*** spare (part); *fig* ***pezzo grosso*** big shot; ***andare in -i*** break into pieces; ***in -i da cento mila lire*** in denominations of one hundred thousand lira
ph *m* pH
piacente attractive
piacere **1** *v/i* ⟨2k⟩: ***le piace il vino?*** do you like wine?; ***non mi piace il cioccolato*** I don't like chocolate; ***non mi piacciono i tuoi amici*** I don't like your friends; ***mi piacerebbe saperlo*** I'd really like to know; ***faccio come mi pare e piace*** I do as I please **2** *m* pleasure; (*favore*) favo(u)r; ***piacere!*** pleased to meet you!; ***viaggio*** *m* ***di piacere*** pleasure trip; ***aver piacere di*** be delighted to; ***mi fa piacere*** I'm happy to; ***con piacere*** with pleasure; ***per piacere*** please; ***serviti a piacere*** take as much as you like
piacevole pleasant
piacimento *m*: ***a piacimento*** as much as you like
piaga *f* (*pl* -ghe) (*ferita*) wound; *fig* scourge; ***agitare il coltello nella piaga*** rub salt into the wound
pialla *f* plane
piallare ⟨1a⟩ plane
piana *f* plain
pianerottolo *m* landing
pianeta *m* planet
piangere ⟨3d⟩ **1** *v/i* cry, weep **2** *v/t* mourn
pianificare ⟨1m & d⟩ plan
pianificazione *f* planning
pianista *m/f* (*mpl* -i) pianist
piano **1** *agg* flat **2** *avv* (*adagio*) slowly; (*a voce bassa*) quietly, in a low voice **3** *m* plan; (*pianura*) plane; *di edificio* floor; MUS piano; ***piano rialzato*** mezzanine (floor); ***primo piano*** foreground; PHOT close-up
pianoforte *m* piano; ***pianoforte a coda*** grand piano
pianta *f* plant; *di città* map; *del piede* sole; ***pianta di appartamento*** house plant; ***pianta medicinale*** medicinal plant; ***di sana pianta*** from start to finish
piantare ⟨1a⟩ plant; *chiodo* hammer in; F ***piantala!*** cut that out! F; F ***piantare qu*** dump s.o. F; ***piantare grane*** make difficulties
piantarsi F: ***si sono piantati*** they've split up F
pianterreno *m* ground floor, *Am* first floor

P

pianto 1 *pp* → ***piangere*** **2** *m* crying, weeping; (*lacrime*) tears
pianura *f* plain
piastra *f* plate
piastrella *f* tile
piattaforma *f* platform; ***piattaforma di lancio*** launch pad
piattino *m* saucer
piatto 1 *agg* flat **2** *m* plate; GASTR dish; MUS ***-i*** *pl* cymbals; ***piatto forte*** main course; ***piatto fondo*** soup plate; ***piatto nazionale*** national dish; ***piatto piano*** flat plate; ***primo piatto*** first course; ***piatto del giorno*** day's special
piazza *f* square; COM market(place); *fig* ***fare piazza pulita*** make a clean sweep
piazzale *m* large square; *in autostrada* toll-booth area
piazzare ⟨1a⟩ place, put; (*vendere*) sell
piazzista *m/f* salesman; *donna* saleswoman
piazzola *f* small square; ***piazzola di sosta*** layby
piccante spicy, hot
picchiare ⟨1a⟩ beat
picchiata *f* AVIA nosedive
picchio *m* (*pl* -cchi); ZO woodpecker
piccionaia *f* TEA gods
piccione *m* pigeon; ***piccione viaggiatore*** carrier pigeon; ***prendere due -i con una fava*** kill two birds with one stone
picco *m* (*pl* -cchi) peak; MAR ***colare a picco*** sink
piccolezza *f* smallness; (*inezia*) trifle; *fig* pettiness, small-mindedness
piccolo 1 *agg* small, little; *di statura* short; *meschino* petty **2** *m*, **-a** *f* child; ***la gatta con i suoi -i*** the cat and her young; ***da piccolo*** as a child; ***fin da piccolo*** since I/he was a child
piccozza *f* ice ax(e)
picnic *m inv* picnic; ***fare un picnic*** have a picnic, picnic
pidocchio *m* (*pl* -cchi) louse
piede *m* foot; ***-i*** *pl* ***piatti*** flat feet; P cops P, flatfoots P; ***a -i*** on foot; ***su due -i*** suddenly; ***stare in -i*** stand; ***a piede libero*** at large; ***a -i nudi*** barefoot, with bare feet
piedistallo *m* pedestal
piega *f* (*pl* -ghe) wrinkle; *di pantaloni* crease; *di gonna* pleat; ***a -ghe*** *gonna* pleated
piegare ⟨1b & e⟩ **1** *v/t* bend; (*ripiegare*) fold **2** *v/i* bend
piegarsi bend; *fig* ***piegarsi a*** comply with
pieghevole *sedia* folding
Piemonte *m* Piedmont
piemontese *agg*, *m/f* Piedmontese
piena *f* flood; *a teatro* full house
pienezza *f* fullness
pieno 1 *agg* full (***di*** of); (*non cavo*) solid; ***in pieno giorno*** in broad daylight; ***in -a notte*** in the middle of the night **2** *m*: ***nel pieno dell'inverno*** in the depths of winter; AUTO ***fare il pieno*** fill up
pietà *f* pity (***di*** for); PITT pietà; ***avere pietà di qu*** take pity on s.o.; ***senza pietà*** pitiless, merciless
pietanza *f* dish
pietoso pitiful; (*compassionevole*) merciful
pietra *f* stone; ***pietra focaia*** flint; ***pietra preziosa*** precious stone; ***pietra miliare*** milestone (*anche fig*)
pietrina *f* flint
pietroso stony
pigiama *m* pyjamas *pl*, PJs F
pigiare ⟨1f⟩ crush
pigione *f* rent
pigliare ⟨1g⟩ catch; ***pigliare fiato*** catch one's breath
pigmeo *m*, **-a** *f* pygmy
pigna *f* pinecone
pignolo pedantic, nit-picking F
pignoramento *m* distraint
pignorare ⟨1a⟩ distrain
pigrizia *f* laziness
pigro lazy
PIL *abbr* (= ***prodotto interno lordo***) GDP (= gross domestic product)
pila *f* EL battery; (*catasta*) pile, heap
pilastro *m* pillar
pillola *f* pill; ***pillola (anticoncezionale)*** pill; ***prendere la pillola*** be on the pill
pilone *m* pier; EL pylon
pilota (*pl* -i) **1** *m/f* AVIA, MAR pilot; AUTO driver; ***pilota automatico*** automatic pilot **2** *agg* pilot *attr*
pilotare ⟨1c⟩ pilot; AUTO drive
pinacoteca *f* (*pl* -che) art gallery
pineta *f* pine forest
ping-pong *m* table tennis, ping-pong
pinna *f di pesce* fin; SP flipper
pino *m* pine
pinolo *m* pine nut
pinza *f* pliers *pl*; MED forceps *pl*
pinzare ⟨1a⟩ staple
pinzatrice *f* stapler
pinzette *fpl* tweezers
pio pious
pioggerella *f* drizzle
pioggia *f* (*pl* -gge) rain; ***pioggia acida*** acid rain
piombare ⟨1a⟩ **1** *v/t dente* fill **2** *v/i* fall; *precipitarsi* rush (***su*** at); ***mi è piombato in casa*** he dropped in unexpectedly
piombatura *f di dente* filling
piombino *m* sinker

piombo *m* lead; ***a piombo*** plumb; ***con / senza piombo*** *benzina* leaded / unleaded; *fig* ***andare con i piedi di piombo*** tread carefully
pioniere *m*, **-a** *f* pioneer
pioppo *m* poplar
piovere ⟨3kk⟩ rain; ***piove a dirotto*** it's raining cats and dogs
piovigginare ⟨1m⟩ drizzle
piovigginoso drizzly
piovoso rainy
piovra *f* octopus
pipa *f* pipe; ***fumare la pipa*** smoke a pipe
pipì *f* F pee F; F ***fare la pipì*** go for a pee F
pipistrello *m* bat
piramide *f* pyramid
pirata *m* (*pl* -i) pirate; ***pirata dell'aria*** hijacker; ***pirata della strada*** hit-and-run driver; (*guidatore spericolato*) roadhog
pirofila *f* oven-proof dish
piroscafo *m* steamer, steamship
pirotecnica *f* fireworks *pl*
pirotecnico (*pl* -ci) fireworks *attr*
pisciare ⟨1f⟩ P piss P
piscina *f* (swimming) pool; ***piscina coperta*** indoor pool
pisello *m* pea
pisolino *m* nap
pista *f di atletica* track; *di circo* ring; (*traccia*) trail; *di autostrada* toll-lane; ***pista d'atterraggio*** runway; ***pista da ballo*** dance floor; ***pista da sci*** ski slope; ***pista da sci da fondo*** cross country ski trail; ***pista ciclabile*** bike path
pistacchio *m* (*pl* -cchi) pistachio
pistola *f* pistol; ***pistola ad acqua*** water pistol; ***pistola automatica*** automatic (pistol); ***pistola a spruzzo*** spray gun
pistone *m* piston
pittore *m*, **-trice** *f* painter
pittoresco (*pl* -chi) picturesque
pittura *f* painting
pitturare ⟨1a⟩ paint
più 1 *avv* more (***di, che*** than); *superlativo* most; MAT plus; ***più grande*** bigger; ***il più grande*** the biggest; ***di più*** more; ***non più*** no more; *tempo* no longer; ***più o meno*** more or less; ***per di più*** what's more; ***mai più*** never again; ***al più presto*** as soon as possible; ***al più tardi*** at the latest **2** *agg* more; *superlativo* most; ***più volte*** several times **3** *m* most; MAT plus sign; ***per lo più*** mainly; ***i più, le più*** the majority
piuma *f* feather
piumaggio *m* plumage
piumino *m* down; *giacca* down jacket
piumone *m* Continental quilt, duvet
piuttosto rather
pizza *f* pizza
pizzaiolo *m* pizza maker
pizzeria *f* pizzeria, pizza parlo(u)r
pizzicare ⟨1l & d⟩ **1** *v/t braccio, persona* pinch; F *ladro* catch (redhanded), nick F **2** *v/i* pinch
pizzico *m* (*pl* -chi) pinch
pizzicotto *m* pinch
pizzo *m* (*merletto*) lace
placare ⟨1d⟩ placate; *dolore* ease
placca *f* (*pl* -cche) plate; (*targhetta*) plaque; ***placca dentaria*** plaque
placcare ⟨1d⟩ plate; *nel rugby* tackle; ***placcato d'oro*** gold-plated
placido placid
planare ⟨1a⟩ glide
planata *f*: ***fare una planata*** glide
plancia *f* bridge; (*passerella*) gangway, gangplank
planetario (*pl* -ri) **1** *agg* planetary **2** *m* planetarium
plasma *m* plasma; ***plasma sanguigno*** blood plasma
plasmabile malleable
plasmare ⟨1a⟩ mo(u)ld
plastica *f* plastic; MED plastic surgery; ***posate*** *fpl* ***di plastica*** plastic cutlery
plastico (*pl* -ci) **1** *agg* plastic **2** *m* ARCHI scale model; ***esplosivo*** *m* ***al plastico*** plastic bomb
plastilina® *f* Plasticine®
platano *m* plane (tree)
platea *f* TEA stalls
platino *m* platinum
plausibile plausible
plenilunio *m* (*pl* -ni) full moon
pletora *f fig* plethora
plettro *m* plectrum
pleurite *f* pleurisy
plico *m* (*pl* -chi) envelope; ***in plico separato*** under separate cover
plurale *m/agg* plural
pluripartitico (*pl* -ci) multiparty
plusvalore *m* capital gains; ***tassa*** *f* ***sul plusvalore*** capital gains tax
plutonio *m* plutonium
pneumatico (*pl* -ci) **1** *agg* pneumatic **2** *m* tyre, *Am* tire; ***-i da neve*** *pl* snow tyres (*Am* tires)
PNL *abbr* (= ***prodotto nazionale lordo***) GNP (= gross national product)
po': ***un po'*** a little (***di*** sth), a little bit (***di*** of); ***un bel po'*** quite a lot
poco (*pl* -chi) **1** *agg* little; *con nomi plurali* few **2** *avv* not much; *con aggettivi* not very, not greatly; ***senti un po'!*** just listen!; ***a poco a poco*** little by little, gradually; ***poco fa*** a little while ago; ***fra poco*** in a little while, soon; ***poco dopo*** a little while later, soon after; ***per poco*** cheap;

P

(*quasi*) almost, nearly
podere *m* farm
podio *m* (*pl* -di) podium, dais; MUS podium
podismo *m* walking
poesia *f* poetry; *componimento* poem
poeta *m* (*pl* -i), **-essa** *f* poet
poetico (*pl* -ci) poetic
poggiare ⟨1f & c⟩ lean; (*posare*) put, place
poggiarsi: ***poggiarsi a*** lean on
poggiatesta *m inv* head rest
poggio *m* (*pl* -ggi) mound
poi *avv* then; ***d'ora in poi*** from now on; ***questa poi!*** well I'm blowed!; ***dalle 6 in poi*** from 6 o'clock on(wards); ***prima o poi*** sooner or later
poiché since
poker *m* poker
polacco (*pl* -cchi) **1** *m/agg* Polish **2** *m*, **-a** *f* Pole
polare Polar; ***circolo*** *m* ***polare artico / antartico*** Arctic / Antarctic circle
polarizzare ⟨1a⟩ polarize
polemica *f* (*pl* -che) argument; ***fare -che*** argue
polemico (*pl* -ci) argumentative
polemizzare ⟨1a⟩ argue
polenta *f* polenta, *kind of porridge made from cornmeal*
policlinico *m* (*pl* -ci) general hospital
poliglotta **1** *agg* multilingual **2** *m/f* polyglot
poligono *m* MAT polygon; MIL ***poligono di tiro*** firing range
polio *f* F polio F
poliomielite *f* poliomyelitis
polipo *m* polyp
politica *f* politics; (*strategia*) policy; ***politica estera*** foreign policy; ***politica interna*** domestic policy; ***politica sanitaria*** health policy
politico (*pl* -ci) **1** *agg* political **2** *m*, **-a** *f* politician
polizia *f* police; ***polizia ferroviaria*** transport police; ***polizia stradale*** (o ***della strada***) traffic police, *Am* highway patrol; ***agente*** *m* ***di polizia*** police officer
poliziesco (*pl* -chi) police *attr*; ***romanzo*** *m* ***poliziesco*** detective story
poliziotto **1** *m* policeman **2** *agg*: ***donna*** *f* ***-a*** policewoman; ***cane*** *m* ***poliziotto*** police dog
polizza *f* policy; ***polizza di assicurazione*** insurance policy
pollame *m* poultry
pollice *m* thumb; *unità di misura* inch
polline *m* pollen
pollo *m* chicken; ***pollo arrosto*** roast chicken
polmonare pulmonary
polmone *m* lung
polmonite *f* pneumonia
polo[1] *m* GEOG pole; ***polo nord*** North Pole; ***polo sud*** South Pole
polo[2] **1** *m* SP polo **2** *f inv* polo shirt
Polonia *f* Poland
polpa *f* flesh; *di manzo, vitello* meat
polpaccio *m* (*pl* -cci) calf
polpastrello *m* fingertip
polpetta *f di carne* meatball
polpettone *m* meat loaf
polpo *m* octopus
polposo fleshy
polsino *m* cuff
polso *m* ANAT wrist; *di camicia* cuff; *pulsazione* pulse; ***tastare il polso a qu*** take s.o.'s pulse
poltiglia *f* mush
poltrire ⟨4d⟩ laze around
poltrona *f* armchair; TEA stall (seat)
poltrone *m*, **-a** *f* lazybones
polvere *f* dust; (*sostanza polverizzata*) powder; ***caffè*** *m* ***in polvere*** instant coffee; ***latte*** *m* ***in polvere*** powdered milk
polverina *f* powder
polverizzare ⟨1a⟩ crush, pulverize; *fig* pulverize
polveroso dusty
pomata *f* cream
pomello *m* cheek; *di porta* knob
pomeridiano afternoon *attr*; ***alle tre -e*** at three in the afternoon, at three pm
pomeriggio *m* (*pl* -ggi) afternoon; ***di pomeriggio, nel pomeriggio*** in the afternoon; ***domani pomeriggio*** tomorrow afternoon
pomice *f/agg*: (***pietra*** *f*) ***pomice*** pumice (stone)
pomo *m* knob; ***pomo d'Adamo*** Adam's apple
pomodoro *m* tomato
pompa[1] *f* pomp; ***impresa*** *f* ***di -e funebri*** undertaker's, *Am* mortician
pompa[2] *f* TEC pump
pompelmo *m* grapefruit
pompiere *m* firefighter, *Br* fireman; ***-i*** *pl* firefighters, *Br* fire brigade
pomposo pompous
ponderare ⟨1l & c⟩ ponder
ponderato *decisione*, *scelta* carefully considered; *persona* reflective
pone → ***porre***
ponente *m* west
pongo → ***porre***
ponte *m* bridge; ARCHI scaffolding; MAR deck; ***ponte girevole*** swing bridge; ***ponte sospeso*** suspension bridge; ***ponte ra-***

dio radio link; ***ponte aereo*** airlift; ***fare il ponte*** have a four-day weekend
pontefice *m* pontiff
ponteggio *m* scaffolding
ponticello *m* MUS bridge
pontificio (*pl* -ci) papal; ***Stato** m **pontificio*** Papal States *pl*
pontile *m* jetty
pop: ***musica** f **pop*** pop (music)
popolamento *m di città, Stato* population
popolare 1 *agg* popular; *quartiere* working-class; ***ballo** m **popolare*** folk dance **2** *v/t* ⟨1l⟩populate
popolarità *f* popularity
popolato populated; (*abitato*) inhabited; (*pieno*) crowded
popolazione *f* population
popolo *m* people
poppa *f* MAR stern
porcellana *f* porcelain, china
porcellino *m* piglet; ***porcellino d'India*** guinea-pig
porcheria *f* disgusting thing; *fig* ***una porcheria*** filth; ***mangiare -e*** eat junk food
porchetta *f suckling pig roasted whole in the oven*
porcile *m* pigsty, *Am* pigpen
porcino *m* cep
porco *m* (*pl* -chi) pig
porcospino *m* porcupine
porgere ⟨3d⟩ *mano, oggetto* hold out; *aiuto, saluto ecc* proffer
porno F **1** *agg* porn(o) F **2** *m* porn F
pornografia *f* pornography
pornografico (*pl* -ci) pornographic
poro *m* pore
poroso porous
porre ⟨3ll⟩ place, put; ***porre una domanda*** ask a question; ***poniamo che …*** let's suppose (that) …
porro *m* leek; MED wart
porta *f* door; ***porta scorrevole*** sliding door; ***a -e chiuse*** behind closed doors
portabagagli *m inv* luggage rack; AUTO roof rack
portacenere *m inv* ashtray
portachiavi *m inv* keyring
portacipria *m inv* powder compact
portafinestra *f* (*pl* portefinestre) French window
portafoglio *m* (*pl* -gli) wallet
portafortuna *m inv* good luck charm, talisman
portale *m* door
portalettere *m/f inv* → ***postino***
portamento *m* bearing
portamonete *m inv* purse
portaombrelli *m inv* umbrella stand
portapacchi *m inv di macchina* roof rack; *di bicicletta* carrier
portapenne *m inv* pencil case
portare ⟨1c⟩ (*trasportare*) carry; (*accompagnare*) take; (*avere adosso*) wear; (*condurre*) lead; ***portare via*** take away; ***mi ha portato un regalo*** he brought me a present; ***portale un regalo*** take her a present; ***portare in tavola*** serve; ***essere portato per qc / per fare qc*** have a gift for sth / for doing sth; ***portare fortuna*** be lucky; ***porta bene i propri anni*** he doesn't look his age
portasci *m inv* AUTO ski rack
portasigarette *m inv* cigarette case
portata *f* GASTR course; *di danni* extent; TEC *di camion* load capacity; *di cannocchiale* range; ***alla portata di*** *film, libro ecc* suitable for; ***a portata di mano*** within reach
portatile portable; ***computer** m **portatile*** portable (computer); ***radio** f **portatile*** portable (radio); ***telefono** m **portatile*** mobile (phone), *Am* cell(ular) phone; ***farmacia** f **portatile*** first-aid kit
portatore *m*, **-trice** *f* bearer; *di malattia* carrier
portauovo *m inv* eggcup
portavoce *m/f inv* spokesperson
portico *m* (*pl* -ci) porch; **-i** *pl* arcades
portiera *f* door
portiere *m* doorman; (*portinaio*) caretaker; SP goalkeeper, goalie F
portinaio *m* (*pl* -ai), **-a** *f* caretaker
portineria *f* caretaker's flat (*Am* apartment)
porto[1] *pp* → ***porgere***
porto[2] *m posta* postage; ***porto d'armi*** gun licence (*Am* license)
porto[3] *m* MAR port; ***porto d'imbarco*** port of embarkation
Portogallo *m* Portugal
portoghese *agg*, *m/f* Portuguese
portone *m* main entrance
porzione *f* share; GASTR portion
posa *f di cavi, tubi* laying; FOT exposure; FOT ***mettersi in posa*** pose
posacenere *m inv* ashtray
posare ⟨1c⟩ **1** *v/t* put, place **2** *v/i* (*stare in posa*) pose; ***posare su*** rest on; *fig* ***posare da intellettuale*** pose as an intellectual
posarsi alight
posate *fpl* cutlery *sg*
posato composed
positivo positive
posizione *f* position; ***posizione chiave*** key position
possedere ⟨2o⟩ own, possess
possedimento *m* possession
possessivo possessive

possesso *m* possession
possessore *m* owner, possessor
possiamo → ***potere***
possibile 1 *agg* possible; ***il più presto possibile*** as soon as possible **2** *m*: ***fare il possibile*** do everything one can, do one's best
possibilità *f inv* possibility; (*occasione*) opportunity, chance; ***possibilità di guadagno*** earning potential
possibilmente if possible, if I/you *etc* can
posso → ***potere***
posta *f* mail, *Br* post; (*ufficio postale*) post office; ***posta aerea*** airmail; ***per posta*** by post; ***a giro di posta*** by return of post; INFOR ***posta elettronica*** e-mail; ***fermo posta*** poste restante
postale postal; ***servizio*** *m* ***postale*** postal service; ***cartolina*** *f* ***postale*** postcard
postdatare ⟨1a⟩ postdate
posteggiare ⟨1f⟩ park
posteggio *m* (*pl* -ggi) carpark; ***posteggio dei taxi*** taxi rank
posteriore back *attr*, rear *attr*; (*successivo*) later; ***sedile*** *m* ***posteriore*** back seat
posticipare ⟨1m⟩ postpone
posticipato: ***pagamento*** *m* ***posticipato*** payment in arrears
postino *m*, **-a** *f* postman, *Am* mailman; *donna* postwoman, *Am* mailwoman
posto[1] *pp* → ***porre***; ***posto che*** supposing that
posto[2] *m* place; (*lavoro*) job, position; ***mettere a posto*** *stanza* tidy (up); ***la tua camera è a posto?*** is your room tidy?; ***posto macchina*** parking space; ***posto finestrino / corridoio*** window / aisle seat; ***ho trovato solo un posto in piedi*** I had to stand; ***posto a sedere*** seat; ***posto di guardia*** guard post; INFOR ***posto di lavoro*** workstation; ***posto di polizia*** police station; ***posto di pronto soccorso*** first aid post; ***posto di villeggiatura*** holiday resort; ***vado io al posto tuo*** I'll go in your place, I'll go instead of you; ***fuori posto*** out of place
postoperatorio (*pl* -ri) postoperative
postumo posthumous
potabile fit to drink; ***acqua*** *f* ***potabile*** drinking water
potare ⟨1a⟩ prune
potassio *m* potassium
potente powerful; (*efficace*) potent
potenza *f* power; ***potenza mondiale*** world power; ***potenza del motore*** engine power
potenziare ⟨1a⟩ strengthen
potere 1 *v/i* ⟨2l⟩ can, be able to; ***non posso andare*** I can't go; ***non ho potuto farlo*** I couldn't do it, I was unable to do it; ***posso fumare?*** do you mind if I smoke?; *formale* may I smoke?; ***può essere*** perhaps, maybe; ***può darsi*** perhaps, maybe **2** *m* power; ***potere d'acquisto*** purchasing power; ***essere al potere*** be in power
poveraccio *m* (*pl* -cci), **-a** *f* poor thing, poor creature
poveretto *m*, **poverino** *m* poor man
povero 1 *agg* poor **2** *m*, **-a** *f* poor man; *donna* poor woman; ***i -i*** *pl* the poor
povertà *f* poverty
pozzanghera *f* puddle
pozzo *m* well; ***pozzo petrolifero*** oil well
pp. *abbr* (= ***pagine***) pp (= pages)
p. p. *abbr* (= ***per procura***) pp (= for, on behalf of); (= ***pacco postale***) small parcel
PP.TT. *abbr* (= ***Poste e Telecomunicazioni***) Italian Post Office
pranzare ⟨1a⟩ *a mezzogiorno* have lunch; *la sera* have dinner
pranzo *m a mezzogiorno* lunch; *la sera* dinner
prassi *f inv* standard procedure
prataiolo *m* field mushroom
pratica *f* (*pl* -che) practice; (*esperienza*) experience; (*atto*) file; ***mettere in pratica*** put into practice; ***fare pratica*** gain experience, become more experienced; ***-che*** *pl* papers, documents; ***fare le -che necessarie per qc*** take the necessary steps for sth; ***fare le -che per*** *passaporto* gather together the necessary documentation for; ***in pratica*** in practice; ***avere pratica di qc*** have experience of sth
praticabile *sport* which can be practised; *strada* passable
praticantato *m* apprenticeship
praticare ⟨1l & d⟩ *virtù*, *pazienza* show; *professione*, *sport* practise; *locale* frequent; ***praticare molto sport*** do a lot of sport
pratico (*pl* -ci) practical; ***essere pratico di*** *conoscere bene* know a lot about
prato *m* meadow
preavviso *m* notice
precario (*pl* -ri) precarious
precauzione *f* caution; ***-i*** *pl* precautions
precedente 1 *agg* preceding **2** *m* precedent; ***avere dei -i penali*** have a record
precedenza *f* precedence; AUTO ***diritto*** *m* ***di precedenza*** right of way; ***avere la precedenza*** have precedence; AUTO have right of way; ***dare la precedenza*** give priority; AUTO give way
precedere ⟨3a⟩ precede

precipitare ⟨1m⟩ **1** *v/t* throw; *fig* rush **2** *v/i* fall, plunge
precipitarsi (*affrettarsi*) rush
precipitazione *f* (*fretta*) haste, hurry; ***-i*** *pl* ***atmosferiche*** atmospheric precipitation *sg*
precipitoso hasty
precipizio *m* (*pl* -zi) precipice
precisamente precisely
precisare ⟨1a⟩ specify
precisione *f* precision, accuracy; ***con precisione*** precisely
preciso accurate; *persona* precise; ***alle tre -e*** at three o'clock exactly *o* precisely, at three o'clock sharp
precoce precocious; *pianta* early
precotto *m* ready-made, pre-cooked
preda *f* prey; ***in preda alla disperazione*** in despair
predecessore *m*, **-a** *f* predecessor
predestinare ⟨1a⟩ predestine
predica *f* (*pl* -che) sermon
predicare ⟨1l, b & d⟩ preach
prediletto **1** *pp* → ***prediligere*** **2** *agg* favo(u)rite
predilezione *f* predilection
prediligere ⟨3u⟩ prefer
predire ⟨3t⟩ predict
predisporre ⟨3ll⟩ draw up in advance; ***predisporre a*** encourage, promote
predisposto *pp* → ***predisporre***
predominare ⟨1m & c⟩ predominate
predominio *m* (*pl* -ni) predominance
prefabbricato **1** *agg* prefabricated **2** *m* prefabricated building
prefazione *f* preface
preferenza *f* preference
preferenziale preferential
preferire ⟨4d⟩ prefer
preferito favo(u)rite
prefetto *m* prefect
prefettura *f* prefecture
prefiggersi ⟨3mm⟩ set o.s.
prefisso **1** *pp* → ***prefiggersi*** **2** *m* TELEC code
pregare ⟨1b & e⟩ beg (***di fare*** to do); *divinità* pray to; ***ti prego di ascoltarmi*** please listen to me; ***farsi pregare*** be coaxed; ***prego*** please; ***prego?*** I'm sorry (what did you say)?; ***grazie! – prego!*** thank you! - you're welcome! *or* not at all!
preghiera *f* request; REL prayer
pregiato *metallo*, *pietra* precious
pregio *m* (*qualità*) good point
pregiudicato *m*, **-a** *f* previous offender
pregiudizio *m* (*pl* -zi) prejudice
preg.mo *abbr* (= ***pregiatissimo***) *formal style of address used in correspondence*
pregustare ⟨1a⟩ look forward to
preistoria *f* prehistory
preistorico (*pl* -ci) prehistoric
prelato *m* REL prelate
prelavaggio *m* pre-wash
prelevamento *m di sangue*, *campione* taking; FIN withdrawal; ***prelevamento in contanti*** cash withdrawal
prelevare ⟨1b⟩ *sangue*, *campione* take; *denaro* withdraw
prelibato exquisite
prelievo *m* (*prelevamento*) taking; FIN withdrawal; ***prelievo del sangue*** blood sample
pre-maman **1** *agg* maternity *attr* **2** *m inv* maternity dress
prematrimoniale premarital
prematuro premature
premeditato premeditated
premere ⟨3a⟩ **1** *v/t* press **2** *v/i* press (***su*** on); ***mi preme che*** it is important to me that
premessa *f* introduction
premesso *pp* → ***premettere***
premettere ⟨3ee⟩ say first
premiare ⟨1k & b⟩ give an award *or* prize to; *onestà*, *coraggio* reward
premiato prize-winning, award-winning
premiazione *f* award ceremony
premio *m* (*pl* -mi) prize, award; FIN premium; ***premio Nobel per la pace*** Nobel peace prize; ***assegnare un premio*** award a prize
premura *f* (*fretta*) hurry, rush; ***essere pieno di -e nei confronti di qu*** be very attentive to s.o.; ***mettere premura a qu*** hurry s.o. along; ***non c'è premura*** there's no hurry *o* rush
premuroso attentive
prenatale prenatal
prendere ⟨3c⟩ **1** *v/t* take; *malattia*, *treno* catch; ***cosa prendi?*** what will you have?; ***prendere qu per un italiano*** take *or* mistake s.o. for an Italian; ***andare / venire a prendere qu*** fetch s.o.; ***prendere fuoco*** catch fire; ***prendere il sole*** sunbathe; ***prendere paura*** take fright, get frightened; AVIA ***prendere quota*** gain height; ***prendere in giro qu*** pull s.o.'s leg; ***prendersela*** get upset (***per*** about; ***con*** with); ***che ti prende?*** what's got into you? **2** *v/i* ***prendere a destra*** turn right
prendisole *m inv* sundress
prenotare ⟨1c⟩ book, reserve
prenotato booked, reserved
prenotazione *f* booking, reservation
preoccupare ⟨1m & c⟩ worry, preoccupy
preoccuparsi worry
preoccupato worried, preoccupied

preoccupazione *f* worry
preparare ⟨1a⟩ prepare
prepararsi get ready (***a*** to), prepare (***a*** to)
preparativi *mpl* preparations
preparato **1** *agg* ready, prepared **2** *m* preparation
preparazione *f* preparation
preposizione *f* preposition
prepotente domineering; *bisogno* pressing
prepotenza *f di persona* domineering nature; *di bisogno* pressing nature
presa *f* grip, hold; ***abbandonare la presa*** let go; ***fare una presa*** *presso corriere* call a courier; EL ***presa di corrente*** socket; *fig* ***presa di possesso*** conquest, capture; ***essere alle -e con qc*** be grappling with sth
presagio *m* (*pl* -gi) omen, sign
presalario *m* scholarship
presbite far-sighted, long-sighted
prescindere ⟨3v⟩: ***prescindere da*** have nothing to do with, not be connected with
prescritto *pp* → ***prescrivere***
prescrivere ⟨3tt⟩ prescribe
prescrizione *f* prescription
presentare ⟨1b⟩ *documenti, biglietto* show, present; *domanda* submit; *scuse* make; TEA present; (*contenere*) contain; (*far conoscere*) introduce (***a*** to)
presentarsi look; (*esporre*) show itself; *occasione* present itself, occur
presentatore *m*, **-trice** *f* presenter
presentazione *f* presentation; *di richiesta* submission; ***fare le -i*** make the introductions
presente **1** *agg* present; ***hai presente il negozio ... ?*** do you know the shop ... ? **2** *m* present; GRAM present (tense); ***i -i*** *pl* those present, those in attendance
presentimento *m* premonition
presenza *f* presence; ***alla*** (*o* ***in***) ***presenza di*** in the presence of; ***di bella presenza*** fine-looking
presepe *m*
presepio *m* (pl -pi) crèche
preservare ⟨1b⟩ protect, keep (***da*** from)
preservativo *m* condom
presidente *m/f* chairman; POL ***Presidente dello Stato*** President; ***presidente del Consiglio*** (***dei ministri***) Prime Minister
presidenza *f* chairmanship; POL presidency
preso *pp* → ***prendere***
pressappoco more or less
pressare ⟨1b⟩ crush; TEC press
pressione *f* pressure; ***pressione atmosferica*** atmospheric pressure; ***pressione delle gomme*** tyre pressure; ***pressione sanguigna*** blood pressure; *fig* ***far pressione su*** put pressure on, pressure
presso **1** *prp* (*vicino a*) near; *nella sede di* on the premises of; *posta* care of; ***vive presso i genitori*** he lives with his parents; ***lavoro presso la FIAT*** I work for Fiat **2** *m*: ***nei -i di*** in the vicinity of, in the neighbo(u)rhood of
pressoché almost
prestare ⟨1b⟩ lend; ***prestare ascolto / aiuto a qu*** listen to / help s.o.; ***prestare un servizio*** provide a service
prestarsi offer one's services; (*essere adatto*) lend itself (***a*** to)
prestatore *m di servizio* provider
prestazione *f* service
prestigio *m* prestige
prestito *m* loan; ***in prestito*** on loan; ***dare in prestito*** lend; ***prendere in prestito*** borrow
presto (*fra poco*) soon; (*in fretta*) quickly; (*di buon'ora*) early; ***a presto!*** see you soon!; ***far presto*** be quick
presumere ⟨3h⟩ presume
presuntuoso presumptuous
presunzione *f* presumption
prete *m* priest
pretendente *m/f* claimant
pretendere ⟨3c⟩ claim
pretensioso pretentious
pretesa *f* pretension; ***avanzare -e*** put forward claims; ***senza -e*** unpretentious
pretesto *m* pretext
pretore *m* magistrate
pretura *f* magistrates' court
prevalenza *f* prevalence; ***in prevalenza*** prevalently
prevalere ⟨2r⟩ prevail
prevedere ⟨2s⟩ foresee, predict; *tempo* forecast; *di legge* provide for
prevedibile predictable
prevendita *f* advance sale
prevenire ⟨4p⟩ *domanda, desiderio* anticipate; (*evitare*) prevent
preventivo **1** *agg* preventive **2** *m* estimate
prevenzione *f* prevention
previdente foresighted
previdenza *f* foresight; ***previdenza sociale*** social security, *Am* welfare
previsione *f* forecast; ***-i*** *pl* ***del tempo*** weather forecast *sg*
previsto *pp* → ***prevedere***
prezioso precious
prezzemolo *m* parsley
prezzo *m* price; ***prezzo di listino*** recommended retail price; ***prezzo promozionale*** special introductory price; ***aumento*** *m* ***del prezzo*** price increase; ***a buon***

prezzo cheap; *fig* ***a caro prezzo*** dearly; ***a metà prezzo*** half-price; ***a qualunque prezzo*** at any cost; ***prezzo netto*** net price
prigione *f* prison
prigionia *f* imprisonment
prigioniero *m*, **-a** *f* prisoner; ***fare prigioniero*** take prisoner
prima[1] *avv* before; (*in primo luogo*) first; ***prima di*** before; ***prima di fare qc*** before doing sth; ***prima o poi*** sooner or later; ***prima che*** before; ***quanto prima*** as soon as possible
prima[2] *f* FERR first class; AUTO first gear; TEA first night
primario (*pl* -ri) prime
primavera *f* spring
primaverile spring *attr*
primitivo primitive; (*iniziale*) original
primizia *f* early crop
primo 1 *agg* first; ***primo piano*** *m* first floor; ***in -a visione*** *film* just out **2** *m*, **-a** *f* first; ***ai -i del mese*** at the beginning of the month; ***sulle -e*** in the beginning, at first **3** *m* GASTR first course, starter
primogenito 1 *agg* first-born **2** *m*, **-a** *f* first-born
principale 1 *agg* main **2** *m* boss
principato *m* principality
principe *m* prince
principessa *f* princess
principiante *m/f* beginner
principio *m* (*pl* -pi) (*inizio*) start, beginning; (*norma*) principle; ***al principio*** at the start, in the beginning; ***da principio*** from the start *or* beginning *or* outset; ***per principio*** as a matter of principle; ***in linea di principio*** in theory
privare ⟨1a⟩ deprive (***di*** of)
privarsi deprive o.s. (***di*** of)
privatizzare ⟨1a⟩ privatize
privato 1 *agg* private; ***in privato*** in private **2** *m* private citizen
privazione *f* deprivation; (*sacrificio*) privation
privilegiare ⟨1f⟩ favo(u)r, prefer
privilegiato privileged
privilegio *m* (*pl* -gi) privilege
privo: ***privo di*** lacking in, devoid of; ***privo di sensi*** unconscious
pro 1 *m inv*: ***i pro e i contro*** the pros and cons; ***a che pro?*** what's the point *or* use? **2** *prp* for; ***pro capite*** per capita, each
probabile probable
probabilità *f inv* probability
problema *m* (*pl* -i) problem
problematico (*pl* -ci) problematic
proboscide *f* trunk
procedere ⟨3a⟩ carry on; *fig* (*agire*) proceed; DIR ***procedere contro qu*** take legal proceedings against s.o.
procedimento *m* process
procedura *f* procedure; DIR proceedings *pl*
processare ⟨1b⟩ try
processione *f* procession
processo *m* process; DIR trial; ***processo civile*** civil proceedings; ***processo di fabbricazione*** manufacturing process; ***processo verbale*** minutes *pl*; ***essere sotto processo*** be on trial
processuale DIR trial *attr*
procinto *m*: ***essere in procinto di*** be about to, be on the point of
proclamare ⟨1a⟩ proclaim
proclamazione *f* proclamation
procura *f* power of attorney; ***Procura di Stato*** public prosecutor's office; ***per procura*** by proxy
procurare ⟨1a⟩ (*causare*) cause; ***procurare qc a qu*** cause s.o. sth
procurarsi get hold of, obtain
procuratore *m*, **-trice** *f* person with power of attorney; DIR lawyer for the prosecution; ***procuratore generale*** Attorney General
prodigio *m* (*pl* -gi) prodigy
prodigioso tremendous, prodigious
prodotto 1 *pp* → ***produrre*** **2** *m* product; ***-i** pl **alimentari*** foodstuffs; ***-i** pl **farmaceutici*** pharmaceuticals; ***prodotto finito*** finished product; ***prodotto interno / nazionale lordo*** gross domestic / national product; ***-i** pl **di bellezza*** cosmetics
produco → ***produrre***
produrre ⟨3e⟩ produce; *danni* cause
produttività *f* productivity
produttivo productive
produttore *m*, **-trice** *f* producer
produzione *f* production; ***produzione giornaliera*** daily production *or* output; ***produzione in serie*** mass production
prof. *abbr* (= ***professore***) Prof. (= Professor)
profanare ⟨1a⟩ desecrate
profano 1 *agg* profane **2** *m fig*: ***sono un profano di*** I know nothing about
professionale *esperienza*, *impegno* professional; *scuola*, *corso* vocational
professione *f* profession; ***professione di fede*** profession of faith; ***calciatore** m **di professione*** professional footballer
professionista *m/f* (*mpl* -i) professional, pro F; ***libero professionista*** self-employed person
professore *m*, **-essa** *f* teacher; *d'università* professor
profeta *m* (*pl* -i) prophet

profezia *f* prophecy
proficuo profitable
profilassi *f inv* prophylaxis
profilattico (*pl* -ci) prophylactic
profilo *m* profile
profitto *m* (*vantaggio*) advantage; FIN ***conto -i e perdite*** profit and loss account
profondità *f inv* depth; FOT ***profondità di campo*** depth of field
profondo deep
prof. ssa *abbr* (= ***professoressa***) Prof. (= Professor)
profugo *m* (*pl* -ghi), **-a** *f* refugee
profumare ⟨1a⟩ perfume, scent
profumatamente: ***pagare profumatamente*** pay through the nose, pay a fortune
profumeria *f* perfume shop
profumo *m* perfume
progettare ⟨1b⟩ plan
progettazione *f* design
progetto *m* design; *di costruzione* project; ***progetto pilota*** pilot project; ***progetto di legge*** bill
prognosi *f inv* prognosis
programma *m* (*pl* -i) programme, *Am* program; INFOR program; ***programma applicativo*** application; ***programma di scrittura*** word processor; ***programma televisivo*** TV program(me); ***fuori programma*** unscheduled; ***avere in programma qualcosa*** have something planned
programmare ⟨1a⟩ plan; INFOR program
programmatore *m*, **-trice** *f* programmer
programmazione *f* programming; FIN ***programmazione economica*** economic planning; INFOR ***linguaggio*** *m* ***di programmazione*** programming language
progredire ⟨4d⟩ progress
progredito advanced
progressione *f* progression
progressivo progressive
progresso *m* progress; ***fare -i*** make progress
proibire ⟨4d⟩ ban, prohibit; ***proibire a qu di fare qc*** forbid s.o. to do sth
proibizione *f* ban
proiettare ⟨1b⟩ throw; *film* screen, show; *fig* project
proiettile *m* projectile
proiettore *m* projector; ***proiettore per diapositive*** slide projector
proiezione *f* projection; *di film* screening, showing
prole *f* children, offspring
proletario (*pl* -ri) **1** *agg* proletariat **2** *m* proletarian
pro loco *f inv* local tourist board
prologo *m* (*pl* -ghi) prolog(ue)
prolunga *f* EL extension cord
prolungamento *m* extension
prolungare ⟨1e⟩ *nel spazio* extend; *nel tempo* prolong, extend
prolungarsi *di strada* extend; *di riunione* go on, continue
promemoria *m inv* memo
promessa *f* promise
promesso *pp* → ***promettere***
promettente promising
promettere ⟨3ee⟩ promise; ***promettere bene*** look promising
promontorio *m* (*pl* -ri) promontory, headland
promosso *pp* → ***promuovere***
promozione *f* promotion; EDU year; ***promozione delle vendite*** sales promotion
promuovere ⟨3ff⟩ promote; EDU move up
pronipote *m/f di nonni* great-grandson; *donna, ragazza* great-granddaughter; *di zii* great-nephew; *donna, ragazza* great-niece
pronome *m* pronoun
prontezza *f* readiness, promptness; (*rapidità*) speediness, promptness; ***prontezza di spirito*** quick thinking
pronto (*preparato*) ready (***a fare qc*** to do sth; ***per qc*** for sth); (*rapido*) speedy, prompt; TELEC ***pronto!*** hello!; ***pagamento*** *m* ***-a cassa*** payment in cash, cash payment; ***pronto soccorso*** first aid; *in ospedale* accident and emergency, A&E; ***pronto per l'uso*** ready to use
pronuncia *f* pronunciation
pronunciare ⟨1f⟩ pronounce; ***non ha pronunciato una parola*** he didn't say a word
pronunciarsi give an opinion (***su*** on)
pronunciato *fig* definite, pronounced
propaganda *f* propaganda; POL ***propaganda elettorale*** electioneering
propagare ⟨1e⟩ propagate; *fig* spread
propagarsi spread (*anche fig*)
propano *m* propane
propenso inclined (***a fare qc*** to do sth)
propizio (*pl* -zi) suitable
propongo → ***proporre***
proponimento *m* resolution; ***fare proponimento di fare qc*** decide *or* make up one's mind to do sth
proporre ⟨3ll⟩ propose
proporsi stand (***come*** as); ***proporsi di fare qc*** intend to do sth
proporzionale proportional
proporzionato in proportion (***a*** to)
proporzione *f* proportion; ***in proporzione*** in proportion (***a, con*** to)
proposito *m* intention; ***a che proposito?***

P

what about?; ***a proposito*** by the way; ***a proposito di*** about, with reference to; ***di proposito*** deliberately, on purpose; ***capitare a proposito*** turn up at just the right moment
proposizione *f* GRAM sentence
proposta *f* proposal
proposto *pp* → ***proporre***
propriamente really
proprietà *f inv* property; *diritto* ownership; ***proprietà privata*** private property; ***essere di proprietà di qu*** belong to s.o., be s.o.'s property
proprietario *m* (pl -ri), **-a** *f* owner
proprio (*pl* -ri) **1** *agg* own; (*caratteristico*) typical; (*adatto*) proper; ***nome*** *m* ***proprio*** proper noun; ***amor*** *m* ***proprio*** pride; ***a -e spese*** at one's own expense **2** *avv* (*davvero*) really; ***è proprio lui che me l'ha chiesto*** he's the one who asked me!; ***è proprio impossibile*** that is quite impossible **3** *m* (*beni*) personal property; ***lavorare in proprio*** be self-employed
propulsione *f* propulsion
propulsore *m* propeller
prora *f* prow
proroga *f* (*pl* -ghe) postponement; (*prolungamento*) extension
prorogare ⟨1l, e & c⟩ (*rinviare*) postpone; (*prolungare*) extend
prosa *f* prose
prosciogliere ⟨3ss⟩ release; DIR acquit
prosciugare ⟨1e⟩ drain; *di sole* dry up
prosciutto *m* ham, prosciutto; ***prosciutto cotto*** cooked ham; ***prosciutto crudo*** *salted air-dried ham*
proseguimento *m* continuation
proseguire ⟨4a⟩ **1** *v/t* continue **2** *v/i* continue, carry on, go on
prosperare ⟨1l & c⟩ prosper
prosperità *f* prosperity
prospero prosperous
prospettiva *f* perspective; (*panorama*) view; *fig* point of view; ***senza -e*** without prospects
prospetto *m disegno* elevation; (*facciata*) facade; (*tabella*) table; ***prospetto pubblicitario*** brochure
prossimamente shortly, soon
prossimità *f inv* proximity; ***in prossimità di*** near, close to
prossimo **1** *agg* close; ***la -a volta*** the next time; ***il lavoro è prossimo alla fine*** the work is nearly finished **2** *m* fellow human being, neighbo(u)r
prostituta *f* prostitute
prostituzione *f* prostitution
protagonista *m/f* (*mpl* -i) protagonist
proteggere ⟨3cc⟩ protect (***da*** from)
proteico protein *attr*
proteina *f* protein
protesi *f inv* prosthesis; ***protesi dentaria*** false teeth, dentures
protesta *f* protest
protestante *agg*, *m/f* Protestant
protestare ⟨1b⟩ *v/t & v/i* protest
protettivo protective
protetto *pp* → ***proteggere***
protezione *f* protection; ***protezione degli animali*** prevention of cruelty to animals; ***protezione dell'ambiente*** environmental protection, protection of the environment; ***protezione del paesaggio*** nature conservation; ***protezione delle acque*** prevention of water pollution; INFOR ***protezione dati*** data protection
protocollare **1** *agg* official **2** *v/t* ⟨1c⟩ register
protocollo *m* protocol; (*registro*) register; TEC standard; ***foglio*** *m* ***protocollo*** foolscap; ***mettere a protocollo*** register
prototipo *m* prototype
prova *f* (*esame*) test; (*tentativo*) attempt; (*testimonianza*) proof; *di abito* fitting; SP heat; TEA ***-e*** *pl* rehearsal *sg*; TEA ***-e*** *pl* ***generali*** dress rehearsal *sg*; ***prova di laboratorio*** lab test; ***banco*** *m* ***di prova*** test bench; ***a prova di bomba*** bombproof; ***salvo prova contraria*** unless otherwise stated; ***per insufficienza di -e*** for lack of evidence; ***mettere alla prova*** put to the test
provare ⟨1c⟩ test, try out; *vestito* try (on); (*dimostrare*) prove; TEA rehearse; ***provare a fare qc*** try to do sth
provato proven; *fig* marked (***da*** by)
provengo → ***provenire***
provenienza *f* origin
provenire ⟨4p⟩ come (***da*** from)
proventi *mpl* income *sg*
proverbio *m* (*pl* -i) proverb
provetta *f* test-tube; ***bambino*** *m* ***in provetta*** test-tube baby
provincia *f* (*pl* -ce) province
provinciale **1** *agg* provincial; ***strada*** *f* ***provinciale*** *B road* **2** *m/f* provincial **3** *f B road*
provino *m* screen-test; (*campione*) sample
provocante provocative
provocare ⟨1l, c & d⟩ (*causare*) cause; (*sfidare*) provoke; *invidia* arouse
provvedere ⟨2s⟩ **1** *v/t* provide (***di*** with) **2** *v/i*: ***provvedere a*** take care of
provvedimento *m* measure; ***provvedimento d'urgenza*** emergency measure
provvidenza *f* providence
provvigione *f* commission

provvisorio (*pl* -ri) provisional
provvista *f*: ***fare -e*** go (food) shopping; ***far provvista di qc*** stock up on sth
provvisto 1 *pp* → ***provvedere* 2** *agg*: ***essere provvisto di*** be provided with, have; ***essere ben provvisto di qc*** have lots of sth
prozio *m*, **-a** *f* great-uncle; *donna* great--aunt
prua *f* prow
prudente careful, cautious
prudenza *f* care, caution
prudere ⟨3a⟩: ***mi prude la mano*** my hand itches
prugna *f* plum; ***prugna secca*** prune
prurito *m* itch
P.S. *abbr* (= ***Pubblica Sicurezza***) police; (= ***post scriptum***) PS (= post scriptum)
pseudo ... pseudo ...
pseudonimo *m* pseudonym
psicanalisi *f* psychoanalysis
psicanalista *m/f* (*mpl* -i) psychoanalyst
psiche *f* psyche
psichiatra *m/f* (*mpl* -i) psychiatrist
psichiatria *f* psychiatry
psichiatrico (*pl* -ci) psychiatric
psicologia *f* psychology
psicologico (*pl* -ci) psychological
psicologo *m* (*pl* -gi), **-a** *f* psychologist
psicosi *f inv* psychosis
psicoterapia *f* psychotherapy
P.T.P. *abbr* (= ***Posto Telefonico Pubblico***) public telephone
pubblicare ⟨1l & d⟩ publish
pubblicazione *f* publication; ***-i*** *pl* ***matrimoniali*** banns
pubblicità *f inv* publicity, advertising; *annuncio* ad(vert); ***pubblicità televisiva*** TV ad, *Br* commercial; ***fare pubblicità a*** *evento* publicize; *prodotto* advertise
pubblicitario 1 *agg* advertising **2** *m*, **-a** *f* publicist
pubblico (*pl* -ci) **1** *agg* public; ***Pubblico Ministero*** public prosecutor **2** *m* public; (*spettatori*) audience; ***in pubblico*** in public
pube *m* pubis
pubertà *f* puberty
pudore *m* modesty; ***senza pudore*** shameless, immodest
pugilato *m* boxing; ***incontro*** *m* ***di pugilato*** boxing match
pugile *m* boxer
pugnalare ⟨1a⟩ stab
pugnale *m* dagger
pugno *m* fist; (*colpo*) punch; *quantità* handful; ***di proprio pugno*** in one's own handwriting; ***avere in pugno qc*** have sth in one's grasp; ***ti ho in pugno*** I've got you now; ***rimanere con un pugno di mosche*** come away empty-handed; ***fare a -i*** fight, come to blows
pulce *f* flea
pulcino *m* chick
puledro *m*, **-a** *f* colt; (*femmina*) filly
pulire ⟨4d⟩ clean
pulito clean; *fig* cleaned-out
pulitura *f* cleaning; ***pulitura a secco*** dry cleaning
pulizia *f* cleanliness; *fig* ***pulizia etnica*** ethnic cleansing; ***donna*** *f* ***delle -e*** cleaner; ***fare le -e*** do the cleaning, clean
pullman *m inv* coach, bus
pullover *m inv* pullover
pullulare ⟨1l⟩: ***pullulare di*** be teeming or swarming with
pulpito *m* pulpit
pulsante *m* button
pulsare ⟨1a⟩ pulsate
pulsazione *f* pulsation
pulviscolo *m* dust
pungente *foglia* prickly; *freddo*, *parola* sharp, biting; *desiderio* sharp
pungere ⟨3d⟩ prick; *di ape*, *vespa* sting; ***pungere qu sul vivo*** cut s.o. to the quick
pungiglione *m* sting
punibile punishable (***con*** by)
punire ⟨4d⟩ punish
punizione *f* punishment; SP ***calcio*** *m* ***di punizione*** free kick
punta *f di spillo*, *coltello* point; *di dita*, *lingua* tip; GEOG peak; *fig* touch, trace; ***ora*** *f* ***di punta*** peak hour; ***ce l'ho sulla punta della lingua*** it's on the tip of my tongue; *fig* ***prendere qc di punta*** face sth head--on
puntare ⟨1a⟩ **1** *v/t* pin (***su*** to); (*dirigere*) point (***verso*** at); (*scommettere*) bet (***su*** on); *fig* ***puntare i piedi*** dig one's heels in **2** *v/i* (*dirigersi*) head (***verso*** for); ***puntare a*** *successo*, *matrimonio* aspire to, set one's sights on; ***puntare su*** *contare su* rely on
puntata *f* instal(l)ment; (*scommessa*) bet
punteggiatura *f* punctuation
punteggio *m* score
puntiglio *m* obstinacy
puntiglioso punctilious
puntina *f*; *di giradischi* stylus; ***puntina*** (***da disegno***) drawing pin, *Am* thumbtack
puntino *m* dot; ***a puntino*** perfectly, to perfection
punto 1 *pp* → ***pungere* 2** *m* point; MED, (*maglia*) stitch; ***punto di vista*** point of view, viewpoint; ***punto cardinale*** point of the compass; ***punto culminante*** height; ***punto di partenza*** starting point;

P

punto di fusione melting point; ***fino a che punto sei arrivato?*** how far have you got?; ***alle dieci in punto*** at ten o'clock exactly *or* on the dot; ***punto fermo*** full stop, *Am* period; ***due -i*** colon; ***punto e virgola*** semi-colon; ***punto esclamativo*** exclamation mark; ***punto interrogativo*** question mark; ***di punto in bianco*** suddenly, without warning; ***essere sul punto di fare qc*** be on the point of doing sth, be about to do sth

puntuale punctual

puntualità *f* punctuality

puntualizzare ⟨1a⟩ make clear

puntura *f di ape, vespa* sting; *di ago* prick; MED injection; ***puntura d'insetto*** insect bite

punzecchiare ⟨1k⟩ prick; *fig* (*provocare*) tease

può, **puoi** → ***potere***

pupazzo *m* puppet; ***pupazzo di neve*** snowman

pupilla *f* pupil

purché provided, on condition that

pure 1 *cong* even if; (*tuttavia*) (and) yet **2** *avv* too, as well; ***pur di*** in order to; ***venga pure avanti!*** do come in!

purè *m* puree

purezza *f* purity

purga *f* (*pl* -ghe) purge

purgante *m* laxative

puro pure

purtroppo unfortunately

pus *m* pus

pustola *f* pimple

putrefare ⟨3aa⟩ rot, putrefy

puttana *f* P whore P

puzza *f* stink

puzzare ⟨1a⟩ stink (***di*** of)

puzzo *m* stink

puzzola *f* ZO polecat

puzzolente stinking, evil-smelling

p.v. *abbr* (= ***prossimo venturo***) next

P

Q

q *abbr* (= ***quintale***) 100 kilograms
qua here; ***passa di qua*** come this way; ***al di qua di*** on this side of
quaderno *m* exercise book
quadrangolare four-sided
quadrangolo *m* quadrangle
quadrante *m* quadrant; *di orologio* dial
quadrare ⟨1a⟩ **1** *v/t* MAT square; *conti* balance **2** *v/i di conti* balance, square F; *fig* ***i conti non quadrano*** there's something fishy going on
quadrato 1 *agg* square; *fig persona* rational **2** *m* square; *tabella ecc* list
quadrifoglio *m* (*pl* -gli) four-leaf clover
quadro 1 *agg* square **2** *m* painting, picture; MAT square; *fig* ***nel quadro di*** as part of; ***quadro*** (***sinottico***) table; ***-i*** *pl* ***direttivi*** senior executives, senior management *sg*; ***quadro di comando*** control panel; ***quadro a olio*** oil painting; ***a -i*** check *attr*
quadruplo *m/agg* quadruple
quaggiù down here
quaglia *f* quail
qualche a few; (*un certo*) some; *interrogativo* any; ***rimango qualche giorno*** I'm staying for a few days; ***qualche giorno usciamo insieme*** we'll go out some day; ***qualche cosa*** something; ***qualche volta*** sometime; *alcune volte* a few times; *a volte* sometimes; ***in qualche luogo*** somewhere; ***qualche mese fa*** a few months ago; ***in qualche modo*** somehow
qualcheduno someone, somebody
qualcosa something; *interrogativo* anything, something; ***qualcos'altro*** something else; ***qualcosa da mangiare*** something to eat; ***qualcosa di bello*** something beautiful
qualcuno someone, somebody; *in interrogazioni anche* anyone, anybody; ***qualcun'altro*** someone *or* somebody else; ***c'è qualcuno?*** (is) anybody *or* anyone home?
quale 1 *agg* what; ***quale libro vuoi?*** which book do you want?; ***città quale Roma*** cities like Rome **2** *pron*: ***prendi un libro – quale?*** take a book - which one?; ***il / la quale*** *persona* who, that; *cosa* which, that; ***la persona della quale stai parlando*** the person you're talking about **3** *avv* as
qualifica *f* (*pl* -che) qualification; ***qualifica professionale*** profession
qualificare ⟨1m & d⟩ qualify; (*definire*) describe
qualificarsi give one's name (***come*** as); *a esame, gara* qualify
qualificato qualified
qualificazione *f* qualification
qualità *f inv* quality; ***merce*** *f* ***di prima qualità*** top quality goods; ***qualità della vita*** quality of life
qualora in the event that
qualsiasi any; *non importa quale* whatever; ***qualsiasi persona*** anyone; ***qualsiasi cosa faccia*** whatever I do
qualunque any; ***uno qualunque*** any one; ***qualunque cosa*** anything; ***qualunque cosa faccia*** whatever I do; ***in qualunque stagione*** whatever the season; ***l'uomo qualunque*** the man in the street
qualvolta: ***ogni qualvolta*** every time that
quando when; ***per quando?*** when?; ***da quando?*** how long?; ***quando vengo*** when I come; *ogni volta che* whenever I come; ***di quando in quando*** now and then, from time to time
quantità *f inv* quantity, amount
quantitativo *m* quantity, amount
quanto 1 *agg* how much; *con nomi plurali* how many; ***tutto quanto il libro*** the whole book; ***tutti -i*** *pl* every single one *sg*; ***-i ne abbiamo oggi?*** what is the date today?, what is today's date? **2** *avv*: ***quanto dura ancora?*** how long will it go on for?; ***quanto a me*** as for me; ***quanto costa?*** how much is it?; ***quanto prima*** as soon as possible; ***in quanto*** since, because; ***per quanto ne sappia*** as far as I know **3** *m*: ***teoria*** *f* ***dei -i*** quantum theory
quaranta forty
quarantena *f* quarantine
quarantenne 1 *agg* forty or so **2** *m/f* person in his / her forties
quarantesimo *m/agg* fortieth
quaresima *f* Lent
quarta *f* AUTO fourth (gear)
quartiere *m* district; MIL quarters *pl*; ***quartiere generale*** headquarters
quarto 1 *agg* fourth **2** *m* fourth; (*quarta parte*) quarter; ***quarto d'ora*** quarter of an hour; ***sono le due e un quarto*** it's (a) quarter past two; ***un quarto di rosso*** a quarter-litre (*Am* liter) of red; ***-i di finale*** quarter-finals
quarzo *m* quartz; ***orologio*** *m* ***al quarzo***

quartz watch
quasi almost; ***quasi mai*** hardly ever
quassù up here
quattordicesimo *m/agg* fourteenth
quattordici fourteen
quattrini *mpl* money *sg*, cash *sg*
quattro four; ***al quattro per cento*** at four per cent; ***fare quattro passi*** go for a stroll; ***farsi in quattro per fare qc*** go to a lot of trouble to do sth
quattrocchi *m inv*: ***a quattrocchi*** in private
quattrocento 1 *agg* four hundred **2** *m*: ***il* Quattrocento** the fifteenth century
quattromila four thousand
quegli, **quei** → ***quello***
quello 1 *agg* that, *pl* those **2** *pron* that (one), *pl* those (ones); ***quello che*** the one that; ***tutto quello che*** all (that), everything (that)
quercia *f* (*pl* -ce) oak
querela *f* legal action; ***sporgere querela contro qc*** take legal action against s.o., sue s.o.; ***querela per diffamazione*** action for slander
quesito *m* question
questi → ***questo***
questionario *m* (*pl* -ri) questionnaire
questione *f* question; ***questione di fiducia*** question *or* matter of trust; ***qui non è questione di*** it is not a question *or* matter of; ***è questione di fortuna*** it's a matter of luck; ***è fuori questione*** it is out of the question; ***mettere qc in questione*** cast doubt on sth
questo 1 *agg* this, *pl* these; ***quest'oggi*** today **2** *pron* this (one), *pl* these (ones); ***questo qui*** this one here; ***con questo*** with that; ***per questo*** for that reason; ***quest'oggi*** today; ***-a poi!*** well I'm blowed!; ***ci mancherebbe anche -a!*** that's all we'd need!; ***-a non me l'aspettavo*** I wasn't expecting this
questore *m chief of police*
questura *f offices of the chief of police*
qui here; ***qui vicino*** near here; ***fin qui*** up to here; ***passa di qui!*** come this way!; ***voglio uscire di qui*** I want to get out of here; ***di qui a un mese*** a month from now, in a month's time
quietanza *f* receipt
quiete *f* peace and quiet
quieto quiet
quindecismo *m/agg* fifteenth
quindi 1 *avv* then **2** *cong* therefore
quindici fifteen; ***tra quindici giorni*** in two weeks (time), *Br* in a fortnight('s time)
quindicina *f*: ***una quindicina*** about fifteen; ***una quindicina di giorni*** about two weeks, *Br* about a fortnight
quinta *f* AUTO fifth (gear); TEA ***le -e*** the wings; *fig* ***dietro le -e*** behind the scenes
quintale *m* hundred kilos; ***mezzo quintale*** fifty kilos
quinto *m/agg* fifth
quota *f* (*parte*) share, quota; (*altitudine*) altitude; ***perdere quota*** lose altitude; ***prendere quota*** gain altitude
quotare ⟨1c⟩ (*valutare*) value; FIN ***azioni*** *pl* ***quotate in borsa*** shares listed *or* quoted on the Stock Exchange
quotato respected
quotazione *f di azioni* value, price; ***quotazione d'acquisto*** bid price; ***quotazione di vendita*** offer price
quotidianamente daily
quotidiano 1 *agg* daily **2** *m* daily (newspaper)
quoziente *m*: ***quoziente d'intelligenza*** IQ

R

R. *abbr* (= ***raccomandata***) recorded delivery, *Am* certified mail
rabarbaro *m* rhubarb
rabbia *f* rage; (*stizza*) anger; MED rabies; ***accesso*** *m* ***di rabbia*** fit of rage; ***fare rabbia a qu*** make s.o. cross
rabbino *m* rabbi
rabbioso *gesto*, *sguardo* of rage; *cane* rabid
rabbrividire ⟨4d⟩ shudder; *per paura* shiver
rabbuiarsi ⟨1i⟩ get dark, darken; *fig* darken
racc. *abbr* (= ***raccomandata***) recorded delivery, *Am* certified mail
raccapricciante appalling, sickening
raccattare ⟨1a⟩ (*tirar su*) pick up
racchetta *f* racquet; ***racchetta da sci*** ski pole
racchiudere ⟨3b⟩ contain
raccogliere ⟨3ss⟩ (*tirar su*) pick up; (*radunare*) gather, collect; AGR harvest; ***raccogliere i frutti di qc*** reap the benefits of sth
raccoglitore *m* ring binder; ***raccoglitore del vetro*** bottle bank
raccolgo → ***raccogliere***
raccolta *f* collection; AGR harvest; ***fare raccolta di francobolli*** collect stamps
raccolto **1** *pp* → ***raccogliere*** **2** *m* harvest
raccomandabile: ***un tipo poco raccomandabile*** a shady character
raccomandare ⟨1a⟩ **1** *v/t* recommend **2** *v/i*: ***raccomandare a qu di fare qc*** tell s.o. to do sth
raccomandata *f* recorded delivery (letter), *Am* certified mail
raccomandazione *f* recommendation
raccontare ⟨1a⟩ tell; ***raccontare per filo e per segno*** tell in great detail
racconto *m* story
raccordo *m* TEC connection; *strada* slip road; ***raccordo anulare*** ring road; ***raccordo autostradale*** junction
rada *f* roads *pl*, roadstead
radar *m inv* radar; ***impianto*** *m* ***radar*** radar installation; ***uomini*** *pl* ***radar*** air traffic controllers
raddolcire ⟨4d⟩ sweeten; *fig* soften
raddolcirsi *di aria* grow milder; *di carattere* mellow
raddoppiare ⟨1k⟩ double; *sforzi* redouble
raddrizzare ⟨1a⟩ straighten
raddrizzarsi straighten up
radere ⟨3b⟩ shave; *sfiorare* skim; ***radere al suolo*** raze (to the ground)
radersi shave
radiare ⟨1k⟩ strike off
radiatore *m* radiator
radiazione *f* radiation
radicale radical
radice *f* root; ***radice quadrata*** square root; ***mettere -i*** put down roots
radio *f inv* radio; (*stazione*) radio station; ***giornale*** *m* ***radio*** (radio) news; ***via radio*** by radio; ***ascoltare la radio*** listen to the radio
radioascoltatore *m*, **-trice** *f* (radio) listener
radioattività *f* radioactivity
radioattivo radioactive
radiocronaca *f* (radio) commentary
radiocronista *m/f* (*pl* -i) (radio) commentator
radiodramma *m* (*pl* -i) (radio) play
radiofonico radio *attr*
radiografia *f* x-ray
radiografico (*pl* -ci): ***esame*** *m* ***radiografico*** x-ray
radioregistratore *m* radio cassette recorder
radioso radiant
radiosveglia *f* clock radio
radiotaxi *m inv* taxi, cab
radiotelefono *m* radio
radioterapia *f* radiation treatment
radiotrasmittente *f apparecchio* radio transmitter; *stazione* radio station
rado *pettine* wide-toothed; *alberi*, *capelli* sparse; ***di rado*** seldom
radunare ⟨1a⟩ collect, gather
radunarsi collect, gather
raduno *m* rally
rafano *m* horseradish
raffermo *pane* stale
raffica *f* (*pl* -che) gust; *di mitragliatrice* burst
raffigurare ⟨1a⟩ represent
raffinare ⟨1a⟩ refine
raffinatezza *f* refinement; ***gli piacciono le -e*** he likes the finer things in life
raffinato *fig* refined
raffineria *f* refinery
rafforzare ⟨1c⟩ strengthen
raffreddamento *m* cooling; ***raffreddamento ad acqua*** water cooling
raffreddare ⟨1a⟩ cool

raffreddarsi cool down; MED catch cold
raffreddato *fig*: ***essere molto raffreddato*** have a very bad cold
raffreddore *m* cold; ***raffredddore da fieno*** hay fever
rag. *abbr* (= ***ragioniere***) accountant
ragazza *f* girl; ***la mia ragazza*** my girlfriend; ***ragazza alla pari*** au pair; ***nome m da ragazza*** maiden name
ragazzo *m* boy; ***il mio ragazzo*** my boyfriend
raggio *m* (*pl* -ggi) ray; MAT radius; ***raggio d'azione*** range; *fig* duties, responsibilities; ***raggio di sole*** ray of sunshine; ***-i pl X*** x-rays; ***-i pl infrarossi / ultravioletti*** infrared / ultraviolet rays
raggirare ⟨1a⟩ fool, take in
raggiro *m* trick
raggiungere ⟨3d⟩ *luogo* reach, get to; *persona* join; *scopo* achieve
raggomitolare ⟨1n⟩ wind *or* roll into a ball
raggomitolarsi curl up
raggrinzito wrinkled
ragionamento *m* reasoning
ragionare ⟨1a⟩ reason; ***ragionare di*** talk about, discuss
ragione *f* reason; (*diritto*) right; ***ragione sociale*** company name; ***per -i di salute*** for health reasons; ***aver ragione*** be right; ***dare ragione a qu*** admit that s.o. is right; ***a ragione, con ragione*** rightly; ***senza ragione*** for no reason
ragioneria *f* book-keeping; EDU *high school specializing in business studies*
ragionevole reasonable
ragioniere *m*, **-a** *f* accountant
ragnatela *f* spider's web
ragno *m* spider
ragù *m inv meat sauce for pasta*
RAI-TV *abbr* (= ***Radio Televisione Italiana***) Italian state radio and television
rallegramenti *mpl* congratulations
rallegrare ⟨1a⟩ cheer up, brighten up
rallegrarsi cheer up, brighten up; ***rallegrarsi con qu di qc*** congratulate s.o. on sth
rallentare ⟨1b⟩ slow down; *fig* ***rallentare il lavoro*** ease off in one's work
rallentatore *m*: ***al rallentatore*** in slow motion
ramanzina *f* lecture
rame *m* copper
ramificarsi ⟨1m & d⟩ *di fiume* branch
ramificazione *f* ramification
ramino *m* (*gioco*) rummy
rammaricare ⟨1m & d⟩ disappoint
rammaricarsi be disappointed (***di*** at)
rammarico *m* (*pl* -chi) regret
rammendare ⟨1a⟩ darn
rammendo *m* darn
rammollire ⟨4d⟩ *v/t & v/i* soften
ramo *m* branch
ramoscello *m* twig
rampa *f* flight; ***rampa di carico*** loading ramp; ***rampa d'accesso*** slip road; ***rampa di lancio*** launch(ing) pad
rampicante 1 *agg* climbing; ***pianta f rampicante*** climber **2** *m* climber
rampone *m* crampon
rana *f* frog; ***uomo m rana*** frogman
rancido rancid
rancore *m* ranco(u)r
randagio (*pl* -gi) stray
randello *m* club
rango *m* (*pl* -ghi) rank
rannicchiarsi ⟨1k⟩ huddle up
rannuvolamento *m* clouding over
rannuvolarsi ⟨1m⟩ cloud over
ranocchio *m* (*pl* -cchi) frog
rapa *f* turnip
rapace 1 *m* bird of prey **2** *agg fig* predatory; ***uccello m rapace*** bird of prey
rapida *f* rapids *pl*
rapidità *f* speed, rapidity
rapido 1 *agg* quick, fast; *crescita, aumento* rapid **2** *m* (***treno*** *m*)***rapido*** intercity train
rapimento *m* abduction, kidnap(p)ing
rapina *f* robbery
rapinare ⟨1a⟩ rob
rapinatore *m*, **-trice** *f* robber
rapire ⟨4d⟩ abduct, kidnap
rapitore *m*, **-trice** *f* abductor, kidnap(p)er
rappacificare ⟨1n & d⟩ reconcile
rappacificazione *f* reconciliation
rappezzare ⟨1b⟩ patch; *fig discorso, articolo* cobble together
rappezzo *m* patch
rapporto *m resoconto* report; *relazione* relationship; *nesso* connection, link; ***-i pl interpersonali*** personal relationships; ***avere -i pl di lavoro con qu*** be a colleague of s.o., work with s.o.; ***in rapporto a*** in connection with; ***le due cose sono in rapporto*** the two things are related *or* connected
rappresentante *m/f* representative
rappresentanza *f* agency; ***rappresentanza esclusiva*** sole agency
rappresentare ⟨1b⟩ represent; TEA perform
rappresentazione *f* representation; TEA performance
rarità *f inv* rarity
raro rare
rasare ⟨1a⟩ shave
rasatura *f* shaving

raschiare ⟨1k⟩ scrape; *ruggine*, *sporco* scrape off
raschiarsi: ***raschiarsi la gola*** clear one's throat
rasentare ⟨1b⟩ (*sfiorare*) scrape; *fig* (*avvicinarsi*) verge on; ***rasentare il muro*** hug the wall
rasente: ***rasente a*** very close to
rasoio *m* (*pl* -oi) razor; ***rasoio di sicurezza*** safety razor; ***rasoio elettrico*** electric razor
raspo *m* cluster
rassegna *f* festival; *di pittura ecc* exhibition; ***passare in rassegna*** review
rassegnarsi ⟨1a⟩ resign o.s (***a*** to)
rassegnato resigned
rassegnazione *f* resignation
rasserenare ⟨1a⟩ calm down
rasserenarsi *di cielo*, *tempo* clear up
rassicurare ⟨1a⟩ reassure
rassicurarsi feel reassured
rassomigliante similar
rassomiglianza *f* resemblance
rassomigliare ⟨1g⟩: ***rassomigliare a*** look like, resemble
rassomigliarsi look like *or* resemble each other
rastrellare ⟨1b⟩ rake; *fig* comb
rastrelliera *f* rack; ***rastrelliera per biciclette*** bike rack
rastrello *m* rake
rata *f* instal(l)ment; ***a -e*** in instalments; ***rata qc a rate*** buy sth on hire purchase *or Am* the installment plan
rateale: ***pagamento*** *m* ***rateale*** payment in insta(l)lments; ***vendita*** *f* ***rateale*** hire purchase, *Am* installment plan
ratificare ⟨1m & d⟩ ratify
ratto *m* zo rat
rattoppare ⟨1c⟩ patch
rattoppo *m* patch
rattrappire ⟨4d⟩, **rattrappirsi** go stiff
rattrappito stiff
rattristare ⟨1a⟩ sadden, make sad
rattristarsi become sad
raucedine *f* hoarseness
rauco (*pl* -chi) hoarse
ravanello *m* radish
ravioli *mpl* ravioli *sg*
ravvicinamento *m* approach; *fig* reconciliation
ravvicinare ⟨1a⟩ move closer; *fig* (*confrontare*) compare; (*riappacificare*) reconcile
ravvivare ⟨1a⟩ revive
razionale rational
razionalizzare ⟨1a⟩ rationalize
razionare ⟨1a⟩ ration
razione *f* ration
razza *f* race; *fig* sort, kind; zo breed
razzia *f* raid
razziale racial
razzismo *m* racism
razzista *agg*, *m/f* (*mpl* -i) racist
razzo *m* rocket; ***come un razzo*** like greased lightning, like a bat out of hell
re *m inv* king; MUS D
reagire ⟨4d⟩ react (***a*** to)
reale *vero* real; *regale* royal
realismo *m* realism
realista *m/f* (*mpl* -i) realist
realistico (*pl* -ci) realistic
realizzabile feasible
realizzare ⟨1a⟩ realize; *piano*, *progetto* carry out
realizzarsi *di sogno* come true; *di persona* find o.s., find fulfilment
realizzazione *f* fulfilment; (*cosa realizzata*) achievement
realmente really
realtà *f* reality; ***in realtà*** in fact, actually; ***realtà virtuale*** virtual reality
reato *m* (criminal) offence (*Am* offense); ***-i*** *pl* ***minori*** minor offences
reattore *m* AVIA jet engine; *aereo* jet; ***reattore nucleare*** nuclear reactor
reazionario (*pl* -ri) **1** *agg* reactionary **2** *m*, **-a** *f* reactionary
reazione *f* reaction
recapitare ⟨1m⟩ deliver
recapito *m* delivery; (*indirizzo*) address; ***recapito telefonico*** phone number
recare ⟨1d⟩ *portare* bring; *arrecare* cause
recarsi go
recensione *f* review
recensire ⟨4d⟩ review
recensore *m* reviewer, critic
recente recent
recentemente recently
recintare ⟨1a⟩ enclose
recinto *m* enclosure; *per animali* pen, enclosure; *steccato* fence
recipiente *m* container, recipient
reciproco (*pl* -ci) mutual, reciprocal
recita *f* performance
recitare ⟨1l & b⟩ **1** *v/t* recite; TEA play (the part of); *preghiera* say **2** *v/i* act
reclamare ⟨1a⟩ **1** *v/i* complain **2** *v/t* claim
réclame *f inv* advert
reclamizzare ⟨1a⟩ advertise
reclamo *m* complaint
reclusione *f* seclusion
recluso *m* prisoner
recluta *f* recruit
record *m inv* record; ***stabilire il record*** set the record; ***a tempo di record*** in record time
recuperare → ***ricuperare***

R

recupero → ***ricupero***
redatto *pp* → ***redigere***
redattore *m*, **-trice** *f* editor; *di articolo* writer; ***trice capo*** editor-in-chief
redazione *f* editorial staff; *di articolo* writing
redditizio (*pl* -zi) profitable
reddito *m* income; ***reddito annuo*** annual income
Redentore *m* REL Redeemer
redigere ⟨3oo⟩ *testo*, *articolo* write; *lista* draw up
redini *fpl* reins
reduce *m/f* ex-serviceman
referendum *m inv* referendum
referenza *f* reference
referto *m* (official) report
refettorio *m* (*pl* -ri) refectory
refill *m inv* refill
refrigerante cooling
refrigerare ⟨1m⟩ refrigerate
refrigerio *m* (*pl* -ri) coolness
refurtiva *f* stolen property
regalare ⟨1a⟩ give; ***regalarsi qc*** treat o.s. to sth
regale regal
regalino *m* gift, present, little something F
regalo *m* gift, present; ***articolo*** *m* ***da regalo*** gift
regata *f* (boat) race
reggere ⟨3cc⟩ **1** *v/t* (*sostenere*) support; (*tenere in mano*) hold; (*sopportare*) bear; GRAM take **2** *v/i di tempo* last; *di ragionamento* stand up; *fig* ***non reggo più*** I can't take any more
reggersi stand
reggia *f* (*pl* -gge) palace
reggicalze *m inv* suspender belt
reggipetto *m*, **reggiseno** *m* bra, *Am* brassiere
regia *f* production; *di film* direction
regime *m* régime; MED diet; MED ***essere a regime*** be on a diet
regina *f* queen
regionale regional
regione *f* region
regista *m/f* director; TEA producer
registrare ⟨1a⟩ *in un registro* enter, record, register; *rilevare* show, register; *canzone*, *messaggio* record
registratore *m*: ***registratore*** (***a cassetta***) cassette recorder; ***registratore a nastro*** tape recorder; ***registratore di cassa*** cash register
registrazione *f* recording
registro *m* register
regnare ⟨1a⟩ reign
regno *m* kingdom; *periodo* reign
regola *f* rule; ***in regola*** in order; ***di regola*** as a rule
regolabile adjustable
regolamento *m* regulation; ***regolamento dei conti*** settling of accounts
regolare 1 *v/t* ⟨1l & b⟩ regulate; *spese*, *consumo* cut down on; TEC adjust; *questione* sort out, settle; *conto*, *debito* settle **2** *agg* regular
regolarità *f* regularity
regolarizzare ⟨1a⟩ *situazione* sort out, put in order
regredire ⟨4d⟩ regress
regressione *f* regression
regressivo regressive
regresso *m* regression
reimpiego *m* (*pl* -ghi) *di capitali* re-investment; *di personale* re-employment
relatività *f* relativity; ***teoria*** *f* ***della relatività*** theory of relativity
relativo relative (***a*** to); (*corrispondente*) relevant
relatore *m*, **-trice** *f* speaker
relazione *f legame* relationship; *esposizione* report; ***avere una relazione con qu*** have an affair *or* a relationship with s.o.; ***in relazione a*** with reference to; ***-i pubbliche*** public relations, PR
religione *f* religion
religiosa *f* nun
religiosità *f* religion
religioso 1 *agg* religious **2** *m* monk
relitto *m* wreck
remare ⟨1b⟩ row
rematore *m* rower
remo *m* oar
remoto remote
remunerare ⟨1m⟩ pay
remunerativo remunerative, well-paid; ***non remunerativo*** unpaid
remunerazione *f* payment, remuneration
rendere ⟨3c⟩ *restituire* give back, return; *fruttare* yield; *senso*, *idea* render; ***rendere un servizio a qu*** do s.o. a favo(u)r; ***rendere conto a qu di qc*** account to s.o. for sth; ***rendere felice*** make happy
rendimento *m di macchina*, *impiegato* performance; ***rendimento giornaliero*** daily output *or* production
rendita *f* income; ***rendita vitalizia*** annuity; ***vivere di rendita*** have private means
rene *m* kidney
reparto *m* department
repentaglio *m*: ***mettere a repentaglio*** risk, endanger
reperibile available; ***difficilmente reperibile*** difficult to find
reperire ⟨4d⟩ find
reperto *m* find; DIR exhibit
repertorio *m* (*pl* -ri) TEA, MUS repertory

replica *f* (*pl* -che). (*copia*) replica; TV repeat; TEA repeat performance; (*risposta*) answer, response; ***il suo tono non ammette -e*** his tone of voice leaves no room for discussion
replicare ⟨1l, b & d⟩ *ripetere* repeat; *ribattere* reply, answer
reportage *m inv* report
reporter *m/f inv* reporter, journalist
repressione *f* repression
repressivo repressive
represso *pp* → ***reprimere***
reprimere ⟨3r⟩ repress
repubblica *f* (*pl* -che) republic
Repubblica Ceca *f* Czech Republic
repubblicano republican
repulsione *f* repulsion
reputare ⟨1l & b⟩ consider, deem
reputarsi consider o.s.
reputazione *f* reputation
requisire ⟨4d⟩ requisition
requisito *m* requirement
resa *f* surrender; *restituzione* return; ***resa dei conti*** settling of accounts
residence *m inv* block of service flats (*Am* apartments)
residente resident
residenza *f* (official) address; *sede* seat; *soggiorno* stay
residenziale residential; ***zona*** *f* ***residenziale*** residential area
residuo *m* remainder
resina *f* resin
resistente sturdy, strong; ***resistente al fuoco*** fire-resistant
resistenza *f* resistance; *instancabilità* stamina
resistere ⟨3f⟩ *al freddo ecc* stand up to; *opporsi* resist; ***non resisto più*** I can't take any more
reso *pp* → ***rendere***
resoconto *m* report
respingere ⟨3d⟩ *richiesta*, *pretendente* reject, turn down; *nemico*, *attacco* repel
respinto *pp* → ***respingere***
respirare ⟨1a⟩ **1** *v/t* breathe (in) **2** *v/i* breathe; *fig* draw breath
respiratore *m* respirator; *per apnea* snorkel
respirazione *f* breathing; ***respirazione artificiale*** artificial respiration
respiro *m* breathing; ***trattenere il respiro*** hold one's breath; *fig* ***un attimo di respiro*** a moment's rest
responsabile responsible (***di*** for); DIR liable (***di*** for)
responsabilità *f inv* responsibility; DIR liability; ***responsabilità civile*** civil liability; ***responsabilità limitata*** limited liability
ressa *f* crowd
restare ⟨1b⟩ stay, remain; *avanzare* be left; ***restare indietro*** stay behind; ***restare perplesso / vedovo*** be puzzled / widowed; ***restarci male*** be hurt
restaurare ⟨1a⟩ restore
restauratore *m*, **-trice** *f* restorer
restauro *m* restoration; ***chiuso per -i*** closed for restoration
restituire ⟨4d⟩ return; *saluto* restore
restituzione *f* return
resto *m* rest, remainder; (*soldi*) change; ***-i*** *pl* remains; ***del resto*** anyway, besides
restringere ⟨3d⟩ narrow; *vestito*, *giacca* take in
restringersi *di strada* narrow; *di stoffa* shrink
restrizione *f* restriction
rete *f per pescare ecc* net; SP goal; INFOR, TELEC, FERR network; ***rete autostradale*** road network
retina *f* ANAT retina
retribuire ⟨4d⟩ pay
retribuzione *f* payment
retroattivo retroactive
retrobottega *m inv* back shop
retrocedere ⟨3l⟩ retreat; *fig* lose ground
retrodatare ⟨1a⟩ backdate
retrogrado reactionary
retromarcia *f* (*pl* -ce) AUTO reverse (gear)
retroscena *mpl fig* background *sg*
retrospettivo *mostra* retrospective
retroterra *m inv* hinterland
retrovisivo: specchietto *m* ~ rearview mirror
retta[1] *f somma* fee
retta[2] *f* MAT straight line
retta[3] *f*: ***dare retta a qu*** listen to s.o.
rettangolare rectangular
rettangolo *m* rectangle
rettifica *f* (*pl* -che) correction
rettificare ⟨1m & d⟩ correct
rettile *m* reptile
rettilineo straight
rettorato *m* rectorship
rettore *m* rector
reumatico (*pl* -ci) rheumatic
reumatismo *m* rheumatism
revisionare ⟨1a⟩ *conti* audit; AUTO MOT, put through the MOT test; *testo* revise
revisione *f di conti* audit; AUTO MOT; *di testo* revision
revoca *f* (*pl* -che) repeal
revocare ⟨1l, b & d⟩ repeal, revoke
R.I. *abbr* (= ***Repubblica Italiana***) Italian Republic
ri- *prefisso* re-.
riabilitare ⟨1n⟩ rehabilitate

riabilitazione *f* rehabilitation

riacquistare ⟨1a⟩ get back, regain; *casa* buy back

riagganciare ⟨1f⟩ TELEC hang up

riallacciare ⟨1f⟩ refasten; TELEC reconnect

rialzare ⟨1a⟩ *alzare di nuovo* pick up; *aumentare* raise, increase

rialzo *m* rise, increase

rianimare ⟨1m⟩ *speranze, entusiasmo* revive; (*rallegrare*) cheer up; MED resuscitate

rianimarsi revive

rianimazione *f* resuscitation; ***centro*** *m* ***di rianimazione*** intensive care unit, ICU

riapertura *f* reopening

riaprire ⟨4f⟩ reopen

riarmare ⟨1a⟩ rearm

riarmo *m* rearmament

riassettare ⟨1b⟩ tidy up

riassetto *m* tidy-up

riassumere ⟨3h⟩ re-employ; (*riepilogare*) summarize

riassunto 1 *pp* → ***riassumere*** **2** *m* summary

riavere ⟨2b⟩ get back, regain; ***ho riavuto il raffreddore*** I've got another cold

riaversi recover (***da*** from), get over (***da*** sth)

riavviare ⟨1h⟩ INFOR reboot

ribaltabile folding

ribaltare ⟨1a⟩ **1** *v/t* overturn **2** *v/i di macchina, barca* turn over

ribassare ⟨1a⟩ **1** *v/t* lower **2** *v/i* fall, drop

ribasso *m* fall, drop; *sconto* discount; ***essere in ribasso*** be falling *or* dropping

ribattere ⟨3a⟩ **1** *v/t argomento* refute **2** *v/i* (*replicare*) answer back; (*insistere*) insist; ***ribattere a un'accusa*** deny an accusation

ribellarsi ⟨1b⟩ rebel (***a*** against)

ribelle 1 *agg* rebellious **2** *m/f* rebel

ribellione *f* rebellion

ribes *m inv* currant; ***ribes nero*** blackcurrant; ***ribes rosso*** redcurrant

ribrezzo *m* horror; ***fare ribrezzo a*** disgust

ricadere ⟨2c⟩ fall; *cadere di nuovo* fall back; *fig* relapse

ricaduta *f* relapse

ricamare ⟨1a⟩ embroider

ricambiare ⟨1k⟩ change; *contraccambiare* return, reciprocate

ricambio *m* change; (*sostituzione*) replacement; *pezzo* (spare) part; ***pezzo*** *m* ***di ricambio*** spare part

ricamo *m* embroidery

ricapitolare ⟨1n⟩ sum up, recapitulate

ricaricare ⟨1m & d⟩ *batteria* recharge

ricattare ⟨1a⟩ blackmail

ricattatore *m*, **-trice** *f* blackmailer

ricatto *m* blackmail

ricavare ⟨1a⟩ derive; *denaro* get

ricavato *m di vendita* proceeds

ricchezza *f* wealth

riccio[1] *m* (*pl* -cci) ZO hedgehog; BOT *spiny outer casing of the chestnut*; ***riccio di mare*** sea urchin

riccio[2] (*pl* -cci) **1** *agg* curly **2** *m* curl

ricciolo *m* curl

ricco (*pl* -cchi) **1** *agg* rich, wealthy; ***ricco di*** rich in **2** *m*, **-a** *f* rich *or* wealthy man / woman; ***i -i*** *pl* the rich

ricerca *f* (*pl* -che) research; *di persona scomparsa, informazione ecc* search (***di*** for); EDU project; ***alla ricerca di*** in search of

ricercare ⟨1d⟩ (*cercare di nuovo*) look again for; (*cercare con cura*) search *or* look for

ricercato 1 *agg oggetto, artista* sought-after **2** *m* man wanted by the police

ricercatore *m*, **-trice** *f* researcher

ricetta *f* prescription; GASTR recipe

ricevere ⟨3a⟩ receive; *di medico* see patients; ***ricevere gente*** have guests

ricevimento *m* receipt; *festa* reception

ricevitore *m* receiver

ricevuta *f* receipt; ***accusare ricevuta*** acknowledge receipt

richiamare ⟨1a⟩ (*chiamare di nuovo*) call again; (*chiamare indietro*) call back; *attirare* draw; *fig rimproverare* rebuke, reprimand; ***richiamare l'attenzione di qu*** draw s.o.'s attention (***su*** to); ***richiamare qu all'ordine*** call s.o. to order

richiamarsi: ***richiamarsi a*** refer to

richiedente *m/f* applicant

richiedere ⟨3k⟩ ask for again; (*necessitare di*) take, require; *documento* apply for

richiesta *f* request (***di qc*** for sth); FIN demand; ***a*** (*o* ***su***) ***richiesta di*** at the request of; ***più informazioni saranno disponibili su richiesta*** further information on request

richiesto 1 *pp* → ***richiedere*** **2** *agg*: ***molto richiesto*** much in demand, much sought after

riciclaggio *m* (*pl* -ggi) recycling

riciclare ⟨1a⟩ recycle

ricompensa *f* reward

ricompensare ⟨1b⟩ reward (***qu di qc*** s.o. for sth)

riconciliare ⟨1g⟩ reconcile

riconciliazione *f* reconciliation

ricondurre ⟨3e⟩ (*riportare*) take back (***a*** to); (*imputare*) attribute (***a*** to)

riconoscente grateful; ***mostrarsi riconoscente*** show one's gratitude

riconoscenza *f* gratitude; ***per riconoscenza*** out of gratitude
riconoscere ⟨3n⟩ recognise; *ammettere* acknowledge; ***riconosco che*** I admit that; ***non si riconosce più*** he's unrecognisable
riconoscibile recognizable
riconoscimento *m* recognition
riconquistare ⟨1a⟩ reconquer
ricordare ⟨1c⟩ remember; (*menzionare*) mention; ***ricordare qc a qu*** remind s.o. of sth
ricordarsi remember (***di qc*** sth; ***di fare qc*** to do sth)
ricordo *m* memory; *oggetto* memento; ***ricordo di viaggio*** souvenir
ricorrente recurrent, recurring
ricorrenza *f* recurrence; *di evento* anniversary
ricorrere ⟨3o⟩ *di date, di festa* take place, happen; ***ricorrere a qu*** turn to s.o.; ***ricorrere a qc*** have recourse to sth; ***oggi ricorre l'aniversario del nostro matrimonio*** today is our wedding anniversary
ricorso 1 *pp* → ***ricorrere* 2** *m* DIR appeal; ***avere ricorso a*** *avvocato, medico* see; ***avere ricorso all'aiuto di qu*** ask for s.o.'s help; ***presentare ricorso*** appeal
ricostruire ⟨4d⟩ rebuild; *fig* reconstruct
ricostruzione *f* rebuilding; *fig* reconstruction
ricotta *f* ricotta, *soft cheese made from ewe's milk*
ricoverare ⟨1m & c⟩ admit
ricoverato 1 *agg* admitted **2** *m*, **-a** *f in ospedale* patient
ricovero *m in ospedale* admission; (*refugio*) shelter
ricreazione *f* recreation; *nelle scuole* break, recreation, *Am* recess
ricredersi ⟨3a⟩ change one's mind
ricuperare ⟨1m⟩ **1** *v/t* get back, recover; *libertà, fiducia* regain; *spazio* gain; *tempo* make up; ***ricuperare il tempo perso*** make up for lost time **2** *v/i* catch up
ricupero *m* recovery; ***ricupero del centro storico*** development of the old part of town; ***ricupero di debiti*** debt collection; EDU ***corso** m **di ricupero*** remedial course; ***materiale** m **di ricupero*** scrap; SP ***partita** f **di ricupero*** rescheduled match
ricurvo bent, crooked
ridare ⟨1r⟩ *restituire* give back, return; *fiducia, forze* restore
ridere ⟨3b⟩ laugh (***di*** at); ***far ridere di sé*** make a fool of o.s.; ***se la ride del parere degli altri*** he couldn't care less what people think
ridicolizzare ⟨1a⟩ ridicule
ridicolo 1 *agg* ridiculous **2** *m* ridicule; ***mettere qu in ridicolo, gettare il ridicolo su qu*** ridicule s.o.
ridimensionare ⟨1a⟩ downsize; *fig* get into perspective
ridotto 1 *pp* → ***ridurre* 2** *agg*: ***a prezzi -i*** at reduced prices
riduco → ***ridurre***
ridurre ⟨3e⟩ reduce (***a*** to); *prezzi, sprechi* reduce, cut; *personale* reduce, cut back; ***ridurre al silenzio*** reduce to silence
ridursi decrease, diminish; ***ridursi a fare qc*** be reduced to doing sth; ***ridursi male*** be in a bad way; ***ridursi in miseria*** ruin o.s.
riduzione *f* reduction, cut; ***riduzione del personale*** staff cutbacks
riempire ⟨4g⟩ fill (up); *formulario* fill in
rientrare ⟨1a⟩ come back; *a casa* come home; ***questo non rientrava nei miei piani*** that was not part of the plan
rientro *m* return; ***al tuo rientro*** when you get back
rifare ⟨3aa⟩ do again; (*rinnovare*) do up; *stanza* tidy (up); *letto* make
rifarsi *vita* rebuild; *casa* renovate; *guardaroba* replace; ***rifarsi di qc*** make up for sth
riferimento *m* reference; ***punto** m **di riferimento*** point of reference; ***con riferimento a*** with reference to
riferire ⟨4d⟩ report
riferirsi: ***riferirsi a*** refer to
rifiutare ⟨1a⟩ *e* **rifiutarsi** refuse
rifiuto *m* refusal; ***-i** pl* waste *sg*, refuse *sg*; (*spazzatura*) rubbish *sg*; ***-i tossici*** toxic waste
riflessione *f* thought, reflection; FIS reflection
riflessivo thoughtful; GRAM reflexive
riflesso 1 *pp* → ***riflettere* 2** *m* reflection; (*gesto istintivo*) reflex (movement); ***ho agito di riflesso*** it was a reflex action, I did it automatically
riflettere ⟨3qq⟩ **1** *v/t* reflect **2** *v/i* think; ***riflettere su qc*** think about sth, reflect on sth
riflettersi be reflected
riflettore *m* floodlight
riflusso *m* ebb
riforma *f* reform; REL Reformation; ***riforma monetaria*** monetary reform
riformare ⟨1a⟩ (*rifare*) re-shape, re-form; (*cambiare*) reform; MIL declare unfit
riformato REL Reformed; MIL declared unfit
rifornimento *m* AVIA refuelling; ***-i** pl* supplies, provisions; ***fare rifornimento di ci-***

R

bo stock up on food; ***fare rifornimento di benzina*** fill up
rifornire ⟨4d⟩ *macchina* fill (up); *frigo* restock, fill (***di*** with); ***rifornire il magazzino*** restock
rifornirsi stock up (***di*** on)
rifugiarsi ⟨1f⟩ take refuge
rifugiato *m*, **-a** *f* refugee; ***rifugiato politico*** political refugee
rifugio *m* (*pl* -gi) shelter; ***rifugio alpino*** mountain hut; ***rifugio antiaereo*** air-raid shelter
riga *f* (*pl* -ghe) *f* line; (*fila*) row; (*regolo*) rule; *in stoffa* stripe; *nei capelli* parting, *Am* part; ***stoffa** f **a -ghe*** striped fabric
rigatoni *mpl* rigatoni *sg*
rigenerare ⟨1m & b⟩ regenerate
rigenerazione *f* regeneration
rigetto *m* MED rejection; *fig* mental block
rigido (*duro*) rigid; *muscolo*, *articolazione* stiff; *clima* harsh; *fig*: *severo* strict
rigirare ⟨1a⟩ **1** *v/i* walk around **2** *v/t* turn over and over; *denaro* launder; ***rigirare il discorso*** change the subject
rigirarsi turn round; *nel letto* toss and turn
rigo *m* (*pl* -ghi) line; ***rigo musicale*** staff, stave
rigoglioso lush, luxuriant
rigore *m di clima* harshness; (*severità*) strictness; SP (*anche* ***calcio** m **di rigore***) penalty (kick); ***area** f **di rigore*** penalty area; ***di rigore*** compulsory
rigoroso rigorous
riguardante about, regarding
riguardare ⟨1a⟩ look at again; (*rivedere*) review, look at; (*riferirsi*) be about, concern; ***per quanto riguarda …*** as far as … is concerned; ***non ti riguarda*** it's none of your business, it doesn't concern you
riguardarsi take care of o.s.
riguardo *m* (*attenzione*) care; (*rispetto*) respect; ***mancanza** f **di riguardo*** lack of respect; ***di riguardo*** important; ***riguardo a*** as regards, about; ***senza riguardo*** carelessly
rilasciare ⟨1f⟩ release; *documento* issue
rilascio *m* release; *di passaporto* issue
rilassamento *m* relaxation
rilassare ⟨1a⟩ *e* **rilassarsi** relax
rilassato relaxed
rilegare ⟨1e⟩ *libro* bind
rilegatore *m* bookbinder
rilegatura *f* binding
rilevare ⟨1b⟩ (*ricavare*) find; (*osservare*) note, notice; *ditta* acquire, buy up; ***da quanto è successo si rileva che …*** from what has happened, we can gather that …
rilievo *m* relief; *fig* ***dare rilievo a qc, mettere qc in rilievo*** emphasize *or* highlight sth; ***di rilievo*** important; ***di nessun rilievo*** of no importance
rima *f* rhyme; ***far rima*** rhyme
rimandare ⟨1a⟩ send again; (*restituire*) send back, return; *palla* return; (*rinviare*) postpone
rimanente **1** *agg* remaining **2** *m* rest, balance
rimanenza *f* remainder
rimanere ⟨2m⟩ stay, remain; (*avanzare*) be left (over); ***rimanerci male*** be hurt; ***come siete rimasti per stasera?*** what arrangements did you make for this evening?
rimango → ***rimanere***
rimarginare ⟨1m⟩ *e* **rimarginarsi** heal
rimasto *pp* → ***rimanere***
rimbalzare ⟨1a⟩ bounce
rimbalzo *m* bounce
rimboccare ⟨1d⟩ *coperte* tuck in; ***rimboccarsi le maniche*** roll up one's sleeves
rimborsare ⟨1a⟩ reimburse, refund, pay back
rimborso *m* reimbursement, repayment; ***rimborso spese*** reimbursement of expenses; ***contro rimborso*** COD, cash on delivery
rimboschimento *m* reforestation
rimboschire ⟨4d⟩ reforest
rimediare ⟨1k & b⟩ **1** *v/i* ***rimediare a*** make up for, remedy; ***come posso rimediare?*** how can I put things right? **2** *v/t* find, scrape together
rimedio *m* (*pl* -di) remedy; MED medicine; ***senza rimedio*** hopeless
rimescolare ⟨1m⟩ mix again; *più volte* mix thoroughly; *caffè* stir again
rimessa *f di auto* garage; *degli autobus* depot; FIN remittance; SP ***rimessa laterale*** throw-in
rimettere ⟨3ee⟩ put back, return; (*affidare*) refer; *vomitare* bring up; ***rimettere a posto*** put back; ***rimettere in ordine*** tidy up; ***ci ho rimesso molti soldi*** I lost a lot of money
rimettersi *di tempo* improve; ***rimettersi da qc*** get over sth; ***rimettersi a qu*** put o.s. in s.o.'s hands
rimmel® *m inv* mascara
rimodernare ⟨1b⟩ modernize
rimorchiare ⟨1k & c⟩ AUTO tow (away)
rimorchiatore *m* tug
rimorchio *m* AUTO tow; *veicolo* trailer
rimorso *m* remorse
rimozione *f* removal
rimpatriare ⟨1k & m⟩ **1** *v/t* repatriate **2** *v/i* return *or* go home
rimpatrio *m* (*pl* -ri) repatriation

rimpiangere ⟨3d⟩ regret (***di avere fatto qc*** doing sth); *tempi passati, giovinezza* miss
rimpianto **1** *pp* → ***rimpiangere*** **2** *m* regret
rimpiazzare ⟨1a⟩ replace
rimpicciolire ⟨4d⟩ **1** *v/t* make smaller **2** *v/i* become smaller, shrink
rimproverare ⟨1m & c⟩ scold; *impiegato* reprimand; ***rimproverare qc a qu*** reproach s.o. for sth
rimprovero *m* scolding; *dal capo* reprimand; ***-i*** *pl* reproaches
rimuovere ⟨3ff⟩ remove; *muovere di nuovo* move again
rinascere ⟨3gg⟩ be born again; *di passione, speranza* be revived; *fig* ***sentirsi rinascere*** feel rejuvenated
Rinascimento *m* Renaissance
rincarare ⟨1a⟩ **1** *v/t* increase, put up; ***rincarare la dose*** make matters worse **2** *v/i* increase in price
rincaro *m* increase in price
rincasare ⟨1a⟩ *venire* come home; *andare* go home
rinchiudere ⟨3b⟩ shut up
rinchiudersi shut o.s. up
rincorrere ⟨3o⟩ run *or* chase after
rincorsa *f* run-up
rincorso *pp* → ***rincorrere***
rincrescere ⟨3n⟩: ***mi rincresce*** I'm sorry; ***se non ti rincresce*** if you don't mind
rincrescimento *m* regret
rinfacciare ⟨1f⟩: ***rinfacciare qc a qu*** cast sth up to s.o.
rinforzare ⟨1c⟩ strengthen
rinforzarsi get stronger
rinforzo *m* reinforcement; MIL ***-i*** *pl* reinforcements
rinfrescare ⟨1d⟩ **1** *v/t* cool down, make cooler; (*ristorare*) refresh; (*rinnovare*) freshen up; ***rinfrescare la memoria a qu*** refresh s.o.'s memory **2** *v/i* cool down
rinfrescarsi freshen up
rinfresco *m* (*pl* -chi) buffet (party)
rinfusa: ***alla rinfusa*** any which way, all higgledy-piggledy
ringhiare ⟨1k⟩ growl
ringhiera *f* railing
ringiovanire ⟨4d⟩ **1** *v/t* make feel younger; *di aspetto* make look younger **2** *v/i* feel younger; *di aspetto* look younger
ringraziamento: ***un ringraziamento*** a word of thanks; ***lettera*** *f* ***di ringraziamento*** thank you letter, letter of thanks; ***i miei -i*** *pl* my thanks
ringraziare ⟨1g⟩ thank (***di*** for)
rinnovamento *m* change; *di contratto, tessera* renewal
rinnovare ⟨1c⟩ renovate; *guardaroba* replace; *abbonamento* renew; (*ripetere*) renew, repeat
rinnovarsi renew itself; (*ripetersi*) be repeated, happen again
rinnovo *m* renovation; *di guardaroba* replacement; *di abbonamento* renewal; *di richiesta* repetition
rinsavire ⟨4d⟩ **1** *v/t*: ***rinsavire qu*** bring s.o. back to his / her senses **2** *v/i* come to one's senses
rintanarsi ⟨1a⟩ hide, go to earth
rintracciare ⟨1f⟩ track down
rinuncia *f* (*pl* -ce) renunciation (***a*** of)
rinunciare ⟨1f⟩ give up (***a*** sth)
rinunzia → ***rinuncia***
rinvenimento *m* recovery; *di resti* discovery
rinvenire ⟨4p⟩ **1** *v/t* recover; *resti* discover **2** *v/i* regain consciousness, come round
rinviare ⟨1h⟩ (*mandare indietro*) return; (*posticipare*) postpone, put off; *a letteratura* refer
rinvio *m* (*pl* -vii) return; *di riunione* postponement; *in un testo* cross-reference
rione *m* district
riordinare ⟨1m⟩ tidy up; ***riordinare le idee*** set one's ideas in order
riorganizzare ⟨1a⟩ reorganize
riorganizzazione *f* reorganization
riparare ⟨1a⟩ **1** *v/t* (*proteggere*) protect (***da*** from); (*aggiustare*) repair; *un torto* make up for **2** *v/i* escape
ripararsi *dalla pioggia* shelter, take shelter (***da*** from)
riparato sheltered
riparazione *f* repair; *fig di torta, ingiustizia* putting right, reparation; ***officina*** *f* ***-i*** garage
riparo *m* shelter; ***mettersi al riparo*** take shelter
ripartire[1] *v/i* ⟨4a⟩ leave again
ripartire[2] *v/t* ⟨4d⟩ divide (up)
ripartizione *f* division
ripassare ⟨1a⟩ **1** *v/i* → ***passare*** **2** *v/t col ferro* iron; *lezione* revise, *Am* review
ripensamento *m*: ***avere un ripensamento*** have second thoughts
ripensare ⟨1b⟩ *riflettere* think; ***ripensare a qc*** think about sth again; ***ci ho ripensato*** I've changed my mind
ripetere ⟨3a⟩ repeat; ***ti ho ripetuto mille volte la stessa cosa*** I've told you the same thing a thousand times
ripetizione *f* repetition; ***dare -i a qu*** tutor s.o.
ripetuto repeated
ripido steep
ripiegare ⟨1b & e⟩ **1** *v/t* fold (up) again **2** *v/i* fall back

R

ripiego *m* (*pl* -ghi) makeshift (solution)
ripieno 1 *agg* full; GASTR stuffed **2** *m* stuffing
riporre ⟨3ll⟩ put away; *speranze* place
riportare ⟨1c⟩ take back; (*riferire*) report; *vittoria, successo* achieve; MAT carry over; *tasche* sew on; *danni, ferite* sustain
riporto *m* amount carried over
riposare ⟨1c⟩ *v/t & v/i* rest
riposarsi rest
riposato: ***a mente -a*** once I've / you've had some rest
riposo *m* rest; ***giorno*** *m* ***di riposo*** day off; ***collocare a riposo*** retire; ***senza riposo*** non-stop
ripostiglio *m* (*pl* -gli) boxroom, storeroom
riprendere ⟨3c⟩ take again; (*prendere indietro*) take back; *lavoro* go back to; FOT record; ***riprendere coscienza*** regain consciousness; ***riprendere a fare qc*** start doing sth again
riprendersi: ***riprendersi da qc*** get over sth
ripresa *f* resumption; *di vestito* alteration; *film* shot; AUTO acceleration; RAD, TV ***in ripresa diretta*** (broadcast) live; ***a più -e*** several times, on several occasions
riproduco → ***riprodurre***
riprodurre ⟨3e⟩ reproduce
riprodursi *di animali* breed, reproduce; *di situazione* happen again
riproduzione *f* reproduction; ***riproduzione vietata*** copyright
riprovare ⟨1c⟩ **1** *v/t* feel again; *vestito* try on again **2** *v/i* try again
ripugnante disgusting, repugnant
ripugnanza *f* disgust, repugnance
ripugnare ⟨1a⟩: ***ripugnare a qu*** disgust s.o.
ripulire ⟨4d⟩ clean again; (*rimettere in ordine*) tidy (up); *spir* empty, clean out
risa *fpl* laughter *sg*
risaia *f* rice field
risalire ⟨4m⟩ **1** *v/t scale* go back up **2** *v/i* (*rincarare*) go up again; ***risalire alle origini*** go back to source
risalita *f* ascent; ***impianti*** *mpl* ***di risalita*** ski lifts
risaltare ⟨1a⟩ stand out
risalto *m*: ***fare risalto*** stand out; ***mettere in risalto, dare risalto a*** highlight
risanamento *m* redevelopment; FIN improvement; ***risanamento del deficit pubblico*** reduction in the public deficit
risanare ⟨1a⟩ redevelop; FIN improve
risarcimento *m* compensation
risarcire ⟨4d⟩ *persona* compensate (***di*** for); *danno* compensate for
risata *f* laugh
riscaldamento *m* heating; ***riscaldamento centrale*** central heating system (*for a block of flats*)
riscaldare ⟨1a⟩ heat *or* warm up
riscaldarsi warm o.s.
rischiararsi ⟨1a⟩ clear (up); *cielo* clear (up); ***rischiararsi in volto*** cheer up
rischiare ⟨1k⟩ **1** *v/t* risk **2** *v/i*: ***rischiare di sbagliare*** risk making a mistake
rischio *m* (*pl* -chi) risk; ***a rischio della propria vita*** risking one's own life; ***mettere a rischio*** put at risk
rischioso risky
riscontrare ⟨1a⟩ (*confrontare*) compare; (*controllare*) check; (*incontrare*) come up against; *errori* come across
riscontro *m* comparison; check; ***in riscontro alla Vostra*** in response to yours
riscuotere ⟨3ff⟩ FIN *soldi* draw; *assegno* cash; *fig* earn
risentimento *m* resentment
risentire ⟨4b⟩ **1** *v/t* hear again **2** *v/i* feel the effects (***di*** of)
risentirsi TELEC talk again; (*offendersi*) take offence (*Am* offense)
riserbo *m* reserve; ***senza riserbo*** openly
riserva *f* reserve; (*scorta*) stock, reserve; *fig* reservation; AUTO ***essere in riserva*** be running out of fuel; ***fondo*** *m* ***di riserva*** reserve stock; ***avere delle -e*** *pl* ***su qc*** have reservations about sth; ***senza -e*** without reservation, wholeheartedly; ***riserva naturale*** nature reserve; ***fare riserva di*** stock up on
riservare ⟨1b⟩ keep; (*prenotare*) book, reserve
riservarsi reserve; ***mi riservo di non accettare*** I reserve the right not to accept
riservatezza *f* reserve
riservato reserved; (*confidenziale*) confidential
risiedere ⟨3a⟩ be resident, reside
riso[1] **1** *pp* → ***ridere*** **2** *m* laughing
riso[2] *m* rice
risolto *pp* → ***risolvere***
risolutezza *f* determination, resolution; ***con risolutezza*** with determination
risoluto determined
risoluzione *f* resolution; (*soluzione*) solution; ***risoluzione d'un contratto*** cancellation of a contract; ***prendere una risoluzione*** make a decision
risolvere ⟨3g⟩ solve; (*decidere*) resolve
risolversi be solved; (*decidersi*) decide, resolve; ***risolversi in nulla*** come to nothing
risonanza *f* MUS resonance; *fig*: *di scandolo* reverberations *pl*

R

risorgere ⟨3d⟩ rise; *fig*: *di industria ecc* experience a rebirth
Risorgimento *m* Risorgimento, *the reunification of Italy*
risorsa *f* resource
risotto *m* risotto
risparmiare ⟨1k⟩ save; *fig* spare
risparmiarsi conserve one's energy
risparmiatore *m* saver
risparmio *m* (*pl* -mi) saving; ***-i*** *pl* savings; ***cassa*** *f* ***di risparmio*** savings bank
rispecchiare ⟨1k⟩ reflect
rispettare ⟨1b⟩ respect; *legge*, *contratto* abide by
rispettivo respective
rispetto **1** *m* respect **2** *prp*: ***rispetto a*** (*confronto a*) compared with; (*in relazione a*) as regards
risplendere ⟨3a⟩ shine, glitter
rispondere ⟨3hh⟩ answer (***a*** sth), reply (***a*** to); (*reagire*) respond; *saluto* acknowledge; ***rispondere alle speranze*** come up to expectations; ***rispondere di qc*** be accountable for sth (***a*** to); ***rispondere male*** answer back; TELEC ***non risponde*** there's no answer
risposta *f* answer, reply; (*reazione*) response; ***risposta pagata*** reply paid
rissa *f* brawl
ristabilimento *m di ordine* restoration; *di regolamento* re-introduction; (*guarigione*) recovery
ristabilire ⟨4d⟩ *ordine* restore; *regolamento* re-introduce; ***ristabilire la verità*** set the record straight
ristabilirsi recover
ristampa *f* reprint
ristampare ⟨1a⟩ reprint
ristorante *m* restaurant
ristrettezza *f di idee* narrowness; ***vivere nelle -e*** live in straitened circumstances
ristretto: ***caffè*** *m inv* ***ristretto*** very strong coffee
ristrutturare ⟨1a⟩ *azienda* restructure
ristrutturazione *f* restructuring
risultare ⟨1a⟩ (*derivare*) result; (*rivelarsi*) turn out; ***mi risulta che ...*** as far as I know ...
risultato *m* result; ***senza risultato*** unsuccessfully
risurrezione *f* REL Resurrection
risvegliare ⟨1g⟩, **risvegliarsi** *fig* reawaken
risveglio *m* (*pl* -gli) awakening; *fig* reawakening; ***al mio risveglio*** when I woke
ritardare ⟨1a⟩ **1** *v/t* delay **2** *v/i* be late; *orologio* be slow
ritardatario *m* (*pl* -ri), **-a** *f* latecomer
ritardo *m* delay; ***senza ritardo*** without delay; ***essere in ritardo*** be late
ritenere ⟨2q⟩ (*credere*) believe
ritenersi: ***si ritiene molto intelligente*** he thinks he is very intelligent
ritenuta *f* deduction (***su*** from); ***ritenuta alla fonte*** deduction at source
ritirare ⟨1a⟩ withdraw, pull back; (*tirare di nuovo*) throw again; *proposta* withdraw; (*prelevare*) collect, pick up
ritirarsi (*restringersi*) shrink; ***ritirarsi a vita privata*** retire into private life; ***ritirarsi da*** *gara*, *esame ecc* withdraw from
ritiro *m* withdrawal
ritmo *m* rhythm
rito *m* ceremony; ***essere di rito*** be customary
ritoccare ⟨1d⟩ touch up
ritornare ⟨1a⟩ **1** *v/i venire* get back, come back, return; *andare* go back, return; *su argomento* go back (***su*** over); ***ritornare verde*** turn green again; ***ritornare in sé*** come to one's senses **2** *v/t* return
ritornello *m* refrain
ritorno *m* return; ***far ritorno*** come back, return; ***essere di ritorno*** be back; ***viaggio*** *m* ***di ritorno*** return trip
ritrarre ⟨3xx⟩ pull away; PITT paint; (*rappresentare*) depict
ritrattare ⟨1a⟩ retract
ritrattazione *f* retraction
ritratto *m* portrait; *fig* ***il ritratto di qu*** the spitting image of s.o.
ritrovare ⟨1c⟩ find; (*riacquistare*) regain
ritrovarsi meet again; (*capitare*) find o.s.; (*orientarsi*) get one's bearings
ritrovo *m* meeting; *luogo* meeting place; ***ritrovo notturno*** nightclub
ritto straight
riunificazione *f* reunification
riunione *f* meeting; *di amici*, *famiglia* reunion
riunire ⟨4d⟩ gather
riunirsi meet
riuscire ⟨4o⟩ succeed; (*essere capace*) manage; ***non riesco a capire*** I can't understand; ***riuscire bene / male*** be a success/a failure; *di foto* come out well / badly; ***riuscire in qc*** be successful in sth
riuscita *f* success
riuscito successful
riutilizzare ⟨1a⟩ re-use
riutilizzazione *f* re-use
riva *f* shore
rivale **1** *agg* rival *attr* **2** *m/f* rival
rivaleggiare ⟨1f⟩ compete
rivalità *f* rivalry
rivalutare ⟨1a⟩ revalue; *persona* change

R

one's mind about
rivalutazione *f* revaluation
rivedere ⟨2s⟩ see again; (*ripassare*) review, look at again; (*verificare*) check
rivelare ⟨1a⟩ reveal
rivelazione *f* revelation
rivendere ⟨3a⟩ resell
rivendicare ⟨1m & d⟩ demand
rivendicazione *f* demand; ***-i** pl* ***salariali*** wage demands
rivendita *f negozio* retail outlet
rivenditore *m*, **-trice** *f* retailer; ***rivenditore specializzato*** dealer
rivestimento *m* covering
rivestire ⟨4b⟩ (*foderare*) cover; *ruolo* play; *carica* fill
rivestirsi get dressed again
rivincita *f* return match; ***prendersi la rivincita*** get one's revenge
rivista *f* magazine; TEA revue; MIL review; ***rivista di moda*** fashion magazine
rivolgere ⟨3d⟩ turn; *domanda* address (***a qu*** to s.o.); ***non mi rivolge mai il saluto*** he never acknowledges me; ***rivolgere la parola a qu*** speak to s.o., address s.o.; ***rivolgere l'attenzione a qc*** turn one's attention to sth
rivolgersi: ***rivolgersi a qu*** apply to s.o. (***per*** for)
rivolgimento *m fig* upheaval
rivolta *f* revolt
rivoltare ⟨1c⟩ turn; (*mettere sottosopra*) turn upside down; (*disgustare*) revolt
rivoltella *f* revolver
rivoluzionario (*pl* -ri) revolutionary
rivoluzione *f* revolution
rizzare ⟨1a⟩ put up; *bandiera* raise; *orecchie* prick up
rizzarsi straighten up; ***mi si sono rizzati i capelli in testa*** my hair stood on end
roba *f* things *pl*, stuff; ***roba da mangiare*** food, things *or* stuff to eat; ***roba da matti!*** would you believe it!
robot *m inv* robot; *da cucina* food processor
robustezza *f* sturdiness
robusto sturdy
rocca *f* (*pl* -cche) fortress
roccia *f* (*pl* -cce) rock
rocciatore *m* rock climber
roccioso rocky
rock *m inv* MUS rock; ***concerto** m* ***rock*** rock concert
rockettaro *m*, **-a** *f* rocker
roco (*pl* -chi) hoarse
rodaggio *m* running in; *fig* ***sono ancora in rodaggio*** I'm still finding my feet; ***in rodaggio*** running in
rodere ⟨3b⟩ gnaw at
rodersi: ***rodersi dalla gelosia*** be eaten up with jealousy
roditore *m* rodent
rogna *f* F *di cane* mange; *problema* hassle
rognone *m di animale* kidney
Roma *f* Rome
romanico (*pl* -ci) Romanesque
romano 1 *agg* Roman; ***fare alla -a*** go Dutch **2** *m*, **-a** *f* Roman
romanticismo *m* Romanticism
romantico (*pl* -ci) **1** *agg* romantic **2** *m*, **-a** *f* romantic
romanziere *m* novelist
romanzo 1 *agg* Romance **2** *m* novel; ***romanzo giallo*** thriller
rombare ⟨1a⟩ rumble
rombo[1] *m* rumble
rombo[2] *m* ZO turbot
rombo[3] *m* MAT rhombus
romeno 1 *agg* Romanian **2** *m*, **-a** *f* Romanian
rompere ⟨3rr⟩ **1** *v/t* break; F ***rompere le scatole a qu*** get on s.o.'s nerves F **2** *v/i* F be a pain F; *fig* ***rompere con qu*** break it off with s.o.
rompersi break; ***rompersi un braccio*** break one's arm
rompicapo *m inv* puzzle; (*problema*) headache
rompighiaccio *m inv* ice-breaker; ALP ice-pick
rondine *f* swallow
ronzare ⟨1a⟩ buzz
ronzio *m* buzzing
rosa 1 *f* rose; ***rosa selvatica*** wild rose; ***rosa dei venti*** wind rose **2** *m/agg inv* pink
rosaio *m* (*pl* -ai) *pianta* rosebush
rosario *m* (*pl* -ri) REL rosary
rosato *m* rosé
rosbif *m inv* roast beef
roseo pink; *avvenire* rosy
roseto *m* rose garden
rosmarino *m* rosemary
rosolare ⟨1l & c⟩ brown
rosolia *f* German measles *sg*
rosone *m* ARCHI rose window
rospo *m* toad; *fig* F ***ingoiare il rospo*** lump it F
rossastro reddish
rossetto *m* lipstick
rossiccio (*pl* -cci) reddish
rosso 1 *agg* red **2** *m* red; ***rosso d'uovo*** egg yolk; ***fermarsi al rosso*** stop at a red light; ***passare col rosso*** go through a red light
rossore *m* red patch
rosticceria *f* rotisserie (*shop selling roast meat*)
rotaia *f* rail

rotare ⟨1o⟩ rotate
rotatoria *f* roundabout, *Am* traffic circle
rotazione *f* rotation
rotella *f* castor
rotocalco *m* (*pl* -chi) magazine
rotolare ⟨1l & c⟩ *v/t & v/i* roll
rotolarsi roll (around)
rotolino *m* FOTO film
rotolo *m* roll; FOTO film; ***andare a -i*** go to rack and ruin; ***mandare a -i*** ruin
rotondo round
rotta *f* MAR, AVIA course; *fig* (*giusta direzione*) straight and narrow; ***cambiare rotta*** change course; ***a rotta di collo*** at breakneck speed
rottame *m* wreck
rotto 1 *pp* → ***rompere* 2** *agg* broken
rottura *f* breaking; F *tra innamorati* break-up; F ***che rottura!*** what a pain! F
rotula *f* kneecap
roulotte *f inv* caravan
routine *f* routine
rovesciare ⟨1f & b⟩ *liquidi* spill; *oggetto* knock over; (*capovolgere*) overturn, upset; *fig* turn upside down
rovesciarsi overturn, capsize
rovesciata *f calcio* bicycle kick
rovescio (*pl* -sci) reverse; *in tennis* backhand; *fig* ***rovescio d'acqua*** downpour, cloudburst; ***rovescio di fortuna*** reversal of fortune; ***il rovescio della medaglia*** the other side of the coin; ***mettersi una maglia al rovescio*** put a sweater on inside out
rovina *f* ruin; ***andare in -e*** go to rack and ruin; ***mandare in -e*** ruin; ***-e*** *pl* ruins
rovinare ⟨1a⟩ ruin
rovinarsi ruin o.s.
rovo *m* bramble
rozzo rough and ready
RSM *abbr* (= ***Repubblica di San Marino***) Republic of San Marino
R.U. *abbr* (= ***Regno Unito***) UK (= United Kingdom)
ruba *f*: ***andare a ruba*** sell like hot cakes, walk out the door
rubare ⟨1a⟩ steal
rubinetto *m* tap; ***rubinetto dell'acqua calda*** hot water tap
rubino *m* ruby
rubrica *f* (*pl* -che) *di libro* table of contents; *quaderno* address book; *di giornale* column; TV report
rude rough and ready
rudere *m* ruin; **-i** *pl* ruins
rudimentale rudimentary, basic
rudimenti *mpl* basics, rudiments
ruga *f* (*pl* -ghe) wrinkle, line
ruggine *f* rust
ruggire ⟨4d⟩ roar
ruggito *m* roar
rugiada *f* dew
rugoso rough; *pelle* wrinkled; *albero* gnarled
rullare ⟨1a⟩ MAR roll; AVIA taxi
rullino *m* FOTO film
rullio *m* roll
rullo *m* roll; ***rullo compressore*** steam roller
rum *m* rum
ruminare ⟨1a⟩ chew the cud; *fig* ruminate
rumore *m* noise; ***far rumore*** make a noise, be noisy
rumoreggiare ⟨1f⟩ be noisy; *di tuono* growl, rumble; *di folla* mutter
rumoroso noisy
ruolo *m* role; ***personale*** *m* ***di ruolo*** (permanent) members of staff
ruota *f* wheel; ***ruota anteriore*** front wheel; ***ruota dentata*** cog; ***ruota posteriore*** back wheel; ***ruota motrice*** drive wheel; ***ruota di scorta*** spare wheel; *fig* ***mettere i bastoni tra le -e a qu*** put a spoke in s.o.'s wheel
rupe *f* cliff
rupestre *inv* rock *attr*; ***arte*** *f* ***rupestre*** wall painting
ruscello *m* stream
russare ⟨1a⟩ snore
Russia *f* Russia
russo 1 *agg* Russian **2** *m*, **-a** *f* Russian
rustico (*pl* -ci) rural, rustic; *fig* unsophisticated
ruttare ⟨1a⟩ belch; *di bambino* burp
ruttino *m* burp
rutto *m* belch
ruvidezza *f* roughness
ruvido rough
ruzzolare ⟨1l⟩ fall
ruzzolone *m* fall; ***fare un ruzzolone*** fall, have a fall

S

S *abbr* (= ***sud***) S (= south)
S. *abbr* (= ***santo***) St (= Saint)
s *abbr* (= ***secondo***) s, sec (= second)
S.A. *abbr* (= ***Società Anonima***) Ltd (= Limited)
sa → ***sapere***
sabato *m* Saturday; ***di sabato*** on Saturdays; ***è meglio uscire di sabato*** it's better to go out on a Saturday
sabbia *f* sand
sabbioso sandy
sabotaggio *m* sabotage
sabotare ⟨1a⟩ sabotage
sabotatore *m*, **-trice** *f* saboteur
sacca *f* (*pl* -cche) bag; ANAT, BIO sac
saccarina *f* saccharin
saccheggiare ⟨1f⟩ sack; *spir* raid
saccheggio *m* (*pl* -ggi) sack, sacking
sacchetto *m* bag
sacco *m* (*pl* -cchi) sack; *fig* F ***un sacco di*** piles of F; ***costa un sacco*** it costs a fortune; ***sacco a pelo*** sleeping bag; ***sacco da montagna*** backpack, rucksack; *fig* ***vuotare il sacco*** spill the beans; *confidarsi* pour one's heart out
saccopelista *m/f* backpacker, hiker
sacerdote *m* priest
sacramento *m* sacrament
sacrificare ⟨1m & d⟩ sacrifice
sacrificarsi sacrifice o.s.
sacrificio *m* (*pl* -ci) sacrifice
sacrilegio *m* sacrilege
sacro sacred; ***osso*** *m* ***sacro*** sacrum
sadico (*pl* -ci) **1** *agg* sadistic **2** *m*, **-a** *f* sadist
sadismo *m* sadism
safari *m inv* safari; ***safari fotografico*** photo safari
saggezza *f* wisdom
saggiare ⟨1f⟩ test
saggio[1] (*pl* -ggi) **1** *agg* wise **2** *m* wise man, sage
saggio[2] *m* (*pl* -ggi) test; (*campione*) sample; *scritto* essay; *di danza*, *musica* end of term show; ***saggio d'interesse*** interest rate, rate of interest; ***saggio di sconto*** discount rate
saggista *m/f* essayist
saggistica *f* essay-writing
Sagittario *m* ASTR Sagittarius
sahariana *f* safari jacket
sala *f* room; (*soggiorno*) living room; ***sala d'aspetto*** waiting room; ***sala da pranzo*** dining room; ***sala di lettura*** reading room; ***sala giochi*** amusement arcade; ***sala operatoria*** (operating) theatre, *Am* operating room
salamandra *f* salamander
salame *m* salami
salamoia *f*: ***in salamoia*** in brine
salare ⟨1a⟩ salt
salariale pay *attr*
salariato *m* employee
salario *m* (*pl* -ri) salary, wages; ***salario base*** basic salary *or* wage
salatino *m* savo(u)ry
salato savo(u)ry; *acqua* salt; *cibo* salted; F (*caro*) steep F; ***troppo salato*** salty
saldare ⟨1a⟩ weld; *ossa* set; *fattura* pay (off)
saldatura *f* welding; ***una saldatura*** a weld
saldo 1 *agg* steady, secure; *fig* ***essere saldo nelle proprie convizioni*** be unshakeable in one's beliefs; ***tenersi saldo*** hold on tight **2** *m* payment; *in svendita* sale item; (*resto*) balance; **-i** *pl* ***di fine stagione*** end-of-season sales; ***articolo in saldo*** sale item; ***saldo attivo*** net assets; ***saldo passivo*** net liabilities
sale *m* salt; ***ha poco sale in zucca*** he's not very bright
salgo → ***salire***
salice *m* willow; ***salice piangente*** weeping willow
saliera *f* salt cellar
salina *f* salt works
salire ⟨4m⟩ **1** *v/i* climb; *di livello*, *prezzi*, *temperatura*, rise; ***salire in*** *macchina* get in; ***salire su*** *scala* climb; *treno*, *autobus* get on **2** *v/t*: ***salire le scale*** *andare* go up, climb; *venire* come up, climb
saliscendi *m inv*: ***finestra*** *f* ***a saliscendi*** sash window
salita *f* climb; *strada* slope; ***strada*** *f* ***in salita*** steep street
saliva *f* saliva
salma *f* corpse, body
salmastro 1 *agg* briny **2** *m* salt
salmone *m* salmon; ***salmone affumicato*** smoked salmon
salmonella *f* salmonella (poisoning)
salone *m* living room; (*esposizione*) show; ***salone dell'automobile*** motor show; ***salone di bellezza*** beauty salon
salotto *m* lounge
salpare ⟨1a⟩ sail
salsa *f* sauce; ***salsa di pomodoro*** tomato

sauce
salsiccia *f* (*pl* -cce) sausage
saltare ⟨1a⟩ **1** *v/t* jump; (*omettere*) skip; ***saltare*** (***in padella***) sauté **2** *v/i* jump; *di bottone* come off; *di fusibile* blow; F *di impegno* be cancelled; ***saltare*** (***giù***) ***dal letto*** jump out of bed; ***saltare dalla gioia*** jump for joy; ***è saltata la corrente*** there's been a power cut; ***saltare / far saltare in aria*** blow up; ***saltare fuori*** turn up
saltellare ⟨1b⟩ hop
saltimbocca *m inv fried veal topped with prosciutto and a sage leaf*
salto *m* jump; (*dislivello*) change in level; ***salto mortale*** somersault; ***salto in alto*** high jump; ***salto in lungo*** long jump; *fig* ***salto nel buio*** leap in the dark; ***faccio un salto da te*** I'll drop by *or* in
saltuariamente occasionally
saltuario (*pl* -ri) occasional; ***lavoro*** *m* ***saltuario*** casual work
salubre healthy
salumeria *f* shop that sells salumi
salumi *mpl* cold meat *sg*
salutare **1** *agg* healthy; *fig discussione* helpful **2** *v/t* ⟨1a⟩ say hello to, greet; ***salutami la tua famiglia*** say hello to the family for me
salute *f* health; ***salute!*** cheers!; ***alla tua salute!*** cheers!, here's to you!
salutista *m/f* (*mpl* -i) health fanatic
saluto *m* wave; ***tanti -i*** greetings
salvagente *m inv* lifebelt; *giubbotto* life jacket; *per bambini* ring; (*isola spartitraffico*) traffic island
salvaguardare ⟨1a⟩ protect, safeguard
salvaguardia *f* protection
salvare ⟨1a⟩ save, rescue
salvataggio *m* (*pl* -ggi) salvage; ***barca*** *f* ***di salvataggio*** lifeboat
salve! hello!
salvezza *f* salvation
salvia *f* sage
salvietta *f* napkin, *Br* serviette
salvo **1** *agg* safe **2** *prp* except; ***salvo che*** unless; ***salvo imprevisti*** barring accidents, all being well **3** *m*: ***mettersi in salvo*** take shelter
sambuco *m* (*pl* -chi) elder
San = ***Santo***
sanare ⟨1a⟩ heal; FIN, ARCHI restore
sanatorio *m* (*pl* -ri) sanatorium, *Am* sanitarium
sandalo *m* sandal; BOT sandalwood
sangue *m* blood; ***a sangue freddo*** in cold blood; ***donare il sangue*** give blood; GASTR ***al sangue*** rare
sanguigno: ***gruppo*** *m* ***sanguigno*** blood group; ***vaso*** *m* ***sanguigno*** blood vessel
sanguinare ⟨1l⟩ bleed; ***mi sanguina il naso*** my nose is bleeding
sanguinoso bloody
sanguisuga *f* (*pl* -ghe) leech
sanità *f* health; *amministrazione* health care
sanitario (*pl* -ri) health *attr*; ***assistenza*** *f* ***-a*** health care
sanno → ***sapere***
sano healthy; ***sano e salvo*** safe and sound
santo **1** *agg* holy; ***acqua*** *f* ***-a*** holy water; ***tutto il santo giorno*** the whole blessed day **2** *m*, **-a** *f* saint; *davanti al nome* St
santuario *m* (*pl* -ri) sanctuary
sanzione *f* sanction
sapere ⟨2n⟩ **1** *v/t* know; (*essere capace di*) be able to; (***venire a***) ***sapere*** hear; ***sai nuotare?*** can you swim?; ***lo so*** I know **2** *v/i*: ***far sapere qc a qu*** let s.o. know sth; ***saperla lunga*** know all about it; ***non si sa mai*** you never know; ***per quel che ne so*** as far as I know; ***sapere di*** (*avere sapore di*) taste of; ***non sa di nulla*** it doesn't taste of anything **3** *m* knowledge
sapiente **1** *agg* wise **2** *m/f* (*scienzato*) scientist
sapienza *f* wisdom
sapone *m* soap
saponetta *f* toilet soap
sapore *m* taste (***di*** of); ***-i*** *pl* aromatic herbs; ***avere sapore di qc*** taste of sth; ***senza sapore*** tasteless
saporito tasty
saracinesca *f* (*pl* -sche) roller shutter
sarcasmo *m* sarcasm; ***non fare sarcasmo!*** don't be sarcastic!
sarcastico (*pl* -ci) sarcastic
sarcofago *m* (*pl* -gi e -ghi) sarcophagus
Sardegna *f* Sardinia
sardina *f* sardine
sardo **1** *agg* Sardinian **2** *m*, **-a** *f* Sardinian
sarò → ***essere***
sarto *m*, **-a** *f* tailor; *per donne* dressmaker
sartoria *f* tailor's; *per donne* dressmaker's
sasso *m* stone; ***restare di sasso*** be thunderstruck
sassofonista *m/f* (*mpl* -i) saxophone player, saxophonist
sassofono *m* saxophone
satellite **1** *m* satellite **2** *agg* satellite *attr*; ***città*** *f* ***satellite*** satellite town
satira *f* satire
satirico (*pl* -ci) satirical
saturare ⟨1l⟩ saturate (***di*** with)
saturazione *f* saturation
saturo saturated

S

sauna *f* sauna
saziare ⟨1g⟩ satiate
saziarsi eat one's fill; ***non saziarsi mai di fare qc*** never get tired of doing sth
sazietà *f*: ***mangiare a sazietà*** eat one's fill
sazio (*pl* -zi) full (up)
sbadato absent-minded
sbadigliare ⟨1g⟩ yawn
sbadiglio *m* (*pl* -gli) yawn
sbagliare ⟨1g⟩ **1** *v/i e* **sbagliarsi** make a mistake; ***hai sbagliato a dirle la verità*** you were wrong to tell her the truth **2** *v/t* make a mistake in; ***sbagliarsi persona*** have the wrong person; ***sbagliarsi strada*** go the wrong way
sbagliato wrong
sbaglio *m* (*pl* -gli) mistake; ***per sbaglio*** by mistake; ***senza -i*** flawless
sbalordimento *m* amazement, stupefaction
sbalordire ⟨4d⟩ stun, amaze
sbalorditivo amazing, incredible
sbalzare ⟨1a⟩ throw; *temperatura* change
sbalzo *m* jump; ***sbalzo di temperatura*** change in temperature
sbandare ⟨1a⟩ AUTO skid; FERR, *fig* go off the rails
sbandata *f* AUTO skid; F ***prendersi una sbandata per qu*** develop a crush on s.o.
sbarazzare ⟨1a⟩ clear
sbarazzarsi: ***sbarazzarsi di*** get rid of
sbarcare ⟨1d⟩ **1** *v/t merci* unload; *persone* disembark; *fig* ***sbarcare il lunario*** make ends meet **2** *v/i* disembark
sbarco *m* (*pl* -chi) *di merce* unloading; *di persone* disembarkation
sbarra *f* bar; ***essere alla sbarra*** be on trial
sbarramento *m* fence; (*ostacolo*) barrier
sbarrare ⟨1a⟩ bar; *assegno* cross; *occhi* open wide
sbarrato *assegno* crossed; *occhi* wide open
sbattere ⟨3a⟩ **1** *v/t porta* slam, bang; (*urtare*) bang; GASTR beat; ***sbattere la porta in faccia a qu*** close the door in s.o.'s face **2** *v/i* bang
sbattitore *m* hand mixer
sbendare ⟨1b⟩ take the bandage(s) off
sberla *f* F slap
sbiadire ⟨4d⟩ fade
sbiadito faded; *stile* colo(u)rless
sbiancare ⟨1d⟩ **1** *v/t* bleach **2** *v/i* turn pale
sbilanciare ⟨1f⟩ unbalance, throw off balance
sbilanciarsi lose one's balance; *fig* commit o.s.
sbizzarrirsi ⟨4d⟩ indulge o.s.
sbloccare ⟨1c & d⟩ clear; *macchina* unblock; *prezzi* deregulate
sblocco *m* (*pl* -cchi) *f* clearing; *di macchina* unblocking; *di prezzi* deregulation
sboccare ⟨1d⟩: ***sboccare in*** *di fiume* flow into; *di strada* lead to
sbocciare ⟨1f & c⟩ open (out)
sbocco *m* (*pl* -cchi) FIN outlet; *di situazione* way out; ***strada*** *f* ***senza sbocco*** dead end, cul-de-sac
sbornia *f* F hangover; ***prendersi una sbornia*** get drunk
sborsare ⟨1a⟩ F cough up F
sbottonare ⟨1a⟩ unbutton
sbottonarsi *fig* open up (***con*** to); ***sbottonarsi la giacca*** unbutton one's jacket
sbozzare ⟨1c⟩ draft, rough out
sbraitare ⟨1a⟩ shout, yell
sbranare ⟨1a⟩ tear apart
sbriciolare ⟨1l⟩ spread crumbs
sbrigare ⟨1e⟩ attend to
sbrigarsi hurry up
sbrigativo (*rapido*) hurried, rushed; (*brusco*) brusque
sbrinare ⟨1a⟩ *frigorifero* defrost
sbrinatore *m* defrost control
sbrogliare ⟨1g & c⟩ untangle, disentangle; ***sbrogliarsela*** sort things out
sbronza *f* F hangover
sbronzarsi ⟨1a⟩ F get drunk
sbronzo F tight F, sloshed F
sbucare ⟨1d⟩ emerge; ***da dove sei sbucato?*** where did you spring from?
sbucciare ⟨1f⟩ *frutta, patate* peel; ***sbucciarsi le ginocchia*** skin one's knees
sbucciato peeled; *ginocchio* skinned
sbucciatura *f* graze
s.c. *abbr* (= ***sopra citato***) above-mentioned
scabroso rough, uneven; *fig* offensive
scacchiera *f* chessboard
scacciare ⟨1f⟩ chase away
scacco *m* (*pl* -cchi) (chess) piece; *fig* setback; ***scacco matto*** checkmate; ***-cchi*** *pl* chess *sg*; ***giocare a -cchi*** play chess; ***a -cchi*** checked
scadente 1 → ***scadere*** **2** *agg* second-rate
scadenza *f* deadline; *su alimento* best before date; ***scadenza del termine*** deadline, last date; ***a breve scadenza*** short-term; ***a lunga scadenza*** long-term
scadere ⟨2c⟩ *di passaporto* expire; *di cambiale* fall due; (*perdere valore*) decline (in quality)
scaduto expired; *alimento* past its sell-by date
scaffale *m* shelves *pl*
scaglia *f* flake; *di legno* chip; *di pesce* scale
scagliare ⟨1g⟩ hurl

scagliarsi: ***scagliarsi contro*** attack
scala *f* staircase; GEOG scale; ***scala (a pioli)*** ladder; ***scala mobile*** escalator; FIN sliding scale; ***scala musicale*** (musical) scale; ***disegno*** *m* ***in scala*** scale drawing; ***su larga scala*** on a large scale; ***su scala nazionale*** country-wide; ***fare le -e*** climb the stairs
scalare ⟨1a⟩ climb
scalata *f* climb; ***scalata al successo*** rise to fame
scalatore *m*, **-trice** *f* climber
scaldabagno *m* water heater
scaldare ⟨1a⟩ heat (up); *fig* ***scaldare la testa a qu*** get s.o. worked up
scaldarsi warm up; *fig* get worked up, get excited
scaldavivande *m inv* food warmer
scalinata *f* steps *pl*
scalino *m* step
scalo *m* AVIA stop; MAR port of call; ***volo*** *m* ***senza scalo*** nonstop flight; ***fare scalo a*** call at
scalogna *f* bad luck; ***portare scalogna*** be unlucky
scalognato unlucky
scaloppina *f* escalope
scalpello *m* chisel
scaltro shrewd
scalzo barefoot
scambiare ⟨1k⟩ (*confondere*) mistake (***per*** for); (*barattare*) exchange, swap F (***con*** for)
scambio *m* (*pl* -bi) exchange; *di persona* mistake; FERR points *pl*; ***-i*** *pl* ***commerciali*** trade *sg*; ***scambio di lettere*** exchange of letters; ***scambio d'opinioni*** exchange of views; ***-i*** *pl* ***culturali*** cultural exchange *sg*; ***libero scambio*** free trade
scampagnata *f* day out in the country
scampanellare ⟨1b⟩ ring
scampanellata *f* ring
scampi *mpl* zo scampi
scampo *m* escape, way out
scampolo *m* remnant
scandagliare ⟨1g⟩ sound; *fig* sound out
scandalistico (*pl* -ci) scandal-mongering
scandalizzare ⟨1a⟩ scandalize, shock
scandalizzarsi be scandalized *or* shocked (***di*** by)
scandalizzato scandalized
scandalo *m* scandal
scandaloso scandalous
scandinavo 1 *agg* Scandinavian **2** *m*, **-a** *f* Scandinavian
scanner *m inv* INFOR scanner
scannerizzare ⟨1a⟩ INFOR scan
scansafatiche *m/f inv* lazybones
scansare ⟨1a⟩ (*allontanare*) move; (*evitare*) avoid
scansarsi move out of the way
scansia *f* bookcase
scantinato *m* cellar
scapito *m*: ***a scapito di*** to the detriment of
scapola *f* shoulder blade, ANAT scapula
scapolo 1 *agg* single, unmarried **2** *m* bachelor
scappamento *m* TEC exhaust
scappare ⟨1a⟩ (*fuggire*) run away; (*affrettarsi*) rush, run; ***lasciarsi scappare l'occasione*** let the opportunity slip; ***mi è scappata la pazienza*** I lost patience
scappatella *f di bambino* escapade; ***fare delle -lle*** get into mischief
scappatoia *f* way out
scarabocchiare ⟨1k & c⟩ scribble
scarabocchio *m* (*pl* -cchi) scribble
scarafaggio *m* (*pl* -ggi) cockroach
scaraventare ⟨1b⟩ throw, hurl
scaraventarsi throw *or* hurl o.s. (***contro*** at)
scarcerare ⟨1l⟩ release
scarcerazione *f* release
scardinare ⟨1l⟩ take off the hinges
scarica *f* (*pl* -che) discharge
scaricare ⟨1l & d⟩ unload; *batteria* run down; *rifiuti*, *sostanze nocive* dump; *responsabilità* offload, get rid of; ***scaricarearsi la coscienza*** ease one's conscience; F ***scaricare qu*** get rid of s.o.; INFOR ***scaricare dalla rete*** download; INFOR ***scaricare su dischetto*** download to disk
scaricarsi relax, unwind F; *di batteria* run down
scarico (*pl* -chi) **1** *agg camion* empty; *batteria* run-down **2** *m di merce* unloading; *luogo* dump; *di responsabilità* offloading; ***gas*** *m* ***di scarico*** exhaust (fumes); ***tubo*** *m* ***di scarico*** exhaust (pipe); ***divieto di scarico*** no dumping; ***-chi*** *pl* ***industriali*** industrial waste *sg*
scarlattina *f* scarlet fever
scarpa *f* shoe; ***-e*** *pl* ***da uomo / da donna*** men's/women's shoes
scarpata *f* (*burrone*) escarpment
scarpetta *f* shoe; ***-e*** *pl* ***da ginnastica*** trainers
scarpinare ⟨1a⟩ trek
scarpinata *f* trek
scarpone *m* (heavy) boot; ***scarpone da sci*** ski boot
scarseggiare ⟨1f⟩ become scarce; ***scarseggiare di qc*** not have much of sth, be short of sth
scarsezza *f*, **scarsità** *f* shortage, scarcity; ***scarsezza di viveri*** food shortage

scarso scarce, in short supply; ***essere scarso di qc*** be lacking in sth; ***quattro chilometri -si*** barely four kilometres
scartare ⟨1a⟩ (*svolgere*) unwrap; (*eliminare*) reject
scarto *m* rejection; (*cosa scartata*) reject; ***merce** f **di scarto*** imperfect goods
scassare ⟨1a⟩ F ruin, wreck
scassarsi F give up the ghost F
scassato F done for F
scassinare ⟨1a⟩ force open
scassinatore *m*, **-trice** *f* burglar
scasso *m* forced entry; ***furto** m **con scasso*** breaking and entering, burglary
scatenare ⟨1a⟩ *fig* unleash
scatenarsi *fig*: *di tempesta* break; *di collera* break out; *di persona* let one's hair down
scatenato unrestrained
scatola *f* box; *di tonno, piselli* tin, can; ***in scatola*** *cibo* tinned, canned; AVIA ***scatola nera*** black box
scattare ⟨1a⟩ **1** *v/t* FOT take **2** *v/i* go off; *di serratura* catch; (*arrabbiarsi*) lose one's temper; *di atleta* put on a spurt; ***scattare in piedi*** jump up; ***far scattare*** activate
scatto *m* click; SP spurt; FOTO exposure; *di foto* taking; TELEC unit; FOTO ***scatto automatico*** automatic timer; ***uno scatto di rabbia*** an angry gesture; ***scatto di stipendio*** automatic raise
scavalcare ⟨1d⟩ *muro* climb (over)
scavare ⟨1a⟩ *con pala* dig; *con trivella* excavate
scavi *mpl archeologici* dig *sg*
scegliere ⟨3ss⟩ choose, pick, select
scelgo → ***scegliere***
scelta *f* choice, selection; ***di prima scelta*** first-rate; ***prendine uno a scelta*** take your pick
scelto 1 *pp* → ***scegliere*** **2** *agg* handpicked; *merce, pubblico* (specially) selected
scemo 1 *agg* stupid, idiotic **2** *m*, **-a** *f* idiot
scena theatre, *Am* theater; (*scenata*) scene; *fig* ***colpo** m **di scena*** coup de théâtre; ***mettere in scena*** produce; *fig* ***fare scena muta*** be struck dumb
scenario *m* (*pl* -ri) screenplay; *fig* scenery
scenata *f* scene; ***fare una scenata*** (***a qu***) make a scene
scendere ⟨3c⟩ **1** *v/i andare* go down, descend; *venire* come down, descend; *da cavallo* get down, dismount; *dal treno, dall' autobus* get off; *dalla macchina* get out; *di temperatura, prezzi* go down, drop; ***scendere a terra*** come (back) down to earth **2** *v/t*: ***scendere le scale*** *andare* go down the stairs; *venire* come down the stairs
scendiletto *m* bedside rug
sceneggiatura *f* screenplay
scenografia *f* sets *pl*
scenografo *m*, **-a** *f* set designer
scetticismo *m* scepticism, *Am* skepticism
scettico 1 *agg* sceptical, *Am* skeptical **2** *m*, **-a** *f* sceptic, *Am* skeptic
scheda *f* card; (*formulario*) form; ***scheda elettorale*** ballot (paper); INFOR ***scheda grafica*** graphics card; ***scheda telefonica*** phonecard
schedario *m* (*pl* -ri) file
schedina *f* pools coupon
scheggia *f* (*pl* -gge) sliver
scheletro *m* skeleton
schema *m* (*pl* -i) diagram; (*abbozzo*) outline
schematico (*pl* -ci) general; *disegno* schematic
schematizzare ⟨1a⟩ outline
scherma *f* fencing; ***tirare di scherma*** fence
schermo *m* screen; (*riparo*) shield
scherzare ⟨1a⟩ play; (*burlare*) joke
scherzo *m* joke; MUS scherzo; ***essere uno scherzo*** (*facile*) be child's play; ***-i a parte*** joking aside; ***per scherzo*** *fare, dire qc* as a joke
scherzoso playful
schiaccianoci *m inv* pair of nutcrackers, nutcrackers *pl*
schiacciare ⟨1f⟩ **1** *v/t* crush; *noce* crack; ***schiacciare un piede a qu*** step on s.o.'s toes; F ***schiacciare un sonnellino*** have a snooze F, have forty winks F **2** *v/i* SP smash
schiacciato crushed, squashed
schiaffeggiare ⟨1f⟩ slap
schiaffo *m* slap
schiamazzare ⟨1a⟩ make a din
schiamazzo *m* yell, scream
schiantare ⟨1a⟩ **1** *v/t* crash, smash **2** *v/i e* **schiantarsi** crash
schianto *m* crash
schiarire ⟨4d⟩ lighten
schiarirsi brighten up
schiarita *f* bright spell
schiavitù *f* slavery
schiavo 1 *agg*: ***essere schiavo di*** be a slave to **2** *m*, **-a** *f* slave
schiena *f* back; ***mal** m **di schiena*** back ache
schienale *m di sedile* back
schiera *f* group; ***a schiera*** in ranks
schierare ⟨1b⟩ line up
schierarsi: ***schierarsi in favore di qu*** come out in favo(u)r of s.o.
schietto pure; *fig* frank

schifezza *f*: ***che schifezza!*** how disgusting!
schifo *m* disgust; ***fare schifo a qu*** disgust s.o.
schifoso disgusting; (*pessimo*) dreadful
schioppo *m* shotgun
schiuma *f* foam; ***schiuma da bagno*** bubble bath; ***schiuma da barba*** shaving foam
schiumoso foamy
schivare ⟨1a⟩ avoid, dodge F
schivo shy
schizzare ⟨1a⟩ **1** *v/t* (*spruzzare*) squirt; (*abbozzare*) sketch **2** *v/i* squirt; (*saltare*) jump
schizzinoso fussy
schizzo *m* squirt; (*abbozzo*) (lightning) sketch
sci *m inv* ski; *attività* skiing; ***sci acquatico*** water ski / skiing; ***sci di fondo*** cross-country ski / skiing
sciacquare ⟨1a⟩ rinse
sciacquatura *f* rinse
sciagura *f* disaster
sciagurato *giorno*, *evento* unfortunate
scialle *m* shawl
scialuppa *f* dinghy; ***scialuppa di salvataggio*** lifeboat
sciame *m* swarm
sciare ⟨1h⟩ ski
sciarpa *f* scarf
sciatica *f* sciatica
sciatore *m*, **-trice** *f* skier
sciatteria *f* untidiness, sloppiness F
sciatto untidy, sloppy F
scientifico (*pl* -ci) scientific
scienza *f* science; ***-e** pl **naturali*** natural science
scienziato *m*, **-a** *f* scientist
scimmia *f* monkey
scimmiottare ⟨1c⟩ ape
scimpanzè *m inv* chimpanzee, chimp F
scintilla *f* spark
scintillante sparkling
scintillare ⟨1a⟩ sparkle
scintillio *m* sparkle
sciocchezza *f* (*idiozia*) stupidity; ***è solo una sciocchezza*** it's nothing
sciocco (*pl* -cchi) **1** *agg* silly **2** *m*, **-a** *f* silly thing
sciogliere ⟨3ss⟩ untie; *capelli* undo, let down; *matrimonio* dissolve; *neve* melt; *dubbio*, *problema* clear up
sciogliersi *di corda*, *nodo* come undone; *di burro*, *neve* melt; *di questione*, *problema* resolve itself
scioglilingua *m inv* tongue-twister
scioltezza *f* nimbleness; *fisica* agility
sciolto **1** *pp* → ***sciogliere*** **2** *agg neve*, *ghiaccio* melted; *matrimonio* dissolved; ***a briglia -a*** at breakneck speed
scioperante *m/f* striker
scioperare ⟨1l & c⟩ strike
sciopero *m* strike; ***fare sciopero*** go on strike; ***sciopero bianco*** work-to-rule; ***sciopero generale*** general strike; ***sciopero della fame*** hunger strike
sciovia *f* ski-lift
sciovinismo *m* chauvinism
sciovinista *m/f* (*mpl* -i) chauvinist
scipito bland
scippatore *m*, **-trice** *f* bag-snatcher
scippo *m* bag-snatching
scirocco *m* sirocco
sciroppo *m* syrup
scissione *f* splitting
scisto *m* GEOL schist
sciupare ⟨1a⟩ (*logorare*) wear out; *salute* ruin; *tempo*, *denaro* waste, fritter away
sciupato *persona* drawn; *cosa* worn out
scivolare ⟨1l⟩ slide; (*cadere*) slip
scivolo *m* slide; (*caduta*) slip; *gioco* chute; ***scivolo d'emergenza*** escape chute
scivoloso slippery
sclerosi *f inv* MED sclerosis
sclerosi multipla multiple sclerosis, MS
scocciare F ⟨1f⟩ bother, annoy, hassle F
scocciatore F *m*, **-trice** *f* pest F, nuisance F
scocciatura F *f* nuisance F
scodella *f* bowl
scogliera *f* cliff
scoglio *m* (*pl* -gli) rock; *fig* stumbling block
scoiattolo *m* squirrel
scolapasta *m inv* colander
scolare ⟨1a⟩ drain
scolaro *m*, **-a** *f* schoolboy; *ragazza* schoolgirl
scolastico (*pl* -ci) school *attr*
scoliosi *f inv* curvature of the spine
scollato low-necked; *donna* wearing a low neck
scollatura *f* neck(line)
scollo *m* neck
scolo *m* drainage
scolorire ⟨4d⟩ **1** *v/t* fade **2** *v/i e* **scolorirsi** fade
scolorito faded
scolpire ⟨4d⟩ *marmo*, *statua* sculpt; *legno* carve; *fig* engrave
scommessa *f* bet
scommesso *pp* → ***scommettere***
scommettere ⟨3ee⟩ bet
scomodare ⟨1l & c⟩ disturb
scomodarsi put o.s. out; ***non si scomodi*** please don't go to any bother

scomodo uncomfortable; (*non pratico*) inconvenient
scomparire ⟨4e⟩ disappear
scomparsa *f* disappearance
scomparso *pp* → ***scomparire***
scompartimento *m* compartment; FERR ***scompartimento per (non) fumatori*** (non-)smoking compartment
scompenso *m* imbalance; ***scompenso cardiaco*** cardiac insufficiency
scompigliare ⟨1g⟩ *persona* ruffle the hair of; *capelli* ruffle
scompiglio *m* (*pl* -gli) confusion
scomponibile flat pack *attr*, modular
scomporre ⟨3ll⟩ break down
scomporsi: ***senza scomporsi*** without showing any emotion
sconcertante disconcerting
sconcio (*pl* -ci) indecent; *parola* disgusting, filthy
sconclusionato incoherent
sconfiggere ⟨3cc⟩ defeat
sconfinare ⟨1a⟩ trespass; MIL cross the border
sconfinato vast, boundless
sconfitta *f* defeat
sconfitto *pp* → ***sconfiggere***
sconfortante discouraging, disheartening
sconfortare ⟨1c⟩ discourage, dishearten
sconforto *m* discouragement
scongelare ⟨1b⟩ thaw
scongiurare ⟨1a⟩ beg; *pericolo* avert
sconosciuto 1 *agg* unknown **2** *m*, **-a** *f* stranger
sconsigliare ⟨1g⟩ advise against; ***sconsigliare qc a qu*** advise s.o. against sth
sconsolato disconsolate
scontare ⟨1a⟩ FIN deduct, discount; *pena* serve
scontato discounted; (*previsto*) expected; ***scontato del 30%*** 30% discount *or* deduction
scontento 1 *agg* unhappy, not satisfied (***di*** with) **2** *m* unhappiness, dissatisfaction
sconto *m* discount; ***praticare uno sconto*** give a discount
scontrarsi ⟨1a⟩ collide (***con*** with); *fig* clash (***con*** with)
scontrino *m* receipt; ***fare lo scontrino alla cassa*** please pay at the cash desk before ordering
scontro *m* AUTO collision; *fig* clash
scontroso unpleasant, disagreeable
sconveniente inappropriate, unacceptable
sconvolgente upsetting, distressing; ***di un'intelligenza sconvolgente*** incredibly intelligent
sconvolgere ⟨3d⟩ upset
sconvolto 1 *pp* → ***sconvolgere*** **2** *agg paese* in upheaval
scooter *m inv* scooter
scopa *f* broom
scopare ⟨1a⟩ sweep; P shag P
scoperchiare ⟨1k⟩ *pentola* take the lid off
scoperta *f* discovery
scoperto 1 *pp* → ***scoprire*** **2** *agg pentola* uncovered; ***a capo scoperto*** bareheaded; ***assegno*** *m* ***scoperto*** bad cheque, rubber cheque F **3** *m* FIN overdraft; ***allo scoperto*** in the open
scopo *m* aim, purpose; ***allo scopo di fare qc*** in order to do sth; ***senza scopo*** aimlessly
scoppiare ⟨1k & c⟩ *di bomba, petardo* explode; *di palloncino, pneumatico* burst; ***scoppiare in lacrime*** burst into tears; ***scoppiare a ridere*** burst out laughing; ***scoppiare di caldo*** be boiling hot
scoppio *m* (*pl* -ppi) explosion; *di palloncino* bursting; *fig* outbreak
scoprire ⟨4f⟩ *contenitore* take the lid off; (*denudare*) uncover; *piani, verità* discover, find out
scoraggiare ⟨1f⟩ discourage, dishearten
scoraggiarsi become discouraged, lose heart
scoraggiato discouraged, disheartened
scorciatoia *f* short cut
scordare ⟨1c⟩, **scordarsi di** forget
scordato MUS out of tune
scoreggia *f* (*pl* -gge) F fart F
scoreggiare ⟨1f⟩ F fart F
scorgere ⟨3d⟩ see, make out; ***non farsi scorgere*** not let o.s. be seen
scoria *f* waste
scorpione *m* scorpion; ASTR ***Scorpione*** Scorpio
scorrere ⟨3o⟩ **1** *v/i* flow, run; *di tempo* go past, pass **2** *v/t giornale* skim
scorretto (*errato*) incorrect; (*non onesto*) unfair
scorrevole *porta* sliding; *stile* flowing
scorso 1 *pp* → ***scorrere*** **2** *agg*: ***l'anno scorso*** last year
scorta *f* escort; (*provvista*) supply, stock
scortare ⟨1c⟩ escort
scortese rude, discourteous
scortesia *f* rudeness, lack of courtesy
scorto *pp* → ***scorgere***
scorza *f* peel; *fig* exterior
scossa *f* shake; ***scossa di terremoto*** (earth) tremor; ***scossa elettrica*** electric shock
scosso *pp* → ***scuotere***
scostare ⟨1c⟩ move away (***da*** from)
scostarsi move (aside); *fig* ***scostarsi del-***

la retta via leave the straight and narrow
scottante delicate
scottare ⟨1c⟩ **1** *v/t* burn; GASTR *verdure* blanch; ***mi sono scottato le dita*** I burned my fingers **2** *v/i* burn; ***scotta!*** it's hot!
scottato *verdure* blanched
scottatura *f* burn; ***ho già avuto troppe -e*** I've had my fingers burned once too often
scozzese 1 *agg* Scottish **2** *m/f* Scot
Scozia *f* Scotland
screditare ⟨1l⟩ discredit
scremato skimmed; ***parzialmente scremato*** semi-skimmed
screpolare ⟨1l & b⟩ *e* **screpolarsi** crack
screpolatura *f* crack
scricchiolare ⟨1l⟩ creak
scricchiolio *m* (*pl* -ii) creak
scricciolo *m* ZO wren
scritta *f* inscription
scritto 1 *pp* → ***scrivere* 2** *m* writing; ***per scritto*** in writing
scrittore *m*, **-trice** *f* writer
scrittura *f* writing; REL scripture
scritturare ⟨1a⟩ engage, sign F
scrivania *f* desk
scrivere ⟨3tt⟩ write; (*annotare*) write down; ***come si scrive ... ?*** how do you spell … ?
scroccare ⟨1c & d⟩ F scrounge F
scrofa *f* sow
scrollare ⟨1c⟩ shake; ***scrollare le spalle*** shrug (one's shoulders)
scrosciare ⟨1f & c⟩ *di pioggia* fall in torrents
scrupolo *m* scruple; ***senza -i*** unscrupulous
scrupolosità *f* scrupulousness
scrupoloso scrupulous
scrutare ⟨1a⟩ look at intently; *orrizonte* scan
scrutatore *m*, **-trice** *f* POL person counting votes
scrutinio *m* (*pl* -ni) POL counting; EDU *teachers' meeting to discuss pupils' performance*
scucire ⟨4a⟩ unpick; F ***scuci i soldi!*** cough up! F
scucirsi come apart at the seams
scuderia *f* stable
scudetto *m* SP championship
scudo *m* shield
sculacciare ⟨1f⟩ spank
scultore *m*, **-trice** *f* sculptor
scultura *f* sculpture
scuola *f* school; ***scuola di lingue*** language school; ***scuola elementare*** primary school; ***scuola media*** secondary school; ***scuola parificata*** *private school officially recognized by the state*; ***scuola serale*** evening classes *pl*; ***scuola superiore*** high school; ***scuola guida*** driving school; ***andare a scuola*** go to school
scuotere ⟨3ff⟩ shake
scuotersi shake off
scure *f* ax(e)
scurire ⟨4d⟩ *v/t & v/i* darken
scuro 1 *agg* dark **2** *m* darkness; ***essere allo scuro di qc*** be in the dark about sth
scusa *f* excuse; ***chiedere scusa*** apologize
scusare ⟨1a⟩ forgive; (*giustificare*) excuse; ***mi scusi*** I'm sorry; ***scusi, scusa*** excuse me
scusarsi apologize
S.C.V. *abbr* (= ***Stato della Città del Vaticano***) Vatican City
s.d. *abbr* (= ***senza data***) undated
sdebitarsi ⟨1l⟩ pay one's debts
sdegnare ⟨1a⟩ (*disprezzare*) despise; (*fare arrabbiarre*) incense
sdegnarsi get angry (***con*** with)
sdegno *m* moral indignation
sdentato toothless
sdoganamento *m* customs clearance
sdoganare ⟨1a⟩ clear through customs
sdolcinato sloppy
sdraiare ⟨1i⟩ lay
sdraiarsi lie down
sdraiato lying down
sdraio *m*: (***sedia*** *f* ***a***) ***sdraio*** deck chair
se[1] *cong* if; ***se mai*** if need be; ***se mai arrivasse ...*** should he arrive …; ***come se*** as if; ***se no*** if not
se[2] *pron* = ***si*** *in front of* ***lo, la, li, le, ne***
sé oneself; *lui* himself; *lei* herself; *loro* themselves; *esso*, *essa* itself; ***da sé*** (by) himself / herself / themselves
sebbene even though, although; ***sebbene abbia detto la verità*** even though he told the truth
secca *f* (*pl* -cche) shallows
seccante *fig* annoying
seccare ⟨1d⟩ **1** *v/t* dry; *fig* annoy **2** *v/i e* **seccarsi** dry; *fig* get annoyed
seccatore *m*, **-trice** *f* nuisance, pest
seccatura *f* nuisance
secchio *m* (*pl* -cchi) bucket, pail
secco (*pl* -cchi) **1** *agg* dry; *fiori*, *pomodori* dried; *risposta*, *tono* curt; ***frutta*** *f* ***-a*** dried fruit; (*noci*) nuts *pl* **2** *m*: ***rimanere a secco*** run out of petrol; *fig* run out of money; ***pulire a secco*** dryclean
secolare *albero*, *tradizione* hundred-year old
secolo *m* century; ***ti ho aspettato un secolo!*** I waited hours for you!

S

seconda *f* AUTO second (gear); FERR second class; EDU second year
secondario (*pl* -ri) secondary
secondo 1 *agg* second; ***di -a mano*** second-hand; ***secondo fine*** ulterior motive, hidden agenda **2** *prp* according to; ***secondo me*** in my opinion; ***secondo le istruzioni*** as per instructions **3** *m* second; GASTR main course
secrétaire *m inv mobile* writing desk
sedano *m* celery
sedare ⟨1b⟩ calm (down)
sedativo *m* sedative
sede *f* headquarters; ***la Santa Sede*** the Holy See
sedentario (*pl* -ri) sedentary
sedere 1 *m* F rear end F **2** *v/i* ⟨2o⟩ *e* **sedersi** sit down
sedia *f* chair; ***sedia a sdraio*** deck chair; ***sedia a dondolo*** rocking chair; ***sedia a rotelle*** wheelchair
sedicesimo *m/agg* sixteenth
sedicente so-called, self-styled
sedici sixteen
sedile *m* seat; AUTO ***sedile posteriore*** back seat
seducente attractive
sedurre ⟨3e⟩ seduce; (*attrarre*) attract
seduta *f* session; (*posa*) sitting; ***seduta plenaria*** plenary session
seduto seated
seduttore *m*, **-trice** *f* seducer; *donna* seductress
seduzione *f* seduction
S.E. e O. *abbr* (= ***salvo errori e omissioni***) E & OE (= errors and omissions excepted)
seg. *abbr* (= ***seguente***) foll. (= following)
sega *f* (*pl* -ghe) saw
segale *f* rye; ***pane*** *m* ***di segale*** rye bread
segare ⟨1e⟩ saw
segatura f sawdust
seggio *m* (*pl* -ggi) seat; ***seggio*** (***elettorale***) polling station
seggiola *f* chair
seggiolino *m di macchina*, *bicicletta* child's seat
seggiolone *m* high chair
seggiovia *f* chair lift
seggo → ***sedere***
segnalare ⟨1a⟩ signal; (*annunciare*) report
segnale *m* signal; (*segno*) sign; ***segnale d'allarme*** alarm; ***segnale orario*** (***alla radio***) time signal; ***segnale stradale*** road sign
segnaletica *f* signs *pl*; ***segnaletica stradale*** road signs *pl*
segnalibro *m* bookmark
segnare ⟨1a⟩ (*marcare*) mark; (*annotare*) note down; SP score; ***segnare a dito qu*** point s.o. out, point to s.o.; ***sentirsi segnato a dita*** feel the finger pointed at you; ***ha segnato due gol*** he scored two goals
segno *m* sign; (*traccia*) mark, trace; (*cenno*) gesture, sign; ***-i*** *pl* ***caratteristici*** distinguishing marks; *fig* ***non dar -i di vita*** not get in touch; ***cogliere nel segno*** hit the nail on the head; ***segno zodiacale*** sign of the zodiac; ***farsi il segno de la croce*** cross o.s.; ***lasciare il segno*** leave a mark
segretaria *f* secretary; ***segretaria di direzione*** executive secretary
segretariato *m* secretariat
segretario *m* (*pl* -ri) secretary; POL ***segretario di partito*** party leader
segreteria *f carica* secretaryship; *ufficio* administrative office; *attività* secretarial duties *pl*; ***segreteria telefonica*** answering machine, answerphone
segreto 1 *agg* secret **2** *m* secret; ***segreto professionale*** confidentiality
seguace *m/f* disciple, follower
seguente next, following
seguire ⟨4a⟩ **1** *v/t* follow; *corso* take **2** *v/i* follow (***a qc*** sth); ***come segue*** as follows
seguitare ⟨1l⟩: ***seguitare a fare qc*** carry on doing sth
seguito *m persone* retinue; (*sostenitori*) followers; *di film* sequel; ***di seguito*** one after the other, in succession; ***in seguito*** after that; ***in seguito a*** following, in the wake of
sei[1] → ***essere***
sei[2] six
seicento 1 *agg* six hundred **2** *m*: ***il Seicento*** the seventeenth century
selciato *m* paving
selezione *f* selection
self-service *m inv* self-service
sella *f* saddle
sellino *m* saddle
seltz *m*: ***acqua*** *f* ***di seltz*** soda (water)
selva *f* forest
selvaggina *f* game
selvaggio (*pl* -ggi) **1** *agg animale*, *fiori* wild; *tribù*, *omicidio* savage **2** *m*, **-a** *f* savage
selvatico (*pl* -ci) wild
semaforo *m* traffic lights
sembrare ⟨1a⟩ seem; (*assomigliare a*) resemble, look like
seme *m* seed
semestre *m* six months; EDU term
semicerchio *m* (*pl* -chi) semi-circle, half-moon

semicircolare semi-circular
semiconduttore *m* EL semi-conductor
semifinale *f* semi-final
semifreddo *m soft ice cream*
semilavorato *m* semi-finished
semina *f* sowing
seminare ⟨1l⟩ sow
seminario *m* (*pl* -ri) seminar
seminudo half-naked
seminuovo practically new
semisfera *f* hemisphere
semolino *m* semolina
semplice simple; (*non doppio*) single; (*spontaneo*) natural
semplicità *f* simplicity
semplificare ⟨1m & d⟩ simplify
semplificazione *f* simplification
sempre always; ***ci conosciamo da sempre*** we've known each other practically for ever; ***è quello di sempre*** he's the same as always; ***per sempre*** for ever; ***sempre più*** more and more; ***sempre più vecchio*** older and older; ***piove sempre di più*** the rain's getting heavier and heavier; ***sempre che*** as long as, on condition that
sen. *abbr* (= ***senatore***) Sen (= senator)
senape *f* mustard
senato *m* senate
senatore *m*, **-trice** *f* senator
senile senile
senno *m* common sense; ***uscire di senno*** lose one's mind; (*arrabbiarsi*) lose control
seno *m* breast; GEOG inlet; MAT sine; ***in seno a*** in
sensato sensible
sensazionale sensational
sensazione *f* sensation, feeling; (*impressione*) feeling; ***fare sensazione*** cause a sensation; ***ho la sensazione che*** I have a feeling that
sensibile sensitive; (*evidente*) significant, substantial
sensibilità *f* sensitivity
sensibilizzare ⟨1a⟩ make more aware (***a*** of)
senso *m* sense; (*significato*) meaning; (*direzione*) direction; ***buon senso*** common sense; ***senso unico*** one way; ***senso vietato*** no entry; ***in senso orario*** clockwise; ***privo di -i*** unconscious; ***perdere i -i*** faint
sensore *m* TEC sensor
sensuale sensual
sensualità *f* sensuality
sentenza *f* DIR verdict; ***sentenza di morte*** death sentence
sentenziare ⟨1g⟩ *fig* pass judgment
sentiero *m* path
sentimentale sentimental
sentimento *m* feeling, sentiment
sentinella *f* sentry
sentire ⟨4b⟩ feel; (*udire*) hear; (*ascoltare*) listen to; *odore* smell; *cibo* taste
sentirsi feel; ***sentirsela di fare qc*** feel up to doing sth
senza without; ***senz'altro*** definitely; ***senza dubbio*** more than likely, probably; ***senza impegno*** (with) no obligation *or* commitment; ***senza di me*** without me
senzatetto *m/f inv* homeless person; ***i -i*** *pl* the homeless
separare ⟨1a or 1l & b⟩ separate
separarsi separate, split up F
separazione *f* separation; ***separazione dei beni*** division of property
sepolto *pp* → ***seppellire***
sepoltura *f* burial
seppellire ⟨4d⟩ bury
seppia *f* cuttle fish
seppure even if
sequestrare ⟨1b⟩ confiscate; DIR impound, seize; (*rapire*) kidnap
sequestro *m* kidnap(ping); DIR impounding, seizure
sera *f* evening; ***di sera*** in the evenings; ***questa sera*** this evening; ***verso sera*** towards evening
serale evening *attr*
serata *f* evening; (*festa*) party; ***serata danzante*** dance; ***serata di gala*** gala (evening)
serbatoio *m* (*pl* -oi) tank; ***serbatoio di riserva*** reserve tank
serbo[1] **1** *agg* Serbian **2** *m*, **-a** *f* Serb
serbo[2] *m*: ***tenere in serbo*** keep; ***avere qc in serbo*** have sth in store
serenata *f* serenade
serenità *f* serenity
sereno serene; *fig* relaxed, calm
serial *m inv* serial
seriale INFOR serial; ***porta*** *f* ***seriale*** serial port
sericoltura *f* silk-worm farming
serie *f inv* series; ***articolo*** *m* ***di serie*** mass produced item; ***produzione*** *f* ***in serie*** mass production
serietà *f* seriousness
serigrafia *f* silk-screen printing
serio (*pl* -ri) **1** *agg* serious; (*affidabile*) reliable **2** *m*: ***sul serio*** seriously
sermone *m* sermon
serpe *f* grass snake
serpeggiare ⟨1f⟩ wind
serpente *m* snake
serpentina *f linea* wavy line; *strada* wind-

S

ing street
serra *f* greenhouse
serramanico *m*: ***coltello*** *m* ***a serramanico*** flick knife
serranda *f* shutter
serrare ⟨1b⟩ close; *denti*, *pugni* clench; ***serrare il ritmo*** step up the pace
serrata *f* lock-out
serratura *f* lock; ***serratura a combinazione*** combination lock
servire ⟨4b⟩ **1** *v/i* be useful; ***non mi serve*** I don't need it; ***a che serve questo?*** what's this for?; ***servire da bere a qu*** pour s.o. a drink **2** *v/t* serve; ***mi serve aiuto*** I need help
servirsi (*usare*) use (***di*** sth); ***prego, si serva!*** *a tavola* please help yourself!
servitù *f* slavery, servitude; (*personale*) servants *pl*
servizio *m* (*pl* -zi) service; (*favore*) favo(u)r; (*dipartimento*) department; *in giornale* feature (story); ***lavorare a mezzo servizio*** work part-time; ***servizio assistenza tecnica*** after-sales service; ***servizio civile*** *community service in lieu of military service*; ***servizio militare*** military service; ***servizio d'emergenza*** emergency service; ***servizio da tavola*** dinner service; ***di servizio*** on duty; ***fuori servizio*** out of order; ***in servizio*** on duty; ***-zi*** *pl* services
servofreno *m* servo brake
servosterzo *m* power steering
sesamo *m* sesame
sessanta sixty
sessantenne sixty-year-old
sessantesimo *m/agg* sixtieth
sessantina *f*: ***una sessantina*** about sixty (***di*** sth); ***sulla sessantina*** about sixty
sesso *m* sex
sessuale sexual
sessualità *f* sexuality
sesto *m/agg* sixth
seta *f* silk; ***seta artificiale*** artificial silk
sete *f* thirst; ***aver sete*** be thirsty
setola *f* bristle
setta *f* sect
settanta seventy
settantenne seventy-year-old
settantesimo *m/agg* seventieth
settantina *f*: ***una settantina*** about seventy (***di*** sth); ***sulla settantina*** about seventy
settare ⟨1a⟩ *macchina*, *computer* set up
sette seven
settecento **1** *agg* seven hundred **2** *m*: ***il Settecento*** the eighteenth century
settembre *m* September
settentrionale **1** *agg* northern **2** *m/f* northerner
settentrione *m* north
setticemia *f* septic(a)emia
settimana *f* week; ***settimana corta*** five-day week; ***settimana santa*** Easter week
settimanale *m/agg* weekly
settimo *m/agg* seventh
settore *m* sector
severità *f* severity
severo severe
sezione *f* section
sfaccendato idle
sfacchinata *f* backbreaking job
sfacciato cheeky
sfacelo *m* ruin
sfamare ⟨1a⟩ feed
sfarfallio *m* flicker
sfarzo *m* splendo(u)r
sfarzoso magnificent
sfasciare ⟨1f⟩ smash; MED unbandage
sfasciarsi smash
sfaticato *m*, **-a** *f* idler
sfavillare ⟨1a⟩ *di occhi* sparkle; *di fuoco* flicker
sfavillio *m di occhi* sparkle
sfavore *m* disadvantage
sfavorevole unfavourable
sfera *f* sphere; ***sfera d'azione*** responsibilities, duties; ***sfera di competenza*** area of expertise
sferico (*pl* -ci) spherical
sfida *f* challenge
sfidare ⟨1a⟩ challenge
sfiducia *f* distrust, mistrust; ***voto*** *m* ***di sfiducia*** vote of no confidence
sfiduciato discouraged, disheartened
sfigurare ⟨1a⟩ **1** *v/t* disfigure **2** *v/i* look out of place
sfigurato disfigured
sfilare ⟨1a⟩ **1** *v/t* unthread; (*togliere*) take off **2** *v/i* parade
sfilata *f*: ***sfilata di moda*** fashion show
sfinimento *m* exhaustion
sfinito exhausted
sfiorare ⟨1a⟩ brush; *argomento* touch on
sfiorire ⟨4d⟩ fade, wither
sfitto empty, not let
sfocato *foto* blurred
sfociare ⟨1f⟩ flow
sfogare ⟨1e⟩ *rabbia*, *frustrazione* vent, get rid of (***con, su*** on)
sfogarsi vent one's feelings; ***non ti sfogare su di me*** don't take it out on me; ***sfogarsi con qu*** confide in s.o., pour one's heart out to s.o.
sfoglia: ***pasta*** *f* ***sfoglia*** puff pastry
sfogliare ⟨1g & c⟩ *libro* leaf through
sfogo *m* (*pl* -ghi) outlet; MED rash
sfoltire ⟨4d⟩ thin

sfondare ⟨1a⟩ break; *porta* break down; *muro* knock down; *pavimento* break through
sfondo *m* background
sformare ⟨1a⟩ stretch out of shape
sformato *m* GASTR soufflé
sfornito: ***essere sfornito di qc*** be out of sth
sfortuna *f* bad luck, misfortune
sfortunatamente unfortunately
sfortunato unlucky, unfortunate
sforzare ⟨1c⟩ strain
sforzarsi try very hard, make every effort
sforzo *m* effort; *fisico* strain; ***fare uno sforzo*** make an effort; *fisicamente* strain o.s.; ***senza sforzo*** effortlessly
sfracellarsi ⟨1b⟩ break into pieces, shatter
sfrattare ⟨1a⟩ evict
sfratto *m* eviction; *avviso* notice to quit
sfregare ⟨1e⟩ rub
sfrenato unrestrained
sfrontato insolent
sfruttamento *m* exploitation
sfruttare ⟨1a⟩ exploit
sfuggevole fleeting
sfuggire ⟨4a⟩ (*scampare*) escape (***a*** from); ***mi è sfuggito di mente*** it slipped my mind
sfuggita *f*: ***di sfuggita*** in passing
sfumatura *f* nuance; *di colore* shade
sfuriata *f* (angry) tirade
sfuso loose; *burro* melted; *vino* in bulk
sgabello *m* stool
sgabuzzino *m* cupboard
sgambetto *m*: ***fare lo sgambetto a qu*** trip s.o. up
sganciare ⟨1f⟩ unhook; FERR uncouple; F *soldi* fork out F
sganciarsi become unhooked; *di persona* release o.s.; *fig* free o.s.
sgarbato rude
sgarbo *m* discourtesy
sgelare ⟨1b⟩ thaw
sgelo *m* thaw
sghembo crooked; ***di sghembo*** crookedly, not in a straight line
sgobbare ⟨1c⟩ slave
sgobbone *m*, **-a** *f* F swot F
sgocciolare ⟨1l⟩ *v/t & v/i* drip
sgomberare ⟨1l⟩ → ***sgombrare***
sgombero *m di strada* clearing; (*trasloco*) removal
sgombrare ⟨1a⟩ *strada*, *stanza* clear; *ostacolo* remove; *appartamento* clear out, empty
sgombro[1] *agg strada*, *stanza* empty
sgombro[2] *m* mackerel
sgomentare ⟨1a⟩ frighten
sgomentarsi be frightened
sgomento *m* fear
sgonfiare ⟨1k⟩ **1** *v/t* let the air out of **2** *v/i e* **sgonfiarsi** become deflated; ***il braccio si è sgonfiato*** the swelling in the arm has gone down
sgonfio (*pl* -fi) flat; MED not swollen
sgradevole unpleasant
sgradito unwelcome
sgranchire ⟨4d⟩, **sgranchirsi**: ***sgranchire le gambe*** stretch one's legs
sgraziato awkward
sgridare ⟨1a⟩ scold, tell off F
sgridata *f* scolding, telling off F
sguaiato raucous
sgualdrina *f* tart
sguardo *m* look; (*occhiata*) glance; ***al primo sguardo*** at first glance
sguazzare ⟨1a⟩ splash about; *fig* F ***sguazzare nei soldi*** be rolling (in it) F
sgusciare ⟨1f⟩ **1** *v/t* shell **2** *v/i* slip away; ***mi è sgusciato di mano*** it slipped out of my hand
shampoo *m inv* shampoo
shock *m inv* shock; ***shock culturale*** culture shock
si[1] *pron* oneself; *lui* himself; *lei* herself; *esso*, *essa* itself; *loro* themselves; *reciproco* each other; ***spazzolarsi i capelli*** brush one's hair; ***si è spazzolato i capelli*** he brushed his hair; ***si dice*** they say; ***cosa si può dire?*** what can one say?, what can I say?; ***si capisce da sé*** it's self-evident
si[2] *m* MUS B
sì *avv* yes; ***dire di sì*** say yes; ***sì e no*** yes and no; ***penso di sì*** I think so
sia: ***sia ... sia ...*** both ... and ...; (*o l'uno o l'altro*) either ... or ...; ***sia che ... sia che ...*** whether ... or whether ...
siamo → ***essere***
sibilare ⟨1l⟩ hiss; *di vento* whistle
sibilo *m* hiss; *di vento* whistle
sicario *m* hired killer, hit man F
sicché (and) so
siccità *f* drought
siccome since
Sicilia *f* Sicily
siciliano **1** *agg* Sicilian **2** *m*, **-a** *f* Sicilian
sicura *f* safety catch
sicurezza *f* security; (*protezione*) safety; (*certezza*) certainty; ***pubblica sicurezza*** police; ***cintura** f **di sicurezza*** safety belt; ***misure** fpl **di sicurezza*** safety measures
sicuro **1** *agg luogo* safe; *investimento* sound, safe; (*certo*) sure; ***sicuro di sé*** self-confident, sure of o.s.; ***di sicuro*** definitely **2** *m*: ***essere al sicuro da qc*** be safe from sth; ***mettere al sicuro*** put in

a safe place
siderurgia *f* iron and steel industry
sidro *m* cider
siedo → ***sedere***
siepe *f* hedge
siero *m* MED serum
sieropositivo HIV positive
siesta *f* siesta
siete → ***essere***
sifilide *f* MED syphilis
sig. *abbr* (= ***signore***) Mr (= mister)
sigaretta *f* cigarette; ***sigaretta col filtro*** filter tip
sigaro *m* cigar
sigg. *abbr* (= ***signori***) Messrs
sigillare ⟨1a⟩ seal
sigillo *m* seal
sigla *f* initials *pl*; *musicale* theme (tune)
sig.na *abbr* (= ***signorina***) Miss, Ms
significare ⟨1m & d⟩ mean
significativo significant
significato *m* meaning
signora *f* lady; ***mi scusi, signora!*** excuse me!; ***la signora Rossi*** Mrs Rossi; ***-e e signori*** ladies and gentlemen
signore *m* gentleman; ***mi scusi, signore!*** excuse me!; ***il signor Rossi*** Mr Rossi; ***i -i Rossi*** Mr and Mrs Rossi
signorile *appartamento* luxury; *modi* gentlemanly
signorina *f* young lady; ***è ancora signorina*** she's not married; ***la signorina Rossi*** Miss Rossi
sig.ra *abbr* (= ***signora***) Mrs
silenziatore *m* silencer, *Am* muffler
silenzio *m* silence; ***fare silenzio*** be quiet; ***silenzio!*** silence!, quiet!
silenzioso silent
sillaba *f* syllable
sillabare ⟨1l⟩ split into syllables
silo *m* silo
siluro *m* MAR torpedo
simboleggiare ⟨1f⟩ symbolize
simbolico (*pl* -ci) symbolic
simbolismo *m* symbolism
simbolo *m* symbol
simile similar
simmetria *f* symmetry
simmetrico (*pl* -ci) symmetric(al)
simpatia *f* liking; (*affinità*) sympathy; ***avere simpatia per qu*** like s.o.
simpatico (*pl* -ci) likeable
simpatizzare ⟨1a⟩ become friends
simposio *m* (*pl* -si) symposium
simulare ⟨1l⟩ feign; TEC simulate
simulazione *f* pretence, *Am* pretense; TECH simulation; ***simulazione elettronica*** electronic simulation
sinagoga *f* (*pl* -ghe) synagogue
sinceramente sincerely; (*in verità*) honestly
sincerarsi ⟨1b⟩ make sure
sincerità *f* sincerity
sincero sincere
sincronizzare ⟨1a⟩ synchronize
sindacalista *m/f* (*mpl* -i) trade unionist
sindacato *m* trade union
sindaco *m* (*pl* -ci) mayor
sinfonia *f* symphony
sinfonico (*pl* -ci) symphonic
singhiozzare ⟨1a⟩ sob
singhiozzo *m*: ***avere il singhiozzo*** have hiccups; ***-zi*** *pl* sobs
single *m/f inv* single
singolare 1 *agg* singular; (*insolito*) unusual; (*strano*) strange **2** *m* singular; SP singles
singolo 1 *agg* individual; *camera*, *letto* single **2** *m* individual; SP singles
sinistra *f* left; ***a sinistra*** on the left; *andare* to the left
sinistro 1 *agg* left, left-hand; *fig* sinister **2** *m* accident
sino → ***fino***
sinonimo 1 *agg* synonymous **2** *m* synonym
sintesi *f inv* synthesis; (*riassunto*) summary
sintetico (*pl* -ci) synthetic; (*riassunto*) brief; ***materiale*** *m* ***sintetico*** synthetic (material)
sintetizzare ⟨1a⟩ synthesize; (*riassumere*) summarize, sum up
sintomo *m* symptom
sintonia *f* RAD tuning; *fig* ***essere in sintonia*** be on the same wavelength (***con*** as)
sintonizzare ⟨1a⟩ RAD tune
sintonizzarsi tune in (***su*** to)
sinusite *f* sinusitis
sipario *m* (*pl* -ri) curtain
sirena *f* siren; *mitologica* mermaid; ***sirena d'allarme*** alarm
siringa *f* (*pl* -ghe) MED syringe; ***siringa monouso*** disposable syringe
sismico (*pl* -ci) seismic
sistema *m* (*pl* -i) system; ***sistema antibloccaggio*** anti-lock braking system; ***sistema elettorale proporzionale*** proportional representation; ***sistema immunitario*** immune system; ***sistema monetario*** monetary system; INFOR ***sistema operativo*** operating system
sistemare ⟨1b⟩ put; (*mettere in ordine*) arrange; *casa* do up
sistemarsi tidy o.s. up; (*trovare casa*, *sposarsi*) settle down
sistematico (*pl* -ci) systematic
sistemazione *f* place; (*lavoro*) job; *in al-*

bergo accommodation
sito site; ***in sito*** on the premises
situare ⟨1l⟩ locate, find
situato: ***essere situato*** be situated
situazione *f* situation
slacciare ⟨1f⟩ undo
slalom *m* slalom
slanciato slender
slancio *m* (*pl* -ci) impulse
slavo 1 *agg* Slav, Slavonic **2** *m*, **-a** *f* Slav
sleale disloyal
slealtà *f* disloyalty
slegare ⟨1e⟩ untie
slegarsi free o.s.
slegato *fig* incoherent, disjointed
slip *m inv* underpants; *da donna* knickers; ***slip da bagno*** bathing trunks
slitta *f* sledge
slittino *m* sled; SP bobsleigh
s.l.m. *abbr* (= ***sul livello del mare***) above sea level
slogan *m inv* slogan
slogare ⟨1e⟩ dislocate
slogarsi: ***slogarsi una caviglia*** sprain one's ankle
slogatura *f* sprain
sloggiare ⟨1f⟩ move out
smacchiare ⟨1k⟩ take the stains out of
smacchiatore *m* stain remover
smagliatura *f* ladder, *Am* run; MED stretch mark
smaltare ⟨1a⟩ enamel
smaltimento *m* FIN disposal of stock; *di rifiuti tossici* disposal
smaltire ⟨4d⟩ dispose of
smalto *m* enamel; *per ceramiche* glaze; ***smalto per unghie*** nail varnish *or* polish
smantellamento *m* dismantling
smantellare ⟨1b⟩ dismantle
smarrimento *m* loss
smarrire ⟨4d⟩ lose
smarrirsi get lost
smarrito 1 *pp* → ***smarrire*** **2** *agg* lost
smascherare ⟨1l⟩ unmask
Sme *abbr* (= ***Sistema monetario europeo***) EMS (= European Monetary System)
smemorato forgetful
smentire ⟨4d⟩ prove to be wrong; ***non si smentisce mai!*** he doesn't change!
smentita *f* denial
smeraldo 1 *m* emerald **2** *agg* emerald (green)
smercio *m* (*pl* -ci) sale
smesso *pp* → ***smettere***
smettere ⟨3ee⟩ **1** *v/t* stop; *abiti* stop wearing **2** *v/i* stop (***di fare qc*** doing sth)
smilitarizzare ⟨1a⟩ demilitarize
smilitarizzazione *f* demilitarization
sminuire ⟨4d⟩ *problema* downplay; *persona* belittle
smistamento *m* FERR shunting
smistare ⟨1a⟩ FERR shunt
smisurato boundless
smodato excessive
smog *m* smog
smontabile which can be taken apart, *Am* knockdown
smontaggio *m* dismantling
smontare ⟨1a⟩ **1** *v/i* (*da cavallo*) dismount **2** *v/t* dismantle; *persona* deflate
smorfia *f* grimace
smorfioso affected, simpering
smorto *persona* deathly pale; *colore* dull
smorzare ⟨1c⟩ *colore* tone down; *luce* dim; *entusiasmo* dampen
smuovere ⟨3ff⟩ shift, move
snellezza *f* slenderness
snellire ⟨4d⟩ slim down; *fig* pare down
snello slim, slender
snervante irritating, wearing on the nerves
snob 1 *agg* snobbish **2** *m/f inv* snob
SO *abbr* (= ***sud-ovest***) SW (= southwest)
so → ***sapere***
sobborgo *m* (*pl* -ghi) suburb
sobrietà *f* sobriety
sobrio (*pl* -ri) sober
Soc. *abbr* (= ***società***) Co (= company); soc. (= society)
socchiudere ⟨3b⟩ half-close
socchiuso 1 *pp* → ***socchiudere*** **2** *agg* half-closed; *porta* ajar
soccombere ⟨3a⟩ succumb
soccorrere ⟨3o⟩ help
soccorritore *m* rescue worker
soccorso 1 *pp* → ***soccorrere*** **2** *m* rescue; ***venire in soccorso a qu*** come to s.o.'s rescue; ***pronto soccorso*** first aid; ***soccorso stradale*** breakdown service, *Am* wrecking service; ***segnale*** *m* ***di soccorso*** distress signal
sociale social
socialismo *m* socialism
socialista (*mpl* -i) *agg*, *m/f* socialist
socializzare ⟨1a⟩ socialize
società *f inv* company; (*associazione*) society; ***società a responsabilità limitata*** limited liability company; ***società in nome collettivo*** general partnership; ***società per azioni*** joint stock company; ***società del benessere*** welfare society; ***società dei consumi*** consumer society
socievole sociable
socio *m* (*pl* -ci), **-a** *f* member; FIN partner
sociologia *f* sociology
sociologo *m* (*pl* -gi), **-a** *f* sociologist
soddisfacente satisfying

soddisfare ⟨3aa⟩ satisfy
soddisfatto 1 *pp* → ***soddisfare* 2** *agg* satisfied; ***essere soddisfatto di qu*** be satisfied with s.o.
soddisfazione *f* satisfaction
sodio *m* sodium
sodo *uovo* hard-boiled; *fig* ***venire al sodo*** get down to brass tacks
sofà *m inv* sofa
sofferente suffering
sofferenza *f* suffering
soffermare ⟨1a⟩ *attenzione* turn
soffermarsi dwell (***su*** on)
sofferto *pp* → ***soffrire***
soffiare ⟨1k⟩ blow; F swipe F; ***soffiarsi il naso*** blow one's nose
soffice soft
soffio *m* puff
soffitta *f* attic
soffitto *m* ceiling
soffocante suffocating
soffocare ⟨1l, c & d⟩ suffocate
soffriggere ⟨3cc⟩ fry gently
soffrire ⟨4f⟩ **1** *v/t* suffer; *persone* bear, stand **2** *v/i* suffer (***di*** from)
sofisticato sophisticated
software *m inv* software
softwarista *m/f* software engineer
soggettivo subjective
soggetto 1 *agg* subject; ***soggetto a tassa*** subject to tax; ***andare soggetto a qc*** suffer from sth **2** *m* GRAM subject
soggezione *f* subjection
soggiornare ⟨1a⟩ stay
soggiorno *m* stay; ***permesso*** *m* ***di soggiorno*** residence permit
soglia *f* threshold
sogliola *f* sole
sognare ⟨1a⟩ *e* **sognarsi** dream (***di*** about, of)
sognatore *m*, **-trice** *f* dreamer
sogno *m* dream; ***neppure per sogno!*** in your dreams!
soia *f* soya
sol *m inv* MUS G
solaio *m* (*pl* -ai) attic, loft
solamente only; ***solamente ieri*** just yesterday
solare solar
solarium *m inv* solarium
solco *m* (*pl* -chi) furrow
soldato *m* soldier
soldi *mpl* money *sg*
sole *m* sun; ***c'è il sole*** it's sunny; ***colpo*** *m* ***di sole*** sunstroke; ***prendere il sole*** sunbathe
soleggiare ⟨1f⟩ dry in the sun
soleggiato sun-dried
solenne solemn
solennità *f inv* solemnity
solere ⟨2p⟩: ***solere fare*** be in the habit of doing
soletta *f* insole
solforico (*pl* -ci) sulphur, *Am* sulfur *attr*; ***acido*** *m* ***solforico*** sulphuric, *Am* sulfuric acid
solidale *fig* in agreement
solidarietà *f* solidarity
solidarizzare ⟨1a⟩ agree, be in agreement
solidità *f* solidity
solido solid; (*robusto*) sturdy
solista *m/f* (*mpl* -i) soloist
solitario (*pl* -ri) **1** *agg* solitary; *luogo* lonely; *navigatore* solo **2** *m* solitaire; *gioco* patience
solito usual, same; ***al*** *o* ***di solito*** usually; ***come al solito*** as usual; ***più del solito*** more than usual
solitudine *f* solitude, being alone
sollecitare ⟨1m⟩ (*stimolare*) urge; *risposta* ask (again) for
sollecito 1 *agg persona* diligent; *risposta, reazione* prompt; ***lettera*** *f* ***di sollecito*** reminder **2** *m* reminder
sollecitudine *f di persona* diligence; *di risposta* promptness
solleticare ⟨1m & d⟩ tickle; *appetito* whet
solletico *m* tickling; ***fare il solletico a qu*** tickle s.o.; ***soffrire il solletico*** be ticklish
sollevamento *m* lifting; (*insurrezione*) rising; ***sollevamento pesi*** weightlifting
sollevare ⟨1b⟩ lift; *problema, obiezione* bring up
sollevarsi *di popolo* rise up; AVIA climb, rise
sollievo *m* relief
solo 1 *agg* lonely; (*non accompagnato*) alone; (*unico*) only; MUS solo; ***da solo*** by myself / yourself etc, on my / your *etc* own **2** *avv* only **3** *m* MUS solo
solstizio *m* (*pl* -zi) solstice
soltanto only; ***soltanto ieri*** only yesterday
solubile soluble
soluzione *f* solution; ***soluzione provvisoria*** stopgap
solvente 1 *agg* FIN solvent **2** *m* CHIM solvent
somigliante similar
somiglianza *f* resemblance
somigliare ⟨1g⟩: ***somigliare a qu*** resemble s.o.
somma *f* (*addizione*) addition; *risultato* sum; (*importo*) amount (of money), sum; ***fare la somma di*** add (up); *fig* ***tirare le -e*** sum up
sommare ⟨1a⟩ add; ***sommare a*** total, come to

sommario (*pl* -ri) **1** *agg* summary **2** *m* summary; *di libro* table of contents
sommato: ***tutto sommato*** all things considered, on the whole
sommergere ⟨3uu⟩ submerge; *fig* overwhelm (***di*** with)
sommergersi submerge, dive
sommergibile *m* submarine
sommerso *città* submerged; *strade* inches deep in water
sommesso *voce* quiet
somministrare ⟨1a⟩ MED administer
sommo 1 *agg* supreme **2** *m* summit; *fig* height
sommossa *f* uprising
sondaggio *m* (*pl* -ggi): ***sondaggio*** (***d'opinione***) (opinion) poll
sondare ⟨1a⟩ sound; *fig* test
sonnambulo *m*, **-a** *f* sleepwalker
sonnecchiare ⟨1k⟩ doze
sonnifero *m* sleeping tablet
sonno *m* sleep; ***aver sonno*** be sleepy; ***prendere sonno*** fall asleep
sonnolento drowsy
sonnolenza *f* drowsiness
sono → ***essere***
sonorità *f inv* sonority
sonoro sound *attr*; *risa*, *applausi* loud; ***colonna*** *f* **-a** sound-track
sontuosità *f* magnificence
sontuoso sumptuous, magnificent
soppesare ⟨1a⟩ weigh; *fig* weigh up
sopportabile bearable, tolerable
sopportare ⟨1c⟩ *peso* bear; *fig* bear, stand F
soppressione *f* deletion; *di regola* abolition
soppresso *pp* → ***sopprimere***
sopprimere ⟨3r⟩ delete; *regola* abolish
sopra 1 *prp* on; (*più in alto di*) above; (*riguardo a*) about, on; ***sopra il tavolo*** on the table; ***l'uno sopra l'altro*** one on top of the other; ***i bambini sopra cinque anni*** children over five; ***5 gradi sopra zero*** 5 degrees above zero; ***al di sopra di qc*** over sth **2** *avv* on top; (*al piano superiore*) upstairs; ***dormirci sopra*** sleep on it; ***vedi sopra*** see above; ***la parte di sopra*** the top *or* upper part
soprabito *m* (over)coat
sopracciglio *m* (*fpl* -a) eyebrow
sopraccoperta *f di letto* bedspread; *di libro* dustjacket
sopraffare ⟨3aa⟩ overwhelm
sopraggiungere ⟨3d⟩ *di persona* turn up, arrive on the scene; *di difficoltà* arise, come up F
sopralluogo *m* (*pl* -ghi) inspection (of the site)
soprammobile *m* ornament
soprannaturale supernatural
soprannome *m* nickname
soprannumero *m*: ***in soprannumero*** overcrowded
soprano *m* soprano; ***mezzo soprano*** mezzo(-soprano)
soprappensiero → ***sovrappensiero***
soprassalto: *di soprassalto* with a start
soprattassa *f* surcharge
soprattutto particularly, (e)specially, above all
sopravvalutare ⟨1a⟩ overvalue; *fig* overestimate
sopravvenire ⟨4p⟩ turn up, appear
sopravvento *m*: ***avere*** *o* ***prendere il sopravvento*** have the upper hand
sopravvissuto 1 *agg* surviving **2** *m*, **-a** *f* survivor
sopravvivenza *f* survival
sopravvivere ⟨3zz⟩ survive, outlive (***a qu*** s.o.)
soprintendente *m/f* supervisor
sopruso *m* abuse of power
soqquadro *m*: ***mettere a soqquadro*** turn upside down
sorbetto *m* sorbet
sorbire ⟨4d⟩ sip
sorbirsi put up with
sorcio *m* (*pl* -ci) mouse
sordina *f* mute; ***in sordina*** in secret, on the quiet F
sordità *f* deafness
sordo deaf
sordomuto deaf and dumb
sorella *f* sister
sorellastra *f* stepsister
sorgente *f* spring; *fig* source
sorgere ⟨3d⟩ *di sole* rise, come up; *fig* arise, come up
sormontare ⟨1a⟩ *difficoltà* overcome, surmount
sorpassare ⟨1a⟩ go past; AUTO pass, overtake; *fig* exceed
sorpassato out of date
sorpasso *m*: ***divieto di sorpasso*** no passing, no overtaking; ***fare un sorpasso*** pass, overtake
sorprendente surprising
sorprendere ⟨3c⟩ surprise; (*cogliere sul fatto*) catch
sorpresa *f* surprise
sorpreso *pp* → ***sorprendere***
sorridere ⟨3b⟩ smile
sorriso 1 *pp* → ***sorridere* 2** *m* smile
sorseggiare ⟨1f⟩ sip
sorso *m* mouthful
sorta *f* sort, kind
sorte *f* fate; ***tirare a sorte*** draw lots

sorteggiare ⟨1f⟩ draw
sorteggio *m* (*pl* -ggi) draw
sorto *pp* → ***sorgere***
sorveglianza *f* supervision; *di edificio* security
sorvegliare ⟨1g⟩ supervise; *edificio* provide security for; *bagagli ecc* look after, take care of
sorvolare ⟨1a⟩ **1** *v/t* AVIA fly over **2** *v/i fig*: ***sorvolare su*** skim over, skip
sosia *m inv* double
sospendere ⟨3c⟩ suspend; (*appendere*) hang
sospensione *f* suspension
sospeso 1 *pp* → ***sospendere* 2** *agg* hanging; *fig questione* pending; ***tenere in sospeso*** *persona* keep in suspense
sospettare ⟨1b⟩ suspect; ***sospettare qu*** o ***di qu*** suspect s.o.
sospetto 1 *agg* suspicious **2** *m*, **-a** *f* suspect
sospettoso suspicious
sospirare ⟨1a⟩ **1** *v/i* sigh **2** *v/t* long for
sospiro *m* sigh
sosta *f* stop; (*pausa*) break, pause; ***senza sosta*** nonstop; ***divieto di sosta*** no parking
sostantivo *m* noun
sostanza *f* substance; ***in sostanza*** in short, to sum up
sostare ⟨1c⟩ stop
sostegno *m* support; ***a sostegno di*** in support of
sostenere ⟨2q⟩ support; (*affermare*) maintain
sostengo → ***sostenere***
sostenitore *m*, **-trice** *f* supporter
sostentamento *m* support
sostenuto *stile* formal; *velocità* high
sostituibile which can be replaced, replaceable
sostituire ⟨4d⟩: ***sostituire X con Y*** replace X with Y, substitute Y for X
sostituto *m*, **-a** *f* substitute, replacement
sostituzione *f* substitution, replacement
sottaceti *mpl* pickles
sottana *f* slip, underskirt; (*gonna*) skirt; REL cassock
sotterranea *f* underground
sotterraneo 1 *agg* underground *attr* **2** *m* cellar
sotterrare ⟨1b⟩ bury
sottile fine; *fig* subtle; *udito* keen
sottintendere ⟨3c⟩ imply
sottinteso 1 *pp* → ***sottintendere* 2** *m* allusion
sotto 1 *prp* under; ***i bambini sotto cinque anni*** children under five; ***5 gradi sotto zero*** 5 degrees below (zero); ***sotto la pioggia*** in the rain; ***al di sotto di qc*** under sth **2** *avv* below; (*più in basso*) lower down; (*al di sotto*) underneath; (*al piano di sotto*) downstairs
sottobanco under the counter
sottobraccio: ***camminare sottobraccio*** walk arm-in-arm; ***prendere qu sottobraccio*** take s.o.'s arm
sottocchio: ***tenere sottocchio qc*** keep an eye on sth
sottochiave under lock and key
sottocosto at less than cost price
sottoesposto FOT underexposed
sottofondo *m* background
sottolineare ⟨1n⟩ underline; *fig* emphasize, underline
sottomarino 1 *agg* underwater *attr* **2** *m* submarine
sottomesso 1 *pp* → ***sottomettere* 2** *agg* submissive; *popolo* subject *attr*
sottomettere ⟨3ee⟩ submit; *popolo* subdue
sottomissione *f* submission
sottopassaggio *m* (*pl* -ggi) underpass
sottoporre ⟨3ll⟩ submit
sottoporsi: ***sottoporsi a*** undergo
sottoscritto 1 *pp* → ***sottoscrivere* 2** *m* undersigned
sottoscrivere ⟨3tt⟩ *documento* sign; *teoria* subscribe to; *abbonamento* take out
sottoscrizione *f* signing; (*abbonamento*) subscription
sottosopra *fig* upside-down
sottosuolo *m* subsoil; ***ricchezze*** *fpl* ***del sottosuolo*** mineral wealth; ***nel sottosuolo*** underground
sottosviluppato underdeveloped
sottovalutare ⟨1a⟩ undervalue; *persona* underestimate
sottoveste *f* slip, underskirt
sottovoce quietly, sotto voce
sottrarre ⟨3xx⟩ MAT subtract; *denaro* embezzle
sottrarsi: ***sottrarsi a qc*** avoid sth
sottratto *pp* → ***sottrarre***
sottrazione *f* MAT subtraction; *di denaro* embezzlement
sottufficiale *m* non-commissioned officer, NCO
souvenir *m inv* souvenir
sovietico (*pl* -ci) Soviet
sovrabbondante overabundant
sovrabbondanza *f* overabundance
sovrabbondare ⟨1a⟩ be overabundant; ***sovrabbondare di*** have an overabundance of
sovraccarico 1 *agg* overloaded (***di*** with) **2** *m* overload
sovrano 1 *agg* sovereign **2** *m*, **-a** *f* sovereign

sovrappensiero: ***essere sovrappensiero*** be lost in thought
sovrappeso 1 *agg* overweight **2** *m* excess weight
sovrappopolato overpopulated
sovrapporre ⟨3ll⟩ overlap
sovrapposizione *f* overlapping
sovrapproduzione *f* overproduction
sovrastare ⟨1a⟩ overlook, dominate
sovrintendente *m/f* → ***soprintendente***
sovrumano superhuman
sovvenzionare ⟨1a⟩ give a grant to
sovvenzione *f* grant
sovversivo subversive
S.P. *abbr* (= ***Strada Provinciale***) B road
S.p.A. *abbr* (= ***Società per Azioni***) joint stock company
spaccare ⟨1d⟩ break in two; *legna* split, chop
spaccarsi break in two
spaccatura *f* crevice
spacciare ⟨1f⟩ *droga* deal in, push F; ***siamo spacciati!*** we've had it!
spacciarsi: ***spacciarsi per*** pass o.s. off as
spacciatore *m*, **-trice** *f di droga* dealer
spaccio *m* (*pl* -cci) *di droga* dealing; *negozio* general store
spacco *m* (*pl* -cchi) *in gonna* slit; *in giacca* vent
spaccone *m*, **-a** *f* braggart
spada *f* sword
spadroneggiare ⟨1f⟩ throw one's weight around
spaesato disorient(at)ed, confused
spaghetti *mpl* spaghetti *sg*
Spagna *f* Spain
spagnolo 1 *m/agg* Spanish **2** *m*, **-a** *f* Spaniard
spago *m* (*pl* -ghi) string
spalancare ⟨1d⟩ open wide
spalla *f* shoulder; ***girare le -e a qu*** turn one's back on s.o.; ***era di -e*** he had his back to me; ***stringersi nelle -e*** shrug; ***vivere alle -e di qu*** live off s.o.
spalleggiare ⟨1f⟩ support, back up
spalliera *f* wallbars
spallina *f* shoulder pad
spalmare ⟨1a⟩ spread
spalti *mpl* terraces
spandere ⟨3a⟩ spread
spandersi spread
spanto *pp* → ***spandere***
sparare ⟨1a⟩ **1** *v/i* shoot (***a*** at) **2** *v/t*: ***sparare un colpo*** fire a shot
sparatoria *f* gunfire, series of shots
sparecchiare ⟨1k⟩ clear
spareggio *m* SP play-off
spargere ⟨3uu⟩ spread; *lagrime*, *sangue* shed
sparire ⟨4d or 4e⟩ disappear
sparizione *f* disappearance
sparo *m* (gun)shot
sparpagliare ⟨1g⟩ scatter
sparso 1 *pp* → ***spargere* 2** *agg* scattered
spartiacque *m inv* watershed
spartire ⟨4d⟩ divide (up), split F
spartito *m* score
spartitraffico *m* (*pl* -ci) traffic island
spartizione *f* division
spasimante *m/f* admirer
spasimo *m* agony
spasmo *m* MED spasm
spasso *m* fun; ***andare a spasso*** go for a walk; *fig* ***essere a spasso*** be out of work, be unemployed; ***è uno spasso*** he / it's a good laugh; ***per spasso*** as a joke, for fun
spassoso very funny
spastico (*pl* -ci) spastic
spaurito frightened
spavaldo cocky, over-confident
spaventapasseri *m inv* scarecrow
spaventare ⟨1b⟩ frighten, scare
spaventarsi be frightened, be scared
spavento *m* fright; ***mi sono preso uno spavento*** I got a fright
spaventoso frightening
spaziale space *attr*
spazientirsi ⟨4d⟩ get impatient, lose one's patience
spazio *m* (*pl* -zi) space; ***spazio aereo*** airspace
spazioso spacious
spazzacamino *m* chimney sweep
spazzaneve *m inv* snowplough, *Am* -plow
spazzare ⟨1a⟩ sweep
spazzatura *f* rubbish, garbage
spazzino *m*, **-a** *f* street sweeper
spazzola *f* brush
spazzolare ⟨1l⟩ brush
spazzolino *m* brush; ***spazzolino da denti*** toothbrush
specchiarsi ⟨1k⟩ look at o.s.; (*riflettersi*) be mirrored, be reflected
specchietto *m* mirror; (*prospetto*) table; AUTO ***specchietto retrovisore*** rear-view mirror
specchio *m* (*pl* -cchi) mirror
speciale special
specialista *m/f* (*mpl* -i) specialist
specialità *f inv* special(i)ty
specializzarsi ⟨1a⟩ specialize
specialmente especially, particularly
specie 1 *f inv* species; ***una specie di*** a sort *or* kind of **2** *avv* especially
specificare ⟨1m & d⟩ specify
specifico (*pl* -ci) specific
speculare ⟨1l & b⟩ speculate (***in*** in, ***su***

S

on)
speculativo speculative
speculatore *m*, **-trice** *f* speculator
speculazione *f* speculation
spedire ⟨4d⟩ send
spedito fast
spedizione *f* dispatch, sending; *di merce* shipping; (*viaggio*) expedition; ***agenzia*** *f* ***di spedizione*** shipping agency; ***spese*** *pl* ***di spedizione*** shipping costs
spedizioniere *m* courier
spegnere ⟨3vv⟩ put out; *luce*, *motore*, *radio* turn off, switch off
spegnersi *di fuoco* go out; *di motore* stop, die F
spellare ⟨1a⟩ skin
spellarsi peel
spelonca *f* (*pl* -che) cave
spendere ⟨3c⟩ spend; *fig* invest
spennare ⟨1a⟩ *pollo* pluck
spensierato carefree
spento *pp* → ***spegnere***
speranza *f* hope; ***senza speranza*** hopeless
sperare ⟨1b⟩ **1** *v/t* hope for **2** *v/i* trust (***in*** in)
sperduto lost; *luogo* remote, isolated
spergiuro **1** *m* perjury **2** *m*, **-a** *f* perjurer
sperimentale experimental
sperimentare ⟨1a⟩ try; *in laboratorio* test; *fig*: *fatica*, *dolore* feel; *droga* experiment with
sperma *m* sperm
sperperare ⟨1l & b⟩ fritter away, squander
sperpero *m* frittering away, squandering
spesa *f* expense; ***fare la spesa*** do the shopping; ***fare -e*** go shopping; ***-e*** *pl* ***di produzione*** production costs; ***-e*** *pl* ***di pubblicità*** advertising costs; ***-e*** *pl* ***vive*** incidental expenses; ***a proprie -e*** at one's own expense
spesso **1** *agg* thick; ***-e volte*** many times, often **2** *avv* often, frequently
spessore *m* thickness
spett. *abbr* (= ***spettabile***) Messrs; *in lettera* **Spett. Ditta** Dear Sirs
spettacolare spectacular
spettacolo *m* show; (*panorama*) spectacle, sight; ***spettacolo teatrale*** show
spettare ⟨1b⟩: ***questo spetta a te*** this is yours; ***non spetta a te giudicare*** it's not up to you to judge
spettatore *m*, **-trice** *f* spectator; TEA member of the audience
spettinare ⟨1l & b⟩: ***spettinare qu*** ruffle s.o.'s hair
spettro *m* ghost; FIS spectrum
spezie *fpl* spices
spezzare ⟨1b⟩ break in two
spezzarsi break
spezzatino *m* stew
spezzato **1** *agg* broken (in two) **2** *m* co-ordinated two-piece suit
spezzettare ⟨1a⟩ break up
spia *f* spy; TEC pilot light; ***fare la spia*** tell, sneak
spiacente: ***essere spiacente*** be sorry; ***sono molto spiacente*** I am very sorry
spiacere ⟨2k⟩: ***mi spiace*** I am sorry
spiacevole unpleasant
spiaggia *f* (*pl* -gge) beach
spianare ⟨1a⟩ roll
spiare ⟨1h⟩ spy on
spiazzo *m* empty space; *in bosco* clearing
spiccato strong
spicchio *m* (*pl* -cchi) *di frutto* section; ***spicchio d'aglio*** clove of garlic
spicciarsi ⟨1f⟩ hurry up
spiccioli *mpl* (small) change *sg*
spiedo *m* spit; ***allo spiedo*** spit-roasted
spiegabile possible to explain
spiegare ⟨1b & e⟩ (*stendere*) spread; (*chiarire*) explain
spiegarsi explain what one means; ***mi spiego?*** have I made myself clear?; ***non so se mi spiego*** I don't know if I make myself clear
spiegazione *f* explanation
spiegazzare ⟨1a⟩ crease
spietato merciless, pitiless
spiga *f* (*pl* -ghe) *di grano* ear
spigato herring-bone *attr*
spigliato confident
spigola *f* sea bass
spigolo *m* corner
spilla *f gioiello* brooch; ***spilla da balia*** safety pin
spillo *m* pin; ***spillo di sicurezza*** safety pin
spina *f* BOT thorn; ZO spine; *di pesce* bone; EL plug; ANAT ***spina dorsale*** spine; ***parcheggio*** *m* ***a spina di pesce*** angle parking; ***birra*** *f* ***alla spina*** draught beer, beer on tap; *fig* ***stare sulle -e*** be on tenterhooks
spinaci *mpl* spinach *sg*
spinale spinal
spinello F *m* joint F
spingere ⟨3d⟩ push; *fig* drive
spino *m* thorn
spinoso thorny
spinta *f* push
spinterogeno *m* AUTO distributor
spinto *pp* → ***spingere***
spionaggio *m* (*pl* -ggi) espionage
spiraglio *m* (*pl* -gli) crack; *di luce*, *speranza* gleam, glimmer

spirale *f* spiral; *contraccettivo* coil
spirare ⟨1a⟩ blow; *fig* die
spirito *m* spirit; (*disposizione*) mind; (*umorismo*) wit; ***avere spirito d'osservazione*** be observant; ***fare dello spirito*** be witty
spiritoso witty
spirituale spiritual
splendere ⟨3a⟩ shine
splendente bright
splendido wonderful, splendid
splendore *m* splendo(u)r
spogliare ⟨1g⟩ undress; (*rubare*) rob
spogliarsi undress, strip; ***spogliarsi di qc*** give sth up
spogliarello *m* striptease
spogliatoio *m* (*pl* -oi) dressing room, locker room
spoglio (*pl* -gli) bare
spola *f*: ***fare la spola da un posto all'altro*** shuttle backwards and forwards between two places
spolverare ⟨1l⟩ dust
spolverizzare ⟨1a⟩ dust (***di*** with)
sponda *f di letto* edge, side; *di fiume* bank; *nel biliardo* cushion
sponsor *m inv* sponsor
sponsorizzare ⟨1a⟩ sponsor
spontaneità *f* spontaneity
spontaneo spontaneous
sporadico (*pl* -ci) sporadic
sporcare ⟨1c & d⟩ dirty
sporcarsi get dirty
sporcizia *f* dirt
sporco (*pl* -chi) **1** *agg* dirty **2** *m* dirt
sporgere ⟨3d⟩ **1** *v/t* hold out; *denuncia* make **2** *v/i* jut out
sporgersi lean out
sport *m inv* sport; ***sport****pl* ***invernali*** winter sports; ***fare dello sport*** do sport; ***per sport*** for fun
sporta *f* shopping bag; *di vimini* shopping basket
sportello *m* door; ***sportello automatico*** automatic teller machine, cash dispenser
sportivo **1** *agg* sports *attr*; *persona* sporty; ***campo*** *m* ***sportivo*** playing field **2** *m*, **-a** *f* sportsman; *donna* sportswoman
sporto *pp* → ***sporgere***
sposa *f* bride; ***abito*** *m* ***da sposa*** wedding dress
sposare ⟨1c⟩ marry
sposarsi get married
sposato married
sposo *m* bridegroom; ***-i*** *pl* newlyweds
spostare ⟨1a⟩ (*trasferire*) move, shift; (*rimandare*) postpone
spostarsi move
S.P.Q.R. *abbr* (= ***Senatus Populusque Romanus***) the Senate and People of Rome
spranga *f* (*pl* -ghe) bar
sprangare ⟨1e⟩ bar
sprecare ⟨1b & d⟩ waste, squander
spreco *m* (*pl* -chi) waste
spregevole contemptible, despicable
spregiudicato unprejudiced, unbiased; *spreg* unscrupulous
spremere ⟨3a⟩ squeeze
spremilimoni *m inv* lemon squeezer
spremuta *f* juice; ***spremuta di limone*** lemon juice; ***spremuta d'arancia*** orange juice
sprizzare ⟨1a⟩ spurt; *fig* exude
sprofondare ⟨1a⟩ sink; *fig* ***sprofondare dalla vergogna*** be overcome with embarrassment
spronare ⟨1a⟩ spur on
sprone *m* spur
sproporzionato disproportionate (***a*** to), out of proportion (***a*** to)
sproposito *m* blunder; ***fare uno sproposito*** do something silly; ***costare uno sproposito*** cost a fortune; ***a sproposito*** out of turn
sprovveduto inexperienced
sprovvisto: ***sprovvisto di*** lacking; ***sono sprovvisto di …*** I don't have any …; ***alla -a*** unexpectedly
spruzzare ⟨1a⟩ spray
spruzzatore *m* spray
spruzzo *m* spray; *fango* splatter
spudorato shameless
spugna *f* sponge
spuma *f* foam
spumante: (***vino*** *m*) ***spumante*** sparkling wine
spumeggiante frothy; *persona* bubbly
spuntare ⟨1a⟩ stick out; BOT come up; *di sole* appear; *di giorno* break; ***gli è spuntato un dente*** he has cut a tooth
spuntino *m* snack
spunto *m* suggestion; ***prendere spunto da*** be inspired by
sputare ⟨1a⟩ **1** *v/i* spit **2** *v/t* spit out
sputo *m* spittle
squadra *f strumento* set square; (*gruppo*) squad; SP team; ***squadra volante*** flying squad
squalifica *f* (*pl* -che) disqualification
squalificare ⟨1m & d⟩ disqualify
squallido squallid
squallore *m* squalor
squalo *m* shark
squama *f* flake; *di pesce* scale
squarcio *m* (*pl* -ci) *in stoffa* rip, tear; *in nuvole* break
squilibrato **1** *agg* insane **2** *m*, **-a** *f* lunatic

squilibrio *m* (*pl* -ri) imbalance
squillare ⟨1a⟩ ring
squillo *m* ring; ***ragazza*** *f* ***squillo*** callgirl
squisito *cibo* delicious
sradicare ⟨1l & d⟩ uproot; *fig* (*eliminare*) eradicate, uproot
S.r.l. *abbr* (= ***Società a responsabilità limitata***) Ltd (= limited)
SS. *abbr* (= ***santi***) Saints
S.S. *abbr* (= ***Sua Santità***) His Holiness (the Pope); (= ***Strada Statale***) A road
stabile 1 *agg* steady; (*duraturo*) stable; *tempo* settled **2** *m* building
stabilimento *m* (*fabbrica*) plant, *Br* factory; ***stabilimento balneare*** lido
stabilire ⟨4d⟩ *data*, *obiettivi*, *record* set; (*decidere*) decide, settle
stabilirsi settle
stabilità *f* steadiness; *di relazione*, *moneta* stability
stabilizzare ⟨1a⟩ stabilize
staccare ⟨1d⟩ remove, detach; EL unplug; TELEC ***staccare il ricevitore*** lift the receiver
stadio *m* (*pl* -di) stage; SP stadium
staffa *f* stirrup; ***perdere le -e*** blow one's top
staffetta *f* SP relay; ***corsa*** *f* ***a staffetta*** relay race
stage *m inv* training period
stagionale seasonal
stagionare ⟨1a⟩ age, mature; *legno* season
stagionato aged, mature; *legno* seasoned
stagione *f* season; ***alta stagione*** high season; ***bassa stagione*** low season; ***stagione morta*** off-season; ***frutta*** *f* ***di stagione*** fruit in season, seasonal fruit
stagnare ⟨1a⟩ *dell'acqua* grow stagnant; FIN stagnate
stagnante stagnant
stagno 1 *m* pond; TEC tin **2** *agg* watertight
stalla *f per bovini* cowshed; *per cavalli* stable
stamani, **stamattina** this morning
stambecco *m* (*pl* -cchi) ibex
stampa *f* press; *tecnica* printing; FOT print; *posta* ***-e*** *pl* printed matter; ***libro*** *m* ***in corso di stampa*** book that has gone to press; ***stampa locale*** local press; ***stampa scandalistica*** tabloids, gutter press; ***libertà*** *f* ***di stampa*** freedom of the press
stampante *f* INFOR printer; ***stampante a getto di inchiostro*** ink-jet printer; ***stampante laser*** laser printer
stampare ⟨1a⟩ print
stampatello *m* block letters *pl*
stampato *m* INFOR printout, hard copy
stampella *f* crutch
stampo *m* mo(u)ld
stancare ⟨1d⟩ tire (out)
stancarsi get tired, tire
stanchezza *f* tiredness, fatigue
stanco (*pl* -chi) tired; ***stanco morto*** dead beat
stand *m inv* stand
standard *m/agg inv* standard
standardizzare ⟨1a⟩ standardize
standardizzazione *f* standardization
stanga *f* (*pl* -ghe) bar
stanghetta *f* leg
stanotte tonight; (*la notte scorsa*) last night
stantuffo *m* piston
stanza *f* room
stanziare ⟨1g⟩ *somma di denaro* allocate, earmark
stanzino *m* boxroom
stappare ⟨1a⟩ take the top off
star *f inv* star
stare ⟨1q⟩ be; (*restare*) stay; (*abitare*) live; ***stare in piedi*** stand; ***stare bene*** be well; *di vestiti* suit; ***stare per fare qc*** be about to do sth; ***stammi a sentire*** listen to me; ***lascialo stare*** leave him alone, let him be; ***stare telefonando*** be on the phone, be making a phonecall; ***come sta?*** how are you?, how are things?; ***ben ti sta!*** serves you right!; ***ci sto!*** here I am!; ***sta bene*** all right, ok
starnutire ⟨4d⟩ sneeze
starnuto *m* sneeze
start *m inv* off
starter *m inv* SP starter; AUTO choke
stasera this evening, tonight
statale 1 *agg* state *attr* **2** *m/f* (*gen* pl -i) civil servant **3** *f* main road
Stati Uniti d'America *mpl* United States of America, USA
statistica *f* (*pl* -che) statistics
statizzare ⟨1a⟩ nationalize
stato 1 *pp* → ***essere*** *e* ***stare*** **2** *m anche* POL state; ***stato assistenziale*** Welfare State; ***stato civile*** marital status; ***stato maggiore*** general staff; ***stato di salute*** state of health, condition; ***essere in stato di fare*** be in a position to do; ***essere in stato interessante*** be pregnant
statua *f* statue
statunitense 1 *agg* US *attr*, American **2** *m/f* US citizen, citizen of the United States
statura *f* height; *fig* stature
statuto *m* statute
stavolta this time
stazionamento *m* parking
stazionare ⟨1a⟩ be parked

stazionario (*pl* -ri) stationary
stazione *f* station; ***stazione di servizio*** service station; ***stazione balneare*** seaside resort; ***stazione centrale*** main station; ***stazione climatica*** health resort; ***stazione termale*** spa; ***stazione trasmittente*** radio station
stecca *f* (*pl* -cche) *di biliardo* cue; *di sigarette* carton; MED splint; MUS wrong note
stecchino *m* toothpick
stella *f* star; ***stella alpina*** edelweiss; ***stella polare*** North Star, Pole Star; ***stella cadente*** shooting star; ***stella di mare*** starfish; *fig* ***vedere le -e*** see stars
stelo *m* stem, stalk
stemma *m* (*pl* -i) coat of arms
stendere ⟨3c⟩ spread; *braccio* stretch out; *biancheria* hang out, hang up; *verbale* draw up
stendersi stretch out
stendibiancheria *m inv* clothes dryer
stenodattilografa *f* shorthand typist
stenodattilografia *f* shorthand typing
stenografare ⟨1m & c⟩ take down in shorthand
stenografia *f* shorthand
stentare ⟨1b⟩: ***stentare a fare qc*** find it hard to do sth, have difficulty doing sth
stento *m*: ***a stento*** with difficulty; ***-i*** *pl* hardship
stereo *m inv* stereo
stereotipo 1 *agg* stereotypical **2** *m* stereotype
sterile sterile
sterilità *f* sterility
sterilizzare ⟨1a⟩ sterilize
sterilizzazione *f* sterilization
sterlina *f* sterling
sterminare ⟨1l & b⟩ exterminate
sterminato vast
sterminio *m* (*pl* -ni) extermination
sterno *m* breastbone, ANAT sternum
sterzare ⟨1b⟩ steer; ***sterzare a sinistra*** turn left
sterzata *f* swerve
sterzo *m* AUTO steering
steso *pp* → ***stendere***
stesso same; ***lo stesso, la stessa*** the same one; ***è lo stesso*** it's all the same; ***oggi stesso*** this very day; ***io stesso*** myself; ***se stesso*** himself; ***l'ho visto coi miei stessi occhi*** I saw it with my very own eyes
stile *m* style; SP ***stile libero*** freestyle
stilografica *f* fountain pen
stima *f* (*ammirazione*) esteem; (*valutazione*) estimate
stimare ⟨1a⟩ *persona* esteem; *oggetto* value, estimate (the value of); (*ritenere*) think, consider
stimarsi think *or* consider o.s.
stimato respected
stimolante 1 *agg* stimulating **2** *m* stimulant
stimolare ⟨1l⟩ stimulate
stimolo *m* stimulus
stinco *m* (*pl* -chi) shin
stingere ⟨3d⟩ **1** *v/t* fade **2** *v/i e* **stingersi** fade
stinto *pp* → ***stingere***
stipare ⟨1a⟩ cram
stipato crammed (***di*** with)
stipendiato *m*, **-a** *f* person on a salary
stipendio *m* (*pl* -di) salary
stipulare ⟨1l⟩ stipulate
stipulazione *f* stipulation
stiramento *m* MED pulled muscle
stirare ⟨1a⟩ iron; ***non si stira*** it's non-iron
stirarsi pull
stiratura *f* ironing
stiro *m*: ***ferro*** *m* ***da stiro*** iron; ***non stiro*** non-iron
stirpe *f* (*origine*) birth
stitichezza *f* constipation
stivale *m* boots; ***-i*** *pl* ***di gomma*** rubber boots, *Br* wellingtons
sto → ***stare***
stoccafisso *m* stockfish (*air-dried cod*)
stoccaggio *m* (*pl* -ggi) stocking
stoffa *f* material; *fig* ***avere stoffa*** be talented
stomaco *m* (*pl* -chi) stomach; ***dolori*** *mpl* ***di stomaco*** stomach pains; ***mi sono tolto un peso dallo stomaco*** I got it off my chest
stonare ⟨1c⟩ *di cantante* sing out of tune; *fig* be out of place; *di colori* clash
stonato *persona* tone deaf; *nota* false; *strumento* out of tune
stop *m inv* AUTO brake light; *cartello* stop sign
stoppare ⟨1c⟩ stop
storcere ⟨3d⟩ twist; ***storcere il naso*** make a face
storcersi bend; ***storcersi un piede*** twist one's ankle
stordimento *m* dizziness
stordire ⟨4d⟩ stun
stordito stunned
storia *f* history; (*narrazione*) story; ***storia dell'arte*** history of art; ***non far -e!*** don't make a fuss *or* scene!
storico (*pl* -ci) **1** *agg* historical; (*memorabile*) historic **2** *m*, **-a** *f* historian
storiografia *f* historiography
storiografo *m*, **-a** *f* historigrapher
storione *m* sturgeon
stormo *m di uccelli* flock

stornare ⟨1a⟩ *pericolo* avert
storno *m uccello* starling
storpio (*pl* -pi) **1** *agg* crippled **2** *m* **-a** *f* cripple
storta *f*: ***prendere una storta al piede*** twist one's ankle
storto crooked
stoviglie *fpl* dishes
strabico (*pl* -ci) cross-eyed
strabismo *m* strabismus
stracarico (*pl* -chi) overloaded
stracaro exceedingly expensive
stracciare ⟨1f⟩ tear up
stracciatella *f type of soup*; *gelato* chocolate chip
stracciato in shreds
straccio (*pl* -cci) **1** *m per pulire* cloth; *per spolverare* duster **2** *agg*: ***carta*** *f* ***-a*** waste paper
strada *f* road; ***per strada*** down the road; ***sono*** (***già***) ***per strada*** I'm coming, I'm on my way; ***strada provinciale*** B road; ***strada a senso unico*** one-way street; ***strada statale*** A road; ***farsi strada*** push one's way through; *nella vita* get on in life; ***a mezza strada*** half-way
stradale road *attr*; ***incidente*** *m* ***stradale*** road accident; ***polizia*** *f* ***stradale*** traffic police; ***regolamento*** *m* ***stradale*** rule of the road; ***rete*** *f* ***stradale*** road network
stradario *m* street-finder, street map
strafare ⟨3aa⟩ exaggerate
strage *f* slaughter; ***fare strage di cuori*** be a heartbreaker
stragrande: ***la stragrande maggioranza*** the vast majority
stranezza *f* strangeness
strangolare ⟨1l⟩ strangle
straniero **1** *agg* foreign **2** *m*, **-a** *f* foreigner
strano strange
straordinario (*pl* -ri) **1** *agg* special; *eccezionale* extraordinary **2** *m* overtime
strapazzare ⟨1a⟩ treat badly; ***uova*** *fpl* ***strapazzate*** scrambled eggs
strapazzarsi overdo it
strapazzo *m* strain; ***essere uno strapazzo*** be exhausting; ***da strapazzo*** third-rate
strapieno crowded
strapiombo *m*: ***a strapiombo*** overhanging
strappare ⟨1a⟩ tear, rip; (*staccare*) tear down; (*togliere*) grab, snatch (***a qu*** out of s.o.'s hands)
strappo *m* tear, rip; MED torn ligament; *fig* ***uno strappo alla regola*** an exception to the rule
straricco (*pl* -cchi) extremely rich
straripare ⟨1a⟩ flood, overflow its banks
strascico *m* (*pl* -chi) train; *fig* after-effects
stratagemma *m* (*pl* -i) stratagem
strategia *f* strategy
strategico (*pl* -ci) strategic
strato *m* layer; ***strato d'ozono*** ozone layer; ***strato protettivo*** protective coating; ***strato sociale*** social stratum
stravagante extravagant
stravaganza *f* extravagance
stravecchio (*pl* -cchi) ancient
stravedere ⟨2s⟩: ***stravedere per qu*** worship s.o.
stravincere ⟨3d⟩ win by a mile
stravolgere ⟨3d⟩ change radically; (*travisare*) twist; (*stancare*) exhaust
stravolto **1** *pp* → ***stravolgere*** **2** *agg* (*stanco*) exhausted
strazio *m* (*pl* -zi): ***era uno strazio*** it was painful
strega *f* (*pl* -ghe) witch
stregare ⟨1e⟩ bewitch
stregone *m* wizard
stremare ⟨1b⟩ exhaust
stremato exhausted
stress *m inv* stress
stressante stressful
stressare ⟨1b⟩ stress
stretta *f* hold; ***stretta di mano*** handshake; ***mettere qu alle -e*** put s.o. in a tight corner
strettamente closely; ***tenere qc strettamente*** (***in mano***) clutch sth (in one's hand)
strettezza *f* narrowness
stretto **1** *pp* → ***stringere*** **2** *agg* narrow; *vestito*, *scarpe* too tight; ***lo stretto necessario*** the bare minimum **3** *m* GEOG strait
strettoia *f* bottleneck
stridere ⟨3a⟩ *di porta* squeak; *di colori* clash
stridulo shrill
strillare ⟨1a⟩ scream
strillo *m* scream
striminzito skimpy
strimpellare ⟨1b⟩ strum
stringa *f* (*pl* -ghe) lace
stringere ⟨3d⟩ **1** *v/t* make narrower; *abito* take in; *vite* tighten; ***stringere amicizia*** become friends **2** *v/i di tempo* press
stringersi *intorno a tavolo* squeeze up
striscia *f* (*pl* -sce) strip; *dipinta* stripe; ***-sce*** *pl* ***pedonali*** pedestrian crossing *sg*, *Br* zebra crossing *sg*; ***a -sce*** striped
strisciare ⟨1f⟩ **1** *v/t piedi* scrape; (*sfiorare*) brush, smear (***contro*** against) **2** *v/i* crawl
striscio *m* MED smear
striscione *m* banner
strizzare ⟨1a⟩ wring; ***strizzare l'occhio a***

S

qu wink at s.o.
strofa *f* verse
strofinaccio *m* (*pl* -cci) dish towel
strofinare ⟨1a⟩ rub
stroncare ⟨1d⟩ *albero* knock down; *vita* snuff out; F *idea* shoot down
stropicciare ⟨1f⟩ crush, wrinkle
strozzare ⟨1c⟩ strangle
strozzatura *f* narrowing
strozzino *m*, **-a** *f* loan shark F
struggente all-consuming
struggere ⟨3cc⟩ consume
strumentalizzare make use of
strumento *m* instrument; ***strumento musicale*** musical instrument; ***strumento ad arco/a fiato*** string / wind instrument
strutto *m* lard
struttura *f* structure
strutturale structural
strutturare ⟨1a⟩ structure
struzzo *m* zo ostrich
stuccare ⟨1d⟩ plaster
stucco *m* (*pl* -cchi) plaster; ***rimanere di stucco*** be thunderstruck, *Br* be gobsmacked F
studente *m*, **-essa** *f* student; ***casa f dello studente*** hall of residence
studiare ⟨1k⟩ study
studio *m* (*pl* -di) study; *di artista*, RAD, TV studio; *di professionista* office; *di medico* surgery; ***borsa f di studio*** bursary
studioso 1 *agg* studious **2** *m*, **-a** *f* scholar
stufa *f* stove; ***stufa elettrica/a gas*** electric / gas fire
stufare ⟨1a⟩ GASTR stew; *fig* bore
stufarsi get bored (***di*** with)
stufato *m* stew
stufo: ***essere stufo di qc*** be bored with sth
stuolo *m* host
stupefacente 1 *agg* amazing, stupefying **2** *m* narcotic
stupefatto amazed, stupefied
stupendo stupendous
stupidaggine *f* stupidity; ***è una stupidaggine*** (*cosa senza importanza*) it's nothing
stupidità *f* stupidity
stupido 1 *agg* stupid **2** *m*, **-a** *f* idiot
stupire ⟨4d⟩ **1** *v/t* amaze **2** *v/i e* **stupirsi** be amazed
stupore *m* amazement
stuprare ⟨1a⟩ rape
stupratore *m* rapist
stupro *m* rape
sturare ⟨1a⟩ clear, unblock
stuzzicadenti *m inv* toothpick
stuzzicare ⟨1l & d⟩ tease; ***stuzzicare l'appetito*** whet the appetite

su 1 *prp* on; *argomento* about; (*circa*) (round) about; ***sul tavolo*** on the table; ***sul mare*** by the sea; ***sulle tremila lire*** round about three thousand lire; ***su misura*** made to measure; ***nove volte su dieci*** nine times out of ten **2** *avv* up; (*al piano di sopra*) upstairs; ***su!*** come on!; ***avere su*** *vestito* have on; ***guardare in su*** look up
sub *m/f inv* skin diver
subacqueo 1 *agg* underwater **2** *m*, **-a** *f* skin diver
subaffittare ⟨1a⟩ sublet
subaffitto *m* sublet
subdolo underhand
subentrare ⟨1a⟩: ***subentrare a qu*** replace s.o., take s.o.'s place
subire ⟨4d⟩ *danni*, *perdita* suffer
subito immediately
subordinare ⟨1m⟩ subordinate
suburbano suburban
succedere ⟨3a or 3l⟩ (*accadere*) happen; ***succedere a*** *in carica* succeed; ***che succede?*** what's going on?
successione *f* succession
successivo successive
successo 1 *pp* → ***succedere*** **2** *m* success; ***di successo*** successful
successore *m* successor
succhiare ⟨1k⟩ suck
succo *m* (*pl* -cchi) juice; ***succo d'arancia*** orange juice
succoso juicy
succursale *f* branch
sud *m* south; ***sud ovest*** south-west; ***sud est*** south-east; ***al sud di*** (to the) south of
sudare ⟨1a⟩ perspire, sweat
sudata *f* perspiration, sweat
sudato sweaty
suddividere ⟨3q⟩ subdivide
suddivisione *f* subdivision
sudicio (*pl* -ci) **1** *agg* dirty **2** *m* dirt
sudiciume *m* dirt
sudore *m* perspiration, sweat
sufficiente sufficient
sufficienza *f* sufficiency; ***a sufficienza*** enough
suffragio *m* (*pl* -gi) suffrage; ***suffragio universale*** universal suffrage
suggerimento *m* suggestion
suggerire ⟨4d⟩ suggest; TEA prompt
suggeritore *m* TEA prompter
suggestionare ⟨1a⟩ influence
suggestione *f* influence
suggestivo picturesque
sughero *m* cork
sugli *prp* ***su*** and *art* ***gli***
sugo *m* (*pl* -ghi) sauce; *di arrosto* juice; ***al sugo*** with sauce

sui *prp* ***su*** and *art* ***i***
suicida *m/f* suicide (victim)
suicidarsi ⟨1a⟩ commit suicide, kill o.s.
suicidio *m* (*pl* -di) suicide
suino pork *attr*
sul *prp* ***su*** and *art* ***il***
sull', **sulla**, **sulle**, **sullo** *prp* ***su*** and *art* ***l', la, le, lo***
suo 1 *agg* his; *di cosa* its; ***-a*** *f* her; *di cosa* its; ***il suo maestro*** his teacher; ***i suoi amici*** his friends; ***questo libro è suo*** this is his book; ***Suo*** your **2** *pron*: ***il suo*** his; *di cosa* its; ***la -a*** *f* hers; *di cosa* its
suocera *f* mother-in-law
suocero *m* father-in-law; ***-i*** *pl* mother- and father-in-law, in-laws F
suola *f* sole
suolo *m* ground; (*terreno*) soil
suonare ⟨1o⟩ **1** *v/t* play; *campanello* ring **2** *v/i* play; *alla porta* ring
suono *m* sound
suora *f* REL nun
super *f inv* F 4-star
superare ⟨1l⟩ go past; *fig* overcome; *esame* pass
superato out of date
superbia *f* haughtiness
superbo haughty
superficiale superficial
superficie *f* surface; ***in superficie*** on the surface
superfluo superfluous
superiora *f* Mother Superior
superiore 1 *agg* top; *qualità* superior; ***superiore alla media*** better than average **2** *m* superior
superiorità *f* superiority
superlativo *m/agg* superlative
supermarket *m inv*, **supermercato** *m* supermarket
superstite 1 *agg* surviving **2** *m/f* survivor
superstizione *f* superstition
superstizioso superstitious
superstrada *f* motorway, *Am* highway (*with no tolls*)
superuomo *m* (*pl* -uomini) superman
suppergiù about
supplementare additional, supplementary
supplemento *m* supplement; ***supplemento intercity*** intercity supplement; FERR ***fare il supplemento*** pay a supplement
supplente *m/f* replacement; EDU supply teacher
supplenza *f* supply teaching
supplicare ⟨1l & d⟩ beg
supplizio *m* (*pl* -zi) torture
suppongo → ***supporre***
supporre ⟨3ll⟩ suppose
supporto *m* TEC support; INFOR ***supporto dati*** data support
supposizione *f* supposition
supposta *f* MED suppository
supposto *pp* → ***supporre***
suppurare ⟨1a⟩ MED suppurate
suppurazione *f* suppuration
supremazia *f* supremacy
supremo supreme
surf *m inv* surfboard; ***fare surf*** surf, go surfing
surfista *m/f* (*mpl* -i) surfer
surgelare ⟨1b⟩ freeze
surgelato 1 *agg* frozen **2** *m*: ***-i*** *pl* frozen food *sg*
surriscaldare ⟨1a⟩ overheat
surrogato *m* substitute
suscettibile touchy; ***è suscettibile di miglioramento*** it's likely to improve
suscettibilità *f* touchiness
suscitare ⟨1l⟩ arouse
susina *f* plum
susino *m* plum (tree)
sussidio *m* (*pl* -di) grant, allowance; ***sussidio di disoccupazione*** unemployment benefit
sussultare ⟨1a⟩ start, jump
sussulto *m* start, jump
sussurrare ⟨1a⟩ *v/t & v/i* whisper
sussurro *m* whisper
sutura *f* MED stitches *pl*
svagarsi ⟨1e⟩ take one's mind off things
svago *m* (*pl* -ghi) distraction; ***per svago*** to take one's mind off things
svaligiare ⟨1f⟩ burgle, *Am* burglarize
svalutare ⟨1a⟩ devalue
svalutazione *f* devaluation
svanire ⟨4d⟩ vanish
svantaggio *m* (*pl* -ggi) disadvantage
svantaggioso disadvantageous
svariato varied
svedese 1 *m/agg* Swedish **2** *m/f* Swede
sveglia *f* alarm clock
svegliare ⟨1g⟩ waken (up)
svegliarsi waken up
sveglio awake; *fig* alert
svelare ⟨1a⟩ *segreto* reveal
svelto quick; ***alla -a*** quickly
svendere ⟨3a⟩ sell at a reduced price
svendita *f* clearance
svenimento *m* fainting fit
svenire ⟨4p⟩ faint
sventolare ⟨1l & b⟩ *v/t & v/i* wave
sventura *f* misfortune
sventurato unfortunate
svenuto *pp* → ***svenire***
svergognato shameless
svernare ⟨1b⟩ spend the winter in

svestire ⟨4b⟩ undress
svestirsi get undressed, undress
Svezia *f* Sweden
sviare ⟨1h⟩ deflect; *fig* divert
svignarsela ⟨1a⟩ slip away
sviluppare ⟨1a⟩ develop
svilupparsi develop
sviluppato developed
sviluppo *m* development
svincolo *m di strada* junction
svista *f* oversight; ***per svista*** by some oversight
svitare ⟨1a⟩ unscrew
svitato unscrewed; *fig* ***essere svitato*** have a screw loose
Svizzera *f* Switzerland
svizzero 1 *agg* Swiss **2** *m*, **-a** *f* Swiss
svogliatezza *f* laziness
svogliato lazy
svolazzare ⟨1a⟩ flutter
svolgere ⟨3d⟩ *rotolo* unwrap; *tema* develop; *attività* carry out
svolgersi happen; *di commedia, film* be set (***in*** in)
svolgimento *m* course; *di tema* development
svolta *f* (*curva*) turning; *fig* turning point
svoltare ⟨1c⟩: ***svoltare a destra*** turn right
svolto *pp* → ***svolgere***
svuotare ⟨1c⟩ empty

S

T

t *abbr* (= ***tonnellata***) t (= tonne)
tabaccaio *m* (*pl* -ai), **-a** *f* tobacconist
tabaccheria *f* tobacconist's
tabacco *m* (*pl* -cchi) tobacco
tabagismo *m* smoking
tabella *f* table; ***tabella dei prezzi*** price list; *fig* ***tabella di marcia*** schedule
tabellina *f* multiplication table
tabellone *m* board; *per avvisi* notice board; ***tabellone pubblicitario*** billboard
tabernacolo *m* tabernacle
tabù *m/agg inv* taboo
tabulato *m* printout
TAC *abbr* (= ***Tomografia Assiale Computerizzata***) CAT (= computerized axial tomography)
taccagno mean, stingy F
taccheggio *m* shoplifting
tacchino *m* turkey
tacco *m* (*pl* -cchi) heel
taccuino *m* notebook
tacere ⟨2k⟩ **1** *v/t* keep quiet about, say nothing about **2** *v/i* not say anything, be silent
tachicardia *f* tachycardia
tachimetro *m* speedometer
tacitare ⟨1l⟩ *scandalo* hush up
tacito tacit
taciturno taciturn
tafano *m* ZO horsefly
tafferuglio *m* (*pl* -gli) scuffle
taglia *f* (*misura*) size; ***di taglia media*** medium; ***taglia forte*** outsize; ***taglia unica*** one size
tagliacarte *m inv* paper-knife
tagliando *m* coupon; AUTO service; ***fare il tagliando*** have the vehicle serviced
tagliare ⟨1g⟩ cut; *albero* cut down; *legna* chop; ***tagliare i capelli*** have one's hair cut; *fig* ***tagliare la strada a qu*** cut in front of s.o.
tagliarsi cut o.s.; ***mi sono tagliata un dito*** I've cut my finger
tagliatelle *fpl* tagliatelle *sg*
tagliente sharp
tagliere *m* chopping board
taglierini *mpl type of noodles*
taglio *m* (*pl* -gli) cut; ***taglio cesareo*** C(a)esarean (section)
tailleur *m inv* suit
talco *m* (*pl* -chi) talc, talcum powder
tale such a; *-**i** pl* such; ***tale e quale*** just like; ***un tale*** someone; ***il signor tal dei -i*** Mr So-and-so
talento *m* talent
tallonare ⟨1a⟩ *persona* follow close behind; *nel rugby* heel
talloncino *m* coupon
tallone *m* heel
talmente so
talora sometimes
talpa *f* mole
talvolta sometimes
tamburo *m* drum
tamponamento *m* AUTO collision; ***tamponamento a catena*** multi-vehicle pile-up
tamponare ⟨1a⟩ *falla* plug; AUTO collide with, crash into
tampone *m* MED swab; *per donne* tampon; *per timbri* (ink) pad; INFOR buffer
tana *f* den
tandem *m inv* tandem
tangente *f* MAT tangent; F (*percentuale illecita*) kickback F; F (*bustarella*) bribe; F (*pizzo*) protection money
tangenziale *f* ring road
tanica *f* container; MAR *per fuoribordo* tank
tanto 1 *agg* so much; ***-i*** *pl* so many; ***-i saluti*** best wishes; ***-e grazie*** thank you so much, many thanks **2** *pron* much; ***-i*** *pl* many **3** *avv* (*così*) so; *con verbi* so much; ***di tanto in tanto*** from time to time; ***tanto quanto*** as much as; ***è da tanto*** (***tempo***) ***che non lo vedo*** I haven't seen him for a long time; ***tanto per cambiare*** for a change
tappa *f* stop; *di viaggio* stage
tappare ⟨1a⟩ plug; *bottiglia* put the cork in
tapparella *f* rolling shutter
tappeto *m* carpet
tappezzare ⟨1a⟩ (wall)paper
tappezzeria *f di pareti* wallpaper; *di sedili* upholstery
tappo *m* cap, top; *di sughero* cork; *di lavandini, vasche* plug
tarare ⟨1a⟩ TEC calibrate
tarchiato stocky
tardare ⟨1a⟩ **1** *v/t* delay **2** *v/i* be late
tardi late; ***più tardi*** later (on); ***al più tardi*** at the latest; ***a più tardi!*** see you!; ***far tardi*** (*arrivare in ritardo*) be late; (*stare alzato*) stay up late; *in ufficio* work late
tardivo late; *fig* retarded, slow
tardo late
targa *f* (*pl* -ghe) nameplate; AUTO number-

plate
targhetta *f* tag; *su porta* nameplate
tariffa *f* rate; *nei trasporti* fare; *doganale* tariff
tarlato worm-eaten
tarlo *m* woodworm
tarma *f* (clothes) moth
tartaro *m* tartar
tartaruga *f* (*pl* -ghe) *terrestre* tortoise; *aquatica* turtle
tartina *f* canapé
tartufo *m* truffle
tasca *f* (*pl* -che) pocket; ***ne ho piene le -che*** I'm fed up with this
tascabile 1 *agg* pocket *attr* **2** *m* paperback
tassa *f* tax; ***tassa di circolazione*** road tax; ***tassa di soggiorno*** visitor tax; ***esente da tassa*** tax free; ***soggetto a tassa*** subject to tax
tassametro *m* meter, clock F
tassare ⟨1a⟩ tax
tassello *m nel muro* plug
tassista *m/f* (*mpl* -i) taxi driver
tasso[1] *m* FIN rate; ***tasso d'inflazione*** inflation rate, rate of inflation; ***tasso d'interesse*** interest rate; ***tasso di sconto*** discount rate
tasso[2] *m* ZO badger
tasso[3] *m* BOT yew
tastare ⟨1a⟩ feel; *fig* ***tastare il terreno*** test the water, see how the land lies
tastiera *f* keyboard
tastierista *m/f* (*mpl* -i) keyboarder
tasto *m* key; INFOR ***tasto operativo*** function key
tattica *f* (*pl* -che) tactics *pl*
tattico (*pl* -ci) tactical
tatto *m* (*senso*) touch; *fig* tact; ***mancanza f di tatto*** tactlessness, lack of tact
tatuaggio *m* (*pl* -ggi) tattoo
tatuare ⟨1l⟩ tattoo
taverna *f country-style restaurant*
tavola *f* table; (*asse*) plank, board; *in libro* plate; ***tavola calda*** snackbar; ***tavola rotonda*** round table; SP ***tavola a vela*** sailboard; ***mettersi a tavola*** sit down to eat; ***a tavola!*** lunch / dinner is ready!, come and get it! F
tavoletta *f*: ***tavoletta di cioccolata*** bar of chocolate
tavolo *m* table
taxi *m inv* taxi
tazza *f* cup
tazzina *f* espresso cup
tbc, **TBC** *abbr* (= ***tubercolosi***) TB (= tuberculosis)
TCI *abbr* (= ***Touring Club Italiano***) Italian motoring organization
te you; ***te l'ho venduto*** I sold it to you
tè *m* tea; ***tè freddo*** iced tea; ***sala f da tè*** tearoom; ***tazza f da tè*** teacup
teatrale theatre, *Am* theater; *fig* theatrical; ***rappresentazione f teatrale*** play
teatro *m* theatre, *Am* theater; *fig* (*luogo*) scene; ***teatro all'aperto*** open air theatre (*Am* theater); ***teatro lirico*** opera (house)
tecnica *f* (*pl* -che) technique; (*tecnologia*) technology
tecnico (*pl* -ci) **1** *agg* technical **2** *m* technician
tecnologia *f* technology; ***alta tecnologia*** high technology, high tech F
tecnologico (*pl* -ci) technological
tedesco (*pl* -chi) **1** *m/agg* German **2** *m*, **-a** *f* German
tegame *m* (sauce)pan
teglia *f* baking tin
tegola *f* tile
teiera *f* teapot
tel. *abbr* (= ***telefono***) tel (= telephone)
tela *f* cloth; PITT canvas; ***tela cerata*** oilcloth
telaio *m* (*pl* -ai) loom; *di automobile* chassis; *di bicicletta*, *finestra* frame
telecamera *f* television camera
telecomando *m* remote control
telecomunicazioni *fpl* telecommunications, telecomms
telefax *m inv* fax
teleferica *f* (*pl* -che) cableway
telefilm *m inv* film made for television
telefonare ⟨1m & b⟩ (tele)phone, ring (***a qu*** s.o.)
telefonata *f* (tele)phone call; ***telefonata interurbana*** long-distance (phone) call; ***telefonata urbana*** local call; ***fare una telefonata a qu*** ring *or* phone s.o.
telefonico (*pl* -ci) (tele)phone *attr*
telefonista *m/f* (*mpl* -i) (switchboard) operator
telefonino *m* mobile (phone), *Am* cell(ular) phone
telefono *m* (tele)phone; ***telefono a gettoni*** *telephone that takes tokens*; ***telefono a scheda*** (***magnetica***) cardphone; ***telefono a tastiera*** push-button (tele)phone; ***telefono cellulare*** cellphone, cellular (tele)phone; ***dare un colpo di telefono a qu*** give s.o. a ring
telegiornale *m* news *sg*
telegrafare ⟨1m & b⟩ telegraph
telegrafico (*pl* -ci) *stile* telegraphic; *risposta* very brief
telegrafo *m* telegraph
telegramma *m* (pl -i) telegram
teleguidato remote controlled
telelavoro *m* teleworking
teleobiettivo *m* telephoto lens

telepatia *f* telepathy
teleschermo *m* TV screen
telescopio *m* (*pl* -pi) telescope
teleselezione *f* STD
telespettatore *m*, **-trice** *f* TV viewer
televisione *f* television, TV; ***televisione via cavo*** cable television *or* TV; ***televisione via satellite*** satellite television *or* TV
televisivo television *attr*, TV *attr*
televisore *m* television (set), TV (set); ***televisore a colori*** colo(u)r TV
telex *m inv* telex
telone *m* tarpaulin; TEA curtain
tema *m* theme, subject
temerario (*pl* -ri) reckless
temere ⟨2a⟩ be afraid *or* frightened of
temperamatite *m inv* pencil sharpener
temperamento *m* temperament
temperare ⟨1l & b⟩ *acciaio* temper; *matita* sharpen
temperato *acciaio* tempered; *matita* sharp; *clima* temperate
temperatura *f* temperature; ***temperatura ambiente*** room temperature
tempesta *f* storm
tempestoso stormy
tempia *f* temple
tempio *m* (*pl* -pli) temple
tempo *m* time; METEO weather; ***tempo libero*** free time; ***a tempo parziale*** part-time; ***a tempo perso*** in one's spare time; ***a tempo pieno*** full-time; SP ***-i*** *pl* ***supplementari*** extra time *sg*, *Am* overtime *sg*; ***a tempo, in tempo*** in time; ***col tempo*** in time, eventually; ***un tempo*** once, long ago; ***per tempo*** (*presto*) in good time; (*di buon'ora*) early; ***non ho tempo*** I don't have (the) time; ***lavora da molto tempo*** he has been working for a long time; ***fa bel / brutto tempo*** the weather is lovely / nasty
temporale *m* thunderstorm
temporaneo temporary
tenace *materiali*, *sostanze* strong; *fig* tenacious
tenacia *f fig* tenacity
tenaglie *fpl* pincers *pl*
tenda *f* curtain; *da campeggio* tent
tendenza *f* tendency
tendere ⟨3c⟩ **1** *v/t molla*, *elastico*, *muscoli* stretch; *corde del violino* tighten; *mano* hold out, stretch out; *fig trappola* lay; ***tendere un braccio per fare qc*** reach out to do sth; ***tendere le braccia a qu*** hold one's arms out to s.o. **2** *v/i*: ***tendere a*** (*aspirare a*) aim at; (*essere portati a*) tend to; (*avvicinarsi a*) verge on
tendina *f* net curtain
tendine *m* tendon
tenebre *fpl* darkness *sg*
tenente *m* lieutenant
tenere ⟨2q⟩ **1** *v/t* hold; (*conservare*, *mantenere*) keep; (*gestire*) run; *spazio* take up; *conferenza* give; ***tenere d'occhio*** keep an eye on, watch **2** *v/i* hold (on); ***tenere a*** (*dare importanza a*) care about; SP support
tenerezza *f* tenderness
tenero tender; *pietra*, *legno* soft
tenersi (*reggersi*) hold on (***a*** to); (*mantenersi*) keep o.s.; ***tenersi in piedi*** stand (up)
tengo → ***tenere***
tennis *m* tennis; ***tennis da tavolo*** table tennis
tennista *m/f* (*mpl* -i) tennis player
tenore *m* MUS tenor; ***tenore di vita*** standard of living
tensione *f* voltage; *fig* tension
tentare ⟨1b⟩ try, attempt; (*allettare*) tempt; ***tentare tutto il possibile*** do everything possible
tentativo *m* attempt
tentazione *f* temptation
tenue *colore* pale; *luce*, *speranza* faint
tenuta *f* (*capacità*) capacity; (*resistenza*) stamina; (*divisa*) uniform; (*abbigliamento*) outfit; AGR estate; ***a tenuta d'aria*** airtight; AUTO ***tenuta di strada*** roadholding ability
teologia *f* theology
teologico (*pl* -ci) theological
teologo *m* (*pl* -gi), **-a** *f* theologian
teorema *m* (*pl* -i) theorem
teoria *f* theory
teorico (*pl* -ci) theoretical
tepore *m* warmth
teppista *m/f* (*pl* -i) hooligan
terapia *f* therapy
tergicristallo *m* AUTO windscreen (*Am* windshield) wiper
termale thermal; ***stazione*** *f* ***termale*** spa; ***stabilimento*** *m* ***termale*** baths *pl*
terme *fpl* baths
terminal *m inv* AVIA air terminal, terminal building
terminale **1** *agg* terminal; ***stazione*** *f* ***terminale*** terminus **2** *m* INFOR, EL terminal
terminare ⟨1l & b⟩ *v/t & v/i* end, finish, terminate
termine *m* end; (*confine*) limit; FIN (*scadenza*) deadline; (*parola*) term; ***-i*** *pl* ***di consegna*** terms of delivery; ***termine tecnico*** technical term; ***a breve / lungo termine*** in the short / long term; ***in altri -i*** in other words; ***volgere al termine*** come to an end

termocoperta *f* electric blanket
termometro *m* thermometer
termos *m inv* thermos®
termosifone *m* radiator
termostato *m* thermostat
terra *f* earth; (*regione, proprietà, terreno agricolo*) land; (*superficie del suolo*) ground; (*pavimento*) floor; ***a terra*** on the ground; AVIA, MAR ***scendere a terra*** get off; TEC ***mettere a terra*** earth; ***cadere a o per terra*** fall (down)
terracotta *f* (*pl* terrecotte) terracotta
terraferma *f* dry land, terra firma
terrapieno *m* embankment
terrazza *f*, **terrazzo** *m* balcony, terrace
terremoto *m* earthquake
terreno 1 *agg* earthly; *piano* ground, *Am* first **2** *m* (*superficie*) ground; (*suolo, materiale*) soil; (*appezzamento*) plot of land; *fig* (*settore, tema*) field, area; ***perdere / guadagnare terreno*** lose / gain ground; ***terreno fabbricabile*** land that may be built on
terrestre land *attr*, terrestrial; *della Terra* of the Earth; ***globo*** *m* ***terrestre*** globe
terribile terrible
terrina *f* bowl
territoriale territorial
territorio *m* (*pl* -ri) territory
terrore *m* terror
terrorismo *m* terrorism
terrorista *m/f* (*mpl* -i) terrorist
terrorizzare ⟨1a⟩ terrorize
terza *f* AUTO third (gear)
terziario *m* (*pl* -ri) tertiary sector, services *pl*
terzino *m* SP back
terzo 1 *agg* third; ***il terzo mondo*** the Third World; ***-a pagina*** arts page **2** *m* third
teschio *m* (*pl* -chi) skull
tesi *f inv*: ***tesi*** (***di laurea***) thesis
teso 1 *pp* → ***tendere*** **2** *agg* taut; *fig* tense
tesoro *m* treasure; (*tesoreria*) treasury
tessera *f* card; ***tessera d'abbonamento*** season ticket
tessile 1 *agg* textile **2** ***-i*** *mpl* textiles
tessuto *m* fabric, material; ***tessuto di lana*** wool; ***-i*** *pl* fabrics, material *sg*
test *m inv* test
testa *f* head; ***a testa*** each, a head; ***alla testa di*** at the head of; ***essere in testa*** lead
testamento *m* will
testardaggine *f* stubbornness
testardo stubborn
testata *f* (*giornale*) newspaper; *di letto* headboard; AUTO cylinder head; ***testata nucleare*** nuclear warhead
teste *m/f* witness
testicolo *m* testicle
testimone *m/f* witness; ***testimone oculare*** eyewitness; ***Testimoni*** *pl* ***di Geova*** Jehovah's Witnesses
testimonianza *f* testimony; (*prova*) proof
testimoniare ⟨1k & c⟩ **1** *v/i* testify, give evidence **2** *v/t fig* testify to; DIR ***testimoniare il falso*** commit perjury
testo *m* text
tetano *m* tetanus
tetro gloomy
tetto *m* roof
tettoia *f* roof
Tevere *m* Tiber
TG *abbr* (= ***Telegiornale***) TV news
thermos → ***termos***
ti you; *riflessivo* yourself
tibia *f* shinbone, tibia
tic *m inv di orologio* tick; MED tic
ticchettio *m di orologio* ticking; *di pioggia* patter
ticket *m inv* MED charge
tiene → ***tenere***
tiepido lukewarm, tepid; *fig* half-hearted, lukewarm
tifo *m* MED typhus; *fig* ***fare il tifo per una squadra*** be a fan *or* supporter of a team
tifoso *m*, **-a** *f* fan, supporter
tiglio *m* (*pl* -gli) lime tree
tigre *f* tiger
timbrare ⟨1a⟩ stamp
timbro *m* stamp; MUS timbre; ***timbro postale*** postage stamp
timidezza *f* shyness, timidity
timido shy, timid
timo *m* BOT thyme
timone *m* MAR, AVIA rudder; *fig* helm
timoniere *m* helmsman
timore *m* fear
timoroso timorous
timpano *m* MUS kettledrum; ANAT eardrum
tingere ⟨3d⟩ dye
tinta *f* (*colorante*) dye; (*colore*) colo(u)r
tintarella *f* (sun)tan
tinto *pp* → ***tingere***
tintoria *f* dry-cleaner's
tintura *f* dyeing; (*colorante*) dye; ***tintura di iodio*** iodine
tipico (*pl* -ci) typical
tipo *m* sort, kind, type; F *fig* guy
tipografia *f* printing; *stabilimento* printer's
tipografo *m* printer
tipografico typographical
tir *m* heavy goods vehicle, HGV
tiranneggiare ⟨1f⟩ tyrannize
tirannia *f* tyranny

tiranno 1 *agg* tyrannical **2** *m* tyrant
tirare ⟨1a⟩ **1** *v/t* pull; (*tendere*) stretch; (*lanciare*) throw; (*sparare*) fire; (*tracciare*) draw; ***tirare fuori*** take out; ***tirare su*** *da terra* pick up; *bambino* bring up; ***tirare giù*** take down **2** *v/i* pull; *di abito* be too tight; *di vento* blow; (*sparare*) shoot; ***tirare avanti*** (*arrangiarsi*) get by, manage; (*continuare*) keep going; ***tirare dritto*** go straight on; ***tirare a sorte*** draw lots
tirarsi: ***tirarsi indietro*** back off; *fig* back out
tiratore *m*, **-trice** *f* shot
tiratura *f di libro* print run; *di giornale* circulation
tirchio (*pl* -chi) **1** *agg* mean, stingy F **2** *m*, **-a** *f* miser, skinflint F
tiro *m* (*lancio*) throw; (*sparo*) shot; ***tiro con l'arco*** archery; *fig* ***un brutto tiro*** a nasty trick; ***essere a tiro*** be within range
tirocinante *m/f* trainee
tirocinio *m* (*pl* -ni) training
tiroide *f* thyroid
tirolese *agg*, *m/f* Tyrolean, Tyrolese
Tirolo *m* Tyrol
tisana *f* herbal tea, tisane
titolare *m/f* owner
titolo *m* title; *dei giornali* headline; FIN security; ***titolo a reddito fisso*** fixed income security; ***a titolo di*** as; ***titolo di studio*** qualification
titubare ⟨1l⟩ hesitate
tizio *m*, **-a** *f*: ***un tizio*** somebody, some man; ***una -a*** somebody, some woman
toccare ⟨1d⟩ **1** *v/t* touch; (*riguardare*) concern, be about **2** *v/i* happen (***a*** to); ***gli tocca metà dell'eredità*** half the estate is going to him; ***tocca a me*** it's my turn; ***mi tocca partire*** I must go, I have to go
tocco *m* (*pl* -cchi) touch
togliere ⟨3ss⟩ take (away), remove; (*eliminare*) take off; (*tirare fuori*) take out, remove; (*revocare*) lift, raise; *dente* take out, extract; ***togliere di mezzo*** get rid of; ***ciò non toglie che*** the fact remains that
togliersi *giacca* take off, remove; (*spostarsi*) take o.s. off; ***togliersi dai piedi*** get out of the way
tolgo → ***togliere***
tollerante tolerant
tolleranza *f* tolerance
tollerare ⟨1l & c⟩ tolerate
tolto *pp* → ***togliere***
tomba *f* grave
tombola *f* bingo
tomografia *f* MED tomography; ***tomografia assiale computerizzata*** computerized axial tomography
tonaca *f* (*pl* -che) habit
tonalità *f inv* tonality
tondeggiante roundish
tondo round; (*grassoccio*) plump; ***chiaro e tondo*** quite clearly
tonfo *m in acqua* splash
tonico *m* (*pl* -ci) tonic
tonificare ⟨1m & d⟩ tone up
tonnellata *f* tonne
tonno *m* tuna
tono *m* tone; ***rispondere a tono*** (*a proposito*) answer to the point; *per le rime* answer back
tonsille *fpl* ANAT tonsils
tonsillite *f* tonsillitis
topazio *m* (*pl* -zi) topaz
topo *m* mouse
topografia *f* topography
Topolino *m* Mickey Mouse
toppa *f* (*serratura*) keyhole; (*rattoppo*) patch
torace *m* chest
torbido *liquid* cloudy
torcere ⟨3d⟩ twist; *biancheria* wring
torchio *m* (*pl* -chi) press
torcia *f* (*pl* -ce) *f* torch
torcicollo *m* stiff neck
tordo *m* thrush
torinese of Turin, Turin *attr*
Torino *f* Turin
tormenta *f* snowstorm
tormentare ⟨1a⟩ torment
tormentarsi torment o.s.
tormento *m* torment
tornaconto *m* benefit
tornante *m* hairpin bend
tornare ⟨1a⟩ *venire* come back, return; *andare* go back, return; (*quadrare*) balance; ***tornare utile*** prove useful; ***tornare a fare / dire qc*** do / say sth again; ***ben tornato!*** welcome back!; ***tornare in sé*** come to one's senses
torneo *m* tournament; ***Torneo delle Sei Nazioni*** Six Nations Cup
tornio *m* (*pl* -ni) lathe
toro *m* bull; ASTR ***Toro*** Taurus
torpedine *m* ZO electric ray
torpore *m* torpor
torre *f* tower
torrefare ⟨3aa⟩ roast
torrefazione *f* roasting
torreggiare ⟨1f⟩ tower (***su*** over)
torrente *m* stream
torrido torrid
torrone *m* nougat
torsione *f* twisting; TEC torsion
torso *m* torso
torsolo *m* core
torta *f* cake

tortellini *mpl* tortellini *sg*
torto *m* wrong; ***aver torto*** be wrong; ***a torto*** wrongly
tortora *f* turtledove
tortuoso (*sinuoso*) winding; (*ambiguo*) devious
tortura *f* torture
torturare ⟨1a⟩ torture
torvo *sguardo* dark, black
tosaerba *f e m* lawnmower
tosare ⟨1a⟩ *pecore* shear
Toscana *f* Tuscany
toscano Tuscan
tosse *f* cough; ***tosse canina*** whooping cough; ***aver la tosse*** have a cough
tossico (*pl* -ci) **1** *agg* toxic **2** *m*, **-a** *f* F druggie F
tossicodipendente *m/f* drug addict
tossicodipendenza *f* drug addiction
tossicomane *m/f* drug addict
tossire ⟨4a & d⟩ cough
tostapane *m* toaster
tostare ⟨1c⟩ *pane* toast; *caffè* roast
tot 1 *agg* so many **2** *pron* so much
totale *m/agg* total
totalità *f* (*interezza*) entirety, totality; ***nella totalità dei casi*** in all cases
totip *m competition similar to football pools, based on horse racing*
totocalcio *m competition similar to football pools*
tovaglia *f* tablecloth
tovagliolo *m* napkin, serviette
tozzo 1 *agg* stocky **2** *m di pane* crust
tra → ***fra***
traballare ⟨1a⟩ stagger; *mobile* wobble
traboccare ⟨1d⟩ overflow (*anche fig*)
traccia *f* (*pl* -cce) (*orma*) footprint; *di veicolo* track; (*indizio*) clue; (*segno*) trace; (*abbozzo*) sketch
tracciare ⟨1f⟩ *linea* draw; (*delineare*) outline; (*abbozzare*) sketch
trachea *f* windpipe
tracolla *f* (shoulder) strap; ***a tracolla*** slung over one's shoulder; ***borsa*** *f* ***a tracolla*** shoulder bag
tracollo *m* collapse
tradimento *m* betrayal; POL treason; ***a tradimento*** treacherously
tradire ⟨4d⟩ betray; *coniuge* be unfaithful to
tradirsi give o.s. away
traditore 1 *agg* (*infedele*) unfaithful **2** *m*, **-trice** *f* traitor
tradizionale traditional
tradizione *f* tradition
tradotto *pp* → ***tradurre***
tradurre ⟨3e⟩ translate; ***tradurre in inglese*** translate into English
traduttore *m*, **-trice** *f* translator
traduzione *f* translation
trafficante *m/f spreg* dealer; ***trafficante di droga*** drug dealer
trafficare ⟨1l & d⟩ deal, trade (***in*** in); *spreg* traffic (***in*** in); (*armeggiare*) tinker; (*affaccendarsi*) bustle about
traffico *m* (*pl* -chi e -ci) traffic; ***traffico aereo*** air traffic; ***traffico stradale*** road traffic; ***densità*** *f* ***del traffico*** volume of traffic
traforo *m* tunnel
tragedia *f* tragedy
traghettare ⟨1a⟩ ferry
traghetto *m* ferry
tragico (*pl* -ci) tragic
tragitto *m* journey
traguardo *m* finishing line
traiettoria *f* trajectory
trainare ⟨1l⟩ (*rimorchiare*) tow; *di animali* pull, draw
traino *m* towing; *veicolo* vehicle on tow; ***a traino*** on tow
tralasciare ⟨1f⟩ (*omettere*) omit, leave out; (*interrompere*) interrupt
traliccio *m* (*pl* -cci) EL pylon; TEC trellis
tram *m inv* tram
trama *f fig* plot
tramandare ⟨1a⟩ hand down
tramare ⟨1a⟩ *fig* plot
trambusto *m* (*confusione*) bustle; (*tumulto*) uproar, commotion
tramezzino *m* sandwich
tramezzo *m* partition
tramite 1 *m* (*collegamento*) link; (*intermediario*) go-between **2** *prep* through
tramontana *f* north wind
tramontare ⟨1a⟩ set
tramonto *m* sunset; *fig* decline
trampolino *m* diving board; SCI ski jump
tranello *m* trap
tranne except
tranquillante *m* tranquil(l)izer
tranquillità *f* peacefulness, tranquillity
tranquillizzare ⟨1a⟩: ***tranquillizzare qu*** set s.o.'s mind at rest
tranquillo calm, peaceful
transatlantico (*pl* -ci) **1** *agg* transatlantic **2** *m* liner
transazione *f* DIR settlement; FIN transaction
transenna *f* barrier
transistor *m inv* transistor
transitabile *strada* passable
transitare ⟨1l⟩ pass
transitivo GRAM transitive
transito *m* transit; ***divieto di transito*** no thoroughfare
transitorio (*pl* -ri) transitory

transizione *f* transition
transoceanico (*pl* -ci) ocean *attr*
trantran *m* F routine
tranviere *m* (*manovratore*) tram driver; (*controllore*) tram conductor
trapanare ⟨1l⟩ drill
trapano *m* drill; ***trapano a percussione*** percussion drill
trapezio *m* (*pl* -zi) trapeze; MAT trapezium
trapezista *m/f* (*mpl* -i) trapeze artist
trapiantare ⟨1a⟩ transplant
trapianto *m* transplant
trappola *f* trap
trapunta *f* quilt
trarre ⟨3xx⟩ *conclusioni* draw; *vantaggio* derive; ***tratto da un libro di*** taken from a book by
trasalire ⟨4m⟩ jump
trasandato scruffy; *lavoro* slipshod
trasbordare ⟨1a⟩ transfer
trasbordo *m* transfer
trascinare ⟨1a⟩ drag; (*travolgere*) sweep away; *fig* (*entusiasmare*) carry away
trascorrere ⟨3o⟩ **1** *v/t* spend **2** *v/i* pass, go by
trascorso *pp* → ***trascorrere***
trascrivere ⟨3tt⟩ transcribe
trascrizione *f* transcription
trascurabile unimportant
trascurare ⟨1a⟩ neglect; (*tralasciare*) ignore; ***trascurare di fare qc*** fail to do sth
trascuratezza *f* negligence
trascurato careless, negligent; (*trasandato*) slovenly; (*ignorato*) neglected
trasferibile transferable
trasferimento *m* transfer
trasferire ⟨4d⟩ transfer
trasferirsi move
trasferta *f* transfer; SP away game
trasformare ⟨1a⟩ transform; TEC process; *nel rugby* convert
trasformarsi change, turn (***in*** into)
trasformatore *m* transformer
trasformazione *f* transformation
trasfusione *f* transfusion
trasgredire ⟨4d⟩ disobey
trasgressione *f* disobedience
trasgressore *m* transgressor
traslocare ⟨1c & d⟩ *v/t & v/i* move
trasloco *m* (*pl* -chi) move
trasmettere ⟨3ee⟩ pass on; RAD, TV broadcast, transmit; DIR *diritti* transfer
trasmissibile transmissible
trasmissione *f* transmission; RAD, TV broadcast, transmission; (*programma*) programme, *Am* program; RAD, TV ***trasmissione in diretta*** live broadcast; INFOR ***trasmissione dati*** data transmission
trasognato dreamy
trasparente 1 *agg* transparent **2** *m* transparency
trasparenza *f* transparency
trasportare ⟨1c⟩ transport
trasporto *m* transport; ***trasporto combinato rotaia-strada*** piggyback transport; ***-i** pl* ***pubblici*** public transport *sg*
trasversale 1 *agg* transverse **2** *f* MAT transversal
tratta *f* trade; FIN draft
trattamento *m* treatment
trattare ⟨1a⟩ **1** *v/t* treat; TEC treat, process; FIN deal in; (*negoziare*) negotiate **2** *v/i* deal; ***trattare di*** be about; FIN ***trattare in*** deal in
trattarsi: ***di che si tratta?*** what's it about?
trattative *fpl* negotiations, talks
trattato *m* treatise; DIR, POL treaty; ***trattato di pace*** peace treaty
trattenere ⟨2q⟩ (*far restare*) keep, hold; (*far perder tempo*) hold up; (*frenare*) restrain; *fiato, respiro* hold; *lacrime* hold back; *somma* withhold
trattenersi (*rimanere*) stay; (*frenarsi*) restrain o.s.; ***trattenersi dal fare qc*** refrain from doing sth
trattenuta *f* deduction
trattino *m* dash; *in parole composte* hyphen
tratto 1 *pp* → ***trarre*** **2** *m di spazio, tempo* stretch; *di penna* stroke; (*linea*) line; ***a un tratto*** all of a sudden; ***-i*** *pl* (*lineamenti*) features; ***a -i*** at intervals
trattore *m* tractor
trattoria *f* restaurant
trauma *m* (*pl* -i) trauma
traumatico (*pl* -ci) traumatic
travaglio *m*: MED ***travaglio di parto*** labo(u)r
travasare ⟨1a⟩ decant
trave *f* beam
traversa *f* crossbeam
traversare ⟨1b⟩ cross
traversata *f* crossing
traverso: ***flauto*** *m* ***traverso*** flute; ***andare di traverso*** *di cibi* go down the wrong way; ***per vie -e*** by devious means
travestimento *m* disguise
travestire ⟨4b⟩ disguise
travestirsi disguise o.s., dress up (***da*** as)
travestito *m* transvestite
travolgere ⟨3d⟩ carry away (*anche fig*); *con un veicolo* run over
travolto *pp* → ***travolgere***
trazione *f* TEC traction; AUTO ***trazione anteriore / posteriore*** front-/rear-wheel drive
tre three
trebbiare ⟨1k⟩ AGR thresh

treccia *f* (*pl* -cce) plait

trecento 1 *agg* three hundred **2** *m*: ***il Trecento*** the fourteenth century

tredicesimo *m/agg* thirteenth

tredici thirteen

tregua *f* truce; *fig* break, let-up

trekking *m* hiking

tremante trembling, shaking

tremare ⟨1b⟩ tremble, shake (***di, per*** with)

tremendo terrible, tremendous

tremila three thousand

treno *m* train; ***treno intercity*** intercity train; ***treno merci*** goods train; ***in treno*** by train

trenta thirty

trentenne *agg*, *m/f* thirty-year-old

trentesimo *m/agg* thirtieth

trentina: ***una trentina*** about thirty; ***essere sulla trentina*** be about thirty, be in one's thirties

treppiedi *m inv* tripod

treruote *m inv* three-wheeler

triangolare triangular

triangolo *m* triangle; AUTO warning triangle

tribù *f inv* tribe

tribuna *f* platform

tribunale *m* court; ***tribunale per i minorenni*** juvenile court

tributario (*pl* -ri) tax

tributo *m* tax; *fig* tribute

tricheco *m* (*pl* -chi) walrus

triciclo *m* tricycle

tricolore 1 *agg* tricolo(u)r(ed) **2** *m* tricolo(u)r

triennale *contratto*, *progetto* three-year; *mostra*, *festival* three-yearly

triennio *m* (*pl* -nni) three-year period

triestino of Trieste, Trieste *attr*

trifoglio *m* (*pl* -gli) clover

triglia *f* red mullet

trilaterale trilateral

trillare ⟨1a⟩ trill

trillo *m* trill

trim. *abbr* (= ***trimestre***) term

trimestrale quarterly

trimestre *m* quarter; EDU term

trincea *f* trench

trincerare ⟨1b⟩ entrench

trincerarsi entrench o.s.

trinchetto *m* foremast

trinciare ⟨1f⟩ cut up, chop

Trinità *f* Trinity

trio *m* trio

trionfare ⟨1a⟩ triumph (***su*** over)

trionfo *m* triumph

triplicare ⟨1l & d⟩ triple

triplice triple

triplo 1 *agg* triple **2** *m*: ***il triplo*** three times as much (***di*** as)

trippa *f* tripe

triste sad

tristezza *f* sadness

tritacarne *m inv* mincer

tritare ⟨1a⟩ mince

tritatutto *m inv* mincer

trito minced; *fig* ***trito e ritrito*** rehashed

trittico *m* (*pl* -ci) triptych

triturare ⟨1a⟩ grind

trivellare ⟨1b⟩ drill

trivella *f* drill

triviale trivial

trofeo *m* trophy

tromba *f* MUS trumpet; AUTO horn; ***tromba d'aria*** whirlwind; ***tromba delle scale*** stairwell

trombone *m* trombone

trombosi *f* thrombosis

troncare ⟨1d⟩ cut off; *fig* break off

tronco *m* (*pl* -chi) ANAT, BOT trunk; FERR section; ***licenziare in tronco*** fire on the spot *or* there and then

trono *m* throne

tropicale tropical

tropici *mpl* tropics

troppo 1 *agg* too much; ***-i*** *pl* too many **2** *avv* too much; ***non troppo*** not too much; ***è troppo tardi*** it's too late

trota *f* trout

trottare ⟨1c⟩ trot

trotto *m* trot

trottola *f* (spinning) top

trovare ⟨1c⟩ find; (*inventare*) find, come up with; ***andare a trovare qu*** (go and) see s.o.

trovarsi be; ***trovarsi bene*** be happy

trovata *f* good idea

truccare ⟨1d⟩ make up; *motore* soup up; *partita*, *elezioni* fix

truccarsi put on one's make-up

truccatore *m*, **-trice** *f* make-up artist

trucco *m* (*pl* -cchi) make-up; (*inganno*, *astuzia*) trick

truce fierce; (*crudele*) cruel

truffa *f* fraud

truffare ⟨1a⟩ defraud (***di*** of)

truffatore *m*, **-trice** *f* trickster, con artist F

truppa *f* troops *pl*; *fig* horde

tu you; ***dammi del tu*** call me 'tu'; ***sei tu?*** is that you?

tuba *f* tuba

tubatura *f*, **tubazione** *f* pipes *pl*, piping

tubercolosi *f* tuberculosis

tubero *m* tuber

tubetto *m* tube

tubo *m* pipe; *flessibile* hose; AUTO ***tubo di***

scappamento exhaust (pipe); ***tubo fluorescente*** fluorescent light
tuffare ⟨1a⟩ dip
tuffarsi (*immergersi*) dive; (*buttarsi dentro*) throw o.s. (*anche fig*)
tuffo *m* dip; SP dive
tugurio *m* (*pl* -ri) hovel
tulipano *m* tulip
tumore *m* tumo(u)r
tumulto *m* riot
tumultuoso tumultuous
tunica *f* (*pl* -che) tunic
Tunisia *f* Tunisia
tunisino 1 *agg* Tunisian **2** *m*, **-a** *f* Tunisian
tunnel *m inv* tunnel; ***tunnel dell'orrore*** ghost train
tuo (*pl* tuoi) **1** *agg* your; ***il tuo amico*** your friend; ***un tuo amico*** a friend of yours **2** *pron*: ***il tuo*** yours
tuonare ⟨1c⟩ thunder
tuono *m* thunder
tuorlo *m* yolk
turare ⟨1a⟩ stop; *bottiglia* put the top on
turbamento *m* perturbation
turbante *m* turban
turbare ⟨1a⟩ upset, disturb
turbina *f* turbine
turbine *m* whirlwind
turbo ... *nelle parole composte* turbo ...
turbolenza *f* turbulence
turboreattore *m* turbojet
turchese *m/agg* turquoise
Turchia *f* Turkey
turco (*pl* -chi) **1** *m/agg* Turkish **2** *m*, **-a** *f* Turk
turismo *m* tourism; ***turismo di massa*** mass tourism
turista *m/f* (*mpl* -i) tourist
turistico (*pl* -ci) tourist; ***assegno*** *m* ***turistico*** traveller's cheque, *Am* traveler's check
turno *m* turn; *di lavoro* shift; ***a turno*** in turn; ***di turno*** on duty; ***è il mio turno*** it's my turn; ***turno di riposo*** rest day; ***darsi il turno*** take turns
tuta *f da lavoro* boiler suit, overalls; ***tuta da ginnastica*** track suit; ***tuta da sci*** salopettes
tutela *f* protection; DIR guardianship
tutelare ⟨1b⟩ protect
tutore *m*, **-trice** *f* guardian
tuttavia still
tutto 1 *agg* whole; ***-i, -e*** *pl* all; ***tutto il libro*** the whole book; ***-i i giorni*** every day; ***-i e tre*** all three; ***noi -i*** all of us **2** *avv* all; ***era tutto solo*** he was all alone; ***del tutto*** quite; ***in tutto*** altogether, in all **3** *pron* all; *gente* everybody, everyone; *cose* everything; ***lo ha mangiato tutto*** he ate it all
tuttora still
TV *abbr* (= ***televisione***) TV (= television)

T

U

ubbidiente obedient
ubbidienza *f* obedience
ubbidire ⟨4d⟩ obey; ***ubbidire ai genitori*** obey one's parents
ubriacare ⟨1d⟩: ***ubriacare qu*** get s.o. drunk
ubriacarsi get drunk
ubriachezza *f* drunkenness
ubriaco (*pl* -chi) **1** *agg* drunk **2** *m*, **-a** *f* drunk
uccello *m* bird; ***uccello rapace*** bird of prey
uccidere ⟨3q⟩ kill
uccidersi kill o.s.
ucciso *pp* → ***uccidere***
uccisione *f* killing
udienza *f* (audience) audience; DIR hearing
udire ⟨4n⟩ hear
udito *m* hearing
uditorio *m* (*pl* -ri) audience
Ue *abbr* (= ***Unione europea***) EU (= European Union)
Uem *abbr* (= ***Unione economica e monetaria europea***) EMU (= Economic and Monetary Union)
ufficiale 1 *agg* official; ***non ufficiale*** unofficial **2** *m* official; MIL officer
ufficio *m* (*pl* -ci) office; ***ufficio cambi*** bureau de change; ***ufficio oggetti smarriti*** lost property; ***ufficio postale*** post office; ***ufficio stampa*** press office; ***ufficio di collocamento*** Jobcentre
ufficio *turistico* tourist information office
ufficioso unofficial
ufo[1] *m*: ***a ufo*** at other people's expense, free (of charge)
ufo[2] *m* UFO
uguaglianza *f* equality
uguagliare ⟨1g⟩ make equal; (*livellare*) level; (*essere pari a*) equal
uguale equal; *lo stesso* the same; *terreno* level
UIL *abbr* (= ***Unione Italiana del Lavoro***) Italian trade union organization
ulcera *f* ulcer; ***ulcera gastrica*** gastric ulcer
ulteriore further
ultimamente recently
ultimare ⟨1l⟩ complete
ultimatum *m inv* ultimatum
ultimo 1 *agg* last; *più recente* latest; ***ultimo piano*** top floor **2** *m*, **-a** *f* last; ***fino all'ultimo*** till the end
ultracorto: onde *fpl* **-e** ultrashort waves
ultrasuono *m* ultrasound
ultravioletto ultraviolet
ululare ⟨1l⟩ howl
ululato *m* howl
umanità *f* humanity
umanitario (*pl* -ri) humanitarian
umano human; *trattamento ecc* humane
Ume *abbr* (= ***unione monetaria*** (***europea***)) EMU (= European Monetary Union)
umidificatore *m* humidifier
umidità *f* dampness
umido 1 *agg* damp **2** *m* dampness; GASTR ***in umido*** stewed
umile (*modesto*) humble; *mestiere* menial
umiliante humiliating
umiliare ⟨1g⟩ humiliate
umiliazione *f* humiliation
umiltà *f* humility
umore *m* mood; ***di buon umore*** in a good mood; ***di cattivo umore*** in a bad mood
umorismo *m* humo(u)r
umorista *m/f* (*mpl* -i) humorist
un, una → ***uno***
unanime unanimous
unanimità *f* unanimity; ***all'unanimità*** unanimously
uncinetto *m* crochet hook; ***lavorare all'uncinetto*** crochet
uncino *m* hook
undicesimo *m/agg* eleventh
undici eleven
ungere ⟨3d⟩ grease
ungherese *agg*, *m/f* Hungarian
Ungheria *f* Hungary
unghia *f* nail
unguento *m* ointment, cream
unico (*pl* -ci) only; (*senza uguali*) unique; ***moneta*** *f* ***-a*** single currency
unifamiliare: ***casa*** *f* ***unifamiliare*** detached house
unificare ⟨1m & d⟩ unify
unificazione *f* unification
uniformare ⟨1a⟩ standardize
uniformarsi: ***uniformarsi a*** conform to; *regole*, *direttive* comply with
uniforme *f/agg* uniform
uniformità *f* uniformity
unione *f* union; *fig* unity; ***Unione economica e monetaria*** Economic and Monetary Union; ***Unione europea*** European Union; ***Unione monetaria*** (***europea***) (European) Monetary Union
unire ⟨4d⟩ unite; *congiungere* join

unirsi unite; ***unirsi in matrimonio*** marry
unità *f inv* unit; ***unità monetaria*** monetary unit; ***unità di misura*** unit of measurement; INFOR ***unità a dischi flessibili*** disk drive; ***unità*** *pl* ***periferiche*** peripherals
unito united
universale universal
università *f inv* university
universitario (*pl* -ri) **1** *agg* university *attr* **2** *m*, **-a** *f* university student; (*professore*) university lecturer
universo *m* universe
uno 1 *art* a; *before a vowel or silent h* an; ***un' uovo*** an egg **2** *agg* a, one **3** *m* one; ***uno e mezzo*** one and a half **4** *pron* one; ***a uno a uno*** one by one; ***l'uno dopo l'altro*** one after the other; ***l'un l'altro*** each other, one another
unto 1 *pp* → ***ungere*** **2** *agg* greasy **3** *m* grease
unzione *f*: ***estrema unzione*** last rites
uomo *m* (*pl* uomini) man; ***uomo d'affari*** businessman; ***uomo di fiducia*** right-hand man; ***uomo qualunque*** man in the street; ***da uomo*** *abbigliamento ecc* for men, men's
uovo *m* (*pl* le -a) egg; ***uovo alla coque*** soft-boiled egg; ***uovo di Pasqua*** Easter egg; ***uovo sodo*** hard-boiled egg; ***uovo al tegame*** fried egg; ***-a*** *pl* ***strapazzate*** scrambled eggs
uragano *m* hurricane
uranio *m* uranium
urbanistica *f* town planning
urbano urban; *fig* urbane
uretra *f* urethra
urgente urgent
urgenza *f* urgency; ***in caso d'urgenza*** in an emergency
urina *f* urine
urlare ⟨1a⟩ scream
urlo *m* (*pl anche* le -a) scream
urna *f* urn; *elettorale* ballot box
urologo *m* (*pl* -gi), **-a** *f* urologist
urrà! hooray!
urtare ⟨1a⟩ bump into, collide with; *con un veicolo* hit; *fig* offend; ***urtare i nervi a qu*** get on s.o.'s nerves
urto *m* bump; (*scontro*) collision
u.s. *abbr* (= ***ultimo scorso***) last, ult.
USA *abbr* (= ***Stati uniti d'America***) USA (= United States of America)
usa: ***usa e getta*** disposable
usanza *f* custom, tradition
usare ⟨1a⟩ **1** *v/t* use **2** *v/i* use; (*essere di moda*) be in fashion
usato used; (*di seconda mano*) second-hand
uscire ⟨4o⟩ come out; (*andare fuori*) go out
uscita *f* exit, way out; INFOR output; ***uscita di sicurezza*** emergency exit; ***via d'uscita*** way out
usignolo *m* nightingale
uso *m* use; (*abitudine*) custom; ***pronto per l'uso*** ready to use; ***fuori uso*** out of use; ***uso indebito*** misuse; ***per uso interno*** for internal use; ***per uso esterno*** not to be taken internally
US(S)L, Us(s)l *abbr* (= ***Unità*** (***Socio-***)***sanitaria Locale***) local health authority
ustionarsi ⟨1a⟩ burn o.s.
ustione *f* burn
usuale usual
usufruire ⟨4d⟩: ***usufruire di qc*** have the use of sth
usura *f di denaro* illegal money lending; (*logorio*) wear and tear
usuraio *m* (*pl* -i) loan shark
utensile 1 *agg*: ***macchina*** *f* ***utensile*** machine tool **2** *m* utensil
utente *m/f* user; ***utente della strada*** road user
utero *m* womb
utile 1 *agg* useful; ***in tempo utile*** within the time limit **2** *m* FIN profit; ***unire l'utile al dilettevole*** combine business with pleasure; ***utile netto*** net profit; ***utile d'esercizio*** operating profit
utilità *f* usefulness
utilitaria *f* economy car
utilizzare ⟨1a⟩ use
utilizzazione *f* use
utopia *f* utopia
utopista *m/f* (*mpl* -i) dreamer
uva *f* grapes *pl*; ***uva passa*** raisins *pl*; ***uva spina*** gooseberry

V

V *abbr* (= ***volt***) V (= volt)
V. *abbr* (= ***via***) St (= street)
v. *abbr* (= ***vedi***) see
va → ***andare***
vacante vacant
vacanza *f* holiday; ***-e*** *pl* ***estive*** summer holiday(s); ***andare in vacanza*** go on holiday
vacca *f* (*pl* -cche) cow
vaccinare ⟨1a⟩ vaccinate
vaccinazione *f* vaccination; ***vaccinazione antitetanica*** tetanus injection *or* shot
vaccino *m* vaccine
vado → ***andare***
vagabondare ⟨1a⟩ wander
vagabondo 1 *agg* (*girovago*) wandering; (*fannullone*) idle **2** *m*, **-a** *f* (*giramondo*) wanderer; (*fannullone*) idler, layabout F; (*barbone*) tramp
vagare ⟨1e⟩ wander (aimlessly)
vagina *f* ANAT vagina
vaglia *m inv*: ***vaglia*** (***postale***) postal order; ***vaglia bancario*** bill of exchange, draft
vago (*pl* -ghi) vague
vagone *m* carriage; ***vagone letto*** sleeper; ***vagone merci*** goods wagon; ***vagone ristorante*** dining car
vai → ***andare***
vaiolo *m* smallpox
valanga *f* (*pl* -ghe) avalanche
valere ⟨2r⟩ be worth; (*essere valido*) be valid; ***non vale nulla*** it's worthless, it isn't worth anything; ***far valere*** *diritti*, *autorità* assert; ***non vale!*** that's not fair!
valersi: ***valersi di qc*** avail o.s. of sth
valeriana *f* valerian
valevole valid
valgo → ***valere***
valico *m* (*pl* -chi) pass
validità *f* validity
valido valid; *persona* fit; ***non valido*** invalid
valigia *f* (*pl* -gie) suitcase; ***fare le -e*** pack
valle *f* valley
valore *m* value; (*coraggio*) bravery, valo(u)r; ***valore aggiunto*** added value; ***valore commerciale*** market value; ***valore corrente*** current value; ***valore energetico*** energy value; ***-i*** *pl* securities; ***di valore*** valuable; ***senza valore*** worthless
valorizzare ⟨1a⟩ increase the value of; (*far risaltare*) show off
valoroso courageous
valuta *f* currency; ***stabilità*** *f* ***della valuta*** monetary stability
valutare ⟨1a⟩ value
valutario monetary
valutazione *f* valuation
valvola *f* valve; EL fuse; ***valvola dell'aria*** air valve
valzer *m inv* waltz
vandalismo *m* vandalism
vandalo *m* vandal
vanga *f* (*pl* -ghe) spade
vangelo *m* gospel
vaniglia *f* vanilla
vanità *f* vanity
vanitoso vain
vanno → ***andare***
vano 1 *agg minacce*, *promesse* empty; (*inutile*) vain **2** *m* (*spazio vuoto*) hollow; (*stanza*) room; AUTO ***vano portaoggetti*** glove compartment
vantaggio *m* (*pl* -ggi) advantage; *in gara* lead
vantaggioso advantageous
vantare ⟨1a⟩ speak highly of; *possedere* boast
vantarsi boast (***di*** of)
vanto *m* boast
vapore *m* vapo(u)r; MAR steamer; ***vapore*** (***d'acqua***) steam
vaporetto *m* water bus
vaporizzare ⟨1a⟩ (*nebulizzare*) spray
vaporoso floaty; (*vago*) woolly
variabile 1 *agg* changeable **2** *f* MAT variable
variare ⟨1k⟩ *v/t & v/i* vary
variazione *f* variation
varice *f* varicose vein
varicella *f* chickenpox
varietà 1 *f inv* variety **2** *m inv* variety, *Am* vaudeville; (***spettacolo*** *m* ***di***) ***varietà*** variety (*Am* vaudeville) show
vario (*pl* -ri) varied; ***-ri*** *pl* various
variopinto multicolo(u)red
vasca *f* (*pl* -che) (*serbatoio*, *cisterna*) tank; (*lunghezza di piscina*) length; *di fontana* basin; ***vasca*** (***da bagno***) bath, (bath)tub
vaselina *f* vaseline
vasellame *m* dishes
vaso *m* pot; ANAT vessel
vassoio *m* (*pl* -oi) tray
vasto vast
V.d.F. *abbr* (= ***vigili del fuoco***) fire brigade, *Am* fire department
ve = ***vi*** *before* ***lo, la, li, le, ne***

vecchiaia *f* old age
vecchio (*pl* -cchi) **1** *agg* old **2** *m*, **-a** *f* old man; *donna* old woman
vece *f*: ***in vece di*** instead of; ***fare le -i di qu*** take s.o.'s place
vedere ⟨2s⟩ see; ***far vedere*** show; ***stare a vedere*** watch
vedovo 1 *agg* widowed **2** *m*, **-a** *f* widower; *donna* widow
veduta *f* view (***su*** of); ***veduta aerea*** aerial view; *fig* ***larghezza*** *f* ***di -e*** broadmindedness
vegetale 1 *agg* vegetable *attr*; *regno*, *vita* plant *attr* **2** *m* plant
vegetare ⟨1l & b⟩ vegetate
vegetariano 1 *agg* vegetarian *attr* **2** *m*, **-a** *f* vegetarian
vegetazione *f* vegetation
vegeto *vecchio* spry; ***vivo e vegeto*** hale and hearty
veggente *m/f* (*chiaroveggente*) clairvoyant
veglia *f* (*l'essere svegli*) wakefulness; (*il vegliare*) vigil; ***essere tra la veglia e il sonno*** be half asleep
vegliare ⟨1g⟩ **1** *v/i* keep watch **2** *v/t*: ***vegliare qu*** watch over s.o.
veicolo *m* vehicle; ***veicolo spaziale*** spaceship
vela *f* sail; *attività* sailing; ***fare vela*** set sail; ***tutto è andato a gonfie -e*** everything went swimmingly
veleggiare ⟨1f⟩ sail
veleno *m* poison; *di animali* venom (*anche fig*)
velenoso poisonous; *fig* venomous
veliero *m* sailing ship
velina: ***carta*** *f* ***velina*** *per imballaggio* tissue paper
velismo *m* sailing
velista *m/f* sailor
velivolo *m* aircraft
velluto *m* velvet; ***velluto a coste*** corduroy
velo *m* veil
veloce fast, quick
velocemente quickly
velocità *f inv* speed; ***limite*** *m* ***di velocità*** speed limit; ***eccesso*** *m* ***di velocità*** speeding; ***velocità della luce*** speed of light; ***velocità di crociera*** cruising speed
velodromo *m* velodrome
vena *f* vein; ***essere in vena*** be in the mood
vendemmia *f* (grape) harvest
vendemmiare ⟨1k⟩ *v/t v/i* harvest
vendere ⟨3a⟩ sell; ***vendere all'ingrosso*** sell wholesale; ***vendere al minuto*** retail
vendetta *f* revenge
vendicare ⟨1f & d⟩ avenge
vendicarsi get one's revenge (***di qu*** on s.o.; ***di qc*** for sth)
vendita *f* sale; ***vendita di fine stagione*** end-of-season sale; ***vendita diretta*** direct selling
venditore *m*, **-trice** *f* salesman; *donna* saleswoman
venerare ⟨1l & b⟩ revere
venerazione *f* veneration
venerdì *m inv* Friday; ***Venerdì Santo*** Good Friday
Venere *f* Venus
Venezia *f* Venice
veneziano 1 *agg* of Venice, Venetian **2** *m*, **-a** *f* Venetian
vengo → ***venire***
venire ⟨4p⟩ come; (*riuscire*) turn out; *come ausiliare* be; ***i suoi disegni vengono ammirati da tutti*** his drawings are admired by all; ***venire a costare*** total, work out at; ***venire a sapere qc*** learn sth, find sth out; ***venire al dunque*** get to the point; ***mi sta venendo fame*** I'm getting hungry
ventaglio *m* (*pl* -gli) fan
ventenne *agg*, *m/f* twenty-year-old
ventesimo *m/agg* twentieth
venti twenty
ventilatore *m* fan
ventilazione *f* ventilation
ventina *f*: ***una ventina*** about twenty
ventiquattrore *f inv* (*valigetta*) overnight bag
vento *m* wind; ***c'è vento*** it's windy
ventoso windy
ventre *m* stomach; ***basso ventre*** lower abdomen
venturo next
venuta *f* arrival
venuto 1 *pp* → ***venire*** **2** *m*, **-a** *f*: ***il primo venuto*** just anyone; ***non è certo il primo venuto*** he's not just anyone
veramente really
veranda *f* veranda
verbale 1 *agg* verbal **2** *m* record; *di riunione* minutes *pl*
verbalizzare ⟨1a⟩ record (in writing), take down; *riunione* take the minutes of; (*esprimere a parole*) verbalize
verbalmente verbally
verbo *m* GRAM verb
verde 1 *agg* green; *benzina* unleaded; ***numero verde*** freephone number; ***essere al verde*** be broke **2** *m* green; POL ***i -i*** *pl* the Greens
verdetto *m* verdict
verdura *f* vegetables *pl*
vergine 1 *agg* virgin *attr* **2** *f* virgin; ASTR

Vergine Virgo
verginità *f* virginity
vergogna *f* shame; (*timidezza*) shyness
vergognarsi ⟨1a⟩ be ashamed; (*essere timido*) be shy
vergognoso ashamed; (*timido*) shy; *azione* shameful
verifica *f* (*pl* -che) check
verificare ⟨1m & d⟩ check
verificarsi (*accadere*) occur, take place; (*avverarsi*) come true
verità *f* truth
verme *m* worm; ***verme solitario*** tapeworm
vermut *m* vermouth
vernice *f* paint; *trasparente* varnish; *pelle* patent leather; *fig* veneer; ***vernice antiruggine*** rust-proofing paint; ***vernice fresca*** wet paint; ***vernice protettiva*** protective coating
verniciare ⟨1f⟩ paint; *con vernice trasparente* varnish; ***verniciato di fresco*** wet paint
verniciatura *f* painting; *con vernice trasparente* varnishing; *fig* veneer
vero 1 *agg* (*rispondente a verità*) true; (*autentico*) real; ***sei contento, vero?*** you're happy, aren't you?; ***ti piace il gelato, vero?*** you like ice cream, don't you?; ***fosse vero!*** if only (it were true)! **2** *m* truth; PITT ***dal vero*** from life
veronese 1 *agg* of Verona **2** *m/f* inhabitant of Verona
verosimile likely
verruca *f* (*pl* -che) wart
versamento *m* payment; ***ricevuta f di versamento*** receipt for payment
versante *m* slope
versare ⟨1b⟩ **1** *v/t vino* pour; *denaro* pay; (*rovesciare*) spill **2** *v/i* (*trovarsi*, *essere*) be
versione *f* version; (*traduzione*) translation; ***in versione originale*** original language version
verso 1 *prp* towards; ***andare verso casa*** head for home; ***verso le otto*** about eight o'clock **2** *m di poesie* verse; (*modo*) manner; ***non c'è verso*** there is no way
vertebra *f* vertebra
vertebrale: ***colonna f vertebrale*** spinal column
verticale 1 *agg* vertical **2** *f* vertical (line); *in ginnastica* handstand
vertice *m* summit; ***incontro m al vertice*** summit (meeting)
vertigine *f* vertigo, dizziness; ***ho le -i*** I feel dizzy
vertiginoso *altezza* dizzy; *prezzi* staggering, sky-high; *velocità* breakneck
verza *f* savoy (cabbage)
vescica *f* (*pl* -che) ANAT bladder
vescovo *m* bishop
vespa *f* ZO wasp
vespaio *m* (*pl* -ai) wasps' nest; *fig* hornets' nest
vestaglia *f* dressing gown, *Am* robe
veste *f fig* (*capacità*, *funzione*) capacity; ***in veste ufficiale*** in an offical capacity
vestiario *m* wardrobe
vestire ⟨4b⟩ dress; (*portare*) wear
vestirsi get dressed; *in un certo modo* dress; ***vestirsiirsi da*** (*travestirsi*) dress up as
vestito *m da uomo* suit; *da donna* dress; (*capo di vestiario*) item of clothing, garment; ***-i*** *pl* clothes; ***-i*** *pl* ***da uomo*** men's wear
veterinario *m* (*pl* -ri), **-a** *f* veterinary surgeon, vet F
veto *m* veto; ***porre il veto a*** veto
vetraio *m* (*pl* -i), (*installatore*) glazier
vetrata *f finestra* large window; *porta* glass door; *di chiesa* stained-glass window
vetreria *f* (*fabbrica*) glass works; (*negozio*) glazier's
vetrina *f* (shop) window; *mobile* display cabinet; *di museo*, *fig* showcase
vetrinista *m/f* (*mpl* -i) window dresser
vetro *m* glass; *di finestra*, *porta* pane; ***di vetro*** glass *attr*; ***vetro armato*** reinforced glass; ***vetro smerigliato*** frosted glass
vetta *f* top; *di montagna* peak
vettura *f* AUTO car; FERR carriage; ***vettura da corsa*** racing car; ***in vettura!*** all aboard!
vi 1 *pron* you; *riflessivo* yourselves; *reciproco* each other **2** *avv* → ***ci***
via 1 *f* street, road; *fig* way; ***via Marconi*** Marconi St; ***lettera f (per) via aerea*** airmail letter; ***Via lattea*** Milky Way; ***ricorrere alle -e legali*** take legal action; ***in via eccezionale*** as an exception; ***per via di*** by; (*a causa di*) because of **2** *m* off, starting signal; SP ***dare il via*** give the off; *fig* ***dare il via a qc*** get sth under way **3** *avv* away; ***andar via*** go away, leave; ***via via*** (*gradualmente*) little by little, gradually; (*man mano*) as (and when); ***e così via*** and so on; ***via!*** *per scacciare* go away!, scram! F; (*suvvia*) come on! **4** *prp* via, by way of
viabilità *f* road conditions *pl*; (*rete stradale*) road network; (*traffico stradale*) road traffic
viadotto *m* viaduct
viaggiare ⟨1f⟩ travel; ***viaggiare per affari*** travel on business
viaggiatore *m*, **-trice** *f* travel(l)er
viaggio *m* (*pl* -ggi) journey; ***viaggio ae-***

reo flight; ***viaggio per mare*** voyage; ***viaggio di nozze*** honeymoon; ***viaggio in comitiva*** group travel; ***viaggio in treno*** train journey; ***viaggio d'affari*** business trip; ***viaggio di studio*** study trip; ***cestino*** *m* ***da viaggio*** packed meal; ***mettersi in viaggio*** set out; ***essere in viaggio*** be away, be travelling
viale *m* avenue
viavai *m inv* coming and going
vibrare ⟨1a⟩ vibrate
vibrazione *f* vibration
vice- *prefisso* vice-
vice *m/f inv* deputy
vicedirettore *m* assistant manager
vicenda *f* (*episodio*) event; (*storia*) story; ***alterne vicende*** changing fortunes; ***a vicenda*** (*a turno*) in turn; (*scambievolmente*) each other, one another
viceversa vice versa
vicinanza *f* nearness, proximity; ***-e*** *pl* neighbo(u)rhood *sg*, vicinity *sg*
vicinato *m* neighbo(u)rhood; (*persone*) neighbo(u)rs *pl*
vicino 1 *agg* near, close; ***vicino a*** near, close to; (*accanto a*) next to; ***da vicino*** *esaminare* closely; *visto* close up **2** *avv* nearby, close by **3** *m*, **-a** *f* neighbo(u)r
vicolo *m* lane; ***vicolo cieco*** dead end
videata *f* INFOR display
video *m* video; F (*schermo*) screen
videocamera *f* videocamera
videocassetta *f* video (cassette)
videocontrollo *m* video surveillance
videogioco *m* video game
videoregistratore *m* video (recorder)
videoteca *f* video library; (*negozio*) video shop
videotel *m inv Italian Videotex®*
videotelefono *m* videophone, viewphone
vietare ⟨1b⟩ forbid; ***vietare a qu di fare qc*** forbid s.o. to do sth
vietato: ***vietato fumare*** no smoking
vigente in force
vigilante *m* security guard
vigilanza *f* vigilance; ***sotto vigilanza*** under surveillance
vigilare ⟨1l⟩ *persone* watch (over); (*pattugliare*) patrol
vigile 1 *agg* watchful **2** *m/f*: ***vigile*** (***urbano***) local police officer; ***vigile del fuoco*** firefighter
vigilia *f* night before, eve; ***vigilia di Natale*** Christmas Eve
vigliacco (*pl* -cchi) **1** *agg* cowardly **2** *m*, **-a** *f* coward
vigna *f* (small) vineyard
vigneto *m* vineyard
vignetta *f* cartoon
vigore *m* vigo(u)r
vigoroso vigorous
vile 1 *agg* vile; (*codardo*) cowardly **2** *m* coward
villa *f* villa
villaggio *m* (*pl* -ggi) village; ***villaggio turistico*** holiday village
villeggiatura *f* holiday
villino *m* house
vincere ⟨3d⟩ **1** *v/t* win; *avversario, nemico* defeat, beat; *difficoltà* overcome **2** *v/i* win
vincersi (*dominarsi*) control o.s.
vincita *f* win
vincitore *m*, **-trice** *f* winner
vincolare ⟨1l⟩ bind; *capitale* tie up
vincolo *m* bond
vino *m* wine; ***vino bianco*** white wine; ***vino rosso*** red wine; ***vino da pasto*** table wine
vinto *pp* → ***vincere***
viola *f* MUS viola; BOT violet; ***viola del pensiero*** pansy
violare ⟨1l⟩ violate; *legge* break
violazione *f* violation; *di leggi, patti, accordi* breach; ***violazione di domicilio*** unlawful entry
violentare ⟨1b⟩ rape
violentatore *m* rapist
violento violent
violenza *f* violence
violinista *m/f* (*mpl* -i) violinist
violino *m* violin
violoncello *m* cello
vipera *f* viper
virgola *f* comma; MAT decimal point
virile manly, virile
virtù *f inv* virtue
virtuoso 1 *agg* virtuous **2** *m* virtuoso
virus *m inv* virus
viscere *fpl* insides; *fig*: *della terra* bowels
vischio *m* (*pl* -chi) mistletoe
viscido slimy
viscosa *f* viscose
viscoso viscous
visibile visible
visibilità *f* visibility
visiera *f di berretto* peak; *di casco* visor
visione *f* sight, vision; ***prendere visione di qc*** have a look at sth; ***in visione*** for examination
visita *f* visit; ***visita medica*** medical (examination); ***far visita a qu*** visit s.o.
visitare ⟨1l⟩ visit; MED examine
visitatore *m*, **-trice** *f* visitor
visivo visual
viso *m* face
visone *m* mink
vissuto *pp* → ***vivere***

vista *f* (*senso*) sight; (*capacità visiva*) eyesight; (*veduta*) view; ***a prima vista*** at first sight; MUS at sight; ***in vista di*** in sight of; *fig* in view of; ***conoscere qu di vista*** know s.o. by sight; *fig* ***perdere qu di vista*** lose touch with s.o.
visto 1 *pp* → ***vedere***; ***visto che*** seeing that **2** *m* visa; ***visto d'entrata*** entry visa; ***visto di transito*** transit visa; ***visto d'uscita*** exit visa
vistoso eye-catching
visuale 1 *agg* visual **2** *f* (*veduta*) view
vita *f* life; (*durata della vita*) lifetime; ANAT waist; ***a vita*** for life; ***costo*** *m* ***della vita*** cost of living; ***senza vita*** lifeless
vitale vital; *persona* lively, full of life
vitalità *f inv* vitality
vitamina *f* vitamin
vite[1] *f* TEC screw
vite[2] *f* AGR vine
vitello *m* calf; GASTR veal
viticoltore *m* vinegrower
viticoltura *f* vinegrowing
vitreo *fig*: *sguardo*, *occhio* glazed, glassy
vittima *f* victim
vitto *m* diet food; ***vitto e alloggio*** bed and board
vittoria *f* victory
vittorioso victorious
vivace lively; *colore* bright
vivacità *f* liveliness; *di colori* brightness
vivaio *m di pesci* tank; *di piante* nursery; *fig* breeding ground
vivanda *f* food
viva voce *m inv* speakerphone
vivente living
vivere ⟨3zz⟩ **1** *v/i* live (***di*** on) **2** *v/t* (*passare*, *provare*) experience; ***vivere una vita tranquilla*** live quietly, lead a quiet life
viveri *mpl* food (supplies)
vivisezione *f* vivisection
vivo 1 *agg* (*in vita*) alive; (*vivente*) living; *colore* bright; ***farsi vivo*** get in touch; (*arrivare*) turn up; ***vivo e vegeto*** hale and hearty **2** *m*: ***dal vivo*** *trasmissione*, *concerto* live; ***entrare nel vivo della questione*** get to the heart of the matter; ***i -i*** *pl* the living
viziare ⟨1g⟩ *persona* spoil
viziato *persona* spoiled; ***aria*** *f* ***-a*** stale air
vizio *m* (*pl* -zi) vice; (*cattiva abitudine*) (bad) habit; (*dipendenza*) addiction; ***vizio cardiaco*** heart defect
vizioso *persona* dissolute; ***circolo*** *m* ***vizioso*** vicious circle
v.le *abbr* (= ***viale***) St (= street)
vocabolario *m* (*pl* -ri) (*lessico*) vocabulary; (*dizionario*) dictionary
vocabolo *m* word
vocale 1 *agg* vocal **2** *f* vowel
vocazione *f* vocation
voce *f* voice; *fig* rumo(u)r; *in dizionario*, *elenco* entry; ***ad alta voce*** in a loud voice, loudly; ***a bassa voce*** in a low voice, quietly; ***spargere la voce*** spread rumo(u)rs
voglia *f* (*desiderio*) wish, desire; (*volontà*) will; *sulla pelle* birthmark; ***avere voglia di fare qc*** feel like doing sth; ***morire dalla voglia di fare qc*** be dying to do sth; ***contro voglia, di mala voglia*** unwillingly, reluctantly
voglio → ***volere***
voi you; *riflessivo* yourselves; *reciproco* each other; ***a voi*** to you; ***senza di voi*** without you
vol. *abbr* (= ***volume***) vol (= volume)
volano *m* shuttlecock
volante 1 *agg* flying **2** *m* AUTO (steering) wheel **3** *f* flying squad
volantino *m* leaflet
volare ⟨1a⟩ fly
volata *f* SP final sprint; ***di volata*** in a rush
volenteroso willing
volentieri willingly; ***volentieri!*** with pleasure!
volere 1 ⟨2t⟩ *v/t & v/i* want; ***vorrei ...*** I would *or* I'd like ...; ***vorrei partire*** I'd like to leave; ***volere dire*** mean; ***volere bene a qu*** (*amare*) love s.o.; ***ci vogliono dieci mesi*** it takes ten months; ***senza volere*** without meaning to **2** *m* will
volgare vulgar
volgarità *f* vulgarity
volgere ⟨3d⟩ **1** *v/t*: ***volgere le spalle*** turn one's back **2** *v/i*: ***volgere al termine*** draw to a close; ***il tempo volge al brutto*** the weather is getting worse; ***volgere al peggio*** take a turn for the worse
volo *m* flight; (*caduta*) fall; ***prendere il volo*** *di uccello* fly away; *di persona* run away; ***volo a vela*** gliding; ***volo diretto*** direct flight; ***volo di linea*** scheduled flight; ***volo internazionale*** international flight; ***volo nazionale*** domestic flight; ***volo senza scalo*** nonstop flight; *fig* ***afferrare qc al volo*** be quick to grasp sth
volontà *f* will; ***a volontà*** as much as you like; ***buona volontà*** goodwill
volontariato *m* voluntary work
volontario (*pl* -ri) **1** *agg* voluntary **2** *m*, **-a** *f* volunteer
volpe *f* fox; *femmina* vixen
volt *m inv* volt
volta *f* time; (*turno*) turn; ARCHI vault; ***una volta*** once; ***due volte*** twice; ***qualche volta*** sometimes; ***questa volta*** this time; ***ogni volta*** every time; ***una volta per***

sempre once and for all; ***poco per volta*** little by little; ***un'altra volta*** *ancora una volta* one more time; ***lo faremo un'altra volta*** we'll do it some other time; ***molte -e*** many times, often
voltaggio *m* (*pl* -ggi) voltage
voltare ⟨1c⟩ **1** *v/t* turn; *pagina* turn (over); ***voltare le spalle a qu*** *azione* turn one's back on s.o.; *posizione* have one's back to s.o. **2** *v/i* turn; ***voltare a destra*** turn right
voltarsi turn (round)
volto[1] *m* face
volto[2] *pp* → ***volgere***
volume *m* volume
voluminoso bulky
voluttà *f* voluptuousness
vomitare ⟨1l & c⟩ vomit, throw up F; *fig* ***mi fa vomitare*** it makes me sick
vomito *m* vomit
vongola *f* ZO, GASTR clam
voragine *f* chasm, abyss
vortice *m* whirl; *in acqua* whirlpool; *di vento* whirlwind
vostro 1 *agg* your; ***i -i amici*** your friends **2** *pron*: ***il vostro*** yours; ***questi libri sono -i*** these books are yours
votare ⟨1a⟩ vote
votazione *f* vote
voto *m* POL vote; EDU mark; REL, *fig* vow; ***mettere qc ai -i*** put sth to the vote, take a vote on sth
v.r. *abbr* (= ***vedi retro***) see over
Vs. *abbr* (= ***vostro***) your
v.s. *abbr* (= ***vedi sopra***) see above
V.U. *abbr* (= ***Vigili Urbani***) police
vulcanico (*pl* -ci) volcanic
vulcano *m* volcano
vulnerabile vulnerable
vuole → ***volere***
vuotare ⟨1c⟩ empty
vuotarsi empty
vuoto 1 *agg* empty; (*non occupato*) vacant; (*privo*) devoid (***di*** of) **2** *m* (*spazio*) empty space; (*recipiente*) empty; FIS vacuum; *fig* void; ***vuoto d'aria*** air pocket; ***vuoto a perdere*** non-returnable container; ***vuoto a rendere*** returnable container; ***andare a vuoto*** fall through; (***confezionato***) ***sotto vuoto*** vacuum-packed

W

W *abbr* (= ***watt***) W (= watt); (= ***viva***) long live
walkman *m inv* Walkman®
watt *m inv* watt
WC *abbr* (= ***gabinetto***) WC (= water closet)
week-end *m inv* weekend
western *m inv* Western; ***western all'italiana*** spaghetti Western
whisky *m inv* whisky
windsurf *m inv* (*tavola*) sailboard; *attività* windsurfing; ***fare windsurf*** go windsurfing
W.L. *abbr* (= ***vagone letto***) sleeping car

X, Y

X, x *f* x; ***raggi*** *mpl* ***X*** X-rays
xenofobia *f* xenophobia
xenofobo 1 *agg* xenophobic **2** *m*, **-a** *f* xenophobe
xilofono *m* xylophone
yacht *m inv* yacht
yoga *m* yoga
yogurt *m inv* yoghurt
yugoslavo 1 *agg* Yugoslav(ian) **2** *m*, **-a** *f* Yugoslav(ian)

Z

zabaione *m* zabaglione
zafferano *m* saffron
zaffiro *m* sapphire
zagara *f* orange blossom
zaino *m* rucksack
zampa *f* ZO (*piede*) paw; *di uccello* claw; (*zoccolo*) hoof; (*arto*) leg; GASTR *di maiale* trotter; *fig* ***giù le -e!*** hands off!; ***a zampa di elefante*** flared
zampillare ⟨1a⟩ gush
zampillo *m* spurt
zampone *m* GASTR stuffed pig's trotter
zanzara *f* mosquito
zanzariera *f* mosquito net; *su finestre* insect screen
zappa *f* hoe
zappare ⟨1a⟩ hoe
zapping *m inv*: ***fare lo zapping*** zap
zattera *f* raft
zavorra *f* ballast
zebra *f* zebra
zecca[1] *f* (*pl* -cche) ZO tick
zecca[2] *f* (*pl* -cche) Mint; ***nuovo di zecca*** brand-new
zelante zealous
zelo *m* zeal
zenit *m* zenith
zenzero *m* ginger
zeppo: ***pieno zeppo*** crammed (***di*** with)
zerbino *m* doormat
zero *m* zero; *nel tennis* love; *nel calcio* nil; *fig* ***partire da zero*** start from scratch; ***2 gradi sotto zero*** 2 degrees below zero
zigomo *m* cheekbone
zigzag *m inv* zigzag
zimbello *m* decoy; *fig* laughing stock
zinco *m* zinc
zingaro *m*, **-a** *f* gipsy
zio *m*, **-a** *f* uncle; *donna* aunt
zitto quiet; ***sta zitto!*** be quiet!; *in tono minaccioso* keep your mouth shut! F
zoccolo *m* clog; ZO hoof; ARCHI base
zodiacale : ***segni*** *mpl* ***-i*** signs of the Zodiac
zodiaco *m* Zodiac
zolfo *m* sulphur, *Am* sulfur
zona *f* zone, area; ***zona di libero scambio*** free trade area; ***zona disco*** short-stay parking area; ***zona industriale*** industrial area; ***zona pedonale*** pedestrian precinct; ***zona residenziale*** residential area; ***zona verde*** green belt
zonzo: ***andare a zonzo*** wander around
zoo *m inv* zoo
zoppicare ⟨1l, c & d⟩ limp; *di mobile* wobble
zoppo lame; (*zoppicante*) limping; *mobile* wobbly
zucca *f* (*pl* -cche) marrow; *fig* F (*testa*) bonce F, nut F
zuccherare ⟨1l⟩ sugar
zuccheriera *f* sugar bowl
zucchero *m* sugar; ***zucchero greggio*** brown sugar; ***zucchero vanigliato*** vanilla sugar; ***zucchero in zollette*** sugar cubes
zucchini *mpl* courgettes, *Am* zucchini(s)
zuffa *f* scuffle
zuppa *f* soup; ***zuppa di verdura*** vegetable soup; ***zuppa di pesce*** fish soup; ***zuppa inglese*** trifle
zuppiera *f* tureen
zuppo soaked, wet through

Activity & Reference Section

The following section contains three parts, each of which will help you in your learning:

Games and puzzles to help you learn to use this dictionary and practice your Italian-language skills. You'll learn about the different features of this dictionary and how to look something up effectively.

Basic words and expressions to reinforce your learning and help you master the basics.

A short grammar reference to help you use the language correctly.

Using Your Dictionary

Using a bilingual dictionary is important if you want to speak, read or write in a foreign language. Unfortunately, if you don't understand the symbols in your dictionary or the format of the entries, you'll make mistakes.

What kind of mistakes? Think of some of the words you know in English that sound or look alike. For example, think about the word *ring*. How many meanings can you think of for this word, *ring*? Try to list at least three.

a. ______________________________

b. ______________________________

c. ______________________________

Now look up *ring* in the English side of the dictionary. There are more than ten Italian words that correspond to the single English word *ring*. Some of these Italian words are listed below in scrambled form.

Unscramble the jumbled Italian words, then draw a line connecting each Italian word with the appropriate English meaning.

Italian jumble	***English meanings***
1. RUSNOAE =	**a.** a circle around something
2. ONALLE =	**b.** the action a bell or telephone does; to ring
3. ATSPI =	**c.** jewelry worn on the finger
4. AMAHICRE =	**d.** the boxing venue
5. GNRI =	**e.** one of the venues at a circus
6. CORECHI =	**f.** to call someone

With so many Italian words, each meaning something different, you must be careful to choose the right one. Using the wrong definition can obscure your meaning. Imagine the bizarre and misleading sentences you would make if you never looked beyond the first definition.

For example:

The boxer wearily entered the circle.

She always wore the circle left to her by her grandmother.

I was waiting for the phone circle when there was a knock at the door.

If you choose the wrong definition, you simply won't be understood. Mistakes like these are easy to avoid, once you know what to look for when using your dictionary. The following pages will review the structure of your bilingual dictionary and show you how to pick the right word when you use it. Read the tips and guidelines, then complete the puzzles and exercises to practice what you have learned.

Identifying Headwords

If you are looking for a single word in the dictionary, you simply look for that word's location in alphabetical order. However, if you are looking for a phrase, or an object that is described by several words, you will have to decide which word to look up.

Two-word terms are listed by their first word. If you are looking for the Italian equivalent of *shooting star*, you will find it under *shooting*.

So-called phrasal verbs in English are found in a block under the main verb. The phrasal verbs *go ahead*, *go back*, *go off*, *go on*, *go out*, and *go up* are all found in a block after *go*.

Idiomatic expressions are found under the key word in the expression. The phrase *give someone a ring*, meaning to call someone, is found in the entry for *ring*.

Feminine headwords that are variants of a masculine headword and share a meaning with the masculine word will be found in alphabetical order with their masculine counterpart. In Italian a male painter is called a **pittore** and a female painter is a **pittrice**. Both of the words are found in alphabetical order under the masculine form, **pittore**.

Find the following words and phrases in your bilingual dictionary. Identify the headword under which you should look for each. Then, try to find all of the headwords in the word-search puzzle on the next page.

1. in the middle of

2. be in shock

3. break in

4. dog

5. bring up

6. string someone along

7. be in jeopardy

8. get something done

9. that's a relief

10. take advantage of

11. attore

12. dare del lei a qualcuno

13. le ultime notizie

14. domestico

15. segreteria telefonica

z	h	r	ù	o	v	ò	l	x	q	r	è	r	p	o	u	j	k
u	g	è	d	u	a	v	c	l	x	f	ì	u	e	t	è	c	i
ì	a	e	z	ò	v	c	d	e	z	ú	i	a	j	l	j	k	u
m	e	q	t	b	a	h	g	l	w	a	r	à	e	p	i	r	y
e	é	w	c	i	o	a	p	f	m	u	r	g	o	h	r	e	s
k	n	k	b	g	t	y	z	o	g	ù	n	i	p	a	s	h	f
c	f	w	i	n	g	b	s	i	z	i	d	r	a	t	i	g	e
ì	s	é	a	d	n	r	f	è	r	è	a	à	r	t	y	n	t
u	e	v	o	l	u	e	r	t	a	è	l	d	d	o	o	o	r
s	d	e	n	u	m	a	s	è	m	s	e	z	y	r	è	t	y
a	h	d	s	o	i	k	b	r	i	n	g	w	o	e	l	i	s
ï	e	o	d	q	m	i	d	d	l	e	j	d	l	u	r	z	q
b	d	g	c	o	r	g	l	e	y	l	n	i	o	t	u	i	l
e	z	g	n	k	z	w	a	c	s	e	n	s	e	i	e	a	f
l	w	y	u	f	v	è	ò	o	i	i	a	i	l	q	r	t	g
c	è	f	g	i	r	a	m	l	o	r	c	e	d	u	i	à	a
a	n	r	y	t	e	i	s	e	g	r	e	t	e	r	i	a	w
u	z	a	c	a	s	n	e	l	e	h	s	e	s	g	r	d	ë

Alphabetization

The entries in a bilingual dictionary are in alphabetical order. They are ordered from A to Z for each language. If words begin with the same letter or letters, they are alphabetized from A to Z using the first unique letter in each word.

Practice alphabetizing the following words. Rewrite the words in alphabetical order, using the space provided below. Next to each word also write the number that is associated with it. Then follow that order to connect the dots on the next page. Not all of the dots will be used; only those whose numbers appear in the word list.

festa	**1**	calcio	**53**
treno	**4**	proprio	**55**
finora	**6**	cellulare	**56**
forza	**7**	incidente	**59**
giro	**9**	difficoltà	**61**
caldo	**11**	sicurezza	**62**
vero	**20**	ancora	**65**
bicchiere	**21**	zucchero	**65**
magari	**23**	pena	**77**
rosso	**28**	qualcuno	**82**
pane	**29**	smettere	**83**
riso	**32**	tavola	**93**
regola	**35**	ospite	**96**
oggi	**38**	domani	**97**
esaurito	**47**	pesca	**98**
lingua	**50**	ricordo	**99**

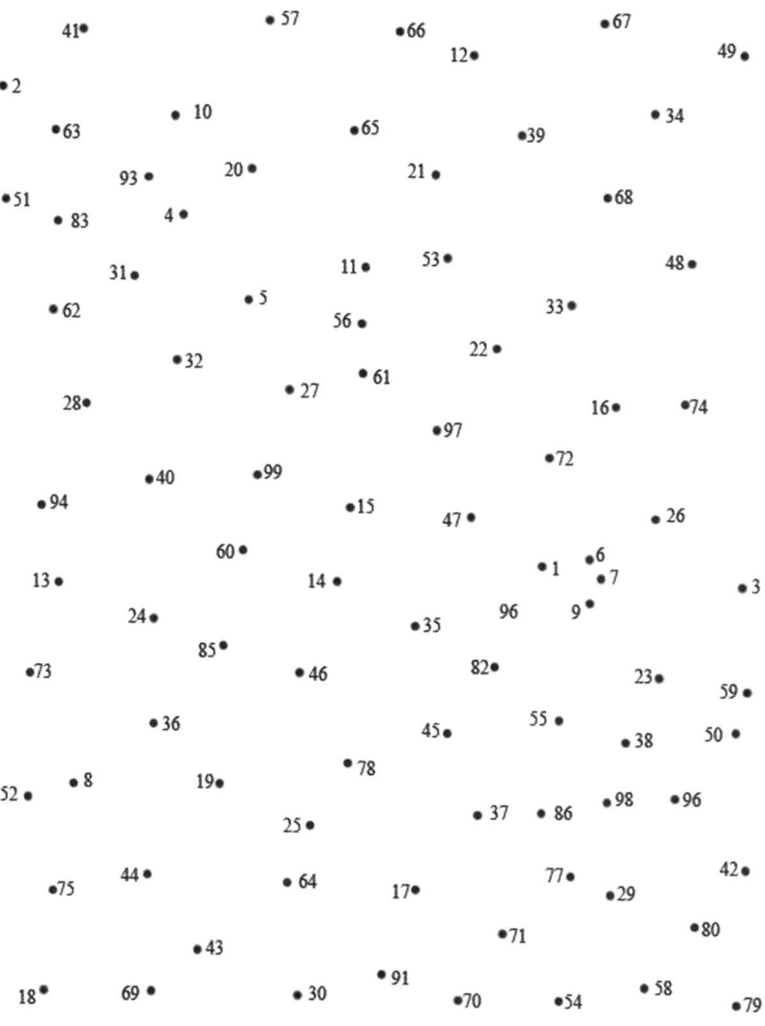

Quale paese vede?

________ ________ ________ ________ ________ ________

Spelling

Like any dictionary, a bilingual dictionary will tell you if you have spelled a word right. But how can you look up a word if you don't know how to spell it? Though it may be time consuming, the only way to check your spelling with a dictionary is to take your best guess, or your best guesses, and look to see which appears in the dictionary.

Practice checking your spelling using the words below. Each group includes one correct spelling and three incorrect spellings. Look up the words and cross out the misspelled versions (the ones you do not find in the dictionary). Rewrite the correct spelling in the blanks on the next page. When you have filled in all of the blanks, use the circled letters to reveal a mystery message.

1. fummeto	fumetto	phumeto	vumetto
2. giornale	gournale	jiornale	journale
3. chiamra	chamra	camera	samera
4. caminarre	camminare	chaminare	ciaminare
5. peede	peide	phide	piede
6. giuda	guiba	guica	guida
7. baeto	beato	beeto	biato
8. leabreia	leebrira	libreria	lipreria
9. besogno	besonnu	bisogno	bisonno
10. scoura	scuola	scuora	shuola
11. spasso	spaeso	speeso	spesso

1. (___) ___ ___ ___ ___ ___ ___

2. ___ ___ (___) ___ ___ ___ ___ ___

3. ___ ___ ___ ___ (___) ___

4. ___ ___ (___) ___ ___ ___ ___ ___ ___

5. ___ (___) ___ ___ ___

6. ___ ___ ___ (___) ___

7. ___ ___ (___) ___ ___

8. ___ ___ (___) ___ ___ ___ ___ ___

9. ___ (___) ___ ___ ___ ___ ___

10. ___ ___ ___ ___ (___) ___

11. ___ ___ (___) ___ ___ ___

___ ___ ___ ___ ___ ___ ___ ___ ___ ___ ___ !

1 2 3 4 5 6 7 8 9 10 11

Entries in Context

In addition to the literal translation of each headword in the dictionary, entries sometimes include phrases using that word.

Solve the crossword puzzle below using the correct word in context.

Hint: Each clue contains key words that will help you find the answer. Look up the key words in each clue.

ACROSS

1. He plans to be in the lead soon. **Pensa di essere in** ______________ .
4. Good night. **Buona** ______________**! See you again tomorrow.**
7. Grazie? Oh, don't mention it. **Non c'è di** ______________ .
10. The sticker in the no smoking section read "______________ **fumare**."
11. The weather is very nice. The sun is shining and the skies are clear. **Fa bel** ______________ .
13. The exchange students participating in the ______________ **culturale** live with host families.
15. **In primo** ______________, he got off to a rough start. And in the second place, the competition was stiff.
17. They have open-air seating on the patio, if you'd prefer to dine *all'* ______________.

DOWN

2. A pet, or **un** ______________ **domestico**, can be a caring companion.
3. Oh, no! **Che** ______________. What a shame!
5. I can't wait for you to come home. I miss you. **Mi** ______________ **tanto!**

6. The food was vacuum packed. **Era confezionato sotto** ________________ .

8. The schedule said 1:30, but the train arrived late. **Era in** ________________ .

9. The sign marking the one-way street read "**strada a** ________________ **unico**."

10. Tonight she will pick out her clothes and pack her bags (**fare le** ________________). Tomorrow she is leaving on vacation.

12. The line is too long today, but we'll have time to wait tomorrow. **Domani possiamo fare la** ___________ .

14. Hey! That's none of your business! **Fatti gli** ________________ **tuoi**.

16. I wondered what time it was; I asked a friend, "**Che** ________________ **è**?"

18. You wonder if all the trouble we went through is worth it? I think so. **Secondo me, ne vale la** ________________ .

1 2 3 4 5 6 7 8 9 10 11 12 13 14 15 16 17 18

Word Families

Some English words have several related meanings that are represented by different words in Italian. These related meanings belong to the same word family and are grouped together under a single English headword. Other words, while they look the same, do not belong to the same word family. These words are written under a separate headword.

Think back to our first example, *ring*. The translations **cerchio**, **anello**, and **pista** all refer to related meanings of *ring* in English. They are all circular things, though in different contexts. **Trillo**, **chiamare**, and **suonare**, however, refer to a totally different meaning of *ring* in English: the sound a bell or phone makes.

The word family for circles, with all of its nuanced Italian translations, is grouped together under *ring*[1]. The word family for sounds is grouped together under *ring*[2].

Study the lists of words below. Each group includes three Italian translations belonging to one word family, and one Italian translation of an identical-looking but unrelated English word. Eliminate the translation that is not in the same word family as the others. Then rewrite the misfit word in the corresponding blanks. When you have filled in all of the blanks, use the circled letters to reveal a bonus message.

Hint: Look up the Italian words to find out what they mean. Then look up those translations in the English-Italian side of your dictionary to find the word family that contains the Italian words.

1. bloccare	ficcare	ingorgo	marmellata
2. abbinare	fiammifero	partita	uguagliare
3. profondo	solido	suono	valido
4. anello	cerchio	pista	trillo
5. accendere	illuminare	leggero	luce

1. ___ ___ ___ (___) ___ ___ ___ ___ ___ ___

2. ___ ___ ___ ___ ___ (___) ___ ___ ___ ___

3. (___) ___ ___ ___ ___

4. (___) ___ ___ ___ ___ ___

5. ___ ___ ___ ___ ___ ___ (___)

___ ___ ___ ___ ___ !
1 2 3 4 5

Pronunciation

You can determine the sound of an Italian word from its spelling. Words are pronounced the way they are spelled. However, some letters represent different sounds in Italian than in English.

In English, 'ch' makes a soft sound at the front of your mouth, as in the word *cherry*, and 'k' makes a hard sound in the throat, like *kite*. Italian also has hard and soft combinations.

In Italian, to make the soft sound found in the English word *cherry*, you do not use an h. Use the following spellings:

ci
ce

Italian does not have the letter 'k'. To make the sound from the English word *kite*, use the following spellings:

chi
che
ca
co
cu

There is a similar rule for the sounds that 'g' makes in the English words *judge* and *gate*.

In Italian, to make the soft sound found in the English word *judge*, use the following spellings:

gi
ge

To make the sound from the English word *gate*, use the following spellings:

ghi
ghe
ga
go
gu

Look up the Italian translations for the following words and fill in the crossword puzzle.

ACROSS

2. sack
5. because
6. church
7. cat
9. place
11. dog

DOWN

1. kiss
3. today
4. frozen
7. day
8. cherry
10. dinner
11. certain

Which of these words have soft sounds in the front of the mouth, like English *cherry* or *judge*?

Which of these words have hard sounds in the back of the mouth, like English *kite* or *gate*?

Running Heads

Running heads are the words printed in blue at the top of each page. The running head on the left tells you the first headword on the left-hand page. The running head on the right tells you the last headword on the right-hand page. All the words that fall in alphabetical order between the two running heads appear on those two dictionary pages.

Look up the running head on the page where each headword appears, and write it in the space provided. Then unscramble the jumbled running heads and match them with what you wrote.

Headword	***Running head***	***Jumbled running head***
1. arrosto	ARMISTIZIO	REATNEMMCO
2. battimano	______________	OMNA
3. comodo	______________	TENEIN
4. fastidio	______________	ZZARAEIMRAB
5. immerso	______________	ENEPLA
6. lezione	______________	ZIOSITMAIR
7. mancino	______________	MEDOINA
8. mentire	______________	SEZAZSAB
9. negozio	______________	ZOLNOEZUR
10. pentola	______________	TIAPLEET
11. rovina	______________	ZOIENEL
12. televisione	______________	NELLUOFANN

Parts of Speech

In Italian and English, words are categorized into different ***parts of speech***. These labels tell us what function a word performs in a sentence. In this dictionary, the part of speech is given before a word's definition.

Nouns are things. ***Verbs*** describe actions. ***Adjectives*** describe nouns in sentences. For example, the adjective *pretty* tells you about the noun *girl* in the phrase *a pretty girl*. ***Adverbs*** also describe, but they modify verbs, adjectives, and other adverbs. The adverb *quickly* tells you more about how the action is carried out in the phrase *ran quickly*.

Prepositions specify relationships in time and space. They are words such as *in*, *on*, *before*, or *with*. ***Articles*** are words that accompany nouns. Words like *the* and *a* or *an* modify the noun, marking it as specific or general, and known or unknown.

Conjunctions are words like *and*, *but*, and *if* that join phrases and sentences together. ***Pronouns*** take the place of nouns in a sentence.

The following activity uses words from the dictionary in a Sudoku-style puzzle. In Sudoku puzzles, the numbers 1 to 9 are used to fill in grids. All digits 1 to 9 must appear, but cannot be repeated, in each square, row, and column.

In the following puzzles, you are given a set of words for each part of the grid. Look up each word to find out its part of speech. Then arrange the words within the square so that, in the whole puzzle, you do not repeat any part of speech within a column or row.

Hint: If one of the words given in the puzzle is a noun, then you know that no other nouns can be put in that row or column of the grid. Use the process of elimination to figure out where the other parts of speech can go.

Let's try a small puzzle first. You will use the categories noun *n*, verb *v*, adjective *adj*, and preposition *prp* to solve this puzzle.

Part 1

bere, cane, **corretto**, da

Part 2

di, **doccia**, fare, formidabile

Part 3

giocare, grosso, **in**, itinerario

Part 4

lotteria, malato, **mettere**, su

	corretto		
			doccia
		mettere	
in			

Now try a larger puzzle. For this puzzle, you will use the categories noun *n*, verb *v*, adjective *adj*, preposition *prp*, article *art*, and pronoun *pron*.

Part 1

ascensore, attraente, **bisognare**, loro, la, nei

Part 2

altro, davanti, **educare**, **faccia**, gli, voi

Part 3

bello, con, disoccupazione, **entrare**, **noi**, **una**

Part 4

cultura, **esclusivo**, lui, un, leggere, senza

Part 5

dopo, diverso, esempio, esercitare, **io**, **uno**

Part 6

famiglia, **lei**, lo, nazionale, **sotto**, marcare

		bisognare	**faccia**		
ascensore					**educare**
	entrare			**cultura**	
una	**noi**			**esclusivo**	
dopo		**uno**			**lei**
		io	**sotto**		

Gender

Italian nouns belong to one of two groups: feminine or masculine. A noun's gender is indicated in an entry after the headword or pronunciation with **m** for masculine, **f** for feminine, and **m/f** if the same form of the word can be used for a man or a woman.

In some cases, the masculine and feminine forms of one word mean two different things. For example, the masculine **un partito** means *a political party*. The feminine **una partita** means *a game* or *match*. The gender associated with each meaning follows the headword in the dictionary entry.

Look up the words in the grids below. Circle the feminine words. Put an **X** through the masculine words.

piede	stazione	mano
dente	sacco	persona
paura	porco	pomodoro

donna	regalo	mela
carta	mosca	cinema
testa	video	pisolino

mondo	sciopero	ferrovia
strada	parola	tavola
scherzo	mente	lavoro

Think of these as tic-tac-toe grids. Does masculine or feminine win more matches?

Adjectives

Adjectives in Italian change form to agree in gender and number with the noun they modify. In many cases, the feminine singular ends in –**a**, and the masculine singular ends in –**o**. The feminine plural ends in –**e** and the masculine plural ends in –**i**. If the base form of an adjective ends in –**e**, the plural ends in –**i**, for either gender. Some adjectives have irregular forms; in this case, the irregular forms are written out after the headword.

Use the dictionary to determine whether the nouns in the following phrases are masculine or feminine, singular or plural. Then write in the correct inflected form of the adjective. Check your answers against the word search. The correct forms are found in the puzzle.

1. a blonde woman = una donna ____________

2. a difficult exam = un esame ____________

3. two important messages = due messaggi ______________

4. secondary school = la scuola _________________

5. three green cars = tre macchine ______________

6. a funny boy = un ragazzo _______________

7. a beautiful girl = una _________ ragazza

8. an interesting book = un libro ________________

9. the first time = la _____________ volta

10. Italian guides = guide _____________

11. a red bag = una borsa ____________

t	r	v	g	m	l	u	o	b	p	o	à	o	a	e	l	è	ò
f	e	à	i	f	ì	n	l	ù	b	i	e	ù	t	u	é	n	i
k	p	a	i	c	o	b	v	m	h	t	a	i	l	ù	q	a	r
p	r	c	b	ù	g	m	s	i	n	i	t	a	l	i	a	n	e
g	i	b	e	u	m	c	é	a	d	e	ù	w	e	k	s	g	u
q	m	i	l	r	d	e	s	y	o	i	i	g	ì	f	k	e	é
ê	a	s	l	d	o	s	e	à	c	z	f	b	e	m	f	o	b
n	a	à	a	à	e	s	i	e	u	e	ù	f	i	o	n	d	e
n	i	ò	n	r	u	è	i	a	ù	ù	p	l	i	u	t	i	ò
u	s	e	e	p	ì	j	e	a	c	r	v	m	c	c	o	u	ï
ì	é	t	o	r	o	s	s	a	t	e	l	j	e	é	i	à	d
p	n	c	i	t	s	e	c	o	n	d	a	r	i	a	u	l	v
i	u	o	a	b	i	o	n	d	a	è	a	o	g	h	g	è	e
r	o	v	à	p	k	i	x	p	h	a	r	w	g	a	h	g	ä
ë	w	ô	ì	d	d	ü	e	i	m	p	o	r	t	a	n	t	i
è	s	u	z	r	e	v	c	g	u	o	à	ù	o	i	è	v	u
v	o	n	e	i	e	n	ï	z	ö	ê	i	v	u	h	o	k	ì
p	z	v	i	n	d	i	m	e	n	t	i	c	b	u	f	f	o
i	s	c	f	a	i	p	e	t	k	ò	i	f	é	e	a	g	u
é	e	e	d	i	v	c	i	o	s	è	h	s	r	r	f	z	é

Verbs

Verbs are listed in the dictionary in their infinitive form. To use the verb in a sentence, you must conjugate it and use the form that agrees with the sentence's subject.

Most verbs fall into categories with other verbs that are conjugated in the same way. In the verb appendix of this dictionary, you will find an example of each category, along with conjugations of common irregular verbs.

For this puzzle, conjugate the given verbs in the present tense. Use the context and the subject pronoun to determine the person and number of the form you need. The correct answer fits in the crossword spaces provided.

Hint: The verb class code given in the verb's dictionary entry tells you which model conjugation to follow.

ACROSS

1. Lei ______________ la porta quando arriva a casa. **chiudere**
3. Io ho un gatto, e lui _______ un cane. **avere**
5. Voi ______________ una parola nel dizionario? **cercare**
7. Cristina e Caterina _____________ sempre il lavoro. **finire**
9. Tutti _____________ bene in Italia. **mangiare**
12. Voi _____________ visitare il Vaticano? **volere**
15. Io ___________ in Europa quest'estate! **viaggiare**
19. Voi ______________ l'autobus alla fermata. **aspettare**
20. I ragazzi ______________ bene. **stare**

DOWN

2. L'uomo d'affari _________ dall'ufficio alle sei. **uscire**
4. Noi _____________ spesso al cinema. **andare**
6. Gli studenti? Loro _______________ al professore. **rispondere**
7. Paolo ______ le valige prima di partire in vacanze. **fare**

8. La squadra italiana __________ la partita! **vincere**

10. Voi ___________ il giornale a tavola? **leggere**

11. Io ____________ un panino al caffè. **prendere**

13. In genere, lui __________ l'acqua minerale. **bere**

14. _____________ amici. Diamoci del tu. **essere**

16. I bambini ____________ a palla. **giocare**

17. Tu ________ alla festa, vero? **andare**

18. Io __________ sempre le chiavi. **perdere**

1 2 3 4 5 6 7 8 9 10 11 12 13 14 15 16 17 18 19 20

When reading Italian, you face a different challenge. You see a conjugated verb in context and need to determine what its infinitive is in order to understand its meaning.

For the next puzzle, you will see conjugated verbs in the sentences. Figure out which verb the conjugated form represents, and write the infinitive (the headword form) in the puzzle.

ACROSS

1. Cosa mi **consiglia**?
4. Il gatto **dorme** al sole.
6. Io **suonavo** uno strumento da giovane.
7. Le donne **preparano** la cena.
8. Il re **morì**.
10. **Vendono** molti gusti di gelato.
13. **Vissero** per sempre felici e contenti.
14. Non **ubbidisci** mai ai genitori.
16. **Mangeranno** a casa.
18. Gli studenti **hanno dato** l'esame.
19. Ai bambini **piacciono** i videogiochi.

DOWN

1. Non **capisco** cosa dite.
2. Il giovane **nascose** i cioccolatini.
3. Maria e Doriana **arriveranno** alle sei.
5. **Abbiamo vinto**!
9. La chiesa **era** bella e grande.
11. Lui **dividerebbe** il panino con gli amici.
12. **Ti abbronzerai** al mare.
15. **Parlavate** spesso agli amici.
17. Voglio che voi **facciate** i compiti.

1 2 3 4 5 6 7 8 9 10 11 12 13 14 15 16 17 18 19

Riddles

Solve the following riddles in English. Give the Italian word for the riddle's solution.

1. This cold season is followed by spring.

___ ___ ___ ___ ___ ___ ___
15 27 25 5 6 27 16

2. These winter objects hang off roofs and gutters in snowy weather.

___ ___ ___ ___ ___ ___ ___ ___ ___ ___
11 2 15 9 24 24 15 16 18 16

3. This thing protects you from the rain, but it's bad luck to open it indoors!

___ ___ ___ ___ ___ ___ ___ ___
16 26 28 6 5 18 18 16

4. Many people enjoy this hot caffeinated beverage in the morning.

___ ___ ___ ___ ___
24 9 12 12 21

5. This is the number that follows three and precedes five.

___ ___ ___ ___ ___ ___ ___
4 14 9 1 1 6 16

6. If you are injured or very ill, you should go to this place.

___ ___ ___ ___ ___ ___ ___ ___
16 10 17 5 13 9 18 5

7. This mode of transportation has only two wheels. It is also good exercise!

___ ___ ___ ___ ___ ___ ___ ___ ___ ___
28 15 24 15 24 18 5 1 1 9

8. This large mammal lives in the ocean.

___ ___ ___ ___ ___ ___

28 9 18 5 27 9

9. This person is your mother's mother.

___ ___ ___ ___ ___

27 16 27 27 9

10. There are twelve of these in a year.

___ ___ ___ ___

26 5 10 15

11. Wearing this in the car is a safety precaution.

___ ___ ___ ___ ___ ___ ___

24 15 27 1 14 6 9

12. Snow White bit into this red fruit and fell into a long slumber.

___ ___ ___ ___

26 5 18 9

13. This professional brings letters and packages to your door.

___ ___ ___ ___ ___ ___ ___

17 16 10 1 15 27 16

14. This midday meal falls between breakfast and dinner.

___ ___ ___ ___ ___ ___

17 6 9 27 22 16

15. A very young dog is referred to as this.

___ ___ ___ ___ ___ ___ ___ ___

24 14 24 24 15 6 18 16

Cryptogram

Use the number-to-letter correspondence from the riddles to fill in the hidden message. When you are done, translate the Italian message into English. What does it say?

18	9		24	16	10	1	15	1	14	22	15	16	27	5
15	1	9	18	15	9	27	9		13	15	24	5	:	
18	‘	15	1	9	18	15	9		5		14	27	9	
			6	5	17	14	28	28	18	15	24	9		
		13	5	26	16	24	6	9	1	15	24	9		
		12	16	27	13	9	1	9		10	14	18		
						18	9	25	16	6	16			

Translation:

________ ________________ __________________ _________:

________________ ________ ______ __________________________

________________________ ______________ _____ ____________.

Answer Key

Using Your Dictionary

a–b. Answers will vary

1. suonare, b
2. anello, c
3. pista, e
4. chiamare, f
5. ring, d
6. cerchio, a

Identifying Headwords

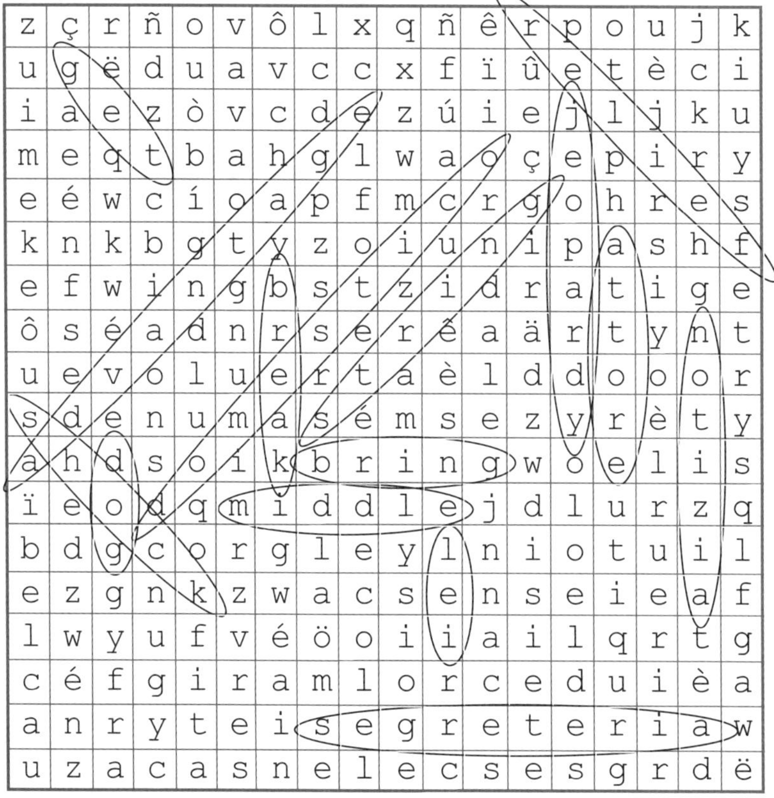

z	ç	r	ñ	o	v	ô	l	x	q	ñ	ê	r	p	o	u	j	k
u	g	ë	d	u	a	v	c	c	x	f	ï	û	e	t	è	c	i
i	a	e	z	ò	v	c	d	e	z	ú	i	e	j	l	j	k	u
m	e	q	t	b	a	h	g	l	w	a	o	ç	e	p	i	r	y
e	é	w	c	í	o	a	p	f	m	c	r	g	o	h	r	e	s
k	n	k	b	g	t	y	z	o	i	u	n	i	p	a	s	h	f
e	f	w	i	n	g	b	s	t	z	i	d	r	a	t	i	g	e
ô	s	é	a	d	n	r	s	e	r	ê	a	ä	r	t	y	n	t
u	e	v	o	l	u	e	r	t	a	è	l	d	d	o	o	o	r
s	d	e	n	u	m	a	s	é	m	s	e	z	y	r	è	t	y
a	h	d	s	o	i	k	b	r	i	n	g	w	o	e	l	i	s
ï	e	o	d	q	m	i	d	d	l	e	j	d	l	u	r	z	q
b	d	g	c	o	r	g	l	e	y	l	n	i	o	t	u	i	l
e	z	g	n	k	z	w	a	c	s	e	n	s	e	i	e	a	f
l	w	y	u	f	v	é	ö	o	i	i	a	i	l	q	r	t	g
c	é	f	g	i	r	a	m	l	o	r	c	e	d	u	i	è	a
a	n	r	y	t	e	i	s	e	g	r	e	t	e	r	i	a	w
u	z	a	c	a	s	n	e	l	e	c	s	e	s	g	r	d	ë

Alphabetization

ancora, bicchiere, calcio, caldo, cellulare, difficoltà, domani, esaurito, festa, finora, forza, giro, incidente, lingua, magari, oggi, ospite, pane, pena, pesca, proprio, qualcuno, regola, ricordo, riso, rosso, sicurezza, smettere, tavola, treno, vero, zucchero

I T A L I A

Spelling

1. fumetto
2. giornale
3. camera
4. camminare
5. piede
6. guida
7. beato
8. libreria
9. bisogno
10. scuola
11. spesso

F O R M I D A B I L E!

Entries in Context

1 TESTA
2 ANIMALE
3 PECCATO
4 NOTTE
5 MANCHI
6 VUOTO
7 CHE
8 RITARDO
9 SENSO
10 VIETATO
10 VALIGIE
11 TEMPO
12 FILA
13 SCAMBIO
14 AFFARI
15 LUOGO
16 ORA
17 APERTO
18 PENA

Word Families

1. marmellata
2. fiammifero
3. suono
4. trillo
5. leggero

M I S T O!

Pronunciation

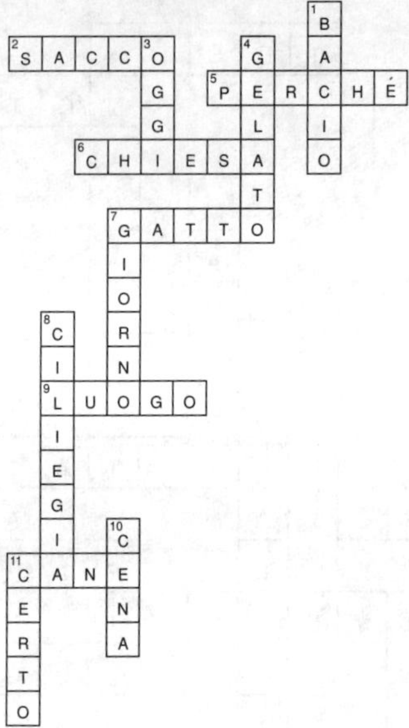

The DOWN words have soft sounds in the front of the mouth, like English *cherry* or *judge*. The ACROSS words have hard sounds in the back of the mouth, like English *kite* or *gate*.

Running Heads

Headword	*Running head*	*Jumbled running head*
1. arrosto	ARMISTIZIO	REATNEMMCO
2. battimano	BASSEZZA	OMNA
3. comodo	COMMENTARE	TENEIN
4. fastidio	FANNULLONE	ZZARAEIMRAB
5. immerso	IMBARAZZARE	ENEPLA
6. lezione	LEZIONE	ZIOSITMAIR
7. mancino	MANO	MEDOINA
8. mentire	MEDIANO	SEZAZSAB
9. negozio	NIENTE	ZOLNOEZUR
10. pentola	PENALE	TIAAPLEET
11. rovina	RUZZOLONE	ZOIENEL
12. televisione	TELEPATIA	NELLUOFANN

Parts of Speech

cane	**corretto**	di	fare
bere	da	formidabile	**doccia**
grosso	itinerario	**mettere**	su
in	giocare	lotteria	malato

loro	la	**bisognare**	**faccia**	davanti	altro
ascensore	nei	attraente	gli	voi	**educare**
bello	**entrare**	con	lui	**cultura**	un
una	**noi**	disoccupazione	leggere	**esclusivo**	senza
dopo	esempio	**uno**	nazionale	marcare	**lei**
esercitare	diverso	**io**	**sotto**	lo	famiglia

Gender

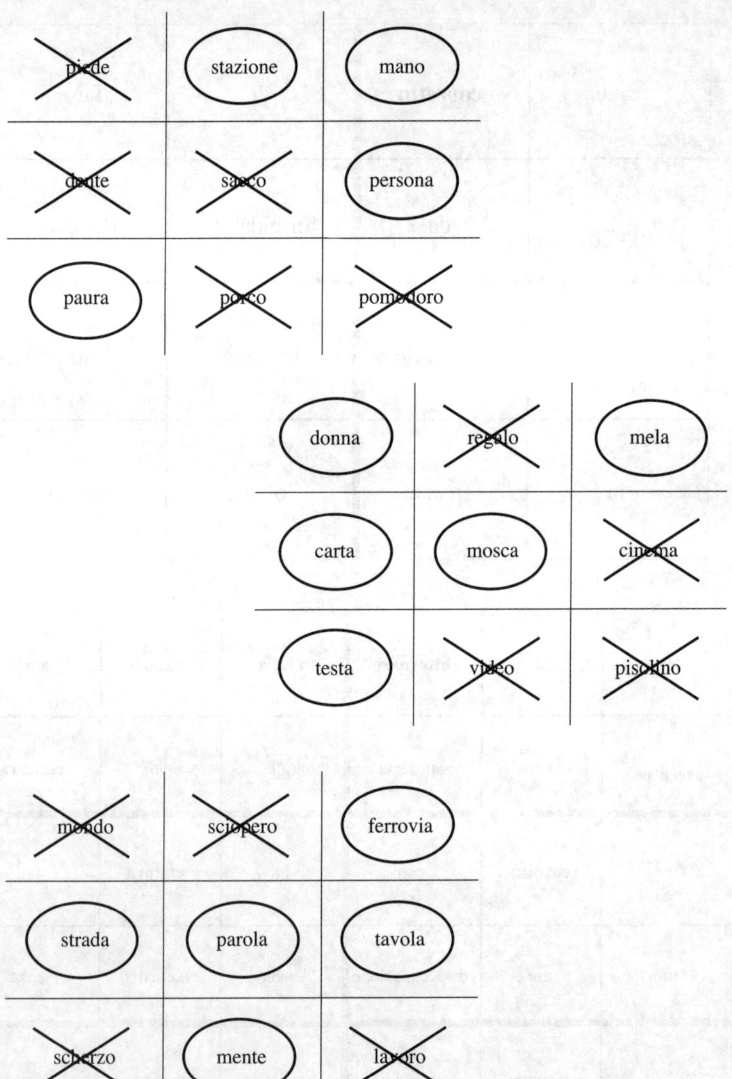

Feminine wins the most matches.

Adjectives

1. una donna **bionda**
2. un esame **difficile**
3. due messaggi **importanti**
4. la scuola **secondaria**
5. tre macchine **verdi**
6. un ragazzo **buffo**
7. una **bella** ragazza
8. un libro **interessante**
9. la **prima** volta
10. guide **italiane**
11. una borsa **rossa**

t	r	v	g	m	l	u	o	b	p	o	á	o	a	e	l	é	ó
f	e	á	i	f	í	n	l	ú	b	i	é	ú	t	u	é	n	i
k	p	a	i	c	o	b	v	m	h	t	a	i	l	ú	q	a	r
p	r	c	b	ú	g	m	s	i	n	i	t	a	l	i	a	n	e
g	I	b	e	u	m	c	é	a	d	e	ú	w	e	k	s	g	u
q	m	i	l	r	d	e	s	y	o	i	i	g	í	f	k	e	é
á	a	s	l	d	o	s	é	á	c	z	f	b	e	m	f	o	b
n	a	á	a	á	e	s	i	e	u	e	ú	f	i	o	n	d	e
n	i	ó	n	r	u	é	i	a	ú	ú	p	l	i	u	t	i	ó
u	s	e	e	p	í	j	e	a	c	r	v	m	c	c	o	u	í
í	é	t	o	r	o	s	s	a	t	e	l	j	e	é	i	á	d
p	n	c	i	t	s	e	c	o	n	d	a	r	i	a	u	l	v
í	u	o	a	b	i	o	n	d	a	é	a	o	g	h	g	é	e
r	o	v	á	p	k	i	x	p	h	a	r	w	g	a	h	g	a
é	w	ó	í	d	d	u	e	i	m	p	o	r	t	a	n	t	i
é	s	u	z	r	e	v	c	g	u	o	á	ú	o	i	é	v	u
v	o	n	e	i	e	n	i	z	é	e	i	v	u	h	o	k	í
p	z	v	i	n	d	i	m	e	n	t	i	v	b	u	f	f	o
i	s	c	f	a	i	p	e	t	k	ó	i	f	é	e	a	g	u
é	e	e	d	i	v	c	i	o	s	é	h	s	r	r	f	z	é

Verbs

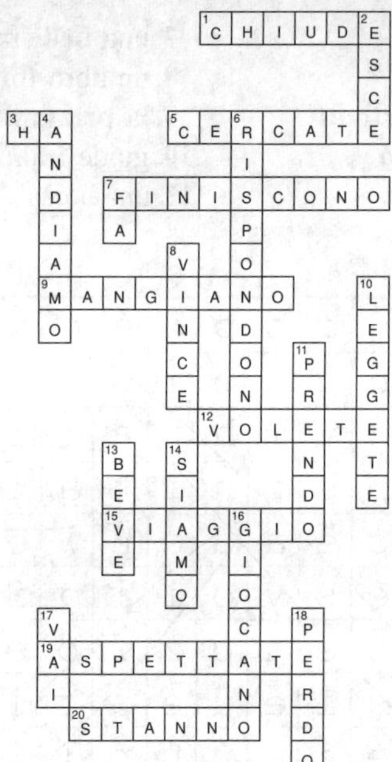
CHIUDE
ESCE
HA
ANDIAMO
CERCATE
RISPONDONO
FINISCONO
FA
VINCE
MANGIANO
LEGGETE
PRENDO
VOLETE
BEVE
SIAMO
VIAGGIO
GIOCATANO
VAI
ASPETTATE
PERDO
STANNO

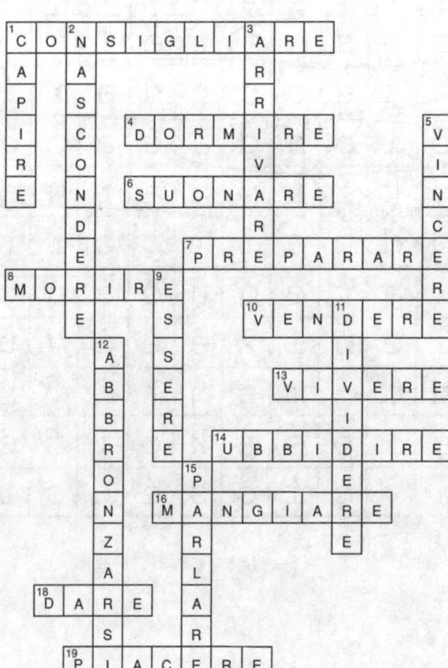
CONSIGLIARE
APRIRE
NASCONDERE
ARRIVARE
DORMIRE
VINCERE
SUONARE
PREPARARE
MORIRE
ESSERE
VENDERE
DIVIDERE
ABBRONZARSI
VIVERE
UBBIDIRE
PARLARE
MANGIARE
DARE
PIACERE

Riddles

1. inverno
2. ghiacciolo
3. ombrello
4. caffè
5. quattro
6. ospedale
7. bicicletta
8. balena
9. nonna
10. mesi
11. cintura
12. mela
13. postino
14. pranzo
15. cucciolo

Cryptogram

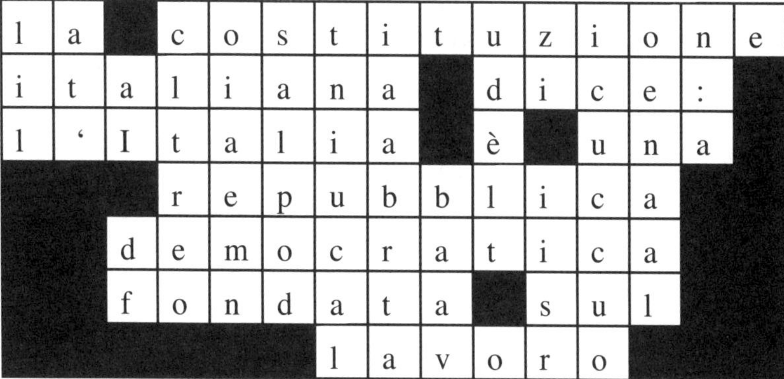

l	a		c	o	s	t	i	t	u	z	i	o	n	e
i	t	a	l	i	a	n	a		d	i	c	e	:	
l	‘	I	t	a	l	i	a		è		u	n	a	
			r	e	p	u	b	b	l	i	c	a		
		d	e	m	o	c	r	a	t	i	c	a		
		f	o	n	d	a	t	a		s	u	l		
						l	a	v	o	r	o			

The Italian constitution says: Italy is a democratic republic, founded on labor.

BASIC ITALIAN PHRASES & GRAMMAR

Pronunciation

In this section we have used a simplified phonetic system to represent the sounds of Italian. Simply read the pronunciation as if it were English.

BASIC PHRASES

Essential

Hello / Hi!	**Ciao!**	chah-oh
Good morning!	**Buongiorno!**	bwohn-johrnoh
Good afternoon!	**Buona sera!**	bwohnah sehrah
Good evening!	**Buona sera!**	bwohnah sehrah
Goodbye!	**Arrivederci!**	ahr-reeveh-dehrchee
…, please!	**…, per favore!**	pehr fah-vohreh
Thank you!	**Grazie!**	grahtzee-eh
Yes.	**Sì.**	see
No.	**No.**	noh
Sorry!	**Scusi!**	skoozee
Where are the restrooms?	**Dov'è la toilette?**	dohveh lah twah-leht
When?	**Quando?**	kwahndoh
What?	**Che cosa?**	keh kohzah
Where?	**Dove?**	dohveh
Here.	**Qui.**	kwee
There.	**Là.**	lah
On the right.	**A destra.**	ah dehstrah
On the left.	**A sinistra.**	ah seeneestrah
Do you have …?	**Ha …?**	ah
I'd like …	**Vorrei …**	vohr-ray
How much is that?	**Quanto costa?**	kwahntoh kohstah
Where is …?	**Dov'è …?**	dohveh
Where can I get …?	**Dove trovo …?**	dohveh trohvoh

Communication Difficulties

Do you speak English?	**Parla inglese?**	pahrlah eenglehzeh
Does anyone here speak English?	**C'è qualcuno qui che parla inglese?**	cheh kwahl-koonoh kwee keh pahrlah eenglehzeh
Did you understand that?	**Ha capito?**	ah kahpeetoh
I understand.	**Ho capito. / Capisco.**	oh kahpeetoh / kah-peeskoh
I didn't understand that.	**Non ho capito.**	nohn oh kahpeetoh
Could you speak a bit more slowly, please?	**Potrebbe parlare più lentamente, per favore?**	pohtrehb-beh pahrlahreh pew lehntah-mehnteh pehr fahvohreh
Could you please repeat that?	**Potrebbe ripetere, per favore?**	pohtrehb-beh reepeh-tehreh pehr fahvohreh
What does … mean?	**Che cosa significa …?**	keh kohzah seenyee-feekah …

Greetings

Hello, Hi!	**Salve! / Ciao!**	sahlveh / chah-oh
Good morning!	**Buongiorno!**	bwohn-johrnoh
Good afternoon / evening!	**Buona sera!**	bwohnah-sehrah
How are you?	**Come sta / stai?**	kohmeh stah / stah-ee
How are things?	**Come va?**	kohmeh vah
Fine, thanks. And you?	**Bene, grazie. E Lei / tu?**	behneh grahtzee-eh eh lay / too
I'm afraid I have to go now.	**Mi dispiace, ma devo andare.**	mee deespee-ahcheh mah dehvoh ahndahreh
Goodbye!	**Arrivederci!**	ahr-reeveh-dehrchee
See you soon / tomorrow!	**A presto / domani!**	ah prehstoh / dohmahnee
Bye!	**Ciao! / Arrivederci!**	chah-oh / ahr-reeveh-dehrchee
It was nice meeting you.	**Piacere di averLa conosciuto** (m) / **conosciuta** (f).	pee-ahchehreh dee ahvehrlah kohnoh-shootoh / kohnoh-shootah

Thank you for a lovely evening / day.	**Grazie per la bella serata / giornata.**	grahtzee-eh pehr lah behl-lah sehrah-tah / johrnahtah
Have a good trip!	**Buon viaggio!**	bwohn vee-ah-djoh

Meeting People

What's your name?	**Come si chiama?**	kohmeh see key-ahmah
My name is …	**Mi chiamo …**	mee key-ahmoh …
May I introduce …	**Posso presentarLe …**	pohs-soh prehzehn-tahrleh
– my my husband?	**mio marito?**	mee-oh mahreetoh
– my my wife?	**mia moglie?**	mee-ah moh-lee-eh
– my my boyfriend?	**il mio ragazzo?**	eel mee-oh rahgah-tzoh
– my my girlfriend?	**la mia ragazza?**	lah mee-ah rahgah-tzah
Where are you from?	**Di dov'è?**	dee dohveh
I'm from …	**Vengo …**	vehngoh
– the US.	**dagli Stati Uniti.**	dah-lee stahtee ooneetee
– Canada.	**dal Canada.**	dahl kahnahdah
– the UK.	**dall'Inghilterra.**	dahl-leen-gheel-tehrrah

Expressing Likes and Dislikes

Very good!	**Benissimo!**	behnees-seemoh
I'm very happy.	**Sono molto contento** (m) / **contenta** (f).	sohnoh mohltoh kohntehntoh / kohntehnta
I like that.	**Mi piace.**	mee pee-ahcheh
What a shame!	**Che peccato!**	keh pehk-kahtoh
I'd rather …	**Preferirei …**	prehfeh-reeray …
I don't like it.	**Non mi piace.**	nohn mee pee-ahcheh
I'd rather not.	**Preferirei di no.**	prehfeh-reeray dee noh
Certainly not.	**Assolutamente no.**	ahs-sohlootah-mehn-teh noh

Expressing Requests and Thanks

Thank you very much.	**Grazie mille.**	grahtzee-eh meel-leh
Thanks, you too.	**Grazie, altrettanto.**	grahtzee-eh ahltreht-tahntoh
May I?	**Posso?**	pohs-soh
Please, …	**Per favore, … / Prego, …**	pehr fahvohreh / prehgoh
No, thank you.	**No, grazie.**	noh grahtzee-eh
Could you help me, please?	**Mi potrebbe aiutare, per favore?**	mee pohtrehb-beh ahyou-tahreh pehr fahvohreh
Thank you, that's very nice of you.	**Grazie, molto gentile da parte Sua.**	grahtzee-eh mohltoh jehnteeleh dah pahrteh sooah
Thank you very much for all your trouble / help.	**Grazie mille per il disturbo / l'aiuto.**	grahtzee-eh meel-leh pehr eel deestoorboh / lahy-outoh
You're welcome.	**Prego.**	prehgoh

Apologies

Sorry!	**Scusi!**	skoozee
Excuse me!	**Scusi!**	skoozee
I'm sorry about that.	**Mi dispiace.**	mee deespee-ahcheh
Don't worry about it!	**Non fa niente! / Non importa!**	nohn fah nee-ehnteh / nohn eem-pohrtah
How embarrassing!	**Che figura!**	keh feegoorah
It was a misunderstanding.	**È stato un malinteso.**	eh stahtoh oon mahleen-tehzoh

GRAMMAR

Regular Verbs and Their Tenses

There are three verb types that follow a regular pattern, their infinitives ending in **-are**, **-ere** and **-ire**, e.g. *to speak* **parlare**, *to sell* **vendere**, *to finish* **finire**. Here are the most common present, past and future forms:

	Present	***Past***	***Future***
io *I*	**parlo**	**ho parlato**	**parlerò**
tu *you (inform.)*	**parli**	**hai parlato**	**parlerai**
lui/lei/Lei *he/she/ you (form.)*	**parla**	**ha parlato**	**parlerà**
noi *we*	**parliamo**	**abbiamo parlato**	**parleremo**
voi *you (pl. inform.)*	**parlate**	**avete parlato**	**parlerete**
loro/Loro *they /you (form.)*	**parlano**	**hanno parlato**	**parleranno**
io *I*	**vendo**	**ho venduto**	**venderò**
tu *you (inform.)*	**vendi**	**hai venduto**	**venderai**
lui/lei/Lei *he/she /you (form.)*	**vende**	**ha venduto**	**venderà**
noi *we*	**vendiamo**	**abbiamo venduto**	**venderemo**
voi *you (pl. inform.)*	**vendete**	**avete venduto**	**venderete**
loro/Loro *they/you (form.)*	**vendono**	**hanno venduto**	**venderanno**
io *I*	**finisco**	**ho finito**	**finirò**
tu *you (inform.)*	**finisci**	**hai finito**	**finirai**
lui/lei/Lei *he/she/ you (form.)*	**finisce**	**ha finito**	**finirà**
noi *we*	**finiamo**	**abbiamo finito**	**finiremo**
voi *you (pl. inform.)*	**finite**	**avete finito**	**finirete**
loro/Loro *they/you (form.)*	**finiscono**	**hanno finito**	**finiranno**

Very often, people omit the pronoun, using only the verb form.

Examples:	**Vivo a Roma.**	*I live in Rome.*
	Parla italiano?	*Do you speak Italian?*

There are many irregular verbs whose forms differ considerably. The most common way to express the past is by using the conjugated form of *to have* **avere** and the past participle of the verb as demonstrated on the previous page. Many verbs, especially verbs related to movement are conjugated with *to be* **essere**. In that case the participle agrees with number and gender of the subject.

avere *to have*	**essere** *to be*
io ho *I have*	**io sono** *I am*
tu hai *you have*	**tu sei** *you are*
lui/lei/Lei ha *he/she has; you have*	**lui/lei/Lei è** *he/she is; you are*
noi abbiamo *we have*	**noi siamo** *we are*
voi avete *you have*	**voi siete** *you are*
loro/Loro hanno *they/you have*	**loro/Loro sono** *they/you are*

Examples:

Ho lavorato.	*I worked.*
Lei è andata a Palermo.	*She went to Palermo.*
Siamo andate in autobus.	*We (f) went by bus.*

Nouns and Articles

Generally nouns ending in **-o** are masculine, their plural ending changing to **-i**. Nouns ending in **-a** are usually feminine, their plural ending changing to **-e**. Nouns ending in **-e** can be either gender.

The definite articles are **il** (m) and **la** (f). The plural forms are **i** for masculine and **le** for feminine nouns. When a masculine noun begins with the vowels, **z-**, **sc-**, **sp-**, **st-** or **gn-**, the singular article changes to **lo**, the plural to **gli**.

Examples:

Singular	***Plural***
il treno *the train*	**i treni** *the trains*
lo studio *the studio*	**gli studi** *the studios*
la casa *the house*	**le case** *the houses*

The indefinite articles also indicate gender: **un** (m), or **uno** when a masculine noun begins with a **z-**, **sc-**, **sp-**, **st-** or **gn-**. Feminine nouns take **una** for words beginning with a consonant and **un'** when the noun begins with a vowel.

Examples:	***Singular***		***Plural***	
	un treno	*a train*	**treni**	*trains*
	uno studio	*a studio*	**studi**	*studios*
	una casa	*a house*	**case**	*houses*
	un'ora	*an hour*	**ore**	*hours*

Possessive Determiners

Possessives are used to show that the noun belongs to something or someone. They must agree with the noun in gender and number.

	Singular		***Plural***	
	Masc.	***Fem.***	***Masc.***	***Fem.***
my	**il mio**	**la mia**	**i miei**	**le mie**
your (inf.)	**il tuo**	**la tua**	**i tuoi**	**le tue**
your (form.)	**il Suo**	**la Sua**	**i Suoi**	**le Sue**
his/her/its	**il suo**	**la sua**	**i suoi**	**le sue**
our	**il nostro**	**la nostra**	**i nostri**	**le nostre**
your (pl., inf.)	**il vostro**	**la vostra**	**i vostri**	**le vostre**
your (pl., form.)	**il Loro**	**la Loro**	**i Loro**	**le Loro**
their	**il loro**	**la loro**	**i loro**	**le loro**

Examples:	**Dov'è il Suo biglietto?**	*Where is your ticket?*
	La vostra corriera parte alle 8.	*Your bus leaves at 8.*
	La tua casa è bella.	*Your (singular) house is pretty.*

Word Order

The conjugated verb generally comes after the subject.

Examples: **Lui vorrebbe una birra.** *He'd like a beer.*

Questions are formed by simply raising your voice at the end of the sentence or by reversing the order of subject and verb when using key question words like **when** or **where** .

Negations

Negative sentences are generally formed by putting **non** *not* before the verb that is being negated.

Examples:	**Non fumiamo.**	*We don't smoke.*
	Non capisco.	*I don't understand.*
	Il treno non arriva.	*The train doesn't arrive.*

Adjectives

Adjectives describe nouns and agree with them in gender and number. Singular forms end in **-o** (m), **-a** (f) or **-e** (m/f). Plural forms end in **-i** (m), **-e** (f) and **-i** (m/f).

Examples:	**un ristorante grande**	*a large restaurant*
	una camicia bianca	*a white shirt*
	le scarpe italiane	*the Italian shoes*

Sometimes adjectives precede the noun.

Examples:	**un bel giardino**	*a beautiful garden*
	la piccola casa	*the little house*
	una larga strada	*a wide street*

Adjectives linked to the subject with a verb also agree in number and gender with the noun they relate to.

Examples:	**Il clima è mite.**	*The climate is mild.*
	Il nostro capo è simpatico.	*Our boss is nice.*

Comparisons and Superlatives

Adjective	***Comparative***	***Superlative***
ricco	**più ricco**	**il più ricco**
rich	*richer*	*the richest*
vecchio	**meno vecchio**	**il meno vecchio**
old	*less old*	*the least old*

Examples:	**Ha qualcosa di meno caro?**	*Do you have anything cheaper?*

Adverbs and Adverbial Expressions

Adverbs describe verbs. In Italian, the majority are formed by adding **-mente** to the feminine form of the adjective.

Adjective	***Comparative***	***Superlative***
lento *slow*	**lenta** *slow*	**lentamente** *slowly*

Adjectives ending in **-re** or **-le** drop the final **-e** before adding **-mente**. Like in English, there are a number of exceptions to the rule, e.g. *good* **buono** / *well* **bene**.

Examples: **Maria guida lentamente.** *Maria drives slowly.*
Roberto guida normalmente. *Robert drives normally.*
Parlo bene italiano. *I speak Italian well.*

Some common adverbial time expressions:
attualmente *presently*
ancora *still*
non ancora *not yet*
finalmente *finally*

Part 2

English-Italian Dictionary

a [ə] *stressed* [eɪ] *art* un *m*, una *f*; *masculine before s + consonant, gn, ps, z* uno; *feminine before vowel* un'; ***a cat*** un gatto; ***a joke*** uno scherzo; ***a girl*** una ragazza; ***an island*** un'isola; ***£5 a ride*** una corsa 5 sterline; ***£2 a litre*** 2 sterline al litro; ***five flights a day*** cinque voli al giorno

a•back [ə'bæk] *adv*: ***taken aback*** preso alla sprovvista

a•ban•don [ə'bændən] *v/t* abbandonare; *hope, scheme* rinunciare a

a•bashed [ə'bæʃt] *adj* imbarazzato

a•bate [ə'beɪt] *v/i of storm, flood waters* calmarsi

ab•at•toir ['æbətwɑː(r)] mattatoio *m*

ab•bey ['æbɪ] abbazia *f*

ab•bre•vi•ate [ə'briːvɪeɪt] *v/t* abbreviare

ab•bre•vi•a•tion [əbriːvɪ'eɪʃn] abbreviazione *f*

ab•di•cate ['æbdɪkeɪt] *v/i* abdicare

ab•di•ca•tion [æbdɪ'keɪʃn] abdicazione *f*

ab•do•men ['æbdəmən] addome *m*

ab•dom•i•nal [æb'dɒmɪnl] *adj* addominale

ab•duct [əb'dʌkt] *v/t* sequestrare, rapire

ab•duc•tion [əb'dʌkʃn] sequestro *m*, rapimento *m*

ab•hor•rence [əb'hɒrəns] *fml* orrore *m*

ab•hor•rent [əb'hɒrənt] *adj fml* ripugnante

◆ **abide by** [ə'baɪd] *v/t* attenersi a

a•bil•i•ty [ə'bɪlətɪ] abilità *f inv*

a•blaze [ə'bleɪz] *adj* in fiamme

a•ble ['eɪbl] *adj* (*skilful*) capace; ***be able to*** essere capace a; ***I wasn't able to see / hear*** non ero in grado di vedere / sentire

a•ble-bod•ied [eɪbl'bɒdiːd] *adj* robusto; MIL abile

ab•nor•mal [æb'nɔːml] *adj* anormale

ab•nor•mal•ly [æb'nɔːməlɪ] *adv* in modo anomalo

a•board [ə'bɔːd] **1** *prep* a bordo di **2** *adv*: ***be aboard*** essere a bordo; ***go aboard*** salire a bordo

a•bol•ish [ə'bɒlɪʃ] *v/t* abolire

ab•o•li•tion [æbə'lɪʃn] abolizione *f*

a•bort [ə'bɔːt] *v/t mission, rocket launch* annullare; COMPUT: *program* interrompere

a•bor•tion [ə'bɔːʃn] aborto *m*; ***have an abortion*** abortire

a•bor•tive [ə'bɔːtɪv] *adj* fallito; ***the plan proved abortive*** il piano si è rivelato un fallimento

a•bout [ə'baʊt] **1** *prep* (*concerning*) su; ***I'll tell you all about it*** ti dirò tutto al riguardo; ***talk about sth*** parlare di qc; ***be angry about sth*** essere arrabbiato per qc; ***there's nothing you can do about it*** non ci puoi fare niente; ***what's it about?*** *of book, film* di cosa parla?; *of complaint, problem* di cosa si tratta? **2** *adv* (*roughly*) intorno a, verso; (*nearly*) quasi; ***it's about ready*** è quasi pronto; ***be about to …*** (*be going to*) essere sul punto di …; ***be about*** (*somewhere near*) essere nei paraggi; ***there are a lot of people about*** c'è un sacco di gente qui

a•bove [ə'bʌv] **1** *prep* (*higher than*) sopra; (*more than*) sopra, oltre; ***above all*** soprattutto **2** *adv* sopra; ***on the floor above*** al piano di sopra

a•bove-men•tioned [əbʌv'menʃnd] *adj* suddetto

ab•ra•sion [ə'breɪʒn] abrasione *f*

ab•ra•sive [ə'breɪsɪv] *adj personality* ruvido

a•breast [ə'brest] *adv* fianco a fianco; ***keep abreast of*** tenere al corrente di

a•bridge [ə'brɪdʒ] *v/t* ridurre

a•broad [ə'brɔːd] *adv* all'estero

a•brupt [ə'brʌpt] *adj departure* improvviso; *manner* brusco

a•brupt•ly [ə'brʌptlɪ] *adv leave* improvvisamente; *say* bruscamente

ab•scess ['æbsɪs] ascesso *m*

ab•sence ['æbsəns] assenza *f*

ab•sent ['æbsənt] *adj* assente

ab•sen•tee [æbsən'tiː] *n* assente *m/f*

ab•sen•tee•ism [æbsən'tiːɪzm] assenteismo *m*

ab•sent-mind•ed [æbsənt'maɪndɪd] *adj* distratto

ab•sent-mind•ed•ly [æbsənt'maɪndɪdlɪ] *adv* distrattamente

ab•so•lute ['æbsəluːt] *adj power* assoluto; *idiot* totale

ab•so•lute•ly ['æbsəluːtlɪ] *adv* (*completely*) assolutamente; ***absolutely not!*** assolutamente no!; ***do you agree? – absolutely*** sei d'accordo? – assolutamente sì

ab•so•lu•tion [æbsə'luːʃn] REL assoluzione *f*

ab•solve [əb'zɒlv] *v/t* assolvere

ab•sorb [əb'sɔːb] *v/t* assorbire; ***absorbed in …*** assorto in …

ab•sorb•en•cy [əb'sɔːbənsɪ] assorbenza *f*

ab•sorb•ent [əb'sɔːbənt] *adj* assorbente
ab•sorb•ing [əb'sɔːbɪŋ] *adj* avvincente
ab•stain [əb'steɪn] *v/i from voting* astenersi
ab•sten•tion [əb'stenʃn] *in voting* astensione *f*
ab•sti•nence ['æbstɪnəns] astinenza *f*
ab•stract ['æbstrækt] *adj* astratto
ab•struse [əb'struːs] *adj* astruso
ab•surd [əb'sɜːd] *adj* assurdo
ab•surd•i•ty [əb'sɜːdətɪ] assurdità *f*
ab•surd•ly [əb'sɜːdlɪ] *adv* in modo assurdo
a•bun•dance [ə'bʌndəns] abbondanza *f*
a•bun•dant [ə'bʌndənt] *adj* abbondante
a•buse[1] [ə'bjuːs] *n* abuso *m*; (*ill treatment*) maltrattamento *m*; (*insults*) insulti *mpl*
a•buse[2] [ə'bjuːz] *v/t* abusare di; (*treat badly*) maltrattare; (*insult*) insultare
a•bu•sive [ə'bjuːsɪv] *adj language* offensivo; ***become abusive*** diventare aggressivo
a•bys•mal [ə'bɪʒml] *adj* F (*very bad*) pessimo
a•byss [ə'bɪs] abisso *m*
AC ['eɪsiː] *abbr* (= ***alternating current***) c.a. (corrente *f* alternata)
ac•a•dem•ic [ækə'demɪk] **1** *n* docente *m/f* universitario, -a **2** *adj* accademico; *person* portato per lo studio
a•cad•e•my [ə'kædəmɪ] accademia *f*
ac•cede [ək'siːd] *v/i*: ***accede to*** *throne* salire a
ac•cel•e•rate [ək'seləreɪt] *v/t & v/i* accelerare
ac•cel•e•ra•tion [əkselə'reɪʃn] *of car* accelerazione *f*
ac•cel•e•ra•tor [ək'seləreɪtə(r)] *of car* acceleratore *m*
ac•cent ['æksənt] accento *m*
ac•cen•tu•a•te [ək'sentjʊeɪt] *v/t* accentuare
ac•cept [ək'sept] *v/t* accettare
ac•cep•ta•ble [ək'septəbl] *adj* accettabile
ac•cept•ance [ək'septəns] accettazione *f*
ac•cess ['ækses] **1** *n* accesso *m*; ***have access to*** *computer* avere accesso a; *child* avere il permesso di vedere **2** *v/t* accedere a
'ac•cess code COMPUT codice *m* di accesso
ac•ces•si•ble [ək'sesəbl] *adj* accessibile
ac•ces•sion [ək'seʃn] ascesa *f*
ac•ces•so•ry [ək'sesərɪ] *for wearing* accessorio *m*; LAW complice *m/f*
'ac•cess road svincolo *m*
'ac•cess time COMPUT tempo *m* di accesso
ac•ci•dent ['æksɪdənt] incidente *m*; ***by accident*** per caso
ac•ci•den•tal [æksɪ'dentl] *adj* accidentale
ac•ci•den•tal•ly [æksɪ'dentlɪ] *adv* accidentalmente
ac•claim [ə'kleɪm] **1** *n* consenso *m* **2** *v/t* acclamare
ac•cla•ma•tion [æklə'meɪʃn] acclamazioni *fpl*
ac•cli•mate, ac•cli•ma•tize [ə'klaɪmət, ə'klaɪmətaɪz] **1** *v/t* acclimatare **2** *v/i* acclimatarsi
ac•com•mo•date [ə'kɒmədeɪt] *v/t* ospitare; *special requirements* tenere conto di
ac•com•mo•da•tion [əkɒmə'deɪʃn] sistemazione *f*
ac•com•pa•ni•ment [ə'kʌmpənɪmənt] MUS accompagnamento *m*
ac•com•pa•nist [ə'kʌmpənɪst] MUS: ***with Gerald Moore as his accompanist*** con l'accompagnamento di Gerald Moore
ac•com•pa•ny [ə'kʌmpənɪ] *v/t* (*pret & pp* ***-ied***) accompagnare
ac•com•plice [ə'kʌmplɪs] complice *m/f*
ac•com•plish [ə'kʌmplɪʃ] *v/t task* compiere; *goal* conseguire
ac•com•plished [ə'kʌmplɪʃt] *adj* dotato
ac•com•plish•ment [ə'kʌmplɪʃmənt] *of a task* realizzazione *f*; (*talent*) talento *m*; (*achievement*) risultato *m*
accord [ə'kɔːd] accordo *m*; ***of his / my own accord*** di sua / mia spontanea volontà
ac•cord•ance [ə'kɔːdəns]: ***in accordance with*** conformemente a
ac•cord•ing [ə'kɔːdɪŋ] *adv*: ***according to*** secondo
ac•cord•ing•ly [ə'kɔːdɪŋlɪ] *adv* di conseguenza
ac•cor•di•on [ə'kɔːdɪən] fisarmonica *f*
ac•cor•di•on•ist [ə'kɔːdɪənɪst] fisarmonicista *m/f*
ac•count [ə'kaʊnt] *financial* conto *m*; (*report, description*) resoconto *m*; ***give an account of*** fare un resoconto di; ***on no account*** per nessuna ragione; ***on account of*** a causa di; ***take ... into account, take account of ...*** tenere conto di ...
◆ **account for** *v/t* (*explain*) giustificare; (*make up, constitute*) ammontare a
ac•count•abil•i•ty [əkaʊntə'bɪlətɪ] responsabilità *f*
ac•coun•ta•ble [ə'kaʊntəbl] *adj* responsabile; ***be held accountable*** essere considerato responsabile
ac•coun•tant [ə'kaʊntənt] contabile *m/f*; *running own business* commercialista *m/f*

ac'count holder titolare *m/f* di conto; *of current account* correntista *m/f*
ac'count num•ber numero *m* di conto
ac•counts [ə'kaʊnts] *npl* contabilità *f*
ac•cu•mu•late [ə'kjuːmjʊleɪt] **1** *v/t* accumulare **2** *v/i* accumularsi
ac•cu•mu•la•tion [əkjuːmjʊ'leɪʃn] accumulazione *f*
ac•cu•ra•cy ['ækjʊrəsɪ] precisione *f*
ac•cu•rate ['ækjʊrət] *adj* preciso
ac•cu•rate•ly ['ækjʊrətlɪ] *adv* con precisione
ac•cu•sa•tion [ækjuː'zeɪʃn] accusa *f*
ac•cuse [ə'kjuːz] *v/t* accusare; ***he accused me of lying*** mi ha accusato di mentire; ***be accused of …*** LAW essere accusato di …
ac•cused [ə'kjuːzd] *n* LAW accusato *m*, -a *f*
ac'cus•ing [ə'kjuːzɪŋ] *adj* accusatorio
ac'cus•ing•ly [ə'kjuːzɪŋlɪ] *adv look, point* con aria accusatoria; *say* con tono accusatorio
ac•cus•tom [ə'kʌstəm] *v/t*: ***get accustomed to*** abituarsi a; ***be accustomed to*** essere abituato a
ace [eɪs] *in cards* asso *m*; (*in tennis*: *shot*) ace *m inv*
ache [eɪk] **1** *n* dolore *m* **2** *v/i* fare male; ***my head aches*** mi fa male la testa
a•chieve [ə'tʃiːv] *v/t* realizzare; *success, fame* ottenere
a•chieve•ment [ə'tʃiːvmənt] *of ambition* realizzazione *f*; (*thing achieved*) successo *m*
ac•id ['æsɪd] *n* acido *m*
a•cid•i•ty [ə'sɪdətɪ] *also fig* acidità *f*
ac•id 'rain pioggia *f* acida
'ac•id test *fig* prova *f* della verità
ac•knowl•edge [ək'nɒlɪdʒ] *v/t* riconoscere; *by smile, nod* far capire di aver notato; ***he acknowledged the applause with a smile*** ha risposto all'applauso con un sorriso; ***acknowledge (receipt of) a letter*** accusare ricezione di una lettera
ac•knowl•edg(e)•ment [ək'nɒlɪdʒmənt] riconoscimento *m*; (*smile, nod*) cenno *m*; (*letter*) lettera *f* di accusata ricezione; ***in acknowledg(e)ment of*** *thanking* come pegno di riconoscenza di; ***acknowledg(e)ments*** (*in book*) ringraziamenti *mpl*
ac•ne ['æknɪ] MED acne *m*
a•corn ['eɪkɔːn] BOT ghianda *f*
a•cous•tics [ə'kuːstɪks] acustica *f*
ac•quaint [ə'kweɪnt] *v/t*: ***be acquainted with*** *fml* conoscere
ac•quaint•ance [ə'kweɪntəns] *person* conoscenza *f*
ac•qui•esce [ækwɪ'es] *v/i fml* acconsentire
ac•qui•es•cence [ækwɪ'esns] *fml* consentimento *m*
ac•quire [ə'kwaɪə(r)] *v/t* acquisire
ac•qui•si•tion [ækwɪ'zɪʃn] acquisizione *f*
ac•quis•i•tive [ə'kwɪzətɪv] *adj* avido
ac•quit [ə'kwɪt] *v/t* LAW assolvere
ac•quit•tal [ə'kwɪtl] LAW assoluzione *f*
a•cre ['eɪkə(r)] acro *m*
a•cre•age ['eɪkrɪdʒ] estensione *f* in acri
ac•rid ['ækrɪd] *adj smell* acre
ac•ri•mo•ni•ous [ækrɪ'məʊnɪəs] *adj* aspro
ac•ro•bat ['ækrəbæt] acrobata *m/f*
ac•ro•bat•ic [ækrə'bætɪk] *adj* acrobatico
ac•ro•bat•ics [ækrə'bætɪks] *npl* acrobazie *fpl*
ac•ro•nym ['ækrənɪm] acronimo *m*
a•cross [ə'krɒs] **1** *prep on other side of* dall'altro lato di; ***sail across the Atlantic*** attraversare l'Atlantico in barca a vela; ***walk across the street*** attraversare la strada; ***a bridge across the river*** un ponte sul fiume; ***across Europe*** *all over* in tutta Europa **2** *adv to other side* dall'altro lato; ***10 m across*** largo 10 m; ***they came to the river and swam across*** sono arrivati al fiume e l'hanno attraversato a nuoto
a•cryl•ic [ə'krɪlɪk] *adj* acrilico
act [ækt] **1** *v/i* agire; THEA recitare; (*pretend*) fare finta; ***act as*** fare le funzioni di **2** *n* (*deed*) atto *m*; *of play* atto *m*; *in variety show* numero *m*; (*pretence*) finta *f*; (*law*) atto *m*; ***act of God*** causa *f* di forza maggiore
act•ing ['æktɪŋ] **1** *n* recitazione *f*; ***she went into acting*** si è data alla recitazione **2** *adj* (*temporary*) facente funzione; ***the acting president*** il facente funzione di presidente
ac•tion ['ækʃn] azione *f*; ***out of action*** (*not functioning*) fuori uso; ***take action*** agire; ***bring an action against*** LAW fare causa a
ac•tion 're•play TV replay *m inv*
ac•tive ['æktɪv] *adj* attivo; GRAM attivo
ac•tiv•ist ['æktɪvɪst] POL attivista *m/f*
ac•tiv•i•ty [æk'tɪvətɪ] attività *f*
ac•tor ['æktə(r)] attore *m*
ac•tress ['æktrɪs] attrice *f*
ac•tu•al ['æktʃʊəl] *adj* reale; *cost* effettivo; ***the actual ceremony starts at 10*** la cerimonia vera e propria comincia alle 10
ac•tu•al•ly ['æktʃʊəlɪ] *adv* (*in fact, to tell the truth*) in realtà; *expressing surprise* veramente; ***actually I do know him*** *stressing the converse* a dire il vero, lo

conosco
ac•u•punc•ture ['ækjʊpʌŋktʃə(r)] agopuntura *f*
a•cute [ə'kjuːt] *adj pain, sense* acuto; *shortage* estremo
a•cute•ly [ə'kjuːtlɪ] *adv* (*extremely*) estremamente
AD [eɪ'diː] *abbr* (*= **anno domini***) d.C. (= dopo Cristo)
ad [æd] → ***advertisement***
ad•a•mant ['ædəmənt] *adj* categorico
ad•a•mant•ly ['ædəməntlɪ] *adv* categoricamente
Ad•am's ap•ple [ædəmz'æpəl] pomo *m* di Adamo
a•dapt [ə'dæpt] **1** *v/t* adattare **2** *v/i of person* adattarsi
a•dapt•a•bil•i•ty ['ədæptə'bɪlətɪ] adattabilità *f*
a•dap•ta•ble [ə'dæptəbl] *adj* adattabile
a•dap•ta•tion [ædæp'teɪʃn] *of play etc* adattamento *m*
a•dapt•or [ə'dæptə(r)] *electrical* adattatore *m*
add [æd] **1** *v/t* aggiungere; MATH addizionare **2** *v/i of person* fare le somme
◆ **add on** *v/t 15% etc* aggiungere
◆ **add up 1** *v/t* sommare **2** *v/i fig* quadrare
ad•der ['ædə(r)] vipera *f* rossa
ad•dict ['ædɪkt] *to football, chess* maniaco *m*, -a *f*; ***drug addict*** tossicomane *m/f*, tossicodipendente *m/f*; ***heroin addict*** eroinomane *m/f*; ***TV addict*** teledipendente *m/f*
ad•dic•ted [ə'dɪktɪd] *adj* dipendente; ***be addicted to*** *drugs, alcohol* essere dedito a; *football, computer games etc* essere un maniaco di
ad•dic•tion [ə'dɪkʃn] *to drugs* dipendenza *f*, assuefazione *f*; *to TV, chocolate etc* dipendenza *f*
ad•dic•tive [ə'dɪktɪv] *adj*: ***be addictive*** *of drugs* provocare dipendenza *o* assuefazione; *of TV, chocolate etc* provocare dipendenza
ad•di•tion [ə'dɪʃn] MATH addizione *f*; *to list, company etc* aggiunta *f*; ***in addition to*** in aggiunta a
ad•di•tion•al [ə'dɪʃnl] *adj* aggiuntivo
ad•di•tive ['ædɪtɪv] additivo *m*
add-on ['ædɒn] complemento *m*
ad•dress [ə'dres] **1** *n* indirizzo *m*; ***form of address*** appellativo *m* **2** *v/t letter* indirizzare; *audience* tenere un discorso a; *person* rivolgersi a
ad'dress book indirizzario *m*
ad•dress•ee [ædre'siː] destinatario *m*, -a *f*
ad•ept [ə'dept] *adj* esperto; ***be adept at*** essere esperto in
ad•e•quate ['ædɪkwət] *adj* adeguato
ad•e•quate•ly ['ædɪkwətlɪ] *adv* adeguatamente
ad•here [əd'hɪə(r)] *v/i* aderire
◆ **adhere to** *v/t surface* aderire a; *rules* attenersi a
ad•he•sive [əd'hiːsɪv] *n* adesivo *m*
ad•he•sive 'plas•ter cerotto *m*
ad•he•sive 'tape nastro *m* adesivo
ad•ja•cent [ə'dʒeɪsnt] *adj* adiacente
ad•jec•tive ['ædʒɪktɪv] aggettivo *m*
ad•join [ə'dʒɔɪn] *v/t* essere adiacente a
ad•join•ing [ə'dʒɔɪnɪŋ] *adj* adiacente
ad•journ [ə'dʒɜːn] *v/i* aggiornare
ad•journ•ment [ə'dʒɜːnmənt] aggiornamento *m*
ad•just [ə'dʒʌst] *v/t* regolare; ***adjust o.s. to*** adattarsi a
ad•just•a•ble [ə'dʒʌstəbl] *adj* regolabile
ad•just•ment [ə'dʒʌstmənt] regolazione *f*; *psychological* adattamento *m*
ad lib [æd'lɪb] **1** *adj & adv* a braccio F **2** *v/i* (*pret & pp* ***-bed***) improvvisare
ad•min•is•ter [əd'mɪnɪstə(r)] *v/t medicine* somministrare; *company* amministrare; *country* governare
ad•min•is•tra•tion [ədmɪnɪ'streɪʃn] amministrazione *f*; (*government*) governo *m*
ad•min•is•tra•tive [ədmɪnɪ'strətɪv] *adj* amministrativo
ad•min•is•tra•tor [əd'mɪnɪstreɪtə(r)] amministratore *m*, -trice *f*
ad•mi•ra•ble ['ædmərəbl] *adj* ammirevole
ad•mi•ra•bly ['ædmərəblɪ] *adv* ammirevolmente
ad•mi•ral ['ædmərəl] ammiraglio *m*
ad•mi•ra•tion [ædmə'reɪʃn] ammirazione *f*
ad•mire [əd'maɪə(r)] *v/t* ammirare
ad•mir•er [əd'maɪərə(r)] ammiratore *m*, -trice *f*
ad•mir•ing [əd'maɪərɪŋ] *adj* ammirativo
ad•mir•ing•ly [əd'maɪərɪŋlɪ] *adv* con ammirazione
ad•mis•si•ble [əd'mɪsəbl] *adj* ammissibile
ad•mis•sion [əd'mɪʃn] (*confession*) ammissione *f*; ***admission free*** entrata *f* libera
ad•mit [əd'mɪt] *v/t* (*pret & pp* ***-ted***) ammettere; *to a place* lasciare entrare; *to school, club etc* ammettere; *to hospital* ricoverare
ad•mit•tance [əd'mɪtəns]: ***no admittance*** vietato l'accesso
ad•mit•ted•ly [əd'mɪtedlɪ] *adv* effettivamente
ad•mon•ish [əd'mɒnɪʃ] *v/t fml* ammonire
a•do [ə'duː]: ***without further ado*** senza

ulteriori indugi
ad•o•les•cence [ædə'lesns] adolescenza *f*
ad•o•les•cent [ædə'lesnt] **1** *n* adolescente *m/f* **2** *adj* adolescenziale
a•dopt [ə'dɒpt] *v/t* adottare
a•dop•tion [ə'dɒpʃn] adozione *f*
adop•tive par•ents [ədɒptɪv 'peərənts] *npl* genitori *mpl* adottivi
a•dor•a•ble [ə'dɔːrəbl] *adj* adorabile
ad•o•ra•tion [ædə'reɪʃn] adorazione *f*
a•dore [ə'dɔː(r)] *v/t* adorare
a•dor•ing [ə'dɔːrɪŋ] *adj* in adorazione
ad•ren•al•in [ə'drenəlɪn] adrenalina *f*
a•drift [ə'drɪft] *adj* alla deriva; *fig* sbandato
ad•u•la•tion [ædjʊ'leɪʃn] adulazione *f*
ad•ult ['ædʌlt] **1** *n* adulto *m*, -a *f* **2** *adj* adulto
ad•ult ed•u'ca•tion corsi *mpl* per adulti
a•dul•ter•ous [ə'dʌltərəs] *adj relationship* extraconiugale
a•dul•ter•y [ə'dʌltərɪ] adulterio *m*
'adult film *euph* film *m inv* per adulti
ad•vance [əd'vɑːns] **1** *n* (*money*) anticipo *m*; *in science etc* progresso *m*; MIL avanzata *f*; ***in advance*** in anticipo; ***make advances*** (*progress*) fare progressi; *sexually* fare delle avances **2** *v/i* MIL avanzare; (*make progress*) fare progressi **3** *v/t theory* avanzare; *sum of money* anticipare; *human knowledge, a cause* fare progredire
ad•vance 'book•ing prenotazione *f*
ad•vanced [əd'vɑːnst] *adj country, level* avanzato; *learner* di livello avanzato
ad•vance 'no•tice preavviso *m*
ad•vance 'pay•ment pagamento *m* anticipato
ad•van•tage [əd'vɑːntɪdʒ] vantaggio *m*; ***it's to your advantage*** è a tuo vantaggio; ***take advantage of*** *opportunity* approfittare di
ad•van•ta•geous [ædvən'teɪdʒəs] *adj* vantaggioso
ad•vent ['ædvent] *fig* avvento *m*
'ad•vent cal•en•dar *calendario m dell'Avvento con finestrelle numerate che i bambini aprono giorno per giorno*
ad•ven•ture [əd'ventʃə(r)] avventura *f*
ad•ven•tur•ous [əd'ventʃərəs] *adj* avventuroso
ad•verb ['ædvɜːb] avverbio *m*
ad•ver•sa•ry ['ædvəsərɪ] avversario *m*, -a *f*
ad•verse ['ædvɜːs] *adj* avverso
ad•vert ['ædvɜːt] → ***advertisement***
ad•ver•tise ['ædvətaɪz] **1** *v/t job* mettere un annuncio per; *product* reclamizzare **2** *v/i for job* mettere un annuncio; *for product* fare pubblicità
ad•ver•tise•ment [əd'vɜːtɪsmənt] annuncio *m*, inserzione *f*; *for product* pubblicità *f inv*
ad•ver•tis•er ['ædvətaɪzə(r)] acquirente *m/f* di uno spazio pubblicitario; *in magazine, newspaper* inserzionista *m/f*
ad•ver•tis•ing ['ædvətaɪzɪŋ] pubblicità *f inv*
'ad•ver•tis•ing a•gen•cy agenzia *f* pubblicitaria
'ad•ver•tis•ing budg•et budget *m inv* per la pubblicità
'ad•ver•tis•ing cam•paign campagna *f* pubblicitaria
'ad•ver•tis•ing rev•e•nue proventi *mpl* della pubblicità
ad•vice [əd'vaɪs] consigli *mpl*; *legal, financial* consulenza *f*; ***a bit of advice*** un consiglio; ***take s.o.'s advice*** seguire il consiglio di qu
ad•vis•a•ble [əd'vaɪzəbl] *adj* consigliabile
ad•vise [əd'vaɪz] *v/t person* consigliare a; *caution etc* consigliare; ***advise s.o. to …*** consigliare a qu di …
ad•vis•er [əd'vaɪzə(r)] consulente *m/f*
ad•vo•cate ['ædvəkeɪt] *v/t* propugnare
aer•i•al ['eərɪəl] *n* antenna *f*
aer•i•al 'pho•to•graph fotografia *f* aerea
aer•o•bics [eə'rəʊbɪks] *nsg* aerobica *f*
aer•o•dy•nam•ic [eərəʊdaɪ'næmɪk] *adj* aerodinamico
aer•o•nau•ti•cal [eərəʊ'nɔːtɪkl] *adj* aeronautico
aer•o•plane ['eərəpleɪn] aeroplano *m*
aer•o•sol ['eərəsɒl] spray *m inv*
aer•o•space in•dus•try ['eərəspeɪs ɪndʌstrɪ] industria *f* aerospaziale
aes•thet•ic [iːs'θetɪk] *adj* estetico
af•fa•ble ['æfəbl] *adj* affabile
af•fair [ə'feə(r)] (*matter*) affare *m*; (*event*) caso *m*; (*business*) affare *m*; (*love*) relazione *f*; ***foreign affairs*** affari *mpl* esteri; ***have an affair with*** avere una relazione con
affect [ə'fekt] *v/t* MED colpire; (*influence*) influire su; (*concern*) riguardare; (*cause feelings to*) colpire
af•fec•tion [ə'fekʃn] affetto *m*
af•fec•tion•ate [ə'fekʃnət] *adj* affettuoso
af•fec•tion•ate•ly [ə'fekʃnətlɪ] *adv* affettuosamente
af•fin•i•ty [ə'fɪnətɪ] affinità *f inv*
af•fir•ma•tive [ə'fɜːmətɪv] *adj* affermativo; ***answer in the affirmative*** rispondere affermativamente
af•flict [ə'flɪkt] *v/t* tormentare; ***be afflicted with*** soffrire di
af•flu•ence ['æflʊəns] benessere *m*

af•flu•ent ['æfluənt] *adj* benestante; ***affluent society*** società *f inv* del benessere
af•ford [ə'fɔːd] *v/t*: ***be able to afford sth*** *financially* potersi permettere qc; ***I can't afford the time*** non ne ho il tempo; ***it's a risk we can't afford to take*** è un rischio che non possiamo permetterci di correre
af•ford•a•ble [ə'fɔːdəbl] *adj* abbordabile
af•front [ə'frʌnt] *n* affronto *m*
a•float [ə'fləʊt] *adj boat* a galla; ***keep the company afloat*** tenere a galla l'azienda
a•fraid [ə'freɪd] *adj*: ***be afraid*** avere paura; ***be afraid of*** avere paura di; ***I'm afraid*** *expressing regret* sono spiacente; ***I'm afraid so*** temo che sia così; ***I'm afraid not*** purtroppo no
a•fresh [ə'freʃ] *adv* da capo
Af•ri•ca ['æfrɪkə] Africa *f*
Af•ri•can ['æfrɪkən] **1** *n* africano *m*, -a *f* **2** *adj* africano
af•ter ['ɑːftə(r)] **1** *prep* dopo; ***after her / me / you*** dopo di lei / me / te; ***after all*** dopo tutto; ***after that*** dopo; ***the day after tomorrow*** dopodomani **2** *adv* dopo; ***the day after*** il giorno dopo
af•ter•math ['ɑːftəmɑːθ]: ***the aftermath of war*** il dopoguerra; ***in the aftermath of*** nel periodo immediatamente successivo a
afternoon [ɑːftə'nuːn] pomeriggio *m*; ***in the afternoon*** nel pomeriggio; ***this afternoon*** oggi pomeriggio; ***good afternoon*** buon giorno
'af•ter sales serv•ice servizio *m* dopovendita
'af•ter•shave dopobarba *m inv*
'af•ter•taste retrogusto *m*
af•ter•wards ['ɑːftəwədz] *adv* dopo
a•gain [ə'geɪn] *adv* di nuovo; ***I never saw him again*** non l'ho mai più visto
a•gainst [ə'geɪnst] *prep lean* contro; ***America against Brazil*** SP America contro Brasile; ***I'm against the idea*** sono contrario all'idea; ***what do you have against her?*** cos'hai contro di lei?; ***against the law*** contro la legge
age [eɪdʒ] **1** *n* (*also era*) età *f inv*; ***at the age of*** all'età di; ***under age*** minorenne; ***she's five years of age*** ha cinque anni; ***I've been waiting for ages*** F ho aspettato un secolo F **2** *v/i* invecchiare
aged[1] [eɪdʒd] *adj*: ***a boy aged 16*** un ragazzo di 16 anni; ***he was aged 16*** aveva 16 anni
aged[2] ['eɪdʒɪd] **1** *adj*: ***her aged parents*** i suoi anziani genitori **2** *n*: ***the aged*** gli anziani
'age group fascia *f* d'età
'age lim•it limite *m* d'età
a•gen•cy ['eɪdʒənsɪ] agenzia *f*
a•gen•da [ə'dʒendə] ordine *m* del giorno; ***on the agenda*** all'ordine del giorno
a•gent ['eɪdʒənt] agente *m/f*
ag•gra•vate ['ægrəveɪt] *v/t* aggravare; (*annoy*) seccare
ag•gre•gate ['ægrɪgət] *n* insieme *m*; ***in (the) aggregate*** nel complesso; ***win on aggregate*** SP vincere ai punti
ag•gres•sion [ə'greʃn] aggressione *f*
ag•gres•sive [ə'gresɪv] *adj* (*also dynamic*) aggressivo
ag•gres•sive•ly [ə'gresɪvlɪ] *adv* con aggressività
ag•gro ['ægrəʊ] P grane *fpl*
a•ghast [ə'gɑːst] *adj* inorridito
ag•ile ['ædʒaɪl] *adj* agile
a•gil•i•ty [ə'dʒɪlətɪ] agilità *f*
ag•i•tate ['ædʒɪteɪt] *v/i*: ***agitate for / against*** mobilitarsi per / contro
ag•i•tat•ed ['ædʒɪteɪtɪd] *adj* agitato
ag•i•ta•tion [ædʒɪ'teɪʃn] agitazione *f*
ag•i•ta•tor [ædʒɪ'teɪtə(r)] agitatore *m*, -trice *f*
AGM [eɪdʒiː'em] *abbr* (= ***annual general meeting***) assemblea *f* annuale
ag•nos•tic [æg'nɒstɪk] *n* agnostico *m*, -a *f*
a•go [ə'gəʊ] *adv*: ***2 days ago*** due giorni fa; ***long ago*** molto tempo fa; ***how long ago?*** quanto tempo fa?
ag•o•nize ['ægənaɪz] *v/i* angosciarsi; ***agonize over*** angosciarsi per
ag•o•niz•ing ['ægənaɪzɪŋ] *adj* angosciante
ag•o•ny ['ægənɪ] agonia *f*; *mental* angoscia *f*
a•gree [ə'griː] **1** *v/i* essere d'accordo; *of figures, accounts* quadrare; (*reach agreement*) mettersi d'accordo; ***I agree*** sono d'accordo; ***it doesn't agree with me*** *of food* mi fa male **2** *v/t price* concordare; ***agree that sth should be done*** concordare che si dovrebbe fare qc
a•gree•a•ble [ə'griːəbl] *adj* (*pleasant*) piacevole; ***be agreeable*** (*in agreement*) essere d'accordo
a•gree•ment [ə'griːmənt] (*consent, contract*) accordo *m*; ***reach agreement on*** trovare un accordo su
ag•ri•cul•tur•al [ægrɪ'kʌltʃərəl] *adj* agricolo
ag•ri•cul•ture ['ægrɪkʌltʃə(r)] agricoltura *f*
ahead [ə'hed] *adv* davanti; (*in advance*) avanti; ***200 m ahead*** 200 m più avanti; ***be ahead of*** essere davanti a; ***plan / think ahead*** programmare per tempo; ***arrive ahead of the others*** arrivare prima degli altri

aid [eɪd] **1** *n* aiuto *m* **2** *v/t* aiutare
aide [eɪd] assistente *m/f*
Aids [eɪdz] Aids *m*
ail•ing ['eɪlɪŋ] *adj economy* malato
ail•ment ['eɪlmənt] disturbo *m*
aim [eɪm] **1** *n in shooting* mira *f*; (*objective*) obiettivo *m*; ***take aim*** prendere la mira; **2** *v/i in shooting* mirare; ***aim at doing sth, aim to do sth*** aspirare a fare qc **3** *v/t*: ***be aimed at*** *of remark etc* essere rivolto a; ***be aimed at*** *of guns* essere puntato contro
aim•less ['eɪmlɪs] *adj* senza obiettivi; *wandering* senza meta
air [eə(r)] **1** *n* aria *f*; ***by air*** *travel* in aereo; *send mail* per via aerea; ***in the open air*** all'aperto; ***on the air*** RAD, TV in onda **2** *v/t room* arieggiare; *fig*: *views* rendere noto
'**air•bag** airbag *m inv*
'**air•base** base *f* aerea
'**air-con•di•tioned** *adj* con aria condizionata
'**air-con•di•tion•ing** aria *f* condizionata
'**air•craft** aereo *m*
'**air•craft car•ri•er** portaerei *f inv*
'**air fare** tariffa *f* aerea
'**air•field** campo *m* d'aviazione
'**air force** aeronautica *f* militare
'**air host•ess** hostess *f inv*
'**air let•ter** aerogramma *m*
'**air•lift 1** *n* ponte *m* aereo **2** *v/t* trasportare per via aerea
'**air•line** compagnia *f* aerea
'**air•lin•er** aereo *m* di linea
'**air•mail**: ***by airmail*** per via aerea
'**air•plane** aeroplano *m*
'**air•pock•et** vuoto *m* d'aria
'**air pol•lu•tion** inquinamento *m* atmosferico
'**air•port** aeroporto *m*
'**air•sick**: ***get airsick*** soffrire il mal d'aereo *o* l'aereo
'**air•space** spazio *m* aereo
'**air ter•mi•nal** terminale *m*
'**air•tight** *adj container* ermetico
'**air traf•fic** traffico *m* aereo
'**air-traf•fic con•trol** controllo *m* del traffico aereo
air-traf•fic con'trol•ler controllore *m* di volo
air•y ['eərɪ] *adj room* arieggiato; *attitude* noncurante
aisle [aɪl] corridoio *m*; *in supermarket* corsia *f*; *in church* navata *f* laterale
'**aisle seat** posto *m* corridoio
a•jar [ə'dʒɑː(r)] *adj*: ***be ajar*** essere socchiuso
a•lac•ri•ty [ə'lækrətɪ] alacrità *f*
a•larm [ə'lɑːm] **1** *n* allarme *m*; ***raise the alarm*** dare l'allarme **2** *v/t* allarmare
a'larm clock sveglia *f*
a•larm•ing [ə'lɑːmɪŋ] *adj* allarmante
a•larm•ing•ly [ə'lɑːmɪŋlɪ] *adv* in modo allarmante
al•bum ['ælbəm] *for photographs*, (*record*) album *m inv*
al•co•hol ['ælkəhɒl] alcol *m*; ***alcohol-free*** analcolico
al•co•hol•ic [ælkə'hɒlɪk] **1** *n* alcolizzato *m*, -a *f* **2** *adj* alcolico
a•lert [ə'lɜːt] **1** *n* (*signal*) allarme *m*; ***be on the alert*** stare all'erta; *of troops, police* essere in stato di allerta **2** *v/t* mettere in guardia **3** *adj* all'erta *inv*
A-lev•el ['eɪlevl] *diploma f di scuola media superiore in Gran Bretagna che permettere di accedere all'università*
al•ge•bra ['ældʒɪbrə] algebra *f*
al•i•bi ['ælɪbaɪ] alibi *m inv*
a•li•en ['eɪlɪən] **1** *n* (*foreigner*) straniero *m*, -a *f*; *from space* alieno *m*, -a *f* **2** *adj* estraneo; ***be alien to s.o.*** essere estraneo a qu
a•li•en•ate ['eɪlɪəneɪt] *v/t* alienarsi
a•light [ə'laɪt] *adj*: ***be alight*** essere in fiamme; ***set sth alight*** dare fuoco a qc
a•lign [ə'laɪn] *v/t* allineare
a•like [ə'laɪk] **1** *adj* simile; ***be alike*** assomigliarsi **2** *adv*: ***it appeals to old and young alike*** attira vecchi e giovani allo stesso tempo
al•i•mo•ny ['ælɪmənɪ] alimenti *mpl*
a•live [ə'laɪv] *adj*: ***be alive*** essere vivo; ***alive and kicking*** vivo e vegeto
all [ɔːl] **1** *adj* tutto; (*any whatever*) qualsiasi; ***all day / month*** tutto il giorno / mese; ***beyond all doubt*** al di là di qualsiasi dubbio **2** *pron* tutto; ***all of us / them*** tutti noi / loro; ***he ate all of it*** lo ha mangiato tutto; ***that's all, thanks*** è tutto, grazie; ***for all I care*** per quello che me ne importa; ***for all I know*** per quel che ne so; ***all at once*** tutto in una volta; (*suddenly*) tutt'a un tratto; ***all but*** (*nearly*) quasi; ***all but John agreed*** (*except*) erano tutti d'accordo tranne John; ***all the better*** molto meglio; ***all the time*** tutto il tempo; ***they're not at all alike*** non si assomigliano affatto; ***not at all!*** niente affatto!; ***two all*** SP due pari; ***all right*** → ***alright***
al•lay [ə'leɪ] *v/t* attenuare
al•le•ga•tion [ælɪ'geɪʃn] accusa *f*
al•lege [ə'ledʒ] *v/t* dichiarare
al•leged [ə'ledʒd] *adj* presunto
al•leg•ed•ly [ə'ledʒɪdlɪ] *adv* a quanto si suppone
al•le•giance [ə'liːdʒəns] fedeltà *f*
al•ler•gic [ə'lɜːdʒɪk] *adj* allergico; ***be al-***

lergic to essere allergico a
al•ler•gy ['ælədʒɪ] allergia *f*
al•le•vi•ate [ə'li:vɪeɪt] *v/t* alleviare
al•ley ['ælɪ] vicolo *m*
al•li•ance [ə'laɪəns] alleanza *f*
al•lied ['ælaɪd] MIL alleato
al•lo•cate ['æləkeɪt] *v/t* assegnare
al•lo•ca•tion [ælə'keɪʃn] assegnazione *f*; (*amount*) parte *f*
al•lot [ə'lɒt] *v/t* (*pret & pp* ***-ted***) assegnare
al•lot•ment [ə'lɒtmənt] *Br* lotto *m* da coltivare
al•low [ə'laʊ] *v/t* (*permit*) permettere; (*calculate for*) calcolare; ***be allowed*** essere autorizzato; ***it's not allowed*** è vietato; ***passengers are not allowed to smoke*** è vietato ai passeggeri fumare; ***dogs not allowed*** vietato l'ingresso ai cani; ***allow s.o. to ...*** permettere a qu di ...
◆ **allow for** *v/t* tenere conto di
al•low•ance [ə'laʊəns] (*money*) sussidio *m*; (*pocket money*) paghetta *f*; ***make allowances for sth*** tenere conto di qc; ***make allowances for s.o.*** essere indulgente con qu
al•loy ['ælɔɪ] lega *m*
'all-pur•pose *adj* multiuso *inv*
'all-round *adj improvement* generale; *person* eclettico
'all-time: ***be at an all-time low*** *of inflation, unemployment* aver raggiunto il minimo storico
◆ **allude to** [ə'lu:d] *v/t* alludere a
al•lur•ing [ə'lu:rɪŋ] *adj* attraente
al•lu•sion [ə'lu:ʒn] allusione *f*
al•ly ['ælaɪ] *n* alleato *m*, -a *f*
Al•might•y [ɔ:l'maɪtɪ]: ***the Almighty*** l'Onnipotente
al•mond ['ɑ:mənd] mandorla *f*
al•most ['ɔ:lməʊst] *adv* quasi
a•lone [ə'ləʊn] *adj* solo
a•long [ə'lɒŋ] **1** *prep* lungo; ***walk along the street*** camminare lungo la strada **2** *adv*: ***along with*** insieme con; ***all along*** (*all the time*) per tutto il tempo; ***we're going, would you like to come along?*** noi andiamo, vuoi venire con noi?
a•long•side [əlɒŋ'saɪd] *prep* di fianco a; *person* al fianco di; ***draw up alongside*** accostare; ***draw up alongside s.o.*** accostare vicino a qu; ***alongside him*** al suo fianco
a•loof [ə'lu:f] *adj* in disparte
a•loud [ə'laʊd] *adv* ad alta voce; *laugh, call* forte
al•pha•bet ['ælfəbet] alfabeto *m*
al•pha•bet•i•cal [ælfə'betɪkl] *adj* alfabetico
al•pine ['ælpaɪn] *adj* alpino
Alps [ælps] *npl* Alpi *fpl*
al•read•y [ɔ:l'redɪ] *adv* già
al•right [ɔ:l'raɪt] *adj*: ***it's alright*** va bene; ***are you alright?*** (*not hurt*) stai bene?; ***I'm alright*** (*not hurt*) sto bene; (*have got enough*) va bene così; ***is the monitor alright?*** (*in working order*) funziona il monitor?; ***is it alright with you if I ...?*** ti va bene se ...?; ***alright, you can have one!*** va bene, puoi averne uno!; ***alright, I heard you!*** sì, ti ho sentito!; ***everything is alright now between them*** adesso va tutto bene tra di loro; ***that's alright*** (*don't mention it*) non c'è di che; (*I don't mind*) non fa niente; ***alright, that's enough!*** basta così!
Al•sa•tian [æl'seɪʃn] *Br* pastore *m* tedesco
al•so ['ɔ:lsəʊ] *adv* anche
al•tar ['ɒltə(r)] REL altare *m*
al•ter ['ɒltə(r)] *v/t* modificare; *clothes* aggiustare
al•ter•a•tion [ɒltə'reɪʃn] modifica *f*
al•ter•nate ['ɒltəneɪt] **1** *v/i* alternare **2** *adj* ['ɒltənət] alternato; ***on alternate days*** a giorni alterni; ***on alternate Mondays*** un lunedì su due
al•ter•nat•ing 'cur•rent [ɒltəneɪtɪŋ] corrente *f* alternata
al•ter•na•tive [ɒl'tɜ:nətɪv] **1** *n* alternativa *f* **2** *adj* alternativo
al•ter•na•tive•ly [ɒl'tɜ:nətɪvlɪ] *adv* alternativamente
al•though [ɔ:l'ðəʊ] *conj* benché, sebbene
al•ti•tude ['æltɪtju:d] altitudine *f*
al•to•geth•er [ɔ:ltə'geðə(r)] *adv* (*completely*) completamente; (*in all*) complessivamente
al•tru•ism ['æltru:ɪzm] altruismo *m*
al•tru•is•tic [æltru:'ɪstɪk] *adj* altruistico
a•lu•min•i•um [æljʊ'mɪnɪəm], *Am* **a•lu•mi•num** [ə'lu:mɪnəm] alluminio *m*
al•ways ['ɔ:lweɪz] *adv* sempre
a. m. [eɪ'em] *abbr* (= ***ante meridiem***) di mattina
a•mal•gam•ate [ə'mælgəmeɪt] *v/i of companies* fondersi
a•mass [ə'mæs] *v/t* accumulare
am•a•teur ['æmətə(r)] *n* (*unskilled*) dilettante *m/f*; SP non professionista *m/f*
am•a•teur•ish ['æmətərɪʃ] *adj pej* dilettantesco
a•maze [ə'meɪz] *v/t* stupire
a•mazed [ə'meɪzd] *adj* stupito
a•maze•ment [ə'meɪzmənt] stupore *m*
a•maz•ing [ə'meɪzɪŋ] *adj* (*surprising*) sorprendente; F (*very good*) incredibile
a•maz•ing•ly [ə'meɪzɪŋlɪ] *adv* incredibilmente

am•bas•sa•dor [æm'bæsədə(r)] ambasciatore *m*, -trice *f*
am•ber ['æmbə(r)] *n* ambra *f*; ***at amber*** giallo
am•bi•dex•trous [æmbɪ'dekstrəs] *adj* ambidestro
am•bi•ence ['æmbɪəns] atmosfera *f*
am•bi•gu•i•ty [æmbɪ'gjuːətɪ] ambiguità *f*
am•big•u•ous [æm'bɪgjʊəs] *adj* ambiguo
am•bi•tion [æm'bɪʃn] ambizione *f*
am•bi•tious [æm'bɪʃəs] *adj* ambizioso
am•biv•a•lent [æm'bɪvələnt] *adj* ambiguo
am•ble ['æmbl] *v/i* camminare con calma; ***we were ambling along the riverbank*** stavamo passeggiando lungo il fiume
am•bu•lance ['æmbjʊləns] ambulanza *f*
am•bush ['æmbʊʃ] **1** *n* agguato *m* **2** *v/t* tendere un agguato a; ***be ambushed by*** subire un agguato da parte di
a•mend [ə'mend] *v/t* emendare
a•mend•ment [ə'mendmənt] emendamento *m*
a•mends [ə'mendz]: ***make amends*** fare ammenda
a•men•i•ties [ə'miːnətɪz] *npl* comodità *fpl*
A•mer•i•ca [ə'merɪkə] America *f*
A•mer•i•can [ə'merɪkən] **1** *n* americano *m*, -a *f* **2** *adj* americano
a•mi•a•ble ['eɪmɪəbl] *adj* amichevole
a•mi•ca•ble ['æmɪkəbl] *adj* amichevole
a•mi•ca•bly ['æmɪkəblɪ] *adv* amichevolmente
am•mu•ni•tion [æmjʊ'nɪʃn] munizioni *fpl*; *fig* arma *f*
am•ne•sia [æm'niːzɪə] amnesia *f*
am•nes•ty ['æmnəstɪ] amnistia *f*
a•mong(st) [ə'mʌŋ(st)] *prep* tra
a•mor•al [eɪ'mɒrəl] *adj* amorale
a•mount [ə'maʊnt] quantità *f inv*; (*sum of money*) importo *m*
◆ **amount to** *v/t of income, sum* ammontare a; (*be equal to*) equivalere a
am•phib•i•an [æm'fɪbɪən] anfibio *m*
am•phib•i•ous [æm'fɪbɪəs] *adj animal* anfibio; *vehicle* anfibio
am•phi•the•a•ter *Am*, **am•phi•the•a•tre** ['æmfɪθɪətə(r)] anfiteatro *m*
am•ple ['æmpl] *adj* abbondante; (*more than enough*) in abbondanza
am•pli•fi•er ['æmplɪfaɪə(r)] amplificatore *m*
am•pli•fy ['æmplɪfaɪ] *v/t* (*pret & pp* ***-ied***) *sound* amplificare
am•pu•tate ['æmpjʊteɪt] *v/t* amputare
am•pu•ta•tion [æmpjʊ'teɪʃn] amputazione *f*
a•muse [ə'mjuːz] *v/t* (*make laugh etc*) divertire; (*entertain*) intrattenere
a•muse•ment [ə'mjuːzmənt] (*merriment*) divertimento *m*; (*entertainment*) intrattenimento *m*; ***amusements*** (*games*) divertimenti *mpl*; ***to our great amusement*** con nostro grande divertimento
a'muse•ment ar•cade sala *f* giochi
a'muse•ment park parco *m* giochi
a•mus•ing [ə'mjuːzɪŋ] *adj* divertente
an [æn] → ***a***
an•a•bol•ic 'ster•oid [ænəbɒlɪk] anabolizzante *m*
an•ae•mi•a [ə'niːmɪə] anemia *f*
an•aem•ic [ə'niːmɪk] *adj* anemico
an•aes•thet•ic [ænəs'θetɪk] *n* anestetico *m*
an•aes•the•tist [ə'niːsθətɪst] anestesista *m/f*
an•a•log ['ænəlɒg] *adj* COMPUT analogico
a•nal•o•gy [ə'nælədʒɪ] analogia *f*
an•a•lyse ['ænəlaɪz] *v/t* analizzare; (*psychoanalyse*) psicanalizzare
an•a•lysis [ə'næləsɪs] (*pl* ***analyses*** [ə'næləsiːz]) analisi *f inv*
an•a•lyst ['ænəlɪst] *also* PSYCH analista *m/f*
an•a•lyt•i•cal [ænə'lɪtɪkl] *adj* analitico
an•a•lyze *Am* → ***analyse***
an•arch•y ['ænəkɪ] anarchia *f*
a•nat•o•my [ə'nætəmɪ] anatomia *f*
an•ces•tor ['ænsestə(r)] antenato *m*, -a *f*
an•chor ['æŋkə(r)] **1** *n* NAUT ancora *f* **2** *v/i* NAUT gettare l'ancora
'an•chor•man TV presentatore *m*, anchorman *m inv*
an•cient ['eɪnʃənt] *adj* antico
an•cil•lar•y [æn'sɪlərɪ] *adj staff* ausiliario
and [ənd] *stressed* [ænd] *conj* e; ***5 and 5 makes 10*** 5 più 5 fa 10; ***three hundred and sixty*** trecentosessanta; ***worse and worse*** sempre peggio; ***I'll come and pick you up*** vengo a prenderti
an•ec•dote ['ænɪkdəʊt] aneddoto *m*
a•ne•mi•a *etc Am* → ***anaemia*** *etc*
an•es•thet•ic *etc Am* → ***anaesthetic*** *etc*
an•gel ['eɪndʒl] REL, *fig* angelo *m*
an•ger ['æŋgə(r)] **1** *n* rabbia *f* **2** *v/t* fare arrabbiare
an•gi•na [æn'dʒaɪnə] angina *f* (pectoris)
an•gle ['æŋgl] *n* angolo *m*; (*position, fig*) angolazione *f*
an•gler ['æŋglə(r)] pescatore *m*, -trice *f* (con amo e lenza)
An•gli•can ['æŋglɪkən] REL **1** *adj* anglicano **2** *n* anglicano *m*, -a *f*
An•glo-Sax•on [æŋgləʊ'sæksn] **1** *adj* anglosassone **2** *n person* anglosassone *m/f*
an•gry ['æŋgrɪ] *adj* arrabbiato; ***be angry with s.o.*** essere arrabbiato con qu
an•guish ['æŋgwɪʃ] angoscia *f*

an•gu•lar ['æŋgjʊlə(r)] *adj face, shape* spigoloso
an•i•mal ['ænɪml] animale *m*
an•i•mated ['ænɪmeɪtɪd] *adj* animato
an•i•ma•ted car'toon cartone *m* animato
an•i•ma•tion [ænɪ'meɪʃn] animazione *f*
an•i•mos•i•ty [ænɪ'mɒsətɪ] animosità *f*
an•kle ['æŋkl] caviglia *f*
an•nex [ə'neks] *v/t state* annettere
an•nexe ['æneks] *n* (*building*) edificio *m* annesso; *to document* annesso *m*
an•ni•hi•late [ə'naɪəleɪt] *v/t* annientare
an•ni•hi•la•tion [ənaɪə'leɪʃn] annientamento *m*
an•ni•ver•sa•ry [ænɪ'vɜːsərɪ] (*wedding anniversary*) anniversario *m*
an•no•tate ['ænəteɪt] *v/t report* annotare
an•nounce [ə'naʊns] *v/t* annunciare
an•nounce•ment [ə'naʊnsmənt] annuncio *m*
an•nounc•er [ə'naʊnsə(r)] TV, *Radio* annunciatore *m*, -trice *f*
an•noy [ə'nɔɪ] *v/t* infastidire; ***be annoyed*** essere infastidito
an•noy•ance [ə'nɔɪəns] (*anger*) irritazione *f*; (*nuisance*) fastidio *m*
an•noy•ing [ə'nɔɪɪŋ] *adj* irritante
an•nu•al ['ænjʊəl] *adj* annuale
an•nu•al gen•er•al 'meet•ing assemblea *f* annuale
an•nu•i•ty [ə'njuːətɪ] rendita *f* annuale
an•nul [ə'nʌl] *v/t* (*pret & pp* ***-led***) *marriage* annullare
an•nul•ment [ə'nʌlmənt] annullamento *m*
a•non•y•mous [ə'nɒnɪməs] *adj* anonimo
an•o•rak ['ænəræk] *Br* giacca *f* a vento
an•o•rex•i•a [ænə'reksɪə] anoressia *f*
an•o•rex•ic [ænə'reksɪk] *adj* anoressico
an•oth•er [ə'nʌðə(r)] **1** *adj* un altro *m*, un'altra *f* **2** *pron* un altro *m*, un'altra *f*; ***one another*** l'un l'altro; ***do they know one another?*** si conoscono?
ans•wer ['ɑːnsə(r)] **1** *n to letter, person, problem* risposta *f* **2** *v/t letter, person* rispondere a; ***answer the door*** aprire la porta; ***answer the telephone*** rispondere al telefono
◆ **answer back 1** *v/t person* ribattere a **2** *v/i* ribattere
◆ **answer for** *v/t* rispondere di
an•swer•ing ma•chine ['ɑːnsərɪŋ] TELEC segreteria *f* telefonica
ans•wer•phone ['ɑːnsəfəʊn] segreteria *f* telefonica
ant [ænt] formica *f*
an•tag•o•nis•m [æn'tægənɪzm] antagonismo *m*
an•tag•o•nis•tic [æntægə'nɪstɪk] *adj* ostile
an•tag•o•nize [æn'tægənaɪz] *v/t* contrariare
Ant•arc•tic [ænt'ɑːktɪk] *n* Antartico *m*
an•te•lope ['æntɪləʊp] antilope *f*
an•te•na•tal [æntɪ'neɪtl] *adj* durante la gravidanza; ***antenatal classes*** corso *m* di preparazione al parto; ***antenatal clinic*** clinica *f* per gestanti
an•ten•na [æn'tenə] antenna *f*
an•thol•o•gy [æn'θɒlədʒɪ] antologia *f*
an•thro•pol•o•gy [ænθrə'pɒlədʒɪ] antropologia *f*
an•ti•bi•ot•ic [æntɪbaɪ'ɒtɪk] *n* antibiotico *m*
an•ti•bod•y ['æntɪbɒdɪ] anticorpo *m*
an•tic•i•pate [æn'tɪsɪpeɪt] *v/t* prevedere
an•tic•i•pa•tion [æntɪsɪ'peɪʃn] previsione *f*
an•ti•clock•wise ['æntɪklɒkwaɪz] *Br* **1** *adj* antiorario **2** *adv* in senso antiorario
an•tics ['æntɪks] *npl* buffonate *fpl*
an•ti•dote ['æntɪdəʊt] antidoto *m*
an•ti•freeze ['æntɪfriːz] antigelo *m inv*
an•tip•a•thy [æn'tɪpəθɪ] antipatia *f*
an•ti•quat•ed ['æntɪkweɪtɪd] *adj* antiquato
an•tique [æn'tiːk] *n* pezzo *m* d'antiquariato
an'tique dealer antiquario *m*, -a *f*
an•tiq•ui•ty [æn'tɪkwətɪ] antichità *f inv*
an•ti•sep•tic [æntɪ'septɪk] **1** *adj* antisettico **2** *n* antisettico *m*
an•ti•so•cial [æntɪ'səʊʃl] *adj* asociale
an•ti•vi•rus pro•gram [æntɪ'vaɪrəs] COMPUT programma *m* antivirus
anx•i•e•ty [æŋ'zaɪətɪ] ansia *f*
anx•ious ['æŋkʃəs] *adj* ansioso; ***be anxious for ...*** *for news etc* essere ansioso di avere ...
an•y ['enɪ] **1** *adj* qualche; ***are there any diskettes / glasses?*** ci sono dei dischetti / bicchieri?; ***is there any bread?*** c'è del pane?; ***is there any improvement?*** c'è qualche miglioramento?; ***there aren't any diskettes / glasses*** non ci sono dischetti / bicchieri; ***there isn't any bread*** non c'è pane; ***there isn't any improvement*** non c'è nessun miglioramento; ***have you any idea at all?*** hai qualche idea?; ***take any one you like*** prendi quello che vuoi **2** *pron*: ***do you have any?*** ne hai?; ***there aren't any left*** non ce ne sono più; ***there isn't any left*** non ce n'è più; ***any of them could be guilty*** chiunque di loro potrebbe essere colpevole **3** *adv* un po'; ***is that any better / easier?*** è un po' meglio / più facile?; ***I don't like it any more*** non mi piace più

an•y•bod•y ['enɪbɒdɪ] *pron* qualcuno; *with negative* nessuno; (*whoever*) chiunque; ***is there anybody there?*** c'è qualcuno?; ***there wasn't anybody there*** non c'era nessuno; ***anybody could do it*** lo potrebbe fare chiunque

an•y•how ['enɪhaʊ] comunque; ***if I can help you anyhow, let me know*** se ti posso aiutare in qualsiasi modo, fammi sapere

an•y•one ['enɪwʌn] → ***anybody***

an•y•thing ['enɪθɪŋ] *pron* qualcosa; *with negatives* niente, nulla; ***I didn't hear anything*** non ho sentito niente *o* nulla; ***anything but*** per niente; ***she was anything but helpful*** non è stata per niente d'aiuto; ***anything else?*** qualcos'altro?

an•y•way ['enɪweɪ] → ***anyhow***

an•y•where ['enɪweə(r)] *adv* da qualche parte; *with negative* da nessuna parte; (*wherever*) dovunque; ***I can't find it anywhere*** non riesco a trovarlo da nessuna parte

a•part [ə'pɑːt] *adv in distance* distante; ***the two cities are 250 miles apart*** le due città distano 250 miglia l'una dall'altra; ***live apart*** *of people* vivere separati; ***apart from*** (*excepting*) a parte, tranne; (*in addition to*) oltre a

a•part•ment [ə'pɑːtmənt] appartamento *m*

a'part•ment block *Am* palazzo *m* (d'appartamenti)

ap•a•thet•ic [æpə'θetɪk] *adj* apatico

ap•a•thy ['æpəθɪ] apatia *f*

ape [eɪp] scimmia *f*

a•pe•ri•tif [ə'perɪtiːf] aperitivo *m*

ap•er•ture ['æpətʃə(r)] PHOT apertura *f*

a•piece [ə'piːs] *adv* l'uno *m*, l'una *f*; ***you can have one apiece*** potete averne uno a testa

a•pol•o•get•ic [əpɒlə'dʒetɪk] *adj letter, smile* di scuse; ***he was very apologetic for being late*** si è scusato molto di essere in ritardo

a•pol•o•gize [ə'pɒlədʒaɪz] *v/i* scusarsi; ***apologize to s.o.*** scusarsi con qu

a•pol•o•gy [ə'pɒlədʒɪ] scusa *f*; ***make an apology to s.o.*** fare le proprie scuse a qu

a•pos•tle [ə'pɒsl] REL apostolo *m*

a•pos•tro•phe [ə'pɒstrəfɪ] GRAM apostrofo *m*

ap•pal [ə'pɔːl] *v/t* sconvolgere

ap•pal•ling [ə'pɔːlɪŋ] *adj* sconvolgente; *language* scioccante

ap•pa•ra•tus [æpə'reɪtəs] apparecchio *m*

ap•par•ent [ə'pærənt] *adj* evidente; (*seeming real*) apparente; ***become apparent that …*** diventare evidente che …

ap•par•ent•ly [ə'pærəntlɪ] *adv* apparentemente

ap•pa•ri•tion [æpə'rɪʃn] (*ghost*) apparizione

ap•peal [ə'piːl] **1** *n* (*charm*) attrattiva *f*; *for funds etc*, LAW appello *m* **2** *v/i* LAW fare appello

◆ **appeal to** (*be attractive to*) attirare

◆ **appeal for** *v/t blood, help* fare un appello per ottenere; ***the President appealed for calm*** il Presidente ha fatto appello alla calma

ap•peal•ing [ə'piːlɪŋ] *adj idea, offer* allettante; *glance* supplichevole

ap•pear [ə'pɪə(r)] *v/i* apparire, comparire; *in film etc* apparire; *of new product* comparire; *in court* comparire; (*look, seem*) apparire; ***it appears that …*** sembra che …

ap•pear•ance [ə'pɪərəns)] (*arrival*) apparizione *f*, comparsa *f*; *in film etc* apparizione *f*; *in court* comparizione *f*; (*look*) aspetto *m*; ***put in an appearance*** fare un salto; ***judge by appearances*** giudicare dalle apparenze

ap•pease [ə'piːz] *v/t gods, anger* placare; *tyrant* compiacere

ap•pen•di•ci•tis [əpendɪ'saɪtɪs] appendicite *f*

ap•pen•dix [ə'pendɪks] MED, *of book etc* appendice *f*

ap•pe•tite ['æpɪtaɪt] appetito *m*; ***appetite for sth*** *fig* sete *f* di qc

ap•pe•tiz•er ['æpɪtaɪzə(r)] *food* stuzzichino *m*; *drink* aperitivo *m*

ap•pe•tiz•ing ['æpɪtaɪzɪŋ] *adj* appetitoso

ap•plaud [ə'plɔːd] **1** *v/i* applaudire **2** *v/t also fig* applaudire

ap•plause [ə'plɔːz] applauso *m*; (*praise*) approvazione *f*

ap•ple ['æpl] mela *f*

ap•ple 'pie torta *f* di mele

ap•ple 'sauce composta *f* di mele

appliance [ə'plaɪəns] apparecchio *m*; *household* elettrodomestico *m*

ap•plic•a•ble [ə'plɪkəbl] *adj* applicabile

ap•pli•cant ['æplɪkənt] candidato *m*, -a *f*

ap•pli•ca•tion [æplɪ'keɪʃn] *for job etc* candidatura *f*; *for passport, visa* domanda *f*, richiesta *f*; *for university* domanda *f* di iscrizione

ap•pli'ca•tion form modulo *m* di richiesta; *for passport, visa* modulo *f* di richiesta; *for university* modulo *f* di richiesta di iscrizione

ap•ply [ə'plaɪ] (*pret & pp* **-ied**) **1** *v/t* applicare **2** *v/i of rule, law* applicarsi

◆ **apply for** *v/t job, passport* fare domanda per; *university* fare domanda di iscri-

zione a
◆ **apply to** *v/t* (*contact*) rivolgersi a; (*affect*) applicarsi a
ap•point [ə'pɔɪnt] *v/t to position* nominare
ap•point•ment [ə'pɔɪntmənt] *to position* nomina *f*; (*meeting*) appuntamento *m*
ap'point•ments di•a•ry agenda *f* degli appuntamenti
ap•prais•al [ə'preɪz(ə)l] valutazione *f*
ap•pre•cia•ble [ə'priːʃəbl] *adj* notevole
ap•pre•ci•ate [ə'priːʃɪeɪt] **1** *v/t* apprezzare; (*acknowledge*) rendersi conto di; ***thanks, I appreciate it*** grazie, te ne sono grato; ***I appreciate that …*** mi rendo conto che … **2** *v/i* FIN rivalutarsi
ap•pre•ci•a•tion [əpriːʃɪ'eɪʃn] *of kindness etc* riconoscenza *f*; *of music etc* apprezzamento *m*
ap•pre•ci•a•tive [ə'priːʃətɪv] *adj* (*showing gratitude*) riconoscente; (*showing pleasure*) soddisfatto
ap•pre•hen•sion [æprɪ'henʃn] apprensione *f*
ap•pre•hen•sive [æprɪ'hensɪv] *adj* apprensivo
ap•pren•tice [ə'prentɪs] apprendista *m/f*
ap•pren•tice•ship [ə'prentɪsʃɪp] apprendistato *m*
ap•proach [ə'prəʊʧ] **1** *n* avvicinamento *m*; (*proposal*) contatto *m*; *to problem* approccio *m* **2** *v/t* (*get near to*) avvicinarsi a; (*contact*) contattare; *problem* abbordare
ap•proach•a•ble [ə'preʊʧəbl] *adj person* abbordabile
ap•pro•pri•ate[1] [ə'prəʊprɪət] *adj* appropriato
ap•pro•pri•ate[2] [ə'prəʊprɪeɪt] *v/t also euph* appropriarsi di
ap•prov•al [ə'pruːvl] approvazione *f*
ap•prove [ə'pruːv] *v/t & v/i* approvare
◆ **approve of** *v/t* approvare
ap•prox•i•mate [ə'prɒksɪmət] *adj* approssimativo
ap•prox•i•mate•ly [ə'prɒksɪmətlɪ] *adv* approssimativamente
ap•prox•i•ma•tion [əprɒksɪ'meɪʃn] approssimazione *f*
APR [eɪpiː'ɑː] *abbr* (= ***annual percentage rate***) tasso *m* di interesse annuale
a•pri•cot ['eɪprɪkɒt] albicocca *f*
A•pril ['eɪprəl] aprile *m*
a•pron ['eɪprən] grembiule *m*
apt [æpt] *adj pupil* portato; *remark* appropriato; ***be apt to …*** avere tendenza a …
ap•ti•tude ['æptɪtjuːd] attitudine *f*
'ap•ti•tude test test *m inv* attitudinale
aq•ua•lung ['ækwəlʌŋ] autorespiratore *m*
a•quar•i•um [ə'kweərɪəm] acquario *m*
A•quar•i•us [ə'kweərɪəs] ASTR Acquario *m*
a•quat•ic [ə'kwætɪk] *adj* acquatico
Ar•ab ['ærəb] **1** *n* arabo *m*, -a *f* **2** *adj* arabo
Ar•a•bic ['ærəbɪk] **1** *n* arabo *m* **2** *adj* arabo
ar•a•ble ['ærəbl] *adj* coltivabile
ar•bi•tra•ry ['ɑːbɪtrərɪ] *adj* arbitrario
ar•bi•trate ['ɑːbɪtreɪt] *v/i* arbitrare
ar•bi•tra•tion [ɑːbɪ'treɪʃn] arbitrato *m*
ar•bi•tra•tor ['ɑːbɪ'treɪtə(r)] arbitro *m*
ar•cade [ɑː'keɪd] (*games arcade*) sala *f* giochi
arch [ɑːʧ] *n* arco *m*
ar•chae•o•log•i•cal [ɑːkɪə'lɒdʒɪkl] *adj* archeologico
ar•chae•ol•o•gist [ɑːkɪ'ɒlədʒɪst] archeologo *m*, -a *f*
ar•chae•ol•o•gy [ɑːkɪ'ɒlədʒɪ] archeologia *f*
ar•cha•ic [ɑː'keɪɪk] *adj* arcaico
arch•bish•op [ɑːʧ'bɪʃəp] arcivescovo *m*
ar•che•ol•o•gy *etc Am* → ***archaeology*** *etc*
ar•cher [ɑːʧə(r)] arciere *m*, -a *f*
ar•chi•tec•t ['ɑːkɪtekt] architetto *m*
ar•chi•tec•tur•al [ɑːkɪ'tekʧərəl] *adj* architettonico
ar•chi•tec•ture ['ɑːkɪtekʧə(r)] architettura *f*
ar•chives ['ɑːkaɪvz] *npl* archivi *mpl*
arch•way ['ɑːʧweɪ] arco *m*
Arc•tic ['ɑːktɪk] *n* Artico *m*
ar•dent ['ɑːdənt] *adj* ardente
ar•du•ous ['ɑːdjʊəs] *adj* arduo
ar•e•a ['eərɪə] area *f*; (*region*) zona *f*
'ar•e•a code *Am* TELEC prefisso *m* telefonico; *official name* indicativo *m* distrettuale
a•re•na [ə'riːnə] SP arena *f*
Ar•gen•ti•na [ɑːdʒən'tiːnə] Argentina *f*
Ar•gen•tin•i•an [ɑːdʒən'tɪnɪən] **1** *adj* argentino **2** *n* argentino *m*, -a *f*
ar•gu•a•bly ['ɑːgjʊəblɪ] *adv* probabilmente; ***he's arguably the best*** si può dire che è il migliore
ar•gue ['ɑːgjuː] **1** *v/i* (*quarrel*) litigare; (*reason*) sostenere **2** *v/t*: ***argue that …*** sostenere che …
ar•gu•ment ['ɑːgjʊmənt] (*quarrel*) litigio *m*; (*reasoning*) argomento *m*
ar•gu•ment•a•tive [ɑːgjʊ'mentətɪv] *adj* polemico
a•ri•a ['ɑːrɪə] MUS aria *f*
ar•id ['ærɪd] *adj land* arido
Ar•i•es ['eəriːz] ASTR Ariete *m*
a•rise [ə'raɪz] *v/i* (*pret* ***arose***, *pp* ***arisen***) *of situation*, *problem* emergere
a•ris•en [ə'rɪzn] *pp* → ***arise***
ar•is•toc•ra•cy [ærɪ'stɒkrəsɪ] aristocrazia

f

ar•is•to•crat ['ærɪstəkræt] aristocratico *m*, -a *f*

a•ris•to•crat•ic [ærɪstə'krætɪk] *adj* aristocratico

a•rith•me•tic [ə'rɪθmətɪk] aritmetica *f*

arm[1] [ɑːm] *n of person* braccio *m*; *of chair* bracciolo *m*

arm[2] [ɑːm] *v/t* armare; ***arm s.o./sth with sth*** armare qu / qc di qc

ar•ma•ments ['ɑːməmənts] *npl* armamenti *mpl*

arm•chair ['ɑːmʧeə(r)] poltrona *f*

armed [ɑːmd] *adj* armato

armed 'forc•es *npl* forze *fpl* armate

armed 'rob•ber•y rapina *f* a mano armata

ar•mor *Am*, **ar•mour** ['ɑːmə(r)] armatura *f*; (*metal plates*) blindatura *f*

ar•mored ve•hi•cle *Am*, **ar•moured ve•hi•cle** [ɑːməd'viːɪkl] veicolo *m* blindato

arm•pit ['ɑːmpɪt] ascella *f*

arms [ɑːmz] *npl* (*weapons*) armi *fpl*

ar•my ['ɑːmɪ] esercito *m*

a•ro•ma [ə'rəʊmə] aroma *m*

a•rose [ə'rəʊz] *pret* → ***arise***

a•round [ə'raʊnd] **1** *prep* (*in circle, roughly*) intorno a; *room, world* attraverso; ***it's around the corner*** è dietro l'angolo **2** *adv* (*in the area*) qui intorno; (*encircling*) intorno; ***he lives around here*** abita da queste parti; ***walk around*** andare in giro; ***she has been around*** (*has travelled, is experienced*) ha girato; ***he's still around*** F (*alive*) è ancora in circolazione

a•rouse [ə'raʊz] *v/t* suscitare; (*sexually*) eccitare

ar•range [ə'reɪndʒ] *v/t* (*put in order*) sistemare; *music* arrangiare; *meeting, party etc* organizzare; *time and place* combinare; ***I've arranged to meet her*** ho combinato di incontrarla

◆ **arrange for** *v/t* provvedere a; ***I've arranged for him to meet us*** ho provveduto affinché ci incontrasse

ar•range•ment [ə'reɪndʒmənt] (*agreement*) accordo *m*; *of party, meeting* organizzazione *f*; (*layout: of furniture etc*) disposizione *f*; *of music* arrangiamento *m*; ***arrangements*** *for party, meeting* preparativi *mpl*; ***make arrangements*** prendere disposizioni

ar•rears [ə'rɪəz] *npl* arretrati *mpl*; ***be in arrears*** *of person* essere in arretrato; ***be paid in arrears*** *for job* essere pagato a lavoro effettuato

ar•rest [ə'rest] **1** *n* arresto *m*; ***be under arrest*** essere in arresto **2** *v/t* arrestare

ar•riv•al [ə'raɪvl] arrivo *m*; ***arrivals*** *at airport* arrivi *mpl*

ar•rive [ə'raɪv] *v/i* arrivare

◆ **arrive at** *v/t place, decision* arrivare a

ar•ro•gance ['ærəgəns] arroganza *f*

ar•ro•gant ['ærəgənt] *adj* arrogante

ar•ro•gant•ly ['ærəgəntlɪ] *adv* con arroganza

ar•row ['ærəʊ] freccia *f*

arse [ɑːs] V culo *m* V

ar•se•nic ['ɑːsənɪk] arsenico *m*

ar•son ['ɑːsn] incendio *m* doloso

ar•son•ist ['ɑːsənɪst] piromane *m/f*

art [ɑːt] arte *f*; ***the arts*** l'arte

ar•te•ry ['ɑːtərɪ] MED arteria *f*

'art gal•ler•y galleria *f* d'arte

ar•thri•tis [ɑː'θraɪtɪs] artrite *f*

ar•ti•choke ['ɑːtɪʧəʊk] carciofo *m*

ar•ti•cle ['ɑːtɪkl] articolo *m*

ar•tic•u•late [ɑː'tɪkjʊlət] *adj speech* chiaro; ***be articulate*** *of person* esprimersi bene

ar•tic•u•lat•ed 'lor•ry [ɑːtɪkjʊleɪtɪd] *Br* autoarticolato *m*

ar•ti•fi•cial [ɑːtɪ'fɪʃl] *adj* artificiale; (*not sincere*) finto

ar•ti•fi•cial in'tel•li•gence intelligenza *f* artificiale

ar•til•le•ry [ɑː'tɪlərɪ] artiglieria *f*

ar•ti•san ['ɑːtɪzæn] artigiano *m*, -a *f*

ar•tist ['ɑːtɪst] artista *m/f*

ar•tis•tic [ɑː'tɪstɪk] *adj* artistico

'arts de•gree laurea *f* in discipline umanistiche

as [æz] **1** *conj* (*while, when*) mentre; (*because*) dato che; (*like*) come; ***as he grew older, …*** diventando più vecchio, …; ***as if*** come se; ***as usual*** come al solito; ***as necessary*** in base alla necessità; **2** *adv*: ***as high / pretty as …*** alto / carino come …; ***as much as that?*** così tanto?; ***run as fast as you can*** corri più veloce che puoi **3** *prep* come; ***as a child*** da bambino; ***as a schoolgirl*** quando andava a scuola; ***I'm talking to you as a friend*** ti parlo come amico; ***dressed as a policeman*** vestito da poliziotto; ***work as a teacher / translator*** essere insegnante / traduttore; ***as for*** quanto a; ***as Hamlet*** nel ruolo di Amleto

asap ['eɪzæp] *abbr* (= ***as soon as possible***) quanto prima

as•bes•tos [æz'bestɒs] amianto *m*

As•cen•sion [ə'senʃn] REL Ascensione *f*

as•cent [ə'sent] *path* salita *f*; *of mountain* ascensione *f*; *fig* ascesa *f*

ash [æʃ] cenere *f*; ***ashes*** ceneri *fpl*

a•shamed [ə'ʃeɪmd] *adj*: ***be ashamed of*** vergognarsi di; ***you should be ashamed of yourself*** dovresti vergognarti

a•shore [ə'ʃɔː(r)] *adv* a terra; ***go ashore***

sbarcare
ash•tray ['æʃtreɪ] posacenere *m*, portacenere *m*
Ash 'Wednes•day mercoledì *m inv* delle Ceneri
A•sia ['eɪʃə] Asia *f*
A•sian ['eɪʃən] **1** *n* asiatico *m*, -a *f*; (*Indian*, *Pakistani*) indiano *m*, -a *f* **2** *adj* asiatico; (*Indian*, *Pakistani*) indiano
a•side [ə'saɪd] *adv* da parte; ***take s.o. aside*** prendere a parte qu; ***joking aside*** scherzi a parte; ***aside from*** a parte
ask [ɑːsk] **1** *v/t person* chiedere a; (*invite*) invitare; *question* fare; *favour* chiedere; ***can I ask you something?*** posso chiederti una cosa?; ***ask s.o. about sth*** chiedere a qu di qc; ***ask s.o. for …*** chiedere a qu …; ***ask s.o. to …*** chiedere a qu di … **2** *v/i* chiedere
◆ **ask after** *v/t person* chiedere di
◆ **ask for** *v/t* chiedere; *person* chiedere di
◆ **ask out** *v/t for a drink*, *night out* chiedere di uscire a
ask•ing price ['ɑːskɪŋpraɪs] prezzo *m* di domanda
a•sleep [ə'sliːp]: *adj*: ***he's (fast) asleep*** sta dormendo (profondamente); ***fall asleep*** addormentarsi
as•par•a•gus [ə'spærəgəs] asparagi *mpl*
as•pect ['æspekt] aspetto *m*
as•phalt ['æsfælt] *n* asfalto *m*
as•phyx•i•ate [æ'sfɪksɪeɪt] *v/t* asfissiare
as•phyx•i•a•tion [əsfɪksɪ'eɪʃn] asfissia *f*
as•pi•ra•tion [æspə'reɪʃn] aspirazione *f*
as•pi•rin ['æsprɪn] aspirina *f*
ass [æs] F (*idiot*) cretino *m*, -a; *Am* P (*backside*) culo *m* P
as•sai•lant [ə'seɪlənt] assalitore *m*, -trice *f*
as•sas•sin [ə'sæsɪn] assassino *m*, -a *f*
as•sas•sin•ate [ə'sæsɪneɪt] *v/t* assassinare
as•sas•sin•a•tion [əsæsɪ'neɪʃn] assassinio *m*
as•sault [ə'sɒlt] **1** *n* assalto *m*; LAW aggressione *f* **2** *v/t* aggredire
as•sem•ble [ə'sembl] **1** *v/t parts* assemblare, montare **2** *v/i of people* radunarsi
as•sem•bly [ə'semblɪ] assemblea *f*; *of parts* assemblaggio *m*
as'sem•bly line catena *f* di montaggio
as'sem•bly plant officina *f* di montaggio
as•sent [ə'sent] *v/i* acconsentire
as•sert [ə'sɜːt]: *v/t*: ***assert o.s.*** farsi valere
as•ser•tive [ə'sɜːtɪv] *adj person* sicuro di sé
as•sess [ə'ses] *v/t* valutare
as•sess•ment [ə'sesmənt] valutazione *f*
as•set ['æset] FIN attivo *m*; *fig*: *thing* vantaggio *m*; *person* elemento *m* prezioso
as•sign [ə'saɪn] *v/t*: *person* destinare; *thing* assegnare
as•sign•ment [ə'saɪnmənt] (*task*, *study*) compito *m*
as•sim•i•late [ə'sɪmɪleɪt] *v/t information* assimilare; *person into group* integrare
as•sist [ə'sɪst] *v/t* assistere
as•sist•ance [ə'sɪstəns] assistenza *f*
as•sis•tant [ə'sɪstənt] assistente *m/f*; *in shop* commesso *m*, -a *f*
as•sis•tant di'rec•tor vice-direttore *m*; *of film* aiuto-regista *m/f*
as•sis•tant 'man•ag•er *of business* vice-responsabile *m/f*; *of hotel*, *restaurant* vice-direttore *m*
as•so•ci•ate [ə'səʊʃɪeɪt] **1** *v/t* associare **2** *v/i*: ***associate with*** frequentare **3** *n* [ə'səʊʃɪət] socio *m*, -a *f*
as•so•ci•ate pro'fes•sor professore *m* associato, professoressa *f* associata
as•so•ci•a•tion [əsəʊsɪ'eɪʃn] associazione *f*; ***in association with*** in associazione con
as•sort•ed [ə'sɔːtɪd] *adj* assortito
as•sort•ment [ə'sɔːtmənt] assortimento *m*; ***there was a whole assortment of people*** c'era gente di tutti i tipi
as•sume [ə'sjuːm] *v/t* (*suppose*) supporre
as•sump•tion [ə'sʌmpʃn] supposizione *f*; ***The Assumption*** REL l'Assunzione *f*
as•sur•ance [ə'ʃʊərəns] assicurazione *f*, garanzia *f*; (*confidence*) sicurezza *f*; ***he gave me his personal assurance that …*** mi ha assicurato personalmente che …
as•sure [ə'ʃʊə(r)] *v/t* (*reassure*): ***assure s.o. of sth*** assicurare qc a qu
as•sured [ə'ʃʊəd] *adj* (*confident*) sicuro
as•ter•isk ['æstərɪsk] asterisco *m*
asth•ma ['æsmə] asma *f*
asth•mat•ic [æs'mætɪk] *adj* asmatico
as•ton•ish [ə'stɒnɪʃ] *v/t* sbalordire; ***be astonished*** essere sbalordito
as•ton•ish•ing [ə'stɒnɪʃɪŋ] *adj* sbalorditivo
as•ton•ish•ing•ly [ə'stɒnɪʃɪŋlɪ] *adv* in modo sbalorditivo
as•ton•ish•ment [ə'stɒnɪʃmənt] stupore *m*
as•tound [ə'staʊnd] *v/t* stupefare
as•tound•ing [ə'staʊndɪŋ] *adj* stupefacente
a•stray [ə'streɪ] *adv*: ***go astray*** smarrirsi; *morally* uscire dalla retta via
a•stride [ə'straɪd] **1** *adv* a cavalcioni **2** *prep* a cavalcioni di
as•trol•o•ger [ə'strɒlədʒə(r)] astrologo *m*, -a *f*

as•trol•o•gy [ə'strɒlədʒɪ] astrologia *f*
as•tro•naut ['æstrənɔːt] astronauta *m/f*
as•tron•o•mer [ə'strɒnəmə(r)] astronomo *m*, -a *f*
as•tro•nom•i•cal [æstrə'nɒmɪkl] *adj price etc* astronomico
as•tron•o•my [ə'strɒnəmɪ] astronomia *f*
as•tute [ə'stjuːt] *adj* astuto
a•sy•lum [ə'saɪləm] *mental* manicomio *m*; *political* asilo *m*
at [ət] *stressed* [æt] *prep* (*with places*) a; ***he works at the hospital*** lavora in ospedale; ***at the baker's*** dal panettiere *o* in panetteria; ***at Joe's*** da Joe; ***at the door*** alla porta; ***at 10 pounds*** a 10 sterline; ***at the age of 18*** all'età di 18 anni; ***at 5 o'clock*** alle cinque; ***at war*** in guerra; ***at night*** di notte; ***at the moment you called*** nel momento in cui hai chiamato; ***at 150 km/h*** a 150 km/h; ***be good / bad at sth*** essere / non essere bravo in qc
ate [eɪt] *pret of* **eat**
a•the•is•m ['eɪθɪɪzm] ateismo *m*
a•the•ist ['eɪθɪɪst] ateo *m*, -a *f*
ath•lete ['æθliːt] atleta *m/f*
ath•let•ic [æθ'letɪk] *adj* atletico
ath•let•ics [æθ'letɪks] *nsg* atletica *f*
At•lan•tic [ət'læntɪk] *n* Atlantico *m*
at•las ['ætləs] atlante *m*
at•mos•phere ['ætməsfɪə(r)] *of earth, mood* atmosfera *f*
at•mos•pher•ic pol•'lu•tion [ætməsferɪk] inquinamento *m* atmosferico
at•om ['ætəm] atomo *m*
'at•om bomb bomba *f* atomica
a•tom•ic [ə'tɒmɪk] *adj* atomico
a•tom•ic 'en•er•gy energia *f* nucleare
a•tom•ic 'waste scorie *fpl* nucleari
a•tom•iz•er ['ætəmaɪzə(r)] vaporizzatore *m*
a•tone [ə'təʊn] *v/i*: ***atone for*** scontare
a•tro•cious [ə'trəʊʃəs] *adj* atroce
a•troc•i•ty [ə'trɒsətɪ] atrocità *f inv*
at•tach [ə'tætʃ] *v/t* attaccare; *importance* attribuire; *document, file* allegare; ***be attached to*** (*fond of*) essere attaccato a
at•tach•ment [ə'tætʃmənt] (*fondness*) attaccamento *m*; *to email* allegato *m*
at•tack [ə'tæk] **1** *n* aggressione *f*; MIL attacco *m* **2** *v/t* aggredire; MIL attaccare
at•tempt [ə'tempt] **1** *n* tentativo *m* **2** *v/t* tentare
at•tend [ə'tend] *v/t wedding, funeral* partecipare a; *school, classes* frequentare
◆ **attend to** *v/t* (*deal with*) sbrigare; *customer* servire; *patient* assistere
at•tend•ance [ə'tendəns] partecipazione *f*; *at school* frequenza *f*
at•tend•ant [ə'tendənt] *in museum etc* sorvegliante *m/f*
at•ten•tion [ə'tenʃn] attenzione *f*; ***bring sth to s.o.'s attention*** informare qu di qc; ***your attention please*** attenzione; ***pay attention*** fare attenzione; ***for the attention of*** *in faxes etc* alla cortese attenzione di
at•ten•tive [ə'tentɪv] *adj listener* attento
at•tic ['ætɪk] soffitta *f*
at•ti•tude ['ætɪtjuːd] atteggiamento *m*
attn *abbr* (= ***attention***) c.a. (= alla cortese attenzione di)
at•tor•ney [ə'tɜːnɪ] avvocato *m*; ***power of attorney*** delega *f*
at•tract [ə'trækt] *v/t* attirare; ***be attracted to s.o.*** essere attirato da qu
at•trac•tion [ə'trækʃn] attrazione *f*
at•trac•tive [ə'træktɪv] *adj* attrattivo; *person* attraente
at•trib•ute[1] [ə'trɪbjuːt] *v/t* attribuire; ***attribute sth to …*** attribuire qc a …
at•trib•ute[2] ['ætrɪbjuːt] *n* attributo *m*
au•ber•gine ['əʊbəʒiːn] melanzana *f*
auc•tion ['ɔːkʃn] **1** *n* asta *f* **2** *v/t* mettere all'asta
◆ **auction off** *v/t* vendere all'asta
auc•tio•neer [ɔːkʃə'nɪə(r)] banditore *m*, -trice *f*
au•da•cious [ɔː'deɪʃəs] *adj* audace
au•dac•i•ty [ɔː'dæsətɪ] audacia *f*
au•di•ble ['ɔːdəbl] *adj* udibile
au•di•ence ['ɔːdɪəns] pubblico *m*; TV telespettatori *mpl*; *with the Pope etc* udienza *f*
au•di•o ['ɔːdɪəʊ] *adj* audio *inv*
au•di•o•vi•su•al [ɔːdɪəʊ'vɪʒjʊəl] *adj* audiovisivo
au•dit ['ɔːdɪt] **1** *n of accounts* revisione *f o* verifica *f* contabile; ***software audit*** inventario *m* dei software **2** *v/t* verificare
au•di•tion [ɔː'dɪʃn] **1** *n* audizione *f* **2** *v/i* fare un'audizione
au•di•tor ['ɔːdɪtə(r)] revisore *m* contabile
au•di•to•ri•um [ɔːdɪ'tɔːrɪəm] *of theatre etc* sala *f*
Au•gust ['ɔːgəst] agosto *m*
aunt [ɑːnt] zia *f*
au pair (girl) [əʊ'peə(r)] ragazza *f* alla pari
au•ra ['ɔːrə]: ***she has an aura of confidence*** emana sicurezza
aus•pic•es ['ɔːspɪsɪz]: ***under the auspices of*** sotto l'egida di
aus•pi•cious [ɔː'spɪʃəs] *adj* propizio
aus•tere [ɔː'stɪə(r)] *adj* austero
aus•ter•i•ty [ɒs'terətɪ] *economic* austerità *f*
Aus•tra•li•a [ɒ'streɪlɪə] Australia *f*
Aus•tra•li•an [ɒ'streɪlɪən] **1** *adj* australiano **2** *n* australiano *m*, -a *f*

Aus•tri•a ['ɒstrɪə] Austria *f*
Aus•tri•an ['ɒstrɪən] **1** *adj* austriaco **2** *n* austriaco *m*, -a *f*
au•then•tic [ɔː'θentɪk] *adj* autentico
au•then•tic•i•ty [ɔːθen'tɪsətɪ] autenticità *f*
au•thor ['ɔːθə(r)] autore *m*, autrice *f*
au•thor•i•tar•i•an [ɔːθɒrɪ'teərɪən] *adj* autoritario
au•thor•i•ta•tive [ɔː'θɒrɪtətɪv] *adj* autoritario; *information* autorevole
au•thor•i•ty [ɔː'θɒrətɪ] autorità *f inv*; (*permission*) autorizzazione *f*; ***be in authority*** avere l'autorità; ***be an authority on*** essere un'autorità in materia di; ***the authorities*** le autorità
au•thor•i•za•tion [ɔːθəraɪ'zeɪʃn] autorizzazione *f*
au•thor•ize ['ɔːθəraɪz] *v/t* autorizzare; ***be authorized to …*** essere autorizzato a …
au•tis•tic [ɔː'tɪstɪk] *adj* autistico
au•to•bi•og•ra•phy [ɔːtəbaɪ'ɒgrəfɪ] autobiografia *f*
au•to•crat•ic [ɔːtə'krætɪk] *adj* autocratico
au•to•graph ['ɔːtəgrɑːf] autografo *m*
au•to•mate ['ɔːtəmeɪt] *v/t* automatizzare
au•to•mat•ic [ɔːtə'mætɪk] **1** *adj* automatico **2** *n car* macchina *f* con il cambio automatico; *gun* pistola *f* automatica; *washing machine* lavatrice *f* automatica
au•to•mat•i•cal•ly [ɔːtə'mætɪklɪ] *adv* automaticamente
au•to•ma•tion [ɔːtə'meɪʃn] automazione *f*
au•to•mo•bile ['ɔːtəməbiːl] automobile *f*
au•ton•o•mous [ɔː'tɒnəməs] *adj* autonomo
au•ton•o•my [ɔː'tɒnəmɪ] autonomia *f*
au•to•pi•lot ['ɔːtəʊpaɪlət] pilota *m* automatico
au•top•sy ['ɔːtɒpsɪ] autopsia *f*
au•tumn ['ɔːtəm] autunno *m*
aux•il•ia•ry [ɔːg'zɪlɪərɪ] *adj* ausiliario
a•vail [ə'veɪl] **1** *n*: ***to no avail*** invano **2** *v/t*: ***avail o.s. of*** avvalersi di
a•vai•la•ble [ə'veɪləbl] *adj* disponibile
av•a•lanche ['ævəlɑːnʃ] valanga *f*
av•a•rice ['ævərɪs] avarizia *f*
a•venge [ə'vendʒ] *v/t* vendicare
av•e•nue ['ævənjuː] corso *m*; *fig* strada *f*
av•e•rage ['ævərɪdʒ] **1** *adj* medio; (*of mediocre quality*) mediocre **2** *n* media *f*; ***above / below average*** sopra / sotto la media; ***on average*** in media, mediamente **3** *v/t* raggiungere in media
◆ **average out** *v/t* fare la media di
◆ **average out at** *v/t* risultare in media a
a•verse [ə'vɜːs] *adj*: ***not be averse to*** non avere niente contro
a•ver•sion [ə'vɜːʃn] avversione *f*; ***have an aversion to*** avere un'avversione per
a•vert [ə'vɜːt] *v/t one's eyes* distogliere; *crisis* evitare
a•vi•a•ry ['eɪvɪərɪ] voliera *f*
a•vi•a•tion [eɪvɪ'əɪʃn] aviazione *f*; ***aviation industry*** industria *f* aeronautica
av•id ['ævɪd] *adj* avido
av•o•ca•do [ævə'kɑːdəʊ] avocado *m inv*
a•void [ə'vɔɪd] *v/t* evitare
a•void•a•ble [ə'vɔɪdəbl] *adj* evitabile
a•wait [ə'weɪt] *v/t* attendere
a•wake [ə'weɪk] *adj* sveglio; ***it's keeping me awake*** mi impedisce di dormire
a•ward [ə'wɔːd] **1** *n* (*prize*) premio *m* **2** *v/t* assegnare; *damages* riconoscere; ***she was awarded the Nobel Prize for …*** le hanno assegnato il premio Nobel per …
a•ware [ə'weə(r)] *adj* conscio, consapevole; ***be aware of sth*** essere conscio *o* consapevole di qc; ***become aware of sth*** rendersi conto di qc
a•ware•ness [ə'weənɪs] consapevolezza *f*
a•way [ə'weɪ] *adv* via; SP fuori casa; ***be away*** *travelling, sick etc* essere via; ***go / run away*** andare / correre via; ***look away*** guardare da un'altra parte; ***it's 2 miles away*** dista 2 miglia; ***Christmas is still six weeks away*** mancano ancora sei settimane a Natale; ***take sth away from s.o.*** togliere qc a qu; ***put sth away*** mettere via qc
a'way match SP partita *f* fuori casa
awe [ɔː] soggezione *f*
awe•some ['ɔːsm] *adj* F (*terrific*) fantastico
aw•ful ['ɔːfl] *adj* tremendo, terribile; ***I feel awful*** F sto da cani F
aw•ful•ly ['ɔːflɪ] *adv* F (*very*) da matti F
awk•ward ['ɔːkwəd] *adj* (*clumsy*) goffo; (*difficult*) difficile; (*embarrassing*) scomodo; ***feel awkward*** sentirsi a disagio
awn•ing ['ɔːnɪŋ] tenda *f*
ax *Am*, **axe** [æks] **1** *n* scure *f*, accetta *f* **2** *v/t project*, *job* sopprimere
ax•le ['æksl] asse *f*

B

BA [biː'eɪ] *abbr* (= **Bachelor of Arts**) (*degree*) *laurea f in lettere*; (*person*) *laureato m, -a f in lettere*
ba•by ['beɪbɪ] *n* bambino *m*, -a *f*
'**baby boom** baby boom *m inv*
ba•by•ish ['beɪbɪɪʃ] *adj* infantile
'**bab•y-sit** *v/i* (*pret & pp* **-sat**) fare il / la baby-sitter
'**bab•y-sit•ter** baby-sitter *m/f inv*
bach•e•lor ['bætʃələ(r)] scapolo *m*
back [bæk] **1** *n of person* schiena *f*; *of animal, hand* dorso *m*; *of car, bus* parte *f* posteriore; *of book, house* retro *m*; *of clothes* rovescio *m*; *of drawer* fondo *m*; *of chair* schienale *m*; SP terzino *m*; ***in the back*** (***of the car***) (nei sedili) di dietro; ***at the back of the bus*** in fondo all'autobus; ***back to front*** al contrario; ***at the back of beyond*** in capo al mondo **2** *adj door, steps* di dietro; *wheels, legs* posteriore; *garden, room* sul retro; *payment, issue* arretrato; ***back road*** strada secondaria **3** *adv*: ***please move / stand back*** indietro, per favore; ***2 metres back from the edge*** a 2 metri dal bordo; ***back in 1935*** nel 1935; ***give sth back to s.o.*** restituire qc a qu; ***she'll be back tomorrow*** sarà di ritorno domani; ***when are you coming back?*** quando torni?; ***take sth back to the store*** *because unsatisfactory* riportare qc indietro al negozio; ***they wrote / phoned back*** hanno risposto alla lettera / telefonata; ***he hit me back*** mi ha restituito il colpo **4** *v/t* (*support*) appoggiare; *car* guidare in retromarcia; *horse* puntare su; ***back the car into the garage*** mettere la macchina in garage in retromarcia **5** *v/i of driver* fare retromarcia
◆ **back away** *v/i* indietreggiare
◆ **back down** *v/i fig* fare marcia indietro
◆ **back off** *v/i* spostarsi indietro; *from danger* tirasi indietro
◆ **back onto** *v/t* dare su
◆ **back out** *v/i fig* tirarsi indietro
◆ **back up 1** *v/t* (*support*) confermare; *claim, argument* supportare; *file* fare un backup di; ***back s.o. up*** spalleggiare qu; ***be backed up*** *of traffic* essere congestionato **2** *v/i in car* fare retromarcia
'**back•ache** mal *m inv* di schiena
back•bench•er [bæk'bentʃə(r)] parlamentare *m/f* ordinario, -a
'**back•bit•ing** maldicenze *fpl*
'**back•bone** *also fig* spina *f* dorsale
'**back-break•ing** *adj* massacrante
back '**burn•er**: ***put sth on the back burner*** accantonare qc
'**back•date** *v/t* retrodatare
'**back•door** porta *f* di dietro
back•er ['bækə(r)] FIN finanziatore *m*, -trice *f*
back'fire *v/i fig* avere effetto contrario; ***backfire on s.o.*** ritorcersi contro qu
'**back•ground** *n* sfondo *m*; *fig*: *of person* background *m inv*; *of story, event* retroscena *mpl*
'**back•hand** *n in tennis* rovescio *m*
back•hand•er ['bækhændə(r)] F bustarella *f* F
'**back•ing** ['bækɪŋ] *n moral* appoggio *m*; *financial* finanziamento *m*; MUS accompagnamento *m*
'**back•ing group** MUS gruppo *m* d'accompagnamento
'**back•lash** reazione *f* violenta
'**back•log**: ***backlog of work*** lavoro *m* arretrato; ***backlog of unanswered letters*** corrispondenza *f* arretrata
'**back•pack 1** *n* zaino *m* **2** *v/i viaggiare con zaino e sacco a pelo*
'**back•pack•er** saccopelista *m/f*
'**back•pack•ing** *il viaggiare con zaino e sacco a pelo*
'**back•ped•al** *v/i fig* fare marcia indietro
'**back seat** *of car* sedile *m* posteriore
back-seat '**driv•er**: ***you're a terrible back-seat driver!*** smettila di dire come si deve guidare!
'**back•side** F sedere *m*
'**back•space** (**key**) (tasto di) ritorno *m*
'**back•stairs** *npl* scala *f* di servizio
'**back streets** *npl* vicoli *mpl*
'**back•stroke** SP dorso *m*
'**back•track** *v/i* tornare indietro
'**back•up** (*support*) rinforzi *mpl*; COMPUT backup *m inv*
'**back•up disk** COMPUT disco *m* di backup
back•ward ['bækwəd] *adj child* tardivo; *society* arretrato; *glance* all'indietro
backwards ['bækwədz] *adv* indietro
back'yard cortile *m*; ***not in my backyard*** *fig* non in casa mia
ba•con ['beɪkn] pancetta *f*
bac•te•ri•a [bæk'tɪərɪə] batteri *mpl*
bad [bæd] *adj news, manners* cattivo; *weather, cold, headache* brutto; *mistake, accident* grave; *egg, food* guasto; ***smoking is bad for you*** il fumo fa male; ***it's not***

bad non è male; ***that's too bad*** *shame* peccato!; ***feel bad about sth*** (*guilty*) sentirsi in colpa per qc; ***be bad at*** essere negato per; ***Friday's bad, how about Thursday?*** venerdì non posso, che ne dici di giovedì?

bad 'debt debito *m* insoluto

badge [bædʒ] distintivo *m*

bad•ger ['bædʒə(r)] *v/t* tasso *m*

bad 'lan•guage parolacce *fpl*

bad•ly ['bædlɪ] *adv* male; *injured, damaged* gravemente; ***he badly needs a haircut / rest*** ha urgente bisogno di tagliarsi i capelli / riposare; ***he is badly off*** (*poor*) è povero

bad-man•nered [bæd'mænəd] *adj* maleducato

bad•min•ton ['bædmɪntən] badminton *m inv*

bad-tem•pered [bæd'tempəd] *adj* irascibile

baf•fle ['bæfl] *v/t*: ***be baffled*** essere perplesso

baf•fling ['bæflɪŋ] *adj* sconcertante

bag [bæg] borsa *f*; *plastic, paper* busta *f*

bag•gage ['bægɪdʒ] bagagli *mpl*

bag•gage re•claim ['riːkleɪm] ritiro *m* bagagli

'bag•gage trol•ley carrello *m*

bag•gy ['bægɪ] *adj* senza forma

'bag•pipes *npl* cornamusa *fsg*

bail [beɪl] *n* LAW cauzione *f*; ***on bail*** su cauzione

◆ **bail out 1** *v/t* LAW scarcerare su cauzione; *fig* tirare fuori dai guai **2** *v/i of aeroplane* lanciarsi col paracadute

bai•liff ['beɪlɪf] *ufficiale m giudiziario*

bait [beɪt] *n* esca *f*

bake [beɪk] *v/t* cuocere al forno

baked 'beans [beɪkt] *npl fagioli mpl in salsa rossa*

baked po'ta•toes *npl patate fpl cotte al forno con la buccia*

bak•er ['beɪkə(r)] fornaio *m*, -a *f*

bak•er's ['beɪkəz] panetteria *f*

bak•er•y ['beɪkərɪ] panetteria *f*

bak•ing pow•der ['beɪkɪŋ] lievito *m*

bal•ance ['bæləns] **1** *n* equilibrio *m*; (*remainder*) resto *m*; *of bank account* saldo *m* **2** *v/t* tenere in equilibrio; ***balance the books*** fare il bilancio **3** *v/i* stare in equilibrio; *of accounts* quadrare

bal•anced ['bælənst] *adj* (*fair*) obiettivo; *diet, personality* equilibrato

bal•ance of 'pay•ments bilancia *f* dei pagamenti

bal•ance of 'trade bilancia *f* commerciale

'bal•ance sheet bilancio *m* (di esercizio)

bal•co•ny ['bælkənɪ] *of house* balcone *m*; *in theatre* prima galleria *f*

bald [bɔːld] *adj man* calvo; ***he's going bald*** sta perdendo i capelli

bald•ing ['bɔːldɪŋ] *adj* stempiato

Bal•kan ['bɔːlkən] *adj* balcanico

Bal•kans ['bɔːlkənz] *npl*: ***the Balkans*** i Balcani *mpl*

ball[1] [bɔːl] palla *f*; *football* pallone *m*; ***be on the ball*** essere sveglio; ***play ball*** *fig* collaborare; ***the ball's in his court*** la prossima mossa è sua

ball[2] [bɔːl] (*dance*) ballo *m*

bal•lad ['bæləd] ballata *f*

ball 'bear•ing cuscinetto *m* a sfere

bal•le•ri•na [bælə'riːnə] ballerina *f*

bal•let ['bæleɪ] *art* danza *f* classica; *dance* balletto *m*

'bal•let danc•er ballerino *m* classico, ballerina *f* classica

'ball game F: ***that's a different ball game*** è un altro paio di maniche

bal•lis•tic mis•sile [bə'lɪstɪk] missile *m* balistico

bal•loon [bə'luːn] *child's* palloncino *m*; *for flight* mongolfiera *f*

bal•loon•ist [bə'luːnɪst] aeronauta *m/f*

bal•lot ['bælət] **1** *n* votazione *f* **2** *v/t members* consultare tramite votazione

'bal•lot box urna *f* elettorale

'bal•lot pa•per scheda *f* elettorale

'ballpark F: ***be in the right ballpark*** essere nell'ordine corretto di cifre

'ballpark fig•ure F cifra *f* approssimativa

'ball•point (pen) penna *f* a sfera

balls [bɔːlz] *npl* V (*also courage*) palle *fpl* V

bam•boo [bæm'buː] *n* bambù *m inv*

ban [bæn] **1** *n* divieto *m* (***on*** di) **2** *v/t* (*pret & pp* ***-ned***) proibire

ba•nal [bə'nɑːl] *adj* banale

ba•na•na [bə'nɑːnə] banana *f*

band [bænd] banda *f*; *pop* gruppo *m*; *of material* nastro *m*

ban•dage ['bændɪdʒ] **1** *n* benda *f* **2** *v/t* bendare

B&B [biːn'biː] *abbr* (= ***bed and breakfast***) pensione *f* familiare, bed and breakfast *m inv*

ban•dit ['bændɪt] brigante *m*

'band•wagon *n*: ***jump on the bandwagon*** seguire la corrente

ban•dy ['bændɪ] *adj legs* storto

bang [bæŋ] **1** *n* colpo *m* **2** *v/t door* chiudere violentemente; (*hit*) sbattere; ***I banged my knee on the table*** ho battuto il ginocchio contro il tavolo **3** *v/i* sbattere; ***the door banged shut*** la porta si è chiusa con un colpo

bang•er ['bæŋə(r)] F (*sausage*) salamino

m; ***an old banger*** (*car*) una vecchia carretta
ban•gle ['bæŋgl] braccialetto *m*
ban•is•ters ['bænɪstəz] *npl* ringhiera *fsg*
ban•jo ['bændʒəʊ] banjo *m inv*
bank[1] [bæŋk] *of river* riva *f*
bank[2] [bæŋk] **1** *n* FIN banca *f* **2** *v/i*: ***bank with*** avere un conto presso **3** *v/t money* mettere in banca
◆ **bank on** *v/t* contare su; ***don't bank on it*** non ci contare; ***bank on s.o. doing sth*** dare per scontato che qu faccia qc
'**bank ac•count** conto *m* bancario
'**bank bal•ance** saldo *m*
bank•er ['bæŋkə(r)] banchiere *m*
'**bank•er's card** carta *f* assegni
bank•er's 'or•der ordine *m* di pagamento
bank 'hol•i•day giorno *m* festivo
bank•ing ['bæŋkɪŋ] professione *f* bancaria
'**bank loan** prestito *m* bancario
'**bank man•ag•er** direttore *m* di banca
'**bank note** banconota *f*
'**bank rate** tasso *m* ufficiale di sconto
'**bank•roll** *v/t* finanziare
bank•rupt ['bæŋkrʌpt] **1** *adj* fallito; ***go bankrupt*** fallire **2** *v/t* portare al fallimento
bank•rupt•cy ['bæŋkrʌpsɪ] bancarotta *f*
'**bank state•ment** estratto *m* conto
ban•ner ['bænə(r)] striscione *m*
banns [bænz] *npl* pubblicazioni *mpl* (matrimoniali)
ban•quet ['bæŋkwɪt] *n* banchetto *m*
ban•ter ['bæntə(r)] *n* scambio *m* di battute
bap•tis•m ['bæptɪzm] battesimo *m*
bap•tize [bæp'taɪz] *v/t* battezzare
bar[1] [bɑː(r)] *n of iron* spranga *f*; *of chocolate* tavoletta *f*; *for drinks* bar *m inv*; (*counter*) bancone *m*; ***a bar of soap*** una saponetta; ***be behind bars*** (*in prison*) essere dietro le sbarre
bar[2] [bɑː(r)] *v/t* (*pret & pp* ***-red***) vietare l'ingresso a; ***he's been barred from the club*** gli hanno vietato l'ingresso al club
bar[3] [bɑː(r)] *prep* (*except*) tranne
bar•bar•i•an [bɑː'beərɪən] barbaro *m*, -a *f*
bar•ba•ric [bɑː'bærɪk] *adj* barbaro
bar•be•cue ['bɑːbɪkjuː] **1** *n* barbecue *m inv* **2** *v/t* cuocere al barbecue
barbed 'wire [bɑːbd] filo *m* spinato
bar•ber ['bɑːbə(r)] barbiere *m*
bar•bi•tu•rate [bɑː'bɪtjʊrət] barbiturico *m*
'**bar code** codice *m* a barre
bare [beə(r)] *adj* (*naked*) nudo; (*empty*: *room*) spoglio; *mountainside* brullo
'**bare•foot** *adj*: ***be barefoot*** essere scalzo
bare-head•ed [beə'hedɪd] *adj* senza cappello
'**bare•ly** ['beəlɪ] *adv* appena
bar•gain ['bɑːgɪn] **1** *n* (*deal*) patto *m*; (*good buy*) affare *m*; ***it's a bargain!*** (*deal*) è un affarone!; ***into the bargain*** per giunta **2** *v/i* tirare sul prezzo
◆ **bargain for** *v/t* (*expect*) aspettarsi; ***he got more than he bargained for*** non se l'aspettava
barge [bɑːdʒ] *n* NAUT chiatta *f*
◆ **barge into** *v/t* piombare su
bar•i•tone ['bærɪtəʊn] *n* baritono *m*
bark[1] [bɑːk] **1** *n of dog* abbaiare *m* **2** *v/i* abbaiare
bark[2] [bɑːk] *of tree* corteccia *f*
bar•ley ['bɑːlɪ] orzo *m*
'**bar•maid** barista *f*
'**bar•man** barista *m*
barm•y ['bɑːmɪ] *adj* F pazzoide F
barn [bɑːn] granaio *m*
ba•rom•e•ter [bə'rɒmɪtə(r)] *also fig* barometro *m*
Ba•roque [bə'rɒk] *adj* barocco
bar•racks ['bærəks] *npl* MIL caserma *fsg*
bar•rage ['bærɑːdʒ] MIL sbarramento *m*; *fig* raffica *f*
bar•rel ['bærəl] (*container*) barile *m*
bar•ren ['bærən] *adj land* arido
bar•ri•cade [bærɪ'keɪd] *n* barricata *f*
bar•ri•er ['bærɪə(r)] barriera *f*; ***language barrier*** l'ostacolo *m* della lingua
bar•ring ['bɑːrɪŋ] *prep*: ***barring accidents*** salvo imprevisti
bar•ris•ter ['bærɪstə(r)] avvocato *m*
bar•row ['bærəʊ] carriola *f*
'**bar ten•der** barista *m/f*
bar•ter ['bɑːtə(r)] **1** *n* baratto *m* **2** *v/i* barattare
base [beɪs] **1** *n* base *f* **2** *v/t* basare; ***base sth on sth*** basare qc su qc; ***be based in*** *in city, country* essere di base a; ***be based on*** essere basato su
'**base•ball** baseball *m inv*
'**base•ball bat** mazza *f* da baseball
'**base•ball cap** berretto *m* da baseball
base•less ['beɪslɪs] *adj* infondato
base•ment ['beɪsmənt] seminterrato *m*
'**base rate** FIN tasso *m* base
bash [bæʃ] **1** *n* F colpo *m* **2** *v/t* F sbattere
ba•sic ['beɪsɪk] *adj knowledge, equipment* rudimentale; *salary* di base; *beliefs* fondamentale
ba•sic•al•ly ['beɪsɪklɪ] *adv* essenzialmente
ba•sics ['beɪsɪks] *npl*: ***the basics*** i rudimenti *mpl*; ***get down to basics*** venire al sodo

bas•il ['bæzɪl] basilico *m*
ba•sil•i•ca [bə'zɪlɪkə] basilica *f*
ba•sin ['beɪsn] *for washing* lavandino *m*
ba•sis ['beɪsɪs] (*pl* **bases** ['beɪsiːz]) base *f*
bask [bɑːsk] *v/i* crogiolarsi
bas•ket ['bɑːskɪt] cestino *m*; *in basketball* cesto *m*
'**bas•ket•ball** basket *m inv*, pallacanestro *f*
bass [beɪs] **1** *n* (*part*) voce *f* di basso; (*singer*) basso *m*; (*double bass*) contrabbasso *m*; (*guitar*) basso *m* **2** *adj* di basso
bas•tard ['bɑːstəd] F bastardo *m*, -a *f* F
bat[1] [bæt] **1** *n* mazza *f*; *for table tennis* racchetta *f* **2** *v/i* (*pret & pp* **-ted**) SP battere
bat[2] [bæt] *v/t* (*pret & pp* **-ted**): ***he didn't bat an eyelid*** non ha battuto ciglio
bat[3] [bæt] (*animal*) pipistrello *m*
batch [bætʃ] *n of students* gruppo *m*; *of goods* lotto *m*; *of bread* infornata *f*
ba•ted ['beɪtɪd] *adj*: ***with bated breath*** col fiato sospeso
bath [bɑːθ] bagno *m*; ***have a bath, take a bath*** fare il bagno
bathe [beɪð] *v/i* (*swim, have bath*) fare il bagno
'**bath•ing cost•ume**, '**bath•ing suit** costume *m* da bagno
'**bath mat** tappetino *m* da bagno
'**bath•robe** accappatoio *m*
'**bath•room** (stanza *f* da) bagno *m*
baths [bɑːðz] *npl Br* bagni *mpl* pubblici
'**bath tow•el** asciugamano *m* da bagno
'**bath•tub** vasca *f* da bagno
bat•on ['bætən] *of conductor* bacchetta *f*
bat•tal•i•on [bə'tæliən] MIL battaglione *m*
bat•ter ['bætə(r)] *n* pastella *f*
bat•tered ['bætəd] *adj* maltrattato; *old hat, suitcase etc* malridotto
bat•ter•y ['bætrɪ] pila *f*; MOT batteria *f*
'**bat•ter•y charg•er** caricabatterie *m inv*
bat•ter•y-op•e•rat•ed [bætrɪ'ɒpəreɪtɪd] *adj* a pile
bat•tle ['bætl] **1** *n also fig* battaglia *f* **2** *v/i against illness etc* lottare
'**bat•tle•field**, '**bat•tle•ground** campo *m* di battaglia
'**bat•tle•ship** corazzata *f*
bawd•y ['bɔːdɪ] *adj* spinto
bawl [bɔːl] *v/i* (*shout*) urlare; (*weep*) strillare
◆ **bawl out** *v/t* F fare una lavata di capo a
bay [beɪ] (*inlet*) baia *f*
bay•o•net ['beɪənet] *n* baionetta *f*
bay '**win•dow** bovindo *m*
BBC [biːbiː'siː] *abbr* (= ***British Broadcasting Corporation***) BBC *f inv*
BC [biː'siː] *abbr* (= ***before Christ***) a. C. (= avanti Cristo)

be [biː] *v/i* (*pret* **was** / **were**, *pp* **been**) essere; ***it's me*** sono io; ***was she there?*** era lì?; ***how much is / are ...?*** quant'è/-quanto sono ...?; ***there is, there are*** c'è, ci sono; ***be careful*** sta' attento; ***don't be sad*** non essere triste; ***how are you?*** come stai?; ***he's very well*** sta bene; ***I'm hot / cold*** ho freddo / caldo; ***it's hot / cold*** fa freddo / caldo; ***he's seven*** ha sette anni ◇ ***has the postman been?*** è passato il postino?; ***I've never been to Japan*** non sono mai stato in Giappone; ***I've been here for hours*** sono qui da tanto
◇ *tags*: ***that's right, isn't it?*** giusto, no?; ***she's American, isn't she?*** è americana, vero?
◇ *v/aux*: ***I am thinking*** sto pensando; ***he was running*** stava correndo; ***you're being silly*** stai facendo lo sciocco; ***he's working in London*** lavora a Londra; ***I'll be waiting for an answer*** aspetterò una risposta
◇ *obligation*: ***you are to do what I tell you*** devi fare quello che ti dico; ***I was to tell you this*** dovevo dirtelo; ***you were not to tell anyone*** non dovevi dirlo a nessuno
◇ *passive* essere, venire (*not with past tenses*); ***he was killed*** è stato ucciso; ***they have been sold*** sono stati venduti; ***it will be sold for £100*** sarà *o* verrà venduto a 100 sterline
◆ **be in for** *v/t* doversi aspettare; ***you're in for a disappointment*** resterai deluso
beach [biːtʃ] *n* spiaggia *f*
'**beach ball** pallone *m* da spiaggia
'**beach•wear** abbigliamento *m* da spiaggia
beads [biːdz] *npl* perline *fpl*
beak [biːk] becco *m*
bea•ker ['biːkə(r)] bicchiere *m*
'**be-all**: ***the be-all and end-all*** la cosa più importante
beam [biːm] **1** *n in ceiling etc* trave *f* **2** *v/i* (*smile*) fare un sorriso radioso **3** *v/t* (*transmit*) trasmettere
bean [biːn] (*vegetable*) fagiolo *m*; *of coffee* chicco *m*; ***be full of beans*** F essere particolarmente vivace
'**bean•bag** *seat* poltrona *f* sacco
bear[1] [beə(r)] *animal* orso *m*
bear[2] [beə(r)] (*pret* **bore**, *pp* **borne**) **1** *v/t weight* portare; *costs* sostenere; (*tolerate*) sopportare; *child* dare alla luce **2** *v/i*: ***bring pressure to bear on*** fare pressione su
◆ **bear out** *v/t* (*confirm*) confermare; ***bear s.o. out*** appoggiare qu

bear•a•ble ['beərəbl] *adj* sopportabile
beard [bɪəd] barba *f*
beard•ed ['bɪədɪd] *adj* con la barba
bear•ing ['beərɪŋ] *in machine* cuscinetto *m*; ***that has no bearing on the case*** ciò non ha alcuna attinenza col caso
'**bear mar•ket** FIN mercato *m* cedente
beast [bi:st] bestia *f*
beat [bi:t] **1** *n of heart* battito *m*; *of music* ritmo *m* **2** *v/i* (*pret* ***beat***, *pp* ***beaten***) *of heart* battere; *of rain* picchiettare; ***beat about the bush*** menar il can per l'aia **3** *v/t* (*pret* ***beat***, *pp* ***beaten***) *in competition* battere; (*hit*) picchiare; *drum* suonare; ***beat it!*** F fila!; ***it beats me*** non capisco
◆ **beat up** *v/t* picchiare
beat•en ['bi:tən] **1** *adj*: ***off the beaten track*** fuori mano **2** *pp* → ***beat***
beat•ing ['bi:tɪŋ] (*physical*) botte *fpl*
beat-up *adj* F malconcio
beau•ti•cian [bju:'tɪʃn] estetista *m/f*
beau•ti•ful ['bju:tɪfʊl] *adj* bello; ***thanks, that's just beautiful!*** grazie, così va bene
beau•ti•ful•ly ['bju:tɪflɪ] *adv* stupendamente
beaut•y ['bju:tɪ] *of woman, sunset* bellezza *f*
'**beaut•y sal•on** istituto *m* di bellezza
◆ **beaver away** *v/i* F sgobbare F
be•came [bɪ'keɪm] *pret* → ***become***
be•cause [bɪ'kɒz] *conj* perché; ***because of*** a causa di
beck•on ['bekn] *v/i* fare cenno
be•come [bɪ'kʌm] *v/i* (*pret* ***became***, *pp* ***become***) diventare; ***what's become of her?*** che ne è stato di lei?
be•com•ing [bɪ'kʌmɪŋ] *adj* grazioso
bed [bed] *n* letto *m*; ***bed of flowers*** aiuola *f*; ***go to bed*** andare a letto; ***he's still in bed*** è ancora a letto; ***go to bed with*** andare a letto con
bed and '**breakfast** pensione *f* familiare, bed and breakfast *m inv*
'**bed•clothes** *npl* coperte e lenzuola *fpl*
bed•ding ['bedɪŋ] *materasso m e lenzuola fpl*
bed•lam ['bedləm] F manicomio *m*
bed•rid•den ['bedrɪdən] *adj* costretto a letto
'**bed•room** camera *f* da letto
'**bed•side**: ***be at the bedside of*** essere al capezzale di
bed•side '**lamp** lampada *f* da comodino
bed•side '**ta•ble** comodino *m*
'**bed-sit**, **bed-**'**sit•ter** *monolocale m*
'**bed•spread** copriletto *m*
'**bed•time** ora *f* di andare a letto
bee [bi:] ape *f*
beech [bi:tʃ] faggio *m*
beef [bi:f] **1** *n* manzo *m*; F (*complaint*) problema *m* **2** *v/i* F (*complain*) lagnarsi
◆ **beef up** *v/t* rinforzare
'**beef•bur•ger** hamburger *m inv*
'**bee•hive** alveare *m*
'**bee•line**: ***make a beeline for*** andare diritto a
been [bi:n] *pp* → ***be***
beep [bi:p] **1** *n* bip *m inv* **2** *v/i* suonare **3** *v/t* (*call on pager*) chiamare sul cercapersone
beep•er ['bi:pə(r)] (*pager*) cercapersone *m inv*
beer [bɪə(r)] birra *f*
bee•tle ['bi:tl] coleottero *m*
beet•root ['bi:tru:t] barbabietola *f*; ***as red as a beetroot*** rosso come un peperone
be•fore [bɪ'fɔ:(r)] **1** *prep* prima di; ***before eight o'clock*** prima delle otto **2** *adv* prima; ***have you been to England before?*** sei già stato in Inghilterra?; ***I've seen this film before*** questo film l'ho già visto **3** *conj* prima che; ***I saw him before he left*** l'ho visto prima che partisse; ***I saw him before I left*** l'ho visto prima di partire
be'**fore•hand** *adv* prima
be•friend [bɪ'frend] *v/t* fare amicizia con
beg [beg] (*pret & pp* ***-ged***) **1** *v/i* mendicare **2** *v/t*: ***beg s.o. to …*** pregare qu di …
be•gan [bɪ'gæn] *pret* → ***begin***
beg•gar ['begə(r)] *n* mendicante *m/f*
be•gin [bɪ'gɪn] *v/t & v/i* (*pret* ***began***, *pp* ***begun***) cominciare; ***to begin with*** per cominciare
be•gin•ner [bɪ'gɪnə(r)] principiante *m/f*
be•gin•ning [bɪ'gɪnɪŋ] inizio *m*; (*origin*) origine *f*
be•grudge [bɪ'grʌdʒ] *v/t* (*envy*) invidiare; (*give reluctantly*) dare malvolentieri
be•gun [bɪ'gʌn] *pp* → ***begin***
be•half: ***on behalf of*** a nome di; ***on my / his behalf*** a nome mio / suo
be•have [bɪ'heɪv] *v/i* comportarsi
behave (o.s.) comportarsi bene; ***behave (yourself)!*** comportati bene!
be•hav•iour [bɪ'heɪvjə(r)] comportamento *m*
be•hind [bɪ'haɪnd] **1** *prep in position* dietro; *in progress* indietro rispetto a; *in order* dietro a; ***be behind*** (*responsible for*) essere dietro a; (*support*) appoggiare **2** *adv* (*at the back*) dietro; ***she had to stay behind*** è dovuta rimanere; ***be behind*** *in match* essere in svantaggio; ***be behind with sth*** essere indietro con qc
beige [beɪʒ] *adj* beige *inv*

be•ing ['biːɪŋ] (*existence*) esistenza *f*; (*creature*) essere *m*
be•lat•ed [bɪ'leɪtɪd] *adj* in ritardo
belch [beltʃ] **1** *n* rutto *m* **2** *v/i* ruttare
Bel•gian ['beldʒən] **1** *adj* belga **2** *n* belga *m/f*
Bel•gium ['beldʒəm] Belgio *m*
be•lief [bɪ'liːf] convinzione *f*; *in God* fede *f*; ***your belief in me*** il fatto che tu creda in me
be•lieve [bɪ'liːv] *v/t* credere
◆ **believe in** *v/t God, person* credere in; *ghost, person* credere a
be•liev•er [bɪ'liːvə(r)] REL credente *m/f*; ***I'm a great believer in …*** credo fermamente in …
be•lit•tle [bɪ'lɪtl] *v/t* sminuire
bell [bel] *in church, school* campana *f*; *on door* campanello *m*
bel•lig•er•ent [bɪ'lɪdʒərənt] *adj* bellicoso
bel•low ['beləʊ] **1** *n* urlo *m*; *of bull* muggito *m* **2** *v/i* urlare; *of bull* muggire
bel•ly ['belɪ] pancia *f*
'**bel•ly•ache** *v/i* F brontolare F
be•long [bɪ'lɒŋ] *v/i*: ***where does this belong?*** dove va questo?; ***I don't belong here*** mi sento un estraneo; ***at last he found a place where he belonged*** finalmente ha trovato un posto adatto a lui
◆ **belong to** *v/t* appartenere a
be•long•ings [bɪ'lɒŋɪŋz] *npl* cose *fpl*
be•lov•ed [bɪ'lʌvɪd] *adj* adorato
be•low [bɪ'ləʊ] **1** *prep* sotto **2** *adv* di sotto; *in text* sotto; ***see below*** vedi sotto; ***10 degrees below*** 10 gradi sotto zero
belt [belt] *n* cintura *f*; ***tighten one's belt*** *fig* stringere la cinghia
◆ **belt up** *v/i* (*fasten seat belt*) allacciare la cintura (di sicurezza); ***belt up!*** F sta' zitto!
be•moan [bɪ'məʊn] *v/t* lamentarsi di
bench [bentʃ] (*seat*) panchina *f*; (*workbench*) banco *m*
'**bench•mark** punto *m* di riferimento
bend [bend] **1** *n* curva *f* **2** *v/t* (*pret & pp* ***bent***) piegare **3** *v/i* (*pret & pp* ***bent***) curvarsi; *of person* inchinarsi
◆ **bend down** *v/i* chinarsi
bend•er ['bendə(r)] F sbronza *f* F
be•neath [bɪ'niːθ] **1** *prep* sotto **2** *adv* di sotto; ***they think he's beneath her*** lo considerano inferiore a lei
ben•e•dic•tion [benɪ'dɪkʃn] benedizione *f*
ben•e•fac•tor ['benɪfæktə(r)] benefattore *m*, -trice *f*
ben•e•fi•cial [benɪ'fɪʃl] *adj* vantaggioso
ben•e•fit ['benɪfɪt] **1** *n* (*advantage*) vantaggio *m*; *payment* indennità *f inv* **2** *v/t* andare a vantaggio di **3** *v/i* trarre vantaggio (***from*** da)
be•nev•o•lence [bɪ'nevələns] benevolenza *f*
be•nev•o•lent [bɪ'nevələnt] *adj* benevolo
be•nign [bɪ'naɪn] *adj* benevolo; MED benigno
bent [bent] **1** *adj* F corrotto **2** *pret & pp* → ***bend***
be•queath [bɪ'kwiːð] *v/t also fig* lasciare in eredità
be•quest [bɪ'kwest] lascito *m*
be•reaved [bɪ'riːvd] **1** *adj* addolorato **2** *n*: ***the bereaved*** i familiari *mpl* del defunto
be•ret ['bereɪ] berretto *m*
ber•ry ['berɪ] bacca *f*
ber•serk [bə'zɜːk] *adv*: ***go berserk*** dare in escandescenze
berth [bɜːθ] *on ship, train* cuccetta *f*; ***give s.o. a wide berth*** stare alla larga da qu
be•seech [bɪ'siːtʃ] *v/t*: ***beseech s.o. to do sth*** implorare qu di fare qc
be•side [bɪ'saɪd] *prep* accanto a; ***be beside o.s.*** essere fuori di sé; ***that's beside the point*** questo non c'entra
be•sides [bɪ'saɪdz] **1** *adv* inoltre **2** *prep* (*apart from*) oltre a
be•siege [bɪ'siːdʒ] *v/t also fig* assediare
best [best] **1** *adj* migliore **2** *adv* meglio; ***it would be best if …*** sarebbe meglio se …; ***I like her best*** lei è quella che mi piace di più **3** *n*: ***do one's best*** fare del proprio meglio; ***the best*** il meglio; (*outstanding thing or person*) il / la migliore; ***they've done the best they can*** hanno fatto tutto il possibile; ***make the best of*** cogliere il lato buono di; ***all the best!*** tanti auguri!
best be'fore date scadenza *f*
best 'man *at wedding* testimone *m* dello sposo
'**best-sell•er** bestseller *m inv*
bet [bet] **1** *n* scommessa *f* **2** *v/i* scommettere; ***you bet!*** ci puoi scommettere!
be•tray [bɪ'treɪ] *v/t* tradire
be•tray•al [bɪ'treɪəl] tradimento *m*
bet•ter ['betə(r)] **1** *adj* migliore; ***get better*** migliorare **2** *adv* meglio; ***you'd better ask permission*** faresti meglio a chiedere il permesso; ***I'd really better not*** sarebbe meglio di no; ***all the better for us*** tanto meglio per noi; ***I like her better*** lei mi piace di più
bet•ter 'off *adj*: ***be better off*** stare meglio finanziariamente; ***the better off*** la classe abbiente
be•tween [bɪ'twiːn] *prep* tra; ***between you and me*** tra me e te
bev•er•age ['bevərɪdʒ] *fml* bevanda *f*
be•ware [bɪ'weə(r)] *v/t*: ***beware of …!***

(stai) attento a …!
be•wil•der [bɪ'wɪldə(r)] *v/t* sconcertare
be•wil•der•ment [bɪ'wɪldəmənt] perplessità *f inv*
be•yond [bɪ'jɒnd] **1** *prep* oltre, al di là di; ***it's beyond me*** (*don't understand*) non capisco; (*can't do it*) va oltre le mie capacità **2** *adv* più in là
bi•as ['baɪəs] *n against* pregiudizio *m*; *in favour of* preferenza *f*
bi•as(s)ed ['baɪəst] *adj* parziale
bib [bɪb] *for baby* bavaglino *m*
Bible ['baɪbl] bibbia *f*
bib•li•cal ['bɪblɪkl] *adj* biblico
bib•li•og•ra•phy [bɪblɪ'ɒgrəfɪ] bibliografia *f*
bi•car•bon•ate of so•da [baɪ'kɑːbəneɪt] bicarbonato *m* di sodio
bi•cen•te•na•ry [baɪsen'tiːnərɪ] bicentenario *m*
bi•ceps ['baɪseps] *npl* bicipiti *mpl*
bick•er ['bɪkə(r)] *v/i* bisticciare
bi•cy•cle ['baɪsɪkl] *n* bicicletta *f*
bid [bɪd] **1** *n at auction* offerta *f*; (*attempt*) tentativo *m* **2** *v/t & v/i* (*pret & pp* ***bid***) *at auction* offrire
bid•der ['bɪdə(r)] offerente *m/f*
bi•en•ni•al [baɪ'enɪəl] *adj* biennale
bi•fo•cals [baɪ'fəʊkəlz] *npl* occhiali *mpl* bifocali
big [bɪg] **1** *adj* grande; ***my big brother / sister*** mio fratello / mia sorella maggiore; ***big name*** nome importante **2** *adv*: ***talk big*** spararle grosse
big•a•mist ['bɪgəmɪst] bigamo *m*, -a *f*
big•a•mous ['bɪgəməs] *adj* bigamo
big•a•my ['bɪgəmɪ] bigamia *f*
'**big•head** F pallone *m* gonfiato F
big-head•ed [bɪg'hedɪd] *adj* F presuntuoso
big•ot ['bɪgət] fanatico *m*, -a *f*
bike [baɪk] **1** *n* F bici *f inv* F **2** *v/i* andare in bici; ***I biked here*** sono venuto in bici
bik•er ['baɪkə(r)] motociclista *m/f*; (*courier*) corriere *m*
bi•ki•ni [bɪ'kiːnɪ] bikini *m inv*
bi•lat•er•al [baɪ'lætərəl] *adj* bilaterale
bi•lin•gual [baɪ'lɪŋgwəl] *adj* bilingue
bill [bɪl] **1** *n in hotel, restaurant* conto *m*; (*gas / electricity bill*) bolletta *f*; (*invoice*) fattura *f*; *Am*: *money* banconota *f*; POL disegno *m* di legge; (*poster*) avviso *m* **2** *v/t* (*invoice*) mandare la fattura a
'**bill•fold** *Am* portafoglio *m*
bil•li•ards ['bɪljədz] *nsg* biliardo *m*
bil•li•on ['bɪljən] (*1,000,000,000*) miliardo *m*
bill of ex'change FIN cambiale *f*
bill of 'sale atto *m* di vendita
bin [bɪn] *n* bidone *m*
bi•na•ry ['baɪnərɪ] *adj* binario
bind [baɪnd] *v/t* (*pret & pp* ***bound***) *also fig* legare; (LAW: *oblige*) obbligare
bind•ing ['baɪndɪŋ] **1** *adj agreement, promise* vincolante **2** *n of book* rilegatura *f*; *of ski* attacco *m*
bin•go ['bɪŋgəʊ] tombola *f*
bi•noc•u•lars [bɪ'nɒkjʊləz] *npl* binocolo *msg*
bi•o•chem•ist [baɪəʊ'kemɪst] biochimico *m*, -a *f*
bi•o•chem•is•try [baɪəʊ'kemɪstrɪ] biochimica *f*
bi•o•de•grad•a•bil•i•ty [baɪəʊdɪgreɪdə'bɪlətɪ] biodegradabilità *f inv*
bi•o•de•gra•da•ble [baɪəʊdɪ'greɪdəbl] *adj* biodegradabile
bi•og•ra•pher [baɪ'ɒgrəfə(r)] biografo *m*, -a *f*
bi•og•ra•phy [baɪ'ɒgrəfɪ] biografia *f*
bi•o•log•i•cal [baɪə'lɒdʒɪkl] *adj* biologico
bi•ol•o•gist [baɪ'ɒlədʒɪst] biologo *m*, -a *f*
bi•ol•o•gy [baɪ'ɒlədʒɪ] biologia *f*
bi•o•tech•nol•o•gy [baɪəʊtek'nɒlədʒɪ] biotecnologia *f*
bird [bɜːd] uccello *m*
'**bird•cage** gabbia *f* per uccelli
bird of 'prey (uccello *m*) rapace *m*
'**bird sanc•tu•a•ry** rifugio *m* per uccelli
bird's eye 'view vista *f* a volo d'uccello
bi•ro® ['baɪrəʊ] biro *f*
birth [bɜːθ] *also fig* nascita *f*; (*labour*) parto *m*; ***give birth to*** *child* partorire; ***date of birth*** data di nascita
'**birth cer•tif•i•cate** certificato *m* di nascita
'**birth con•trol** controllo *m* delle nascite
'**birth•day** compleanno *m*; ***happy birthday!*** buon compleanno!
'**birth•mark** voglia *f*
'**birth•place** luogo *m* di nascita
'**birth•rate** tasso *m* di nascita
bis•cuit ['bɪskɪt] biscotto *m*
bi•sex•u•al ['baɪseksjʊəl] **1** *adj* bisessuale **2** *n* bisessuale *m/f*
bish•op ['bɪʃəp] vescovo *m*
bit[1] [bɪt] *n* (*piece*) pezzo *m*; (*part*) parte *f*; COMPUT bit *m inv*; ***a bit*** (*a little*) un po'; ***a bit of*** (*a little*) un po' di; ***a bit of news / advice*** una notizia / un consiglio; ***bit by bit*** poco a poco; ***I'll be there in a bit*** (*in a little while*) sarò lì tra poco
bit[2] [bɪt] *for a horse* morso *m*
bit[3] [bɪt] *pret* → ***bite***
bitch [bɪʧ] **1** *n dog* cagna *f*; F *woman* bastarda *f* F, stronza *f* V **2** *v/i* F (*complain*) lamentarsi
bitch•y ['bɪʧɪ] *adj* F *person, remark* vele-

noso

bite [baɪt] **1** *n* morso *m*; ***let's have a bite (to eat)*** mangiamo un boccone; ***he didn't get a bite*** *of angler* non ha abboccato neanche un pesce **2** *v/t* (*pret* ***bit***, *pp* ***bitten***) mordere; *one's nails* mangiarsi **3** *v/i* (*pret* ***bit***, *pp* ***bitten***) mordere; *of fish* abboccare

bit•ten ['bɪtn] *pp* → ***bite***

bit•ter ['bɪtə(r)] **1** *adj taste* amaro; *person* amareggiato; *weather* gelido; *argument* aspro **2** *n beer* birra *f* amara

bit•ter•ly ['bɪtəlɪ] *adv resent* profondamente; ***bitterly cold*** gelido

bi•zarre [bɪ'zɑː(r)] *adj* bizzarro

blab [blæb] *v/i* (*pret & pp* ***-bed***) F spifferare F

blab•ber•mouth ['blæbəmaʊθ] F spione *m*, -a *f*

black [blæk] **1** *adj also fig* nero; *person* negro, nero; *tea* senza latte **2** *n* (*colour*) nero *m*; (*person*) nero *m*, -a *f*; ***in the black*** FIN in attivo; ***in black and white*** *fig* nero su bianco

◆ **black out** *v/i* svenire

'**black•ber•ry** mora *f* di rovo

'**blackbird** merlo *m*

'**black•board** lavagna *f*

black 'box scatola *f* nera

black e'con•o•my economia *f* sommersa

black•en ['blækn] *v/t fig*: *person's name* infangare

black 'eye occhio *m* nero

'**black•head** punto *m* nero, comedone *m*

black 'ice ghiaccio *m* (sulla strada)

'**black•list 1** *n* lista *f* nera **2** *v/t* mettere sulla lista nera

'**black•mail 1** *n also fig* ricatto *m* **2** *v/t* ricattare

'**black•mail•er** ricattatore *m*, -trice *f*

black 'mar•ket mercato *m* nero

black•ness ['blæknɪs] *of night* oscurità *f inv*

'**black•out** ELEC black-out *m inv*; MED svenimento *m*

black 'pud•ding *sanguinaccio m*

'**black•smith** fabbro *m* ferraio

blad•der ['blædə(r)] vescica *f*

blade [bleɪd] *of knife*, *sword* lama *f*; *of helicopter* pala *f*; *of grass* filo *m*

blame [bleɪm] **1** *n* colpa *f*; (*responsibility*) responsabilità *f inv* **2** *v/t* biasimare; ***blame s.o. for sth*** ritenere qu responsabile di qc

bland [blænd] *adj smile*, *answer* insulso; *food* insipido

blank [blæŋk] **1** *adj* (*not written on*) bianco; *tape* vergine; *look* vuoto **2** *n* (*empty space*) spazio *m*; ***my mind's a blank*** ho la testa vuota

blank 'check *Am*, **blank 'cheque** assegno *m* in bianco

blan•ket ['blæŋkɪt] *n also fig* coperta *f*

blare [bleə(r)] *v/i* suonare a tutto volume

◆ **blare out 1** *v/i* strepitare **2** *v/t* fare rimbombare

blas•pheme [blæs'fiːm] *v/i* bestemmiare

blas•phe•my ['blæsfəmɪ] bestemmia *f*

blast [blɑːst] **1** *n* (*explosion*) esplosione *f*; (*gust*) raffica *f* **2** *v/t* far esplodere; ***blast!*** accidenti!

◆ **blast off** *v/i of rocket* essere lanciato

blast fur•nace altoforno *m*

'**blast-off** lancio *m*

bla•tant ['bleɪtənt] *adj* palese

blaze [bleɪz] **1** *n* (*fire*) incendio *m*; ***a blaze of colour*** un'esplosione di colore **2** *v/i of fire* ardere

◆ **blaze away** *v/i with gun* sparare a raffica

blaz•er ['bleɪzə(r)] blazer *m inv*

bleach [bliːtʃ] **1** *n for clothes* varechina *f*; *for hair* acqua *f* ossigenata **2** *v/t hair* ossigenarsi

bleak [bliːk] *adj countryside* desolato; *weather* cupo; *future* deprimente

blear•y-eyed ['blɪərɪaɪd] *adj*: ***be bleary-eyed*** avere lo sguardo appannato

bleat [bliːt] *v/i of sheep* belare

bled [bled] *pret & pp* → ***bleed***

bleed [bliːd] (*pret & pp* ***bled***) **1** *v/i* sanguinare **2** *v/t fig* dissanguare

bleed•ing ['bliːdɪŋ] *n* emorragia *f*

bleep [bliːp] **1** *n* blip *m inv* **2** *v/i* suonare **3** *v/t* (*call on pager*) chiamare sul cercapersone

bleep•er ['bliːpə(r)] (*pager*) cercapersone *m inv*

blem•ish ['blemɪʃ] **1** *n on skin* imperfezione *f*; *on fruit* ammaccatura *f* **2** *v/t reputation* infangare

blend [blend] **1** *n* miscela *f* **2** *v/t* miscelare

◆ **blend in 1** *v/i* inserirsi; (*look good*) armonizzare **2** *v/t in cooking* incorporare

blend•er ['blendə(r)] *machine* frullatore *m*

bless [bles] *v/t* benedire; (***God***) ***bless you!*** Dio ti benedica!; ***bless you!*** (*in response to sneeze*) salute!; ***bless me!, bless my soul!*** santo cielo!; ***be blessed with*** godere di

bless•ing ['blesɪŋ] *also fig* benedizione *f*

blew [bluː] *pret* → ***blow***

blind [blaɪnd] **1** *adj* cieco; ***be blind to*** *fig* non vedere **2** *n*: ***the blind*** i ciechi **3** *v/t* accecare

blind 'al•ley vicolo *m* cieco

blind 'date appuntamento *m* al buio

'**blind•fold** **1** *n* benda *f* **2** *v/t* bendare (gli occhi a) **3** *adv* con gli occhi bendati
blind•ing ['blaɪndɪŋ] *adj* atroce; *light* accecante, abbagliante
blind•ly ['blaɪndlɪ] *adv feel, grope* a tastoni; *fig* ciecamente
'**blind spot** *in road* punto *m* cieco; (*ability that is lacking*) punto *m* debole
blink [blɪŋk] *v/i of person* sbattere le palpebre; *of light* tremolare
blink•ered ['blɪŋkəd] *adj fig* ottuso
blip [blɪp] *on radar screen* segnale *m*; *fig* battuta *f* d'arresto
bliss [blɪs] felicità *f inv*
blis•ter ['blɪstə(r)] **1** *n* vescichetta *f* **2** *v/i* formare una vescichetta; *of paint* formare delle bolle
blis•ter pack blister *m inv*
bliz•zard ['blɪzəd] bufera *f* di neve
bloat•ed ['bləʊtɪd] *adj* gonfio
blob [blɒb] *of liquid* goccia *f*
bloc [blɒk] POL blocco *m*
block [blɒk] **1** *n* blocco *m*; *in town* isolato *m*; *of shares* pacchetto *m*; (*blockage*) blocco *m*; ***block of flats*** palazzo *m* (d'appartamenti) **2** *v/t* bloccare
◆ **block in** *v/t with vehicle* bloccare la macchina di; ***somebody's car was blocking me in*** qualcuno ha bloccato la mia macchina parcheggiando la sua
◆ **block out** *v/t light* impedire
◆ **block up** *v/t sink etc* otturare
block•ade [blɒ'keɪd] **1** *n* blocco *m* **2** *v/t* bloccare
block•age ['blɒkɪdʒ] ingorgo *m*
block•bust•er ['blɒkbʌstə(r)] successone *m*
block '**let•ters** *npl* maiuscole *fpl*
bloke [bləʊk] F tipo *m* F
blond [blɒnd] *adj* biondo
blonde [blɒnd] *n* (*woman*) bionda *f*
blood [blʌd] sangue *m*; ***in cold blood*** a sangue freddo
'**blood al•co•hol lev•el** concentrazione *f* di alcol etilico nel sangue
'**blood bank** banca *f* del sangue
'**blood bath** bagno *m* di sangue
'**blood do•nor** donatore *m*, -trice *f* di sangue
'**blood group** gruppo *m* sanguigno
blood•less ['blʌdlɪs] *adj coup* senza spargimento di sangue
'**blood poi•son•ing** setticemia *f*
'**blood pres•sure** pressione *f* del sangue
'**blood re•la•tion**, '**blood rel•a•tive** consanguineo *m*, -a *f*
'**blood sam•ple** prelievo *m* di sangue
'**blood•shed** spargimento *m* di sangue
'**blood•shot** *adj* iniettato di sangue
'**blood•stain** macchia *f* di sangue
'**blood•stain•ed** *adj* macchiato di sangue
'**blood•stream** circolazione *f* (del sangue)
'**blood test** analisi *f inv* del sangue
'**blood•thirst•y** *adj* assetato di sangue
'**blood trans•fu•sion** trasfusione *f* di sangue
'**blood ves•sel** vaso *m* sanguigno
blood•y ['blʌdɪ] **1** *adj hands etc* insanguinato; *battle* sanguinoso; F maledetto; ***bloody hell!*** porca miseria! F; ***it's a bloody nuisance*** è una gran rottura F; ***you're a bloody genius!*** sei un geniaccio! F **2** *adv*: ***that's bloody difficult / easy!*** è facile / difficile da morire!; ***I'm bloody tired*** sono stanco morto; ***you'll bloody well do it!*** eccome se lo farai!
blood•y-mind•ed [blʌdɪ'maɪndɪd] *adj* F ostinato
bloom [blu:m] **1** *n* fiore *m*; ***in full bloom*** in piena fioritura **2** *v/i also fig* fiorire
blos•som ['blɒsəm] **1** *n* fiori *mpl* **2** *v/i also fig* fiorire
blot [blɒt] **1** *n* macchia *f* **2** *v/t* (*pret & pp* ***-ted***) (*dry*) asciugare
◆ **blot out** *v/t memory* cancellare; *view* nascondere
blotch [blɒtʃ] chiazza *f*
blotch•y ['blɒtʃɪ] *adj* coperto di chiazze
blouse [blaʊz] camicetta *f*
blow [bləʊ] **1** *n* colpo *m* **2** *v/t* (*pret* **blew**, *pp* **blown**) *of wind* spingere; *smoke* soffiare; F (*spend*) sperperare; F *opportunity* mandare all'aria; ***blow a whistle*** fischiare; ***blow one's nose*** soffiarsi il naso **3** *v/i* (*pret* **blew**, *pp* **blown**) *of wind, person* soffiare; *of fuse* saltare; *of tyre* scoppiare; ***the whistle blew for half-time*** è stato fischiato l'intervallo
◆ **blow off** **1** *v/t* portar via **2** *v/i* volar via
◆ **blow out** **1** *v/t candle* spegnere **2** *v/i of candle* spegnersi
◆ **blow over** **1** *v/t* abbattere **2** *v/i* rovesciarsi; *of storm, argument* calmarsi
◆ **blow up** **1** *v/t with explosives* far saltare; *balloon* gonfiare; *photograph* ingrandire **2** *v/i also fig* esplodere
'**blow-dry** *v/t* (*pret & pp* ***-ied***) asciugare col phon
'**blow job** V pompino *m* V
'**blow-out** *of tyre* scoppio *m*; F (*big meal*) abbuffata *f*
'**blow-up** *of photo* ingrandimento *m*
blown [bləʊn] *pp* → ***blow***
blue [blu:] **1** *adj* blu; F *film* porno **2** *n* blu *m inv*
blue '**chip** *adj* sicuro; *company* di alto livello
blue-'**col•lar work•er** operaio *m*, -a *f*

'**blue•print** cianografia *f*; (*fig*: *plan*) programma *m*
blues [bluːz] *npl* MUS blues *m inv*; ***have the blues*** essere giù
'**blues sing•er** cantante *m/f* blues
bluff [blʌf] **1** *n* (*deception*) bluff *m inv* **2** *v/i* bluffare
blun•der ['blʌndə(r)] **1** *n* errore *m* **2** *v/i* fare un errore
blunt [blʌnt] *adj* spuntato; *person* diretto
blunt•ly ['blʌntlɪ] *adv speak* senza mezzi termini
blur [blɜː(r)] **1** *n* massa *f* indistinta **2** *v/t* (*pret & pp* ***-red***) offuscare
blurb [blɜːb] *on book* note *fpl* di copertina
◆ **blurt out** [blɜːt] *v/t* spiattellare
blush [blʌʃ] **1** *n* rossore *m* **2** *v/i* arrossire
blusher ['blʌʃə(r)] *cosmetic* fard *m inv*
blus•ter ['blʌstə(r)] *v/i* protestare
blus•ter•y ['blʌstərɪ] *adj* ventoso
BO [biː'əʊ] *abbr* (= ***body odour***) odori *mpl* corporei
board [bɔːd] **1** *n* asse *f*; *for game* scacchiera *f*; *for notices* tabellone *m*; ***board*** (***of directors***) consiglio *m* (d'amministrazione); ***on board*** (*plane*, *train*, *boat*) a bordo; ***take on board*** *comments etc* prendere in esame; ***take on board*** (*fully realize truth of*) accettare; ***across the board*** a tutti i livelli **2** *v/t aeroplane etc* salire a bordo di **3** *v/i of passengers* salire a bordo
◆ **board up** *v/t* chiudere con assi
◆ **board with** *v/t* essere a pensione da
board and 'lodg•ing vitto e alloggio *m*
board•er ['bɔːdə(r)] pensionante *m/f*; EDU convittore *m*, -trice *f*
'**board game** gioco *m* da tavolo
'**board•ing card** carta *f* d'imbarco
'**board•ing house** pensione *f*
'**board•ing pass** carta *f* d'imbarco
'**board•ing school** collegio *m*
'**board meet•ing** riunione *f* di consiglio
'**board room** sala *f* del consiglio
boast [bəʊst] **1** *n* vanteria *f* **2** *v/i* vantarsi
boat [bəʊt] (*small*, *for leisure*) barca *f*; (*ship*) nave *f*; ***go by boat*** andare in nave
bob[1] [bɒb] (*haircut*) caschetto *m*
bob[2] [bɒb] *v/i* (*pret & pp* ***-bed***) *of boat etc* andare su e giù
◆ **bob up** *v/i* spuntare
'**bob•sleigh**, '**bob•sled** bob *m inv*
bod•ice ['bɒdɪs] corpetto *m*
bod•i•ly ['bɒdɪlɪ] **1** *adj* corporale **2** *adv eject* di peso
bod•y ['bɒdɪ] corpo *m*; *dead* cadavere *m*; ***body of water*** massa *f* d'acqua; ***body*** (***suit***) (*undergarment*) body *m inv*
'**bod•y ar•mour** giubbotto *m* antiproiettile
'**body•guard** guardia *f* del corpo
'**body lan•guage** linguaggio *m* del corpo
'**bod•y o•dour** odori *mpl* corporei
'**bod•y pierc•ing** piercing *m inv*
'**body shop** MOT carrozzeria *f*
'**bod•y stock•ing** body *m inv*
'**body•work** MOT carrozzeria *f*
bog palude *f*
bog•gle ['bɒgl] *v/i*: ***the mind boggles!*** è incredibile!
bo•gus ['bəʊgəs] *adj* fasullo
boil[1] [bɔɪl] *n* (*swelling*) foruncolo *m*
boil[2] [bɔɪl] **1** *v/t* far bollire **2** *v/i* bollire
◆ **boil down to** *v/t* ridursi a
◆ **boil over** *v/i of milk etc* traboccare bollendo
boil•er ['bɔɪlə(r)] caldaia *f*
boil•ing point ['bɔɪlɪŋ] *of liquid* punto *m* d'ebollizione; ***reach boiling point*** *fig* perdere le staffe
bois•ter•ous ['bɔɪstərəs] *adj* turbolento
bold [bəʊld] **1** *adj* (*brave*) audace **2** *n* (*print*) neretto *m*; ***in bold*** in neretto
bol•ster ['bəʊlstə(r)] *v/t confidence* rafforzare
bolt [bəʊlt] **1** *n on door* catenaccio *m*; (*metal pin*) bullone *m*; *of lightning* fulmine *m*; ***like a bolt from the blue*** come un fulmine a ciel sereno **2** *adv*: ***bolt upright*** diritto come un fuso **3** *v/t* (*fix with bolts*) fissare con bulloni; (*close*) chiudere col catenaccio **4** *v/i* (*run off*) scappare via
bomb [bɒm] **1** *n* bomba *f* **2** *v/t* bombardare; (*blow up*) fare esplodere una bomba in, far saltare
bom•bard [bɒm'bɑːd] *v/t* (*attack*) bombardare; ***bombard with questions*** bombardare di domande
'**bomb attack** attacco *m* dinamitardo
bomb•er ['bɒmə(r)] (*aeroplane*) bombardiere *m*; (*terrorist*) dinamitardo *m*, -a *f*
'**bomb•er jack•et** bomber *m inv*
'**bomb•proof** *adj* a prova di bomba
'**bomb scare** allarme-bomba *m*
'**bomb•shell** (*fig*: *news*) bomba *f*
bond [bɒnd] **1** *n* (*tie*) legame *m*; FIN obbligazione *f*; ***government bonds*** titoli *mpl* di Stato **2** *v/i* aderire
bone [bəʊn] **1** *n* osso *m* **2** *v/t meat* disossare; *fish* togliere la lisca a
bon•fire ['bɒnfaɪə(r)] falò *m inv*
bonk [bɒŋk] *v/t & v/i* P scopare P
bon•net ['bɒnɪt] *of car* cofano *m*
bo•nus ['bəʊnəs] (*money*) gratifica *f*; (*something extra*) vantaggio *m* in più
boo [buːb] **1** *n* fischio *m* **2** *v/t & v/i actor*, *speaker* fischiare

boob[1] [buːb] **1** *n* F (*mistake*) errore *m* **2** *v/i* F (*make a mistake*) fare un errore
boob[2] [buːb] *n* P (*breast*) tetta *f* P
boo•boo ['buːbuː] *n* F → ***boob***[1]
book [bʊk] **1** *n* libro *m*; ***book of matches*** bustina *f* di fiammiferi **2** *v/t* (*reserve*) prenotare; *of policeman* multare; SP ammonire **3** *v/i* (*reserve*) prenotare
◆ **book in 1** *v/i* prenotare una camera; (*check in*) registrarsi **2** *v/t* prenotare una camera per
'**book•case** scaffale *m*
booked up [bʊkt'ʌp] *adj* tutto esaurito; *person* occupatissimo
book•ie ['bʊkɪ] F allibratore *m*
book•ing ['bʊkɪŋ] (*reservation*) prenotazione *f*
'**book•ing clerk** impiegato *m* della biglietteria
'**book•ing of•fice** biglietteria *f*
'**book•keep•er** contabile *m/f*
'**book•keep•ing** contabilità *f inv*
book•let ['bʊklɪt] libretto *m*
'**book•mak•er** allibratore *m*
books [bʊks] *npl* (*accounts*) libri *mpl* contabili; ***do the books*** tenere la contabilità; ***cook the bookss*** falsificare i libri contabili
'**book•sell•er** libraio *m*, -a *f*
'**book•shelf** mensola *f*
'**book•shop** libreria *f*
'**book•stall** edicola *f*
'**book to•ken** buono *m* libro
boom[1] [buːm] **1** *n* boom *m inv* **2** *v/i of business* andare a gonfie vele
boom[2] [buːm] **1** *n* (*bang*) rimbombo *m* **2** *v/i* rimbombare
boor [bɔː(r)] zotico *m*
boor•ish ['bɔːrɪʃ] *adj* da zotico
boost [buːst] **1** *n* spinta *f* **2** *v/t production, sales* incrementare; *confidence* aumentare
boot[1] [buːt] *n* stivale *m*; (*climbing boot*) scarpone *m*; *for football* scarpetta *m*
boot[2] [buːt] *of car* bagagliaio *m*
◆ **boot out** *v/t* F sbattere fuori F
◆ **boot up** *v/t & v/i* COMPUT inizializzare
booth [buːð] *at market, fair* bancarella *f*; (*telephone booth*) cabina *f*
booze [buːz] *n* F alcolici *mpl*
booz•er ['buːzə(r)] F (*pub*) pub *m inv*; (*person*) beone *m*, -a *f* F
'**booze-up** F bevuta *f*
bor•der ['bɔːdə(r)] **1** *n between countries* confine *m*; (*edge*) bordo *m* **2** *v/t country* confinare con
◆ **border on** *country* confinare con; (*be almost*) rasentare
'**bor•der•line** *adj* al limite; ***a borderline case*** un caso limite
bore[1] [bɔː(r)] *v/t hole* praticare
bore[2] [bɔː(r)] **1** *n* (*person*) persona *f* noiosa; ***it's such a bore*** è una seccatura **2** *v/t* annoiare
bore[3] [bɔː(r)] *pret* → ***bear***[2]
bored [bɔːd] *adj* annoiato; ***I'm bored*** mi sto annoiando
bore•dom ['bɔːdəm] noia *f*
bor•ing ['bɔːrɪŋ] *adj* noioso
born [bɔːn] *adj*: ***be born*** essere nato; ***where were you born?*** dove sei nato?; ***be a born …*** essere un … nato
borne [bɔːn] *pp* → ***bear***[2]
bor•row ['bɒrəʊ] *v/t* prendere in prestito
bos•om ['bʊzm] *of woman* seno *m*
boss [bɒs] boss *m inv*
◆ **boss about** *v/t* dare ordini a
boss•y ['bɒsɪ] *adj* prepotente
bo•tan•i•cal [bə'tænɪkl] *adj* botanico
bo•tan•ic(•al) gar•dens *npl* orto *m* botanico
bot•a•nist ['bɒtənɪst] botanico *m*, -a *f*
bot•a•ny ['bɒtənɪ] botanica *f*
botch [bɒtʃ] *v/t* fare un pasticcio con
both [bəʊθ] **1** *adj pron* entrambi, tutti *mpl* e due, tutte *fpl* e due, tutt'e due; ***I know both (of the) brothers*** conosco tutt'e due i fratelli; ***both (of the) brothers were there*** tutt'e due i fratelli erano lì; ***both of them*** entrambi **2** *adv*: ***both my mother and I*** sia mia madre che io; ***is it business or pleasure? – both*** per piacere o per affari? - tutt'e due
both•er ['bɒðə(r)] **1** *n* disturbo *m*; ***it's no bother*** non c'è problema **2** *v/t* (*disturb*) disturbare; (*worry*) preoccupare **3** *v/i*: ***don't bother*** (*you needn't do it*) non preoccuparti; ***you needn't have bothered!*** non dovevi!
bot•tle ['bɒtl] **1** *n* bottiglia *f*; *for baby* biberon *m* **2** *v/t* imbottigliare
◆ **bot•tle out** *v/i* P tirarsi indietro
◆ **bottle up** *v/t feelings* reprimere
'**bot•tle bank** contenitore *m* per la raccolta del vetro
bot•tled wa•ter ['bɒtld] acqua *f* in bottiglia
'**bot•tle•neck** *n* ingorgo *m*
'**bot•tle-o•pen•er** apribottiglie *m inv*
bot•tom ['bɒtəm] **1** *adj* più basso **2** *n* fondo *m*; (*buttocks*) sedere *m*; ***at the bottom of the screen*** in basso sullo schermo; ***at the bottom of the page / street*** in fondo alla pagina / strada; ***she started at the bottom and she's a manager now*** ha cominciato dal basso e ora è dirigente
◆ **bottom out** *v/i* toccare il fondo
bot•tom 'line (*fig: financial outcome*) risultato *m* finanziario; ***the bottom line***

(*the real issue*) l'essenziale *m*
bought [bɔːt] *pret & pp* → **buy**
boul•der ['bəʊldə(r)] macigno *m*
bounce [baʊns] **1** *v/t ball* far rimbalzare **2** *v/i of ball* rimbalzare; *on sofa etc* saltare; *of cheque* essere protestato
bounc•er ['baʊnsə(r)] buttafuori *m inv*
bouncy ['baʊnsɪ] *adj ball* che rimbalza bene; *chair* molleggiato
bound[1] [baʊnd] *adj*: ***be bound to do sth*** (*sure to*) dover fare per forza qc; (*obliged to*) essere obbligato a fare qc; ***the train is bound to be late*** il treno sarà senz'altro in ritardo
bound[2] [baʊnd] *adj*: ***be bound for*** *of ship* essere diretto a
bound[3] [baʊnd] **1** *n* (*jump*) balzo *m* **2** *v/i* saltellare
bound[4] [baʊnd] *pret & pp* → **bind**
bound•a•ry ['baʊndərɪ] confine *m*
bound•less ['baʊndlɪs] *adj* illimitato
bou•quet [bʊ'keɪ] bouquet *m inv*
bour•bon ['bɜːbən] bourbon *m inv*
bout [baʊt] MED attacco *m*; *in boxing* incontro *m*
bou•tique [buː'tiːk] boutique *f inv*
bo•vine spon•gi•form en•ceph•alo•pa•thy [bəʊvaɪnspʌdʒɪfɔːmensefə'lɒpəθɪ] encefalite *f* spongiforme bovina
bow[1] [baʊ] **1** *n as greeting* inchino *m* **2** *v/i* inchinarsi **3** *v/t head* chinare
bow[2] [bəʊ] (*knot*) fiocco *m*; MUS archetto *m*
bow[3] [baʊ] *of ship* prua *f*
bow•els ['baʊəlz] *npl* intestino *msg*
bowl[1] [bəʊl] (*container*) bacinella *f*; *for soup, cereal* ciotola *f*; *for cooking, salad* terrina *f*; *plastic* contenitore *m* di plastica
bowl[2] [bəʊl] **1** *n ball* boccia *f* **2** *v/i in bowling* lanciare
◆ **bowl over** *v/t* (*fig*: *astonish*) strabiliare
bowl•er ['bəʊlə(r)] (*hat*) bombetta *f*; *in cricket* lanciatore *m*
bowl•ing ['bəʊlɪŋ] bowling *m inv*
'**bowl•ing al•ley** pista *f* da bowling
bowls [bəʊlz] *nsg* (*game*) bocce *fpl*
bow 'tie (cravatta *f* a) farfalla *f*
box[1] [bɒks] *n container* scatola *f*; *on form* casella *f*
box[2] [bɒks] *v/i do boxing* fare pugilato; ***he boxed well*** ha combattuto bene
box•er ['bɒksə(r)] pugile *m*
'**box•er shorts** *npl* boxer *mpl*
box•ing ['bɒksɪŋ] pugilato *m*, boxe *f inv*
'**Box•ing Day** *Br* Santo Stefano
'**box•ing glove** guantone *m* da pugile
'**box•ing match** incontro *m* di pugilato
'**box•ing ring** quadrato *m*, ring *m inv*
'**box num•ber** *at post office* casella *f*
'**box of•fice** botteghino *m*
boy [bɔɪ] *child* bambino *m*; *youth* ragazzo *m*; *son* figlio *m*
boy•cott ['bɔɪkɒt] **1** *n* boicottaggio *m* **2** *v/t* boicottare
'**boy•friend** ragazzo *m*
boy•ish ['bɔɪɪʃ] *adj* da ragazzo
boy'scout boy-scout *m inv*
bra [brɑː] reggiseno *m*
brace [breɪs] *on teeth* apparecchio *m* (ai denti)
brace•let ['breɪslɪt] braccialetto *m*
brac•es ['breɪsɪs] *npl* bretelle *fpl*
brack•et ['brækɪt] *for shelf* staffa *f*; *in text* parentesi *f inv*
brag [bræg] *v/i* (*pret & pp* **-ged**) vantarsi
braid [breɪd] (*trimming*) passamaneria *f*
braille [breɪl] braille *m*
brain [breɪn] cervello *m*; ***use your brain*** usa il cervello
'**brain dead** *adj* MED cerebralmente morto
brain•less ['breɪnlɪs] *adj* F deficiente
brains [breɪnz] *npl* (*intelligence*) cervello *msg*
'**brain•storm** *Br* attacco *m* di follia
brain•storm•ing ['breɪnstɔːmɪŋ] brain-storming *m inv*
'**brain sur•geon** neurochirurgo *m*
'**brain sur•ger•y** neurochirurgia *f*
'**brain tu•mour** tumore *m* al cervello
'**brain•wash** *v/t* fare il lavaggio del cervello a; ***we've been brainwashed into believing that …*** ci hanno fatto il lavaggio del cervello per convincerci che …
'**brain•wave** (*brilliant idea*) lampo *m* di genio
brain•y ['breɪnɪ] *adj* F geniale
brake [breɪk] **1** *n* freno *m* **2** *v/i* frenare
'**brake flu•id** MOT liquido *m* dei freni
'**brake light** MOT fanalino *m* d'arresto
'**brake ped•al** MOT pedale *m* del freno
branch [brɑːntʃ] *n of tree* ramo *m*; *of bank, company* filiale *f*
◆ **branch off** *v/i of road* diramarsi
◆ **branch out** *v/i* diversificarsi
brand [brænd] **1** *n* marca *f*; **2** *v/t*: ***be branded a traitor*** essere tacciato di tradimento
brand 'im•age brand image *f inv*
bran•dish ['brændɪʃ] *v/t* brandire
brand 'lead•er marca *f* leader di mercato
brand 'loy•al•ty fedeltà *f inv* alla marca
'**brand name** marca *f*
brand-'new *adj* nuovo di zecca
bran•dy ['brændɪ] brandy *m inv*
brass [brɑːs] (*alloy*) ottone *m*; ***the brass*** MUS gli ottoni
brass 'band fanfara *f*
bras•sière [brə'zɪə(r)] *Am* reggiseno *m*

brat [bræt] *pej* marmocchio *m*
bra•va•do [brə'vɑːdəʊ] spavalderia *f*
brave [breɪv] *adj* coraggioso
brave•ly ['breɪvlɪ] *adv* coraggiosamente
brav•er•y ['breɪvərɪ] coraggio *m*
brawl [brɔːl] **1** *n* rissa *f* **2** *v/i* azzuffarsi
brawn•y ['brɔːnɪ] *adj* muscoloso
Bra•zil [brə'zɪl] Brasile *m*
Bra•zil•ian [brə'zɪlɪən] **1** *adj* brasiliano **2** *n* brasiliano *m*, -a *f*
breach [briːtʃ] *n* (*violation*) violazione *f*; *in party* rottura *f*
breach of 'con•tract LAW inadempienza *f* di contratto
bread [bred] *n* pane *m*
'bread•crumbs *npl for cooking* pane *msg* grattato; *for bird* briciole *fpl*
'bread knife coltello *m* per il pane
breadth [bredθ] larghezza *f*
'bread•win•ner: ***be the breadwinner*** mantenere la famiglia
break [breɪk] **1** *n also fig* rottura *f*; (*rest*) pausa *f*; ***give s.o. a break*** F (*opportunity*) dare un'opportunità a qu; ***take a break*** fare una pausa; ***without a break*** *work*, *travel* senza sosta; ***lucky break*** colpo di fortuna **2** *v/t* (*pret* ***broke***, *pp* ***broken***) *china*, *egg*, *bone* rompere; *rules*, *law* violare; *promise* non mantenere; *news* comunicare; *record* battere **3** *v/i* (*pret* ***broke***, *pp* ***broken***) *of china*, *egg*, *toy* rompersi; *of news* diffondersi; *of storm* scoppiare; *of boy's voice* cambiare
◆ **break away** *v/i* scappare; *from organization*, *tradition* staccarsi
◆ **break down 1** *v/i of vehicle*, *machine* avere un guasto; *of talks* arenarsi; *in tears* scoppiare in lacrime; (*mentally*) avere un esaurimento **2** *v/t door* buttare giù; *figures* analizzare
◆ **break even** *v/i* COM coprire le spese
◆ **break in** *v/i* (*interrupt*) interrompere; *of burglar* entrare con la forza
◆ **break off 1** *v/t* staccare; *engagement* rompere; ***they've broken it off*** si sono lasciati **2** *v/i* (*stop talking*) interrompersi
◆ **break out** *v/i* (*start up*) scoppiare; *of prisoners* evadere; ***he broke out in a rash*** gli è venuta l'orticaria
◆ **break up 1** *v/t* (*into component parts*) scomporre; *fight* far cessare **2** *v/i of ice* spaccarsi; *of couple* separarsi; *of band*, *meeting* sciogliersi
break•a•ble ['breɪkəbl] *adj* fragile
break•age ['breɪkɪdʒ] danni *mpl*
'break•down *of vehicle*, *machine* guasto *m*; *of talks* rottura *f*; (*nervous breakdown*) esaurimento *m* (nervoso); *of figures* analisi *f inv*
'break•down ser•vice servizio *m* di soccorso stradale
'break•down truck carro *m* attrezzi
break-'e•ven point punto *m* di rottura di pareggio
break•fast ['brekfəst] *n* colazione *f*; ***have breakfast*** fare colazione
'break•fast tel•e•vi•sion programmi *mpl* televisivi del mattino
'break-in furto *m* (con scasso)
'break•through *in plan*, *negotiations* passo *m* avanti; *of science*, *technology* scoperta *f*
'break•up *of marriage*, *partnership* rottura *f*
breast [brest] *of woman* seno *m*
'breast•feed *v/t* (*pret & pp* ***breastfed***) allattare
'breast•stroke nuoto *m* a rana
breath [breθ] respiro *m*; ***there wasn't a breath of air*** non c'era un filo d'aria; ***be out of breath*** essere senza fiato; ***take a deep breath*** fai un respiro profondo
breath•a•lyse ['breθəlaɪz] *v/t* sottoporre ad alcoltest
breath•a•lys•er® ['breθəlaɪzə(r)] alcoltest *m inv*
breathe [briːð] *v/t & v/i* respirare
◆ **breathe in 1** *v/i* inspirare **2** *v/t* respirare
◆ **breathe out** *v/i* espirare
breath•ing ['briːðɪŋ] *n* respiro *m*
breath•less ['breθlɪs] *adj* senza fiato
breath•less•ness ['breθlɪsnɪs] fiato *m* corto
breath•tak•ing ['breθteɪkɪŋ] *adj* mozzafiato
bred [bred] *pret & pp* → ***breed***
breed [briːd] **1** *n* razza *f* **2** *v/t* (*pret & pp* ***bred***) allevare; *fig* generare **3** *v/i* (*pret & pp* ***bred***) *of animals* riprodursi
breed•er ['briːdə(r)] allevatore *m*, -trice *f*
breed•ing ['briːdɪŋ] allevamento *m*; *of person* educazione *f*
breed•ing ground *fig* terreno *m* fertile
breeze [briːz] brezza *f*
breez•i•ly ['briːzɪlɪ] *adv fig* con disinvoltura
breez•y ['briːzɪ] *adj* ventoso; *fig* brioso
brew [bruː] **1** *v/t beer* produrre; *tea* fare **2** *v/i of storm* prepararsi; ***there's trouble brewing*** ci sono guai in vista
brew•er ['bruːə(r)] produttore *m* di birra
brew•er•y ['bruːərɪ] fabbrica *f* di birra
bribe [braɪb] **1** *n* bustarella *f* **2** *v/t* corrompere
brib•er•y ['braɪbərɪ] corruzione *f*
brick [brɪk] mattone *m*
'brick•lay•er muratore *m*
brid•al suite ['braɪdl] suite *f inv* nuziale

bride [braɪd] sposa *f*
'**bride•groom** sposo *m*
'**brides•maid** damigella *f* d'onore
bridge[1] [brɪdʒ] **1** *n* ponte *m*; *of ship* ponte *m* di comando; ***bridge of the nose*** setto *m* nasale; **2** *v/t gap* colmare
bridge[2] [brɪdʒ] (*card game*) bridge *m inv*
bri•dle ['braɪdl] briglia *f*
brief[1] [briːf] *adj* breve
brief[2] [briːf] **1** *n* (*mission*) missione *f*; (P: *lawyer*) avvocato *m* **2** *v/t*: ***brief s.o. on sth*** *instruct* dare istruzioni a qu su qc; *inform* mettere qu al corrente di qc
'**brief•case** valigetta *f*
brief•ing ['briːfɪŋ] briefing *m inv*
brief•ly ['briːflɪ] *adv* (*for a short period of time*) brevemente; (*in a few words, to sum up*) in breve
briefs [briːfs] *npl* slip *m inv*
bright [braɪt] *adj colour* vivace; *smile, future* radioso; (*sunny*) luminoso; (*intelligent*) intelligente; ***bright red*** rosso vivo
◆ **brighten up** ['braɪtn] **1** *v/t* ravvivare; **2** *v/i of weather* schiarirsi; *of face, person* rallegrarsi
bright•ly ['braɪtlɪ] *adv smile* in modo radioso; *shine, lit* intensamente; *coloured* in modo sgargiante
bright•ness ['braɪtnɪs] luminosità *f inv*
bril•liance ['brɪljəns] *of person* genialità *f inv*; *of colour* vivacità *f inv*
bril•liant ['brɪljənt] *adj sunshine etc* sfolgorante; (*very good*) eccezionale; (*very intelligent*) brillante
brim [brɪm] *of container* orlo *m*; *of hat* falda *f*
brim•ful ['brɪmfʊl] *adj* colmo
bring [brɪŋ] *v/t* (*pret & pp* ***brought***) portare; ***bring it here, will you*** portalo qui, per favore; ***can I bring a friend?*** posso portare un amico?
◆ **bring about** *v/t* causare
◆ **bring around** *v/t from a faint* far rinvenire; (*persuade*) convincere
◆ **bring back** *v/t* (*return*) restituire; (*re-introduce*) reintrodurre; *memories* risvegliare
◆ **bring down** *v/t tree, government, aeroplane* abbattere; *rates, inflation, price* far scendere
◆ **bring in** *v/t interest, income* rendere; *legislation* introdurre; *verdict* emettere; (*involve*) coinvolgere
◆ **bring on** *v/t illness* provocare
◆ **bring out** *v/t* (*produce*: *book*) pubblicare; *new product* lanciare
◆ **bring to** *v/t from a faint* far rinvenire
◆ **bring up** *v/t child* allevare; *subject* sollevare; (*vomit*) vomitare

brink [brɪŋk] *also fig* orlo *m*
brisk [brɪsk] *adj person, tone* spiccio; *walk* svelto; *trade* vivace
brist•les ['brɪslz] *npl* peli *mpl*
brist•ling ['brɪslɪŋ] *adj*: ***be bristling with*** brulicare di
Brit [brɪt] F britannico *m*, -a *f*
Brit•ain ['brɪtn] Gran Bretagna *f*
Brit•ish ['brɪtɪʃ] **1** *adj* britannico **2** *n*: ***the British*** i britannici
Brit•on ['brɪtn] britannico *m*, -a *f*
brit•tle ['brɪtl] *adj* fragile
broach [brəʊtʃ] *v/t subject* affrontare
broad [brɔːd] *adj* largo; (*general*) generale; ***in broad daylight*** in pieno giorno
'**broad•cast** **1** *n* trasmissione *f* **2** *v/t* trasmettere
'**broad•cast•er** giornalista *m/f* radiotelevisivo, -a
'**broad•cast•ing** diffusione *f* radiotelevisiva
broad•en ['brɔːdn] **1** *v/i* allargarsi **2** *v/t* allargare
broad•ly ['brɔːdlɪ] *adv*: ***broadly speaking*** parlando in senso lato
broad•mind•ed [brɔːd'maɪndɪd] *adj* di larghe vedute
broad•mind•ed•ness [brɔːd'maɪndɪdnɪs] larghezza *f* di vedute
broc•co•li ['brɒkəlɪ] broccoli *mpl*
bro•chure ['brəʊʃə(r)] dépliant *m inv*, opuscolo *m*
broke [brəʊk] **1** *adj* al verde; ***go broke*** (*go bankrupt*) andare sul lastrico **2** *pret* → ***break***
bro•ken ['brəʊkn] **1** *adj* rotto; *English* stentato; *marriage* fallito; ***she's from a broken home*** i suoi sono separati **2** *pp* → ***break***
bro•ken-heart•ed [brəʊkn'hɑːtɪd] *adj* col cuore spezzato
bro•ker ['brəʊkə(r)] mediatore *m*, -trice *f*
brol•ly ['brɒlɪ] F ombrello *m*
bron•chi•tis [brɒŋ'kaɪtɪs] bronchite *f*
bronze [brɒnz] *n* bronzo *m*
brooch [brəʊtʃ] spilla *f*
brood [bruːd] *v/i of person* rimuginare
broom [bruːm] scopa *f*
broth [brɒθ] (*soup*) minestra *f*; (*stock*) brodo *m*
broth•el ['brɒθl] bordello *m*
broth•er ['brʌðə(r)] fratello *m*; ***they're brothers*** sono fratelli; ***brothers and sisters*** fratelli e sorelle
'**broth•er-in-law** (*pl* ***brothers-in-law***) cognato *m*
broth•er•ly ['brʌðəlɪ] *adj* fraterno
brought [brɔːt] *pret & pp* → ***bring***
brow [braʊ] (*forehead*) fronte *f*; *of hill* ci-

ma *f*
brown [braʊn] **1** *n* marrone *m*; *eyes, hair* castano **2** *adj* marrone; (*tanned*) abbronzato **3** *v/t in cooking* rosolare **4** *v/i in cooking* rosolarsi
Brown•ie ['braʊnɪ] giovane esploratrice *f*
brown 'pa•per carta *f* da pacchi
brown pa•per 'bag sacchetto *m* di carta
'brown sug•ar zucchero *m* non raffinato
browse [braʊz] *v/i in shop* curiosare; ***browse through a book*** sfogliare un libro
brows•er ['braʊzə(r)] COMPUT browser *m inv*
bruise [bruːz] **1** *n* livido *m*; *on fruit* ammaccatura *f* **2** *v/t person* fare un livido a; *fruit* ammaccare **3** *v/i of person* coprirsi di lividi; *of fruit* ammaccarsi
bruis•ing ['bruːzɪŋ] *adj fig* doloroso
brunch [brʌntʃ] brunch *m inv*
bru•nette [bruː'net] *n* brunetta *f*
brunt [brʌnt] *n*: ***bear the brunt of …*** subire il peggio di …
brush [brʌʃ] **1** *n* spazzola *f*; (*paintbrush*) pennello *m*; (*toothbrush*) spazzolino *m* da denti; (*conflict*) scontro *m* **2** *v/t* spazzolare; (*touch lightly*) sfiorare; (*move away*) spostare; ***brush your teeth*** lavati i denti
◆ **brush against** *v/t* sfiorare
◆ **brush aside** *v/t* ignorare
◆ **brush off** *v/t* spazzolare via; *criticism* ignorare
◆ **brush up** *v/t* ripassare
'brush•off: ***give s.o. the brushoff*** F rispondere picche a qu F
'brush•work PAINT pennellata *f*
brusque [brʊsk] *adj* brusco
Brus•sels ['brʌslz] Bruxelles *f inv*
Brus•sels 'sprout cavolino *m* di Bruxelles
bru•tal ['bruːtl] *adj* brutale
bru•tal•i•ty [bruː'tælətɪ] brutalità *f inv*
bru•tal•ly ['bruːtəlɪ] *adv* brutalmente
brute [bruːt] bruto *m*
'brute force forza *f* bruta
BSE [biːes'iː] *abbr* (= ***bovine spongiform encephalopathy***)
bub•ble ['bʌbl] *n* bolla *f*
'bub•ble bath bagnoschiuma *m inv*
'bub•ble gum gomma *f* da masticare
'bub•ble wrap *n* involucro *m* a bolle
bub•bly ['bʌblɪ] *n* F (*champagne*) champagne *m inv*
buck[1] [bʌk] *n Am* F (*dollar*) dollaro *m*
buck[2] [bʌk] *v/i of horse* sgroppare
buck[3] [bʌk] *n*: ***pass the buck*** scaricare la responsabilità
buck•et ['bʌkɪt] *n* secchio *m*
'buck•et shop *agenzia f di viaggi che pratica forti sconti*
buck•le[1] ['bʌkl] **1** *n* fibbia *f* **2** *v/t belt* allacciare
buck•le[2] ['bʌkl] *v/i of wood, metal* piegarsi
◆ **buck•le down** *v/i* mettersi a lavorare
bud [bʌd] *n* BOT bocciolo *m*
bud•dy ['bʌdɪ] F amico *m*, -a *f*
budge [bʌdʒ] **1** *v/t* smuovere; (*make reconsider*) far cambiare idea a **2** *v/i* muoversi; (*change one's mind*) cambiare idea
bud•ger•i•gar ['bʌdʒərɪgɑː(r)] pappagallino *m*
bud•get ['bʌdʒɪt] **1** *n* budget *m inv*; *of company* bilancio *m* preventivo; *of state* bilancio *m* dello Stato; ***I'm on a budget*** devo stare attento ai soldi **2** *v/i* prevedere le spese
◆ **budget for** *v/t* preventivare
bud•gie ['bʌdʒɪ] F pappagallino *m*
buff[1] [bʌf] *adj* (*colour*) beige *inv*
buff[2] [bʌf] *n* appassionato *m*, -a *f*
buf•fa•lo ['bʌfələʊ] bufalo *m*
buff•er ['bʌfə(r)] RAIL respingente *m*; COMPUT buffer *m inv*; *fig* cuscinetto *m*
buf•fet[1] ['bʊfeɪ] *n* (*meal*) buffet *m inv*
buf•fet[2] ['bʌfɪt] *v/t of wind* sballottare
bug [bʌg] **1** *n* (*insect*) insetto *m*; (*virus*) virus *m inv*; (*spying device*) microspia *f*; COMPUT bug *m inv* **2** *v/t* (*pret & pp* **-ged**) *room* installare microspie in; *telephone* mettere sotto controllo; F (*annoy*) seccare
bug•gy ['bʌgɪ] *for baby* passeggino *m*
build [bɪld] **1** *n of person* corporatura *f* **2** *v/t* (*pret & pp* **built**) costruire
◆ **build up 1** *v/t relationship* consolidare; *collection* mettere insieme **2** *v/i of tension, traffic* aumentare; ***build up one's strength*** rimettersi in forze
'build•er ['bɪldə(r)] *person* muratore *m*; *company* impresario *m* edile
'build•ing ['bɪldɪŋ] edificio *m*, palazzo *m*; (*activity*) costruzione *f*
'build•ing blocks *npl for child* mattoncini *mpl*
'build•ing site cantiere *m* edile
'build•ing so•ci•e•ty *Br istituto m di credito immobiliare*
'build•ing trade edilizia *f*
'build-up *of traffic, pressure* aumento *m*; *of arms, forces* ammassamento *m*; (*publicity*) pubblicità *f inv*
built [bɪlt] *pret & pp* → ***build***
built-in ['bɪltɪn] *adj wardrobe* a muro; *flash* incorporato
built-up 'ar•e•a abitato *m*
bulb [bʌlb] BOT bulbo *m*; (*light bulb*)

lampadina *f*

bulge [bʌldʒ] **1** *n* rigonfiamento *m* **2** *v/i* sporgere

bu•lim•i•a [bʊ'lɪmɪə] bulimia *f*

bulk [bʌlk] grosso *m*; ***in bulk*** in grande quantità; *wholsesale* all'ingrosso

bulk•y ['bʌlkɪ] *adj* voluminoso

bull [bʊl] toro *m*

bull•doze ['bʊldəʊz] *v/t* (*demolish*) abbattere con il bulldozer; ***bulldoze s.o. into sth*** *fig* costringere qu a fare qc

bull•doz•er ['bʊldəʊzə(r)] bulldozer *m inv*

bul•let ['bʊlɪt] proiettile *m*, pallottola *f*

bul•le•tin ['bʊlɪtɪn] bollettino *m*

'**bul•le•tin board** COMPUT bulletin board *m inv*; *Am*: *on wall* bacheca *f*

'**bul•let-proof** *adj* a prova di proiettile

'**bull mar•ket** FIN mercato *m* in ascesa

'**bull's-eye** centro *m* del bersaglio; ***hit the bull's-eye*** fare centro

'**bull•shit** **1** *n* V stronzate *fpl* V **2** *v/i* (*pret & pp* ***-ted***) V dire stronzate V

bul•ly ['bʊlɪ] **1** *n* prepotente *m/f* **2** *v/t* (*pret & pp* ***-ied***) tiranneggiare

bul•ly•ing ['bʊlɪɪŋ] *n* prepotenze *fpl*

bum [bʌm] **1** *n* F *worthless person* mezza calzetta *f* F; (*Br*: *bottom*) sedere *m*; (*Am*: *tramp*) barbone *m* **2** *adj* F (*useless*) del piffero **3** *v/t* (*pret & pp* ***-med***) F *cigarette etc* scroccare

◆ **bum around**, **bum about** *v/i* F (*travel*) vagabondare; (*be lazy*) oziare

'**bum•bag** F marsupio *m*

bum•ble•bee ['bʌmblbiː] bombo *m*

bump [bʌmp] **1** *n* (*swelling*) gonfiore *m*; (*lump*) bernoccolo *m*; *on road* cunetta *f*; ***get a bump on the head*** prendere un colpo in testa **2** *v/t* battere

◆ **bump into** *v/t* *table* battere contro; (*meet*) incontrare

◆ **bump off** *v/t* F (*murder*) far fuori F

◆ **bump up** *v/t* F (*prices*) aumentare

bump•er ['bʌmpə(r)] **1** *n* MOT paraurti *m inv*; ***the traffic was bumper to bumper*** c'era una coda di macchine **2** *adj* (*extremely good*) eccezionale

bumph [bʌmf] *Br* F scartoffie *fpl*

'**bump-start** *v/t* *car* mettere in moto a spinte; (*fig*: *economy*) dare una spinta a

bump•y ['bʌmpɪ] *adj* *road* accidentato; *flight* movimentato

bun [bʌn] *hairstyle* chignon *m inv*; *for eating* panino *m* dolce

bunch [bʌntʃ] *of people* gruppo *m*; *of keys*, *flowers* mazzo *m*; ***a bunch of grapes*** un grappolo d'uva

bun•dle ['bʌndl] *of clothes* fagotto *m*; *of wood* fascina *f*

◆ **bundle up** *v/t* fare un fagotto di; (*dress warmly*) coprire bene

bung [bʌŋ] *v/t* F buttare

bun•ga•low ['bʌŋgələʊ] bungalow *m inv*

bun•gee jump•ing ['bʌndʒɪdʒʌmpɪŋ] salto *m* con l'elastico

bun•gle ['bʌŋgl] *v/t* pasticciare

bunk [bʌŋk] cuccetta *f*

bunk beds *npl* letti *mpl* a castello

buoy [bɔɪ] *n* NAUT boa *f*

buoy•ant ['bɔɪənt] *adj* (*cheerful*) allegro; *fig*: *economy* sostenuto

bur•den ['bɜːdn] **1** *n also fig* peso *m* **2** *v/t*: ***burden s.o. with sth*** *fig* opprimere qu con qc

bur•eau ['bjʊərəʊ] (*office*) ufficio *m*

bu•reauc•ra•cy [bjʊə'rɒkrəsɪ] burocrazia *f*

bu•reau•crat ['bjʊərəkræt] burocrate *m/f*

bu•reau•crat•ic [bjʊərə'krætɪk] *adj* burocratico

burg•er ['bɜːgə(r)] hamburger *m inv*

bur•glar ['bɜːglə(r)] ladro *m*

'**bur•glar a•larm** antifurto *m*

bur•glar•ize ['bɜːgləraɪz] *v/t* *Am* svaligiare

bur•glar•y ['bɜːglərɪ] furto *m* (con scasso)

bur•gle ['bɜːgl] *v/t* svaligiare

bur•i•al ['berɪəl] sepoltura *f*

bur•ly ['bɜːlɪ] *adj* robusto

burn [bɜːn] **1** *n* bruciatura *f*; *superficial* scottatura *f*; *very serious* ustione *f* **2** *v/t* (*pret & pp* ***burnt***) bruciare; *of sun* scottare **3** *v/i* (*pret & pp* ***burnt***) ardere; *of house* bruciare; *of toast* bruciarsi; (*get sunburnt*) scottarsi, bruciarsi; ***burn to death*** morire carbonizzato

◆ **burn down** **1** *v/t* dare alle fiamme **2** *v/i* essere distrutto dal fuoco

◆ **burn out** *v/t* **:** ***burn o.s. out*** esaurirsi; ***a burned-out car*** un'auto bruciata

burnt [bɜːnt] *pret & pp* → ***burn***

burp [bɜːp] **1** *n* rutto *m* **2** *v/i* ruttare **3** *v/t* *baby* far fare il ruttino a

burst [bɜːst] **1** *n in water pipe* rottura *f*; *of gunfire* raffica *f*; ***a burst of energy*** un'esplosione d'energia **2** *adj* *tyre* bucato **3** *v/t* (*pret & pp* ***burst***) *balloon* far scoppiare **4** *v/i* (*pret & pp* ***burst***) *of balloon*, *tyre* scoppiare; ***burst into a room*** irrompere in una stanza; ***burst into tears*** scoppiare in lacrime; ***burst out laughing*** scoppiare a ridere

bur•y ['berɪ] *v/t* (*pret & pp* ***-ied***) seppellire; *hide* nascondere; ***bury o.s. in work*** immergersi nel lavoro

bus [bʌs] **1** *n* (*local*) autobus *m inv*; (*long distance*) pullman *m inv* **2** *v/t* (*pret & pp* ***-sed***) trasportare in autobus

'**bus driv•er** autista *m/f* di autobus

bush [bʊʃ] (*plant*) cespuglio *m*; (*land*) boscaglia *f*
bushed [bʊʃt] *adj* F (*tired*) distrutto
bush•y ['bʊʃɪ] *adj eyebrows* irsuto
busi•ness ['bɪznɪs] (*trade*) affari *mpl*; (*company*) impresa *f*; (*work*) lavoro *m*; (*affair, matter*) faccenda *f*; (*as subject of study*) economia *f* aziendale; ***in the insurance business*** nel campo delle assicurazioni; ***on business*** per affari; ***that's none of your business!, mind your own business!*** fatti gli affari tuoi!
'**busi•ness card** biglietto *m* da visita (della ditta)
'**busi•ness class** business class *f inv*
'**busi•ness hours** *npl* orario *msg* di apertura
busi•ness•like ['bɪznɪslaɪk] *adj* efficiente
'**busi•ness lunch** pranzo *m* d'affari
'**busi•ness•man** uomo *m* d'affari
'**busi•ness meet•ing** riunione *f* d'affari
'**busi•ness school** istituto *m* commerciale
'**busi•ness stud•ies** *nsg* (*course*) economia *f* aziendale
'**busi•ness trip** viaggio *m* d'affari
'**busi•ness•wom•an** donna *f* d'affari
busk•er ['bʌskə(r)] musicista *m/f* ambulante
'**bus lane** corsia *f* riservata (ai mezzi pubblici)
'**bus shel•ter** pensilina *f* (dell'autobus)
'**bus sta•tion** autostazione *f*
'**bus stop** fermata *f* dell'autobus
'**bus tick•et** biglietto *m* dell'autobus
bust[1] [bʌst] *n of woman* petto *m*
bust[2] [bʌst] **1** *adj* F (*broken*) scassato; ***go bust*** fallire **2** *v/t* scassare
◆ **bus•tle about** ['bʌsl] affaccendarsi
'**bust-up** F rottura *f*
bust•y ['bʌstɪ] *adj* prosperoso
bus•y ['bɪzɪ] **1** *adj* occupato; *day* intenso; *street* animato; *shop*, *restaurant* affollato; TELEC occupato; ***be busy doing sth*** essere occupato a fare qc; ***I'm busy talking to Gran*** sto parlando con la nonna **2** *v/t* (*pret & pp* ***-ied***): ***busy o.s. with*** tenersi occupato con
'**bus•y•bod•y** impiccione *m*, -a *f*
but [bʌt] *unstressed* [bət] **1** *conj* ma; ***but then*** (***again***) d'altra parte **2** *prep*: ***all but him*** tutti tranne lui; ***the last but one*** il penultimo; ***the next but one*** il secondo; ***but for you*** se non fosse per te; ***nothing but the best*** solo il meglio
butch•er ['bʊtʃə(r)] macellaio *m*, -a *f*
butch•er's ['bʊtʃəz] macelleria *f*
butt [bʌt] **1** *n of cigarette* mozzicone *m*; *of joke* bersaglio *m*; *Am* P (*backside*) culo *m* P **2** *v/t* dare una testata a; *of goat*, *bull* dare una cornata a
◆ **butt in** *v/i* interrompere
but•ter ['bʌtə(r)] **1** *n* burro *m* **2** *v/t* imburrare
◆ **butter up** *v/t* F arruffianarsi F
'**but•ter•cup** ranuncolo *m*
'**but•ter•fly** *also swimming* farfalla *f*
but•tocks ['bʌtəks] *npl* natiche *fpl*
but•ton ['bʌtn] **1** *n* bottone *m*; *on machine* pulsante *m* **2** *v/t* abbottonare
◆ **button up** → ***button***
'**but•ton•hole 1** *n in suit* occhiello *m* **2** *v/t* attaccare un bottone a
but•tress ['bʌtrəs] contrafforte *m*
bux•om ['bʌksəm] *adj* formoso
buy [baɪ] **1** *n* acquisto *m* **2** *v/t* (*pret & pp* ***bought***) comprare; ***can I buy you a drink?*** posso offrirti da bere?; ***£5 doesn't buy much*** con 5 sterline non si compra granché
◆ **buy off** *v/t* (*bribe*) comprare
◆ **buy out** *v/t* COM rilevare
◆ **buy up** *v/t* accaparrarsi
buy•er ['baɪə(r)] acquirente *m/f*; *for department store, supermarket* buyer *m inv*
buzz [bʌz] **1** *n* ronzio *m*; F (*thrill*) emozione *f* **2** *v/i of insect* ronzare; *with buzzer* suonare **3** *v/t with buzzer* chiamare
◆ **buzz off** *v/i* F levarsi di torno F
buzz•er ['bʌzə(r)] cicalino *m*
by [baɪ] **1** *prep agency* da; (*near, next to*) vicino a, accanto a; (*no later than*) entro, per; (*past*) davanti a; (*mode of transport*) in; ***side by side*** fianco a fianco; ***by day / night*** di giorno / notte; ***by bus / train*** in autobus / treno; ***by the hour / ton*** a ore / tonnellate; ***by my watch*** secondo il mio orologio; ***a book by …*** un libro di …; ***murdered by her husband*** assassinata dal marito; ***by o.s.*** da solo; ***pay by cheque*** pagare con un assegno; ***by a couple of minutes*** per pochi minuti; ***2 by 4*** (*measurement*) 2 per 4; ***by this time tomorrow*** domani a quest'ora **2** *adv*: ***by and by*** (*soon*) tra breve
bye(-bye) [baɪ] ciao
'**by-e•lec•tion** *elezione f straordinaria di un parlamentare*
by•gone ['baɪgɒn] **1** *n*: ***let bygones be bygones*** metterci una pietra sopra **2** *adj*: ***in bygone days*** nei giorni andati
'**by•pass 1** *n* (*road*) circonvallazione *f*; MED by-pass *m inv* **2** *v/t* aggirare
'**by-prod•uct** sottoprodotto *m*
by•stand•er ['baɪstændə(r)] astante *m/f*
byte [baɪt] byte *m inv*
'**by•word** *n*: ***be a byword for*** essere sinonimo di

C

C

cab [kæb] (*taxi*) taxi *m inv*; *of truck* cabina *f*; ***cab driver*** tassista *m/f*
cab•a•ret ['kæbəreɪ] spettacolo *m* di cabaret
cab•bage ['kæbɪdʒ] cavolo *m*
cab•in ['kæbɪn] *of plane*, *ship* cabina *f*
'**cab•in at•tend•ant** assistente *m/f* di volo
'**cab•in crew** equipaggio *m* di volo
cab•i•net ['kæbɪnɪt] armadietto *m*; POL Consiglio *m* dei ministri; ***display cabinet*** vetrina *f*; ***drinks cabinet*** mobile *m* bar
'**cab•i•net mak•er** ebanista *m/f*
'**cab•i•net meet•ing** riunione *f* del Consiglio dei ministri
'**cab•i•net min•is•ter** membro *m* del Consiglio dei ministri
'**cab•i•net re•shuf•fle** rimpasto *m* del governo
ca•ble ['keɪbl] ELEC, *for securing* cavo *m*; ***cable*** (***TV***) tv *f* via cavo
'**ca•ble car** cabina *f* (di funivia)
'**ca•ble tel•e•vi•sion** televisione *f* via cavo
cac•tus ['kæktəs] cactus *m inv*
CAD-CAM ['kædkæm] *abbr* (= ***computer assisted design-computer assisted manufacture***) CAD-CAM *m*
cad•die ['kædɪ] **1** *n in golf* portamazze *m inv* **2** *v/i* portare le mazze
ca•det [kə'det] cadetto *m*
cadge [kædʒ] *v/t*: ***cadge sth from s.o.*** scroccare qc a qu
Cae•sar•e•an [sɪ'zeərɪən] *n* parto *m* cesareo
caf•é ['kæfeɪ] caffè *m inv*, bar *m*
caf•e•te•ri•a [kæfə'tɪərɪə] tavola *f* calda
caf•feine ['kæfiːn] caffeina *f*
cage [keɪdʒ] gabbia *f*
ca•gey ['keɪdʒɪ] *adj* evasivo
ca•hoots [kə'huːts] F: ***be in cahoots with*** essere in combutta con
ca•jole [kə'dʒəʊl] *v/t* convincere con le lusinghe
cake [keɪk] **1** *n* dolce *m*, torta *f*; ***be a piece of cake*** F essere un gioco da ragazzi **2** *v/i of mud*, *blood* indurirsi
ca•lam•i•ty [kə'læmətɪ] calamità *f inv*
cal•ci•um ['kælsɪəm] calcio *m*
cal•cu•late ['kælkjʊleɪt] *v/t* calcolare
cal•cu•lat•ing ['kælkjʊleɪtɪŋ] *adj* calcolatore
cal•cu•la•tion [kælkjʊ'leɪʃn] calcolo *m*
cal•cu•la•tor ['kælkjʊleɪtə(r)] calcolatrice *f*
cal•en•dar ['kælɪndə(r)] calendario *m*
calf[1] [kɑːf] (*pl* ***calves*** [kɑːvz]) *young cow* vitello *m*
calf[2] [kɑːf] (*pl* ***calves*** [kɑːvz]) *of leg* polpaccio *m*
'**calf•skin** *n* vitello *m*
cal•i•ber *Am*, **cal•i•bre** ['kælɪbə(r)] *of gun* calibro *m*; ***a man of his caliber*** un uomo del suo calibro
call [kɔːl] **1** *n* (*phone call*) telefonata *f*; (*shout*) grido *m*; (*demand*) richiesta *f*; (*visit*) visita *f*; ***be on call*** *of doctor* essere di guardia; ***pay s.o. a call*** far visita a qu **2** *v/t on phone* chiamare; (*summon*) chiamare; (*shout*) gridare; (*describe as*) definire; *meeting*, *election* indire, convocare; ***what have they called the baby?*** come hanno chiamato il bambino?; ***call s.o. as a witness*** citare qu a testimoniare; ***call a flight*** annunciare un volo; ***call s.o. names*** dare dei titoli a qu **3** *v/i on phone* chiamare; (*shout*) gridare; (*visit*) passare
◆ **call at** (*stop at*) passare da
◆ **call back 1** *v/t also* TELEC richiamare **2** *v/i on phone* richiamare; (*make another visit*) ripassare
◆ **call for** *v/t* (*collect*) passare a prendere; (*demand*) reclamare; (*require*) richiedere
◆ **call in 1** *v/t* (*summon*) far venire **2** *v/i on phone* chiamare; ***call in sick*** chiamare per dire di essere ammalato
◆ **call off** *v/t strike* revocare; *wedding*, *appointment* disdire
◆ **call on** *v/t* (*urge*) sollecitare; (*visit*) visitare
◆ **call out** *v/t* (*shout*) chiamare ad alta voce; (*summon*) chiamare
◆ **call up** *v/t on phone* chiamare; COMPUT aprire
'**call box** cabina *f* telefonica
'**call cen•tre** centro *m* chiamate
call•er ['kɔːlə(r)] *on phone* persona *f* che ha chiamato; (*visitor*) visitatore *m*, -trice *f*
'**call girl** squillo *f inv*
cal•lous ['kæləs] *adj* freddo, insensibile
cal•lous•ly ['kæləslɪ] *adv* freddamente, insensibilmente
cal•lous•ness ['kæləsnɪs] freddezza *f*, insensibilità *f*
calm [kɑːm] **1** *adj* calmo **2** *n* calma *f*
◆ **calm down 1** *v/t* calmare **2** *v/i* calmarsi
calm•ly ['kɑːmlɪ] *adv* con calma
cal•o•rie ['kælərɪ] caloria *f*

cam•cor•der ['kæmkɔːdə(r)] videocamera *f*
came [keɪm] *pret* → ***come***
cam•e•ra ['kæmərə] macchina *f* fotografica; (*video camera*) videocamera *f*; (*television camera*) telecamera *f*
'**cam•e•ra•man** cameraman *m inv*
cam•ou•flage ['kæməflɑːʒ] **1** *n* mimetizzazione *f*; *of soldiers* tuta *f* mimetica **2** *v/t* mimetizzare; *fig* mascherare
camp [kæmp] **1** *n* campo *m*; ***make camp*** accamparsi **2** *v/i* accamparsi
cam•paign [kæm'peɪn] **1** *n* campagna *f* **2** *v/i* militare
cam•paign•er [kæm'peɪnə(r)] militante *m/f*
camp•er ['kæmpə(r)] *person* campeggiatore *m*, -trice *f*; *vehicle* camper *m inv*
camp•ing ['kæmpɪŋ] campeggio *m*; ***go camping*** andare in campeggio
'**camp•site** camping *m inv*, campeggio *m*
cam•pus ['kæmpəs] campus *m inv*
can[1] [kæn] *unstressed* [kən] *v/aux* (*pret* ***could***) ◇ (*ability*) potere; ***can you hear me?*** mi senti?; ***I can't see*** non vedo; ***can you speak French?*** sai parlare il francese?; ***can he call me back?*** mi può richiamare?; ***as fast as you can*** più veloce che puoi; ***as well as you can*** meglio che puoi
◇ (*permission*) potere; ***can I help you?*** posso aiutarla?; ***can you help me?*** mi può aiutare?; ***can I have a beer / coffee?*** posso avere una birra / un caffè?; ***that can't be right*** non può essere giusto
can[2] [kæn] **1** *n for drinks* lattina *f*; *for food* scatola *f* **2** *v/t* (*pret & pp* ***-ned***) inscatolare
Can•a•da ['kænədə] Canada *m*
Ca•na•di•an [kə'neɪdɪən] **1** *adj* canadese **2** *n* canadese *m/f*
ca•nal [kə'næl] (*waterway*) canale *m*
ca•nar•y [kə'neərɪ] canarino *m*
can•cel ['kænsl] *v/t* annullare
can•cel•la•tion [kænsə'leɪʃn] annullamento *m*
can•cel'la•tion fee penalità *f* (per annullamento)
can•cer ['kænsə(r)] cancro *m*
Can•cer ['kænsə(r)] ASTR Cancro *m*
can•cer•ous ['kænsərəs] *adj* canceroso
c&f *abbr* (= ***cost and freight***) c&f
can•did ['kændɪd] *adj* franco
can•di•da•cy ['kændɪdəsɪ] candidatura *f*
can•di•date ['kændɪdət] candidato *m*, -a *f*
can•did•ly ['kændɪdlɪ] *adv* francamente
can•died ['kændiːd] *adj* candito
can•dle ['kændl] candela *f*
'**can•dle•stick** portacandele *m inv*
can•dor *Am*, **can•dour** ['kændə(r)] franchezza *f*
can•dy ['kændɪ] *Am* (*sweet*) caramella *f*; (*sweets*) dolciumi *mpl*
can•dy•floss ['kændɪflɒs] zucchero *m* filato
cane [keɪn] canna *f*; *for walking* bastone *m*
can•is•ter ['kænɪstə(r)] barattolo *m*; *spray* bombola *f*
can•na•bis ['kænəbɪs] hashish *m*
canned [kænd] *adj fruit*, *tomatoes* in scatola; (*recorded*) registrato
can•ni•bal•ize ['kænɪbəlaɪz] *v/t* riciclare parti di
can•not ['kænɒt] → ***can***[1]
can•ny ['kænɪ] *adj* (*astute*) arguto
ca•noe [kə'nuː] canoa *f*
'**can o•pen•er** apriscatole *m inv*
can't [kɑːnt] → ***can***[1]
can•tan•ker•ous [kæn'tæŋkərəs] *adj* irascibile
can•teen [kæn'tiːn] *in factory* mensa *f*
can•vas ['kænvəs] tela *f*
can•vass ['kænvəs] **1** *v/t* (*seek opinion of*) fare un sondaggio tra **2** *v/i* POL fare propaganda elettorale
can•yon ['kænjən] canyon *m inv*
cap [kæp] (*hat*) berretto *m*; *of bottle*, *jar* tappo *m*; *of pen* cappuccio *m*; *for lens* coperchio *m*
ca•pa•bil•i•ty [keɪpə'bɪlətɪ] *of person* capacità *f inv*; MIL potenziale *m*
ca•pa•ble ['keɪpəbl] *adj* (*efficient*) capace; ***be capable of*** essere capace di
ca•pac•i•ty [kə'pæsətɪ] capacità *f inv*; *of car engine* potenza *f*; *of factory* capacità *f inv* produttiva; ***in my capacity as …*** in qualità di …
cap•i•tal ['kæpɪtl] *n of country* capitale *f*; (*capital letter*) maiuscola *f*; *money* capitale *m*
cap•i•tal ex'pend•i•ture spese *fpl* in conto capitale
cap•i•tal 'gains tax imposta *f* sui redditi di capitale
cap•i•tal 'growth aumento *m* del capitale
cap•i•tal•is•m ['kæpɪtəlɪzm] capitalismo *m*
'**cap•i•tal•ist** ['kæpɪtəlɪst] **1** *adj* capitalista **2** *n* capitalista *m/f*
◆ **cap•i•tal•ize on** ['kæpɪtəlaɪz] *v/t* trarre vantaggio da
cap•i•tal 'let•ter lettera *f* maiuscola
cap•i•tal 'pun•ish•ment pena *f* capitale
ca•pit•u•late [kə'pɪtjʊleɪt] *v/i* capitolare
ca•pit•u•la•tion [kæpɪtjʊ'leɪʃn] capitolazione *f*
Cap•ri•corn ['kæprɪkɔːn] ASTR Capricor-

C

no *m*

cap•size [kæp'saɪz] **1** *v/i* ribaltarsi **2** *v/t* far ribaltare

cap•sule ['kæpsjʊl] *of medicine* cachet *m inv*; (*space capsule*) capsula *f*

cap•tain ['kæptɪn] *n* capitano *m*

cap•tion ['kæpʃn] *n* didascalia *f*

cap•ti•vate ['kæptɪveɪt] *v/t* affascinare

cap•tive ['kæptɪv] *adj* prigioniero

cap•tiv•i•ty [kæp'tɪvətɪ] cattività *f*

cap•ture ['kæptʃə(r)] **1** *n of building*, *city* occupazione *f*; *of city* presa *f*; *of criminal*, *animal* cattura *f* **2** *v/t person*, *animal* catturare; *city*, *building* occupare; *city* prendere; *market share* conquistare; (*portray*) cogliere

car [kɑː(r)] macchina *f*, auto *f inv*; *of train* vagone *m*; ***by car*** in macchina

ca•rafe [kə'ræf] caraffa *f*

car•a•mel ['kærəmel] *sweet* caramella *f* morbida

car•at ['kærət] carato *m*

car•a•van ['kærəvæn] roulotte *f inv*

'car•a•van site campeggio *m* per roulotte

car•bo•hy•drate [kɑːbə'haɪdreɪt] carboidrato *m*

'car bomb autobomba *f*

car•bon mon•ox•ide [kɑːbənmɒn'ɒksaɪd] monossido *m* di carbonio

car•bu•ret•or [kɑːbjʊ'retə(r)] carburatore *m*

car•cass ['kɑːkəs] carcassa *f*

car•cin•o•gen ['kɑːsɪnədʒen] cancerogeno *m*

car•cin•o•genic [kɑːsɪnə'dʒenɪk] *adj* cancerogeno

card [kɑːd] *to mark special occasion* biglietto *m*; (*postcard*) cartolina *f*; (*business card*) biglietto *m* (da visita); (*playing card*) carta *f*; COMPUT scheda *f*; *material* cartoncino *m*

'card•board cartone *m*

card•board 'box scatola *f* di cartone

car•di•ac ['kɑːdɪæk] *adj* cardiaco

car•di•ac ar'rest arresto *m* cardiaco

car•di•gan ['kɑːdɪgən] cardigan *m inv*

car•di•nal ['kɑːdɪnl] *n* REL cardinale *m*

'card in•dex schedario *m*

'card key tessera *f* magnetica

'card phone telefono *m* a scheda

care [keə(r)] **1** *n of baby*, *pet* cure *fpl*; *of the elderly* assistenza *f*; *of the sick* cura *f*; (*worry*) preoccupazione *f*; ***take care*** (*be cautious*) fare attenzione; ***take care (of yourself)!*** (*goodbye*) stammi bene; ***take care of*** (*look after*: *baby*, *dog*) prendersi cura di; *tool*, *house*, *garden* tenere bene; (*deal with*) occuparsi di; ***(handle) with care!*** *on label* maneggiare con cura **2** *v/i* interessarsi; ***I don't care!*** non mi importa; ***I couldn't care less*** non potrebbe importarmene di meno

care of → ***c/o***

◆ **care about** *v/t* interessarsi a

◆ **care for** *v/t* (*look after*) prendersi cura di; ***I don't care for your tone*** non mi piace il tuo tono; ***would you care for a tea?*** *fml* gradirebbe un tè?

ca•reer [kə'rɪə(r)] (*profession*) carriera *f*; (*path through life*) vita *f*

ca'reers of•fi•cer consulente *m/f* professionale

'care•free *adj* spensierato

care•ful ['keəfʊl] *adj* (*cautious*) attento; (*thorough*) attento; ***(be) careful!*** (stai) attento!

care•ful•ly ['keəfʊlɪ] *adv* con cautela

care•less ['keəlɪs] *adj* incurante; *driver*, *worker* sbadato; *work* fatto senza attenzione; *error* di disattenzione; ***you are so careless!*** sei così sbadato!

care•less•ly ['keəlɪslɪ] *adv* senza cura

carer ['keərə(r)] accompagnatore *m*, -trice *f*

ca•ress [kə'res] **1** *n* carezza *f* **2** *v/t* accarezzare

care•tak•er ['keəteɪkə(r)] custode *m/f*

'care•worn *adj* provato

'car fer•ry traghetto *m* (per le macchine)

car•go ['kɑːgəʊ] carico *m*

'car hire autonoleggio *m*

'car hire com•pa•ny compagnia *f* di autonoleggio

car•i•ca•ture ['kærɪkətjʊə(r)] *n* caricatura *f*

car•ing ['keərɪŋ] *adj* premuroso

'car me•chan•ic meccanico *m* per auto

car•nage ['kɑːnɪdʒ] carneficina *f*

car•na•tion [kɑː'neɪʃn] garofano *m*

car•ni•val ['kɑːnɪvl] carnevale *m*

car•ol ['kærəl] *n* canzone *f* di Natale

car•ou•sel [kærə'sel] *at airport* nastro *m* trasportatore; *for slide projector* carrello *m*

'car park parcheggio *m*

'car park at•tend•ant parcheggiatore *m*, -trice *f*

car•pen•ter ['kɑːpɪntə(r)] falegname *m*

car•pet ['kɑːpɪt] tappeto *m*; (*fitted carpet*) moquette *f inv*

'car phone telefono *m* da automobile

'car•pool *n uso m condiviso della macchina dell'uno o dell'altro tra un gruppo di persone*

'car port posto *m* auto coperto

car 'ra•di•o autoradio *f inv*

car•riage ['kærɪdʒ] carrozza *f*; COM trasporto *m*

car•ri•er ['kærɪə(r)] (*company*) compagnia *f* di trasporto; *of disease* portatore *m* sano, portatrice *f* sana
'**car•ri•er bag** sacchetto *m*
car•rot ['kærət] carota *f*
car•ry ['kærɪ] (*pret & pp* ***-ied***) **1** *v/t* portare; *of pregnant woman* portare in grembo; *of ship, plane, bus etc* trasportare; *proposal* approvare; ***get carried away*** farsi prendere dall'entusiasmo **2** *v/i of sound* sentirsi
◆ **carry on 1** *v/i* (*continue*) andare avanti, continuare; (*make a fuss*) fare storie; (*have an affair*) avere una storia **2** *v/t* (*conduct*) portare avanti
◆ **carry out** *v/t survey etc* effettuare; *orders etc* eseguire
'**car•ry•cot** porte-enfant *m inv*
'**car seat** *for child* seggiolino *m* per auto
cart [kɑːt] carretto *m*
car•tel [kɑː'tel] cartello *m*
car•ton ['kɑːtn] *for storage, transport* cartone *m*; *of cigarettes* stecca *f*
car•toon [kɑː'tuːn] *in newspaper, magazine* fumetto *m*; *on TV, film* cartone *m* animato
car•toon•ist [kɑː'tuːnɪst] *for newspaper etc* vignettista *m/f*
car•tridge ['kɑːtrɪdʒ] *for gun, printer* cartuccia *f*
carve [kɑːv] *v/t meat* tagliare; *wood* intagliare
carv•ing ['kɑːvɪŋ] *figure* scultura *f*
'**car wash** lavaggio *m* per auto
case¹ [keɪs] *for glasses, pen* astuccio *m*; *of whisky, wine* cassa *f*; (*suitcase*) valigia *f*; ***glass case*** teca *f*
case² [keɪs] *n* (*instance, for police*), MED caso *m*; (*argument*) argomentazione *f*; LAW causa *f*; ***in case …*** in caso …; ***take an umbrella in case it rains*** prendi un ombrello in caso piovesse; ***in any case*** in ogni caso; ***in that case*** in questo caso
'**case his•to•ry** MED cartella *f* clinica
'**case•load** numero *m* di assistiti; ***my doctor's caseload*** il numero dei pazienti del mio dottore
cash [kæʃ] **1** *n* contanti *mpl*; F (*money*) soldi *mpl*; ***cash down*** in contanti; ***pay (in) cash*** pagare in contanti; ***cash in advance*** pagamento *m* anticipato; ***cash on delivery*** → ***COD*** **2** *v/t cheque* incassare
◆ **cash in on** *v/t* guadagnare su
'**cash card** carta *f* per prelievi
'**cash cow** vacca *f* da mungere
'**cash desk** cassa *f*
cash 'dis•count sconto *m* su pagamento in contanti
'**cash di•spens•er** (sportello *m*) Bancomat® *m*
'**cash flow** flusso *m* di cassa
cash•ier [kæ'ʃɪə(r)] *n in shop etc* cassiere *m*, -a *f*
'**cash ma•chine** (sportello *m*) Bancomat® *m*
cash•mere ['kæʃmɪər] *adj* cashemere *m inv*
'**cash•point** (sportello *m*) Bancomat® *m*
'**cash re•gis•ter** cassa *f*
ca•si•no [kə'siːnəʊ] casinò *m inv*
ca•sket ['kæskɪt] *Am* (*coffin*) bara *f*
cas•se•role ['kæsərəʊl] *n meal* stufato *m*; *container* casseruola *f*
cas•sette [kə'set] cassetta *f*
cas'sette play•er mangiacassette *m inv*
cas'sette re•cord•er registratore *m* (a cassette)
cast [kɑːst] **1** *n of play* cast *m inv*; (*mould*) stampo *m* **2** *v/t* (*pret & pp* ***cast***) *doubt, suspicion* far sorgere (**on** su); *shadow* proiettare; *metal* colare (in uno stampo); *play* assegnare le parti per; ***cast s.o. as …*** *for play* far fare a qu il ruolo di …; ***he was cast as Romeo*** gli è stata assegnata la parte di Romeo; ***cast a glance at s.o./sth*** gettare uno sguardo su qu / qc
◆ **cast off** *v/i of ship* sciogliere gli ormeggi
caste [kɑːst] casta *f*
cast•er ['kɑːstə(r)] *on chair etc* rotella *f*
'**cast•er sug•ar** zucchero *m* raffinato
cast 'iron ghisa *f*
cast-'iron *adj* di ghisa
cas•tle ['kɑːsl] castello *m*
'**cast•or** ['kɑːstə(r)] → ***caster***
cas•trate [kæ'streɪt] *v/t* castrare
cas•tra•tion [kæ'streɪʃn] castrazione *f*
cas•u•al ['kæʒʊəl] *adj* (*chance*) casuale; (*offhand*) disinvolto; (*irresponsible*) noncurante; *remark* poco importante; *clothes* casual *inv*; (*not permanent*) occasionale; ***casual sex*** rapporti *mpl* occasionali
cas•u•al•ly ['kæʒʊəlɪ] *adv dressed* (in modo) casual; *say* con disinvoltura
cas•u•al•ty ['kæʒʊəltɪ] *dead person* vittima *f*; *injured* ferito *m*
'**cas•u•al wear** abbigliamento *m* casual
cat [kæt] gatto *m*; *wild* felino *m*
cat•a•log *Am*, **cat•a•logue** ['kætəlɒg] *n* catalogo *m*
cat•a•lyst ['kætəlɪst] catalizzatore *m*
cat•a•lyt•ic con'vert•er [kætə'lɪtɪk] marmitta *f* catalitica
cat•a•pult ['kætəpʌlt] **1** *v/t fig*: *to fame, stardom* catapultare **2** *n* catapulta *f*; *toy* fionda *f*
cat•a•ract ['kætərækt] MED cataratta *f*

C

ca•tas•tro•phe [kə'tæstrəfɪ] catastrofe *f*
cat•a•stroph•ic [kætə'strɒfɪk] *adj* catastrofico
catch [kætʃ] **1** *n* presa *f*; *of fish* pesca *f*; *on handbag, box* chiusura *f*; *on door, window* fermo *m*; *on brooch* fermaglio *m*; (*problem*) inghippo *m* **2** *v/t* (*pret & pp* **caught**) *ball, escaped prisoner* prendere; *bus, train* prendere; *fish* prendere; (*in order to speak to*) trovare; (*hear*) afferrare; *illness* prendere; ***catch (a) cold*** prendere un raffreddore; ***catch s.o.'s eye*** *of person, object* attirare l'attenzione di qu; ***catch sight of, catch a glimpse of*** intravedere; ***catch s.o. doing sth*** sorprendere qu a fare qc
◆ **catch on** *v/i* (*become popular*) fare presa; (*understand*) afferrare
◆ **catch up** *v/i* recuperare; ***catch up with s.o.*** raggiungere qu; ***catch up with sth*** *work, studies* mettersi in pari con qc
◆ **catch up on** *v/t* recuperare
catch-22 [kætʃtwentɪ'tuː]: ***it's a catch-22 situation*** è una situazione senza via d'uscita
catch•ing ['kætʃɪŋ] *adj also fig* contagioso
catch•y ['kætʃɪ] *adj tune* orecchiabile
cat•e•go•ric [kætə'gɒrɪk] *adj* categorico
cat•e•gor•i•cal•ly [kætə'gɒrɪklɪ] *adv* categoricamente
cat•e•go•ry ['kætɪgərɪ] categoria *f*
◆ **cater for** ['keɪtə(r)] *v/t* (*meet the needs of*) rispondere alle esigenze di; (*provide food for*) organizzare rinfreschi per
ca•ter•er ['keɪtərə(r)] ristoratore *m*, -trice *f*
ca•ter•pil•lar ['kætəpɪlə(r)] bruco *m*
ca•the•dral [kə'θiːdrl] cattedrale *f*, duomo *m*
Cath•o•lic ['kæθəlɪk] **1** *adj* cattolico **2** *n* cattolico *m*, -a *f*
Ca•thol•i•cism [kə'θɒlɪsɪzm] cattolicesimo *m*
'**cat•nap 1** *n* pisolino *m* **2** *v/i* (*pret & pp* **-ped**) schiacciare un pisolino
'**cat's eye** *on road* catarifrangente *m*
cat•tle ['kætl] bestiame *m*
cat•ty ['kætɪ] *adj* maligno
'**cat•walk** passerella *f*
caught [kɔːt] *pret & pp* → ***catch***
cau•li•flow•er ['kɒlɪflaʊə(r)] cavolfiore *m*
cause [kɔːz] **1** *n* causa *f*; (*grounds*) motivo *m*; (*objective*) causa *f* **2** *v/t* causare; ***what caused you to leave so early?*** perché sei andato via così presto?
caus•tic ['kɔːstɪk] *adj fig* caustico
cau•tion ['kɔːʃn] **1** *n* (*carefulness*) cautela *f*, prudenza *f*; ***caution is advised*** si raccomanda la prudenza **2** *v/t* (*warn*) mettere in guardia
cau•tious ['kɔːʃəs] *adj* cauto, prudente
cau•tious•ly ['kɔːʃəslɪ] *adv* con cautela
cave [keɪv] caverna *f*, grotta *f*
◆ **cave in** *v/i of roof* crollare
cav•i•ar ['kævɪɑː(r)] caviale *m*
cav•i•ty ['kævətɪ] cavità *f inv*; *in tooth* carie *f inv*
cc [siː'siː] **1** *abbr* (= ***carbon copy***) cc (= copia *f* carbone); (= ***cubic centimetres***) cc *m inv* (= centimetri cubici); MOT cilindrata *f* **2** *v/t memo* fare una copia di; *person* mandare una copia per conoscenza a
CD [siː'diː] *abbr* (= ***compact disc***) CD *m inv*
CD play•er lettore *m* CD
CD-ROM [siːdiː'rɒm] CD-ROM *m inv*
CD-ROM drive drive *m inv* per CD-ROM
cease [siːs] *v/t & v/i* cessare
'**cease-fire** cessate il fuoco *m inv*
cei•ling ['siːlɪŋ] *of room* soffitto *m*; (*limit*) tetto *m*, plafond *m inv*
cel•e•brate ['selɪbreɪt] **1** *v/i* festeggiare **2** *v/t* celebrare, festeggiare; (*observe*) festeggiare
cel•e•brat•ed ['selɪbreɪtɪd] *adj* acclamato; ***be celebrated for*** essere famoso per
cel•e•bra•tion [selɪ'breɪʃn] celebrazione *f*, festeggiamento *m*
ce•leb•ri•ty [sɪ'lebrətɪ] celebrità *f inv*
cel•e•ry ['selərɪ] sedano *m*
cel•i•ba•cy ['selɪbəsɪ] celibato *m*
cel•i•bate ['selɪbət] *adj man* celibe; *woman* nubile
cell [sel] *for prisoner* cella *f*; BIO cellula *f*; *in spreadsheet* casella *f*, cella *f*
cel•lar ['selə(r)] *of house* cantina *f*; *of wine* collezione *f* di vini
cel•list ['tʃelɪst] violoncellista *m/f*
cel•lo ['tʃeləʊ] violoncello *m*
cel•lo•phane ['seləfeɪn] cellofan *m inv*
cel•lu•lar phone [seljuːlər'fəʊn] telefono *m* cellulare, cellulare *m*
cel•lu•lite ['seljuːlaɪt] cellulite *f*
ce•ment [sɪ'ment] **1** *n* cemento *m*; (*adhesive*) mastice *m* **2** *v/t* cementare; *friendship* consolidare
cem•e•tery ['semətrɪ] cimitero *m*
cen•sor ['sensə(r)] *v/t* censurare
cen•sor•ship ['sensəʃɪp] censura *f*
cen•sus ['sensəs] censimento *m*
cent [sent] centesimo *m*
cen•te•na•ry [sen'tiːnərɪ] centenario *m*
cen•ter *Am* → ***centre***
cen•ti•grade ['sentɪgreɪd] *adj* centigrado; ***10 degrees centigrade*** 10 gradi centigradi
cen•ti•me•ter *Am*, **cen•ti•me•tre** ['sentɪmiːtə(r)] centimetro *m*

cen•tral ['sentrəl] *adj location, flat* centrale; (*main*) principale, centrale; ***central London / France*** il centro di Londra / della Francia; ***be central to sth*** essere fondamentale per qc
cen•tral 'heat•ing riscaldamento *m* autonomo
cen•tral•ize ['sentrəlaɪz] *v/t decision making* accentrare
cen•tral 'lock•ing MOT chiusura *f* centralizzata
cen•tral 'pro•ces•sing u•nit unità *f inv* centrale
cen•tral res•er'va•tion MOT banchina *f* spartitraffico
cen•tre ['sentə(r)] **1** *n* centro *m*; ***in the centre of*** al centro di **2** *v/t* centrare
◆ **centre on** *v/t* essere incentrato su
cen•tre of 'grav•i•ty centro *m* di gravità
cen•tu•ry ['sentʃərɪ] secolo *m*
CEO [siːiː'əʊ] *abbr* (= ***Chief Executive Officer***) direttore *m* generale
ce•ram•ic [sɪ'ræmɪk] *adj* ceramico
ce•ram•ics [sɪ'ræmɪks] (*pl*: *objects*) ceramiche *fpl*; (*sg*: *art*) ceramica *f*
ce•re•al ['sɪərɪəl] (*grain*) cereale *m*; (*breakfast cereal*) cereali *mpl*
cer•e•mo•ni•al [serɪ'məʊnɪəl] **1** *adj* da cerimonia **2** *n* cerimoniale *m*
cer•e•mo•ny ['serɪmənɪ] (*event*) cerimonia *f*; (*ritual*) cerimonie *fpl*
cer•tain ['sɜːtn] *adj* (*sure, particular*) certo; ***it's certain that …*** è certo che …; ***a certain Mr S.*** un certo Sig S.; ***make certain*** accertarsi; ***know / say for certain*** sapere / dire con certezza
cer•tain•ly ['sɜːtnlɪ] *adv* certamente; ***certainly not!*** certo che no!
cer•tain•ty ['sɜːtntɪ]) certezza *f*; ***it's a certainty*** è una cosa certa; ***he's a certainty to win*** vincerà di certo
cer•tif•i•cate [sə'tɪfɪkət] *qualification* certificazione *f*; *official paper* certificato *m*
cer•ti•fy ['sɜːtɪfaɪ] *v/t* (*pret & pp* ***-ied***) dichiarare ufficialmente
Ce•sar•e•an *Am* → ***Caesarean***
ces•sa•tion [se'seɪʃn] cessazione *f*
c/f *abbr* (= ***cost and freight***) c/f
CFC [siːef'siː] *abbr* (= ***chlorofluorocarbon***) CFC *m inv* (= clorofluorocarburi *mpl*)
chain [tʃeɪn] **1** *n* catena *f* **2** *v/t*: ***chain sth/ s.o. to sth*** incatenare qc / qu a qc
chain re'ac•tion reazione *f* a catena
'chain smoke *v/i* fumare una sigaretta dopo l'altra
'chain smok•er fumatore *m*, -trice *f* incallito
'chain store *store* negozio *m* di una catena; *company* catena *f* di negozi
chair [tʃeə(r)] **1** *n* sedia *f*; (*arm chair*) poltrona *f*; *at university* cattedra *f*; ***the chair*** (*electric chair*) la sedia elettrica; *at meeting* presidente *m/f*; ***take the chair*** presiedere **2** *v/t meeting* presiedere
'chair lift seggiovia *f*
'chair•man presidente *m*
chair•man•ship ['tʃeəmənʃɪp] presidenza *f*
'chair•per•son presidente *m/f*
'chair•wom•an presidente *f*
cha•let ['ʃæleɪ] chalet *m inv*
chal•ice ['tʃælɪs] REL calice *m*
chalk [tʃɔːk] gesso *m*
chal•lenge ['tʃælɪndʒ] **1** *n* sfida *f* **2** *v/t* sfidare; (*call into question*) mettere alla prova
chal•len•ger ['tʃælɪndʒə(r)] sfidante *m/f*
chal•len•ging ['tʃælɪndʒɪŋ] *adj job, undertaking* stimolante
cham•ber•maid ['tʃeɪmbəmeɪd] cameriera *f*
'cham•ber mu•sic musica *f* da camera
Cham•ber of 'Com•merce Camera *f* di Commercio
cham•ois (leather) ['ʃæmɪ] camoscio *m*
cham•pagne [ʃæm'peɪn] champagne *m inv*
cham•pi•on ['tʃæmpɪən] **1** *n* SP campione *m*, -essa *f*; *of cause* difensore *m*, -a *f* **2** *v/t* (*cause*) difendere
cham•pi•on•ship ['tʃæmpɪənʃɪp] *event* campionato *m*; *title* titolo *m* di campione; *of cause* difesa *f*
chance [tʃɑːns] (*possibility*) probabilità *f inv*; (*opportunity*) opportunità *f inv*, occasione *f*; (*risk*) rischio *m*; (*luck*) caso *m*; ***by chance*** per caso; ***take a chance*** correre un rischio; ***I'm not taking any chances*** non voglio correre nessun rischio; ***you don't stand a chance*** non hai nessuna possibilità
Chan•cel•lor ['tʃɑːnsələ(r)] *in Germany* cancelliere *m*; ***Chancellor (of the Exchequer)*** *in Britain* ministro *m* del tesoro
chan•de•lier [ʃændə'lɪə(r)] lampadario *m*
change [tʃeɪndʒ] **1** *n* cambiamento *m*; *small coins* moneta *f*; *from purchase* resto *m*; ***for a change*** per cambiare; ***a change of clothes*** un ricambio di vestiti **2** *v/t* (*alter*) cambiare; *one's clothes* cambiarsi **3** *v/i* cambiare; (*put on different clothes*) cambiarsi; ***you change at Crewe*** devi cambiare a Crewe
change•a•ble ['tʃeɪndʒəbl] *adj* incostante; *weather* variabile
'change•o•ver passaggio *m*; *period* fase *f*

C

di transizione; *in relay race* passaggio *m* del testimone
chang•ing room ['ʧeɪndʒɪŋ] SP spogliatoio *m*; *in shop* camerino *m*
chan•nel ['ʧænl] *on TV*, *in water* canale *m*
Chan•nel 'Tun•nel tunnel *m* della Manica
chant [ʧɑːnt] **1** *n* slogan *m inv*; REL canto *m* **2** *v/i* gridare; *of demonstrators* gridare slogan; REL cantare
cha•os ['keɪɒs] caos *m inv*
cha•ot•ic [keɪ'ɒtɪk] *adj* caotico
chap [ʧæp] *n* F tipo *m* F
chap•el ['ʧæpl] cappella *f*
chapped [ʧæpt] *adj* screpolato
chap•ter ['ʧæptə(r)] *of book* capitolo *m*; *of organization* filiale *f*
char•ac•ter ['kærɪktə(r)] (*nature*) carattere *m*; (*person*) tipo *m*; *in book*, *play* personaggio *m*; *in writing* carattere *m*; ***he's a real character*** è un tipo speciale
char•ac•ter•is•tic [kærɪktə'rɪstɪk] **1** *n* caratteristica *f* **2** *adj* caratteristico
char•ac•ter•is•ti•cal•ly [kærɪktə'rɪstɪklɪ] *adv* in modo caratteristico; ***he was characteristically rude*** era maleducato, come al solito
char•ac•ter•ize ['kærɪktəraɪz] *v/t* caratterizzare
cha•rade [ʃə'rɑːd] *fig* farsa *f*
char•coal ['ʧɑːkəʊl] *for barbecue* carbonella *f*; *for drawing* carboncino *m*
charge [ʧɑːdʒ] **1** *n* (*fee*) costo *m*; LAW accusa *f*; ***free of charge*** gratis; ***be in charge*** essere responsabile; ***take charge*** assumersi l'incombenza; ***take charge of sth*** farsi carico di qc **2** *v/t sum of money* far pagare; *person* far pagare a; (*put on account*) addebitare; LAW accusare; *battery* caricare; ***how much do you charge for ...?*** quanto prende per ...? **3** *v/i* (*attack*) attaccare
'charge ac•count conto *m* (spese)
'charge card carta *f* di addebito
cha•ris•ma [kə'rɪzmə] carisma *m*
char•is•ma•tic [kærɪz'mætɪk] *adj* carismatico
char•i•ta•ble ['ʧærɪtəbl] *adj institution* di beneficenza; *donation* in beneficenza; *person* caritatevole
char•i•ty ['ʧærətɪ] *assistance* carità *f*; *organization* associazione *f* di beneficenza
char•la•tan ['ʃɑːlətən] ciarlatano *m*, -a *f*
charm [ʧɑːm] **1** *n appealing quality* fascino *m*; *on bracelet etc* ciondolo *m* **2** *v/t* (*delight*) conquistare
charm•ing ['ʧɑːmɪŋ] *adj* affascinante; *house*, *village* incantevole
charred [ʧɑːd] *adj* carbonizzato
chart [ʧɑːt] *diagram* diagramma *m*; *for ship* carta *f* nautica; *for aeroplane* carta *f* aeronautica; ***the charts*** MUS l'hit parade *f inv*
char•ter ['ʧɑːtə(r)] *v/t plane*, *boat* noleggiare
'char•ter flight volo *m* charter *inv*
chase [ʧeɪs] **1** *n* inseguimento *m* **2** *v/t* inseguire
◆ **chase away** *v/t* cacciare (via)
chas•er ['ʧeɪsə(r)] *alcolico m bevuto dopo un altro di diverso tipo*
chas•sis ['ʃæsɪ] *of car* telaio *m*
chat [ʧæt] **1** *n* chiacchierata *f*; *useless talk* chiacchiere *fpl* **2** *v/i* (*pret & pp* ***-ted***) chiacchierare
◆ **chat up** *v/t* F abbordare F
'chat room stanza *f* di chat
'chat show talk show *m inv*
'chat show host conduttore *m*, -trice *f* di un talk show
chat•ter ['ʧætə(r)] **1** *n* parlantina *f* **2** *v/i talk* fare chiacchiere; *of teeth* battere
'chat•ter•box chiacchierone *m*, -a *f*
chat•ty ['ʧætɪ] *adj person* chiacchierone; *letter* familiare
chauf•feur ['ʃəʊfə(r)] *n* autista *m/f*
'chauf•feur-driv•en *adj* con autista
chau•vin•ist ['ʃəʊvɪnɪst] *n* sciovinista *m/f*; (*male chauvinist*) maschilista *m*
chau•vin•ist•ic [ʃəʊvɪ'nɪstɪk] *adj* sciovinista
cheap [ʧiːp] *adj* (*inexpensive*) economico; (*nasty*) cattivo; (*mean*) tirchio
cheat [ʧiːt] **1** *n person* imbroglione *m*, -a *f*; *in cards* baro *m*; (*deception*) truffa *f* **2** *v/t* imbrogliare; ***cheat s.o. out of sth*** estorcere qc a qu con l'inganno **3** *v/i* imbrogliare; *in cards* barare; ***cheat on one's wife*** tradire la propria moglie
check[1] [ʧek] **1** *adj shirt* a quadri **2** *n* quadro *m*
check[2] [ʧek] **1** *n to verify sth* verifica *f*; ***keep in check, hold in check*** tenere sotto controllo; ***keep a check on*** tenere sotto controllo **2** *v/t* (*verify*) verificare; (*restrain*) controllare; (*stop*) bloccare; *with a tick* marcare **3** *v/i* verificare; ***did you check for signs of forced entry?*** hai guardato se c'erano segni di infrazione?
◆ **check in** *v/i* registrarsi
◆ **check off** *v/t* segnare
◆ **check on** *v/t* controllare
◆ **check out 1** *v/i of hotel* saldare il conto **2** *v/t* (*look into*) verificare; *club*, *restaurant etc* provare
◆ **check up on** *v/t* fare dei controlli su
◆ **check with** *v/i of person* verificare con; (*tally*) combaciare con

check[3] [ʧek] *Am* → ***cheque***
checked [ʧekt] *adj material* a quadri
checkers ['ʧekəz] *nsg Am*: *game* dama *f*
'**check-in** (**coun•ter**) banco *m* dell'accettazione
'**check•ing ac•count** *Am* conto *m* corrente
'**check-in time** check in *m inv*
'**check•list** lista *f* di verifica
'**check•mark** *Am* segno *m*
'**check•mate** *n* scacco *m* matto
'**check-out** cassa *f*
'**check-out time** *from hotel* ora *f* di check-out
'**check•point** *military*, *police* posto *m* di blocco
'**check•room** *Am for coats* guardaroba *m inv*
'**check•up** *medical* check up *m inv*; *dental* visita *f* di controllo
cheek [ʧiːk] guancia *f*; (*impudence*) sfacciataggine *f*
'**cheek•bone** zigomo *m*
cheek•i•ly ['ʧiːkɪlɪ] *adv* sfacciatamente
cheek•y ['ʧiːkɪ] *adj* sfacciato
cheer [ʧɪə(r)] **1** *n* acclamazione *f*; ***three cheers for ...*** hip, hip, hurrà per ...; ***cheers!*** (*toast*) salute!; ***cheers!*** F (*thanks*) grazie! **2** *v/t* acclamare **3** *v/i* fare acclamazioni
◆ **cheer on** *v/t* incitare
◆ **cheer up** **1** *v/i* consolarsi; ***cheer up!*** su con la vita! **2** *v/t* tirare su
cheer•ful ['ʧɪəfʊl] *adj* allegro
cheer•ing ['ʧɪərɪŋ] *n* acclamazioni *fpl*
cheer•i•o [ʧɪərɪ'əʊ] F ciao F
cheer•y ['ʧɪərɪ] *adj* → ***cheerful***
cheese [ʧiːz] formaggio *m*
'**cheese•burg•er** cheeseburger *m inv*
'**cheese•cake** dolce *m* al formaggio
chef [ʃef] chef *m/f inv*
chem•i•cal ['kemɪkl] **1** *adj* chimico **2** *n* sostanza *f* chimica
chem•i•cal '**war•fare** guerra *f* chimica
chemist ['kemɪst] *in laboratory* chimico *m*, -a *f*; *who dispenses medicine* farmacista *m/f*
chem•is•try ['kemɪstrɪ] chimica *f*; *fig* alchimia *f*
'**chem•ist's** (**shop**) farmacia *f*
chem•o•ther•a•py [kiːməʊ'θerəpɪ] chemioterapia *f*
cheque [ʧek] assegno *m*
'**cheque•book** libretto *m* degli assegni
cheque (**guar•an'tee**) **card** carta *f* assegni
cher•ish ['ʧerɪʃ] *v/t* avere a cuore
cher•ry ['ʧerɪ] *fruit* ciliegia *f*; *tree* ciliegio *m*
cher•ub ['ʧerəb] cherubino *m*
chess [ʧes] scacchi *mpl*
'**chess•board** scacchiera *f*
'**chess•man**, **chess•piece** pezzo *m* degli scacchi
chest [ʧest] *of person* petto *m*; (*box*) cassa *f*; ***I'm glad I've got that off my chest*** sono contento di essermi tolto questo peso dallo stomaco
chest•nut ['ʧesnʌt] castagna *f*; *tree* castagno *m*
chest of '**drawers** comò *m inv*, cassettone *m*
chew [ʧuː] *v/t* masticare; *of dog*, *rats* rosicchiare
chew•ing gum ['ʧuːɪŋ] gomma *f* da masticare
chic [ʃiːk] *adj* chic *inv*
chick [ʧɪk] pulcino *m*; F (*girl*) ragazza *f*
chick•en ['ʧɪkɪn] **1** *n* pollo *m*; F fifone *m*, -a *f* F **2** *adj* F (*cowardly*) fifone
◆ **chicken out** *v/i* F tirarsi indietro per la fifa F
'**chick•en•feed** F una bazzecola
'**chick•en•pox** varicella *f*
chief [ʧiːf] **1** *n* (*head*) principale *m/f*; *of tribe* capo *m* **2** *adj* principale
chief•ly ['ʧiːflɪ] *adv* principalmente
chil•blain ['ʧɪlbleɪn] gelone *m*
child [ʧaɪld] (*pl* ***children*** ['ʧɪldrən]) *also pej* bambino *m*, -a *f*; ***they have two children*** hanno due figli
'**child a•buse** violenza *f* sui minori
'**child•birth** parto *m*
child•hood ['ʧaɪldhʊd] infanzia *f*
child•ish ['ʧaɪldɪʃ] *adj pej* infantile, puerile
child•ish•ness ['ʧaɪldɪʃnɪs] *pej* puerilità *f inv*
child•ish•ly ['ʧaɪldɪʃlɪ] *adv pej* puerilmente
child•less ['ʧaɪldlɪs] *adj* senza figli
child•like ['ʧaɪldlaɪk] *adj* innocente
'**child•mind•er** baby-sitter *m/f inv*
'**child•ren** ['ʧɪldrən] *pl* → ***child***
Chil•e ['ʧɪlɪ] Cile *m*
Chil•e•an ['ʧɪlɪən] **1** *adj* cileno **2** *n* cileno *m*, -a *f*
chill [ʧɪl] **1** *n in air* freddo *m*; *illness* colpo *m* di freddo; ***there's a chill in the air*** l'aria è fredda **2** *v/t wine* mettere in fresco
◆ **chill out** *v/i* P rilassarsi
chilli (**pepper**) ['ʧɪlɪ] peperoncino *m*
chill•y ['ʧɪlɪ] *adj weather*, *welcome* freddo; ***I'm feeling a bit chilly*** ho un po' freddo; ***it's a bit chilly this morning*** sta freddino stamattina
chime [ʧaɪm] *v/i* suonare
chim•ney ['ʧɪmnɪ] camino *m*
chim•pan•zee [ʧɪmpæn'ziː] scimpanzé *m*

C

inv
chin [ʧɪn] mento *m*
Chi•na ['ʧaɪnə] Cina *f*
chi•na ['ʧaɪnə] porcellana *f*
Chi•nese [ʧaɪ'niːz] **1** *adj* cinese **2** *n language* cinese *m*; *person* cinese *m/f*
chink [ʧɪŋk] *gap* fessura *f*; *sound* tintinnio *m*
chip [ʧɪp] **1** *n fragment* scheggia *f*; *damage* scheggiatura *f*; *in gambling* fiche *f inv*; COMPUT chip *m inv*; ***chips*** patate *fpl* fritte; *Am* patatine *fpl* **2** *v/t* (*pret & pp* ***-ped***) *damage* scheggiare
◆ **chip in** *v/i* (*interrupt*) intervenire; *with money* contribuire
chi•rop•o•dist [kɪ'rɒpədɪst] pedicure *m/f inv*
chi•ro•prac•tor ['kaɪrəʊpræktə(r)] chiroterapeuta *m/f*
chirp [ʧɜːp] *v/i* cinguettare
chis•el ['ʧɪzl] *n* scalpello *m*
chit•chat ['ʧɪʧæt] chiacchiere *fpl*
chiv•al•rous ['ʃɪvlrəs] *adj* cavalleresco
chive [ʧaɪv] erba *f* cipollina
chlo•rine ['klɔːriːn] cloro *m*
chlor•o•form ['klɒrəfɔːm] *n* cloroformio *m*
choc•a•hol•ic [ʧɒkə'hɒlɪk] *n* F fanatico *m*, -a *f* del cioccolato
chock-a-block [ʧɒkə'blɒk] *adj* F pieno zeppo
chock-full [ʧɒk'fʊl] *adj* F strapieno
choc•o•late ['ʧɒkələt] cioccolato *m*; *in box* cioccolatino *m*; ***hot chocolate*** cioccolata *f* calda
'**choc•o•late cake** dolce *m* al cioccolato
choice [ʧɔɪs] **1** *n* scelta *f*; ***I had no choice*** non avevo scelta **2** *adj* (*top quality*) di prima scelta
choir ['kwaɪə(r)] coro *m*
'**choir•boy** corista *m*
choke [ʧəʊk] **1** *n* MOT starter *m inv* **2** *v/i* soffocare; ***he choked on a bone*** si è strozzato con un osso **3** *v/t* soffocare
cho•les•te•rol [kə'lestərɒl] colesterolo *m*
choose [ʧuːz] *v/t & v/i* (*pret* ***chose***, *pp* ***chosen***) scegliere
choos•ey ['ʧuːzɪ] *adj* F selettivo
chop [ʧɒp] **1** *n action* colpo *m*; *meat* braciola *f* **2** *v/t* (*pret & pp* ***-ped***) *wood* spaccare; *meat*, *vegetables* tagliare a pezzi
◆ **chop down** *v/t tree* abbattere
chop•per ['ʧɒpə(r)] *tool* accetta *f*; F (*helicopter*) elicottero *m*
chop•ping board ['ʧɒpɪŋ] tagliere *m*
'**chop•sticks** *npl* bastoncini *mpl* (cinesi)
cho•ral ['kɔːrəl] *adj* corale
chord [kɔːd] MUS accordo *m*
chore [ʧɔː(r)] *household* faccenda *f* domestica
chor•e•o•graph ['kɒrɪəgrɑːf] *v/t* coreografare
chor•e•og•ra•pher [kɒrɪ'ɒgrəfə(r)] coreografo *m*, -a *f*
chor•e•og•ra•phy [kɒrɪ'ɒgrəfɪ] coreografia *f*
cho•rus ['kɔːrəs] *singers*, *of song* coro *m*
chose [tʃəʊz] *pret* → ***choose***
cho•sen ['ʧəʊzn] *pp* → ***choose***
Christ [kraɪst] Cristo *m*; ***Christ!*** Cristo!
chris•ten ['krɪsn] *v/t* battezzare
chris•ten•ing ['krɪsnɪŋ] battesimo *m*
Chris•tian ['krɪsʧən] **1** *n* cristiano *m*, -a *f* **2** *adj* cristiano; *attitude* da cristiano
Chris•ti•an•i•ty [krɪstɪ'ænətɪ] cristianesimo *m*
'**Chris•tian name** nome *m* di battesimo
Christ•mas ['krɪsməs] Natale *m*; ***at Christmas*** a Natale; ***Merry Christmas!*** Buon Natale!
'**Christ•mas card** biglietto *m* di auguri natalizi
Christ•mas 'Day giorno *m* di Natale
Christ•mas 'Eve vigilia *f* di Natale
'**Christ•mas present** regalo *m* di Natale
'**Christ•mas tree** albero *m* di Natale
chrome, **chro•mi•um** [krəʊm, 'krəʊmɪəm] cromo *m*
chro•mo•some ['krəʊməsəʊm] cromosomo *m*
chron•ic ['krɒnɪk] *adj* cronico
chron•o•log•i•cal [krɒnə'lɒdʒɪkl] *adj* cronologico; ***in chronological order*** in ordine cronologico
chrys•an•the•mum [krɪ'sænθəməm] crisantemo *m*
chub•by ['ʧʌbɪ] *adj* paffuto
chuck [ʧʌk] *v/t* F buttare
◆ **chuck out** *v/t* F *object* buttare via; *person* buttare fuori
chuck•ing-out time ['ʧʌkɪŋ'aʊt] F ora *f* di chiusura
chuck•le ['ʧʌkl] **1** *n* risatina *f* **2** *v/i* ridacchiare
chum [ʧʌm] amico *m*, -a *f*
chum•my ['ʧʌmɪ] *adj* F pappa e ciccia F; ***be chummy with*** essere pappa e ciccia con
chunk [ʧʌŋk] pezzo *m*
chunk•y ['ʧʌŋkɪ] *adj sweater* spesso; *tumbler* tozzo; *person*, *build* tarchiato
church [ʧɜːʧ] chiesa *f*
church 'hall sala *f* parrocchiale
church 'serv•ice funzione *f* religiosa
'**church•yard** cimitero *m* (di una chiesa)
churl•ish ['ʧɜːlɪʃ] *adj* sgarbato
chute [ʃuːt] scivolo *m*; *for waste disposal* canale *m* di scarico

CIA [siːaɪ'eɪ] *abbr* (= ***Central Intelligence Agency***) CIA *f*
ci•der ['saɪdə(r)] sidro *m*
CIF [siːaɪ'ef] *abbr* (= ***cost insurance freight***) CIF
ci•gar [sɪ'gɑː(r)] sigaro *m*
cig•a•rette [sɪgə'ret] sigaretta *f*
cig•a'rette end mozzicone *m* di sigaretta
cig•a,rette light•er accendino *m*
cig•a,rette pa•per carta *f* per sigarette
cin•e•ma ['sɪnɪmə] cinema *m*
cin•na•mon ['sɪnəmən] canella *f*
cir•cle ['sɜːkl] **1** *n* cerchio *m*; (*group*) cerchia *f* **2** *v/t* (*draw circle around*) cerchiare **3** *v/i of plane* girare in tondo; *of bird* volteggiare
cir•cuit ['sɜːkɪt] ELEC circuito *m*; (*lap*) giro *m*
'cir•cuit board COMPUT circuito *m* stampato
'cir•cuit break•er ELEC interruttore *m* automatico
'cir•cuit train•ing SP percorso *m* ginnico
cir•cu•lar ['sɜːkjʊlə(r)] **1** *n giving information* circolare *f* **2** *adj* circolare
cir•cu•late ['sɜːkjʊleɪt] **1** *v/i* circolare **2** *v/t memo* far circolare
cir•cu•la•tion [sɜːkjʊ'leɪʃn] BIO circolazione *f*; *of newspaper, magazine* tiratura *f*
cir•cum•fer•ence [sə'kʌmfərəns] circonferenza *f*
cir•cum•stances ['sɜːkəmstənsɪs] *npl* circostanze *fpl*; (*financial*) situazione *fsg* (economica); ***under no circumstances*** in nessuna circostanza; ***under the circumstances*** date le circostanze
cir•cus ['sɜːkəs] circo *m*
cir•rho•sis (of the liv•er) [sɪ'rəʊsɪs] cirrosi *f* (epatica)
cis•tern ['sɪstən] cisterna *f*; *of WC* serbatoio *m*
cite [saɪt] *v/t* citare
cit•i•zen ['sɪtɪzn] cittadino *m*, -a *f*
cit•i•zen•ship ['sɪtɪznʃɪp] cittadinanza *f*
citr•us fruit ['sɪtrəs] agrume *m*
cit•y ['sɪtɪ] città *f inv*
city 'centre centro *m* (della città)
city 'hall sala *f* municipale
civ•ic ['sɪvɪk] *adj* civico
civ•il ['ʃɪvl] *adj* civile
civ•il en•gi'neer ingegnere *m* civile
ci•vil•i•an [sɪ'vɪljən] **1** *n* civile *m/f* **2** *adj clothes* civile
ci•vil•i•ty [sɪ'vɪlɪtɪ] civiltà *f*
civ•i•li•za•tion [sɪvəlaɪ'zeɪʃn] civilizzazione *f*
civ•i•lize ['sɪvəlaɪz] *v/t person* civilizzare
civ•il 'rights *npl* diritti *mpl* civili
civ•il 'ser•vant impiegato *m*, -a *f* statale
civ•il 'ser•vice pubblica amministrazione *f*
civ•il 'war guerra *f* civile
claim [kleɪm] **1** *n* (*request*) richiesta *f*; (*right*) diritto *m*; (*assertion*) affermazione *f* **2** *v/t* (*ask for as a right*) rivendicare; *damages* richiedere; (*assert*) affermare; *lost property* reclamare; ***they have claimed responsibility for the attack*** hanno rivendicato l'attentato
claim•ant ['kleɪmənt] richiedente *m/f*
clair•voy•ant [kleə'vɔɪənt] *n* chiaroveggente *m/f*
clam [klæm] vongola *f*
◆ **clam up** *v/i* (*pret & pp* ***-med***) F chiudersi come un riccio
clam•ber ['klæmbə(r)] *v/i* arrampicarsi
clam•my ['klæmɪ] *adj hands* appiccicaticcio; *weather* afoso
clam•or *Am*, **clam•our** ['klæmə(r)] *noise* clamore *m*; (*outcry*) protesta *f*
◆ **clamour for** *v/t* chiedere a gran voce
clamp [klæmp] **1** *n fastener* morsa *f*; *for wheel* ceppo *m* (bloccaruote) **2** *v/t fasten* bloccare (con una morsa); *fig*: *hand etc* stringere; *car* mettere i ceppi a
◆ **clamp down** *v/i* usare il pugno di ferro
◆ **clamp down on** *v/t* mettere un freno a
clan [klæn] clan *m inv*
clan•des•tine [klæn'destɪn] *adj* clandestino
clang [klæŋ] **1** *n* suono *m* metallico **2** *v/i*: ***clang shut*** chiudersi con un suono metallico
clang•er ['klæŋə(r)] F gaffe *f inv*; ***drop a clanger*** fare una gaffe
clap [klæp] *v/t & v/i* (*pret & pp* ***-ped***) (*applaud*) applaudire
clar•et ['klærɪt] *wine* claret *m inv*
clar•i•fi•ca•tion [klærɪfɪ'keɪʃn] chiarimento *m*
clar•i•fy ['klærɪfaɪ] *v/t* (*pret & pp* ***-ied***) chiarire
clar•i•net [klærɪ'net] clarinetto *m*
clar•i•ty ['klærətɪ] chiarezza *f*
clash [klæʃ] **1** *n* scontro *m* **2** *v/i* scontrarsi; *of opinions* essere in contrasto; *of colours* stonare; *of events* coincidere
clasp [klɑːsp] **1** *n fastener* chiusura *f* **2** *v/t in hand* stringere
class [klɑːs] **1** *n* (*lesson*) lezione *f*; (*group of people, category*) classe *f*; ***social class*** classe *f* sociale **2** *v/t* classificare
clas•sic ['klæsɪk] **1** *adj* (*typical*) classico; (*definitive*) eccellente; ***she wrote the classic biography of …*** la sua biografia di … è un classico **2** *n* classico *m*
clas•si•cal ['klæsɪkl] *adj* classico

clas•si•fi•ca•tion [klæsɪfɪ'keɪʃn] classificazione *f*
clas•si•fied ['klæsɪfaɪd] *adj information* riservato
'**clas•si•fied ad(•ver•tise•ment)** inserzione *f*, annuncio *m*
clas•si•fy ['klæsɪfaɪ] *v/t* (*pret & pp* ***-ied***) (*categorize*) classificare
'**class•mate** compagno *m*, -a *f* di classe
'**class•room** aula *f*
'**class war•fare** lotta *f* di classe
classy ['klɑːsɪ] *adj* F d'alta classe
clat•ter ['klætə(r)] **1** *n* frastuono *m* **2** *v/i* fare baccano; ***clatter down the stairs*** scendere rumorosamente le scale
clause [klɔːz] *in agreement* articolo *m*; GRAM proposizione *f*
claus•tro•pho•bi•a [klɔːstrə'fəʊbɪə] claustrofobia *f*
claw [klɔː] **1** *n* artiglio *m*; *of lobster* chela *m* **2** *v/t* (*scratch*) graffiare
clay [kleɪ] argilla *f*
clean [kliːn] **1** *adj* pulito **2** *adv* F (*completely*) completamente **3** *v/t* pulire; *teeth* lavarsi; *car, hands, face* lavare; *clothes* lavare *o* pulire a secco
◆ **clean out** *v/t room, cupboard* pulire a fondo; *fig* ripulire
◆ **clean up 1** *v/t also fig* ripulire **2** *v/i* pulire; (*wash*) ripulirsi; *on stock market etc* fare fortuna
clean•er ['kliːnə(r)] *male* uomo *m* delle pulizie; *female* donna *f* delle pulizie; (*dry cleaner*) lavanderia *f*, tintoria *f*
'**clean•ing wom•an** donna *f* delle pulizie
cleanse [klenz] *v/t skin* detergere
cleans•er ['klenzə(r)] *for skin* detergente *m*
cleans•ing cream ['klenzɪŋ] latte *f* detergente
clear [klɪə(r)] **1** *adj* chiaro; *weather, sky* sereno; *water, eyes* limpido; *skin* uniforme; *conscience* pulito; ***I'm not clear about it*** non l'ho capito bene; ***I didn't make myself clear*** non mi sono spiegato bene; ***I made it clear to him*** gliel'ho fatto capire **2** *adv*: ***loud and clear*** forte e chiaro; ***stand clear of*** stare lontano da; ***steer clear of*** stare alla larga da **3** *v/t roads etc* sgomb(e)rare; (*acquit*) scagionare; (*authorize*) autorizzare; (*earn*) guadagnare al netto; *fence* scavalcare con un salto; *debt* saldare; ***clear one's throat*** schiarirsi la gola; ***clear the table*** sparecchiare (la tavola) **4** *v/i of sky* schiarirsi; *of mist* diradarsi
◆ **clear away** *v/t* mettere via
◆ **clear off** *v/i* F filarsela F
◆ **clear out 1** *v/t cupboard* sgomb(e)rare **2** *v/i* sparire
◆ **clear up 1** *v/i* (*tidy up*) mettere in ordine; *of weather* schiarirsi; *of illness, rash* sparire **2** *v/t* (*tidy*) mettere in ordine; *mystery, problem* risolvere
clear•ance ['klɪərəns] *space* spazio *m* libero; (*authorization*) autorizzazione *f*
clear•ance sale liquidazione *f*
clear•ing ['klɪərɪŋ] *in woods* radura *f*
clear•ly ['klɪəlɪ] *adv* chiaramente
cleav•age ['kliːvɪdʒ] décolleté *m inv*
cleav•er ['kliːvə(r)] mannaia *f*
clem•en•cy ['klemənsɪ] clemenza *f*
clench [klentʃ] *v/t* serrare
cler•gy ['klɜːdʒɪ] clero *m*
cler•gy•man ['klɜːdʒɪmæn] ecclesiastico *m*
clerk [klɑːk, *Am* klɜːrk] impiegato *m*, -a *f*; *Am*: *in shop* commesso *m*, -a *f*
clev•er ['klevə(r)] *adj* intelligente; *gadget, device* ingegnoso; ***don't get clever with me*** non fare il furbo con me
clev•er•ly ['klevəlɪ] *adv* intelligentemente
cli•ché ['kliːʃeɪ] frase *f* stereotipata
cli•chéd ['kliːʃeɪd] *adj* stereotipato
click [klɪk] **1** *n* COMPUT click *m inv* **2** *v/i of camera etc* scattare
◆ **click on** *v/t* COMPUT cliccare su
cli•ent ['klaɪənt] cliente *m/f*
cli•en•tele [kliːən'tel] clientela *f*
cliff [klɪf] scogliera *f*
cli•mate ['klaɪmət] clima *m*
'**cli•mate change** mutazione *f* climatica
cli•mat•ic [klaɪ'mætɪk] *adj* climatico
cli•max ['klaɪmæks] *n* punto *m* culminante
climb [klaɪm] **1** *n up mountain* scalata *f*, arrampicata *f* **2** *v/t* salire su; *clamber up* arrampicarsi su; *mountaineering* scalare **3** *v/i of plane, road, inflation* salire; *clamber* arrampicarsi
◆ **climb down** *v/i* scendere; *fig* fare marcia indietro
climb•er ['klaɪmə(r)] *person* alpinista *m/f*
climb•ing ['klaɪmɪŋ] alpinismo *m*
climb•ing wall *parete f artificiale per esercitarsi nella scalata*
clinch [klɪntʃ] *v/t deal* concludere; ***that clinches it*** questo risolve la questione
cling [klɪŋ] *v/i* (*pret & pp* ***clung***) *of clothes* essere attillato
◆ **cling to** *v/t of child* avvinghiarsi a; *ideas, tradition* aggrapparsi a
'**cling•film** pellicola *f* trasparente
cling•y ['klɪŋɪ] *adj child, boyfriend* appiccicoso
clin•ic ['klɪnɪk] clinica *f*
clin•i•cal ['klɪnɪkl] *adj* clinico
clink [klɪŋk] **1** *n noise* tintinnio *m* **2** *v/i* tin-

tinnare

clip[1] [klɪp] **1** *n fastener* fermaglio *m*; *for hair* molletta *f*; *for paper* graffetta *f* **2** *v/t* (*pret & pp* ***-ped***): ***clip sth to sth*** attaccare qc a qc

clip[2] [klɪp] **1** *n from film* spezzone *f* **2** *v/t* (*pret & pp* ***-ped***) *hair, hedge, grass* tagliare

'**clip•board** fermablocco *m inv*

clip•pers ['klɪpəz] *npl for hair* rasoio *m*; *for nails* tronchesina *f*; *for gardening* tosasiepi *fpl*

clip•ping ['klɪpɪŋ] *from newspaper* ritaglio *m*

clique [kliːk] combriccola *f*

cloak *n* cappa *f*

'**cloak•room** guardaroba *m inv*; (*euph: toilet*) servizi *mpl*

clock [klɒk] orologio *m*; F (*speedometer*) contachilometri *m inv*

'**clock ra•di•o** radiosveglia *f*

'**clockwise** *adv* in senso orario

'**clockwork** meccanismo *m* di orologio; ***it went like clockwork*** è andato liscio come l'olio

◆ **clog up** [klɒg] (*pret & pp* ***-ged***) **1** *v/i* intasarsi **2** *v/t* intasare

clone [kləʊn] **1** *n* clone *m* **2** *v/t* clonare

close[1] [kləʊs] **1** *adj family, friend* intimo; *resemblance* stretto; ***we are very close*** siamo molto uniti; ***be close to s.o.*** *emotionally* essere vicino a qu **2** *adv* vicino; ***close at hand*** a portata di mano; ***close by*** nelle vicinanze

close[2] [kləʊz] **1** *v/t* chiudere **2** *v/i of door, eyes* chiudersi; *of shop* chiudere

◆ **close down** *v/t & v/i* chiudere

◆ **close in** *v/i* circondare; *of fog, night* calare

◆ **close up 1** *v/t building* chiudere **2** *v/i* (*move closer*) avvicinarsi

closed [kləʊzd] *adj* chiuso

closed-cir•cuit '**tel•e•vi•sion** televisione *f* a circuito chiuso

'**close-knit** *adj* affiatato

close•ly ['kləʊslɪ] *adv listen, watch* attentamente; *cooperate* fianco a fianco

clos•et ['klɒzɪt] *Am* armadio *m*

close-up ['kləʊsʌp] primo piano *m*

clos•ing date ['kləʊzɪŋ] termine *m*

clos•ing time ['kləʊzɪŋ] ora *f* di chiusura

clo•sure ['kləʊʒə(r)] chiusura *f*

clot [klɒt] **1** *n of blood* grumo *m* **2** *v/i* (*pret & pp* ***-ted***) *of blood* coagularsi

cloth [klɒθ] (*fabric*) tessuto *m*; *for cleaning* straccio *m*

clothes [kləʊðz] *npl* vestiti *mpl*

'**clothes brush** spazzola *f* per vestiti

'**clothes hang•er** attaccapanni *m inv*

'**clothes•horse** stendibiancheria *m inv*

'**clothes•line** filo *m* stendibiancheria *inv*

'**clothes peg** molletta *f* per i panni

cloth•ing ['kləʊðɪŋ] abbigliamento *m*

cloud [klaʊd] *n* nuvola *f*; ***a cloud of smoke / dust*** una nuvola di fumo / polvere

◆ **cloud over** *v/i of sky* rannuvolarsi

'**cloud•burst** temporale *m*

cloud•less ['klaʊdlɪs] *adj sky* sereno

cloud•y ['klaʊdɪ] *adj* nuvoloso

clout [klaʊt] F (*blow*) botta *f*; (*fig: influence*) impatto *m*

clove of '**gar•lic** [kləʊv] spicchio *m* d'aglio

clown [klaʊn] *in circus* pagliaccio *m*; (*joker, also pej*) pagliaccio *m*

club [klʌb] *n weapon* clava *f*; *in golf* mazza *f*; *organization* club *m inv*

clue [kluː] indizio *m*; ***I haven't a clue*** F non ne ho la minima idea; ***he hasn't a clue*** (*is useless*) non ci capisce niente

clued-up [kluːd'ʌp] *adj* F beninformato

clump [klʌmp] *n of earth* zolla *f*; *group* gruppo *m*

clum•si•ness ['klʌmzɪnɪs] goffaggine *f*

clum•sy ['klʌmzɪ] *adj person* goffo, maldestro

clung [klʌŋ] *pret & pp* → ***cling***

clus•ter ['klʌstə(r)] **1** *n* gruppo *m* **2** *v/i of people* raggrupparsi; *of houses* essere raggruppato

clutch [klʌtʃ] **1** *n* MOT frizione *f* **2** *v/t* stringere

◆ **clutch at** *v/t* cercare di afferrare

clut•ter ['klʌtə(r)] **1** *n* oggetti *mpl* alla rinfusa **2** *v/t* (*also*: ***clutter up***) ingombrare

Co. *abbr* (= ***Company***) C.ia (= compagnia)

c/o *abbr* (= ***care of***) presso

coach [kəʊtʃ] **1** *n* (*trainer*) allenatore *m*, -trice *f*; *of singer etc* maestro *m*, -a *f*; *on train* vagone *m*; (*Br: bus*) pullman *m inv* **2** *v/t* allenare; *singer, actor* dare lezioni a

coach•ing ['kəʊtʃɪŋ] allenamento *m*; *of singer, actor* lezioni *fpl*

'**coach par•ty** gruppo *m* di turisti

'**coach sta•tion** stazione *f* dei pullman

'**coach tour** viaggio *m* turistico in pullman

co•ag•u•late [kəʊ'ægjʊleɪt] *v/i of blood* coagularsi

coal [kəʊl] carbone *m*

co•a•li•tion [kəʊə'lɪʃn] coalizione *f*

'**coal•mine** miniera *f* di carbone

coarse [kɔːs] *adj skin, fabric* ruvido; *hair* spesso; (*vulgar*) grossolano

coarse•ly ['kɔːslɪ] *adv* (*vulgarly*) grossolanamente; *ground* a grani grossi

coast [kəʊst] *n* costa *f*; ***at the coast*** sulla costa
coast•al ['kəʊstl] *adj* costiero
coast•er ['kəʊstə(r)] *for glass* sottobicchiere *m*; *for bottle* sottobottiglia *m*
'**coast•guard** *organization, person* guardia *f* costiera
'**coast•line** costa *f*, litorale *m*
coat [kəʊt] **1** *n* (*overcoat*) cappotto *m*; *of animal* pelliccia *f*; *of paint etc* mano *f* **2** *v/t* (*cover*) ricoprire
'**coat•hang•er** attaccapanni *m inv*, gruccia *f*
coat•ing ['kəʊtɪŋ] strato *m*
co-au•thor ['kəʊɔːθə(r)] **1** *n* co-autore *m*, -trice *f* **2** *v/t* scrivere insieme
coax [kəʊks] *v/t* convincere con le moine; ***coax sth out of s.o.*** ottenere qc da qu con le moine
cob•bled ['kɒbld] *adj* lastricato (a ciottoli)
cob•ble•stone ['kɒblstəʊn] ciottolo *m*
cob•web ['kɒbweb] ragnatela *f*
co•caine [kə'keɪn] cocaina *f*
cock [kɒk] *n chicken* gallo *m*; *any male bird* maschio *m* (di uccelli); V (*penis*) cazzo *m* V
cock•eyed [kɒk'aɪd] *adj* F *idea etc* strampalato
'**cock•pit** *of plane* cabina *f* (di pilotaggio)
cock•roach ['kɒkrəʊtʃ] scarafaggio *m*
'**cock•tail** cocktail *m inv*
'**cock•tail par•ty** cocktail party *m inv*
'**cock•tail shak•er** shaker *m inv*
cock•y ['kɒkɪ] *adj* F arrogante
co•coa ['kəʊkəʊ] *drink* cioccolata *f* calda
co•co•nut ['kəʊkənʌt] cocco *m*
co•co•nut palm palma *f* di cocco
COD [siːəʊ'diː] *abbr* (= ***cash on delivery***) pagamento *m* contrassegno
cod•dle ['kɒdl] *v/t sick person* coccolare; *pej*: *child* viziare
code [kəʊd] *n* codice *m*
co•ed•uca•tion•al [kəʊedjʊ'keɪʃnl] *adj* misto
co•erce [kəʊ'ɜːs] *v/t* costringere
co•ex•ist [kəʊɪg'zɪst] *v/i* coesistere
co•ex•ist•ence [kəʊɪg'zɪstəns] coesistenza *f*
cof•fee ['kɒfɪ] caffè *m inv*
'**cof•fee bar** caffè *m inv*
'**cof•fee bean** chicco *m* di caffè
'**cof•fee break** pausa *f* per il caffè
'**cof•fee cup** tazza *f* da caffè
'**cof•fee grind•er** ['graɪndə(r)] macinacaffè *m inv*
'**cof•fee mak•er** caffettiera *f*
'**cof•fee pot** caffettiera *f*
'**cof•fee shop** caffetteria *f*
'**cof•fee ta•ble** tavolino *m*
cof•fin ['kɒfɪn] bara *f*
cog [kɒg] dente *m*
co•gnac ['kɒnjæk] cognac *m inv*
'**cog•wheel** ruota *f* dentata
co'hab•it [kəʊ'hæbɪt] *v/i* convivere
co•her•ent [kəʊ'hɪərənt] *adj* coerente
coil [kɔɪl] **1** *n of rope* rotolo *m* **2** *v/t*: ***coil*** (***up***) avvolgere
coin [kɔɪn] *n* moneta *f*
co•in•cide [kəʊɪn'saɪd] *v/i* coincidere
co•in•ci•dence [kəʊ'ɪnsɪdəns] coincidenza *f*
coke [kəʊk] P (*cocaine*) coca P *f*
Coke® [kəʊk] Coca® *f*
cold [kəʊld] **1** *adj* freddo; ***I'm*** (***feeling***) ***cold*** ho freddo; ***it's cold*** *of weather* fa freddo; ***in cold blood*** a sangue freddo; ***get cold feet*** F farsi prendere dalla fifa F **2** *n* freddo *m*; MED raffreddore *m*; ***I have a cold*** ho il raffreddore
cold-blood•ed [kəʊld'blʌdɪd] *adj also murder* a sangue freddo; *person* spietato
cold 'call•ing porta-a-porta *m*; *by phone* televendite *fpl*
'**cold cuts** *npl* affettati *mpl*
cold•ly ['kəʊldlɪ] *adv* freddamente
cold 'meat affettati *mpl*
cold•ness ['kəʊldnɪs] *fig* freddezza *f*
'**cold sore** febbre *f* del labbro
cole•slaw ['kəʊlslɔː] *insalata f di cavolo, carote, cipolle tritati e maionese*
col•ic ['kɒlɪk] colica *f*
col•lab•o•rate [kə'læbəreɪt] *v/i* collaborare
col•lab•o•ra•tion [kəlæbə'reɪʃn] collaborazione *f*; *with enemy* collaborazionismo *m*
col•lab•o•ra•tor [kə'læbəreɪtə(r)] collaboratore *m*, -trice *f*; *with enemy* collaborazionista *m/f*
col•lapse [kə'læps] *v/i* crollare; *of person* accasciarsi
col•lap•si•ble [kə'læpsəbl] *adj* pieghevole
col•lar ['kɒlə(r)] collo *m*, colletto *m*; *of dog, cat* collare *m*
'**col•lar-bone** clavicola *f*
col•league ['kɒliːg] collega *m/f*
col•lect [kə'lekt] **1** *v/t person*: *go* andare a prendere; *person*: *come* venire a prendere; *tickets, cleaning etc* ritirare; *as hobby* collezionare; (*gather*) raccogliere **2** *v/i* (*gather together*) radunarsi **3** *adv Am*: ***call collect*** telefonare a carico del destinatario
col•lect•ed [kə'lektɪd] *adj person* controllato; ***the collected works of …*** l'opera omnia di …
col•lec•tion [kə'lekʃn] collezione *f*; *in*

church colletta *f*; *of poems, stories* raccolta *f*

col•lec•tive [kə'lektɪv] *adj* collettivo

col•lec•tive 'bar•gain•ing trattative *fpl* sindacali

col•lec•tor [kə'lektə(r)] collezionista *m/f*

col•lege ['kɒlɪdʒ] istituto *m* parauniversitario; *at Oxford and Cambridge* college *m inv*

col•lide [kə'laɪd] *v/i* scontrarsi

col•li•sion [kə'lɪʒn] collisione *f*, scontro *m*

col•lo•qui•al [kə'ləʊkwɪəl] *adj* colloquiale

co•lon ['kəʊlən] *punctuation* due punti *mpl*; ANAT colon *m inv*

colo•nel ['kɜːnl] colonnello *m*

co•lo•ni•al [kə'ləʊnɪəl] *adj* coloniale

co•lo•nize ['kɒlənaɪz] *v/t country* colonizzare

co•lo•ny ['kɒlənɪ] colonia *f*

col•or *etc Am* → ***colour*** *etc*

co•los•sal [kə'lɒsl] *adj* colossale

col•our ['kʌlə(r)] **1** *n* colore *m*; *in cheeks* colorito *m*; ***in colour*** *film etc* a colori; ***colours*** MIL bandiera *f* **2** *v/t* colorare; *one's hair* tingere **3** *v/i* (*blush*) diventare rosso

'col•our-blind *adj* daltonico

col•oured ['kʌləd] *adj person* di colore

'col•our fast *adj* con colori resistenti

col•our•ful ['kʌləfʊl] *adj* pieno di colori; *account* pittoresco

col•our•ing ['kʌlərɪŋ] colorito *m*

'col•our pho•to•graph fotografia *f* a colori

'col•our scheme abbinamento *m* dei colori

'col•our TV tv *f inv* a colori

colt [kəʊlt] puledro *m*

col•umn ['kɒləm] colonna *f*; (*newspaper feature*) rubrica *f*

col•umn•ist ['kɒləm(n)ɪst] *giornalista m/f che cura una rubrica*

co•ma ['kəʊmə] coma *m inv*

comb [kəʊm] **1** *n* pettine *m* **2** *v/t* pettinare; *area* rastrellare

com•bat ['kɒmbæt] **1** *n* combattimento *m* **2** *v/t* combattere

com•bi•na•tion [kɒmbɪ'neɪʃn] combinazione *f*

com•bine [kəm'baɪn] **1** *v/t* unire; *ingredients* mescolare **2** *v/i of chemical elements* combinarsi

com•bine har•vest•er [kɒmbaɪn'hɑːvɪstə(r)] mietitrebbia *f*

com•bus•ti•ble [kəm'bʌstɪbl] *adj* combustibile

com•bus•tion [kəm'bʌstʃn] combustione *f*

come [kʌm] *v/i* (*pret* ***came***, *pp* ***come***) venire; *of train, bus* arrivare; ***you'll come to like it*** finirà per piacerti; ***how come?*** F come mai? F

◆ **come about** *v/i* (*happen*) succedere

◆ **come across 1** *v/t* (*find*) trovare **2** *v/i of idea, humour* essere capito; ***she comes across as ...*** dà l'impressione di essere ...

◆ **come along** *v/i* (*come too*) venire; (*turn up*) presentarsi; (*progress*) fare progressi; ***how is it coming along?*** come sta andando?; ***your Italian has come along a lot*** il tuo italiano è migliorato molto

◆ **come apart** *v/i* smontarsi; (*break*) andare in pezzi

◆ **come away** *v/i of person, button* venire via

◆ **come back** *v/i* ritornare; ***it came back to me*** mi è tornato in mente

◆ **come by 1** *v/i* passare **2** *v/t* (*acquire*) ottenere

◆ **come down** *v/i* venire giù; *in price, amount etc* scendere; *of rain, snow* cadere; ***he came down the stairs*** è sceso dalle scale

◆ **come for** *v/t* (*attack*) assalire; (*collect*) venire a prendere

◆ **come forward** *v/i* (*present o.s.*) farsi avanti

◆ **come from** *v/t* venire da; ***where do you come from?*** di dove sei?

◆ **come in** *v/i* entrare; *of train, in race* arrivare; *of tide* salire; ***come in!*** entra!

◆ **come in for** *v/t* attirare; ***come in for criticism*** attirare delle critiche

◆ **come in on** *v/t* partecipare a; ***come in on a deal*** stare a un accordo

◆ **come off** *v/i of handle etc* staccarsi

◆ **come on** *v/i* (*progress*) fare progressi; ***how's the work coming on?*** come sta venendo il lavoro?; ***come on!*** dai!; *in disbelief* ma dai!

◆ **come out** *v/i of person, book, sun* uscire; *of results, product* venir fuori; *of stain* venire via; *of gay* rendere nota la propria omosessualità

◆ **come round** *v/i to s.o.'s home* passare; (*regain consciousness*) rinvenire

◆ **come to 1** *v/t place, position* arrivare a; ***that comes to £70*** fanno 70 sterline **2** *v/i* (*regain consciousness*) rinvenire

◆ **come up** *v/i* salire; *of sun* sorgere; ***something has come up*** si è presentato qualcosa

◆ **come up with** *v/t new idea etc* venir fuori con

'come•back ritorno *m*; ***make a come-***

back tornare alla ribalta
co•me•di•an [kəˈmiːdɪən] comico *m*, -a *f*; *pej* buffone *m*
ˈ**come•down** passo *m* indietro
com•e•dy [ˈkɒmədɪ] commedia *f*
com•et [ˈkɒmɪt] cometa *f*
come•up•pance [kʌmˈʌpəns] *n* F: ***he'll get his comeuppance*** avrà quello che si merita
com•fort [ˈkʌmfət] **1** *n* comodità *f inv*; (*consolation*) conforto *m* **2** *v/t* confortare
ˈ**com•for•ta•ble** [ˈkʌmfətəbl] *adj chair, room* comodo; ***be comfortable*** *in chair* stare comodo; *in situation* essere a proprio agio; (*financially*) essere agiato
com•fy [ˈkʌmfɪ] *adj* F → ***comfortable***
com•ic [ˈkɒmɪk] **1** *n to read* fumetto *m*; (*comedian*) comico *m*, -a *f* **2** *adj* comico
com•i•cal [ˈkɒmɪkl] *adj* comico
com•ic book fumetto *m*
com•ic strip striscia *f* (di fumetti)
com•ma [ˈkɒmə] virgola *f*
com•mand [kəˈmɑːnd] **1** *n* comando *m* **2** *v/t person* comandare a
com•man•deer [kɒmənˈdɪə(r)] *v/t* appropriarsi di
com•mand•er [kəˈmɑːndə(r)] comandante *m*
com•mand•er-in-ˈchief comandante *m* in capo
com•mand•ing of•fi•cer [kəˈmɑːndɪŋ] ufficiale *m* comandante
com•mand•ment [kəˈmɑːndmənt]: ***the Ten Commandments*** REL i Dieci Comandamenti
com•mem•o•rate [kəˈmeməreɪt] *v/t* commemorare
com•mem•o•ra•tion [kəmeməˈreɪʃn]: ***in commemoration of*** in commemorazione di
com•mence [kəˈmens] *v/t* & *v/i* cominciare
com•mend [kəˈmend] *v/t* (*praise*) lodare; (*recommend*) raccomandare
com•mend•able [kəˈmendəbl] *adj* lodevole
com•men•da•tion [kɒmenˈdeɪʃn] *for bravery* riconoscimento *m*
com•men•su•rate [kəˈmenʃərət] *adj*: ***commensurate with*** commisurato a
com•ment [ˈkɒment] **1** *n* commento *m*; ***no comment!*** no comment! **2** *v/i* fare commenti
com•men•ta•ry [ˈkɒməntrɪ] cronaca *f*
com•men•tate [ˈkɒmənteɪt] *v/i* commentare
com•men•ta•tor [ˈkɒmənteɪtə(r)] *on TV* telecronista *m/f*; *on radio* radiocronista *m/f*
com•merce [ˈkɒmɜːs] commercio *m*
com•mer•cial [kəˈmɜːʃl] **1** *adj* commerciale **2** *n* (*advert*) pubblicità *f inv*
com•mer•cial ˈ**break** interruzione *f* pubblicitaria
com•mer•cial•ize [kəˈmɜːʃlaɪz] *v/t Christmas etc* commercializzare
com•mer•cial ˈ**tel•e•vi•sion** televisione *f* privata
com•mer•cial ˈ**trav•el•ler** rappresentante *m/f*
com•mis•e•rate [kəˈmɪzəreɪt] *v/i* esprimere rincrescimento (***with*** a)
com•mis•sion [kəˈmɪʃn] **1** *n* (*payment, committee*) commissione *f*; (*job*) incarico *m* **2** *v/t for a job* incaricare
com•mis•sion•aire [kəmɪʃəˈneə(r)] portiere *m*
Com•mis•sion•er [kəˈmɪʃənə(r)] *in European Union* Commissario *m*, -a *f*
com•mit [kəˈmɪt] *v/t* (*pret* & *pp* ***-ted***) *crime* commettere; *money* assegnare; ***commit o.s.*** impegnarsi
com•mit•ment [kəˈmɪtmənt] impegno *m*
com•mit•tee [kəˈmɪtɪ] comitato *m*
com•mod•i•ty [kəˈmɒdətɪ] prodotto *m*
com•mon [ˈkɒmən] *adj* comune; ***in common*** in comune; ***have sth in common with s.o.*** avere qc in comune con qu
com•mon•er [ˈkɒmənə(r)] persona *f* non nobile
com•mon ˈ**law husband / wife** *convivente al quale spettano legalmente i diritti di una moglie / un marito*
com•mon•ly [ˈkɒmənlɪ] *adv* comunemente
Com•mon ˈ**Mar•ket** Mercato *m* Comune
ˈ**com•mon•place** *adj* luogo *m* comune
Com•mons [ˈkɒmənz] *npl*: ***the Commons*** la Camera dei Comuni
com•mon ˈ**sense** buon senso *m*
com•mo•tion [kəˈməʊʃn] confusione *f*
com•mu•nal [ˈkɒmjʊnl] *adj* comune
com•mu•nal•ly [ˈkɒmjʊnəlɪ] *adv* in comune
com•mu•ni•cate [kəˈmjuːnɪkeɪt] *v/t* & *v/i* comunicare
com•mu•ni•ca•tion [kəmjuːnɪˈkeɪʃn] comunicazione *f*
com•mu•niˈca•tions *npl* comunicazioni *fpl*
com•mu•niˈca•tions sat•el•lite satellite *m* per telecomunicazioni
com•mu•ni•ca•tive [kəˈmjuːnɪkətɪv] *adj person* comunicativo
Com•mu•nion [kəˈmjuːnɪən] REL comunione *f*
com•mu•ni•qué [kəˈmjuːnɪkeɪ] comunicato *m* ufficiale

C

Com•mu•nis•m ['kɒmjʊnɪzm] comunismo *m*
Com•mu•nist ['kɒmjʊnɪst] **1** *adj* comunista **2** *n* comunista *m/f*
com•mu•ni•ty [kə'mju:nətɪ] comunità *f inv*
com'mu•ni•ty cen•tre centro *m* comunitario
com'mu•ni•ty serv•ice servizio *m* civile (come pena per reati minori)
com•mute [kə'mju:t] **1** *v/i* fare il / la pendolare **2** *v/t* LAW commutare
com•mut•er [kə'mju:tə(r)] pendolare *m/f*
com'mut•er traf•fic traffico *m* dei pendolari
com'mut•er train treno *m* dei pendolari
com•pact [kəm'pækt] **1** *adj* compatto **2** *n* ['kɒmpækt] *for powder* portacipria *m inv*
com•pact 'disc → ***CD***
com•pan•ion [kəm'pænjən] compagno *m*, -a *f*
com•pan•ion•ship [kəm'pænjənʃɪp] compagnia *f*
com•pa•ny ['kʌmpənɪ] COM società *f inv*; (*ballet company*, *theatre company*) compagnia *f*; (*companionship*, *guests*) compagnia *f*
com•pa•ny: ***keep s.o. company*** fare compagnia a qu
com•pa•ny 'car auto *f inv* della ditta
com•pa•ny 'law diritto *m* societario
com•pa•ra•ble ['kɒmpərəbl] *adj* paragonabile; (*similar*) simile
com•par•a•tive [kəm'pærətɪv] **1** *adj* (*relative*) relativo; *study*, *method* comparato; GRAM comparativo **2** *n* GRAM comparativo *m*
com•par•a•tive•ly [kəm'pærətɪvlɪ] *adv* relativamente
com•pare [kəm'peə(r)] **1** *v/t* paragonare; ***compare sth with sth/s.o. with s.o.*** paragonare qc a qc / qu a qu; ***compared with …*** rispetto a … **2** *v/i* reggere il confronto; ***how did he compare?*** com'era rispetto agli altri?
com•pa•ri•son [kəm'pærɪsn] paragone *m*, confronto *m*; ***in comparison with*** in confronto a; ***there's no comparison*** non c'è paragone
com•part•ment [kəm'pɑ:tmənt] scomparto *m*; RAIL scompartimento *m*
com•pass ['kʌmpəs] bussola *f*; (***pair of***) ***compasses*** *for geometry* compasso *m*
com•pas•sion [kəm'pæʃn] compassione *f*
com•pas•sion•ate [kəm'pæʃənət] *adj* compassionevole
com•pas•sion•ate leave congedo *m* per motivi familiari
com•pat•i•bil•i•ty [kəmpætə'bɪlɪtɪ] compatibilità *f inv*
com•pat•i•ble [kəm'pætəbl] *adj also* COMPUT compatibile; ***we're not compatible*** siamo incompatibili
com•pel [kəm'pel] *v/t* (*pret & pp* ***-led***) costringere
com•pel•ling [kəm'pelɪŋ] *adj argument* convincente; *film*, *book* avvincente
com•pen•sate ['kɒmpənseɪt] **1** *v/t with money* risarcire **2** *v/i*: ***compensate for*** compensare
com•pen•sa•tion [kɒmpən'seɪʃn] *money* risarcimento *m*; *reward* vantaggio *m*; *comfort* consolazione *f*
com•père ['kɒmpeə(r)] presentatore *m*, -trice *f*
com•pete [kəm'pi:t] *v/i* competere; (*take part*) gareggiare; ***compete for*** contendersi
com•pe•tence ['kɒmpɪtəns] competenza *f*
com•pe•tent ['kɒmpɪtənt] *adj* competente
com•pe•tent•ly ['kɒmpɪtəntlɪ] *adv* con competenza
com•pe•ti•tion [kɒmpə'tɪʃn] (*contest*) concorso *m*; SP gara *f*; (*competing*, *competitors*) concorrenza *f*
com•pet•i•tive [kəm'petətɪv] *adj* competitivo; *sport* agonistico; *price*, *offer* concorrenziale
com•pet•i•tive•ly [kəm'petətɪvlɪ] *adv*: ***competitively priced*** a prezzi concorrenziali
com•pet•i•tive•ness competitività *f inv*
com•pet•i•tor [kəm'petɪtə(r)] *in contest* concorrente *m/f*; ***our competitors*** COM la concorrenza
com•pile [kəm'paɪl] *v/t* compilare
com•pla•cen•cy [kəm'pleɪsənsɪ] autocompiacimento *m*
com•pla•cent [kəm'pleɪsənt] *adj* compiaciuto; ***be complacent about sth*** compiacersi di qc
com•plain [kəm'pleɪn] *v/i* lamentarsi; *to shop*, *manager* reclamare; ***complain of*** MED accusare
com•plaint [kəm'pleɪnt] lamentela *f*; *to shop* reclamo *m*; MED disturbo *m*
com•ple•ment ['kɒmplɪmənt] *v/t* completare; ***they complement each other*** si completano bene
com•ple•men•ta•ry [kɒmplɪ'mentərɪ] *adj* complementare
com•plete [kəm'pli:t] **1** *adj* (*total*) completo; (*finished*) terminato; ***I made a complete fool of myself*** mi sono comportato da perfetto idiota **2** *v/t task*, *building etc* completare; *form* compilare

com•plete•ly [kəm'pliːtlɪ] *adv* completamente
com•ple•tion [kəm'pliːʃn] completamento *m*; ***payment on completion*** pagamento a conclusione lavori
com•plex ['kɒmpleks] **1** *adj* complesso **2** *n also* PSYCH complesso *m*
com•plex•ion [kəm'plekʃn] *facial* carnagione *f*
com•plex•i•ty [kəm'pleksɪtɪ] complessità *f inv*
com•pli•ance [kəm'plaɪəns] conformità *f inv*
com•pli•cate ['kɒmplɪkeɪt] *v/t* complicare
com•pli•cat•ed ['kɒmplɪkeɪtɪd] *adj* complicato
com•pli•ca•tion [kɒmplɪ'keɪʃn] complicazione *f*; ***complications*** MED complicazioni
com•pli•ment ['kɒmplɪmənt] **1** *n* complimento *m* **2** *v/t* fare i complimenti a
com•pli•men•ta•ry [kɒmplɪ'mentərɪ] *adj* lusinghiero; (*free*) in omaggio
'com•pli•ments slip ['kɒmplɪmənts] biglietto *m* intestato della ditta
com•ply [kəm'plaɪ] *v/i* (*pret & pp* ***-ied***) ubbidire; ***comply with*** osservare; *of products*, *equipment* essere conforme a
com•po•nent [kəm'pəʊnənt] componente *m*
com•pose [kəm'pəʊz] *v/t also* MUS comporre; ***be composed of*** essere composto da; ***compose o.s.*** ricomporsi
com•posed [kəm'pəʊzd] *adj* (*calm*) calmo
com•pos•er [kəm'pəʊzə(r)] MUS compositore *m*, -trice *f*
com•po•si•tion [kɒmpə'zɪʃn] *also* MUS composizione *f*; (*essay*) tema *m*
com•po•sure [kəm'pəʊʒə(r)] calma *f*
com•pound ['kɒmpaʊnd] *n* CHEM composto *m*
com•pound 'in•ter•est interesse *m* composto
com•pre•hend [kɒmprɪ'hend] *v/t* (*understand*) capire
com•pre•hen•sion [kɒmprɪ'henʃn] comprensione *f*
com•pre•hen•sive [kɒmprɪ'hensɪv] *adj* esauriente
com•pre•hen•sive in'sur•ance polizza *f* casco
com•pre•hen•sive•ly [kɒmprɪ'hensɪvlɪ] *adv* in modo esauriente
com•pre'hen•sive school scuola *f* secondaria
com•press ['kɒmpres] **1** *n* MED impacco *m* **2** *v/t* [kəm'pres] *air*, *gas* comprimere; *information* condensare
com•prise [kəm'praɪz] *v/t* comprendere; (*make-up*) costituire; ***be comprised of*** essere composto da
com•pro•mise ['kɒmprəmaɪz] **1** *n* compromesso *m* **2** *v/i* arrivare a un compromesso **3** *v/t* (*jeopardize*) compromettere; ***compromise o.s.*** compromettersi
com•pul•sion [kəm'pʌlʃn] PSYCH coazione *f*
com•pul•sive [kəm'pʌlsɪv] *adj behaviour* patologico; *reading*, *viewing* avvincente
com•pul•so•ry [kəm'pʌlsərɪ] *adj* obbligatorio; ***compulsory education*** scuola *f* dell'obbligo
com•put•er [kəm'pjuːtə(r)] computer *m inv*; ***have sth on computer*** avere qc sul computer
com•put•er-aid•ed de'sign progettazione *f* assistita dall'elaboratore
com•put•er-aid•ed man•uˌfacture produzione *f* computerizzata
com•put•er-conˌtrolled *adj* controllato dal computer
comˌputer game computer game *m inv*
com•put•er•ize [kəm'pjuːtəraɪz] *v/t* computerizzare
com•put•er 'lit•er•ate *adj* che ha dimestichezza con il computer
comput•er 'sci•ence informatica *f*
com•put•er 'sci•en•tist informatico *m*, -a *f*
com•put•ing [kəm'pjuːtɪŋ] *n* informatica *f*
com•rade ['kɒmreɪd] *also* POL compagno *m*, -a *f*
com•rade•ship ['kɒmreɪdʃɪp] cameratismo *m*
con [kɒn] **1** *n* F truffa *f* **2** *v/t* (*pret & pp* ***-ned***) F truffare; ***con s.o. into doing sth*** far fare qc a qu con l'inganno
con•ceal [kən'siːl] *v/t* nascondere
con•ceal•ment [kən'siːlmənt] occultazione *f*
con•cede [kən'siːd] *v/t* (*admit*) ammettere; *goal* concedere
con•ceit [kən'siːt] presunzione *f*
con•ceit•ed [kən'siːtɪd] *adj* presuntuoso
con•cei•va•ble [kən'siːvəbl] *adj* concepibile
con•ceive [kən'siːv] *v/i of woman* concepire; ***conceive of*** (*imagine*) immaginare
con•cen•trate ['kɒnsəntreɪt] **1** *v/i* concentrarsi **2** *v/t one's attention*, *energies* concentrare
con•cen•trat•ed ['kɒnsəntreɪtɪd] *adj juice etc* concentrato
con•cen•tra•tion [kɒnsən'treɪʃn] concentrazione *f*
con•cept ['kɒnsept] concetto *m*

con•cep•tion [kən'sepʃn] *of child* concepimento *m*
con•cern [kən'sɜːn] **1** *n* (*anxiety*) preoccupazione *f*; (*care*) interesse *m*; (*business*) affare *m*; (*company*) impresa *f*; ***there's no cause for concern*** non c'è motivo di preoccuparsi; ***it's none of your concern*** non sono affari tuoi **2** *v/t* (*involve*) riguardare; (*worry*) preoccupare; ***concern o.s. with*** preoccuparsi di
con•cerned [kən'sɜːnd] *adj* (*anxious*) preoccupato; (*caring*) interessato; (*involved*) in questione; ***as far as I'm concerned*** per quanto mi riguarda
con•cern•ing [kən'sɜːnɪŋ] *prep* riguardo a
con•cert ['kɒnsət] concerto *m*
con•cert•ed [kən'sɜːtɪd] *adj* (*joint*) congiunto
con•cer•to [kən'tʃeətəʊ] concerto *m*
con•ces•sion [kən'seʃn] (*compromise*) concessione *f*
con•cil•i•a•to•ry [kənsɪlɪ'eɪtərɪ] *adj* conciliatorio
con•cise [kən'saɪs] *adj* conciso
con•clude [kən'kluːd] **1** *v/t* concludere; ***conclude sth from sth*** concludere qc da qc **2** *v/i* concludere
con•clu•sion [kən'kluːʒn] conclusione *f*; ***in conclusion*** in conclusione
con•clu•sive [kən'kluːsɪv] *adj* conclusivo
con•coct [kən'kɒkt] *v/t meal*, *drink* mettere insieme; *excuse*, *story* inventare
con•coc•tion [kən'kɒkʃn] *food*, *drink* intruglio *m*
con•crete[1] ['kɒŋkriːt] *adj* concreto
con•crete[2] ['kɒŋkriːt] *n* calcestruzzo *m*; ***concrete jungle*** giungla *f* di cemento
con•cur [kən'kɜː(r)] *v/i* (*pret & pp* ***-red***) essere d'accordo
con•cus•sion [kən'kʌʃn] commozione *f* cerebrale
con•demn [kən'dem] *v/t action* condannare; *building* dichiarare inagibile; (*doom*) condannare
con•dem•na•tion [kɒndəm'neɪʃn] *of action* condanna *f*
con•den•sa•tion [kɒnden'seɪʃn] *on walls*, *windows* condensa *f*
con•dense [kən'dens] **1** *v/t* (*make shorter*) condensare **2** *v/i of steam* condensarsi
con•densed 'milk [kən'densd] latte *m* condensato
con•de•scend [kɒndɪ'send] *v/i*: ***he condescended to speak to me*** si è degnato di rivolgermi la parola
con•de•scend•ing [kɒndɪ'sendɪŋ] *adj* (*patronizing*) borioso
con•di•tion [kən'dɪʃn] **1** *n* condizione *f*; MED malattia *f*; ***conditions*** (*circumstances*) condizioni; ***on condition that*** a condizione che; ***in / out of condition*** in / fuori forma **2** *v/t* PSYCH condizionare
con•di•tion•al [kən'dɪʃnl] **1** *adj acceptance* condizionale **2** *n* GRAM condizionale *m*
con•di•tion•er [kən'dɪʃnə(r)] *for hair* balsamo *m*; *for fabric* ammorbidente *m*
con•di•tion•ing [kən'dɪʃnɪŋ] PSYCH condizionamento *m*
con•do•lences [kən'dəʊlənsɪz] *npl* condoglianze *fpl*
con•dom ['kɒndəm] preservativo *m*
con•done [kən'dəʊn] *v/t actions* scusare
con•du•cive [kən'djuːsɪv] *adj*: ***be conducive to*** favorire
con•duct ['kɒndʌkt] **1** *n* (*behaviour*) condotta *f* **2** *v/t* [kən'dʌkt] (*carry out*) condurre; ELEC condurre; MUS dirigere; ***conduct o.s.*** comportarsi
con•duct•ed tour [kən'dʌktɪd] visita *f* guidata
con•duc•tor [kən'dʌktə(r)] MUS direttore *m* d'orchestra; *on bus* bigliettaio *m*; PHYS conduttore *m*
con•duc•tress [kən'dʌktrɪs] bigliettaia *f*
cone [kəʊn] cono *m*; *of pine tree* pigna *f*; *on motorway* birillo *m*
◆ **cone off** *v/t* chiudere al traffico
con•fec•tion•er [kən'fekʃənə(r)] pasticciere *m*, -a *f*
con•fec•tion•e•ry [kən'fekʃənərɪ] dolciumi *mpl*
con•fed•e•ra•tion [kənfedə'reɪʃn] confederazione *f*
con•fer [kən'fɜː(r)] (*pret & pp* ***-red***) **1** *v/t* (*bestow*) conferire **2** *v/i* (*discuss*) confabulare
con•fe•rence ['kɒnfərəns] congresso *m*; ***family conference*** consiglio *m* di famiglia
'**con•fe•rence cen•tre** centro *m* congressi
'**con•fe•rence room** sala *f* riunioni
con•fess [kən'fes] **1** *v/t sin*, *crime* confessare **2** *v/i* confessare; REL confessarsi; ***confess to sth*** confessare qc; ***confess to a weakness for sth*** confessare di avere un debole per qc
con•fes•sion [kən'feʃn] confessione *f*
con•fes•sion•al [kən'feʃnl] REL confessionale *m*
con•fes•sor [kən'fesə(r)] REL confessore *m*
con•fide [kən'faɪd] **1** *v/t* confidare **2** *v/i*: ***confide in s.o.*** confidarsi con qu
con•fi•dence ['kɒnfɪdəns] (*assurance*) sicurezza *f* (di sé); (*trust*) fiducia *f*; ***in confidence*** in confidenza

con•fi•dent ['kɒnfɪdənt] *adj* sicuro; *person* sicuro di sé
con•fi•den•tial [kɒnfɪ'denʃl] *adj* riservato, confidenziale; *adviser* di fiducia
con•fi•den•tial•ly [kɒnfɪ'denʃlɪ] *adv* in confidenza
con•fi•dent•ly ['kɒnfɪdəntlɪ] *adv* con sicurezza
con•fine [kən'faɪn] *v/t* (*imprison*) richiudere; (*restrict*) limitare; ***be confined to one's bed*** essere costretto a letto
con•fined [kən'faɪnd] *adj space* ristretto
con•fine•ment [kən'faɪnmənt] (*imprisonment*) reclusione *f*; MED parto *m*
con•firm [kən'fɜːm] *v/t* confermare
con•fir•ma•tion [kɒnfə'meɪʃn] conferma *f*
con•firmed [kɒn'fɜːmd] *adj bachelor* incallito
con•fis•cate ['kɒnfɪskeɪt] *v/t* sequestrare
con•flict ['kɒnflɪkt] **1** *n* conflitto *m* **2** *v/i* [kən'flɪkt] *of statements*, *accounts* essere in conflitto; *of dates* coincidere
con•form [kən'fɔːm] *v/i* conformarsi; ***conform to*** *of products*, *acts etc* essere conforme a
con•form•ist [kən'fɔːmɪst] *n* conformista *m/f*
con•front [kən'frʌnt] *v/t* (*face*) affrontare; ***confront s.o. with sth*** mettere qu di fronte a qc; ***the problems confronting us*** i problemi che dobbiamo affrontare
con•fron•ta•tion [kɒnfrən'teɪʃn] scontro *m*
con•fuse [kən'fjuːz] *v/t*) confondere; ***confuse s.o. with s.o.*** confondere qu con qu
con•fused [kən'fjuːzd] *adj* confuso
con•fus•ing [kən'fjuːzɪŋ] *adj* che confonde
con•fu•sion [kən'fjuːʒn] confusione *f*
con•geal [kən'dʒiːl] *v/i of blood*, *fat* rapprendersi
con•gen•ial [kən'dʒiːnɪəl] *adj* (*pleasant*) simpatico
con•gen•i•tal [kən'dʒenɪtl] *adj* MED congenito
con•gest•ed [kən'dʒestɪd] *adj* congestionato
con•ges•tion [kən'dʒestʃn] congestione *f*; ***traffic congestion*** la congestione del traffico
con•grat•u•late [kən'grætjʊleɪt] *v/t* congratularsi con
con•grat•u•la•tions [kəngrætjʊ'leɪʃnz] *npl* congratulazioni *fpl*; ***congratulations on …*** congratulaizioni per …
con•grat•u•la•to•ry [kəngrætjʊ'leɪtərɪ] *adj* di congratulazioni
con•gre•gate ['kɒŋgrɪgeɪt] *v/i* (*gather*) riunirsi
con•gre•ga•tion [kɒŋgrɪ'geɪʃn] REL fedeli *mpl*
con•gress ['kɒŋgres] (*conference*) congresso *m*; ***Congress*** *in US* il Congresso
Con•gres•sion•al [kən'greʃnl] *adj* del Congresso
Con•gress•man ['kɒŋgresmən] membro *m* del Congresso
co•ni•fer ['kɒnɪfə(r)] conifera *f*
con•jec•ture [kən'dʒektʃə(r)] *n* (*speculation*) congettura *f*
con•ju•gate ['kɒndʒʊgeɪt] *v/t* GRAM coniugare
con•junc•tion [kən'dʒʌŋkʃn] GRAM congiunzione *f*; ***in conjunction with*** insieme a
con•junc•ti•vi•tis [kəndʒʌŋktɪ'vaɪtɪs] congiuntivite *f*
◆ **con•jure up** ['kʌndʒə(r)] *v/t* (*produce*) far apparire (come) per magia; (*evoke*) evocare
con•jur•er, con•jur•or ['kʌndʒərə(r)] (*magician*) prestigiatore *m*, -trice *f*
'con•jur•ing tricks ['kʌndʒərɪŋ] *npl* giochi *mpl* di prestigio
con man ['kɒnman] F truffatore *m*
con•nect [kə'nekt] *v/t* (*join*, *link*) collegare; *to power supply* allacciare; ***connect s.o. with s.o.*** TELEC mettere in comunicazione qu con qu
con•nect•ed [kə'nektɪd] *adj*: ***be well-connected*** avere conoscenze influenti; ***be connected with …*** essere collegato con; *by marriage* essere imparentato con
con•nect•ing flight [kə'nektɪŋ] coincidenza *f* (volo)
con•nec•tion [kə'nekʃn] (*link*) collegamento *m*; *when travelling* coincidenza *f*; (*personal contact*) conoscenza *f*; ***in connection with*** a proposito di
con•nois•seur [kɒnə'sɜː(r)] intenditore *m*, -trice *f*
con•quer ['kɒŋkə(r)] *v/t* conquistare; *fig*: *fear etc* vincere
con•quer•or ['kɒŋkərə(r)] conquistatore *m*, -trice *f*
con•quest ['kɒŋkwest] conquista *f*
con•science ['kɒnʃəns] coscienza *f*; ***have a guilty / clear conscience*** avere la coscienza sporca/a posto; ***on one's conscience*** sulla coscienza
con•sci•en•tious [kɒnʃɪ'enʃəs] *adj* coscienzioso
con•sci•en•tious•ness [kɒnʃɪ'enʃəsnəs] coscienziosità *f inv*
con•sci•en•tious ob'ject•or obiettore *m*

di coscienza
con•scious ['kɒnʃəs] *adj* (*aware*) consapevole; (*deliberate*) conscio; MED cosciente; ***be / become conscious of*** rendersi conto di
con•scious•ly ['kɒnʃəslɪ] *adv* consapevolmente
con•scious•ness ['kɒnʃəsnɪs] (*awareness*) consapevolezza *f*; MED conoscenza *f*; ***lose / regain consciousness*** perdere / riprendere conoscenza
con•sec•u•tive [kən'sekjʊtɪv] *adj* consecutivo
con•sen•sus [kən'sensəs] consenso *m*
con•sent [kən'sent] **1** *n* consenso *m* **2** *v/i* acconsentire
con•se•quence ['kɒnsɪkwəns] (*result*) conseguenza *f*
con•se•quent•ly ['kɒnsɪkwəntlɪ] *adv* (*therefore*) di conseguenza
con•ser•va•tion [kɒnsə'veɪʃn] (*preservation*) tutela *f*
con•ser'va•tion area *area f soggetta a vincoli urbanistici e ambientali*
con•ser•va•tion•ist [kɒnsə'veɪʃnɪst] ambientalista *m/f*
con•ser•va•tive [kən'sɜːvətɪv] **1** *adj* (*conventional*) conservatore; *clothes* tradizionale; *estimate* cauto; ***Conservative*** *Br* POL conservatore **2** *n Br* POL ***Conservative*** conservatore *m*, -trice *f*
con•ser•va•to•ry [kən'sɜːvətrɪ] veranda *f*; MUS conservatorio *m*
con•serve ['kɒnsɜːv] **1** *n* (*jam*) marmellata *f* **2** *v/t* [kən'sɜːv] *energy, strength* risparmiare
con•sid•er [kən'sɪdə(r)] *v/t* (*regard*) considerare; (*show regard for*) tener conto di; (*think about*) pensare a; ***consider doing sth*** prendere in considerazione la possibilità di fare qc; ***it is considered to be his best work*** è considerata la sua opera migliore
con•sid•e•ra•ble [kən'sɪdrəbl] *adj* considerevole
con•sid•e•ra•bly [kən'sɪdrəblɪ] *adv* considerevolmente
con•sid•er•ate [kən'sɪdərət] *adj person, attitude* premuroso; ***be considerate of*** avere riguardo per
con•sid•er•ate•ly [kən'sɪdərətlɪ] *adv* premurosamente
con•sid•e•ra•tion [kənsɪdə'reɪʃn] (*thought*) considerazione *f*; (*thoughtfulness, concern*) riguardo *m*; (*factor*) fattore *m*; ***take sth into consideration*** prendere in considerazione qc; ***under consideration*** in esame
con•sign•ment [kən'saɪnmənt] COM consegna *f*
◆ **con•sist of** [kən'sɪst] *v/t* consistere in
con•sis•ten•cy [kən'sɪstənsɪ] (*texture*) consistenza *f*; (*unchangingness*) coerenza *f*
con•sis•tent [kən'sɪstənt] *adj* (*unchanging*) coerente
con•sis•tent•ly [kən'sɪstəntlɪ] *adv* in modo coerente; *always* costantemente
con•so•la•tion [kɒnsə'leɪʃn] consolazione *f*
con•sole [kən'səʊl] *v/t* consolare
con•sol•i•date [kən'sɒlɪdeɪt] *v/t* consolidare
con•so•nant ['kɒnsənənt] *n* GRAM consonante *f*
con•sor•ti•um [kən'sɔːtɪəm] consorzio *m*
con•spic•u•ous [kən'spɪkjʊəs] *adj*: ***be / look conspicuous*** spiccare; ***feel conspicuous*** sentirsi fuori posto
con•spi•ra•cy [kən'spɪrəsɪ] cospirazione *f*
con•spi•ra•tor [kən'spɪrətə(r)] cospiratore *m*, -trice *f*
con•spire [kən'spaɪə(r)] *v/i* cospirare
con•stant ['kɒnstənt] *adj* (*continuous*) costante
con•stant•ly ['kɒnstəntlɪ] *adv* costantemente
con•ster•na•tion [kɒnstə'neɪʃn] costernazione *f*
con•sti•pat•ed ['kɒnstɪpeɪtɪd] *adj* stitico
con•sti•pa•tion [kɒnstɪ'peɪʃn] stitichezza *f*
con•sti•tu•en•cy [kən'stɪtjʊənsɪ] *Br* POL circoscrizione *f* elettorale
con•sti•tu•ent [kən'stɪtjʊənt] *n* (*component*) componente *m*; *Br* POL elettore *m*, -trice *f*
con•sti•tute ['kɒnstɪtjuːt] *v/t* costituire
con•sti•tu•tion [kɒnstɪ'tjuːʃn] *also* POL costituzione *f*
con•sti•tu•tion•al [kɒnstɪ'tjuːʃənl] *adj* POL costituzionale
con•straint [kən'streɪnt] (*restriction*) restrizione *f*
con•struct [kən'strʌkt] *v/t building etc* costruire
con•struc•tion [kən'strʌkʃn] costruzione *f*; ***under construction*** in costruzione
con'struc•tion in•dus•try edilizia *f*
con,struc•tion site cantiere *m* edile
con,struc•tion work•er operaio *m* edile
con•struc•tive [kən'strʌktɪv] *adj* costruttivo
con•sul ['kɒnsl] console *m*
con•su•late ['kɒnsjʊlət] consolato *m*
con•sult [kən'sʌlt] *v/t* (*seek the advice of*) consultare

con•sul•tan•cy [kən'sʌltənsɪ] (*company*) società *f inv* di consulenza; (*advice*) consulenza *f*
con•sul•tant [kən'sʌltənt] *n* (*adviser*) consulente *m/f*
consultation [kɒnsəl'teɪʃn] consultazione *f*
con•sult•ing hours orario *m* di visita
con•sult•ing room ambulatorio *m*
con•sume [kɒn'sjuːm] *v/t* consumare
con•sum•er [kən'sjuːmə(r)] (*purchaser*) consumatore *m*, -trice *f*
con•sum•er 'con•fi•dence fiducia *f* dei consumatori
con'sum•er goods *npl* beni *mpl* di consumo
con'sum•er so•ci•e•ty società *f inv* dei consumi
con•sump•tion [kən'sʌmpʃn] consumo *m*
con•tact ['kɒntækt] **1** *n* contatto *m*; (*person*) conoscenza *f*; ***keep in contact with s.o.*** mantenere i contatti con qu **2** *v/t* mettersi in contatto con
'con•tact lens lente *f* a contatto
'con•tact num•ber *numero m presso cui si è reperibili*
con•ta•gious [kən'teɪdʒəs] *adj also fig* contagioso
con•tain [kən'teɪn] *v/t* (*hold*) contenere; *flood*, *disease*, *revolt* contenere; ***contain o.s.*** contenersi
con•tain•er [kən'teɪnə(r)] (*recipient*) contenitore *m*; COM container *m inv*
con'tain•er ship nave *f* portacontainer
con•tam•i•nate [kən'tæmɪneɪt] *v/t* contaminare
con•tam•i•na•tion [kəntæmɪ'neɪʃn] contaminazione *f*
con•tem•plate ['kɒntəmpleɪt] *v/t* (*look at*) contemplare; (*think about*) considerare; ***contemplate doing sth*** considerare la possibilità di fare qc
con•tem•po•ra•ry [kən'tempərərɪ] **1** *adj* contemporaneo **2** *n* coetaneo *m*, -a *f*
con•tempt [kən'tempt] disprezzo *m*; ***be beneath contempt*** essere spregevole
con•temp•ti•ble [kən'temptəbl] *adj* spregevole
con•temp•tu•ous [kən'temptjʊəs] *adj* sprezzante
con•tend [kən'tend] *v/i*: ***contend for sth*** contendersi qc; ***contend with s.o./sth*** confrontarsi con qc / qu
con•tend•er [kən'tendə(r)] *in sport*, *competition* concorrente *m/f*; *against champion* sfidante *m/f*; POL candidato *m*, -a *f*
con•tent¹ ['kɒntent] *n* contenuto *m*
con•tent² [kən'tent] **1** *adj* contento **2** *v/t*: ***content o.s. with*** accontentarsi di
con•tent•ed [kən'tentɪd] *adj* contento
con•ten•tion [kən'tenʃn] (*assertion*) opinione *f*; ***be in contention for*** essere in lizza per
con•ten•tious [kən'tenʃəs] *adj* polemico
con•tent•ment [kən'tentmənt] soddisfazione *f*
con•tents ['kɒntents] *npl of house*, *letter*, *bag etc* contentuto *m*
con•test¹ ['kɒntest] *n* (*competition*) concorso *m*; (*struggle*, *for power*) lotta *f*
con•test² [kən'test] *v/t leadership etc* essere in lizza per; *will* impugnare
con•tes•tant [kən'testənt] concorrente *m/f*
con•text ['kɒntekst] contesto *m*; ***look at sth in context / out of context*** considerare qc in / fuori contesto
con•ti•nent ['kɒntɪnənt] *n* continente *m*; ***the continent*** l'Europa continentale
con•ti•nen•tal [kɒntɪ'nentl] *adj* continentale
con•ti•nen•tal 'break•fast *colazione f a base di caffè, pane, burro e marmellata*
con•tin•gen•cy [kən'tɪndʒənsɪ] eventualità *f inv*
con•tin•u•al [kən'tɪnjʊəl] *adj* continuo
con•tin•u•al•ly [kən'tɪnjʊəlɪ] *adv* continuamente
con•tin•u•a•tion [kəntɪnjʊ'eɪʃn] seguito *m*
con•tin•ue [kən'tɪnjuː] **1** *v/t* continuare; ***continue doing sth*** continuare a fare qc; ***to be continued*** continua ... **2** *v/i* continuare
con•ti•nu•i•ty [kɒntɪ'njuːətɪ] continuità *f inv*; *in films* ordine *m* della sceneggiatura
con•tin•u•ous [kən'tɪnjʊəs] *adj* ininterrotto
con•tin•u•ous•ly [kən'tɪnjʊəslɪ] *adv* ininterrottamente
con•tort [kən'tɔːt] *v/t* contorcere
con•tour ['kɒntʊə(r)] profilo *m*; *on map* curva *f* di livello
con•tra•cep•tion [kɒntrə'sepʃn] contraccezione *f*
con•tra•cep•tive [kɒntrə'septɪv] *n* anticoncezionale *m*, contraccettivo *m*
con•tract¹ ['kɒntrækt] *n* contratto *m*
con•tract² [kən'trækt] **1** *v/i* (*shrink*) contrarsi **2** *v/t illness* contrarre
con•trac•tor [kən'træktə(r)] appaltatore *m*, -trice *f*; ***building contractor*** ditta *f* di appalti (edili)
con•trac•tu•al [kən'træktjʊəl] *adj* contrattuale
con•tra•dict [kɒntrə'dɪkt] *v/t* contraddire
con•tra•dic•tion [kɒntrə'dɪkʃn] contraddizione *f*

con•tra•dic•to•ry [kɒntrə'dɪktrɪ] *adj account* contraddittorio
con•trap•tion [kən'træpʃn] F aggeggio *m*
con•trar•y[1] ['kɒntrərɪ] **1** *adj* contrario; ***contrary to*** contrariamente a **2** *n*: ***on the contrary*** al contrario
con•tra•ry[2] [kən'treərɪ] *adj*: ***be contrary*** (*perverse*) essere un bastian contrario
con•trast ['kɒntrɑːst] **1** *n* contrasto *m*; ***by contrast*** invece **2** *v/t* [kən'trɑːst] confrontare **3** *v/i* contrastare
con•trast•ing [kən'trɑːstɪŋ] *adj* contrastante
con•tra•vene [kɒntrə'viːn] *v/t* contravvenire a
con•trib•ute [kən'trɪbjuːt] **1** *v/i with money, material, time* contribuire; *to magazine, paper* collaborare (***to*** con); *to discussion* intervenire (***to*** in); (*help to cause*) contribuire a creare **2** *v/t money* contribuire con
con•tri•bu•tion [kɒntrɪ'bjuːʃn] *money* offerta *f*; *to political party, church* donazione *f*; *of time, effort* contributo *m*; *to debate* intervento *m*; *to magazine* collaborazione *f*
con•trib•u•tor [kən'trɪbjʊtə(r)] *of money* finanziatore *m*, -trice *f*; *to magazine* collaboratore *m*, -trice *f*
con•trol [kən'trəʊl] **1** *n* controllo *m*; ***take control of*** assumere il controllo di; ***lose control of*** perdere il controllo di; ***lose control of o.s.*** perdere il controllo; ***circumstances beyond our control*** cause indipendenti dalla nostra volontà; ***be in control of sth*** tenere qc sotto controllo; ***get out of control*** diventare incontrollabile; ***the situation is under control*** la situazione è sotto controllo; ***bring a blaze under control*** circoscrivere un incendio; ***controls*** *of aircraft, vehicle* comandi; ***controls*** (*restrictions*) restrizioni **2** *v/t* (*pret & pp* ***-led***) (*govern*) controllare; *traffic* dirigere; (*restrict*) contenere; (*regulate*) regolare; ***control o.s.*** controllarsi
con'trol cen•ter *Am*, **con,trol centre** centro *m* di controllo
con'trol freak F *persona f che vuole avere tutto e tutti sotto controllo*
con•trolled 'sub•stance [kən'trəʊld] sostanza *f* stupefacente
con•trol•ling 'in•ter•est [kən'trəʊlɪŋ] FIN maggioranza *f* delle azioni
con'trol pan•el quadro *m* dei comandi
con'trol tow•er torre *f* di controllo
con•tro•ver•sial [kɒntrə'vɜːʃl] *adj* controverso
con•tro•ver•sy ['kɒntrəvɜːsɪ] polemica *f*
con•va•lesce [kɒnvə'les] *v/i* rimettersi (in salute)
con•va•les•cence [kɒnvə'lesns] convalescenza *f*
con•vene [kən'viːn] *v/t* indire
con•ve•ni•ence [kən'viːnɪəns] *of having sth, location* comodità *f inv*; ***at my / your convenience*** a mio / tuo comodo; ***all*** (***modern***) ***conveniences*** tutti i comfort
con've•ni•ence food *scatolame m, cibi precotti ecc*
con've•ni•ence store negozio *m* alimentari
con•ve•ni•ent [kən'viːnɪənt] *adj location, device* comodo; ***whenever it's convenient*** quando ti va bene
con•ve•ni•ent•ly [kən'viːnɪəntlɪ] *adv* comodamente
con•vent ['kɒnvənt] convento *m*
con•ven•tion [kən'venʃn] (*tradition*) convenzione *f*; (*conference*) congresso *m*
con•ven•tion•al [kən'venʃnl] *adj person, ideas* convenzionale; *method* tradizionale
◆ **con•verge on** [kən'vɜːdʒ] *v/t* convergere su
con•ver•sant [kən'vɜːsənt] *adj*: ***be conversant with*** essere pratico di
con•ver•sa•tion [kɒnvə'seɪʃn] conversazione *f*
con•ver•sa•tion•al [kɒnvə'seɪʃnl] *adj* colloquiale
con•verse ['kɒnvɜːs] *n* (*opposite*) contrario *m*
con•verse•ly [kən'vɜːslɪ] *adv* per contro
con•ver•sion [kən'vɜːʃn] conversione *f*; *of house* trasformazione *f*
con'ver•sion ta•ble tabella *f* di conversione
con•vert ['kɒnvɜːt] **1** *n* convertito *m*, -a *f* **2** *v/t* [kən'vɜːt] convertire **3** *v/i* trasformarsi (***into*** in); *house, room* trasformare
con•ver•ti•ble [kən'vɜːtəbl] *n car* cabriolet *f inv*, decappottabile *f*
con•vey [kən'veɪ] *v/t* (*transmit*) comunicare; (*carry*) trasportare
con'vey•or belt [kən'veɪə(r)] nastro *m* trasportatore
con•vict ['kɒnvɪkt] **1** *n* carcerato *m*, -a *f* **2** *v/t* [kən'vɪkt] LAW condannare; ***convict s.o. of sth*** condannare qu per qc
con•vic•tion [kən'vɪkʃn] LAW condanna *f*; (*belief*) convinzione *f*
con•vince [kən'vɪns] *v/t* convincere
con•vinc•ing [kən'vɪnsɪŋ] *adj* convincente
con•viv•i•al [kən'vɪvɪəl] *adj* (*friendly*) gioviale
con•voy ['kɒnvɔɪ] convoglio *m*
con•vul•sion [kən'vʌlʃn] MED convul-

sione *f*

cook [kʊk] **1** *n* cuoco *m*, -a *f*; ***I'm a good cook*** cucino bene **2** *v/t vegetables, meat* cucinare; *meal, dinner* preparare; ***a cooked meal*** un pasto caldo; ***cook the books*** F falsificare i registri **3** *v/i of person* cucinare; *of vegetables, meat* cuocere

ˈ**cook•book** ricettario *m*

cook•er [ˈkʊkə(r)] cucina *f*

cook•e•ry [ˈkʊkərɪ] cucina *f*

ˈ**cook•e•ry book** ricettario *m*

cook•ie [ˈkʊkɪ] *Am* biscotto *m*

cook•ing [ˈkʊkɪŋ] *food* cucina *f*; ***he does all the cooking*** è lui che cucina

cool [kuːl] **1** *n* F: ***keep / lose one's cool*** conservare / perdere la calma **2** *adj weather, breeze, drink* fresco; (*calm*) calmo; (*unfriendly*) freddo **3** *v/i of food* raffreddarsi; *of tempers* calmarsi; *of interest* raffreddarsi **4** *v/t* F: ***cool it!*** calma!

◆ **cool down 1** *v/i* raffreddarsi; *of weather* rinfrescare; *fig*: *of tempers* calmarsi **2** *v/t food* raffreddare; *fig* calmare

cool•ing-ˈoff pe•ri•od periodo *m* di riflessione

co•op•e•rate [kəʊˈɒpəreɪt] *v/i* cooperare

co•op•e•ra•tion [kəʊɒpəˈreɪʃn] cooperazione *f*

co•op•e•ra•tive [kəʊˈɒpərətɪv] **1** *n* COM cooperativa *f* **2** *adj* COM cooperativo; (*helpful*) disponibile (a collaborare)

co•or•di•nate [kəʊˈɔːdɪneɪt] *v/t* coordinare

co•or•di•na•tion [kəʊɔːdɪˈneɪʃn] *of activities* coordinamento *m*; *of body* coordinazione *f*

cop [kɒp] *n* F poliziotto *m*

cope [kəʊp] *v/i* farcela; ***cope with*** farcela con

cop•i•er [ˈkɒpɪə(r)] *machine* fotocopiatrice *f*

co•pi•lot [ˈkəʊpaɪlət] secondo pilota *m*

co•pi•ous [ˈkəʊpɪəs] *adj* abbondante

cop•per [ˈkɒpə(r)] *n metal* rame *m*

cop•y [ˈkɒpɪ] **1** *n* copia *f*; *written material* materiale *m*; ***fair copy*** bella copia *f*; ***rough copy*** brutta copia *f*; ***make a copy of a file*** fare una copia di un file **2** *v/t* (*pret & pp* ***-ied***) copiare

ˈ**cop•y cat** F copione *m*, -a *f* F

cop•y•cat ˈ**crime** *reato m a imitazione di un altro*

ˈ**cop•y•right** *n* diritti *mpl* d'autore, copyright *m inv*

ˈ**cop•y-writ•er** *in advertising* copywriter *m*

cor•al [ˈkɒrəl] corallo *m*

cord [kɔːd] (*string*) corda *f*; (*cable*) filo *m*

cor•di•al [ˈkɔːdɪəl] *adj* cordiale

cord•less ˈ**phone** [ˈkɔːdlɪs] cordless *m inv*

cor•don [ˈkɔːdn] cordone *m*

◆ **cor•don off** *v/t* transennare; *put cordon around* recintare

cords [kɔːdz] *npl trousers* pantaloni *mpl* di velluto a coste

cor•du•roy [ˈkɔːdərɔɪ] velluto *m* a coste

core [kɔː(r)] **1** *n of fruit* torsolo *m*; *of problem* nocciolo *m*; *of organization, party* cuore *m* **2** *v/t fruit* togliere il torsolo a **3** *adj issue, meaning* essenziale

cork [kɔːk] *in bottle* tappo *m* di sughero; (*material*) sughero *m*

ˈ**cork•screw** *n* cavatappi *m inv*

corn [kɔːn] *grain* frumento *m*; *Am* (*maize*) granturco *m*

cor•ner [ˈkɔːnə(r)] **1** *n of page, room, street* angolo *m*; *of table* spigolo *m*; *in football* calcio *m* d'angolo, corner *m inv*; ***in the corner*** nell'angolo; ***on the corner*** *of street* all'angolo; ***around the corner*** dietro l'angolo **2** *v/t person* bloccare; ***corner a market*** prendersi il monopolio di un mercato **3** *v/i of driver, car* affrontare una curva

ˈ**cor•ner kick** *in football* calcio *m* d'angolo

ˈ**cor•ner shop** piccola drogheria *f*

ˈ**corn•flakes** *npl* fiocchi *mpl* di granturco, cornflakes *mpl*

ˈ**corn•flour** farina *f* di granturco

corn•y [ˈkɔːnɪ] *adj* F scontato; *sentimental* sdolcinato

cor•o•na•ry [ˈkɒrənərɪ] **1** *adj* coronario **2** *n* infarto *m*

cor•o•ner [ˈkɒrənə(r)] *ufficiale m pubblico che indaga sui casi di morte sospetta*

cor•po•ral [ˈkɔːpərəl] *n* caporale *m* maggiore

cor•po•ral ˈ**pun•ish•ment** punizione *f* corporale

cor•po•rate [ˈkɔːpərət] *adj* COM aziendale; ***corporate image*** corporate image *f inv*; ***sense of corporate loyalty*** corporativismo *m*

cor•po•ra•tion [kɔːpəˈreɪʃn] (*business*) corporation *f inv*

corps [kɔː(r)] *nsg* corpo *m*

corpse [kɔːps] cadavere *m*

cor•pu•lent [ˈkɔːpjʊlənt] *adj* corpulento

cor•pus•cle [ˈkɔːpʌsl] globulo *m*

cor•rect [kəˈrekt] **1** *adj* giusto; *behaviour* corretto; ***she's correct*** ha ragione **2** *v/t* correggere

cor•rec•tion [kəˈrekʃn] correzione *f*

cor•rect•ly [kəˈrektlɪ] *adv* giustamente; *behave* correttamente

cor•re•spond [kɒrɪˈspɒnd] *v/i* (*match, write*) corrispondere; ***correspond to*** corrispondere a; ***correspond with*** cor-

rispondere con
cor•re•spon•dence [kɒrɪ'spɒndəns] (*agreement, letters*) corrispondenza *f*
cor•re•spon•dent [kɒrɪ'spɒndənt] corrispondente *m/f*
cor•re•spon•ding [kɒrɪ'spɒndɪŋ] *adj* (*equivalent*) corrispondente
cor•ri•dor ['kɒrɪdɔː(r)] *in building* corridoio *m*
cor•rob•o•rate [kə'rɒbəreɪt] *v/t* corroborare
cor•rode [kə'rəʊd] *v/t & v/i* corrodere
cor•ro•sion [kə'rəʊʒn] corrosione *f*
cor•ru•gated 'card•board ['kɒrəgeɪtɪd] cartone *m* ondulato
cor•ru•gated 'i•ron lamiera *f* (di ferro) ondulata
cor•rupt [kə'rʌpt] **1** *adj also* COMPUT corrotto **2** *v/t morals, youth* traviare; (*bribe*) corrompere
cor•rup•tion [kə'rʌpʃn] corruzione *f*
Cor•si•ca ['kɔːsɪkə] Corsica *f*
Cor•si•can ['kɔːsɪkən] **1** *adj* corso **2** *n* corso *m*, -a *f*
cos•met•ic [kɒz'metɪk] *adj* cosmetico; *surgery* estetico; *fig* di facciata
cos•met•ics [kɒz'metɪks] *npl* cosmetici *mpl*
cos•met•ic 'sur•geon chirurgo *m* estetico
cos•met•ic 'sur•ger•y chirurgia *f* estetica
cos•mo•naut ['kɒzmənɔːt] cosmonauta *m/f*
cos•mo•pol•i•tan [kɒzmə'pɒlɪtən] *adj city* cosmopolitano
cost[1] [kɒst] **1** *n also fig* costo *m*; ***at all costs*** a ogni costo; ***I've learnt to my cost*** l'ho imparato a mie spese; ***costs*** LAW spese **2** *v/t* (*pret & pp* ***cost***) costare; FIN: *proposal, project* fare il preventivo di; ***how much does it cost?*** quanto costa?; ***it cost me my health*** ci ho rimesso la salute
cost[2] [kɒst] *v/t* (*pret & pp* ***costed***) FIN: *proposal, project* fare il preventivo di
cost and 'freight COM costo e nolo
'cost-con•scious *adj*: ***be cost-conscious*** fare attenzione ai consumi
'cost-ef•fec•tive *adj* conveniente
'cost, insurance and freight COM costo, assicurazione e nolo
cost•ly ['kɒstlɪ] *adj mistake* costoso; ***it would be a costly mistake*** potresti pagarla cara
cost of 'liv•ing costo *m* della vita
cost 'price prezzo *m* di costo
cos•tume ['kɒstjuːm] *for actor* costume *m*
cos•tume 'jew•el•lery, *Am* **costume 'jew•el•ry** bigiotteria *f*
co•sy *adj* (*comfortable*) gradevole; (*intimate and friendly*) intimo; ***be nice and cosy in bed*** starsene al calduccio a letto; ***a nice cosy little job*** un lavoretto tranquillo
cot [kɒt] *for child* lettino *m*
cott•age ['kɒtɪdʒ] cottage *m inv*
cot•tage 'cheese fiocchi *mpl* di latte
cot•ton ['kɒtn] **1** *n* cotone *m* **2** *adj* di cotone
◆ **cotton on** *v/i* F afferrare F
◆ **cotton on to** *v/t* F afferrare F
cot•ton 'wool ovatta *f*
couch [kaʊtʃ] *n* divano *m*
'couch po•ta•to F teledipendente *m/f*
cou•chette [kuː'ʃet] cuccetta *f*
cough [kɒf] **1** *n* tosse *f*; *to get attention* colpetto *m* di tosse **2** *v/i* tossire; *to get attention* tossicchiare
◆ **cough up 1** *v/t blood etc* sputare; F *money* cacciar fuori F **2** *v/i* F (*pay*) cacciare i soldi F
'cough medicine, 'cough syrup sciroppo *m* per la tosse
could[1] [kʊd] *v/aux*: ***could I have my key?*** mi dà la chiave?; ***could you help me?*** mi puoi dare una mano?; ***this could be our bus*** questo potrebbe essere il nostro autobus; ***you could be right*** magari hai ragione; ***I couldn't say for sure*** non potrei giurarci; ***he could have got lost*** può darsi che si sia smarrito; ***you could have warned me!*** *in indignation* avresti potuto avvisarmi!
could[2] [kʊd] *pret* → ***can***
coun•cil ['kaʊnsl] *n* (*assembly*) consiglio *m*; (*city council*) comune *m*
'coun•cil house casa *f* popolare
coun•cil•lor ['kaʊnsələ(r)] consigliere *m*, -a *f* (comunale)
'coun•cil tax imposta *f* comunale sugli immobili
coun•sel ['kaʊnsl] **1** *n* (*advice*) consiglio *m*; (*lawyer*) avvocato *m* **2** *v/t course of action* consigliare; *person* offrire consulenza a
coun•sel•ing *Am*, **coun•sel•ling** ['kaʊnslɪŋ] terapia *f*
coun•sel•lor, *Am* **coun•sel•or** ['kaʊnslə(r)] (*adviser*) consulente *m/f*
count[1] [kaʊnt] *aristrocrat* conte *m*
count[2] [kaʊnt] **1** *n* conteggio *m*; ***keep / lose count of*** tenere / perdere il conto di; ***what's your count?*** quanti ne hai contati? **2** *v/i* contare; ***that doesn't count*** questo non conta **3** *v/t* contare; ***count yourself lucky*** considerati fortunato
◆ **count on** *v/t* contare su
'count•down conto *m* alla rovescia
coun•te•nance ['kaʊntənəns] *v/t* appro-

C

vare

coun•ter[1] ['kaʊntə(r)] *in shop, café* banco *m*; *in game* segnalino *m*

coun•ter[2] ['kaʊntə(r)] **1** *v/t* neutralizzare **2** *v/i* (*retaliate*) rispondere

coun•ter[3] ['kaʊntə(r)] *adv*: ***run counter to*** andare contro

'coun•ter•act *v/t* neutralizzare

coun•ter-at'tack 1 *n* contrattacco *m* **2** *v/i* contrattaccare

'coun•terbal•ance 1 *n* contrappeso *m* **2** *v/t* fare da contrappeso a

coun•ter'es•pi•o•nage controspionaggio *m*

coun•ter•feit ['kaʊntəfɪt] **1** *v/t* falsificare **2** *adj* falso

coun•ter•foil ['kaʊntəfɔɪl] matrice *f*

'coun•ter•part *person* omologo *m*, -a *f*

coun•ter•pro'duc•tive *adj* controproducente

'coun•ter•sign *v/t* controfirmare

coun•tess ['kaʊntes] contessa *f*

count•less ['kaʊntlɪs] *adj* innumerevole

coun•try ['kʌntrɪ] **1** *n* (*nation*) paese *m*; *as opposed to town* campagna *f*; ***in the country*** in campagna **2** *adj roads, life* di campagna

coun•try and 'west•ern MUS country and western *m inv*

'country•man (*fellow countryman*) connazionale *m*

'coun•try•side campagna *f*

coun•ty ['kaʊntɪ] contea *f*

coup [kuː] POL colpo *m* di stato, golpe *m inv*; *fig* colpo *m*

cou•ple ['kʌpl] *n* coppia *f*; ***just a couple*** solo un paio; ***a couple of*** un paio di

cou•pon ['kuːpɒn] buono *m*

cour•age ['kʌrɪdʒ] coraggio *m*

cou•ra•geous [kə'reɪdʒəs] *adj* coraggioso

cou•ri•er ['kʊrɪə(r)] (*messenger*) corriere *m*; *with tourist party* accompagnatore *m* turistico, accompagnatrice *f* turistica

course [kɔːs] *n series of lessons* corso *m*; *part of meal* portata *f*; *of ship, plane* rotta *f*; *for golf* campo *m*; *for race, skiing* pista *f*; ***of course*** (*certainly*) certo; (*naturally*) ovviamente; ***of course not*** certo che no; ***first course*** primo *m*; ***second course*** secondo *m*; ***course of action*** linea *f* di condotta; ***course of treatment*** cura *f*; ***in the course of*** nel corso di

court [kɔːt] *n* LAW corte *f*; (*courthouse*) tribunale *m*; SP campo *m*; ***take s.o. to court*** fare causa a qu; ***out of court*** in via amichevole

'court case caso *m* (giudiziario)

cour•te•ous ['kɜːtɪəs] *adj* cortese

cour•te•sy ['kɜːtəsɪ] cortesia *f*

'court•house tribunale *m*, palazzo *m* di giustizia

court 'mar•tial 1 *n* corte *f* marziale **2** *v/t* processare in corte marziale

'court or•der ingiunzione *f* del tribunale

'court•room aula *f* del tribunale

'court•yard cortile *m*

cous•in ['kʌzn] cugino *m*, -a *f*

cove [kəʊv] *small bay* cala *f*

cov•er ['kʌvə(r)] **1** *n protective* fodera *f*; *of book, magazine* copertina *f*; (*shelter*) riparo *m*; *insurance* copertura *f*; ***covers*** *for bed* coperte *fpl*; ***take cover*** ripararsi **2** *v/t* coprire; *distance* percorrere; *of journalist* fare un servizio su; ***we're not covered for theft*** non siamo coperti contro i furti

◆ **cover up 1** *v/t* coprire; *fig* insabbiare **2** *v/i*: ***cover up for s.o.*** *fig* coprire qu

cov•er•age ['kʌvərɪdʒ] *by media* copertura *f*; ***the trial got a lot of coverage*** il processo ha avuto molta risonanza

cov•er•ing let•ter ['kʌvrɪŋ] lettera *f* d'accompagnamento

cov•ert [kəʊ'vɜːt] *adj* segreto

'cov•er-up insabbiamento *m*; ***it looks like a cover-up*** sembra che qualcuno stia cercando di insabbiare le prove

cow [kaʊ] mucca *f*

cow•ard ['kaʊəd] vigliacco *m*, -a *f*

cow•ard•ice ['kaʊədɪs] vigliaccheria *f*

cow•ard•ly ['kaʊədlɪ] *adj* vile

'cow•boy cow-boy *m inv*

cow•er ['kaʊə(r)] *v/i* rannicchiarsi

coy [kɔɪ] *adj* (*evasive*) evasivo; (*flirtatious*) civettuolo

'coz•y *Am* → ***cosy***

CPU [siːpiː'juː] *abbr* (= ***central processing unit***) unità *f* centrale di elaborazione

crab [kræb] *n* granchio *m*

crack [kræk] **1** *n* crepa *f*; (*joke*) battuta *f* **2** *v/t cup, glass* incrinare; *nut* schiacciare; *code* decifrare; F (*solve*) risolvere; ***crack a joke*** fare una battuta **3** *v/i* incrinarsi; ***get cracking*** F darsi una mossa F

◆ **crack down on** *v/t* prendere serie misure contro

◆ **crack up** *v/i* (*have breakdown*) avere un esaurimento; F (*laugh*) scoppiare a ridere

'crack•brained *adj* F pazzoide *f*

'crack•down intensificazione *f* dei controlli (***on*** su)

cracked [krækt] *adj cup, glass* incrinato; F (*crazy*) tocco F

crack•er ['krækə(r)] *to eat* cracker *m inv*

crack•le ['krækl] *v/i of fire* schioppettare

cra•dle ['kreɪdl] *n for baby* culla *f*

craft[1] [krɑːft] NAUT imbarcazione *f*

craft[2] [krɑːft] (*skill*) attività *f inv* artigiana; (*trade*) mestiere *m*
crafts•man ['krɑːftsmən] artigiano *m*
craft•y ['krɑːftɪ] *adj* astuto
crag [kræg] *rock* rupe *f*
cram [kræm] *v/t papers, food* infilare; *people* stipare
cramp [kræmp] *n* crampo *m*
cramped [kræmpt] *adj room, flat* esiguo
cran•ber•ry ['krænbərɪ] mirtillo *m*
crane [kreɪn] **1** *n machine* gru *f inv* **2** *v/t*: ***crane one's neck*** allungare il collo
crank [krænk] *n strange person* tipo *m* strambo
'**crank•shaft** albero *m* a gomiti
crash [kræʃ] **1** *n noise* fragore *m*; *accident* incidente *m*; COM crollo *m*; COMPUT crash *m inv* **2** *v/i fall noisily* fracassarsi; *of thunder* rombare; *of car* schiantarsi; *of two cars* scontrarsi, schiantarsi; *of plane* precipitare; COM: *of market* crollare; COMPUT fare un crash; F (*sleep*) dormire **3** *v/t car* avere un incidente con
◆ **crash out** *v/i* F (*fall asleep*) addormentarsi; *without meaning to* crollare F
'**crash bar•ri•er** barriera *f* protettiva
'**crash course** corso *m* intensivo
'**crash di•et** dieta *f* lampo
'**crash hel•met** casco *m* (di protezione)
'**crash-land** *v/i* fare un atterraggio di fortuna
'**crash land•ing** atterraggio *m* di fortuna
crate [kreɪt] (*packing case*) cassetta *f*
cra•ter ['kreɪtə(r)] *of volcano* cratere *m*
crave [kreɪv] *v/t* smaniare dalla voglia di
crav•ing ['kreɪvɪŋ] voglia *f*; *pej* smania *f*
crawl [krɔːl] **1** *n in swimming* crawl *m*, stile *m* libero; ***at a crawl*** (*very slowly*) a passo d'uomo **2** *v/i on floor* andare (a) carponi; (*move slowly*) avanzare lentamente
◆ **crawl with** *v/t* brulicare di
cray•on ['kreɪən] *n* matita *f* colorata; *wax* pastello *m* a cera
craze [kreɪz] moda *f*
cra•zy ['kreɪzɪ] *adj* pazzo; ***be crazy about s.o.*** essere pazzo di qu; ***be crazy about sth*** andare matto per qc
creak [kriːk] **1** *n* scricchiolio *m* **2** *v/i* scricchiolare
creak•y ['kriːkɪ] *adj* che scricchiola
cream [kriːm] **1** *n for skin* crema *f*; *for coffee, cake* panna *f*; (*colour*) color *m* panna **2** *adj* color panna
cream '**cheese** formaggio *m* fresco da spalmare
creamer ['kriːmə(r)] *for coffee* panna *f* liofilizzata
cream•y ['kriːmɪ] *adj with lots of cream* cremoso
crease [kriːs] **1** *n accidental* grinza *f*; *deliberate* piega *f* **2** *v/t accidentally* sgualcire
cre•ate [kriː'eɪt] *v/t* creare
cre•a•tion [kriː'eɪʃn] creazione *f*
cre•a•tive [kriː'eɪtɪv] *adj* creativo
cre•a•tor [kriː'eɪtə(r)] creatore *m*, -trice *f*; ***the Creator*** REL il Creatore
crea•ture ['kriːtʃə(r)] creatura *f*
crèche [kreʃ] *for children* asilo *m* nido; REL presepe *m*
cred•i•bil•i•ty [kredə'bɪlətɪ] credibilità *f inv*
cred•i•ble ['kredəbl] *adj* credibile
cred•it ['kredɪt] **1** *n* FIN credito *m*; (*honour*) merito *m*; ***be in credit*** avere un saldo attivo; ***get the credit for sth*** prendersi il merito di qc **2** *v/t* (*believe*) credere; ***credit an amount to an account*** accreditare una cifra su un conto
cred•i•ta•ble ['kredɪtəbl] *adj* lodevole
'**cred•it card** carta *f* di credito
'**cred•it lim•it** limite *m* di credito
cred•i•tor ['kredɪtə(r)] creditore *m*, -trice *f*
'**cred•it•wor•thy** *adj* solvibile
cred•u•lous ['kredjʊləs] *adj* credulo
creed [kriːd] credo *m inv*
creep [kriːp] **1** *n pej* tipo *m* odioso **2** *v/i* (*pret & pp* ***crept***) *quietly* avanzare quatto quatto; *slowly* avanzare lentamente
creep•er ['kriːpə(r)] BOT rampicante *m*
creeps [kriːps] *npl* F: ***the house / he gives me the creeps*** la casa / lui mi fa venire la pelle d'oca
creep•y ['kriːpɪ] *adj* F che dà i brividi; ***be creepy*** F far paura
cre•mate [krɪ'meɪt] *v/t* cremare
cre•ma•tion [krɪ'meɪʃn] cremazione *f*
cre•ma•to•ri•um [kremə'tɔːrɪəm] crematorio *m*
crept [krept] *pret & pp* → ***creep***
cres•cent ['kresənt] *n shape* mezzaluna *f*
crest [krest] *of hill, bird* cresta *f*
crest•fal•len *adj* abbattuto
cre•vasse [krə'væs] voraggine *f*
crev•ice ['krevɪs] crepa *f*
crew [kruː] *n of ship, plane* equipaggio *m*; *of workers etc* squadra *f*; (*film crew*) troupe *f inv*; (*crowd, group*) ghenga *f*
'**crew cut** taglio *m* a spazzola
'**crew neck** girocollo *m*
crick [krɪk] *n*: ***crick in the neck*** torcicollo *m*
crick•et ['krɪkɪt] *insect* grillo *m*; *game* cricket *m inv*
crime [kraɪm] (*offence*) reato *m*; (*criminality*) criminalità *f inv*; (*shameful act*) crimine *m*

C

crim•i•nal ['krɪmɪnl] **1** *n* delinquente *m/f* **2** *adj* LAW penale; (*shameful*) vergognoso; ***a criminal offence*** un reato
crim•son ['krɪmzn] *adj* cremisi *inv*
cringe [krɪndʒ] *v/i* morire di vergogna
crip•ple ['krɪpl] **1** *n* (*disabled person*) invalido *m*, -a *f* **2** *v/t person* rendere invalido; *fig* paralizzare
cri•sis ['kraɪsɪs] (*pl* ***crises*** ['kraɪsiːz]) crisi *f inv*
crisp [krɪsp] *adj weather, air, lettuce, new shirt* fresco; *bacon, toast* croccante; *bank notes* nuovo di zecca
crisps [krɪsps] *npl Br* patatine *fpl*
cri•te•ri•on [kraɪ'tɪərɪən] criterio *m*
crit•ic ['krɪtɪk] critico *m*, -a *f*
crit•i•cal ['krɪtɪkl] *adj* critico
crit•i•cal•ly ['krɪtɪklɪ] *adv speak etc* criticamente; ***critically ill*** gravemente malato
crit•i•cis•m ['krɪtɪsɪzm] critica *f*
crit•i•cize ['krɪtɪsaɪz] *v/t* criticare
croak [krəʊk] **1** *n of frog* gracidio *m*; *of person* rantolo *m* **2** *v/i of frog* gracidare; *of person* parlare con voce rauca
cro•chet ['krəʊʃeɪ] **1** *n* lavoro *m* all'uncinetto **2** *v/t* lavorare all'uncinetto
crock•e•ry ['krɒkərɪ] stoviglie *fpl*
croc•o•dile ['krɒkədaɪl] coccodrillo *m*
cro•cus ['krəʊkəs] croco *m*
cro•ny ['krəʊnɪ] F amico *m*, -a *f*
crook [krʊk] *n* truffatore *m*, -trice *f*
crook•ed ['krʊkɪd] *adj streets* tortuoso; *picture* storto; (*dishonest*) disonesto
crop [krɒp] **1** *n* raccolto *m*; *type of grain etc* coltura *f*; *fig* scaglione *m* **2** *v/t* (*pret & pp* ***-ped***) *hair, photo* tagliare
◆ **crop up** *v/i* venir fuori
cross [krɒs] **1** *adj* (*angry*) arrabbiato **2** *n* croce *f* **3** *v/t* (*go across*) attraversare; ***cross o.s.*** REL farsi il segno della croce; ***cross one's legs*** accavallare le gambe; ***keep one's fingers crossed*** fare gli scongiuri; ***it never crossed my mind*** non mi è passato per la testa **4** *v/i* (*go across*) attraversare; *of lines* intersecarsi
◆ **cross off**, **cross out** *v/t* depennare
'**cross•bar** *of goal* traversa *f*; *of bicycle* canna *f*; *in high jump* asticella *f*
'**cross•check 1** *n* controllo *m* incrociato **2** *v/t* fare un controllo incrociato su
cross-'coun•try corsa *f* campestre
cross-coun•try ('skiing) sci *m inv* di fondo
crossed 'check *Am*, **crossed 'cheque** [krɒst] assegno *m* sbarrato
cross-ex•am•i'na•tion LAW interrogatorio *m* in contraddittorio
cross-ex'am•ine *v/t* LAW interrogare in contraddittorio
cross-eyed ['krɒsaɪd] *adj* strabico
cross•ing ['krɒsɪŋ] NAUT traversata *f*; *for pedestrians* attraversamento *m* pedonale
'**cross•roads** *nsg* incrocio *m*; *fig* bivio *m*
'**cross-sec•tion** *of people* campione *m* rappresentativo
'**cross-walk** *Am* passaggio *m* pedonale
'**cross•word (puz•zle)** cruciverba *m inv*
crotch [krɒtʃ] *of person* inguine *m*; *of trousers* cavallo *m*
crouch [kraʊtʃ] *v/i* accovacciarsi
crow [krəʊ] *n bird* corvo *m*; ***as the crow flies*** in linea d'aria
'**crow•bar** piede *m* di porco
crowd [kraʊd] *n* folla *f*
crowd•ed ['kraʊdɪd] *adj* affollato
crown [kraʊn] **1** *n* corona *f*; *on tooth* capsula *f* **2** *v/t king* incoronare; *tooth* incapsulare
cru•cial ['kruːʃl] *adj* essenziale
cru•ci•fix ['kruːsɪfɪks] crocifisso *m*
cru•ci•fix•ion [kruːsɪ'fɪkʃn] crocifissione *f*
cru•ci•fy ['kruːsɪfaɪ] *v/t* (*pret & pp* ***-ied***) REL crocifiggere; *fig* fare a pezzi
crude [kruːd] **1** *adj* (*vulgar*) volgare; (*unsophisticated*) rudimentale **2** *n*: ***crude (oil)*** (petrolio *m*) greggio *m*
crude•ly ['kruːdlɪ] *adv speak* volgarmente; *made* rozzamente
cru•el ['kruːəl] *adj* crudele
cru•el•ty ['kruːəltɪ] crudeltà *f inv*
cruise [kruːz] **1** *n* crociera *f* **2** *v/i of people* fare una crociera; *of car, plane* viaggiare a velocità di crociera
'**cruise lin•er** nave *f* da crociera
cruis•ing speed ['kruːzɪŋ] *also fig* velocità *f inv* di crociera
crumb [krʌm] briciola *f*
crum•ble ['krʌmbl] **1** *v/t* sbriciolare **2** *v/i of bread* sbriciolarsi; *of stonework* sgretolarsi; *fig*: *of opposition etc* crollare
crum•bly ['krʌmblɪ] *adj* friabile
crum•ple ['krʌmpl] **1** *v/t* (*crease*) sgualcire **2** *v/i* (*collapse*) accasciarsi
crunch [krʌntʃ] **1** *n* F: ***when it comes to the crunch*** al momento cruciale **2** *v/i of snow, gravel* scricchiolare
cru•sade [kruː'seɪd] *n also fig* crociata *f*
crush [krʌʃ] **1** *n crowd* ressa *f*; ***have a crush on*** avere una cotta per **2** *v/t* schiacciare; (*crease*) sgualcire; ***they were crushed to death*** sono morti schiacciati **3** *v/i* (*crease*) sgualcire
crust [krʌst] *on bread* crosta *f*
crust•y ['krʌstɪ] *adj bread* croccante
crutch [krʌtʃ] *for injured person* stampella *f*
cry [kraɪ] **1** *n* (*call*) grido *m*; ***have a cry***

piangere **2** *v/t* (*pret & pp* ***-ied***) (*call*) gridare **3** *v/i* (*pret & pp* ***-ied***) (*weep*) piangere
◆ **cry out** *v/t & v/i* gridare
◆ **cry out for** *v/t* (*need*) aver fortemente bisogno di
cryp•tic ['krɪptɪk] *adj* sibillino
crys•tal ['krɪstl] **1** *n mineral* cristallo *m*; *glass* cristalli *mpl* **2** *adj* di cristallo
crys•tal•lize ['krɪstlaɪz] **1** *v/t* concretizzare **2** *v/i of thoughts etc* concretizzarsi
cub [kʌb] cucciolo *m*
Cu•ba ['kjuːbə] Cuba *f*
Cu•ban ['kjuːbən] **1** *adj* cubano **2** *n* cubano *m*, -a *f*
cube [kjuːb] *shape* cubo *m*
cu•bic ['kjuːbɪk] *adj* cubico
cu•bic ca'pac•i•ty TECH cilindrata *f*
cu•bi•cle ['kjuːbɪkl] (*changing room*) cabina *f*
cu•cum•ber ['kjuːkʌmbə(r)] cetriolo *m*
cud•dle ['kʌdl] **1** *n* coccole *fpl* **2** *v/t* coccolare
cud•dly ['kʌdlɪ] *adj kitten etc* tenero; *liking cuddles* coccolone
cue [kjuː] *n for actor etc* imbeccata *f*; *for billiards* stecca *f*
cuff [kʌf] **1** *n of shirt* polsino *m*; (*blow*) schiaffo *m*; *Am* (*of trousers*) risvolto *m*; ***off the cuff*** improvvisando **2** *v/t hit* dare uno schiaffo a
'cuff link gemello *m*
'cul-de-sac ['kʌldəsæk] vicolo *m* cieco
cu•li•nar•y ['kʌlɪnərɪ] *adj* culinario
cul•mi•nate ['kʌlmɪneɪt] *v/i* culminare; ***culminate in*** culminare in
cul•mi•na•tion [kʌlmɪ'neɪʃn] culmine *m*
cu•lottes ['kjuːlɒt] *npl* gonna *f* pantalone
cul•prit ['kʌlprɪt] colpevole *m/f*
cult [kʌlt] culto *m*
cul•ti•vate ['kʌltɪveɪt] *v/t land* coltivare; *person* coltivarsi
cul•ti•vat•ed ['kʌltɪveɪtɪd] *adj person* colto
cul•ti•va•tion [kʌltɪ'veɪʃn] *of land* coltivazione *f*
cul•tu•ral ['kʌltʃərəl] *adj* culturale
cul•ture ['kʌltʃə(r)] *n* cultura *f*
cul•tured ['kʌltʃəd] *adj* (*cultivated*) colto
'cul•ture shock shock *m inv* culturale
cum•ber•some ['kʌmbəsəm] *adj* ingombrante; *procedure* macchinoso
cu•mu•la•tive ['kjuːmjʊlətɪv] *adj* cumulativo
cun•ning ['kʌnɪŋ] **1** *n* astuzia *f* **2** *adj* astuto
cup [kʌp] *n* tazza *f*; (*trophy*) coppa *f*; ***a cup of tea*** una tazza di tè
cup•board ['kʌbəd] armadio *m*
'cup fi•nal finale *f* di coppa
cu•po•la ['kjuːpələ] cupola *f*
'cup tie partita *f* di coppa
cu•ra•ble ['kjʊərəbl] *adj* curabile
cu•ra•tor [kjʊə'reɪtə(r)] direttore *m*, -trice di museo
curb [kɜːb] **1** *n on powers etc* freno *m* **2** *v/t* tenere a freno
cur•dle ['kɜːdl] *v/i of milk* cagliare
cure [kjʊə(r)] **1** *n* MED cura *f* **2** *v/t* MED guarire; *by drying* essiccare; *by salting* salare; *by smoking* affumicare
cur•few ['kɜːfjuː] coprifuoco *m*
cu•ri•os•i•ty [kjʊərɪ'ɒsətɪ] curiosità *f inv*
cu•ri•ous ['kjʊərɪəs] *adj* (*inquisitive*) curioso; (*strange*) strano
cu•ri•ous•ly ['kjʊərɪəslɪ] *adv* (*inquisitively*) con curiosità; (*strangely*) stranamente; ***curiously enough ...*** sembrerà strano ma ...
curl [kɜːl] **1** *n in hair* ricciolo *m*; *of smoke* spirale *f* **2** *v/t* arricciare **3** *v/i of hair* arricciarsi; *of leaf, paper etc* accartocciarsi
◆ **curl up** *v/i* acciambellarsi
curl•y ['kɜːlɪ] *adj hair* riccio; *tail* a ricciolo
cur•rant ['kʌrənt] (*dried fruit*) uva *f* passa
cur•ren•cy ['kʌrənsɪ] *money* valuta *f*; ***foreign currency*** valuta estera
cur•rent ['kʌrənt] **1** *n* corrente *f* **2** *adj* (*present*) attuale
'cur•rent ac•count conto *m* corrente
cur•rent af'fairs, cur•rent e,vents *npl* attualità *f inv*
cur•rent af'fairs pro•gramme programma *m* di attualità
cur•rent•ly ['kʌrəntlɪ] *adv* attualmente
cur•ric•u•lum [kə'rɪkjʊləm] programma *m* (scolastico)
cur•ric•u•lum vi•tae ['viːtaɪ] curriculum *m inv* vitae
cur•ry ['kʌrɪ] *dish* piatto *m* al curry; *spice* curry *m inv*
curse [kɜːs] **1** *n spell* maledizione *f*; (*swearword*) imprecazione *f* **2** *v/t* maledire; (*swear at*) imprecare contro **3** *v/i* (*swear*) imprecare
cur•sor ['kɜːsə(r)] COMPUT cursore *m*
cur•so•ry ['kɜːsərɪ] *adj* di sfuggita
curt [kɜːt] *adj* brusco
cur•tail [kɜː'teɪl] *v/t trip etc* accorciare
cur•tain ['kɜːtn] tenda *f*; THEA sipario *m*
curve [kɜːv] **1** *n* curva *f* **2** *v/i* (*bend*) fare una curva
cush•ion ['kʊʃn] **1** *n for couch etc* cuscino *m* **2** *v/t blow, fall* attutire
cus•tard ['kʌstəd] crema *f* (pasticciera)
cus•to•dy ['kʌstədɪ] *of children* custodia *f*; ***in custody*** LAW in detenzione preventiva
cus•tom ['kʌstəm] (*tradition*) usanza *f*;

C

COM clientela *f*; ***as was his custom*** com'era suo solito

cus•tom•a•ry ['kʌstəmərɪ] *adj* consueto; ***it is customary to ...*** è consuetudine ...

cus•tom•er ['kʌstəmə(r)] cliente *m/f*

cus•tom•er re'la•tions *npl* relazione *f* clienti

cus•tom•er 'serv•ice servizio *m* assistenza al cliente

cus•toms ['kʌstəmz] *npl* dogana *f*

Cus•toms and 'Ex•cise Ufficio *m* Dazi e Dogana

'cus•toms clearance sdoganamento *m*

'cus•toms in•spec•tion controllo *m* doganale

'cus•toms of•fi•cer doganiere *m*, -a *f*

cut [kʌt] **1** *n with knife*, *of hair*, *clothes* taglio *m*; (*reduction*) riduzione *f*; *in public spending* taglio *m*; ***my hair needs a cut*** devo tagliarmi i capelli **2** *v/t* (*pret & pp* ***cut***) tagliare; (*reduce*) ridurre; ***get one's hair cut*** tagliarsi i capelli; ***I cut my finger*** mi sono tagliato un dito

◆**cut back 1** *v/i in costs* limitare le spese **2** *v/t employees* ridurre

◆**cut down 1** *v/t tree* abbattere **2** *v/i in smoking etc* limitarsi

◆**cut down on** *v/t cigarettes*, *chocolate* ridurre la quantità di; ***cut down on smoking*** fumare di meno

◆**cut off** *v/t with knife*, *scissors etc* tagliare; (*isolate*) isolare; ***I've been cut off*** TELEC è caduta la linea

◆**cut out** *v/t with scissors* ritagliare; (*eliminate*) eliminare; ***cut that out!*** F smettila!; ***be cut out for sth*** essere tagliato per qc

◆**cut up** *v/t meat etc* sminuzzare

cut•back *in production* riduzione *f*; *in public spending* taglio *m*

cute [kjuːt] *adj* (*pretty*) carino; (*smart*, *clever*) furbo

cu•ti•cle ['kjuːtɪkl] pellicina *f*

cut•le•ry ['kʌtlərɪ] posate *fpl*

'cut-off date scadenza *f*

cut-'price *adj goods* a prezzo ridotto; *store* di articoli scontati

'cut-throat *adj competition* spietato

cut•ting ['kʌtɪŋ] **1** *n from newspaper etc* ritaglio *m* **2** *adj remark* tagliente

CV [siː'viː] *abbr* (= ***curriculum vitae***) CV *m inv* (= curriculum *m inv* vitae)

'cy•ber•space ['saɪbəspeɪs] ciberspazio *m*

cy•cle ['saɪkl] **1** *n* (*bicycle*) bicicletta *f*; *of events* ciclo *m* **2** *v/i to work* andare in bicicletta

'cy•cle path pista *f* ciclabile

cy•cling ['saɪklɪŋ] ciclismo *m*; ***he's taken up cycling*** ha cominciato ad andare in bicicletta

cy•clist ['saɪklɪst] ciclista *m/f*

cyl•in•der ['sɪlɪndə(r)] cilindro *m*

cy•lin•dri•cal [sɪ'lɪndrɪkl] *adj* cilindrico

cyn•ic ['sɪnɪk] cinico *m*, -a *f*

cyn•i•cal ['sɪnɪkl] *adj* cinico

cyn•i•cal•ly ['sɪnɪklɪ] *adv* cinicamente

cyn•i•cism ['sɪnɪsɪzm] cinismo *m*

cy•press ['saɪprəs] cipresso *m*

cyst [sɪst] cisti *f inv*

Czech [tʃek] **1** *adj* ceco; ***the Czech Republic*** la Repubblica Ceca **2** *n person* ceco *m*, -a *f*; *language* ceco *m*

D

dab [dæb] **1** *n* (*small amount*) tocco *m*, pochino *m* **2** *v/t* (*remove*) (*pret & pp* **-bed**) tamponare; (*apply*) applicare; ***dab a cut with ointment*** applicare una pomata sul taglio

◆ **dabble in** *v/t* dilettarsi di

dad [dæd] papà *m inv*

dad•dy ['dædɪ] papà *m inv*

dad•dy long•legs zanzarone *m*

daf•fo•dil ['dæfədɪl] trombone *m*

daft [dɑːft] *adj* stupido

dag•ge r ['dægə(r)] pugnale *m*

dai•ly ['deɪlɪ] **1** *n* (*paper*) quotidiano *m*; (*cleaning woman*) domestica *f* **2** *adj* quotidiano

dain•ty ['deɪntɪ] *adj* aggraziato

dair•y cat•tle ['deərɪ] vacche *fpl* da latte

'dair•y farm•ing produzione *f* di latticini

'dair•y prod•ucts *npl* latticini *mpl*

dais ['deɪɪs] palco *m*

dai•sy ['deɪzɪ] margherita *f*

dam [dæm] **1** *n for water* diga *f* **2** *v/t* (*pret & pp* **-med**) *river* costruire una diga su

dam•age ['dæmɪdʒ] **1** *n also fig* danno *m* **2** *v/t* danneggiare; *fig*: *reputation etc* compromettere

dam•ages ['dæmɪdʒɪz] *npl* LAW risarcimento *msg*

dam•ag•ing ['dæmɪdʒɪŋ] *adj* nocivo

dame [deɪm] *Am* F (*woman*) tizia *f* F; ***she's quite a dame!*** che donna!

damn [dæm] **1** *int* F accidenti **2** *n*: F ***I don't give a damn!*** non me ne frega niente! F **3** *adj* F maledetto **4** *adv* F incredibilmente **5** *v/t* (*condemn*) maledire; ***damn it!*** F accidenti!; ***I'm damned if I will*** F non me lo sogno nemmeno

damned [dæmd] → **damn** *adj & adv*

damn•ing ['dæmɪŋ] *adj evidence* schiacciante; *report* incriminante

damp [dæmp] *adj* umido

damp•en ['dæmpən] *v/t* inumidire

dance [dɑːns] **1** *n* ballo *m* **2** *v/i* ballare; *of ballerina* danzare; ***would you like to dance?*** ti va di ballare?; *fml* posso invitarla a ballare?

danc•er ['dɑːnsə(r)] (*performer*) ballerino *m*, -a *f*; ***be a good dancer*** ballare bene

danc•ing ['dɑːnsɪŋ] ballo *m*, danza *f*

dan•de•lion ['dændɪlaɪən] dente *m* di leone

dan•druff ['dændrʌf] forfora *f*

dan•druff sham'poo shampoo *m inv* antiforfora *inv*

Dane [deɪn] danese *m/f*

dan•ger ['deɪndʒə(r)] pericolo *m*; ***be in danger*** essere in pericolo; ***out of danger*** *of patient* fuori pericolo

dan•ger•ous ['deɪndʒərəs] *adj* pericoloso

dan•ger•ous 'driv•ing guida *f* pericolosa

dan•ger•ous•ly ['deɪndʒərəslɪ] *adv drive* spericolatamente; ***dangerously ill*** gravemente malato

dan•gle ['dæŋgl] **1** *v/t* dondolare **2** *v/i* pendere

Da•nish ['deɪnɪʃ] **1** *adj* danese **2** *n* (*language*) danese *m*

Da•nish ('**pastry**) *dolcetto m ripieno*

dare [deə(r)] **1** *v/i* osare; ***dare to do sth*** osare fare qc; ***how dare you!*** come osi! **2** *v/t*: ***dare s.o. to do sth*** sfidare qu a fare qc

dare•dev•il ['deədevɪl] scavezzacollo *m*

dar•ing ['deərɪŋ] *adj* audace

dark [dɑːk] **1** *n* buio *m*, oscurità *f*; ***after dark*** dopo il calare della notte; ***keep s.o. in the dark*** *fig* tenere qu all'oscuro **2** *adj room, night* buio; *hair, eyes, colour* scuro; ***dark green / blue*** verde / blu scuro

dark•en ['dɑːkn] *v/i of sky* oscurarsi

dark 'glasses *npl* occhiali *mpl* scuri

dark•ness ['dɑːknɪs] oscurità *f*

'dark•room PHOT camera *f* oscura

dar•ling ['dɑːlɪŋ] **1** *n* tesoro *m*; ***be a darling and …*** sii carino e … **2** *adj* caro

darn [dɑːn] **1** *n* (*mend*) rammendo *m* **2** *v/t* (*mend*) rammendare

dart [dɑːt] **1** *n for throwing* freccetta *f* **2** *v/i* scagliarsi

darts [dɑːts] *nsg* (*game*) freccette *fpl*

'dart(s)•board tabellone *m* delle freccette

dash [dæʃ] **1** *n in punctuation* trattino *m*, lineetta *f*; *of whisky, milk* goccio *m*; *of salt* pizzico *m*; (MOT: *dashboard*) cruscotto *m*; ***make a dash for*** precipitarsi su **2** *v/i* precipitarsi; ***I must dash*** devo scappare **3** *v/t hopes* stroncare

◆ **dash off 1** *v/i* scappare **2** *v/t* (*write quickly*) buttare giù

'dash•board cruscotto *m*

data ['deɪtə] dati *mpl*

'data•base base *f* dati

da•ta ˌcapture inserimento *f* dati

da•ta 'pro•cess•ing elaborazione *f* dati

da•ta proˌtec•tion protezione *f* dati

da•ta 'stor•age memorizzazione *f* dati,

archiviazione *f* dati
date[1] [deɪt] (*fruit*) dattero *m*
date[2] [deɪt] **1** *n* data *f*; (*meeting*) appuntamento *m*; ***your date is here*** è arrivato il tuo ragazzo, è arrivata la tua ragazza; ***what's the date today?*** quanti ne abbiamo oggi?; ***out of date*** *clothes* fuori moda; *passport* scaduto; ***up to date*** aggiornato; (*fashionable*) attuale **2** *v/t letter, cheque* datare; (*go out with*) uscire con; ***that dates you*** (*shows your age*) quanto sei vecchio
dat•ed ['deɪtɪd] *adj* superato
daub [dɔːb] *v/t*: ***daub paint on a wall*** imbrattare il muro di vernice
daugh•ter ['dɔːtə(r)] figlia *f*
'**daugh•ter-in-law** (*pl* ***daughters-in-law***) nuora *f*
daunt [dɔːnt] *v/t* scoraggiare
daw•dle ['dɔːdl] *v/i* ciondolare
dawn [dɔːn] **1** *n* alba *f*; *fig*: *of new age* albori *mpl* **2** *v/i*: ***it dawned on me that …*** mi sono reso conto che …
day [deɪ] giorno *m*; ***what day is it today?*** che giorno è oggi?; ***day off*** giorno *m* di ferie; ***by day*** di giorno; ***day by day*** giorno per giorno; ***the day after*** il giorno dopo; ***the day after tomorrow*** dopodomani; ***the day before*** il giorno prima; ***the day before yesterday*** l'altro ieri; ***day in day out*** senza tregua; ***in those days*** a quei tempi; ***one day*** un giorno; ***the other day*** (*recently*) l'altro giorno; ***let's call it a day!*** lasciamo perdere!
'**day boy** alunno *m* esterno
'**daybreak**: ***at daybreak*** allo spuntare del giorno
'**day care** asilo *m*
'**day•dream 1** *n* sogno *m* ad occhi aperti **2** *v/i* essere sovrappensiero
'**day dream•er** sognatore *m*, -trice *f*
'**day girl** alunna *f* esterna
day re'turn biglietto *m* di andata e ritorno in giornata
'**day•time**: ***in the daytime*** durante il giorno
day•light 'sav•ing time ora *f* legale
'**day•trip** gita *f* di un giorno
daze [deɪz] *n*: ***in a daze*** sbalordito
dazed [deɪzd] *adj by good / bad news* sbalordito; *by a blow* stordito
daz•zle ['dæzl] *v/t of light*, *fig* abbagliare
DC [diː'siː] *abbr* (= ***direct current***) c.c.; (=corrente *f* continua); ***District of Columbia***) DC
dead [ded] **1** *adj person, plant* morto; *battery* scarica; *phone* muto; *light bulb* bruciato; ***be dead*** F *of place* essere un mortorio F **2** *adv* F (*very*) da matti F; ***dead beat, dead tired*** stanco morto; ***that's dead right*** è assolutamente vero; ***it's dead interesting*** è interessante da matti **3** *n*: ***the dead*** (*dead people*) i morti; ***in the dead of night*** nel cuore della notte
dead•en ['dedn] *v/t pain* attenuare; *sound* attutire
dead 'end (*street*) vicolo *m* cieco
dead-'end job lavoro *m* senza prospettive
dead 'heat pareggio *m*
'**dead•line** scadenza *f*; *for newspaper, magazine* termine *m* per l'invio in stampa
'**dead•lock** *n in talks* punto *m* morto
dead•ly ['dedlɪ] *adj* (*fatal*) mortale; F (*boring*) di una noia mortale F
deaf [def] *adj* sordo
deaf-and-'dumb *adj* sordomuto
deaf•en ['defn] *v/t* assordare
deaf•en•ing ['defnɪŋ] *adj* assordante
deaf•ness ['defnɪs] sordità *f inv*
deal [diːl] **1** *n* accordo *m*; ***it's a deal!*** affare fatto!; ***a good deal*** (*bargain*) un affare; (*a lot*) molto; ***a great deal of*** (*lots*) un bel po' di; ***it's your deal*** *in games* tocca a te **2** *v/t* (*pret & pp* ***dealt***) *cards* distribuire; ***deal a blow to*** inferire un duro colpo a
◆ **deal in** *v/t* (*trade in*) trattare; *drugs* trafficare
◆ **deal out** *v/t cards* distribuire
◆ **deal with** *v/t* (*handle*) occuparsi di; *situation* gestire; (*do business with*) trattare con
deal•er ['diːlə(r)] (*merchant*) commerciante *m/f*; (*drug dealer*) spacciatore *m*, -trice *f*
deal•ing ['diːlɪŋ] (*drug dealing*) spaccio *m*
deal•ings ['diːlɪŋz] *npl* (*business*) rapporti *mpl*
dealt [delt] *pret & pp* → ***deal***
dean [diːn] *of college* preside *m*
dear [dɪə(r)] *adj* caro; ***Dear Sir*** Egregio Signore; ***Dear Richard / Dear Margaret*** caro Richard / cara Margareth; **(*oh*) *dear!, dear me!*** povero/a me!
dear•ly ['dɪərlɪ] *adv love* teneramente
death [deθ] morte *f*
'**death cer•tif•i•cate** certificato *m* di decesso
'**death pen•al•ty** pena *f* di morte
'**death toll** numero *m* delle vittime
de•ba•ta•ble [dɪ'beɪtəbl] *adj* discutibile
de•bate [dɪ'beɪt] **1** *n* dibattimento *m*; POL dibattito *m*; ***after much debate*** dopo molto dibattere **2** *v/i* dibattere; ***debate with o.s. whether …*** considerare se … **3** *v/t* dibattere su
de•bauch•er•y [dɪ'bɔːtʃərɪ] depravazione *f*

deb•it ['debɪt] **1** *n* addebito *m* **2** *v/t*: ***debit £150 to s.o.'s account*** addebitare £ 150 a qu; ***debit an account with £ 150*** addebitare £ 150 su un conto
'**deb•it card** carta *f* di debito
deb•ris ['debriː] *of plane* rottami *mpl*; *of building* macerie *fpl*
debt [det] debito *m*; ***be in debt*** (*financially*) avere dei debiti
debt•or ['detə(r)] debitore *m*, -trice *f*
de•bug [diː'bʌg] *v/t* (*pret & pp* ***-ged***) *room* togliere le microspie da; COMPUT togliere gli errori da
dé•but ['deɪbjuː] *n* debutto *m*
dec•ade ['dekeɪd] decennio *m*, decade *f*
dec•a•dence ['dekədəns] decadenza *f*
dec•a•dent ['dekədənt] *adj* decadente
de•caf•fein•at•ed [dɪ'kæfɪneɪtɪd] *adj* decaffeinato
de•cant•er [dɪ'kæntə(r)] caraffa *f*
de•cap•i•tate [dɪ'kæpɪteɪt] *v/t* decapitare
de•cay [dɪ'keɪ] **1** *n of organic matter* decomposizione *f*; *of civilization* declino *m*; (*decayed matter*) marciume *m*; *in teeth* carie *f inv* **2** *v/i of organic matter* decomporsi; *of civilization* declinare; *of teeth* cariarsi
de•ceased [dɪ'siːst]: ***the deceased*** il defunto *m*, la defunta *f*
de•ceit [dɪ'siːt] falsità *f*, disonestà *f*
de•ceit•ful [dɪ'siːtfʊl] *adj* falso, disonesto
de•ceive [dɪ'siːv] *v/t* ingannare
De•cem•ber [dɪ'sembə(r)] dicembre *m*
de•cen•cy ['diːsənsɪ] decenza *f*; ***he had the decency to …*** ha avuto la decenza di …
de•cent ['diːsənt] *adj price*, *proposition* corretto; *meal*, *sleep* decente; (*adequately dressed*) presentabile; ***a decent guy*** un uomo per bene; ***that's very decent of you*** è molto gentile da parte tua
de•cen•tral•ize [diː'sentrəlaɪz] *v/t* decentralizzare
de•cep•tion [dɪ'sepʃn] inganno *m*
de•cep•tive [dɪ'septɪv] *adj* ingannevole
de•cep•tive•ly [dɪ'septɪvlɪ] *adv*: ***it looks deceptively simple*** sembra semplice solo all'apparenza
dec•i•bel ['desɪbel] decibel *m inv*
de•cide [dɪ'saɪd] **1** *v/t* (*make up one's mind*) decidere; (*conclude*, *settle*) risolvere **2** *v/i* decidere; ***you decide*** decidi tu
de•cid•ed [dɪ'saɪdɪd] *adj* (*definite*) deciso
de•cid•er [dɪ'saɪdə(r)]: ***be the decider*** *of match etc* essere decisivo
dec•i•du•ous [dɪ'sɪdjʊəs] *adj* che perde le foglie in inverno
dec•i•mal ['desɪml] *n* decimale
dec•i•mal 'point *punto m che separa i decimali*; *in Italy* virgola *f*
dec•i•mate ['desɪmeɪt] *v/t* decimare
de•ci•pher [dɪ'saɪfə(r)] *v/t* decifrare
de•ci•sion [dɪ'sɪʒn] decisione *f*; (*conclusion*) risoluzione *f*; ***come to a decision*** prendere una decisione
de'ci•sion-mak•er responsabile *m/f*; ***be a decision-maker*** (*be able to make decisions*) saper prendere delle decisioni
de•ci•sive [dɪ'saɪsɪv] *adj* risoluto; (*crucial*) decisivo
deck [dek] *of ship* ponte *m*; *of bus* piano *m*; *of cards* mazzo *m*
'**deck•chair** sedia *f* a sdraio, sdraio *f inv*
dec•la•ra•tion [deklə'reɪʃn] dichiarazione *f*
de•clare [dɪ'kleə(r)] *v/t* dichiarare
de•cline [dɪ'klaɪn] **1** *n in number*, *standards* calo *m*; *in health* peggioramento *m* **2** *v/t invitation* declinare; ***decline to comment / accept*** esimersi dal commentare / accettare **3** *v/i* (*refuse*) declinare; (*decrease*) diminuire; *of health* peggiorare
de•clutch [diː'klʌtʃ] *v/i* lasciare andare la frizione
de•code [diː'kəʊd] *v/t* decodificare
de•com•pose [diːkəm'pəʊz] *v/i* decomporsi
dé•cor ['deɪkɔː(r)] arredamento *m*
dec•o•rate ['dekəreɪt] *v/t with paint* imbiancare; *with paper* tappezzare; (*adorn*), MIL decorare
dec•o•ra•tion [dekə'reɪʃn] *paint* vernice *f*; *paper* tappezzeria *f*; (*ornament*) addobbi *mpl*; MIL decorazione *f*
dec•o•ra•tive ['dekərətɪv] *adj* decorativo
dec•o•ra•tor ['dekəreɪtə(r)] (*interior decorator*) imbianchino *m*
de•co•rum [dɪ'kɔːrəm] decoro *m*
de•coy ['diːkɔɪ] *n* esca *f*
de•crease ['diːkriːs] **1** *n* diminuzione *f* **2** *v/t* ridurre **3** *v/i* ridursi
de•crep•it [dɪ'krepɪt] *adj* decrepito
ded•i•cate ['dedɪkeɪt] *v/t book etc* dedicare; ***dedicate o.s. to …*** consacrarsi a …
ded•i•ca•ted ['dedɪkeɪtɪd] *adj* dedito
ded•i•ca•tion [dedɪ'keɪʃn] *in book* dedica *f*; *to cause*, *work* dedizione *f*
de•duce [dɪ'djuːs] *v/t* dedurre
de•duct [dɪ'dʌkt] *v/t* detrarre; ***deduct sth from sth*** detrarre qc da qc
de•duc•tion [dɪ'dʌkʃn] *from salary* trattenuta *f*; (*conclusion*) deduzione *f*; ***deduction at source*** ritenuta *f* alla fonte
dee•jay ['diːdʒeɪ] F dj *m/f inv*
deed [diːd] *n* (*act*) azione *f*; LAW atto *m*
deem [diːm] *v/t* ritenere
deep [diːp] *adj hole*, *water*, *voice*, *thinker*

D

profondo; *colour* intenso; ***you're in deep trouble*** sei davvero nei guai
deep•en ['diːpn] **1** *v/t* rendere più profondo **2** *v/i* diventare più profondo; *of crisis* aggravarsi; *of mystery* infittirsi
'**deep freeze** *n* congelatore *m*
'**deep-froz•en food** surgelati *mpl*
'**deep-fry** *v/t* (*pret & pp* **-ied**) friggere (immergendo nell'olio)
deep 'fry•er padella *f* (per friggere); *electric* friggitrice *f*
deer [dɪə(r)] (*pl* **deer**) cervo *m*
de•face [dɪ'feɪs] *v/t* vandalizzare
def•a•ma•tion [defə'meɪʃn] diffamazione *f*
de•fam•a•to•ry [dɪ'fæmətərɪ] *adj* diffamatorio
de•fault ['dɪfɒlt] *adj* COMPUT di default
de•feat [dɪ'fiːt] **1** *n* sconfitta *f* **2** *v/t* sconfiggere; ***this problem defeats me*** questo problema è troppo grande per me
defeatist [dɪ'fiːtɪst] *adj attitude* disfattista
de•fect ['diːfekt] *n* difetto *m*
de•fec•tive [dɪ'fektɪv] *adj* difettoso
de•fend [dɪ'fend] *v/t* difendere
de•fend•ant [dɪ'fendənt] accusato *m*, -a *f*; *in criminal case* imputato *m*, -a *f*
de•fence [dɪ'fens] difesa *f*; ***come to s.o.'s defence*** venire in aiuto a qu
de'fence budg•et POL budget *m inv* della difesa
de'fence law•yer avvocato *m* difensore
de•fence•less [dɪ'fenslɪs] *adj* indifeso
de'fence play•er SP difensore *m*
de'fence wit•ness LAW testimone *m*/*f* della difesa
de'fense *etc Am* → ***defence*** *etc*
de•fen•sive [dɪ'fensɪv] **1** *n*: ***on the defensive*** sulla difensiva; ***go on the defensive*** mettersi sulla difensiva **2** *adj weaponry* difensivo; *person* sulla difensiva
de•fen•sive•ly [dɪ'fensɪvlɪ] *adv* sulla difensiva; ***play defensively*** SP ritirarsi in difesa
de•fer [dɪ'fɜː(r)] *v/t* (*pret & pp* **-red**) (*postpone*) rinviare
de•fer•ence ['defərəns] deferenza *f*
def•er•en•tial [defə'renʃl] *adj* deferente
de•fi•ance [dɪ'faɪəns] sfida *f*; ***in defiance of*** a dispetto di
de•fi•ant [dɪ'faɪənt] *adj* provocatorio
de•fi•cien•cy [dɪ'fɪʃənsɪ] (*lack*) carenza *f*
de•fi•cient [dɪ'fɪʃənt] *adj* carente; ***be deficient in ...*** essere carente di ...
def•i•cit ['defɪsɪt] deficit *m inv*
de•fine [dɪ'faɪn] *v/t* definire
def•i•nite ['defɪnɪt] *adj date, time, answer* preciso; *improvement* netto; (*certain*) certo; ***are you definite about that?*** ne sei sicuro?; ***nothing definite has been arranged*** non è stato previsto niente di preciso
def•i•nite 'ar•ti•cle GRAM articolo *m* determinativo
def•i•nite•ly ['defɪnɪtlɪ] *adv* senza dubbio; *smell, hear* distintamente
def•i•ni•tion [defɪ'nɪʃn] definizione *f*
def•i•ni•tive [dɪ'fɪnətɪv] *adj biography* più completo; *performance* migliore
de•flect [dɪ'flekt] *v/t ball, blow* deviare; sviare; ***be deflected from*** essere sviato da
de•for•est•a•tion [dɪfɒrɪs'teɪʃn] disboscamento *m*
de•form [dɪ'fɔːm] *v/t* deformare
de•for•mi•ty [dɪ'fɔːmɪtɪ] deformità *f inv*
de•fraud [dɪ'frɔːd] *v/t* defraudare; *Inland Revenue* frodare
de•frost [diː'frɒst] *v/t food* scongelare; *fridge* sbrinare
deft [deft] *adj* agile
de•fuse [diː'fjuːz] *v/t bomb* disinnescare; *situation* placare
de•fy [dɪ'faɪ] *v/t* (*pret & pp* **-ied**) (*disobey*) disobbedire a
de•gen•e•rate [dɪ'dʒenəreɪt] *v/i* degenerare; ***degenerate into*** degenerare in
de•grade [dɪ'greɪd] *v/t* degradare
de•grad•ing [dɪ'greɪdɪŋ] *adj position, work* degradante
de•gree [dɪ'griː] *from university* laurea *f*; *of temperature, angle, latitude* grado *m*; ***a degree of*** (*amount*) un po' di; ***by degrees*** per gradi; ***to a certain degree*** fino a un certo punto; ***there is a degree of truth in that*** c'è del vero in questo; ***get one's degree*** prendere la laurea
de•hy•drat•ed [diːhaɪ'dreɪtɪd] *adj* disidratato
de-ice [diː'aɪs] *v/t* togliere il ghiaccio da
de-ic•er [diː'aɪsə(r)] (*spray*) antigelo *m inv*
deign [deɪn] *v/i*: ***deign to ...*** degnarsi di ...
de•i•ty ['diːɪtɪ] divinità *f inv*
de•jec•ted [dɪ'dʒektɪd] *adj* sconfortato
de•lay [dɪ'leɪ] **1** *n* ritardo **2** *v/t* ritardare; ***be delayed*** (*be late*) essere in ritardo; ***delay doing sth*** tardare a fare qc; ***sorry, I've been delayed*** scusa, sono stato trattenuto **3** *v/i* tardare
del•e•gate ['delɪgət] **1** *n* delegato *m*, -a *f* **2** *v/t* ['delɪgeɪt] *task, person* delegare
del•e•ga•tion [delɪ'geɪʃn] *of task* delega *f*; (*people*) delegazione *f*
de•lete [dɪ'liːt] *v/t* cancellare
de'lete key COMPUT tasto *m* 'cancella'
de•le•tion [dɪ'liːʃn] *act* cancellazione *f*; *that deleted* cancellatura *f*

D

del•i ['delɪ] → ***delicatessen***
de•lib•e•rate [dɪ'lɪbərət] **1** *adj* deliberato **2** *v/i* [dɪ'lɪbəreɪt] riflettere
de•lib•e•rate•ly [dɪ'lɪbərətlɪ] *adv* deliberatamente
del•i•ca•cy ['delɪkəsɪ] delicatezza *f*; (*food*) prelibatezza *f*
del•i•cate ['delɪkət] *adj* delicato
del•i•ca•tes•sen [delɪkə'tesn] gastronomia *f*
del•i•cious [dɪ'lɪʃəs] *adj* delizioso, ottimo
de•light [dɪ'laɪt] *n* gioia *f*; ***to my great delight*** con mio grande piacere
de•light•ed [dɪ'laɪtɪd] *adj* lieto
de•light•ful [dɪ'laɪtfʊl] *adj* molto piacevole
de•lim•it [diː'lɪmɪt] *v/t* delimitare
de•lin•quen•cy [dɪ'lɪŋkwənsɪ] delinquenza *f* (minorile)
de•lin•quent [dɪ'lɪŋkwənt] *n* delinquente *m/f*
de•lir•i•ous [dɪ'lɪrɪəs] *adj* MED delirante; (*ecstatic*) in delirio
de•liv•er [dɪ'lɪvə(r)] *v/t* consegnare; *message* trasmettere; *baby* far nascere; ***deliver a speech*** tenere un discorso
de•liv•er•y [dɪ'lɪvərɪ] *of goods, mail* consegna *f*; *of baby* parto *m*
de'liv•ery charge: ***there is no delivery charge*** la consegna è gratuita
de'liv•er•y date termine *m* di consegna
de'livery man fattorino *m*
de'liv•er•y note bolla *f*, documento *m* di trasporto
de'liv•ery serv•ice consegna *f* a domicilio
de'liv•er•y van furgone *m* delle consegne
de•lude [dɪ'luːd] *v/t* ingannare; ***delude s.o. into believing sth*** far credere qc a qu; ***you're deluding yourself*** ti sbagli
de•luge ['deljuːdʒ] **1** *n* temporale *m*; *fig* valanga *f* **2** *v/t fig* sommergere
de•lu•sion [dɪ'luːʒn] illusione *f*; *of others* inganno *m*
de luxe [də'lʌks] *adj* di lusso
◆ **delve into** [delv] *v/t* addentrarsi in; *s.o.'s past* scavare in
de•mand [dɪ'mɑːnd] **1** *n* rivendicazione *f*; COM domanda *f*; ***in demand*** richiesto **2** *v/t* esigere; (*require*) richiedere
de•mand•ing [dɪ'mɑːndɪŋ] *adj job* impegnativo; *person* esigente
de•mean•ing [dɪ'miːnɪŋ] *adj* avvilente
de•men•ted [dɪ'mentɪd] *adj* demente
de•mise [dɪ'maɪz] scomparsa *f*
dem•o ['deməʊ] (*protest*) manifestazione *f*; *of video etc* dimostrazione *f*
de•moc•ra•cy [dɪ'mɒkrəsɪ] democrazia *f*
dem•o•crat ['deməkræt] democratico *m*, -a *f*; ***Democrat*** POL democratico *m*, -a *f*
dem•o•crat•ic [demə'krætɪk] *adj* democratico
dem•o•crat•ic•ally [demə'krætɪklɪ] *adv* democraticamente
'dem•o disk disco *m* dimostrativo
de•mo•graph•ic [deməʊ'græfɪk] *adj* demografico
de•mol•ish [dɪ'mɒlɪʃ] *v/t* demolire
dem•o•li•tion [demə'lɪʃn] demolizione *f*
de•mon ['diːmən] demone *m*
dem•on•strate ['demənstreɪt] **1** *v/t* (*prove*) dimostrare; *machine* fare una dimostrazione di **2** *v/i politically* manifestare
dem•on•stra•tion [demən'streɪʃn] dimostrazione *f*; (*protest*) manifestazione *f*
de•mon•stra•tive [dɪ'mɒnstrətɪv] *adj* espansivo
de•mon•stra•tor ['demənstreɪtə(r)] (*protester*) manifestante *m/f*
de•mor•al•ized [dɪ'mɒrəlaɪzd] *adj* demoralizzato
de•mor•al•iz•ing [dɪ'mɒrəlaɪzɪŋ] *adj* demoralizzante
de•mote [diː'məʊt] *v/t* retrocedere; MIL degradare
de•mure [dɪ'mjʊə(r)] *adj* contegnoso
den [den] (*study*) studio *m*
de•ni•al [dɪ'naɪəl] *of rumour, accusation* negazione *f*; *of request, right* negazione *f*, rifiuto *m*
den•im ['denɪm] denim *m inv*
den•ims ['denɪmz] *npl* (*jeans*) jeans *m inv*
Den•mark ['denmɑːk] Danimarca *f*
de•nom•i•na•tion [dɪnɒmɪ'neɪʃn] *of money* banconota *f*; REL confessione *f*; ***money in small denominations*** denaro *m* in banconote di piccolo taglio
de•nounce [dɪ'naʊns] *v/t* denunciare
dense [dens] *adj* fitto; (*stupid*) ottuso
dense•ly ['denslɪ] *adv*: ***densely populated*** densamente popolato
den•si•ty ['densɪtɪ] *of population* densità *f inv*
dent [dent] **1** *n* ammaccatura *f* **2** *v/t* ammaccare
den•tal ['dentl] *adj treatment* dentario, dentale; *hospital* dentistico
den•ted ['dentɪd] *adj* ammaccato
den•tist ['dentɪst] dentista *m/f*
den•tist•ry ['dentɪstrɪ] odontoiatria *f*
den•tures ['dentʃəz] *npl* dentiera *f*
de•ny [dɪ'naɪ] *v/t* (*pret & pp* ***-ied***) negare; *rumour* smentire; ***I was denied the right to …*** mi è stato negato il diritto di …
de•o•do•rant [diː'əʊdərənt] deodorante *m*
de•part [dɪ'pɑːt] *v/i* partire; ***depart from*** (*deviate from*) allontanarsi da
de•part•ment [dɪ'pɑːtmənt] *of university*

dipartimento *m*; *of government* ministero *m*; *of store*, *company* reparto *m*
de'part•ment store grande magazzino *m*
de•par•ture [dɪ'pɑːtʃə(r)] partenza *f*; (*deviation*) allontanamento *m*; ***a new departure*** *for government*, *organization* una svolta
de'par•ture lounge sala *f* partenze
de'par•ture time ora *f* di partenza
de•pend [dɪ'pend] *v/i*: ***that depends*** dipende; ***it depends on the weather*** dipende dal tempo; ***I am depending on you*** conto su di te
de•pen•da•ble [dɪ'pendəbl] *adj* affidabile
de•pen•dant [dɪ'pendənt] → ***dependent***
de•pen•dence, de•pen•den•cy [dɪ'pendəns, dɪ'pendənsɪ] dipendenza *f*
de•pen•dent [dɪ'pendənt] **1** *n* persona *f* a carico; ***a married man with dependents*** un uomo sposato con famiglia a carico **2** *adj* dipendente; ***dependent children*** figli *mpl* a carico
de•pict [dɪ'pɪkt] *v/t in painting*, *writing* raffigurare
de•plete [dɪ'pliːt] *v/t* intaccare
de•plor•a•ble [dɪ'plɔːrəbl] *adj* deplorevole
de•plore [dɪ'plɔː(r)] *v/t* deplorare, lamentarsi di
de•ploy [dɪ'plɔɪ] *v/t* (*use*) spiegare; (*position*) schierare
de•pop•u•la•tion [diːpɒpjʊ'leɪʃn] spopolamento *m*
de•port [dɪ'pɔːt] *v/t* deportare
de•por•ta•tion [diːpɔː'teɪʃn] deportazione *f*
de•por'ta•tion or•der ordine *m* di deportazione
de•pose [dɪ'pəʊz] *v/t* deporre
de•pos•it [dɪ'pɒzɪt] **1** *n in bank* versamento *m*, deposito *m*; *of mineral* deposito *m*; *on purchase* acconto *m*; (*against loss, damage*) cauzione *f* **2** *v/t money* versare, depositare; (*put down*) lasciare; *silt*, *mud* depositare
de'pos•it ac•count libretto *m* di risparmio
dep•ot ['depəʊ] (*train station*) stazione *f* ferroviaria; (*bus station*) rimessa *f* degli autobus; *for storage* magazzino *m*
de•praved [dɪ'preɪvd] *adj* depravato
de•pre•ci•ate [dɪ'priːʃɪeɪt] *v/i* FIN svalutarsi
de•pre•ci•a•tion [dɪpriːʃɪ'eɪʃn] FIN svalutazione *f*
de•press [dɪ'pres] *v/t person* deprimere
de•pressed [dɪ'prest] *adj person* depresso
de•press•ing [dɪ'presɪŋ] *adj* deprimente
de•pres•sion [dɪ'preʃn] depressione *f*
dep•ri•va•tion [deprɪ'veɪʃn] privazione *f*; (*lack*: *of sleep*, *food*) carenza *f*
de•prive [dɪ'praɪv] *v/t*: ***deprive s.o. of sth*** privare qu di qc
de•prived [dɪ'praɪvd] *adj* socialmente svantaggiato
depth [depθ] profondità *f inv*; ***in depth*** (*thoroughly*) a fondo; ***in the depths of winter*** in pieno inverno; ***be out of one's depth*** *in water* non toccare (il fondo); ***when they talk about politics I'm out of my depth*** la politica va al di là della mia comprensione
dep•u•ta•tion [depjʊ'teɪʃn] deputazione *f*
◆ **deputize for** ['depjʊtaɪz] *v/t* fare le veci di
dep•u•ty ['depjʊtɪ] vice *m/f inv*
'dep•u•ty lead•er *of party* vice segretario *m*
de•rail [dɪ'reɪl] *v/t*: ***be derailed*** *of train* essere deragliato
de•ranged [dɪ'reɪndʒd] *adj* squilibrato
de•reg•u•late [dɪ'regjʊleɪt] *v/t* deregolamentare
de•reg•u•la•tion [dɪregjʊ'leɪʃn] deregolamentazione *f*
der•e•lict ['derəlɪkt] *adj* desolato
de•ride [dɪ'raɪd] *v/t* deridere
de•ri•sion [dɪ'rɪʒn] derisione *f*
de•ri•sive [dɪ'raɪsɪv] *adj remarks*, *laughter* derisorio
de•ri•sive•ly [dɪ'raɪsɪvlɪ] *adv* con aria derisoria
de•ri•so•ry [dɪ'raɪsərɪ] *adj amount*, *salary* irrisorio
de•riv•a•tive [dɪ'rɪvətɪv] *adj* (*not original*) derivato
de•rive [dɪ'raɪv] *v/t* trarre; ***be derived from*** *of word* derivare da
der•ma•tol•o•gist [dɜːmə'tɒlədʒɪst] dermatologo *m*, -a *f*
de•rog•a•tory [dɪ'rɒgətrɪ] *adj* peggiorativo
de•scend [dɪ'send] **1** *v/t* scendere; ***be descended from*** discendere da **2** *v/i* scendere; *of mood*, *darkness* calare
de•scen•dant [dɪ'sendənt] discendente *m/f*
de•scent [dɪ'sent] discesa *f*; (*ancestry*) discendenza *f*; ***of Chinese descent*** di origini cinesi
de•scribe [dɪ'skraɪb] *v/t* descrivere; ***describe sth as sth*** descrivere qc come qc
de•scrip•tion [dɪ'skrɪpʃn] descrizione *f*
des•e•crate ['desɪkreɪt] *v/t* profanare
des•e•cra•tion [desɪ'kreɪʃn] profanazione *f*
de•seg•re•gate [diː'segrəgeɪt] eliminare

la segregazione in
des•ert[1] ['dezət] *n also fig* deserto *m*
des•ert[2] [dɪ'zɜːt] **1** *v/t* (*abandon*) abbandonare **2** *v/i of soldier* disertare
des•ert•ed [dɪ'zɜːtɪd] *adj* deserto
de•sert•er [dɪ'zɜːtə(r)] MIL disertore *m*
de•ser•ti•fi•ca•tion [dɪzɜːtɪfɪ'keɪʃn] desertificazione *f*
de•ser•tion [dɪ'zɜːʃn] (*abandoning*) abbandono *m*; MIL diserzione *f*
des•ert 'is•land isola *f* deserta
de•serve [dɪ'zɜːv] *v/t* meritare
de•sign [dɪ'zaɪn] **1** *n* design *m*; *technical* progettazione *f*; (*drawing*) progetto *m*, disegno *m*; (*pattern*) motivo *m*; ***the machine's unique design*** la concezione unica della macchina **2** *v/t house, car* progettare; *clothes* disegnare; ***this machine is not designed for …*** questa macchina non è stata concepita per …
des•ig•nate ['dezɪgneɪt] *v/t person* designare; ***it has been designated a no smoking area*** quest'area è riservata ai non fumatori
de•sign•er [dɪ'zaɪnə(r)] designer *m/f inv*; *of building, car, ship* progettista *m/f*; ***costume designer*** costumista *m/f*; ***fashion designer*** stilista *m/f*; ***interior designer*** arredatore *m*, -trice *f*
de'sign•er clothes *npl* abiti *mpl* firmati
de'sign fault difetto *m* di concezione
de'sign school scuola *f* di design
de•sir•a•ble [dɪ'zaɪrəbl] *adj* desiderabile; (*advisable*) preferibile
de•sire [dɪ'zaɪə(r)] *n* desiderio *m*
desk [desk] scrivania *f*; *in hotel* reception *f inv*
'desk clerk *Am* receptionist *m/f inv*
'desk di•a•ry agenda *f* da tavolo
'desk•top scrivania *f*; (*computer*) computer *m inv* da tavolo; (*screen*) desktop *m inv*
desk•top 'publish•ing editoria *f* elettronica
des•o•late ['desələt] *adj place* desolato
de•spair [dɪ'speə(r)] **1** *n* disperazione *f*; ***in despair*** disperato **2** *v/i* disperare; ***despair of sth/s.o.*** aver perso la fiducia in qc / qu; ***despair of doing sth*** disperare di fare qc
des•per•ate ['despərət] *adj* disperato; ***be desperate for a cigarette / drink*** morire dalla voglia di una sigaretta / bere qualcosa
des•per•a•tion [despə'reɪʃn] disperazione *f*
des•pic•a•ble [dɪs'pɪkəbl] *adj* deplorevole
de•spise [dɪ'spaɪz] *v/t* disprezzare
de•spite [dɪ'spaɪt] *prep* malgrado, nonostante
de•spon•dent [dɪ'spɒndənt] *adj* abbattuto
des•pot ['despɒt] despota *m*
des•sert [dɪ'zɜːt] dolce *m*, dessert *m inv*
des•ti•na•tion [destɪ'neɪʃn] destinazione *f*
des•tined ['destɪnd] *adj*: ***be destined for*** *fig* essere destinato a
des•ti•ny ['destɪnɪ] destino *m*
des•ti•tute ['destɪtjuːt] *adj* indigente
de•stroy [dɪ'strɔɪ] *v/t* distruggere
de•stroy•er [dɪ'strɔɪə(r)] NAUT cacciatorpediniere *m*
de•struc•tion [dɪ'strʌkʃn] distruzione *f*
de•struc•tive [dɪ'strʌktɪv] *adj* distruttivo; *child* scalmanato
de•tach [dɪ'tætʃ] *v/t* staccare
de•tach•a•ble [dɪ'tætʃəbl] *adj* staccabile
de•tached [dɪ'tætʃt] *adj* (*objective*) distaccato
de'tached house villetta *f*
de•tach•ment [dɪ'tætʃmənt] (*objectivity*) distacco *m*
de•tail ['diːteɪl] *n* dettaglio *m*; ***in detail*** dettagliatamente
de•tailed ['diːteɪld] *adj* dettagliato
de•tain [dɪ'teɪn] *v/t* (*hold back*) trattenere; *as prisoner* trattenere
de•tain•ee [diːteɪn'iː] detenuto *m*, -a *f*
de•tect [dɪ'tekt] *v/t* rilevare; *anxiety, irony* cogliere
de•tec•tion [dɪ'tekʃn] *of criminal, crime* investigazione *f*; *of smoke etc* rilevamento *m*
de•tec•tive [dɪ'tektɪv] (*policeman*) agente *m/f* investigativo
de'tec•tive nov•el romanzo *m* giallo, giallo *m*
de•tec•tor [dɪ'tektə(r)] rilevatore *m*
dé•tente ['deɪtɒnt] POL distensione *f*
de•ten•tion [dɪ'tenʃn] (*imprisonment*) detenzione *f*
de•ter [dɪ'tɜː(r)] *v/t* (*pret & pp* ***-red***) dissuadere; ***deter s.o. from doing sth*** dissuadere qu dal fare qc
de•ter•gent [dɪ'tɜːdʒənt] detergente *m*
de•te•ri•o•rate [dɪ'tɪərɪəreɪt] *v/i* deteriorarsi
de•te•ri•o•ra•tion [dɪtɪərɪə'reɪʃn] deterioramento *m*
de•ter•mi•na•tion [dɪtɜːmɪ'neɪʃn] (*resolution*) determinazione *f*
de•ter•mine [dɪ'tɜːmɪn] *v/t* (*establish*) determinare
de•ter•mined [dɪ'tɜːmɪnd] *adj* determinato, deciso
de•ter•rent [dɪ'terənt] *n* deterrente *m*

de•test [dɪ'test] *v/t* detestare
de•test•a•ble [dɪ'testəbl] *adj* detestabile
de•to•nate ['detəneɪt] **1** *v/t* fare detonare **2** *v/i* detonare
de•to•na•tion [detə'neɪʃn] detonazione *f*
de•tour ['diːtʊə(r)] *n* deviazione *f*
◆ **de•tract from** [dɪ'trækt] *v/t merit*, *value* sminuire; *enjoyment* rovinare; *room*, *décor* rovinare l'effetto di
de•tri•ment ['detrɪmənt]: ***to the detriment of*** a scapito di
de•tri•men•tal [detrɪ'mentl] *adj* nocivo
deuce [djuːs] *in tennis* 40 pari *m inv*
de•val•u•a•tion [diːvælju'eɪʃn] *of currency* svalutazione *f*
de•val•ue [diː'væljuː] *v/t currency* svalutare
dev•a•state ['devəsteɪt] *v/t also fig* devastare
dev•a•stat•ing ['devəsteɪtɪŋ] *adj* devastante
de•vel•op [dɪ'veləp] **1** *v/t film*, *business* sviluppare; *land*, *site* valorizzare; (*originate*) scoprire; *illness*, *cold* contrarre **2** *v/i* (*grow*) svilupparsi; ***develop into*** diventare
de•vel•op•er [dɪ'veləpə(r)] *of property* impresario *m*, a *f* edile
de'vel•op•ing coun•try paese *m* in via di sviluppo
de•vel•op•ment [dɪ'veləpmənt] sviluppo *m*; *of land*, *site* valorizzazione *f*; (*origination*) scoperta *f*
de•vice [dɪ'vaɪs] (*tool*) dispositivo *m*
dev•il ['devl] diavolo *m*
de•vi•ous ['diːvɪəs] (*sly*) subdolo
de•vise [dɪ'vaɪz] *v/t* escogitare
de•void [dɪ'vɔɪd] *adj*: ***be devoid of*** essere privo di
dev•o•lu•tion [diːvə'luːʃn] POL decentramento *m*
de•vote [dɪ'vəʊt] *v/t time*, *effort*, *money* dedicare
de•vot•ed [dɪ'vəʊtɪd] *adj son etc* devoto; ***be devoted to a person*** essere molto attaccato a una persona
dev•o•tee [dɪvəʊ'tiː] appassionato *m*, -a *f*
de•vo•tion [dɪ'vəʊʃn] *to a person* attaccamento *m*; *to one's job* dedizione *f*
de•vour [dɪ'vaʊə(r)] *v/t food*, *book* divorare
de•vout [dɪ'vaʊt] *adj* devoto; ***a devout Catholic*** un cattolico fervente
dew [djuː] rugiada *f*
dex•ter•i•ty [dek'sterətɪ] destrezza *f*
di•a•be•tes [daɪə'biːtiːz] *nsg* diabete *m*
di•a•bet•ic [daɪə'betɪk] **1** *n* diabetico *m*, -a *f* **2** *adj* diabetico; *foods* per diabetici
di•a•bol•i•cal [daɪə'bɒlɪkl] *adj* P (*very bad*) penoso
di•ag•nose ['daɪəgnəʊz] *v/t* diagnosticare
di•ag•no•sis [daɪəg'nəʊsɪs] (*pl* ***diagnoses*** [daɪəg'nəʊsiːz]) diagnosi *f inv*
di•ag•o•nal [daɪ'ægənl] *adj* diagonale
di•ag•o•nal•ly [daɪ'ægənlɪ] *adv* diagonalmente
di•a•gram ['daɪəgræm] diagramma *m*
di•al ['daɪəl] **1** *n of clock*, *meter* quadrante *m*; TELEC disco *m* combinatore **2** *v/i* (*pret & pp* ***-led***, *Am* ***-ed***) TELEC comporre il numero **3** *v/t* (*pret & pp* ***-led***, *Am* ***-ed***) TELEC *number* comporre
di•a•lect ['daɪəlekt] dialetto *m*
di•al•ling code ['daɪlɪŋ] prefisso *m*
'di•al•ling tone, *Am* **'dial tone** segnale *m* di linea libera
di•a•log *Am*, **di•a•logue** ['daɪəlɒg] dialogo *m*
di•a•logue box COMPUT riquadro *m* di dialogo
di•am•e•ter [daɪ'æmɪtə(r)] diametro *m*
di•a•met•ri•cal•ly [daɪə'metrɪkəlɪ] *adv*: ***diametrically opposed*** diametricalmente opposto
di•a•mond ['daɪəmənd] (*jewel*) diamante *m*; (*shape*) losanga *f*; ***diamonds*** *in cards* quadri *mpl*
di•a•per ['daɪəpər] *Am* pannolino *m*
di•a•phragm ['daɪəfræm] diaframma *m*
di•ar•rhe•a *Am*, **di•ar•rhoe•a** [daɪə'riːə] diarrea *f*
di•a•ry ['daɪərɪ] *for thoughts* diario *m*; *for appointments* agenda *f*
dice [daɪs] **1** *n* dado *m* **2** *v/t* (*cut*) tagliare a dadini
di•chot•o•my [daɪ'kɒtəmɪ] dicotomia *f*
dic•ta•te [dɪk'teɪt] *v/t letter*, *novel* dettare; *course of action* imporre
dic•ta•tion [dɪk'teɪʃn] dettatura *f*
dic•ta•tor [dɪk'teɪtə(r)] POL dittatore *m*
dic•ta•tori•al [dɪktə'tɔːrɪəl] *adj* dittatoriale
dic•ta•tor•ship [dɪk'teɪtəʃɪp] dittatura *f*
dic•tion•a•ry ['dɪkʃənrɪ] dizionario *m*
did [dɪd] *pret* → ***do***
die [daɪ] *v/i* morire; ***die of cancer / Aids*** morire di cancro / AIDS; ***I'm dying to know / leave*** muoio dalla voglia di sapere / andare via
◆ **die away** *v/i of noise* estinguersi
◆ **die down** *v/i of noise*, *fire* estinguersi; *of storm*, *excitement* placarsi
◆ **die out** *v/i of custom* scomparire; *of species* estinguersi
die•sel ['diːzl] (*fuel*) diesel *m*
di•et ['daɪət] **1** *n* dieta *f* **2** *v/i to lose weight* essere a dieta
di•e•ti•tian [daɪə'tɪʃn] dietologo *m*, -a *f*

dif•fer ['dɪfə(r)] *v/i* (*be different*) differire, essere differente; (*disagree*) non essere d'accordo

dif•fe•rence ['dɪfrəns] differenza *f*; (*disagreement*) divergenza *f*; ***it doesn't make any difference*** non fa nessuna differenza

dif•fe•rent ['dɪfrənt] *adj* diverso, differente

dif•fe•ren•ti•ate [dɪfə'renʃɪeɪt]: *v/i* distinguere; ***differentiate between*** *things* distinguere tra; *people* fare distinzioni tra

dif•fe•rent•ly ['dɪfrəntlɪ] *adv* diversamente, differentemente

dif•fi•cult ['dɪfɪkəlt] *adj* difficile

dif•fi•cul•ty ['dɪfɪkəltɪ] difficoltà *f inv*; ***with difficulty*** a fatica

dif•fi•dence ['dɪfɪdəns] diffidenza *f*

dif•fi•dent ['dɪfɪdənt] *adj* diffidente

dig [dɪg] (*pret & pp* ***dug***) **1** *v/t* scavare **2** *v/i*: ***it was digging into me*** mi si stava conficcando dentro

◆ **dig out** *v/t* tirar fuori

◆ **dig up** *v/t garden* scavare; *buried object* dissotterare; *tree* sradicare; *information* scovare

di•gest [daɪ'dʒest] *v/t also fig* digerire

di•gest•i•ble [daɪ'dʒestəbl] *adj food* digeribile

di•ges•tion [daɪ'dʒestʃn] digestione *f*

di•ges•tive [daɪ'dʒestɪv] *adj* digestivo; ***digestive juices*** succhi *mpl* gastrici; ***digestive system*** apparato *m* digerente

dig•ger ['dɪgə(r)] (*machine*) scavatrice *f*

di•git ['dɪdʒɪt] (*number*) cifra *f*; ***a 4 digit number*** un numero di 4 cifre

di•gi•tal ['dɪdʒɪtl] *adj* digitale

dig•ni•fied ['dɪgnɪfaɪd] *adj* dignitoso

dig•ni•ta•ry dignitario *m*

dig•ni•ty ['dɪgnɪtɪ] dignità *f*

di•gress [daɪ'gres] *v/i* fare una digressione

di•gres•sion [daɪ'greʃn] digressione *f*

digs [dɪgz] *npl* camera *f* in affitto

dike [daɪk] *along a river* argine *m*; *across a river* diga *f*

di•lap•i•dat•ed [dɪ'læpɪdeɪtɪd] *adj* rovinato; *house* cadente

di•late [daɪ'leɪt] *v/i of pupils* dilatarsi

di•lem•ma [dɪ'lemə] dilemma *m*; ***be in a dilemma*** trovarsi in un dilemma

dil•et•tante [dɪle'tæntɪ] dilettante *m/f*

dil•i•gent ['dɪlɪdʒənt] *adj* diligente

di•lute [daɪ'lu:t] *v/t* diluire

dim [dɪm] **1** *adj room* buio; *light* fioco; *outline* indistinto; (*stupid*) idiota; *prospects* vago **2** *v/t* (*pret & pp* ***-med***): ***dim the headlights*** abbassare le luci **3** *v/i* (*pret & pp* ***-med***) *of lights* abbassarsi

di•men•sion [daɪ'menʃn] (*measurement*) dimensione *f*

di•min•ish [dɪ'mɪnɪʃ] *v/t & v/i* diminuire

di•min•u•tive [dɪ'mɪnjʊtɪv] **1** *n* diminutivo *m* **2** *adj* minuscolo

dim•ple ['dɪmpl] fossetta *f*

din [dɪn] *n* baccano *m*

dine [daɪn] *v/i fml* cenare

din•er ['daɪnə(r)] *in a restaurant* cliente *m/f*; ***fellow diner*** commensale *m/f*

din•ghy ['dɪŋgɪ] *small yacht* dinghy *m*; *rubber boat* gommone *m*

din•gy ['dɪndʒɪ] *adj atmosphere* offuscato; (*dirty*) sporco

din•ing car ['daɪnɪŋ] RAIL vagone *m* ristorante

'**din•ing room** *in house* sala *f* da pranzo; *in hotel* sala *f* ristorante

'**din•ing ta•ble** tavolo *m* da pranzo

din•ner ['dɪnə(r)] *in the evening* cena *f*; *at midday* pranzo *m*; *formal gathering* ricevimento *m*

'**din•ner guest** invitato *m*, -a

'**dinner jack•et** smoking *m inv*

'**dinner par•ty** cena *f*

'**din•ner serv•ice** servizio *m* (di piatti)

di•no•saur ['daɪnəsɔ:(r)] dinosauro *m*

dip [dɪp] **1** *n* (*swim*) tuffo *m*; *for food* salsa *f*; *in road* pendenza *f* **2** *v/t* (*pret & pp* ***-ped***) immergere; ***dip the headlights*** abbassare le luci **3** *v/i* (*pret & pp* ***-ped***) *of road* scendere

di•plo•ma [dɪ'pləʊmə] diploma *m*

di•plo•ma•cy [dɪ'pləʊməsɪ] diplomazia *f*

di•plo•mat ['dɪpləmæt] diplomatico *m*, -a *f*

di•plo•mat•ic [dɪplə'mætɪk] *adj* diplomatico

dip•lo•mat•i•cal•ly [dɪplə'mætɪklɪ] *adv* con diplomazia

dip•lo•mat•ic im'mu•ni•ty immunità *f* diplomatica

dire ['daɪə(r)] *adj* tremendo

di•rect [daɪ'rekt] **1** *adj* diretto **2** *v/t play* mettere in scena; *film* curare la regia di; *attention* dirigere; ***could you please direct me to ...?*** mi può per favore indicare la strada per ...?

di•rect 'cur•rent ELEC corrente *f* continua

di•rect 'deb•it FIN ordine *m* di addebito automatico

di•rec•tion [dɪ'rekʃn] direzione *f*; *of film, play* regia *f*; ***directions*** (*instructions*), *to a place* indicazioni *fpl*; *for use* istruzioni *fpl*

di•rec•tion 'in•di•ca•tor MOT freccia *f*

di•rec•tive [dɪ'rektɪv] *of EU etc* direttiva *f*

di•rect•ly [dɪ'rektlɪ] **1** *adv* (*straight*) direttamente; (*soon, immediately*) immedia-

tamente **2** *conj* (non) appena; ***I'll do it directly I've finished this*** lo faccio (non) appena ho finito questo
di•rec•tor [dɪ'rektə(r)] *of company* direttore *m*, -trice *f*; *of play, film* regista *m/f*
di•rec•to•ry [dɪ'rektərɪ] elenco *m*; TELEC guida *f* telefonica
dirt [dɜːt] sporco *m*, sporcizia *f*
'**dirt cheap** *adj* F a un prezzo stracciato
dirt•y ['dɜːtɪ] **1** *adj* sporco; (*pornographic*) sconcio **2** *v/t* (*pret & pp* ***-ied***) sporcare
dirt•y 'trick tiro *m* mancino
dis•a•bil•i•ty [dɪsə'bɪlətɪ] handicap *m inv*, invalidità *f inv*
dis•a•bled [dɪs'eɪbld] **1** *n* handicappato *m*, -a *f*; ***the disabled*** i disabili **2** *adj* handicappato
dis•ad•van•tage [dɪsəd'vɑːntɪdʒ] (*drawback*) svantaggio *m*; ***be at a disadvantage*** essere svantaggiato
dis•ad•van•taged [dɪsəd'vɑːntɪdʒd] *adj* penalizzato
dis•ad•van•ta•geous [dɪsədvən'teɪdʒəs] *adj* svantaggioso
dis•a•gree [dɪsə'griː] *v/i of person* non essere d'accordo
◆ **disagree with** *v/t of person* non essere d'accordo con; *of food* fare male a
dis•a•gree•a•ble [dɪsə'griːəbl] *adj* sgradevole
dis•a•gree•ment [dɪsə'griːmənt] disaccordo *m*; (*argument*) discussione *f*
dis•al•low [dɪsə'laʊ] *v/t goal* annullare
dis•ap•pear [dɪsə'pɪə(r)] *v/i* sparire, scomparire
dis•ap•pear•ance [dɪsə'pɪərəns] sparizione *f*, scomparsa *f*
dis•ap•point [dɪsə'pɔɪnt] *v/t* deludere
dis•ap•point•ed [dɪsə'pɔɪntɪd] *adj* deluso
dis•ap•point•ing [dɪsə'pɔɪntɪŋ] *adj* deludente
dis•ap•point•ment [dɪsə'pɔɪntmənt] delusione *f*
dis•ap•prov•al [dɪsə'pruːvl] disapprovazione *f*
dis•ap•prove [dɪsə'pruːv] *v/i* disapprovare; ***disapprove of*** disapprovare
dis•ap•prov•ing [dɪsə'pruːvɪŋ] *adj look* di disapprovazione
dis•ap•prov•ing•ly [dɪsə'pruːvɪŋlɪ] *adv* con disapprovazione
dis•arm [dɪs'ɑːm] **1** *v/t* disarmare **2** *v/i* disarmarsi
dis•ar•ma•ment [dɪs'ɑːməmənt] disarmo *m*
dis•arm•ing [dɪs'ɑːmɪŋ] *adj* disarmante
dis•as•ter [dɪ'zɑːstə(r)] disastro *m*
di'sas•ter ar•e•a area *f* disastrata; (*fig: person*) disastro *m*
di•sas•trous [dɪ'zɑːstrəs] *adj* disastroso
dis•band [dɪs'bænd] **1** *v/t* sciogliere **2** *v/i* sciogliersi
dis•be•lief [dɪsbə'liːf] incredulità *f*; ***in disbelief*** con incredulità
disc [dɪsk] disco *m*
dis•card [dɪ'skɑːd] *v/t* sbarazzarsi di
di•scern [dɪ'sɜːn] *v/t improvement, intentions* percepire; *outline* distinguere
di•scern•i•ble [dɪ'sɜːnəbl] *adj improvement* percepibile; *outline* distinguibile
di•scern•ing [dɪ'sɜːnɪŋ] *adj person* perspicace; ***the car for the discerning driver*** la macchina per i guidatori che sanno fare la differenza
dis•charge ['dɪstʃɑːdʒ] **1** *n from hospital* dimissione *f*; *from army* congedo *m* **2** *v/t* [dɪs'tʃɑːdʒ] *from hospital* dimettere; *from army* congedare; *from job* licenziare; LAW prosciogliere
di•sci•ple [dɪ'saɪpl] discepolo *m*, -a *f*
dis•ci•pli•nar•y [dɪsɪ'plɪnərɪ] *adj* disciplinare
dis•ci•pline ['dɪsɪplɪn] **1** *n* disciplina *f* **2** *v/t child, dog* imporre disciplina a; *employee* applicare provvedimenti disciplinari a
'**disc jock•ey** disc jockey *m/f inv*
dis•claim [dɪs'kleɪm] *v/t* negare; *responsibility* declinare
dis•close [dɪs'kləʊs] *v/t* svelare, rivelare
dis•clo•sure [dɪs'kləʊʒə(r)] rivelazione *f*
dis•co ['dɪskəʊ] discoteca *f*
dis•col•or *Am*, **dis•col•our** [dɪs'kʌlə(r)] *v/i* scolorire
dis•com•fort [dɪs'kʌmfət] *n* disagio *m*; (*pain*) fastidio *m*
dis•con•cert [dɪskən'sɜːt] *v/t* sconcertare
dis•con•cert•ed [dɪskən'sɜːtɪd] *adj* sconcertato
dis•con•nect [dɪskə'nekt] *v/t* (*detach*) sconnettere; *supply, telephones* staccare; ***they'll disconnect you if you don't pay your phone bill*** ti staccheranno il telefono se non paghi la bolletta; ***I was disconnected*** TELEC è caduta la linea
dis•con•so•late [dɪs'kɒnsələt] *adj* sconsolato
dis•con•tent [dɪskən'tent] malcontento *m*
dis•con•tent•ed [dɪskən'tentɪd] *adj* scontento
dis•con•tin•ue [dɪskən'tɪnjuː] *v/t* interrompere; ***be a discontinued line*** essere fuori produzione
dis•cord ['dɪskɔːd] MUS dissonanza *f*; *in relations* contrasto *m*
dis•co•theque ['dɪskətek] discoteca *f*
dis•count ['dɪskaʊnt] **1** *n* sconto *m*; ***a 10% discount*** uno sconto del 10% **2** *v/t* [dɪ-

s'kaʊnt] *goods* scontare; *theory* trascurare

dis•cour•age [dɪs'kʌrɪdʒ] *v/t* (*dissuade*) scoraggiare

dis•cour•age•ment [dɪs'kʌrɪdʒmənt] *being disheartened* scoraggiamento *m*; ***meet with discouragement*** non avere incoraggiamento

dis•cov•er [dɪ'skʌvə(r)] *v/t* scoprire

dis•cov•er•er [dɪ'skʌvərə(r)] scopritore *m*, -trice *f*

dis•cov•e•ry [dɪ'skʌvərɪ] scoperta *f*

dis•cred•it [dɪs'kredɪt] *v/t* screditare

di•screet [dɪ'skriːt] *adj* discreto

di•screet•ly [dɪ'skriːtlɪ] *adv* discretamente

di•screp•an•cy [dɪ'skrepənsɪ] incongruenza *f*

di•scre•tion [dɪ'skreʃn] discrezione *f*; ***at your discretion*** a tua discrezione

di•scrim•i•nate [dɪ'skrɪmɪneɪt] *v/i*: ***discriminate against*** discriminare; ***discriminate between*** (*distinguish between*) distinguere tra

di•scrim•i•nat•ing [dɪ'skrɪmɪneɪtɪŋ] *adj* esigente

di•scrim•i•na•tion [dɪ'skrɪmɪneɪʃn] *sexual, racial etc* discriminazione *f*

dis•cus ['dɪskəs] SP: *object* disco *m*; SP: *event* lancio *m* del disco

di•scuss [dɪ'skʌs] *v/t* discutere; *of article* trattare di; ***the article discusses whether …*** l'articolo esamina se …

di•scus•sion [dɪ'skʌʃn] discussione *f*

'**dis•cus throw•er** lanciatore *m*, -trice *f* di disco

dis•dain [dɪs'deɪn] *n* sdegno *m*

dis•ease [dɪ'ziːz] malattia *f*

dis•em•bark [dɪsəm'bɑːk] *v/i* sbarcare

dis•en•chant•ed [dɪsən'tʃɑːntɪd] *adj* disincantato; ***disenchanted with*** disilluso di

dis•en•gage [dɪsən'geɪdʒ] *v/t* svincolare

dis•en•tan•gle [dɪsən'tæŋgl] *v/t* districare

dis•fig•ure [dɪs'fɪgə(r)] *v/t* sfigurare; *fig* deturpare

dis•grace [dɪs'greɪs] **1** *n* vergogna *f*; ***it's a disgrace*** è una vergogna; ***in disgrace*** in disgrazia **2** *v/t* disonorare

dis•grace•ful [dɪs'greɪsfʊl] *adj behaviour, situation* vergognoso

dis•grunt•led [dɪs'grʌntld] *adj* scontento

dis•guise [dɪs'gaɪz] **1** *n* travestimento *m*; ***be in disguise*** essere travestito **2** *v/t one's voice, handwriting* camuffare; *fear, anxiety* dissimulare; ***disguise o.s. as*** travestirsi da; ***he was disguised as a woman*** era travestito da donna

dis•gust [dɪs'gʌst] **1** *n* disgusto *m*; ***in disgust*** disgustato **2** *v/t* disgustare

dis•gust•ing [dɪs'gʌstɪŋ] *adj* disgustoso

dish [dɪʃ] *part of meal* piatto *m*; *for serving* piatto *m*; *for cooking* recipiente *m*

'**dish•cloth** strofinaccio *m*

dis•heart•en•ed [dɪs'hɑːtnd] *adj* demoralizzato

dis•heart•en•ing [dɪs'hɑːtnɪŋ] *adj* demoralizzante

di•shev•eled [dɪ'ʃevld] *adj person, appearance* arruffato; *after effort* scompigliato

dis•hon•est [dɪs'ɒnɪst] *adj* disonesto

dis•hon•est•y [dɪs'ɒnɪstɪ] disonestà *f*

dis•hon•or *etc Am* → ***dishonour*** *etc*

dis•hon•our [dɪs'ɒnə(r)] *n* disonore *m*; ***bring dishonour on*** coprire di disonore

dis•hon•our•a•ble [dɪs'ɒnərəbl] *adj* disdicevole

'**dish•wash•er** *machine* lavastoviglie *f inv*; *person* lavapiatti *m/f inv*

'**dish•wash•ing liq•uid** *Am* detersivo *m* per i piatti

'**dish•wa•ter** acqua *f* dei piatti

dis•il•lu•sion [dɪsɪ'luːʒn] *v/t* disilludere

dis•il•lu•sion•ment [dɪsɪ'luːʒnmənt] disillusione *f*

dis•in•clined [dɪsɪn'klaɪnd] *adj* restio (**to** a)

dis•in•fect [dɪsɪn'fekt] *v/t* disinfettare

dis•in•fec•tant [dɪsɪn'fektənt] disinfettante *m*

dis•in•her•it [dɪsɪn'herɪt] *v/t* diseredare

dis•in•te•grate [dɪs'ɪntəgreɪt] *v/i* disintegrarsi; *of marriage, building* andare in pezzi

dis•in•ter•est•ed [dɪs'ɪntərestɪd] *adj* (*unbiased*) disinteressato

dis•joint•ed [dɪs'dʒɔɪntɪd] *adj* sconnesso

disk [dɪsk] disco *m*; (*diskette*) dischetto *m*; ***on disk*** su dischetto *m*

'**disk drive** COMPUT lettore *m o* drive *m inv* di dischetti

disk•ette [dɪs'ket] dischetto *m*

dis•like [dɪs'laɪk] **1** *n* antipatia *f*; ***take a dislike to s.o.*** prendere qu in antipatia **2** *v/t*: ***I dislike cats*** non mi piacciono i gatti; ***I dislike watching TV*** non mi piace guardare la TV

dis•lo•cate ['dɪsləkeɪt] *v/t shoulder* lussare

dis•lodge [dɪs'lɒdʒ] *v/t* rimuovere

dis•loy•al [dɪs'lɔɪəl] *adj* sleale

dis•loy•al•ty [dɪs'lɔɪəltɪ] slealtà *f*

dis•mal ['dɪzməl] *adj weather, news* deprimente; *person* (*sad*), *failure* triste; *person* (*negative*) ombroso

dis•man•tle [dɪs'mæntl] *v/t* smontare; *organization* demolire

dis•may [dɪs'meɪ] **1** *n* costernazione *f* **2** *v/t*

D

costernare
dis•miss [dɪs'mɪs] *v/t employee* licenziare; *suggestion*, *possibility* scartare; *idea*, *thought* accantonare
dis•miss•al [dɪs'mɪsl] *of employee* licenziamento *m*
dis•mount [dɪs'maʊnt] *v/i* smontare
dis•o•be•di•ence [dɪsə'biːdɪəns] disobbidienza *f*
dis•o•be•di•ent [dɪsə'biːdɪənt] *adj* disobbidiente
dis•o•bey [dɪsə'beɪ] *v/t* disobbedire a
dis•or•der [dɪs'ɔːdə(r)] (*untidiness*) disordine *m*; (*unrest*) disordini *mpl*; MED disturbo *m*
dis•or•der•ly [dɪs'ɔːdəlɪ] *adj room*, *desk* in disordine; *mob* turbolento
dis•or•gan•ized [dɪs'ɔːgənaɪzd] *adj* disorganizzato
dis•o•ri•ent•ed [dɪs'ɔːrɪəntɪd], **dis•o•ri•en•tat•ed** [dɪs'ɔːrɪənteɪtɪd] *adj* disorientato
dis•own [dɪs'əʊn] *v/t* disconoscere
di•spar•ag•ing [dɪ'spærɪdʒɪŋ] *adj* dispregiativo
di•spar•i•ty [dɪ'spærətɪ] disparità *f inv*
dis•pas•sion•ate [dɪ'spæʃənət] *adj* (*objective*) spassionato
di•spatch [dɪ'spætʃ] *v/t* (*send*) spedire
di•spen•sa•ry [dɪ'spensərɪ] *in pharmacy* dispensario *m*
◆ **di•spense with** [dɪ'spens] *v/t* fare a meno di
di•sperse [dɪ'spɜːs] **1** *v/t* dissipare **2** *v/i of crowd* disperdersi; *of mist* dissiparsi
di•spir•it•ed [dɪs'pɪrɪtɪd] *adj* abbattuto
dis•place [dɪs'pleɪs] *v/t* (*supplant*) rimpiazzare
di•splay [dɪ'spleɪ] **1** *n* esposizione *f*, mostra *f*; *in shop window* articoli *mpl* in esposizione; COMPUT visualizzazione *f*; ***be on display*** *at exhibition* essere in esposizione *o* mostra; (*be for sale*) essere esposto in vendita **2** *v/t emotion* manifestare; *at exhibition* esporre; (*for sale*) esporre in vendita; COMPUT visualizzare
di'splay cab•i•net *in museum* teca *f*; *in shop* vetrinetta *f*
dis•please [dɪs'pliːs] *v/t* contrariare; ***they were displeased with her*** erano contrariati con lei
dis•plea•sure [dɪs'pleʒə(r)] disappunto *m*
dis•po•sa•ble [dɪ'spəʊzəbl] *adj* usa e getta *inv*
dis•po•sa•ble 'in•come reddito *m* disponibile
dis•pos•al [dɪ'spəʊzl] (*getting rid of*) eliminazione *f*; *of pollutants*, *nuclear waste* smaltimento *m*; ***I am at your disposal*** sono a tua disposizione; ***put sth at s.o.'s disposal*** mettere qc a disposizione di qu
◆ **dis•pose of** [dɪ'spəʊz] *v/t* (*get rid of*) sbarazzarsi di
dis•posed [dɪ'spəʊzd] *adj*: ***be disposed to do sth*** (*willing*) essere disposto a fare qc; ***be well disposed towards*** essere ben disposto verso
dis•po•si•tion [dɪspə'zɪʃn] (*nature*) indole *f*
dis•pro•por•tion•ate [dɪsprə'pɔːʃənət] *adj* sproporzionato
dis•prove [dɪs'pruːv] *v/t* smentire
di•spute [dɪ'spjuːt] **1** *n* controversia *f*; (*industrial*) contestazione *f*; ***be in dispute*** essere controverso **2** *v/t* contestare; (*fight over*) contendersi
dis•qual•i•fi•ca•tion [dɪskwɒlɪfɪ'keɪʃn] squalifica *f*; ***it's a disqualification*** è penalizzante
dis•qual•i•fy [dɪs'kwɒlɪfaɪ] *v/t* (*pret & pp **-ied***) squalificare
dis•re•gard [dɪsrə'gɑːd] **1** *n* mancanza *f* di considerazione **2** *v/t* ignorare
dis•re•pair [dɪsrə'peə(r)]: ***in a state of disrepair*** in cattivo stato
dis•rep•u•ta•ble [dɪs'repjʊtəbl] *adj* depravato; *area* malfamato
dis•re•spect [dɪsrə'spekt] mancanza *f* di rispetto
dis•re•spect•ful [dɪsrə'spektfʊl] *adj* irriverente
dis•rupt [dɪs'rʌpt] *v/t train service* creare disagi a; *meeting*, *class* disturbare; (*intentionally*) creare scompiglio in
dis•rup•tion [dɪs'rʌpʃn] *of train service* disagio *m*; *of meeting*, *class* disturbo *m*; (*intentional*) scompiglio *m*
dis•rup•tive [dɪs'rʌptɪv] *adj influence* deleterio; ***he's very disruptive in class*** è un elemento di disturbo nella classe
dis•sat•is•fac•tion [dɪssætɪs'fækʃn] insoddisfazione *f*
dis•sat•is•fied [dɪs'sætɪsfaɪd] *adj* insoddisfatto
dis•sen•sion [dɪ'senʃn] dissenso *m*
dis•sent [dɪ'sent] **1** *n* dissenso *m* **2** *v/i* ***dissent from*** dissentire da
dis•si•dent ['dɪsɪdənt] *n* dissidente *m/f*
dis•sim•i•lar [dɪs'sɪmɪlə(r)] *adj* dissimile
dis•so•ci•ate [dɪ'səʊʃɪeɪt] *v/t*: ***dissociate o.s. from*** dissociarsi da
dis•so•lute ['dɪsəluːt] *adj* dissoluto
dis•so•lu•tion ['dɪsəluːʃn] POL scioglimento *m*
dis•solve [dɪ'sɒlv] **1** *v/t substance* sciogliere **2** *v/i of substance* sciogliersi

dis•suade [dɪ'sweɪd] *v/t* dissuadere; ***dissuade s.o. from doing sth*** dissuadere qu dal fare qc
dis•tance ['dɪstəns] **1** *n* distanza *f*; ***in the distance*** in lontananza **2** *v/t*: ***distance o.s. from*** prendere le distanze da
dis•tant ['dɪstənt] *adj* lontano
dis•taste [dɪs'teɪst] avversione *f*
dis•taste•ful [dɪs'teɪstfʊl] *adj* spiacevole
dis•till•er•y [dɪs'tɪlərɪ] distilleria *f*
dis•tinct [dɪ'stɪŋkt] *adj* (*clear*) netto; (*different*) distinto; ***as distinct from*** contrariamente a
dis•tinc•tion [dɪ'stɪŋkʃn] (*differentiation*) distinzione *f*; ***hotel / product of distinction*** hotel / prodotto d'eccezione
dis•tinc•tive [dɪ'stɪŋktɪv] *adj* caratteristico
dis•tinct•ly [dɪ'stɪŋktlɪ] *adv* distintamente; (*decidedly*) decisamente
dis•tin•guish [dɪ'stɪŋgwɪʃ] *v/t* (*see*) distinguere; ***distinguish between X and Y*** distinguere tra X e Y
dis•tin•guished [dɪ'stɪŋgwɪʃt] *adj* (*famous*) insigne; (*dignified*) distinto
dis•tort [dɪ'stɔːt] *v/t* distorcere
dis•tract [dɪ'strækt] *v/t person* distrarre; *attention* distogliere
dis•tract•ed [dɪ'stræktɪd] *adj* assente
dis•trac•tion [dɪ'strækʃn] *of attention* distrazione *f*; ***drive s.o. to distraction*** fare impazzire qu
dis•traught [dɪ'strɔːt] *adj* affranto
dis•tress [dɪ'stres] **1** *n* sofferenza *f*; ***in distress*** *of ship*, *aircraft* in difficoltà **2** *v/t* (*upset*) angosciare
dis•tress•ing [dɪ'stresɪŋ] *adj* sconvolgente
dis'tress sig•nal segnale *m* di pericolo
dis•trib•ute [dɪ'strɪbjuːt] *v/t* distribuire
dis•tri•bu•tion [dɪstrɪ'bjuːʃn] distribuzione *f*
dis•trib•u•tor [dɪs'trɪbjuːtə(r)] COM distributore *m*
dis•trict ['dɪstrɪkt] quartiere *m*
dis•trust [dɪs'trʌst] **1** *n* diffidenza *f* **2** *v/t* non fidarsi di
dis•turb [dɪ'stɜːb] *v/t* disturbare; ***do not disturb*** non disturbare
dis•turb•ance [dɪ'stɜːbəns] (*interruption*) fastidio *m*; ***disturbances*** (*civil unrest*) disordini *mpl*
dis•turbed [dɪ'stɜːbd] *adj* (*concerned, worried*) turbato; *psychologically* malato di mente
dis•turb•ing [dɪ'stɜːbɪŋ] *adj* inquietante
dis•used [dɪs'juːzd] *adj* inutilizzato
ditch [dɪtʃ] **1** *n* fosso *m* **2** *v/t* F *boyfriend* scaricare F; F *car* sbarazzarsi di
dith•er ['dɪθə(r)] *v/i* titubare
di•van [dɪ'væn] (*bed*) divano *m*
dive [daɪv] **1** *n* tuffo *m*; (*underwater*) immersione *f*; *of plane* picchiata *f*; F (*bar etc*) bettola *f* F; ***take a dive*** F *of sterling etc* crollare **2** *v/i* tuffarsi; (*underwater*) fare immersione; *of submarine* immergersi; *of plane* scendere in picchiata; ***the goalie dived for the ball*** il portiere si è tuffato per prendere la palla
div•er ['daɪvə(r)] *off board* tuffatore *m*, -trice *f*; (*underwater*) sub *m/f inv*, sommozzatore *m*, -trice *f*
di•verge [daɪ'vɜːdʒ] *v/i* divergere
di•verse [daɪ'vɜːs] *adj* svariato
di•ver•si•fi•ca•tion [daɪvɜːsɪfɪ'keɪʃn] COM diversificazione *f*
di•ver•si•fy [daɪ'vɜːsɪfaɪ] *v/i* (*pret & pp* ***-ied***) COM diversificare
di•ver•sion [daɪ'vɜːʃn] *for traffic* deviazione *f*; *to distract attention* diversivo *m*
di•ver•si•ty [daɪ'vɜːsətɪ] varietà *f inv*
di•vert [daɪ'vɜːt] *v/t traffic* deviare; *attention* sviare, distogliere
di•vest [daɪ'vest] *v/t*: ***divest s.o. of sth*** privare qu di qc
di•vide [dɪ'vaɪd] *v/t* dividere
div•i•dend ['dɪvɪdend] FIN dividendo *m*; ***pay dividends*** *fig* dare i suoi frutti
di•vine [dɪ'vaɪn] *adj* REL, F divino
div•ing ['daɪvɪŋ] *from board* tuffi *mpl*; (*scuba diving*) immersione *f*
'div•ing board trampolino *m*
di•vis•i•ble [dɪ'vɪzəbl] *adj* divisibile
di•vi•sion [dɪ'vɪʒn] divisione *f*; *of company* sezione *f*
di•vorce [dɪ'vɔːs] **1** *n* divorzio *m*; ***get a divorce*** divorziare **2** *v/t* divorziare da; ***get divorced*** divorziare **3** *v/i* divorziare
di•vorced [dɪ'vɔːst] *adj* divorziato
di•vor•cee [dɪvɔː'siː] divorziato *m*, -a *f*
di•vulge [daɪ'vʌldʒ] *v/t* divulgare
DIY [diːaɪ'waɪ] *abbr* (= ***do it yourself***) fai da te *m inv*, bricolage *m*
DI'Y store negozio *m* di bricolage; *smaller shop* ferramenta *f*
diz•zi•ness ['dɪzɪnɪs] giramento *m* di testa, vertigini *fpl*
diz•zy ['dɪzɪ] *adj* stordito; ***I feel dizzy*** mi gira la testa
DJ [diː'dʒeɪ] *abbr* (= ***disc jockey***) dj *m/f inv*; (= ***dinner jacket***) smoking *m inv*
DNA [diːen'eɪ] *abbr* (= ***deoxyribonucleic acid***) DNA *m inv* (= acido *m* deossiribonucleico)
do [duː] (*pret* ***did***, *pp* ***done***) **1** *v/t* fare; *one's hair* farsi; *100mph etc* andare a; ***do the ironing / cooking*** stirare / cucinare; ***what are you doing tonight?*** cosa

D

fai stasera?; ***I don't know what to do*** non so cosa fare; ***no, I'll do it*** no, lo faccio; *stress on I* no, lo faccio io; ***do it right now!*** fallo subito!; ***have you done this before?*** lo hai già fatto?; ***have one's hair done*** farsi fare i capelli **2** *v/i* (*be suitable, enough*) andare bene; ***that will do!*** basta così!; ***do well*** (*do a good job*) essere bravo; (*be in good health*) stare bene; *of business* andare bene; ***well done!*** (*congratulations!*) bravo!; ***how do you do?*** molto piacere **3** *v/aux*: ***do you know him?*** lo conosci?; ***I don't know*** non (lo) so; ***do be quick*** sii veloce; ***do you like London? – yes I do*** ti piace Londra? - sì (mi piace); ***he works hard, doesn't he?*** lavora sodo, no?; ***don't you believe me?*** non mi credi?; ***you do believe me, don't you?*** mi credi, non è vero?; ***you don't know the answer, do you? – no I don't*** non sai la risposta, vero? - no, non la so

◆ **do away with** *v/t* (*abolish*) abolire

◆ **do in** *v/t* F (*exhaust*) stravolgere F; ***I'm done in*** sono stravolto

◆ **do out of** *v/t*: ***do s.o. out of sth*** F fregare qc a qu F

◆ **do up** *v/t* (*renovate*) restaurare; (*fasten*) allacciare; ***do up your buttons*** abbottonati; ***do up your shoe-laces*** allacciati le scarpe

◆ **do with** *v/t*: ***I could do with ...*** mi ci vorrebbe ...; ***he won't have anything to do with it*** (*won't get involved*) non vuole averci niente a che fare

◆ **do without 1** *v/i* farne a meno **2** *v/t* fare a meno di

do•cile ['dəʊsaɪl] *adj* docile

dock¹ [dɒk] **1** *n* NAUT bacino *m* **2** *v/i of ship* entrare in porto; *of spaceship* agganciarsi

dock² [dɒk] LAW banco *m* degli imputati

dock•er ['dɒkə(r)] portuale *m*

'**dock•yard** cantiere *m* navale

doc•tor ['dɒktə(r)] *n* MED dottore *m*, -essa *f*

doc•tor•ate ['dɒktərət] dottorato *m*

doc•trine ['dɒktrɪn] dottrina *f*

doc•u•dra•ma ['dɒkjʊdrɑːmə] ricostruzione *f* filmata

doc•u•ment ['dɒkjʊmənt] *n* documento *m*

doc•u•men•ta•ry [dɒkjʊ'mentərɪ] *n programme* documentario *m*

doc•u•men•ta•tion [dɒkjʊmen'teɪʃn] documentazione *f*

dodge [dɒdʒ] *v/t blow* schivare; *person, issue* evitare; *question* aggirare

dodg•ems ['dɒdʒəms] *npl* autoscontro *m*

dog [dɒg] **1** *n* cane *m* **2** *v/t* (*pret & pp* **-ged**) *of bad luck* perseguitare

'**dog catch•er** accalappiacani *m inv*

dog-eared ['dɒgɪəd] *adj book* con le orecchie

dog•ged ['dɒgɪd] *adj* accanito

dog•gie ['dɒgɪ] *in children's language* cagnolino *m*

dog•gy bag ['dɒgɪbæg] *pacchetto m con gli avanzi di una cena al ristorante per l'asporto*

'**dog•house**: ***be in the doghouse*** F essere nei casini F

dog•ma ['dɒgmə] dogma *m*

dog•mat•ic [dɒg'mætɪk] *adj* dogmatico

do-good•er [duː'gʊdə(r)] *pej* impiccione *m*, -a *f*

dogs•body ['dɒgzbɒdɪ] F bestia *m* da soma

'**dog-tired** *adj* F stravolto

do-it-your•self [duːɪtjə'self] fai da te *m inv*

dol•drums ['dɒldrəmz]: ***be in the doldrums*** *of economy* essere in stallo; *of person* essere giù di corda

dole [dəʊl] *Br* F assegno *m* di disoccupazione; ***be on the dole*** ricevere l'assegno di disoccupazione

'**dole money** *Br* F assegni *mpl* di disoccupazione

◆ **dole out** *v/t* distribuire

doll [dɒl] *toy*, F *woman* bambola *f*

◆ **doll up** *v/t*: ***get dolled up*** mettersi in ghingheri

dol•lar ['dɒlə(r)] dollaro *m*

dol•lop ['dɒləp] *n* F cucchiaiata *f*

dol•phin ['dɒlfɪn] delfino *m*

dome [dəʊm] *of building* cupola *f*

do•mes•tic [də'mestɪk] *adj* domestico; *news, policy* interno

do•mes•tic 'an•i•mal animale *m* domestico

do•mes•ti•cate [də'mestɪkeɪt] *v/t animal* addomesticare; ***be domesticated*** *of person* essere incline a fare i lavori di casa

do'mes•tic flight volo *m* nazionale

dom•i•nant ['dɒmɪnənt] *adj* dominante; *member* principale

dom•i•nate ['dɒmɪneɪt] *v/t* dominare

dom•i•na•tion [dɒmɪ'neɪʃn] dominio *m*

dom•i•neer•ing [dɒmɪ'nɪərɪŋ] *adj* autoritario

dom•i•no ['dɒmɪnəʊ] domino *m*; ***play dominos*** giocare a domino

do•nate [dəʊ'neɪt] *v/t* donare

do•na•tion [dəʊ'neɪʃn] donazione *f*

done [dʌn] *pp* → ***do***

don•key ['dɒŋkɪ] asino *m*

do•nor ['dəʊnə(r)] donatore *m*, -trice *f*

do•nut ['dəʊnʌt] *Am* → ***doughnut***

doo•dle ['du:dl] *v/i* scarabbocchiare
doom [du:m] *n* (*fate*) destino *f*; (*ruin*) rovina *f*
doomed [du:md] *adj project* condannato al fallimento; ***we are doomed*** siamo condannati; ***the doomed ship*** la nave destinata ad affondare; ***the doomed plane*** l'aereo destinato a cadere
door [dɔ:(r)] porta *f*; *of car* portiera *f*; ***there's someone at the door*** stanno suonando alla porta
'**door•bell** campanello *m*
'**doorknob** pomello *m* della porta
'**doorman** usciere *m*
'**door•mat** zerbino *m*
'**door•step** gradino *m* della porta
'**door•way** vano *m* della porta
dope [dəʊp] **1** *n* (*drugs*) droga *f* leggera; *in sport* doping *m inv*; F (*idiot*) cretino *m*, -a *f*; F (*information*) soffiata *f* **2** *v/t* dopare
dor•mant ['dɔ:mənt] *adj*: ***dormant volcano*** vulcano *m* inattivo; ***lie dormant*** *of plant* rimanere latente
dor•mi•to•ry ['dɔ:mɪtrɪ] dormitorio *m*
dos•age ['dəʊsɪdʒ] dosaggio *m*
dose [dəʊs] *n* dose *f*
dot [dɒt] *n* puntino *m*; *in email address* punto *m*; ***on the dot*** (*exactly*) in punto
◆ **dote on** [dəʊt] *v/t* stravedere per
dot•ing ['dəʊtɪŋ] *adj* adorante
dot•ted line ['dɒtɪd] linea *f* tratteggiata
dot•ty ['dɒtɪ] *adj* F svitato
doub•le ['dʌbl] **1** *n* (*amount*) doppio; (*person*) sosia *m inv*; *of film star* controfigura *f*; (*room with two beds*) doppio; (*room with double bed*) matrimoniale **2** *adj* doppio; ***in double figures*** a due cifre **3** *adv*: ***double the amount*** il doppio della quantità **4** *v/t* raddoppiare **5** *v/i* raddoppiare
◆ **double back** *v/i* (*go back*) fare dietrofront
◆ **double up** *v/i in pain* piegarsi in due; (*share a room*) dividere la stanza
doub•le-'bass contrabbasso *m*
doub•le 'bed letto *m* matrimoniale
doub•le-'breast•ed *adj* a doppio petto
doub•le'check *v/t & v/i* ricontrollare
doub•le 'chin doppio mento *m*
doub•le'cross *v/t* fare il doppio gioco con
doub•le deck•er 'bus autobus *m inv* a due piani
doub•le 'glaz•ing doppi vetri *mpl*
doub•le'park *v/i* parcheggiare in doppia fila
'**doub•le-quick** *adj*: ***in double-quick time*** in un batter d'occhio
'**doub•le room** *with two beds* camera *f* doppia; *with double bed* camera *f* matrimoniale
doub•les ['dʌblz] *npl in tennis* doppio *msg*
doubt [daʊt] **1** *n* dubbio *m*; ***be in doubt*** essere in dubbio; ***no doubt*** (*probably*) senz'altro **2** *v/t*: ***doubt s.o./sth*** dubitare di qu / qc; ***doubt that …*** dubitare che …
doubt•ful [daʊtfʊl] *adj remark*, *look* dubbio; ***be doubtful*** *of person* essere dubbioso; ***it is doubtful whether …*** è in dubbio se …
doubt•ful•ly [daʊtflɪ] *adv* con aria dubbiosa
doubt•less [daʊtlɪs] *adj* senza dubbio
dough [dəʊ] impasto *m*; F (*money*) quattrini *mpl*
dough•nut [dəʊnʌt] bombolone *m*, krapfen *m inv*
dove [dʌv] colomba *f*; *fig* pacifista *m/f*
dow•dy ['daʊdɪ] *adj* scialbo
down[1] [daʊn] *n* (*feathers*) piuma *f*, piumino *m*
down[2] [daʊn] **1** *adv* (*downwards*) giù; ***down there*** laggiù; ***fall down*** cadere giù; ***die down*** calmarsi; ***£200 down*** (*as deposit*) un acconto di £200; ***down south*** a sud; ***be down*** *of price*, *rate* essere diminuito; (*not working*) non funzionare; F (*depressed*) essere giù **2** *prep* giù da; (*along*) lungo; ***I looked down the list*** ho scorso la lista; ***the third door down this corridor*** la terza porta lungo questo corridoio; ***walk down a street*** percorrere una strada **3** *v/t* (*swallow*) buttare giù; (*destroy*) abbattere
'**down-and-out** *n* senza tetto *m/f inv*
'**down•cast** *adj* (*dejected*) abbattuto
'**down•fall** rovina *f*; *of politician*, *government* caduta *f*
'**down•grade** *v/t* ridimensionare; *employee* retrocedere di livello
down•heart•ed [daʊn'hɑ:tɪd] *adj* abbattuto
down'hill *adv* in discesa; ***go downhill*** *fig* peggiorare
'**down•hill ski•ing** discesa *f* libera
'**down•load** *v/t* COMPUT scaricare
'**down•mark•et** *adj* di fascia medio-bassa
'**down pay•ment** deposito *m*, acconto *m*
'**down•play** *v/t* minimizzare
'**down•pour** acquazzone *m*
'**down•right** **1** *adj*: ***it's a downright lie*** è una bugia bella e buona; ***he's a downright idiot*** è un perfetto idiota **2** *adv dangerous*, *stupid etc* assolutamente
'**downside** (*disadvantage*) contropartita *f*
'**down•size** **1** *v/t*: *company* ridimensionare; ***the downsized version*** *of car* la versione ridotta **2** *v/i of company* ridi-

D

mensionarsi
'**down•stairs** *adj & adv* al piano di sotto
down-to-'earth *adj approach* pratico; ***she's very down-to-earth about it*** ha i piedi molto per terra al riguardo
'**down-town** *adj & adv* in centro
'**down•turn** *in economy* flessione *f*
'**down•wards** *adj & adv* verso il basso
doze [dəʊz] **1** *n* sonnellino *m* **2** *v/i* fare un sonnellino
◆ **doze off** *v/i* assopirsi
doz•en ['dʌzn] dozzina *f*; ***dozens of ...*** F un sacco di ... F
drab [dræb] *adj* scialbo
draft [drɑːft] *of document* bozza *f*; *Am* MIL leva *f*; *Am* → ***draught*** **2** *v/t document* fare una bozza di; *Am* MIL arruolare
'**draft dodg•er** *Am* MIL renitente *m* alla leva
drag [dræg] **1** *n*: ***it's a drag having to ...*** F è una rottura dover ... F; ***he's a drag*** F è una pizza F; ***the main drag*** P il corso principale; ***in drag*** vestito da donna; ***a man in drag*** un travestito **2** *v/t* (*pret & pp* ***-ged***) (*pull*) trascinare; (*search*) dragare **3** *v/i* (*pret & pp* ***-ged***) *of time* non passare mai; *of show*, *film* trascinarsi; ***drag s.o. into sth*** (*involve*) tirare in ballo qu in qc; ***drag sth out of s.o.*** (*get information from*) tirare fuori qc da qu
◆ **drag away** *v/t*: ***drag o.s. away from the TV*** staccarsi dalla TV
◆ **drag in** *v/t into conversation* tirare fuori
◆ **drag on** *v/i* (*last long time*) trascinarsi
◆ **drag out** *v/t* (*prolong*) tirare per le lunghe
◆ **drag up** *v/t* F (*mention*) rivangare
drag•on ['drægn] drago *m*; *fig* strega *f*
drain [dreɪn] **1** *n* (*pipe*) tubo *m* di scarico; *under street* tombino *m*; ***a drain on resources*** un salasso per le risorse **2** *v/t water* fare colare; *oil* fare uscire; *vegetables* scolare; *land* drenare; *glass*, *tank* svuotare; (*exhaust*: *person*) svuotare **3** *v/i of dishes* scolare
◆ **drain away** *v/i of liquid* defluire
◆ **drain off** *v/t water* fare defluire
drain•age ['dreɪnɪdʒ] (*drains*) fognatura *f*; *of water from soil* drenaggio *m*
'**drain•pipe** tubo *m* di scarico
dra•ma ['drɑːmə] (*art form*) arte *f* drammatica; (*acting*) recitazione *f*; (*excitement*) dramma *m*; (*play*: *on* TV) sceneggiato *m*; ***drama classes*** corso *m* di recitazione
dra•mat•ic [drə'mætɪk] *adj* drammatico; (*exciting*) sorprendente; *gesture* teatrale
dra•mat•i•cal•ly [drə'mætɪklɪ] *adv say* drammaticamente; *decline*, *rise*, *change etc* drasticamente
dram•a•tist ['dræmətɪst] drammaturgo *m*, -a *f*
dram•a•ti•za•tion [dræmətaɪ'zeɪʃn] (*play*) adattamento *m* teatrale
dram•a•tize ['dræmətaɪz] *v/t story* adattare; *fig* drammatizzare
drank [dræŋk] *pret* → ***drink***
drape [dreɪp] *v/t cloth*, *coat* appoggiare; ***draped in*** (*covered with*) avvolto in
drap•er•y ['dreɪpərɪ] drappeggio *m*
drapes [dreɪps] *npl Am* tende *fpl*
dras•tic ['dræstɪk] *adj* drastico
draught [drɑːft] **1** *n of air* corrente *f* (d'aria); ***draught*** (***beer***), ***beer on draught*** birra *f* alla spina
draughts [drɑːfts] *nsg game* dama *f*
draughts•man ['drɑːftsmən] disegnatore *m* industriale; *of plan* disegnatore *m*, -trice *f*
draught•y ['drɑːftɪ] *adj* pieno di correnti d'aria
draw [drɔː] **1** *n in match*, *competition* pareggio *m*; *in lottery* estrazione *f*, sorteggio *m*; (*attraction*) attrazione *f* **2** *v/t t* (*pret* ***drew***, *pp* ***drawn***) *picture*, *map* disegnare; *cart*, *curtain*, tirare; *in lottery*, *gun*, *knife* estrarre; (*attract*) attirare; (*lead*) tirare; *from bank account* ritirare **3** *v/i t* (*pret* ***drew***, *pp* ***drawn***) disegnare; *in match*, *competition* pareggiare; ***draw near*** avvicinarsi
◆ **draw back 1** *v/i* (*recoil*) tirarsi indietro **2** *v/t hand* ritirare; *curtains* aprire
◆ **draw on 1** *v/i* (*approach*) avvicinarsi **2** *v/t* (*make use of*) attingere a
◆ **draw out** *v/t wallet etc* estrarre; *money from bank* ritirare
◆ **draw up 1** *v/t document* redigere; *chair* accostare **2** *v/i of vehicle* fermarsi; ***draw up alongside s.o.*** accostarsi a qu
'**draw•back** inconveniente *m*
draw•er[1] [drɔː(r)] *of desk etc* cassetto *m*
draw•er[2] [drɔː(r)] (*person*) disegnatore *m*, -trice *f*; ***she's a good drawer*** disegna bene
draw•ing ['drɔːɪŋ] disegno *m*
'**draw•ing board** tecnigrafo *m*; ***go back to the drawing board*** *fig* ricominciare da capo
'**draw•ing pin** puntina *f*
drawl [drɔːl] *n* pronuncia *f* strascicata
drawn [drɔːn] *pp* → ***draw***
dread [dred] *v/t* aver il terrore di; ***I dread him finding it out*** ho il terrore che lo scopra
dread•ful ['dredfʊl] *adj* terribile
dread•ful•ly ['dredflɪ] *adv* F (*extremely*) terribilmente; *behave* malissimo

dream [driːm] **1** *n* sogno *m* **2** *adj* F *house etc* dei sogni **3** *v/t* sognare **4** *v/i* sognare; ***I dreamt about you*** ti ho sognato

◆ **dream up** *v/t* sognare

dream•er ['driːmə(r)] (*daydreamer*) sognatore *m*, -trice *f*

dream•y ['driːmɪ] *adj voice, look* sognante

drear•y ['drɪərɪ] *adj* deprimente; (*boring*) noioso

dredge [dredʒ] *v/t harbour, canal* dragare

◆ **dredge up** *v/t fig* scovare

dregs [dregz] *npl of coffee* fondi *mpl*; ***the dregs of society*** la feccia della società

drench [drentʃ] *v/t* inzuppare; ***get drenched*** inzupparsi; ***I'm drenched*** sono fradicio

dress [dres] **1** *n for woman* vestito *m*; (*clothing*) abbigliamento *m* **2** *v/t person* vestire; *wound* medicare; *salad* condire; ***get dressed*** vestirsi **3** *v/i* vestirsi; ***dress in red*** vestirsi di rosso

◆ **dress up** *v/i* vestirsi elegante; (*wear a disguise*) travestirsi; ***dress up as a ghost*** travestirsi da fantasma

'**dress cir•cle** prima galleria *f*

dress•er ['dresə(r)] *in kitchen* credenza *f*

dress•ing ['dresɪŋ] *for salad* condimento *m*; *for wound* medicazione *f*

dress•ing 'down sgridata *f*

'**dressing gown** vestaglia *f*

'**dress•ing room** *in theatre* spogliatoio *m*

'**dress•ing ta•ble** toilette *f inv*

'**dress•mak•er** sarto *m*, -a *f*

'**dress re•hears•al** prova *f* generale

dress•y ['dresɪ] *adj* F sull'elegante F

drew [druː] *pret* → ***draw***

drib•ble ['drɪbl] *v/i of person* sbavare; *of water* gocciolare; SP dribblare

dried [draɪd] *adj fruit etc* essicato

dri•er ['draɪə(r)] → ***dryer***

drift [drɪft] **1** *n of snow* cumulo *m* **2** *v/i of snow* accumularsi; *of ship* andare alla deriva; (*go off course*) uscire dalla rotta; *of person* vagabondare

◆ **drift apart** *v/i of couple* allontanarsi (l'uno dall'altro)

drift•er ['drɪftə(r)] vagabondo *m*, -a *f*

drill [drɪl] **1** *n* (*tool*) trapano *m*; (*exercise*), MIL esercitazione *f* **2** *v/t tunnel* scavare; ***drill a hole*** fare un foro col trapano **3** *v/i for oil* trivellare; MIL addestrarsi

dril•ling rig ['drɪlɪŋrɪg] (*platform*) sonda *f*

dri•ly ['draɪlɪ] *adv remark* ironicamente

drink [drɪŋk] **1** *n* bevanda *f*; ***non-alcoholic drink*** bibita *f* (analcolica); ***a drink of ...*** un bicchiere di ...; ***go for a drink*** andare a bere qualcosa **2** *v/t & v/i* (*pret* ***drank***, *pp* ***drunk***) bere; ***I don't drink*** non bevo

◆ **drink up 1** *v/i* (*finish drink*) finire il bicchiere **2** *v/t* (*drink completely*) finire di bere

drink•a•ble ['drɪŋkəbl] *adj* potabile

drink 'driv•ing guida *f* in stato di ebbrezza

drink•er ['drɪŋkə(r)] bevitore *m*, -trice *f*

drink•ing ['drɪŋkɪŋ] *of alcohol* consumo *m* di alcolici; ***he has a drinking problem*** beve troppi alcolici

'**drink•ing wa•ter** acqua *f* potabile

'**drinks ma•chine** distributore *m* di bevande

drip [drɪp] **1** *n action* gocciolamento *m*; *amount* goccia *f*; MED flebo *f inv* **2** *v/i* (*pret & pp* ***-ped***) gocciolare

'**drip-dry** *adj* non-stiro

drip•ping ['drɪpɪŋ] *adv*: ***dripping wet*** fradicio

drive [draɪv] **1** *n* percorso *m* in macchina; (*outing*) giro *m* in macchina; (*driveway*) viale *m*; (*energy*) grinta *f*; COMPUT lettore *m*; (*campaign*) campagna *f*; ***left-/right--hand drive*** MOT guida *f* a sinistra / destra **2** *v/t* (*pret* ***drove***, *pp* ***driven***) *vehicle* guidare; (*take in car*) portare (in macchina); TECH azionare; ***that noise / this man is driving me mad*** questo rumore / quest'uomo mi fa diventare matto **3** *v/i* (*pret* ***drove***, *pp* ***driven***) guidare; ***I drive to work*** vado al lavoro in macchina

◆ **drive at** *v/t*: ***what are you driving at?*** dove vuoi andare a parare?

◆ **drive away 1** *v/t* portare via (in macchina); (*chase off*) cacciare **2** *v/i* andare via (in macchina)

◆ **drive in** *v/t nail* piantare

◆ **drive off** → ***drive away***

driv•el ['drɪvl] *n* sciocchezze *fpl*

driv•en ['drɪvn] *pp* → ***drive***

driv•er ['draɪvə(r)] guidatore *m*, -trice *f*, conducente *m/f*; *of train* macchinista *m/f*; COMPUT driver *m inv*

'**driv•er's li•cense** *Am* patente *f* (di guida)

'**drive•way** viale *m*

driv•ing ['draɪvɪŋ] **1** *n* guida *f* **2** *adj rain* violento

driv•ing 'force elemento *m* motore

'**driving in•struct•or** istruttore *m*, -trice *f* di guida

'**driv•ing les•son** lezione *f* di guida

'**driv•ing li•cence** patente *f* (di guida)

'**driv•ing school** scuola *f* guida

'**driv•ing test** esame *m* di guida

driz•zle ['drɪzl] **1** *n* pioggerella *f* **2** *v/i* piovvigginare

drone [drəʊn] *n* (*noise*) ronzio *m*

droop [druːp] *v/i* abbassarsi; *of plant* af-

D

flosciarsi
drop [drɒp] **1** *n of rain* goccia *f*; (*small amount*) goccio *m*; *in price, temperature* calo *m*; *in number* calo *m* **2** *v/t* (*pret & pp* ***-ped***) far cadere; *from plane* sganciare; *person from car* lasciare; *person from team* scartare; (*stop seeing*) smettere di frequentare; *charges, demand etc* abbandonare; (*give up*) lasciare perdere; ***drop a line to*** scrivere due righe a **3** *v/i* (*pret & pp* ***-ped***) cadere; (*decline*) calare
◆ **drop in** *v/i* (*visit*) passare
◆ **drop off** **1** *v/t person, goods* lasciare **2** *v/i* (*fall asleep*) addormentarsi; (*decline*) calare
◆ **drop out** *v/i from competition, school* ritirarsi
'**drop•out** (*from school*) *persona f che ha abbandonato gli studi*; (*from society*) emarginato *m*, -a *f*
drops [drɒps] *npl for eyes* collirio *m*
drought [draʊt] siccità *f*
drove [drəʊv] *pret* → ***drive***
drown [draʊn] **1** *v/i* annegare **2** *v/t person* annegare; *sound* coprire; ***be drowned*** annegare
drow•sy ['draʊzɪ] *adj* sonnolento
drudg•e•ry ['drʌdʒərɪ] lavoro *m* ingrato
drug [drʌg] **1** *n* droga *f*; ***be on drugs*** drogarsi **2** *v/t* (*pret & pp* ***-ged***) drogare
'**drug addict** tossicodipendente *m/f*
'**drug deal•er** spacciatore *m*, -trice *f* (di droga)
'**drug•store** *esp Am negozio-bar m che vende articoli vari, inclusi medicinali*
'**drug traf•fick•ing** traffico *m* di droga
drum [drʌm] *n* MUS tamburo *m*; (*container*) bidone *m*; ***drums*** *in pop music* batteria *f*
◆ **drum into** *v/t* (*pret & pp* ***-med***): ***drum sth into s.o.*** inculcare qc in qu
◆ **drum up** *v/t*: ***drum up support*** cercare supporto
drum•mer [drʌmə(r)] batterista *m/f*; *in brass band* percussionista *m/f*
'**drum•stick** MUS bacchetta *f*; *of poultry* coscia *f*
drunk [drʌŋk] **1** *n* ubriacone *m*, -a *f* **2** *adj* ubriaco; ***get drunk*** ubriacarsi **3** *pp* → ***drink***
drunk•en [drʌŋkn] *voices, laughter* da ubriaco; ***drunken party*** festa *f* in cui si beve molto
drunk 'driv•ing guida *f* in stato di ebbrezza
dry [draɪ] **1** *adj* secco; (*ironic*) ironico; *clothes* asciutto; (*where alcohol is banned*) *dove la vendita e il consumo di alcolici sono illegali* **2** *v/t & v/i* (*pret & pp* ***-ied***) asciugare
◆ **dry out** *v/i* asciugare; *of alcoholic* disintossicarsi
◆ **dry up** *v/i of river* prosciugarsi; F (*be quiet*) stare zitto
'**dry•clean** *v/t* pulire *o* lavare a secco
'**dry clean•er** tintoria *f*
'**dryclean•ing** (*clothes*) abiti *mpl* portati in tintoria
dry•er ['draɪə(r)] (*machine*) asciugatrice *f*
DTP [diːtiː'piː] *abbr* (= ***desk-top publishing***) desk-top publishing *m*, impaginazione *f* elettronica
du•al ['djuːəl] *adj* doppio
du•al 'car•riage•way *Br* carreggiata *f* a due corsie
dub [dʌb] *v/t* (*pret & pp* ***-bed***) *film* doppiare
du•bi•ous ['djuːbɪəs] *adj* equivoco; (*having doubts*) dubbioso
duch•ess ['dʌtʃis] duchessa *f*
duck [dʌk] **1** *n* anatra *f* **2** *v/i* piegarsi **3** *v/t one's head* piegare; *question* aggirare
dud [dʌd] *n* F (*false note*) falso *m*
due [djuː] *adj* (*owed, proper*) dovuto; ***be due*** *of train, baby etc* essere previsto; ***I'm due to meet him*** dovrei incontrarlo; ***due to*** (*because of*) a causa di; ***be due to*** (*be caused by*) essere dovuto a; ***in due course*** a tempo debito
dues [djuːz] *npl* quota *fsg*
du•et [djuː'et] MUS duetto *m*
dug [dʌg] *pret & pp* → ***dig***
duke [djuːk] duca *m*
dull [dʌl] *adj weather* grigio; *sound, pain* sordo; (*boring*) noioso
du•ly ['djuːlɪ] *adv* (*as expected*) come previsto; (*properly*) debitamente
dumb [dʌm] *adj* (*mute*) muto; F (*stupid*) stupido
dumb•found•ed [dʌm'faundɪd] *adj* ammutolito
dum•my ['dʌmɪ] *for clothes* manichino *m*; *for baby* succhiotto *m*
dump [dʌmp] **1** *n for rubbish* discarica *f*; (*unpleasant place*) postaccio *m* **2** *v/t* (*deposit*) lasciare; (*dispose of*) scaricare; *toxic waste etc* sbarazzarsi di
dump•ling ['dʌmplɪŋ] *fagotto m di pasta ripieno, sia dolce che salato*
dune [djuːn] duna *f*
dung [dʌŋ] sterco *m*
dun•ga•rees [dʌŋgə'riːz] *npl* salopette *f inv*
dunk [dʌŋk] *v/t in coffee etc* inzuppare
du•o ['djuːəʊ] MUS duo *m inv*
du•pli•cate ['djuːplɪkət] **1** *n* duplicato *m*; ***in duplicate*** in duplicato **2** *v/t* ['djuːplɪ-

keɪt] (*copy*) duplicare; (*repeat*) rifare
du•pli•cate 'key chiave *f* di scorta
du•ra•ble ['djʊərəbl] *adj material* resistente; *relationship* durevole
du•ra•tion [djʊə'reɪʃn] durata *f*
du•ress [djʊə'res]: ***under duress*** sotto costrizione
dur•ing ['djʊərɪŋ] *prep* durante
dusk [dʌsk] crepuscolo *m*
dust [dʌst] **1** *n* polvere *f* **2** *v/t* spolverare; ***dust sth with sth*** (*sprinkle*) spolverare qc con qc
'dust•bin bidone *m* della spazzatura
'dust cov•er *for book* sopraccoperta *f*
duster ['dʌstə(r)] (*cloth*) straccio *m* (per spolverare)
'dust jack•et *of book* sopraccoperta *f*
'dust•man spazzino *m*
'dust•pan paletta *f*
dust•y ['dʌstɪ] *adj table* impolverato; *road* polveroso
Dutch [dʌtʃ] **1** *adj* olandese; ***go Dutch*** F fare alla romana F **2** *n language* olandese *m*; ***the Dutch*** gli Olandesi
du•ty ['dju:tɪ] dovere *m*; *on goods* tassa *f* doganale, dazio *m*; ***be on duty*** essere di servizio; ***be off duty*** essere fuori servizio
du•ty 'free 1 *adj* duty free *inv* **2** *n* acquisto *m* fatto in un duty free
du•ty free al'low•ance limite *m* di acquisto in un duty free
du•ty'free shop duty free *m inv*
dwarf [dwɔ:f] **1** *n* nano *m*, -a *f* **2** *v/t* fare scomparire
◆ **dwell on** [dwel] *v/t* rimuginare
dwin•dle ['dwɪndl] *v/i* diminuire
dye [daɪ] **1** *n* tintura *f*; *for food* colorante *m* **2** *v/t* colorare, tingere
dy•ing ['daɪɪŋ] *adj person* morente; *industry, tradition* in via di disparizione; ***his dying day*** il giorno della sua morte
dy•nam•ic [daɪ'næmɪk] *adj person* dinamico
dy•na•mism ['daɪnəmɪzm] dinamismo *m*
dy•na•mite ['daɪnəmaɪt] *n* dinamite *f*
dy•na•mo ['daɪnəməʊ] TECH dinamo *f inv*
dy•nas•ty ['dɪnəstɪ] dinastia *f*
dys•lex•i•a [dɪs'leksɪə] dislessia *f*
dys•lex•ic [dɪs'leksɪk] **1** *adj* dislessico **2** *n* dislessico *m*, -a *f*

E

each [iːʧ] **1** *adj* ogni **2** *adv* ciascuno; ***they're £1.50 each*** costano £1,50 ciascuno **3** *pron* ciascuno *m*, -a *f*, ognuno *m*, -a *f*; ***each other*** l'un l'altro *m*, l'una l'altra *f*; ***we know each other*** ci conosciamo; ***we drive each other's car*** guidiamo l'uno la macchina dell'altro

ea•ger ['iːgə(r)] *adj* entusiasta; ***be eager to do sth*** essere ansioso di fare qc; ***be eager for*** essere desideroso di

ea•ger 'bea•ver F fanatico *m*, -a *f* F

ea•ger•ly ['iːgəlɪ] *adv* ansiosamente

ea•ger•ness ['iːgənɪs] smania *f*

ea•gle ['iːgl] aquila *f*

ea•gle-eyed [iːgl'aɪd] *adj*: ***be eagle-eyed*** avere l'occhio di falco

ear¹ [ɪə(r)] *of person*, *animal* orecchio *m*

ear² [ɪə(r)] *of corn* spiga *f*

'ear•ache mal *m* d'orecchi

'ear•drum timpano *m*

earl [ɜːl] conte *m*

'ear•lobe lobo *m* dell'orecchio

ear•ly ['ɜːlɪ] **1** *adj* (*not late*) primo; *arrival* anticipato; (*farther back in time*) antico; ***in the early hours*** nelle prime ore; ***in the early stages*** nelle fasi iniziali; ***in early spring*** all'inizio della primavera; ***early October*** inizio ottobre; ***at an early age*** in giovane età; ***I'm an early riser*** mi alzo sempre presto; ***let's have an early supper*** ceniamo presto; ***an early Picasso*** un Picasso primo periodo; ***the early Romans*** gli antichi Romani; ***early music*** musica *f* primitiva; ***I look forward to an early reply*** resto in attesa di una sollecita risposta **2** *adv* (*not late*) presto; (*ahead of time*) in anticipo; ***it's too early*** è troppo presto; ***you're a bit early*** sei un po' in anticipo

'ear•ly bird persona *f* mattiniera; *planning ahead* persona *f* previdente

ear•mark ['ɪəmɑːk] *v/t* riservare; ***earmark sth for sth*** riservare qc a qc

earn [ɜːn] *v/t* guadagnare; *of interest* fruttare; *holiday*, *drink etc* guadagnarsi; ***earn one's living*** guadagnarsi da vivere; ***his honesty earned him everybody's respect*** la sua onestà gli è valsa il rispetto di tutti

ear•nest ['ɜːnɪst] serio; ***in earnest*** sul serio

earn•ings ['ɜːnɪŋz] *npl* guadagno *m*

'ear•phones *npl* cuffie *fpl* (d'ascolto)

'ear-pierc•ing *adj* perforante

'ear•ring orecchino *m*

'ear•shot: ***within earshot*** a portata d'orecchio; ***out of earshot*** fuori dalla portata d'orecchio

earth [ɜːθ] (*soil*, *planet*) terra *f*; ***where on earth have you been?*** F dove cavolo sei stato? F

earth•en•ware ['ɜːθnweə(r)] *n* terracotta *f*

earth•ly ['ɜːθlɪ] *adj* terreno; ***it's no earthly use ...*** F è perfettamente inutile ...

earth•quake ['ɜːθkweɪk] terremoto *m*

earth-shat•ter•ing ['ɜːθʃætərɪŋ] *adj* sconvolgente

ease [iːz] **1** *n* facilità *f*; ***be at (one's) ease, feel at ease*** essere *o* sentirsi a proprio agio; ***be or feel ill at ease*** essere *o* sentirsi a disagio **2** *v/t* (*relieve*) alleviare; ***it will ease my mind*** mi darà sollievo **3** *v/i of pain* alleviarsi

◆ **ease off 1** *v/t* (*remove*) togliere con cautela **2** *v/i of pain*, *rain* diminuire

ea•sel ['iːzl] cavalletto *m*

eas•i•ly ['iːzəlɪ] *adv* (*with ease*) facilmente; (*by far*) di gran lunga

east [iːst] **1** *n* est *m* **2** *adj* orientale **3** *adv travel* a est

Eas•ter ['iːstə(r)] Pasqua *f*

Eas•ter 'Day il giorno *o* la domenica di Pasqua

'Eas•ter egg uovo *m* di Pasqua

eas•ter•ly ['iːstəlɪ] *adj*: ***easterly wind*** vento *m* dell'est; ***in an easterly direction*** verso est

Eas•ter 'Mon•day lunedì *m inv* di Pasqua, Pasquetta *f*

east•ern ['iːstən] *adj* orientale

east•ward(s) ['iːstwəd(z)] *adv* verso est

eas•y ['iːzɪ] *adj* facile; (*relaxed*) tranquillo; ***take things easy*** (*slow down*) prendersela con calma; ***take it easy!*** (*calm down*) calma!; ***I've had it easy*** ho avuto una vita facile

'eas•y chair poltrona *f*

eas•y-go•ing ['iːzɪgəʊɪŋ] *adj*: ***he's very easy-going*** gli va bene quasi tutto

eat [iːt] *v/t & v/i* (*pret* **ate**, *pp* **eaten**) mangiare

◆ **eat out** *v/i* mangiare fuori

◆ **eat up** *v/t finish* finire di mangiare; *fig* mangiare; *with jealousy* consumare; ***eat up your beans*** *eat them all* mangia tutti i fagioli

eat•a•ble ['iːtəbl] *adj* commestibile; *lunch*, *dish* mangiabile

eat•en ['iːtn] *pp* → ***eat***
eau de Co•logne [əʊdəkə'ləʊn] acqua *f* di Colonia
eaves [iːvz] *npl* cornicione *m*
eaves•drop ['iːvzdrɒp] *v/i* (*pret & pp* ***-ped***) origliare; ***eavesdrop on s.o./sth*** origliare qu / qc
ebb [eb] *v/i of tide* rifluire
◆ **ebb away** *v/i fig*: *of courage, strength* venire meno
ec•cen•tric [ɪk'sentrɪk] **1** *adj* eccentrico **2** *n* eccentrico *m*, -a *f*
ec•cen•tric•i•ty [ɪksen'trɪsɪtɪ] eccentricità *f inv*
ech•o ['ekəʊ] **1** *n* eco *f* **2** *v/i* risuonare **3** *v/t words* ripetere; *views* condividere
e•clipse [ɪ'klɪps] **1** *n* eclissi *f inv* **2** *v/t fig* eclissare
e•co•lo•gi•cal [iːkə'lɒdʒɪkl] *adj* ecologico; ***ecological bal•ance*** equilibrio *m* ecologico
e•co•lo•gi•cal•ly [iːkə'lɒdʒɪklɪ] *adv* ecologicamente
e•co•lo•gi•cal•ly 'friend•ly *adj* ecologico
e•col•o•gist [ɪ'kɒlədʒɪst] ecologista *m/f*
e•col•o•gy [ɪ'kɒlədʒɪ] ecologia *f*
ec•o•nom•ic [iːkə'nɒmɪk] *adj* economico
ec•o•nom•i•cal [iːkə'nɒmɪkl] *adj* (*cheap*) economico; (*thrifty*) parsimonioso
ec•o•nom•i•cal•ly [iːkə'nɒmɪklɪ] *adv* (*in terms of economics*) economicamente; (*thriftily*) con parsimonia
ec•o•nom•ics [iːkə'nɒmɪks] *science* economia *f*; *financial aspects* aspetti *mpl* economici
e•con•o•mist [ɪ'kɒnəmɪst] economista *m/f*
e•con•o•mize [ɪ'kɒnəmaɪz] *v/i* risparmiare, fare economia
◆ **economize on** *v/t* risparmiare su
e•con•o•my [ɪ'kɒnəmɪ] *of a country* economia *f*; (*saving*) risparmio *m*, economia *f*
e'con•o•my class classe *f* economica
e'con•o•my drive regime *m* di risparmio
e'con•o•my size confezione *f* famiglia
e•co•sys•tem ['iːkəʊsɪstm] ecosistema *m*
e•co•tour•ism ['iːkəʊtʊərɪzm] agriturismo *m*
ec•sta•sy ['ekstəsɪ] estasi *f*
ec•sta•t•ic [ɪk'stætɪk] *adj* in estasi
ec•ze•ma ['eksmə] eczema *m*
edge [edʒ] **1** *n of knife* filo *m*; *of table, seat, lawn* bordo *m*; *of road* ciglio *m*; *of cliff* orlo *m*; *in voice* sfumatura *f* tagliente; ***there's an edge of cynicism in his voice*** c'è una punta di cinismo nella sua voce; ***on edge*** → ***edgy*** **2** *v/t* profilare **3** *v/i* (*move slowly*) muoversi con cautela
edge•ways ['edʒweɪz] *adv*: ***I couldn't get a word in edgeways*** non sono riuscito a piazzare una parola
edg•y ['edʒɪ] *adj* teso
ed•i•ble ['edɪbl] *adj* commestibile
ed•it ['edɪt] *v/t text* rivedere; *prepare for publication* curare; *newspaper* dirigere; *TV program, film* montare; COMPUT editare
e•di•tion [ɪ'dɪʃn] edizione *f*
ed•i•tor ['edɪtə(r)] *of text* revisore *m*; *of publication* curatore *m*, -trice *f*; *of newspaper* direttore *m*, -trice; *of TV program* responsabile *m/f* del montaggio; *of film* tecnico *m* del montaggio; ***sports editor*** redattore *m*, -trice sportivo, -a; *in charge* caporedattore *m*, -trice *f* sportivo, -a
ed•i•to•ri•al [edɪ'tɔːrɪəl] **1** *adj* editoriale; ***the editorial staff*** la redazione **2** *n* editoriale *m*, articolo *m* di fondo
EDP [iːdiː'piː] *abbr* (= ***electronic data processing***) EDP (= elaborazione *f* elettronica dei dati)
ed•u•cate ['edjʊkeɪt] *v/t child* istruire; *consumers* educare; ***he was educated at Cambridge*** ha studiato a Cambridge
ed•u•cat•ed ['edjʊkeɪtɪd] *adj person* istruito
ed•u•ca•tion [edjʊ'keɪʃn] istruzione *f*; ***the education system*** la pubblica istruzione
ed•u•ca•tion•al [edjʊ'keɪʃnl] *adj* didattico; (*informative*) istruttivo
eel [iːl] anguilla *f*
ee•rie ['ɪərɪ] *adj* inquietante
ef•fect [ɪ'fekt] effetto *m*; ***take effect*** *of medicine, drug* fare effetto; ***come into effect*** *of law* entrare in vigore
ef•fec•tive [ɪ'fektɪv] *adj* (*efficient*) efficace; (*striking*) d'effetto; ***effective May 1*** con decorrenza dal 1 maggio; ***a very effective combination*** un abbinamento di grande effetto
ef•fem•i•nate [ɪ'femɪnət] *adj* effeminato
ef•fer•ves•cent [efə'vesnt] *adj also fig* effervescente
ef•fi•cien•cy [ɪ'fɪʃənsɪ] efficienza *f*; *of machine* rendimento *m*
ef•fi•cient [ɪ'fɪʃənt] *adj* efficiente; *machine* ad alto rendimento
ef•fi•cient•ly [ɪ'fɪʃəntlɪ] *adv* con efficienza
ef•flu•ent ['eflʊənt] scarichi *mpl*
ef•fort ['efət] sforzo *m*; ***make an effort to do sth*** fare uno sforzo per fare qc
ef•fort•less ['efətlɪs] *adj* facile
ef•fron•te•ry [ɪ'frʌntərɪ] sfrontatezza *f*, sfacciataggine *f*
ef•fu•sive [ɪ'fjuːsɪv] *adj thanks, welcome*

caloroso
e.g. [iː'dʒiː] ad *o* per esempio
e•gal•i•tar•i•an [ɪgælɪ'teərɪən] *adj* egualitario
egg [eg] uovo *m*; *of woman* ovulo *m*
◆ **egg on** *v/t* istigare
'egg•cup portauovo *m inv*
'egghead F intellettualoide *m/f*
'eggplant *Am* melanzana *f*
'egg•shell guscio *m* d'uovo
'egg tim•er *timer m per misurare il tempo di cottura delle uova*
e•go ['iːgəʊ] ego *m*
e•go•cen•tric [iːgəʊ'sentrɪk] *adj* egocentrico
e•go•ism ['iːgəʊɪzm] egoismo *m*
e•go•ist ['iːgəʊ'ɪst] egoista *m/f*
E•gypt ['iːdʒɪpt] Egitto *m*
E•gyp•tian [ɪ'dʒɪpʃn] **1** *adj* egiziano **2** *n* egiziano *m*, -a *f*
ei•der•down ['aɪdədaʊn] (*quilt*) piumino *m*
eight [eɪt] otto
eigh•teen [eɪ'tiːn] diciotto
eigh•teenth [eɪ'tiːnθ] *n & adj* diciottesimo, -a
eighth [eɪtθ] *n & adj* ottavo, -a
eigh•ti•eth ['eɪtɪɪθ] *n & adj* ottantesimo, -a
eigh•ty ['eɪtɪ] ottanta
ei•ther ['aɪðə(r)] **1** *adj* l'uno o l'altro; (*both*) entrambi *pl*; ***at either side of the street*** da entrambi i lati della strada **2** *pron* l'uno o l'altro *m*, l'una o l'altra *f* **3** *adv* nemmeno, neppure; ***I won't go either*** non vado nemmeno *o* neppure io **4** *conj*: ***either my mother or my sister*** mia madre o mia sorella; ***he doesn't like either wine or beer*** non gli piacciono né il vino, né la birra; ***either you write or phone*** o scrivi, o telefoni
e•ject [ɪ'dʒekt] **1** *v/t* espellere **2** *v/i from plane* eiettarsi
◆ **eke out** [iːk] *v/t* usare con parsimonia; *grant etc* arrotondare
elaborate [ɪ'læbərət] **1** *adj* elaborato **2** *v/i* [ɪ'læbəreɪt] fornire particolari
e•lab•o•rate•ly [ɪ'læbəreɪtlɪ] *adv* in modo elaborato
e•lapse [ɪ'læps] *v/i* trascorrere
e•las•tic [ɪ'læstɪk] **1** *adj* elastico **2** *n* elastico *m*
e•las•ti•ca•ted [ɪ'læstɪkeɪtɪd] *adj* elasticizzato
e•las•tic 'band elastico *m*
e•las•ti•ci•ty [ɪlæs'tɪsətɪ] elasticità *f*
E•las•to•plast® [ɪ'læstəplɑːst] cerotto *m*
e•lat•ed [ɪ'leɪtɪd] *adj* esultante
el•at•ion [ɪ'leɪʃn] esultanza *f*
el•bow ['elbəʊ] **1** *n* gomito *m* **2** *v/t*: ***elbow out of the way*** allontanare a spintoni
el•der ['eldə(r)] **1** *adj* maggiore **2** *n* maggiore *m/f*; ***she's two years my elder*** è più vecchia di me di due anni
el•der•ly ['eldəlɪ] *adj* anziano
el•dest ['eldəst] **1** *adj* maggiore **2** *n* maggiore *m/f*; ***the eldest*** il / la maggiore
e•lect [ɪ'lekt] **1** *v/t* eleggere; ***elect to ...*** decidere di ... **2** *adj*: ***the president elect*** il futuro presidente
e•lec•tion [ɪ'lekʃn] elezione *f*
e'lec•tion cam•paign campagna *f* elettorale
e'lec•tion day giorno *m* delle elezioni
e•lec•tor [ɪ'lektə(r)] elettore *m*, -trice *f*
e•lec•to•ral sys•tem [ɪ'lektərəlsɪstm] sistema *m* elettorale
e•lec•tive [ɪ'lektɪv] *adj* facoltativo
e•lec•to•rate [ɪ'lektərət] elettorato *m*
e•lec•tric [ɪ'lektrɪk] *adj also fig* elettrico
e•lec•tri•cal [ɪ'lektrɪkl] *adj* elettrico
e•lec•tri•cal en•gi'neer ingegnere *m* elettrico
e•lec•tri•cal en•gi'neer•ing ingegneria *f* elettrica
e•lec•tric 'blan•ket coperta *f* elettrica
e•lec•tric 'chair sedia *f* elettrica
e•lec•tri•cian [ɪlek'trɪʃn] elettricista *m/f*
e•lec•tri•ci•ty [ɪlek'trɪsətɪ] elettricità *f*
e•lec•tric 'ra•zor rasoio *m* elettrico
e•lec•tri•fy [ɪ'lektrɪfaɪ] *v/t* (*pret & pp* **-ied**) elettrificare; *fig* elettrizzare
e•lec•tro•cute [ɪ'lektrəkjuːt] *v/t* fulminare
e•lec•trode [ɪ'lektrəʊd] elettrodo *m*
e•lec•tron [ɪ'lektrɒn] elettrone *m*
e•lec•tron•ic [ɪlek'trɒnɪk] *adj* elettronico
e•lec•tron•ic da•ta 'pro•ces•sing elaborazione *f* elettronica dei dati
e•lec•tron•ic 'mail posta *f* elettronica
e•lec•tron•ics [ɪlek'trɒnɪks] elettronica *f*
el•e•gance ['elɪgəns] eleganza *f*
el•e•gant ['elɪgənt] *adj* elegante
el•e•gant•ly ['elɪgəntlɪ] *adv* elegantemente
el•e•ment ['elɪmənt] elemento *m*
el•e•men•ta•ry [elɪ'mentərɪ] *adj* (*rudimentary*) elementare
el•e'men•ta•ry school *Am* scuola *f* elementare
el•e'men•ta•ry teacher maestro *m*, -a *f* elementare
el•e•phant ['elɪfənt] elefante *m*
el•e•vate ['elɪveɪt] *v/t* elevare
el•e•va•tion [elɪ'veɪʃn] (*altitude*) altitudine *f*
el•e•va•tor ['elɪveɪtə(r)] *Am* ascensore *m*
el•e•ven [ɪ'levn] undici

el•e•venth [ɪ'levnθ] *n & adj* undicesimo, -a; ***at the eleventh hour*** all'ultima ora, all'ultimo momento
el•i•gi•ble ['elɪdʒəbl] *adj*: ***be eligible to do sth*** avere il diritto di fare qc; ***be eligible for sth*** avere diritto a qc
el•i•gi•ble 'bach•e•lor buon partito *m*
e•lim•i•nate [ɪ'lɪmɪneɪt] *v/t* eliminare; ***be eliminated*** *from competition* essere eliminato
e•lim•i•na•tion [ɪ'lɪmɪneɪʃn] eliminazione *f*
e•lite [eɪ'li:t] **1** *n* elite *f inv* **2** *adj* elitario
el•lipse [ɪ'lɪps] ellisse *f*
elm [elm] olmo *m*
e•lope [ɪ'ləʊp] *v/i* scappare (per sposarsi)
el•o•quence ['eləkwəns] eloquenza *f*
el•o•quent ['eləkwənt] *adj* eloquente
el•o•quent•ly ['eləkwəntlɪ] *adv* con eloquenza
else [els] *adv*: ***anything else*** qualcos'altro; ***anything else?*** *in shop* (desidera) altro?; ***nothing else*** nient'altro; ***if you've got nothing else to do*** se non hai altro da fare; ***nobody else*** nessun altro; ***everyone else is going*** tutti gli altri vanno; ***who else was there?*** chi altro c'era?; ***someone else*** qualcun altro; ***something else*** qualcos'altro; ***let's go somewhere else*** andiamo da qualche altra parte; ***or else*** altrimenti
else•where ['elsweə(r)] *adv* altrove
e•lude [ɪ'lu:d] *v/t* (*escape from*) sfuggire a; (*avoid*) sfuggire a; ***the name eludes me*** il nome mi sfugge
e•lu•sive [ɪ'lu:sɪv] *adj person* difficile da trovare; *quality* raro; *criminal* inafferrabile
e•ma•ci•ated [ɪ'meɪsɪeɪtɪd] *adj* emaciato
e-mail ['i:meɪl] **1** *n* e-mail *m inv* **2** *v/t person* mandare un e-mail a; *text* mandare per e-mail
'e-mail ad•dress indirizzo *m* e-mail
e•man•ci•pat•ed [ɪ'mænsɪpeɪtɪd] *adj woman* emancipato
e•man•ci•pa•tion [ɪmænsɪ'peɪʃn] emancipazione *f*
em•balm [ɪm'bɑ:m] *v/t* imbalsamare
em•bank•ment [ɪm'bænkmənt] *of river* argine *m*; RAIL massicciata *f*
em•bar•go [em'bɑ:gəʊ] embargo *m inv*
em•bark [ɪm'bɑ:k] *v/i* imbarcarsi
◆ **embark on** *v/t* imbarcarsi in
em•bar•rass [ɪm'bærəs] *v/t* imbarazzare
em•bar•rassed [ɪm'bærəst] *adj* imbarazzato
em•bar•rass•ing [ɪm'bærəsɪŋ] *adj* imbarazzante
em•bar•rass•ment [ɪm'bærəsmənt] imbarazzo *m*
em•bas•sy ['embəsɪ] ambasciata *f*
em•bel•lish [ɪm'belɪʃ] *v/t* ornare; *story* ricamare su
em•bers ['embəz] *npl* brace *fsg*
em•bez•zle [ɪm'bezl] *v/t* appropriarsi indebitamente di
em•bez•zle•ment [ɪm'bezlmənt] appropriazione *f* indebita
em•bez•zler [ɪm'bezlə(r)] malversatore *m*, -trice *f*
em•bit•ter [ɪm'bɪtə(r)] *v/t* amareggiare
em•blem ['embləm] emblema *f*
em•bod•i•ment [ɪm'bɒdɪmənt] incarnazione *f*
em•bod•y [ɪm'bɒdɪ] *v/t* (*pret & pp* ***-ied***) incarnare
em•bo•lis•m ['embəlɪzm] embolia *f*
em•boss [ɪm'bɒs] *v/t metal* lavorare a sbalzo; *paper*, *fabric* stampare in rilievo
em•brace [ɪm'breɪs] **1** *n* abbraccio *m* **2** *v/t* (*hug*, *include*) abbracciare **3** *v/i of two people* abbracciarsi
em•broi•der [ɪm'brɔɪdə(r)] *v/t* ricamare; *fig* ricamare su
em•broi•der•y [ɪm'brɔɪdərɪ] ricamo *m*
em•bry•o ['embrɪəʊ] embrione *m*
em•bry•on•ic [embrɪ'ɒnɪk] *adj fig* embrionale
em•e•rald ['emərəld] *precious stone* smeraldo *m*; *colour* verde *m* smeraldo
e•merge [ɪ'mɜ:dʒ] *v/i* (*appear*) emergere; ***it has emerged that …*** è emerso che …
e•mer•gen•cy [ɪ'mɜ:dʒənsɪ] emergenza *f*; ***in an emergency*** in caso di emergenza
emer•gen•cy 'ex•it uscita *f* di sicurezza
e'mer•gen•cy land•ing atterraggio *m* di fortuna
e'mer•gen•cy serv•ices *npl* servizi *mpl* di soccorso
em•er•y board ['emərɪbɔ:d] limetta *f* (da unghie)
em•i•grant ['emɪgrənt] emigrante *m/f*
em•i•grate ['emɪgreɪt] *v/i* emigrare
em•i•gra•tion [emɪ'greɪʃn] emigrazione *f*
Em•i•nence ['emɪnəns]: REL ***His Eminence*** Sua Eminenza
em•i•nent ['emɪnənt] *adj* eminente
em•i•nent•ly ['emɪnəntlɪ] *adv* decisamente
e•mis•sion [ɪ'mɪʃn] *of gases* emanazione *f*
e•mit [ɪ'mɪt] *v/t* (*pret & pp* ***-ted***) *heat*, *gases* emanare; *light*, *smoke* emettere; *smell* esalare
e•mo•tion [ɪ'məʊʃn] emozione *f*
e•mo•tion•al [ɪ'məʊʃnl] *adj problems*, *development* emozionale; (*causing emotion*) commovente; (*showing emotion*) commosso

E

em•pa•thize ['empəθaɪz] *v/i* immedesimarsi; ***empathize with s.o.*** immedesimarsi con qu; ***empathize with sth*** capire qc
em•pe•ror ['empərə(r)] imperatore *m*
em•pha•sis ['emfəsɪs] enfasi *f*; *on word* rilievo *m*
em•pha•size ['emfəsaɪz] *v/t* enfatizzare; *word* dare rilievo a
em•phat•ic [ɪm'fætɪk] *adj* enfatico
em•pire ['empaɪə(r)] impero *m*
em•ploy [ɪm'plɔɪ] *v/t* dare lavoro a; (*take on*) assumere; (*use*) impiegare; ***she's employed as a secretary*** lavora come segretaria; ***he hasn't been employed for six months*** non lavora da sei mesi
em•ploy•ee [emplɔɪ'iː] dipendente *m/f*
em•ploy•er [em'plɔɪ'ə(r)] datore *m*, -trice *f* di lavoro
em•ploy•ment [em'plɔɪmənt] occupazione *f*; (*work*) impiego *m*; ***be seeking employment*** essere in cerca di occupazione
em'ploy•ment a•gen•cy agenzia *f* di collocamento
em•press ['emprɪs] imperatrice *f*
emp•ti•ness ['emptɪnɪs] vuoto *m*
emp•ty ['emptɪ] **1** *adj* vuoto **2** *v/t* (*pret & pp* ***-ied***) vuotare **3** *v/i* (*pret & pp* ***-ied***) *of room*, *street* svuotarsi
em•u•late ['emjʊleɪt] *v/t* emulare
e•mul•sion [ɪ'mʌlʃn] *n paint* emulsione *f*
en•a•ble [ɪ'neɪbl] *v/t person* permettere a; *thing* permettere; ***enable s.o. to do sth*** permettere a qu di fare qc
en•act [ɪ'nækt] *v/t law* emanare; THEA rappresentare
e•nam•el [ɪ'næml] smalto *m*
enc *abbr* (= ***enclosure(s)***) all. (= allegato *m*)
en•chant [ɪn'tʃɑːnt] *v/t* (*delight*) incantare
en•chant•ing [ɪn'tʃɑːntɪŋ] *adj smile*, *village*, *person* incantevole
en•cir•cle [ɪn'sɜːkl] *v/t* circondare
encl *abbr* (= ***enclosure(s)***) all. (= allegato *m*)
en•close [ɪn'kləʊz] *v/t in letter* allegare; *area* recintare; ***please find enclosed …*** in allegato, …
en•clo•sure [ɪn'kləʊʒə(r)] *with letter* allegato *m*
en•core ['ɒŋkɔː(r)] bis *m inv*
en•coun•ter [ɪn'kaʊntə(r)] **1** *n* incontro *m* **2** *v/t* incontrare
en•cour•age [ɪn'kʌrɪdʒ] *v/t* incoraggiare
en•cour•age•ment [ɪn'kʌrɪdʒmənt] incoraggiamento *m*
en•cour•ag•ing [ɪn'kʌrɪdʒɪŋ] *adj* incoraggiante
◆ **encroach on** [ɪn'krəʊtʃ] *v/t land*, *time* invadere; *rights* violare
en•cy•clo•pe•di•a [ɪnsaɪklə'piːdɪə] enciclopedia *f*
end [end] **1** *n* (*extremity*) estremità *f inv*; (*conclusion*) fine *f*; (*purpose*) fine *m*; ***in the end*** alla fine; ***for hours on end*** senza sosta; ***stand sth on end*** mettere qc verticale; ***at the end of July*** alla fine di luglio; ***put an end to*** mettere fine a **2** *v/t* terminare **3** *v/i* finire
◆ **end up** *v/i* finire; ***I'll end up doing it myself*** finirò per farlo io stesso
en•dan•ger [ɪn'deɪndʒə(r)] *v/t* mettere in pericolo
en'dan•gered spe•cies specie *f* in via d'estinzione
en•dear•ing [ɪn'dɪərɪŋ] *adj* accattivante
en•deav•our [ɪn'devə(r)] **1** *n* tentativo *m* **2** *v/t* tentare
en•dem•ic [ɪn'demɪk] *adj* endemico
end•ing ['endɪŋ] finale *m*; GRAM desinenza *f*
end•less ['endlɪs] *adj* interminabile
en•dorse [en'dɔːs] *v/t cheque* girare; *candidacy* appoggiare; *product* fare pubblicità a
en•dorse•ment [en'dɔːsmənt] *of cheque* girata *f*; *of candidacy* appoggio *m*; *of product* pubblicità *f*
end 'prod•uct prodotto *m* finale
end re'sult risultato *m* finale
en•dur•ance [ɪn'djʊrəns] resistenza *f*
en•dure [ɪn'djʊə(r)] **1** *v/t* sopportare **2** *v/i* (*last*) resistere
en•dur•ing [ɪn'djʊərɪŋ] *adj* durevole
end-us•er [end'juːzə(r)] utilizzatore *m* finale
en•e•my ['enəmɪ] nemico *m*, -a *f*
en•er•get•ic [enə'dʒetɪk] *adj* energico
en•er•get•ic•ally [enə'dʒetɪklɪ] *adv* con energia
en•er•gy ['enədʒɪ] energia *f*
en•er•gy-sav•ing ['enədʒɪseɪvɪŋ] *adj device* per risparmiare energia
'e•ner•gy sup•ply rifornimento *m* di energia elettrica
en•force [ɪn'fɔːs] *v/t* far rispettare
en•gage [ɪn'geɪdʒ] **1** *v/t* (*hire*) ingaggiare **2** *v/i* TECH ingranare
◆ **engage in** *v/t* occuparsi di; *conversation* coinvolgere in
en•gaged [ɪn'geɪdʒd] *adj to be married* fidanzato; ***get engaged*** fidanzarsi
en'gaged tone *Br* TELEC segnale *m* d'occupato
en•gage•ment [ɪn'geɪdʒmənt] (*appointment*) impegno *m*; *to be married* fidanzamento *m*; MIL scontro *m*

en'gage•ment ring anello *m* di fidanzamento
en•gag•ing [ɪn'geɪdʒɪŋ] *adj smile, person* accattivante
en•gine ['endʒɪn] motore *m*
en•gi•neer [endʒɪ'nɪə(r)] **1** *n* ingegnere *m*; *for sound, software* tecnico *m*; NAUT macchinista *m* **2** *v/t fig: meeting etc* macchinare, architettare
en•gi•neer•ing [endʒɪ'nɪərɪŋ] ingegneria *f*
En•gland ['ɪŋglənd] Inghilterra *f*
En•glish ['ɪŋglɪʃ] **1** *adj* inglese **2** *n* (*language*) inglese *m*; ***the English*** gli inglesi
En•glish 'Chan•nel Manica *f*
'En•glish•man inglese *m*
'En•glish•wom•an inglese *f*
en•grave [ɪn'greɪv] *v/t* incidere
en•grav•ing [ɪn'greɪvɪŋ] (*drawing*) stampa *f*; (*design*) incisione *f*
en•grossed [ɪn'grəʊst] *adj*: ***engrossed in*** assorto in
en•gulf [ɪn'gʌlf] *v/t* avvolgere
en•hance [ɪn'hɑːns] *v/t* accrescere; *performance, reputation* migliorare
e•nig•ma [ɪ'nɪgmə] enigma *m*
e•nig•mat•ic [enɪg'mætɪk] *adj* enigmatico
en•joy [ɪn'dʒɔɪ] *v/t*: ***did you enjoy the film?*** ti è piaciuto il film?; ***I enjoy reading*** mi piace leggere; ***enjoy your meal!*** buon appetito!; ***enjoy o.s.*** divertirsi
en•joy•a•ble [ɪn'dʒɔɪəbl] *adj* piacevole
en•joy•ment [ɪn'dʒɔɪmənt] piacere *m*, divertimento *m*
en•large [ɪn'lɑːdʒ] *v/t* ingrandire
en•large•ment [ɪn'lɑːdʒmənt] ingrandimento *m*
en•light•en [ɪn'laɪtn] *v/t* illuminare
en•list [ɪn'lɪst] **1** *v/i* MIL arruolarsi **2** *v/t*: ***enlist the help of …*** ottenere l'appoggio di …
en•liv•en [ɪn'laɪvn] *v/t* animare
en•mi•ty ['enmətɪ] inimicizia *f*
e•nor•mi•ty [ɪ'nɔːmətɪ] enormità *f inv*
e•nor•mous [ɪ'nɔːməs] *adj* enorme
e•nor•mous•ly [ɪ'nɔːməslɪ] *adv* enormemente
e•nough [ɪ'nʌf] **1** *adj* sufficiente, abbastanza *inv* **2** *pron* abbastanza; ***will £50 be enough?*** saranno sufficienti £50?; ***I've had enough!*** ne ho abbastanza!; ***thanks, I've had enough*** *food, drinks* grazie, basta così; ***that's enough, calm down!*** adesso basta, calmati! **3** *adv* abbastanza; ***strangely enough*** per quanto strano
en•quire [ɪn'kwaɪə(r)] *v/i* chiedere informazioni, informarsi; ***enquire about sth*** chiedere informazioni su qc; ***enquire into sth*** fare delle ricerche su qc
en•quir•ing [ɪn'kwaɪərɪŋ] *adj*: ***have an enquiring mind*** avere una mente curiosa
en•quir•y [ɪn'kwaɪərɪ] richiesta *f* di informazioni; (*public enquiry*) indagine *f*
en•raged [ɪn'reɪdʒd] *adj* arrabbiato
en•rich [ɪn'rɪtʃ] *v/t* arricchire
en•roll [ɪn'rəʊl] *v/i* iscriversi
en•rol•ment [ɪn'rəʊlmənt] iscrizione *f*
en•sue [ɪn'sjuː] *v/i* seguire
en suite (**bath•room**) ['ɒnswiːt] bagno *m* in camera
en•sure [ɪn'ʃʊə(r)] *v/t* assicurare
en•tail [ɪn'teɪl] *v/t* comportare
en•tan•gle [ɪn'tæŋgl] *v/t in rope* impigliare; ***become entangled in*** impigliarsi in; *in love affair* invischiarsi in
en•ter ['entə(r)] **1** *v/t room, house* entrare in; *competition* inscriversi a; *person, horse in race* iscrivere; (*write down*) registrare; COMPUT inserire **2** *v/i* entrare; THEA entrare in scena; *in competition* iscriversi **3** *n* COMPUT invio *m*
en•ter•prise ['entəpraɪz] (*initiative*) intraprendenza *f*; (*venture*) impresa *f*
en•ter•pris•ing ['entəpraɪzɪŋ] *adj* intraprendente
en•ter•tain [entə'teɪn] **1** *v/t* (*amuse*) intrattenere; (*consider: idea*) considerare **2** *v/i* (*have guests*) ricevere
en•ter•tain•er [entə'teɪnə(r)] artista *m/f*
en•ter•tain•ing [entə'teɪnɪŋ] *adj* divertente
en•ter•tain•ment [entə'teɪnmənt] *adj* divertimento *m*
en•thrall [ɪn'θrɔːl] *v/t* affascinare
en•thu•si•as•m [ɪn'θjuːzɪæzm] entusiasmo *m*
en•thu•si•ast [ɪn'θjuːzɪ'æst] appassionato *m*, -a *f*
en•thu•si•as•tic [ɪnθjuːzɪ'æstɪk] *adj* entusiasta
en•thu•si•as•tic•al•ly [ɪnθjuːzɪ'æstɪklɪ] *adv* con entusiasmo
en•tice [ɪn'taɪs] *v/t* attirare
en•tire [ɪn'taɪə(r)] *adj* intero
en•tire•ly [ɪn'taɪəlɪ] *adv* interamente
en•ti•tle [ɪn'taɪtl] *v/t* dare il diritto a; ***be entitled to do sth*** avere il diritto di fare qc
en•ti•tled [ɪn'taɪtld] *adj book* intitolato
en•trance ['entrəns] entrata *f*, ingresso *m*; THEA entrata *f* in scena; (*admission*) ammissione *f*
'en•trance ex•am•(i•na•tion) esame *m* di ammissione
en•tranced [ɪn'trɑːnst] *adj* incantato
'en•trance fee quota *f* di ingresso

E

E

en•trant ['entrənt] concorrente *m/f*
en•treat [ɪn'triːt] *v/t* supplicare; ***entreat s.o. to do sth*** supplicare qu di fare qc
en•trenched [ɪn'trentʃt] *adj attitudes* radicato
en•tre•pre•neur [ɒntrəprə'nɜː] imprenditore *m*, -trice *f*
en•tre•pre•neur•i•al [ɒntrəprə'nɜːrɪəl] *adj* imprenditoriale
en•trust [ɪn'trʌst] *v/t* affidare; ***entrust s.o. with sth, entrust sth to s.o.*** affidare qc a qu
en•try ['entrɪ] (*way in*) entrata *f*; (*admission*) ingresso *m*; *in diary* annotazione *f*; *in accounts*, *dictionary* voce *f*
'en•try form modulo *m* d'iscrizione
'en•try•phone citofono *m*
'en•try vi•sa visto *m* d'ingresso
e•nu•me•rate [ɪ'njuːməreɪt] *v/t* enumerare
en•vel•op [ɪn'veləp] *v/t* avviluppare
en•ve•lope ['envələʊp] busta *f*
en•vi•a•ble ['envɪəbl] *adj* invidiabile
en•vi•ous ['envɪəs] *adj* invidioso; ***be envious of s.o.*** essere invidioso di qu
en•vi•ron•ment [ɪn'vaɪərənmənt] ambiente *m*
en•vi•ron•men•tal [ɪnvaɪərən'məntl] *adj* ambientale
en•vi•ron•men•tal•ist [ɪnvaɪərən'məntəlɪst] ambientalista *m/f*
en•vi•ron•men•tal•ly friend•ly [ɪnvaɪərən'məntəlɪ] *adj* ecologico
en•vi•ron•men•tal pol'lu•tion inquinamento *m* ambientale
en•vi•ron•men•tal pro'tec•tion tutela *f* dell'ambiente
en•vi•rons [ɪn'vaɪərənz] *npl* dintorni *mpl*
en•vis•age [ɪn'vɪzɪdʒ] *v/t* prevedere
en•voy ['envɔɪ] inviato *m*, -a *f*
en•vy ['envɪ] **1** *n* invidia *f*; ***be the envy of*** essere invidiato da **2** *v/t* (*pret & pp* ***-ied***): ***envy s.o. sth*** invidiare qc a qu
e•phem•er•al *adj* effimero
ep•ic ['epɪk] **1** *n* epopea *f* **2** *adj journey* mitico; ***a task of epic proportions*** un'impresa titanica
ep•i•cen•tre ['epɪsentr] epicentro *m*
ep•i•dem•ic [epɪ'demɪk] epidemia *f*
ep•i•lep•sy ['epɪlepsɪ] epilessia *f*
ep•i•lep•tic [epɪ'leptɪk] epilettico *m*, -a *f*
ep•i•lep•tic 'fit attacco *m* epilettico
ep•i•log *Am*, **ep•i•logue** ['epɪlɒg] epilogo *m*
ep•i•sode ['epɪsəʊd] episodio *m*
ep•i•taph ['epɪtɑːf] epitaffio *m*
e•poch ['iːpɒk] epoca *f*
e•poch-mak•ing ['iːpɒkmeɪkɪŋ] *adj* che fa epoca
e•qual ['iːkwl] **1** *adj* uguale, pari *inv*; ***be equal to*** *task* essere all'altezza di **2** *n*: ***be the equal of*** essere equivalente a; ***treat s.o. as his equal*** trattare qualcuno alla pari **3** *v/t* (*pret & pp* ***-led***, *Am* ***-ed***) (*be as good as*) uguagliare; ***4 times 12 equals 48*** 4 per 12 fa 48
e•qual•i•ty [ɪ'kwɒlətɪ] uguaglianza *f*, parità *f*
e•qual•ize ['iːkwəlaɪz] **1** *v/t* uniformare **2** *v/i Br* SP pareggiare
e•qual•iz•er ['iːkwəlaɪzə(r)] *Br* SP gol *m inv* del pareggio
e•qual•ly ['iːkwəlɪ] *adv* ugualmente; ***equally, ...*** allo stesso modo, ...
e•qual 'rights *npl* parità *f* di diritti
e•quate [ɪ'kweɪt] *v/t* equiparare; ***equate sth with sth*** equiparare qc e qc
e•qua•tion [ɪ'kweɪʒn] MATH equazione *f*
e•qua•tor [ɪ'kweɪtə(r)] equatore *m*
e•qui•lib•ri•um [iːkwɪ'lɪbrɪəm] equilibrio *m*
e•qui•nox ['iːkwɪnɒks] equinozio *m*
e•quip [ɪ'kwɪp] *v/t* (*pret & pp* ***-ped***) equipaggiare; ***equip s.o./sth with sth*** equipaggiare qu / qc di qc; ***he's not equipped to handle it*** *fig* non ha la capacità di gestirlo
e•quip•ment equipaggiamento *m*; *electrical*, *electronic* apparecchiature *fpl*
eq•ui•ty ['ekwətɪ] FIN capitale *m* azionario
e•quiv•a•lent [ɪ'kwɪvələnt] **1** *adj* equivalente; ***be equivalent to*** essere equivalente a **2** *n* equivalente *m*
e•ra ['ɪərə] era *f*
e•rad•i•cate [ɪ'rædɪkeɪt] *v/t* sradicare
e•rase [ɪ'reɪz] *v/t* cancellare
e•ras•er [ɪ'reɪzə(r)] gomma *f* (da cancellare)
e•rect [ɪ'rekt] **1** *adj* eretto **2** *v/t* erigere
e•rec•tion [ɪ'rekʃn] erezione *f*
er•go•nom•ic [ɜːgəʊ'nɒmɪk] *adj furniture* ergonomico
e•rode [ɪ'rəʊd] *v/t* erodere; *of acid* corrodere; *fig*: *rights*, *power* eliminare
e•ro•sion [ɪ'rəʊʒn] erosione *f*; *of acid* corrosione *f*; *fig* eliminazione *f*
e•rot•ic [ɪ'rɒtɪk] *adj* erotico
e•rot•i•cism [ɪ'rɒtɪsɪzm] erotismo *m*
er•rand ['erənd] commissione *f*; ***run errands*** fare commissioni
er•rat•ic [ɪ'rætɪk] *adj* irregolare
er•ror ['erə(r)] errore *m*
'er•ror mes•sage COMPUT messaggio *m* di errore
e•rupt [ɪ'rʌpt] *v/i of volcano* eruttare; *of violence* esplodere; *of person* dare in escandescenze

e•rup•tion [ɪ'rʌpʃn] *of volcano* eruzione *f*; *of violence* esplosione *f*
es•ca•late ['eskəleɪt] *v/i of costs* aumentare; *of war* intensificarsi
es•ca•la•tion [eskə'leɪʃn] escalation *f inv*
es•ca•la•tor ['eskəleɪtə(r)] scala *f* mobile
es•cape [ɪ'skeɪp] **1** *n of prisoner, animal, gas* fuga *f*; ***have a narrow escape*** scamparla per un pelo **2** *v/i of prisoner, animal* scappare, fuggire; *of gas* fuoriuscire **3** *v/t*: ***the word escapes me*** la parola mi sfugge
es'cape chute AVIA scivolo *m*
es•cort ['eskɔːt] **1** *n* accompagnatore *m*, -trice *f*; (*guard*) scorta *f* **2** *v/t* [ɪ'skɔːt] *socially* accompagnare; *act as guard to* scortare
es•pe•cial [ɪ'speʃl] → ***special***
es•pe•cial•ly [ɪ'speʃlɪ] *adv* specialmente
es•pi•o•nage ['espɪənɑːʒ] spionaggio *m*
es•pres•so (cof•fee) [es'presəʊ] espresso *m*
es•say ['eseɪ] *n* saggio *m*; *in school* tema *m*
es•sen•tial [ɪ'senʃl] *adj* essenziale
es•sen•tial•ly [ɪ'senʃlɪ] *adv* essenzialmente
es•tab•lish [ɪ'stæblɪʃ] *v/t company* fondare; (*create, determine*) stabilire; ***establish o.s. as*** imporsi come
es•tab•lish•ment [ɪ'stæblɪʃmənt] *firm* azienda *f*; *hotel, restaurant* struttura *f*; ***the Establishment*** la classe dirigente
es•tate [ɪ'steɪt] (*area of land*) tenuta *f*; (*possessions of dead person*) patrimonio *m*
es'tate a•gen•cy agenzia *f* immobiliare
es,tate a•gent agente *m/f* immobiliare
es,tate car giardiniera *f*
es•thet•ic *etc Am* → ***aesthetic*** *etc*
es•ti•mate ['estɪmət] **1** *n* stima *f*, valutazione *f*; COM preventivo *m* **2** *v/t* stimare
es•ti•ma•tion [estɪ'meɪʃn] stima *f*; ***he has gone up / down in my estimation*** è salito / sceso nella mia stima; ***in my estimation*** (*opinion*) a mio giudizio
es•tranged [ɪs'treɪndʒd] *adj wife, husband* separato
es•tu•a•ry ['estjʊərɪ] estuario *m*
ETA [iːtiː'eɪ] *abbr* (= ***estimated time of arrival***) ora *f* d'arrivo prevista
etc [et'setrə] *abbr* (= ***et cetera***) ecc. (= eccetera)
etch•ing ['etʃɪŋ] acquaforte *f*
e•ter•nal [ɪ'tɜːnl] *adj* eterno
e•ter•ni•ty [ɪ'tɜːnətɪ] eternità *f*
eth•i•cal ['eθɪkl] *adj* etico
eth•ics ['eθɪks] etica *f*
eth•nic ['eθnɪk] *adj* etnico
eth•nic 'group gruppo *m* etnico, etnia *f*
eth•nic mi'nor•i•ty minoranza *f* etnica
EU [iː'juː] *abbr* (= ***European Union***) UE *f* (= Unione *f* europea)
eu•phe•mism ['juːfəmɪzm] eufemismo *m*
eu•pho•ri•a [juː'fɔːrɪə] euforia *f*
eu•ro ['jʊərəʊ] euro *m inv*
'Eu•ro•cheque Eurocheque *m inv*
Eu•ro•crat ['jʊərəʊkræt] funzionario *m*, -a *f* della Commissione europea
'Eu•ro MP eurodeputato *m*, -a *f*
Eu•rope ['jʊərəp] Europa *f*
Eu•ro•pe•an [jʊərə'pɪən] **1** *adj* europeo **2** *n* europeo *m*, -a *f*
Eu•rope•an Com'mis•sion Commissione *f* europea
Eu•ro•pe•an Com'mission•er Commissario *m* europeo
Eu•ro•pe•an 'Par•lia•ment Parlamento *m* europeo
Eu•ro•pe•an 'Un•ion Unione *f* europea
eu•tha•na•si•a [jʊθə'neɪzɪə] eutanasia *f*
e•vac•u•ate [ɪ'vækjʊeɪt] *v/t* evacuare
e•vade [ɪ'veɪd] *v/t* eludere; *taxes* evadere
e•val•u•ate [ɪ'væljʊeɪt] *v/t* valutare
e•val•u•a•tion [ɪvæljʊ'eɪʃn] valutazione *f*
e•van•gel•ist [ɪ'vændʒəlɪst] evangelizzatore *m*, -trice *f*
e•vap•o•rate [ɪ'væpəreɪt] *v/i of water* evaporare; *of confidence* svanire
e•vap•o•ra•tion [ɪvæpə'reɪʃn] *of water* evaporazione *f*
e•va•sion [ɪ'veɪʒn] elusione *f*; *of taxes* evasione *f*
e•va•sive [ɪ'veɪsɪv] *adj* evasivo
eve [iːv] vigilia *f*
e•ven ['iːvn] **1** *adj* (*regular*) omogeneo; *breathing* regolare; *surface* piano; *hem* diritto; (*number*) pari *inv*; *players, game* alla pari; ***get even with …*** farla pagare a … **2** *adv* persino; ***the car even has a CD player*** la macchina ha persino un lettore CD; ***even bigger*** ancora più grande; ***even better / worse*** ancora meglio / peggio; ***not even*** nemmeno, neppure; ***even so*** nonostante questo; ***even if*** anche se **3** *v/t*: ***even the score*** pareggiare
eve•ning ['iːvnɪŋ] sera *f*; ***in the evening*** di sera; ***this evening*** stasera; ***good evening*** buona sera
'eve•ning class corso *m* serale
'eve•ning dress *for woman* vestito *m* da sera; *for man* abito *m* scuro
eve•ning 'pa•per giornale *m* della sera
e•ven•ly ['iːvnlɪ] *adv* (*regularly*) in modo omogeneo; *breathe* regolarmente
e•vent [ɪ'vent] evento *m*, avvenimento *m*; *social* manifestazione *f*; SP prova *f*; ***at all events*** ad ogni modo

E

E

e•vent•ful [ɪ'ventfʊl] *adj* movimentato
e•ven•tu•al [ɪ'ventjʊəl] *adj* finale
e•ven•tu•al•ly [ɪ'ventjʊəlɪ] *adv* finalmente, alla fine
ev•er ['evə(r)] *adv* mai; ***have you ever been to ...?*** sei mai stato in ...?; ***for ever*** per sempre; ***as ever*** come sempre; ***ever more*** sempre di più; ***ever since he left I have been worried*** da quando è partito sono preoccupato; ***ever since his sister's death*** dalla morte di sua sorella; ***he's been depressed ever since*** è depresso da allora
ev•er•green ['evəgriːn] *n* sempreverde *m*
ev•er•last•ing [evə'lɑːstɪŋ] *adj* eterno
ev•ery ['evrɪ] *adj* ogni; ***one in every ten houses*** una casa su dieci; ***every other day*** un giorno sì, uno no; ***every now and then*** ogni tanto
ev•ery•bod•y ['evrɪbɒdɪ] → ***everyone***
ev•ery•day ['evrɪdeɪ] *adj* di tutti i giorni
ev•ery•one ['evrɪwʌn] *pron* tutti *pl*
ev•ery•thing ['evrɪθɪŋ] *pron* tutto
ev•ery•where ['evrɪweə(r)] *adv* dovunque, dappertutto; (*wherever*) dovunque
e•vict [ɪ'vɪkt] *v/t* sfrattare
ev•i•dence ['evɪdəns] prova *f*; ***give evidence*** testimoniare
ev•i•dent ['evɪdənt] *adj* evidente
ev•i•dent•ly ['evɪdəntlɪ] *adv* evidentemente
e•vil ['iːvl] **1** *adj* cattivo **2** *n* male *m*
e•voke [ɪ'vəʊk] *v/t image* evocare
ev•o•lu•tion [iːvə'luːʃn] evoluzione *f*
e•volve [ɪ'vɒlv] *v/i* evolvere
ewe [juː] pecora *f* femmina
ex- [eks] *pref* ex-
ex [eks] F (*former wife*) ex *f inv* F; (*former husband*) ex *m inv* F
ex•act [ɪg'zækt] *adj* esatto
ex•act•ing [ɪg'zæktɪŋ] *adj task* impegnativo; *employer* esigente; *standards* rigido
ex•act•ly [ɪg'zæktlɪ] *adv* esattamente; ***exactly!*** esatto!, esattamente!; ***not exactly*** non esattamente
ex•ag•ge•rate [ɪg'zædʒəreɪt] *v/t & v/i* esagerare
ex•ag•ge•ra•tion [ɪgzædʒə'reɪʃn] esagerazione *f*
ex•am [ɪg'zæm] esame *m*; ***sit an exam*** dare *o* sostenere un esame; ***pass an exam*** passare *o* superare un esame; ***fail an exam*** essere bocciato a un esame
ex•am•i•na•tion [ɪgzæmɪ'neɪʃn] esame *m*; *of patient* visita *f*
ex•am•ine [ɪg'zæmɪn] *v/t* esaminare; *patient* visitare
ex•am•in•er [ɪg'zæmɪnə(r)] EDU esaminatore *m*, -trice *f*
ex•am•ple [ɪg'zɑːmpl] esempio *m*; ***for example*** ad *o* per esempio; ***set a good / bad example*** dare il buon / cattivo esempio
ex•as•pe•rat•ed [ɪg'zæspəreɪt] *adj* esasperato
ex•as•pe•rat•ing [ɪg'zæspəreɪtɪŋ] *adj* esasperante
ex•ca•vate ['ekskəveɪt] *v/t* (*dig*) scavare; *of archaeologist* riportare alla luce
ex•ca•va•tion [ekskə'veɪʃn] scavo *m*
ex•ca•va•tor ['ekskəveɪtə(r)] escavatrice *f*
ex•ceed [ɪk'siːd] *v/t* (*be more than*) eccedere, superare; (*go beyond*) oltrepassare, superare
ex•ceed•ing•ly [ɪk'siːdɪŋlɪ] *adj* estremamente
ex•cel [ɪk'sel] (*pret & pp* **-led**) **1** *v/i* eccellere; ***excel at*** eccellere in **2** *v/t*: ***excel o.s.*** superare se stesso
ex•cel•lence ['eksələns] eccellenza *f*
ex•cel•lent ['eksələnt] *adj* eccellente
ex•cept [ɪk'sept] *prep* eccetto; ***except for*** fatta eccezione per; ***except that ...*** eccetto che ...
ex•cep•tion [ɪk'sepʃn] eccezione *f*; ***with the exception of*** con l'eccezione di; ***take exception to*** avere da ridire su; (*be offended by*) risentirsi per
ex•cep•tion•al [ɪk'sepʃnl] *adj* eccezionale
ex•cep•tion•al•ly [ɪk'sepʃnlɪ] *adv* (*extremely*) eccezionalmente
ex•cerpt ['eksɜːpt] estratto *m*
ex•cess [ɪk'ses] **1** *n* eccesso *m*; ***eat / drink to excess*** mangiare / bere all'eccesso; ***be in excess of*** eccedere **2** *adj* in eccesso
ex•cess 'bag•gage eccedenza *f* di bagaglio
ex•cess 'fare supplemento *m* tariffa
ex•ces•sive [ɪk'sesɪv] *adj* eccessivo
ex•change [ɪks'tʃeɪndʒ] **1** *n of views, information* scambio *m*; *between schools* scambio *m* culturale; ***in exchange*** (***for***) in cambio (di) **2** *v/t* cambiare; ***exchange sth for sth*** cambiare qc con qc
ex'change rate FIN tasso *m* di cambio
ex•ci•ta•ble [ɪk'saɪtəbl] *adj* eccitabile
ex•cite [ɪk'saɪt] *v/t* (*make enthusiastic*) eccitare
ex•cit•ed [ɪk'saɪtɪd] *adj* eccitato; ***get excited*** eccitarsi; ***get excited about sth*** eccitarsi per qc
ex•cite•ment [ɪk'saɪtmənt] eccitazione *f*
ex•cit•ing [ɪk'saɪtɪŋ] *adj* eccitante, emozionante
ex•claim [ɪk'skleɪm] *v/t* esclamare
ex•cla•ma•tion [eksklə'meɪʃn] esclamazione *f*

ex•cla'ma•tion mark punto *m* esclamativo
ex•clude [ɪk'sklu:d] *v/t* escludere
ex•clud•ing [ɪk'sklu:dɪŋ] *prep* ad esclusione di
ex•clu•sive [ɪk'sklu:sɪv] *adj* esclusivo
ex•com•mu•ni•cate [ekskə'mju:nɪkeɪt] *v/t* REL scomunicare
ex•cru•ci•a•ting [ɪk'skru:ʃɪeɪtɪŋ] *adj pain* lancinante
ex•cur•sion [ɪk'skɜ:ʃn] escursione *f*, gita *f*
ex•cuse [ɪk'skju:s] **1** *n* scusa *f* **2** *v/t* [ɪk'skju:z] scusare; ***excuse s.o. from sth*** dispensare qu da qc; ***excuse me*** *to get attention, interrupting* scusami, mi scusi *fml*; *to get past* permesso
ex-di'rec•to•ry: *Br* ***be ex-directory*** non comparire sull'elenco telefonico
e•x•e•cute ['eksɪkju:t] *v/t criminal* giustiziare; *plan* attuare
ex•e•cu•tion [eksɪ'kju:ʃn] *of criminal* esecuzione *f*; *of plan* attuazione *f*
ex•e•cu•tion•er [eksɪ'kju:ʃnə(r)] carnefice *m*
ex•ec•u•tive [ɪg'zekjʊtɪv] dirigente *m/f*
ex•ec•u•tive 'brief•case ventiquattrore *f inv*
ex•ec•u•tive 'wash•room bagno *m* della direzione
ex•em•pla•ry [ɪg'zemplərɪ] *adj* esemplare
ex•empt [ɪg'zempt] *adj*: ***be exempt from*** essere esente da
ex•er•cise ['eksəsaɪz] **1** *n* (*physical*), EDU esercizio *m*; MIL esercitazione *f*; ***take exercise*** fare esercizio **2** *v/t muscle* fare esercizio con; *dog* far fare esercizio a; *caution, restraint* adoperare **3** *v/i* fare esercizio
'ex•er•cise bike cyclette *f inv*
'ex•er•cise book EDU quaderno *m* di esercizi
'ex•er•cise class esercitazione *f*
ex•ert [ɪg'zɜ:t] *v/t authority* esercitare; ***exert o.s.*** sforzarsi
ex•er•tion [ɪg'zɜ:ʃn] sforzo *m*
ex•hale [eks'heɪl] *v/t* esalare
ex•haust [ɪg'zɔ:st] **1** *n fumes* gas *mpl* di scarico; *pipe* tubo *m* di scappamento **2** *v/t* (*tire*) estenuare; (*use up*) esaurire
ex'haust fumes *npl* gas *mpl* di scarico
ex•haust•ed [ɪg'zɔ:stɪd] *adj* (*tired*) esausto
ex•haust•ing [ɪg'zɔ:stɪŋ] *adj* estenuante
ex•haus•tion [ɪg'zɔ:stʃn] spossatezza *f*
ex•haus•tive [ɪg'zɔ:stɪv] *adj* esauriente
ex'haust pipe tubo *m* di scappamento
ex•hib•it [ɪg'zɪbɪt] **1** *n in exhibition* oggetto *m* esposto; LAW prova *f* **2** *v/t of gallery, artist* esporre; (*give evidence of*) manifestare
exhibition [eksɪ'bɪʃn] esposizione *f*; *of bad behaviour* manifestazione *f*; *of skill* dimostrazione *f*
ex•hi•bi•tion•ist [eksɪ'bɪʃnɪst] esibizionista *m/f*
ex•hil•a•rat•ing [ɪg'zɪləreɪtɪŋ] *adj* emozionante
ex•ile ['eksaɪl] **1** *n* esilio *m*; *person* esiliato *m*, -a *f* **2** *v/t* esiliare
ex•ist [ɪg'zɪst] *v/i* esistere; ***exist on*** vivere di
ex•ist•ence [ɪg'zɪstəns] esistenza *f*; ***in existence*** esistente; ***come into existence*** nascere
ex•ist•ing [ɪg'zɪstɪŋ] *adj* attuale
ex•it ['eksɪt] **1** *n* uscita *f* **2** *v/i* COMPUT uscire
ex•on•e•rate [ɪg'zɒnəreɪt] *v/t* scagionare
ex•or•bi•tant [ɪg'zɔ:bɪtənt] *adj* esorbitante
ex•ot•ic [ɪg'zɒtɪk] *adj* esotico
ex•pand [ɪk'spænd] **1** *v/t* espandere **2** *v/i* espandersi; *of metal* dilatarsi
◆ **expand on** *v/t* dilungarsi su
ex•panse [ɪk'spæns] distesa *f*
ex•pan•sion [ɪk'spænʃn] espansione *f*; *of metal* dilatazione *f*
ex•pat•ri•ate [eks'pætrɪət] **1** *adj* residente all'estero **2** *n* residente *m/f* all'estero
ex•pect [ɪk'spekt] **1** *v/t* aspettare; (*suppose, demand*) aspettarsi **2** *v/i*: ***be expecting*** aspettare un bambino; ***I expect so*** immagino di sì
ex•pec•tant [ɪk'spektənt] *adj* pieno di aspettativa
ex•pec•tant 'moth•er donna *f* in stato interessante
ex•pec•ta•tion [ekspek'teɪʃn] aspettativa *f*; ***expectations*** (*demands*) aspettative *fpl*
ex•pe•dient [ɪk'spi:dɪənt] *n* espediente *m*
ex•pe•di•tion [ekspɪ'dɪʃn] spedizione *f*; ***go on a shopping / sightseeing expedition*** andare a fare spese / in giro a visitare
ex•pel [ɪk'spel] *v/t* (*pret & pp* ***-led***) espellere
ex•pend [ɪk'spend] *v/t energy* spendere
ex•pend•a•ble [ɪk'spendəbl] *adj person* sacrificabile
ex•pen•di•ture [ɪk'spendɪtʃə(r)] spesa *f*
ex•pense [ɪk'spens] spesa *f*; ***at the company's expense*** a spese della società; ***a joke at my expense*** uno scherzo a mie spese; ***at the expense of his health*** a spese della sua salute
ex'pense ac•count nota *f* spese
ex•pen•ses [ɪk'spensɪz] *npl* spese *fpl*

E

ex•pen•sive [ɪk'spensɪv] *adj* caro
ex•pe•ri•ence [ɪk'spɪərɪəns] **1** *n* esperienza *f* **2** *v/t pain, pleasure* provare; *problem, difficulty* incontrare
ex•pe•ri•enced [ɪk'spɪərɪənst] *adj* con esperienza; ***he's experienced in teaching*** ha esperienza nell'insegnamento
ex•per•i•ment [ɪk'sperɪmənt] **1** *n* sperimento *m* **2** *v/i* fare esperimenti; ***experiment on*** *animals* sperimentare su; ***experiment with*** (*try out*) sperimentare
ex•per•i•men•tal [ɪksperɪ'mentl] *adj* sperimentale
ex•pert ['ekspɜːt] **1** *adj* esperto **2** *n* esperto *m*, -a *f*
ex•pert ad'vice parere *m* di un esperto
ex•pert•ise [ekspɜː'tiːz] competenza *f*
ex•pire [ɪk'spaɪə(r)] *v/i* scadere
ex•pi•ry [ɪk'spaɪərɪ] scadenza *f*
ex'pi•ry date data *f* di scadenza
ex•plain [ɪk'spleɪn] **1** *v/t* spiegare **2** *v/i* spiegarsi
ex•pla•na•tion [eksplə'neɪʃn] spiegazione *f*
ex•plic•it [ɪk'splɪsɪt] *adj instructions* esplicito
ex•plic•it•ly [ɪk'splɪsɪtlɪ] *adv state, forbid* esplicitamente
ex•plode [ɪk'spləʊd] **1** *v/i of bomb* esplodere **2** *v/t bomb* fare esplodere
ex•ploit[1] ['eksplɔɪt] *n* exploit *m inv*
ex•ploit[2] [ɪk'splɔɪt] *v/t person, resources* sfruttare
ex•ploi•ta•tion [eksplɔɪ'teɪʃn] sfruttamento *m*
ex•plo•ra•tion [eksplə'reɪʃn] esplorazione *f*
ex•plor•a•to•ry [ɪk'splɒrətərɪ] *adj surgery* esplorativo
ex•plore [ɪk'splɔː(r)] *v/t country, possibility etc* esplorare
ex•plo•rer [ɪk'splɔːrə(r)] esploratore *m*, -trice *f*
ex•plo•sion [ɪk'spləʊʒn] esplosione *f*; ***a population explosion*** un'esplosione demografica
ex•plo•sive [ɪk'spləʊsɪv] *n* esplosivo *m*
ex•port ['ekspɔːt] **1** *n action* esportazione *f*; *item* prodotto *m* di esportazione **2** *v/t goods*, COMPUT esportare
'ex•port cam•paign campagna *f* per l'esportazione
ex•port•er ['ekspɔːtə(r)] esportatore *m*, -trice *f*
ex•pose [ɪk'spəʊz] *v/t* (*uncover*) scoprire; *scandal, person* denunciare; ***expose sth to sth*** esporre qc a qc
ex•po•sure [ɪk'spəʊʒə(r)] esposizione *f*; *to cold weather* esposizione *f* prolungata al freddo; *of dishonest behaviour* denuncia *f*; PHOT posa *f*
ex•press [ɪk'spres] **1** *adj* (*fast, explicit*) espresso **2** *n* (*train*) espresso *m* **3** *v/t* (*speak of, voice*) esprimere; ***express o.s. well / clearly*** esprimersi bene / chiaramente; ***express o.s.*** (*emotionally*) esprimersi
ex•pres•sion [ɪk'spreʃn] espressione *f*; (*expressiveness*) espressività *f*
ex•pres•sive [ɪk'spresɪv] *adj* espressivo
ex•press•ly [ɪk'spreslɪ] *adv* espressamente
ex•press•way [ɪk'spresweɪ] autostrada *f*
ex•pul•sion [ɪk'spʌlʃn] espulsione *f*
ex•qui•site [ek'skwɪzɪt] *adj* (*beautiful*) squisito
ex•tend [ɪk'stend] **1** *v/t* estendere; *house, repertoire* ampliare; *runway, path* prolungare; *contract, visa* prorogare; *thanks, congratulations* porgere **2** *v/i of garden etc* estendersi
ex•ten•sion [ɪk'stenʃn] *to house* annesso *m*; *of contract, visa* proroga *f*; TELEC interno *m*
ex'ten•sion ca•ble prolunga *f*
ex•ten•sive [ɪk'stensɪv] *adj* ampio
ex•tent [ɪk'stent] ampiezza *f*, portata *f*; ***to such an extent that*** a un punto tale che; ***to a certain extent*** fino a un certo punto
ex•ten•u•at•ing cir•cum•stances [ɪk'stenjʊeɪtɪŋ] *npl* circostanze *fpl* attenuanti
ex•te•ri•or [ɪk'stɪərɪə(r)] **1** *adj* esterno **2** *n of building* esterno *m*; *of person* aspetto *m* esteriore
ex•ter•mi•nate [ɪk'stɜːmɪneɪt] *v/t* sterminare
ex•ter•nal [ɪk'stɜːnl] *adj* (*outside*) esterno
ex•tinct [ɪk'stɪŋkt] *adj species* estinto
ex•tinc•tion [ɪk'stɪŋkʃn] *of species* estinzione *f*
ex•tin•guish [ɪk'stɪŋgwɪʃ] *v/t* spegnere
ex•tin•guish•er [ɪk'stɪŋgwɪʃə(r)] estintore *m*
extort [ɪk'stɔːt] *v/t* estorcere; ***extort money from …*** estorcere denaro da …
ex•tor•tion [ɪk'stɔːʃn] estorsione *f*
ex•tor•tion•ate [ɪk'stɔːʃənət] *adj prices* esorbitante; ***that's extortionate!*** è un furto!
ex•tra ['ekstrə] **1** *n* extra *m inv* **2** *adj* in più; ***be extra*** (*cost more*) essere a parte **3** *adv* particolarmente; ***an extra special day*** un giorno particolarmente speciale
ex•tra 'charge costo *m* aggiuntivo
ex•tract[1] ['ekstrækt] *n* estratto *m*
ex•tract[2] [ɪk'strækt] *v/t* estrarre; *information* estorcere
ex•trac•tion [ɪk'strækʃn] estrazione *f*

ex•tra•dite ['ekstrədaɪt] *v/t* estradare
ex•tra•di•tion [ekstrə'dɪʃn] estradizione *f*
ex•tra'di•tion trea•ty accordo *m* di estradizione
ex•tra•mar•i•tal [ekstrə'mærɪtl] *adj* extraconiugale
ex•tra•or•di•nar•i•ly [ekstrɔːdɪn'eərɪlɪ] *adv* eccezionalmente
ex•tra•or•di•na•ry [ɪk'strɔːdɪnərɪ] *adj* straordinario
ex•tra 'time SP tempi *mpl* supplementari
ex•trav•a•gance [ɪk'strævəgəns] stravaganza *f*
ex•trav•a•gant [ɪk'strævəgənt] *adj with money* stravagante
ex•treme [ɪk'striːm] **1** *n* estremo *m* **2** *adj* estremo
ex•treme•ly [ɪk'striːmlɪ] *adv* estremamente
ex•trem•ist [ɪk'striːmɪst] estremista *m/f*
ex•tri•cate ['ekstrɪkeɪt] *v/t* districare
ex•tro•vert ['ekstrəvɜːt] *n/adj* estroverso *m*, -a *f*
ex•u•be•rant [ɪg'zjuːbərənt] *adj* esuberante
ex•ult [ɪg'zʌlt] *v/i* esultare
eye [aɪ] **1** *n* occhio *m*; *of needle* cruna *f*; ***keep an eye on*** tenere d'occhio **2** *v/t* scrutare
'eye•ball bulbo *m* oculare
'eye•brow sopracciglio *m*
'eyecatch•ing *adj* appariscente
'eyelash ciglio *m*
'eye•lid palpebra *f*
'eye•lin•er eyeliner *m inv*
'eyesha•dow ombretto *m*
'eye•sight vista *f*
'eye•sore pugno *m* in un occhio
'eye strain affaticamento *m* della vista
'eye•wit•ness testimone *m/f* oculare

E

F

F *abbr* (= ***Fahrenheit***) F (= Fahrenheit)
fab•ric ['fæbrɪk] (*material*) tessuto *m*
fab•u•lous ['fæbjʊləs] *adj* fantastico
fab•u•lous•ly ['fæbjʊləslɪ] *adv* incredibilmente
fa•çade [fə'sɑːd] *of building, person* facciata *f*
face [feɪs] **1** *n* viso *m*, faccia *f*; ***face to face*** faccia a faccia; ***lose face*** perdere la faccia **2** *v/t person, the sea etc* essere di fronte a; *facts, truth* affrontare
◆ **face up to** *v/t* affrontare
'**face•cloth** guanto *m* di spugna
'**face•lift** lifting *m inv* del viso
'**face pack** maschera *f* di bellezza
face 'val•ue valore *m* nominale; ***take sth at face value*** giudicare qc dalle apparenze
fa•cial ['feɪʃl] *n* pulizia *f* del viso
fa•cil•i•tate [fə'sɪlɪteɪt] *v/t* facilitare
fa•cil•i•ties [fə'sɪlətɪz] *npl* strutture *fpl*
fact [fækt] fatto *m*; ***in fact, as a matter of fact*** in realtà
faction ['fækʃn] fazione *f*
fac•tor ['fæktə(r)] fattore *m*
fac•to•ry ['fæktərɪ] fabbrica *f*
fac•ul•ty ['fækəltɪ] facoltà *f inv*
fad [fæd] mania *f* passeggera
fade [feɪd] *v/i of colours* sbiadire; *of light* smorzarsi; *of memories* svanire
fad•ed ['feɪdɪd] *adj colour, jeans* sbiadito
fag [fæg] F (*cigarette*) sigaretta *f*
'**fag end** F (*cigarette end*) mozzicone *m* di sigaretta
Fahr•en•heit ['færənhaɪt] *adj* Fahrenheit
fail [feɪl] **1** *v/i* fallire **2** *v/t test, exam* essere bocciato a; ***he failed to arrive in time*** non è riuscito ad arrivare in tempo; ***he never fails to write*** non manca mai di scrivere **2** *n*: ***without fail*** con certezza
fail•ing ['feɪlɪŋ] *n* difetto *m*
fail•ure ['feɪljə(r)] fallimento *m*
faint [feɪnt] **1** *adj* vago **2** *v/i* svenire
faint•ly ['feɪntlɪ] *adv* vagamente
fair[1] [feə(r)] *n* (*fun fair*) luna park *m inv*; COM fiera *f*
fair[2] [feə(r)] *adj hair* biondo; *complexion* chiaro; (*just*) giusto; ***it's not fair*** non è giusto *adv*: ***fair enough*** e va bene
fair•ly ['feəlɪ] *adv treat* giustamente; (*quite*) piuttosto
fair•ness ['feənɪs] *of treatment* giustizia *f*
fai•ry ['feərɪ] fata *f*
'**fai•ry tale** fiaba *f*, favola *f*
faith [feɪθ] fede *f*
faith•ful ['feɪθfl] *adj* fedele; ***be faithful to one's partner*** essere fedele al proprio compagno
faith•ful•ly ['feɪθflɪ] *adv* fedelmente; ***Yours faithfully*** distinti saluti
fake [feɪk]? **1** *n* falso *m* **2** *adj* falso **3** *v/t* (*forge*) falsificare; (*feign*) simulare
fall[1] [fɔːl] *n Am* autunno *m*
fall[2] [fɔːl] **1** *v/i* (*pret* ***fell***, *pp* ***fallen***) *of person, government, night* cadere; *of prices, temperature* calare; ***it falls on a Tuesday*** cade di martedì; ***fall ill*** ammalarsi **2** *n of person, government* caduta *f*; *in price, temperature* calo *m*
◆ **fall back on** *v/t* ricorrere a
◆ **fall behind** *v/i with work, studies* rimanere indietro
◆ **fall down** *v/i* cadere
◆ **fall for** *v/t* (*fall in love with*) innamorarsi di; (*be deceived by*) abboccare a
◆ **fall out** *v/i of hair* cadere; (*argue*) litigare
◆ **fall over** *v/i* cadere
◆ **fall through** *v/i of plans* andare a monte
fal•len ['fɔːlən] *pp* → ***fall***
fal•li•ble ['fæləbl] *adj* fallibile
'**fallout** precipitazione *f*
false [fɔːls] *adj* falso
false a'larm falso allarme *m*
false•ly ['fɔːlslɪ] *adv*: ***be falsely accused of sth*** essere ingiustamente accusato di qc
false 'start *in race* falsa partenza *f*
false 'teeth *npl* dentiera *f*
fal•si•fy ['fɔːlsɪfaɪ] *v/t* (*pret & pp* ***-ied***) falsificare
fame [feɪm] fama *f*
fa•mil•i•ar [fə'mɪljə(r)] *adj* (*intimate*) intimo; *form of address*, (*well-known*) familiare; ***be familiar with sth*** conoscere bene qc; ***that looks / sounds familiar*** ha un'aria familiare
fa•mil•i•ar•i•ty [fəmɪlɪ'ærɪtɪ] *with subject etc* buona conoscenza *f*
fa•mil•i•ar•ize [fəm'ɪljəraɪz] *v/t* familiarizzare; ***familiarize o.s. with …*** familiarizzarsi con …
fam•i•ly ['fæməlɪ] famiglia *f*
fam•i•ly 'doc•tor medico *m* di famiglia
fam•i•ly 'name cognome *m*
fam•i•ly 'plan•ning pianificazione *f* familiare

fam•i•ly 'plan•ning clinic consultorio *m* per la pianificazione familiare
fam•i•ly 'tree albero *m* genealogico
fam•ine ['fæmɪn] fame *f*
fam•ished ['fæmɪʃt] *adj* F affamato
fa•mous ['feɪməs] *adj* famoso; ***be famous for ...*** essere noto per ...
fan[1] [fæn] *n* (*supporter*) fan *m/f*
fan[2] [fæn] **1** *n for cooling*: *electric* ventilatore *m*; *handheld* ventaglio *m* **2** *v/t* (*pret & pp* **-ned**): ***fan o.s.*** farsi aria
fa•nat•ic [fə'nætɪk] *n* fanatico *m*, -a *f*
fa•nat•i•cal [fə'nætɪkl] *adj* fanatico
fa•nat•i•cism [fə'nætɪsɪzm] fanatismo *m*
'fan belt MOT cinghia *f* della ventola
'fan club fan club *m inv*
fan•cy ['fænsɪ] **1** *adj design* stravagante **2** *n*: ***as the fancy takes you*** quanto ti va; ***take a fancy to s.o.*** prendere a benvolere qu **3** *v/t* (*pret & pp* **-ied**) F avere voglia di; ***I'm sure he fancies you*** sono sicuro che gli piaci
fan•cy 'dress costume *m*
fan•cy-'dress par•ty festa *f* in maschera
fang [fæŋ] dente *m* aguzzo
'fan mail lettere *fpl* dei fans
fan•ta•size ['fæntəsaɪz] *v/i* fantasticare
fan•tas•tic [fæn'tæstɪk] *adj* (*very good*) fantastico; (*very big*) enorme
fan•tas•tic•al•ly [fæn'tæstɪklɪ] *adv* (*extremely*) incredibilmente
fan•ta•sy ['fæntəsɪ] fantasia *f*
far [fɑː(r)] *adv* lontano; (*much*) molto; ***far away*** lontano; ***how far is it to ...?*** quanto dista ...?; ***as far as the corner / hotel*** fino all'angolo / hotel; ***as far as I can see*** per quanto posso vedere; ***as far as I know*** per quanto ne so; ***you've gone too far*** *in behaviour* sei andato troppo oltre; ***so far so good*** fin qui tutto bene
farce [fɑːs] farsa *f*
fare [feə(r)] *n for travel* tariffa *f*
Far 'East Estremo Oriente *m*
fare•well [feə'wel] *n* addio *m*
fare'well par•ty festa *f* d'addio
far•fetched [fɑː'fetʃt] *adj* inverosimile
farm [fɑːm] *n* fattoria *f*
farm•er ['fɑːmə(r)] agricoltore *m*, -trice *f*
'farm•house cascina *f*
farm•ing ['fɑːmɪŋ] *n* agricoltura *f*
'farm•work•er bracciante *m/f*
'farm•yard cortile *m* di una cascina
far-'off *adj* lontano
far•sight•ed [fɑː'saɪtɪd] *adj* previdente; *Am* OPT presbite
fart [fɑːt] **1** *n* F scoreggia *f* F, peto *m* **2** *v/i* F scoreggiare F, petare
far•ther ['fɑːðə(r)] *adv* più lontano
far•thest ['fɑːðəst] *adv travel etc* più lontano
fas•ci•nate ['fæsɪneɪt] *v/t* affascinare; ***I always was fascinated by the idea of ...*** mi ha sempre affascinato l'idea di ...
fas•ci•nat•ing ['fæsɪneɪtɪŋ] *adj* affascinante
fas•ci•na•tion [fæsɪ'neɪʃn] *with subject* fascino *m*
fas•cis•m ['fæʃɪzm] fascismo *m*
fas•cist ['fæʃɪst] **1** *n* fascista *m/f* **2** *adj* fascista
fash•ion ['fæʃn] *n* moda *f*; (*manner*) maniera *f*, modo *m*; ***in fashion*** alla moda; ***out of fashion*** fuori moda
fash•ion•a•ble ['fæʃnəbl] *adj* alla moda
fash•ion•a•bly ['fæʃnəblɪ] *adv dressed* alla moda
'fash•ion-con•scious *adj* fanatico della moda
'fash•ion de•sign•er stilista *m/f*
'fash•ion mag•a•zine rivista *f* di moda
'fash•ion show sfilata *f* di moda
fast[1] [fɑːst] **1** *adj* veloce, rapido; ***be fast*** *of clock* essere avanti **2** *adv* velocemente; ***stuck fast*** fissato saldamente; ***fast asleep*** profondamente addormentato
fast[2] [fɑːst] *n not eating* digiuno *m*
fas•ten ['fɑːsn] **1** *v/t* chiudere; *dress*, *seat-belt* allacciare; ***fasten sth onto sth*** attaccare qc a qc; *brooch* appuntare qc su qc **2** *v/i of dress etc* allacciarsi
fas•ten•er ['fɑːsnə(r)] chiusura *f*
fast 'food fast food *m*
fast•food 'res•tau•rant fast food *m inv*
fast 'for•ward **1** *n on video etc* riavvolgimento *m* rapido **2** *v/i* riavvolgere rapidamente
'fast lane *on road* corsia *f* di sorpasso; ***in the fast lane*** *fig*: *of life* a cento all'ora
'fast train rapido *m*
fat [fæt] **1** *adj* grasso **2** *n* grasso *m*
fa•tal ['feɪtl] *adj* fatale
fa•tal•i•ty [fə'tælətɪ] fatalità *f inv*
fa•tal•ly ['feɪtəlɪ] *adv*: ***fatally injured*** ferito a morte
fate [feɪt] fato *m*
fat•ed ['feɪtɪd] *adj*: ***be fated to do sth*** essere destinato a fare qc
fa•ther ['fɑːðə(r)] *n* padre *m*; ***Father Martin*** REL padre Martin
Fa•ther 'Christ•mas Babbo *m* Natale
fa•ther•hood ['fɑːðəhʊd] paternità *f*
'fa•ther-in-law (*pl* **fathers-in-law**) suocero *m*
fa•ther•ly ['fɑːðəlɪ] *adj* paterno
fath•om ['fæðəm] *n* NAUT fathom *m inv*
◆ **fathom out** *v/t fig* spiegarsi; ***I just can't fathom you out*** proprio non ti capisco
fa•tigue [fə'tiːg] *n* stanchezza *f*

F

fat•so ['fætsəʊ] *n* F ciccione *m*, -a *f* F
fat•ten ['fætn] *v/t animal* ingrassare
fat•ty ['fætɪ] **1** *adj* grasso **2** *n* F *person* ciccione *m*, -a *f* F
fau•cet ['fɔːsɪt] *Am* rubinetto *m*
fault [fɔːlt] *n* (*defect*) difetto *m*; ***it's your / my fault*** è colpa tua / mia; ***find fault with*** criticare
fault•less ['fɔːltlɪs] *adj person, performance* impeccabile
fault•y ['fɔːltɪ] *adj goods* difettoso
fa•vor *etc Am* → ***favour*** *etc*
fa•vour ['feɪvə(r)] **1** *n* favore *m*; ***do s.o. a favour*** fare un favore a qu; ***do me a favour!*** (*don't be stupid*) fammi il piacere!; ***in favour of ...*** a favore di ...; ***be in favour of ...*** essere a favore di ... **2** *v/t* (*prefer*) preferire, prediligere
fa•vou•ra•ble ['feɪvərəbl] *adj reply etc* favorevole
fa•vou•rite ['feɪvərɪt] **1** *n* prediletto *m*, -a *f*; (*food*) piatto *m* preferito; *in race, competition* favorito *m*, -a *f* **2** *adj* preferito
fa•vour•it•ism ['feɪvrɪtɪzm] favoritismo *m*
fax [fæks] **1** *n* fax *m inv*; ***send sth by fax*** inviare qc per fax **2** *v/t* inviare per fax; ***fax sth to s.o.*** inviare qc per fax a qc
FBI *abbr* (= ***Federal Bureau of Investigation***) FBI *f*
fear [fɪə(r)] **1** *n* paura *f* **2** *v/t* avere paura di
fear•less ['fɪəlɪs] *adj* intrepido
fear•less•ly ['fɪəlɪslɪ] *adv* intrepidamente
fea•si•bil•i•ty stud•y [fiːzə'bɪlətɪ] studio *m* di fattibilità
fea•si•ble ['fiːzəbl] *adj* fattibile
feast [fiːst] *n* banchetto *m*
feat [fiːt] prodezza *f*
fea•ther ['feðə(r)] piuma *f*
fea•ture ['fiːtʃə(r)] **1** *n on face* tratto *m*; *of city, building, plan, style* caratteristica *f*; *in paper* servizio *m*; (*film*) lungometraggio *m*; ***make a feature of ...*** mettere l'accento su ... **2** *v/t of film* avere come protagonista
'fea•ture film lungometraggio *m*
Feb•ru•a•ry ['februərɪ] febbraio *m*
fed [fed] *pret & pp* → ***feed***
fed•e•ral ['fedərəl] *adj* federale
fed•e•ra•tion [fedə'reɪʃn] federazione *f*
fed 'up *adj* F stufo F; ***be fed up with ...*** essere stufo di ...
fee [fiː] tariffa *f*; *of lawyer, doctor etc* onorario *m*
fee•ble ['fiːbl] *adj* debole
feed [fiːd] *v/t* (*pret & pp* ***fed***) nutrire; *family* mantenere; *baby* dare da mangiare a
'feed•back *n* riscontro *m*, feedback *m inv*
feel [fiːl] (*pret & pp* ***felt***) **1** *v/t* (*touch*) toccare; (*sense*) sentire; *pain, pleasure, sensation* sentire; (*think*) pensare **2** *v/i* sentirsi; ***it feels like silk / cotton*** sembra seta / cotone al tatto; ***your hand feels hot / cold*** la tua mano è calda / fredda; ***I feel hungry*** ho fame; ***I feel tired*** sono stanco; ***how are you feeling today?*** come ti senti oggi?; ***how does it feel to be rich?*** che sensazione fa essere ricchi?; ***do you feel like a drink / meal?*** hai voglia di bere / mangiare qualcosa?; ***I feel like going / staying*** ho voglia di andare / rimanere; ***I don't feel like it*** non ne ho voglia
◆ **feel up to** *v/t* sentirsi in grado di
feel•er ['fiːlə(r)] *of insect* antenna *f*
'feel•good fac•tor fattore *m* tranquillizzante
feel•ing ['fiːlɪŋ] sentimento *m*; (*emotion*) sensazione *f*; (*sensation*) sensibilità *f*; ***what are your feelings about it?*** quali sono le tue impressioni in proposito?; ***I have mixed feelings about him*** ho sensazioni contrastanti nei suoi riguardi; ***I have this feeling that ...*** ho la sensazione che ...
feet [fiːt] *pl* → ***foot***
fe•line ['fiːlaɪn] *adj* felino
fell [fel] *pret* → ***fall***
fel•low ['feləʊ] *n* (*man*) tipo *m*
fel•low 'cit•i•zen concittadino *m*, -a *f*
fel•low 'coun•try•man compatriota *m/f*
fel•low 'man prossimo *m*
fel•o•ny ['felənɪ] *Am* delitto *m*
felt[1] [felt] *n* feltro *m*
felt[2] [felt] *pret & pp* → ***feel***
felt 'tip, felt-tip(•ped) 'pen pennarello *m*
fe•male ['fiːmeɪl] **1** *adj* femmina; *typical of women* femminile **2** *n* femmina *f*; F (*woman*) donna *f*
fem•i•nine ['femɪnɪn] **1** *adj* femminile **2** *n* GRAM femminile *m*
fem•i•nis•m ['femɪnɪzm] femminismo *m*
fem•i•nist ['femɪnɪst] **1** *n* femminista *f* **2** *adj* femminista
fence [fens] *n round garden etc* recinto *m*; F *criminal* ricettatore *m*, -trice *f*; ***sit on the fence*** non prendere partito
◆ **fence in** *v/t land* recintare
fenc•ing ['fensɪŋ] SP scherma *f*
fend [fend] *v/i*: ***fend for o.s.*** badare a se stesso
fer•ment[1] [fə'ment] *v/i of liquid* fermentare
fer•ment[2] ['fɜːment] *n* (*unrest*) fermento *m*
fer•men•ta•tion [fɜːmen'teɪʃn] fermentazione *f*
fern [fɜːn] felce *f*

fe•ro•cious [fə'rəʊʃəs] *adj* feroce
fer•ry ['ferɪ] *n* traghetto *m*
fer•tile ['fɜːtaɪl] *adj* fertile
fer•til•i•ty [fɜː'tɪlətɪ] fertilità *f*
fer'til•i•ty drug cura *f* per sviluppare la fertilità
fer•ti•lize ['fɜːtəlaɪz] *v/t ovum* fecondare
fer•ti•liz•er ['fɜːtəlaɪzə(r)] *for soil* fertilizzante *m*
fer•vent ['fɜːvənt] *adj admirer* fervente
fer•vent•ly ['fɜːvəntlɪ] *adv* ardentemente
fes•ter ['festə(r)] *v/i of wound* fare infezione
fes•ti•val ['festɪvl] festival *m inv*
fes•tive ['festɪv] *adj* festivo; ***the festive season*** le festività
fes•tiv•i•ties [fe'stɪvətɪz] *npl* festeggiamenti *mpl*
fe•tal ['fiːtl] *adj* fetale
fetch [fetʃ] *v/t* (*go and fetch*) andare a prendere; (*come and fetch*) venire a prendere; *thing* prendere; *price* rendere
fe•tus ['fiːtəs] feto *m*
feud [fjuːd] **1** *n* faida *f* **2** *v/i* litigare
fe•ver ['fiːvə(r)] febbre *f*
fe•ver•ish ['fiːvərɪʃ] *adj also fig* febbrile; ***I'm feeling feverish*** mi sento la febbre
few [fjuː] **1** *adj* (*not many*) pochi; ***a few ...*** alcuni ...; ***a few people*** alcune persone, qualche persona; ***a few books*** alcuni libri, qualche libro; ***quite a few, a good few*** (*a lot*) parecchi **2** *pron* (*not many*) pochi; ***a few*** (*some*) alcuni; ***quite a few, a good few*** (*a lot*) parecchi
fewer ['fjuːə(r)] *adj* meno; ***fewer than ...*** meno di ...
fi•an•cé [fɪ'ɒnseɪ] fidanzato *m*
fi•an•cée [fɪ'ɒnseɪ] fidanzata *f*
fi•as•co [fɪ'æskəʊ] fiasco *m*
fib [fɪb] *n* frottola *f*
fi•ber *Am* → ***fibre***
fi•bre ['faɪbə(r)] *n* fibra *f*
'fi•bre•glass *n* fibra *f* di vetro
fi•bre 'op•tic *adj* fibra *f* ottica
fi•bre 'op•tics tecnologia *f* delle fibre ottiche
fick•le ['fɪkl] *adj* incostante
fic•tion ['fɪkʃn] *n* (*novels*) narrativa *f*; (*made-up story*) storia *f*
fic•tion•al ['fɪkʃnl] *adj* immaginario
fic•ti•tious [fɪk'tɪʃəs] *adj* fittizio
fid•dle ['fɪdl] **1** *n* F (*violin*) violino *m*; ***it's a fiddle*** F (*cheat*) è una fregatura F **2** *v/i*: ***fiddle with ...*** giocherellare con ...; ***fiddle around with ...*** trafficare con ... **3** *v/t accounts, results* truccare
fi•del•i•ty [fɪ'delətɪ] fedeltà *f*
fid•get ['fɪdʒɪt] *v/i* agitarsi
fid•get•y ['fɪdʒɪtɪ] *adj* in agitazione; ***get fidgety*** mettersi in agitazione
field [fiːld] campo *m*; (*competitors in race*) formazione *f*; ***that's not my field*** non è il mio campo
field•er ['fiːldə(r)] *in cricket* esterno *m*
'field e•vents *npl* atletica *f* leggera (escluse le specialità su pista)
fierce [fɪəs] *adj animal* feroce; *wind, storm* violento
fierce•ly ['fɪəslɪ] *adv* ferocemente; ***say sth fiercely*** dire qc in tono aggressivo
fi•er•y ['faɪərɪ] *adj personality, temper* focoso
fif•teen [fɪf'tiːn] quindici
fif•teenth [fɪf'tiːnθ] *n & adj* quindicesimo, -a
fifth [fɪfθ] *n & adj* quinto, -a
fifth•ly ['fɪfθlɪ] *adv* al quinto posto
fif•ti•eth ['fɪftɪɪθ] *n & adj* cinquantesimo, -a
fif•ty ['fɪftɪ] cinquanta
fif•ty-'fif•ty *adv* metà e metà; ***go fifty-fifty with s.o.*** fare a metà con qu
fig [fɪg] fico *m*
fight [faɪt] **1** *n* lotta *f*; *in war* combattimento *m*; (*argument*) litigio *m*; *in boxing* incontro *m* **2** *v/t* (*pret & pp* ***fought***) (*brawl*) azzuffare; *in war* combattere; *in boxing* battersi contro; *disease, injustice* combattere **3** *v/i* (*pret & pp* ***fought***) *in war* combattere; *of drunks, schoolkids* azzuffarsi; (*argue*) litigare
◆ **fight for** *v/t one's rights, a cause* lottare per
fight•er ['faɪtə(r)] combattente *m/f*; *aeroplane* caccia *m inv*; (*boxer*) pugile *m*; ***she's a fighter*** è combattiva
fight•ing ['faɪtɪŋ] *n* risse *fpl*; ***he's always in trouble for fighting*** è sempre nei guai perché scatena risse
fig•u•ra•tive ['fɪgjərətɪv] *adj use of word* figurato; *art* figurativo
fig•ure ['fɪgə(r)] *n* (*digit*) cifra *f*; *of person* linea *f*; (*form, shape*) figura *f*
◆ **figure out** *v/t* (*understand*) capire; *calculation* calcolare
'fig•ure skat•er pattinatore *m*, -trice *f* artistico, -a
'fig•ure skat•ing pattinaggio *m* artistico
file[1] [faɪl] **1** *n for papers* raccoglitore *m*; *contents* dossier *m inv*, pratica *f*; COMPUT file *m inv*; ***on file*** in archivio **2** *v/t documents* schedare
◆ **file away** *v/t documents* archiviare
file[2] [faɪl] *n for wood, fingernails* lima *f*
'file man•ag•er COMPUT file manager *m inv*
fi•li•al ['fɪlɪəl] *adj* filiale
fil•ing cab•i•net ['faɪlɪŋkæbɪnət] schedar-

F

io *m*
fill [fɪl] **1** *v/t* riempire; *tooth* otturare **2** *n*: ***eat one's fill*** mangiare a sazietà
◆ **fill in** *v/t form* compilare; *hole* riempire; ***fill s.o. in*** mettere al corrente qu
◆ **fill in for** *v/t* sostituire temporaneamente
◆ **fill out 1** *v/t form* compilare **2** *v/i* (*get fatter*) arrotondarsi
◆ **fill up 1** *v/t* riempire **2** *v/i of stadium, theatre* riempirsi

F

fil•let ['fɪlɪt] *n* filetto *m*
fil•let 'steak filetto *m*
fill•ing ['fɪlɪŋ] **1** *n in sandwich* ripieno *m*; *in tooth* otturazione *f* **2** *adj food* pesante
'fill•ing sta•tion stazione *f* di rifornimento
film [fɪlm] **1** *n for camera* pellicola *f*; *at cinema* film *m inv* **2** *v/t person, event* riprendere, filmare; *scene* girare
'film-mak•er regista *m/f*
'film star stella *f* del cinema
fil•ter ['fɪltə(r)] **1** *n* filtro *m* **2** *v/t coffee, liquid* filtrare
◆ **filter through** *v/i of news, reports* diffondersi
'fil•ter pa•per carta *f* filtrante
'fil•ter tip (*cigarette*) filtro *m*
filth [fɪlθ] sporcizia *f*; (*obscenities*) sconcezze *fpl*
filth•y [fɪlθɪ] *adj* sporco; *language etc* volgare
fin [fɪn] *of fish* pinna *f*
fi•nal ['faɪnl] **1** *adj* finale **2** *n* SP finale *f*
fi•na•le [fɪ'nɑːlɪ] finale *m*
fi•nal•ist ['faɪnəlɪst] finalista *m/f*
fi•nal•ize ['faɪnəlaɪz] *v/t plans, design* mettere a punto
fi•nal•ly ['faɪnəlɪ] *adv* infine; (*at last*) finalmente
fi•nals ['faɪnəlz] *npl* EDU esami *mpl* finali
fi•nance ['faɪnæns] **1** *n* finanza *f* **2** *v/t* finanziare
fi•nan•ces ['faɪnænsɪz] *npl* finanze *fpl*
fi•nan•cial [faɪ'nænʃl] *adj* finanziario
fi•nan•cial•ly [faɪ'nænʃəlɪ] *adv* finanziariamente
fi•nan•cial 'year esercizio *m* (finanziario)
fi•nan•cier [faɪ'nænsɪə(r)] *n* finanziatore *m*, -trice *f*
find [faɪnd] *v/t* (*pret & pp* ***found***) trovare; ***if you find it too hot / cold*** se lo trovi troppo caldo / freddo; ***find a person innocent / guilty*** LAW giudicare una persona innocente / colpevole
◆ **find out** *v/t & v/i* scoprire
find•ings ['faɪndɪŋz] *npl of report* conclusioni *fpl*
fine[1] [faɪn] *adj day, weather, city* bello; *wine, performance* buono; *distinction, line* sottile; ***how's that? – that's fine*** com'è? – va benissimo; ***that's fine by me*** a me sta bene; ***how are you? – fine*** come stai? – bene
fine[2] [faɪn] **1** *n penalty* multa *f* **2** *v/t* multare
fine-'tooth comb: ***go through sth with a fine-tooth comb*** passare qc al setaccio
fine-'tune *v/t also fig* mettere a punto
fin•ger ['fɪŋgə(r)] **1** *n* dito *m* **2** *v/t* passare le dita su
'fin•ger•nail unghia *f*
'fin•ger•print 1 *n* impronta *f* digitale **2** *v/t* prendere le impronte digitali di
'fin•ger•tip punta *f* del dito; ***have sth at one's fingertips*** *knowledge* sapere qc a menadito
fin•i•cky ['fɪnɪkɪ] *adj person* pignolo; *design, pattern* complicato
fin•ish ['fɪnɪʃ] **1** *v/t* finire; ***finish doing sth*** finire di fare qc **2** *v/i* finire **3** *n of product* finitura *f*; *finishing line* traguardo *m*
◆ **finish off** *v/t* finire
◆ **finish up** *v/t food* finire; ***he finished up liking London*** Londra ha finito per piacergli
◆ **finish with** *v/t boyfriend etc* lasciare
fin•ish•ing line ['fɪnɪʃɪŋ] traguardo *m*
Fin•land ['fɪnlənd] Finlandia *f*
Finn [fɪn] finlandese *m/f*
Finn•ish ['fɪnɪʃ] **1** *adj* finlandese, finnico **2** *n language* finlandese *m*
fir [fɜː(r)] abete *m*
fire ['faɪə(r)] **1** *n* fuoco *m*; (*blaze*) incendio *m*; (*bonfire, campfire etc*) falò *m inv*; ***be on fire*** essere in fiamme; ***catch fire*** prendere fuoco; ***set sth on fire, set fire to sth*** dare fuoco a qc **2** *v/i* (*shoot*) sparare **3** *v/t* F (*dismiss*) licenziare
'fire a•larm allarme *m* antincendio
'fire•arm arma *f* da fuoco
'fire bri•gade vigili *mpl* del fuoco
'fire•crack•er petardo *m*
'fire door porta *f* taglia-fuoco
'fire drill esercitazione *f* antincendio
'fire en•gine autopompa *f*
'fire es•cape scala *f* antincendio
fire ex•tin•guish•er ['faɪərɪkstɪŋgwɪʃə(r)] estintore *m*
'fire fight•er pompiere *m*
'fire•guard parafuoco *m inv*
'fire•man pompiere *m*
'fire•place camino *m*
'fire sta•tion caserma *f* dei pompieri
'fire truck *Am* autopompa *f*
'fire•wood legna *f* da ardere
'fire•works *npl* fuochi *mpl* d'artificio
firm[1] [fɜːm] *adj grip, handshake* energico;

flesh, muscles sodo; *voice, parents* deciso; *decision* risoluto; *date, offer* definitivo; *control* rigido; *foundations* solido; *believer* convinto; ***a firm deal*** un accordo definito
firm[2] [fɜːm] *n* COM azienda *f*
first [fɜːst] **1** *adj* primo; ***who's first please?*** chi è il primo, per favore? **2** *n* primo *m*, -a *f* **3** *adv arrive, finish* per primo; (*beforehand*) prima; ***first of all*** (*for one reason*) innanzitutto; ***at first*** in un primo tempo, al principio
first 'aid pronto soccorso *m*
first-'aid box, first-'aid kit cassetta *f* del pronto soccorso
'first•born *adj* primogenito
'first class 1 *adj* di prima classe **2** *adv travel* in prima classe
first 'floor primo piano *m*; *Am* piano *m* terra
first'hand *adj* diretto
First 'La•dy *of US* First Lady *f inv*
first•ly ['fɜːstlɪ] *adv* in primo luogo
first 'name nome *m* di battesimo
first 'night prima serata *f*
first of'fend•er delinquente *m/f* non pregiudicato, -a
first-'rate *adj* di prima qualità
fis•cal ['fɪskl] *adj* fiscale
fish [fɪʃ] **1** *n* (*pl* ***fish***) pesce *m*; ***drink like a fish*** F bere come una spugna F; ***feel like a fish out of water*** sentirsi come un pesce fuor d'acqua **2** *v/i* pescare
fish and 'chips *npl pesce e patate fritte*
'fish•bone lisca *f*
fish•er•man ['fɪʃəmən] pescatore *m*
fish 'fin•ger bastoncino *m* di pesce
fish•ing ['fɪʃɪŋ] pesca *f*
'fish•ing boat peschereccio *m*
'fish•ing line lenza *f*
'fish•ing rod canna *f* da pesca
fish•mon•ger ['fɪʃmʌŋgə(r)] pescivendolo *m*
fish•y ['fɪʃɪ] *adj* F (*suspicious*) sospetto
fist [fɪst] pugno *m*
fit[1] [fɪt] *n* MED attacco *m*; ***a fit of rage / jealousy*** un accesso di rabbia / gelosia
fit[2] [fɪt] *adj physically* in forma; *morally* adatto; ***keep fit*** tenersi in forma
fit[3] [fɪt] **1** *v/t* (*pret & pp* ***-ted***) *of clothes* andare bene a; (*attach*) installare **2** *v/i* (*pret & pp* ***-ted***) *of clothes* andare bene; *of piece of furniture etc* starci **3** *n*: ***it is a good fit*** *of piece of furniture etc* ci sta perfettamente; *of clothes* calza a pennello; ***it's a tight fit*** *of piece of furniture etc* ci sta appena; *of clothes* va giusto giusto
◆ **fit in 1** *v/i of person in group* integrarsi; ***it fits in with our plans*** si concilia con i nostri programmi **2** *v/t*: ***fit s.o. in*** *into schedule* fissare un appuntamento a qu
fit•ful ['fɪtfʊl] *adj sleep* a tratti
fit•ness ['fɪtnɪs] *physical* forma *f*
'fit•ness cen•ter *Am*, **'fit•ness cen•tre** palestra *f*
fit•ted 'car•pet ['fɪtɪd] moquette *f inv*
fit•ted 'kitch•en cucina *f* componibile
fit•ted 'sheet lenzuolo *m* con gli angoli
fit•ter ['fɪtə(r)] *n* assemblatore *m*, -trice *f*
fit•ting ['fɪtɪŋ] *adj* appropriato
fit•tings ['fɪtɪŋz] *npl* equipaggiamento *msg*
five [faɪv] cinque
fiv•er ['faɪvə(r)] F banconota *f* da cinque sterline
fix [fɪks] **1** *n* (*solution*) soluzione *f*; ***be in a fix*** F essere nei casini F **2** *v/t* (*attach*) fissare; (*repair*) aggiustare; (*arrange*: *meeting etc*) fissare; *lunch* preparare; *dishonestly*: *match etc* manipolare; ***fix sth onto sth*** attaccare qc a qc; ***I'll fix you a drink*** ti preparo da bere
◆ **fix up** *v/t meeting* fissare; ***it's all fixed up*** è tutto stabilito
fixed [fɪkst] *adj in one position* fisso; *timescale, exchange rate* stabilito
fix•tures ['fɪkstʃəz] *npl in room* installazioni *fpl* fisse; SP incontro *m*
◆ **fiz•zle out** ['fɪzl] *v/i* F sfumare F
fiz•zy ['fɪzɪ] *adj drink* gassato
flab [flæb] *on body* ciccia *f*
flab•ber•gast ['flæbəgɑːst] *v/t* F: ***be flabbergasted*** cadere dalle nuvole
flab•by ['flæbɪ] *adj muscles, stomach* flaccido
flag[1] [flæg] *n* bandiera *f*
flag[2] [flæg] *v/i* (*pret & pp* ***-ged***) (*tire*) soccombere
'flag•pole asta *f*
fla•grant ['fleɪgrənt] *adj* flagrante
'flag•ship *fig* cavallo *m* di battaglia
'flag•staff asta *f*
'flag•stone lastra *f* di pietra
flair [fleə(r)] *n* (*talent*) talento *m*; (*style*) stile *m*
flake [fleɪk] *n of snow* fiocco *m*; *of paint, plaster* scaglia *f*
◆ **flake off** *v/i* squamarsi
flak•y ['fleɪkɪ] *adj* squamato
flak•y 'pas•try pasta *f* sfoglia
flam•boy•ant [flæm'bɔɪənt] *adj personality* esuberante
flam•boy•ant•ly [flæm'bɔɪəntlɪ] *adv dressed* in modo vistoso
flame [fleɪm] *n* fiamma *f*; ***go up in flames*** incendiarsi
flam•ma•ble ['flæməbl] *adj* infiammabile
flan [flæn] sformato *m*

flank [flæŋk] **1** *n* fianco *m* **2** *v/t*: ***be flanked by*** essere affiancato da
flan•nel ['flænl] *n for washing* guanto *m* di spugna
flap [flæp] **1** *n of envelope*, *pocket* falda *f*; *of table* ribalta *f*; ***be in a flap*** F essere in fibrillazione F **2** *v/t* (*pret & pp* **-ped**) *wings* sbattere **3** *v/i* (*pret & pp* **-ped**) *of flag etc* sventolare; F (*panic*) andare in fibrillazione F
flare [fleə(r)] **1** *n* (*distress signal*) razzo *m*; *in dress* svasatura *f*; ***flares*** *trousers* pantaloni *mpl* a zampa di elefante **2** *v/t nostrils* allargare
◆ **flare up** *v/i of violence*, *illness*, *temper* esplodere; *of fire* divampare
flash [flæʃ] **1** *n of light* lampo *m*; PHOT flash *m inv*; ***in a flash*** F in un istante; ***have a flash of inspiration*** avere un lampo di genio; ***flash of lightning*** lampo *m* **2** *v/i of light* lampeggiare **3** *v/t*: ***flash one's headlights*** lampeggiare
'**flash•back** *in film* flashback *m inv*
flash•er ['flæʃə(r)] MOT freccia *f*; F *person* esibizionista *m*
'**flash•light** *esp Am* pila *f*; PHOT flash *m inv*
flash•y ['flæʃɪ] *adj pej* appariscente
flask [flɑːsk] (*vacuum flask*) termos *m inv*
flat[1] [flæt] **1** *adj surface*, *land*, *tone* piatto; *beer* sgassato; *battery*, *tyre* a terra; *shoes* basso; ***A/B flat*** MUS la / si bemolle; ***and that's flat*** F punto e basta F **2** *adv* MUS sotto tonalità; ***flat out*** *work*, *run*, *drive* a tutto gas **3** *n* gomma *f* a terra
flat[2] [flæt] *n Br* (*apartment*) appartamento *m*
flat-chest•ed [flæ'tʃestɪd] *adj* piatto
flat•ly ['flætlɪ] *adv refuse*, *deny* risolutamente
'**flat•mate** *persona f con cui si divide la casa*
'**flat rate** tariffa *f* forfettaria
flat•ten ['flætn] *v/t land*, *road* livellare; *by bombing*, *demolition* radere al suolo
flat•ter ['flætə(r)] *v/t* adulare
flat•ter•er ['flætərə(r)] adulatore *m*, -trice *f*
flat•ter•ing ['flætərɪŋ] *adj comments* lusinghiero; ***Jane's dress is very flattering*** il vestito di Jane le dona molto
flat•ter•y ['flætərɪ] adulazione *f*
flat•u•lence ['flætjʊləns] flatulenza *f*
flat•ware ['flætweər] *Am* stoviglie *fpl*
flau•tist ['flɔːtɪst] flautista *m/f*
fla•vor *etc Am* → ***flavour*** *etc*
fla•vour ['fleɪvə(r)] **1** *n* gusto *m* **2** *v/t food* insaporire
fla•vour•ing ['fleɪvərɪŋ] *n* aroma *m*
flaw [flɔː] *n* difetto *m*
flaw•less ['flɔːlɪs] *adj* perfetto
flea [fliː] *n* pulce *f*
fleck [flek] puntino *m*
fled [fled] *pret & pp* → ***flee***
flee [fliː] *v/i* (*pret & pp* **fled**) scappare
fleece [fliːs] *v/t* F fregare F
fleet [fliːt] *n* NAUT flotta *f*; *of taxis*, *trucks* parco *m* macchine
fleet•ing ['fliːtɪŋ] *adj visit etc* di sfuggita; ***catch a fleeting glimpse of*** vedere di sfuggita
flesh [fleʃ] carne *f*; *of fruit* polpa *f*; ***meet / see a person in the flesh*** incontrare / vedere una persona in carne e ossa
flex [fleks] **1** *v/t muscles* flettere **2** *n* ELEC cavo *m*
flex•i•bil•i•ty [fleksə'bɪlətɪ] flessibilità *f*
flex•i•ble ['fleksəbl] *adj* flessibile; ***I'm quite flexible*** *about arrangements*, *timing* sono abbastanza flessibile
flex•(i)•time ['fleks(ɪ)taɪm] orario *m* flessibile
flew [fluː] *pret* → ***fly***
flick [flɪk] *v/t tail* agitare; ***he flicked a fly off his hand*** ha cacciato via una mosca dalla mano; ***she flicked her hair out of her eyes*** si è tolta i capelli dagli occhi con un gesto
◆ **flick through** *v/t book*, *magazine* sfogliare
flick•er ['flɪkə(r)] *v/i of light* tremolare
'**flick-knife** coltello *m* a scatto
fli•er ['flaɪə(r)] (*circular*) volantino *m*
flies [flaɪz] *npl on trousers* patta *f*
flight [flaɪt] volo *m*; (*fleeing*) fuga *f*; ***flight (of stairs)*** rampa *f* (di scale)
'**flight at•tend•ant** assistente *m/f* di volo
'**flight crew** equipaggio *m* di volo
'**flight deck** *in aeroplane* cabina *f* di pilotaggio; *of aircraft carrier* ponte *m* di decollo
'**flight num•ber** numero *m* di volo
'**flight path** rotta *f* (di volo)
'**flight re•cord•er** registratore *m* di volo
'**flight time** *departure* orario *m* di volo; *duration* durata *f* di volo
flight•y ['flaɪtɪ] *adj* volubile
flim•sy ['flɪmzɪ] *adj structure*, *furniture* leggero; *dress*, *material* sottile; *excuse* debole
flinch [flɪntʃ] *v/i* sobbalzare
fling [flɪŋ] **1** *v/t* (*pret & pp* **flung**) scagliare; ***fling o.s. into a chair*** buttarsi su una sedia **2** *n* F (*affair*) avventura *f*
◆ **flip through** [flɪp] *v/t* (*pret & pp* **-ped**) *book*, *magazine* sfogliare
flip•per ['flɪpə(r)] *for swimming* pinna *f*
flirt [flɜːt] **1** *v/i* flirtare **2** *n* flirt *m inv*

flir•ta•tious [flɜːˈteɪʃəs] *adj* civettuolo
float [fləʊt] *v/i* galleggiare; FIN fluttuare
float•ing vot•er [ˈfləʊtɪŋ] *elettore che cambia spesso opinione*
flock [flɒk] **1** *n of sheep* gregge *m* **2** *v/i* accorrere in massa
flog [flɒg] *v/t* (*pret & pp* ***-ged***) (*whip*) fustigare; F (*sell*) vendere
flood [flʌd] **1** *n* inondazione *f* **2** *v/t of river* inondare; ***flood its banks*** *of river* straripare
◆ **flood in** *v/i* affluire
flood•ing [ˈflʌdɪŋ] inondazione *f*
ˈ**flood•light** *n* riflettore *m*
flood•lit [ˈflʌdlɪt] *adj match* illuminato da riflettori
flood wa•ters [ˈflʌdwɔːtəz] *npl* acque *fpl* di inondazione
floor [flɔː(r)] *n* pavimento *m*; (*storey*) piano *m*
ˈ**floor•board** asse *f* del pavimento
ˈ**floor cloth** straccio *m* per lavare per terra
ˈ**floor•lamp** *Am* lampada *f* a stelo
flop [flɒp] **1** *v/i* (*pret & pp* ***-ped***) crollare; F (*fail*) fare fiasco **2** *n* F (*failure*) fiasco *m*
flop•py [ˈflɒpɪ] *adj not stiff* floscio; (*weak*) moscio
flop•py (ˈ**disk**) floppy *m inv*, floppy disk *m inv*
Flor•ence [ˈflɒrəns] Firenze
Flor•en•tine [ˈflɒrəntaɪn] **1** *adj* fiorentino **2** *n* fiorentino *m*, -a *f*
flor•ist [ˈflɒrɪst] fiorista *m/f*
floss [flɒs] **1** *n for teeth* filo *m* interdentale **2** *v/t*: ***floss one's teeth*** passare il filo interdentale
flour [ˈflaʊə(r)] farina *f*
flour•ish [ˈflʌrɪʃ] *v/i* fiorire; *of business, civilization* prosperare
flour•ish•ing [ˈflʌrɪʃɪŋ] *adj business, trade* prospero
flow [fləʊ] **1** *v/i of river, traffic, current* scorrere; *of work* procedere **2** *n of river, ideas* flusso *m*
ˈ**flow•chart** diagramma *m* (di flusso)
flow•er [ˈflaʊə(r)] **1** *n* fiore *m* **2** *v/i* fiorire
ˈ**flow•er•bed** aiuola *f*
ˈ**flow•er•pot** vaso *m* per fiori
ˈ**flow•er show** esposizione *f* floreale
flow•er•y [ˈflaʊərɪ] *adj pattern* a fiori; *style of writing* fiorito
flown [fləʊn] *pp* → ***fly***
flu [fluː] influenza *f*
fluc•tu•ate [ˈflʌktjʊeɪt] *v/i* oscillare
fluc•tu•a•tion [flʌktjʊˈeɪʃn] oscillazione *f*
flu•en•cy [ˈfluːənsɪ] *in a language* scioltezza *f*
flu•ent [ˈfluːənt] *adj* fluente; ***he speaks fluent Spanish*** parla correntemente lo spagnolo
flu•ent•ly [ˈfluːəntlɪ] *adv speak, write* correntemente
fluff [flʌf] *material* lanugine *f*; ***a bit of fluff*** un po' di lanugine
fluff•y [ˈflʌfɪ] *adj material, hair* lanuginoso; *clouds* soffice; ***fluffy toy*** peluche *m inv*
fluid [ˈfluːɪd] *n* fluido *m*
flung [flʌŋ] *pret & pp* → ***fling***
flunk [flʌŋk] *v/t Am* F essere bocciato a
flu•o•res•cent [flʊəˈresnt] *adj light* fluorescente
flur•ry [ˈflʌrɪ] *of snow* raffica *f*
flush [flʌʃ] **1** *v/t toilet* tirare l'acqua di; ***flush sth down the toilet*** buttare qc giù dal water **2** *v/i* (*go red in the face*) diventare rosso; ***the toilet won't flush*** lo sciacquone del bagno non funziona **3** *adj* (*level*) a filo; ***be flush with ...*** a filo con ...
◆ **flush away** *v/t down toilet* buttare giù dal water
◆ **flush out** *v/t rebels etc* scovare
flus•ter [ˈflʌstə(r)] *v/t* mettere in agitazione; ***get flustered*** mettersi in agitazione
flute [fluːt] MUS flauto *m* traverso; *glass* flute *m inv*
flut•ter [ˈflʌtə(r)] **1** *v/i of bird* sbattere le ali; *of wings* sbattere; *of flag* sventolare; *of heart* battere forte **2** *n* F (*bet*) piccola scommessa *f*
fly[1] [flaɪ] *n insect* mosca *f*
fly[2] [flaɪ] *n on trousers* patta *f*
fly[3] [flaɪ] (*pret* ***flew***, *pp* ***flown***) **1** *v/i* volare; *of flag* sventolare; (*rush*) precipitarsi; ***fly into a rage*** perdere le staffe **2** *v/t aeroplane* pilotare; *airline* volare con; (*transport by air*) spedire per via aerea
◆ **fly away** *v/i of bird, plane* volare via
◆ **fly back** *v/i* (*travel back*) ritornare (in aereo)
◆ **fly in 1** *v/i of plane, passengers* arrivare **2** *v/t supplies etc* mandare per via aerea
◆ **fly off** *v/i of hat etc* volare via
◆ **fly out** *v/i* partire in aereo
◆ **fly past** *v/i in formation* volare in formazione; *of time* volare
fly•ing [ˈflaɪɪŋ] *n* volare *m*
fly•ing ˈ**sau•cer** disco *m* volante
ˈ**fly•o•ver** MOT cavalcavia *m inv*
foam [fəʊm] *n on liquid* schiuma *f*
foam ˈ**rub•ber** gommapiuma® *f*
FOB [efəʊˈbiː] *abbr* (= ***free on board***) FOB
fo•cus [ˈfəʊkəs] **1** *n of attention* centro *m*; PHOT fuoco *m*; ***be in focus / be out of focus*** PHOT essere a fuoco / non essere a

fuoco **2** *v/t*: ***focus one's attention on*** focalizzare l'attenzione su **3** *v/i* mettere a fuoco

◆ **focus on** *v/t problem, issue* focalizzare l'attenzione su; PHOT mettere a fuoco

fod•der ['fɒdə(r)] foraggio *m*

foe•tal ['fiːtl] *adj* → ***fetal***

foe•tus ['fiːtəs] → ***fetus***

fog [fɒg] nebbia *f*

◆ **fog up** *v/i* (*pret & pp* ***-ged***) appannarsi

'**fog•bound** *adj* bloccato dalla nebbia

fog•gy ['fɒgɪ] *adj* nebbioso; ***I haven't the foggiest*** (***idea***) non ne ho la più pallida idea

foi•ble ['fɔɪbl] fisima *f*

foil[1] [fɔɪl] *n* carta *f* stagnola

foil[2] [fɔɪl] *v/t* (*thwart*) sventare

fold[1] [fəʊld] **1** *v/t paper etc* piegare; ***fold one's arms*** incrociare le braccia **2** *v/i of business* chiudere i battenti **3** *n in cloth etc* piega *f*

◆ **fold up 1** *v/t chairs etc* chiudere; *clothes* piegare **2** *v/i of chair, table* chiudere

fold[2] [fəʊld] *n for sheep etc* ovile *m*

fold•er ['fəʊldə(r)] *for documents* cartellina *f*; COMPUT directory *f inv*

fold•ing ['fəʊldɪŋ] *adj* pieghevole; ***folding chair*** sedia *f* pieghevole

fo•li•age ['fəʊlɪɪdʒ] fogliame *m*

folk [fəʊk] (*people*) gente *f*; ***my folk*** (*family*) i miei parenti; ***come in, folks*** F entrate, gente F

'**folk dance** danza *f* popolare

'**folk mu•sic** musica *f* folk

'**folk sing•er** cantante *m/f* folk

'**folk song** canzone *f* popolare

fol•low ['fɒləʊ] **1** *v/t* (*also understand*) seguire **2** *v/i* seguire; *logically* quadrare; ***it follows from this that …*** ne consegue che …; ***as follows*** quanto segue

◆ **follow up** *v/t letter, inquiry* dare seguito a

fol•low•er ['fɒləʊə(r)] *of politician etc* seguace *m/f*; *of football team* tifoso *m*, -a *f*; ***are you a follower of …?*** *of TV programme* segui …?

fol•low•ing ['fɒləʊɪŋ] **1** *adj* seguente **2** *n people* seguito *m*; ***the following*** quanto segue

'**fol•low-up meet•ing** riunione *f* ulteriore

'**fol•low-up vis•it** *to doctor etc* visita *f* successiva

fol•ly ['fɒlɪ] (*madness*) follia *f*

fond [fɒnd] *adj* (*loving*) affezionato; *memory* caro; ***he is fond of travel*** gli piace viaggiare

fon•dle ['fɒndl] *v/t* accarezzare

fond•ness ['fɒndnɪs] *for person* affetto *m*; *for wine, food* gusto *m*

font [fɒnt] *for printing* carattere *m*; *in church* fonte *f* battesimale

food [fuːd] cibo *m*; ***I like Italian food*** mi piace la cucina italiana; ***there's no food in the house*** non c'è niente da mangiare in casa

'**food chain** catena *f* alimentare

food•ie ['fuːdɪ] F buongustaio *m*, -a *f*

'**food mix•er** mixer *m inv*

food poi•son•ing ['fuːdpɔɪznɪŋ] intossicazione *f* alimentare

fool [fuːl] **1** *n* pazzo *m*, -a *f*; ***make a fool of o.s.*** rendersi ridicolo **2** *v/t* ingannare; ***fool s.o. into believing that …*** far credere a qu che …

◆ **fool about**, **fool around** *v/i* fare lo sciocco; *sexually* avere l'amante

◆ **fool around with** *v/t knife, drill etc* trastullarsi con; *s.o.'s wife* avere una relazione con

'**fool•har•dy** *adj* temerario

fool•ish ['fuːlɪʃ] *adj* sciocco

fool•ish•ly ['fuːlɪʃlɪ] *adv* scioccamente

'**fool•proof** *adj* a prova di idiota

foot [fʊt] (*pl* ***feet*** [fiːt]) *also measurement* piede *m*; ***on foot*** a piedi; ***I've been on my feet all day*** sono stato in piedi tutto il giorno; ***be back on one's feet*** essere di nuovo in piedi; ***at the foot of the page*** a piè di pagina; ***at the foot of the hill*** ai piedi della collina; ***put one's foot in it*** F fare una gaffe

foot•age ['fʊtɪdʒ] pellicola *f* cinematografica

'**foot•ball** (*soccer*) calcio *m*; *American style* football *m* americano; (*ball*) pallone *m* da calcio; *for American football* pallone *m* da football americano

foot•bal•ler ['fʊtbɔːlə(r)] calciatore *m*, -trice *f*

'**foot•ball hoo•li•gan** teppista *m* del calcio

'**foot•ball pitch** campo *m* da calcio

'**foot•ball play•er** *soccer* calciatore *m*, -trice *f*; *American style* giocatore *m* di football americano

'**foot•bridge** passerella *f*

foot•er ['fʊtə(r)] COMPUT piè *m* di pagina

foot•hills ['fʊthɪlz] *npl* colline *fpl* pedemontane

'**foot•hold** *in climbing* punto *m* d'appoggio; ***gain a foothold*** *fig* conquistarsi uno spazio

foot•ing ['fʊtɪŋ] (*basis*) presupposti *mpl*; ***lose one's footing*** perdere il punto d'appoggio; ***be on the same footing/a different footing*** essere sullo stesso piano / su un piano diverso; ***be on a friendly footing with …*** avere rapporti amichevoli con …

foot•lights ['fʊtlaɪts] *npl* luci *fpl* della ribalta
'**foot•mark** impronta *f* di piede
'**foot•note** nota *f* a piè di pagina
'**foot•path** sentiero *m*
'**foot•print** impronta *f* di piede
'**foot•step** passo *m*; ***follow in s.o.'s footsteps*** seguire i passi di qu
'**foot•stool** sgabello *m* per i piedi
'**foot•wear** calzatura *f*
for [fə(r)], [fɔː(r)] *prep* ◇ *purpose*, *destination etc* per; ***a train for …*** un treno per …; ***clothes for children*** abbigliamento *m* per bambini; ***it's too big / small for you*** è troppo grande / piccolo per te; ***here's a letter for you*** c'è una lettera per te; ***this is for you*** questo è per te; ***what is there for lunch?*** cosa c'è per pranzo?; ***the steak is for me*** la bistecca è per me; ***what is this for?*** a cosa serve?; ***what for?*** a che scopo?, perché?;
◇ *time* per; ***for three days / two hours*** per tre giorni / due ore; ***I have been waiting for an hour*** ho aspettato (per) un'ora; ***please get it done for Monday*** per favore, fallo per lunedì;
◇ *distance* per; ***I walked for a mile*** ho camminato per un miglio; ***it stretches for 100 miles*** si estende per 100 miglia;
◇ (*in favour of*) per; ***campaign for*** fare una campagna per; ***I am for the idea*** sono a favore dell'idea;
◇ (*instead of*, *on behalf of*) per; ***let me do that for you*** lascia che te lo faccia io, lascia che faccia questo per te; ***we are agents for …*** siamo rappresentanti di …;
◇ (*in exchange for*) per; ***I bought it for £25*** l'ho comprato per 25 sterline; ***how much did you sell it for?*** a quanto l'hai venduto?
for•bade [fə'bæd] *pret* → ***forbid***
for•bid [fə'bɪd] *v/t* (*pret* **forbade**, *pp* **forbidden**) vietare, proibire; ***forbid s.o. to do sth*** vietare *o* proibire a qu di fare qc
for•bid•den [fə'bɪdn] **1** *adj* vietato, proibito; ***smok•ing forbidden*** vietato fumare; ***park•ing forbidden*** divieto di sosta **2** *pp* → ***forbid***
for•bid•ding [fə'bɪdɪŋ] *adj* ostile
force [fɔːs] **1** *n* (*violence*) forza *f*; ***come into force*** *of law etc* entrare in vigore; ***the forces*** MIL le forze armate **2** *v/t door*, *lock* forzare; ***force s.o. to do sth*** forzare *o* costringere qu a fare qc; ***force sth open*** aprire qc con la forza
◆ **force back** *v/t tears etc* trattenere
forced [fɔːst] *adj laugh*, *smile* forzato
forced 'land•ing atterraggio *m* d'emergenza
force•ful ['fɔːsfʊl] *adj argument*, *speaker* convincente; *character* energico
force•ful•ly ['fɔːsflɪ] *adv* in modo energico
for•ceps ['fɔːseps] *npl* MED forcipe *f*
for•ci•ble ['fɔːsəbl] *adj entry* forzato; *argument* convincente
for•ci•bly ['fɔːsəblɪ] *adv restrain* con la forza
ford [fɔːd] *n* guado *m*
fore [fɔː(r)] *n*: ***come to the fore*** salire alla ribalta
'**fore•arm** avanbraccio *m*
fore•bears ['fɔːbeəz] *npl* antenati *mpl*
fore•bod•ing [fə'bəʊdɪŋ] presentimento *m*
'**fore•cast** **1** *n* previsione *f* **2** *v/t* (*pret & pp* ***forecast***) prevedere
'**fore•court** *of garage* area *f* di rifornimento
fore•fa•thers ['fɔːfɑːðəz] *npl* antenati *mpl*
'**fore•fin•ger** indice *m*
'**fore•front**: ***be in the forefront of*** essere all'avanguardia in
'**fore•gone** *adj*: ***that's a foregone conclusion*** è una conclusione scontata
'**fore•ground** primo piano *m*
'**fore•hand** *in tennis* diritto *m*
'**fore•head** fronte *f*
for•eign ['fɒrən] *adj* straniero; *trade*, *policy* estero
for•eign af•fairs *npl* affari *mpl* esteri
for•eign 'aid aiuti *mpl* ad altri paesi
for•eign 'bod•y corpo *m* estraneo
for•eign 'cur•ren•cy valuta *f* estera
for•eign•er ['fɒrənə(r)] straniero *m*, -a *f*
for•eign ex'change cambio *m* valutario
for•eign 'lan•guage lingua *f* straniera
'**For•eign Of•fice** *in UK* Ministero *m* degli esteri
for•eign 'pol•i•cy politica *f* estera
For•eign 'Sec•re•ta•ry *in UK* ministro *m* degli esteri
'**fore•man** caposquadra *m*
'**fore•most** **1** *adv* (*uppermost*) soprattutto **2** *adj* (*leading*) principale
fo•ren•sic 'medi•cine [fə'renzɪk] medicina *f* legale
fo•ren•sic 'scien•tist medico *m* legale
'**fore•run•ner** precursore *m*
fore•ˌsaw *pret* → ***foresee***
foreˌsee *v/t* (*pret* **foresaw**, *pp* **foreseen**) prevedere
fore•see•a•ble [fə'siːəbl] *adj* prevedibile; ***in the foreseeable future*** per quanto si possa prevedere in futuro
foreˌseen *pp* → ***foresee***

F

'fore•sight lungimiranza *f*
for•est ['fɒrɪst] foresta *f*
for•est•er ['fɒrɪstə(r)] guardaboschi *m/f*
for•est•ry ['fɒrɪstrɪ] scienze *fpl* forestali
'fore•taste anteprima *m*, assaggio *m*
fore'tell *v/t* (*pret & pp* ***foretold***) predire
fore'told *pret & pp* → ***foretell***
for•ev•er [fə'revə(r)] *adv* per sempre; ***it is forever raining here*** piova continuamente qui
for•gave [fə'geɪv] *pret* → ***forgive***
fore•word ['fɔːwɜːd] prefazione *f*
for•feit ['fɔːfɪt] *v/t right, privilege etc* perdere
forge [fɔːdʒ] *v/t* (*counterfeit*) contraffare; *signature* falsificare
◆ **forge ahead** *v/i* prendere il sopravvento
forg•er ['fɔːdʒə(r)] falsario *m*, -a *f*
forg•er•y ['fɔːdʒərɪ] (*banknote*) falsificazione *f*; (*document*) falso *m*
for•get [fə'get] *v/t* (*pret* ***forgot***, *pp* ***forgotten***) dimenticare; ***forget him, he's a waste of time*** lascialo perdere, ti fa solo perdere tempo
for•get•ful [fə'getfʊl] *adj* smemorato
for'get-me-not non-ti-scordar-di-me *m inv*
for•give [fə'gɪv] *v/t & v/i* (*pret* ***forgave***, *pp* ***forgiven***) perdonare
for•given [fə'gɪvn] *pp* → ***forgive***
for•give•ness [fə'gɪvnɪs] perdono *m*
for•got [fə'gɒt] *pret* → ***forget***
for•got•ten [fə'gɒtn] *pp* → ***forget***
fork [fɔːk] *n for eating* forchetta *f*; *for gardening* forca *f*; *in road* biforcazione *f*
◆ **fork out** *v/t & v/i* F (*pay*) sborsare F
fork•lift 'truck muletto *m*
form [fɔːm] **1** *n* (*shape*) forma *f*; (*document*) modulo *m*; *in school* classe *f*; ***be on / off form*** essere in / fuori forma; ***in the form of*** sotto forma di **2** *v/t in clay etc* modellare; *friendship* creare; *opinion* formarsi; *past tense etc* formare; (*constitute*) costituire **3** *v/i* (*take shape*, *develop*) formarsi
form•al ['fɔːml] *adj* formale
for•mal•i•ty [fə'mælətɪ] formalità *f inv*; ***it's just a formality*** è solo una formalità; ***the formalities*** le formalità
for•mal•ly ['fɔːməlɪ] *adv* formalmente
for•mat ['fɔːmæt] **1** *v/t* (*pret & pp* ***-ted***) *diskette* formattare; *document* impaginare **2** *n* (*size*: *of magazine etc*) formato *m*; (*makeup*: *of programme*) formula *f*
for•ma•tion [fɔː'meɪʃn] formazione *f*
for•ma•tive ['fɔːmətɪv] *adj* formativo; ***in his formative years*** nei suoi anni formativi
for•mer ['fɔːmə(r)] *adj wife*, *president* ex *inv*; *statement*, *arrangement* precedente; ***the former*** quest'ultimo
for•mer•ly ['fɔːməlɪ] *adv* precedentemente
for•mi•da•ble ['fɔːmɪdəbl] *adj* imponente
for•mu•la ['fɔːmjʊlə] formula *f*
for•mu•late ['fɔːmjʊleɪt] *v/t* (*express*) formulare
for•ni•cate ['fɔːnɪkeɪt] *v/i fml* fornicare
for•ni•ca•tion [fɔːnɪ'keɪʃn] *fml* fornicazione *f*
fort [fɔːt] MIL forte *m*
forth [fɔːθ] *adv*: ***back and forth*** avanti e indietro; ***and so forth*** eccetera; ***from that day forth*** da quel giorno in poi
forth•com•ing ['fɔːθkʌmɪŋ] *adj* (*future*) prossimo; *personality* comunicativo
'forth•right *adj* schietto
for•ti•eth ['fɔːtɪɪθ] *n & adj* quarantesimo, -a
fort•night ['fɔːtnaɪt] due settimane
for•tress ['fɔːtrɪs] MIL fortezza *f*
for•tu•nate ['fɔːtʃʊnət] *adj* fortunato
for•tu•nate•ly ['fɔːtʃʊnətlɪ] *adv* fortunatamente
for•tune ['fɔːtʃuːn] sorte *f*; (*lot of money*) fortuna *f*; ***tell s.o.'s fortune*** predire il futuro a qu
'for•tune-tell•er chiromante *m/f*
for•ty ['fɔːtɪ] quaranta; ***have forty winks*** F fare un pisolino F
Fo•rum ['fɔːrəm] *Roman* foro *m*
fo•rum ['fɔːrəm] *fig* foro *m*
for•ward ['fɔːwəd] **1** *adv* avanti **2** *adj pej*: *person* diretto **3** *n* SP attaccante *m* **4** *v/t letter* inoltrare
'for•ward•ing ad•dress ['fɔːwədɪŋ] recapito *m*
'for•ward•ing a•gent COM spedizioniere *m*
'for•ward-look•ing *adj* progressista
fos•sil ['fɒsəl] fossile *m*
fos•sil•ized ['fɒsəlaɪzd] *adj* fossilizzato
fos•ter ['fɒstə(r)] *v/t child* avere in affidamento; *attitude*, *belief* incoraggiare
'fos•ter child figlio *m*, -a *f* in affidamento
'fos•ter home famiglia *f* di accoglienza
'fos•ter par•ents *npl* genitori *mpl* con affidamento
fought [fɔːt] *pret & pp* → ***fight***
foul [faʊl] **1** *n* SP fallo *m* **2** *adj smell*, *taste* pessimo; *weather* orribile **3** *v/t* SP fare un fallo contro
found[1] [faʊnd] *v/t school etc* fondare
found[2] [faʊnd] *pret & pp* → ***find***
foun•da•tion [faʊn'deɪʃn] *of theory etc* fondamenta *fpl*; (*organization*) fondazione *f*; *make-up* fondotinta *m*

foun•da•tions [faʊn'deɪʃnz] *npl of building* fondamenta *fpl*
found•er ['faʊndə(r)] *n* fondatore *m*, -trice *f*
found•ing ['faʊndɪŋ] *n* fondazione *f*
foun•dry ['faʊndrɪ] fonderia *f*
foun•tain ['faʊntɪn] fontana *f*
'**foun•tain pen** penna *f* stilografica
four [fɔː(r)] **1** *adj* quattro **2** *n*: ***on all fours*** a quattro zampe
four-let•ter '**word** parolaccia *f*
four-post•er ('**bed**) letto *m* a baldacchino
'**four-star** *adj hotel etc* a quattro stelle
four-star ('**pet•rol**) super *f*
four•teen [fɔː'tiːn] quattordici
four•teenth ['fɔːtiːnθ] *n & adj* quattordicesimo, -a
fourth [fɔːθ] *n & adj* quarto, -a
four-wheel '**drive** MOT quattro per quattro *m inv*
fowl [faʊl] pollame *m*
fox [fɒks] **1** *n* volpe *f* **2** *v/t* (*puzzle*) mettere in difficoltà
foy•er ['fɔɪeɪ] atrio *m*
frac•tion ['frækʃn] frazione *f*
frac•tion•al•ly ['frækʃnəlɪ] *adv* lievemente
frac•ture ['fræktʃə(r)] **1** *n* frattura *f* **2** *v/t* fratturare
fra•gile ['frædʒaɪl] *adj* fragile
frag•ment ['frægmənt] *n* frammento *m*
frag•men•tar•y [fræg'mentərɪ] *adj* frammentario
fra•grance ['freɪgrəns] fragranza *f*
fra•grant ['freɪgrənt] *adj* profumato
frail [freɪl] *adj* gracile
frame [freɪm] **1** *n of picture, window* cornice *f*; *of glasses* montatura *f*; *of bicycle* telaio *m*; ***frame of mind*** stato *m* d'animo **2** *v/t picture* incorniciare; F *person* incastrare F
'**frame-up** F montatura *f*
'**frame•work** struttura *f*
France [frɑːns] Francia *f*
fran•chise ['fræntʃaɪz] *n for business* concessione *f*
frank [fræŋk] *adj* franco
frank•furt•er ['fræŋkfɜːtə(r)] wurstel *m inv*
frank•ly ['fræŋklɪ] *adv* francamente
frank•ness ['fræŋknɪs] franchezza *f*
fran•tic ['fræntɪk] *adj search, attempt* frenetico; (*worried*) agitatissimo
fran•ti•cal•ly ['fræntɪklɪ] *adv* freneticamente
fra•ter•nal [frə'tɜːnl] *adj* fraterno
fraud [frɔːd] frode *f*; *person* impostore *m*, -trice *f*
fraud•u•lent ['frɔːdjʊlənt] *adj* fraudolento
fraud•u•lent•ly ['frɔːdjʊləntlɪ] *adv* in modo fraudolento
frayed [freɪd] *adj cuffs* liso
freak [friːk] **1** *n unusual event* fenomeno *m* anomalo; *two-headed person, animal etc* scherzo *m* di natura; F *strange person* tipo *m*, -a *f* strambo, -a; ***movie / jazz freak*** F (*fanatic*) fanatico *m*, -a *f* del cinema / del jazz **2** *adj wind, storm etc* violento

F

freck•le ['frekl] lentiggine *f*
free [friː] **1** *adj* (*at liberty, not occupied*) libero; (*no cost*) gratuito; ***are you free this afternoon?*** sei libero oggi pomeriggio?; ***free and easy*** spensierato; ***for free*** *travel, get sth* gratis **2** *v/t prisoners* liberare
free•bie ['friːbɪ] F omaggio *m*
free•dom ['friːdəm] libertà *f*
free•dom of '**speech** libertà *f* di parola
free•dom of the '**press** libertà *f* di stampa
free '**en•ter•prise** liberalismo *m* economico
free '**kick** *in soccer* calcio *m* di punizione
free•lance ['friːlɑːns] **1** *adj* free lance *inv* **2** *adv work* free lance *inv*
free•lanc•er ['friːlɑːnsə(r)] free lance *m/f inv*
free•ly ['friːlɪ] *adv admit* apertamente
free mar•ket e'con•o•my economia *f* del libero mercato
free-range '**chick•en** pollo *m* ruspante
free-range '**eggs** *npl* uova *fpl* di galline ruspanti
free '**sam•ple** campione *m* gratuito
free '**speech** libertà *f* di espressione
'**free•way** *Am* autostrada *f*
free'wheel *v/i on bicycle* andare a ruota libera
freeze [friːz] (*pret* **froze**, *pp* **frozen**) **1** *v/t food, river* gelare; *wages, account* congelare; *video* bloccare **2** *v/i of water* gelare
◆ **freeze over** *v/i of river* gelare
'**freeze-dried** *adj* liofilizzato
freez•er ['friːzə(r)] freezer *m inv*, congelatore *m*
freez•ing ['friːzɪŋ] **1** *adj* gelato; ***it's freezing out here*** si gela qui fuori; ***it's freezing*** (***cold***) *of weather* si gela; *of water* è gelata; ***I'm freezing*** (***cold***) sono congelato **2** *n*: ***10 below freezing*** 10 gradi sotto zero
'**freez•ing com•part•ment** freezer *m inv*
'**freez•ing point** punto *m* di congelamento
freight [freɪt] *n* carico *m*; *costs* trasporto *m*
freight•er ['freɪtə(r)] *ship* nave *f* da cari-

co; *aeroplane* aereo *f* da carico
French [frentʃ] **1** *adj* francese **2** *n* (*language*) francese *m*; ***the French*** i francesi
French 'bread baguette *fpl*
'French fries *npl* patate *fpl* fritte
'French•man francese *m*
French 'stick baguette *f inv*
French 'win•dows *npl* vetrata *f*
'French•wom•an francese *f*

F

fren•zied ['frenzɪd] *adj attack, activity* frenetico; *mob* impazzito
fren•zy ['frenzɪ] frenesia *f*
fre•quen•cy ['friːkwənsɪ] frequenza *f*
fre•quent¹ ['friːkwənt] *adj* frequente
fre•quent² [frɪ'kwent] *v/t bar etc* frequentare
fre•quent•ly ['frɪkwentlɪ] *adv* frequentemente
fres•co ['freskəʊ] affresco *m*
fresh [freʃ] *adj fruit, meat etc*, (*cold*) fresco; (*new: start*) nuovo
fresh 'air aria *f* fresca
fresh•en ['freʃn] *v/i of wind* rinfrescare
◆ **freshen up 1** *v/i* rinfrescarsi **2** *v/t room, paintwork* rinfrescare
'fresh•er ['freʃə(r)] matricola *f*
fresh•ly ['freʃlɪ] *adv* appena
fresh•ness ['freʃnɪs] *of fruit, meat, climate* freschezza *f*; *of style, approach* novità *f*
fresh 'or•ange spremuta *f* d'arancia
'fresh•wa•ter *adj* d'acqua dolce
fret [fret] *v/i* (*pret & pp* ***-ted***) agitarsi
Freud•i•an ['frɔɪdɪən] *adj* freudiano
fric•tion ['frɪkʃn] PHYS frizione *f*; *between people* attrito *m*
Fri•day ['fraɪdeɪ] venerdì *m inv*
fridge [frɪdʒ] frigo *m*
fried 'egg [fraɪd] uovo *m* fritto
fried po'ta•toes *npl* patate *fpl* saltate
friend [frend] amico *m*, -a *f*; ***make friends*** fare amicizia; ***make friends with s.o.*** fare amicizia con qu
friend•li•ness ['frendlɪnɪs] amichevolezza *f*
friend•ly ['frendlɪ] **1** *adj* amichevole; (*easy to use*) facile da usare; ***be friendly with s.o.*** (*be friends*) essere in rapporti d'amicizia con qu; ***they're very friendly*** *with each other* sono molto in confidenza; ***he started getting too friendly*** ha cominciato a prendersi troppa confidenza **2** *n* SP amichevole *f*
'friend•ship ['frendʃɪp] amicizia *f*
fries [fraɪz] *npl* patate *fpl* fritte
fright [fraɪt] paura *f*; ***give s.o. a fright*** far paura a qu
fright•en ['fraɪtn] *v/t* spaventare; ***be frightened*** (***of***) aver paura (di); ***don't be frightened*** non aver paura
◆ **frighten away** *v/t* far scappare
fright•en•ing ['fraɪtnɪŋ] *adj* spaventoso
fri•gid ['frɪdʒɪd] *adj sexually* frigido
frill [frɪl] *on dress etc* volant *m inv*; ***frills*** (*fancy extras*) fronzoli *mpl*
frill•y ['frɪlɪ] *adj* pieno di volant
fringe [frɪndʒ] frangia *f*; (*edge*) margini *mpl*
fringe ben•e•fits *npl* benefici *mpl* accessori
frisk [frɪsk] *v/t* F frugare F
frisk•y ['frɪskɪ] *adj puppy etc* vivace
◆ **fritter away** ['frɪtə(r)] *v/t time, fortune* sprecare
fri•vol•i•ty [frɪ'vɒlətɪ] frivolezza *f*
friv•o•lous ['frɪvələs] *adj person, pleasures* frivolo
frizz•y ['frɪzɪ] *adj hair* crespo
frog [frɒg] rana *f*
'frog•man sommozzatore *m*, -trice *f*
from [frɒm] *prep* ◇ *in time* da; ***from 9 to 5*** (***o'clock***) dalle 9 alle 5; ***from the 18th century*** dal XVIII secolo; ***from today on*** da oggi in poi; ***from next Tuesday*** da martedì della prossima settimana ◇ *in space* da; ***from here to there*** da qui a lì; ***we drove here from Paris*** siamo venuti qui in macchina da Parigi ◇ *origin* di; ***a letter from Jo*** una lettera di Jo; ***a gift from the management*** un regalo della direzione; ***it doesn't say who it's from*** non c'è scritto di chi è; ***I am from Liverpool*** sono di Liverpool; ***made from bananas*** fatto di banane ◇ (*because of*) di; ***tired from the journey*** stanco del viaggio; ***it's from overeating*** è a causa del troppo mangiare
front [frʌnt] **1** *n of building* lato *m* principale; *of car, statue* davanti *m inv*; *of book* copertina *f*; (*cover organization*) facciata *f*; MIL, *of weather* fronte *m*; ***in front*** davanti; ***in front of*** davanti a; ***at the front*** davanti; ***at the front of*** *of bus etc* nella parte anteriore di **2** *adj wheel, seat* anteriore **3** *v/t TV programme* presentare
front 'bench POL *principali esponenti mpl del governo e dell'opposizione nel Parlamento*
front 'cov•er copertina *f*
front 'door porta *f* principale
front 'en•trance entrata *f* principale
fron•tier ['frʌntɪə(r)] *also fig* frontiera *f*
'front 'line MIL fronte *m*
front 'page *of newspaper* prima pagina *f*
front page 'news *nsg* notizia *f* di prima pagina
front 'row prima fila *f*
front seat 'pas•sen•ger *in car* passeggero

m davanti
front-wheel 'drive trazione *f* anteriore
frost [frɒst] *n* brina *f*
'frost•bite congelamento *m*
'frost•bit•ten *adj* congelato
frosted glass ['frɒstɪd] vetro *m* smerigliato
frost•y ['frɒstɪ] *adj also fig* gelido
froth [frɒθ] *n* spuma *f*
froth•y ['frɒθɪ] *adj cream etc* spumoso
frown [fraʊn] **1** *n* cipiglio *m* **2** *v/i* aggrottare le sopracciglia
froze [frəʊz] *pret* → ***freeze***
fro•zen ['frəʊzn] **1** *adj* gelato; *wastes* gelido; *food* surgelato; ***I'm frozen*** F sono congelato F **2** *pp* → ***freeze***
fro•zen 'food cibi *mpl* surgelati
fruit [fruːt] frutto *m*; *collective* frutta *f*
'fruit cake *dolce f con frutta candita*
fruit•ful ['fruːtfʊl] *adj discussions etc* fruttuoso
'fruit juice succo *m* di frutta
'fruit ma•chine slot machine *f inv*
fruit 'sal•ad macedonia *f*
frus•trate [frʌ'streɪt] *v/t person* frustrare; *plans* scombussolare
frus•trat•ed [frʌ'streɪtɪd] *adj look, sigh* frustrato
frus•trat•ing [frʌ'streɪtɪŋ] *adj* frustrante
frus•trat•ing•ly [frʌ'streɪtɪŋlɪ] *adv slow, hard* in modo frustrante
frus•tra•tion [frʌ'streɪʃn] frustrazione *f*; ***sexual frustration*** insoddisfazione *f* sessuale; ***the frustrations of modern life*** le frustrazioni della vita moderna
fry [fraɪ] *v/t* (*pret & pp* ***-ied***) friggere
fry•ing pan ['fraɪɪŋ] padella *f*
fuck [fʌk] *v/t* V scopare V; ***fuck!*** cazzo!
◆ **fuck off** *v/i* V andare affanculo V; ***fuck off!*** vaffanculo!
fuck•ing ['fʌkɪŋ] **1** *adj* V del cazzo V **2** *adv* V; ***I'm fucking late!*** V sono in ritardo, cazzo!; ***I'm fucking tired*** cazzo, come sono stanco
fu•el ['fjuːəl] **1** *n* carburante *m* **2** *v/t fig* alimentare
fu•gi•tive ['fjuːdʒətɪv] *n* fuggiasco *m*, -a *f*
ful•fil, *Am* **ful•fill** [fʊl'fɪl] *v/t* (*pret & pp* ***-led***) *dreams* realizzare; *needs, expectations* soddisfare; *contract* eseguire; *requirements* corrispondere a; ***feel fulfillled*** *in job, life* sentirsi soddisfatto
ful•fil•ment, *Am* **ful•fill•ment** [fʊl'fɪlmənt] *of contract* esecuzione *f*; *of dreams* realizzazione *f*; *moral, spiritual* soddisfazione *f*
full [fʊl] *adj* pieno (***of*** di); *account, report* esauriente; *life* intenso; ***full up*** *hotel, with food* pieno; ***in full*** *write* per intero; ***pay in full*** saldare il conto
full 'board pensione *f* completa
'full-grown *adj* adulto; ***full-grown adult*** *person* adulto in età matura; *animal* adulto completamente sviluppato
'full-length *adj dress* lungo; ***full-length film*** lungometraggio *m*
full 'moon luna *f* piena
full 'stop punto *m* fermo
full-'time *adj & adv worker, job* a tempo pieno
ful•ly ['fʊlɪ] *adv booked, recovered* completamente; *understand, explain* perfettamente; *describe* ampiamente
fum•ble ['fʌmbl] *v/t catch* farsi sfuggire
◆ **fumble about** *v/i in bags, pockets* frugare; *move in the dark* andare a tastoni; *search in the dark* cercare a tastoni
fume [fjuːm] *v/i*: ***be fuming*** F (*be very angry*) essere nero F
fumes [fjuːmz] *npl* esalazioni *fpl*
fun [fʌn] divertimento *m*; ***it was great fun*** era molto divertente; ***bye, have fun!*** ciao, divertiti!; ***for fun*** per divertirsi; (*joking*) per scherzo; ***make fun of*** prendere in giro
func•tion ['fʌŋkʃn] **1** *n* (*purpose*) funzione *f*; (*reception etc*) cerimonia *f* **2** *v/i* funzionare; ***function as*** servire da
func•tion•al ['fʌŋkʃnl] *adj* funzionale
fund [fʌnd] **1** *n* fondo *m* **2** *v/t project etc* finanziare
fun•da•men•tal [fʌndə'mentl] *adj* fondamentale
fun•da•men•tal•ist [fʌndə'mentlɪst] *n* fondamentalista *m/f*
fun•da•men•tal•ly [fʌndə'mentlɪ] *adv* fondamentalmente
fund•ing ['fʌndɪŋ] *money* fondi *mpl*
fu•ne•ral ['fjuːnərəl] funerale *m*
'fu•ne•ral di•rec•tor impresario *m* delle pompe funebri
'fu•ne•ral home *Am*, **'fu•ne•ral par•lour** obitorio *m*
'fun•fair luna park *m inv*
fun•gus ['fʌŋgəs] fungo *m*
fu•nic•u•lar ('rail•way) [fjuː'nɪkjʊlə(r)] funicolare *f*
fun•nel ['fʌnl] *n of ship* imbuto *m*
fun•ni•ly ['fʌnɪlɪ] *adv* (*oddly*) stranamente; (*comically*) in modo divertente; ***funnily enough*** per quanto strano
fun•ny ['fʌnɪ] *adj* (*comical*) divertente; (*odd*) strano
'fun•ny bone osso *m* del gomito
fur [fɜː(r)] pelliccia *f*; *on animal* pelo *m*
fu•ri•ous ['fjʊərɪəs] *adj* (*angry*) furioso; (*intense*) spaventoso; ***at a furious pace*** a tutta velocità

fur•nace ['fɜːnɪs] forno *m*
fur•nish ['fɜːnɪʃ] *v/t room* arredare; (*supply*) fornire
fur•ni•ture ['fɜːnɪtʃə(r)] mobili *mpl*; ***a piece of furniture*** un mobile
fur•ry ['fɜːrɪ] *adj animal* coperto di pelliccia
fur•ther ['fɜːðə(r)] **1** *adj* (*additional*) ulteriore; (*more distant*) più lontano; ***until further notice*** fino a nuovo avviso; ***have you anything further to say?*** ha qualcosa da aggiungere? **2** *adv walk, drive* oltre; ***further, I want to say ...*** inoltre, volevo dire ...; ***two miles further*** (***on***) due miglia più avanti **3** *v/t cause etc* favorire
fur•ther ed•u'ca•tion *istruzione f universitaria o para-universitaria*
fur•ther'more *adv* inoltre
fur•thest ['fɜːðɪst] **1** *adj* più lontano **2** *adv*: ***this is the furthest north*** è il punto più a nord; ***the furthest man has travelled in space*** il punto più lontano che si è raggiunto nello spazio
fur•tive ['fɜːtɪv] *adj glance* furtivo
fur•tive•ly ['fɜːtɪvlɪ] *adv* furtivamente
fu•ry ['fjʊərɪ] (*anger*) furore *m*

F

fuse [fjuːz] **1** *n* ELEC fusibile *m* **2** *v/i* ELEC bruciarsi **3** *v/t* ELEC bruciare
'fuse•box scatola *f* dei fusibili
fu•se•lage ['fjuːzəlɑːʒ] fusoliera *f*
'fuse wire filo *m* per fusibili
fu•sion ['fjuːʒn] fusione *f*
fuss [fʌs] *n* agitazione *f*; *about film, event* scalpore *m*; ***make a fuss*** *complain* fare storie; *behave in exaggerated way* agitarsi; ***make a fuss of*** *be very attentive to* colmare qu di attenzioni
fuss•y ['fʌsɪ] *adj person* difficile; *design etc* complicato; ***be a fussy eater*** essere schizzinoso nel mangiare
fu•tile ['fjuːtaɪl] *adj* futile
fu•til•i•ty [fjuː'tɪlətɪ] futilità *f inv*
fu•ture ['fjuːtʃə(r)] **1** *n* futuro *m*; ***in future*** in futuro **2** *adj* futuro
fu•tures ['fjuːtʃəz] *npl* FIN titoli *mpl* a termine
'fu•tures mar•ket FIN mercato *m* dei titoli a termine
fu•tur•is•tic [fjuːtʃə'rɪstɪk] *adj design* futuristico
fuzz•y ['fʌzɪ] *adj hair* crespo; (*out of focus*) sfuocato

G

gab [gæb] *n*: ***have the gift of the gab*** F avere la parlantina F
gab•ble ['gæbl] *v/i* parlare troppo in fretta
◆ **gad about** [gæd] *v/i* (*pret & pp* ***-ded***) andarsene in giro
gad•get ['gædʒɪt] congegno *m*
Gael•ic ['geɪlɪk] *n language* gaelico *m*
gaffe [gæf] gaffe *f inv*
gag [gæg] **1** *n* bavaglio *m*; (*joke*) battuta *f* **2** *v/t* (*pret & pp* ***-ged***) *person* imbavagliare; *the press* azzittire
gai•ly ['geɪlɪ] *adv* (*blythely*) allegramente
gain [geɪn] *v/t* (*acquire*) acquisire, acquistare; ***gain speed*** acquistare velocità; ***gain 10 pounds*** aumentare di 10 libbre
ga•la ['gɑːlə] *concert etc* serata *f* di gala
gal•ax•y ['gæləksɪ] AST galassia *f*
gale [geɪl] bufera *f*
gal•lant ['gælənt] *adj* galante
gall blad•der ['gɔːlblædə(r)] cistifellea *f*
gal•le•ry ['gælərɪ] galleria *f*
gal•ley ['gælɪ] *on ship* cambusa *f*
◆ **gal•li•vant around** ['gælɪvænt] *v/i* andarsene a spasso
gal•lon ['gælən] gallone *m*; ***gallons of tea*** F litri *mpl* di tè
gal•lop ['gæləp] *v/i* galoppare
gal•lows ['gæləʊz] *npl* forca *fsg*
gall•stone ['gɔːlstəʊn] calcolo *m* biliare
ga•lore [gə'lɔ(r)] *adj*: ***apples / novels galore*** mele / romanzi a iosa
gal•va•nize ['gælvənaɪz] *v/t* TECH galvanizzare; *fig* stimolare
gam•ble ['gæmbl] *v/i* giocare (d'azzardo)
gam•bler ['gæmblə(r)] giocatore *m*, -trice *f* (d'azzardo)
gam•bling ['gæmblɪŋ] *n* gioco *m* (d'azzardo)
game [geɪm] *n* gioco *m*; (*match, in tennis*) partita *f*
'**game•keep•er** guardacaccia *m/f inv*
'**game re•serve** riserva *f* di caccia
gam•mon ['gæmən] coscia *f* di maiale affumicata
gang [gæŋ] banda *f*
◆ **gang up on** *v/t* mettersi contro
'**gang rape 1** *n* stupro *m* collettivo **2** *v/t* stuprare in massa
gan•grene ['gæŋgriːn] MED cancrena *f*
gang•ster ['gæŋstə(r)] malvivente *m*, gangster *m inv*
'**gang war•fare** guerra *f* tra bande
'**gang•way** passaggio *m*; *for ship* passerella *f*
gaol [dʒeɪl] → ***jail***
gap [gæp] *in wall, for parking* buco *m*; *in conversation, life* vuoto *m*; *in time* intervallo *m*; *in story, education* lacuna *f*; *between two people's characters* scarto *m*
gape [geɪp] *v/i of person* rimanere a bocca aperta; *of hole* spalancarsi
◆ **gape at** *v/t* guardare a bocca aperta
gap•ing ['geɪpɪŋ] *adj hole* spalancato
'**gap year** *anno m tra la fine del liceo e l'inizio dell'università dedicato ad altre attività*
gar•age ['gærɪdʒ] *n for parking* garage *m inv*; *for petrol* stazione *f* di servizio; *for repairs* officina *f*
gar•bage ['gɑːbɪdʒ] rifiuti *mpl*; (*fig: nonsense*) idiozie *fpl*
gar•bled ['gɑːbld] *adj message* ingarbugliato
gar•den ['gɑːdn] giardino *m*; *for vegetables* orto *m*
'**gar•den cen•ter** *Am*, '**gar•den cen•tre** centro *m* per il giardinaggio
gar•den•er ['gɑːdnə(r)] giardiniere *m*, -a *f*
gar•den•ing ['gɑːdnɪŋ] giardinaggio *m*
gar•gle ['gɑːgl] *v/i* fare i gargarismi
gar•goyle ['gɑːgɔɪl] ARCHI gargouille *f inv*
gar•ish ['geərɪʃ] *adj* sgargiante
gar•land ['gɑːlənd] *n* ghirlanda *f*
gar•lic ['gɑːlɪk] aglio *m*
gar•lic '**bread** pane *m* all'aglio
gar•ment ['gɑːmənt] capo *m* d'abbigliamento
gar•nish ['gɑːnɪʃ] *v/t* guarnire
gar•ret ['gærɪt] soffitta *f*
gar•ri•son ['gærɪsn] *n* guarnigione *f*
gar•ter ['gɑːtə(r)] giarrettiera *f*
gas [gæs] *n* gas *m inv*; (*esp Am: gasoline*) benzina *f*
'**gas bill** bolletta *f* del gas
gash [gæʃ] *n* taglio *m*
gas•ket ['gæskɪt] guarnizione *f*
'**gas man** impiegato *m* del gas
'**gas me•ter** contatore *m* del gas
gas•o•line ['gæsəliːn] *Am* benzina *f*
gasp [gɑːsp] **1** *n* sussulto *m* **2** *v/i* rimanere senza fiato; ***gasp for breath*** essere senza fiato; ***he collapsed gasping for breath*** si è accasciato senza fiato
'**gas pipe•line** gasdotto *m*
'**gas ped•al** *Am* acceleratore *m*
'**gas sta•tion** *Am* stazione *f* di rifornimento
'**gas stove** cucina *f* a gas

gas•tric ['gæstrɪk] *adj* MED gastrico
gas•tric 'flu MED influenza *f* intestinale
gas•tric 'juices *npl* succhi *mpl* gastrici
gas•tric 'ul•cer MED ulcera *f* gastrica
gate [geɪt] cancello *m*; *of city, castle, at airport* porta *f*
ga•teau ['gætəʊ] torta *f*
'gate•crash *v/t* intrufolarsi in
'gate•way ingresso *m*; *fig* via *f* d'accesso
gath•er ['gæðə(r)] **1** *v/t facts, information* raccogliere; ***gather speed*** acquistare velocità; ***am I to gather that …?*** devo dedurre che …? **2** *v/i* (*understand*) dedurre
◆ **gather up** *v/t possessions* radunare
gather•ing ['gæðərɪŋ] *n* (*group of people*) raduno *m*
gau•dy ['gɔːdɪ] *adj* pacchiano
gauge [geɪdʒ] **1** *n* indicatore *m* **2** *v/t pressure* misurare; *opinion* valutare
gaunt [gɔːnt] *adj* smunto
gauze [gɔːz] garza *f*
gave [geɪv] *pret* → ***give***
gaw•ky ['gɔːkɪ] *adj* impacciato
gawp [gɔːp] *v/i* F fissare come un ebete F; ***gawp at sth*** fissare qc con aria inebetita
gay [geɪ] **1** *n* (*homosexual*) omosessuale *m/f* **2** *adj* omosessuale; *club* gay *inv*
gaze [geɪz] **1** *n* sguardo *m* **2** *v/i* fissare
◆ **gaze at** *v/t* fissare
GB [dʒiː'biː] *abbr* (= ***Great Britain***) GB (= Gran Bretagna *f*)
GDP [dʒiːdiː'piː] *abbr* (= ***gross domestic product***) PIL *m* (= prodotto *m* interno lordo)
gear [gɪə(r)] *n* (*equipment*) equipaggiamento *m*; *in vehicles* marcia *f*
'gear•box MOT scatola *f* del cambio
'gear le•ver, **'gear shift** MOT leva *f* del cambio
geese [giːs] *pl* → ***goose***
gel [dʒel] *for hair, shower* gel *m inv*
gel•a•tine ['dʒelətiːn] gelatina *f*
gel•ig•nite ['dʒelɪgnaɪt] gelignite *f*
gem [dʒem] gemma *f*; *fig*: *book etc* capolavoro *m*; *person* perla *f* rara
Gem•i•ni ['dʒemɪnaɪ] ASTR Gemelli *mpl*
gen•der ['dʒendə(r)] genere *m*
gene [dʒiːn] gene *m*; ***it's in his genes*** è una sua caratteristica innata
gen•e•ral ['dʒenrəl] **1** *n* MIL generale *m*; ***in general*** in generale **2** *adj* generale
gen•e•ral e'lec•tion elezioni *fpl* politiche
gen•er•al•i•za•tion [dʒenrəlaɪ'zeɪʃn] generalizzazione *f*
gen•e•ral•ize ['dʒenrəlaɪz] *v/i* generalizzare
gen•er•al•ly ['dʒenrəlɪ] *adv* generalmente; ***generally speaking*** in generale
gen•e•ral prac'ti•tion•er medico *m* generico
gen•e•rate ['dʒenəreɪt] *v/t* generare; *in linguistics* formare
gen•e•ra•tion [dʒenə'reɪʃn] generazione *f*
gen•e'ra•tion gap scarto *m* generazionale
gen•e•ra•tor ['dʒenəreɪtə(r)] ELEC generatore *m*
ge•ner•ic drug [dʒə'nerɪk] MED *medicina f senza una marca specifica*
gen•e•ros•i•ty [dʒenə'rɒsɪtɪ] generosità *f*
gen•e•rous ['dʒenərəs] *adj* generoso
ge•net•ic [dʒɪ'netɪk] *adj* genetico
ge•net•i•cal•ly [dʒɪ'netɪklɪ] *adv* geneticamente; ***genetically modified*** transgenico
ge•net•ic 'code codice *m* genetico
ge•net•ic en•gi'neer•ing ingegneria *f* genetica
ge•net•ic 'fin•ger•print esame *m* del DNA
ge•net•i•cist [dʒɪ'netɪsɪst] genetista *m/f*
ge•net•ics [dʒɪ'netɪks] genetica *f*
ge•ni•al ['dʒiːnɪəl] *adj person, company* gioviale
gen•i•tals ['dʒenɪtlz] *npl* genitali *mpl*
ge•ni•us ['dʒiːnɪəs] genio *m*
Gen•o•a ['dʒenəʊə] Genova *f*
gen•o•cide ['dʒenəsaɪd] genocidio *m*
gen•tle ['dʒentl] *adj* delicato; *breeze, slope* dolce
gen•tle•man ['dʒentlmən] signore *m*; ***he's a real gentleman*** è un vero gentleman
gen•tle•ness ['dʒentlnɪs] delicatezza *f*; *of breeze, slope* dolcezza *f*
gen•tly ['dʒentlɪ] *adv* delicatamente; *blow, slope* dolcemente
gents [dʒents] *toilet* bagno *m* degli uomini
gen•u•ine ['dʒenjʊɪn] *adj* autentico; (*sincere*) sincero
gen•u•ine•ly ['dʒenjʊɪnlɪ] *adv* sinceramente
ge•o•graph•i•cal [dʒɪə'græfɪkl] *adj* geografico
ge•og•ra•phy [dʒɪ'ɒgrəfɪ] geografia *f*
ge•o•log•i•cal [dʒɪə'lɒdʒɪkl] *adj* geologico
ge•ol•o•gist [dʒɪ'ɒlədʒɪst] geologo *m*, -a *f*
ge•ol•o•gy [dʒɪ'ɒlədʒɪ] geologia *f*
ge•o•met•ric, **ge•o•met•ri•cal** [dʒɪə'metrɪk(l)] *adj* geometrico
ge•om•e•try [dʒɪ'ɒmətrɪ] geometria *f*
ge•ra•ni•um [dʒə'reɪnɪəm] geranio *m*
ger•i•at•ric [dʒerɪ'ætrɪk] **1** *adj* geriatrico **2** *n* anziano *m*, -a *f*
germ [dʒɜːm] *also fig* germe *m*
Ger•man ['dʒɜːmən] **1** *adj* tedesco **2** *n person* tedesco *m*, -a *f*; *language* tedesco *m*
Ger•man 'mea•sles *nsg* rosolia *f*

Ger•man 'shep•herd pastore *m* tedesco
Germany ['dʒɜːmənɪ] Germania *f*
ger•mi•nate ['dʒɜːmɪneɪt] *v/i of seed* germogliare
germ 'war•fare guerra *f* batteriologica
ges•tic•u•late [dʒe'stɪkjʊleɪt] *v/i* gesticolare
ges•ture ['dʒestʃə(r)] *n also fig* gesto *m*
get [get] *v/t* (*pret & pp* **got**) (*obtain*) prendere; (*fetch*) andare a prendere; (*receive*: *letter*) ricevere; (*receive*: *knowledge, respect etc*) ottenere; (*catch*: *bus, train, flu*) prendere; (*become*) diventare; (*arrive*) arrivare; (*understand*) afferrare; ***get sth done*** *causative* farsi fare qc; ***get s.o. to do sth*** far fare qc a qu; ***I'll get him to do it*** glielo faccio fare; ***get to do sth*** *have opportunity* avere occasione di fare qc; ***get one's hair cut*** tagliarsi i capelli; ***get sth ready*** preparare qc; ***get going*** (*leave*) andare via; ***have got*** avere; ***I have got to study / see him*** devo studiare / vederlo; ***I don't want to, but I've got to*** non voglio, ma devo; ***get to know*** venire a sapere
◆ **get about** *v/i* (*travel*) andare in giro; (*be mobile*) muoversi
◆ **get along** *v/i* (*progress*) procedere; ***how is he getting along at school?*** come se la cava a scuola?; *come to party etc* venire; *with s.o.* andare d'accordo
◆ **get at** *v/t* (*criticize*) prendersela con; (*imply, mean*) volere arrivare a; ***I don't understand what you're getting at*** non capisco dove vuoi arrivare
◆ **get away 1** *v/i* (*leave*) andare via **2** *v/t*: ***get sth away from s.o.*** togliere qc a qu
◆ **get away with** *v/t* cavarsela per
◆ **get back 1** *v/i* (*return*) ritornare; ***I'll get back to you on that*** ti faccio sapere **2** *v/t* (*obtain again*) recuperare
◆ **get by** *v/i* (*pass*) passare; *financially* tirare avanti
◆ **get down 1** *v/i from ladder etc* scendere; (*duck etc*) abbassarsi **2** *v/t* (*depress*) buttare giù
◆ **get down to** *v/t* (*start*: *work*) mettersi a; (*reach*: *real facts*) arrivare a; ***let's get down to business*** parliamo d'affari
◆ **get in 1** *v/i* (*arrive*: *of train, plane*) arrivare; (*come home*) arrivare a casa; *to car* salire; ***how did they get in?*** *of thieves, mice etc* come sono entrati? **2** *v/t to suitcase etc* far entrare
◆ **get off 1** *v/i from bus etc* scendere; (*finish work*) finire; (*not be punished*) cavarsela **2** *v/t* (*remove*) togliere; *clothes, hat, footgear* togliersi; ***get off the grass!*** togliti dal prato!
◆ **get off with** *v/t* F *sexually* rimorchiare F; ***get off with a small fine*** cavarsela con una piccola multa
◆ **get on 1** *v/i to bike, bus, train* salire; (*be friendly*) andare d'accordo; (*advance*: *of time*) farsi tardi; (*become old*) invecchiare; (*make progress*) procedere; ***he's getting on well at school*** se la sta cavando bene a scuola; ***it's getting on*** *getting late* si sta facendo tardi; ***he's getting on*** *getting old* sta invecchiando; ***he's getting on for 50*** va per i 50 anni **2** *v/t*: ***get on the bus / one's bike*** salire sull'autobus / sulla bici; ***get one's hat on*** mettersi il cappello; ***I can't get these trousers on*** non riesco a mettermi questi pantaloni
◆ **get out 1** *v/i of car etc* scendere; *of prison* uscire; ***get out!*** fuori!; ***let's get out of here*** usciamo da qui; ***I don't get out much these days*** non esco molto in questi giorni **2** *v/t* (*extract*: *nail, something jammed*) tirare fuori; (*remove*: *stain*) mandare via; (*pull out*: *gun, pen*) tirare fuori
◆ **get over** *v/t fence, disappointment etc* superare; *lover etc* dimenticare
◆ **get over with** *v/t* togliersi; ***let's get it over with*** togliamocelo
◆ **get through** *v/i on telephone* prendere la linea; (*make self understood*) farsi capire; ***get through to s.o.*** (*make self understood*) farsi capire da qu; ***I called you all day but I didn't manage to get through*** ti ho chiamato tutto il giorno, ma era sempre occupato
◆ **get up 1** *v/i of person, wind* alzarsi **2** *v/t* (*climb*: *hill*) salire su
'get•a•way *from robbery* fuga *f*
'get•a•way car macchina *f* per la fuga
'get-to•geth•er ritrovo *m*
ghast•ly ['gɑːstlɪ] *adj colour, experience, person etc* orrendo; ***you look ghastly*** hai un aspetto orribile
gher•kin ['gɜːkɪn] cetriolino *m* sotto aceto
ghet•to ['getəʊ] ghetto *m*
ghost [gəʊst] fantasma *m*, spettro *m*
ghost•ly ['gəʊstlɪ] *adj* spettrale
'ghost town città *f inv* fantasma
ghoul [guːl] persona *f* morbosa
ghoul•ish ['guːlɪʃ] *adj* macabro
gi•ant ['dʒaɪənt] **1** *n* gigante *m* **2** *adj* gigante
gib•ber•ish ['dʒɪbərɪʃ] F bestialità *fpl* F
gibe [dʒaɪb] *n* frecciatina *f*
gib•lets ['dʒɪblɪts] *npl* frattaglie *fpl* (di volatili)
gid•di•ness ['gɪdɪnɪs] giramenti *mpl* di testa
gid•dy ['gɪdɪ] *adj*: ***I feel giddy*** mi gira la

testa
gift [gɪft] regalo *m*
gift•ed ['gɪftɪd] *adj* dotato
'**gift to•ken**, '**gift voucher** buono *m* d'aquisto
'**gift•wrap 1** *n* carta *f* da regalo **2** *v/t* (*pret & pp* ***-ped***) impacchettare; ***would you like it giftwrapped?*** le faccio un pacco regalo?
gig [gɪg] F concerto *m*
gi•ga•byte ['gɪgəbaɪt] COMPUT gigabyte *m inv*
gi•gan•tic [dʒaɪ'gæntɪk] *adj* gigante
gig•gle ['gɪgl] **1** *v/i* ridacchiare **2** *n* risatina *f*
gig•gly ['gɪglɪ] *adj* ridacchiante
gill [gɪl] *of fish* branchia *f*
gilt [gɪlt] *n* doratura *f*; ***gilts*** FIN titoli *mpl* obbligazionari
gim•mick ['gɪmɪk] trovata *f*
gim•mick•y ['gɪmɪkɪ] *adj* appariscente
gin [dʒɪn] gin *m inv*; ***gin and tonic*** gin and tonic *m inv*
gin•ger ['dʒɪndʒə(r)] **1** *n spice* zenzero *m* **2** *adj hair* rosso carota; *cat* rosso
gin•ger '**beer** bibita *f* allo zenzero
'**gin•ger•bread** pan *m* di zenzero
gin•ger•ly ['dʒɪndʒəlɪ] *adv* con cautela
gip•sy ['dʒɪpsɪ] zingaro *m*, -a *f*
gi•raffe [dʒɪ'rɑːf] giraffa *f*
gir•der ['gɜːdə(r)] *n* trave *f*
girl [gɜːl] ragazza *f*
'**girl•friend** *of boy* ragazza *f*; *of girl* amica *f*
girl '**guide** giovane esploratrice *f*
girl•ie ['gɜːlɪ] *adj* F da femminuccia F
'**girl•ie mag•a•zine** *pornographic* rivista *f* per soli uomini
girl•ish ['gɜːlɪʃ] *adj* tipicamente femminile
gi•ro ['dʒaɪərəʊ] bonifico *m*
gist [dʒɪst] sostanza *f*
give [gɪv] *v/t* (*pret* ***gave***, *pp* ***given***) dare; *present* fare; (*supply*: *electricity etc*) fornire; *talk*, *groan* fare; *party* dare; *pain*, *appetite* far venire; ***give her my love*** salutala da parte mia
◆ **give away** *v/t as present* regalare; (*betray*) tradire; ***give o.s. away*** tradirsi
◆ **give back** *v/t* restituire
◆ **give in 1** *v/i surrender* arrendersi **2** *v/t* (*hand in*) consegnare
◆ **give off** *v/t smell*, *fumes* emettere
◆ **give onto** *v/t* (*open onto*) dare su
◆ **give out 1** *v/t leaflets etc* distribuire **2** *v/i of supplies*, *strength* esaurirsi
◆ **give up 1** *v/t smoking etc* rinunciare a; ***he gave up smoking*** ha smesso di fumare; ***give o.s. up to the police*** consegnarsi alla polizia **2** *v/i* (*cease habit*) smettere; (*stop making effort*) lasciar perdere
◆ **give way** *v/i of bridge etc* cedere; MOT dare la precedenza
give-and-'**take** concessioni *fpl* reciproche
giv•en ['gɪvn] *pp* → ***give***
'**giv•en name** nome *m* di battesimo
gla•ci•er ['glæsɪə(r)] ghiacciaio *m*
glad [glæd] *adj* contento
glad•ly ['glædlɪ] *adv* volentieri
glam•or *Am* → ***glamour***
glam•or•ize ['glæməraɪz] *v/t* esaltare
glam•or•ous ['glæmərəs] *adj* affascinante
glam•our ['glæmə(r)] fascino *m*
glance [glɑːns] **1** *n* sguardo *m*; ***at first glance*** a prima vista **2** *v/i* dare un'occhiata *o* uno sguardo
◆ **glance at** *v/t* dare un'occhiata *o* uno sguardo a
gland [glænd] ghiandola *f*
glan•du•lar fe•ver ['glændjʊlə(r)] mononucleosi *f*
glare [gleə(r)] **1** *n of sun*, *headlights* luce *f* abbagliante **2** *v/i of sun*, *headlights* splendere di luce abbagliante
◆ **glare at** *v/t* guardare di storto
glar•ing ['gleərɪŋ] *adj mistake* lampante
glar•ing•ly ['gleərɪŋlɪ] *adv*: ***be glaringly obvious*** essere più che ovvio
glass [glɑːs] *material* vetro *m*; *for drink* bicchiere *m*
glass '**case** teca *f*
glasses *npl* occhiali *mpl*
'**glass•house** serra *f*
glaze [gleɪz] *n* smalto *m* trasparente
◆ **glaze over** *v/i of eyes* appannarsi
glazed [gleɪzd] *adj expression* assente
gla•zi•er ['gleɪzɪə(r)] vetraio *m*
glaz•ing ['gleɪzɪŋ] vetri *mpl*
gleam [gliːm] **1** *n* luccichio *m* **2** *v/i* luccicare
glee [gliː] allegria *f*
glee•ful ['gliːfʊl] *adj* allegro
glib [glɪb] *adj* poco convincente
glib•ly ['glɪblɪ] *adv* in modo poco convincente
glide [glaɪd] *v/i of skier*, *boat* scivolare; *of bird*, *plane* planare
glid•er ['glaɪdə(r)] aliante *m*
glid•ing ['glaɪdɪŋ] *n* SP volo *m* planato
glim•mer ['glɪmə(r)] **1** *n of light* barlume *m*; ***glimmer of hope*** barlume *m* di speranza **2** *v/i* emettere un barlume
glimpse [glɪmps] **1** *n* occhiata *f*; ***catch a glimpse of*** intravedere **2** *v/t* intravedere
glint [glɪnt] **1** *n* luccichio *m* **2** *v/i of light*, *eyes* luccicare
glis•ten ['glɪsn] *v/i* scintillare
glit•ter ['glɪtə(r)] *v/i* brillare
glit•ter•ati *npl*: ***the glitterati*** il bel mondo

gloat [gləʊt] *v/i* gongolare
◆ **gloat over** *v/t* compiacersi di
glo•bal ['gləʊbl] *adj* (*worldwide*) mondiale; *without exceptions* globale
glo•bal e'con•o•my economia *f* mondiale
glo•bal 'mar•ket mercato *m* mondiale
glo•bal 'war•ming effetto *m* serra
globe [gləʊb] globo *m*; *model of earth* mappamondo *m*
gloom [gluːm] (*darkness*) penombra *f*; *mood* tristezza *f*
gloom•i•ly ['gluːmɪlɪ] *adv* tristemente
gloom•y ['gluːmɪ] *adj room* buio; *mood, person* triste; *day* grigio
glo•ri•ous ['glɔːrɪəs] *adj weather, day* splendido; *victory* glorioso
glo•ry ['glɔːrɪ] *n* gloria *f*; (*beauty*) splendore *m*
gloss [glɒs] *n* (*shine*) lucido *m*; (*general explanation*) glossa *f*
◆ **gloss over** *v/t* sorvolare su
glos•sa•ry ['glɒsərɪ] glossario *m*
'gloss paint vernice *f* lucida
gloss•y ['glɒsɪ] **1** *adj paper* patinato **2** *n magazine* rivista *f* femminile
glove [glʌv] guanto *m*
'glove com•part•ment *in car* cruscotto *m*
'glove pup•pet burattino *m*
glow [gləʊ] **1** *n of light, fire* bagliore *m*; *in cheeks* colorito *m* vivo; *of candle* luce *f* fioca **2** *v/i of light* brillare; ***her cheeks glowed*** è diventata rossa
glow•er ['glaʊə(r)] *v/i*: ***glower at s.o.*** guardare qu in cagnesco
glow•ing ['gləʊɪŋ] *adj description* entusiastico
glu•cose ['gluːkəʊs] glucosio *m*
glue [gluː] **1** *n* colla *f* **2** *v/t*: ***glue sth to sth*** incollare qc a qc; ***be glued to the TV*** F essere incollato alla TV F
glum [glʌm] *adj* triste
glum•ly ['glʌmlɪ] *adv* tristemente
glut [glʌt] *n* eccesso *m*
glut•ton ['glʌtən] ghiottone *m*, -a *f*
glut•ton•y ['glʌtənɪ] ghiottoneria *f*
GMT [dʒiːem'tiː] *abbr* (= ***Greenwich Mean Time***) ora *f* di Greenwich
gnarled [nɑːld] *adj branch, hands* nodoso
gnat [næt] moscerino *m*
gnaw [nɔː] *v/t bone* rosicchiare
GNP [dʒiːen'piː] *abbr* (= ***gross national product***) PNL *m* (= prodotto *m* nazionale lordo)
go [gəʊ] **1** *n* (*try*) tentativo *m*; ***it's my go*** tocca a me, è il mio turno; ***have a go at sth*** (*try*) fare un tentativo in qc; (*complain about*) lamentarsi di qc; ***be on the go*** essere indaffarato; ***in one go*** *drink, write etc* tutto in una volta **2** *v/i* ◇ (*pret* ***went***, *pp* ***gone***) andare; (*leave: of train, plane*) partire; (*leave: of people*) andare via; (*work, function*) funzionare; (*become*) diventare; (*come out: of stain etc*) andare via; (*cease: of pain etc*) sparire; (*match: of colours etc*) stare bene insieme; ***go shopping / go jogging*** andare a fare spese / andare a correre; ***I must be going*** devo andare; ***let's go!*** andiamo!; ***go for a walk*** andare a fare una passeggiata; ***go to bed*** andare a letto; ***go to school*** andare a scuola; ***how's the work going?*** come va il lavoro?; ***they're going for £50*** (*being sold at*) li vendono a £50; ***be all gone*** (*finished*) essere finito; ***I've gone 15 miles*** ho fatto 15 miglia; ***there are two days to go before ...*** mancano due giorni a ...; ***the story goes that ...*** la storia dice che ...; ***to go*** *Am food* da asporto
◇ *future* ***I'm going to meet him tomorrow*** lo incontrerò domani; ***it's going to snow*** sta per nevicare
◆ **go ahead** *v/i and do sth* andare avanti; ***go ahead!*** (*on you go*) fai pure!
◆ **go ahead with** *v/t plans etc* andare avanti con
◆ **go along with** *v/t suggestion* concordare con
◆ **go at** *v/t* (*attack*) scagliarsi contro
◆ **go away** *v/i of person, pain* andare via; *of rain* smettere
◆ **go back** *v/i* (*return*) ritornare; (*date back*) rimontare; ***we go back a long way*** ci conosciamo da una vita; ***go back to sleep*** tornare a dormire
◆ **go by** *v/i of car, people, time* passare
◆ **go down** *v/i* scendere; *of sun, ship* tramontare; *of ship* affondare; *of swelling* diminuire; ***will it go down well with them?*** la prenderanno bene?
◆ **go for** *v/t* (*attack*) attaccare; ***I don't much go for gin*** non vado matto per il gin; ***she really goes for him*** le piace davvero
◆ **go in** *v/i to room, house* entrare; *of sun* andare via; (*fit: of part etc*) andare
◆ **go in for** *v/t competition, race* iscriversi a; (*like, take part in*) dedicarsi a
◆ **go off 1** *v/i* (*leave*) andarsene; *of bomb* esplodere; *of gun* sparare; *of alarm* scattare; *of light* spegnersi; *of milk etc* andare a male **2** *v/t* (*stop liking*) stufarsi di
◆ **go on** *v/i* (*continue*) andare avanti; (*happen*) succedere; ***go on, do it!*** *encouraging* dai, fallo!; ***what's going on?*** cosa sta succedendo?
◆ **go on at** *v/t* (*nag*) sgridare
◆ **go out** *v/i of person* uscire; *of light, fire*

G

spegnersi
◆ **go out with** *v/t romantically* uscire con
◆ **go over** *v/t* (*check*) esaminare; (*do again*) rifare
◆ **go through** *v/t illness*, *hard times* passare; (*check*) controllare; (*read through*) leggere
◆ **go under** *v/i* (*sink*) affondare; *of company* fallire
◆ **go up** *v/i* salire
◆ **go without 1** *v/t food etc* fare a meno di **2** *v/i* farne a meno
goad [gəʊd] *v/t* spronare
'**go-a•head 1** *n* via libera *m*; ***get the go-ahead*** avere il via libera **2** *adj* (*enterprising*, *dynamic*) intraprendente
goal [gəʊl] (*sport*: *target*) rete *f*; (*sport*: *points*) gol *m inv*; (*objective*) obiettivo *m*
goal•ie ['gəʊlɪ] F portiere *m*
'**goal•keep•er** portiere *m*
'**goal kick** rimessa *f*
'**goal•mouth** area *f* di porta
'**goal•post** palo *m*
goat [gəʊt] capra *f*
gob•ble ['gɒbl] *v/t* trangugiare
◆ **gobble up** *v/t* trangugiare
gob•ble•dy•gook ['gɒbldɪguːk] F linguaggio *m* incomprensibile
'**go-be•tween** mediatore *m*, -trice *f*
gob-smacked ['gɒbsmækt] *adj* P sbigottito
god [gɒd] dio *m*; ***thank god!*** grazie a Dio!; ***oh god!*** Dio mio!
'**god•child** figlioccio *m*, -a *f*
'**god•daugh•ter** figliaccia *f*
god•dess ['gɒdɪs] dea *f*
'**god•fa•ther** *also in mafia* padrino *m*
'**god•for•sak•en** ['gɒdfəseɪkən] *adj place*, *town* dimenticato da Dio
'**god•moth•er** madrina *f*
'**god•pa•rent** *man* padrino *m*; *woman* madrina *f*
'**god•send** benedizione *f*
'**god•son** figlioccio *m*
go•fer ['gəʊfə(r)] F galoppino *m*, -a *f* F
gog•gles ['gɒglz] *npl* occhialini *mpl*
go•ing ['gəʊɪŋ] *adj price etc* corrente; ***going concern*** azienda *f* florida
go•ings-on [gəʊɪŋz'ɒn] *npl* vicende *fpl*
gold [gəʊld] **1** *n* oro *m* **2** *adj* d'oro
gold•en ['gəʊldn] *adj sky*, *hair* dorato
gold•en 'hand•shake buonuscita *f*
gold•en 'wed•ding (an•ni•ver•sa•ry) nozze *fpl* d'oro
'**gold•fish** pesce *m* rosso
'**gold mine** *fig* miniera *f* d'oro
'**gold•smith** orefice *m/f*
golf [gɒlf] golf *m*
'**golf ball** palla *f* da golf
'**golf club** *organization* club *m inv* di golf; *stick* mazza *f* da golf
'**golf course** campo *m* di golf
golf•er ['gɒlfə(r)] giocatore *m*, -trice di golf
gon•do•la ['gɒndələ] gondola *f*
gon•do•lier [gɒndə'lɪə(r)] gondoliere *m*
gone [gɒn] *pp* → ***go***
gong [gɒŋ] gong *m inv*
good [gʊd] **1** *adj* buono; *weather*, *film* bello; *actor*, *child* bravo; ***a good many*** un bel po' (di); ***be good at*** essere bravo in; ***be good for s.o.*** fare bene a qu; ***be good for sth*** andare bene per qc; ***good!*** bene!; ***it's good to see you*** è bello vederti **2** *n* bene *m*; ***it did him no good*** non gli ha fatto bene; ***it did him a lot of good*** gli ha fatto molto bene; ***what good is that to me?*** a che cosa mi serve?; ***the good*** il buono; *people* i buoni
goodbye [gʊd'baɪ] arrivederci; ***say goodbye to s.o., wish s.o. goodbye*** salutare qu
'**good-for-nothing** *n* buono *m*, -a *f* a nulla
Good 'Fri•day venerdì *m inv* santo
good-hu•mored *Am*, **good-hu•moured** [gʊd'hjuːməd] *adj* di buon umore
good-'look•ing [gʊd'lʊkɪŋ] *adj* attraente
good-na•tured [gʊd'neɪʧəd] di buon cuore
good•ness ['gʊdnɪs] bontà *f*; ***thank goodness!*** grazie al cielo
goods [gʊdz] *npl* COM merce *fsg*
good'will buona volontà *f*
good•y-good•y ['gʊdɪgʊdɪ] *n* F santarellino *m*, -a *f* F
goo•ey ['guːɪ] *adj* appiccicoso
goof [guːf] *v/i* F fare una gaffe
goose [guːs] (*pl* ***geese*** [giːs])oca *f*
goose•ber•ry ['gʊzbərɪ] uva *f* spina
'**goose pim•ples** *npl* pelle *f* d'oca
gorge [gɔːdʒ] **1** *n* gola *f* **2** *v/t*: ***gorge o.s. on sth*** strafogarsi di qc
gor•geous ['gɔːdʒəs] *adj* stupendo; *smell* ottimo
go•ril•la [gə'rɪlə] gorilla *m*
gosh [gɒʃ] *int* caspita
go-'slow sciopero *m* bianco
gos•pel ['gɒspl] *in Bible* vangelo *m*
'**gos•pel truth** sacrosanta verità *f inv*
gos•sip ['gɒsɪp] **1** *n* pettegolezzo *m*; *person* pettegolo *m*, -a *f* **2** *v/i* spettegolare
'**gos•sip col•umn** cronaca *f* rosa
'**gos•sip col•um•nist** giornalista *m/f* di cronaca rosa
gossipy ['gɒsɪpɪ] *adj letter* pieno di chiacchiere
got [gɒt] *pret & pp* → ***get***
gour•met ['gʊəmeɪ] *n* buongustaio *m*, -a *f*

gov•ern ['gʌvn] *v/t country* governare
gov•ern•ment ['gʌvnmənt] governo *m*
gov•er•nor ['gʌvənə(r)] governatore *m*
gown [gaʊn] (*long dress*) abito *m* lungo; (*wedding dress*) abito *m* da sposa; *of academic, judge* toga *f*; *of surgeon* camice *m*
GP [dʒiː'piː] *abbr* (= ***General Practitioner***) medico *m* generico
grab [græb] *v/t* (*pret & pp* **-bed**) afferrare; ***grab a bite to eat*** fare uno spuntino rapido; ***grab some sleep*** farsi una dormita
grace [greɪs] *of dancer etc* grazia *f*; *before meals* preghiera *f* (prima di un pasto)
grace•ful ['greɪsfʊl] *adj* aggraziato
grace•ful•ly ['greɪsfʊlɪ] *adv move* con grazia
gra•cious ['greɪʃəs] *adj person* cortese; *style* elegante; *living* agiato; ***good gracious!*** santo cielo!
grade [greɪd] **1** *n* (*quality*) qualità *f inv*; EDU voto *m* **2** *v/t* classificare
'**grade school** *Am* scuola *f* elementare
gra•di•ent ['greɪdɪənt] pendenza *f*
grad•u•al ['grædʒʊəl] *adj* graduale
grad•u•al•ly ['grædʒʊəlɪ] *adv* gradualmente
grad•u•ate ['grædʒʊət] **1** *n* laureato *m*, -a *f* **2** *v/i from university* laurearsi
grad•u•a•tion [grædʒʊ'eɪʃn] laurea *f*; *ceremony* cerimonia *f* di laurea
graf•fi•ti [grə'fiːtiː] graffiti *mpl*
graft [grɑːft] **1** *n* BOT innesto *m*; MED trapianto *m*; F (*hard work*) duro lavoro *m* **2** *v/t* BOT innestare; MED trapiantare
grain [greɪn] cereali *mpl*; *seed* granello *m*; *of rice, wheat* chicco *m*; *in wood* venatura *f*; ***go against the grain*** essere contro natura
gram [græm] grammo *m*
gram•mar ['græmə(r)] grammatica *f*
'**gram•mar school** liceo *m*
gram•mat•i•cal [grə'mætɪkl] *adj* grammaticale
gram•mat•i•cal•ly *adv* grammaticalmente
grand [grænd] **1** *adj* grandioso; F (*very good*) eccezionale **2** *n* F (*£1000*) mille sterline *fpl*
'**gran•dad** ['grændæd] nonno *m*
'**grand•child** nipote *m/f*
'**grand•daugh•ter** nipote *f*
gran•deur ['grændʒə(r)] grandiosità *f*
'**grand•fa•ther** nonno *m*
grand•fa•ther clock pendolo *m*
gran•di•ose ['grændɪəʊs] *adj* grandioso
'**grand•ma** F nonna *f*
'**grand•moth•er** nonna *f*
'**grand•pa** F nonno *m*
'**grand•par•ents** *npl* nonni *mpl*
grand pi'an•o pianoforte *m* a coda
grand 'slam grande slam *m inv*
'**grand•son** nipote *m*
'**grand•stand** tribuna *f*
gran•ite ['grænɪt] granito *m*
gran•ny ['grænɪ] F nonna *f*
'**gran•ny flat** appartamento *m* annesso
grant [grɑːnt] **1** *n money* sussidio *m*; *for university* borsa *f* di studio **2** *v/t visa* assegnare; *permission* concedere; *request, wish* esaudire; ***take sth for granted*** dare qc per scontato; ***he takes his wife for granted*** considera quello che fa sua moglie come dovuto
gran•ule ['grænjuːl] granello *m*
grape [greɪp] acino *m* d'uva; ***grapes*** uva *fsg*
'**grape•fruit** pompelmo *m*
'**grape•fruit juice** succo *m* di pompelmo
'**grape•vine**: ***I heard on the grapevine that …*** ho sentito dire che …
graph [grɑːf] grafico *m*
graph•ic ['græfɪk] **1** *adj* grafico; (*vivid*) vivido **2** *n* COMPUT grafico *m*; ***graphics*** grafica *f*
graph•ic•ally ['græfɪklɪ] *adv describe* in modo vivido
graph•ic de'sign•er grafico *m*, -a *f*
◆ **grap•ple with** ['græpl] *v/t attacker* lottare con; *problem etc* essere alle prese con
grasp [grɑːsp] **1** *n physical* presa *f*; *mental* comprensione *f* **2** *v/t physically, mentally* afferrare
grass [grɑːs] *n* erba *f*
'**grass•hop•per** cavalletta *f*
grass roots *npl people* massa *f* popolare
grass 'wid•ow *donna f il cui marito è spesso assente*
grass 'wid•ow•er *uomo m la cui moglie è spesso assente*
gras•sy ['grɑːsɪ] *adj* erboso
grate[1] [greɪt] *n metal* grata *f*
grate[2] [greɪt] **1** *v/t in cooking* grattugiare **2** *v/i of sounds* stridere
grate•ful ['greɪtfʊl] *adj* grato; ***be grateful to s.o.*** essere grato a qu
grate•ful•ly ['greɪtfʊlɪ] *adv* con gratitudine
grat•er ['greɪtə(r)] grattugia *f*
grat•i•fy ['grætɪfaɪ] *v/t* (*pret & pp* **-ied**) soddisfare
grat•ing ['greɪtɪŋ] **1** *n* grata *f* **2** *adj sound, voice* stridente
grat•i•tude ['grætɪtjuːd] gratitudine *f*
gra•tu•i•tous [grə'tjuːɪtəs] *adj* gratuito
gra•tu•i•ty [grə'tjuːətɪ] (*tip*) mancia *f*
grave[1] [greɪv] *n* tomba *f*
grave[2] [greɪv] *adj* (*serious*) grave

grav•el ['grævl] *n* ghiaia *f*
'grave•stone lapide *f*
'grave•yard cimitero *m*
◆ **grav•i•tate towards** ['grævɪteɪt] *v/t* gravitare intorno a
grav•i•ty ['grævətɪ] PHYS forza *f* di gravità
gra•vy ['greɪvɪ] sugo *m* della carne
gray *Am* → ***grey***
graze[1] [greɪz] *v/i of cow, horse* brucare
graze[2] [greɪz] **1** *v/t arm etc* graffiare **2** *n* graffio *m*
grease [gri:s] *n* grasso *m*
grease•proof 'pa•per carta *f* oleata
greas•y ['gri:sɪ] *adj food, hair, skin* grasso; *hands, plate* unto
great [greɪt] *adj* grande; F (*very good*) fantastico; ***great to see you!*** sono contento di vederti!
Great 'Brit•ain Gran Bretagna *f*
great-'grand•child pronipote *m/f*
great-'grand•daugh•ter pronipote *f*
great-'grand•fa•ther bisnonno *m*
great-'grand•moth•er bisnonna *f*
great-'grand•par•ents *npl* bisnonni *mpl*
great-'grand•son pronipote *m*
great•ly ['greɪtlɪ] *adv* molto
great•ness ['greɪtnɪs] grandezza *f*
Greece [gri:s] Grecia *f*
greed [gri:d] avidità *f*; *for food* ingordigia *f*
greed•i•ly ['gri:dɪlɪ] *adv* con avidità; *eat* con ingordigia
greed•y ['gri:dɪ] *adj* avido; *for food* ingordo
Greek [gri:k] **1** *n* greco *m*, -a *f*; *language* greco *m* **2** *adj* greco
green [gri:n] *adj* verde; *environmentally* ecologico; ***the Greens*** POL i verdi
green 'beans *npl* fagiolini *mpl*
'green belt *zona f verde tutt'intorno ad una città*
'green card *driving insurance* carta *f* verde
green 'fin•gers: ***have green fingers*** avere il pollice verde
'green•gro•cer fruttivendolo *m*, -a *f*
'green•horn F pivello *m*, -a *f* F
'green•house serra *f*
'green•house ef•fect effetto *m* serra
'green•house gas gas *m inv* inquinante
green 'pep•per *vegetable* peperone *m*
greens [gri:nz] *npl* verdura *f*
greet [gri:t] *v/t* salutare
greet•ing ['gri:tɪŋ] saluto *m*
'greet•ings card biglietto *m* d'auguri
gre•gar•i•ous [grɪ'geərɪəs] *adj person* socievole
gre•nade [grɪ'neɪd] granata *f*
grew [gru:] *pret* → ***grow***
grey [greɪ] *adj* grigio; *hair* bianco; ***be going grey*** cominciare ad avere i capelli bianchi
grey-'haired [greɪ'heəd] *adj* con i capelli bianchi
'grey•hound levriero *m*
grid [grɪd] grata *f*; *on map* reticolato *m*
'grid•lock *in traffic* ingorgo *m*
grief [gri:f] dolore *m*
grief-strick•en ['gri:fstrɪkn] *adj* addolorato
griev•ance ['gri:vəns] rimostranza *f*
grieve [gri:v] *v/i* essere addolorato; ***grieve for s.o.*** essere addolorato per qu
grill [grɪl] **1** *n for cooking* grill *m inv*; *metal frame* griglia *f*; *dish* grigliata *f*; *on window* grata *f* **2** *v/t food* fare alla griglia; (*interrogate*) mettere sotto torchio
grille [grɪl] grata *f*
grim [grɪm] *adj* cupo; *determination* accanito
gri•mace ['grɪməs] *n* smorfia *f*
grime [graɪm] sporcizia *f*
grim•ly ['grɪmlɪ] *adv* con aria grave
grim•y ['graɪmɪ] *adj* sudicio
grin [grɪn] **1** *n* sorriso *m* **2** *v/i* (*pret & pp* ***-ned***) sorridere
grind [graɪnd] *v/t* (*pret & pp* ***ground***) *coffee, meat* macinare; ***grind one's teeth*** digrignare i denti
grip [grɪp] **1** *n on rope etc* presa *f*; ***he's losing his grip*** *losing skills* sta perdendo dei colpi; ***get to grips with sth*** affrontare qc **2** *v/t* (*pret & pp* ***-ped***) afferrare; *of brakes* fare presa su; ***be gripped by sth*** *by panic* essere preso da qc
gripe [graɪp] **1** *n* lamentela *f* **2** *v/i* lamentarsi
grip•ping ['grɪpɪŋ] *adj* avvincente
gris•tle ['grɪsl] cartilagine *f*
grit [grɪt] **1** *n* (*dirt*) granelli *mpl*; *for roads* sabbia *f* **2** *v/t* (*pret & pp* ***-ted***): ***grit one's teeth*** stringere i denti
grit•ty ['grɪtɪ] *adj* F *book, film etc* realistico
groan [grəʊn] **1** *n* gemito *m* **2** *v/i* gemere
gro•cer ['grəʊsə(r)] droghiere *m*; ***at the grocer's*** (***shop***) dal droghiere
gro•cer•ies ['grəʊsərɪz] *npl* generi *mpl* alimentari
gro•cer•y store ['grəʊsərɪ] drogheria *f*
grog•gy ['grɒgɪ] *adj* F intontito
groin [grɔɪn] ANAT inguine *m*
groom [gru:m] **1** *n for bride* sposo *m*; *for horse* stalliere *m* **2** *v/t horse* strigliare; (*train, prepare*) preparare; ***well groomed*** *in appearance* ben curato
groove [gru:v] scanalatura *f*
grope [grəʊp] **1** *v/i in the dark* brancolare

2 *v/t sexually* palpeggiare
◆ **grope for** *v/t door handle* cercare a tastoni; *the right word* cercare di trovare
gross [grəʊs] *adj* (*coarse, vulgar*) volgare; *exaggeration* madornale; FIN lordo
gross do•mes•tic 'prod•uct prodotto *m* interno lordo
gross na•tion•al 'prod•uct prodotto *m* nazionale lordo
grot•ty ['grɒtɪ] *adj* F *street, flat* squallido; ***I feel grotty*** sto da schifo F
ground[1] [graʊnd] **1** *n* suolo *m*; (*area, for sport*) terreno *m*; (*reason*) motivo *m*, ragione *f*; ELEC terra *f*; ***on the ground*** per terra; ***on the grounds of*** a causa di **2** *v/t* ELEC mettere a terra
ground[2] [graʊnd] *pret & pp* → ***grind***
'ground con•trol controllo *m* da terra
'ground crew personale *m* di terra
'ground floor pianoterra *m inv*
ground•ing ['graʊndɪŋ] *in subject* basi *fpl*; ***have a good grounding in*** avere delle buoni basi di
ground•less ['graʊndlɪs] *adj* infondato
'ground plan pianta *f* del piano terra
'ground staff SP *personale m addetto alla manutenzione dei campi sportivi*; *at airport* personale *m* di terra
'ground•work lavoro *m* di preparazione
group [gruːp] **1** *n* gruppo *m* **2** *v/t* raggruppare
group•ie ['gruːpɪ] F *ragazza f che segue un gruppo o cantante rock in tutti i concerti*
group 'ther•a•py terapia *f* di gruppo
grouse[1] [graʊs] (*pl* ***grouse***) *bird* gallo *m* cedrone
grouse[2] [graʊs] **1** *n* F lamentela *f* **2** *v/i* F brontolare
grov•el ['grɒvl] *v/i fig* umiliarsi
grow [grəʊ] (*pret* ***grew***, *pp* ***grown***) **1** *v/i of child, animal, plant* crescere; *of number, amount* aumentare; *of business* svilupparsi; ***let one's hair grow*** farsi crescere i capelli; ***grow old / tired*** invecchiare / stancarsi; ***grow into sth*** diventare qc **2** *v/t flowers* coltivare
◆ **grow up** *of person* crescere; *of city* svilupparsi; ***grow up!*** comportati da adulto!
growl [graʊl] **1** *n* grugnito *m* **2** *v/i* ringhiare
grown [grəʊn] *pp* → ***grow***
grown-up ['grəʊnʌp] **1** *n* adulto *m*, -a *f* **2** *adj* adulto
growth [grəʊθ] *of person* crescita *f*; *of company* sviluppo *m*; (*increase*) aumento *m*; MED tumore *m*
grub[1] [grʌb] *of insect* larva *f*
grub[2] [grʌb] F (*food*) mangiare *m*
grub•by ['grʌbɪ] *adj* sporco
grudge [grʌdʒ] **1** *n* rancore *m*; ***bear s.o. a grudge*** portare rancore a qu **2** *v/t* dare a malincuore; ***grudge s.o. sth*** invidiare qc a qu
grudg•ing ['grʌdʒɪŋ] *adj* riluttante
grudg•ing•ly ['grʌdʒɪŋlɪ] *adv* a malincuore
gru•el•ing *Am*, **gru•ell•ing** ['gruːəlɪŋ] *adj climb, task* estenuante
gruff [grʌf] *adj* burbero
grum•ble ['grʌmbl] *v/i* brontolare
grum•bler ['grʌmblə(r)] brontolone *m*, -a *f*
grump•y ['grʌmpɪ] *adj* scontroso
grunt [grʌnt] **1** *n* grugnito *m* **2** *v/i* grugnire
guar•an•tee [gærən'tiː] **1** *n* garanzia *f*; ***guarantee period*** periodo *m* di garanzia **2** *v/t* garantire
guar•an•tor [gærən'tɔː(r)] garante *m*
guard [gɑːd] **1** *n* guardia *m*; ***be on one's guard against*** stare in guardia contro **2** *v/t* fare la guardia a
◆ **guard against** *v/t* guardarsi da
'guard dog cane *m* da guardia
guard•ed ['gɑːdɪd] *adj reply* cauto
guard•i•an ['gɑːdɪən] LAW tutore *m*, -trice *f*
guard•i•an 'an•gel angelo *m* custode
guer•ril•la [gə'rɪlə] guerrigliero *m*, -a *f*
guer•ril•la 'war•fare guerriglia *f*
guess [ges] **1** *n* supposizione *f*; ***I give you three guesses*** ti do tre possibilità di indovinare **2** *v/t the answer* indovinare; ***I guess so*** suppongo di sì; ***I guess not*** suppongo di no **3** *v/i correctly* indovinare; ***I was just guessing*** ho tirato a indovinare
'guess•work congettura *f*
guest [gest] ospite *m/f*
'guest•house pensione *f*
'guest•room camera *f* degli ospiti
guf•faw [gʌ'fɔː] **1** *n* sghignazzata *f* **2** *v/i* sghignazzare
guid•ance ['gaɪdəns] consigli *mpl*
guide [gaɪd] **1** *n person, book* guida *f* **2** *v/t* guidare
'guide•book guida *f* turistica
guid•ed mis•sile ['gaɪdɪd] missile *m* guidato
'guide dog cane *m* per ciechi
guid•ed 'tour visita *f* guidata
guide•lines ['gaɪdlaɪnz] *npl* direttive *fpl*
guilt [gɪlt] colpa *f*; LAW colpevolezza *f*
guilt•y ['gɪltɪ] *adj also* LAW colpevole; ***have a guilty conscience*** avere la coscienza sporca
guin•ea pig ['gɪnɪpɪg] porcellino *m* d'india; *for experiments, fig* cavia *f*
guise [gaɪz]: ***under the guise of*** dietro la

maschera di
gui•tar [gɪ'tɑː(r)] chitarra *f*
gui'tar case custodia *f* della chitarra
gui•tar•ist [gɪ'tɑːrɪst] chitarrista *m/f*
gui'tar play•er chitarrista *m/f*
gulf [gʌlf] golfo *m*; *fig* divario *m*; ***the Gulf*** il Golfo
gull [gʌl] *n bird* gabbiano *m*
gul•let ['gʌlɪt] ANAT esofago *m*
gul•li•ble ['gʌlɪbl] *adj* credulone
gulp [gʌlp] **1** *n of water* sorso *m*; *of air* boccata *f* **2** *v/i in surprise* deglutire
◆ **gulp down** *v/t drink* ingoiare; *food* trangugiare
gum[1] [gʌm] *in mouth* gengiva *f*
gum[2] [gʌm] *n* (*glue*) colla *f*; (*chewing gum*) gomma *f*
gump•tion ['gʌmpʃn] F sale *m* in zucca F
gun [gʌn] *pistol*, *revolver*, *rifle* arma *f* da fuoco; (*cannon*) cannone *m*
◆ **gun down** *v/t* (*pret & pp* ***-ned***) sparare a morte a
'gun•fire spari *mpl*
'gun•man uomo *m* armato; *robber* rapinatore *m*
'gun•point: ***at gunpoint*** con un'arma puntata addosso
'gun•shot sparo *m*
'gun•shot wound ferita *f* da arma da fuoco
gur•gle ['gɜːgl] *v/i of baby*, *drain* gorgogliare
gu•ru ['guru] *fig* guru *m inv*
gush [gʌʃ] *v/i of liquid* sgorgare
gush•y ['gʌʃɪ] *adj* F (*enthusiastic*) iper-entusiastico
gust [gʌst] raffica *f*
gus•to ['gʌstəʊ]: ***with gusto*** con slancio
gust•y ['gʌstɪ] *of weather* ventoso; ***gusty wind*** vento a raffiche
gut [gʌt] **1** *n* intestino *m*; F (*stomach*) pancia *f* **2** *v/t* (*pret & pp* ***-ted***) (*destroy*) sventrare
guts [gʌts] *npl* F (*courage*) fegato *m* F
guts•y ['gʌtsɪ] *adj* F *person* che ha fegato; F *thing to do* che richiede fegato
gut•ter ['gʌtə(r)] *on pavement* canaletto *m* di scolo; *on roof* grondaia *f*
'gutter•press *pej* stampa *f* scandalistica
guv [gʌv] F capo *m*, -a *f* F
guy [gɑɪ] F tipo *m* F; ***hey, you guys*** ei, gente
guz•zle ['gʌzl] *v/t* ingozzarsi di
gym [dʒɪm] palestra *f*; (*activity*) ginnastica *f*
'gym class educazione *f* fisica
gym•na•si•um [dʒɪm'neɪzɪəm] palestra *f*
gym•nast ['dʒɪmnæst] ginnasta *m/f*
gym•nas•tics [dʒɪm'næstɪks] *nsg* ginnastica *f*
'gym shoes *npl* scarpe *fpl* da ginnastica
'gym teacher insegnante *m/f* di educazione fisica
gy•ne•col•o•gy *etc Am* → ***gynaecology etc***
gy•nae•col•o•gy [gaɪnɪ'kɒlədʒɪ] ginecologia *f*
gy•nae•col•ogist [gaɪnɪ'kɒlədʒɪst] ginecologo *m*, -a *f*
gyp•sy ['dʒɪpsɪ] zingaro *m*, -a *f*

H

hab•it ['hæbɪt] abitudine *f*; ***get into the habit of doing sth*** prendere l'abitudine di fare qc
hab•it•a•ble ['hæbɪtəbl] *adj* abitabile
hab•i•tat ['hæbɪtæt] habitat *m inv*
ha•bit•u•al [hə'bɪtjʊəl] *adj* solito; *smoker, drinker* incallito
hack [hæk] *n* (*poor writer*) scribacchino *m*
hack•er ['hækə(r)] COMPUT hacker *m/f inv*
hack•neyed ['hæknɪd] *adj* trito
had [hæd] *pret & pp* → ***have***
had•dock ['hædək] haddock *m inv*
haem•or•rhage ['hemərɪdʒ] **1** *n* emorragia *f* **2** *v/i* avere un'emorragia
hag•gard ['hægəd] *adj* tirato
hag•gle ['hægl] *v/i* contrattare
hail [heɪl] *n* grandine *f*
'**hail•stone** chicco *m* di grandine
'**hail•storm** grandinata *f*
hair [heə(r)] capelli *mpl*; *single* capello *m*; *on body, of animal* pelo *m*
'**hair•brush** spazzola *f* per capelli
'**hair•cut** taglio *m* di capelli
'**hair•do** F pettinatura *f*
'**hair•dress•er** parrucchiere *m*, -a *f*; ***at the hairdresser's*** dal parrucchiere
'**hair•dri•er**, '**hair•dry•er** fon *m inv*
hair•less ['heəlɪs] *adj* glabro
'**hair•pin** forcina *f*
hair•pin '**bend** tornante *m*
hair-rais•ing ['heəreɪzɪŋ] *adj* terrificante
hair re•mov•er [heərɪ'mu:və(r)] crema *f* depilatoria
'**hair's breadth** *fig*: ***by a hair's breadth*** per un pelo
hair-split•ting ['heəsplɪtɪŋ] *n* pedanteria *f*
'**hair spray** lacca *f* per capelli
'**hair•style** acconciatura *f*
'**hair•styl•ist** parrucchiere *m*, -a *f*
hair•y ['heərɪ] *adj arm, animal* peloso; F (*frightening*) preoccupante
half [hɑ:f] **1** *n* (*pl* ***halves*** [hɑ:vz]) metà *f inv*, mezzo *m*; ***half past ten*** le dieci e mezza; ***half an hour*** mezz'ora; ***half a pound*** mezza libbra; ***go halves with s.o. on sth*** fare a metà di qc con qu **2** *adj* mezzo **3** *adv* a metà
half-heart•ed [hɑ:f'hɑ:tɪd] *adj* poco convinto
half '**term** *vacanza f a metà trimestre*
half '**time** **1** *n* SP intervallo *m* **2** *adj*: ***half time job*** lavoro a metà giornata; ***half time score*** risultato alla fine del primo tempo
half'**way** **1** *adj stage, point* intermedio **2** *adv also fig* a metà strada; ***halfway finished*** fatto a metà
hall [hɔ:l] *large room* sala *f*; *hallway in house* ingresso *m*
Hal•low•e'en [hæləʊ'i:n] vigilia *f* d'Ognissanti
halo ['heɪləʊ] aureola *f*
halt [hɔ:lt] **1** *v/i* fermarsi **2** *v/t* fermare **3** *n*: ***come to a halt*** arrestarsi
halve [hɑ:v] *v/t* dimezzare
ham [hæm] prosciutto *m*
ham•burg•er ['hæmbɜ:gə(r)] hamburger *m inv*
ham•mer ['hæmə(r)] **1** *n* martello *m* **2** *v/i* martellare; ***hammer at the door*** picchiare alla porta
ham•mock ['hæmək] amaca *f*
ham•per[1] ['hæmpə(r)] *n for food* cestino *m*
ham•per[2] ['hæmpə(r)] *v/t* (*obstruct*) ostacolare
ham•ster ['hæmstə(r)] criceto *m*
hand [hænd] *n* mano *m*; *of clock* lancetta *f*; (*worker*) operaio *m*; ***at hand, to hand*** a portata di mano; ***at first hand*** di prima mano; ***by hand*** a mano; ***on the one hand ..., on the other hand ...*** da un lato ..., dall'altro ...; ***in hand*** (*being done*) in corso; ***on your right hand*** sulla tua destra; ***hands off!*** giù le mani!; ***hands up!*** mani in alto!; ***change hands*** cambiare di mano; ***give s.o. a hand*** dare una mano a qu
◆ **hand down** *v/t* passare
◆ **hand in** *v/t* consegnare
◆ **hand on** *v/t* passare
◆ **hand out** *v/t* distribuire
◆ **hand over** *v/t* consegnare; *child to parent etc* dare
'**hand•bag** borsetta *f*
'**hand•book** manuale *m*
'**hand•brake** freno *m* a mano
'**hand•cuff** *v/t* ammanettare
hand•cuffs ['hæn(d)kʌfs] *npl* manette *fpl*
hand•i•cap ['hændɪkæp] handicap *m inv*
hand•i•capped ['hændɪkæpt] *adj also fig* handicappato
hand•i•craft ['hændɪkrɑ:ft] artigianato *m*
hand•i•work ['hændɪwə:k] opera *f*
hand•ker•chief ['hæŋkətʃɪf] fazzoletto *m*
han•dle ['hændl] **1** *n* maniglia *f* **2** *v/t goods* maneggiare; *case, deal* trattare; *difficult person* prendere; ***let me handle this*** la-

scia fare a me; ***be able to handle s.o.*** saperci fare con qu
han•dle•bars ['hændlbɑːz] *npl* manubrio *msg*
'**hand lug•gage** bagaglio *m* a mano
hand•made [hæn(d)'meɪd] *adj* fatto a mano
'**hand•rail** corrimano *m inv*
'**hand•shake** stretta *f* di mano
hands-off [hændz'ɒf] *adj approach* teorico
he has a hands-off style of management non partecipa direttamente agli aspetti pratici della gestione
hand•some ['hænsəm] *adj* bello
hands-on [hændz'ɒn] *adj experience* pratico
he has a hands-on style of management partecipa direttamente agli aspetti pratici della gestione
'**hand•writ•ing** calligrafia *f*
hand•writ•ten ['hændrɪtn] *adj* scritto a mano
hand•y ['hændɪ] *adj tool*, *device* pratico; ***it's handy for the shops*** è comodo per i negozi; ***it might come in handy*** potrebbe tornare utile
hang [hæŋ] **1** *v/t* (*pret & pp* **hung**) *picture* appendere; *person* impiccare **2** *v/i* (*pret & pp* **hung**) *of dress*, *hair* cadere; ***his coat was hanging behind the door*** il suo cappotto era appeso dietro la porta **3** *n*: ***get the hang of sth*** F capire qc
◆ **hang about** *v/i on streets* gironzolare; ***hang about a minute!*** F un attimo!
◆ **hang on** *v/i* (*wait*) aspettare
◆ **hang on to** *v/t* (*keep*) tenere
◆ **hang up** *v/i* TELEC riattaccare
han•gar ['hæŋə(r)] hangar *m inv*
hang•er ['hæŋə(r)] *for clothes* gruccia *f*
hang glid•er ['hæŋglaɪdə(r)] deltaplano *m*
hang glid•ing ['hæŋglaɪdɪŋ] deltaplano *m*
'**hang•o•ver** postumi *mpl* della sbornia
◆ **hanker after** ['hæŋkə(r)] *v/t* desiderare
han•kie, han•ky ['hæŋkɪ] F fazzoletto *m*
hap•haz•ard [hæp'hæzəd] *adj* a casaccio
hap•pen ['hæpn] *v/i* succedere; ***if you happen to see him*** se ti capita di vederlo; ***what has happened to you?*** cosa ti è successo?
◆ **happen across** *v/t* trovare per caso
hap•pen•ing ['hæpnɪŋ] avvenimento *m*
hap•pi•ly ['hæpɪlɪ] *adv* allegramente; (*gladly*) volentieri; (*luckily*) per fortuna
hap•pi•ness ['hæpɪnɪs] felicità *f inv*
hap•py ['hæpɪ] *adj* felice
hap•py-go-'luck•y *adj* spensierato
'**hap•py hour** *orario m in cui le consumazioni costano meno*
har•ass [hə'ræs] *v/t* tormentare; *sexually* molestare
har•assed [hər'æst] *adj* stressato
har•ass•ment [hə'ræsmənt] persecuzione *f*; ***sexual harassment*** molestie *fpl* sessuali
har•bor *Am*, **har•bour** ['hɑːbə(r)] **1** *n* porto *m* **2** *v/t criminal* dar rifugio a; *grudge* covare
hard [hɑːd] *adj* duro; (*difficult*) difficile; *facts*, *evidence* concreto; *drug* pesante; ***hard of hearing*** duro d'orecchio
'**hard•back** *n* libro *m* con copertina rigida
hard-boiled [hɑːd'bɔɪld] *adj egg* sodo
'**hard cop•y** copia *f* stampata
'**hard core** *n* (*pornography*) pornografia *f* hard-core
hard 'cur•ren•cy valuta *f* forte
hard 'disk hard disk *m inv*
hard•en ['hɑːdn] **1** *v/t* indurire **2** *v/i of glue* indurirsi; *of attitude* irrigidirsi
'**hard hat** casco *m*; (*construction worker*) muratore *m*
hard•head•ed [hɑːd'hedɪd] *adj* pratico
hard•heart•ed [hɑːd'hɑːtɪd] *adj* dal cuore duro
hard 'line linea *f* dura
hard'lin•er sostenitore *m*, -trice *f* della linea dura
hard•ly ['hɑːdlɪ] *adv* a malapena; ***hardly ever*** quasi mai; ***you can hardly expect him to …*** non puoi certo aspettarti che lui …; ***hardly!*** ci mancherebbe!
hard•ness ['hɑːdnɪs] durezza *f*; (*difficulty*) difficoltà *f inv*
hard•'sell tecnica *f* aggressiva di vendita
hard•ship ['hɑːdʃɪp] difficoltà *fpl* economiche
hard 'shoul•der corsia *f* di emergenza
hard 'up *adj* al verde
'**hard•ware** ferramenta *fpl*; COMPUT hardware *m inv*
'**hard•ware store** negozio *m* di ferramenta
hard-work•ing [hɑːd'wɜːkɪŋ] *adj* che lavora duro
har•dy ['hɑːdɪ] *adj* resistente
hare [heə(r)] lepre *f*
hare•brained ['heəbreɪnd] *adj* pazzo
harm [hɑːm] **1** *n* danno *m*; ***it wouldn't do any harm to …*** non sarebbe una cattiva idea … **2** *v/t* danneggiare
harm•ful ['hɑːmfʊl] *adj* dannoso
harm•less ['hɑːmlɪs] *adj* innocuo
har•mo•ni•ous [hɑː'məʊnɪəs] *adj* armonioso
har•mo•nize ['hɑːmənaɪz] *v/i* armonizzare

har•mo•ny ['hɑːmənɪ] armonia *f*
harp [hɑːp] *n* arpa *f*
◆ **harp on about** *v/t* F menarsela su F
har•poon [hɑː'puːn] arpione *m*
harsh [hɑːʃ] *adj criticism, words* duro; *colour, light* troppo forte
harsh•ly ['hɑːʃlɪ] *adv* duramente
har•vest ['hɑːvɪst] *n* raccolto *m*
hash [hæʃ] *n* F: ***make a hash of*** fare un pasticcio di
hash•ish ['hæʃiːʃ] hashish *m inv*
'**hash mark** cancelletto *m*
haste [heɪst] *n* fretta *f*
has•ten ['heɪsn] *v/i*: ***hasten to do sth*** affrettarsi a fare qc
hast•i•ly ['heɪstɪlɪ] *adv* in fretta
hast•y ['heɪstɪ] *adj* frettoloso
hat [hæt] cappello *m*
hatch [hætʃ] *n for serving food* passavivande *m inv*; *on ship* boccaporto *m*
◆ **hatch out** *v/i of eggs* schiudersi
hatch•et ['hætʃɪt] ascia *f*; ***bury the hatchet*** seppellire l'ascia di guerra
hate [heɪt] **1** *n* odio *m* **2** *v/t* odiare
ha•tred ['heɪtrɪd] odio *m*
haugh•ty ['hɔːtɪ] *adj* altezzoso
haul [hɔːl] **1** *n of fish* pescata *f* **2** *v/t* (*pull*) trascinare
haul•age ['hɔːlɪdʒ] autotrasporto *m*
'**haul•age com•pa•ny** impresa *f* di autotrasporto
haul•i•er ['hɔːlɪə(r)] autotrasportatore *m*
haunch [hɔːntʃ] anca *f*
haunt [hɔːnt] **1** *v/t*: ***this place is haunted*** questo posto è infestato dai fantasmi **2** *n* ritrovo *m*
haunt•ing ['hɔːntɪŋ] *adj tune* indimenticabile
have [hæv] (*pret & pp* ***had***) **1** *v/t* ◇ avere; *breakfast, shower* fare; ***can I have ...?*** posso avere ...?; ***I'll have a coffee*** prendo un caffè; ***have lunch / dinner*** pranzare / cenare; ***do you have ...?*** ha ...?
◇ *must*: ***have (got) to*** dovere; ***I have (got) to go*** devo andare
◇ *causative*: ***have sth done*** far fare qc; ***I had the printer fixed*** ho fatto riparare la stampante; ***I had my hair cut*** mi sono tagliata i capelli **2** *v/aux* avere; *with verbs of motion* essere; ***have you seen her?*** l'hai vista?; ***I have come*** sono venuto
◆ **have back** *v/t*: ***when can I have it back?*** quando posso riaverlo?
◆ **have on** *v/t* (*wear*) portare, indossare; ***do you have anything on tonight?*** (*have planned*) hai programmi per stasera?
ha•ven ['heɪvn] *fig* oasi *f inv*
hav•oc ['hævək] caos *m inv*; ***play havoc with*** scombussolare
hawk [hɔːk] *also fig* falco *m*
hay [heɪ] fieno *m*
'**hay fe•ver** raffreddore *m* da fieno
hay stack pagliaio *m*
haz•ard ['hæzəd] *n* rischio *m*
'**haz•ard lights** *npl* MOT luci *fpl* di emergenza
haz•ard•ous ['hæzədəs] *adj* rischioso
haze [heɪz] foschia *f*
ha•zel ['heɪzl] *n* (*tree*) nocciolo *m*
'**ha•zel•nut** nocciola *f*
haz•y ['heɪzɪ] *adj view, image* indistinto; *memories* vago; ***I'm a bit hazy about it*** non ne sono certo
he [hiː] *pron* lui; ***he's French*** è francese; ***you're funny, he's not*** tu sei spiritoso, lui no; ***there he is*** eccolo
head [hed] **1** *n* testa *f*; (*boss, leader*) capo *m*; *of primary school* direttore *m*, -trice *f*; *of secondary school* preside *m/f*; *on beer* schiuma *f*; *of nail* capocchia *f*; *of queue, line* inizio *m*; *of tape recorder* testina *f*; ***£15 a head*** 15 sterline a testa; ***heads or tails?*** testa o croce?; ***at the head of the list*** in cima alla lista; ***head over heels*** *fall* a capofitto; ***head over heels in love*** pazzamente innamorato; ***lose one's head*** (*go crazy*) perdere la testa **2** *v/t* (*lead*) essere a capo di; *ball* colpire di testa
'**head•ache** mal *m* di testa
'**head•band** fascia *f* per i capelli
head•er ['hedə(r)] *in soccer* colpo *m* di testa; *in document* intestazione *f*
'**head•hunt** *v/t* COM: ***be headhunted*** essere selezionato da un cacciatore di teste
'**head•hunt•er** COM cacciatore *m* di teste
head•ing ['hedɪŋ] *in list* titolo *m*
'**head•lamp** fanale *m*
'**head•land** promontorio *m*
'**head•light** fanale *m*
'**head•line** *n in newspaper* titolo; ***make the headlines*** fare titolo
'**head•long** *adv fall* a testa in giù
'**head•mas•ter** *in primary school* direttore *m*; *in secondary school* preside *m*
'**head•mis•tress** *in primary school* direttrice *f*; *in secondary school* preside *f*
head '**of•fice** *of company* sede *f* centrale
head-'on **1** *adv crash* frontalmente **2** *adj crash* frontale
'**head•phones** *npl* cuffie *fpl*
'**head•quar•ters** *npl* sede *fsg*; MIL quartier *msg* generale
'**head•rest** poggiatesta *m inv*
'**head•room** *for vehicle under bridge* altezza *f* utile; *in car* altezza *f* dell'abitacolo
'**head•scarf** foulard *m inv*

ˈ**head•strong** *adj* testardo
head ˈ**teach•er** *in primary school* direttore *m*, -trice *f*; *in secondary school* preside *m/f*
head ˈ**wait•er** capocameriere *m*
ˈ**head•wind** vento *m* di prua
head•y [ˈhedɪ] *adj drink, wine etc* inebriante
heal [hiːl] *v/t v/i* guarire
◆ **heal up** *v/i* cicatrizzarsi
health [helθ] salute *f*; (*public health*) sanità *f inv*; ***your health!*** (alla) salute!
ˈ**health care** assistenza *f* sanitaria
ˈ**health farm** beauty farm *f inv*
ˈ**health food** alimenti *mpl* macrobiotici
ˈ**health food store** negozio *m* di macrobiotica
ˈ**health in•su•rance** assicurazione *f* contro le malattie
ˈ**health re•sort** stazione *f* termale
health•y [ˈhelθɪ] *adj also fig* sano
heap [hiːp] *n* mucchio *m*
◆ **heap up** *v/t* ammucchiare
hear [hɪə(r)] *v/t & v/i* (*pret & pp* ***heard***) sentire
◆ **hear about** *v/t* sapere di
◆ **hear from** *v/t* (*have news from*) avere notizie di
heard [hɜːd] *pret & pp* → ***hear***
hear•ing [ˈhɪərɪŋ] udito *m*; LAW udienza *f*; ***be within / out of hearing*** essere / non essere a portata di voce
ˈ**hear•ing aid** apparecchio *m* acustico
ˈ**hear•say** diceria *f*; ***by hearsay*** per sentito dire
hearse [hɜːs] carro *m* funebre
heart [hɑːt] cuore *m*; *of problem etc* nocciolo *m*; ***know sth by heart*** sapere qc a memoria
ˈ**heart at•tack** infarto *m*
ˈ**heart•beat** battito *m* cardiaco
heart•break•ing [ˈhɑːtbreɪkɪŋ] *adj* straziante
ˈ**heart•brok•en** *adj* affranto
ˈ**heart•burn** bruciore *m* di stomaco
ˈ**heart fail•ure** infarto *m*
heart•felt [ˈhɑːtfelt] *adj sympathy* sentito
hearth [hɑːθ] focolare *m*
heart•less [ˈhɑːtlɪs] *adj* spietato
heart•rend•ing [ˈhɑːtrendɪŋ] *adj plea, sight* straziante
hearts [hɑːts] *npl in cards* cuori *mpl*
ˈ**heart throb** F idolo *m*
ˈ**heart trans•plant** trapianto *m* cardiaco
heart•y [ˈhɑːtɪ] *adj appetite* robusto; *meal* sostanzioso; *person* gioviale
heat [hiːt] calore *m*; (*hot weather*) caldo *m*
◆ **heat up** *v/t* riscaldare
heat•ed [ˈhiːtɪd] *adj swimming pool* riscaldato; *discussion* animato
heat•er [ˈhiːtə(r)] *radiator* termosifone *m*; *electric*, *gas* stufa *f*; *in car* riscaldamento *m*
heath [hiːθ] brughiera *f*
hea•then [ˈhiːðn] *n* pagano *m*, -a *f*
heath•er [ˈheðə(r)] erica *f*
heat•ing [ˈhiːtɪŋ] riscaldamento *m*
ˈ**heat•proof**, ˈ**heat-re•sis•tant** *adj* termoresistente
ˈ**heat•stroke** colpo *m* di calore
ˈ**heat•wave** ondata *f* di caldo
heave [hiːv] *v/t* (*lift*) sollevare
heav•en [ˈhevn] paradiso *m*; ***good heavens!*** santo cielo!
heav•en•ly [ˈhevənlɪ] *adj* F divino
heav•y [ˈhevɪ] *adj* pesante; *cold*, *rain*, *accent* forte; *traffic* intenso; *food* pesante; *smoker* accanito; *drinker* forte; *financial loss*, *casualties* ingente; ***be a heavy sleeper*** avere il sonno pesante
heav•y-ˈ**du•ty** *adj* resistente
ˈ**heav•y•weight** *adj* SP di pesi massimi
heck•le [ˈhekl] *v/t* interrompere di continuo
hec•tic [ˈhektɪk] *adj* frenetico
hedge [hedʒ] *n* siepe *f*
hedge•hog [ˈhedʒhɒg] riccio *m*
hedge•row [ˈhedʒrəʊ] siepe *f*
heed [hiːd] *v/t*: ***pay heed to …*** ascoltare …
heel [hiːl] *of foot* tallone *m*, calcagno *m*; *of shoe* tacco *m*
ˈ**heel bar** calzoleria *f* istantanea
hef•ty [ˈheftɪ] *adj* massiccio
height [haɪt] altezza *f*; *of aeroplane* altitudine *f*; ***at the height of summer*** nel pieno dell'estate
height•en [ˈhaɪtn] *v/t effect*, *tension* aumentare
heir [eə(r)] erede *m*
heir•ess [ˈeərɪs] ereditiera *f*
held [held] *pret & pp* → ***hold***
hel•i•cop•ter [ˈhelɪkɒptə(r)] elicottero *m*
hell [hel] inferno *m*; ***what the hell are you doing / do you want?*** F che diavolo fai / vuoi? F; ***go to hell!*** F va' all'inferno! F; ***a hell of a lot*** F un casino F; ***one hell of a nice guy*** F un tipo in gambissima
hel•lo [həˈləʊ] *int informal* ciao; *more formal* buongiorno; buona sera; TELEC pronto; ***say hello to s.o.*** salutare qu
helm [helm] NAUT timone *m*
hel•met [ˈhelmɪt] *of motorcyclist* casco *m*; *of soldier* elmetto *m*
help [help] **1** *n* aiuto *m* **2** *v/t* aiutare; ***help o.s.*** *to food* servirsi; ***I can't help it*** non ci posso far niente; ***I couldn't help laughing*** non ho potuto fare a meno di ri-

dere
help•er ['helpə(r)] aiutante *m/f*
help•ful ['helpfʊl] *adj person* di aiuto; *advice* utile; ***he was very helpful*** mi è stato di grande aiuto
help•ing ['helpɪŋ] *of food* porzione *f*
help•less ['helplɪs] *adj* (*unable to cope*) indifeso; (*powerless*) impotente
help•less•ly ['helplɪslɪ] *adv*: ***we watched helplessly*** guardavamo impotenti
help•less•ness ['helplɪsnɪs] impotenza *f*
'**help me•nu** COMPUT menu *m inv* della guida in linea
hem [hem] *n of dress etc* orlo *m*
hem•i•sphere ['hemɪsfɪə(r)] emisfero *m*
'**hem•line** orlo *m*
hen [hen] gallina *f*
hench•man ['hentʃmən] *pej* scagnozzo *m*
'**hen par•ty** *equivalente m al femminile della festa d'addio al celibato*
hen•pecked ['henpekt] *adj*: ***henpecked husband*** marito *m* succube della moglie
hep•a•ti•tis [hepə'taɪtɪs] epatite *f*
her [hɜː(r)] **1** *adj* il suo *m*, la sua *f*, i suoi *mpl*, le sue *fpl*; ***her ticket*** il suo biglietto; ***her brother / sister*** suo fratello / sua sorella **2** *pron direct object* la; *indirect object* le; *after prep* lei; ***I know her*** la conosco; ***I gave her the keys*** le ho dato le chiavi; ***this is for her*** questo è per lei; ***who? – her*** chi? - lei
herb [hɜːb] *for medicines* erba *f* medicinale; *for flavouring* erba *f* aromatica
herb(al) '**tea** ['hɜːb(əl)] tisana *f*
herd [hɜːd] *n* mandria *f*
here [hɪə(r)] *adv* qui, qua; ***here's to you!*** *as toast* salute!; ***here you are*** *giving sth* ecco qui; ***here!*** *in roll-call* presente!
he•red•i•ta•ry [hə'redɪtərɪ] *adj disease* ereditario
he•red•i•ty [hə'redɪtɪ] ereditarietà *f inv*
her•i•tage ['herɪtɪdʒ] patrimonio *m*
her•mit ['hɜːmɪt] eremita *m/f*
her•ni•a ['hɜːnɪə] MED ernia *f*
he•ro ['hɪərəʊ] eroe *m*
he•ro•ic [hɪ'rəʊɪk] *adj* eroico
he•ro•i•cal•ly [hɪ'rəʊɪklɪ] *adv* eroicamente
her•o•in ['herəʊɪn] eroina *f*
'**her•o•in ad•dict** eroinomane *m/f*
her•o•ine ['herəʊɪn] eroina *f*
her•o•ism ['herəʊɪzm] eroismo *m*
her•on ['herən] airone *m*
her•pes ['hɜːpiːz] MED herpes *m*
her•ring ['herɪŋ] aringa *f*
hers [hɜːz] *pron* il suo *m*, la sua *f*, i suoi *mpl*, le sue *fpl*; ***a friend of hers*** un suo amico
her•self [hɜː'self] *pron reflexive* si; *emphatic* se stessa; *after prep* sé, se stessa; ***she must be proud of herself*** dev'essere fiera di sé *o* se stessa; ***she hurt herself*** si è fatta male; ***she told me so herself*** me l'ha detto lei stessa; ***by herself*** da sola
hes•i•tant ['hezɪtənt] *adj* esitante
hes•i•tant•ly ['hezɪtəntlɪ] *adv* con esitazione
hes•i•tate ['hezɪteɪt] *v/i* esitare
hes•i•ta•tion [hezɪ'teɪʃn] esitazione *f*
het•er•o•sex•u•al [hetərəʊ'seksjʊəl] *adj* eterosessuale
hey•day ['heɪdeɪ] tempi *mpl* d'oro
hi [haɪ] *int* ciao
hi•ber•nate ['haɪbəneɪt] *v/i* andare in letargo
hic•cup ['hɪkʌp] *n* singhiozzo *m*; (*minor problem*) intoppo *m*; ***have the hiccups*** avere il singhiozzo
hid [hɪd] *pret* → ***hide***
hid•den ['hɪdn] **1** *adj* nascosto **2** *pp* → ***hide***
hid•den a'gen•da *fig* secondo fine *m*
hide[1] [haɪd] (*pret* ***hid***, *pp* ***hidden***) **1** *v/t* nascondere **2** *v/i* nascondersi
hide[2] [haɪd] *n of animal* pelle *f*
hide-and-'seek nascondino *m*
'**hide•a•way** rifugio *m*
hid•e•ous ['hɪdɪəs] *adj face*, *weather* orrendo; *crime* atroce
hid•ing[1] ['haɪdɪŋ] (*beating*) batosta *f*
hid•ing[2] ['haɪdɪŋ] *n*: ***be in hiding*** tenersi nascosto; ***go into hiding*** darsi alla macchia
'**hid•ing place** nascondiglio *m*
hi•er•ar•chy ['haɪərɑːkɪ] gerarchia *f*
hi-fi ['haɪfaɪ] hi-fi *m inv*
high [haɪ] **1** *adj building*, *price*, *mountain*, *note*, *temperature*, *salary* alto; *wind*, *speed* forte; *quality*, *hopes* buono; (*on drugs*) fatto F; ***high in the sky*** in alto nel cielo; ***have a very high opinion of …*** stimare molto …; ***it is high time he left*** sarebbe ora che se ne andasse **2** *n in statistics* livello *m* record **3** *adv* in alto
'**high•brow** *adj* intellettuale
'**high•chair** seggiolone *m*
high•'class *adj* di (prima) classe
High 'Court Corte *f* Suprema
high 'div•ing tuffo *m*
high-'fre•quen•cy *adj* ad alta frequenza
high-'grade *adj* di buona qualità
high-hand•ed [haɪ'hændɪd] *adj* autoritario
high-heeled [haɪ'hiːld] *adj* col tacco alto
'**high jump** salto *m* in alto
high-'lev•el *adj* ad alto livello
'**high life** bella vita *f*

H

'high•light 1 *n* (*main event*) clou *m inv*; *in hair* colpo *m* di sole **2** *v/t with pen* evidenziare; COMPUT selezionare
'high•light•er *pen* evidenziatore *m*
high•ly ['haɪlɪ] *adv desirable*, *likely* molto; ***be highly paid*** essere pagato profumatamente; ***think highly of s.o.*** stimare molto qu
high•ly 'strung *adj* nervoso
high per'form•ance *adj drill*, *battery* ad alto rendimento
high-pitched [haɪ'pɪtʃt] *adj* acuto
'high point clou *m inv*
high-pow•ered [haɪ'paʊəd] *adj engine* potente; *intellectual* di prestigio
high 'pres•sure 1 *n weather* alta pressione *f* **2** *adj* TECH ad alta pressione; *salesman* aggressivo
high 'priest gran sacerdote *m*
'high•rise palazzone *m*
'high school scuola *f* superiore
high so'ci•e•ty alta società *f inv*
high-speed 'train treno *m* ad alta velocità
'high street via *f* principale
high 'tech 1 *n* high-tech *m inv* **2** *adj* high tech
high 'tide alta marea *f*
high-'volt•age alta tensione *f*
high 'wa•ter alta marea *f*
High•way 'Code Codice *m* stradale
hi•jack ['haɪdʒæk] **1** *v/t* dirottare **2** *n* dirottamento *m*
hi•jack•er ['haɪdʒækə(r)] dirottatore *m*, -trice *f*
hike[1] [haɪk] **1** *n* camminata *f* **2** *v/i* fare camminate
hike[2] [haɪk] *n in prices* aumento *m*
hik•er ['haɪkə(r)] escursionista *m/f*
hik•ing ['haɪkɪŋ] escursionismo *m*
'hik•ing boots *npl* scarponcini *mpl* da camminata
hi•lar•i•ous [hɪ'leərɪəs] *adj* divertentissimo
hill [hɪl] collina *f*; (*slope*) altura *f*
hill•side ['hɪlsaɪd] pendio *m*
hill•top ['hɪltɒp] cima *f* della collina
hill•y ['hɪlɪ] *adj* collinoso
hilt [hɪlt] impugnatura *f*
him [hɪm] *pron direct object* lo; *indirect object* gli; *after prep* lui; ***I know him*** lo conosco; ***I gave him the keys*** gli ho dato le chiavi; ***this is for him*** questo è per lui; ***who? – him*** chi? - lui
him•self [hɪm'self] *pron* se stesso; *after prep* sé, se stesso; ***he must be proud of himself*** dev'essere fiero di sé *o* se stesso; ***he hurt himself*** si è fatto male; ***he told me so himself*** me l'ha detto lui stesso; ***by himself*** da solo
hind [haɪnd] *adj* posteriore
hin•der ['hɪndə(r)] *v/t* intralciare
hin•drance ['hɪndrəns] intralcio *m*
hind•sight ['haɪndsaɪt]: ***with hindsight*** con il senno di poi
hinge [hɪndʒ] cardine *m*
◆ **hinge on** *v/t* dipendere da
hint [hɪnt] *n* (*clue*) accenno *m*; (*piece of advice*) consiglio *m*; (*implied suggestion*) allusione *f*; *of red*, *sadness etc* punta *f*
hip [hɪp] *n* fianco *m*
hip 'pock•et tasca *f* posteriore
hip•po•pot•a•mus [hɪpə'pɒtəməs] ippopotamo *m*
hire ['haɪə(r)] *v/t room*, *hall* affittare; *workers*, *staff* assumere; *conjuror etc* ingaggiare
hire 'pur•chase acquisto *m* rateale
his [hɪz] **1** *adj* il suo *m*, la sua *f*, i suoi *mpl*, le sue *fpl*; ***his bag*** la sua valigia; ***his brother / sister*** suo fratello / sua sorella **2** *pron* il suo *m*, la sua *f*, i suoi *mpl*, le sue *fpl*; ***a friend of his*** un suo amico
hiss [hɪs] *v/i* sibilare
his•to•ri•an [hɪ'stɔːrɪən] storico *m*, -a *f*
his•tor•ic [hɪ'stɒrɪk] *adj* storico
his•tor•i•cal [hɪ'stɒrɪkl] *adj* storico
his•to•ry ['hɪstərɪ] storia *f*
hit [hɪt] **1** *v/t* (*pret & pp* ***hit***) colpire; (*collide with*) sbattere contro; ***I hit my knee*** ho battuto il ginocchio; ***he was hit by a bullet*** è stato colpito da un proiettile; ***it suddenly hit me*** (*I realized*) improvvisamente ho realizzato; ***hit town*** (*arrive*) arrivare (in città) **2** *n* (*blow*) colpo *m*; (*success*) successo *m*
◆ **hit back** *v/i* reagire
◆ **hit on** *v/t idea* trovare
◆ **hit out at** *v/t* (*criticize*) attaccare
hit-and-run *adj*: ***hit-and-run accident*** *incidente m con omissione di soccorso*
hitch [hɪtʃ] **1** *n* (*problem*) contrattempo *m*; ***without a hitch*** senza contrattempi **2** *v/t*: ***hitch sth to sth*** legare qc a qc; *with hook* agganciare qc a qc; ***hitch a lift*** chiedere un passaggio **3** *v/i* (*hitchhike*) fare l'autostop
◆ **hitch up** *v/t wagon*, *trailer* attaccare
'hitch•hike *v/i* fare l'autostop
'hitch•hik•er autostoppista *m/f*
'hitch•hik•ing autostop *m inv*
hi-'tech 1 *n* high-tech *m inv* **2** *adj* high tech
'hit•list libro *m* nero
'hit•man sicario *m*
hit-or-'miss *adj*: ***on a hit-or-miss basis*** affidandosi al caso
'hit squad commando *m*
HIV [eɪtʃaɪ'viː] *abbr* (= ***human immuno-***

deficiency virus) HIV *m*
hive [haɪv] *for bees* alveare *m*
◆ **hive off** *v/t* (COM: *separate off*) separare
HIV-'pos•i•tive sieropositivo
hoard [hɔːd] **1** *n* provvista *f*; ***hoard of money*** gruzzolo *m* **2** *v/t* accumulare
hoard•er ['hɔːdə(r)] *persona f che non butta mai niente*
hoarse [hɔːs] *adj* rauco
hoax [həʊks] *n* scherzo *m*; *malicious* falso allarme *m*
hob [hɒb] *on cooker* piano *m* di cottura
hob•ble ['hɒbl] *v/i* zoppicare
hob•by ['hɒbɪ] hobby *m inv*
hock•ey ['hɒkɪ] hockey *m* (su prato)
hoist [hɔɪst] **1** *n* montacarichi *m inv* **2** *v/t* (*lift*) sollevare; *flag* issare
hold [həʊld] **1** *v/t* (*pret & pp* **held**) *in hand* tenere; (*support, keep in place*) reggere; *passport, licence* avere; *prisoner, suspect* trattenere; (*contain*) contenere; *job, post* occupare; *course* tenere; ***hold hands*** tenersi per mano; ***hold one's breath*** trattenere il fiato; ***he can hold his drink*** regge bene l'alcol; ***hold s.o. responsible*** ritenere qu responsabile; ***hold that ...*** (*believe, maintain*) sostenere che ...; ***hold the line*** TELEC resti in linea **2** *n in ship, plane* stiva *f*; ***catch hold of sth*** afferrare qc; ***lose one's hold on sth*** *on rope etc* perdere la presa su qc
◆ **hold against** *v/t*: ***hold sth against s.o.*** volerne a qu per qc
◆ **hold back 1** *v/t crowds* contenere; *facts, information* nascondere **2** *v/i* (*hesitate*) esitare; ***he's holding back*** *not telling all* non sta dicendo tutta la verità
◆ **hold on** *v/i* (*wait*) attendere; TELEC restare in linea; ***now hold on a minute!*** aspetta un attimo!
◆ **hold on to** *v/t* (*keep*) tenere; *belief* aggrapparsi a
◆ **hold out 1** *v/t hand* tendere; *prospect* offrire **2** *v/i of supplies* durare; *of trapped miners etc* resistere
◆ **hold up 1** *v/t hand* alzare; *bank etc* rapinare; (*make late*) trattenere; ***hold sth up as an example*** portare qc ad esempio
◆ **hold with** *v/t* (*approve of*) essere d'accordo con
'hold•all borsone *m*
hold•er ['həʊldə(r)] (*container*) contenitore *m*; *of passport* titolare *m*; *of ticket* possessore *m*; *of record* detentore *m*, -trice *f*
'hold•ing com•pa•ny holding *f inv*
'hold•up (*robbery*) rapina *f*; (*delay*) ritardo *m*
hole [həʊl] buco *m*
hol•i•day ['hɒlədeɪ] vacanza *f*; *public* giorno *m* festivo; (*day off*) giorno *m* di ferie; ***go on holiday*** andare in vacanza
hol•i•day•mak•er ['hɒlədeɪmeɪkə(r)] vacanziere *m*, -a *f*
Hol•land ['hɒlənd] Olanda *f*
hol•low ['hɒləʊ] *adj object* cavo, vuoto; *cheeks* infossato
hol•ly ['hɒlɪ] agrifoglio *m*
hol•o•caust ['hɒləkɔːst] olocausto *m*
hol•o•gram ['hɒləgræm] ologramma *m*
hol•ster ['həʊlstə(r)] fondina *f*
ho•ly ['həʊlɪ] *adj* santo
Ho•ly 'Spir•it Spirito *m* Santo
'Ho•ly Week settimana *f* santa
home [həʊm] **1** *n* casa *f*; (*native country*) patria *f*; *for old people* casa *f* di riposo; *for children* istituto *m*; ***at home*** a casa; ***make yourself at home*** fai come a casa tua; ***at home*** SP in casa; ***work from home*** lavorare da casa **2** *adv* a casa; ***go home*** andare a casa; ***is she home yet?*** è tornata?
'home ad•dress indirizzo *m* di casa
home 'bank•ing home-banking *m inv*
'home•com•ing ritorno *m*
home com'put•er computer *m inv* (per casa)
home•less ['həʊmlɪs] *adj* senza tetto; ***the homeless*** i senzacasa
'home•lov•ing *adj* casalingo
home•ly ['həʊmlɪ] *adj* semplice; (*welcoming*) accogliente
home'made *adj* fatto in casa, casalingo
'home match incontro *m* casalingo
home 'mov•ie filmino *m* (casalingo)
'Home Of•fice Ministero *m* degli Interni
ho•me•op•a•thy [həʊmɪ'ɒpəθɪ] omeopatia *f*
'home page home page *f*
Home 'Sec•ret•ar•y Ministro *m* degli Interni
'home•sick *adj*: ***be homesick*** avere nostalgia di casa
'home town città *f inv* natale
home•ward ['həʊmwəd] *adv* verso casa
'home•work EDU compiti *mpl* a casa
'home•work•ing COM telelavoro *m inv*
hom•i•cide ['hɒmɪsaɪd] *crime* omicidio *m*; *Am*: *police department* (squadra *f*) omicidi *f*
hom•o•graph ['hɒməgræf] omografo *m*
ho•mo•pho•bi•a [hɒmə'fəʊbɪə] omofobia *f*
ho•mo•sex•u•al [hɒmə'seksjʊəl] **1** *adj* omosessuale **2** *n* omosessuale *m/f*
hon•est ['ɒnɪst] *adj* onesto
hon•est•ly ['ɒnɪstlɪ] *adv* onestamente; ***honestly!*** ma insomma!

hon•es•ty ['ɒnɪstɪ] onestà *f inv*
hon•ey ['hʌnɪ] miele *m*; F (*darling*) tesoro *m*
'**hon•ey•comb** favo *m*
'**hon•ey•moon** *n* luna *f* di miele
honk [hɒŋk] *v/t horn* suonare
hon•or *etc Am* → ***honour*** *etc*
hon•our ['ɒnə(r)] **1** *n* onore *m* **2** *v/t* onorare
hon•our•a•ble ['ɒnrəbl] *adj* onorevole
hood [hʊd] *over head* cappuccio *m*; *over cooker* cappa *f*; MOT: *on convertible* capote *f inv*
hood•lum ['huːdləm] gangster *m inv*
hoof [huːf] zoccolo *m*
hook [hʊk] gancio *m*; *for fishing* amo *m*; ***off the hook*** TELEC staccato
hooked [hʊkt] *adj*: ***be hooked on s.o./-sth*** essere fanatico di qu / qc; ***be hooked on sth*** *on drugs* essere assuefatto a qc
hook•er ['hʊkə(r)] F prostituta *f*; *in rugby* tallonatore *m*
hoo•li•gan ['huːlɪgən] teppista *m/f*
hoo•li•gan•is•m ['huːlɪgənɪzm] teppismo *m*
hoop [huːp] cerchio *m*
hoot [huːt] **1** *v/t horn* suonare **2** *v/i of car* suonare il clacson; *of owl* gufare
hoo•ver® ['huːvə(r)] **1** *n* aspirapolvere *m* **2** *v/t carpets*, *room* pulire con l'aspirapolvere
hop[1] [hɒp] *n plant* luppolo *m*
hop[2] [hɒp] *v/i* (*pret & pp* ***-ped***) saltare
hope [həʊp] **1** *n* speranza *f*; ***there's no hope of that*** non farci conto **2** *v/i* sperare; ***hope for sth*** augurarsi qc; ***I hope so*** spero di sì; ***I hope not*** spero di no **3** *v/t*: ***I hope you like it*** spero che ti piaccia
hopeful ['həʊpfʊl] *adj person* ottimista; (*promising*) promettente
hope•ful•ly ['həʊpflɪ] *adv say*, *wait* con ottimismo; (*I/we hope*) si spera
hope•less ['həʊplɪs] *adj position*, *prospect* senza speranza; (*useless*: *person*) negato F
ho•ri•zon [hə'raɪzn] orizzonte *m*
hor•i•zon•tal [hɒrɪ'zɒntl] *adj* orizzontale
hor•mone ['hɔːməʊn] ormone *m*
horn [hɔːn] *of animal* corno *m*; MOT clacson *m inv*
hor•net ['hɔːnɪt] calabrone *m*
horn-rimmed '**spec•ta•cles** [hɔːnrɪmd] *npl* occhiali *mpl* con montatura di tartaruga
horn•y ['hɔːnɪ] *adj* F *sexually* arrapato P
hor•o•scope ['hɒrəskəʊp] oroscopo *m*
hor•ri•ble ['hɒrɪbl] *adj* orribile
hor•ri•fy ['hɒrɪfaɪ] *v/t* (*pret & pp* ***-ied***) inorridire; ***I was horrified*** ero scioccato
hor•ri•fy•ing ['hɒrɪfaɪɪŋ] *adj experience* terrificante; *idea*, *prices* allucinante
hor•ror ['hɒrə(r)] orrore *m*; ***the horrors of war*** le atrocità della guerra
'**hor•ror mov•ie** film *m* dell'orrore
hors d'oeu•vre [ɔː'dɜːvr] antipasto *m*
horse [hɔːs] cavallo *m*
'**horse•back** *n*: ***on horseback*** a cavallo
horse '**chest•nut** ippocastano *m*
'**horse•pow•er** cavallo-vapore *m*
'**horse•shoe** ferro *m* di cavallo
hor•ti•cul•ture ['hɔːtɪkʌltʃə(r)] orticoltura *f*
hose [həʊz] *n* tubo *m* di gomma
hos•pice ['hɒspɪs] ospedale *m* per i malati terminali
hos•pi•ta•ble [hɒ'spɪtəbl] *adj* ospitale
hos•pi•tal ['hɒspɪtl] ospedale *m*; ***go into hospital*** essere ricoverato (in ospedale)
hos•pi•tal•i•ty [hɒspɪ'tælətɪ] ospitalità *f inv*
host [həʊst] *n at party*, *reception* padrone *m* di casa; *of TV programme* presentatore *m*, -trice *f*
hos•tage ['hɒstɪdʒ] ostaggio *m*; ***be taken hostage*** essere preso in ostaggio
hos•tel ['hɒstl] *for students* pensionato *m*; (*youth hostel*) ostello *m* (della gioventù)
hos•tess ['həʊstɪs] *at party*, *reception* padrona *f* di casa; *on aeroplane* hostess *f inv*
hos•tile ['hɒstaɪl] *adj* ostile
hos•til•i•ty [hɒ'stɪlətɪ] ostilità *f inv*
hot [hɒt] *adj weather*, *water* caldo; (*spicy*) piccante; F (*good*) bravo (***at sth*** in qc); ***it's hot*** fa caldo; ***I'm hot*** ho caldo
'**hot dog** hot dog *m inv*
ho•tel [həʊ'tel] albergo *m*
'**hot•plate** piastra *f* riscaldante
'**hot spot** *military*, *political* zona *f* calda
hour ['aʊə(r)] ora *f*
hour•ly ['aʊəlɪ] *adj pay*, *rate* a ora; ***at hourly intervals*** ad ogni ora
house [haʊs] **1** *n* casa *f*; POL camera *f*; THEA sala *f*; ***at your house*** a casa tua, da te **2** *v/t* [haʊz] alloggiare
'**house•boat** house boat *f inv*
'**house•break•ing** furto *m* con scasso
'**house•hold** famiglia *f*
house•hold '**name** nome *m* conosciuto
'**house hus•band** casalingo *m*
'**house•keep•er** governante *f*
'**house•keep•ing** *activity* governo *m* della casa; *money* soldi *mpl* per le spese di casa
house•warm•ing (party) ['haʊswɔːmɪŋ] *festa f per inaugurare la nuova casa*
'**house•wife** casalinga *f*
'**house•work** lavori *mpl* domestici
hous•ing ['haʊzɪŋ] alloggi *mpl*; TECH al-

loggiamento *m*
hov•el ['hɒvl] tugurio *m*
hov•er ['hɒvə(r)] *v/i* librarsi
'**hov•er•craft** hovercraft *m inv*
how [haʊ] *adv* come; ***how are you?*** come stai?; ***how about …?*** che ne dici di …?; ***how much?*** quanto?; ***how much is it?*** *of cost* quant'è?; ***how many?*** quanti?; ***how often?*** ogni quanto?; ***how odd / lovely!*** che strano / bello!
how'ev•er *adv* comunque; ***however big / rich they are*** per quanto grandi / ricchi siano
howl [haʊl] *v/i of dog* ululare; *of person in pain* urlare; ***howl with laughter*** sbellicarsi dalle risate
howl•er ['haʊlə(r)] *mistake* strafalcione *m*
hub [hʌb] *of wheel* mozzo *m*
'**hub•cap** coprimozzo *m*
◆ **huddle together** ['hʌdl] *v/i* stringersi l'un l'altro
hue [hjuː] tinta *f*
huff [hʌf]: ***be in a huff*** essere imbronciato
hug [hʌg] **1** *v/t* (*pret & pp* ***-ged***) abbracciare **2** *n* abbraccio *m*
huge [hjuːdʒ] *adj* enorme
hull [hʌl] scafo *m*
hul•la•ba•loo [hʌləbə'luː] baccano *m*
hum [hʌm] (*pret & pp* ***-med***) **1** *v/t song, tune* canticchiare **2** *v/i of person* canticchiare; *of machine* ronzare
hu•man ['hjuːmən] **1** *n* essere *m* umano **2** *adj* umano; ***human error*** errore *m* umano
hu•man 'be•ing essere *m* umano
hu•mane [hjuː'meɪn] *adj* umano
hu•man•i•tar•i•an [hjuːmænɪ'teərɪən] *adj* umanitario
hu•man•i•ty [hjuː'mænətɪ] umanità *f inv*
hu•man 'race genere *m* umano
hu•man re'sources *npl* risorse *fpl* umane
hum•ble ['hʌmbl] *adj origins, person* umile; *house* modesto
hum•drum ['hʌmdrʌm] *adj* monotono
hu•mid ['hjuːmɪd] *adj* umido
hu•mid•i•fi•er [hjuː'mɪdɪfaɪə(r)] umidificatore *m*
hu•mid•i•ty [hjuː'mɪdətɪ] umidità *f inv*
hu•mil•i•ate [hjuː'mɪlɪeɪt] *v/t* umiliare
hu•mil•i•at•ing [hjuː'mɪlɪeɪtɪŋ] *adj* umiliante
hu•mil•i•a•tion [hjuːmɪlɪ'eɪʃn] umiliazione *f*
hu•mil•i•ty [hjuː'mɪlətɪ] umiltà *f inv*
hu•mor *Am* → ***humour***
hu•mor•ous ['hjuːmərəs] *adj person* spiritoso; *story* umoristico
hu•mour ['hjuːmə(r)] umorismo *m*; (*mood*) umore *m*; ***sense of humour*** senso dell'umorismo
hump [hʌmp] **1** *n of camel, person* gobba *f*; *on road* dosso *m* **2** *v/t* F (*carry*) portare
hunch [hʌntʃ] (*idea*) impressione *f*; *of detective* intuizione *f*
hun•dred ['hʌndrəd] cento *m*; ***a hundred …*** cento …
hun•dredth ['hʌndrəθ] *n & adj* centesimo, -a
'**hun•dred•weight** cinquanta chili (*circa*)
hung [hʌŋ] *pret & pp* → ***hang***
Hun•gar•i•an [hʌŋ'geərɪən] **1** *adj* ungherese **2** *n person* ungherese *m/f*; *language* ungherese *m*
Hun•ga•ry ['hʌŋgərɪ] Ungheria *f*
hun•ger ['hʌŋgə(r)] fame *f*
hung-o•ver [hʌŋ'əʊvə(r)] *adj*: ***feel hung-over*** avere i postumi della sbornia
hun•gry ['hʌŋgrɪ] *adj* affamato; ***I'm hungry*** ho fame
hunk [hʌŋk] *n* tocco *m*; F (*man*) fusto *m* F
hun•ky-do•ry [hʌŋkɪ'dɔːrɪ] *adj* F: ***everything's hunky-dory*** tutto va a meraviglia
hunt [hʌnt] **1** *n for animals* caccia *f*; *for job, house, missing child* ricerca *f* **2** *v/t animal* cacciare
◆ **hunt for** *v/t* cercare
hunt•er ['hʌntə(r)] cacciatore *m*, -trice *f*
hunt•ing ['hʌntɪŋ] caccia *f*
hur•dle ['hɜːdl] *also fig* ostacolo *m*
hur•dler ['hɜːdlə(r)] SP ostacolista *m/f*
hur•dles *npl* SP: ***100 metres hurdles*** i cento metri a ostacoli
hurl [hɜːl] *v/t* scagliare
hur•ray [hʊ'reɪ] *int* urrà!
hur•ri•cane ['hʌrɪkən] uragano *m*
hur•ried ['hʌrɪd] *adj* frettoloso
hur•ry ['hʌrɪ] **1** *n* fretta *f*; ***be in a hurry*** avere fretta **2** *v/i* (*pret & pp* ***-ied***) sbrigarsi
◆ **hurry up 1** *v/i* sbrigarsi; ***hurry up!*** sbrigati! **2** *v/t* fare fretta a
hurt [hɜːt] (*pret & pp* ***hurt***) **1** *v/i* far male; ***does it hurt?*** ti fa male? **2** *v/t physically* far male a; *emotionally* ferire
hus•band ['hʌzbənd] marito *m*
hush [hʌʃ] *n* silenzio *m*; ***hush!*** silenzio!
◆ **hush up** *v/t scandal etc* mettere a tacere
husk [hʌsk] pula *m*
hus•ky ['hʌskɪ] *adj voice* roco
hus•tle ['hʌsl] **1** *n*: ***hustle and bustle*** trambusto *m* **2** *v/t person* spingere
hut [hʌt] capanno *m*
hy•a•cinth ['haɪəsɪnθ] giacinto *m*
hy•brid ['haɪbrɪd] *n plant, animal* ibrido *m*
hy•drant ['haɪdrənt] idrante *m*
hy•draul•ic [haɪ'drɔːlɪk] *adj* idraulico
hy•dro•e'lec•tric [haɪdrəʊɪ'lektrɪk] *adj* idroelettrico

'hy•dro•foil ['haɪdrəfɔɪl] *boat* aliscafo *m*
hy•dro•gen ['haɪdrədʒən] idrogeno *m*
'hy•dro•gen bomb bomba *f* H
hy•giene ['haɪdʒiːn] igiene *f*
hy•gien•ic [haɪ'dʒiːnɪk] *adj* igienico
hymn [hɪm] inno *m* (sacro)
hype [haɪp] *n* pubblicità *f inv*
hy•per•ac•tive [haɪpər'æktɪv] *adj* iperattivo
hy•per•mar•ket ['haɪpəmɑːkɪt] ipermercato *m*
hy•per•sen•si•tive [haɪpə'sensɪtɪv] *adj* ipersensibile
hy•per•ten•sion [haɪpə'tenʃn] ipertensione *f*
hy•per•text ['haɪpətekst] COMPUT ipertesto *m*
hy•phen ['haɪfn] trattino *m*
hyp•no•sis [hɪp'nəʊsɪs] ipnosi *f*
hyp•no•ther•a•py [hɪpnəʊ'θerəpɪ] ipnoterapia *f*
hyp•no•tize ['hɪpnətaɪz] *v/t* ipnotizzare
hy•po•chon•dri•ac [haɪpə'kɒndrɪæk] *n* ipocondriaco *m*, -a *f*
hy•poc•ri•sy [hɪ'pɒkrəsɪ] ipocrisia *f*
hyp•o•crite ['hɪpəkrɪt] ipocrita *m/f*
hyp•o•crit•i•cal [hɪpə'krɪtɪkl] *adj* ipocrita
hy•po•ther•mi•a [haɪpəʊ'θɜːmɪə] ipotermia *f*
hy•poth•e•sis [haɪ'pɒθəsɪs] (*pl* ***hypotheses*** [haɪ'pɒθəsiːz]) ipotesi *f inv*
hy•po•thet•i•cal [haɪpə'θetɪkl] *adj* ipotetico
hys•ter•ec•to•my [hɪstə'rektəmɪ] isterectomia *f*
hys•te•ri•a [hɪ'stɪərɪə] isteria *f*
hys•ter•i•cal [hɪ'sterɪkl] *adj person, laugh* isterico; F (*very funny*) buffissimo; ***become hysterical*** avere una crisi isterica
hys•ter•ics [hɪ'sterɪks] *npl laughter* attacco *m* di risa; MED crisi *f* isterica

I

I [aɪ] *pron* io; ***I am English*** sono inglese; ***you're crazy, I'm not*** tu sei pazzo, io no
ice [aɪs] ghiaccio *m*; ***break the ice*** *fig* rompere il ghiaccio
◆ **ice up** *v/i of engine, wings* ghiacciarsi
ice•berg ['aɪsbɜːg] iceberg *m inv*
'**ice•box** *Am* frigo *m*
'**ice•break•er** *ship* rompighiaccio *m inv*
'**ice cream** gelato *m*
'**ice cream par•lor** *Am*, '**ice cream parlour** gelateria *f*
'**ice cube** cubetto *m* di ghiaccio
iced [aɪst] *adj drink* ghiacciato; *cake* glassato
iced '**cof•fee** caffè *m inv* freddo
'**ice hock•ey** hockey *m inv* sul ghiaccio
'**ice lol•ly** ghiacciolo *m*
'**ice rink** pista *f* di pattinaggio
'**ice skate** pattinare (sul ghiaccio)
'**ice skat•ing** pattinaggio *m* (sul ghiaccio)
i•ci•cle ['aɪsɪkl] ghiacciolo *m*
i•cing ['aɪsɪŋ] glassa *f*
i•con ['aɪkɒn] *cultural* mito *m*; COMPUT icona *f*
icy ['aɪsɪ] *adj road, surface* ghiacciato; *welcome* glaciale
ID [aɪ'diː] *abbr* (= ***identity***): ***have you got any ID on you?*** ha un documento d'identità?
idea [aɪ'dɪə] idea *f*; ***good idea!*** ottima idea!; ***I have no idea*** non ne ho la minima idea; ***it's not a good idea to …*** non è una buona idea …
i•deal [aɪ'dɪəl] *adj* (*perfect*) ideale; ***it's not ideal but we'll take it*** non è l'ideale ma lo prendiamo lo stesso
i•deal•is•tic [aɪdɪə'lɪstɪk] *adj person* idealista; *views* idealistico
i•deal•ly [aɪ'dɪəlɪ] *adv*: ***the hotel is ideally situated*** l'albergo si trova in una posizione ideale; ***ideally, we would do it like this*** l'ideale sarebbe farlo così
i•den•ti•cal [aɪ'dentɪkl] *adj* identico; ***identical twins*** gemelli *mpl* monozigotici
i•den•ti•fi•ca•tion [aɪdentɪfɪ'keɪʃn] identificazione *f*, riconoscimento *m*; *papers etc* documento *m* di riconoscimento *o* d'identità
i•den•ti•fy [aɪ'dentɪfaɪ] *v/t* (*pret & pp* ***-ied***) (*recognize*) identificare, riconoscere; (*point out*) individuare
i•den•ti•ty [aɪ'dentətɪ] identità *f inv*; ***identity card*** carta *f* d'identità; ***a case of mistaken identity*** uno scambio di persona
i•de•o•log•i•cal [aɪdɪə'lɒdʒɪkl] *adj* ideologico
i•de•ol•o•gy [aɪdɪ'ɒlədʒɪ] ideologia *f*
id•i•om ['ɪdɪəm] (*saying*) locuzione *f* idiomatica
id•i•o•mat•ic [ɪdɪə'mætɪk] *adj* naturale
id•i•o•syn•cra•sy [ɪdɪə'sɪŋkrəsɪ] piccola mania *f*
id•i•ot ['ɪdɪət] idiota *m/f*
id•i•ot•ic [ɪdɪ'ɒtɪk] *adj* idiota
i•dle ['aɪdl] **1** *adj person* disoccupato; *threat* vuoto; *machinery* inattivo; ***in an idle moment*** in un momento libero **2** *v/i of engine* girare al minimo
◆ **idle away** *v/t the time etc* trascorrere oziando
i•dol ['aɪdl] idolo *m*
i•dol•ize ['aɪdəlaɪz] *v/t* idolatrare
i•dyl•lic [ɪ'dɪlɪk] *adj* idilli(a)co
if [ɪf] *conj* se; ***if only you had told me*** se (solo) me l'avessi detto
ig•nite [ɪg'naɪt] *v/t* dar fuoco a
ig•ni•tion [ɪg'nɪʃn] *in car* accensione *f*; ***ignition key*** chiave *f* dell'accensione
ig•no•rance ['ɪgnərəns] ignoranza *f*
ig•no•rant ['ɪgnərənt] *adj* (*rude*) cafone; ***be ignorant of sth*** ignorare qc
ig•nore [ɪg'nɔː(r)] *v/t* ignorare
ill [ɪl] *adj* ammalato; ***fall ill, be taken ill*** ammalarsi; ***feel ill*** sentirsi male; ***look ill*** avere una brutta cera; ***feel ill at ease*** sentirsi a disagio
il•le•gal [ɪ'liːgl] *adj* illegale
il•le•gi•ble [ɪ'ledʒəbl] *adj* illeggibile
il•le•git•i•mate [ɪlɪ'dʒɪtɪmət] *adj child* illegittimo
ill-fat•ed [ɪl'feɪtɪd] *adj* sfortunato
il•li•cit [ɪ'lɪsɪt] *adj copy, imports* illegale; *pleasure, relationship* illecito
il•lit•e•rate [ɪ'lɪtərət] *adj* analfabeta
ill-man•nered [ɪl'mænəd] *adj* maleducato
ill-na•tured [ɪl'neɪtʃəd] *adj* d'indole cattiva
ill•ness ['ɪlnɪs] malattia *f*
il•log•i•cal [ɪ'lɒdʒɪkl] *adj* illogico
ill-tem•pered [ɪl'tempəd] *adj* irascibile
ill'**treat** *v/t* maltrattare
il•lu•mi•nate [ɪ'luːmɪneɪt] *v/t building etc* illuminare
il•lu•mi•nat•ing [ɪ'luːmɪneɪtɪŋ] *adj remarks etc* chiarificatore
il•lu•sion [ɪ'luːʒn] illusione *f*
il•lus•trate ['ɪləstreɪt] *v/t* illustrare

il•lus•tra•tion [ɪlə'streɪʃn] (*picture*) illustrazione *f*; *with examples* esemplificazione *f*
il•lus•tra•tor [ɪlə'streɪtə(r)] illustratore *m*, -trice *f*
ill 'will rancore *m*
im•age ['ɪmɪdʒ] immagine *f*; (*exact likeness*) ritratto *m*
'im•age-con•scious *adj* attento all'immagine
i•ma•gi•na•ble [ɪ'mædʒɪnəbl] *adj* immaginabile; ***the biggest / smallest size imaginable*** la misura più grande / piccola che si possa immaginare
i•ma•gi•na•ry [ɪ'mædʒɪnərɪ] *adj* immaginario
i•ma•gi•na•tion [ɪmædʒɪ'neɪʃn] immaginazione *f*, fantasia *f*; ***it's all in your imagination*** è tutto frutto della tua immaginazione
i•ma•gi•na•tive [ɪ'mædʒɪnətɪv] *adj* fantasioso
i•ma•gine [ɪ'mædʒɪn] *v/t* immaginare; ***I can just imagine it*** me l'immagino; ***you're imagining things*** è frutto della tua immaginazione
im•be•cile ['ɪmbəsiːl] ebete *m/f*
IMF [aɪem'ef] *abbr* (= ***International Monetary Fund***) FMI *m* (= Fondo *m* Monetario Internazionale)
im•i•tate ['ɪmɪteɪt] *v/t* imitare
im•i•ta•tion [ɪmɪ'teɪʃn] imitazione *f*; ***learn by imitation*** imparare copiando
im•mac•u•late [ɪ'mækjʊlət] *adj* immacolato
im•ma•te•ri•al [ɪmə'tɪərɪəl] *adj* (*not relevant*) irrilevante
im•ma•ture [ɪmə'tʃʊə(r)] *adj* immaturo
im•me•di•ate [ɪ'miːdɪət] *adj* immediato; ***the immediate family*** i familiari più stretti; ***the immediate problem*** il problema più immediato; ***in the immediate neighbourhood*** nelle immediate vicinanze
im•me•di•ate•ly [ɪ'miːdɪətlɪ] *adv* immediatamente; ***immediately after the bank / church*** subito dopo la banca / chiesa
im•mense [ɪ'mens] *adj* immenso
im•merse [ɪ'mɜːs] *v/t* immergere; ***immerse o.s. in*** immergersi in
im•mer•sion heat•er [ɪ'mɜːʃn] scaldabagno *m* elettrico
im•mi•grant ['ɪmɪgrənt] *n* immigrato *m*, -a *f*
im•mi•grate ['ɪmɪgreɪt] *v/i* immigrare
im•mi•gra•tion [ɪmɪ'greɪʃn] *act* immigrazione *f*; ***Immigration*** *government department* ufficio *m* stranieri
im•mi•nent ['ɪmɪnənt] *adj* imminente
im•mo•bi•lize [ɪ'məʊbɪlaɪz] *v/t factory, person, car* immobilizzare
im•mo•bi•liz•er [ɪ'məʊbɪlaɪzə(r)] *on car* immobilizzatore *m*
im•mod•e•rate [ɪ'mɒdərət] *adj* smodato
im•mor•al [ɪ'mɒrəl] *adj* immorale
im•mor•al•i•ty [ɪmɒ'rælɪtɪ] immoralità *f inv*
im•mor•tal [ɪ'mɔːtl] *adj* immortale
im•mor•tal•i•ty [ɪmɔː'tælɪtɪ] immortalità *f inv*
im•mune [ɪ'mjuːn] *adj to illness, infection* immune; *from ruling, requirement* esente
im'mune sys•tem MED sistema *m* immunitario
im•mu•ni•ty [ɪ'mjuːnətɪ] *to infection* immunità *f inv*; *from ruling* esenzione *f*; ***diplomatic immunity*** immunità *f inv* diplomatica
im•pact ['ɪmpækt] *n of meteorite, vehicle* urto *m*; *of new manager etc* impatto *m*; (*effect*) effetto *m*
im•pair [ɪm'peə(r)] *v/t* danneggiare
im•paired [ɪm'peəd] *adj* danneggiato
im•par•tial [ɪm'pɑːʃl] *adj* imparziale
im•pass•a•ble [ɪm'pɑːsəbl] *adj road* impraticabile
im•passe ['æmpɑːs] *in negotations etc* impasse *m inv*
im•pas•sioned [ɪm'pæʃnd] *adj speech, plea* appassionato
im•pas•sive [ɪm'pæsɪv] *adj* impassibile
im•pa•tience [ɪm'peɪʃəns] impazienza *f*
im•pa•tient [ɪm'peɪʃənt] *adj* impaziente
im•pa•tient•ly [ɪm'peɪʃəntlɪ] *adv* con impazienza
im•peach [ɪm'piːtʃ] *v/t President* mettere in stato d'accusa
im•pec•ca•ble [ɪm'pekəbl] *adj* impeccabile
im•pec•ca•bly [ɪm'pekəblɪ] *adv* impeccabilmente
im•pede [ɪm'piːd] *v/t* ostacolare
im•ped•i•ment [ɪm'pedɪmənt] *in speech* difetto *m*
im•pend•ing [ɪm'pendɪŋ] *adj* imminente
im•pen•e•tra•ble [ɪm'penɪtrəbl] *adj* impenetrabile
im•per•a•tive [ɪm'perətɪv] **1** *adj* essenziale **2** *n* GRAM imperativo *m*
im•per•cep•ti•ble [ɪmpɜː'septɪbl] *adj* impercettibile
im•per•fect [ɪm'pɜːfekt] **1** *adj* imperfetto **2** *n* GRAM imperfetto *m*
im•pe•ri•al [ɪm'pɪərɪəl] *adj* imperiale
im•per•son•al [ɪm'pɜːsənl] *adj* impersonale
im•per•so•nate [ɪm'pɜːsəneɪt] *v/t as a jo-*

ke imitare; *illegally* fingersi
im•per•ti•nence [ɪm'pɜːtɪnəns] impertinenza *f*
im•per•ti•nent [ɪm'pɜːtɪnənt] *adj* impertinente
im•per•tur•ba•ble [ɪmpə'tɜːbəbl] *adj* imperturbabile
im•per•vious [ɪm'pɜːvɪəs] *adj*: ***impervious to*** indifferente a
im•pe•tu•ous [ɪm'petjʊəs] *adj* impetuoso
im•pe•tus ['ɪmpɪtəs] *of campaign etc* impeto *m*
im•ple•ment ['ɪmplɪmənt] **1** *n* utensile *m* **2** *v/t* implementare; *measures* attuare, implementare
im•pli•cate ['ɪmplɪkeɪt] *v/t* implicare; ***implicate s.o. in sth*** implicare qu in qc
im•pli•ca•tion [ɪmplɪ'keɪʃn] conseguenza *f* possibile; ***by implication*** implicitamente
im•pli•cit [ɪm'plɪsɪt] *adj* implicito; *trust* assoluto
im•plore [ɪm'plɔː(r)] *v/t* implorare
im•ply [ɪm'plaɪ] *v/i* (*pret & pp* ***-ied***) implicare; ***are you implying I was lying?*** stai insinuando che ho mentito?
im•po•lite [ɪmpə'laɪt] *adj* maleducato
im•port ['ɪmpɔːt] **1** *n* importazione *f*; *item* articolo *m* d'importazione **2** *v/t* importare
im•por•tance [ɪm'pɔːtəns] importanza *f*
im•por•tant [ɪm'pɔːtənt] *adj* importante
im•por•ter [ɪm'pɔːtə(r)] importatore *m*, -trice *f*
im•pose [ɪm'pəʊz] *v/t tax* imporre; ***impose o.s. on s.o.*** disturbare qu
im•pos•ing [ɪm'pəʊzɪŋ] *adj* imponente
im•pos•si•bil•i•ty [ɪmpɒsɪ'bɪlɪtɪ] impossibilità *f inv*
im•pos•sible [ɪm'pɒsɪbəl] *adj* impossibile
im•pos•tor [ɪm'pɒstə(r)] impostore *m*, -a *f*
im•po•tence ['ɪmpətəns] impotenza *f*
im•po•tent ['ɪmpətənt] *adj* impotente
im•pov•e•rished [ɪm'pɒvərɪʃt] *adj* impoverito
im•prac•ti•cal [ɪm'præktɪkəl] *adj person* senza senso pratico; *suggestion* poco pratico
im•press [ɪm'pres] *v/t* fare colpo su; ***be impressed by s.o./sth*** essere colpito da qu / qc; ***$500 an hour? – I'm impressed*** 500 dollari all'ora? - però; ***terrible work, I'm not impressed*** pessimo lavoro, vergogna
im•pres•sion [ɪm'preʃn] impressione *f*; (*impersonation*) imitazione *f*; ***make a good / bad impression on s.o.*** fare buona / cattiva impressione su qu; ***I get the impression that …*** ho l'impressione che …
im•pres•sion•a•ble [ɪm'preʃənəbl] *adj* impressionabile
im•pres•sive [ɪm'presɪv] *adj* notevole
im•print ['ɪmprɪnt] *n of credit card* impressione *f*
im•pris•on [ɪm'prɪzn] *v/t* incarcerare
im•pris•on•ment [ɪm'prɪznmənt] carcerazione *f*; ***15 years' imprisonment*** 15 anni di carcere *o* reclusione
im•prob•a•ble [ɪm'prɒbəbəl] *adj* improbabile
im•prop•er [ɪm'prɒpə(r)] *adj behaviour* sconveniente; *use* improprio
im•prove [ɪm'pruːv] *v/t & v/i* migliorare
im•prove•ment [ɪm'pruːvmənt] miglioramento *m*
im•pro•vise ['ɪmprəvaɪz] *v/i* improvvisare
im•pu•dent ['ɪmpjʊdənt] *adj* impudente
im•pulse ['ɪmpʌls] impulso *m*; ***do sth on an impulse*** fare qc d'impulso
'impulse buy acquisto *m* d'impulso
im•pul•sive [ɪm'pʌlsɪv] *adj* impulsivo
im•pu•ni•ty [ɪm'pjuːnətɪ]: ***with impunity*** impunemente
im•pure [ɪm'pjʊə(r)] *adj* impuro
in [ɪn] **1** *prep* ◇ ***in Birmingham / Milan*** a Birmingham / Milano; ***in the street*** per strada; ***in the box*** nella scatola; ***put it in your pocket*** mettitelo in tasca; ***wounded in the leg / arm*** ferito alla gamba / al braccio
◇ ***in 1999*** nel 1999; ***in two hours*** *from now* tra due ore; *over period of* in due ore; ***in the morning*** la mattina; ***in the summer*** d'estate; ***in September*** a *o* in settembre
◇ ***in English / Italian*** in inglese / italiano; ***in a loud voice*** a voce alta; ***in his style*** nel suo stile; ***in yellow*** di giallo
◇ ***in crossing the road*** (*while*) mentre attraversava la strada; ***in agreeing to this*** (*by virtue of*) accettando questo
◇ ***in his first novel*** nel suo primo romanzo; ***in Dante*** in Dante
◇ ***three in all*** tre in tutto; ***one in ten*** uno su dieci **2** *adv*: ***be in*** *at home* essere a casa; *in the building etc* esserci; *arrived*: *of train* essere arrivato; *in its position* essere dentro; ***is she in?*** c'è?; ***in here / there*** qui / lì (dentro) **3** *adj* (*fashionable, popular*) in, di moda
in•a•bil•i•ty [ɪnə'bɪlɪtɪ] incapacità *f inv*
in•ac•ces•si•ble [ɪnək'sesɪbl] *adj* inaccessibile
in•ac•cu•rate [ɪn'ækjʊrət] *adj* inaccurato
in•ac•tive [ɪn'æktɪv] *adj* inattivo
in•ad•e•quate [ɪn'ædɪkwət] *adj* inadeguato

in•ad•vis•a•ble [ɪnəd'vaɪzəbl] *adj* sconsigliabile
in•an•i•mate [ɪn'ænɪmət] *adj* inanimato
in•ap•pro•pri•ate [ɪnə'prəʊprɪət] *adj* inappropriato
in•ar•tic•u•late [ɪnɑː'tɪkjʊlət] *adj* che si esprime male
in•at•ten•tive [ɪnə'tentɪv] *adj* disattento
in•au•di•ble [ɪn'ɔːdɪbl] *adj* impercettibile
in•au•gu•ral [ɪ'nɔːgjʊrəl] *adj speech* inaugurale
in•au•gu•rate [ɪ'nɔːgjʊreɪt] *v/t* inaugurare
in•born ['ɪnbɔːn] *adj* innato
in•breed•ing ['ɪnbriːdɪŋ] unioni *fpl* tra consanguinei
in•cal•cul•a•ble [ɪn'kælkjʊləbl] *adj damage* incalcolabile
in•ca•pa•ble [ɪn'keɪpəbl]] *adj* incapace; ***be incapable of doing sth*** essere incapace di fare qc
in•cen•di•a•ry de'vice [ɪn'sendɪərɪ] ordigno *m* incendiario
in•cense[1] ['ɪnsens] *n* incenso *m*
in•cense[2] [ɪn'sens] *v/t* fare infuriare
in•cen•tive [ɪn'sentɪv] incentivo *m*
in•ces•sant [ɪn'sesnt] *adj* incessante
in•ces•sant•ly [ɪn'sesntlɪ] *adv* incessantemente
in•cest ['ɪnsest] incesto *m*
inch [ɪnʧ] pollice *m*
in•ci•dent ['ɪnsɪdənt] incidente *m*
in•ci•den•tal [ɪnsɪ'dentl] *adj* casuale; ***incidental expenses*** spese accessorie
in•ci•den•tal•ly [ɪnsɪ'dentlɪ] *adv* (*by the way*) a proposito
in•cin•e•ra•tor [ɪn'sɪnəreɪtə(r)] inceneritore *m*
in•ci•sion [ɪn'sɪʒn] incisione *f*
in•ci•sive [ɪn'saɪsɪv] *adj mind, analysis* acuto
in•cite [ɪn'saɪt] *v/t* incitare; ***incite s.o. to do sth*** istigare qu a fare qc
in•clem•ent [ɪn'klemənt] *adj weather* inclemente
in•cli•na•tion [ɪnklɪ'neɪʃn] *tendency, liking* inclinazione *f*
in•cline [ɪn'klaɪn] *v/t*: ***be inclined to believe sth*** essere propenso a credere qc; ***be inclined to do sth*** avere la tendenza di fare qc
in•close, in•clos•ure → ***enclose, enclosure***
in•clude [ɪn'kluːd] *v/t* includere, comprendere
in•clud•ing [ɪn'kluːdɪŋ] *prep* compreso, incluso
in•clu•sive [ɪn'kluːsɪv] **1** *adj price* tutto compreso **2** *prep*: ***inclusive of VAT*** IVA compresa **3** *adv*: ***from Monday to Thursday inclusive*** dal lunedì al giovedì compreso
in•co•her•ent *adj* incoerente
in•come ['ɪnkəm] reddito *m*
'in•come tax imposta *f* sul reddito
in•com•ing ['ɪnkʌmɪŋ] *adj flight, phonecall, mail* in arrivo; *tide* montante; *president* entrante
in•com•pa•ra•ble [ɪn'kɒmprəbl] *adj* incomparabile
in•com•pat•i•bil•i•ty [ɪnkəmpætɪ'bɪlɪtɪ] incompatibilità *f inv*
in•com•pat•i•ble [ɪnkəm'pætɪbl] *adj* incompatibile
in•com•pe•tence [ɪn'kɒmpɪtəns] incompetenza *f*
in•com•pe•tent [ɪn'kɒmpɪtənt] *adj* incompetente
in•com•plete [ɪnkəm'pliːt] *adj* incompleto
in•com•pre•hen•si•ble [ɪnkɒmprɪ'hensɪbl] *adj* incomprensibile
in•con•cei•va•ble [ɪnkən'siːvəbl] *adj* inconcepibile
in•con•clu•sive [ɪnkən'kluːsɪv] *adj* inconcludente
in•con•gru•ous [ɪn'kɒŋgrʊəs] *adj* fuori luogo
in•con•sid•er•ate [ɪnkən'sɪdərət] *adj* poco gentile
in•con•sis•tent [ɪnkən'sɪstənt] *adj* incoerente
in•con•so•la•ble [ɪnkən'səʊləbl] *adj* inconsolabile
in•con•spic•u•ous [ɪnkən'spɪkjʊəs] *adj* poco visibile; ***make o.s. inconspicuous*** passare inosservato
in•con•ve•ni•ence [ɪnkən'viːnɪəns] *n* inconveniente *m*
in•con•ve•ni•ent [ɪnkən'viːnɪənt] *adj* scomodo; *time* poco opportuno
in•cor•po•rate [ɪn'kɔːpəreɪt] *v/t* includere
in•cor•rect [ɪnkə'rekt] *adj answer* errato; *behaviour* scorretto; ***am I incorrect in thinking …?*** sbaglio a pensare che …?
in•cor•rect•ly [ɪnkə'rektlɪ] *adv* in modo errato
in•cor•ri•gi•ble [ɪn'kɒrɪdʒəbl] *adj* incorreggibile
in•crease [ɪn'kriːs] **1** *v/t & v/i* aumentare **2** *n* ['ɪnkriːs] aumento *m*; ***on the increase*** in aumento
in•creas•ing [ɪn'kriːsɪŋ] *adj* crescente
in•creas•ing•ly [ɪn'kriːsɪŋlɪ] *adv* sempre più
in•cred•i•ble [ɪn'kredɪbl] *adj* (*amazing, very good*) incredibile
in•crim•i•nate [ɪn'krɪmɪneɪt] *v/t* compro-

mettere; ***incriminate o.s.*** compromettersi
in•cu•ba•tor ['ɪŋkjʊbeɪtə(r)] incubatrice *f*
in•cur [ɪn'kɜː(r)] *v/t* (*pret & pp* ***-red***) *costs* affrontare; *debts* contrarre; *s.o.'s anger* esporsi a
in•cu•ra•ble [ɪn'kjʊrəbl] *adj* incurabile
in•debt•ed [ɪn'detɪd] *adj*: ***be indebted to s.o.*** essere (molto) obbligato a qu
in•de•cent [ɪn'diːsnt] *adj* indecente
in•de•ci•sive [ɪndɪ'saɪsɪv] *adj* indeciso
in•de•ci•sive•ness [ɪndɪ'saɪsɪvnɪs] indecisione *f*
in•deed [ɪn'diːd] *adv* (*in fact*) in effetti; (*yes, agreeing*) esatto; ***very much indeed*** moltissimo; ***thank you very much indeed*** grazie mille
in•de•fi•na•ble [ɪndɪ'faɪnəbl] *adj* indefinibile
in•def•i•nite [ɪn'defɪnɪt] *adj* indeterminato; ***indefinite article*** GRAM articolo *m* indeterminativo
in•def•i•nite•ly [ɪn'defɪnɪtlɪ] *adv* a tempo indeterminato
in•del•i•cate [ɪn'delɪkət] *adj* indelicato
in•dent ['ɪndent] **1** *n in text* rientro *m* a margine **2** *v/t* [ɪn'dent] *line* rientrare il margine di
in•de•pen•dence [ɪndɪ'pendəns] indipendenza *f*
in•de•pen•dent [ɪndɪ'pendənt] *adj* indipendente
in•de•pen•dent•ly [ɪndɪ'pendəntlɪ] *adv* indipendentemente; ***independently of*** indipendentemente da
in•de•scri•ba•ble [ɪndɪ'skraɪbəbl] *adj* indescrivibile
in•de•scrib•a•bly [ɪndɪ'skraɪbəblɪ] *adv*: ***indescribably beautiful*** di una bellezza indescrivibile; ***indescribably bad*** pessimo
in•de•struc•ti•ble [ɪndɪ'strʌktəbl] *adj* indistruttibile
in•de•ter•mi•nate [ɪndɪ'tɜːmɪnət] *adj* indeterminato
in•dex ['ɪndeks] indice *m*
'in•dex card scheda *f*
'in•dex fin•ger indice *m*
in•dex-'linked *adj* indicizzato
In•di•a ['ɪndɪə] India *f*
In•di•an ['ɪndɪən] **1** *adj* indiano **2** *n person* indiano *m*, -a *f*; *American* indiano *m*, -a *f* d'America
In•di•an 'sum•mer estate *f* di San Martino
in•di•cate ['ɪndɪkeɪt] **1** *v/t* indicare **2** *v/i when driving* segnalare (il cambiamento di direzione)
in•di•ca•tion [ɪndɪ'keɪʃn] indicazione *f*
in•di•ca•tor ['ɪndɪkeɪtə(r)] *on car* indicatore *m* di direzione, freccia *f* F
in•dict [ɪn'daɪt] *v/t* incriminare
in•dif•fer•ence [ɪn'dɪfrəns] indifferenza *f*
in•dif•fer•ent [ɪn'dɪfrənt] *adj* indifferente; (*mediocre*) mediocre
in•di•ges•ti•ble [ɪndɪ'dʒestɪbl] *adj* indigesto
in•di•ges•tion [ɪndɪ'dʒestʃn] indigestione *f*
in•dig•nant [ɪn'dɪgnənt] *adj* indignato
in•dig•na•tion [ɪndɪg'neɪʃn] indignazione *f*
in•di•rect [ɪndɪ'rekt] *adj* indiretto
in•di•rect•ly [ɪndɪ'rektlɪ] *adv* indirettamente
in•dis•creet [ɪndɪ'skriːt] *adj* indiscreto
in•dis•cre•tion [ɪndɪ'skreʃn] indiscrezione *f*; *sexual* scappatella *f*
in•dis•crim•i•nate [ɪndɪ'skrɪmɪnət] *adj* indiscriminato
in•dis•pen•sa•ble [ɪndɪ'spensəbl] *adj* indispensabile
in•dis•posed [ɪndɪ'spəʊzd] *adj* (*not well*) indisposto
in•dis•pu•ta•ble [ɪndɪ'spjuːtəbl] *adj* indiscutibile
in•dis•pu•ta•bly [ɪndɪ'spjuːtəblɪ] *adv* indiscutibilmente
in•dis•tinct [ɪndɪ'stɪŋkt] *adj* indistinto
in•dis•tin•guish•a•ble [ɪndɪ'stɪŋgwɪʃəbl] *adj* indistinguibile
in•di•vid•u•al [ɪndɪ'vɪdjʊəl] **1** *n* individuo *m* **2** *adj* (*separate*) singolo; (*personal*) individuale
in•di•vid•u•a•list [ɪndɪ'vɪdjʊəlɪst] *adj* individualista
in•di•vid•u•al•ly [ɪndɪ'vɪdjʊəlɪ] *adv* individualmente
in•di•vis•i•ble [ɪndɪ'vɪzɪbl] *adj* indivisibile
in•doc•tri•nate [ɪn'dɒktrɪneɪt] *v/t* indottrinare
in•do•lence ['ɪndələns] indolenza *f*
in•do•lent ['ɪndələnt] *adj* indolente
In•do•ne•sia [ɪndə'niːʒə] Indonesia *f*
In•do•ne•sian [ɪndə'niːʒən] **1** *adj* indonesiano **2** *n person* indonesiano *m*, -a *f*
in•door ['ɪndɔː(r)] *adj activities, games* al coperto; *arena, swimming pool* coperto
in•doors [ɪn'dɔːz] *adv in building* all'interno; *at home* in casa
in'duc•tion course [ɪn'dʌkʃn] corso *m* d'avviamento
in•dulge [ɪn'dʌldʒ] **1** *v/t o.s., one's tastes* soddisfare **2** *v/i*: ***indulge in sth*** lasciarsi andare a qc; *in joke* permettersi qc
in•dul•gence [ɪn'dʌldʒəns] *of tastes, appetite etc* soddisfazione *f*; (*laxity*) indulgenza *f*

in•dul•gent [ɪn'dʌldʒənt] *adj (not strict enough)* indulgente
in•dus•tri•al [ɪn'dʌstrɪəl] *adj* industriale
in•dus•tri•al 'ac•tion agitazione *f* sindacale
in•dus•tri•al dis'pute vertenza *f* sindacale
in•dus•tri•al es'tate zona *f* industriale
in•dus•tri•al•ist [ɪn'dʌstrɪəlɪst] industriale *m*
in•dus•tri•al•ize [ɪn'dʌstrɪəlaɪz] **1** *v/t* industrializzare **2** *v/i* industrializzarsi
in•dus•tri•al 'waste scorie *fpl* industriali
in•dus•tri•ous [ɪn'dʌstrɪəs] *adj* diligente
in•dus•try ['ɪndəstrɪ] industria *f*
in•ef•fec•tive [ɪnɪ'fektɪv] *adj* inefficace
in•ef•fec•tu•al [ɪnɪ'fektʃʊəl] *adj person* inetto
in•ef•fi•cient [ɪnɪ'fɪʃənt] *adj* inefficiente
in•eli•gi•ble [ɪn'elɪdʒɪbl] *adj*: ***be ineligible for sth*** non avere diritto a qc
in•ept [ɪ'nept] *adj* inetto
in•e•qual•i•ty [ɪnɪ'kwɒlɪtɪ] disuguaglianza *f*
in•es•ca•pa•ble [ɪnɪ'skeɪpəbl] *adj* inevitabile
in•es•ti•ma•ble [ɪn'estɪməbl] *adj* inestimabile
in•ev•i•ta•ble [ɪn'evɪtəbl] *adj* inevitabile; ***the inevitable bottle of …*** l'immancabile bottiglia di …
in•ev•i•ta•bly [ɪn'evɪtəblɪ] *adv* inevitabilmente
in•ex•cu•sa•ble [ɪnɪk'skjuːzəbl] *adj* imperdonabile
in•ex•haus•ti•ble [ɪnɪg'zɔːstəbl] *adj supply* inesauribile
in•ex•pen•sive [ɪnɪk'spensɪv] *adj* poco costoso, economico
in•ex•pe•ri•enced [ɪnɪk'spɪərɪənst] *adj* inesperto
in•ex•plic•a•ble [ɪnɪk'splɪkəbl] *adj* inspiegabile
in•ex•pres•si•ble [ɪnɪk'spresɪbl] *adj* inesprimibile
in•fal•li•ble [ɪn'fælɪbl] *adj* infallibile
in•fa•mous ['ɪnfəməs] *adj* famigerato
in•fan•cy ['ɪnfənsɪ] *of person* infanzia *f*; *of state, institution* stadio *m* iniziale
in•fant ['ɪnfənt] bambino *m* piccolo, bambina *f* piccola
in•fan•tile ['ɪnfəntaɪl] *adj pej* infantile
in•fan•try ['ɪnfəntrɪ] fanteria *f*
in•fan•try 'sol•dier fante *m*
'in•fant school scuola *f* elementare
in•fat•u•at•ed [ɪn'fætʃʊeɪtɪd] *adj*: ***be infatuated with s.o.*** essere infatuato di qu
in•fect [ɪn'fekt] *v/t of person* contagiare; *food, water* contaminare; ***become infected*** *of wound* infettarsi; *of person* contagiarsi
in•fec•tion [ɪn'fekʃn] infezione *f*
in•fec•tious [ɪn'fekʃəs] *adj disease* infettivo, contagioso; *fig*: *laughter* contagioso
in•fer [ɪn'fɜː(r)] *v/t (pret & pp* **-red**): ***infer sth from sth*** dedurre qc da qc
in•fe•ri•or [ɪn'fɪərɪə(r)] *adj quality, workmanship* inferiore; *in rank* subalterno
in•fe•ri•or•i•ty [ɪnfɪərɪ'ɒrətɪ] *in quality* inferiorità *f inv*
in•fe•ri'or•i•ty com•plex complesso *m* d'inferiorità
in•fer•tile [ɪn'fɜːtaɪl] *adj* sterile
in•fer•til•i•ty [ɪnfə'tɪlɪtɪ] sterilità *f inv*
in•fi•del•i•ty [ɪnfɪ'delɪtɪ] infedeltà *f inv*
in•fil•trate ['ɪnfɪltreɪt] *v/t* infiltrare
in•fi•nite ['ɪnfɪnət] *adj* infinito
in•fin•i•tive [ɪn'fɪnətɪv] GRAM infinito *m*
in•fin•i•ty [ɪn'fɪnətɪ] infinito *m*
in•firm [ɪn'fɜːm] *adj* infermo
in•fir•ma•ry [ɪn'fɜːmərɪ] infermeria *f*
in•fir•mi•ty [ɪn'fɜːmətɪ] infermità *f inv*
in•flame [ɪn'fleɪm] *v/t passions* accendere
in•flam•ma•ble [ɪn'flæməbl] *adj* infiammabile
in•flam•ma•tion [ɪnflə'meɪʃn] MED infiammazione *f*
in•flat•a•ble [ɪn'fleɪtəbl] *adj dinghy* gonfiabile
inflate [ɪn'fleɪt] *v/t tyre, dinghy* gonfiare; *economy* inflazionare
in•fla•tion [ɪn'fleɪʃən] inflazione *f*
in•fla•tion•a•ry [ɪn'fleɪʃənərɪ] *adj* inflazionistico
in•flec•tion [ɪn'flekʃn] *of voice* intonazione *f*
in•flex•i•ble [ɪn'fleksɪbl] *adj attitude, person* inflessibile
in•flict [ɪn'flɪkt] *v/t*: ***inflict sth on s.o.*** *punishment* infliggere qc a qu; *wound, suffering* procurare qc a qu
'in-flight *adj*: ***in-flight entertainment*** intrattenimento a bordo
in•flu•ence ['ɪnflʊəns] **1** *n* influenza *f*; ***be a good / bad influence on s.o.*** avere una buona / cattiva influenza su qu; ***people who have influence*** persone influenti; ***who were your main influences?*** chi si è ispirato principalmente? **2** *v/t s.o.'s thinking* esercitare un'influenza su; *decision* influenzare
in•flu•en•tial [ɪnflʊ'enʃl] *adj writer, philosopher, film-maker* autorevole; ***she knows influential people*** conosce gente influente
in•flu•en•za [ɪnflʊ'enzə] influenza *f*
in•form [ɪn'fɔːm] **1** *v/t* informare; ***inform s.o. about sth*** informare qu di qc; ***please keep me informed*** tienimi informato

2 *v/i* denunciare; ***inform on s.o.*** denunciare qu
in•for•mal [ɪn'fɔːməl] *adj* informale
in•for•mal•i•ty [ɪnfɔː'mælɪtɪ] informalità *f inv*
in•form•ant [ɪn'fɔːmənt] informatore *m*, -trice *f*
in•for•ma•tion [ɪnfə'meɪʃn] informazione *f*; ***a bit of information*** un'informazione
in•for•ma•tion 'sci•ence informatica *f*
in•for•ma•tion 'sci•en•tist informatico *m*, -a *f*
in•for•ma•tion tech'nol•o•gy informatica *f*
in•for•ma•tive [ɪn'fɔːmətɪv] *adj article etc* istruttivo; ***he wasn't very informative*** non è stato di grande aiuto
in•form•er [ɪn'fɔːmə(r)] informatore *m*, -trice *f*
infra-red [ɪnfrə'red] *adj* infrarosso
in•fra•struc•ture ['ɪnfrəstrʌktʃə(r)] infrastruttura *f*
in•fre•quent [ɪn'friːkwənt] *adj* raro
in•fu•ri•ate [ɪn'fjʊərɪeɪt] *v/t* far infuriare
in•fu•ri•at•ing [ɪn'fjʊərɪeɪtɪŋ] *adj* esasperante
in•fuse [ɪn'fjuːz] *v/i*: ***let the tea infuse*** lasciare in infusione il tè
in•fu•sion [ɪn'fjuːʒn] (*herb tea*) infuso *m*
in•ge•ni•ous [ɪn'dʒiːnɪəs] *adj* ingegnoso
in•ge•nu•i•ty [ɪndʒɪ'njuːətɪ] ingegnosità *f inv*
in•got ['ɪŋgət] lingotto *m*
in•gra•ti•ate [ɪn'greɪʃɪeɪt] *v/t*: ***ingratiate o.s. with s.o.*** ingraziarsi qu
in•grat•i•tude [ɪn'grætɪtjuːd] ingratitudine *f*
in•gre•di•ent [ɪn'griːdɪənt] *for cooking* ingrediente *m*; *fig*: *for success* elemento *m*
in•hab•it [ɪn'hæbɪt] *v/t* abitare
in•hab•it•a•ble [ɪn'hæbɪtəbl] *adj* abitabile
in•hab•i•tant [ɪn'hæbɪtənt] abitante *m/f*
in•hale [ɪn'heɪl] **1** *v/t* inalare **2** *v/i when smoking* aspirare
in•ha•ler [ɪn'heɪlə(r)] inalatore *m*
in•her•it [ɪn'herɪt] *v/t* ereditare
in•her•i•tance [ɪn'herɪtəns] eredità *f inv*
in•hib•it [ɪn'hɪbɪt] *v/t growth, conversation etc* inibire
in•hib•it•ed [ɪn'hɪbɪtɪd] *adj* inibito
in•hi•bi•tion [ɪnhɪ'bɪʃn] inibizione *f*
in•hos•pi•ta•ble [ɪnhɒ'spɪtəbl] *adj* inospitale
'in-house **1** *adj* aziendale **2** *adv work* all'interno dell'azienda
in•hu•man [ɪn'hjuːmən] *adj* disumano
i•ni•tial [ɪ'nɪʃl] **1** *adj* iniziale **2** *n* iniziale *f* **3** *v/t* (*write initials on*) siglare (con le iniziali)
i•ni•tial•ly [ɪ'nɪʃlɪ] *adv* inizialmente
i•ni•ti•ate [ɪ'nɪʃɪeɪt] *v/t* avviare
i•ni•ti•a•tion [ɪnɪʃɪ'eɪʃn] avviamento *m*
i•ni•tia•tive [ɪ'nɪʃətɪv] iniziativa *f*; ***do sth on one's own initiative*** fare qc di propria iniziativa
take the initiative prendere l'iniziativa
in•ject [ɪn'dʒekt] *v/t medicine, drug, fuel* iniettare; *capital* investire
in•jec•tion [ɪn'dʒekʃn] MED, *of fuel* iniezione *f*; *of capital* investimento *m*
'in-joke: ***it's an in-joke*** è una battuta tra di noi / loro
in•jure ['ɪndʒə(r)] *v/t* ferire; ***injure o.s.*** ferirsi
in•jured ['ɪndʒəd] **1** *adj leg* ferito; *feelings* offeso **2** *npl* feriti *mpl*
in•ju•ry ['ɪndʒərɪ] ferita *f*
'in•jury time SP minuti *mpl* di recupero
in•jus•tice [ɪn'dʒʌstɪs] ingiustizia *f*
ink [ɪŋk] inchiostro *m*
ink•jet ('prin•ter) stampante *f* a getto d'inchiostro
in•land ['ɪnlənd] *adj areas* dell'interno; *mail* nazionale; *sea* interno
In•land 'Rev•e•nue fisco *m*
in-laws ['ɪnlɔːz] *npl famiglia fsg della moglie / del marito*; (*wife's / husband's parents*) suoceri *mpl*
in•lay ['ɪnleɪ] *n* intarsio *m*
in•let ['ɪnlet] *of sea* insenatura *f*; *in machine* presa *f*
in•mate ['ɪnmeɪt] *of prison* detenuto *m*, -a *f*; *of mental hospital* ricoverato *m*, -a *f*
inn [ɪn] locanda *f*
in•nate [ɪ'neɪt] *adj* innato
in•ner ['ɪnə(r)] *adj* interno
in•ner 'cit•y *centro m in degrado di una zona urbana*; ***inner city decay*** degrado del centro urbano
'in•ner•most *adj thoughts etc* più intimo
in•ner 'tube camera *f* d'aria
in•nings ['ɪnɪŋz] *nsg in cricket* turno *m* di battuta
in•no•cence ['ɪnəsəns] innocenza *f*
in•no•cent ['ɪnəsənt] *adj* innocente
in•no•cu•ous [ɪ'nɒkjʊəs] *adj* innocuo
in•no•va•tion [ɪnə'veɪʃn] innovazione *f*
in•no•va•tive ['ɪnəvətɪv] *adj* innovativo
in•no•va•tor ['ɪnəveɪtə(r)] innovatore *m*, -trice *f*
in•nu•me•ra•ble [ɪ'njuːmərəbl] *adj* innumerevole
i•noc•u•late [ɪ'nɒkjʊleɪt] *v/t* vaccinare
i•noc•u•la•tion [ɪ'nɒkjʊ'leɪʃn] vaccinazione *f*
in•of•fen•sive [ɪnə'fensɪv] *adj* inoffensivo
in•or•gan•ic [ɪnɔː'gænɪk] *adj* inorganico

I

'in-pa•tient degente *m/f*
in•put ['ɪnpʊt] **1** *n* contributo *m*; COMPUT input *m inv* **2** *v/t* (*pret & pp* **-ted** *or* **input**) *into project* contribuire con; COMPUT inserire
in•quest ['ɪnkwest] inchiesta *f* giudiziaria
in•quire [ɪn'kwaɪə(r)] *v/i* domandare; ***inquire into sth*** svolgere indagini su qc
in•quir•y [ɪn'kwaɪərɪ] richiesta *f* di informazioni; (*public inquiry*) indagine *f*
in•quis•i•tive [ɪn'kwɪzətɪv] *adj* curioso
in•sane [ɪn'seɪn] *adj* pazzo
in•san•i•ta•ry [ɪn'sænɪtrɪ] *adj* antigienico
in•san•i•ty [ɪn'sænɪtɪ] infermità *f* mentale
in•sa•tia•ble [ɪn'seɪʃəbl] *adj* insaziabile
in•scrip•tion [ɪn'skrɪpʃn] iscrizione *f*
in•scru•ta•ble [ɪn'skru:təbl] *adj* imperscrutabile
in•sect ['ɪnsekt] insetto *m*
in•sec•ti•cide [ɪn'sektɪsaɪd] insetticida *m*
'in•sect re•pel•lent insettifugo *m*
in•se•cure [ɪnsɪ'kjʊə(r)] *adj* insicuro
in•se•cu•ri•ty [ɪnsɪ'kjʊərɪtɪ] insicurezza *f*
in•sen•si•tive [ɪn'sensɪtɪv] *adj* insensibile
in•sen•si•tiv•i•ty [ɪnsensɪ'tɪvɪtɪ] insensibilità *f inv*
in•sep•a•ra•ble [ɪn'seprəbl] *adj two issues* inscindibile; *two people* inseparabile
in•sert ['ɪnsɜ:t] **1** *n in magazine etc* inserto *m* **2** *v/t* [ɪn'sɜ:t] inserire; ***insert sth into sth*** inserire qc in qc
in•ser•tion [ɪn'sɜ:ʃn] (*act*) inserimento *m*
in•side [ɪn'saɪd] **1** *n of house, box* interno *m*; *of road* destra *f*; sinistra *f*; ***someone on the inside at Lloyds*** qualcuno che lavora ai Lloyds; ***inside out*** a rovescio; ***turn sth inside out*** rivoltare qc; ***know sth inside out*** sapere qc a menadito **2** *prep* dentro; ***inside of 2 hours*** in meno di due ore **3** *adv stay, remain, go, carry* dentro; ***I've never been inside*** non sono mai entrato **4** *adj* interno; ***inside information*** informazioni riservate; ***inside lane*** SP corsia *f* interna; *on road* corsia *f* di marcia; ***inside pocket*** tasca *f* interna
in•sid•er [ɪn'saɪdə(r)]: ***an insider from the Department ...*** un impiegato del Ministero ...
in•sid•er 'deal•ing FIN insider trading *m inv*
in•sides [ɪn'saɪdz] *npl* pancia *fsg*; *intestines* budella *fpl*
in•sid•i•ous [ɪn'sɪdɪəs] *adj* insidioso
in•sight ['ɪnsaɪt]: ***it offers an insight into ...*** permette di capire ...; ***full of insight*** molto intuitivo
in•sig•nif•i•cant [ɪnsɪg'nɪfɪkənt] *adj* insignificante
in•sin•cere [ɪnsɪn'sɪə(r)] *adj* falso
in•sin•cer•i•ty [ɪnsɪn'serɪtɪ] falsità *f inv*
in•sin•u•ate [ɪn'sɪnjʊeɪt] *v/t* (*imply*) insinuare
in•sist [ɪn'sɪst] *v/i* insistere; ***please keep it, I insist*** tienilo, ci tengo!
◆ **insist on** *v/t* esigere; ***insist on doing sth*** insistere per fare qc
in•sis•tent [ɪn'sɪstənt] *adj* insistente
in•so•lent ['ɪnsələnt] *adj* insolente
in•sol•u•ble [ɪn'sɒljʊbl] *adj problem* insolvibile; *substance* insolubile
in•sol•vent [ɪn'sɒlvənt] *adj* insolvente
in•som•ni•a [ɪn'sɒmnɪə] insonnia *f*
in•som•ni•ac [ɪn'sɒmnɪæk] persona *f* che soffre di insonnia
in•spect [ɪn'spekt] *v/t work, tickets, baggage* controllare; *building, factory, school* ispezionare
in•spec•tion [ɪn'spekʃn] *of work, tickets, baggage* controllo *m*; *of building, factory, school* ispezione *f*
in•spec•tor [ɪn'spektə(r)] *in factory* ispettore *m*, -trice *f*; *on buses* controllore *m*; *of police* ispettore *m*
in•spi•ra•tion [ɪnspə'reɪʃn] ispirazione *f*; (*very good idea*) lampo *m* di genio
in•spire [ɪn'spaɪə(r)] *v/t respect etc* suscitare; ***be inspired by s.o./sth*** essere ispirato da qu / qc
in•sta•bil•i•ty [ɪnstə'bɪlɪtɪ] *of character, economy* instabilità *f inv*
in•stall [ɪn'stɔ:l] *v/t computer, telephones, software* installare
in•stal•la•tion [ɪnstə'leɪʃn] *of new equipment, software* installazione *f*; ***military installation*** struttura *f* militare
in•stal•ment, **in•stall•ment** *Am* [ɪn'stɔ:lmənt] *of story, TV drama etc* puntata *f*; (*payment*) rata *f*
in•stance ['ɪnstəns] (*example*) esempio *m*; ***for instance*** per esempio
in•stant ['ɪnstənt] **1** *adj* immediato **2** *n* istante *m*; ***in an instant*** in un attimo
in•stan•ta•ne•ous [ɪnstən'teɪnɪəs] *adj* immediato
in•stant 'cof•fee caffè *m inv* istantaneo *o* solubile
in•stant•ly ['ɪnstəntlɪ] *adv* istantaneamente
in•stead [ɪn'sted] *adv* invece; ***instead of*** invece di
in•step ['ɪnstep] collo *m* del piede
in•stinct ['ɪnstɪŋkt] istinto *m*
in•stinc•tive [ɪn'stɪŋktɪv] *adj* istintivo
in•sti•tute ['ɪnstɪtju:t] **1** *n* istituto *m* **2** *v/t new law* introdurre; *enquiry* avviare
in•sti•tu•tion [ɪnstɪ'tju:ʃn] *governmental* istituto *m*; *sth traditional* istituzione *f*; (*setting up*) avviamento *m*

in•struct [ɪn'strʌkt] *v/t* (*order*) dare istruzioni a; (*teach*) istruire; ***instruct s.o. to do sth*** (*order*) dare istruzioni a qu di fare qc
in•struc•tion [ɪn'strʌkʃn] istruzione *f*; ***instructions for use*** istruzioni per l'uso
in'struc•tion man•u•al libretto *m* d'istruzioni
in•struc•tive [ɪn'strʌktɪv] *adj* istruttivo
in•struc•tor [ɪn'strʌktə(r)] istruttore *m*, -trice *f*
in•stru•ment ['ɪnstrʊmənt] strumento *m*
in•sub•or•di•nate [ɪnsə'bɔːdɪnət] *adj* insubordinato
in•suf•fi•cient [ɪnsə'fɪʃnt] *adj* insufficiente
in•su•late ['ɪnsjʊleɪt] *v/t* ELEC isolare; *against cold* isolare termicamente
'in•su•lat•ing tape nastro *m* isolante
in•su•la•tion [ɪnsjʊ'leɪʃn] ELEC isolamento *m*; *against cold* isolamento *m* termico
in•su•lin ['ɪnsjʊlɪn] insulina *f*
in•sult ['ɪnsʌlt] **1** *n* insulto *m* **2** *v/t* [ɪn'sʌlt] insultare
in•sur•ance [ɪn'ʃʊərəns] assicurazione *f*
in'sur•ance com•pa•ny compagnia *f* di assicurazioni
in,sur•ance pol•i•cy polizza *f* di assicurazione
in,sur•ance premi•um premio *m* assicurativo
in•sure [ɪn'ʃʊə(r)] *v/t* assicurare
in•sured [ɪn'ʃʊəd] **1** *adj* assicurato; ***be insureded*** essere assicurato **2** *n*: ***the insured*** l'assicurato
in•sur•moun•ta•ble [ɪnsə'maʊntəbl] *adj* insormontabile
in•tact [ɪn'tækt] *adj* (*not damaged*) intatto
in•take ['ɪnteɪk] *of college etc* (numero *m* di) iscrizioni *fpl*
in•te•grate ['ɪntɪgreɪt] *v/t* integrare
in•te•grat•ed 'cir•cuit ['ɪntɪgreɪtɪd] *adj* circuito *m* integrato
in•teg•ri•ty [ɪn'tegrətɪ] integrità *f inv*
in•tel•lect ['ɪntəlekt] intelletto *m*
in•tel•lec•tual [ɪntə'lektjʊəl] **1** *adj* intellettuale **2** *n* intellettuale *m/f*
in•tel•li•gence [ɪn'telɪdʒəns] intelligenza *f*; (*information*) informazioni *fpl*
in'tel•li•gence of•fi•cer agente *m/f* dei servizi segreti
in'tel•li•gence ser•vice servizi *mpl* segreti
in•tel•li•gent [ɪn'telɪdʒənt] *adj* intelligente
in•tel•li•gi•ble [ɪn'telɪdʒəbl] *adj* intelligibile
in•tend [ɪn'tend] *v/t*: ***intend to do sth*** (*do on purpose*) volere fare qc; (*plan to do*) avere intenzione di fare qc; ***that's not what I intended*** non è quello che intendevo
in•tense [ɪn'tens] *adj pleasure, heat, pressure* intenso; *concentration* profondo; ***he's too intense*** è troppo serio
in•ten•si•fy [ɪn'tensɪfaɪ] (*pret & pp* **-ied**) **1** *v/t effect, pressure* intensificare **2** *v/i of pain* acuirsi; *of fighting* intensificarsi
in•ten•si•ty [ɪn'tensətɪ] intensità *f inv*
in•ten•sive [ɪn'tensɪv] *adj* intensivo
in•ten•sive 'care (u•nit) MED (reparto *m* di) terapia *f* intensiva
in•ten•sive 'course corso *m* intensivo
in•tent [ɪn'tent] *adj* ***be intent on doing sth*** (*determined to do*) essere deciso a fare qc; (*concentrating on*) essere intento a fare qc
in•ten•tion [ɪn'tenʃn] intenzione *f*; ***I have no intention of …*** (*refuse to*) non ho intenzione di …
in•ten•tion•al [ɪn'tenʃənl] *adj* intenzionale
in•ten•tion•al•ly [ɪn'tenʃnlɪ] *adv* intenzionalmente
in•ter•ac•tion [ɪntər'ækʃn] interazione *f*
in•ter•ac•tive [ɪntər'æktɪv] *adj* interattivo
in•ter•cede [ɪntə'siːd] *v/i* intercedere
in•ter•cept [ɪntə'sept] *v/t* intercettare
in•ter•change ['ɪntətʃeɪndʒ] *Am* MOT interscambio *m*
in•ter•change•a•ble [ɪntə'tʃeɪndʒəbl] *adj* interscambiabile
in•ter•com ['ɪntəkɒm] citofono *m*
in•ter•course ['ɪntəkɔːs] *sexual* rapporto *m* sessuale
in•ter•de•pend•ent [ɪntədɪ'pendənt] *adj* interdipendente
in•ter•est ['ɪntrəst] **1** *n* interesse *m*; FIN: *rate* interesse *m*; *money paid/received* interessi *mpl*; ***take an interest in sth*** interessarsi di qc **2** *v/t* interessare; ***does that offer interest you?*** t'interessa l'offerta?
in•terest•ed ['ɪntrəstɪd] *adj* interessato; ***be interested in sth*** interessarsi di qc; ***thanks, but I'm not interested*** grazie, non mi interessa
in•terest-free 'loan prestito *m* senza interessi
in•terest•ing ['ɪntrəstɪŋ] *adj* interessante
'in•terest rate FIN tasso *m* d'interesse
interface ['ɪntəfeɪs] **1** *n* interfaccia *f* **2** *v/i* interfacciarsi
in•ter•fere [ɪntə'fɪə(r)] *v/i* interferire
◆ **interfere with** *v/t* manomettere; *plans* intralciare
in•ter•fer•ence [ɪntə'fɪərəns] interferenza

f; *on radio* interferenze *fpl*
in•te•ri•or [ɪn'tɪərɪə(r)] **1** *adj* interno **2** *n of house* interno *m*; *of country* entroterra *m*
in•te•ri•or 'dec•o•ra•tor arredatore *m*, -trice *f*
in•te•ri•or de'sign architettura *f* d'interni
in•te•ri•or de'sign•er architetto *m* d'interni
in•ter•lude ['ɪntəluːd] *at theatre*, *concert* intervallo *m*; (*period*) parentesi *f*
in•ter•mar•ry [ɪntə'mærɪ] *v/i* (*pret & pp* ***-ied***) fare matrimoni misti
in•ter•me•di•ar•y [ɪntə'miːdɪərɪ] *n* intermediario *m*, -a *f*
in•ter•me•di•ate [ɪntə'miːdɪət] *adj* intermedio
in•ter•mis•sion [ɪntə'mɪʃn] *in theatre*, *cinema* intervallo *m*
in•tern [ɪn'tɜːn] *v/t* internare
in•ter•nal [ɪn'tɜːnl] *adj* interno
in•ter•nal com'bus•tion en•gine motore *m* a scoppio
in•ter•nal•ly [ɪn'tɜːnəlɪ] *adv*: ***he's bleeding internally*** ha un'emorragia interna; ***not to be taken internally*** per uso esterno
in•ter•na•tion•al [ɪntə'næʃnl] **1** *adj* internazionale **2** *n match* partita *f* internazionale; *player* giocatore *m*, -trice *f* della nazionale
In•ter•na•tion•al Court of 'Jus•tice Corte *f* Internazionale di Giustizia
in•ter•na•tion•al•ly [ɪntə'næʃnəlɪ] *adv* a livello internazionale
In•ter•na•tion•al 'Mon•e•tar•y Fund Fondo *m* Monetario Internazionale
In•ter•net ['ɪntənet] Internet *m inv*; ***on the Internet*** su Internet; ***Internet service provider*** provider *m inv* di servizi Internet
in•ter•pret [ɪn'tɜːprɪt] **1** *v/t linguistically* tradurre; *piece of music*, *comment etc* interpretare **2** *v/i* fare da interprete
in•ter•pre•ta•tion [ɪntɜːprɪ'teɪʃn] *linguistic* traduzione *f*; *of piece of music*, *meaning* interpretazione *f*
in•ter•pret•er [ɪn'tɜːprɪtə(r)] interprete *m/f*
in•ter•re•lat•ed [ɪntərɪ'leɪtɪd] *adj* correlato
in•ter•ro•gate [ɪn'terəgeɪt] *v/t* interrogare
in•ter•ro•ga•tion [ɪnterə'geɪʃn] interrogatorio *m*
in•ter•rog•a•tive [ɪntə'rɒgətɪv] *n* GRAM forma *f* interrogativa
in•ter•ro•ga•tor [ɪnterə'geɪtə(r)] interrogante *m/f*
in•ter•rupt [ɪntə'rʌpt] *v/t & v/i* interrompere
in•ter•rup•tion [ɪntə'rʌpʃn] interruzione *f*
in•ter•sect [ɪntə'sekt] **1** *v/t* intersecare **2** *v/i* intersecarsi
in•ter•sec•tion ['ɪntəsekʃn] (*crossroads*) incrocio *m*
in•ter•val ['ɪntəvl] intervallo *m*; ***sunny intervals*** schiarite
in•ter•vene [ɪntə'viːn] *v/i of person*, *police etc* intervenire; *of time* trascorrere
in•ter•ven•tion [ɪntə'venʃn] intervento *m*
in•ter•view ['ɪntəvjuː] **1** *n on TV*, *in paper* intervista *f*; *for job* intervista *f* d'assunzione, colloquio *m* di lavoro **2** *v/t on TV*, *for paper* intervistare; *for job* sottoporre a intervista
in•ter•view•ee [ɪntəvjuː'iː] *on TV* intervistato *m*, -a *f*; *for job* candidato *m*, -a *f*
in•ter•view•er ['ɪntəvjuːə(r)] *on TV*, *for paper* intervistatore *m*, -trice *f*; (*for job*) *persona f che conduce un'intervista d'assunzione*
in•testine [ɪn'testɪn] intestino *m*
in•ti•ma•cy ['ɪntɪməsɪ] intimità *f inv*
in•ti•mate ['ɪntɪmət] *adj friend*, *thoughts* intimo; ***be intimate with s.o.*** *sexually* avere rapporti intimi con qu
in•tim•i•date [ɪn'tɪmɪdeɪt] *v/t* intimidire
in•tim•i•da•tion [ɪntɪmɪ'deɪʃn] intimidazione *f*
in•to ['ɪntʊ] *prep* in; ***he put it into his suitcase*** l'ha messo in valigia; ***translate into English*** tradurre in inglese; ***be into sth*** F (*like*) amare qc; (*be involved with*) interessarsi di qc; ***be into drugs*** fare uso di droga; ***when you're into the job*** quando sei pratico del lavoro
in•tol•e•ra•ble [ɪn'tɒlərəbl] *adj* intollerabile
in•tol•e•rant [ɪn'tɒlərənt] *adj* intollerante
in•tox•i•cat•ed [ɪn'tɒksɪkeɪtɪd] *adj* ubriaco
in•tran•si•tive [ɪn'trænsɪtɪv] *adj* intransitivo
in•tra•ve•nous [ɪntrə'viːnəs] *adj* endovenoso
in•trep•id [ɪn'trepɪd] *adj* intrepido
in•tri•cate ['ɪntrɪkət] *adj* complicato
in•trigue ['ɪntriːg] **1** *n* intrigo *m* **2** *v/t* [ɪn'triːg] intrigare; ***I would be intrigued to know ...*** m'interesserebbe molto sapere ...
in•trigu•ing [ɪn'triːgɪŋ] *adj* intrigante
in•tro•duce [ɪntrə'djuːs] *v/t person* presentare; *new technique etc* introdurre; ***may I introduce ...?*** permette che le presenti ...?
in•tro•duc•tion [ɪntrə'dʌkʃn] *to person* presentazione *f*; *to a new food*, *sport*

etc approccio *m*; *in book, of new technique* introduzione *f*
in•tro•vert ['ɪntrəvɜːt] introverso *m*, -a *f*
in•trude [ɪn'truːd] *v/i* importunare
in•trud•er [ɪn'truːdə(r)] intruso *m*, -a *f*
in•tru•sion [ɪn'truːʒn] intrusione *f*
in•tu•i•tion [ɪntjuː'ɪʃn] intuito *m*
in•vade [ɪn'veɪd] *v/t* invadere
in•val•id[1] [ɪn'vælɪd] *adj* non valido
in•va•lid[2] ['ɪnvəlɪd] *n* MED invalido *m*, -a *f*
in•val•i•date [ɪn'vælɪdeɪt] *v/t claim, theory* invalidare
in•val•u•a•ble [ɪn'væljʊbl] *adj help, contributor* prezioso
in•var•i•a•bly [ɪn'veɪrɪəblɪ] *adv* (*always*) invariabilmente
in•va•sion [ɪn'veɪʒn] invasione *f*
in•vent [ɪn'vent] *v/t* inventare
in•ven•tion [ɪn'venʃn] invenzione *f*
in•ven•tive [ɪn'ventɪv] *adj* fantasioso
in•ventor [ɪn'ventə(r)] inventore *m*, -trice *f*
in•ven•tory ['ɪnvəntrɪ] inventario *m*
in•verse [ɪn'vɜːs] *adj order* inverso
in•vert [ɪn'vɜːt] *v/t* invertire
in•vert•ed 'com•mas [ɪn'vɜːtɪd] *npl* virgolette *fpl*
in•ver•te•brate [ɪn'vɜːtɪbrət] *n* invertebrato *m*
invest [ɪn'vest] *v/t & v/i* investire
in•ves•ti•gate [ɪn'vestɪgeɪt] *v/t* indagare su
in•ves•ti•ga•tion [ɪnvestɪ'geɪʃn] indagine *f*
in•ves•ti•ga•tive 'jour•nal•ism [ɪn'vestɪgətɪv] giornalismo *m* investigativo
in•vest•ment [ɪn'vestmənt] investimento *m*
in•ves•tor [ɪn'vestə(r)] investitore *m*, -trice
in•vig•or•at•ing [ɪn'vɪgəreɪtɪŋ] *adj climate* tonificante
in•vin•ci•ble [ɪn'vɪnsəbl] *adj* invincibile
in•vis•i•ble [ɪn'vɪzɪbl] *adj* invisibile
in•vi•ta•tion [ɪnvɪ'teɪʃn] invito *m*
in•vite [ɪn'vaɪt] *v/t* invitare; ***can I invite you for a meal?*** posso invitarti a pranzo?
◆ **invite in** *v/t* invitare a entrare
invoice ['ɪnvɔɪs] **1** *n* fattura *f* **2** *v/t customer* fatturare
in•vol•un•ta•ry [ɪn'vɒləntrɪ] *adj* involontario
in•volve [ɪn'vɒlv] *v/t hard work, expense* comportare; (*concern*) riguardare; ***what does it involve?*** che cosa comporta?; ***get involved with sth*** entrare a far parte di qc; ***get involved with s.o.*** *emotionally, romantically* legarsi a qu
in•volved [ɪn'vɒlvd] *adj* (*complex*) complesso
in•volve•ment [ɪn'vɒlvmənt] *in a project etc* partecipazione *f*; *in a crime, accident* coinvolgimento *m*
in•vul•ne•ra•ble [ɪn'vʌlnərəbl] *adj* invulnerabile
in•ward ['ɪnwəd] **1** *adj direction* verso l'interno; *feeling, thoughts* intimo **2** *adv* verso l'interno
in•ward•ly ['ɪnwədlɪ] *adv* dentro di sé
i•o•dine ['aɪədiːn] iodio *m*
IOU [aɪəʊ'juː] *abbr* (= ***I owe you***) pagherò *m*
IQ [aɪ'kjuː] *abbr* (= ***intelligence quotient***) quoziente *m* d'intelligenza
I•ran [ɪ'rɑːn] Iran *m*
I•ra•ni•an [ɪ'reɪnɪən] **1** *adj* iraniano **2** *n person* iraniano *m*, -a *f*
I•raq [ɪ'ræːk] Iraq *m*
I•ra•qi [ɪ'ræːkɪ] **1** *adj* iracheno **2** *n person* iracheno *m*, -a *f*
Ire•land ['aɪələnd] Irlanda *f*
i•ris ['aɪərɪs] *of eye* iride *f*; *flower* iris *m inv*
I•rish ['aɪərɪʃ] *adj* irlandese
'I•rish•man irlandese *m*
'I•rish•wom•an irlandese *f*
i•ron ['aɪən] **1** *n substance* ferro *m*; *for clothes* ferro *m* da stiro **2** *v/t shirts etc* stirare
i•ron•ic(al) [aɪ'rɒnɪk(l)] *adj* ironico
i•ron•ing ['aɪənɪŋ]: ***do the ironing*** stirare
'i•ron•ing board asse *m* da stiro
'i•ron•works stabilimento *m* siderurgico
i•ron•y ['aɪərənɪ] ironia *f*
ir•ra•tion•al [ɪ'ræʃənl] *adj* irrazionale
ir•rec•on•ci•la•ble [ɪrekən'saɪləbl] *adj* inconciliabile
ir•re•cov•e•ra•ble [ɪrɪ'kʌvərəbl] *adj* irrecuperabile
ir•re•gu•lar [ɪ'regʊlə(r)] *adj* irregolare
ir•rel•e•vant [ɪ'reləvənt] *adj* non pertinente
ir•rep•a•ra•ble [ɪ'repərəbl] *adj* irreparabile
ir•re•place•a•ble [ɪrɪ'pleɪsəbl] *adj object, person* insostituibile
ir•re•pres•si•ble [ɪrɪ'presəbl] *adj sense of humour* incontenibile; *person* che non si lascia abbattere
ir•re•proa•cha•ble [ɪrɪ'prəʊʧəbl] *adj* irreprensibile
ir•re•sis•ti•ble [ɪrɪ'zɪstəbl] *adj* irresistibile
ir•re•spec•tive [ɪrɪ'spektɪv] *adj*: ***irrespective of*** a prescindere da
ir•re•spon•si•ble [ɪrɪ'spɒnsəbl] *adj* irresponsabile
ir•re•trie•va•ble [ɪrɪ'triːvəbl] *adj* irrecuperabile
ir•rev•e•rent [ɪ'revərənt] *adj* irriverente
ir•rev•o•ca•ble [ɪ'revəkəbl] *adj* irrevoca-

bile
ir•ri•gate ['ɪrɪgeɪt] *v/t* irrigare
ir•ri•ga•tion [ɪrɪ'geɪʃn] irrigazione *f*
ir•ri•ga•tion ca'nal canale *m* d'irrigazione
ir•ri•ta•ble ['ɪrɪtəbl] *adj* irritabile
ir•ri•tate ['ɪrɪteɪt] *v/t* irritare
ir•ri•tat•ing ['ɪrɪteɪtɪŋ] *adj* irritante
ir•ri•ta•tion [ɪrɪ'teɪʃn] irritazione *f*
Is•lam ['ɪzlɑːm] Islam *m*
Is•lam•ic [ɪz'læmɪk] *adj* islamico
is•land ['aɪlənd] isola *f*; (***traffic***) ***island*** isola *f* spartitraffico
is•land•er ['aɪləndə(r)] isolano *m*, -a *f*
i•so•late ['aɪsəleɪt] *v/t* isolare
i•so•lat•ed ['aɪsəleɪtɪd] *adj house*, *occurrence* isolato
i•so•la•tion [aɪsə'leɪʃn] *of a region* isolamento *m*; ***in isolation*** *taken etc* da solo
i•so'la•tion ward reparto *m* d'isolamento
ISP [aɪes'piː] *abbr* (= ***Internet service provider***) provider *m inv* di servizi Internet
Is•rael ['ɪzreɪl] Israele *m*
Is•rae•li [ɪz'reɪlɪ] **1** *adj* israeliano **2** *n person* israeliano *m*, -a *f*
is•sue ['ɪʃuː] **1** *n* (*matter*) questione *f*; (*result*) risultato *m*; *of magazine* numero *m*; ***the point at issue*** il punto in discussione; ***take issue with s.o./sth*** prendere posizione contro qu / qc **2** *v/t passports*, *visa* rilasciare; *supplies* distribuire; *coins* emettere; *warning* dare
it [ɪt] *pron* ◇ *as subject*: ***what colour is it? – it is red*** di che colore è? - è rosso; ***it's raining*** piove; ***it's me / him*** sono io/è lui; ***it's Charlie here*** TELEC sono Charlie; ***that's it!*** (*that's right*) proprio così!; (*finished*) finito!
◇ *as object* lo *m*, la *f*; ***I broke it*** l'ho rotto, -a; ***I can't eat it all*** non posso mangiarla tutta
IT [aɪ'tiː] *abbr* (= ***information technology***) IT *f*
I•tal•i•an [ɪ'tæljən] **1** *adj* italiano **2** *n person* italiano *m*, -a *f*; *language* italiano *m*
i•tal•ic [ɪ'tælɪk] *adj* in corsivo
I•ta•ly ['ɪtəlɪ] Italia *f*
itch [ɪtʃ] **1** *n* prurito *m* **2** *v/i* prudere
i•tem ['aɪtəm] *on agenda* punto *m* (all'ordine del giorno); *on shopping list* articolo *m*; *in accounts* voce *f*; ***news item*** notizia *f*; ***item of clothing*** capo *m* di vestiario
i•tem•ize ['aɪtəmaɪz] *v/t invoice* dettagliare
i•tin•e•ra•ry [aɪ'tɪnərərɪ] itinerario *m*
its [ɪts] *adj* il suo *m*, la sua *f*, i suoi *mpl*, le sue *fpl*
it's [ɪts] = ***it is***; ***it has***
it•self [ɪt'self] *pron reflexive* si; *emphatic* di per sé; ***by itself*** (*alone*) da solo; (*automatically*) da sé
i•vo•ry ['aɪvərɪ] avorio *m*
i•vy ['aɪvɪ] edera *f*

J

jab [dʒæb] *v/t* (*pret & pp* ***-bed***) conficcare
jab•ber ['dʒæbə(r)] *v/i* parlare fitto fitto
jack [dʒæk] *n* MOT cric *m inv*; *in cards* fante *m*
◆ **jack up** *v/t* MOT sollevare con il cric
jack•et ['dʒækɪt] *n* giacca *f*; *of book* copertina *f*
jack•et po'ta•to patata *f* al forno con la buccia
'**jack-knife 1** *n* coltello *m* a serramanico **2** *v/i*: ***the lorry jack-knifed*** il rimorchio dell'articolato si è messo di traverso
'**jack•pot** primo premio *m*; ***hit the jackpot*** vincere il primo premio; *fig* fare un terno al lotto
jade [dʒeɪd] giada *f*
jad•ed ['dʒeɪdɪd] *adj* spossato
jag•ged ['dʒægɪd] *adj* frastagliato
jail [dʒeɪl] *n* prigione *f*
jam[1] [dʒæm] *for bread* marmellata *f*
jam[2] [dʒæm] **1** *n* MOT ingorgo *m*; ***be in a jam*** F (*difficulty*) essere in difficoltà **2** *v/t* (*pret & pp* ***-med***) (*ram*) ficcare; (*cause to stick*) bloccare; *broadcast* disturbare; ***be jammed*** *of roads* essere congestionato; *of door, window* essere bloccato **3** *v/i* (*pret & pp* ***-med***) (*stick*) bloccarsi; (*squeeze*) stiparsi
◆ **jam on** *v/t*: ***jam on the brakes*** inchiodare
jam-'packed *adj* F pieno zeppo
jan•i•tor ['dʒænɪtə(r)] custode *m*
Jan•u•a•ry ['dʒænjʊərɪ] gennaio *m*
Ja•pan [dʒə'pæn] Giappone *m*
Jap•a•nese [dʒæpə'ni:z] **1** *adj* giapponese **2** *n person* giapponese *m/f*; *language* giapponese *m*
jar[1] [dʒɑ:(r)] *n container* barattolo *m*
jar[2] [dʒɑ:(r)] *v/i* (*pret & pp* ***-red***) *of noise* stridere; ***jar on*** dar fastidio a
jar•gon ['dʒɑ:gən] gergo *m*
jaun•dice ['dʒɔ:ndɪs] itterizia *f*
jaun•diced ['dʒɔ:ndɪst] *adj fig* cinico
jaunt [dʒɔ:nt] gita *f*
jaunt•y ['dʒɔ:ntɪ] *adj* sbarazzino
jav•e•lin ['dʒævlɪn] (*spear*) giavellotto *m*; *event* lancio *m* del giavellotto
jaw [dʒɔ:] *n* mascella *m*
jay•walk•er ['dʒeɪwɔ:kə(r)] pedone *m* indisciplinato
jazz [dʒæz] jazz *m inv*
◆ **jazz up** *v/t* F ravvivare
jeal•ous ['dʒeləs] *adj* geloso; ***be jealous of …*** essere geloso di …
jeal•ous•ly ['dʒeləslɪ] *adv* gelosamente
jeal•ous•y ['dʒeləsɪ] gelosia *f*
jeans [dʒi:nz] *npl* jeans *mpl*
jeep [dʒi:p] jeep *f inv*
jeer [dʒɪə(r)] **1** *n* scherno *m* **2** *v/i* schernire; ***jeer at*** schernire
jel•ly ['dʒelɪ] gelatina *f*
'**jel•ly ba•by** bonbon *m inv* di gelatina
'**jel•ly bean** bonbon *m inv* di gelatina
'**jel•ly•fish** medusa *f*
jeop•ar•dize ['dʒepədaɪz] *v/t* mettere in pericolo
jeop•ar•dy ['dʒepədɪ]: ***be in jeopardy*** essere in pericolo
jerk[1] [dʒɜ:k] **1** *n* scossone *m* **2** *v/t* dare uno strattone
jerk[2] [dʒɜ:k] F idiota *m/f*
jerk•y ['dʒɜ:kɪ] *adj movement* a scatti
jer•sey ['dʒɜ:zɪ] (*sweater*) maglia *f*; *fabric* jersey *m inv*
jest [dʒest] **1** *n* scherzo *m*; ***in jest*** per scherzo **2** *v/i* scherzare
Je•sus ['dʒi:zəs] Gesù *m*
jet [dʒet] **1** *n of water* zampillo *m*; (*nozzle*) becco *m*; *airplane* jet *m inv* **2** *v/i* (*pret & pp* ***-ted***) *travel* volare
jet-'black *adj* (nero) corvino
'**jet en•gine** motore *m* a reazione
'**jet•lag** jet-lag *m inv*
jet•ti•son ['dʒetɪsn] *v/t* gettare; *fig* abbandonare
jet•ty ['dʒetɪ] molo *m*
Jew [dʒu:] ebreo *m*, -a *f*
jew•el ['dʒu:əl] gioiello *m*; *fig*: *person* perla *f*
jew•el•er *Am*, **jew•el•ler** ['dʒu:lə(r)] gioielliere *m*
jew•el•lery, jew•el•ry *Am* ['dʒu:lrɪ] gioielli *mpl*
Jew•ish ['dʒu:ɪʃ] *adj* ebraico; *people* ebreo
jif•fy [dʒɪfɪ] F: ***in a jiffy*** in un batter d'occhio, in un attimo
jig•saw (**puzzle**) ['dʒɪgsɔ:] puzzle *m inv*
jilt [dʒɪlt] *v/t* piantare F
jin•gle ['dʒɪŋgl] **1** *n song* jingle *m inv* **2** *v/i* *of keys, coins* tintinnare
jinx [dʒɪŋks] *n person* iettatore *m*, -trice *f*; (*bad luck*) ***there's a jinx on this project*** questo progetto è iellato
jit•ters ['dʒɪtəz] *npl* F: ***get the jitters*** avere fifa F
jit•ter•y ['dʒɪtərɪ] *adj* F nervoso
job [dʒɒb] (*employment*) lavoro *m*; (*task*)

compito *m*; ***out of a job*** senza lavoro; ***it's a good job you …*** meno male che tu …; ***you'll have a job*** (*it'll be difficult*) sarà un'impresa

'job cen•tre *Br* ufficio *m* di collocamento

'job de•scrip•tion elenco *m* delle mansioni

'job hunt: ***be job hunting*** cercare lavoro

job•less ['dʒɒblɪs] *adj* disoccupato

job sat•is'fac•tion soddisfazione *f* nel lavoro

jock•ey ['dʒɒkɪ] *n* fantino *m*

jog ['dʒɒg] **1** *n* corsa *f*; ***go for a jog*** andare a fare footing **2** *v/i* (*pret & pp* ***-ged***) *as exercise* fare footing **3** *v/t* (*pret & pp* ***-ged***) *elbow etc* urtare; ***jog s.o.'s memory*** rinfrescare la memoria a qu

◆**jog along** *v/i* F procedere

jog•ger ['dʒɒgə(r)] *person* persona *f* che fa footing; *Am shoe* scarpa *f* da ginnastica

jog•ging ['dʒɒgɪŋ] footing *m inv*; ***go jogging*** fare footing

'jog•ging suit tuta *f* da ginnastica

join [dʒɔɪn] **1** *n* giuntura *f* **2** *v/i of roads, rivers* unirsi; (*become a member*) iscriversi **3** *v/t* (*connect*) unire; *person* unirsi a; *club* iscriversi a; (*go to work for*) entrare in; *of road* congiungersi a

◆**join in** *v/i* partecipare

◆**join up** *v/i* MIL arruolarsi

join•er ['dʒɔɪnə(r)] *n* falegname *m*

joint [dʒɔɪnt] **1** *n* ANAT articolazione *f*; *in woodwork* giunto *m*; *of meat* arrosto *m*; F *place* locale *m*; *of cannabis* spinello *m* **2** *adj* (*shared*) comune

joint ac'count conto *m* comune

joint 'ven•ture joint venture *f inv*

joke [dʒəʊk] **1** *n story* barzelletta *f*; (*practical joke*) scherzo *m*; ***play a joke on*** fare uno scherzo a; ***it's no joke*** non è uno scherzo **2** *v/i* (*pretend*) scherzare

jok•er ['dʒəʊkə(r)] *in cards* jolly *m inv*; F burlone *m*, -a *f*

jok•ing ['dʒəʊkɪŋ]: ***joking apart*** scherzi a parte

jok•ing•ly ['dʒəʊkɪŋlɪ] *adv* scherzosamente

jol•ly ['dʒɒlɪ] *adj* allegro; ***jolly good*** benissimo

jolt [dʒɒlt] **1** *n* (*jerk*) scossone *m* **2** *v/t* (*push*) urtare

jos•tle ['dʒɒsl] *v/t* spintonare

◆**jot down** [dʒɒt] *v/t* (*pret & pp* ***-ted***) annotare

jour•nal ['dʒɜːnl] *magazine* rivista *f*; *diary* diario *m*

jour•nal•is•m ['dʒɜːnəlɪzm] giornalismo *m*

jour•nal•ist ['dʒɜːnəlɪst] giornalista *m/f*

jour•ney ['dʒɜːnɪ] *n* viaggio *m*

jo•vi•al ['dʒəʊvɪəl] *adj* gioviale

joy [dʒɔɪ] gioia *f*

'joy•stick COMPUT joystick *m inv*

ju•bi•lant ['dʒuːbɪlənt] *adj* esultante

ju•bi•la•tion [dʒuːbɪ'leɪʃn] giubilo *m*

judge [dʒʌdʒ] **1** *n* giudice *m* **2** *v/t* giudicare; *competition* fare da giudice a **3** *v/i* giudicare

judg(e)•ment ['dʒʌdʒmənt] *n* giudizio *m*; ***I agreed, against my better judg(e)ment*** ho accettato, pur pensando che fosse sbagliato; ***an error of judg(e)ment*** un errore di valutazione

'Judg(e)•ment Day il giorno *m* del giudizio

ju•di•cial [dʒuː'dɪʃl] *adj* giudiziario

ju•di•cious [dʒuː'dɪʃəs] *adj* giudizioso

ju•do ['dʒuːdəʊ] judo *m inv*

jug [dʒʌg] brocca *f*

jug•ger•naut ['dʒʌgənɔːt] bisonte *m* della strada F

jug•gle [dʒʌgl] *v/t* fare giochi di destrezza con; *fig*: *conflicting demands* destreggiarsi fra; *figures* manipolare

jug•gler ['dʒʌglə(r)] giocoliere *m*

juice [dʒuːs] succo *m*

juic•y ['dʒuːsɪ] *adj* succoso; *news, gossip* piccante

juke•box ['dʒuːkbɒks] juke-box *m inv*

Ju•ly [dʒʊ'laɪ] luglio *m*

jum•ble ['dʒʌmbl] mucchio *m*

◆**jumble up** *v/t* mescolare

'jum•ble sale vendita *f* di beneficenza

jum•bo (jet) ['dʒʌmbəʊ] jumbo *m* (jet)

'jum•bo-sized *adj* gigante

jump [dʒʌmp] **1** *n* salto *m*; (*increase*) impennata *f*; ***give a jump*** *of surprise* sobbalzare **2** *v/i* saltare; (*increase*) aumentare rapidamente, avere un'impennata; *in surprise* sobbalzare; ***jump to one's feet*** balzare in piedi; ***jump to conclusions*** arrivare a conclusioni affrettate **3** *v/t fence etc* saltare; F (*attack*) aggredire; ***jump the queue*** non rispettare la fila; ***jump the lights*** passare col rosso

◆**jump at** *v/t opportunity* prendere al balzo, cogliere al volo

jump•er[1] ['dʒʌmpə(r)] golf *m inv*

jump•er[2] ['dʒʌmpə(r)] SP saltatore *m*, -trice *f*

jump•y ['dʒʌmpɪ] *adj* nervoso

junc•tion ['dʒʌŋkʃn] *of roads* incrocio *m*

junc•ture ['dʒʌŋktʃə(r)] *fml*: ***at this juncture*** in questo frangente

June [dʒuːn] giugno *m*

jun•gle ['dʒʌŋgl] giungla *f*

ju•ni•or ['dʒuːnɪə(r)] **1** *adj* (*subordinate*)

subalterno; (*younger*) giovane **2** *n in rank* subalterno *m*, -a *f*; ***she is ten years my junior*** ha dieci anni meno di me
'ju•ni•or school scuola *f* elementare
junk [dʒʌŋk] (*rubbish*) robaccia *f*
'junk food alimenti *mpl* poco sani
junk•ie ['dʒʌŋkɪ] *n* F tossico *m*, -a *f* F
'junk mail posta *f* spazzatura
'junk shop negozio *m* di chincaglierie
'junk•yard deposito *m* di robivecchi
jur•is•dic•tion [dʒʊərɪs'dɪkʃn] LAW giurisdizione *f*
ju•ror ['dʒʊərə(r)] *n* giurato *m*, -a *f*
ju•ry ['dʒʊərɪ] *n* giuria *f*
just [dʒʌst] **1** *adj* giusto **2** *adv* (*barely*) appena; (*exactly*) proprio; (*only*) solo; ***I've just seen her*** l'ho appena vista; ***just about*** (*almost*) quasi; ***I was just about to leave when …*** stavo proprio per andarmene quando …; ***a house just like that*** una casa proprio così; ***he left her just like that*** l'ha lasciata così, senza spiegazioni; ***he agreed just like that*** ha accettato così, senza pensarci due volte; ***just now*** (*a few moments ago*) proprio ora; (*at the moment*) al momento; ***just you wait!*** aspetta un po'!; ***just be quiet!*** fai silenzio!; ***just as rich*** altrettanto ricco
jus•tice ['dʒʌstɪs] giustizia *f*
jus•ti•fi•a•ble [dʒʌstɪ'faɪəbl] *adj* giustificabile
jus•ti•fia•bly [dʒʌstɪ'faɪəblɪ] *adv* a ragione
jus•ti•fi•ca•tion [dʒʌstɪfɪ'keɪʃn] giustificazione *f*
jus•ti•fy ['dʒʌstɪfaɪ] *v/t* (*pret & pp* ***-ied***) *also text* giustificare
just•ly ['dʒʌstlɪ] *adv* giustamente
◆ **jut out** [dʒʌt] *v/i* (*pret & pp* ***-ted***) sporgere
ju•ve•nile ['dʒuːvənaɪl] **1** *adj* minorile; *pej* puerile **2** *n fml* minore *m/f*
ju•ve•nile de'lin•quen•cy delinquenza *f* minorile
ju•ve•nile de'lin•quent delinquente *m/f* minorile

K

k [keɪ] *abbr* (= ***kilobyte***) k (=kilobyte *m inv*); (= ***thousand***) mille; ***earn 25K*** guadagnare 25 mila sterline
kan•ga•roo [kæŋgə'ruː] canguro *m*
ka•ra•te [kə'rɑːtɪ] karate *m inv*
ka'ra•te chop colpo *m* di karate
ke•bab [kɪ'bæb] spiedino *m* di carne
keel [kiːl] NAUT chiglia *f*
◆ **keel over** *v/i of boat* capovolgersi; *of structure* crollare; *of person* cascare per terra; *faint* svenire
keen [kiːn] *adj person* entusiasta; *interest, competition* vivo; ***be keen on sth*** essere appassionato di qc; ***I'm not keen on the idea*** l'idea non mi va tanto; ***he's keen on her*** lei gli piace molto; ***be keen to do sth*** aver molta voglia di fare qc
keep [kiːp] **1** *n* (*maintenance*) vitto e alloggio *m*; ***for keeps*** F per sempre **2** *v/t* (*pret & pp* ***kept***) tenere; (*not lose*) mantenere; (*detain*) trattenere; *family* mantenere; *animals* allevare; ***keep a promise*** mantenere una promessa; ***keep s.o. company*** tenere compagnia a qu; ***keep s.o. waiting*** far aspettare qu; ***keep sth to o.s.*** (*not tell*) tenere qc per sé; ***keep sth from s.o.*** nascondere qc a qu; ***keep s.o. from doing sth*** impedire a qu di fare qc; ***keep trying!*** continua a provare!; ***don't keep interrupting!*** non interrompere in continuazione! **3** *v/i* (*pret & pp* ***kept***) (*remain*) rimanere; *of food, milk* conservarsi; ***keep left*** tenere la sinistra; ***keep straight on*** vai sempre dritto; ***keep still*** stare fermo
◆ **keep away 1** *v/i* stare alla larga; ***keep away from …*** stai alla larga da … **2** *v/t* tenere lontano; ***keep s.o. away from sth*** tenere qu lontano da qc
◆ **keep back** *v/t* (*hold in check*) trattenere; *information* nascondere
◆ **keep down** *v/t voice* abbassare; *costs, inflation etc* contenere; *food* trattenere; ***keep the noise down, will you?*** fate meno rumore!
◆ **keep in** *v/t in hospital* trattenere; ***keep a pupil in*** *punire uno studente trattenendolo oltre l'orario scolastico*
◆ **keep off 1** *v/t* (*avoid*) evitare; ***keep off the grass*** non calpestare l'erba **2** *v/i*: ***if the rain keeps off*** se non piove
◆ **keep on 1** *v/i* continuare; ***keep on doing sth*** continuare a fare qc **2** *v/t employee, coat* tenere
◆ **keep on at** *v/t* (*nag*) assillare
◆ **keep out 1** *v/t the cold* proteggere da; *person* escludere **2** *v/i of room* non entrare (***of*** in); *of argument etc* non immischiarsi (***of*** in); ***keep out*** *as sign* vietato l'ingresso; ***you keep out of this!*** non immischiarti!
◆ **keep to** *v/t path, rules* seguire; ***keep to the point*** non divagare
◆ **keep up 1** *v/i when walking, running etc* tener dietro **2** *v/t pace, payments* stare dietro a; *bridge, pants* reggere
◆ **keep up with** *v/t* stare al passo con; (*stay in touch with*) mantenere i rapporti con
keep•ing ['kiːpɪŋ]: ***be in keeping with*** essere in armonia con
'keep•sake ricordo *m*
keg [keg] barilotto *m*
ken•nel ['kenl] canile *m*
ken•nels ['kenlz] *npl* canile *m*
kept [kept] *pret & pp* → **keep**
kerb [kɜːb] orlo *m* del marciapiede
ker•nel ['kɜːnl] nocciolo *m*
ketch•up ['ketʃʌp] ketchup *m inv*
ket•tle ['ketl] bollitore *m*
key [kiː] **1** *n to door, drawer*, MUS chiave *f*; *on keyboard* tasto *m* **2** *adj* (*vital*) chiave **3** *v/t* COMPUT battere
◆ **key in** *v/t data* immettere
'key•board COMPUT, MUS tastiera *f*
'key•board•er COMPUT, MUS tastierista *m/f*
'key•card tessera *f* magnetica
keyed-up [kiːd'ʌp] *adj* agitato
'key•hole buco *m* della serratura
key•note 'speech discorso *m* programmatico
'key•ring portachiavi *m inv*
kha•ki ['kɑːkɪ] *adj colour* cachi *inv*
kick [kɪk] **1** *n* calcio *m*; F (*thrill*) gusto *m*; (***just***) ***for kicks*** F (solo) per il gusto di farlo **2** *v/t* dare un calcio a; F *habit* liberarsi da **3** *v/i* dare calci; SP calciare; *of horse* scalciare
◆ **kick around** *v/t* (*treat harshly*) maltrattare; F (*discuss*) discutere di; ***kick a ball around*** giocare a pallone
◆ **kick in** *v/i* P (*start to operate*) entrare in funzione
◆ **kick off** *v/i* F (*start*) iniziare; *of player* dare il calcio d'inizio
◆ **kick out** *v/t* buttar fuori; ***be kicked out of the company / army*** essere buttato fuori dalla ditta / dall'esercito

◆ **kick up** *v/t*: ***kick up a fuss*** fare una scenata
'**kick•back** F (*bribe*) tangente *f*
'**kick•off** SP calcio *m* d'inizio
kid [kɪd] **1** *n* F (*child*) bambino *m*, -a *f*; F (*young person*) ragazzo *m*, -a *f*; ***kid brother / sister*** fratello / sorella minore **2** *v/t* (*pret & pp* **-ded**) F prendere in giro **3** *v/i* (*pret & pp* **-ded**) F scherzare; ***I was only kidding*** stavo solo scherzando
kid•der ['kɪdə(r)] F burlone *m*, -a *f*
kid 'gloves: ***handle s.o. with kid gloves*** trattare qu coi guanti
kid•nap ['kɪdnæp] *v/t* (*pret & pp* **-ped**) rapire, sequestrare
kid•nap•per ['kɪdnæpə(r)] rapitore *m*,-trice *f*, sequestratore *m*, -trice *f*
'**kid•nap•ping** ['kɪdnæpɪŋ] rapimento *m*, sequestro *m* (di persona)
kid•ney ['kɪdnɪ] ANAT rene *m*; *in cooking* rognone *m*
'**kid•ney bean** fagiolo *m* comune
'**kid•ney ma•chine** MED rene *m* artificiale
kill [kɪl] *v/t* uccidere; *plant*, *time* ammazzare; ***be killed in an accident*** morire in un incidente; ***kill o.s.*** suicidarsi; ***kill o.s. laughing*** F morire dalle risate
kil•ler ['kɪlə(r)] (*murderer*) assassino *m*, -a *f*; (*hired killer*) killer *m/f inv*; ***flu can be a killer*** si può morire d'influenza
kil•ling ['kɪlɪŋ] omicidio *m*; ***make a killing*** F (*lots of money*) fare un pacco di soldi F
kil•ling•ly ['kɪlɪŋlɪ] *adv* F: ***killingly funny*** divertentissimo
kiln [kɪln] fornace *f*
ki•lo ['kiːləʊ] chilo *m*
ki•lo•byte ['kɪləʊbaɪt] COMPUT kilobyte *m inv*
ki•lo•gram ['kɪləʊgræm] chilogrammo *m*
ki•lo•me•ter *Am*, **ki•lo•me•tre** [kɪ'lɒmɪtə(r)] chilometro *m*
kilt [kɪlt] kilt *m inv*
kind[1] [kaɪnd] *adj* gentile
kind[2] [kaɪnd] *n* (*sort*) tipo *m*; (*make, brand*) marca *f*; ***all kinds of people*** gente di tutti i tipi; ***nothing of the kind!*** niente affatto!; ***kind of sad / strange*** F un po' triste / strano
kin•der•gar•ten ['kɪndəgɑːtn] asilo *m*
kind-heart•ed [kaɪnd'hɑːtɪd] *adj* di buon cuore
kind•ly ['kaɪndlɪ] **1** *adj* gentile **2** *adv* gentilmente; (*please*) per cortesia
kind•ness ['kaɪndnɪs] *n* gentilezza *f*
king [kɪŋ] re *m inv*
king•dom ['kɪŋdəm] regno *m*
'**king-size(d)** *adj bed* matrimoniale grande; *cigarettes* lungo
kink [kɪŋk] *in hose etc* attorcigliamento *m*
kink•y ['kɪŋkɪ] *adj* F particolare F
kiosk ['kiːɒsk] edicola *f*
kip [kɪp] P pisolino *m*
kip•per ['kɪpə(r)] aringa *f* affumicata
kiss [kɪs] **1** *n* bacio *m* **2** *v/t* baciare **3** *v/i* baciarsi
kiss of 'life respirazione *f* bocca a bocca
kit [kɪt] kit *m inv*; (*equipment*) attrezzatura *f*; *for assembly* kit *m inv* di montaggio
kitch•en ['kɪʧɪn] cucina *f*
kitch•en•ette [kɪʧɪ'net] cucinino *m*
kitch•en 'sink: ***she packs everything but the kitchen sink*** F si porta dietro tutta la casa
kite [kaɪt] aquilone *m*
kit•ten ['kɪtn] gattino *m*
kit•ty ['kɪtɪ] *money* cassa *f* comune
knack [næk] capacità *f inv*; ***there's a knack to it*** bisogna saperlo fare
knead [niːd] *v/t dough* lavorare
knee [niː] *n* ginocchio *m*
'**knee•cap** *n* rotula *f*
kneel [niːl] *v/i* (*pret & pp* **knelt**) inginocchiarsi
'**knee-length** *adj* al ginocchio
knelt [nelt] *pret & pp* → **kneel**
knew [njuː] *pret* → **know**
knick•ers ['nɪkəz] *npl* mutandine *fpl*; ***get one's knickers in a twist*** P agitarsi
knick-knacks ['nɪknæks] *npl* F ninnoli *mpl*
knife [naɪf] **1** *n* (*pl* **knives** [naɪvz]) coltello *m* **2** *v/t* accoltellare
knight [naɪt] *n* cavaliere *m*
knit [nɪt] (*pret & pp* **-ted**) **1** *v/t* fare a maglia **2** *v/i* lavorare a maglia
◆ **knit together** *v/i of broken bone* saldarsi
knit•ting ['nɪtɪŋ] *sth being knitted* lavoro *m* a maglia; *activity* il lavorare *m* a maglia
'**knit•ting nee•dle** ferro *m* (da calza)
'**knit•wear** maglieria *f*
knob [nɒb] *on door* pomello *m*; *of butter* noce *f*
knock [nɒk] **1** *n on door* colpo *m*; (*blow*) botta *f* **2** *v/t* (*hit*) colpire; *head*, *knee* battere; F (*criticize*) criticare **3** *v/i at the door* bussare (**at** a); ***I knocked my head*** ho battuto la testa
◆ **knock around 1** *v/t* F (*beat*) picchiare **2** *v/i* F (*travel*) vagabondare
◆ **knock down** *v/t of car* investire; *object, building etc* buttar giù; F (*reduce the price of*) scontare
◆ **knock off 1** *v/t* P (*steal*) fregare P **2** *v/i* F (*stop work for the day*) smontare F
◆ **knock out** *v/t* (*make unconscious*) mettere K.O. F; *power lines etc* mettere fuori

K

uso; (*eliminate*) eliminare
◆ **knock over** *v/t* far cadere; *of car* investire
'**knock•down** *adj*: ***a knockdown price*** un prezzo stracciato
knock•er ['nɒkə(r)] *on door* battente *m*
knock-kneed [nɒk'niːd] *adj* con le gambe storte
'**knock•out** *in boxing* K.O. *m inv*
knot [nɒt] **1** *n* nodo *m* **2** *v/t* (*pret & pp **-ted***) annodare
'**knot•ty** ['nɒtɪ] *adj problem* spinoso
know [nəʊ] **1** *v/t* (*pret **knew**, pp **known***) sapere; *person*, *place* conoscere; (*recognize*) riconoscere; ***know how to waltz*** saper ballare il valzer **2** *v/i* (*pret **knew**, pp **known***) sapere; ***I don't know*** non so; ***yes, I know*** sì, lo so **3** *n*: ***be in the know*** F essere beninformato
'**know-all** F sapientone *m*, -a *f*
'**know•how** F know-how *m inv*
know•ing ['nəʊɪŋ] *adj* d'intesa
know•ing•ly ['nəʊɪŋlɪ] *adv* (*wittingly*) deliberatamente; *smile etc* con aria d'intesa
knowl•edge ['nɒlɪdʒ] conoscenza *f*; ***to the best of my knowledge*** per quanto ne sappia; ***have a good knowledge of ...*** àvere una buona conoscenza di ...
knowl•edge•a•ble ['nɒlɪdʒəbl] *adj* ferrato
known [nəʊn] *pp* → ***know***
knuck•le ['nʌkl] nocca *f*
◆ **knuckle down** *v/i* F impegnarsi
◆ **knuckle under** *v/i* F cedere
KO [keɪ'əʊ] (*knockout*) K.O. *m inv*
Ko•ran [kə'rɑːn] Corano *m*
Ko•re•a [kə'riːə] Corea *f*
Ko•re•an [kə'riːən] **1** *adj* coreano **2** *n* coreano *m*, -a *f*; *language* coreano *m*
ko•sher ['kəʊʃə(r)] *adj* REL kasher; F a posto
kow•tow ['kaʊtaʊ] *v/i* F prostrarsi
ku•dos ['kjuːdɒs] gloria *f*

K

L

lab [læb] laboratorio *m*
la•bel ['leɪbl] **1** *n* etichetta *f* **2** *v/t baggage* mettere l'etichetta su
la•bor•a•to•ry [lə'bɒrətrɪ] laboratorio *m*
la•bor•a•to•ry tech'ni•cian tecnico *m* di laboratorio
la•bor *etc Am* → ***labour*** *etc*
la•bo•ri•ous [lə'bɔːrɪəs] *adj* laborioso
'la•bor u•ni•on *Am* sindacato *m*
la•bour ['leɪbə(r)] *n* (*work*) lavoro *m*; *in pregnancy* travaglio *m*; ***be in labour*** avere le doglie *fpl*
la•boured ['leɪbəd] *adj style*, *speech* pesante
la•bour•er ['leɪbərə(r)] manovale *m*
'La•bour Par•ty partito *m* laburista
'la•bour ward MED sala *f* travaglio
lace [leɪs] *n material* pizzo *m*; *for shoe* laccio *m*
◆ **lace up** *v/t shoes* allacciare
lack [læk] **1** *n* mancanza *f* **2** *v/t* mancare di **3** *v/i*: ***be lacking*** mancare
lac•quer ['lækə(r)] *n for hair* lacca *f*
lad [læd] ragazzo *m*
lad•der ['lædə(r)] scala *f* (a pioli); *Br*: *in tights* sfilatura *f*
'lad•der•proof *adj Br* indemagliabile
la•den ['leɪdn] *adj* carico
la•dies (room) ['leɪdiːz] bagno *m* per donne
la•dle ['leɪdl] *n* mestolo *m*
la•dy ['leɪdɪ] signora *f*
'la•dy•bird coccinella *f*
'la•dy•like da signora; ***she's not very ladylike*** non è certo una signora
lag [læg] *v/t* (*pret & pp* ***-ged***) *pipes* isolare
◆ **lag behind** *v/i* essere indietro
la•ger ['lɑːgə(r)] birra *f* (bionda)
la•goon [lə'guːn] laguna *f*
laid [leɪd] *pret & pp* → ***lay***
laid•back [leɪd'bæk] *adj* rilassato
lain [leɪn] *pp* → ***lie***
lake [leɪk] lago *m*
lamb [læm] *animal*, *meat* agnello *m*
lame [leɪm] *adj person* zoppo; *excuse* zoppicante
la•ment [lə'ment] **1** *n* lamento *m* **2** *v/t* piangere
lam•en•ta•ble ['læməntəbl] *adj* deplorevole
lam•i•nat•ed ['læmɪneɪtɪd] *adj surface* laminato; *paper* plastificato
lam•i•nat•ed 'glass vetro *m* laminato
lamp [læmp] lampada *f*
'lamp•post lampione *m*
'lamp•shade paralume *m*
land [lænd] **1** *n* terreno *m* (*shore*) terra *f* (*country*) paese *m*; ***by land*** per via di terra; ***on land*** sulla terraferma; ***work on the land*** *as farmer* lavorare la terra **2** *v/t aeroplane* far atterrare; *job* accaparrarsi **3** *v/i of aeroplane* atterrare; *of ball*, *sth thrown* cadere, finire
land•ing ['lændɪŋ] *n of aeroplane* atterraggio *m*; *top of staircase* pianerottolo *m*
'land•ing field terreno *m* d'atterraggio
'land•ing gear carrello *m* d'atterraggio
'land•ing strip pista *f* d'atterraggio
'land•la•dy *of bar* proprietaria *f*; *of rented room* padrona *f* di casa
'land•lord *of bar* proprietario *m*; *of rented room* padrone *m* di casa
'land•mark punto *m* di riferimento; *fig* pietra *f* miliare
'land own•er proprietario *m*, -a *f* terriero, -a
land•scape ['lændskeɪp] **1** *n* paesaggio *m* **2** *adv print* landscape, orizzontale
'land•slide frana *f*
land•slide 'vic•to•ry vittoria *f* schiacciante
lane [leɪn] *in country* viottolo *m*; (*alley*) vicolo *m*; MOT corsia *f*
lan•guage ['læŋgwɪdʒ] lingua *f*; (*speech*, *style*) linguaggio *m*
'lan•guage lab laboratorio *m* linguistico
lank [læŋk] *adj pej*: *hair* diritto
lank•y ['læŋkɪ] *adj person* allampanato
lan•tern ['læntən] lanterna *f*
lap¹ [læp] *n of track* giro *m* (di pista)
lap² [læp] *n of water* sciabordio *m*
◆ **lap up** *v/t* (*pret & pp* ***-ped***) *drink*, *milk* leccare; *flattery* compiacersi di
lap³ [læp] *n of person* grembo *m*
la•pel [lə'pel] bavero *m*
lapse [læps] **1** *n* (*mistake*, *slip*) mancanza *f*; *of time* intervallo *m*; ***lapse of memory*** vuoto *m* di memoria; ***lapse of taste*** caduta *f* di tono **2** *v/i* scadere; ***lapse into*** cadere in
'lap•top COMPUT laptop *m inv*
lar•ce•ny ['lɑːsənɪ] furto *m*
lard [lɑːd] lardo *m*
lar•der ['lɑːdə(r)] dispensa *f*
large [lɑːdʒ] *adj* grande; ***at large*** in libertà
large•ly ['lɑːdʒlɪ] *adv* (*mainly*) in gran parte
lark [lɑːk] *bird* allodola *f*

lar•va ['lɑːvə] larva *f*
lar•yn•gi•tis [lærɪn'dʒaɪtɪs] laringite *f*
lar•ynx ['lærɪŋks] laringe *f*
la•ser ['leɪzə(r)] laser *m inv*
'**la•ser beam** raggio *m* laser
'**la•ser print•er** stampante *f* laser
lash[1] [læʃ] *v/t with whip* frustare
lash[2] [læʃ] *n* (*eyelash*) ciglio *m*
◆ **lash down** *v/t with rope* assicurare
◆ **lash out** *v/i with fists, words* menare colpi
lass [læs] ragazza *f*
last[1] [lɑːst] **1** *adj in series* ultimo; (*preceding*) precedente; ***last but one*** penultimo; ***last night*** ieri sera; ***last year*** l'anno scorso **2** *adv* ***he finished last*** ha finito per ultimo; *in race* è arrivato ultimo; ***when I last saw him*** l'ultima volta che l'ho visto; ***last but not least*** per finire; ***at last*** finalmente
last[2] [lɑːst] *v/i* durare
last•ing ['lɑːstɪŋ] *adj* duraturo
last•ly ['lɑːstlɪ] *adv* per finire
latch [lætʃ] chiavistello *m*
late [leɪt] **1** *adj* (*behind time*) in ritardo; *in day* tardi; ***it's getting late*** si sta facendo tardi; ***of late*** recentemente; ***the late 19th century*** il tardo XIX secolo **2** *adv* tardi
late•ly ['leɪtlɪ] *adv* recentemente
lat•er ['leɪtə(r)] *adv* più tardi; ***see you later!*** a più tardi; ***later on*** più tardi
lat•est ['leɪtɪst] **1** *adj* ultimo, più recente **2** *n*: ***at the latest*** al più tardi
lathe [leɪð] *n* tornio *m*
la•ther ['lɑːðə(r)] *from soap* schiuma *f*; ***the horse is in a lather*** il cavallo è sudato
Lat•in ['lætɪn] **1** *adj* latino **2** *n* latino *m*
Lat•in A'mer•i•ca America *f* Latina
La•tin A'mer•i•can **1** *n* latino-americano *m*, -a *f* **2** *adj* latino-americano
lat•i•tude ['lætɪtjuːd] *geographical* latitudine *f*; (*freedom to act*) libertà *f inv* d'azione
lat•ter ['lætə(r)] *adj*: ***the latter*** quest'ultimo
laugh [lɑːf] **1** *n* risata *f*; ***it was a laugh*** F ci siamo divertiti **2** *v/i* ridere
◆ **laugh at** *v/t* ridere di
'**laugh•ing stock** zimbello *m*; ***become a laughing stock*** rendersi ridicolo
laugh•ter ['lɑːftə(r)] risata *f*; ***sounds of laughter*** delle risate
launch [lɔːntʃ] **1** *n boat* lancia *f*; *of rocket, product* lancio *m*; *of ship* varo *m* **2** *v/t rocket, product* lanciare; *ship* varare
'**launch cer•e•mo•ny** cerimonia *f* di lancio
launch•(ing) pad rampa *f* di lancio
laun•der ['lɔːndə(r)] *v/t clothes* lavare e stirare; ***launder money*** riciclare denaro sporco
laun•derette [lɔːn'dret] lavanderia *f* automatica
laun•dry ['lɔːndrɪ] *place* lavanderia *f*; *clothes* bucato *m*
lau•rel ['lɒrəl] alloro *m*
lav•a•to•ry ['lævətrɪ] gabinetto *m*
lav•en•der ['lævəndə(r)] lavanda *f*
lav•ish ['lævɪʃ] *adj meal* lauto; *reception, lifestyle* sontuoso
law [lɔː] legge *f*; ***criminal / civil law*** diritto *m* penale / civile; ***against the law*** contro la legge; ***forbidden by law*** vietato dalla legge
law-a•bid•ing ['lɔːəbaɪdɪŋ] *adj* che rispetta la legge
'**law court** tribunale *m*
law•ful ['lɔːfʊl] *adj* legale
law•less ['lɔːlɪs] *adj* senza legge
lawn [lɔːn] prato *m* all'inglese; ***play on the lawn*** giocare sul prato
'**lawn mow•er** tagliaerba *m inv*
'**law•suit** azione *f* legale
law•yer ['lɔːjə(r)] avvocato *m*
lax [læks] *adj* permissivo
lax•a•tive ['læksətɪv] *n* lassativo *m*
lay[1] [leɪ] *pret* → ***lie***
lay[2] [leɪ] *v/t* (*pret & pp* **laid**) (*put down*) posare; *eggs* deporre; V (*sexually*) scopare V
◆ **lay into** *v/t* (*attack*) aggredire
◆ **lay off** *v/t workers* licenziare; *temporarily* mettere in cassa integrazione
◆ **lay on** *v/t* (*provide*) offrire
◆ **lay out** *v/t objects* disporre; *page* impaginare
'**lay•a•bout** F scansafatiche *m/f inv*
'**lay-by** *on road* piazzola *f* di sosta
lay•er ['leɪə(r)] strato *m*
'**lay•man** laico *m*
'**lay-off** licenziamento *m*; ***there have been 50 lay-offs*** *temporary* 50 operai sono stati messi in cassa integrazione
◆ **laze around** [leɪz] *v/i* oziare
la•zy ['leɪzɪ] *adj person* pigro; *day* passato a oziare
lb *abbr* (= ***pound***) libbra *f*
LCD [elsiː'diː] *abbr* (= ***liquid crystal display***) display *m inv* a cristalli liquidi
lead[1] [liːd] **1** *v/t* (*pret & pp* **led**) *procession, race* essere in testa a; *company, team* essere a capo di; (*guide, take*) condurre **2** *v/i* (*pret & pp* **led**) *in race, competition* essere in testa; (*provide leadership*) dirigere; ***a street leading off the square*** una strada che parte dalla piazza; ***a street leading into the square*** una

L

strada che sbocca sulla piazza; ***where is this leading?*** dove vuoi andare a parare? **3** *n in race* posizione *f* di testa; ***be in the lead*** essere in testa; ***take the lead*** passare in testa

◆ **lead on** *v/i* (*go in front*) guidare

◆ **lead up to** *v/t* preludere

lead[2] [liːd] *for dog* guinzaglio *m*

lead[3] [led] *substance* piombo *m*

lead•ed ['ledɪd] *adj petrol* con piombo

lead•er ['liːdə(r)] *person* capo *m*; *in race, on market* leader *m/f inv*; *in newspaper* editoriale *m*

lead•er•ship ['liːdəʃɪp] *of party etc* direzione *f*, leadership *f inv*; ***under his leadership*** sotto la sua direzione; ***leadership skills*** capacità *f* di comando; ***leadership contest*** lotta *f* per la direzione

lead-free ['ledfriː] *adj petrol* senza piombo

lead•ing ['liːdɪŋ] *adj runner* in testa; *company, product* leader *inv*

'**lead•ing-edge** *adj company, technology* all'avanguardia

leaf [liːf] (*pl* ***leaves*** [liːvz]) foglia *f*

◆ **leaf through** *v/t* sfogliare

leaf•let ['liːflət] dépliant *m inv*

league [liːg] lega *f*; SP campionato *m*

leak [liːk] **1** *n of water* perdita *f*; *of gas* fuga *f*; ***there's been a leak*** *of information* c'è stata una fuga di notizie **2** *v/i of pipe* perdere; *of boat* far acqua

◆ **leak out** *v/i of air, gas* fuoriuscire; *of news* trapelare

leak•y ['liːkɪ] *adj pipe* che perde; *boat* che fa acqua

lean[1] [liːn] **1** *v/i be at an angle* pendere; ***lean against sth*** appoggiarsi a qc **2** *v/t* appoggiare; ***lean sth against sth*** appoggiare qc a qc

lean[2] [liːn] *adj meat* magro; *style, prose* asciutto

leap [liːp] **1** *n* salto *m*; ***a great leap forward*** un grande balzo in avanti **2** *v/i* saltare

'**leap year** anno *m* bisestile

learn [lɜːn] **1** *v/t* imparare; (*hear*) apprendere; ***learn how to do sth*** imparare a fare qc **2** *v/i* imparare

learn•er ['lɜːnə(r)] principiante *m/f*

'**learn•er driv•er** principiante *m/f* (alla guida)

learn•ing ['lɜːnɪŋ] *n* (*knowledge*) sapere *m*; (*act*) apprendimento *m*

'**learn•ing curve** processo *m* di apprendimento; ***be constantly on the learning curve*** non finire mai di imparare

lease [liːs] **1** *n* (contratto *m* di) affitto *m* **2** *v/t flat, equipment* affittare

◆ **lease out** *v/t flat, equipment* dare in affitto

lease '**pur•chase** acquisto *m* in leasing

leash [liːʃ] *for dog* guinzaglio *m*

least [liːst] **1** *adj* (*slightest*) minimo; ***I've the least debt*** io ho il debito minore **2** *adv* meno **3** *n* minimo *m*; ***not in the least suprised / disappointed*** per niente sorpreso / deluso; ***at least*** almeno

leath•er ['leðə(r)] **1** *n* pelle *f*, cuoio *m* **2** *adj* di pelle, di cuoio

leave [liːv] **1** *n* (*holiday*) congedo *m*; MIL licenza *f*; ***on leave*** in congedo, in licenza **2** *v/t* (*pret & pp* ***left***) lasciare; *room, house, office* uscire da; *station, airport* partire da; (*forget*) dimenticare; ***leave school*** finire gli studi; ***let's leave things as they are*** lasciamo le cose come stanno; ***how did you leave things with him?*** come sei rimasto d'accordo con lui?; ***leave s.o./sth alone*** lasciare stare qu / qc; ***be left*** rimanere; ***there is nothing left*** non è rimasto niente **3** *v/i* (*pret & pp* ***left***) *of person, plane, bus* partire; ***he's just left*** è appena uscito

◆ **leave behind** *v/t intentionally* lasciare; (*forget*) dimenticare

◆ **leave on** *v/t hat, coat* non togliersi; *TV, computer* lasciare acceso

◆ **leave out** *v/t word, figure* omettere; (*not put away*) lasciare in giro; ***leave me out of this*** non mi immischiare in questa faccenda

'**leav•ing par•ty** festa *f* d'addio

lec•ture ['lektʃə(r)] **1** *n* lezione *f* **2** *v/i at university* insegnare

'**lec•ture hall** aula *f* magna

'**lec•tur•er** ['lektʃərə(r)] professore *m*, -essa universitario, -a

LED [eliː'diː] *abbr* (= ***light-emitting diode***) LED *m inv*

led [led] *pret & pp* → ***lead***[1]

ledge [ledʒ] *of window* davanzale *m*; *on rock face* sporgenza *f*

ledg•er ['ledʒə(r)] COM libro *m* mastro

leek [liːk] porro *m*

leer [lɪə(r)] *n sexual* sguardo *m* libidinoso; *evil* sguardo *m* malvagio

left[1] [left] **1** *adj* sinistro; POL di sinistra **2** *n* sinistra *f*; ***on the left*** a sinistra; ***on the left of sth*** a sinistra di qc; ***to the left*** *turn, look* a sinistra **3** *adv turn, look* a sinistra

left[2] [left] *pret & pp* → ***leave***

'**left-hand** *adj* sinistro

left-hand '**drive** guida *f* a sinistra

left-'**handed** *adj* mancino

left '**luggage** (**office**) deposito *m* bagagli

'**left-overs** *npl food* avanzi *mpl*

L

'**left-wing** *adj* POL di sinistra
leg [leg] *of person* gamba *f*; *of animal* zampa *f*; *of turkey, chicken* coscia *f*; *of lamb* cosciotto *m*; *of journey* tappa *f*; *of competition* girone *m*; ***pull s.o.'s leg*** prendere in giro qu
leg•a•cy ['legəsɪ] eredità *f inv*
le•gal ['li:gl] *adj* legale
le•gal ad'vis•er consulente *m/f* legale
le•gal•i•ty [lɪ'gælətɪ] legalità *f inv*
le•gal•ize ['li:gəlaɪz] *v/t* legalizzare
le•gend ['ledʒənd] leggenda *f*
le•gen•da•ry ['ledʒəndrɪ] *adj* leggendario
le•gi•ble ['ledʒəbl] *adj* leggibile
le•gis•late ['ledʒɪsleɪt] *v/i* legiferare
le•gis•la•tion [ledʒɪs'leɪʃn] legislazione *f*
le•gis•la•tive ['ledʒɪslətɪv] *adj* legislativo
le•gis•la•ture ['ledʒɪslətʃə(r)] POL legislatura *f*
le•git•i•mate [lɪ'dʒɪtɪmət] *adj* legittimo
'**leg room** spazio *m* per le gambe
lei•sure ['leʒə(r)] svago *m*; ***at your leisure*** con comodo
'**lei•sure cen•ter** *Am*, '**lei•sure cen•tre** centro *m* sportivo e ricreativo
lei•sure•ly ['leʒəlɪ] *adj pace, lifestyle* tranquillo
'**lei•sure time** tempo *m* libero
le•mon ['lemən] limone *m*
le•mon•ade [lemə'neɪd] *fizzy* gazzosa *f*; *made from lemon juice* limonata *f*
'**le•mon juice** succo *m* di limone
le•mon 'tea tè *m inv* al limone
lend [lend] *v/t* (*pret & pp* **lent**) prestare; ***lend s.o. sth*** prestare qc a qu
length [leŋθ] lunghezza *f*; *piece*: *of material* taglio *m*; ***at length*** *describe, explain* a lungo; (*eventually*) alla fine
length•en ['leŋθən] *v/t* allungare
length•y ['leŋθɪ] *adj speech, stay* lungo
le•ni•ent ['li:nɪənt] *adj* indulgente
lens [lenz] *of camera* obiettivo *m*; *of spectacles* lente *f*; *of eye* cristallino *m*
'**lens cov•er** *of camera* copriobiettivo *m*
Lent [lent] REL Quaresima *f*
lent [lent] *pret & pp* → **lend**
len•til ['lentl] lenticchia *f*
len•til 'soup minestra *f* di lenticchie
Leo ['li:əʊ] ASTR Leone *m*
leop•ard ['lepəd] leopardo *m*
le•o•tard ['li:ətɑ:d] body *m inv*
les•bi•an ['lezbɪən] **1** *n* lesbica *f* **2** *adj* di / per lesbiche
less [les] *adv* (di) meno; ***eat / talk less*** parlare / mangiare (di) meno; ***less interesting / serious*** meno interessante / serio; ***it costs less*** costa (di) meno; ***less than £200*** meno di £200
less•en ['lesn] *v/t & v/i* diminuire
les•son ['lesn] lezione *f*
let [let] *v/t* (*pret & pp* **let**) (*allow*) lasciare; (*rent*) affittare; ***let s.o. do sth*** lasciar fare qc a qu; ***let me go!*** lasciami andare!; ***let him come in!*** fallo entrare!; ***let's go / stay*** andiamo / restiamo; ***let's not argue*** non litighiamo; ***let alone*** tanto meno; ***let go of sth*** *of rope, handle* mollare qc
◆ **let down** *v/t hair* sciogliersi; *blinds* abbassare; (*disappoint*) deludere; *dress, trousers* allungare
◆ **let in** *v/t to house* far entrare
◆ **let off** *v/t not punish* perdonare; *from car* far scendere
◆ **let out** *v/t of room, building* far uscire; *jacket etc* allargare; *groan, yell* emettere
◆ **let up** *v/i* (*stop*) smettere
le•thal ['li:θl] mortale
leth•ar•gic [lɪ'θɑ:dʒɪk] *adj* fiacco
leth•ar•gy ['leθədʒɪ] fiacchezza *f*
let•ter ['letə(r)] lettera *f*
'**let•ter•box** *on street* buca *f* delle lettere; *in door* cassetta *f* della posta
'**let•ter•head** *heading* intestazione *f*; (*headed paper*) carta *f* intestata
let•ter of 'cred•it COM lettera *f* di credito
let•tuce ['letɪs] lattuga *f*
'**let•up**: ***without a letup*** senza sosta
leu•ke•mia [lu:'ki:mɪə] leucemia *f*
lev•el ['levl] **1** *adj field, surface* piano; *in competition, scores* pari; ***draw level with s.o.*** *in match* pareggiare; ***he drew level with the leading car*** ha raggiunto l'auto in testa **2** *n* livello *m*; ***on the level*** F (*honest*) onesto
lev•el 'cross•ing *Br* passaggio *m* a livello
lev•el-head•ed [levl'hedɪd] *adj* posato
le•ver ['li:və(r)] **1** *n* leva *f* **2** *v/t*: ***lever sth up / off*** sollevare / togliere qc con una leva; ***lever sth open*** aprire qc facendo leva
lev•er•age ['li:vrɪdʒ] forza *f*; (*influence*) influenza *f*
lev•y ['levɪ] *v/t* (*pret & pp* **-ied**) *taxes* imporre
lewd [lu:d] *adj* osceno
li•a•bil•i•ty [laɪə'bɪlətɪ] (*responsibility*) responsabilità *f inv*; F *person* peso *m* morto; F *thing* peso *m*
li•a•ble ['laɪəbl] *adj* (*answerable*) responsabile; ***it's liable to break*** (*likely*) è probabile che si rompa
◆ **liaise with** [lɪ'eɪz] *v/t* tenere i contatti con
li•ai•son [lɪ'eɪzɒn] (*contacts*) contatti *mpl*
li•ar ['laɪə(r)] bugiardo *m*, -a *f*
li•bel ['laɪbl] **1** *n* diffamazione *f* **2** *v/t* diffamare
lib•e•ral ['lɪbrəl] *adj* (*broad-minded*), POL liberale; *portion etc* abbondante; POL lib-

erale
lib•e•rate ['lɪbəreɪt] *v/t* liberare
lib•e•rat•ed ['lɪbəreɪtɪd] *adj woman* emancipato
lib•e•ra•tion [lɪbə'reɪʃn] liberazione *f*
lib•er•ty ['lɪbətɪ] libertà *f inv*; ***at liberty*** *of prisoner etc* in libertà; ***be at liberty to do sth*** poter fare qc
Libra ['li:brə] ASTR Bilancia *f*
li•brar•i•an [laɪ'breərɪən] bibliotecario *m*, -a *f*
li•bra•ry ['laɪbrərɪ] biblioteca *f*
Lib•y•a ['lɪbɪə] Libia *f*
Lib•y•an ['lɪbɪən] **1** *adj* libico **2** *n person* libico *m*, -a *f*
lice [laɪs] *pl* → ***louse***
li•cence ['laɪsns] (*driving licence*) patente *f*; (*road tax licence*) bollo *m* (auto); *for TV* canone *m* (televisivo); *for gun* porto *m* d'armi; *for imports / exports* licenza *f*; *for dog* tassa *f*
li•cense ['laɪsns] **1** *v/t issue license* rilasciare la licenza a; ***be licensed*** *to sell alcohol* essere autorizzato alla vendita di alcolici; ***the car isn't licensed*** la macchina non ha il bollo **2** *n Am* → ***licence***
'**li•cense plate** *Am* targa *f*
lick [lɪk] **1** *n* leccata *f*; ***a lick of paint*** una passata di vernice **2** *v/t* leccare; ***lick one's lips*** leccarsi i baffi
lick•ing ['lɪkɪŋ] F (*defeat*): ***get a licking*** prendere una batosta
lid [lɪd] coperchio *m*
lie[1] [laɪ] **1** *n* bugia *f*; ***tell lies*** dire bugie **2** *v/i* mentire
lie[2] [laɪ] *v/i* (*pret* ***lay***, *pp* ***lain***) *of person* sdraiarsi; *of object* stare; (*be situated*) trovarsi
◆ **lie down** *v/i* sdraiarsi
'**lie-in**: ***have a lie-in*** restare a letto fino a tardi
lieu [lju:] *n*: ***in lieu of*** invece di
lieu•ten•ant [lef'tenənt] tenente *m*
life [laɪf] (*pl* ***lives*** [laɪvz]) vita *f*; *of machine* durata *f*; *of battery* autonomia *f*; ***all her life*** tutta la vita; ***that's life!*** così è la vita!
'**life as•sur•ance** *Br* assicurazione *f* sulla vita
'**life belt** salvagente *m inv*
'**life•boat** lancia *f* di salvataggio
'**life ex•pect•an•cy** aspettativa *f* di vita
'**life•guard** bagnino *m*, -a *f*
'**life his•to•ry** ciclo *m* vitale
life im'pris•on•ment ergastolo *m*
'**life in•sur•ance** assicurazione *f* sulla vita
'**life jack•et** giubbotto *m* di salvataggio
life•less ['laɪflɪs] *adj* senza vita
life•like ['laɪflaɪk] *adj* fedele
'**life•long** di vecchia data
'**life-sav•ing** *adj medical equipment, drug* salvavita
'**life•sized** *adj* a grandezza naturale
'**life-threat•en•ing** *adj* mortale
'**life•time** *n*: ***in my lifetime*** in vita mia
lift [lɪft] **1** *v/t* sollevare **2** *v/i of fog* diradarsi **3** *n Br*: *in building* ascensore *m*; *in car* passaggio *m*; ***give s.o. a lift*** dare un passaggio a qu
◆ **lift off** *v/i of rocket* decollare
'**lift-off** *of rocket* decollo *m*
lig•a•ment ['lɪgəmənt] legamento *m*
light[1] [laɪt] **1** *n* luce *f*; ***in the light of*** alla luce di; ***have you got a light?*** hai da accendere? **2** *v/t* (*pret & pp* ***lit***) *fire, cigarette* accendere; (*illuminate*) illuminare **3** *adj not dark* chiaro
light[2] [laɪt] **1** *adj not heavy* leggero **2** *adv*: ***travel light*** viaggiare leggero
◆ **light up 1** *v/t* (*illuminate*) illuminare **2** *v/i* (*start to smoke*) accendersi una sigaretta
'**light bulb** lampadina *f*
light•en[1] ['laɪtn] *v/t colour* schiarire
light•en[2] ['laɪtn] *v/t load* alleggerire
◆ **lighten up** *v/i of person* rilassarsi
light•er ['laɪtə(r)] *for cigarettes* accendino *m*
light-head•ed [laɪt'hedɪd] *adj* (*dizzy*) stordito
light-ˌheart•ed [laɪt'hɑ:tɪd] *adj film* leggero
'**light•house** faro *m*
light•ing ['laɪtɪŋ] illuminazione *f*
light•ly ['laɪtlɪ] *adv touch* leggermente; ***get off lightly*** cavarsela con poco
light•ness ['laɪtnɪs] leggerezza *f*
light•ning ['laɪtnɪŋ] fulmine *m*
'**light•ning con•duc•tor** parafulmine *m*
'**light pen** penna *f* luminosa
'**light•weight** *in boxing* peso *m* leggero
'**light year** anno *m* luce
like[1] [laɪk] **1** *prep* come; ***like this / that*** così; ***what is she like?*** *in looks, character* com'è?; ***it's not like him*** *not his character* non è da lui; ***look like s.o.*** assomigliare a qu **2** *conj* F (*as*) come; ***like I said*** come ho già detto
like[2] [laɪk] *v/t*: ***I like it / her*** mi piace; ***I would like …*** vorrei …; ***I would like to …*** vorrei …; ***would you like …?*** ti va …?; ***would you like to …?*** ti va di …?; ***he likes swimming*** gli piace nuotare; ***if you like*** se vuoi
like•a•ble ['laɪkəbl] *adj* simpatico
like•li•hood ['laɪklɪhʊd] probabilità *f inv*; ***in all likelihood*** molto probabilmente
like•ly ['laɪklɪ] *adj* (*probable*) probabile;

not likely! difficile!
like•ness ['laɪknɪs] (*resemblance*) somiglianza *f*
'like•wise ['laɪkwaɪz] *adv* altrettanto
lik•ing ['laɪkɪŋ] predilizione *f*; ***is it to your liking?*** *fml* è di tuo gradimento?; ***take a liking to s.o.*** prendere qu in simpatia
li•lac ['laɪlək] *flower* lillà *m inv*; *colour* lilla *m inv*
li•ly ['lɪlɪ] giglio *m*
li•ly of the 'val•ley mughetto *m*
limb [lɪm] arto *m*
lime[1] [laɪm] *fruit* limetta *f*
lime[2] [laɪm] *substance* calce *f*
lime'green *adj* verde *m* acido
'lime•light *n*: ***be in the limelight*** essere in vista
lim•it ['lɪmɪt] **1** *n* limite *m*; ***within limits*** entro certi limiti; ***off limits*** off-limits; ***that's the limit!*** F è il colmo! **2** *v/t* limitare
lim•i•ta•tion [lɪmɪ'teɪʃn] limite *m*
lim•it•ed 'com•pa•ny società *f inv* a responsabilità limitata
li•mo ['lɪməʊ] F limousine *f inv*
lim•ou•sine ['lɪməziːn] limousine *f inv*
limp[1] [lɪmp] *adj* floscio
limp[2] [lɪmp] *n*: ***he has a limp*** zoppica
line[1] [laɪn] *n on paper*, *road* linea *f*; *of people*, *trees* fila *f*; *of text* riga *f*; (*cord*) filo *m*; *of business* settore *m*; TELEC linea *f*; ***the line is busy*** è occupato; ***hold the line*** rimanga in linea; ***draw the line at sth*** non tollerare qc; ***line of inquiry*** pista *f*; ***line of reasoning*** filo *m* del ragionamento; ***stand in line*** *esp Am* fare la fila; ***in line with …*** (*conforming with*) in linea con …
line[2] [laɪn] *v/t* foderare
◆ **line up** *v/i* mettersi in fila
lin•e•ar ['lɪnɪə(r)] *adj* lineare
lin•en ['lɪnɪn] *material* lino *m*; *sheets etc* biancheria *f*
lin•er ['laɪnə(r)] *ship* transatlantico *m*
lines•man ['laɪnzmən] SP guardalinee *m inv*
lin•ger ['lɪŋgə(r)] *v/i of person* attardarsi; *of smell*, *pain* persistere
lin•ge•rie ['lænʒərɪ] lingerie *f inv*
lin•guist ['lɪŋgwɪst] *professional* linguista *m/f*; *person good at languages* poliglotta *m/f*
lin•guis•tic [lɪŋ'gwɪstɪk] *adj* linguistico
lin•ing ['laɪnɪŋ] *of clothes* fodera *f*; *of brakes* guarnizione *f*
link [lɪŋk] **1** *n* (*connection*) legame *m*; *in chain* anello *m* **2** *v/t* collegare
◆ **link up** *v/i* riunirsi; TV collegarsi
li•on ['laɪən] leone *m*
li•on•ess ['laɪənes] leonessa *f*
lip [lɪp] labbro *m*; ***lips*** labbra
'lip•read *v/i* (*pret & pp* ***-read*** [red]) leggere le labbra
'lip•stick rossetto *m*
li•queur [lɪ'kjʊə(r)] liquore *m*
liq•uid ['lɪkwɪd] **1** *n* liquido *m* **2** *adj* liquido
liq•ui•date ['lɪkwɪdeɪt] *v/t* liquidare
liq•ui•da•tion [lɪkwɪ'deɪʃn] liquidazione *f*; ***go into liquidation*** andare in liquidazione
liq•ui•di•ty [lɪ'kwɪdɪtɪ] FIN liquidità *f inv*
liq•uid•ize ['lɪkwɪdaɪz] *v/t* frullare
liq•uid•iz•er ['lɪkwɪdaɪzə(r)] frullatore *m*
liq•uor ['lɪkə(r)] superalcolici *mpl*
liq•uo•rice ['lɪkərɪs] liquirizia *f*
lisp [lɪsp] **1** *n* lisca *f* **2** *v/i* parlare con la lisca
list [lɪst] **1** *n* elenco *m*, lista *f* **2** *v/t* elencare
lis•ten ['lɪsn] *v/i* ascoltare
◆ **listen in** *v/i* ascoltare (di nascosto)
◆ **listen to** *v/t radio*, *person* ascoltare
lis•ten•er ['lɪsnə(r)] *to radio* ascoltatore *m*, -trice *f*; ***he's a good listener*** sa ascoltare
list•ings mag•a•zine ['lɪstɪŋz] guida *f* dei programmi radio / TV
list•less ['lɪstlɪs] *adj* apatico
lit [lɪt] *pret & pp* → ***light***
li•ter *Am* → ***litre***
lit•e•ral ['lɪtərəl] *adj* letterale
lit•e•ral•ly ['lɪtərəlɪ] *adv* letteralmente
lit•e•ra•ry ['lɪtərərɪ] *adj* letterario
lit•e•rate ['lɪtərət] *adj*: ***be literate*** saper leggere e scrivere
lit•e•ra•ture ['lɪtrətʃə(r)] letteratura *f*; F (*leaflets*) opuscoli *mpl*
li•tre ['liːtə(r)] litro *m*
lit•ter ['lɪtə(r)] rifiuti *mpl*; *of animal* cucciolata *f*
'lit•ter bas•ket cestino *m* dei rifiuti
'lit•ter bin bidone *m* dei rifiuti
lit•tle ['lɪtl] **1** *adj* piccolo; ***the little ones*** i piccoli **2** *n*: ***the little I know*** il poco che so; ***a little*** un po'; ***a little bread / wine*** un po' di pane / vino; ***a little is better than nothing*** meglio poco che niente **3** *adv*: ***little by little*** (a) poco a poco; ***a little better / bigger*** un po' meglio / più grande; ***a little before 6*** un po' prima delle 6
live[1] [lɪv] *v/i* (*reside*) abitare; (*be alive*) vivere
◆ **live on 1** *v/t rice*, *bread* vivere di **2** *v/i continue living* sopravvivere
◆ **live up**: ***live it up*** fare la bella vita
◆ **live up to** *v/t* essere all'altezza di
◆ **live with** *v/t* vivere con
live[2] [laɪv] **1** *adj broadcast* dal vivo; *ammunition* carico **2** *adv broadcast* in diret-

ta; *record* dal vivo
live•li•hood ['laɪvlɪhʊd] mezzi *mpl* di sostentamento; ***earn one's livelihood*** guadagnarsi da vivere
live•li•ness ['laɪvlɪnɪs] vivacità *f inv*
live•ly ['laɪvlɪ] *adj* vivace
liv•er ['lɪvə(r)] fegato *m*
live•stock ['laɪvstɒk] bestiame *m*
liv•id ['lɪvɪd] *adj* (*angry*) furibondo
liv•ing ['lɪvɪŋ] **1** *adj* in vita **2** *n*: ***earn one's living*** guadagnarsi da vivere; ***what do you do for a living?*** che lavoro fai?; ***standard of living*** tenore *m* di vita
'**liv•ing room** salotto *m*, soggiorno *m*
liz•ard ['lɪzəd] lucertola *f*
load [ləʊd] **1** *n* carico *m*; ***loads of*** F un sacco di **2** *v/t* caricare; ***load sth onto sth*** caricare qc su qc
load•ed ['ləʊdɪd] *adj* F (*very rich*) ricco sfondato
loaf [ləʊf] *n* (*pl* **loaves** [ləʊvz]): ***a loaf of bread*** una pagnotta
◆ **loaf about** *v/i* F oziare
loaf•er ['ləʊfə(r)] *shoe* mocassino *m*
loan [ləʊn] **1** *n* prestito *m*; ***on loan*** in prestito **2** *v/t*: ***loan s.o. sth*** prestare qc a qu
loathe [ləʊð] *v/t* detestare
loath•ing ['ləʊðɪŋ] disgusto *m*
lob•by ['lɒbɪ] *in hotel*, *theatre* atrio *m*; POL lobby *f inv*
lobe [ləʊb] *of ear* lobo *m*
lob•ster ['lɒbstə(r)] aragosta *f*
lo•cal ['ləʊkl] **1** *adj people*, *bar* del posto; *produce* locale; ***I'm not local*** non sono del posto **2** *n* persona *f* del posto; ***are you a local?*** sei del posto?
'**lo•cal call** TELEC telefonata *f* urbana
lo•cal e'lec•tions *npl* elezioni *fpl* amministrative
lo•cal 'gov•ern•ment amministrazione *f* locale
lo•cal•i•ty [ləʊ'kælətɪ] località *f inv*
lo•cal•ly ['ləʊkəlɪ] *adv live*, *work* nella zona
lo•cal 'pro•duce prodotti *mpl* locali
'**lo•cal time** ora *f* locale
lo•cate [ləʊ'keɪt] *v/t new factory etc* situare; *identify position of* localizzare; ***be located*** essere situato
lo•ca•tion [ləʊ'keɪʃn] (*siting*) ubicazione *f*; *identifying position of* localizzazione *f*; ***on location*** *film* in esterni; ***the film was shot on location in …*** gli esterni del film sono stati girati in …
loch lago *m*
lock[1] [lɒk] *of hair* ciocca *f*
lock[2] [lɒk] **1** *n on door* serratura *f* **2** *v/t door* chiudere a chiave; ***lock sth in position*** bloccare qc
◆ **lock away** *v/t* mettere sottochiave
◆ **lock in** *v/t person* chiudere dentro
◆ **lock out** *v/t of house* chiudere fuori
◆ **lock up** *v/t in prison* mettere dentro
lock•er ['lɒkə(r)] armadietto *m*
'**lock•er room** spogliatoio *m*
lock•et ['lɒkɪt] medaglione *m*
lock•smith ['lɒksmɪθ] fabbro *m* ferraio
lo•cust ['ləʊkəst] locusta *f*
lodge [lɒdʒ] **1** *v/t complaint* presentare **2** *v/i of bullet* conficcarsi
lodg•er ['lɒdʒə(r)] pensionante *m/f*
loft [lɒft] soffitta *f*
loft•y ['lɒftɪ] *adj peak* alto; *ideals* nobile
log [lɒg] *wood* ceppo *m*; *written record* giornale *m*
◆ **log off** *v/i* (*pret & pp* **-ged**) disconnettersi (**from** da)
◆ **log on** *v/i* connettersi
◆ **log on to** *v/t* connettersi a
'**log•book** giornale *m* di bordo
log 'cab•in casetta *f* di legno
log•ger•heads ['lɒgəhedz]: ***be at loggerheads*** essere ai ferri corti
lo•gic ['lɒdʒɪk] logica *f*
lo•gic•al ['lɒdʒɪkl] *adj* logico
lo•gic•al•ly ['lɒdʒɪklɪ] *adv* a rigor di logica; *arrange* in modo logico
lo•gis•tics [lə'dʒɪstɪks] *npl* logistica *f*
lo•go ['ləʊgəʊ] logo *m inv*
loi•ter ['lɔɪtə(r)] *v/i* gironzolare
lol•li•pop ['lɒlɪpɒp] lecca lecca *m inv*
'**lol•li•pop man / wo•man** *Br uomo / donna che aiuta i bambini ad attraversare la strada*
lol•ly ['lɒlɪ] (*ice lolly*) ghiacciolo *m*; F (*money*) grana *f* F
Lon•don ['lʌndən] Londra *f*
lone•li•ness ['ləʊnlɪnɪs] solitudine *f*
lone•ly ['ləʊnlɪ] *adj person* solo; *place* isolato
lon•er ['ləʊnə(r)] persona *f* solitaria
long[1] [lɒŋ] **1** *adj* lungo; ***it's a long way*** è lontano **2** *adv*: ***don't be long*** torna presto ***5 weeks is too long*** 5 settimane è troppo; ***will it take long?*** ci vorrà tanto?; ***that was long ago*** è stato tanto tempo fa; ***long before then*** molto prima di allora; ***before long*** poco tempo dopo; ***we can't wait any longer*** non possiamo attendere oltre; ***he no longer works here*** non lavora più qui; ***so long as*** (*provided*) sempre che; ***so long!*** arrivederci!
long[2] [lɒŋ] *v/i*: ***long for sth*** desiderare ardentemente qc; ***be longing to do sth*** desiderare ardentemente fare qc
long-'dis•tance *adj phonecall* interurbano; *race* di fondo; *flight* intercontinentale
lon•gev•i•ty [lɒn'dʒevɪtɪ] longevità *f inv*

long•ing ['lɒŋɪŋ] *n* desiderio *m*
lon•gi•tude ['lɒŋgɪtjuːd] longitudine *f*
'**long jump** salto *m* in lungo
long-ˌlife milk latte *m* a lunga conservazione
'**long-range** *missile* a lunga gittata; *forecast* a lungo termine
long-sight•ed [lɒŋ'saɪtɪd] *adj* presbite
long-sleeved [lɒŋ'sliːvd] *adj* a maniche lunghe
long-'stand•ing *adj* di vecchia data
'**long-term** *adj plans*, *investment* a lunga scadenza; *relationship* stabile
'**long wave** RAD onde *fpl* lunghe
long•wind•ed [lɒŋ'wɪndɪd] *adj* prolisso
loo [luː] F gabinetto *m*
look [lʊk] **1** *n* (*appearance*) aspetto *m*; (*glance*) sguardo *m*; ***give s.o. / sth a look*** dare uno sguardo a qu / qc; ***have a look at sth*** *examine* dare un'occhiata a qc; ***can I have a look around?*** *in shop etc* posso dare un'occhiata?; ***looks*** (*beauty*) bellezza *f* **2** *v/i* guardare; (*search*) cercare; (*seem*) sembrare; ***you look tired / different*** sembri stanco / diverso
◆ **look after** *v/t* badare a
◆ **look ahead** *v/i fig* pensare al futuro
◆ **look around** *v/i in shop etc* dare un'occhiata in giro; (*look back*) guardarsi indietro
◆ **look at** *v/t* guardare; (*consider*) considerare
◆ **look back** *v/i* guardare indietro
◆ **look down on** *v/t* disprezzare
◆ **look for** *v/t* cercare
◆ **look forward to** *v/t*: ***look forward to doing sth*** non veder l'ora di fare qc; ***I'm looking forward to the holidays*** non vedo l'ora che arrivino le vacanze; ***I'm not looking forward to it*** non ne ho proprio voglia
◆ **look in on** *v/t* (*visit*) passare a trovare
◆ **look into** *v/t* (*investigate*) esaminare
◆ **look on 1** *v/i* (*watch*) rimanere a guardare **2** *v/t*: ***I look on you as a friend*** (*consider*) ti considero un amico
◆ **look onto** *v/t garden*, *street* dare su
◆ **look out** *v/i of window etc* guardare fuori; (*pay attention*) fare attenzione; ***look out!*** attento!
◆ **look out for** *v/t* cercare; (*be on guard against*) fare attenzione a
◆ **look out of** *v/t window* guardare da
◆ **look over** *v/t house*, *translation* esaminare
◆ **look round** *v/t museum*, *city* visitare
◆ **look through** *v/t magazine*, *notes* scorrere
◆ **look to** *v/t* (*rely on*) contare su
◆ **look up 1** *v/i from paper etc* sollevare lo sguardo; (*improve*) migliorare **2** *v/t word*, *phone number* cercare; (*visit*) andare a trovare
◆ **look up to** *v/t* (*respect*) avere rispetto per
lookout *n person* sentinella *f*; *place* posto *m* di guardia; ***be on the lookout*** stare all'erta; ***be on the lookout for*** *accommodation etc* cercare di trovare; *new staff etc* essere alla ricerca di
◆ **loom up** [luːm] *v/i* apparire
loon•y ['luːnɪ] **1** *n* F matto *m*, -a *f* **2** *adj* F matto
loop [luːp] *n* cappio *m*
'**loop•hole** *in law etc* scappatoia *f*
loose [luːs] *adj wire*, *button* allentato; *clothes* ampio; *tooth* che tentenna; *morals* dissoluto; *wording* vago; ***loose change*** spiccioli *mpl*; ***loose ends*** *of problem*, *discussion* aspetti *mpl* da esaminare
loose•ly ['luːslɪ] *adv tied* senza stringere; *worded* vagamente
loos•en ['luːsn] *v/t collar*, *knot* allentare
loot [luːt] **1** *n* bottino *m* **2** *v/t & v/i* saccheggiare
loot•er [luːtə(r)] saccheggiatore *m*, -trice *f*
◆ **lop off** [lɒp] *v/t* (*pret & pp* ***-ped***) tagliar via
lop-sid•ed [lɒp'saɪdɪd] *adj* sbilenco
Lord [lɔːd] (*God*) Signore *m*; ***the (House of) Lords*** la camera dei Lord
Lord's '**Prayer** il Padrenostro *m*
lor•ry ['lɒrɪ] *Br* camion *m inv*
lose [luːz] (*pret & pp* ***lost***) **1** *v/t object* perdere **2** *v/i* SP perdere; *of clock* andare indietro; ***I'm lost*** mi sono perso; ***get lost!*** F sparisci!
◆ **lose out** *v/i* rimetterci
los•er ['luːzə(r)] *in contest* perdente *m/f*; F *in life* sfigato *m*, -a *f* F
loss [lɒs] perdita *f*; ***make a loss*** subire una perdita; ***be at a loss*** essere perplesso
lost [lɒst] **1** *adj* perso **2** *pret & pp* → ***lose***
lost and '**found** *Am*, **lost** '**prop•er•ty office** *Br* ufficio *m* oggetti smarriti
lot [lɒt] *n*: ***the lot*** tutto; ***a lot, lots*** molto; ***a lot of ice cream, lots of ice cream*** molto gelato; ***a lot of ice creams, lots of ice creams*** molti gelati; ***a lot better / easier*** molto meglio / più facile
lo•tion ['ləʊʃn] lozione *f*
lot•te•ry ['lɒtərɪ] lotteria *f*
loud [laʊd] *adj music*, *voice*, *noise* forte; *colour* sgargiante
loud'**speak•er** altoparlante *m*; *for stereo* cassa *f* dello stereo
lounge [laʊndʒ] *in house* soggiorno *m*; *in hotel* salone *m*; *at airport* sala *f* partenze

◆ **lounge about** *v/i* poltrire
'**lounge suit** completo *m* da uomo
louse [laʊs] (*pl* ***lice*** [laɪs]) pidocchio *m*
lous•y ['laʊzɪ] *adj* F schifoso F; ***I feel lousy*** mi sento uno schifo
lout [laʊt] teppista *m/f*
lov•a•ble ['lʌvəbl] *adj* adorabile
love [lʌv] **1** *n* amore *m*; *in tennis* zero *m*; ***be in love*** essere innamorato; ***fall in love*** innamorarsi; ***make love*** fare l'amore; ***make love to*** fare l'amore con; ***yes, my love*** sì, tesoro **2** *v/t person, country, wine* amare; ***love doing sth*** amare fare qc
'**love af•fair** relazione *f*
'**love•life** vita *f* sentimentale
'**love let•ter** lettera *f* d'amore
love•ly ['lʌvlɪ] *adj face, colour, holiday* bello; *meal, smell* buono; ***we had a lovely time*** siamo stati benissimo
lov•er ['lʌvə(r)] amante *m/f*
lov•ing ['lʌvɪŋ] *adj* affettuoso
lov•ing•ly ['lʌvɪŋlɪ] *adv* amorosamente
low [ləʊ] **1** *adj bridge, price, voice* basso; *quality* scarso; ***be feeling low*** sentirsi giù; ***be low on petrol*** avere poca benzina **2** *n in weather* depressione *f*; *in sales, statistics* minimo *m*
low•brow ['ləʊbraʊ] *adj* di scarso spessore culturale
low-ˌcal•o•rie *adj* ipocalorico
'**low-cut** *adj dress* scollato
low•er ['ləʊə(r)] *v/t boat, sth to the ground* calare; *flag, hemline* ammainare; *pressure, price* abbassare
'**low-fat** *adj* magro
'**low•key** *adj* discreto
'**low•lands** *npl* bassopiano *m*
low-'pres•sure ar•e•a area *f* di bassa pressione
'**low sea•son** bassa stagione *f*
'**low tide** bassa marea *f*
loy•al ['lɔɪəl] *adj* leale
loy•al•ly ['lɔɪəlɪ] *adv* lealmente
loy•al•ty ['lɔɪəltɪ] lealtà *f inv*
loz•enge ['lɒzɪndʒ] *shape* rombo *m*; *tablet* pastiglia *f*
LP [el'piː] *abbr* (= ***long-playing record***) LP *m inv* (= long-playing *m inv*)
Ltd *abbr* (= ***limited***) s.r.l. (= società *f inv* a responsabilità limitata)
lu•bri•cant ['luːbrɪkənt] lubrificante *m*
lu•bri•cate ['luːbrɪkeɪt] *v/t* lubrificare
lu•bri•ca•tion [luːbrɪ'keɪʃn] lubrificazione *f*
lu•cid ['luːsɪd] *adj* (*clear*) chiaro; (*sane*) lucido
luck [lʌk] fortuna *f*; ***bad luck*** sfortuna; ***hard luck!*** che sfortuna!; ***good luck*** fortuna *f*; ***good luck!*** buona fortuna!
luck•i•ly ['lʌkɪlɪ] *adv* fortunatamente
luck•y ['lʌkɪ] *adj* fortunato; ***you were lucky*** hai avuto fortuna; ***he's lucky to be alive*** è vivo per miracolo; ***that's lucky!*** che fortuna!
lu•cra•tive ['luːkrətɪv] *adj* redditizio
lu•di•crous ['luːdɪkrəs] *adj* ridicolo
lug [lʌg] *v/t* (*pret & pp* ***-ged***) F trascinare
lug•gage ['lʌgɪdʒ] bagagli *mpl*
'**lug•gage rack** *in train* portabagagli *m inv*
luke•warm ['luːkwɔːm] *adj* tiepido
lull [lʌl] **1** *n in fighting* momento *m* di calma; *in conversation* pausa *f* **2** *v/t*: ***lull s.o. into a false sense of security*** illudersi che tutto vada bene
lul•la•by ['lʌləbaɪ] ninnananna *f*
lum•ba•go [lʌmbeɪgəʊ] lombaggine *f*
lum•ber ['lʌmbə(r)] (*timber*) legname *m*
lu•mi•nous ['luːmɪnəs] *adj* luminoso
lump [lʌmp] *of sugar* zolletta *f*; (*swelling*) nodulo *m*
◆ **lump together** *v/t* mettere insieme
lump 'sum pagamento *m* unico
lump•y ['lʌmpɪ] *adj sauce* grumoso; *mattress* pieno di buchi
lu•na•cy ['luːnəsɪ] pazzia *f*
lu•nar ['luːnə(r)] *adj* lunare
lu•na•tic ['luːnətɪk] *n* pazzo *m*, -a *f*
lunch [lʌntʃ] pranzo *m*; ***have lunch*** pranzare
'**lunch box** cestino *m* del pranzo
'**lunch break** pausa *f* pranzo
'**lunch hour** pausa *f* pranzo
'**lunch•time** ora *f* di pranzo
lung [lʌŋ] polmone *m*
'**lung can•cer** cancro *m* al polmone
◆ **lunge at** [lʌndʒ] *v/t* scagliarsi contro
lurch [lɜːtʃ] *v/i* barcollare
lure [lʊə(r)] **1** *n* attrattiva *f* **2** *v/t* attirare; ***lure s.o. into a trap*** far cadere qu in trappola
lu•rid ['lʊərɪd] *adj colour* sgargiante; *details* scandaloso
lurk [lɜːk] *v/i of person* appostarsi; *of doubt* persistere
lus•cious ['lʌʃəs] *adj* sensuale
lush [lʌʃ] *adj vegetation* lussureggiante
lust [lʌst] *n* libidine *f*
lux•u•ri•ous [lʌg'ʒʊərɪəs] *adj* lussuoso
lux•u•ri•ous•ly [lʌg'ʒʊərɪəslɪ] *adv* lussuosamente
lux•u•ry ['lʌkʃərɪ] **1** *n* lusso *m* **2** *adj* di lusso
LV *abbr* (= ***luncheon voucher***) buono *m* pasto
lymph gland ['lɪmfglænd] ghiandola *f* linfatica
lynch [lɪntʃ] *v/t* linciare
lyr•i•cist ['lɪrɪsɪst] paroliere *m*
lyr•ics ['lɪrɪks] *npl* parole *fpl*, testi *mpl*

M

M [em] *abbr* (= ***medium***) M (= medio)
MA [em'eɪ] *abbr* (= ***Master of Arts***) master *m inv*
ma'am [mæm] *Am* signora *f*
mac [mæk] F (*mackintosh*) impermeabile *m*
ma•chine [mə'ʃiːn] **1** *n* macchina *f* **2** *v/t with sewing machine* cucire a macchina; TECH lavorare a macchina
ma'chine gun mitragliatrice *f*
ma•chine-'read•a•ble *adj* leggibile dalla macchina
ma•chin•e•ry [mə'ʃiːnərɪ] (*machines*) macchinario *m*
ma•chine trans'la•tion traduzione *f* fatta dal computer
ma•chis•mo [mə'kɪzməʊ] machismo *m*
mach•o ['mætʃəʊ] *adj* macho *m*
mack•in•tosh ['mækɪntɒʃ] impermeabile *m*
mac•ro ['mækrəʊ] COMPUT macro *f*
mad [mæd] *adj* (*insane*) pazzo *m*; F (*angry*) furioso; ***be mad about*** F andar matto per; ***drive s.o. mad*** far impazzire qu; ***go mad*** (*become insane*) impazzire; F *with enthusiasm* impazzire; ***like mad*** F *run*, *work* come un matto
mad•am ['mædəm] signora *f*
mad 'cow dis•ease F morbo *m* della mucca pazza
mad•den ['mædən] *v/t* (*infuriate*) esasperare
mad•den•ing ['mædnɪŋ] *adj* esasperante
made [meɪd] *pret & pp* → ***make***
made-to-'meas•ure *adj* su misura
'mad•house *fig* manicomio *m*
mad•ly ['mædlɪ] *adv* come un matto; ***madly in love*** pazzamente innamorato
'mad•man pazzo *m*
mad•ness ['mædnɪs] pazzia *f*
Ma•don•na [mə'dɒnə] Madonna *f*
Ma•fi•a ['mæfɪə] Mafia *f*
mag•a•zine [mægə'ziːn] *printed* rivista *f*
mag•got ['mægət] verme *m*
Ma•gi ['meɪdʒaɪ] REL Re Magi *mpl*
ma•gic ['mædʒɪk] **1** *n* magia *f*; *tricks* giochi *mpl* di prestigio; ***like magic*** come per magia **2** *adj* magico
mag•i•cal ['mædʒɪkl] *adj powers*, *moment* magico
ma•gi•cian [mə'dʒɪʃn] *performer* mago *m*, -a *f*
ma•gic 'spell incantesimo *m*
ma•gic 'trick gioco *m* di prestigio
mag•ic 'wand bacchetta *f* magica
magistrate ['mædʒɪstreɪt] magistrato *m*
mag•nan•i•mous [mæg'nænɪməs] *adj* magnanimo
mag•net ['mægnɪt] calamita *f*, magnete *m*
mag•net•ic [mæg'netɪk] *adj* calamitato; *also fig* magnetico
mag•net•ic 'stripe striscia *f* magnetizzata
mag•net•ism [mæg'netɪzm] *of person* magnetismo *m*
mag•nif•i•cence [mæg'nɪfɪsəns] magnificenza *f*
mag•nif•i•cent [mæg'nɪfɪsənt] *adj* magnifico
mag•ni•fy ['mægnɪfaɪ] *v/t* (*pret & pp* ***-ied***) ingrandire; *difficulties* ingigantire
'mag•ni•fy•ing glass lente *f* d'ingrandimento
mag•ni•tude ['mægnɪtjuːd] *of problem* portata *f*; AST magnitudine *f*
ma•hog•a•ny [mə'hɒgənɪ] mogano *m*
maid [meɪd] *servant* domestica *f*; *in hotel* cameriera *f*
maid•en name ['meɪdn] nome *m* da ragazza
maid•en 'speech discorso *m* inaugurale
maid•en 'voy•age viaggio *m* inaugurale
mail [meɪl] **1** *n* posta *f*; ***put sth in the mail*** spedire qc **2** *v/t letter* spedire; *person* spedire a
'mail•box *Am* buca *f* delle lettere; *Am*: *of house* cassetta *f* delle lettere; COMPUT casella *f* postale
'mail•ing list mailing list *m inv*
'mail•man *Am* postino *m*
mail-ˌor•der cat•a•log *Am*, **mail-ˌor•der cat•a•logue** catalogo *m* di vendita per corrispondenza
mail-ˌor•der firm ditta *f* di vendita per corrispondenza
'mail•shot mailing *m inv*
maim [meɪm] *v/t* mutilare
main [meɪn] *adj* principale
'main course piatto *m* principale
main 'en•trance entrata *f* principale
'main•frame mainframe *m inv*
'main•land terraferma *f*, continente *m*; ***on the mainland*** sul continente
main•ly ['meɪnlɪ] *adv* principalmente
main 'road strada *f* principale
'main street corso *m*
main•tain [meɪn'teɪn] *v/t* mantenere; *pace*, *speed*; *relationship*; *machine*, *house*; *family*; *innocence*, *guilt* sostenere; ***main-***

tain that sostenere che
main•te•nance ['meɪntənəns] *of machine, house* manutenzione *f*; *money* alimenti *mpl*; *of law and order* mantenimento *m*
'**main•te•nance costs** *npl* spese *fpl* di manutenzione
'**main•te•nance staff** addetti *mpl* alla manutenzione
ma•jes•tic [mə'dʒestɪk] *adj* maestoso
maj•es•ty ['mædʒəstɪ] (*grandeur*) maestà *f inv*; ***Her Majesty*** Sua Maestà
ma•jor ['meɪdʒə(r)] **1** *adj* (*significant*) importante, principale; ***in C major*** MUS in Do maggiore **2** *n* MIL maggiore *m*
ma•jor•i•ty [mə'dʒɒrətɪ] *also* POL maggioranza *f*; ***be in the majority*** essere in maggioranza
make [meɪk] **1** *n brand* marca *f* **2** *v/t* (*pret & pp* ***made***) fare; *decision* prendere; (*earn*) guadagnare; MATH fare; ***make s.o. do sth*** (*force to*) far fare qc a qu; (*cause to*) spingere qu a fare qc; ***you can't make me do it!*** non puoi costringermi a farlo!; ***make s.o. happy / angry*** far felice / arrabbiare qu; ***make s.o. happy / sad*** rendere felice / triste qu; ***make a decision*** prendere una decisione; ***make a telephone call*** fare una telefonata; ***made in Japan*** made in Japan; ***make it*** *catch bus, train, come, succeed, survive* farcela; ***what time do you make it?*** che ore fai?; ***make believe*** far finta; ***make do with*** arrangiarsi con; ***what do you make of it?*** cosa ne pensi?
◆ **make for** *v/t* (*go towards*) dirigersi verso
◆ **make off** *v/i* svignarsela
◆ **make off with** *v/t* (*steal*) svignarsela con
◆ **make out** *v/t list* fare; *cheque* compilare; (*see*) distinguere; (*imply*) far capire; ***who shall I make the cheque out to?*** a chi devo intestare l'assegno?
◆ **make over**: ***make sth over to s.o.*** cedere qc a qu
◆ **make up 1** *v/i of woman, actor* truccarsi; *after quarrel* fare la pace **2** *v/t story, excuse* inventare; *face* truccare; (*constitute*) costituire; ***be made up of*** essere composto da; ***make up one's mind*** decidersi; ***make it up*** *after quarrel* fare la pace
◆ **make up for** *v/t* compensare; ***I'll make up for forgetting your birthday*** mi farò perdonare di essermi scordato del tuo compleanno
'**make-be•lieve** *n* finta *f*
mak•er ['meɪkə(r)] *manufacturer* fabbricante *m/f*
make•shift ['meɪkʃɪft] *adj* improvvisato
make-up ['meɪkʌp] (*cosmetics*) trucco *m*
'**make-up bag** trousse *f inv* da trucco
mal•ad•just•ed [mælə'dʒʌstɪd] *adj* disadattato
male [meɪl] **1** *adj* (*masculine*) maschile; *animal, bird, fish* maschio **2** *n man* uomo *m*; *animal, bird, fish* maschio *m*
male 'chau•vin•ism maschilismo *m*
male chau•vin•ist 'pig maschilista *m*
male 'nurse infermiere *m*
ma•lev•o•lent [mə'levələnt] *adj* malevolo
mal•func•tion [mæl'fʌŋkʃn] **1** *n* cattivo *m* funzionamento **2** *v/i* funzionare male
mal•ice ['mælɪs] cattiveria *f*, malvagità *f*
ma•li•cious [mə'lɪʃəs] *adj* cattivo, malvagio
ma•lig•nant [mə'lɪgnənt] *adj tumour* maligno
mall [mæl] (*shopping mall*) centro *m* commerciale
mal•nu•tri•tion [mælnjuː'trɪʃn] denutrizione *f*
mal•prac•tice [mæl'præktɪs] negligenza *f*
malt ('**whis•ky**) [mɔːlt] whisky *m inv* di malto
mal•treat [mæl'triːt] *v/t* maltrattare
mal•treat•ment [mæl'triːtmənt] maltrattamento *m*
mam•mal ['mæml] mammifero *m*
mam•moth ['mæməθ] *adj* (*enormous*) colossale
man [mæn] **1** *n* (*pl* ***men*** [men]) *person, human being* uomo *m*; (*human being*) uomo *m*; *humanity* umanità *f inv*; *in draughts* pedina *f* **2** *v/t* (*pret & pp* ***-ned***) *telephones, front desk* essere di servizio a; ***it was manned by a crew of three*** aveva un equipaggio di tre uomini
man•age ['mænɪdʒ] **1** *v/t business, money* gestire; *money*; *suitcase*; ***can you manage the suitcase?*** ce la fai a portare la valigia?; ***manage to ...*** riuscire a ... **2** *v/i cope, financially* tirare avanti; (*financially*); ***can you manage?*** ce la fai?
man•age•a•ble ['mænɪdʒəbl] *adj suitcase etc* maneggevole; *hair* docile; *able to be done* fattibile
man•age•ment ['mænɪdʒmənt] (*managing*) gestione *f*; (*managers*) direzione *f*; ***under his management*** durante la sua gestione
man•age•ment 'buy•out *acquisizione f di un'impresa da parte dei suoi dirigenti*
man•age•ment con,sult•ant consulente *m/f* di gestione aziendale
'**man•age•ment stud•ies** corso *m* di formazione manageriale

M

'man•age•ment team team *m inv* manageriale
man•ag•er ['mænɪdʒə(r)] manager *m/f inv*, direttore *m*, -trice *f*
man•a•ge•ri•al [mænɪ'dʒɪərɪəl] *adj* manageriale
man•ag•ing di'rec•tor direttore *m* generale
man•da•rin 'or•ange [mændərɪn] mandarino *m*
man•date ['mændeɪt] (*authority, task*) mandato *m*
man•da•to•ry ['mændətrɪ] *adj* obbligatorio
mane [meɪn] *of horse* criniera *f*
ma•neu•ver *Am* → ***manoeuvre***
man•gle ['mæŋgl] *v/t* (*crush*) stritolare
man•han•dle ['mænhændl] *v/t person* malmenare; *object* caricare
man•hood ['mænhʊd] *maturity* età *f inv* adulta; (*virility*) virilità *f inv*
'man-hour ora *f* lavorativa
'man•hunt caccia *f* all'uomo
ma•ni•a ['meɪnɪə] (*craze*) mania *f*
ma•ni•ac ['meɪnɪæk] F pazzo *m*, -a *f*
man•i•cure ['mænɪkjʊə(r)] *n* manicure *f inv*
man•i•fest ['mænɪfest] **1** *adj* palese **2** *v/t* manifestare; ***manifest itself*** manifestarsi
ma•nip•u•late [mə'nɪpjʊleɪt] *v/t person, bones* manipolare; *equipment* maneggiare
ma•nip•u•la•tion [mənɪpjʊ'leɪʃn] *of person, bones* manipolazione *f*; *of bones*
ma•nip•u•la•tive [mə'nɪpjʊlətɪv] *adj* manipolatore
man'kind umanità *f inv*
man•ly ['mænlɪ] *adj* virile
'man-made *adj* sintetico
man•ner ['mænə(r)] *of doing sth* maniera *f*, modo *m*; (*attitude*) modo *m* di fare
man•ners ['mænəz] *npl*: ***good / bad manners*** buone / cattive maniere *fpl*; ***have no manners*** essere maleducato
ma•noeu•vre [mə'nuːvə(r)] **1** *n* manovra *f* **2** *v/t* manovrare
man•or ['mænə(r)] maniero *m*
'man•pow•er manodopera *f*, personale *m*
man•sion ['mænʃn] villa *f*
'man•slaugh•ter omicidio *m* colposo
man•tel•piece ['mæntlpiːs] mensola *f* del caminetto
man•u•al ['mænjʊəl] **1** *adj* manuale **2** *n* manuale *m*
man•u•al•ly ['mænjʊəlɪ] *adv* manualmente
man•u•fac•ture [mænjʊ'fæktʃə(r)] **1** *n* manifattura *f* **2** *v/t equipment* fabbricare
man•u•fac•tur•er [mænjʊ'fæktʃərə(r)] fabbricante *m/f*
man•u•fac•tur•ing [mænjʊ'fæktʃərɪŋ] *adj industry* manifatturiero
ma•nure [mə'njʊə(r)] letame *m*
man•u•script ['mænjʊskrɪpt] manoscritto *m*; *typed* dattiloscritto *m*
man•y ['menɪ] **1** *adj* molti; ***many times*** molte volte; ***not many people / taxis*** poche persone / pochi taxi; ***too many problems / beers*** troppi problemi / troppe birre **2** *pron* molti *m*, molte *f*; ***a great many, a good many*** moltissimi; ***how many do you need?*** quanti te ne servono?; ***as many as 200*** ben 200
'man-year anno / uomo *m*
map [mæp] *n* cartina *f*; (*street map*) pianta *f*, piantina *f*
◆ **map out** *v/t* (*pret & pp* ***-ped***) pianificare
ma•ple ['meɪpl] acero *m*
mar [mɑː(r)] *v/t* (*pret & pp* ***-red***) guastare
mar•a•thon ['mærəθən] *race* maratona *f*
mar•ble ['mɑːbl] *material* marmo *m*
March [mɑːtʃ] marzo *m*
march [mɑːtʃ] **1** *n* marcia *f*; (*demonstration*) dimostrazione *f*, manifestazione *f* **2** *v/i* marciare; *in protest* dimostrare, manifestare; ***march from A to B*** *in protest* sfilare in corteo da A a B
march•er ['mɑːtʃə(r)] dimostrante *m/f*, manifestante *m/f*
mare [meə(r)] cavalla *f*, giumenta *f*
mar•ga•rine [mɑːdʒə'riːn] margarina *f*
mar•gin ['mɑːdʒɪn] *of page* margine *m*; (COM: *profit margin*) margine *m* di guadagno; ***by a narrow margin*** di stretta misura
mar•gin•al ['mɑːdʒɪnl] *adj* (*slight*) leggero
mar•gin•al•ly ['mɑːdʒɪnlɪ] *adv* (*slightly*) leggermente
mar•i•hua•na, mar•i•jua•na [mærɪ'hwɑːnə] marijuana *f*
ma•ri•na [mə'riːnə] porticciolo *m*
mar•i•nade [mærɪ'neɪd] *n* marinata *f*
mar•i•nate ['mærɪneɪt] *v/t* marinare
ma•rine [mə'riːn] **1** *adj* marino **2** *n* MIL marina *f* militare
mar•i•tal ['mærɪtl] *adj* coniugale
mar•i•tal 'sta•tus stato *m* civile
mar•i•time ['mærɪtaɪm] *adj* marittimo
mar•jo•ram ['mɑːdʒərəm] maggiorana *f*
mark[1] [mɑːk] FIN marco *m*
mark[2] [mɑːk] **1** *n* (*stain*) macchia *f*; (*sign, token*) segno *m*; (*trace*); EDU voto *m*; ***leave one's mark*** lasciare un segno **2** *v/t* (*stain*) macchiare; EDU correggere; (*indicate*) indicare; (*commemorate*) celebrare; ***your essays will be marked***

out of ten ai temi sarà assegnata una votazione da 1 a 10 **3** *v/i of fabric* macchiarsi
◆ **mark down** *v/t goods* ribassare
◆ **mark out** *v/t with a line etc* delimitare; (*fig: set apart*) distinguere
◆ **mark up** *v/t price* aumentare; *goods* aumentare il prezzo di
marked [mɑːkt] *adj* (*definite*) spiccato
mark•er ['mɑːkə(r)] (*highlighter*) evidenziatore *m*
mar•ket ['mɑːkɪt] **1** *n* mercato *m*; *for particular commodity*; (*stock market*) mercato *m* azionario; ***on the market*** sul mercato **2** *v/t* vendere
mar•ket•a•ble ['mɑːkɪtəbl] *adj* commercializzabile
mar•ket e'con•o•my economia *f* di mercato
'mar•ket for•ces *npl* forze *fpl* di mercato
mar•ket•ing ['mɑːkɪtɪŋ] marketing *m inv*
'mar•ket•ing cam•paign campagna *f* di marketing
'mar•ket•ing de•part•ment reparto *m* marketing
'mar•ket•ing mix marketing mix *m inv*
'mar•ket•ing strat•e•gy strategia *f* di marketing
mar•ket 'lead•er leader *m inv* del mercato
'mar•ket-place *in town* piazza *f* del mercato; *for commodities* piazza *f*, mercato *m*
mar•ket re'search ricerca *f* di mercato
mar•ket 'share quota *f* di mercato
mark-up ['mɑːkʌp] ricarico *m*
mar•ma•lade ['mɑːməleɪd] marmellata *f* d'arance
mar•quee [mɑː'kiː] padiglione *f*
mar•riage ['mærɪdʒ] matrimonio *m*; *event* nozze *fpl*
'mar•riage cer•tif•i•cate certificato *m* di matrimonio
mar•riage 'guid•ance coun•se•llor consulente *m/f* matrimoniale
mar•ried ['mærɪd] *adj* sposato; ***be married to …*** essere sposato con …
mar•ried 'life vita *f* coniugale
mar•ry ['mærɪ] *v/t* (*pret & pp* ***-ied***) sposare; *of priest* unire in matrimonio; ***get married*** sposarsi
marsh [mɑːʃ] palude *f*
mar•shal ['mɑːʃl] *official* membro *m* del servizio d'ordine
marsh•mal•low [mɑːʃ'mæləʊ] *caramella f soffice e gommosa*
marsh•y ['mɑːʃɪ] *adj* paludoso
mar•tial arts [mɑːʃl'ɑːts] *npl* arti *fpl* marziali
mar•tial 'law legge *f* marziale
mar•tyr ['mɑːtə(r)] martire *m/f*
mar•tyred ['mɑːtəd] *adj fig* da martire
mar•vel ['mɑːvl] meraviglia *f*
◆ **marvel at** *v/t* meravigliarsi di
mar•ve•lous *Am*, **mar•vel•lous** ['mɑːvələs] *adj* meraviglioso
Marx•ism ['mɑːksɪzm] marxismo *m*
Marx•ist ['mɑːksɪst] **1** *adj* marxista **2** *n* marxista *m/f*
mar•zi•pan ['mɑːzɪpæn] marzapane *m*
mas•ca•ra [mæ'skɑːrə] mascara *m inv*
mas•cot ['mæskət] mascotte *f inv*
mas•cu•line ['mæskjʊlɪn] *adj* maschile
mas•cu•lin•i•ty [mæskjʊ'lɪnətɪ] (*virility*) virilità *f inv*
mash [mæʃ] *v/t* passare, schiacciare
mashed po•ta•toes [mæʃt] *npl* purè *m inv* di patate
mask [mɑːsk] **1** *n* maschera *f* **2** *v/t feelings* mascherare
'mask•ing tape *nastro m adesivo di carta*
mas•och•ism ['mæsəkɪzm] masochismo *m*
mas•och•ist ['mæsəkɪst] masochista *m/f*
ma•son ['meɪsn] scalpellino *m*
ma•son•ry ['meɪsnrɪ] muratura *f*
mas•que•rade [mæskə'reɪd] **1** *n fig* messinscena *f* **2** *v/i*: ***masquerade as*** farsi passare per
mass[1] [mæs] **1** *n great amount* massa *f*; ***the masses*** le masse; ***masses of*** F un sacco di F **2** *v/i* radunarsi
mass[2] [mæs] REL messa *f*
mas•sa•cre ['mæsəkə(r)] **1** *n also fig* massacro *m* **2** *v/t also fig* massacrare
mas•sage ['mæsɑːʒ] **1** *n* massaggio *m* **2** *v/t* massaggiare; *figures* manipolare
'mas•sage par•lor *Am*, **'mas•sage parlour** *euph* casa *f* d'appuntamenti
mas•seur [mæ'sɜː(r)] massaggiatore *m*
mas•seuse [mæ'sɜːz] massaggiatrice *f*
mas•sive ['mæsɪv] *adj* enorme; *heart attack* grave
mass 'me•di•a *npl* mass media *mpl*
mass-pro,duce *v/t* produrre in serie
mass pro,duc•tion produzione *f* in serie
mast [mɑːst] *of ship* albero *m*; *for radio signal* palo *m* dell'antenna
mas•ter ['mɑːstə(r)] **1** *n of dog* padrone *m*; *of ship* capitano *m*; ***be a master of*** essere un maestro di **2** *v/t skill*, *language* avere completa padronanza di; *situation* dominare
'mas•ter bed•room camera *f* da letto principale
'mas•ter key passe-partout *m inv*
mas•ter•ly ['mɑːstəlɪ] *adj* magistrale
'mas•ter•mind **1** *n fig* cervello *m* **2** *v/t* ideare

Mas•ter of 'Arts master *m inv*
mas•ter of 'cer•e•mo•nies maestro *m* di cerimonie
'mas•ter•piece capolavoro *m*
'mas•ter's (de•gree) master *m inv*
mas•ter•y ['mɑːstərɪ] padronanza *f*
mas•tur•bate ['mæstəbeɪt] *v/i* masturbarsi
mat [mæt] *for floor* tappetino *m*; SP tappeto *m*; *for table* tovaglietta *f* all'americana
match[1] [mætʃ] *for cigarette* fiammifero *m*; *wax* cerino *m*
match[2] [mætʃ] **1** *n* (*competition*) partita *f*; ***be no match for s.o.*** non poter competere con qu; ***meet one's match*** trovare pane per i propri denti **2** *v/t* (*be the same as*) abbinare; (*equal*) uguagliare **3** *v/i of colours, patterns* intonarsi
'match•box scatola *f* di fiammiferi
match•ing ['mætʃɪŋ] *adj* abbinato
'match stick fiammifero *m*
mate [meɪt] **1** *n of animal* compagno *m*, -a *f*; NAUT secondo *m*; F *friend* amico *m*, -a *f* **2** *v/i* accoppiarsi
ma•te•ri•al [mə'tɪərɪəl] **1** *n fabric* stoffa *f*, tessuto *m*; *substance* materia *f*; ***materials*** occorrente *m* **2** *adj* materiale
ma•te•ri•al•ism [mə'tɪərɪəlɪzm] materialismo *m*
ma•te•ri•al•ist [mətɪərɪə'lɪst] materialista *m/f*
ma•te•ri•al•is•tic [mətɪərɪə'lɪstɪk] *adj* materialistico
ma•te•ri•al•ize [mə'tɪərɪəlaɪz] *v/i* materializzarsi
ma•ter•nal [mə'tɜːnl] *adj* materno
ma•ter•ni•ty [mə'tɜːnətɪ] maternità *f inv*
ma'ter•ni•ty dress vestito *m* prémaman
ma,ter•ni•ty leave congedo *m* per maternità
ma•,ter•ni•ty ward reparto *m* maternità
math *Am* → ***maths***
math•e•mat•i•cal [mæθə'mætɪkl] *adj* matematico
math•e•ma•ti•cian [mæθmə'tɪʃn] matematico *m*, -a *f*
math•e•mat•ics [mæθ'mætɪks] matematica *f*
maths [mæθs] matematica *f*
mat•i•née ['mætɪneɪ] matinée *f inv*
ma•tri•arch ['meɪtrɪɑːk] matriarca *f*
ma•tri•arch•al [meɪtrɪ'ɑːkl] *adj* matriarcale
mat•ri•mo•ny ['mætrɪmənɪ] matrimonio *m*
matt [mæt] *adj* opaco
mat•ter ['mætə(r)] **1** *n* (*affair*) questione *f*, faccenda *f*; PHYS materia *f*; ***as a matter of course*** per abitudine; ***as a matter of fact*** a dir la verità; ***what's the matter?*** cosa c'è?; ***no matter what she says*** qualsiasi cosa dica **2** *v/i* importare; ***it doesn't matter*** non importa
mat•ter-of-'fact *adj* distaccato
mat•tress ['mætrɪs] materasso *m*
ma•ture [mə'tjʊə(r)] **1** *adj* maturo **2** *v/i of person, insurance policy etc* maturare; *of wine* invecchiare
ma•tu•ri•ty [mə'tjʊrətɪ] maturità *f inv*
maul [mɔːl] *v/t also fig* sbranare
max•i•mize ['mæksɪmaɪz] *v/t* massimizzare
max•i•mum ['mæksɪməm] **1** *adj* massimo **2** *n* massimo *m*
May [meɪ] maggio *m*
may [meɪ] *v/aux* ◇ (*possibility*): ***it may rain*** potrebbe piovere, può darsi che piova; ***you may be right*** potresti aver ragione, può darsi che abbia ragione; ***it may not happen*** magari non succederà, può darsi che non succeda
◇ (*permission*): ***may I help / smoke?*** posso aiutare / fumare?; ***you may if you like*** puoi farlo se vuoi
may•be ['meɪbiː] *adv* forse
'May Day il primo maggio
may•on•naise [meɪə'neɪz] maionese *f*
may•or ['meə(r)] sindaco *m*
maze [meɪz] *also fig* dedalo *m*, labirinto *m*
MB *abbr* (= ***megabyte***) MB *m* (= megabyte *m inv*)
MBA [embiː'eɪ] *abbr* (= ***master of business administration***) master *m inv* in amministraztione aziendale
MBO [embiː'əʊ] *abbr* (= ***management buyout***) *acquisizione f di un'impresa da parte dei suoi dirigenti*
MC [em'siː] *abbr* (= ***master of ceremonies***) maestro *m* di cerimonie
MD [em'diː] *abbr* (= ***Doctor of Medicine***) dottore *m* in medicina
me [miː] *pron direct & indirect object* mi; *after prep, stressed* me; ***she knows me*** mi conosce; ***she spoke to me*** mi ha parlato; ***she spoke to me but not to him*** ha parlato a me ma non a lui; ***without me*** senza di me; ***it's me*** sono io; ***who? me?*** chi? io?
mead•ow ['medəʊ] prato *m*
mea•ger *Am*, **mea•gre** ['miːgə(r)] *adj* scarso
meal [miːl] pranzo *m*, pasto *m*; ***enjoy your meal!*** buon appetito!
'meal•time ora *f* di pranzo
mean[1] [miːn] *adj with money* avaro; (*nasty*) cattivo
mean[2] [miːn] (*pret & pp* ***meant***) **1** *v/t* (*signify*) significare, voler dire; ***do you***

mean it? (*intend*) dici sul serio?; ***mean to do sth*** avere l'intenzione di fare qc; ***be meant for*** essere destinato a; *of remark* essere diretto a; ***doesn't it mean anything to you?*** (*doesn't it matter?*) non conta niente per te? **2** *v/i*: ***mean well*** avere buone intenzioni

mean•ing ['mi:nɪŋ] *of word* significato *m*

mean•ing•ful ['mi:nɪŋfʊl] *adj* (*comprehensible*) comprensibile; (*constructive*) costruttivo; *glance* eloquente

mean•ing•less ['mi:nɪŋlɪs] *adj sentence etc* senza senso; *gesture* vuoto

means [mi:nz] *npl financial* mezzi *mpl*; (*nsg*: *way*) modo *m*; ***means of transport*** mezzo *m* di trasporto; ***by all means*** (*certainly*) certamente; ***by no means rich / poor*** lungi dall'essere ricco / povero; ***by means of*** per mezzo di

meant [ment] *pret & pp* → ***mean***[2]

mean•time ['mi:ntaɪm] **1** *adv* intanto **2** *n*: ***in the meantime*** nel frattempo

mean•while ['mi:nwaɪl] **1** *adv* intanto **2** *n*: ***in the meanwhile*** nel frattempo

mea•sles ['mi:zlz] *nsg* morbillo *m*

mea•sure ['meʒə(r)] **1** *n* (*step*) misura *f*, provvedimento *m*; ***a measure of success*** *certain amount* un certo successo **2** *v/t* prendere le misure di **3** *v/i* misurare

◆ **measure out** *v/t amount* dosare; *area* misurare

◆ **measure up to** *v/t* dimostrarsi all'altezza di

mea•sure•ment ['meʒəmənt] *action* misurazione *f*; (*dimension*) misura *f*; ***system of measurement*** sistema *m* di misura

meas•ur•ing jug ['meʒərɪŋ] misurino *m*

'**mea•sur•ing tape** metro *m* a nastro

meat [mi:t] carne *f*

'**meat•ball** polpetta *f*

'**meat•loaf** polpettone *m*

me•chan•ic [mɪ'kænɪk] meccanico *m*

me•chan•i•cal [mɪ'kænɪkl] *adj also fig* meccanico

me•chan•i•cal en•gi'neer ingegnere *m* meccanico

me•chan•i•cal en•gi'neer•ing ingegneria *f* meccanica

me•chan•i•cal•ly [mɪ'kænɪklɪ] *adv also fig* meccanicamente

mech•a•nism ['mekənɪzm] meccanismo *m*

mech•a•nize ['mekənaɪz] *v/t* meccanizzare

med•al ['medl] medaglia *f*

med•a•list *Am*, **med•al•list** ['medəlɪst] vincitore *m*,-trice *f* di una medaglia

med•dle ['medl] *v/i* (*interfere*) immischiarsi; ***meddle with*** (*tinker*) mettere le mani in

me•di•a ['mi:dɪə] *npl*: ***the media*** i mass media *mpl*

'**me•di•a cov•er•age**: ***it was given a lot of media coverage*** gli è stato dato molto spazio in tv e sui giornali; ***an event that got a lot of media coverage*** un avvenimento di grande risonanza

'**me•di•a e•vent** spettacolo *m* sensazionale

me•di•a 'hype montatura *f* della stampa

'**me•d•ia stud•ies** scienze *fpl* delle comunicazioni

med•i•ae•val [medɪ'i:vl] → ***medieval***

me•di•ate ['mi:dɪeɪt] *v/i* fare da mediatore *m*, -trice *f*

me•di•a•tion [mi:dɪ'eɪʃn] mediazione *f*

me•di•a•tor ['mi:dɪeɪtə(r)] mediatore *m*, -trice *f*

med•i•cal ['medɪkl] **1** *adj* medico **2** *n* visita *f* medica

'**med•i•cal cer•tif•i•cate** certificato *m* medico

'**med•i•cal ex•am•i•na•tion** visita *f* medica

'**med•i•cal his•to•ry** anamnesi *f inv*

'**med•i•cal pro•fes•sion** professione *f* medica; corpo *m* medico

'**med•i•cal re•cord** cartella *f* clinica

med•i•cat•ed ['medɪkeɪtɪd] *adj* medicato

med•i•ca•tion [medɪ'keɪʃn] medicina *f*

me•di•ci•nal [mɪ'dɪsɪnl] *adj* medicinale

medi•cine ['medsən] medicina *f*

'**med•i•cine cab•i•net** armadietto *m* dei medicinali

med•i•e•val [medɪ'i:vl] *adj* medievale

me•di•o•cre [mi:dɪ'əʊkə(r)] *adj* mediocre

me•di•oc•ri•ty [mi:dɪ'ɒkrətɪ] mediocrità *f inv*

med•i•tate ['medɪteɪt] *v/i* meditare

med•i•ta•tion [medɪ'teɪʃn] meditazione *f*

Med•i•ter•ra•ne•an [medɪtə'reɪnɪən] **1** *adj* mediterraneo **2** *n*: ***the Mediterranean*** il Mar Mediterraneo; *area* i paesi mediterranei

me•di•um ['mi:dɪəm] **1** *adj* (*average*) medio; *steak* cotto al punto giusto **2** *n in size* media *f*; (*vehicle*) strumento *m*; (*spiritualist*) medium *m/f inv*

me•di•um-sized ['mi:dɪəmsaɪzd] *adj* di grandezza media

me•di•um 'term: ***in the medium term*** a medio termine

'**me•di•um wave** RAD onde *fpl* medie

med•ley ['medlɪ] (*assortment*) misto *m*

meek [mi:k] *adj* mite

meet [mi:t] **1** *v/t* (*pret & pp* ***met***) incontrare; (*get to know*) conoscere; (*collect*)

andare *o* venire a prendere; *in competition* affrontare; *of eyes* incrociare; (*satisfy*) soddisfare; ***I'll meet you there*** ci vediamo lì **2** *v/i* (*pret & pp* ***met***) incontrarsi; *in competition* affrontarsi; *of eyes* incrociarsi; *of committee etc* riunirsi; ***have you two met?*** (*do you know each other?*) vi conoscete? **3** *n Am* SP raduno *m* sportivo
◆ **meet with** *v/t person* avere un incontro con; *opposition, approval etc* incontrare; ***it met with success / failure*** ha avuto successo/è fallito
meet•ing ['mi:tɪŋ] incontro *m*; *of committee, in business* riunione *f*; appuntamento *m*; ***he's in a meeting*** è in riunione
'meet•ing place luogo *m* d'incontro
meg•a•byte ['megəbaɪt] COMPUT megabyte *m inv*
mel•an•chol•y ['melənkəlɪ] *adj* malinconia *f*
mel•low ['meləʊ] **1** *adj* maturo **2** *v/i of person* addolcirsi
me•lo•di•ous [mɪ'ləʊdɪəs] *adj* melodioso
mel•o•dra•mat•ic [melədrə'mætɪk] *adj* melodrammatico
mel•o•dy ['melədɪ] melodia *f*
mel•on ['melən] melone *m*
melt [melt] **1** *v/i* sciogliersi **2** *v/t* sciogliere
◆ **melt away** *v/i fig* svanire
◆ **melt down** *v/t metal* fondere
melt•ing pot ['meltɪŋpɒt] *fig* crogliolo *m* di culture
mem•ber ['membə(r)] *of family* componente *m/f*; *of club* socio *m*; *of organization* membro *m*
Mem•ber of 'Par•lia•ment deputato *m*
mem•ber•ship ['membəʃɪp] iscrizione *f*; *number of members* numero *m* dei soci
'mem•ber•ship card tessera *f* d'iscrizione
mem•brane ['membreɪn] membrana *f*
me•men•to [me'mentəʊ] souvenir *m inv*
mem•o ['meməʊ] circolare *f*
mem•oirs ['memwɑ:z] *npl* memorie *fpl*
'mem•o pad blocco *m* notes
mem•o•ra•ble ['memərəbl] *adj* memorabile
me•mo•ri•al [mɪ'mɔ:rɪəl] **1** *adj* commemorativo **2** *n also fig* memorial *m inv*
mem•o•rize ['meməraɪz] *v/t* memorizzare
mem•o•ry ['memərɪ] (*recollection*) ricordo *m*; *power of recollection* memoria *f*; COMPUT memoria *f*; ***in memory of*** in memoria di
men [men] *pl* → ***man***
men•ace ['menɪs] **1** *n* (*threat*) minaccia *f*; *person* pericolo *m* pubblico; (*nuisance*) peste *f* **2** *v/t* minacciare
men•ac•ing ['menɪsɪŋ] minaccioso
mend [mend] **1** *v/t* riparare **2** *n*: ***be on the mend*** *after illness* essere in via di guarigione
me•ni•al ['mi:nɪəl] *adj* umile
men•in•gi•tis [menɪn'dʒaɪtɪs] meningite *f*
men•o•pause ['menəpɔ:z] menopausa *f*
'men's room *Am* bagno *m* (degli uomini)
men•stru•ate ['menstrʊeɪt] *v/i* avere le mestruazioni
men•stru•a•tion [menstrʊ'eɪʃn] mestruazione *f*
men•tal ['mentl] *adj* mentale; F (*crazy*) pazzo
men•tal a'rith•me•tic calcolo *m* mentale
men•tal 'cru•el•ty crudeltà *f inv* mentale
'men•tal hos•pi•tal ospedale *m* psichiatrico
men•tal 'ill•ness malattia *f* mentale
men•tal•i•ty [men'tælətɪ] mentalità *f inv*
men•tal•ly ['mentəlɪ] *adv inwardly* mentalmente; *calculate etc* a mente
men•tal•ly 'hand•i•capped *adj* handicappato mentale
men•tal•ly 'ill *adj* malato di mente
men•tion ['menʃn] **1** *n* cenno *m*; ***he made no mention of it*** non ne ha fatto cenno **2** *v/t* accennare a; ***she mentioned that …*** ha accennato al fatto che …; ***don't mention it*** (*you're welcome*) non c'è di che
men•tor ['mentɔ:(r)] guida *f* spirituale
men•u ['menju:] *also* COMPUT menu *m inv*
MEP [emi:'pi:] *abbr* (= ***Member of the European Parliament***) eurodeputato *m*
mer•ce•na•ry ['mɜ:sɪnərɪ] **1** *adj* mercenario **2** *n* MIL mercenario *m*
mer•chan•dise ['mɜ:tʃəndaɪz] merce *f*
mer•chant ['mɜ:tʃənt] commerciante *m/f*
mer•chant 'bank banca *f* d'affari
mer•chant 'bank•er banchiere *m* d'affari
mer•ci•ful ['mɜ:sɪfʊl] *adj* misericordioso
mer•ci•ful•ly ['mɜ:sɪflɪ] *adv* (*thankfully*) per fortuna
mer•ci•less ['mɜ:sɪlɪs] *adj* spietato
mer•cu•ry ['mɜ:kjʊrɪ] mercurio *m*
mer•cy ['mɜ:sɪ] misericordia *f*; ***be at s.o.'s mercy*** essere alla mercé di qu
mere [mɪə(r)] *adj* semplice; ***he's a mere child*** è solo un bambino
mere•ly ['mɪəlɪ] *adv* soltanto
merge [mɜ:dʒ] *v/i of two lines etc* unirsi; *of companies* fondersi
merg•er ['mɜ:dʒə(r)] COM fusione *f*
mer•it ['merɪt] **1** *n* (*worth*) merito *m*; (*advantage*) vantaggio *m* **2** *v/t* meritare
mer•ri•ment ['merɪmənt] ilarità *f inv*
mer•ry ['merɪ] *adj* allegro; ***Merry Christmas!*** Buon Natale!
'mer•ry-go-round giostra *f*
mesh [meʃ] *in net* maglia *f*
mess [mes] (*untidiness*) disordine *m*;

M

(*trouble*) pasticcio *m*; ***be a mess*** *of room, desk, hair* essere in disordine; *of situation, s.o.'s life* essere un pasticcio
◆ **mess about, mess around 1** *v/i* (*waste time*) trastullarsi **2** *v/t person* menare per il naso
◆ **mess around with** *v/t* (*play with*) giocare con; (*interfere with*) armeggiare con; *s.o.'s wife* avere una relazione con
◆ **mess up** *v/t room, papers* mettere sottosopra; *task, plans, marriage* rovinare
mes•sage ['mesɪdʒ] *also fig* messaggio *m*
mes•sen•ger ['mesɪndʒə(r)] (*courier*) fattorino *m*, -a *f*
Mes•si•ah [me'saɪə] Messia *m*
mess•y ['mesɪ] *adj room* in disordine; *person* disordinato; *job* sporco; *divorce, situation* antipatico
met [met] *pret & pp* → ***meet***
met•a•bol•ic [metə'bɒlɪk] *adj* metabolico
me•tab•o•lis•m [mətæ'bəlɪzm] metabolismo *m*
met•al ['metl] **1** *adj* in *o* di metallo **2** *n* metallo *m*
me•tal•lic [mɪ'tælɪk] *adj* metallico
met•a•phor ['metəfə(r)] metafora *f*
me•te•or ['miːtɪə(r)] meteora *f*
me•te•or•ic [miːtɪ'ɒrɪk] *adj fig* fulmineo
me•te•or•ite ['miːtɪəraɪt] meteorite *m o f*
me•te•or•o•log•i•cal [miːtɪərə'lɒdʒɪkl] *adj* meteorologico
me•te•or•ol•o•gist [miːtɪə'rɒlədʒɪst] meteorologo *m*, -a *f*
me•te•o•rol•o•gy [miːtɪə'rɒlədʒɪ] meteorologia *f*
me•ter ['miːtə(r)] *for gas etc* contatore *m*; (*parking meter*) parchimetro *m*; *Am*: *length* metro *m*
'**me•ter read•ing** lettura *f* del contatore
meth•od ['meθəd] metodo *m*
me•thod•i•cal [mɪ'θɒdɪkl] *adj* metodico
me•thod•i•cal•ly [mɪ'θɒdɪklɪ] *adv* metodicamente
me•tic•u•lous [mɪ'tɪkjʊləs] *adj* meticoloso
me•tic•u•lous•ly [mɪ'tɪkjʊləslɪ] *adv* meticolosamente
me•tre ['miːtə(r)] metro *m*
met•ric ['metrɪk] *adj* metrico
me•trop•olis [mɪ'trɒpəlɪs] metropoli *f inv*
met•ro•pol•i•tan [metrə'pɒlɪtən] *adj* metropolitano
mew [mjuː] *n & v/i* → ***miaow***
Mex•i•can ['meksɪkən] **1** *adj* messicano **2** *n* messicano *m*, -a *f*
Mex•i•co ['meksɪkəʊ] Messico *m*
mez•za•nine (floor) ['mezəniːn] mezzanino *m*
mi•aow [mɪaʊ] **1** *n* miao *m* **2** *v/i* miagolare
mice [maɪs] *pl* → ***mouse***
mick•ey mouse [mɪkɪ'maʊs] *adj* P *course, qualification* del piffero F
mi•cro•bi•ol•o•gy ['maɪkrəʊ] microbiologia *f*
'**mi•cro•chip** microchip *m inv*
'**mi•cro•cli•mate** microclima *m*
mi•cro•cosm ['maɪkreʊkɒzm] microcosmo *m*
'**mi•cro•e•lec•tron•ics** microelettronica *f*
'**mi•cro•film** microfilm *m inv*
'**mi•cro•or•gan•ism** microrganismo *m*
'**mi•cro•phone** microfono *m*
mi•cro'**pro•ces•sor** microprocessore *m*
'**mi•cro•scope** microscopio *m*
mi•cro•scop•ic [maɪkrə'skɒpɪk] *adj* microscopico
'**mi•cro•wave** *oven* forno *m* a microonde
mid•air [mɪd'eə(r)]: ***in midair*** a mezz'aria
mid•day [mɪd'deɪ] mezzogiorno *m*
mid•dle ['mɪdl] **1** *adj* di mezzo **2** *n* mezzo *m*; ***in the middle of*** *of floor, room* nel centro di, in mezzo a; *of period of time* a metà di; ***be in the middle of doing sth*** stare facendo qc
'**mid•dle-aged** *adj* di mezz'età
'**Mid•dle Ages** *npl* Medioevo *m*
mid•dle '**class** *adj* borghese; ***the middle class class(es)*** *npl* la borghesia *f*
Mid•dle '**East** Medio Oriente *m*
'**mid•dle•man** intermediario *m*
mid•dle '**man•age•ment** quadri *mpl* intermedi
mid•dle '**name** secondo nome *m*
'**mid•dle•weight** *boxer* peso *m* medio
mid•dling ['mɪdlɪŋ] *adj* medio
mid•field•er [mɪd'fiːldə(r)] centrocampista *m*
midge [mɪdʒ] moscerino *m*
midg•et ['mɪdʒɪt] *adj* di dimensioni ridotte
'**Mid•lands** *npl regione f nell'Inghilterra centrale*
'**mid•night** ['mɪdnaɪt] mezzanotte *f*; ***at midnight*** a mezzanotte
'**mid•sum•mer** piena estate *f*
'**mid•way** *adv* a metà strada; ***midway through*** a metà di
'**mid•week** *adv* a metà settimana
'**Mid•west** *regione f medio-occidentale degli USA*
'**mid•wife** ostetrica *f*
'**mid•win•ter** pieno inverno *m*
might[1] [maɪt] *v/aux*: ***I might be late*** potrei far tardi; ***it might rain*** magari piove; ***it might never happen*** potrebbe non succedere mai; ***I might have lost it*** *perhaps I did* forse l'ho perso; *it would have been possible* avrei potuto perderlo; ***he might***

M

have left forse se n'è andato; ***you might as well spend the night here*** tanto vale che passi la notte qui; ***you might have told me!*** potevi dirmelo!
might² [maɪt] (*power*) forze *fpl*
might•y ['maɪtɪ] **1** *adj* potente **2** *adv* F (*extremely*) molto
mi•graine ['miːgreɪn] emicrania *f*
mi•grant work•er ['maɪgrənt] emigrante *m/f*
mi•grate [maɪ'greɪt] *v/i* emigrare; *of birds* migrare
mi•gra•tion [maɪ'greɪʃn] emigrazione *f*; *of birds* migrazione *f*
mike [maɪk] F microfono *m*
Mi•lan [mɪ'læn] Milano *f*
mild [maɪld] *adj weather*, *climate* mite; *cheese*, *person*, *voice* dolce; *curry* poco piccante; *punishment*, *symptoms*, *sedative* leggero
mil•dew ['mɪldjuː] muffa *f*
mild•ly ['maɪldlɪ] *adv* gentilmente; (*slightly*) moderatamente; ***to put it mildly*** a dir poco
mild•ness ['maɪldnɪs] *of weather* mitezza *f*; *of person*, *voice* dolcezza *f*
mile [maɪl] miglio *m*; ***miles better / easier*** F molto meglio / più facile
mile•age ['maɪlɪdʒ] chilometraggio *m*
'mile•stone *also fig* pietra *f* miliare
mil•i•tant ['mɪlɪtənt] **1** *adj* militante **2** *n* militante *m/f*
mil•i•ta•ry ['mɪlɪtrɪ] **1** *adj* militare **2** *n*: ***the military*** l'esercito *m*, le forze *fpl* armate; ***it's run by the military*** è in mano ai militari
mil•i•ta•ry a'cad•e•my accademia *f* militare
mil•i•ta•ry po,lice polizia *f* militare
mil•i•tar•y 'serv•ice servizio *m* militare
mi•li•tia [mɪ'lɪʃə] milizia *f*
milk [mɪlk] **1** *n* latte *m* **2** *v/t* mungere
'milk bot•tle bottiglia *f* del latte
milk 'choc•o•late cioccolato *m* al latte
'milk float furgone *m* del lattaio
'milk jug bricco *m* del latte
'milk•man lattaio *m*
milk of mag'ne•sia latte *m* di magnesia
'milk•shake frappé *m inv*
'milk•y ['mɪlkɪ] *adj* con tanto latte
Milk•y 'Way Via *f* Lattea
mill [mɪl] *for grain* mulino *m*; *for textiles* fabbrica *f*
◆ **mill about**, **mill around** *v/i* brulicare
mil•len•ni•um [mɪ'lenɪəm] millennio *m*
mil•li•gram ['mɪlɪgræm] milligrammo *m*
mil•li•me•ter *Am*, **mil•li•me•tre** ['mɪlɪmiːtə(r)] millimetro *m*
mil•lion ['mɪljən] milione *m*
mil•lion•aire [mɪljə'neə(r)] miliardario *m*, -a *f*
mime [maɪm] *v/t* mimare
mim•ic ['mɪmɪk] **1** *n* imitatore *m*, -trice *f* **2** *v/t* (*pret & pp* **-ked**) imitare
mince [mɪns] *v/t meat* carne *f* tritata
'mince•meat *frutta f secca tritata*
mince 'pie *pasticcino m ripieno di frutta secca tritata*
mind [maɪnd] **1** *n* mente *f*, cervello *m*; ***it's all in your mind*** è solo la tua immaginazione; ***be out of one's mind*** essere matto; ***keep sth in mind*** tenere presente qc; ***I've a good mind to …*** ho proprio voglia di …; ***change one's mind*** cambiare idea; ***it didn't enter my mind*** non mi è passato per la testa; ***give s.o. a piece of one's mind*** cantarne quattro a qu; ***make up one's mind*** decidersi; ***have sth on one's mind*** essere preoccupato per qc; ***keep one's mind on sth*** concentrarsi su qc **2** *v/t* (*look after*) tenere d'occhio; *children* badare a; (*heed*) fare attenzione a; ***I don't mind tea if that's all you've got*** (*object to*) il tè va bene se non hai altro; ***I don't mind what we do*** non importa cosa facciamo; ***do you mind if I smoke?, do you mind my smoking?*** le dispiace se fumo?; ***would you mind opening the window?*** le dispiace aprire la finestra?; ***mind the step!*** attento al gradino!; ***mind your own business!*** fatti gli affari tuoi! **3** *v/i*: ***mind!*** (*be careful*) attenzione!; ***never mind!*** non farci caso!; ***I don't mind*** è uguale *o* indifferente
mind-bog•gling ['maɪndbɒglɪŋ] *adj* incredibile
mind•less ['maɪndlɪs] *adj violence* insensato
mine¹ [maɪn] *pron* il mio *m*, la mia *f*, i miei *mpl*, le mie *fpl*; ***a cousin of mine*** un mio cugino
mine² [maɪn] **1** *n for coal etc* miniera *f* **2** *v/i*: ***mine for*** estrarre
mine³ [maɪn] **1** *n explosive* mina *f* **2** *v/t* minare
'mine•field *also fig* campo *m* minato
min•er ['maɪnə(r)] minatore *m*
min•e•ral ['mɪnərəl] *n* minerale *m*
'min•e•ral wa•ter acqua *f* minerale
'mine•sweep•er NAUT dragamine *m inv*
min•gle ['mɪŋgl] *v/i of sounds*, *smells* mischiarsi; *at party* mescolarsi
min•i ['mɪnɪ] *skirt* mini *f inv*
min•i•a•ture ['mɪnɪʧə(r)] *adj* in miniatura
'min•i•bus minibus *m inv*
'min•i•cab radiotaxi *m inv*
min•i•mal ['mɪnɪməl] *adj* minimo

min•i•mal•ism ['mɪnɪməlɪzm] minimalismo *m*
min•i•mize ['mɪnɪmaɪz] *v/t* minimizzare
min•i•mum ['mɪnɪməm] **1** *adj* minimo **2** *n* minimo *m*
min•i•mum '**wage** salario *m* minimo garantito
min•ing ['maɪnɪŋ] industria *f* mineraria
'**min•i•se•ries** TV miniserie *f inv*
'**min•i•skirt** minigonna *f*
min•is•ter ['mɪnɪstə(r)] POL ministro *m*; REL pastore *m*
min•is•te•ri•al [mɪnɪ'stɪərɪəl] *adj* ministeriale
min•is•try ['mɪnɪstrɪ] POL ministero *m*
mink [mɪŋk] **1** *adj fur* di visone **2** *n coat* visone *m*
mi•nor ['maɪnə(r)] **1** *adj* piccolo; ***in D minor*** MUS in Re minore **2** *n* LAW minorenne *m/f*
mi•nor•i•ty [maɪ'nɒrətɪ] minoranza *f*; ***be in the minority*** essere in minoranza
mint [mɪnt] *n herb* menta *f*; *chocolate* cioccolato *m* alla menta; *sweet* mentina *f*
mi•nus ['maɪnəs] **1** *n* (*minus sign*) meno *m* **2** *prep* meno; ***minus 10 degrees*** 10 gradi sotto zero
mi•nus•cule ['mɪnəskjuːl] *adj* minuscolo
min•ute[1] ['mɪnɪt] *of time* minuto *m*; ***in a minute*** (*soon*) in un attimo; ***just a minute*** un attimo
mi•nute[2] [maɪ'njuːt] *adj* (*tiny*) piccolissimo; (*detailed*) minuzioso; ***in minute detail*** minuziosamente
'**mi•nute hand** lancetta *f* dei minuti
mi•nute•ly [maɪ'njuːtlɪ] *adv* (*in detail*) minuziosamente; (*very slightly*) appena
min•utes ['mɪnɪts] *npl of meeting* verbale *m*
mir•a•cle ['mɪrəkl] miracolo *m*
mi•rac•u•lous [mɪ'rækjʊləs] *adj* miracoloso
mi•rac•u•lous•ly [mɪ'rækjʊləslɪ] *adv* miracolosamente
mi•rage ['mɪrɑːʒ] miraggio *m*
mir•ror ['mɪrə(r)] **1** *n* specchio *m*; MOT specchietto *m* **2** *v/t* riflettere; ***be mirrored in sth*** *in water etc* specchiarsi in qc; *fig* rispecchiarsi in qc
mirth [mɜːθ] ilarità *f inv*
mis•an•thro•pist [mɪ'zænθrəpɪst] misantropo *m*
mis•ap•pre•hen•sion [mɪsæprɪ'henʃn]: ***be under a misapprehension*** sbagliarsi
mis•be•have [mɪsbə'heɪv] *v/i* comportarsi male
mis•be•hav•ior *Am*, **mis•be•hav•iour** [mɪsbə'heɪvjə(r)] comportamento *m* scorretto
mis•cal•cu•late [mɪs'kælkjʊleɪt] *v/t & v/i* calcolare male
mis•cal•cu•la•tion [mɪs'kælkjʊleɪʃn] errore *m* di calcolo
mis•car•riage ['mɪskærɪdʒ] MED aborto *m* spontaneo; ***miscarriage of justice*** errore *m* giudiziario
mis•car•ry ['mɪskærɪ] *v/i* (*pret & pp* **-ied**) *of plan* fallire
mis•cel•la•ne•ous [mɪsə'leɪnɪəs] *adj* eterogeneo
mis•chief ['mɪstʃɪf] (*naughtiness*) birichinate *fpl*
mis•chie•vous ['mɪstʃɪvəs] *adj* (*naughty*) birichino; (*malicious*) perfido
mis•con•cep•tion [mɪskən'sepʃn] idea *f* sbagliata
mis•con•duct [mɪs'kɒndʌkt] reato *m* professionale
mis•con•strue [mɪskən'struː] *v/t* interpretare male
mis•de•mea•nor *Am*, **mis•de•mea•nour** [mɪsdə'miːnə(r)] infrazione *f*
mi•ser ['maɪzə(r)] avaro *m*, -a *f*
mis•e•ra•ble ['mɪzrəbl] *adj* (*unhappy*) infelice; *weather, performance* deprimente
mi•ser•ly ['maɪzəlɪ] *adj person* avaro; *amount* misero
mis•e•ry ['mɪzərɪ] (*unhappiness*) tristezza *f*; (*wretchedness*) miseria *f*
mis•fire [mɪs'faɪə(r)] *v/i of joke, scheme* far cilecca; *of engine* perdere colpi
mis•fit ['mɪsfɪt] *in society* disadattato *m*, -a *f*
mis•for•tune [mɪs'fɔːtʃən] sfortuna *f*
mis•giv•ings [mɪs'gɪvɪŋz] *npl* dubbi *mpl*
mis•guid•ed [mɪs'gaɪdɪd] *adj attempts, theory* sbagliato; ***he was misguided in maintaining that …*** sbagliava a sostenere che …
mis•han•dle [mɪs'hændl] *v/t situation* gestire male
mis•hap ['mɪshæp] incidente *m*
mis•in•form [mɪsɪn'fɔːm] *v/t* informare male
mis•in•ter•pret [mɪsɪn'tɜːprɪt] *v/t* interpretare male
mis•in•ter•pre•ta•tion [mɪsɪntɜːprɪ'teɪʃn] interpretazione *f* errata
mis•judge [mɪs'dʒʌdʒ] *v/t person, situation* giudicare male
mis•lay [mɪs'leɪ] *v/t* (*pret & pp* **-laid**) smarrire
mis•lead [mɪs'liːd] *v/t* (*pret & pp* **-led**) trarre in inganno
mis•lead•ing [mɪs'liːdɪŋ] *adj* fuorviante
mis•man•age [mɪs'mænɪdʒ] *v/t* gestire male
mis•man•age•ment [mɪs'mænɪdʒmənt]

cattiva gestione *f*
mis•match ['mɪsmætʃ] discordanza *f*
mis•placed ['mɪspleɪst] *adj loyalty*, *enthusiasm* malriposto
mis•print ['mɪsprɪnt] refuso *m*
mis•pro•nounce [mɪsprə'naʊns] *v/t* pronunciare male
mis•pro•nun•ci•a•tion [mɪsprənʌnsɪ'eɪʃn] errore *m* di pronuncia
mis•read [mɪs'riːd] *v/t* (*pret & pp* ***-read*** [red]) *word*, *figures* leggere male; *situation* interpretare male
mis•rep•re•sent [mɪsreprɪ'zent] *v/t facts*, *truth* travisare; ***I've been misrepresented*** hanno travisato quello che ho detto
miss[1] [mɪs]: ***Miss Smith*** signorina Smith; ***miss!*** signorina!
miss[2] [mɪs] **1** *n*: ***give the meeting / party a miss*** non andare alla riunione / festa **2** *v/t* (*not hit*) mancare; *emotionally* sentire la mancanza di; *bus*, *train*, *plane* perdere; (*not be present at*) mancare a; ***I miss you*** mi manchi; ***you've just missed him*** *he's just gone* è appena uscito; ***we must have missed the turnoff*** ci dev'essere sfuggito lo svincolo **3** *v/i* fallire
mis•shap•en [mɪs'ʃeɪpən] *adj* deforme
mis•sile ['mɪsaɪl] (*rocket*) missile *m*
miss•ing ['mɪsɪŋ] *adj* scomparso; ***be missing*** *of person*, *plane* essere disperso; ***there's a piece missing*** manca un pezzo
mis•sion ['mɪsŋ] (*task*, *people*) missione *f*
mis•sion•a•ry ['mɪʃənrɪ] REL missionario *m*, -a *f*
mis•spell [mɪs'spel] *v/t* scrivere male
mist [mɪst] foschia *f*
◆ **mist over** *v/i of eyes* velarsi di lacrime
◆ **mist up** *v/i of mirror*, *window* appannarsi
mis•take [mɪ'steɪk] **1** *n* errore *m*, sbaglio *m*; ***make a mistake*** fare un errore, sbagliarsi; ***by mistake*** per errore **2** *v/t* (*pret* ***mistook***, *pp* ***mistaken***) sbagliare; ***mistake sth for sth*** scambiare qc per qc
mis•tak•en [mɪ'steɪkən] **1** *adj* sbagliato; ***be mistaken*** sbagliarsi **2** *pp* → ***mistake***
mis•ter ['mɪstə(r)] → ***Mr***
mis•tress ['mɪstrɪs] *lover* amante *f*; *of servant*, *of dog* padrona *f*
mis•trust [mɪs'trʌst] **1** *n* diffidenza *f* **2** *v/t* diffidare di
mist•y ['mɪstɪ] *adj weather* nebbioso; *eyes* velato
mis•un•der•stand [mɪsʌndə'stænd] *v/t* (*pret & pp* ***-stood***) fraintendere
mis•un•der•stand•ing [mɪsʌndə'stændɪŋ] *mistake* malinteso *m*, equivoco *m*; *argument* dissapore *m*
mis•use [mɪs'juːs] **1** *n* uso *m* improprio **2** *v/t* [mɪs'juːz] usare impropriamente
miti•ga•ting cir•cum•stances ['mɪtɪgeɪtɪŋ] *npl* circostanze *fpl* attenuanti
mit•ten ['mɪtən] muffola *f*
mix [mɪks] **1** *n* (*mixture*) mescolanza *f*; *in cooking* miscuglio *m*; *in cooking*: *ready to use* preparato *m* **2** *v/t* mescolare **3** *v/i socially* socializzare
◆ **mix up** *v/t* confondere; ***mix sth up with sth*** scambiare qc per qc; ***be mixed up*** *emotionally* avere disturbi emotivi; *of figures*, *papers* essere in disordine; ***be mixed up in*** essere coinvolto in; ***get mixed up with*** avere a che fare con
◆ **mix with** *v/t* (*associate with*) frequentare
mixed [mɪkst] *adj* misto; *reactions*, *reviews* contrastante; ***I've got mixed feelings*** sono combattuto
mixed 'mar•riage matrimonio *m* misto
mix•er ['mɪksə(r)] *for food* mixer *m inv*; (*drink*) *bibita f da mischiare a un superalcolico*; ***she's a good mixer*** è molto socievole
mix•ture ['mɪkstʃə(r)] miscuglio *m*; *medicine* sciroppo *m*
mix-up ['mɪksʌp] confusione *f*
moan [məʊn] **1** *n of pain* lamento *m*, gemito *m*; (*complaint*) lamentela *f* **2** *v/i in pain* lamentarsi, gemere; (*complain*) lamentarsi
mob [mɒb] **1** *n* folla *f* **2** *v/t* (*pret & pp* ***-bed***) prendere d'assalto
mo•bile ['məʊbaɪl] **1** *adj that can be moved* mobile; ***she's less mobile now*** non si può muovere tanto, ora **2** *n for decoration* mobile *m inv*; *phone* telefonino *m*
mo•bile 'home casamobile *f*
mo•bile 'phone telefono *m* cellulare
mo•bil•i•ty [mə'bɪlətɪ] mobilità *f inv*
mob•ster ['mɒbstə(r)] gangster *m inv*
mock [mɒk] **1** *adj* finto; *exam*, *election* simulato; ***a mock-Tudor house*** una casa in stile Tudor **2** *v/t* deridere
mock•e•ry ['mɒkərɪ] (*derision*) scherno *m*; (*travesty*) farsa *f*
mock-up ['mɒkʌp] (*model*) modello *m*
mod cons [mɒd'kɒnz] *npl*: ***with all mod cons*** con tutti i comfort
mode [məʊd] *form* mezzo *m*; COMPUT modalità *f inv*
mod•el ['mɒdl] **1** *adj employee*, *husband* modello; *boat*, *plane* in miniatura **2** *n* (*miniature*) modellino *m*; (*pattern*) modello *m*; (*fashion model*) indossatrice *f*; ***male model*** indossatore *m* **3** *v/t* indossare **4** *v/i for designer* fare l'indossatore/-trice; *for artist*, *photographer* posare
mo•dem ['məʊdem] modem *m inv*

mod•e•rate ['mɒdərət] **1** *adj* moderato **2** *n* POL moderato *m*, -a *f* **3** *v/t* ['mɒdəreɪt] moderare **4** *v/i* calmarsi
mod•e•rate•ly ['mɒdərətlɪ] *adv* abbastanza
mod•e•ra•tion [mɒdə'reɪʃn] (*restraint*) moderazione *f*; ***in moderation*** con moderazione
mod•ern ['mɒdn] *adj* moderno
mod•ern•i•za•tion [mɒdənaɪ'zeɪʃn] modernizzazione *f*
mod•ern•ize ['mɒdənaɪz] **1** *v/t* modernizzare **2** *v/i of business, country* modernizzarsi
mod•ern 'lan•guages lingue *fpl* moderne
mod•est ['mɒdɪst] *adj* modesto
mod•es•ty ['mɒdɪstɪ] modestia *f*
mod•i•fi•ca•tion [mɒdɪfɪ'keɪʃn] modifica *f*
mod•i•fy ['mɒdɪfaɪ] *v/t* (*pret & pp* ***-ied***) modificare
mod•u•lar ['mɒdjʊlə(r)] *adj furniture* modulare
mod•ule ['mɒdjuːl] modulo *m*; (*space module*) modulo *m* spaziale
moist [mɔɪst] *adj* umido
moist•en ['mɔɪsn] *v/t* inumidire
mois•ture ['mɔɪsʧə(r)] umidità *f inv*
mois•tur•iz•er ['mɔɪsʧəraɪzə(r)] *for skin* idratante *m*
mo•lar ['məʊlə(r)] molare *m*
mold *etc Am* → ***mould*** *etc*
mole [məʊl] *on skin* neo *m*; *animal, spy* talpa *f*
mo•lec•u•lar [mə'lekjʊlə(r)] *adj* molecolare
mol•e•cule ['mɒlɪkjuːl] molecola *f*
mo•lest [mə'lest] *v/t child, woman* molestare
mol•ly•cod•dle ['mɒlɪkɒdl] *v/t* F coccolare
mol•ten ['məʊltən] *adj* fuso
mo•ment ['məʊmənt] attimo *m*, istante *m*; ***at the moment*** al momento; ***for the moment*** per il momento
mo•men•tar•i•ly [məʊmən'teərɪlɪ] *adv* (*for a moment*) per un momento; (*Am: in a moment*) da un momento all'altro
mo•men•ta•ry ['məʊməntrɪ] *adj* momentaneo
mo•men•tous [mə'mentəs] *adj* importante
mo•men•tum [mə'mentəm] impeto *m*
mon•arch ['mɒnək] monarca *m*
mon•ar•chy ['mɒnəkɪ] monarchia *f*
mon•as•tery ['mɒnəstrɪ] monastero *m*
mo•nas•tic [mə'næstɪk] *adj* monastico
Mon•day ['mʌndeɪ] lunedì *m inv*
mon•e•ta•ry ['mʌnɪtrɪ] *adj* monetario
mon•ey ['mʌnɪ] denaro *m*, soldi *mpl*
'mon•ey belt marsupio *m*
'mon•ey mar•ket mercato *m* monetario
'mon•ey or•der vaglia *m*
mon•grel ['mʌngrəl] cane *m* bastardo
mon•i•tor ['mɒnɪtə(r)] **1** *n* COMPUT monitor *m inv* **2** *v/t* osservare
monk [mʌŋk] frate *m*, monaco *m*
mon•key ['mʌŋkɪ] scimmia *f*; F (*child*) diavoletto *m*
◆ **monkey about with** *v/t* F armeggiare con
'mon•key wrench chiave *f* a rullino
mon•o•gram ['mɒnəgræm] monogramma *m*
mon•o•grammed ['mɒnəgræmd] con il monogramma
mon•o•log *Am*, **mon•o•logue** ['mɒnəlɒg] monologo *m*
mo•nop•o•lize [mə'nɒpəlaɪz] *v/t also fig* monopolizzare
mo•nop•o•ly [mə'nɒpəlɪ] monopolio *m*
mo•not•o•nous [mə'nɒtənəs] *adj* monotono
mo•not•o•ny [mə'nɒtənɪ] monotonia *f*
mon•soon [mɒn'suːn] monsone *m*
mon•ster ['mɒnstə(r)] mostro *m*
mon•stros•i•ty [mɒn'strɒsətɪ] obbrobio *m*
mon•strous ['mɒnstrəs] *adj* mostruoso
month [mʌnθ] mese *m*
month•ly ['mʌnθlɪ] **1** *adj* mensile **2** *adv* mensilmente **3** *n magazine* mensile *m*
mon•u•ment ['mɒnjʊmənt] monumento *m*
mon•u•ment•al [mɒnjʊ'mentl] *adj fig* monumentale
moo [muː] *v/i* muggire
mood [muːd] (*frame of mind*) umore *m*; (*bad mood*) malumore *m*; *of meeting, country* clima *m*; ***be in a good / bad mood*** essere di cattivo / buon umore; ***be in the mood for*** aver voglia di
mood•y ['muːdɪ] *adj* lunatico; (*bad-tempered*) di cattivo umore
moon [muːn] luna *f*
'moon•light **1** *n* chiaro *m* di luna **2** *v/i* F lavorare in nero
'moon•lit *adj night* di luna piena
moor [mʊə(r)] *v/t boat* ormeggiare
moor•ings ['mʊərɪŋz] *npl* ormeggio *m*
moose [muːs] alce *m*
mop [mɒp] **1** *n for floor* mocio® *m*; *for dishes* spazzolino per i piatti **2** *v/t* (*pret & pp* ***-ped***) *floor* lavare; *eyes, face* asciugare
◆ **mop up** *v/t* raccogliere; MIL eliminare
mope [məʊp] *v/i* essere depresso
mo•ped ['məʊped] motorino *m*
mor•al ['mɒrəl] **1** *adj* morale; *person* di

saldi principi morali **2** *n of story* morale *f*; ***morals*** principi *mpl* morali

mo•rale [mə'rɑːl] morale *m*

mo•ral•i•ty [mə'rælətɪ] moralità *f inv*

mor•bid ['mɔːbɪd] *adj* morboso

more [mɔː(r)] **1** *adj* più, altro; ***some more tea?*** dell'altro tè?; ***a few more sandwiches*** qualche altro tramezzino; ***for more information*** per maggiori informazioni; ***more and more students / time*** sempre più studenti / tempo; ***there's no more …*** non c'è più … **2** *adv* più; *with verbs* di più; ***more important*** più importante; ***more often*** più spesso; ***more and more*** sempre di più; ***more or less*** più o meno; ***once more*** ancora una volta; ***more than 100*** oltre 100; ***I don't live there any more*** non abito più lì **3** *pron*: ***do you want some more?*** ne vuoi ancora?, ne vuoi dell'altro; ***a little more*** un altro po'

more•o•ver [mɔː'rəʊvə(r)] *adv* inoltre

morgue [mɔːg] obitorio *m*

morn•ing ['mɔːnɪŋ] mattino *m*, mattina *f*; ***in the morning*** di mattina; (*tomorrow*) domattina; ***this morning*** stamattina; ***tomorrow morning*** domani mattina; ***good morning*** buongiorno

morn•ing 'sick•ness nausee *fpl* mattutine

mo•ron ['mɔːrɒn] F idiota *m/f*

mo•rose [mə'rəʊs] *adj* imbronciato

mor•phine ['mɔːfiːn] morfina *f*

mor•sel ['mɔːsl] pezzetto *m*

mor•tal ['mɔːtl] **1** *adj* mortale **2** *n* mortale *m/f*

mor•tal•i•ty [mɔː'tælətɪ] mortalità *f inv*

mor•tar[1] ['mɔːtə(r)] MIL mortaio *m*

mor•tar[2] ['mɔːtə(r)] *cement* malta *f*

mort•gage ['mɔːgɪdʒ] **1** *n* mutuo *m* ipotecario **2** *v/t* ipotecare

mor•tu•a•ry ['mɔːtjʊərɪ] camera *f* mortuaria

mo•sa•ic [məʊ'zeɪɪk] mosaico *m*

Mos•cow ['mɒskəʊ] Mosca *f*

Mos•lem ['mʊzlɪm] **1** *adj* islamico **2** *n* musulmano *m*, -a *f*

mosque [mɒsk] moschea *f*

mos•qui•to [mɒs'kiːtəʊ] zanzara *f*

moss [mɒs] muschio *m*

moss•y ['mɒsɪ] *adj* coperto di muschio

most [məʊst] **1** *adj* la maggior parte di; ***most Saturdays*** quasi tutti i sabati **2** *adv* (*very*) estremamente; ***the most beautiful / interesting*** il più bello / interessante; ***that's the one I like most*** è quello che mi piace di più; ***most of all*** soprattutto **3** *pron* la maggior parte (***of*** di); ***at*** (***the***) ***most*** al massimo; ***make the most of*** approfittare (al massimo) di

most•ly ['məʊstlɪ] *adv* per lo più

MOT [eməʊ'tiː] *Br revisione f annuale obbligatoria dei veicoli*

mo•tel [məʊ'tel] motel *m inv*

moth [mɒθ] falena *f*; (*clothes moth*) tarma *f*

'moth•ball naftalina *f*

moth•er ['mʌðə(r)] **1** *n* madre *f* **2** *v/t* fare da mamma a

'moth•er•board COMPUT scheda *f* madre

'moth•er•hood maternità *f inv*

Moth•er•ing 'Sun•day → ***Mother's Day***

'moth•er-in-law (*pl* ***mothers-in-law***) suocera *f*

moth•er•ly ['mʌðəlɪ] *adj* materno

moth•er-of-'pearl madreperla *f*

'Moth•er,s Day Festa *f* della mamma

'moth•er tongue madrelingua *f*

mo•tif [məʊ'tiːf] motivo *m*

mo•tion ['məʊʃn] **1** *n* (*movement*) moto *m*; (*proposal*) mozione *f*; ***set things in motion*** metter in moto le cose **2** *v/t*: ***he motioned me forward*** mi ha fatto cenno di avvicinarmi

mo•tion•less ['məʊsnlɪs] *adj* immobile

mo•ti•vate ['məʊtɪveɪt] *v/t person* motivare

mo•ti•va•tion [məʊtɪ'veɪʃn] motivazione *f*

mo•tive ['məʊtɪv] motivo *m*

mo•tor ['məʊtə(r)] motore *m*; *Br* F *car* macchina *f*

'mo•tor•bike moto *f*

'mo•tor•boat motoscafo *m*

mo•tor•cade ['məʊtəkeɪd] corteo *m* di auto

'mo•tor•cy•cle motocicletta *f*

'mo•tor•cy•clist motociclista *m/f*

'mo•tor home casamobile *f*

mo•tor•ist ['məʊtərɪst] automobilista *m/f*

'mo•tor me•chan•ic meccanico *m*

'mo•tor rac•ing automobilismo *m*

'mo•tor•scoot•er scooter *m inv*

'mo•tor show salone *m* dell'automobile

'mo•tor ve•hi•cle autoveicolo *m*

'mo•tor•way *Br* autostrada *f*

mot•to ['mɒtəʊ] motto *m*

mould[1] [məʊld] *on food* muffa *f*

mould[2] [məʊld] **1** *n* stampo *m* **2** *v/t also fig* plasmare

mould•y ['məʊldɪ] *adj food* ammuffito

mound [maʊnd] (*hillock*) collinetta *f*; *in baseball* pedana *f* del lanciatore; (*pile*) mucchio *m*

mount [maʊnt] **1** *n* (*horse*) cavalcatura *f*; ***Mount McKinlay*** il Monte McKinlay **2** *v/t steps* salire; *horse* montare a; *bicycle* montare in; *campaign* organizzare; *jewel* montare; *photo*, *painting* incorniciare **3** *v/i* (*increase*) aumentare

◆ **mount up** *v/i* accumularsi
moun•tain ['maʊntɪn] montagna *f*
'**moun•tain bike** mountain bike *f inv*
moun•tain•eer [maʊntɪ'nɪə(r)] alpinista *m/f*
moun•tain•eer•ing [maʊntɪ'nɪərɪŋ] alpinismo *m*
moun•tain•ous ['maʊntɪnəs] *adj* montuoso
moun•tain 'res•cue serv•ice soccorso *m* alpino
mount•ed po'lice ['maʊntɪd] polizia *f* a cavallo
mourn [mɔːn] **1** *v/t* piangere **2** *v/i*: ***mourn for*** piangere la morte di
mourn•er ['mɔːnə(r)] *persona f che partecipa a un corteo funebre*
mourn•ful ['mɔːnfʊl] *adj* triste
mourn•ing ['mɔːnɪŋ] lutto *m*; ***be in mourning*** essere in lutto; ***wear mourning*** portare il lutto
mouse [maʊs] (*pl* ***mice*** [maɪs]) topo *m*; COMPUT mouse *m inv*
'**mouse mat** COMPUT tappetino *m* del mouse
mous•tache [mə'stɑːʃ] baffi *mpl*
mouth [maʊθ] *of person* bocca *f*; *of river* foce *f*
mouth•ful ['maʊθfʊl] *of food* boccone *m*; *of drink* sorsata *f*
'**mouth•or•gan** armonica *f* a bocca
'**mouth•piece** *of instrument* bocchino *m*; (*spokesperson*) portavoce *m/f*
'**mouth•wash** collutorio *m*
'**mouth•wa•ter•ing** *adj* che fa venire l'acquolina
move [muːv] **1** *n* (*step, action*) mossa *f*; *change of house* trasloco *m*; ***get a move on!*** F spicciati!; ***don't make a move!*** non ti muovere! **2** *v/t object* spostare, muovere; (*transfer*) trasferire; *emotionally* commuovere **3** *v/i* muoversi, spostarsi; (*transfer*) trasferirsi; ***move house*** traslocare
◆ **move around** *v/i in room* muoversi; *from place to place* spostarsi
◆ **move away** *v/i* allontanarsi; *move house* traslocare
◆ **move in** *v/i* trasferirsi
◆ **move on** *v/i* ripartire; *in discussion* andare avanti; ***move on to sth*** passare a qc
◆ **move out** *v/i of house* andare via; *of troops* ritirarsi
◆ **move up** *v/i in league* avanzare; (*make room*) spostarsi
move•ment ['muːvmənt] movimento *m*
mov•ie ['muːvɪ] film *m inv*; ***go to a movie / the movies*** andare al cinema
'**mov•ie thea•ter** *Am* cinema *m inv*
mov•ing ['muːvɪŋ] *adj which can move* mobile; *emotionally* commovente
mow [məʊ] *v/t grass* tagliare, falciare
◆ **mow down** *v/t* falciare
mow•er ['məʊə(r)] tosaerba *m inv*
MP [em'piː] *abbr* (= ***Member of Parliament***) deputato *m*; (= ***Military Policeman***) polizia *f* militare
mph [empiː'eɪtʃ] *abbr* (= ***miles per hour***) miglia *fpl* orarie
Mr ['mɪstə(r)] signor
Mrs ['mɪsɪz] signora
Ms [mɪz] signora *appellativo m usato sia per donne sposate che nubili*
Mt *abbr* (= ***Mount***) M. (= monte *m*)
much [mʌtʃ] **1** *adj* molto; ***so much money*** tanti soldi; ***how much sugar?*** quanto zucchero?; ***as much ... as ...*** tanto ... quanto ... **2** *adv* molto; ***very much*** moltissimo; ***too much*** troppo; ***as much as ...*** tanto quanto ...; ***as much as a million dollars*** addirittura un milione di dollari; ***I thought as much*** me l'aspettavo **3** *pron* molto; ***nothing much*** niente di particolare; ***there's not much left*** non ne è rimasto, -a molto, -a
muck [mʌk] (*dirt*) sporco *m*
mu•cus ['mjuːkəs] muco *m*
mud [mʌd] fango *m*
mud•dle ['mʌdl] **1** *n* disordine *m*; ***I'm in a muddle*** sono confuso **2** *v/t* confondere
◆ **muddle up** *v/t* (*mess up*) mettere in disordine; (*confuse*) confondere
mud•dy ['mʌdɪ] *adj* fangoso; *hands, boots* sporco di fango
mues•li ['muːzlɪ] müsli *m inv*
muf•fle ['mʌfl] *v/t sound* attutire; *voice* camuffare
muf•fler ['mʌflər] *Am* MOT marmitta *f*
◆ **muffle up** *v/i* coprirsi bene
mug[1] [mʌg] *for tea, coffee* tazzone *m*; F (*face*) faccia *f*
mug[2] [mʌg] *v/t* (*pret & pp* ***-ged***) *attack* aggredire
mug•ger ['mʌgə(r)] aggressore *m*
mug•ging ['mʌgɪŋ] aggressione *f*
mug•gy ['mʌgɪ] *adj* afoso
mule [mjuːl] *animal* mulo *m*; (*slipper*) mule *f inv*
◆ **mull over** [mʌl] *v/t* riflettere su
mul•ti•lat•e•ral [mʌltɪ'lætərəl] *adj* POL multilaterale
mul•ti•lin•gual [mʌltɪ'lɪŋgwəl] *adj* multilingue *inv*
mul•ti•me•di•a [mʌltɪ'miːdɪə] **1** *adj* multimediale **2** *n* multimedialità *f inv*
mul•ti•na•tion•al [mʌltɪ'næʃnl] **1** *adj* multinazionale **2** *n* COM multinazionale *f*
mul•ti•ple ['mʌltɪpl] *adj* multiplo

mul•ti•ple 'choice ques•tion esercizio *m* a scelta multipla
mul•ti•ple scle'ro•sis sclerosi *f* multipla
'mul•ti•plex ('cin•e•ma) cinema *m inv* multisale
mul•ti•pli•ca•tion [mʌltɪplɪ'keɪʃn] moltiplicazione *f*
mul•ti•ply ['mʌltɪplaɪ] (*pret & pp* **-ied**) **1** *v/t* moltiplicare **2** *v/i* moltiplicarsi
multi-sto•rey (car park) [mʌltɪ'stɔːrɪ] parcheggio *m* a più piani
mum [mʌm] mamma *f*
mum•ble ['mʌmbl] **1** *n* borbottio *m* **2** *v/t & v/i* borbottare
mum•my ['mʌmɪ] mamma *f*
mumps [mʌmps] *nsg* orecchioni *mpl*
munch [mʌntʃ] *v/t & v/i* sgranocchiare
mu•ni•ci•pal [mjuː'nɪsɪpl] *adj* municipale
mu•ral ['mjʊərəl] murale *m*
mur•der ['mɜːdə(r)] **1** *n* omicidio *m* **2** *v/t person* uccidere; *song* rovinare
mur•der•er ['mɜːdərə(r)] omicida *m/f*
mur•der•ous ['mɜːdrəs] *adj rage, look* omicida
murk•y ['mɜːkɪ] *adj also fig* torbido
mur•mur ['mɜːmə(r)] **1** *n* mormorio *m* **2** *v/t* mormorare
mus•cle ['mʌsl] muscolo *m*
mus•cu•lar ['mʌskjʊlə(r)] *adj pain, strain* muscolare; *person* muscoloso
muse [mjuːz] *v/i* riflettere
mu•se•um [mjuː'zɪəm] museo *m*
mush•room ['mʌʃrʊm] **1** *n* fungo *m* **2** *v/i* crescere rapidamente
mu•sic ['mjuːzɪk] musica *f*; *in written form* spartito *m*
mu•sic•al ['mjuːzɪkl] **1** *adj* musicale; *person* portato per la musica; *voice* melodioso **2** *n* musical *m inv*
'mu•sic(•al) box carillon *m inv*
mu•sic•al 'in•stru•ment strumento *m* musicale
mu•si•cian [mjuː'zɪʃn] musicista *m/f*
mus•sel ['mʌsl] cozza *f*
must [mʌst] *v/aux* ◇ (*necessity*): ***I must be on time*** devo arrivare in orario; ***I must*** devo; ***I mustn't be late*** non devo far tardi
◇ (*probability*): ***it must be about 6 o'clock*** devono essere circa le sei; ***they must have arrived by now*** ormai devono essere arrivati
mus•tache *Am* → ***moustache***
mus•tard ['mʌstəd] senape *f*
must•y ['mʌstɪ] *adj smell* di stantio; *room* che sa di stantio
mute [mjuːt] *adj* muto
mut•ed ['mjuːtɪd] *adj* tenue
mu•ti•late ['mjuːtɪleɪt] *v/t* mutilare
mu•ti•ny ['mjuːtɪnɪ] **1** *n* ammutinamento *m* **2** *v/i* (*pret & pp* **-ied**) ammutinarsi
mut•ter ['mʌtə(r)] *v/t & v/i* farfugliare
mutton ['mʌtn] montone *m*
mu•tu•al ['mjuːtjʊəl] *adj admiration* reciproco; *friend* in comune
muz•zle ['mʌzl] **1** *n of animal* muso *m*; *for dog* museruola *f* **2** *v/t*: ***muzzle the press*** imbavagliare la stampa
my [maɪ] *adj* il mio *m*, la mia *f*, i miei *mpl*, le mie *fpl*; ***my bag*** *said by man / woman* la mia valigia; ***my sister / brother*** mia sorella / mio fratello
my•op•ic [maɪ'ɒpɪk] *adj* miope
my•self [maɪ'self] *pron reflexive* mi; *emphatic* io stesso; *after prep* me stesso; ***I've hurt myself*** mi sono fatto male; ***myself, I'd prefer ...*** quanto a me, preferirei ...; ***by myself*** da solo
mys•te•ri•ous [mɪ'stɪərɪəs] *adj* misterioso
mys•te•ri•ous•ly [mɪ'stɪərɪəslɪ] *adv* misteriosamente
mys•te•ry ['mɪstərɪ] mistero *m*
mys•tic ['mɪstɪk] *adj* mistico
mys•ti•fy ['mɪstɪfaɪ] *v/t* (*pret & pp -ied*) lasciare perplesso
myth [mɪθ] *also fig* mito *m*
myth•i•cal ['mɪθɪkl] *adj* mitico
my•thol•o•gy [mɪ'θɒlədʒɪ] mitologia *f*

N

nab [næb] *v/t* (*pret & pp* ***-bed***) F *take for o.s.* prendere
nag [næg] (*pret & pp* ***-ged***) **1** *v/i of person* brontolare di continuo **2** *v/t* assillare; ***nag s.o. to do sth*** assillare qu perché faccia qc
nag•ging ['nægɪŋ] *adj person* brontolone; *doubt, pain* assillante
nail [neɪl] *for wood* chiodo *m*; *on finger, toe* unghia *f*
'**nail clip•pers** *npl* tagliaunghie *m inv*
'**nail file** limetta *f* per unghie
'**nail pol•ish** smalto *m* per unghie
'**nail pol•ish re•mov•er** solvente *m* per unghie
'**nail scis•sors** *npl* forbicine *fpl* per unghie
'**nail var•nish** smalto *m* per unghie
na•ive [naɪ'iːv] *adj* ingenuo
naked ['neɪkɪd] *adj* nudo; ***to the naked eye*** a occhio nudo
name [neɪm] **1** *n* nome *m*; ***what's your name?*** come ti chiami?; ***call s.o. names*** insultare qu; ***make a name for o.s.*** farsi un nome **2** *v/t* chiamare
◆ **name after** *v/t*: ***they named him after his grandfather*** gli hanno messo il nome del nonno
◆ **name for** *Am* → ***name after***
name•ly ['neɪmlɪ] *adv* cioè
'**name•sake** omonimo *m*, -a *f*
'**name•tag** *on clothing etc* targhetta *f* col nome
nan•ny ['nænɪ] bambinaia *f*
nap [næp] *n* sonnellino *m*; ***have a nap*** farsi un sonnellino
nape [neɪp]: ***nape of the neck*** nuca *f*
nap•kin ['næpkɪn] (*table napkin*) tovagliolo *m*; *Am* (*sanitary napkin*) assorbente *m*
Naples [neɪpəlz] Napoli *f*
nap•py ['næpɪ] pannolino *m*
nar•cot•ic [nɑː'kɒtɪk] *n* narcotico *m*
nar•rate [nə'reɪt] *v/t* raccontare, narrare
nar•ra•tion [nə'reɪʃn] *telling* narrazione *f*
nar•ra•tive ['nærətɪv] **1** *n story* racconto **2** *adj poem, style* narrativo
nar•ra•tor [nə'reɪtə(r)] narratore *m*, -trice *f*
nar•row ['nærəʊ] *adj street, bed etc* stretto; *views, mind* ristretto; *victory* di stretta misura
nar•row•ly ['nærəʊlɪ] *adv win* di stretta misura; ***narrowly escape sth*** scampare a qc per un pelo F
nar•row-mind•ed [nærəʊ'maɪndɪd] *adj* di idee ristrette
na•sal ['neɪzl] *adj voice* nasale
nas•ty ['nɑːstɪ] *adj person, thing to say, smell, weather* cattivo; *cut, wound, disease* brutto
na•tion ['neɪʃn] nazione *f*
na•tion•al ['næʃənl] **1** *adj* nazionale **2** *n* cittadino *m*, -a *f*
na•tion•al 'an•them inno *m* nazionale
na•tion•al 'debt debito *m* pubblico
na•tion•al•ism ['næʃənəlɪzm] nazionalismo *m*
na•tion•al•i•ty [næʃə'nælətɪ] nazionalità *f inv*
na•tion•al•ize ['næʃənəlaɪz] *v/t industry etc* nazionalizzare
na•tion•al 'park parco *m* nazionale
na•tive ['neɪtɪv] **1** *adj* indigeno; ***native language*** madrelingua *f* **2** *n* (*tribesman*) indigeno *m*, -a *f*; ***she's a native of New York*** è originaria di New York; ***she speaks Chinese like a native*** parla cinese come una madrelingua
na•tive 'coun•try patria *f*
na•tive 'speak•er: ***English native speaker*** persona *f* di madrelingua inglese
NATO ['neɪtəʊ] *abbr* (= ***North Atlantic Treaty Organization***) NATO *f*
nat•u•ral ['nætʃrəl] *adj* naturale
nat•u•ral 'gas gas *m inv* naturale
nat•u•ral•ist ['nætʃrəlɪst] naturalista *m/f*
nat•u•ral•ize ['nætʃrəlaɪz] *v/t*: ***become naturalized*** naturalizzarsi
nat•u•ral•ly ['nætʃərəlɪ] *adv* (*of course*) naturalmente; *behave, speak* con naturalezza; (*by nature*) per natura
nat•u•ral 'sci•ence scienze *fpl* naturali
nat•u•ral 'sci•en•tist studioso *m*, -a *f* di scienze naturali
na•ture ['neɪtʃə(r)] natura *f*
na•ture re'serve riserva *f* naturale
naugh•ty ['nɔːtɪ] *adj* cattivo; *photograph, word etc* spinto
nau•se•a ['nɔːzɪə] nausea *f*
nau•se•ate ['nɔːzɪeɪt] *v/t* (*fig: disgust*) disgustare
nau•se•at•ing ['nɔːzɪeɪtɪŋ] *adj smell, taste* nauseante; *person* disgustoso
nau•seous ['nɔːzɪəs] *adj*: ***feel nauseous*** avere la nausea
nau•ti•cal ['nɔːtɪkl] *adj* nautico
'**nau•ti•cal mile** miglio *m* nautico
na•val ['neɪvl] *adj* navale; *officer, uniform*

della marina
'na•val base base *f* navale
na•vel ['neɪvl] ombelico *m*
nav•i•ga•ble ['nævɪgəbl] *adj river* navigabile
nav•i•gate ['nævɪgeɪt] *v/i in ship, in aeroplane* navigare; *in car* fare da navigatore/-trice; COMPUT navigare
nav•i•ga•tion [nævɪ'geɪʃn] navigazione *f*
nav•i•ga•tor ['nævɪgeɪtə(r)] *on ship, in aeroplane* ufficiale *m* di rotta; *in car* navigatore *m*, -trice *f*
na•vy ['neɪvɪ] marina *f* militare
na•vy 'blue 1 *n* blu *m inv* scuro **2** *adj* blu scuro
near [nɪə(r)] **1** *adv* vicino **2** *prep* vicino a; ***near the bank*** vicino alla banca; ***do you go near the bank?*** va dalle parti della banca? **3** *adj* vicino; ***the nearest stop*** la fermata più vicina; ***in the near future*** nel prossimo futuro
near•by [nɪə'baɪ] *adv live* vicino
near•ly ['nɪəlɪ] *adv* quasi
near-sight•ed [nɪə'saɪtɪd] *adj* miope
neat [niːt] *adj room, desk, person* ordinato; *whisky* liscio; *solution* efficace; F (*terrific*) fantastico
ne•ces•sar•i•ly ['nesəserəlɪ] *adv* necessariamente
ne•ces•sa•ry ['nesəsərɪ] *adj* necessario; ***it is necessary to …*** è necessario …, bisogna …
ne•ces•si•tate [nɪ'sesɪteɪt] *v/t* rendere necessario
ne•ces•si•ty [nɪ'sesɪtɪ] necessità *f inv*
neck [nek] collo *m*
neck•lace ['neklɪs] collana *f*
'neck•line *of dress* scollo *m*
née [neɪ] *adj*: ***Lisa Higgins née Smart*** Lisa Higgins nata Smart
need [niːd] **1** *n* bisogno *m*; ***if need be*** se necessario; ***be in need*** (*be needy*) essere bisognoso; ***be in need of sth*** aver bisogno di qc; ***there's no need to be rude / upset*** non c'è bisogno di essere maleducato / triste **2** *v/t* avere bisogno di; ***you'll need to buy one*** dovrai comprarne uno; ***you don't need to wait*** non c'è bisogno che aspetti; ***I need to talk to you*** ti devo parlare; ***need I say more?*** devo aggiungere altro?
nee•dle ['niːdl] *for sewing, on dial* ago *m*; *on record player* puntina *f*
'nee•dle•work cucito *m*
need•y ['niːdɪ] *adj* bisognoso
neg•a•tive ['negətɪv] **1** *adj* negativo **2** *n* ELEC polo *m* negativo; PHOT negativa *f*; ***answer in the negative*** rispondere negativamente
ne•glect [nɪ'glekt] **1** *n* trascuratezza *f* **2** *v/t garden, one's health* trascurare; ***neglect to do sth*** trascurare di fare qc
ne•glect•ed [nɪ'glektɪd] *adj gardens, author* trascurato; ***feel neglected*** sentirsi trascurato
neg•li•gence ['neglɪdʒəns] negligenza *f*
neg•li•gent ['neglɪdʒənt] *adj* negligente
neg•li•gi•ble ['neglɪdʒəbl] *adj quantity, amount* trascurabile
ne•go•ti•a•ble [nɪ'gəʊʃəbl] *adj salary, contract* negoziabile
ne•go•ti•ate [nɪ'gəʊʃɪeɪt] **1** *v/i* trattare **2** *v/t deal, settlement* negoziare; *obstacles* superare; *bend in road* affrontare
ne•go•ti•a•tion [nɪgəʊʃɪ'eɪʃn] negoziato *m*, trattativa *f*
ne•go•ti•a•tor [nɪ'gəʊʃɪeɪtə(r)] negoziatore *m*, -trice *f*
neigh [neɪ] *v/i* nitrire
neigh•bor *etc Am* → ***neighbour*** *etc*
neigh•bour ['neɪbə(r)] vicino *m*, -a *f*
neigh•bour•hood ['neɪbəhʊd] *in town* quartiere *m*; ***in the neighbourhood of*** *fig* intorno a
neigh•bour•ing ['neɪbərɪŋ] *adj house, state* confinante
neigh•bour•ly ['neɪbəlɪ] *adj* amichevole
nei•ther ['naɪðə(r)] **1** *adj*: ***neither player*** nessuno dei due giocatori **2** *pron* nessuno *m* dei due, nessuna *f* delle due, né l'uno né l'altro, né l'una né l'altra **3** *adv*: ***neither … nor …*** né … né … **4** *conj* neanche; ***neither do I*** neanch'io
ne•on light ['niːɒn] luce *f* al neon
neph•ew ['nevjuː] nipote *m* (di zii)
nerd [nɜːd] P fesso *m*, -a *f* P; *in style* tamarro *m* P
nerve [nɜːv] nervo *m*; (*courage*) coraggio *m*; (*impudence*) faccia *f* tosta; ***it's bad for my nerves*** mi mette in agitazione; ***get on s.o.'s nerves*** dare sui nervi a qu
nerve-rack•ing ['nɜːvrækɪŋ] *adj* snervante
ner•vous ['nɜːvəs] *adj* nervoso; ***be nervous about doing sth*** essere ansioso all'idea di fare qc
ner•vous 'break•down esaurimento *m* nervoso
ner•vous 'en•er•gy: ***be full of nervous energy*** essere sovraeccitato
ner•vous•ness ['nɜːvəsnɪs] nervosismo *m*
ner•vous 'wreck: ***be a nervous wreck*** avere i nervi a pezzi
nest [nest] *n* nido *m*
nes•tle ['nesl] *v/i* rannicchiarsi
net[1] [net] *for fishing* retino *m*; *for tennis* rete *f*

net² [net] *adj* COM netto
net 'cur•tain tenda *f* di tulle
net 'pro•fit guadagno *m o* utile *m* netto
net•tle ['netl] ortica *f*
'net•work *of contacts, cells* rete *f*; COMPUT network *m inv*
neu•rol•o•gist [njʊə'rɒlədʒɪst] neurologo *m*, -a *f*
neu•ro•sis [njʊə'rəʊsɪs] nevrosi *f inv*
neu•rot•ic [njʊ'rɒtɪk] *adj* nevrotico
neu•ter ['nju:tə(r)] *v/t animal* sterilizzare
neu•tral ['nju:trl] **1** *adj country* neutrale; *colour* neutro **2** *n gear* folle *m*; ***in neutral*** in folle
neu•tral•i•ty [njʊ'trælətɪ] neutralità *f inv*
neu•tral•ize ['njʊtrəlaɪz] *v/t* neutralizzare
nev•er ['nevə(r)] *adv* mai; ***never!*** *in disbelief* ma va'!; ***you're never going to believe this*** non ci crederesti mai; ***you never promised, did you?*** non l'avrai promesso, spero!
nev•er-'end•ing *adj* senza fine
nev•er•the•less [nevəðə'les] *adv* comunque, tuttavia
new [nju:] *adj* nuovo; ***this system is still new to me*** non sono ancora abituato al sistema; ***I'm new to the job*** sono nuovo del mestiere; ***that's nothing new*** non è una novità
'new•born *adj* neonato
new•com•er ['nju:kʌmə(r)] nuovo arrivato *m*, nuova arrivata *f*
new•ly ['nju:lɪ] *adv* (*recently*) recentemente
ˌnew•ly weds [wedz] *npl* sposini *mpl*
new 'moon luna *f* nuova
news [nju:z] *nsg* notizia *f*; *on TV, radio* notiziario *m*; novità *f inv*; ***any news?*** ci sono novità?; ***that's news to me*** mi giunge nuovo
'news a•gen•cy agenzia *f* di stampa
'news•a•gent giornalaio *m*
'news•cast telegiornale *m*
'news•cast•er giornalista *m/f* televisivo, -a
'news flash notizia *f* flash
'newspaper giornale *m*
'news•read•er giornalista *m/f* radiotelevisivo, -a
'news re•port notiziario *m*
'news•stand edicola *f*
'news•ven•dor edicolante *m/f*
new 'year anno *m* nuovo; ***Happy New Year!*** buon anno!
New Year's 'Day capodanno *m*
New Year's 'Eve San Silvestro *m*
New Zea•land ['zi:lənd] Nuova Zelanda *f*
New Zea•land•er ['zi:ləndə(r)] neozelandese *m/f*
next [nekst] **1** *adj in time* prossimo; *in space* vicino; ***the next week / month he came back again*** la settimana / il mese dopo ritornò; ***who's next?*** a chi tocca? **2** *adv* dopo; ***next to*** (*beside*) accanto a; (*in comparison with*) a paragone di
next 'door 1 *adj*: ***next door neighbour*** vicino *m*, -a *f* di casa **2** *adv live* nella casa accanto
next of 'kin parente *m/f* prossimo
nib•ble ['nɪbl] *v/t* mordicchiare
nice [naɪs] *adj person* carino, gentile; *day, weather, party* bello; *meal, food* buono; ***be nice to your sister!*** sii carino con tua sorella!; ***that's very nice of you*** molto gentile da parte tua!
nice•ly ['naɪslɪ] *adv written, presented* bene
nice•ties ['naɪsətɪz] *npl*: ***social niceties*** convenevoli *mpl*
niche [ni:ʃ] *in market* nicchia *f* (di mercato); *special position* nicchia *f*
nick [nɪk] *n cut* taglietto *m*; ***in the nick of time*** appena in tempo
nick•el ['nɪkl] *material* nichel *m inv*; (*Am: coin*) *moneta f da 5 centesimi di dollaro*
'nick•name *n* soprannome *m*
niece [ni:s] nipote *f* (di zii)
nig•gard•ly ['nɪgədlɪ] *adj amount* misero; *person* tirchio
night [naɪt] notte *f*; (*evening*) sera *f*; ***at night*** di notte / di sera; ***last night*** ieri notte / ieri sera; ***travel by night*** viaggiare di notte; ***during the night*** durante la notte; ***stay the night*** rimanere a dormire; ***a room for 2 nights*** una stanza per due notti; ***work nights*** fare il turno di notte; ***good night*** buona notte; ***in the middle of the night*** a notte fonda
'night•cap (*drink*) *bicchierino m bevuto prima di andare a letto*
'night•club night(-club) *m inv*
'night•dress camicia *f* da notte
'night•fall: ***at nightfall*** al calar della notte
'night flight volo *m* notturno
'night•gown camicia *f* da notte
night•ie ['naɪtɪ] F camicia *f* da notte
nigh•tin•gale ['naɪtɪŋgeɪl] usignolo *m*
'night•life vita *f* notturna
night•ly ['naɪtlɪ] *adj & adv* ogni sera; *late at night* ogni notte
'night•mare *also fig* incubo *m*
'night por•ter portiere *m* notturno
'night school scuola *f* serale
'night shift turno *m* di notte
'night•shirt camicia *f* da notte (*da uomo*)
'night•spot locale *m* notturno
'night•time: ***at nighttime, in the nighttime*** di notte, la notte

nil [nɪl] SP zero *m*
nim•ble ['nɪmbl] *adj* agile
nine [naɪn] nove
nine•teen [naɪn'tiːn] diciannove
nine•teenth [naɪn'tiːnθ] *n & adj* diciannovesimo, -a
nine•ti•eth ['naɪntɪɪθ] *n & adj* novantesimo, -a
nine•ty ['naɪntɪ] novanta
ninth [naɪnθ] *n & adj* nono
nip [nɪp] (*pinch*) pizzico *m*; (*bite*) morso *m*
nip•ple ['nɪpl] capezzolo *m*
ni•tro•gen ['naɪtrədʒn] azoto *m*
no [nəʊ] **1** *adv* no **2** *adj* nessuno; ***there's no coffee / tea left*** non c'è più caffè / tè; ***I have no family / money*** non ho famiglia / soldi; ***I'm no linguist / expert*** non sono un linguista / esperto; ***no parking*** sosta vietata; ***no smoking*** vietato fumare
no•bil•i•ty [nəʊ'bɪlətɪ] nobiltà *f inv*
no•ble ['nəʊbl] *adj* nobile
no•bod•y ['nəʊbədɪ] *pron* nessuno; ***nobody knows*** nessuno lo sa; ***there was nobody at home*** non c'era nessuno in casa
nod [nɒd] **1** *n* cenno *m* del capo **2** *v/i* (*pret & pp* **-ded**) fare un cenno col capo; ***nod in agreement*** annuire
◆ **nod off** *v/i* (*fall asleep*) appisolarsi
no-hop•er [nəʊ'həʊpə(r)] F buono *m*, -a *f* a nulla
noise [nɔɪz] (*sound*) rumore *m*; *loud, unpleasant* chiasso *m*
nois•y ['nɔɪzɪ] *adj* rumoroso; *children, party* chiassoso; ***don't be so noisy*** non fate tanto rumore
nom•i•nal ['nɒmɪnl] *adj amount* simbolico
nom•i•nate ['nɒmɪneɪt] *v/t* (*appoint*) designare; ***nominate s.o. for a post*** proporre qu come candidato per una posizione
nom•i•na•tion [nɒmɪ'neɪʃn] (*appointing*) nomina *f*; (*proposal*) candidatura *f*; *person proposed* candidato *m*, -a *f*
nom•i•nee [nɒmɪ'niː] candidato *m*, -a *f*
non ... [nɒn] non ...
non•al•co'hol•ic *adj* analcolico
non•a'ligned *adj* non allineato
non•cha•lant ['nɒnʃələnt] *adj* noncurante
non•com•mis•sioned 'of•fi•cer sottufficiale *m*
non•com'mit•tal *adj person, response* evasivo
non•de•script ['nɒndɪskrɪpt] *adj* ordinario
none [nʌn] *pron* nessuno *m*, -a *f*; ***none of the students*** nessuno degli studenti; ***none of this money is mine*** neanche una lira di questi soldi è mia; ***there are none left*** non ne sono rimasti; ***there is none left*** non ne è rimasto, non è rimasto niente
non'en•ti•ty nullità *f inv*
none•the•less [nʌnðə'les] *adv* nondimeno
non•ex'ist•ent *adj* inesistente
non'fic•tion opere *fpl* non di narrativa
non•(in)'flam•ma•ble *adj* non infiammabile
non•in•ter'fer•ence, non•in•ter•ˌvention non intervento *m*
non-'i•ron *adj shirt* che non si stira
'no-no: ***that's a no-no*** F non si fa
no-'non•sense *adj approach* pragmatico
non'payment mancato pagamento *m*
non•pol'lut•ing *adj* non inquinante
non'res•i•dent *n in country* non residente *m/f*; (*in hotel*) *persona f chi non è cliente di un albergo*
non•re•turn•a•ble [nɒnrɪ'tɜːnəbl] *adj* a fondo perduto
non•sense ['nɒnsəns] sciocchezze *fpl*; ***don't talk nonsense*** non dire sciocchezze; ***nonsense, it's easy!*** sciocchezze, è facile!
non'skid *adj tyres* antisdrucciolevole
non'slip *adj surface* antiscivolo *inv*
non'smok•er *person* non fumatore *m*, -trice *f*
non'stand•ard *adj* fuori standard, non di serie; *use of a word* che fa eccezione
non'stick *adj pans* antiaderente
non'stop 1 *adj flight, train* diretto; *chatter* continuo **2** *adv fly, travel* senza scalo; *chatter, argue* di continuo
non'swim•mer *persona f chi non sa nuotare*
non'u•nion *adj* non appartenente al sindacato
non'vi•o•lence non violenza *f*
non'vi•o•lent *adj* non violento
noo•dles ['nuːdlz] *npl* spaghetti *mpl* cinesi
nook [nʊk] angolino *m*
noon [nuːn] mezzogiorno *m*; ***at noon*** a mezzogiorno
noose [nuːs] cappio *m*
nor [nɔː(r)] *adv conj* né; ***nor do I*** neanch'io, neanche a me
norm [nɔːm] norma *f*
nor•mal ['nɔːml] *adj* normale
nor•mal•i•ty [nɔː'mælətɪ] normalità *f inv*
nor•mal•ize ['nɔːməlaɪz] *v/t relationships* normalizzare
nor•mal•ly ['nɔːməlɪ] *adv* (*usually*) di solito; *in a normal way* normalmente
north [nɔːθ] **1** *n* nord *m*; ***to the north of*** a

N

nord di **2** *adj* settentrionale, nord *inv* **3** *adv travel* verso nord; ***north of*** a nord di
North Am'er•i•ca America *f* del Nord
North Am'er•i•can 1 *n* nordamericano *m*, -a *f* **2** *adj* nordamericano
north,east *n* nordest
nor•ther•ly ['nɔːðəlɪ] *adj wind* settentrionale; *direction* nord *inv*
nor•thern ['nɔːðən] *adj* settentrionale
nor•thern•er ['nɔːðənə(r)] settentrionale *m/f*
North Ko're•a Corea *f* del Nord
North Ko're•an 1 *adj* nordcoreano **2** *n* nordcoreano *m*, -a *f*
North 'Pole polo *m* nord
north•wards ['nɔːðwədz] *adv travel* verso nord
north•west [nɔːð'west] *n* nordovest *m*
Nor•way ['nɔːweɪ] Norvegia *f*
Nor•we•gian [nɔː'wiːdʒn] **1** *adj* norvegese **2** *n person* norvegese *m/f*; *language* norvegese *m*
nose [nəʊz] naso *m*; ***right under my nose!*** proprio sotto il naso!
◆ **nose about** *v/i* F curiosare
'nose•bleed emorragia *f* nasale
nos•tal•gia [nɒ'stældʒɪə] nostalgia *f*
nos•tal•gic [nɒ'stældʒɪk] *adj* nostalgico
nos•tril ['nɒstrəl] narice *f*
nos•y ['nəʊzɪ] *adj* F curioso
not [nɒt] *adv* non; ***not this one, that one*** non questo, quello; ***not a lot*** non molto; ***I hope not*** spero di no; ***I don't know*** non so; ***I am not American*** non sono americano; ***he didn't help*** non ha aiutato; ***not me*** io no
no•ta•ble ['nəʊtəbl] *adj* notevole
no•ta•ry ['nəʊtərɪ] notaio *m*
notch [nɒtʃ] tacca *f*
note [nəʊt] *n short letter* biglietto *m*; MUS nota *f*; *memo to self* appunto *m*; *comment on text* nota *f*; ***take notes*** prendere appunti; ***take note of sth*** prendere nota di qc
◆ **note down** *v/t* annotare
'note•book taccuino *m*; COMPUT notebook *m inv*
not•ed ['nəʊtɪd] *adj* noto
'note•pad bloc-notes *m inv*
'note•pa•per carta *f* da lettere
noth•ing ['nʌθɪŋ] *pron* niente; ***nothing but*** nient'altro che; ***nothing much*** niente di speciale; ***for nothing*** (*for free*) gratis; (*for no reason*) per un nonnulla; ***I'd like nothing better*** non chiedo di meglio
no•tice ['nəʊtɪs] **1** *n on notice board, in street* avviso *m*; (*advance warning*) preavviso *m*; *in newspaper* annuncio *m*; *to leave job* preavviso *m*; *to leave house* disdetta *f*; ***at short notice*** con un breve preavviso; ***until further notice*** fino a nuovo avviso; ***give s.o. his / her notice*** *to quit job* dare il preavviso a qu; *to leave house* dare la disdetta a qu; ***hand in one's notice*** *to employer* presentare le dimissioni; ***four weeks' notice*** quattro settimane di preavviso; ***take notice of sth*** fare caso a qc; ***take no notice of s.o./sth*** non fare caso a qu / qc **2** *v/t* notare
no•tice•a•ble ['nəʊtɪsəbl] *adj* sensibile
'notice board bacheca *f*
no•ti•fy ['nəʊtɪfaɪ] *v/t* (*pret & pp* ***-ied***) informare
no•tion ['nəʊʃn] idea *f*
no•to•ri•ous [nəʊ'tɔːrɪəs] *adj* famigerato
nou•gat ['nuːgɑː] torrone *m*
nought [nɔːt] zero *m*
noun [naʊn] nome *m*, sostantivo *m*
nou•rish•ing ['nʌrɪʃɪŋ] *adj* nutriente
nou•rish•ment ['nʌrɪʃmənt] nutrimento *m*
nov•el ['nɒvl] *n* romanzo *m*
nov•el•ist ['nɒvlɪst] romanziere *m*, -a *f*
no•vel•ty ['nɒvəltɪ] novità *f inv*
No•vem•ber [nəʊ'vembə(r)] novembre *m*
nov•ice ['nɒvɪs] principiante *m/f*
now [naʊ] *adv* ora, adesso; ***now and again, now and then*** ogni tanto; ***by now*** ormai; ***from now on*** d'ora in poi; ***right now*** subito; ***just now*** (proprio) adesso; ***now, now!*** su, su!; ***now, where did I put it?*** dunque, dove l'ho messo?
now•a•days ['naʊədeɪz] *adv* oggigiorno
no•where ['nəʊweə(r)] *adv* da nessuna parte; ***there's nowhere to sit*** non c'è posto; ***it's nowhere near finished*** è ben lontano dall'essere terminato
noz•zle ['nɒzl] bocchetta *f*
nu•cle•ar ['njuːklɪə(r)] *adj* nucleare
nu•cle•ar 'en•er•gy energia *f* nucleare
nu•cle•ar 'fis•sion fissione *f* nucleare
'nu•cle•ar-free *adj* denuclearizzato
nu•cle•ar 'phys•ics fisica *f* nucleare
nu•cle•ar 'pow•er energia *f* nucleare; POL potenza *f* nucleare
nu•cle•ar 'pow•er sta•tion centrale *f* nucleare
nu•cle•ar re'ac•tor reattore *m* nucleare
nu•cle•ar 'waste scorie *fpl* radioattive
nu•cle•ar 'weap•on arma *f* nucleare
nude [njuːd] **1** *adj* nudo **2** *n painting* nudo *m*; ***in the nude*** nudo
nudge [nʌdʒ] *v/t* dare un colpetto di gomito a
nud•ist ['njuːdɪst] *n* nudista *m/f*
nui•sance ['njuːsns] seccatura *f*; ***make a nuisance of o.s.*** dare fastidio; ***what a***

N

nuisance! che seccatura!
nuke [njuːk] *v/t* F distruggere con armi atomiche
null and 'void [nʌl] *adj* nullo
numb [nʌm] *adj* intirizzito; *emotionally* impietrito
num•ber ['nʌmbə(r)] **1** *n* (*figure*) numero *m*, cifra *f*; (*quantity*) quantità *f inv*; *of hotel room, house, phone number etc* numero *m* **2** *v/t put a number on* contare
'number plate MOT targa *f*
numeral ['njuːmərəl] numero *m*
nu•me•rate ['njuːmərət] *adj*: ***be numerate*** avere buone basi in matematica; *of children* saper contare
nu•me•rous ['njuːmərəs] *adj* numeroso
nun [nʌn] suora *f*
nurse [nɜːs] infermiere *m*, -a *f*
nur•se•ry ['nɜːsərɪ] *school* asilo *m*; *in house* stanza *f* dei bambini; *for plants* vivaio *m*
'nur•se•ry rhyme filastrocca *f*
'nur•se•ry school scuola *f* materna
'nur•se•ry school teach•er insegnante *m/f* di scuola materna
nurs•ing ['nɜːsɪŋ] professione *f* d'infermiere; ***she went into nursing*** è diventata infermiera
'nurs•ing home *for old people* casa *f* di riposo
nut [nʌt] noce *f*; *for bolt* dado *m*; ***nuts*** F (*testicles*) palle *fpl*
'nut•crack•ers *npl* schiaccianoci *m inv*
nu•tri•ent ['njuːtrɪənt] *n* sostanza *f* nutritiva
nu•tri•tion [njuː'trɪʃn] alimentazione *f*
nu•tri•tious [njuː'trɪʃəs] *adj* nutriente
nuts [nʌts] *adj* F (*crazy*) svitato; ***be nuts about s.o.*** essere pazzo di qu
'nut•shell: ***in a nutshell*** in poche parole
nut•ty ['nʌtɪ] *adj taste* di noce; F (*crazy*) pazzo
ny•lon ['naɪlɒn] **1** *n* nylon *m inv* **2** *adj* di nylon

oak [əʊk] *tree* quercia *f*; *wood* rovere *m*
OAP [əʊeɪ'piː] *abbr* (= ***old age pensioner***) pensionato *m*, -a *f*
oar [ɔː(r)] remo *m*
o•a•sis [əʊ'eɪsɪs] (*pl* ***oases*** [əʊ'eɪsiːz]) *also fig* oasi *f inv*
oath [əʊθ] LAW giuramento *m*; (*swear-word*) imprecazione *f*; ***on oath*** sotto giuramento
'oat•meal farina *f* d'avena
oats [əʊts] *npl* avena *f*
o•be•di•ence [ə'biːdɪəns] ubbidienza *f*
o•be•di•ent [ə'biːdɪənt] *adj* ubbidiente
o•be•di•ent•ly [ə'biːdɪəntlɪ] *adv* docilmente
o•bese [əʊ'biːs] *adj* obeso
o•bes•i•ty [əʊ'biːsɪtɪ] obesità *f inv*
o•bey [ə'beɪ] *v/t parents* ubbidire a; *law* osservare
o•bit•u•a•ry [ə'bɪtjʊərɪ] *n* necrologio *m*
ob•ject[1] ['ɒbdʒɪkt] *n* (*thing*) oggetto *m*; (*aim*) scopo *m*; GRAM complemento *m*
ob•ject[2] [əb'dʒekt] *v/i* avere da obiettare
◆ **object to** *v/t* essere contrario a
ob•jec•tion [əb'dʒekʃn] obiezione *f*
ob•jec•tio•na•ble [əb'dʒekʃnəbl] *adj* (*unpleasant*) antipatico
ob•jec•tive [əb'dʒektɪv] **1** *adj* obiettivo **2** *n* obiettivo *m*
ob•jec•tive•ly [əb'dʒektɪvlɪ] *adv* obiettivamente
ob•jec•tiv•i•ty [əb'dʒektɪvətɪ] obiettività *f inv*
ob•li•ga•tion [ɒblɪ'geɪʃn] obbligo *m*; ***be under an obligation to s.o.*** essere in debito con qu
ob•lig•a•to•ry [ə'blɪgətrɪ] *adj* obbligatorio
o•blige [ə'blaɪdʒ] *v/t*: ***much obliged!*** grazie mille!
o•blig•ing [ə'blaɪdʒɪŋ] *adj* servizievole
o•blique [ə'bliːk] **1** *adj reference* indiretto **2** *n in punctuation* barra *f*
o•blit•er•ate [ə'blɪtəreɪt] *v/t city* annientare; *memory* cancellare
o•bliv•i•on [ə'blɪvɪən] oblio *m*; ***fall into oblivion*** cadere in oblio
o•bliv•i•ous [ə'blɪvɪəs] *adj*: ***be oblivious of sth*** essere ignaro di qc
ob•long ['ɒblɒŋ] **1** *adj* rettangolare **2** *n* rettangolo *m*
ob•nox•ious [əb'nɒkʃəs] *adj* offensivo; *smell* sgradevole
ob•scene [əb'siːn] *adj* osceno; *salary, poverty* vergognoso
ob•scen•i•ty [əb'senətɪ] oscenità *f inv*
ob•scure [əb'skjʊə(r)] *adj* oscuro
ob•scu•ri•ty [əb'skjʊərətɪ] oscurità *f inv*
ob•ser•vance [əb'zɜːvns] osservanza *f*
ob•ser•vant [əb'zɜːvnt] *adj* osservante
ob•ser•va•tion [ɒbzə'veɪʃn] osservazione *f*
ob•ser•va•to•ry [əb'zɜːvətrɪ] osservatorio *m*
ob•serve [əb'zɜːv] *v/t* osservare
ob•serv•er [əb'zɜːvə(r)] osservatore *m*, -trice *f*
ob•sess [əb'ses] *v/t*: ***be obsessed by / with*** essere fissato con
ob•ses•sion [əb'seʃn] fissazione *f*
ob•ses•sive [əb'sesɪv] *adj person, behaviour* ossessivo
ob•so•lete ['ɒbsəliːt] *adj model* obsoleto; *word* disusato, antiquato
ob•sta•cle ['ɒbstəkl] *also fig* ostacolo
ob•ste•tri•cian [ɒbstə'trɪʃn] ostetrico *m*, -a *f*
ob•stet•rics [ɒb'stetrɪks] ostetricia *f*
ob•sti•na•cy ['ɒbstɪnəsɪ] ostinazione *f*
ob•sti•nate ['ɒbstɪnət] *adj* ostinato
ob•sti•nate•ly ['ɒbstɪnətlɪ] *adv* ostinatamente
ob•struct [əb'strʌkt] *v/t road, passage* ostruire; *investigation, police* ostacolare
ob•struc•tion [əb'strʌktʃn] *on road etc* ostruzione *f*
ob•struc•tive [əb'strʌktɪv] *adj behaviour, tactics* ostruzionista
ob•tru•sive [əb'truːsɪv] *adj music* invadente; *colour* stonato
ob•tain [əb'teɪn] *v/t* ottenere
ob•tain•a•ble [əb'teɪnəbl] *adj products* reperibile
ob•tuse [əb'tjuːs] *adj fig* ottuso
ob•vi•ous ['ɒbvɪəs] *adj* ovvio, evidente
ob•vi•ous•ly ['ɒbvɪəslɪ] *adv* ovviamente, evidentemente; ***obviously!*** ovviamente!
oc•ca•sion [ə'keɪʒn] occasione *f*
oc•ca•sion•al [ə'keɪʒənl] *adj* sporadico; ***I like the occasional whisky*** bevo un whisky ogni tanto
oc•ca•sion•al•ly [ə'keɪʒnlɪ] *adv* ogni tanto
oc•cult [ɒ'kʌlt] **1** *adj* occulto **2** *n*: ***the occult*** l'occulto *m*
oc•cu•pant ['ɒkjʊpənt] *of vehicle* occupante *m/f*; *of building, flat* abitante *m/f*
oc•cu•pa•tion [ɒkjʊ'peɪʃn] (*job*) profes-

sione *f*; *of country* occupazione *f*
oc•cu•pa•tion•al 'ther•a•pist [ɒkjʊ'peɪʃnl] ergoterapeuta *m/f*
oc•cu•pa•tion•al 'ther•a•py ergoterapia *f*
oc•cu•py ['ɒkjʊpaɪ] *v/t* (*pret & pp* ***-ied***) occupare
oc•cur [ə'kɜː(r)] *v/i* (*pret & pp* ***-red***) accadere; ***it occurred to me that ...*** mi è venuto in mente che ...
oc•cur•rence [ə'kʌrəns] evento *m*
o•cean ['əʊʃn] oceano *m*
o•ce•a•nog•ra•pher [əʊʃn'ɒgrəfə(r)] oceanografo *m*, -a *f*
o•ce•a•nog•ra•phy [əʊʃn'ɒgrəfɪ] oceanografia *f*
o'clock [ə'klɒk]: ***at five / six o'clock*** alle cinque / sei; ***it's one o'clock*** è l'una; ***it's three o'clock*** sono le tre
Oc•to•ber [ɒk'təʊbə(r)] ottobre *m*
oc•to•pus ['ɒktəpəs] polpo *m*
OD [əʊ'diː] *v/i*: F ***OD on*** *drug* fare un'overdose di
odd [ɒd] *adj* (*strange*) strano; (*not even*) dispari; ***the odd one out*** l'eccezione *f*; ***50 odd*** 50 e rotti
'odd•ball F persona *f* stramba; ***he's an oddball*** è un tipo strambo
odds [ɒdz] *npl*: ***be at odds with*** essere in disaccordo con; ***the odds are 10 to one*** le probabilità sono 10 contro una; ***the odds are that ...*** è probabile che ...; ***against all the odds*** contro ogni aspettativa
odds and 'ends *npl objects* cianfrusaglie *fpl*; *things to do* cose *fpl*
'odds-on *adj*: ***the odds-on favourite*** il favorito; ***it's odds-on that ...*** è praticamente scontato che ...
o•di•ous ['əʊdɪəs] *adj* odioso
o•dor *Am*, **o•dour** ['əʊdə(r)] odore *m*
of [ɒv], [əv] *prep* di; ***the works of Dickens*** le opere di Dickens; ***it's made of steel*** è di acciaio; ***die of cancer*** morire di cancro; ***a friend of mine*** un mio amico; ***very nice of him*** molto gentile da parte sua; ***of the three this is ...*** dei tre questo è ...
off [ɒf] **1** *prep*: ***a lane off the main road*** *not far from* un sentiero poco lontano dalla strada principale; *leading off* un sentiero che parte dalla strada principale; ***£20 off the price*** 20 sterline di sconto; ***he's off his food*** ha perso l'appetito **2** *adv*: ***be off*** *of light, TV etc* essere spento; *of gas, tap* essere chiuso; (*cancelled*) essere annullato; *of food* essere finito; ***she was off today*** *not at work* oggi non era al lavoro; ***you've left the lid off*** non hai messo il coperchio; ***we're off tomorrow*** *leaving* partiamo domani; ***I'm off to New York*** vado a New York; ***I must be off*** devo andare; ***with his trousers / hat off*** senza pantaloni / cappello; ***take a day off*** prendere un giorno libero; ***it's 3 miles off*** dista 3 miglia; ***it's a long way off*** è molto lontano; ***drive off*** partire (in macchina); ***walk off*** allontanarsi; ***off and on*** ogni tanto **3** *adj food* andato a male; ***off switch*** interruttore *m* di spegnimento
of•fal ['ɒfl] frattaglie *fpl*
of•fence [ə'fens] LAW reato *m*; ***take offence at sth*** offendersi per qc
of•fend [ə'fend] *v/t* (*insult*) offendere
of•fend•er [ə'fendə(r)] LAW delinquente *m/f*; ***offenders will be prosecuted*** i trasgressori saranno perseguiti a norma di legge
of•fense *Am* → ***offence***
of•fen•sive [ə'fensɪv] **1** *adj behaviour, remark*, offensivo; *smell* sgradevole **2** *n* (MIL: *attack*) offensiva *f*; ***go onto the offensive*** passare all'offensiva
of•fer ['ɒfə(r)] **1** *n* offerta *f* **2** *v/t* offrire; ***offer s.o. sth*** offrire qc a qu
off'hand *adj attitude* disinvolto
of•fice ['ɒfɪs] ufficio *m*; (*position*) carica *f*
'of•fice block complesso *m* di uffici
'of•fice hours *npl* orario *m* d'ufficio
of•fi•cer ['ɒfɪsə(r)] MIL ufficiale *m*; *in police* agente *m/f*
of•fi•cial [ə'fɪʃl] **1** *adj* ufficiale **2** *n* funzionario *m*, -a *f*
of•fi•cial•ly [ə'fɪʃlɪ] *adv* ufficialmente
of•fi•ci•ate [ə'fɪʃɪeɪt] *v/i* officiare
of•fi•cious [ə'fɪʃəs] *adj* invadente
'off-licence *Br negozio m di alcolici*
'off-line *adj & adv* off-line
'off-peak *adj rates* ridotto; ***off-peak electricity*** elettricità *f* a tariffa ridotta
'off-sea•son 1 *adj rates* di bassa stagione **2** *n* bassa stagione *f*
'off•set *v/t* (*pret & pp* ***-set***) *losses, disadvantage* compensare
'off•shore *adj drilling rig, investment* off-shore *inv*
'off•side 1 *adj wheel etc* destro; *on the left* sinistro **2** *adv* SP in fuorigioco
'off•spring figli *mpl*; *of animal* piccoli *mpl*
off-the-'rec•ord *adj* ufficioso
'off-white *adj* bianco sporco
of•ten ['ɒfn] *adv* spesso
oil [ɔɪl] **1** *n* olio *m*; *petroleum* petrolio *m*; *for central heating* nafta *f* **2** *v/t hinges, bearings* oliare
'oil change cambio *m* dell'olio
'oil•cloth tela *f* cerata
'oil com•pa•ny compagnia *f* petrolifera

'**oil•field** giacimento *m* petrolifero
'**oil-fired** *adj central heating* a nafta
'**oil paint•ing** quadro *m* a olio
'**oil-pro•duc•ing coun•try** paese *m* produttore di petrolio
'**oil re•fin•e•ry** raffineria *f* di petrolio
'**oil rig** piattaforma *f* petrolifera
'**oil•skins** *npl* abiti *mpl* di tela cerata
'**oil slick** chiazza *f* di petrolio
'**oil tank•er** petroliera *f*
'**oil well** pozzo *m* petrolifero
oil•y ['ɔɪlɪ] *adj* unto
oint•ment ['ɔɪntmənt] pomata *f*
ok [əʊ'keɪ] *adj*, *adv* F: ***is it ok with you if …?*** ti va bene se …?; ***does that look ok?*** ti sembra che vada bene?; ***that's ok by me*** per me va bene; ***are you ok?*** *well, not hurt* stai bene?; ***are you ok for Friday?*** ti va bene venerdì?; ***he's ok*** (*is a good guy*) è in gamba
old [əʊld] *adj* vecchio; (*previous*) precedente; ***how old are you / is he?*** quanti anni hai / ha?; ***he's getting old*** sta invecchiando
old 'age vecchiaia *f*
old age 'pen•sion pensione *f* di anzianità
old-age 'pen•sion•er pensionato *m*, -a *f*
old 'peo•ple's home casa *f* di riposo (per anziani)
old-'fash•ioned *adj* antiquato
ol•ive ['ɒlɪv] oliva *f*
'**ol•ive oil** olio *m* d'oliva
O•lym•pic 'Games [ə'lɪmpɪk] *npl* Olimpiadi *fpl*, giochi *mpl* olimpici
om•e•let *Am*, **om•e•lette** ['ɒmlɪt] frittata *f*
om•i•nous ['ɒmɪnəs] *adj* sinistro
o•mis•sion [ə'mɪʃn] omissione *f*; *on purpose* esclusione *f*
o•mit [ə'mɪt] *v/t* (*pret & pp* ***-ted***) omettere; *on purpose* escludere; ***omit to do sth*** tralasciare di fare qc
om•nip•o•tent [ɒm'nɪpətənt] *adj* onnipotente
om•nis•ci•ent [ɒm'nɪsɪənt] *adj* onnisciente
on [ɒn] **1** *prep* su; ***on the table / wall*** sul tavolo / muro; ***on the bus / train*** in autobus / treno; ***get on the bus / train*** salire sull'autobus / sul treno; ***on TV / the radio*** alla tv / radio; ***on Sunday*** domenica; ***on Sundays*** di domenica; ***on the 1st of June*** il primo di giugno; ***be on holiday / sale / offer*** essere in vacanza / vendita / offerta; ***I'm on antibiotics*** sto prendendo antibiotici; ***this is on me*** (*I'm paying*) offro io; ***have you any money on you?*** hai dei soldi con te?; ***on his arrival / departure*** al suo arrivo / alla sua partenza; ***on hearing this*** al sentire queste parole **2** *adv*: ***be on*** *of light, TV etc* essere acceso; *of gas, tap* essere aperto; *of machine* essere in funzione; *of handbrake* essere inserito; ***it's on after the news*** *of programme* è dopo il notiziario; ***the meeting is on*** *scheduled to happen* la riunione si fa; ***put the lid on*** metti il coperchio; ***with his jacket / hat on*** con la giacca / il cappello; ***what's on tonight?*** *on TV etc* cosa c'è stasera?; ***I've got something on tonight*** *planned* stasera ho un impegno; ***you're on*** *I accept your offer etc* d'accordo; ***that's not on*** (*not allowed, not fair*) non è giusto; ***on you go*** (*go ahead*) fai pure; ***walk / talk on*** continuare a parlare / camminare; ***and so on*** e così via; ***on and on*** *talk etc* senza sosta **3** *adj*: ***the on switch*** l'interruttore *m* d'accensione
once [wʌns] **1** *adv* (*one time*) una volta; (*formerly*) un tempo; ***once again, once more*** ancora una volta; ***at once*** (*immediately*) subito; ***all at once*** (*suddenly*) improvvisamente; (***all***) ***at once*** (*together*) contemporaneamente; ***once upon a time there was …*** c'era una volta …; ***once in a while*** ogni tanto; ***once and for all*** una volta per tutte; ***for once*** per una volta **2** *conj* non appena; ***once you have finished*** non appena hai finito
one [wʌn] **1** *n* (*number*) uno *m* **2** *adj* uno, -a; ***one day*** un giorno **3** *pron* uno *m*, -a *f*; ***which one?*** quale?; ***that one*** quello *m*, -a *f*; ***this one*** questo *m*, -a *f*; ***one by one*** *enter, deal with* uno alla volta; ***one another*** l'un l'altro, a vicenda; ***what can one say / do?*** cosa si può dire / fare?; ***one would have thought that …*** si sarebbe pensato che …; ***the more one thinks about it …*** più ci si pensa …; ***the little ones*** i piccoli; ***I for one*** per quanto mi riguarda
one-'off **1** *n* fatto *m* eccezionale; *person* persona *f* eccezionale **2** *adj* unico
one-par•ent 'fam•i•ly famiglia *f* monogenitore
one'self *pron reflexive* si; *after prep* se stesso *m*, -a *f*, sé; ***cut oneself*** tagliarsi; ***do sth oneself*** fare qc da sé; ***do sth by oneself*** fare qc da solo
one-sid•ed [wʌn'saɪdɪd] *adj* unilaterale
one-track 'mind *hum*: ***have a one-track mind*** essere fissato col sesso
'**one-way street** strada *f* a senso unico
'**one-way tick•et** biglietto *m* di sola andata
on•ion ['ʌnjən] cipolla *f*
'**on-line** *adj & adv* on-line *inv*
'**on-line serv•ice** COMPUT servizio *m* on-

O

line

on•look•er ['ɒnlʊkə(r)] astante *m*

on•ly ['əʊnlɪ] **1** *adv* solo; ***not only X but also Y*** non solo X ma anche Y; ***only just*** a malapena **2** *adj* unico; ***only son*** unico figlio maschio

'**on•set** inizio *m*

'**onside** *adv* SP non in fuorigioco

on-the-job '**train•ing** training *m inv* sul lavoro

on•to ['ɒntuː] *prep*: ***put sth onto sth*** mettere qc sopra qc

on•wards ['ɒnwədz] *adv* in avanti; ***from ... onwards*** da ... in poi

ooze [uːz] **1** *v/i of liquid, mud* colare **2** *v/t*: ***he oozes charm*** è di una gentilezza esagerata

o•paque [əʊ'peɪk] *glass* opaco

OPEC ['əʊpek] *abbr* (= ***Organization of Petroleum Exporting Countries***) OPEC *f*

o•pen ['əʊpən] **1** *adj* aperto; *flower* sbocciato; (*honest, frank*) aperto, franco; ***in the open air*** all'aria aperta **2** *v/t* aprire **3** *v/i of door, shop* aprirsi; *of flower* sbocciare

◆ **open up** *v/i of person* aprirsi

o•pen-'air *adj meeting, concert* all'aperto; *pool* scoperto

'**o•pen day** *giornata f di apertura al pubblico*

o•pen-'end•ed *adj contract etc* aperto

o•pen•ing ['əʊpənɪŋ] *in wall etc* apertura *f*; *of film, novel etc* inizio *m*; (*job going*) posto *m* vacante

'**o•pen•ing hours** *npl* orario *m* d'apertura

o•pen•ly ['əʊpənlɪ] *adv* (*honestly, frankly*) apertamente

o•pen-mind•ed [əʊpən'maɪndɪd] *adj* aperto

o•pen '**plan of•fice** open space *m inv*

'**o•pen tick•et** biglietto *m* aperto

op•e•ra ['ɒpərə] lirica *f*, opera *f*

'**op•e•ra glass•es** *npl* binocolo *m* da teatro

'**op•e•ra house** teatro *m* dell'opera

'**op•e•ra sing•er** cantante lirico *m*, -a *f*

op•e•rate ['ɒpəreɪt] **1** *v/i of company* operare; *of airline, bus service* essere in servizio; *of machine* funzionare; MED operare, intervenire **2** *v/t machine* far funzionare

◆ **operate on** *v/t* MED operare

'**op•e•rat•ing in•struc•tions** *npl* istruzioni *fpl* per l'uso

'**op•e•rat•ing sys•tem** COMPUT sistema *m* operativo

op•e•ra•tion [ɒpə'reɪʃn] operazione *f*; MED intervento *m* (chirurgico), operazione *f*; *of machine* funzionamento *m*; ***operations*** *of company* operazioni *fpl*; ***have an operation*** MED subire un intervento (chirurgico)

op•e•ra•tor ['ɒpəreɪtə(r)] TELEC centralinista *m/f*; *of machine* operatore *m*, -trice *f*; (*tour operator*) operatore *m* turistico

o•pin•ion [ə'pɪnjən] opinione *f*, parere *m*; ***in my opinion*** a mio parere

o'pin•ion poll sondaggio *m* d'opinione

op•po•nent [ə'pəʊnənt] avversario *m*, -a *f*

op•por•tune ['ɒpətjuːn] *adj fml* opportuno

op•por•tun•ist [ɒpə'tjuːnɪst] opportunista *m/f*

op•por•tu•ni•ty [ɒpə'tjuːnətɪ] opportunità *f inv*

op•pose [ə'pəʊz] *v/t* opporsi a; ***be opposed to ...*** essere contrario a ...; ***as opposed to ...*** piuttosto che ...

op•po•site ['ɒpəzɪt] **1** *adj direction* opposto; *meaning, views* contrario; *house* di fronte; ***the opposite side of the road*** l'altro lato della strada; ***the opposite sex*** l'altro sesso **2** *n* contrario *m*

op•po•site '**num•ber** omologo *m*

op•po•si•tion [ɒpə'zɪʃn] opposizione *f*

op•press [ə'pres] *v/t the people* opprimere

op•pres•sive [ə'presɪv] *adj rule, dictator* oppressivo; *weather* opprimente

opt [ɒpt] *v/t*: ***opt to do sth*** optare per fare qc

op•ti•cal il•lu•sion ['ɒptɪkl] illusione *f* ottica

op•ti•cian [ɒp'tɪʃn] *dispensing* ottico *m*, -a *f*; *ophthalmic* optometrista *m/f*

op•ti•mism ['ɒptɪmɪzm] ottimismo *m*

op•ti•mist ['ɒptɪmɪst] ottimista *m/f*

op•ti•mist•ic [ɒptɪ'mɪstɪk] *adj attitude, view* ottimistico; *person* ottimista

op•timist•ic•ally [ɒptɪ'mɪstɪklɪ] *adv* ottimisticamente

optimum ['ɒptɪməm] **1** *adj* ottimale **2** *n* optimum *m inv*

op•tion ['ɒpʃn] possibilità *f inv*, opzione *f*; ***he had no other option*** non ha avuto scelta

op•tion•al ['ɒpʃnl] *adj* facoltativo

op•tion•al '**ex•tras** *npl* optional *m inv*

or [ɔː(r)] *conj* o; ***he can't hear or see*** non può né sentire né vedere; ***or else!*** o guai a te!

o•ral ['ɔːrəl] *adj* orale

or•ange ['ɒrɪndʒ] **1** *adj colour* arancione **2** *n fruit* arancia *f*; *colour* arancione *m*

or•ange•ade ['ɒrɪndʒeɪd] aranciata *f*

'**or•ange juice** succo *m* d'arancia

or•ange '**squash** aranciata *f* non gasata

or•a•tor ['ɒrətə(r)] oratore *m*, -trice *f*
or•bit ['ɔːbɪt] **1** *n of earth* orbita *f*; ***send sth into orbit*** lanciare in orbita qc **2** *v/t the earth* orbitare intorno a
or•chard ['ɔːʧəd] frutteto *m*
or•ches•tra ['ɔːkɪstrə] orchestra *f*
or•chid ['ɔːkɪd] orchidea *f*
or•dain [ɔː'deɪn] *v/t priest* ordinare
or•deal [ɔː'diːl] esperienza *f* traumatizzante
or•der ['ɔːdə(r)] **1** *n* ordine *m*; *for goods, in restaurant* ordinazione *f*; ***in order to do sth*** così da fare qc; ***he stood down in order that she could get the job*** si è ritirato, così che lei potesse avere il lavoro; ***out of order*** (*not functioning*) fuori servizio; (*not in sequence*) fuori posto; ***he's out of order*** (*not doing the proper thing*) si sta comportando in modo scorretto **2** *v/t* ordinare; ***order s.o. to do sth*** ordinare a qu di fare qc **3** *v/i* ordinare
or•der•ly ['ɔːdəlɪ] **1** *adj room, mind* ordinato; *crowd* disciplinato **2** *n in hospital* inserviente *m/f*
or•di•nal num•ber ['ɔːdɪnl] numero *m* ordinale
or•di•nar•i•ly [ɔːdɪ'neərɪlɪ] *adv* (*as a rule*) normalmente
or•di•nary ['ɔːdɪnərɪ] *adj* normale; *pej* ordinario; ***nothing out of the ordinary*** niente di straordinario
ore [ɔː(r)] minerale *m* grezzo
or•gan ['ɔːgən] ANAT, MUS organo *m*
or•gan•ic [ɔː'gænɪk] *adj food, fertilizer* biologico
or•gan•i•cal•ly [ɔː'gænɪklɪ] *adv grown* biologicamente
or•gan•is•m ['ɔːgənɪzm] organismo *m*
or•gan•i•za•tion [ɔːgənaɪ'zeɪʃn] organizzazione *f*
or•gan•ize ['ɔːgənaɪz] *v/t* organizzare
or•gan•ized 'crime criminalità *f inv* organizzata
or•gan•iz•er ['ɔːgənaɪzə(r)] *person* organizzatore *m*, -trice *f*
or•gas•m ['ɔːgæzm] orgasmo *m*
O•ri•ent ['ɔːrɪənt] Oriente *m*
O•ri•en•tal [ɔːrɪ'entl] **1** *adj* orientale **2** *n* orientale *m/f*
o•ri•en•tate ['ɔːrɪənteɪt] *v/t* (*direct*) orientare; ***orientate o.s.*** (*get bearings*) orientarsi
or•i•gin ['ɒrɪdʒɪn] origine *f*; ***of Chinese origin*** di origine cinese
o•rig•i•nal [ə'rɪdʒənl] **1** *adj* originale **2** *n painting etc* originale *m*
o•rig•i•nal•i•ty [ərɪdʒɪn'ælətɪ] originalità *f inv*
o•rig•i•nal•ly [ə'rɪdʒənəlɪ] *adv* (*at first*) in origine; ***originally he comes from France*** è di origini francesi
o•rig•i•nate [ə'rɪdʒɪneɪt] **1** *v/t scheme, idea* dare origine a **2** *v/i of idea, belief* avere origine
o•rig•i•na•tor [ə'rɪdʒɪneɪtə(r)] *of scheme etc* ideatore *m*, -trice *f*
or•na•ment ['ɔːnəmənt] soprammobile *m*
or•na•men•tal [ɔːnə'mentl] *adj* ornamentale
or•nate [ɔː'neɪt] *adj style, architecture* ornato
or•phan ['ɔːfn] *n* orfano *m*, -a *f*
or•phan•age ['ɔːfənɪdʒ] orfanotrofio *m*
or•tho•dox ['ɔːθədɒks] *adj also fig* ortodosso
or•tho•pe•dic [ɔːθə'piːdɪk] *adj* ortopedico
os•ten•si•bly [ɒ'stensəblɪ] *adv* apparentemente
os•ten•ta•tion [ɒsten'teɪʃn] ostentazione *f*
os•ten•ta•tious [ɒsten'teɪʃəs] *adj* ostentato
os•ten•ta•tious•ly [ɒsten'teɪʃəslɪ] *adv* con ostentazione
os•tra•cize ['ɒstrəsaɪz] *v/t* ostracizzare
oth•er ['ʌðə(r)] **1** *adj* altro; ***the other day*** l'altro giorno; ***every other day*** a giorni alterni; ***every other person*** una persona su due **2** *n* l'altro *m*, -a *f*; ***the others*** gli altri
oth•er•wise ['ʌðəwaɪz] *adv* altrimenti; (*differently*) diversamente
OTT [əʊtiː'tiː] *abbr* F (= ***over the top***) esagerato
ot•ter ['ɒtə(r)] lontra *f*
ought [ɔːt] *v/aux*: ***I/you ought to know*** dovrei / dovresti saperlo; ***you ought to have done it*** avresti dovuto farlo
ounce [aʊns] oncia *f*
our ['aʊə(r)] *adj* il nostro *m*, la nostra *f*, i nostri *mpl*, le nostre *fpl*; ***our brother / sister*** nostro fratello / nostra sorella
ours ['aʊəz] *pron* il nostro *m*, la nostra *f*, i nostri *mpl*, le nostre *fpl*
our•selves [aʊə'selvz] *pron reflexive* ci; *emphatic* noi stessi / nois stesse; *after prep* noi; ***we did it ourselves*** l'abbiamo fatto noi (stessi / stesse); ***we talked about ourselves*** abbiamo parlato di noi; ***by ourselves*** da soli
oust [aʊst] *v/t from office* esautorare
out [aʊt]: ***be out*** *of light, fire* essere spento; *of flower* essere sbocciato; *of sun* splendere; *not at home, not in building* essere fuori; *of calculations* essere sbagliato; (*be published*) essere uscito; *of secret* essere svelato; *no longer in competi-*

O

tion essere eliminato; *of workers* essere in sciopero; (*no longer in fashion*) essere out; ***out here in Dallas*** qui a Dallas; ***he's out in the garden*** è in giardino; (***get***) ***out!*** fuori!; (***get***) ***out of my room!*** fuori dalla mia stanza!; ***that's out!*** (*out of the question*) è fuori discussione!; ***he's out to win*** *fully intends to* è deciso a vincere

out•board 'mo•tor motore *m* fuoribordo

'out•break *of war, disease* scoppio *m*

'out•build•ing annesso *m*

'out•burst *emotional* reazione *f* violenta; ***outburst of anger*** esplosione *f* di rabbia

'out•cast *n* emarginato *m*, -a *f*

'out•come risultato *m*

'out•cry protesta *f*

out'dat•ed *adj* sorpassato

out'do *v/t* (*pret* ***-did***, *pp* ***-done***) superare

out'door *adj toilet, activities, life* all'aperto; *swimming pool* scoperto

out'doors *adv* all'aperto

out•er ['aʊtə(r)] *adj wall etc* esterno

out•er 'space spazio *m* intergalattico

'out•fit (*clothes*) completo *m*; (*company, organization*) organizzazione *f*

'out•go•ing *adj flight, mail* in partenza; *personality* estroverso

out'grow *v/t* (*pret* ***-grew***, *pp* ***-grown***) *bad habits, interests* perdere

out•ing ['aʊtɪŋ] (*trip*) gita *f*

out'last *v/t* durare più di

'out•let *of pipe* scarico *m*; *for sales* punto *m* di vendita

'out•line 1 *n of person, building etc* profilo *m*; *of plan, novel* abbozzo *m* **2** *v/t plans etc* abbozzare

out'live *v/t* sopravvivere a

'out•look (*prospects*) prospettiva *f*

'out•ly•ing *adj areas* periferico

out'num•ber *v/t* superare numericamente

out of *prep* (*motion*) fuori; ***fall out of the window*** cadere fuori dalla finestra ◇ (*position*) da ***20 miles out of Newcastle*** 20 miglia da Newcastle
◇ (*cause*) per; ***out of jealousy / curiosity*** per gelosia / curiosità
◇ (*without*) senza; ***we're out of petrol / beer*** siamo senza benzina / birra
◇ *from a group* su ***5 out of 10*** 5 su 10

out-of-'date *adj passport* scaduto; *values* superato

out-of-the-way *adj* fuori mano

'out•pa•tient paziente *m/f* esterno, -a

'out•pa•tients' (clin•ic) ambulatorio *m*

'out•per•form *v/t of machine, investment* rendere meglio di; *of company, economy* andare meglio di

'out•put 1 *n of factory* produzione *f*; COMPUT output *m inv* **2** *v/t* (*pret & pp* ***-ted*** *or* ***output***) (*produce*) produrre; COMPUT: *signal* emettere

'out•rage 1 *n feeling* sdegno *m*; *act* atrocità *f inv* **2** *v/t* indignare

out•ra•geous [aʊt'reɪdʒəs] *adj acts* scioccante; *prices* scandaloso

'out•right 1 *adj winner* assoluto **2** *adv win* nettamente; *kill* sul colpo

out'run *v/t* (*pret* ***-ran***, *pp* ***-run***) *also fig* superare; *run faster than* correre più veloce di

'out•set *n*: ***at / from the outset*** all'/-dall'inizio

out'shine *v/t* (*pret & pp* ***-shone***) eclissare

'out•side 1 *adj surface, wall, lane* esterno **2** *adv sit, go* fuori **3** *prep* fuori da; (*apart from*) al di fuori di **4** *n of building, case etc* esterno *m*; ***at the outside*** al massimo

out•side 'broad•cast trasmissione *f* in esterni

out•sid•er [aʊt'saɪdə(r)] estraneo *m*, -a *f*; *in election, race* outsider *m inv*

'out•size *adj clothing* di taglia forte

'out•skirts *npl* periferia *f*

out'smart → ***outwit***

out'stand•ing *adj success, writer* eccezionale; FIN: *invoice, sums* da saldare

out•stretched ['autstretʃt] *adj hands* teso

out'vote *v/t* mettere in minoranza

out•ward ['aʊtwəd] *adj appearance* esteriore; ***outward journey*** viaggio *m* d'andata

out•ward•ly ['aʊtwədlɪ] *adv* esteriormente

out'weigh *v/t* contare più di

out'wit *v/t* (*pret & pp* ***-ted***) riuscire a gabbare

o•val ['əʊvl] *adj* ovale

o•va•ry ['əʊvərɪ] ovaia *f*

o•va•tion [əʊ'veɪʃn] ovazione *f*; ***she was given a standing ovation*** il pubblico s'è alzato in piedi per applaudirla

ov•en ['ʌvn] *in kitchen* forno *m*; *in factory* fornace *f*

'ov•en glove, **'ov•en mitt** guanto *m* da forno

'ov•en•proof *adj* pirofilo

'ov•en-read•y *adj* pronto da mettere al forno

o•ver ['əʊvə(r)] **1** *prep* (*above*) sopra, su; (*across*) dall'altra parte; (*more than*) oltre; (*during*) nel corso di; ***over the phone*** al telefono; ***travel all over Brazil*** girare tutto il Brasile; ***you find them all over Brazil*** si trovano dappertutto in Brasile; ***let's talk over a meal*** parliamone a pranzo; ***we're over the worst*** il peggio è passato; ***over and above*** oltre a **2** *adv*: ***be over*** (*finished*) essere finito;

(*left*) essere rimasto; ***over to you*** (*your turn*) tocca a te; ***over in Japan*** in Giappone; ***overhere / there*** qui / lì; ***it hurts all over*** mi fa male dappertutto; ***painted white all over*** tutto dipinto di bianco; ***it's all over*** è finito; ***I've told you over and over again*** te l'ho detto mille volte; ***do sth over again*** rifare qc

o•ver•all ['əʊvərɔːl] **1** *adj length* totale **2** *adv measure* complessivamente; (*in general*) nell'insieme

o•ver•alls ['əʊvərɔːlz] *npl* tuta *f* da lavoro

o•ver'awe *v/t* intimidire; ***be overawed by s.o./sth*** essere intimidito da qu / qc

o•ver'bal•ance *v/i* perdere l'equilibrio

o•ver'bear•ing *adj* autoritario

'o•ver•board *adv*: ***man overboard!*** uomo in mare!; ***go overboard for s.o./sth*** entusiasmarsi per qu / qc

'o•ver•cast *adj day, sky* nuvoloso

o•ver'charge *v/t customer* far pagare più del dovuto a

'o•ver•coat cappotto *m*

o•ver'come *v/t* (*pret* ***-came***, *pp* ***-come***) *difficulties, shyness* superare; ***be overcome by emotion*** essere sopraffatto dall'emozione

o•ver'crowd•ed *adj* sovraffollato

o•ver'do *v/t* (*pret* ***-did***, *pp* ***-done***) (*exaggerate*) esagerare; *in cooking* stracuocere; ***you're overdoing things*** *taking on too much* ti stai strapazzando

o•ver'done *adj meat* stracotto

'o•ver•dose *n* overdose *f inv*

'o•ver•draft scoperto *m* (di conto); ***have an overdraft*** avere il conto scoperto

o•ver'draw *v/t* (*pret* ***-drew***, *pp* ***-drawn***): ***overdraw one's account*** andare allo scoperto; ***be £800 overdrawn*** essere (allo) scoperto di 800 sterline

o•ver'dressed *adj* troppo elegante

'o•ver•drive MOT overdrive *m inv*

o•ver'due *adj bill, rent* arretrato; *train, baby* in ritardo

o•ver'es•ti•mate *v/t abilities, value* sovrastimare

o•ver'ex•pose *v/t photograph* sovraesporre

'o•ver•flow[1] *n pipe* troppopieno *m*

o•ver'flow[2] *v/i of water* traboccare; *of river* straripare

o•ver'grown *adj garden* coperto d'erbacce; ***he's an overgrown baby*** è un bambinone

o•ver'haul *v/t engine* revisionare; *plans* rivedere

'o•ver•head[1] *adj lights, cables* in alto, aereo; *railway* soprelevato

'over•head[2] *Am nsg*, **'over•heads** *npl* FIN costi *mpl* di gestione; ***travel overhead*** spese *fpl* di viaggio

'o•ver•head pro•jec•tor lavagna *f* luminosa

o•ver'hear *v/t* (*pret & pp* ***-heard***) sentire per caso

o•ver'heat•ed *adj room, engine* surriscaldato

o•ver•joyed [əʊvə'dʒɔɪd] *adj* felicissimo

'o•ver•kill: ***that's overkill*** è un'esagerazione

'o•ver•land *adj & adv* via terra

o•ver'lap *v/i* (*pret & pp* ***-ped***) (*partly cover*) sovrapporsi; (*partly coincide*) coincidere

o•ver'leaf: ***see overleaf*** a tergo

o•ver'load *v/t* sovraccaricare

o•ver'look *v/t of tall building etc* dominare, dare su; *deliberately* chiudere un occhio su; *accidentally* non notare; ***the room overlooks the garden*** la stanza dà sul giardino

o•ver•ly ['əʊvəlɪ] *adv* troppo; ***not overly ...*** non particolarmente ...

'o•ver•night *adv travel* di notte; *stay* per la notte

o•ver•night 'bag piccola borsa *f* da viaggio

o•ver'paid *adj* strapagato

o•verpop•u•lat•ed [əʊvə'pɒpjʊleɪtɪd] *adj* sovrappopolato

o•ver'pow•er *v/t physically* sopraffare

o•ver•pow•er•ing [əʊvə'paʊrɪŋ] *adj smell* asfissiante; *sense of guilt* opprimente

o•ver•priced [əʊvə'praɪst] *adj* troppo caro

o•ver•rat•ed [əʊvə'reɪtɪd] *adj* sopravvalutato

o•ver•re'act *v/i* reagire in modo eccessivo

o•ver'ride *v/t* (*pret* ***-rode***, *pp* ***-ridden***) annullare; *person* annullare la decisione di; (*be more important than*) prevalere su

o•ver'rid•ing *adj concern* principale

o•ver'rule *v/t decision* annullare

o•ver'run *v/t* (*pret* ***-ran***, *pp* ***-run***) *country* invadere; *time* sforare; ***be overrun with*** essere invaso da

o•ver'seas *adv & adj* all'estero

o•ver'see *v/t* (*pret* ***-saw***, *pp* ***-seen***) sorvegliare

o•ver'shad•ow *v/t fig* eclissare

'o•ver•sight svista *f*

o•ver•sim•pli•fi'ca•tion semplificazione *f* eccessiva

o•ver'sim•pli•fy *v/t* (*pret & pp* ***-ied***) semplificare troppo

o•ver'sleep *v/i* (*pret & pp* ***-slept***) non svegliarsi in tempo

o•ver'state *v/t* esagerare

o•ver'state•ment esagerazione *f*
o•ver'step *v/t* (*pret & pp* ***-ped***): *fig* ***overstep the mark*** passare il segno
o•ver'take *v/t* (*pret* ***-took***, *pp* ***-taken***) *in work*, *development* superare; MOT sorpassare
o•ver'throw[1] *v/t* (*pret* ***-threw***, *pp* ***-thrown***) *government* rovesciare
'o•verthrow[2] *n of government* rovesciamento *m*
'o•ver•time *Br* **1** *n* straordinario *m* **2** *adv*: ***work overtime*** fare lo straordinario
'o•ver•ture ['əʊvətjʊə(r)] MUS ouverture *f inv*; ***make overtures to*** fare approcci a
o•ver'turn 1 *v/t vehicle*, *object* ribaltare; *government* rovesciare **2** *v/i of vehicle* ribaltarsi
'o•ver•view visione *f* d'insieme
o•ver'weight *adj* sovrappeso
o•ver'whelm [əʊvə'welm] *v/t with work* oberare; *with emotion* sopraffare; ***be overwhelmed by*** *by response* essere colpito da
o•verwhelm•ing [əʊvə'welmɪŋ] *adj feeling* profondo; *majority* schiacciante
o•ver'work 1 *n* lavoro *m* eccessivo **2** *v/i* lavorare troppo **3** *v/t* far lavorare troppo
owe [əʊ] *v/t* dovere; ***owe s.o. £500*** dovere £500 a qu; ***owe s.o. an apology*** dovere delle scuse a qu; ***how much do I owe you?*** quanto le devo?
ow•ing to ['əʊɪŋ] *prep* a causa di
owl [aʊl] gufo *m*
own[1] [əʊn] *v/t* possedere
own[2] [əʊn] **1** *adj* proprio; ***my own car*** la mia macchina; ***my very own mother*** proprio mia madre **2** *pron*: ***a car of my own*** un'auto tutta mia; ***on my/his own*** da solo
◆ **own up** *v/i* confessare
own•er ['əʊnə(r)] proprietario *m*, -a *f*
own•er•ship ['əʊnəʃɪp] proprietà *f inv*
ox [ɒks] bue *m*
ox•ide ['ɒksaɪd] ossido *m*
ox•y•gen ['ɒksɪdʒən] ossigeno *m*
oy•ster ['ɔɪstə(r)] ostrica *f*
oz *abbr* (= ***ounce(s)***) oncia
o•zone ['əʊzəʊn] ozono *m*
'o•zone lay•er fascia *f o* strato *m* d'ozono

P

p [piː] *abbr* (= ***penny***; ***pence***) penny *m inv*
PA [piːˈeɪ] *abbr* (= ***personal assistant***) assistente *m/f* personale
pace [peɪs] **1** *n* (*step*) passo *m*; (*speed*) ritmo *m* **2** *v/i*: ***pace up and down*** camminare su e giù
ˈ**pace•mak•er** MED pacemaker *m inv*; SP battistrada *m inv*
Pa•cif•ic [pəˈsɪfɪk]: ***the Pacific*** (***Ocean***) il Pacifico
pac•i•fism [ˈpæsɪfɪzm] pacifismo *m*
pac•i•fist [ˈpæsɪfɪst] *n* pacifista *m/f*
pac•i•fy [ˈpæsɪfaɪ] *v/t* (*pret & pp* ***-ied***) placare
pack [pæk] **1** *n* (*backpack*) zaino *m*; *of cereal, food* confezione *f*; *of cigarettes* pacchetto *m*; *of peas etc* confezione *f*; *of cards* mazzo *m* **2** *v/t bag* fare; *item of clothing etc* mettere in valigia; *goods* imballare; *groceries* imbustare **3** *v/i* fare la valigia / le valigie
pack•age [ˈpækɪdʒ] **1** *n* (*parcel*) pacco *m*; *of offers etc* pacchetto *m* **2** *v/t* confezionare
ˈ**pack•age deal** *for holiday* offerta *f* tutto compreso
ˈ**pack•age tour** viaggio *m* organizzato
pack•ag•ing [ˈpækɪdʒɪŋ] *also fig* confezione *f*
pack•ed [pækt] *adj* (*crowded*) affollato
pack•et [ˈpækɪt] confezione *f*; *of cigarettes, crisps* pacchetto *m*
pact [pækt] patto *m*
pad[1] [pæd] **1** *n piece of cloth etc* tampone *m*; *for writing* blocchetto *m* **2** *v/t* (*pret & pp* ***-ded***) *with material* imbottire; *speech, report* farcire
pad[2] [pæd] *v/i* (*move quietly*) camminare a passi felpati
pad•ded [ˈpædɪd] *adj jacket, shoulders* imbottito
pad•ding [ˈpædɪŋ] *material* imbottitura *f*; *in speech etc* riempitivo *m*
pad•dle [ˈpædl] **1** *n for canoe* pagaia *f* **2** *v/i in canoe* pagaiare; *in water* sguazzare
pad•dling pool [ˈpædlɪŋpuːl] piscinetta *f* per bambini
pad•dock [ˈpædək] paddock *m inv*
pad•lock [ˈpædlɒk] **1** *n* lucchetto *m* **2** *v/t gate* chiudere col lucchetto; ***padlock X to Y*** fissare col lucchetto X a Y
paed•i•at•ric *etc* → ***pediatric*** *etc*
page[1] [peɪdʒ] *n of book etc* pagina *f*
page[2] [peɪdʒ] *v/t* (*call*) chiamare con l'altoparlante; *with pager* chiamare col cercapersone
pag•er [ˈpeɪdʒə(r)] cercapersone *m inv*
paid [peɪd] *pret & pp* → ***pay***
paid emˈ**ploy•ment** occupazione *f* rimunerata
pail [peɪl] secchio *m*
pain [peɪn] dolore *m*; ***be in pain*** soffrire; ***take pains to …*** fare il possibile per …; ***a pain in the neck*** F una rottura *f* di scatole F
pain•ful [ˈpeɪnfʊl] *adj* (*distressing*) doloroso; (*laborious*) difficile; ***my leg is still painful*** la gamba mi fa ancora male; ***it is my painful duty to inform you …*** siamo addolorati di comunicarle …
pain•ful•ly [ˈpeɪnflɪ] *adv* (*extremely, acutely*) estremamente
pain•kill•er [ˈpeɪnkɪlə(r)] analgesico *m*
pain•less [ˈpeɪnlɪs] *adj* indolore
pains•tak•ing [ˈpeɪnzteɪkɪŋ] *adj* accurato
paint [peɪnt] **1** *n for wall, car* vernice *f*; *for artist* colore *m* **2** *v/t wall etc* pitturare; *picture* dipingere **3** *v/i as art form* dipingere
paint•brush [ˈpeɪntbrʌʃ] pennello *m*
paint•er [ˈpeɪntə(r)] *decorator* imbianchino *m*; *artist* pittore *m*, -trice *f*
paint•ing [ˈpeɪntɪŋ] *activity* pittura *f*; (*picture*) quadro *m*
paint•work [ˈpeɪntwɜːk] vernice *f*
pair [peə(r)] *of objects* paio *m*; *of animals, people* coppia *f*; ***a pair of shoes*** un paio di scarpe
pa•ja•mas *Am* → ***pyjamas***
Pa•ki•stan [pɑːkɪˈstɑːn] Pakistan *m*
Pa•ki•sta•ni [pɑːkɪˈstɑːnɪ] **1** *n* pakistano *m*, -a *f* **2** *adj* pakistano
pal [pæl] F (*friend*) amico *m*, -a *f*
pal•ace [ˈpælɪs] palazzo *m* signorile
pal•ate [ˈpælət] palato *m*
pa•la•tial [pəˈleɪʃl] *adj* sfarzoso
pale [peɪl] *adj person* pallido; ***pale pink*** / ***blue*** rosa / celeste pallido
Pal•e•stine [ˈpæləstaɪn] Palestina *f*
Pal•e•stin•i•an [pæləˈstɪnɪən] **1** *n* palestinese *m/f* **2** *adj* palestinese
pal•let [ˈpælɪt] pallet *m inv*
pal•lor [ˈpælə(r)] pallore *m*
palm[1] [pɑːm] *of hand* palma *f*
palm[2] [pɑːm] *tree* palma *f*
pal•pi•ta•tions [pælpɪˈteɪʃnz] *npl* MED palpitazioni *fpl*
pal•try [ˈpɔːltrɪ] *adj* irrisorio
pam•per [ˈpæmpə(r)] *v/t* viziare

pam•phlet ['pæmflɪt] volantino *m*
pan [pæn] **1** *n for cooking* pentola *f*; *for frying* padella *f* **2** *v/t* (*pret & pp* ***-ned***) F (*criticize*) stroncare F
◆ **pan out** *v/i* (*develop*) sviluppare
pan•cake ['pænkeɪk] crêpe *f inv*
pan•da ['pændə] panda *m inv*
pan•de•mo•ni•um [pændɪ'məʊnɪəm] pandemonio *m*
◆ **pan•der to** ['pændə(r)] *v/t* assecondare
pane [peɪn]: ***pane (of glass)*** vetro *m*
pan•el ['pænl] pannello *m*; *of experts* gruppo *m*; *of judges* giuria *f*
pan•el•ling ['pænəlɪŋ] rivestimento *m* a pannelli
pang [pæŋ] *of remorse* fitta *f*; ***pangs of hunger*** morsi *mpl* della fame
pan•ic ['pænɪk] **1** *n* panico *m* **2** *v/i* (*pret & pp* ***-ked***): ***don't panic*** non farti prendere dal panico
'**pan•ic buy•ing** FIN *acquisto m motivato dal panico*
'**pan•ic sel•ling** FIN *vendita f motivata dal panico*
'**pan•ic-strick•en** *adj* in preda al panico
pan•o•ra•ma [pænə'rɑːmə] panorama *m*
pa•no•ra•mic [pænə'ræmɪk] *adj view* panoramico
pan•sy ['pænzɪ] *flower* viola *f* del pensiero
pant [pænt] *v/i* ansimare
pan•ties ['pæntɪz] *npl* mutandine *fpl*
pants [pænts] *npl* (*underpants*) mutande *fpl*; *esp Am* (*trousers*) pantaloni *mpl*
pan•ty•hose ['pæntɪhəʊz] *Am* collant *mpl*
pa•pal ['peɪpəl] *adj* pontificio
pa•per ['peɪpə(r)] **1** *n material* carta *f*; (*newspaper*) giornale *m*; (*wallpaper*) carta *f* da parati; *academic* relazione *f*; (*examination paper*) esame *m*; ***papers*** (*identity papers, documents*) documenti *mpl*; ***a piece of paper*** un pezzo di carta **2** *adj* di carta **3** *v/t room, walls* tappezzare
'**paperback** tascabile *m*
paper '**bag** sacchetto *m* di carta
'**paper boy** *ragazzo m che recapita i giornali a domicilio*
'**paper clip** graffetta *f*
'**paper cup** bicchiere *m* di carta
'**paperwork** *disbrigo m delle pratiche*
par [pɑː (r)] *in golf* par *m inv*; ***be on a par with*** essere allo stesso livello di; ***feel below par*** non sentirsi bene
par•a•chute ['pærəʃuːt] **1** *n* paracadute *m inv* **2** *v/i* paracadutarsi **3** *v/t troops, supplies* paracadutare
par•a•chut•ist ['pærəʃuːtɪst] paracadutista *m/f*
pa•rade [pə'reɪd] **1** *n* (*procession*) sfilata *f* **2** *v/i* sfilare **3** *v/t knowledge, new car* fare sfoggio di
par•a•dise ['pærədaɪs] paradiso *m*
par•a•dox ['pærədɒks] paradosso *m*
par•a•dox•i•cal [pærə'dɒksɪkl] *adj* paradossale
par•a•dox•i•cal•ly [pærə'dɒksɪklɪ] *adv* paradossalmente
par•a•graph ['pærəgrɑːf] paragrafo *m*
par•al•lel ['pærəlel] **1** *n* (*in geometry*) parallela *f*; GEOG, *fig* parallelo *m*; ***do two things in parallel*** fare due cose in parallelo **2** *adj also fig* parallelo **3** *v/t* (*match*) uguagliare
par•a•lyse ['pærəlaɪz] *v/t also fig* paralizzare
pa•ral•y•sis [pə'ræləsɪs] *also fig* paralisi *f inv*
par•a•med•ic [pærə'medɪk] *n* paramedico *m*, -a *f*
pa•ram•e•ter [pə'ræmɪtə(r)] parametro *m*
par•a•mil•i•tar•y [pærə'mɪlɪtrɪ] **1** *adj* paramilitare **2** *n appartenente m/f ad un'organizzazione paramilitare*
par•a•mount ['pærəmaʊnt] *adj* vitale; ***be paramount*** essere di vitale importanza
par•a•noi•a [pærə'nɔɪə] paranoia *f*
par•a•noid ['pærənɔɪd] *adj* paranoico
par•a•pher•na•li•a [pærəfə'neɪlɪə] armamentario *m*
par•a•phrase ['pærəfreɪz] *v/t* parafrasare
par•a•pleg•ic [pærə'pliːdʒɪk] *n* paraplegico *m*, -a *f*
par•a•site ['pærəsaɪt] *also fig* parassita *m*
par•a•sol ['pærəsɒl] parasole *m*
par•a•troop•er ['pærətruːpə(r)] MIL paracadutista *m*
par•cel ['pɑːsl] *n* pacco *m*
◆ **parcel up** *v/t* impacchettare
parch [pɑːtʃ] *v/t* riardere; ***be parched*** F *of person* essere assetato
par•don ['pɑːdn] **1** *n* LAW grazia *f*; ***I beg your pardon?*** (*what did you say*) prego?; ***I beg your pardon*** (*I'm sorry*) scusi **2** *v/t* scusare; LAW graziare
pare [peə(r)] *v/t* (*peel*) pelare
par•ent ['peərənt] genitore *m*
pa•ren•tal [pə'rentl] *adj* dei genitori
'**par•ent company** società *f inv* madre
par•ent-'teacher association *organizzazione f composta da genitori e insegnanti*
par•ish ['pærɪʃ] parrocchia *f*
park[1] [pɑːk] *n* parco *m*
park[2] [pɑːk] *v/t & v/i* MOT parcheggiare
par•ka ['pɑːkə] parka *m inv*
par•king ['pɑːkɪŋ] MOT parcheggio *m*; ***no parking*** sosta *f* vietata
'**par•king brake** *Am* freno *m* a mano

ˈ**par•king disc** disco *m* orario
ˈ**par•king lot** *Am* parcheggio *m*
ˈ**par•king me•ter** parchimetro *m*
ˈ**par•king place** parcheggio *m*
ˈ**par•king tick•et** multa *f* per sosta vietata
par•lia•ment [ˈpɑːləmənt] parlamento *m*
par•lia•men•ta•ry [pɑːljəˈmentərɪ] *adj* parlamentare
pa•role [pəˈrəʊl] **1** *n* libertà *f inv* vigilata; ***be out on parole*** essere rimesso in libertà vigilata **2** *v/t* concedere la libertà vigilata a
par•rot [ˈpærət] pappagallo *m*
pars•ley [ˈpɑːslɪ] prezzemolo *m*
part [pɑːt] **1** *n* parte *f*; *of machine* pezzo *m*; *Am*: *in hair* riga *f*; ***take part in*** prendere parte in **2** *adv* (*partly*) in parte **3** *v/i* separarsi **4** *v/t*: ***part one's hair*** farsi la riga
◆**part with** *v/t* separarsi da
ˈ**part ex•change** permuta *f*; ***take sth in part exchange*** prendere qc in permuta
par•tial [ˈpɑːʃl] *adj* (*incomplete*) parziale; ***be partial to*** avere un debole per
par•tial•ly [ˈpɑːʃəlɪ] *adv* parzialmente
par•ti•ci•pant [pɑːˈtɪsɪpənt] partecipante *m/f*
par•ti•ci•pate [pɑːˈtɪsɪpeɪt] *v/i* partecipare; ***participate in sth*** partecipare a qc
par•ti•ci•pa•tion [pɑːtɪsɪˈpeɪʃn] partecipazione *f*
par•ti•cle [ˈpɑːtɪkl] PHYS particella *f*; *small amount* briciolo *m*
par•tic•u•lar [pəˈtɪkjʊlə(r)] *adj* (*specific*) particolare; (*fussy*) pignolo; ***in particular*** in particolare
par•tic•u•lar•ly [pəˈtɪkjʊləlɪ] *adv* particolarmente
part•ing [ˈpɑːtɪŋ] *of people* separazione *f*; *in hair* riga *f*
par•ti•tion [pɑːˈtɪʃn] **1** *n* (*screen*) tramezzo *m*; (*of country*) suddivisione *f* **2** *v/t country* suddividere
◆**partition off** *v/t* tramezzare
part•ly [ˈpɑːtlɪ] *adv* in parte
part•ner [ˈpɑːtnə(r)] COM socio *m*, -a *f*; *in relationship* partner *m/f inv*; *in particular activity* compagno *m*, -a *f*
part•ner•ship [ˈpɑːtnəʃɪp] COM società *f inv*; *in particular activity* sodalizio *m*
part of ˈ**speech** GRAM parte *f* del discorso
ˈ**part own•er** comproprietario *m*, -a *f*
ˈ**part-time** *adj & adv* part-time
part-ˈ**tim•er** lavoratore *m*, -trice *f* part-time
par•ty [ˈpɑːtɪ] **1** *n* (*celebration*) festa *f*; POL partito *m*; (*group*) gruppo *m*; ***be a party to*** essere coinvolto in **2** *v/i* (*pret & pp* ***-ied***) F far baldoria
pass [pɑːs] **1** *n for getting into a place* pass *m inv*; SP passaggio *m*; *in mountains* passo *m*; ***make a pass at*** fare avances a **2** *v/t* (*hand*) passare; (*go past*) passare davanti a; (*overtake*) sorpassare; (*go beyond*) superare; (*approve*) approvare; SP passare; ***pass an exam*** superare un esame; ***pass sentence*** LAW emanare la sentenza; ***pass the time*** passare il tempo **3** *v/i* passare; *in exam* essere promosso
◆**pass around** *v/t* far circolare
◆**pass away** *v/i euph* spegnersi *euph*
◆**pass by 1** *v/t* (*go past*) passare davanti a **2** *v/i* (*go past*) passare
◆**pass on 1** *v/t information, book, savings* passare (***to*** a) **2** *v/i* (*euph: die*) mancare *euph*
◆**pass out** *v/i* (*faint*) svenire
◆**pass through** *v/t town* passare per
◆**pass up** *v/t opportunity* lasciarsi sfuggire
pass•a•ble [ˈpɑːsəbl] *adj road* transitabile; (*acceptable*) passabile
pas•sage [ˈpæsɪdʒ] (*corridor*) passaggio *m*; *from poem, book* passo *m*; ***the passage of time*** il passare del tempo
pas•sage•way [ˈpæsɪdʒweɪ] corridoio *m*
pas•sen•ger [ˈpæsɪndʒə(r)] passeggero *m*, -a *f*
ˈ**pas•sen•ger seat** sedile *m* del passeggero
pas•ser-by [pɑːsəˈbaɪ] (*pl* ***passers-by***) passante *m/f*
pas•sion [ˈpæʃn] passione *f*
pas•sion•ate [ˈpæʃnət] *adj* appassionato
pas•sive [ˈpæsɪv] **1** *adj* passivo **2** *n* GRAM passivo *m*; ***in the passive*** al passivo
ˈ**pass mark** EDU voto *m* sufficiente
Pass•o•ver [ˈpɑːsəʊvə(r)] REL Pasqua *f* ebraica
pass•port [ˈpɑːspɔːt] passaporto *m*
ˈ**pass•port control** controllo *m* passaporti
pass•word [ˈpɑːswɜːd] parola *f* d'ordine; COMPUT password *f inv*
past [pɑːst] **1** *adj* (*former*) precedente; ***in the past few days*** nei giorni scorsi; ***that's all past now*** è acqua passata ormai **2** *n* passato *m*; ***in the past*** nel passato **3** *prep in position* oltre; ***it's half past two*** sono le due e mezza; ***it's past seven o'clock*** sono le sette passate **4** *adv*: ***run past*** passare di corsa
pas•ta [ˈpæstə] pasta *f*
paste [peɪst] **1** *n* (*adhesive*) colla *f* **2** *v/t* (*stick*) incollare
pas•tel [ˈpæstl] **1** *n* pastello *m* **2** *adj* pastello
pas•time [ˈpɑːstaɪm] passatempo *m*

past par'ti•ci•ple GRAM participio *m* passato
pas•tra•mi [pæ'strɑːmɪ] *affettato m di carne di manzo speziata*
pas•try ['peɪstrɪ] *for pie* pasta *f* (sfoglia); (*small cake*) pasticcino *m*
'past tense GRAM passato *m*
pas•ty ['peɪstɪ] *adj complexion* smorto
pat [pæt] **1** *n* colpetto *m*; *affectionate* buffetto *m*; ***give s.o. a pat on the back*** *fig* dare una pacca sulla spalla a qu **2** *v/t* (*pret & pp* ***-ted***) dare un colpetto a; *affectionately* dare un buffetto a
patch [pætʃ] **1** *n on clothing* pezza *f*; (*period of time*) periodo *m*; (*area*) zona *f*; ***go through a bad patch*** attraversare un brutto periodo; ***patches of fog*** banchi *mpl* di nebbia; ***be not a patch on*** *fig* non essere niente a paragone di **2** *v/t clothing* rattoppare
◆ **patch up** *v/t* (*repair temporarily*) riparare alla meglio; *quarrel* risolvere
patch•work ['pætʃwɜːk] **1** *n* patchwork *m inv* **2** *adj quilt* patchwork *inv*
patch•y ['pætʃɪ] *adj quality* irregolare; *work*, *performance* discontinuo, disuguale
pâ•té ['pæteɪ] pâté *m inv*
pa•tent ['peɪtnt] **1** *adj* palese **2** *n for invention* brevetto *m* **3** *v/t invention* brevettare
pa•tent 'leath•er vernice *f*
pa•tent•ly ['peɪtntlɪ] *adv* (*clearly*) palesemente
pa•ter•nal [pə'tɜːnl] *adj* paterno
pa•ter•nal•ism [pə'tɜːnlɪzm] paternalismo *m*
pa•ter•nal•is•tic [pətɜːnl'ɪstɪk] *adj* paternalistico
pa•ter•ni•ty [pə'tɜːnɪtɪ] paternità *f inv*
path [pɑːθ] sentiero *m*; *fig* strada *f*
pa•thet•ic [pə'θetɪk] *adj invoking pity* patetico; F (*very bad*) penoso
path•o•log•i•cal [pæθə'lɒdʒɪkl] *adj* patologico
pa•thol•o•gy [pə'θɒlədʒɪ] patologia *f*
pa•thol•o•gist [pə'θɒlədʒɪst] patologo *m*, -a *f*
pa•tience ['peɪʃns] pazienza *f*; *Br*: *card game* solitario *m*
pa•tient ['peɪʃnt] **1** *n* paziente *m/f* **2** *adj* paziente; ***just be patient!*** abbi pazienza!
pa•tient•ly ['peɪʃntlɪ] *adv* pazientemente
pat•i•o ['pætɪəʊ] terrazza *f*
pat•ri•ot ['peɪtrɪət] patriota *m/f*
pat•ri•ot•ic [peɪtrɪ'ɒtɪk] *adj* patriottico
pa•tri•ot•ism ['peɪtrɪətɪzm] patriottismo *m*
pa•trol [pə'trəʊl] **1** *n* pattuglia *f*; ***be on patrol*** essere di pattuglia **2** *v/t* (*pret & pp* ***-led***) *streets*, *border* pattugliare
pa'trol car autopattuglia *f*
pa'trol•man agente *m/f* di pattuglia
pa•tron ['peɪtrən] *of artist* patrocinatore *m*, -trice *f*; *of charity* patrono *m*, -essa *f*; *of shop*, *cinema* cliente *m/f*
pa•tron•age ['peɪtrənɪdʒ] *of artist* patronato *m*; *of charity* patrocinio *m*
pa•tron•ize ['pætrənaɪz] *v/t shop* essere cliente di; *person* trattare con condiscendenza
pa•tron•iz•ing ['pætrənaɪzɪŋ] *adj* condiscendente
pa•tron 'saint patrono *m*, -a *f*
pat•ter ['pætə(r)] **1** *n of rain etc* picchiettio *m*; F *of salesman* imbonimento *m* **2** *v/i* picchiettare
pat•tern ['pætn] *n on wallpaper*, *fabric* motivo *m*, disegno *m*; *for knitting*, *sewing* (carta) modello *m*; *in behaviour*, *events* schema *m*
pat•terned ['pætənd] *adj* fantasia *inv*
paunch [pɔːntʃ] pancia *f*
pause [pɔːz] **1** *n* pausa *f* **2** *v/i* fermarsi **3** *v/t tape* fermare
pave [peɪv] *v/t* pavimentare; ***pave the way for*** *fig* aprire la strada a
pave•ment ['peɪvmənt] *Br* marciapiede *m*
pav•ing stone ['peɪvɪŋ] lastra *f* di pavimentazione
paw [pɔː] **1** *n of animal*, F (*hand*) zampa *f* **2** *v/t* F palpare
pawn[1] [pɔːn] *n in chess* pedone *m*; *fig* pedina *f*
pawn[2] [pɔːn] *v/t* impegnare
'pawn•bro•ker prestatore *m*, -trice *f* su pegno
'pawn•shop monte *m* di pietà
pay [peɪ] **1** *n* paga *f*; ***in the pay of*** al soldo di **2** *v/t* (*pret & pp* ***paid***) pagare; ***pay attention*** fare attenzione; ***pay s.o. a compliment*** fare un complimento a qu **3** *v/i* (*pret & pp* ***paid***) pagare; (*be profitable*) rendere; ***it doesn't pay to ...*** non conviene ...; ***pay for*** *purchase* pagare; ***you'll pay for this!*** *fig* la pagherai!
◆ **pay back** *v/t person* restituire i soldi a; *loan* restituire; (*get revenge on*) farla pagare a
◆ **pay in** *v/t to bank* versare
◆ **pay off 1** *v/t debt* estinguere; *workers* liquidare; *corrupt official* comprare **2** *v/i* (*be profitable*) dare frutti
◆ **pay up** *v/i* pagare
pay•a•ble ['peɪəbl] *adj* pagabile
'pay•day giorno *m* di paga
pay•ee [peɪ'iː] beneficiario *m*, -a *f*
pay•er ['peɪə(r)] pagatore *m*, -trice *f*

pay•ment ['peɪmənt] pagamento *m*
'**pay pack•et** busta *f* paga
'**pay phone** telefono *m* pubblico
'**pay•roll** *money* stipendi *mpl*; *employees* personale *m*; ***be on the payroll*** essere sul libro paga
'**pay•slip** busta *f* paga
PC [piː'siː] *abbr* (= ***personal computer***) PC *m inv*; (= ***politically correct***) politicamente corretto; (= ***police constable***) agente *m* di polizia
pea [piː] pisello *m*
peace [piːs] pace *f*
peace•a•ble ['piːsəbl] *adj person* pacifico
peace•ful ['piːsfʊl] *adj* tranquillo; *demonstration* pacifico
peace•ful•ly ['piːsflɪ] *adv* tranquillamente; *demonstrate* pacificamente
peach [piːʧ] pesca *f*; *tree* pesco *m*
pea•cock ['piːkɒk] pavone *m*
peak [piːk] **1** *n* vetta *f*; *fig* apice *m* **2** *v/i* raggiungere il livello massimo
'**peak con•sump•tion** periodo *m* di massimo consumo
'**peak hours** *npl* ore *fpl* di punta
peak '**view•ing hours** *npl* prima serata *f*
pea•nut ['piːnʌt] arachide *f*; ***get paid peanuts*** F essere pagati una miseria F; ***that's peanuts to him*** sono briciole per lui
pea•nut '**but•ter** burro *m* d'arachidi
pear [peə(r)] pera *f*; *tree* pero *m*
pearl [pɜːl] perla *f*
peas•ant ['peznt] contadino *m*, -a *f*
peb•ble ['pebl] ciottolo *m*
peck [pek] **1** *n* (*bite*) beccata *f*; (*kiss*) bacetto *m* **2** *v/t* (*bite*) beccare; (*kiss*) dare un bacetto a
pe•cu•li•ar [pɪ'kjuːlɪə(r)] *adj* (*strange*) strano; ***peculiar to*** (*special*) caratteristico di
pe•cu•li•ar•i•ty [pɪkjuːlɪ'ærətɪ] (*strangeness*) stranezza *f*; (*special feature*) caratteristica *f*
ped•al ['pedl] **1** *n of bike* pedale *m* **2** *v/i turn pedals* pedalare; (*cycle*) andare in bicicletta
pe•dan•tic [pɪ'dæntɪk] *adj* pedante
ped•dle ['pedl] *v/t drugs* spacciare
ped•es•tal ['pedɪstl] *for statue* piedistallo *m*
pe•des•tri•an [pɪ'destrɪən] *n* pedone *m*
pe•des•tri•an '**cros•sing** passaggio *m* pedonale
pe•des•tri•an '**pre•cinct** zona *f* pedonale
pe•di•at•ric [piːdɪ'ætrɪk] *adj* pediatrico
pe•di•a•tri•cian [piːdɪə'trɪʃn] pediatra *m/f*
pe•di•at•rics [piːdɪ'ætrɪks] pediatria *f*
ped•i•cure ['pedɪkjʊə(r)] pedicure *f inv*
ped•i•gree ['pedɪgriː] **1** *n* pedigree *m inv* **2** *adj* di razza pura
pee [piː] *v/i* F fare pipì F
peek [piːk] **1** *n* sbirciata F **2** *v/i* sbirciare F
peel [piːl] **1** *n* buccia *f*; *of citrus fruit* scorza *f* **2** *v/t fruit, vegetables* sbucciare **3** *v/i of nose, shoulders* spellarsi; *of paint* scrostarsi
◆ **peel off** **1** *v/t wrapper etc* togliere **2** *v/i of wrapper* venir via
peep [piːp] → ***peek***
peep•hole ['piːphəʊl] spioncino *m*
peer[1] [pɪə(r)] *n* (*equal*) pari *m/f inv*
peer[2] [pɪə(r)] *v/i* guardare; ***peer through the mist*** guardare attraverso la foschia; ***peer at*** scrutare
peeved [piːvd] *adj* F seccato
peg [peg] *n for coat* attaccapanni *m inv*; *for tent* picchetto *m*; ***off the peg*** prêt-à--porter
pe•jo•ra•tive [pɪ'dʒɒrətɪv] *adj* peggiorativo
pel•let ['pelɪt] pallina *f*; (*bullet*) pallino *m*
pelt [pelt] **1** *v/t*: ***pelt s.o with sth*** tirare qc a qu **2** *v/i*: ***they pelted along the road*** F sono sfrecciati per strada; ***it's pelting down*** F piove a dirotto
pel•vis ['pelvɪs] pelvi *f inv*
pen[1] [pen] *n* penna *f*
pen[2] [pen] (*enclosure*) recinto *m*
pe•nal•ize ['piːnəlaɪz] *v/t* penalizzare
pen•al•ty ['penəltɪ] ammenda *f*; *in soccer* rigore *m*; *in rugby* punizione *f*; ***take the penalty*** battere il rigore / la punizione
'**pen•al•ty ar•e•a** SP area *f* di rigore
'**pen•al•ty clause** LAW penale *f*
'**pen•al•ty kick** *in soccer* calcio *m* di rigore; *in rugby* calcio *m* di punizione
pen•al•ty '**shoot-out** rigori *mpl*
'**pen•al•ty spot** dischetto *m* di rigore
pence [pens] *npl* penny *m inv*
pen•cil ['pensɪl] matita *f*
pen•cil sharp•en•er temperamatite *m inv*
pen•dant ['pendənt] *necklace* pendaglio *m*
pend•ing ['pendɪŋ] **1** *prep* in attesa di **2** *adj*: ***be pending*** essere in sospeso
pen•e•trate ['penɪtreɪt] *v/t* penetrare in
pen•e•trat•ing ['penɪtreɪtɪŋ] *adj stare, scream* penetrante; *analysis* perspicace
pen•e•tra•tion [penɪ'treɪʃn] penetrazione *f*
'**pen friend** amico *m*, -a *f* di penna
pen•guin ['peŋgwɪn] pinguino *m*
pen•i•cil•lin [penɪ'sɪlɪn] penicillina *f*
pe•nin•su•la [pə'nɪnsjʊlə] penisola *f*
pe•nis ['piːnɪs] pene *m*
pen•i•tence ['penɪtəns] penitenza *f*

P

pen•i•tent ['penɪtənt] *adj* pentito
pen•knife ['pennaɪf] temperino *m*
'pen name pseudonimo *m*
pen•nant ['penənt] gagliardetto *m*
pen•ni•less ['penɪlɪs] *adj* al verde
pen•ny ['penɪ] penny *m inv*
'pen pal amico *m*, -a *f* di penna
pen•sion ['penʃn] pensione *f*
◆ **pension off** *v/t* mandare in pensione
pen•sion•er ['penʃnə(r)] pensionato *m*, -a *f*
'pen•sion fund fondo *m* pensioni
'pen•sion scheme schema *m* pensionistico
pen•sive ['pensɪv] *adj* pensieroso
Pen•ta•gon ['pentəgɒn]: ***the Pentagon*** il Pentagono
pen•tath•lon [pen'tæθlən] pentathlon *m inv*
Pen•te•cost ['pentɪkɒst] Pentecoste *f*
pent•house ['penthaʊs] attico *m*
pent-up ['pentʌp] *adj* represso
pe•nul•ti•mate [pe'nʌltɪmət] *adj* penultimo
peo•ple ['pi:pl] *npl* gente *f*, persone *fpl*; (*nsg*: *race*, *tribe*) popolazione *f*; ***the people*** (*the citizens*) il popolo; ***the American people*** gli americani; ***people say ...*** si dice che ...
pep•per ['pepə(r)] *spice* pepe *m*; *vegetable* peperone *m*
pep•per•mint *sweet* mentina *f*; *flavouring* menta *f*
pep talk ['peptɔ:k] discorso *m* d'incoraggiamento
per [pɜ:(r)] *prep* a; ***100 km per hour*** 100 km all'ora; ***£50 per night*** 50 sterline a notte; ***per annum*** all'anno
per•ceive [pə'si:v] *v/t with senses* percepire; (*view*, *interpret*) interpretare
per•cent [pə'sent] per cento
per•cen•tage [pə'sentɪdʒ] percentuale *f*
per•cep•ti•ble [pə'septəbl] *adj* percettibile
per•cep•ti•bly [pə'septəblɪ] *adv* percettibilmente
per•cep•tion [pə'sepʃn] *through senses* percezione *f*; (*insight*) sensibilità *f inv*
per•cep•tive [pə'septɪv] *adj person*, *remark* perspicace
perch [pɜ:ʧ] **1** *n for bird* posatoio *m* **2** *v/i of bird* posarsi; *of person* appollaiarsi
per•co•late ['pɜ:kəleɪt] *v/i of coffee* filtrare
per•co•la•tor ['pɜ:kəleɪtə(r)] caffettiera *f* a filtro
per•cus•sion [pə'kʌʃn] percussioni *fpl*
per'cus•sion in•stru•ment strumento *m* a percussione

P

pe•ren•ni•al [pə'renɪəl] *n* BOT pianta *f* perenne
per•fect ['pɜ:fɪkt] **1** *n* GRAM passato *m* prossimo **2** *adj* perfetto **3** *v/t* [pə'fekt] perfezionare
per•fec•tion [pə'fekʃn] perfezione *f*; ***to perfection*** alla perfezione
per•fec•tion•ist [pə'fekʃnɪst] perfezionista *m/f*
per•fect•ly ['pɜ:fɪktlɪ] *adv* perfettamente
per•fo•rat•ed ['pɜ:fəreɪtɪd] *adj line* perforato
per•fo•ra•tions [pɜ:fə'reɪʃnz] *npl* linea *fsg* perforata
per•form [pə'fɔ:m] **1** *v/t* (*carry out*) eseguire; *of actors* rappresentare; *of musician* eseguire **2** *v/i of actor*, *musician*, *dancer* esibirsi; *of actor* recitare; ***the car performs well*** la macchina dà ottime prestazioni
per•form•ance [pə'fɔ:məns] *by actor* rappresentazione *f*; *by musician* esecuzione *f*; (*show*) spettacolo *m*; *of employee*, *company etc* rendimento *m*; *of machine* prestazioni *fpl*
per'form•ance car auto *f inv* di alte prestazioni
per•form•er [pə'fɔ:mə(r)] artista *m/f*
per•fume ['pɜ:fju:m] profumo *m*
per•func•to•ry [pə'fʌŋktərɪ] *adj* superficiale
per•haps [pə'hæps] *adv* forse
per•il ['perəl] pericolo *m*
per•il•ous ['perələs] *adj* pericoloso
pe•rim•e•ter [pə'rɪmɪtə(r)] perimetro *m*
pe'rim•e•ter fence recinzione *f*
pe•ri•od ['pɪərɪəd] *time* periodo *m*; (*menstruation*) mestruazioni *fpl*; ***I don't want to, period!*** *Am* non voglio, punto e basta!
pe•ri•od•ic [pɪərɪ'ɒdɪk] *adj* periodico
pe•ri•od•i•cal [pɪərɪ'ɒdɪkl] *n* periodico *m*
pe•ri•od•i•cal•ly [pɪərɪ'ɒdɪklɪ] *adv* periodicamente
pe•riph•e•ral [pə'rɪfərəl] **1** *adj not crucial* marginale **2** *n* COMPUT periferica *f*
pe•riph•e•ry [pə'rɪfərɪ] periferia *f*
per•ish ['perɪʃ] *v/i of rubber* deteriorarsi; *of person* perire
per•ish•a•ble ['perɪʃəbl] *adj food* deteriorabile
per•ish•ing ['perɪʃɪŋ] *adj* F: ***it's perishing*** fa un freddo da cane F
per•jure ['pɜ:dʒə(r)] *v/r*: ***perjure o.s.*** spergiurare
per•ju•ry ['pɜ:dʒərɪ] falso giuramento *m*
perk [pɜ:k] *n of job* vantaggio *m*
◆ **perk up** **1** *v/t* F tirare su di morale **2** *v/i* F animarsi

perk•y ['pɜːkɪ] *adj* F (*cheerful*) allegro
perm [pɜːm] **1** *n* permanente *f* **2** *v/t* fare la permanente a
per•ma•nent ['pɜːmənənt] *adj* permanente; *job*, *address* fisso
per•ma•nent•ly ['pɜːmənəntlɪ] *adv* permanentemente
per•me•a•ble ['pɜːmɪəbl] *adj* permeabile
per•me•ate ['pɜːmɪeɪt] *v/t* permeare
per•mis•si•ble [pə'mɪsəbl] *adj* permesso, ammissibile
per•mis•sion [pə'mɪʃn] permesso *m*
per•mis•sive [pə'mɪsɪv] *adj* permissivo
per•mis•sive so'c•i•ety società *f inv* permissiva
per•mit ['pɜːmɪt] **1** *n* permesso *m* **2** *v/t* [pə'mɪt] (*pret & pp* **-ted**) permettere; ***permit s.o. to do sth*** permettere a qu di fare qc
per•pen•dic•u•lar [pɜːpən'dɪkjʊlə(r)] *adj* perpendicolare
per•pet•u•al *adj* perenne
per•pet•u•al•ly [pə'petjʊəlɪ] *adv* perennemente
per•pet•u•ate [pə'petjʊeɪt] *v/t* perpetuare
per•plex [pə'pleks] *v/t* lasciare perplesso
per•plexed [pə'plekst] *adj* perplesso
per•plex•i•ty [pə'pleksɪtɪ] perplessità *f inv*
per•se•cute ['pɜːsɪkjuːt] *v/t* perseguitare
per•se•cu•tion [pɜːsɪ'kjuːʃn] persecuzione *f*
per•se•cu•tor [pɜːsɪ'kjuːtə(r)] persecutore *m*, -trice *f*
per•se•ver•ance [pɜːsɪ'vɪərəns] perseveranza *f*
per•se•vere [pɜːsɪ'vɪə(r)] *v/i* perseverare
per•sist [pə'sɪst] *v/i* persistere; ***persist in*** persistere in
per•sis•tence [pə'sɪstəns] (*perseverance*) perseveranza *f*; (*continuation*) persistere *m*
per•sis•tent [pə'sɪstənt] *adj person*, *questions* insistente; *rain*, *unemployment etc* continuo
per•sis•tent•ly [pə'sɪstəntlɪ] *adv* (*continually*) continuamente
per•son ['pɜːsn] persona *f*; ***in person*** di persona
per•son•al ['pɜːsənl] *adj* personale; ***don't make personal remarks*** non fare commenti personali
per•son•al as'sist•ant assistente *m/f* personale
'per•son•al col•umn annunci *mpl* personali
per•son•al com'put•er personal computer *m inv*
per•son•al 'hy•giene igiene *f* personale
per•son•al•i•ty [pɜːsə'nælətɪ] personalità *f inv*
per•son•al•ly ['pɜːsənəlɪ] *adv* personalmente; ***don't take it personally*** non offenderti
per•son•al 'or•gan•iz•er agenda *f* elettronica
per•son•al 'pro•noun pronome *m* personale
per•son•al 'ster•e•o Walkman® *m inv*
per•son•i•fy [pə'sɒnɪfaɪ] *v/t* (*pret & pp* **-ied**) *of person* personificare
per•son•nel [pɜːsə'nel] *employees* personale *m*; *department* ufficio *m* del personale
per•son'nel man•a•ger direttore *m*, -trice *f* del personale
per•spec•tive [pə'spektɪv] PAINT prospettiva *f*; ***get sth into perspective*** vedere qc nella giusta prospettiva
per•spi•ra•tion [pɜːspɪ'reɪʃn] traspirazione *f*
per•spire [pə'spaɪə(r)] *v/i* sudare
per•suade [pə'sweɪd] *v/t* persuadere, convincere; ***persuade s.o. to do sth*** persuadere *o* convincere qu a fare qc
per•sua•sion [pə'sweɪʒn] persuasione *f*
per•sua•sive [pə'sweɪsɪv] *adj* persuasivo
per•ti•nent ['pɜːtɪnənt] *adj fml* pertinente
per•turb [pə'tɜːb] *v/t* inquietare
per•turb•ing [pə'tɜːbɪŋ] *adj* inquietante
pe•ruse [pə'ruːz] *v/t fml* leggere
per•va•sive [pə'veɪsɪv] *adj influence*, *ideas* diffuso
per•verse [pə'vɜːs] *adj* ostinato, irragionevole; *sexually* pervertito; ***be perverse*** (*awkward*) essere un bastian contrario; ***take a perverse delight in doing sth*** provare un piacere perverso a fare qc
per•ver•sion [pə'vɜːʃn] *sexual* perversione *f*
per•vert ['pɜːvɜːt] *n sexual* pervertito *m*, -a *f*
pes•si•mis•m ['pesɪmɪzm] pessimismo *m*
pes•si•mist ['pesɪmɪst] pessimista *m/f*
pes•si•mist•ic [pesɪ'mɪstɪk] *adj attitude*, *view* pessimistico; *person* pessimista
pest [pest] animale / insetto *m* nocivo; F *person* peste *f*
pes•ter ['pestə(r)] *v/t* assillare; ***pester s.o. to do sth*** assillare qu perché faccia qc
pes•ti•cide ['pestɪsaɪd] pesticida *m*
pet [pet] **1** *n animal* animale *m* domestico; (*favourite*) favorito *m*, -a *f* **2** *adj* preferito **3** *v/t* (*pret & pp* **-ted**) *animal* accarezzare **4** *v/i* (*pret & pp* **-ted**) *of couple* pomiciare F
pet•al ['petl] petalo *m*

◆ **pe•ter out** ['piːtə(r)] *v/i of rebellion, rain* cessare; *of path* finire
pe•tite [pə'tiːt] *adj* minuta
pe•ti•tion [pə'tɪʃn] *n* petizione *f*
'**pet name** nomignolo *m*
pet•ri•fied ['petrɪfaɪd] *adj* terrorizzato
pet•ri•fy ['petrɪfaɪ] *v/t* (*pret & pp* **-ied**) terrorizzare
pet•ro•chem•i•cal [petrəʊ'kemɪkl] *adj* petrolchimico
pet•rol ['petrl] benzina *f*
pe•tro•le•um [pɪ'trəʊlɪəm] petrolio *m*
'**pet•rol gauge** spia *f* della benzina
'**pet•rol pump** pompa *f* della benzina
'**pet•rol sta•tion** stazione *f* di servizio
pet•ting ['petɪŋ] petting *m inv*
pet•ty ['petɪ] *adj person, behaviour* meschino; *details, problem* insignificante
pet•ty 'cash piccola cassa *f*
pet•u•lant ['petjʊlənt] *adj* petulante
pew [pjuː] banco *m* (di chiesa)
pew•ter ['pjuːtə(r)] peltro *m*
phar•ma•ceu•ti•cal [fɑːmə'sjuːtɪkl] *adj* farmaceutico
phar•ma•ceu•ti•cals [fɑːmə'sjuːtɪklz] *npl* farmaceutici *mpl*
phar•ma•cist ['fɑːməsɪst] farmacista *m/f*
phar•ma•cy ['fɑːməsɪ] farmacia *f*
phase [feɪz] fase *f*
◆ **phase in** *v/t* introdurre gradualmente
◆ **phase out** *v/t* eliminare gradualmente
PhD [piːeɪtʃ'diː] *abbr* (= ***Doctor of Philosophy***) *dottorato m di ricerca*
phe•nom•e•nal [fɪ'nɒmɪnl] *adj* fenomenale
phe•nom•e•nal•ly [fɪ'nɒmɪnlɪ] *adv* straordinariamente
phe•nom•e•non [fɪ'nɒmɪnɒn] fenomeno *m*
phil•an•throp•ic [fɪlən'θrɒpɪk] *adj* filantropico
phi•lan•thro•pist [fɪ'lænθrəpɪst] filantropo *m*, -a *f*
phi•lan•thro•py [fɪ'lænθrəpɪ] filantropia *f*
Phil•ip•pines ['fɪlɪpiːnz] *npl*: ***the Philippines*** le Filippine *fpl*
phil•is•tine ['fɪlɪstaɪn] *n* ignorante *m/f*
phi•los•o•pher [fɪ'lɒsəfə(r)] filosofo *m*, -a *f*
phil•o•soph•i•cal [fɪlə'sɒfɪkl] *adj* filosofico
phi•los•o•phy [fɪ'lɒsəfɪ] filosofia *f*
pho•bi•a ['fəʊbɪə] fobia *f*
phone [fəʊn] **1** *n* telefono *m*; ***be on the phone*** *have one* avere il telefono; *be talking* essere al telefono **2** *v/t* telefonare a **3** *v/i* telefonare
'**phone book** guida *f* telefonica, elenco telefonico *m*
'**phone booth** cabina *f* telefonica
'**phone box** cabina *f* telefonica
'**phone call** telefonata *f*
'**phone card** scheda *f* telefonica
'**phone num•ber** numero *m* di telefono
pho•net•ics [fə'netɪks] fonetica *f*
pho•n(e)y ['fəʊnɪ] *adj* F falso
pho•to ['fəʊtəʊ] *n* foto *f*
'**pho•to al•bum** album *m* fotografico
'**pho•to•cop•i•er** fotocopiatrice *f*
'**pho•to•cop•y** **1** *n* fotocopia *f* **2** *v/t* (*pret & pp* **-ied**) fotocopiare
pho•to•gen•ic [fəʊtəʊ'dʒenɪk] *adj* fotogenico
pho•to•graph ['fəʊtəgrɑːf] **1** *n* fotografia *f* **2** *v/t* fotografare
pho•tog•ra•pher [fə'tɒgrəfə(r)] fotografo *m*, -a *f*
pho•tog•ra•phy [fə'tɒgrəfɪ] fotografia *f*
phrase [freɪz] **1** *n* frase *f* **2** *v/t* esprimere
'**phrase•book** vocabolarietto *m* di frasi utili
phys•i•cal ['fɪzɪkl] **1** *adj* fisico **2** *n* MED visita *f* medica
phys•i•cal 'hand•i•cap *adj* handicap *m inv* fisico
phys•i•cal•ly ['fɪzɪklɪ] *adv* fisicamente
phys•i•cal•ly 'hand•i•cap•ped *adj*: ***be physically handicapped*** essere portatore *m*, -trice *f* di handicap fisico
phy•si•cian [fɪ'zɪʃn] medico *m*
phys•i•cist ['fɪzɪsɪst] fisico *m*, -a *f*
phys•ics ['fɪzɪks] fisica *f*
phys•i•o•ther•a•pist [fɪzɪəʊ'θerəpɪst] fisioterapeuta *m/f*
phys•i•o•ther•a•py [fɪzɪəʊ'θerəpɪ] fisioterapia *f*
phy•sique [fɪ'ziːk] fisico *m*
pi•a•nist ['pɪənɪst] pianista *m/f*
pi•an•o [pɪ'ænəʊ] piano *m*
pick [pɪk] **1** *n*: ***take your pick*** scegli quello che vuoi **2** *v/t* (*choose*) scegliere; *flowers, fruit* raccogliere; ***pick one's nose*** mettersi le dita nel naso **3** *v/i*: ***pick and choose*** fare i difficili
◆ **pick at** *v/t*: ***pick at one's food*** mangiucchiare poco
◆ **pick on** *v/t treat unfairly* prendersela con; (*select*) scegliere
◆ **pick out** *v/t* (*identify*) riconoscere
◆ **pick up** **1** *v/t* prendere; *phone* sollevare; *baby* prendere in braccio; *from ground* raccogliere; (*collect*) andare / venire a prendere; *information* raccogliere; *in car* far salire; *man, woman* rimorchiare F; *language, skill* imparare; *habit, illness* prendere; (*buy*) trovare; *criminal* arrestare; ***pick up the tab*** F pagare (il conto) **2** *v/i* (*improve*) migliorare

P

pick•et ['pɪkɪt] **1** *n of strikers* picchetto *m* **2** *v/t* picchettare
'**pick•et line** cordone *m* degli scioperanti
pick•le ['pɪkl] *v/t* conservare sott'aceto
pick•les ['pɪklz] *npl* sottaceti *mpl*
'**pick•pock•et** borseggiatore *m*, -trice *f*
pick•y ['pɪkɪ] *adj* F difficile (da accontentare)
pic•nic ['pɪknɪk] **1** *n* picnic *m inv* **2** *v/i* (*pret & pp* ***-ked***) fare un picnic
pic•ture ['pɪktʃə(r)] **1** *n photo* foto *f*; *painting* quadro *m*; *illustration* figura *f*; *film* film *m inv*; ***put / keep s.o. in the picture*** mettere / tenere al corrente qu **2** *v/t* immaginare
'**pic•ture book** libro *m* illustrato
pic•ture '**post•card** cartolina *f* illustrata
pic•tures ['pɪktʃəz] *npl* cinema *m*
pic•tur•esque [pɪktʃə'resk] *adj* pittoresco
pie [paɪ] *sweet* torta *f*; *savoury* pasticcio *m*
piece [piːs] pezzo *m*; ***a piece of pie / bread*** una fetta di torta / pane; ***a piece of advice*** un consiglio; ***go to pieces*** crollare; ***take to pieces*** smontare
◆ **piece together** *v/t broken plate* rimettere insieme; *facts*, *evidence* ricostruire
piece•meal ['piːsmiːl] *adv* poco alla volta
piece•work ['piːswɜːk] *n* lavoro *m* a cottimo
pier [pɪə(r)] *at seaside* pontile *m*
pierce [pɪəs] *v/t* (*penetrate*) trapassare; *ears* farsi i buchi in
pierc•ing ['pɪəsɪŋ] *noise* lacerante; *eyes* penetrante; *wind* pungente
pig [pɪg] *also fig* maiale *m*
pi•geon ['pɪdʒɪn] piccione *m*
'**pi•geon•hole 1** *n* casella *f* **2** *v/t person* etichettare; *proposal* archiviare
pig•gy•bank ['pɪgɪbæŋk] salvadanaio *m*
pig•head•ed [pɪg'hedɪd] *adj* testardo
'**pig•skin** pelle *f* di cinghiale
'**pig•sty** *also fig* porcile *m*
'**pig•tail** *plaited* treccina *f*
pile [paɪl] mucchio *m*; F ***a pile of work*** un sacco di lavoro F
◆ **pile up 1** *v/i of work*, *bills* accumularsi **2** *v/t* ammucchiare
piles [paɪlz] *nsg* MED emorroidi *fpl*
pile-up ['paɪlʌp] MOT tamponamento *m* a catena
pil•fer•ing ['pɪlfərɪŋ] piccoli furti *mpl*
pil•grim ['pɪlgrɪm] pellegrino *m*, -a *f*
pil•grim•age ['pɪlgrɪmɪdʒ] pellegrinaggio *m*
pill [pɪl] pastiglia *f*; ***the pill*** la pillola; ***be on the pill*** prendere la pillola
pil•lar ['pɪlə(r)] colonna *f*
'**pil•lar box** buca *f* delle lettere (a colonnina)
pil•lion ['pɪljən] *of motor bike* sellino *m* posteriore
pil•low ['pɪləʊ] *n* guanciale *m*
'**pill•ow•case**, '**pil•low•slip** federa *f*
pi•lot ['paɪlət] **1** *n of aeroplane* pilota *m/f* **2** *v/t aeroplane* pilotare
'**pi•lot plant** stabilimento *m* pilota
'**pi•lot scheme** progetto *m* pilota
pimp [pɪmp] *n* ruffiano *m*
pim•ple ['pɪmpl] brufolo *m*
pin [pɪn] **1** *n for sewing* spillo *m*; *in bowling* birillo *m*; (*badge*) spilla *f*; ELEC spinotto *m* **2** *v/t* (*pret & pp* ***-ned***) (*hold down*) immobilizzare; (*attach*) attaccare; *on lapel* appuntare
◆ **pin down** *v/t*: ***pin s.o. down to a date*** far fissare una data a qu
◆ **pin up** *v/t notice* appuntare
PIN [pɪn] *abbr* (= ***personal identification number***) numero *m* di codice segreto
pin•cers ['pɪnsəz] *npl tool* tenaglie *fpl*; *of crab* chele *fpl*
pinch [pɪntʃ] **1** *n* pizzico *m*; ***at a pinch*** al massimo **2** *v/t* pizzicare **3** *v/i of shoes* stringere
pine[1] [paɪn] *n* pino *m*; ***pine furniture*** mobili *mpl* di pino
pine[2] [paɪn] *v/i*: ***pine for*** soffrire per la mancanza di
pine•ap•ple ['paɪnæpl] ananas *m inv*
ping [pɪŋ] **1** *n* suono *m* metallico **2** *v/i* fare un suono metallico
ping-pong ['pɪngpɒng] ping-pong *m inv*
pink [pɪŋk] *adj* rosa *inv*
pin•na•cle ['pɪnəkl] *fig* apice *m*
'**pin•point** *v/t* indicare con esattezza
pins and '**nee•dles** *npl* formicolio *m*
'**pin•stripe** *adj* gessato
pint [paɪnt] pinta *f*
'**pin-up (girl)** pin-up *f inv*
pi•o•neer [paɪə'nɪə(r)] **1** *n fig* pioniere *m*, -a *f* **2** *v/t* essere il / la pioniere di
pi•o•neer•ing [paɪə'nɪərɪŋ] *adj work* pionieristico
pi•ous ['paɪəs] *adj* pio
pip [pɪp] *n of fruit* seme *m*
pipe [paɪp] **1** *n for smoking* pipa *f*; *for water*, *gas*, *sewage* tubo *m* **2** *v/t* trasportare con condutture
◆ **pipe down** *v/i* F far silenzio
piped mu•sic [paɪpt'mjuːzɪk] musica *f* di sottofondo
pipe•line conduttura *f*; ***in the pipeline*** *fig* in arrivo
pip•ing hot [paɪpɪŋ'hɒt] *adj* caldissimo
pi•rate ['paɪərət] *v/t software* piratare
Pis•ces ['paɪsiːz] ASTR Pesci *m/f inv*
piss [pɪs] **1** *v/i* P (*urinate*) pisciare P **2** *n* (*urine*) piscio *m* P; ***take the piss out***

of s.o. P prendere qu per il culo P
◆ **piss off** *v/i* P sparire; ***piss off!*** levati dalle palle! P
pissed [pɪst] *adj* P (*drunk*) sbronzo F; *Am* (*annoyed*) seccato
pis•tol ['pɪstl] pistola *f*
pis•ton ['pɪstən] pistone *m*
pit [pɪt] *n* (*hole*) buca *f*; (*coal mine*) miniera *f*
pitch[1] [pɪtʃ] *n* MUS intonazione *f*
pitch[2] [pɪtʃ] *v/t tent* piantare; *ball* lanciare
'**pitch black** *adj* buio pesto
pitch•er ['pɪtʃə(r)] *container* brocca *f*
pit•e•ous ['pɪtɪəs] *adj* pietoso
pit•fall ['pɪtfɔːl] tranello *m*
pith [pɪθ] *of citrus fruit* parte *f* bianca della scorza
pit•i•ful ['pɪtɪfʊl] *adj sight* pietoso; *excuse, attempt* penoso
pit•i•less ['pɪtɪləs] *adj* spietato
pits [pɪts] *npl in motor racing* box *m inv*
'**pit stop** *in motor racing* sosta *f* ai box
pit•tance ['pɪtns] miseria *f*
pit•y ['pɪtɪ] **1** *n* pietà *f inv*; ***it's a pity that*** è un peccato che; ***what a pity!*** che peccato!; ***take pity on*** avere pietà di **2** *v/t* (*pret & pp* ***-ied***) *person* avere pietà di
piv•ot ['pɪvət] *v/i* ruotare
piz•za ['piːtsə] pizza *f*
plac•ard ['plækɑːd] cartello *m*
place [pleɪs] **1** *n* posto *m*; *flat, house* casa *f*; ***I've lost my place*** *in book* ho perso il segno; ***at my / his place*** a casa mia / sua; ***in place of*** invece di; ***feel out of place*** sentirsi fuori posto; ***take place*** aver luogo; ***in the first place*** (*firstly*) in primo luogo **2** *v/t* (*put*) piazzare; ***I can't quite place you*** non mi ricordo dove ci siamo concosciuti; ***place an order*** fare un'ordinazione
'**place mat** tovaglietta *f* all'americana
plac•id ['plæsɪd] *adj* placido
pla•gia•rism ['pleɪdʒərɪzm] plagio *m*
pla•gia•rize ['pleɪdʒəraɪz] *v/t* plagiare
plague [pleɪg] **1** *n* peste *f* **2** *v/t* (*bother*) tormentare
plain[1] [pleɪn] *n* pianura *f*
plain[2] [pleɪn] **1** *adj* (*clear, obvious*) chiaro; *not fancy* semplice; *not pretty* scialbo; *not patterned* in tinta unita; (*blunt*) franco; ***plain chocolate*** cioccolato *m* fondente **2** *adv* semplicemente; ***it's plain crazy*** è semplicemente matto
'**plain-clothes**: ***in plain-clothes*** in borghese
plain•ly ['pleɪnlɪ] *adv* (*clearly*) chiaramente; (*bluntly*) francamente; (*simply*) semplicemente
plain-'spo•ken *adj* franco
plain•tiff ['pleɪntɪf] LAW attore *m*, -trice *f*
plain•tive ['pleɪntɪv] *adj* lamentoso
plait [plæt] **1** *n in hair* treccia *f* **2** *v/t hair* intrecciare
plan [plæn] **1** *n* (*project, intention*) piano *m*; (*drawing*) progetto *m* **2** *v/t* (*pret & pp* ***-ned***) (*prepare*) organizzare; (*design*) progettare; ***plan to do, plan on doing*** avere in programma di **3** *v/i* (*pret & pp* ***-ned***) pianificare
plane[1] [pleɪn] *n* (*aeroplane*) aereo *m*
plane[2] [pleɪn] *tool* pialla *f*
plan•et ['plænɪt] pianeta *m*
plank [plæŋk] *of wood* asse *f*; *fig*: *of policy* punto *m*
plan•ning ['plænɪŋ] pianificazione *f*; ***at the planning stage*** allo stadio di progettazione
plant[1] [plɑːnt] **1** *n* pianta *f* **2** *v/t* piantare
plant[2] [plɑːnt] *n* (*factory*) stabilimento *m*; (*equipment*) impianto *m*
plan•ta•tion [plæn'teɪʃn] piantagione *f*
plaque [plæk] *on wall, teeth* placca *f*
plas•ter ['plɑːstə(r)] **1** *n on wall, ceiling* intonaco *m* **2** *v/t wall, ceiling* ***be plastered with*** essere ricoperto di
plas•ter cast ingessatura *f*
plas•tic ['plæstɪk] **1** *n* plastica *f*; F (*money*) carte *fpl* di credito **2** *adj made of plastic* di plastica
plas•tic 'bag sacchetto *m* di plastica
'**plas•tic mon•ey** carte *fpl* di credito
plas•tic 'sur•geon chirurgo *m* plastico
plas•tic 'sur•ge•ry chirurgia *f* plastica
plate [pleɪt] *n for food* piatto *m*; *sheet of metal* lastra *f*
pla•teau ['plætəʊ] altopiano *m*
plat•form ['plætfɔːm] (*stage*) palco *m*; *of railway station* binario *m*; *fig*: *political* piattaforma *f*
plat•i•num ['plætɪnəm] **1** *n* platino *m* **2** *adj* di platino
plat•i•tude ['plætɪtjuːd] banalità *f inv*
pla•ton•ic [plə'tɒnɪk] *adj relationship* platonico
pla•toon [plə'tuːn] *of soldiers* plotone *m*
plat•ter ['plætə(r)] *for meat, fish* vassoio *m*
plau•si•ble ['plɔːzəbl] *adj* plausibile
play [pleɪ] **1** *n in theatre, on TV* commedia *f*; *of children*, TECH, SP gioco *m* **2** *v/i of children*, SP giocare; *of musician* suonare **3** *v/t* MUS suonare; *game* giocare a; *opponent* giocare contro; (*perform*: *Macbeth etc*) rappresentare; *particular role* interpretare; ***play a joke on*** fare uno scherzo a
◆ **play around** *v/i* F (*be unfaithful*): ***his wife's been playing around*** sua moglie

P

lo ha tradito; ***her husband was playing around with his secretary*** suo marito aveva una relazione con la segretaria
◆ **play down** *v/t* minimizzare
◆ **play up** *v/i of machine* dare noie; *of child* fare i capricci; *of tooth, bad back etc* fare male
play•act ['pleɪækt] *v/i* (*pretend*) fare la commedia
play•back ['pleɪbæk] playback *m inv*
play•boy ['pleɪbɔɪ] playboy *m inv*
play•er ['pleɪə(r)] SP giocatore *m*, -trice *f*; *musician* musicista *m/f*; *actor* attore *m*, -trice *f*
play•ful ['pleɪfʊl] *adj punch, mood* scherzoso; *puppy* giocherellone
play•ground ['pleɪgraʊnd] *in school* cortile *m* per la ricreazione; *in park* parco *m* giochi
'**play•group** asilo *m*
play•ing card ['pleɪɪŋkɑːd] carta *f* da gioco
play•ing field ['pleɪɪŋfiːld] campo *m* sportivo
play•mate ['pleɪmeɪt] compagno *m*, -a *f* di gioco
play•wright ['pleɪraɪt] commediografo *m*, -a *f*
plc [piːel'siː] *abbr* (= ***public limited company***) società *f inv* a responsabilità limitata quotata in borsa
plea [pliː] **1** *n* appello *m*
plead 2 *v/i*: ***plead for*** supplicare; ***plead guilty / not guilty*** dichiararsi colpevole / innocente; ***plead with*** supplicare
pleas•ant ['pleznt] *adj* piacevole
please [pliːz] **1** *adv* per favore; ***more tea? – yes, please*** ancora tè? - sì, grazie; ***please do*** fai pure, prego **2** *v/t* far piacere a; ***please yourself*** fai come ti pare
pleased [pliːzd] *adj* contento; ***pleased to meet you*** piacere!
pleas•ing ['pliːzɪŋ] *adj* piacevole
pleas•ure ['pleʒə(r)] (*happiness, satisfaction*) contentezza *f*; (*as opposed to work*) piacere *m*; (*delight*) gioia *f*; ***it's a pleasure*** (*you're welcome*) è un piacere; ***with pleasure*** con vero piacere
pleat [pliːt] *n in skirt* piega *f*
pleat•ed skirt ['pliːtɪd] gonna *f* a pieghe
pledge [pledʒ] **1** *n* (*promise*) promessa *f* **2** *v/t* (*promise*) promettere
plen•ti•ful ['plentɪfʊl] *adj* abbondante
plen•ty ['plentɪ] (*abundance*) abbondanza *f*; ***plenty of*** molto; ***that's plenty*** basta così; ***there's plenty for everyone*** ce n'è per tutti
pli•a•ble *adj* flessibile
pli•ers *npl* pinze *fpl*; ***a pair of pliers*** un paio di pinze
plight [plaɪt] situazione *f* critica
plod [plɒd] *v/i* (*pret & pp* ***-ded***) *walk* trascinarsi
◆ **plod on** *v/i with a job* sgobbare
plod•der ['plɒdə(r)] *at work, school* sgobbone *m*, -a *f*
plot[1] [plɒt] *n land* appezzamento *m*
plot[2] [plɒt] **1** *n* (*conspiracy*) complotto *m*; *of novel* trama *f* **2** *v/t & v/i* (*pret & pp* ***-ted***) complottare
plot•ter ['plɒtə(r)] cospiratore *m*, -trice *f*; COMPUT plotter *m inv*
plough, plow *Am* [plaʊ] **1** *n* aratro *m* **2** *v/t & v/i* arare
◆ **plough back** *v/t profits* reinvestire
pluck [plʌk] *v/t eyebrows* pinzare; *chicken* spennare
◆ **pluck up** *v/t*: ***pluck up courage*** trovare il coraggio
plug [plʌg] **1** *n for sink, bath* tappo *m*; *electrical* spina *f*; (*spark plug*) candela *f*; *for new book etc* pubblicità *f inv* **2** *v/t* (*pret & pp* ***-ged***) *hole* tappare; *new book etc* fare pubblicità a
◆ **plug away** *v/i* F sgobbare
◆ **plug in** *v/t* attaccare (alla presa)
plum [plʌm] **1** *n* susina *f* **2** *adj*: ***plum job*** F un lavoro favoloso
plum•age ['pluːmɪdʒ] piumaggio *m*
plumb [plʌm] *adj* a piombo
◆ **plumb in** *v/t washing machine* collegare all'impianto idraulico
plumb•er ['plʌmə(r)] idraulico *m*
plumb•ing ['plʌmɪŋ] *pipes* impianto *m* idraulico
plume [pluːm] *n* piuma *f*
plum•met ['plʌmɪt] *v/i of aeroplane* precipitare; *of share prices* crollare
plump [plʌmp] *adj person, chicken* in carne; *hands, feet, face* paffuto
◆ **plump for** *v/t* scegliere
plunge [plʌndʒ] **1** *n* caduta *f*; *in prices* crollo *m*; ***take the plunge*** fare il gran passo **2** *v/i* precipitare; *of prices* crollare **3** *v/t knife* conficcare; *tomatoes* immergere; ***the city was plunged into darkness*** la città fu immersa nel buio; ***the news plunged him into despair*** la notizia lo gettò nella disperazione
plung•ing ['plʌndʒɪŋ] *adj neckline* profondo
plu•per•fect ['pluːpɜːfɪkt] *n* GRAM piuccheperfetto *m*
plu•ral ['plʊərəl] **1** *n* plurale *m* **2** *adj* plurale
plus [plʌs] **1** *prep* più **2** *adj*: ***£500 plus*** oltre 500 sterline **3** *n symbol* più *m inv*; (*advantage*) vantaggio *m* **4** *conj* (*moreo-*

ver, in addition) per di più
plush [plʌʃ] *adj* di lusso
'plus sign segno *m* più
ply•wood ['plaɪwʊd] compensato *m*
PM [piː'em] *abbr* (= ***Prime Minister***) primo ministro *m*
p.m. [piː'em] *abbr* (= ***post meridiem***): ***at 2 p.m.*** alle 2 del pomeriggio; ***at 10.30 p.m.*** alle 10.30 di sera
pneu•mat•ic [njuː'mætɪk] *adj* pneumatico
pneu•mat•ic 'drill martello *m* pneumatico
pneu•mo•ni•a [njuː'məʊnɪə] polmonite *f*
poach[1] [pəʊtʃ] *v/t cook* bollire; *egg* fare in camicia
poach[2] [pəʊtʃ] **1** *v/i for game* cacciare di frodo; *for fish* pescare di frodo **2** *v/t* cacciare / pescare di frodo
poached egg [pəʊtʃt'eg] uovo *m* in camicia
poach•er ['pəʊtʃə(r)] *of salmon, game* cacciatore / pescatore *m* di frodo
P.O. Box [piː'əʊbɒks] casella *f* postale
pock•et ['pɒkɪt] **1** *n* tasca *f*; ***line one's pockets*** arricchirsi; ***be out of pocket*** rimetterci **2** *adj* (*miniature*) in miniatura **3** *v/t* intascare
pock•et 'cal•cu•la•tor calcolatrice *f* tascabile
'pocket book *Am* (*wallet*) portafoglio *m*; (*handbag*) borsetta *f*
po•di•um ['pəʊdɪəm] podio *m*
po•em ['pəʊɪm] poesia *f*
po•et ['pəʊɪt] poeta *m*, -essa *f*
po•et•ic [pəʊ'etɪk] *adj person, description* poetico
po•et•ic 'jus•tice giustizia *f* divina
po•et•ry ['pəʊɪtrɪ] poesia *f*
poign•ant ['pɔɪnjənt] *adj* commovente
point [pɔɪnt] **1** *n of pencil, knife* punta *f*; *in competition, exam* punto *m*; (*purpose*) senso *m*; (*moment*) punto *m*; *in argument, discussion* punto *m*; *in decimals* virgola *f*; ***that's beside the point*** non c'entra; ***be on the point of*** stare giusto per; ***get to the point*** venire al dunque; ***that's a point*** questo, in effetti, è vero; ***the point is ...*** il fatto è che ...; ***you've got a point there*** su questo, hai ragione; ***I take your point*** su questo, ti do ragione; ***there's no point in waiting / trying*** non ha senso aspettare / tentare **2** *v/i* indicare **3** *v/t gun* puntare (***at*** contro)
◆ **point at** *v/t with finger* indicare col dito
◆ **point out** *v/t sights, advantages* indicare
◆ **point to** *v/t with finger* additare; (*fig: indicate*) far presupporre
'point-blank 1 *adj refusal, denial* categorico; ***at point-blank range*** a bruciapelo **2** *adv refuse, deny* categoricamente
point•ed ['pɔɪntɪd] *adj remark, question* significativo
point•er ['pɔɪntə(r)] *for teacher* bacchetta *f*; (*hint*) consiglio *m*; (*sign, indication*) indizio *m*
point•less ['pɔɪntləs] *adj* inutile; ***it's pointless trying*** è inutile tentare
'point of sale punto *m* vendita
'point of view punto *m* di vista
poise [pɔɪz] padronanza *f* di sé
poised [pɔɪzd] *adj person* posato
poi•son ['pɔɪzn] **1** *n* veleno *m* **2** *v/t* avvelenare
poi•son•ous ['pɔɪznəs] *adj* velenoso
poke [pəʊk] **1** *n* colpetto *m* **2** *v/t* (*prod*) dare un colpetto a; (*stick*) ficcare; ***poke fun at*** prendere in giro; ***poke one's nose into*** ficcare il naso in
◆ **poke around** *v/i* F curiosare
pok•er ['pəʊkə(r)] *card game* poker *m inv*
pok•y ['pəʊkɪ] *adj* F (*cramped*) angusto
Po•land ['pəʊlənd] Polonia *f*
po•lar ['pəʊlə(r)] *adj* polare
po•lar bear orso *m* polare
po•lar•ize ['pəʊləraɪz] *v/t* polarizzare
Pole [pəʊl] polacco *m*, -a *f*
pole[1] [pəʊl] *of wood, metal* paletto *m*
pole[2] [pəʊl] *of earth* polo *m*
'pole star stella *f* polare
'pole•vault salto *m* con l'asta
'pole-vault•er saltatore *m*, -trice *f* con l'asta
po•lice [pə'liːs] *n* polizia *f*
po'lice car auto *f* della polizia
po,lice•man poliziotto *m*
po,lice state stato *m* di polizia
po,lice sta•tion commissariato *m* di polizia
po,lice•wo•man donna *f* poliziotto
pol•i•cy[1] ['pɒlɪsɪ] politica *f*
pol•i•cy[2] ['pɒlɪsɪ] (*insurance policy*) polizza *f*
po•li•o ['pəʊlɪəʊ] polio *f*
Pol•ish ['pəʊlɪʃ] **1** *adj* polacco **2** *n* polacco *m*
pol•ish ['pɒlɪʃ] **1** *n product* lucido *m*; (*nail polish*) smalto *m* **2** *v/t* lucidare; *speech* rifinire
◆ **polish off** *v/t food* spazzolare F
◆ **polish up** *v/t skill* perfezionare
pol•ished ['pɒlɪʃt] *adj performance* impeccabile
po•lite [pə'laɪt] *adj* cortese
po•lite•ly [pə'laɪtlɪ] *adv* cortesemente
po•lite•ness [pə'laɪtnɪs] cortesia *f*
po•lit•i•cal [pə'lɪtɪkl] *adj* politico

po•lit•i•cal•ly cor•rect [pə'lɪtɪklɪ kə'rekt] *adj* politicamente corretto
pol•i•ti•cian [pɒlɪ'tɪʃn] uomo *m* politico, donna *f* politica
pol•i•tics ['pɒlətɪks] politica *f*; ***what are his politics?*** di che tendenze politiche è?
poll [pəʊl] **1** *n* (*survey*) sondaggio *m*; ***the polls*** (*election*) le elezioni *fpl*; ***go to the polls*** (*vote*) andare alle urne **2** *v/t people* fare un sondaggio tra; *votes* guadagnare
pol•len ['pɒlən] polline *m*
'**pol•len count** concentrazione *f* di polline
'**poll•ing booth** ['pəʊlɪŋ] cabina *f* elettorale
'**poll•ing day** giorno *m* delle elezioni
'**poll•ing sta•tion** seggio *m* elettorale
poll•ster ['pɒlstə(r)] esperto *m*, -a *f* di sondaggi
pol•lu•tant [pə'luːtənt] sostanza *f* inquinante
pol•lute [pə'luːt] *v/t* inquinare
pol•lu•tion [pə'luːʃn] inquinamento *m*
po•lo ['pəʊləʊ] SP polo *m*
'**po•lo neck** *adj sweater* a dolcevita
'**po•lo shirt** polo *f inv*
pol•y•es•ter [pɒlɪ'estə(r)] poliestere *m*
pol•y•sty•rene [pɒlɪ'staɪriːn] polistirolo *m*
pol•y•thene ['pɒlɪθiːn] polietilene *m*
pol•y•thene 'bag sacchetto *m* di plastica
pol•y•un•sat•u•rat•ed [pɒlɪʌn'sætjəreɪtɪd] *adj* polinsaturo
pom•pous ['pɒmpəs] *adj* pomposo
pond [pɒnd] stagno *m*
pon•der ['pɒndə(r)] *v/i* riflettere
pon•tiff ['pɒntɪf] pontefice *m*
pon•y ['pəʊnɪ] pony *m inv*
'**pon•y•tail** coda *f* (di cavallo)
poo•dle ['puːdl] barboncino *m*
pool[1] [puːl] (*swimming pool*) piscina *f*; *of water, blood* pozza *f*
pool[2] [puːl] *game* biliardo *m*
pool[3] [puːl] **1** *n common fund* cassa *f* comune **2** *v/t resources* mettere insieme
'**pool hall** sala *f* da biliardo
pools [puːlz] *npl* totocalcio *m*; ***do the pools*** giocare al totocalcio
'**pool table** tavolo *m* da biliardo
poop•ed [puːpt] *adj* F stanco morto
poor [pʊə(r)] **1** *adj not wealthy, unfortunate* povero; *not good* misero; ***be in poor health*** essere in cattiva salute; ***poor old Tony!*** povero Tony! **2** *n*: ***the poor*** i poveri
poor•ly ['pʊəlɪ] **1** *adv* male **2** *adj* (*unwell*) indisposto
pop[1] [pɒp] **1** *n noise* schiocco *m* **2** *v/i* (*pret & pp* ***-ped***) *of balloon etc* scoppiare **3** *v/t* (*pret & pp* ***-ped***) *cork* stappare; *balloon* far scoppiare
pop[2] [pɒp] **1** *n* MUS pop *m inv* **2** *adj* pop *inv*
pop[3] [pɒp] *v/t* (*pret & pp* ***-ped***) F (*put*) ficcare F; ***pop one's head around the door*** sbucare con la testa dalla porta
◆ **pop in** *v/i* F (*make a brief visit*) entrare un attimo
◆ **pop out** *v/i* F (*go out for a short time*) fare un salto fuori
◆ **pop up** *v/i* F (*appear suddenly*) saltare fuori
'**pop con•cert** concerto *m* pop
pop•corn ['pɒpkɔːn] popcorn *m inv*
pope [pəʊp] papa *m*
'**pop group** gruppo *m* pop
pop•py ['pɒpɪ] papavero *m*
'**pop song** canzone *m* pop
pop•u•lar ['pɒpjʊlə(r)] *adj* popolare; *belief, support* diffuso
pop•u•lar•i•ty [pɒpjʊ'lærətɪ] popolarità *f inv*
pop•u•late ['pɒpjʊleɪt] *v/t* popolare
pop•u•la•tion [pɒpjʊ'leɪʃn] popolazione *f*
porce•lain ['pɔːsəlɪn] **1** *n* porcellana *f* **2** *adj* di porcellana
porch [pɔːtʃ] porticato *m*; *Am* veranda *f*
por•cu•pine ['pɔːkjʊpaɪn] porcospino *m*
pore [pɔː(r)] *of skin* poro *m*
◆ **pore over** *v/t* studiare attentamente
pork [pɔːk] maiale *m*
porn [pɔːn] *n* F porno *m* F
porn(o) [pɔːn, 'pɔːnəʊ] *adj* F porno *inv* F
por•no•graph•ic [pɔːnə'græfɪk] *adj* pornografico
porn•og•ra•phy [pɔː'nɒgrəfɪ] pornografia *f*
po•rous ['pɔːrəs] *adj* poroso
port[1] [pɔːt] *n* (*harbour, drink*) porto *m*
port[2] [pɔːt] *adj* (*left-hand*) babordo; ***on the port side*** a babordo
por•ta•ble ['pɔːtəbl] **1** *adj* portatile **2** *n* portatile *m*
por•ter ['pɔːtə(r)] portiere *m*
port•hole ['pɔːthəʊl] NAUT oblò *m inv*
por•tion ['pɔːʃn] *n* parte *f*; *of food* porzione *f*
por•trait ['pɔːtreɪt] **1** *n* ritratto *m* **2** *adv print* verticale
por•tray [pɔː'treɪ] *v/t of artist, photographer* ritrarre; *of actor* interpretare; *of author* descrivere
por•tray•al [pɔː'treɪəl] *by actor* rappresentazione *f*; *by author* descrizione *f*
Por•tu•gal ['pɔːtjʊgl] Portogallo *m*
Por•tu•guese [pɔːtjʊ'giːz] **1** *adj* portoghese **2** *n person* portoghese *m/f*; *language* portoghese *m*

pose [pəʊz] **1** *n* (*pretence*) posa *f* **2** *v/i for artist, photographer* posare; ***pose as*** farsi passare per **3** *v/t*: ***pose a problem/a threat*** creare un problema / una minaccia
posh [pɒʃ] *adj* F elegante; *pej* snob
po•si•tion [pə'zɪʃn] **1** *n* posizione *f*; ***what would you do in my position?*** cosa faresti al mio posto? **2** *v/t* sistemare, piazzare
pos•i•tive ['pɒzətɪv] *adj* positivo; ***be positive*** (*sure*) essere certo
pos•i•tive•ly ['pɒzətɪvlɪ] *adv* (*downright*) decisamente; (*definitely*) assolutamente; *think* in modo positivo
pos•sess [pə'zes] *v/t* possedere
pos•ses•sion [pə'zeʃn] (*ownership*) possesso *m*; *thing owned* bene *m*; ***possessions*** averi *mpl*
pos•ses•sive [pə'zesɪv] *adj also* GRAM possessivo
pos•si•bil•i•ty [pɒsə'bɪlətɪ] possibilità *f inv*
pos•si•ble ['pɒsəbl] *adj* possibile; ***the shortest / quickest possible ...*** la … più breve / veloce possibile; ***the best possible ...*** la miglior … possibile
pos•si•bly ['pɒsəblɪ] *adv* (*perhaps*) forse; ***that can't possibly be right*** non è possibile che sia giusto; ***could you possibly tell me ...?*** potrebbe per caso dirmi …?
post¹ [pəʊst] **1** *n of wood, metal* palo *m* **2** *v/t notice* affiggere; *profits* annunciare; ***keep s.o. posted*** tenere informato qu
post² [pəʊst] **1** *n* (*place of duty*) posto *m* **2** *v/t soldier, employee* assegnare; *guards* piazzare
post³ [pəʊst] **1** *n* (*mail*) posta *f*; ***by post*** per posta **2** *v/t letter* spedire (per posta); (*put in the mail*) imbucare
post•age ['pəʊstɪdʒ] affrancatura *f*
'**post•age stamp** *fml* francobollo *m*
post•al ['pəʊstl] *adj* postale
'**post•al or•der** vaglia *m* postale
'**post•box** buca *f* delle lettere
'**post•card** cartolina *f*
'**post•code** codice *m* di avviamento postale
'**post•date** *v/t* postdatare
post•er ['pəʊstə(r)] manifesto *m*; *for decoration* poster *m inv*
pos•te•ri•or [pɒ'stɪərɪə(r)] *n* (*hum*: *buttocks*) posteriore *m*
pos•ter•i•ty [pɒ'sterətɪ] posteri *mpl*
post•grad•u•ate ['pəʊstgrædjʊɪt] **1** *n studente m/studentessa f di un corso post-universitario* **2** *adj* post-universitario
post•hu•mous ['pɒstjʊməs] *adj* postumo
post•hu•mous•ly ['pɒstjʊməslɪ] *adv* dopo la sua morte; ***it was published posthumously*** è stato pubblicato postumo
post•ing ['pəʊstɪŋ] (*assignment*) incarico *m*
post•man ['pəʊstmən] postino *m*
post•mark ['pəʊstmɑːk] timbro *m* postale
post•mor•tem [pəʊst'mɔːtəm] autopsia *f*
'**post of•fice** ufficio *m* postale
post•pone [pəʊst'pəʊn] *v/t* rinviare
post•pone•ment [pəʊst'pəʊnmənt] rinvio *m*
pos•ture ['pɒstʃə(r)] posizione *f*
'**post•war** *adj* del dopoguerra
pot¹ [pɒt] *for cooking* pentola *f*; *for coffee* caffettiera *f*; *for tea* teiera *f*; *for plant* vaso *m*
pot² [pɒt] F (*marijuana*) erba *f* F
po•ta•to [pə'teɪtəʊ] patata *f*
po•ta•to chips *Am*, **po•ta•to crisps** *Br npl* patatine *fpl*
'**pot•bel•ly** ['pɒtbelɪ] pancetta F
po•tent ['pəʊtənt] *adj* potente
po•ten•tial [pə'tenʃl] **1** *adj* potenziale **2** *n* potenziale *m*
po•ten•tial•ly [pə'tenʃəlɪ] *adv* potenzialmente
pot•hole ['pɒthəʊl] *in road* buca *f*
pot•ter ['pɒtə(r)] *n* vasaio *m*, -a *f*
pot•ter•y ['pɒtərɪ] *n activity* ceramica *f*; *items* vasellame *m*; *place* laboratorio *m* di ceramica
pot•ty ['pɒtɪ] *n for baby* vasino *m*
pouch [paʊtʃ] (*bag*) borsa *f*
poul•try ['pəʊltrɪ] *birds* volatili *mpl*; *meat* pollame *m*
pounce [paʊns] *v/i of animal* balzare; *fig* piombare
pound¹ [paʊnd] *n weight* libbra *f*; FIN sterlina *f*
pound² [paʊnd] *for strays* canile *m* municipale; *for cars* deposito *m* auto
pound³ [paʊnd] *v/i of heart* battere forte; ***pound on*** (*hammer on*) picchiare su
pound 'ster•ling sterlina *f*
pour [pɔː(r)] **1** *v/t liquid* versare **2** *v/i*: ***it's pouring (with rain)*** sta diluviando
◆ **pour out** *v/t liquid* versare; *troubles* sfogarsi raccontando
pout [paʊt] *v/i* fare il broncio
pov•er•ty ['pɒvətɪ] povertà *f inv*
pov•er•ty-strick•en ['pɒvətɪstrɪkn] *adj* poverissimo
pow•der ['paʊdə(r)] **1** *n* polvere *f*; *for face* cipria *f* **2** *v/t*: ***powder one's face*** mettersi la cipria
'**pow•der room** F toilette *f inv* per signore
pow•er ['paʊə(r)] **1** *n* (*strength*) forza *f*; *of engine* potenza *f*; (*authority*) potere *m*; (*energy*) energia *f*; (*electricity*) elettricità

f inv; ***in power*** POL al potere; ***fall from power*** POL perdere il potere **2** *v/t*: ***powered by atomic energy*** a propulsione atomica
'**pow•er-as•sist•ed steer•ing** servosterzo *m*
'**pow•er cut** interruzione *f* di corrente
'**pow•er fail•ure** guasto *m* alla linea elettrica
pow•er•ful ['paʊəfʊl] *adj* potente
pow•er•less ['paʊəlɪs] *adj* impotente; ***be powerless to …*** non poter far niente per …
'**pow•er line** linea *f* elettrica
'**pow•er sta•tion** centrale *f* elettrica
'**pow•er steer•ing** servosterzo *m*
'**pow•er u•nit** alimentatore *m*
PR [piː'ɑː(r)] *abbr* (= ***public relations***) relazioni *fpl* pubbliche
prac•ti•cal ['præktɪkl] *adj* pratico
prac•ti•cal 'joke scherzo *m*
prac•tic•al•ly ['præktɪklɪ] *adv behave, think* in modo pratico; (*almost*) praticamente
prac•tice ['præktɪs] **1** *n* pratica *f*; (*training*) esercizio *m*; (*rehearsal*) prove *fpl*; (*custom*) consuetudine *f*; ***in practice*** (*in reality*) in pratica; ***be out of practice*** essere fuori allenamento **2** *v/t & v/i Am* → ***practise***
prac•tise ['præktɪs] **1** *v/t* esercitarsi in; *law, medicine* esercitare **2** *v/i* esercitarsi
prag•mat•ic [præg'mætɪk] *adj* pragmatico
prag•ma•tism ['prægmətɪzm] pragmatismo *m*
prai•rie ['preərɪ] prateria *f*
praise [preɪz] **1** *n* lode *f* **2** *v/t* lodare
praise•wor•thy ['preɪzwɜːðɪ] *adj* lodevole
pram [præm] carrozzina *f*
prank [præŋk] *n* birichinata *f*
prat•tle ['prætl] *v/i* cianciare
prawn [prɔːn] gamberetto *m*
pray [preɪ] *v/i* pregare
prayer [preə(r)] preghiera *f*
preach [priːʧ] **1** *v/i* predicare **2** *v/t sermon* predicare
preach•er ['priːʧə(r)] predicatore *m*, -trice *f*
pre•am•ble [priː'æmbl] preambolo *m*
pre•car•i•ous [prɪ'keərɪəs] *adj* precario
pre•car•i•ous•ly [prɪ'keərɪəslɪ] *adv* precariamente
pre•cau•tion [prɪ'kɔːʃn] precauzione *f*
pre•cau•tion•a•ry [prɪ'kɔːʃnrɪ] *adj measure* di precauzione
pre•cede [prɪ'siːd] *v/t* precedere
pre•ce•dence ['presɪdəns] precedenza *f*; ***take precedence over …*** avere la precedenza su …
pre•ce•dent ['presɪdənt] *n* precedente *m*
pre•ce•ding [prɪ'siːdɪŋ] *adj* precedente
pre•cinct ['priːsɪŋkt] (*Am*: *district*) distretto *m*
pre•cious ['preʃəs] *adj* prezioso
pre•cip•i•tate [prɪ'sɪpɪteɪt] *v/t crisis* accelerare
pre•cip•i•ta•tion [prɪsɪpɪ'teɪʃn] *fml* precipitazione *f*
pré•cis ['preɪsiː] *n* riassunto *m*
pre•cise [prɪ'saɪs] *adj* preciso
pre•cise•ly [prɪ'saɪslɪ] *adv* precisamente
pre•ci•sion [prɪ'sɪʒn] precisione *f*
pre•co•cious [prɪ'kəʊʃəs] *adj child* precoce
pre•con•ceived [priːkən'siːvd] *adj idea* preconcetto
pre•con•di•tion [prɪkən'dɪʃn] condizione *f* indispensabile
pred•a•tor ['predətə(r)] *animal* predatore *m*, -trice *f*
pred•a•to•ry ['predətrɪ] *adj* rapace
pre•de•ces•sor ['priːdɪsesə(r)] predecessore *m*
pre•des•ti•na•tion [priːdestɪ'neɪʃn] predestinazione *f*
pre•des•tined [priː'destɪnd] *adj*: ***be predestined to*** essere predestinato a
pre•dic•a•ment [prɪ'dɪkəmənt] situazione *f* difficile
pre•dict [prɪ'dɪkt] *v/t* predire
pre•dict•a•ble [prɪ'dɪktəbl] *adj* prevedibile
pre•dic•tion [prɪ'dɪkʃn] predizione *f*
pre•dom•i•nant [prɪ'dɒmɪnənt] *adj* predominante
pre•dom•i•nant•ly [prɪ'dɒmɪnəntlɪ] *adv* prevalentemente
pre•dom•i•nate [prɪ'dɒmɪneɪt] *v/i* predominare
preen [priːn] *v/t*: ***preen o.s.*** *fig* farsi bello
pre•fab•ri•cat•ed [priː'fæbrɪkeɪtɪd] *adj* prefabbricato
pref•ace ['prefɪs] *n* prefazione *f*
pre•fect ['priːfekt] EDU *studente m/studentessa f dell'ultimo anno di liceo con responsabilità disciplinari*
pre•fer [prɪ'fɜː(r)] *v/t* (*pret & pp* ***-red***) preferire; ***prefer X to Y*** preferire X a Y; ***prefer to do*** preferire fare
pref•e•ra•ble ['prefərəbl] *adj* preferibile
pref•e•ra•bly ['prefərəblɪ] *adv* preferibilmente
pref•e•rence ['prefərəns] preferenza *f*; ***give preference to*** dare *o* accordare la preferenza a
pref•er•en•tial [prefə'renʃl] *adj* preferenziale

pre•fix ['pri:fɪks] prefisso *m*
preg•nan•cy ['pregnənsɪ] gravidanza *f*
preg•nant ['pregnənt] *adj* incinta; ***get pregnant*** restare incinta
pre•heat ['pri:hi:t] *v/t oven* far riscaldare
pre•his•tor•ic [pri:hɪs'tɒrɪk] *adj* preistorico
pre•judge [pri:'dʒʌdʒ] *v/t* giudicare a priori
prej•u•dice ['predʒʊdɪs] **1** *n* pregiudizio *m* **2** *v/t person* influenzare; *chances* pregiudicare
prej•u•diced ['predʒʊdɪst] *adj* prevenuto
prej•u•di•cial [predʒʊ'dɪʃl] *adj*: ***be prejudicial to*** essere pregiudizievole a
pre•lim•i•na•ry [prɪ'lɪmɪnərɪ] *adj* preliminare
prel•ude ['prelju:d] preludio *m*
pre•mar•i•tal [pri:'mærɪtl] *adj* prematrimoniale
pre•ma•ture ['premətjʊə(r)] *adj* prematuro
pre•med•i•tat•ed [pri:'medɪteɪtɪd] *adj* premeditato
prem•i•er ['premɪə(r)] *n* (*Prime Minister*) premier *m inv*
prem•i•ère ['premɪeə(r)] *n* premiere *f inv*, prima *f*
prem•is•es ['premɪsɪz] *npl* locali *mpl*
pre•mi•um ['pri:mɪəm] *n in insurance* premio *m*
pre•mo•ni•tion [premə'nɪʃn] premonizione *f*
pre•oc•cu•pied [prɪ'ɒkjʊpaɪd] *adj* preoccupato
pre•paid ['pri:peɪd] *adj* prepagato
prep•a•ra•tion [prepə'reɪʃn] preparazione *f*; ***in preparation for*** in vista di; ***preparations*** preparativi *mpl*
pre•pare [prɪ'peə(r)] **1** *v/t* preparare; ***be prepared to do sth*** (*willing*) essere preparato a fare qc; ***be prepared for sth*** (*be expecting*) essere preparato per qc **2** *v/i* prepararsi
prep•o•si•tion [prepə'zɪʃn] preposizione *f*
pre•pos•sess•ing [pri:pə'zesɪŋ] *adj* attraente
pre•pos•ter•ous [prɪ'pɒstərəs] *adj* ridicolo
prep school ['prepsku:l] *scuola f privata di preparazione alla scuola superiore*
pre•req•ui•site [pri:'rekwɪzɪt] condizione *f* indispensabile
pre•rog•a•tive [prɪ'rɒgətɪv] prerogativa *f*
pre•scribe [prɪ'skraɪb] *v/t of doctor* prescrivere
pre•scrip•tion [prɪ'skrɪpʃn] MED ricetta *f* medica
pres•ence ['prezns] presenza *f*; ***in the presence of*** in presenza di
pres•ence of 'mind presenza *f* di spirito
pres•ent[1] ['preznt] **1** *adj* (*current*) attuale; ***be present*** essere presente **2** *n*: ***the present*** *also* GRAM il presente; ***at present*** al momento
pres•ent[2] ['preznt] *n* (*gift*) regalo *m*
pre•sent[3] [prɪ'zent] *v/t award* consegnare; *bouquet* offrire; *programme* presentare; ***present s.o. with sth, present sth to s.o.*** offrire qc a qu
pre•sen•ta•tion [prezn'teɪʃn] presentazione *f*
pres•ent-day [preznt'deɪ] *adj* di oggi
pre•sent•er [prɪ'zentə(r)] presentatore *m*, -trice *f*
pres•ent•ly ['prezntlɪ] *adv* (*at the moment*) attualmente; (*soon*) tra breve
'pres•ent tense presente *m*
pres•er•va•tion [prezə'veɪʃn] *of food* conservazione *f*; *of standards, peace etc* mantenimento *m*
pre•ser•va•tive [prɪ'zɜ:vətɪv] *n for wood; in food* conservante *m*
pre•serve [prɪ'zɜ:v] **1** *n* (*domain*) dominio *m* **2** *v/t standards, peace etc* mantenere; *wood etc* proteggere; *food* conservare
pre•serves [prɪ'zɜ:vz] *npl* conserve *fpl*
pre•side [prɪ'zaɪd] *v/i at meeting* presiedere; ***preside over*** *meeting* presiedere a
pres•i•den•cy ['prezɪdənsɪ] presidenza *f*
pres•i•dent ['prezɪdnt] presidente *m*
pres•i•den•tial [prezɪ'denʃl] *adj* presidenziale
press [pres] **1** *n*: ***the press*** la stampa **2** *v/t button* premere; (*urge*) far pressione su; (*squeeze*) stringere; *clothes* stirare; *grapes, olives* spremere **3** *v/i*: ***press for*** fare pressioni per ottenere
'press a•gen•cy agenzia *f* di stampa
'press con•fer•ence conferenza *f* stampa
press•ing ['presɪŋ] *adj* urgente
press-stud ['presstʌd] (bottone *m*) automatico
press-up ['presʌp] flessione *f* sulle braccia
pres•sure ['preʃə(r)] **1** *n* pressione *f*; ***be under pressure*** (***to do***) essere sotto pressione (per fare) **2** *v/t* fare delle pressioni su
'pres•sure cook•er pentola *f* a pressione
'pres•sur•ize ['preʃəraɪz] *v/t person* fare delle pressioni su
pres•tige [pre'sti:ʒ] prestigio *m*
pres•ti•gious [pre'stɪdʒəs] *adj* prestigioso
pre•sum•a•ble [prɪ'zju:məbl] *adj* presumibile

pre•su•ma•bly [prɪ'zjuːməblɪ] *adv* presumibilmente
pre•sume [prɪ'zjuːm] *v/i* presumere; ***presume to do*** *fml* permettersi di fare
pre•sump•tion [prɪ'zʌmpʃn] *of innocence, guilt* presunzione *f*
pre•sump•tu•ous [prɪ'zʌmptjʊəs] *adj* impertinente
pre•sup•pose [priːsə'pəʊs] *v/t* presupporre
pre-tax ['priːtæks] *adj* al lordo d'imposta
pre•tence [prɪ'tens] finta *f*
pre•tend [prɪ'tend] **1** *v/t* fingere **2** *v/i* fare finta
pre•tense *Am* → ***pretence***
pre•ten•tious [prɪ'tenʃəs] *adj* pretenzioso
pre•text ['priːtekst] pretesto *m*
pret•ty ['prɪtɪ] **1** *adj* carino **2** *adv* (*quite*) piuttosto
pre•vail [prɪ'veɪl] *v/i* (*triumph*) prevalere
pre•vail•ing [prɪ'veɪlɪŋ] *adj* prevalente
pre•var•i•cate [prɪ'værɪkeɪt] *v/i* tergiversare
pre•vent [prɪ'vent] *v/t* prevenire; ***prevent s.o. (from) doing sth*** impedire a qu di fare qc
pre•ven•tion [prɪ'venʃn] prevenzione *f*
pre•ven•tive [prɪ'ventɪv] *adj* preventivo
pre•view ['priːvjuː] *n of film, exhibition* anteprima *f*
pre•vi•ous ['priːvɪəs] *adj* precedente; ***previous to*** prima di
pre•vi•ously ['priːvɪəslɪ] *adv* precedentemente
pre-war ['priːwɔː(r)] *adj* dell'anteguerra
prey [preɪ] *n* preda *f*
◆ **prey on** *v/t* far preda di; *fig*: *of conman etc* approfittarsi di; ***prey on s.o.'s mind*** preoccupare qu
price [praɪs] **1** *n* prezzo *m* **2** *v/t* COM fissare il prezzo di
price•less ['praɪslɪs] *adj* (*valuable*) di valore inestimabile
'**price tag** cartellino *m* del prezzo
'**price war** guerra *f* dei prezzi
price•y ['praɪsɪ] *adj* F caro
prick[1] [prɪk] **1** *n pain* puntura *f* **2** *v/t* (*jab*) pungere
prick[2] [prɪk] *n* V (*penis*) cazzo *m* V; *person* testa *f* di cazzo V
◆ **prick up** *v/t*: ***prick up one's ears*** *also fig* drizzare le orecchie
prick•le ['prɪkl] *on plant* spina *f*
prick•ly ['prɪklɪ] *adj plant* spinoso; *beard* ispido; (*irritable*) permaloso
pride [praɪd] **1** *n in person, achievement* orgoglio *m*; (*self-respect*) amor *m* proprio **2** *v/t*: ***pride o.s. on*** vantarsi di
priest [priːst] prete *m*
pri•ma•ri•ly [praɪ'meərɪlɪ] *adv* principalmente
pri•ma•ry ['praɪmərɪ] *adj* principale
'**pri•ma•ry school** scuola *f* elementare
prime [praɪm] **1** *n*: ***be in one's prime*** essere nel fiore degli anni **2** *adj example, reason* principale; (*very good*) ottimo; ***of prime importance*** della massima importanza
prime 'min•is•ter primo ministro *m*
'**prime time TV** TV programmi *mpl* tv di prima serata
prim•i•tive ['prɪmɪtɪv] *adj also fig* primitivo
prim•rose ['prɪmrəʊz] primula *f*
prince [prɪns] principe *m*
prin•cess [prɪn'ses] principessa *f*
prin•ci•pal ['prɪnsəpl] **1** *adj* principale **2** *n of school* preside *m/f*
prin•ci•pal•i•ty [prɪnsɪ'pælətɪ] principato *m*
prin•ci•pal•ly ['prɪnsəplɪ] *adv* principalmente
prin•ci•ple ['prɪnsəpl] principio *m*; ***on principle*** per principio; ***in principle*** in linea di principio
print [prɪnt] **1** *n in book, newspaper etc* caratteri *mpl*; *photograph* stampa *f*; *mark* impronta *f*; ***out of print*** esaurito **2** *v/t* stampare; (*use block capitals*) scrivere in stampatello
◆ **print out** *v/t* stampare
print•ed mat•ter ['prɪntɪdmætə(r)] stampe *fpl*
print•er ['prɪntə(r)] *person* tipografo *m*; *machine* stampante *f*
print•ing press ['prɪntɪŋpres] pressa *f* tipografica
'**print•out** stampato *m*
pri•or ['praɪə(r)] **1** *adj* precedente **2** *prep*: ***prior to*** prima di
pri•or•i•tize [praɪ'ɒrətaɪz] *v/t* (*put in order of priority*) classificare in ordine d'importanza; (*give priority to*) dare precedenza a
pri•or•i•ty [praɪ'ɒrətɪ] priorità *f inv*; ***have priority*** avere la precedenza
pris•on ['prɪzn] prigione *f*
pris•on•er ['prɪznə(r)] prigioniero *m*, -a *f*; ***take s.o. prisoner*** fare prigioniero qu
pris•on•er of 'war prigioniero *m* di guerra
priv•a•cy ['prɪvəsɪ] privacy *f inv*
pri•vate ['praɪvət] **1** *adj* privato **2** *n* MIL soldato *m* semplice; ***in private*** in privato
pri•vate 'en•ter•prise iniziativa *f* privata
pri•vate•ly ['praɪvətlɪ] *adv* (*in private*) in privato; (*inwardly*) dentro di sé; ***privately funded*** finanziato da privati; ***privately owned*** privato

'**pri•vate sec•tor** settore *m* privato
pri•va•ti•za•tion [praɪvətaɪ'zeɪʃn] privatizzazione *f*
pri•va•tize ['praɪvətaɪz] *v/t* privatizzare
priv•i•lege ['prɪvəlɪdʒ] *special treatment* privilegio *m*; (*honour*) onore *m*
priv•i•leged ['prɪvəlɪdʒd] *adj* privilegiato; (*honoured*) onorato
prize [praɪz] **1** *n* premio *m* **2** *v/t* dare molto valore a
prize•win•ner ['praɪzwɪnə(r)] vincitore *m*, -trice *f*
prize•win•ning ['praɪzwɪnɪŋ] *adj* vincente
pro[1] [prəʊ] *n*: ***the pros and cons*** i pro e i contro
pro[2] [prəʊ] → ***professional***
pro[3] [prəʊ] *prep*: ***be pro …*** (*in favour of*) essere a favore di …
prob•a•bil•i•ty [prɒbə'bɪlətɪ] probabilità *f inv*
prob•a•ble ['prɒbəbl] *adj* probabile
prob•a•bly ['prɒbəblɪ] *adv* probabilmente
pro•ba•tion [prə'beɪʃn] *in job* periodo *m* di prova; LAW *libertà f inv vigilata*; ***on probation*** *in job* in prova
pro•'ba•tion of•fi•cer *funzionario m che sorveglia i vigilati*
pro•'ba•tion pe•ri•od *in job* periodo *m* di prova
probe [prəʊb] **1** *n* (*investigation*) indagine *f*; *scientific* sonda *f* **2** *v/t* esplorare; (*investigate*) investigare
prob•lem ['prɒbləm] problema *m*; ***no problem*** non c'è problema
pro•ce•dure [prə'siːdʒə(r)] procedura *f*
pro•ceed [prə'siːd] **1** *v/i of people* proseguire; *of work etc* procedere **2** *v/t*: ***proceed to do sth*** cominciare a fare qc
pro•ceed•ings [prə'siːdɪŋz] *npl* (*events*) avvenimenti *mpl*
pro•ceeds ['prəʊsiːdz] *npl* ricavato *m*
pro•cess ['prəʊses] **1** *n* processo *m*; ***in the process*** *while doing it* nel far ciò **2** *v/t food*, *raw materials* trattare; *data* elaborare; *application etc* sbrigare; ***processed cheese*** formaggio *m* fuso
pro•ces•sion [prə'seʃn] processione *f*
pro•claim [prə'kleɪm] *v/t* proclamare
proc•la•ma•tion [prɒklə'meɪʃn] proclamazione *f*
prod [prɒd] **1** *n* colpetto *m* **2** *v/t* (*pret & pp* ***-ded***) dare un colpetto a
pro•di•gious [prə'dɪdʒəs] *adj* straordinario
prod•i•gy ['prɒdɪdʒɪ]: (***infant***) ***prodigy*** bambino *m*, -a *f* prodigio
prod•uce[1] ['prɒdjuːs] *n* prodotti *mpl*
pro•duce[2] [prə'djuːs] *v/t* produrre; (*bring about*) dare origine a; (*bring out*) tirar fuori; *play* mettere in scena
pro•duc•er [prə'djuːsə(r)] produttore *m*, -trice *f*; *of play* regista *m/f*
prod•uct ['prɒdʌkt] prodotto *m*; (*result*) risultato *m*
pro•duc•tion [prə'dʌkʃn] produzione *f*; *of play* regia *f*; ***a new production of …*** una nuova messa in scena di …
pro'duc•tion ca•pac•i•ty capacità *f inv* produttiva
pro'duc•tion costs *npl* costi *mpl* di produzione
pro•duc•tive [prə'dʌktɪv] *adj* produttivo
pro•duc•tiv•i•ty [prɒdʌk'tɪvətɪ] produttività *f inv*
pro•fane [prə'feɪn] *adj language* sacrilego
pro•fan•i•ty [prə'fænətɪ] (*swearword*) imprecazione *f*
pro•fess [prə'fes] *v/t* dichiarare
pro•fes•sion [prə'feʃn] professione *f*
pro•fes•sion•al [prə'feʃnl] **1** *adj not amateur* professionale; *advice*, *help* di un esperto; *piece of work* da professionista; ***turn professional*** passare al professionismo **2** *n* professionista *m/f*
pro•fes•sion•al•ly [prə'feʃnlɪ] *adv play sport* a livello professionistico; (*well, skilfully*) in modo professionale
pro•fes•sor [prə'fesə(r)] professore *m* (universitario)
pro•fi•cien•cy [prə'fɪʃnsɪ] competenza *f*
pro•fi•cient [prə'fɪʃnt] *adj* competente
pro•file ['prəʊfaɪl] profilo *m*
prof•it ['prɒfɪt] **1** *n* profitto *m* **2** *v/i*: ***profit by, profit from*** trarre profitto da
prof•i•ta•ble ['prɒfɪtəbl] *adj* redditizio
prof•it•a•bil•i•ty [prɒfɪtə'bɪlətɪ] redditività *f inv*
'**prof•it cen•ter** *Am*, '**prof•it cen•tre** centro *m* di profitto
'**prof•it mar•gin** margine *m* di profitto
pro•found [prə'faʊnd] *adj* profondo
pro•found•ly [prə'faʊndlɪ] *adv* profondamente
pro•fuse [prə'fjuːs] *adj* abbondante
pro•fuse•ly [prə'fjuːslɪ] *adv thank* con grande effusione; *bleed* copiosamente
prog•no•sis [prɒg'nəʊsɪs] prognosi *f inv*
pro•gram ['prəʊgræm] **1** *n* COMPUT programma *m* **2** *v/t* (*pret & pp* ***-med***) COMPUT programmare
pro•gram *Am*, **pro•gramme** ['prəʊgræm] **1** *n* programma *m* **2** *v/t* programmare
pro•gram•mer ['prəʊgræmə(r)] COMPUT programmatore *m*, -trice *f*
pro•gress ['prəʊgres] **1** *n* progresso *m*; ***make progress*** fare progressi; ***in progress*** in corso **2** *v/i* [prə'gres] (*advance in time*) procedere; (*move on*) avanzare;

P

(*make progress*) fare progressi; ***how is the work progressing?*** come procede il lavoro?
pro•gres•sive [prəˈgresɪv] *adj* (*enlightened*) progressista; *which progresses* progressivo
pro•gres•sive•ly [prəˈgresɪvlɪ] *adv* progressivamente
pro•hib•it [prəˈhɪbɪt] *v/t* proibire
pro•hi•bi•tion [prəʊhɪˈbɪʃn] proibizione *f*; ***Prohibition*** il Proibizionismo
pro•hib•i•tive [prəˈhɪbɪtɪv] *adj prices* proibitivo
proj•ect[1] [ˈprɒdʒekt] *n* (*plan*) piano *m*; (*undertaking*) progetto *m*; EDU ricerca *f*
pro•ject[2] [prəˈdʒekt] **1** *v/t figures*, *sales* fare una proiezione di; *film* proiettare **2** *v/i* (*stick out*) sporgere in fuori
pro•jec•tion [prəˈdʒekʃn] (*forecast*) proiezione *f*
pro•jec•tor [prəˈdʒektə(r)] *for slides* proiettore *m*
pro•lif•ic [prəˈlɪfɪk] *adj writer*, *artist* prolifico
pro•log *Am*, **pro•logue** [ˈprəʊlɒg] prologo *m*
pro•long [prəˈlɒŋ] *v/t* prolungare
prom•i•nent [ˈprɒmɪnənt] *adj nose*, *chin* sporgente; (*significant*) prominente
prom•is•cu•i•ty [prɒmɪˈskjuːətɪ] promiscuità *f inv*
pro•mis•cu•ous [prəˈmɪskjʊəs] *adj* promiscuo
prom•ise [ˈprɒmɪs] **1** *n* promessa *f* **2** *v/t* promettere; ***promise to …*** promettere di …; ***promise sth to s.o.*** promettere qc a qu **3** *v/i* promettere; ***I promise*** lo prometto
prom•ising [ˈprɒmɪsɪŋ] *adj* promettente
pro•mote [prəˈməʊt] *v/t* promuovere
pro•mot•er [prəˈməʊtə(r)] *of sports event* promoter *m/f inv*
pro•mo•tion [prəˈməʊʃn] promozione *f*; ***get promotion*** essere promosso
prompt [prɒmpt] **1** *adj* (*on time*) puntuale; (*speedy*) tempestivo **2** *adv*: ***at two o'clock prompt*** alle due in punto **3** *v/t* (*cause*) causare; *actor* dare l'imbeccata a **4** *n* COMPUT prompt *m inv*
prompt•ly [ˈprɒmptlɪ] *adv* (*on time*) puntualmente; (*immediately*) prontamente
prone [prəʊn] *adj*: ***be prone to*** essere soggetto a
prong [prɒŋ] dente *m*
pro•noun [ˈprəʊnaʊn] pronome *m*
pro•nounce [prəˈnaʊns] *v/t word* pronunciare; (*declare*) dichiarare
pro•nounced [prəˈnaʊnst] *adj accent* spiccato; *views* preciso
pron•to [ˈprɒntəʊ] *adv* F immediatamente
pro•nun•ci•a•tion [prənʌnsɪˈeɪʃn] pronuncia *f*
proof [pruːf] *n* prova *f*; *of book* bozza *f*
prop [prɒp] **1** *v/t* (*pret & pp* ***-ped***) appoggiare **2** *n* THEA materiale *m* di scena
◆ **prop up** *v/t also fig* sostenere
prop•a•gan•da [prɒpəˈgændə] propaganda *f*
pro•pel [prəˈpel] *v/t* (*pret & pp* ***-led***) spingere; *of engine*, *fuel* azionare
pro•pel•lant [prəˈpelənt] *in aerosol* propellente *m*
pro•pel•ler [prəˈpelə(r)] elica *f*
prop•er [ˈprɒpə(r)] *adj* (*real*) vero e proprio; (*correct*) giusto; (*fitting*) appropriato
prop•er•ly [ˈprɒpəlɪ] *adv* (*correctly*) correttamente; (*fittingly*) in modo appropriato
ˈ**prop•er noun** nome *m* proprio
prop•er•ty [ˈprɒpətɪ] proprietà *f inv*
prop•er•ty deˈvel•op•er impresario *m* edile
proph•e•cy [ˈprɒfəsɪ] profezia *f*
proph•e•sy [ˈprɒfəsaɪ] *v/t* (*pret & pp* ***-ied***) profetizzare
pro•por•tion [prəˈpɔːʃn] proporzione *f*
pro•por•tion•al [prəˈpɔːʃnl] *adj* proporzionale
pro•por•tion•al rep•re•senˈta•tion POL rappresentanza *f* proporzionale
pro•pos•al [prəˈpəʊzl] proposta *f*
pro•pose [prəˈpəʊz] **1** *v/t* (*suggest*) proporre; ***propose to do sth*** (*plan*) proporsi di fare qc **2** *v/i make offer of marriage* fare una proposta di matrimonio
prop•o•si•tion [prɒpəˈzɪʃn] **1** *n* proposta *f* **2** *v/t woman* fare proposte sessuali a
pro•pri•e•tor [prəˈpraɪətə(r)] proprietario *m*, -a *f*
pro•pri•e•tress [prəˈpraɪətrɪs] proprietaria *f*
prose [prəʊz] prosa *f*
pros•e•cute [ˈprɒsɪkjuːt] *v/t* LAW intentare azione legale contro; *of lawyer* sostenere l'accusa contro
pros•e•cu•tion [prɒsɪˈkjuːʃn] LAW azione *f* giudiziaria; (*lawyers*) accusa *f*
pros•pect [ˈprɒspekt] **1** *n* (*chance*, *likelihood*) probabilità *f inv*; *thought of something in the future* prospettiva *f*; ***prospects*** *for company*, *in job* prospettive *fpl* **2** *v/i*: ***prospect for*** *gold* cercare
pro•spec•tive [prəˈspektɪv] *adj* potenziale; *MP* aspirante
pros•per [ˈprɒspə(r)] *v/i* prosperare
pros•per•i•ty [prɒˈsperətɪ] prosperità *f*

inv
pros•per•ous ['prɒspərəs] *adj* prospero
pros•ti•tute ['prɒstɪtju:t] *n* prostituta *f*; ***male prostitute*** prostituto *m*
pros•ti•tu•tion [prɒstɪ'tju:ʃn] prostituzione *f*
pros•trate ['prɒstreɪt] *adj*: ***be prostrate with grief*** essere abbattuto dal dolore
pro•tect [prə'tekt] *v/t* proteggere
pro•tec•tion [prə'tekʃn] protezione *f*
pro'tec•tion mon•ey pizzo *m* F
pro•tec•tive [prə'tektɪv] *adj* protettivo
pro•tec•tive 'cloth•ing indumenti *mpl* protettivi
pro•tec•tor [prə'tektə(r)] protettore *m*, -trice *f*
pro•tein ['prəʊti:n] proteina *f*
pro•test ['prəʊtest] **1** *n* protesta *f* **2** *v/t* [prə'test] protestare **3** *v/i* protestare; POL manifestare, protestare
Prot•es•tant ['prɒtɪstənt] **1** *n* protestante *m/f* **2** *adj* protestante
pro•test•er [prə'testə(r)] dimostrante *m/f*, manifestante *m/f*
pro•to•col ['prəʊtəkɒl] protocollo *m*
pro•to•type ['prəʊtətaɪp] prototipo *m*
pro•tracted [prə'træktɪd] *adj* prolungato
pro•trude [prə'tru:d] *v/i* sporgere
pro•trud•ing [prə'tru:dɪŋ] *adj* sporgente
proud [praʊd] *adj* orgoglioso, fiero; ***be proud of*** essere fiero di
proud•ly ['praʊdlɪ] *adv* con orgoglio
prove [pru:v] *v/t* dimostrare
prov•erb ['prɒvɜ:b] proverbio *m*
pro•vide [prə'vaɪd] *v/t money*, *food* fornire; *opportunity* offrire; ***provide s.o. with sth*** fornire qu di qc
◆ **provide for** *v/t family* provvedere a; *of law etc* contemplare
pro•vi•ded [prə'vaɪdɪd] *conj*: ***provided (that)*** (*on condition that*) a condizione che
prov•ince ['prɒvɪns] provincia *f*
pro•vin•cial [prə'vɪnʃl] *adj also pej* provinciale
pro•vi•sion [prə'vɪʒn] (*supply*) fornitura *f*; *of law*, *contract* disposizione *f*
pro•vi•sion•al [prə'vɪʒnl] *adj* provvisorio
pro•vi•so [prə'vaɪzəʊ] condizione *f*
prov•o•ca•tion [prɒvə'keɪʃn] provocazione *f*
pro•voc•a•tive [prə'vɒkətɪv] *adj* provocatorio; *sexually* provocante
pro•voke [prə'vəʊk] *v/t* (*cause*) causare; (*annoy*) provocare
prow [praʊ] NAUT prua *f*
prow•ess ['praʊɪs] abilità *f inv*
prowl [praʊl] *v/i* aggirarsi
prowl•er ['praʊlə(r)] tipo *m* sospetto
prox•im•i•ty [prɒk'sɪmətɪ] prossimità *f inv*
prox•y ['prɒksɪ] (*authority*) procura *f*; *person* procuratore *m*, -trice *f*, mandatario *m*, -a *f*
prude [pru:d]: ***be a prude*** scandalizzarsi facilmente
pru•dence ['pru:dns] prudenza *f*
pru•dent ['pru:dnt] *adj* prudente
prud•ish ['pru:dɪʃ] *adj* che si scandalizza facilmente
prune[1] [pru:n] *n* prugna *f*
prune[2] [pru:n] *v/t plant* potare; *fig* ridurre
pry [praɪ] *v/i* (*pret & pp* ***-ied***) essere indiscreto
◆ **pry into** *v/t* ficcare il naso in
PS ['pi:es] *abbr* (= ***postscript***) P.S. (= post scriptum *m inv*)
pseu•do•nym ['sju:dənɪm] pseudonimo *m*
psy•chi•at•ric [saɪkɪ'ætrɪk] *adj* psichiatrico
psy•chi•a•trist [saɪ'kaɪətrɪst] psichiatra *m/f*
psy•chi•a•try [saɪ'kaɪətrɪ] psichiatria *f*
psy•chic ['saɪkɪk] *adj* psichico; ***I'm not psychic!*** non sono un indovino!
psy•cho•an•a•lyse [saɪkəʊ'ænəlaɪz] *v/t* psicanalizzare
psy•cho•a•nal•y•sis [saɪkəʊən'æləsɪs] psicanalisi *f*
psy•cho•an•a•lyst [saɪkəʊ'ænəlɪst] psicanalista *m/f*
psy•cho•log•i•cal [saɪkə'lɒdʒɪkl] *adj* psicologico
psy•cho•log•i•cal•ly [saɪkə'lɒdʒɪklɪ] *adv* psicologicamente
psy•chol•o•gist [saɪ'kɒlədʒɪst] psicologo *m*, -a *f*
psy•chol•o•gy [saɪ'kɒlədʒɪ] psicologia *f*
psy•cho•path ['saɪkəpæθ] psicopatico *m*, -a *f*
psy•cho•so•mat•ic [saɪkəʊsə'mætɪk] *adj* psicosomatico
PT [pi:'ti:] *abbr* (= ***physical training***) educazione *f* fisica
PTO [pi:ti:'əʊ] *abbr* (= ***please turn over***) vedi retro
pub [pʌb] pub *m inv*
pu•ber•ty ['pju:bətɪ] pubertà *f inv*
pu•bic hair [pju:bɪk'heə(r)] peli *mpl* del pube
pub•lic ['pʌblɪk] **1** *adj* pubblico **2** *n*: ***the public*** il pubblico; ***in public*** in pubblico
pub•li•ca•tion [pʌblɪ'keɪʃn] pubblicazione *f*
pub•lic 'hol•i•day giorno *m* festivo
pub•lic•i•ty [pʌb'lɪsətɪ] pubblicità *f inv*
pub•li•cize ['pʌblɪsaɪz] *v/t make known*

far sapere in giro; COM reclamizzare
pub•lic 'li•bra•ry biblioteca *f* pubblica
pub•lic lim•it•ed ,com•pa•ny società *f inv* a responsabilità limitata quotata in borsa
pub•lic•ly ['pʌblɪklɪ] *adv* pubblicamente
pub•lic 'pros•e•cu•tor *pubblico ministero m*
pub•lic re'la•tions *npl* relazioni *fpl* pubbliche
'pub•lic school *Br* scuola *f* privata
'pub•lic sec•tor settore *m* pubblico
pub•lic 'trans•port mezzi *mpl* pubblici
pub•lish ['pʌblɪʃ] *v/t* pubblicare
pub•lish•er ['pʌblɪʃə(r)] editore *m*
pub•lish•ing ['pʌblɪʃɪŋ] editoria *f*
'pub•lish•ing com•pa•ny casa *f* editrice
pud•ding ['pʊdɪŋ] *dish* budino *m*; *part of meal* dolce *m*
pud•dle ['pʌdl] *n* pozzanghera *f*
puff [pʌf] **1** *n of wind, smoke* soffio *m* **2** *v/i* (*pant*) ansimare; ***puff on a cigarette*** tirare boccate da una sigaretta
puff•y ['pʌfɪ] *adj eyes, face* gonfio
puke [pju:k] *v/i* F vomitare
pull [pʊl] **1** *n on rope* tirata *f*; F (*appeal*) attrattiva *f*; F (*influence*) influenza *f* **2** *v/t* (*drag*) tirare; (*tug*) dare uno strappo a; *tooth* togliere **3** *v/i* tirare; ***pull a muscle*** farsi uno strappo muscolare
◆ **pull ahead** *v/i in race, competition* portarsi in testa
◆ **pull apart** *v/t* (*separate*) separare
◆ **pull away** *v/t* spostare
◆ **pull down** *v/t* (*lower*) tirar giù; (*demolish*) demolire
◆ **pull in** *v/i of bus, train* arrivare
◆ **pull off** *v/t* togliere; F *deal etc* portare a termine
◆ **pull out 1** *v/t* tirar fuori; *troops* (far) ritirare **2** *v/i of agreement, competition*, MIL ritirarsi; *of ship* partire
◆ **pull over** *v/i of driver* accostarsi
◆ **pull through** *v/i from an illness* farcela F
◆ **pull together 1** *v/i* (*cooperate*) cooperare **2** *v/t*: ***pull o.s. together*** darsi una mossa F
◆ **pull up 1** *v/t* (*raise*) tirar su; *plant, weeds* strappare **2** *v/i of car etc* fermarsi
pul•ley ['pʊlɪ] puleggia *f*
pull•o•ver ['pʊləʊvə(r)] pullover *m inv*
pulp [pʌlp] *soft mass* poltiglia *f*; *of fruit* polpa *f*; *for paper-making* pasta *f*
pul•pit ['pʊlpɪt] pulpito *m*
pul•sate [pʌl'seɪt] *v/i of heart, blood* pulsare; *of rhythm* vibrare
pulse [pʌls] polso *m*
pul•ver•ize ['pʌlvəraɪz] *v/t* polverizzare
pump [pʌmp] **1** *n* pompa *f* **2** *v/t* pompare
◆ **pump up** *v/t* gonfiare
pump•kin ['pʌmpkɪn] zucca *f*
pun [pʌn] gioco *m* di parole
punch [pʌntʃ] **1** *n blow* pugno *m*; *implement* punzonatrice *f* **2** *v/t with fist* dare un pugno a; *hole* perforare; *ticket* forare
'punch line finale *m*
punk (rock) ['pʌŋkrɒk] MUS punk *m inv*
punc•tu•al ['pʌŋktjʊəl] *adj* puntuale
punc•tu•al•i•ty [pʌŋktjʊ'ælətɪ] puntualità *f inv*
punc•tu•al•ly ['pʌŋktjʊəlɪ] *adv* puntualmente
punc•tu•ate ['pʌŋktjʊeɪt] *v/t* mettere la punteggiatura in
punc•tu•a•tion ['pʌŋktjʊ'eɪʃn] punteggiatura *f*
punc•tu'a•tion mark segno *m* d'interpunzione
punc•ture ['pʌŋktʃə(r)] **1** *n* foratura *f* **2** *v/t* forare
pun•gent ['pʌndʒənt] *adj* acre; *taste* aspro
pun•ish ['pʌnɪʃ] *v/t person* punire
pun•ish•ing ['pʌnɪʃɪŋ] *adj pace, schedule* estenuante
pun•ish•ment ['pʌnɪʃmənt] punizione *f*
pu•ny ['pju:nɪ] *adj person* gracile
pup [pʌp] cucciolo *m*
pu•pil[1] ['pju:pl] *of eye* pupilla *f*
pu•pil[2] ['pju:pl] (*student*) allievo *m*, -a *f*
pup•pet ['pʌpɪt] burattino *m*; *with strings* marionetta *f*
'pup•pet gov•ern•ment governo *m* fantoccio
pup•py ['pʌpɪ] cucciolo *m*
pur•chase[1] ['pɜ:tʃəs] **1** *n* acquisto *m* **2** *v/t* acquistare
pur•chase[2] ['pɜ:tʃəs] (*grip*) presa *f*
pur•chas•er ['pɜ:tʃəsə(r)] acquirente *m/f*
pure [pjʊə(r)] *adj* puro; ***pure new wool*** pura lana *f* vergine
pure•ly ['pjʊəlɪ] *adv* puramente
pur•ga•to•ry ['pɜ:gətrɪ] purgatorio *m*
purge [pɜ:dʒ] **1** *n of political party* epurazione *f* **2** *v/t* epurare
pu•ri•fy ['pjʊərɪfaɪ] *v/t* (*pret & pp* ***-ied***) *water* purificare
pu•ri•tan ['pjʊərɪtən] puritano *m*, -a *f*
pu•ri•tan•i•cal [pjʊərɪ'tænɪkl] *adj* puritano
pu•ri•ty ['pjʊərɪtɪ] purezza *f*
pur•ple ['pɜ:pl] *adj* viola *inv*
pur•pose ['pɜ:pəs] (*aim, object*) scopo *m*; ***on purpose*** di proposito
pur•pose•ful ['pɜ:pəsfʊl] *adj* risoluto
pur•pose•ly ['pɜ:pəslɪ] *adv* di proposito
purr [pɜ:(r)] *v/i of cat* far le fusa
purse [pɜ:s] *n for money* borsellino *m*; *Am* (*handbag*) borsetta *f*

pur•sue [pə'sjuː] *v/t person* inseguire; *career* intraprendere; *course of action* proseguire
pur•su•er [pə'sjuːə(r)] inseguitore *m*, -trice *f*
pur•suit [pə'sjuːt] (*chase*) inseguimento *m*; *of happiness etc* ricerca *f*; *activity* occupazione *f*; ***those in pursuit*** gli inseguitori
pus [pʌs] pus *m inv*
push [pʊʃ] **1** *n* (*shove*) spinta *f*; ***at the push of a button*** premendo un pulsante **2** *v/t* (*shove*) spingere; *button* premere; (*pressurize*) fare pressioni su; F *drugs* spacciare; ***be pushed for*** F essere a corto di; ***be pushing 40*** F essere sulla quarantina **3** *v/i* spingere
◆ **push ahead** *v/i* andare avanti
◆ **push along** *v/t cart etc* spingere
◆ **push away** *v/t* respingere
◆ **push off 1** *v/t lid* spingere via **2** *v/i* F (*leave*) andarsene; ***push off!*** sparisci! F
◆ **push on** *v/i* (*continue*) continuare
◆ **push up** *v/t prices* far salire
push-but•ton ['pʊʃbʌtn] *adj* a tastiera
'**push•chair** passeggino *m*
push•er ['pʊʃə(r)] F *of drugs* spacciatore *m*, -trice *f*
push-up ['pʊʃʌp] flessione *f* sulle braccia
push•y ['pʊʃɪ] *adj* F troppo intraprendente
puss, pus•sy (cat) [pʊs, 'pʊsɪ (kæt)] F micio *m*, -a *f*
◆ **pussy foot about** ['pʊsɪfʊt] *v/i* F tentennare
put [pʊt] *v/t* (*pret & pp* **put**) mettere; *question* porre; ***put the cost at …*** stimare il costo intorno a …
◆ **put across** *v/t ideas etc* trasmettere
◆ **put aside** *v/t* mettere da parte
◆ **put away** *v/t in cupboard etc* mettere via; *in institution* rinchiudere; (*consume*) far fuori; *money* mettere da parte
◆ **put back** *v/t* (*replace*) rimettere a posto
◆ **put by** *v/t money* mettere da parte
◆ **put down** *v/t* mettere giù; *deposit* versare; *rebellion* reprimere; *animal* abbattere; (*belittle*) sminuire; *in writing* scrivere; ***put one's foot down*** *in car* accelerare; (*be firm*) farsi valere; ***put X down to Y*** (*attribute*) attribuire X a Y
◆ **put forward** *v/t idea etc* avanzare
◆ **put in** *v/t* inserire; *overtime* fare; *time, effort* dedicare; *request, claim* presentare
◆ **put in for** *v/t* (*apply for*) fare domanda per
◆ **put off** *v/t light, radio, TV* spegnere; (*postpone*) rimandare; (*deter*) scoraggiare; (*repel*) disgustare; ***the accident put me off driving*** l'incidente mi ha fatto passare la voglia di guidare
◆ **put on** *v/t light, radio, TV* accendere; *tape, music* mettere su; *jacket, shoes, glasses* mettersi; *makeup* mettere; (*perform*) mettere in scena; (*assume*) affettare; ***put on the brakes*** frenare; ***put on weight*** ingrassare; ***she's just putting it on*** sta solo fingendo
◆ **put out** *v/t hand* allungare; *fire, light* spegnere
◆ **put through** *v/t*: ***I'll put you through (to him)*** glielo passo; ***I'll put you through to sales*** le passo l'ufficio vendite
◆ **put together** *v/t* (*assemble*) montare; (*organize*) organizzare
◆ **put up** *v/t hand* alzare; *person* ospitare; (*erect*) costruire; *prices* aumentare; *poster, notice* affiggere; *money* fornire; ***put up for sale*** mettere in vendita
◆ **put up with** *v/t* (*tolerate*) sopportare
putt [pʌt] *v/t & v/i* SP pattare
put•ty ['pʌtɪ] mastice *m*
puz•zle ['pʌzl] **1** *n* (*mystery*) mistero *m*; *game* rebus *m inv*; *jigsaw* puzzle *m inv*; *crossword* cruciverba *m inv* **2** *v/t* lasciar perplesso
puz•zling ['pʌzlɪŋ] *adj* inspiegabile
PVC [piːviː'siː] *abbr* (= ***polyvinyl chloride***) PVC *m inv* (= polivinilcloruro *m*)
py•ja•mas [pə'dʒɑːməz] *npl* pigiama *m*
py•lon ['paɪlən] pilone *m*

Q

quack[1] [kwæk] **1** *n of duck* qua qua *m inv* **2** *v/i* fare qua qua
quack[2] [kwæk] F (*bad doctor*) ciarlatano *m*, -a *f*; ***I'm going to see the quack*** vado dal dottore
quad•ran•gle ['kwɒdræŋgl] *figure* quadrilatero *m*; *courtyard* cortile *m*
quad•ru•ped ['kwɒdrʊped] quadrupede *m*
quad•ru•ple ['kwɒdrʊpl] *v/i* quadruplicare
quad•ru•plets ['kwɒdrʊplɪts] *npl* quattro gemelli *mpl*
quads [kwɒdz] *npl* F quattro gemelli *mpl*
quag•mire ['kwɒgmaɪə(r)] *fig* ginepraio *m*
quail [kweɪl] *v/i* perdersi d'animo
quaint [kweɪnt] *adj pretty* pittoresco; *slightly eccentric: ideas etc* curioso
quake [kweɪk] **1** *n* (*earthquake*) terremoto *m* **2** *v/i also fig* tremare
qual•i•fi•ca•tion [kwɒlfɪ'keɪʃn] *from university etc* titolo *m* di studio; *of remark etc* riserva *f*; ***have the right qualifications for a job*** *skills* avere tutti i requisiti per un lavoro
qual•i•fied ['kwɒlɪfaɪd] *adj doctor, engineer etc* abilitato; (*restricted*) con riserva; ***I am not qualified to judge*** non sono in grado di valutare
qual•i•fy ['kwɒlɪfaɪ] (*pret & pp* **-ied**) **1** *v/t of degree, course etc* abilitare; *remark etc* precisare **2** *v/i* (*get certificate etc*) ottenere la qualifica (**as** di); *in competition* qualificarsi; ***our team has qualified for the semi-final*** la nostra squadra è entrata in semifinale; ***that doesn't qualify as …*** non può essere considerato …
qual•i•ty ['kwɒlətɪ] qualità *f inv*
qual•i•ty con'trol controllo *m* (di) qualità
qualm [kwɑːm]: ***have no qualms about …*** non aver scrupoli a …
quan•da•ry ['kwɒndərɪ] *n* dilemma *m*; ***be in a quandary*** avere un dilemma
quan•ti•fy ['kwɒntɪfaɪ] *v/t* (*pret & pp* **-ied**) quantificare
quan•ti•ty ['kwɒntətɪ] quantità *f inv*
quan•tum 'phys•ics ['kwɒntəm] teoria *f* fisica dei quanti
quar•an•tine ['kwɒrəntiːn] *n* quarantena *f*
quar•rel ['kwɒrəl] **1** *n* litigio *m* **2** *v/i* (*pret & pp* **-led**, *Am* **-ed**) litigare
quar•rel•some ['kwɒrəlsʌm] *adj* litigioso
quar•ry[1] ['kwɒrɪ] *in hunt* preda *f*
quar•ry[2] ['kwɒrɪ] *for mining* cava *f*
quart [kwɔːt] quarto *m* di gallone
quar•ter ['kwɔːtə(r)] **1** *n* quarto *m*; *part of town* quartiere *m*; ***a quarter of an hour*** un quarto d'ora; (***a***) ***quarter to 5*** le cinque meno un quarto; (***a***) ***quarter past 5*** le cinque e un quarto **2** *v/t* dividere in quattro parti
quar•ter-'fi•nal partita *f* dei quarti *mpl* di finale
quar•ter-'fi•nal•ist concorrente *m/f* dei quarti di finale
quar•ter•ly ['kwɔːtəlɪ] **1** *adj* trimestrale **2** *adv* trimestralmente
quar•ters ['kwɔːtəz] *npl* MIL quartieri *mpl*
quar•tet [kwɔː'tet] MUS quartetto *m*
quartz [kwɔːts] quarzo *m*
quash [kwɒʃ] *v/t rebellion* reprimere; *court decision* annullare
qua•ver ['kweɪvə(r)] **1** *n in voice* tremolio *m*; MUS croma *f* **2** *v/i of voice* tremolare
quay [kiː] banchina *f*
'quay•side banchina *f*
quea•sy ['kwiːzɪ] *adj* nauseato
queen [kwiːn] regina *f*
queen 'bee ape *f* regina
queer [kwɪə(r)] *adj* (*peculiar*) strano
queer•ly ['kwɪə(r)lɪ] *adv* stranamente
quell [kwel] *v/t* soffocare
quench [kwentʃ] *v/t also fig* spegnere
que•ry ['kwɪərɪ] **1** *n* interrogativo *m* **2** *v/t* (*pret & pp* **-ied**) *express doubt about* contestare; *check* controllare
quest [kwest] *n* ricerca *f*
ques•tion ['kwestʃn] **1** *n* domanda *f*; *matter* questione *f*; ***in question*** *being talked about* in questione; ***in question*** *in doubt* in dubbio; ***it's a question of money / time*** è questione di soldi / tempo; ***that's out of the question*** è fuori discussione **2** *v/t person* interrogare; (*doubt*) dubitare di; ***that's not being questioned*** nessuno lo mette in dubbio
ques•tion•a•ble ['kwestʃnəbl] *adj* discutibile; (*dubious*) dubbio
ques•tion•er ['kwestʃnə(r)] *n* interrogatore *m*, -trice *f*
ques•tion•ing ['kwestʃnɪŋ] **1** *adj look, tone* interrogativo **2** *n* interrogatorio *m*
'ques•tion mark punto *m* interrogativo
'ques•tion mas•ter presentatore *m*, -trice *f* di quiz
ques•tion•naire [kwestʃə'neə(r)] *n* questionario *m*

queue [kjuː] **1** *n* coda *f*, fila *f* **2** *v/i* fare la fila *o* la coda
queue-jump•er ['kjuːdʒʌmpə(r)] persona *f* che non rispetta la coda
quib•ble ['kwɪbl] *v/i* cavillare
quick [kwɪk] *adj person* svelto; *reply*, *change* veloce; ***be quick!*** fai presto!, fai in fretta!; ***let's have a quick drink*** beviamo qualcosina?; ***can I have a quick look?*** posso dare un'occhiatina?; ***that was quick!*** già fatto?
quick•ie ['kwɪkɪ] F: ***have a quickie*** *quick drink* bere qualcosina
quick•ly ['kwɪklɪ] *adv* rapidamente, in fretta
'**quick•sand** sabbie *fpl* mobili
'**quick•sil•ver** mercurio *m*
quick•wit•ted [kwɪk'wɪtɪd] *adj* sveglio
quid [kwɪd] F sterlina *f*; ***50 quid*** 50 sterline
qui•et ['kwaɪət] *adj voice*, *music* basso; *engine* silenzioso; *street*, *life*, *town* tranquillo; ***keep quiet about sth*** tenere segreto qc; ***quiet!*** silenzio!, stai zitto!
◆ **quieten down** ['kwaɪətn] **1** *v/t* calmare **2** *v/i* calmarsi
quiet•ly ['kwaɪətlɪ] *adv not loudly* silenziosamente, senza far rumore; (*without fuss*) semplicemente; (*peacefully*) tranquillamente
quiet•ness ['kwaɪətnɪs] *of night*, *street* tranquillità *f*, calma *f*; *of voice* dolcezza *f*
quilt [kwɪlt] *on bed* piumino *m*
quilt•ed ['kwɪltɪd] *adj* trapuntato
quin•ine ['kwɪniːn] chinino *m*
quin•tet [kwɪn'tet] MUS quintetto *m*
quip [kwɪp] **1** *n* battuta *f* (di spirito) **2** *v/i* (*pret & pp* ***-ped***) scherzare
quirk [kwɜːk] bizzarria *f*
quirk•y ['kwɜːkɪ] *adj* bizzarro
quit [kwɪt] (*pret & pp* ***quit***) **1** *v/t job* mollare F; ***quit doing sth*** smettere di fare qc **2** *v/i* (*leave job*) licenziarsi; COMPUT uscire; ***get one's notice to quit*** *from landlord* ricevere la disdetta
quite [kwaɪt] *adv* (*fairly*) abbastanza; (*completely*) completamente; ***not quite ready*** non ancora pronto; ***I didn't quite understand*** non ho capito bene; ***is that right? – not quite*** giusto? – non esattamente; ***quite!*** esatto!; ***quite a lot*** *drink*, *change* parecchio; ***quite a lot better*** molto meglio; ***quite a few*** un bel po'; ***it was quite a surprise / change*** è stata una bella sorpresa / un bel cambiamento
quits [kwɪts] *adj*: ***be quits with s.o.*** essere pari con qu
quit•ter ['kwɪtə(r)] F rinunciatario *m*, -a *f*
quiv•er ['kwɪvə(r)] *v/i* tremare
quiz [kwɪz] **1** *n* quiz *m inv* **2** *v/t* (*pret & pp* ***-zed***) interrogare
'**quiz mas•ter** conduttore *m*, -trice *f* (di gioco a quiz)
'**quiz pro•gram** *Am*, '**quiz pro•gramme** gioco *m* a quiz
quo•ta ['kwəʊtə] quota *f*
quo•ta•tion [kwəʊ'teɪʃn] *from author* citazione *f*; *price* preventivo *m*; ***give s.o. a quotation for sth*** fare un preventivo a qu per qc
quo'ta•tion marks *npl* virgolette *fpl*
quote [kwəʊt] **1** *n from author* citazione *f*; *price* preventivo *m*; (*quotation mark*) virgoletta *f*; ***in quotes*** tra virgolette **2** *v/t text* citare; *price* stimare; ***quoted on the Stock Exchange*** quotato in Borsa **3** *v/i*: ***quoted from an author*** citare un autore

R

rab•bi ['ræbaɪ] rabbino *m*
rab•bit ['ræbɪt] coniglio *m*
◆ **rab•bit on** *v/i* P blaterare
rab•ble ['ræbl] marmaglia *f*
rab•ble-rous•er ['ræblraʊzə(r)] agitatore *m*, -trice *f*
ra•bies ['reɪbiːz] *nsg* rabbia *f*, idrofobia *f*
race[1] [reɪs] *n of people* razza *f*
race[2] [reɪs] **1** *n* SP gara *f*; ***the races*** (*horse races*) le corse **2** *v/i* (*run fast*) correre; ***he raced against the world champion*** ha gareggiato contro il campione del mondo **3** *v/t*: ***I'll race you*** facciamo una gara
'**race•course** ippodromo *m*
'**race•horse** cavallo *m* da corsa
'**race re•la•tions** *npl* rapporti *mpl* interrazziali
'**race riot** scontri *mpl* razziali
'**race•track** pista *f*; *for horses* ippodromo *m*
ra•cial ['reɪʃl] *adj* razziale; ***racial equality*** parità *f inv* razziale
rac•ing ['reɪsɪŋ] corse *fpl*
'**rac•ing car** auto *f inv* da corsa
'**rac•ing driv•er** pilota *m* automobilistico
ra•cis•m ['reɪsɪzm] razzismo *m*
ra•cist ['reɪsɪst] **1** *n* razzista *m/f* **2** *adj* razzista
rack [ræk] **1** *n for parking bikes* rastrelliera *f*; *for bags on train* portabagagli *m inv*; *for CDs* porta-CD *m inv* **2** *v/t*: ***rack one's brains*** scervellarsi
rack•et[1] ['rækɪt] SP racchetta *f*
rack•et[2] ['rækɪt] (*noise*) baccano *m*; *criminal activity* racket *m inv*
ra•dar ['reɪdɑː(r)] radar *m inv*
'**ra•dar screen** schermo *m* radar
'**ra•dar trap** autovelox® *m*
ra•di•al '**tire** *Am*, **ra•di•al** '**tyre** ['reɪdɪəl] pneumatico *m* radiale
ra•di•ance ['reɪdɪəns] splendore *m*
ra•di•ant ['reɪdɪənt] *adj smile* splendente; *appearance* raggiante
ra•di•ate ['reɪdɪeɪt] *v/i of heat, light* diffondersi
ra•di•a•tion [reɪdɪ'eɪʃn] PHYS radiazione *f*
ra•di•a•tor ['reɪdɪeɪtə(r)] *in room* termosifone *m*; *in car* radiatore *m*
rad•i•cal ['rædɪkl] **1** *adj* radicale **2** *n* radicale *m/f*
rad•i•cal•ism ['rædɪkəlɪzm] POL radicalismo *m*
rad•i•cal•ly ['rædɪklɪ] *adv* radicalmente
ra•di•o ['reɪdɪəʊ] radio *f inv*; ***on the radio*** alla radio; ***by radio*** via radio
ra•di•o•ac•tive [reɪdɪəʊ'æktɪv] *adj* radioattivo
ra•di•o•ac•tive '**waste** scorie *fpl* radioattive
ra•di•o•ac•tiv•i•ty [reɪdɪəʊæk'tɪvətɪ] radioattività *f inv*
ra•di•o a'larm radiosveglia *f*
ra•di•og•ra•phy [reɪdɪ'ɒgrəfɪ] radiografia *f*
ra•di•og•ra•pher [reɪdɪ'ɒgrəfə(r)] radiologo *m*, -a *f*
'**ra•di•o sta•tion** stazione *f* radiofonica, radio *f inv*
'**ra•di•o tax•i** radiotaxi *m inv*
ra•di•o'ther•a•py radioterapia *f*
rad•ish ['rædɪʃ] ravanello *m*
ra•di•us ['reɪdɪəs] raggio *m*
raf•fle ['ræfl] *n* lotteria *f*
raft [rɑːft] zattera *f*
raf•ter ['rɑːftə(r)] travicello *m*
rag [ræg] *n for cleaning etc* straccio *m*; ***dressed in rags*** vestito di stracci
rage [reɪdʒ] **1** *n* rabbia *f*, collera *f*; ***be in a rage*** essere furioso; ***be all the rage*** F essere di moda **2** *v/i of person* infierire; *of storm* infuriare
rag•ged ['rægɪd] *adj* stracciato
raid [reɪd] **1** *n* raid *m inv* **2** *v/t of police, robbers* fare un raid in; *fridge, orchard* fare razzia in
raid•er ['reɪdə(r)] *on bank etc* rapinatore *m*, -trice *f*
rail [reɪl] *n on track* rotaia *f*; (*handrail*) corrimano *m*; (*barrier*) parapetto *m*; ***curtain rail*** bastone *m* per tende; ***towel rail*** portasciugamano *m inv*; ***by rail*** in treno
rail•ings ['reɪlɪŋz] *npl around park etc* inferriata *f*
'**rail•road** *etc Am* → ***railway*** *etc*
rail•way ['reɪlweɪ] ferrovia *f*
'**rail•way line** linea *f* ferroviaria
'**rail•way sta•tion** stazione *f* ferroviaria
rain [reɪn] **1** *n* pioggia *f*; ***in the rain*** sotto la pioggia **2** *v/i* piovere; ***it's raining*** sta piovendo
'**rain•bow** arcobaleno *m*
'**rain•coat** impermeabile *m*
'**rain•drop** goccia *f* di pioggia
'**rain•fall** piovosità *f inv*
'**rain for•est** foresta *f* pluviale
'**rain•proof** *adj fabric* impermeabile
'**rain•storm** temporale *m*
rain•y ['reɪnɪ] *adj day* di pioggia; *weather*

piovoso; ***it's rainy*** piove molto
raise [reɪz] **1** *n esp Am*: *in salary* aumento *m* **2** *v/t shelf*, *question* sollevare; *offer* aumentare; *children* allevare; *money* raccogliere
rai•sin ['reɪzn] uva *f* passa
rake [reɪk] *n for garden* rastrello *m*
◆ **rake up** *v/t leaves* rastrellare; *fig* rivangare
ral•ly ['rælɪ] *n meeting* raduno *m*; MOT rally *m inv*; *in tennis* scambio *m*
◆ **rally round** (*pret & pp* **-ied**) **1** *v/i* offrire aiuto **2** *v/t*: ***rally round s.o.*** aiutare qu
ram [ræm] **1** *n* montone *m* **2** *v/t* (*pret & pp* **-med**) *ship*, *car* sbattere contro
RAM [ræm] *abbr* COMPUT (= ***random access memory***) RAM *f inv*
ram•ble ['ræmbl] **1** *n walk* escursione *f* **2** *v/i walk* fare passeggiate; *in speaking* divagare; *talk incoherently* vaneggiare
ram•bler ['ræmblə(r)] *walker* escursionista *m/f*
ram•bling ['ræmblɪŋ] *adj speech* sconnesso
ramp [ræmp] rampa *f*; *for raising vehicle* ponte *m* idraulico
ram•page ['ræmpeɪdʒ] **1** *v/i* scatenarsi **2** *n*: ***go on the rampage*** scatenarsi
ram•pant ['ræmpənt] *adj inflation* dilagante
ram•part ['ræmpɑːt] bastione *m*
ram•shack•le ['ræmʃækl] *adj* sgangherato
ran [ræn] *pret* → ***run***
ranch [rɑːntʃ] ranch *m inv*
ran•cid ['rænsɪd] *adj* rancido
ran•cour ['ræŋkə(r)] rancore *m*
R&D [ɑːrən'diː] *abbr* (= ***research and development***) ricerca *f* e sviluppo *m*
ran•dom ['rændəm] **1** *adj* casuale; ***random sample*** campione *m* casuale; ***take a random sample*** prendere un campione a caso **2** *n*: ***at random*** a caso
ran•dy ['rændɪ] *adj* F arrapato F
rang [ræŋ] *pret* → ***ring***
range [reɪndʒ] **1** *n of products* gamma *f*; *of missile*, *gun* gittata *f*; *of salary* scala *f*; *of voice* estensione *f*; *of mountains* catena *f*; (*shooting range*) poligono *m* (di tiro); ***at close range*** a distanza ravvicinata **2** *v/i*: ***range from X to Y*** variare da X a Y
rank [ræŋk] **1** *n* MIL grado *m*; *in society* rango *m*; ***the ranks*** MIL la truppa **2** *v/t* classificare
◆ **rank among** *v/t* classificarsi tra
ran•kle ['ræŋkl] *v/i* bruciare
ran•sack ['rænsæk] *v/t* saccheggiare
ran•som ['rænsəm] *n* riscatto *m*; ***hold s.o. to ransom*** tenere in ostaggio qu
'ran•som mon•ey (soldi *mpl* del) riscatto *m*
rant [rænt] *v/i*: ***rant and rave*** inveire
rap [ræp] **1** *n at door etc* colpo *m*; MUS rap *m inv* **2** *v/t* (*pret & pp* **-ped**) *table etc* battere
◆ **rap at** *v/t window etc* bussare a
rape[1] [reɪp] **1** *n* stupro *m* **2** *v/t* violentare
rape[2] [reɪp] *n* BOT colza *f*
'rape vic•tim vittima *f* stupro
rap•id ['ræpɪd] *adj* rapido
ra•pid•i•ty [rə'pɪdətɪ] rapidità *f inv*
rap•id•ly ['ræpɪdlɪ] *adv* rapidamente
rap•ids ['ræpɪdz] *npl* rapide *fpl*
rap•ist ['reɪpɪst] violentatore *m*
rap•port [ræ'pɔː(r)] rapporto *m*
rap•ture ['ræptʃə(r)] *n*: ***go into raptures over*** andare in estasi per
rap•tur•ous ['ræptʃərəs] *adj* entusiastico
rare [reə(r)] *adj* raro; *steak* al sangue
rare•ly ['reəlɪ] *adv* raramente
rar•i•ty ['reərətɪ] rarità *f inv*
ras•cal ['rɑːskl] birbante *m/f*
rash[1] [ræʃ] *n* MED orticaria *f*
rash[2] [ræʃ] *adj action*, *behaviour* avventato
rash•er ['ræʃə(r)] fettina *f*
rash•ly ['ræʃlɪ] *adv* avventatamente
rasp•ber•ry ['rɑːzbərɪ] lampone *m*
rat [ræt] *n* ratto *m*
rate [reɪt] **1** *n of exchange* tasso *m*; *of pay*, *pricing* tariffa *f*; (*speed*) ritmo *m*; ***rate of interest*** FIN tasso *m* d'interesse; ***at this rate*** (*at this speed*) di questo passo; ***at any rate*** in ogni modo **2** *v/t* (*consider*, *rank*) reputare
rather ['rɑːðə(r)] *adv* piuttosto; ***I would rather stay here*** preferirei stare qui; ***or would you rather ...?*** o preferiresti ...?
rat•i•fi•ca•tion [rætɪfɪ'keɪʃn] ratifica *f*
rat•i•fy ['rætɪfaɪ] *v/t* (*pret & pp* **-ied**) ratificare
rat•ings ['reɪtɪŋz] *npl* indice *m* d'ascolto
ra•ti•o ['reɪʃɪəʊ] proporzione *f*
ra•tion ['ræʃn] **1** *n* razione *f* **2** *v/t supplies* razionare
ra•tion•al ['ræʃənl] *adj* razionale
ra•tion•al•i•ty [ræʃə'nælɪtɪ] razionalità *f inv*
ra•tion•al•i•za•tion [ræʃənəlaɪ'zeɪʃn] razionalizzazione *f*
ra•tion•al•ize ['ræʃənəlaɪz] *v/t & v/i* razionalizzare
ra•tion•al•ly ['ræʃənlɪ] *adv* razionalmente
'rat race corsa *f* al successo
rat•tle ['rætl] **1** *n noise* rumore *m*; *toy* sonaglio *m* **2** *v/t* scuotere **3** *v/i* far rumore
◆ **rattle off** *v/t poem*, *list of names* snoc-

ciolare
◆ **rattle through** *v/t* fare di gran carriera
'**rat•tle•snake** serpente *m* a sonagli
rau•cous ['rɔːkəs] *adj* sguaiato
rav•age ['rævɪdʒ] **1** *n*: ***the ravages of time*** le ingiurie del tempo **2** *v/t*: ***ravaged by war*** devastato dalla guerra
rave [reɪv] **1** *v/i* delirare; ***rave about sth*** *be very enthusiastic* entusiasmarsi per qc **2** *n party* rave *m inv*
rave re'view recensione *f* entusiastica
ra•ven ['reɪvn] corvo *m*
rav•e•nous ['rævənəs] *adj* famelico
rav•e•nous•ly ['rævənəslɪ] *adv* voracemente
ra•vine [rə'viːn] burrone *m*
rav•ing ['reɪvɪŋ] *adv*: ***raving mad*** matto da legare
ra•vi•o•li ['rævɪəʊlɪ] *nsg* ravioli *mpl*
rav•ish•ing ['rævɪʃɪŋ] *adj* incantevole
raw [rɔː] *adj meat, vegetable* crudo; *sugar, iron* grezzo
raw ma'te•ri•al materia *f* prima
ray [reɪ] raggio *m*; ***a ray of hope*** un raggio di speranza
raze [reɪz] *v/t*: ***raze to the ground*** radere al suolo
ra•zor ['reɪzə(r)] rasoio *m*
'**ra•zor blade** lametta *f* da barba
re [riː] *prep* COM con riferimento a
reach [riːʧ] **1** *n*: ***within reach*** vicino (***of*** a); *within arm's reach* a portata (di mano); ***out of reach*** non a portata (***of*** di); ***keep out of reach of children*** tenere lontano dalla portata dei bambini **2** *v/t city etc* arrivare a; *decision, agreement, conclusion* raggiungere; ***can you reach it?*** ci arrivi?
◆ **reach out** *v/i* allungare la mano
re•act [rɪ'ækt] *v/i* reagire
re•ac•tion [rɪ'ækʃn] reazione *f*
re•ac•tion•ar•y [rɪ'ækʃnrɪ] **1** *n* POL reazionario *m*, -a *f* **2** *adj* POL reazionario
re•ac•tor [rɪ'æktə(r)] *nuclear* reattore *m*
read [riːd] (*pret & pp* ***read*** [red]) **1** *v/i* leggere; ***read to s.o.*** leggere a qu **2** *v/t* leggere; (*study*) studiare
◆ **read out** *v/t aloud* leggere a voce alta
◆ **read up on** *v/t* documentarsi su
rea•da•ble ['riːdəbl] *adj handwriting* leggibile; *book* di piacevole lettura
read•er ['riːdə(r)] *person* lettore *m*, -trice *f*
read•i•ly ['redɪlɪ] *adv* (*willingly*) volentieri; (*easily*) facilmente
read•i•ness ['redɪnɪs] *for action* disponibilità *f inv*; *to agree* prontezza *f*
read•ing ['riːdɪŋ] *also from meter* lettura *f*
'**read•ing mat•ter** roba *f* da leggere
re•ad•just [riːə'dʒʌst] **1** *v/t equipment, controls* regolare **2** *v/i to conditions* riadattarsi
read-'on•ly file COMPUT file *m inv* di sola lettura
read-'on•ly mem•o•ry COMPUT memoria *f* di sola lettura
read•y ['redɪ] *adj* pronto; ***get (o.s.) ready*** prepararsi; ***get sth ready*** preparare qc
read•y 'cash contanti *mpl*
read•y-made *adj stew etc* precotto; *solution* bell'e pronto
read•y-to-wear *adj* confezionato
real [riːl] *adj* vero
'**real es•tate** proprietà *fpl* immobiliari
re•a•lis•m ['rɪəlɪzm] realismo *m*
re•a•list ['rɪəlɪst] realista *m/f*
re•a•lis•tic [rɪə'lɪstɪk] *adj* realistico
re•a•lis•tic•al•ly [rɪə'lɪstɪklɪ] *adv* realisticamente
re•al•i•ty [rɪ'ælətɪ] realtà *f inv*
re•a•li•za•tion [rɪəlaɪ'zeɪʃn] realizzazione *f*
re•a•lize ['rɪəlaɪz] *v/t* rendersi conto di, realizzare; FIN realizzare; ***I realize now that …*** ora capisco che …
real•ly ['rɪəlɪ] *adv* veramente; ***really?*** davvero?; ***not really*** (*not much*) non proprio
real 'time *n* COMPUT tempo *m* reale
real-time *adj* COMPUT in tempo reale
reap [riːp] *v/t* mietere
re•ap•pear [riːə'pɪər] *v/i* riapparire
reappearance [riːə'pɪərəns] ricomparsa *f*
rear [rɪə(r)] **1** *n of building* retro *m*; *of train* parte *f* posteriore **2** *adj* posteriore
rear 'end F *of person* posteriore *m*
rear-'end *v/t*: ***be rear-ended*** F essere tamponato
rear 'light *of car* fanalino *m* posteriore
re•arm [riː'ɑːm] **1** *v/t* riarmare **2** *v/i* riarmarsi
'**rear•most** *adj* ultimo
re•ar•range [riːə'reɪnʒ] *v/t furniture* spostare; *schedule, meetings* cambiare
rear-view 'mir•ror specchietto *m* retrovisore
rea•son ['riːzn] **1** *n faculty* ragione *f*; (*cause*) motivo *m*; ***see / listen to reason*** ascoltare ragione **2** *v/i*: ***reason with s.o.*** far ragionare con qu
rea•so•na•ble ['riːznəbl] *adj person, price* ragionevole; *weather, health* discreto; ***a reasonable number of people*** un discreto numero di persone
rea•son•a•bly ['riːznəblɪ] *adv act, behave* ragionevolmente; (*quite*) abbastanza
rea•son•ing ['riːznɪŋ] ragionamento *m*
re•as•sure [riːə'ʃʊə(r)] *v/t* rassicurare
re•as•sur•ing [riːə'ʃʊərɪŋ] *adj* rassicurante

re•bate ['riːbeɪt] *money back* rimborso *m*
reb•el ['rebl] **1** *n* ribelle *m/f*; ***rebel forces*** forze *fpl* ribelli **2** *v/i* [rɪ'bel] (*pret & pp* ***-led***) ribellarsi
reb•el•lion [rɪ'belɪən] ribellione *f*
reb•el•lious [rɪ'belɪəs] *adj* ribelle
reb•el•lious•ly [rɪ'belɪəslɪ] *adv* con atteggiamento ribelle
reb•el•lious•ness [rɪ'belɪəsnɪs] spirito *m* di ribellione
re•boot [riː'buːt] *v/t & v/i* COMPUT riavviare
re•bound [rɪ'baʊnd] *v/i of ball etc* rimbalzare
re•buff [rɪ'bʌf] *n* secco rifiuto *m*
re•build ['riːbɪld] *v/t* (*pret & pp* ***-built***) ricostruire
re•buke [rɪ'bjuːk] *v/t* rimproverare
re•call [rɪ'kɔːl] *v/t* richiamare; (*remember*) ricordare
re•cap ['riːkæp] *v/i* (*pret & pp* ***-ped***) F ricapitolare
re•cap•ture [riː'kæptʃə(r)] *v/t criminal* ricatturare; *town* riconquistare
re•cede [rɪ'siːd] *v/i of flood waters* abbassarsi
re•ced•ing [rɪ'siːdɪŋ] *adj forehead, chin* sfuggente; ***have a receding hairline*** essere stempiato
re•ceipt [rɪ'siːt] *for purchase* ricevuta *f*, scontrino *m*; ***acknowledge receipt of sth*** accusare ricevuta di qc; ***receipts*** FIN introiti *mpl*
re•ceive [rɪ'siːv] *v/t* ricevere
re•ceiv•er [rɪ'siːvə(r)] *of letter* destinatario *m*, -a *f*; TELEC ricevitore *m*; *radio* apparecchio *m* ricevente
re•ceiv•er•ship [rɪ'siːvəʃɪp]: ***be in receivership*** essere in amministrazione controllata
re•cent ['riːsnt] *adj* recente
re•cent•ly ['riːsntlɪ] *adv* recentemente
re•cep•tion [rɪ'sepʃn] *in hotel, company* reception *f inv*; *formal party* ricevimento *m*; (*welcome*) accoglienza *f*; *on radio, mobile phone* ricezione *f*
re'cep•tion desk banco *m* della reception
re•cep•tion•ist [rɪ'sepʃnɪst] receptionist *m/f inv*
re•cep•tive [rɪ'septɪv] *adj*: ***be receptive to sth*** essere ricettivo verso qc
re•cess ['riːses] *in wall etc* rientranza *f*; *of parliament* vacanza *f*
re•ces•sion [rɪ'seʃn] *economic* recessione *f*
re•charge [riː'tʃɑːdʒ] *v/t battery* ricaricare
re•ci•pe ['resəpɪ] ricetta *f*
're•ci•pe book ricettario *m*
re•cip•i•ent [rɪ'sɪpɪənt] destinatario *m*, -a *f*
re•cip•ro•cal [rɪ'sɪprəkl] *adj* reciproco
re•cit•al [rɪ'saɪtl] MUS recital *m inv*
re•cite [rɪ'saɪt] *v/t poem* recitare; *details, facts* enumerare
reck•less ['reklɪs] *adj* spericolato
reck•less•ly ['reklɪslɪ] *adv behave, drive* in modo spericolato; *spend* avventatamente
reck•on ['rekən] *v/i* (*think, consider*) pensare
◆ **reckon on** *v/t* contare su
◆ **reckon with** *v/t*: ***have s.o./sth to reckon with*** dover fare i conti con qu / qc
reck•on•ing ['rekənɪŋ] calcoli *mpl*
re•claim [rɪ'kleɪm] *v/t land* bonificare
re•cline [rɪ'klaɪn] *v/i* sdraiarsi
re•clin•er [rɪ'klaɪnə(r)] *chair* poltrona *f* reclinabile
re•cluse [rɪ'kluːs] eremita *m/f*
rec•og•ni•tion [rekəg'nɪʃn] *of state, s.o.'s achievements* riconoscimento *m*; ***have changed beyond recognition*** essere irriconoscibile
rec•og•niz•a•ble [rekəg'naɪzəbl] *adj* riconoscibile
rec•og•nize ['rekəgnaɪz] *v/t* riconoscere; ***it can be recognized by ...*** si riconosce da ...
re•coil [rɪ'kɔɪl] *v/i* indietreggiare
rec•ol•lect [rekə'lekt] *v/t* rammentare
rec•ol•lec•tion [rekə'lekʃn] ricordo *m*
rec•om•mend [rekə'mend] *v/t* consigliare
rec•om•men•da•tion [rekəmen'deɪʃn] consiglio *m*
rec•om•pense ['rekəmpens] *n fml* ricompensa *f*; LAW risarcimento *m*
rec•on•cile ['rekənsaɪl] *v/t people, differences* riconciliare; *facts* conciliare; ***reconcile o.s. to ...*** rassegnarsi a ...; ***they are now reconciled*** si sono riconciliati
rec•on•cil•i•a•tion [rekənsɪlɪ'eɪʃn] *of people, differences* riconciliazione *f*; *of facts* conciliazione *f*
re•con•di•tion [riːkən'dɪʃn] *v/t* ricondizionare
re•con•nais•sance [rɪ'kɒnɪsns] MIL ricognizione *f*
re•con•sid•er [riːkən'sɪdə(r)] **1** *v/t offer, one's position* riconsiderare **2** *v/i* ripensare
re•con•struct [riːkən'strʌkt] *v/t city, crime, life* ricostruire
rec•ord[1] ['rekɔːd] *n* MUS disco *m*; SP *etc* record *m inv*, primato *m*; *written document etc* nota *f*; *in database* record *m inv*; ***records*** archivio *m*; ***say sth off the record*** dire qc ufficiosamente; ***have a criminal record*** avere precedenti penali; ***he has a***

good record for punctuality / reliability è sempre stato puntuale / affidabile
record[2] [rɪ'kɔːd] *v/t electronically* registrare; *in writing* annotare
'rec•ord-break•ing *adj* da record
re•cor•der [rɪ'kɔːdə(r)] MUS flauto *m* dolce
'rec•ord hold•er primatista *m/f*
re•cord•ing [rɪ'kɔːdɪŋ] registrazione *f*
re'cord•ing stu•di•o sala *f* di registrazione
rec•ord play•er ['rekɔːd] giradischi *m inv*
re•count [rɪ'kaʊnt] *v/t* (*tell*) raccontare
re-count ['riːkaʊnt] **1** *n of votes* nuovo conteggio *m* **2** *v/t* (*count again*) ricontare
re•coup [rɪ'kuːp] *v/t financial losses* rifarsi di
re•cov•er [rɪ'kʌvə(r)] **1** *v/t stolen goods* recuperare **2** *v/i from illness* rimettersi
re•cov•er•y [rɪ'kʌvərɪ] *of stolen goods* recupero *m*; *from illness* guarigione *f*; ***he has made a speedy recovery*** è guarito in fretta
rec•re•a•tion [rekrɪ'eɪʃn] ricreazione *f*
rec•re•a•tion•al [rekrɪ'eɪʃnl] *adj done for pleasure* ricreativo
re•cruit [rɪ'kruːt] **1** *n* MIL recluta *f*; *to company* neoassunto *m*, -a *f* **2** *v/t new staff* assumere; *members* arruolare
re•cruit•ment [rɪ'kruːtmənt] assunzione *f*; MIL, POL reclutamento *m*
re'cruit•ment drive campagna *f* di arruolamento
rec•tan•gle ['rektæŋgl] rettangolo *m*
rec•tan•gu•lar [rek'tæŋgjʊlə(r)] *adj* rettangolare
rec•ti•fy ['rektɪfaɪ] *v/t* (*pret & pp* ***-ied***) (*put right*) rettificare
re•cu•pe•rate [rɪ'kjuːpəreɪt] *v/i* recuperare
re•cur [rɪ'kɜː(r)] (*pret & pp* ***-red***) *v/i of error, event* ripetersi; *of symptoms* ripresentarsi
re•cur•rent [rɪ'kʌrənt] *adj* ricorrente
re•cy•cla•ble [riː'saɪkləbl] *adj* riciclabile
re•cy•cle [riː'saɪkl] *v/t* riciclare
re•cy•cling [riː'saɪklɪŋ] riciclo *m*
red [red] *adj* rosso; ***in the red*** FIN in rosso
Red 'Cross Croce *f* Rossa
red•den ['redn] *v/i* (*blush*) arrossire
re•dec•o•rate [riː'dekəreɪt] *v/t* ritinteggiare; *change wallpaper* ritapezzare
re•deem [rɪ'diːm] *v/t debt* estinguere; *sinners* redimere
re•deem•ing [rɪ'diːmɪŋ]: ***redeeming feature*** aspetto *m* positivo
re•demp•tion [rɪ'dempʃn] REL redenzione *f*
re•de•vel•op [riːdɪ'veləp] *v/t part of town* risanare
red-'hand•ed [red'hændɪd] *adj*: ***catch s.o. red-handed*** cogliere qu in flagrante
'red•head rosso *m*, -a *f*
red-'hot *adj* rovente
red-'let•ter day giorno *m* memorabile
red 'light *at traffic lights* rosso *m*
red 'light dis•trict quartiere *m* a luci rosse
red 'meat carni *fpl* rosse
re•dou•ble [riː'dʌbl] *v/t*: ***redouble one's efforts*** intensificare gli sforzi
red 'pep•per peperone *m* rosso
red 'tape F burocrazia *f*
re•duce [rɪ'djuːs] *v/t* ridurre
re•duc•tion [rɪ'dʌkʃn] riduzione *f*
re•dun•dan•cy [rɪ'dʌndənsɪ] *Br at work* licenziamento *m*
re'dun•dan•cy no•tice *Br* avviso *m* di licenziamento
re•'dun•dan•cy pay•ment *Br* indennità *f inv* di licenziamento
re•dun•dant [rɪ'dʌndənt] *adj* (*unnecessary*) superfluo; *Br* ***be made redundant*** *at work* essere licenziato; *Br* ***make s.o. redundant*** licenziare qu
reed [riːd] BOT canna *f*
reef [riːf] *in sea* scogliera *f*
'reef knot nodo *m* piano
reek [riːk] *v/i* puzzare; ***reek of …*** puzzare di …
reel [riːl] *n of film* rullino *m*; *of thread* rocchetto *m*; *of tape* bobina *f*; *of fishing line* mulinello *m*
◆ **reel off** *v/t* snocciolare
re-e'lect *v/t* rieleggere
re-e'lec•tion rielezione *f*
re-'entry *of spacecraft* rientro *m*
ref [ref] F arbitro *m*
re•fer [rɪ'fɜː(r)] **1** *v/t* (*pret & pp* ***-red***): ***refer a decision / problem to s.o.*** rinviare una decisione / un problema a qu **2** *v/i*: ***refer to …*** (*allude to*) riferirsi a …; *dictionary etc* consultare …
ref•er•ee [refə'riː] SP arbitro *m*; *for job* referenza *f*
ref•er•ence ['refərəns] (*allusion*) allusione *f*; *for job* referenza *f*; (*reference number*) (numero *m* di) riferimento *m*; ***with reference to*** con riferimento a
'ref•er•ence book opera *f* di consultazione
'ref•er•ence li•bra•ry biblioteca *f* di consultazione
'ref•er•ence num•ber numero *m* di riferimento
ref•e•ren•dum [refə'rendəm] referendum *m inv*
re•fill ['riːfɪl] *v/t glass* riempire
re•fine [rɪ'faɪn] *v/t* raffinare

re•fined [rɪ'faɪnd] *adj manners, language* raffinato
re•fine•ment [rɪ'faɪnmənt] *to process, machine* miglioramento *m*
re•fin•e•ry [rɪ'faɪnərɪ] raffineria *f*
re•fla•tion ['riːfleɪʃn] reflazione *f*
reflect [rɪ'flekt] **1** *v/t light* riflettere; ***be reflected in …*** riflettersi in … **2** *v/i* (*think*) riflettere
re•flec•tion [rɪ'flekʃn] *in water, glass etc* riflesso *m*; (*consideration*) riflessione *f*; ***on reflection*** dopo averci riflettuto
re•flex ['riːfleks] *in body* riflesso *m*
re•flex re'ac•tion riflesso *m*
re•form [rɪ'fɔːm] **1** *n* riforma *f* **2** *v/t* riformare
re•form•er [rɪ'fɔːmə(r)] riformatore *m*, -trice *f*
re•frain[1] [rɪ'freɪn] *v/i fml*: ***please refrain from smoking*** si prega di non fumare
re•frain[2] [rɪ'freɪn] *n in song* ritornello *m*
re•fresh [rɪ'freʃ] *v/t person* ristorare; ***feel refreshed*** sentirsi ristorato
refresh•er course [rɪ'freʃə(r)] corso *m* di aggiornamento
re•fresh•ing [rɪ'freʃɪŋ] *adj drink* rinfrescante; *experience* piacevole
re•fresh•ments [rɪ'freʃmənts] *npl* rinfreschi *mpl*
re•fri•ge•rate [rɪ'frɪdʒəreɪt] *v/t*: ***keep refrigerated*** conservare in frigo
re•fri•ge•ra•tor [rɪ'frɪdʒəreɪtə(r)] frigorifero *m*
re•fu•el [riːf'juːəl] **1** *v/t aeroplane* rifornire di carburante **2** *v/i of aeroplane, car* fare rifornimento
ref•uge ['refjuːdʒ] rifugio *m*; ***take refuge*** *from storm etc* ripararsi
ref•u•gee [refjʊ'dʒiː] rifugiato *m*, -a *f*, profugo *m*, -a *f*
ref•u'gee camp campo *m* profughi
re•fund ['riːfʌnd] **1** *n* rimborso *m* **2** *v/t* [rɪ'fʌnd] rimborsare

R

re•fus•al [rɪ'fjuːzl] rifiuto *m*
re•fuse[1] [rɪ'fjuːz] *v/t & v/i* rifiutare; ***refuse to do sth*** rifiutare di fare qc
ref•use[2] ['refjuːs] (*garbage*) rifiuti *mpl*
'ref•use col•lec•tion raccolta *f* dei rifiuti
'ref•use dump discarica *f* (dei rifiuti)
re•fute [rɪ'fjuːt] *v/t* confutare
re•gain [rɪ'geɪn] *v/t control, lost territory, the lead* riconquistare
re•gal ['riːgl] *adj* regale
re•gard [rɪ'gɑːd] **1** *n*: ***have great regard for s.o.*** avere molta stima di qu; ***in this regard*** a questo riguardo; ***with regard to*** riguardo a; (***kind***) ***regards*** cordiali saluti; ***give my regards to Paola*** saluti a Paola; ***with no regard for …*** senza alcun riguardo per … **2** *v/t*: ***regard s.o./sth as sth*** considerare qu / qc come qc; ***as regards …*** riguardo a …
re•gard•ing [rɪ'gɑːdɪŋ] *prep* riguardo a
re•gard•less [rɪ'gɑːdlɪs] *adv* lo stesso; ***regardless of*** senza tener conto di
re•gime [reɪ'ʒiːm] (*government*) regime *m*
re•gi•ment ['redʒɪmənt] *n* reggimento *m*
re•gion ['riːdʒən] regione *f*; ***in the region of*** intorno a
re•gion•al ['riːdʒənl] *adj* regionale
re•gis•ter ['redʒɪstə(r)] **1** *n* registro *m* **2** *v/t birth, death: by individual* denunciare; *by authorities* registrare; *vehicle* iscrivere; *letter* assicurare; *emotion* mostrare; ***send a letter registered*** spedire una lettera assicurata **3** *v/i at university* iscriversi; ***I'm registered with Dr Lee*** il mio medico è il dottor Lee
re•gis•tered let•ter ['redʒɪstəd] (lettera *f*) assicurata *f*
reg•is•trar [redʒɪ'strɑː(r)] *of births etc* ufficiale *m* di stato civile
re•gis•tra•tion [redʒɪ'streɪʃn] *Br* (*vehicle number*) numero *m* di targa; *at university* iscrizione *f*
re•gis'tra•tion num•ber *Br* MOT numero *m* di targa
re•gis•try of•fice ['redʒɪstrɪ] ufficio *m* di stato civile
re•gret [rɪ'gret] **1** *v/t* (*pret & pp* **-ted**) rammaricarsi di; *missed opportunity* rimpiangere; ***we regret to inform you that …*** siamo spiacenti di informarla che … **2** *n* rammarico *m*
re•gret•ful [rɪ'gretfəl] *adj* di rammarico
re•gret•ful•ly [rɪ'gretfəlɪ] *adv* con rammarico
re•gret•ta•ble [rɪ'gretəbl] *adj* deplorevole
re•gret•ta•bly [rɪ'gretəblɪ] *adv* purtroppo
reg•u•lar ['regjʊlə(r)] **1** *adj* regolare; (*esp Am: ordinary*) normale **2** *n at bar etc* cliente *m/f* abituale
reg•u•lar•i•ty [regjʊ'lærətɪ] regolarità *f inv*
reg•u•lar•ly ['regjʊlərlɪ] *adv* regolarmente
reg•u•late ['regʊleɪt] *v/t* regolare
reg•u•la•tion [regʊ'leɪʃn] (*rule*) regolamento *m*; *control* controllo *m*
re•hab ['riːhæb] F riabilitazione *f*
re•ha•bil•i•tate [riːhə'bɪlɪteɪt] *v/t ex-criminal* riabilitare
re•hears•al [rɪ'hɜːsl] prova *f*
re•hearse [rɪ'hɜːs] *v/t & v/i* provare
reign [reɪn] **1** *n* regno *m* **2** *v/i* regnare
re•im•burse [riːɪm'bɜːs] *v/t* rimborsare
rein [reɪn] redine *f*
re•in•car•na•tion [riːɪnkɑː'neɪʃn] reincar-

nazione *f*
re•in•force [riːɪn'fɔːs] *v/t* rinforzare
re•in•forced con•crete [riːɪn'fɔːst] cemento *m* armato
re•in•force•ments [riːɪn'fɔːsmənts] *npl* MIL rinforzi *mpl*
re•in•state [riːɪn'steɪt] *v/t* reintegrare
re•it•e•rate [riː'ɪtəreɪt] *v/t fml* ripetere
re•ject [rɪ'dʒekt] *v/t* respingere
re•jec•tion [rɪ'dʒekʃn] rifiuto *m*
re•lapse ['riːlæps] *n* MED ricaduta *f*; ***have a relapse*** avere una ricaduta
re•late [rɪ'leɪt] **1** *v/t story* raccontare; ***relate sth to sth*** collegare qc a qc **2** *v/i*: ***relate to …*** *be connected with* riferirsi a …; ***he doesn't relate to people*** non sa stabilire un rapporto con gli altri
re•lat•ed [rɪ'leɪtɪd] *adj by family* imparentato; *events, ideas etc* collegato
re•la•tion [rɪ'leɪʃn] *in family* parente *m/f*; (*connection*) rapporto *m*; ***business / diplomatic relations*** rapporti d'affari / diplomatici
re•la•tion•ship [rɪ'leɪʃnʃɪp] rapporto *m*
rel•a•tive ['relətɪv] **1** *n* parente *m/f* **2** *adj* relativo; ***X is relative to Y*** X è legato a Y
rel•a•tive•ly ['relətɪvlɪ] *adv* relativamente
re•lax [rɪ'læks] **1** *v/i* rilassarsi; ***relax!, don't get angry*** rilassati! non te la prendere **2** *v/t* rilassare
re•lax•a•tion [riːlæk'seɪʃn] relax *m inv*; *of rules etc* rilassamento *m*
re•laxed [rɪ'lækst] *adj* rilassato
re•lax•ing [rɪ'læksɪŋ] *adj* rilassante
re•lay [riː'leɪ] **1** *v/t* trasmettere **2** *n*: ***relay*** (***race***) (corsa *f* a) staffetta *f*
re•lease [rɪ'liːs] **1** *n from prison* rilascio *m*; *of CD etc* uscita *f*; *of software* versione *f*; ***this film is a new release*** è un film appena uscito **2** *v/t prisoner* rilasciare; *handbrake* togliere; *film, record* far uscire; *information* rendere noto
rel•e•gate ['relɪgeɪt] *v/t* relegare; ***be relegated*** SP essere retrocesso
rel•e•ga•tion [relɪ'geɪʃn] SP retrocessione *f*
re•lent [rɪ'lent] *v/i* cedere
re•lent•less [rɪ'lentlɪs] *adj* incessante, implacabile
re•lent•less•ly [rɪ'lentlɪslɪ] *adv* incessantemente
rel•e•vance ['reləvəns] pertinenza *f*
rel•e•vant ['reləvənt] *adj* pertinente
re•li•a•bil•i•ty [rɪlaɪə'bɪlətɪ] affidabilità *f inv*
re•li•a•ble [rɪ'laɪəbl] *adj* affidabile
re•li•a•bly [rɪ'laɪəblɪ] *adv*: ***I am reliably informed that …*** so da fonte certa che …
re•li•ance [rɪ'laɪəns] dipendenza *f*; ***reliance on s.o./sth*** dipendenza da qu / qc
re•li•ant [rɪ'laɪənt] *adj*: ***be reliant on*** dipendere da
rel•ic ['relɪk] reliquia *f*
re•lief [rɪ'liːf] sollievo *m*; ***that's a relief*** che sollievo; ***in relief*** *in art* in rilievo
re•lieve [rɪ'liːv] *v/t pressure, pain* alleviare; (*take over from*) dare il cambio a; ***be relieved*** *at news etc* essere sollevato
re•li•gion [rɪ'lɪdʒən] religione *f*
re•li•gious [rɪ'lɪdʒəs] *adj* religioso
re•li•gious•ly [rɪ'lɪdʒəslɪ] *adv* (*conscientiously*) religiosamente
re•lin•quish [rɪ'lɪŋkwɪʃ] *v/t* rinunciare a
rel•ish ['relɪʃ] **1** *n sauce* salsa *f*; (*enjoyment*) gusto *m* **2** *v/t idea, prospect* gradire
re•live [riː'lɪv] *v/t* rivivere
re•lo•cate [riːlə'keɪt] *v/i of business, employee* trasferirsi
re•lo•ca•tion [riːlə'keɪʃn] *of business, employee* trasferimento *m*
re•luc•tance [rɪ'lʌktəns] riluttanza *f*
re•luc•tant [rɪ'lʌktənt] *adj* riluttante; ***be reluctant to do sth*** essere restio a fare qc
re•luc•tant•ly [rɪ'lʌktəntlɪ] *adv* a malincuore
◆ **re•ly on** [rɪ'laɪ] *v/t* (*pret & pp* ***-ied***) contare su; ***rely on s.o. to do sth*** contare su qu perché faccia qc
re•main [rɪ'meɪn] *v/i* rimanere
re•main•der [rɪ'meɪndə(r)] **1** *n also* MATH resto *m* **2** *v/t* svendere
re•main•ing [rɪ'meɪnɪŋ] *adj* restante
re•mains [rɪ'meɪnz] *npl of body* resti *mpl*
re•make ['riːmeɪk] *n of film* remake *m inv*
re•mand [rɪ'mɑːnd] **1** *v/t*: ***remand s.o. in custody*** ordinare la custodia cautelare di qu **2** *n*: ***be on remand*** essere in attesa di giudizio
re•mark [rɪ'mɑːk] **1** *n* commento *m* **2** *v/t* osservare
re•mar•ka•ble [rɪ'mɑːkəbl] *adj* notevole
re•mark•a•bly [rɪ'mɑːkəblɪ] *adv* notevolmente
re•mar•ry [riː'marɪ] *v/i* (*pret & pp* ***-ied***) risposarsi
rem•e•dy ['remədɪ] *n* rimedio *m*
re•mem•ber [rɪ'membə(r)] **1** *v/t* ricordare; ***remember to lock the door*** ricordati di chiudere la porta a chiave; ***remember me to her*** dalle i miei saluti **2** *v/i* ricordare, ricordarsi
Re•mem•brance Day [rɪ'membrəns] *11 novembre, commemorazione f dei caduti in guerra*
re•mind [rɪ'maɪnd] *v/t*: ***remind s.o. of s.o./sth*** ricordare qu / qc a qu
re•mind•er [rɪ'maɪndə(r)] promemoria *m*; COM: *for payment* sollecito *m*

rem•i•nisce [remɪ'nɪs] *v/i* rievocare il passato
rem•i•nis•cent [remɪ'nɪsənt] *adj*: ***be reminiscent of sth*** far venire in mente qc
re•miss [rɪ'mɪs] *adj fml* negligente
re•mis•sion [rɪ'mɪʃn] remissione *f*
rem•nant ['remnənt] resto *m*; *of fabric* scampolo *m*
re•morse [rɪ'mɔːs] rimorso *m*
re•morse•less [rɪ'mɔːslɪs] *adj* spietato
re•mote [rɪ'məʊt] *adj village* isolato; *possibility*, *connection* remoto; (*aloof*) distante; *ancestor* lontano
re•mote 'ac•cess COMPUT accesso *m* remoto
re•mote con'trol telecomando *m*
re•mote•ly [rɪ'məʊtlɪ] *adv related*, *connected* lontanamente; ***just remotely possible*** vagamente possibile
re•mote•ness [rɪ'məʊtnəs] isolamento *m*
re•mov•a•ble [rɪ'muːvəbl] *adj* staccabile
re•mov•al [rɪ'muːvl] rimozione *f*; *from home* trasloco
re'mov•al firm ditta *f* di traslochi
re'mov•al van furgone *m* dei traslochi
re•move [rɪ'muːv] *v/t top*, *lid* togliere; MED asportare; *doubt*, *suspicion* eliminare
re•mu•ner•a•tion [rɪmjuːnə'reɪʃn] rimunerazione *f*
re•mu•ner•a•tive [rɪ'mjuːnərətɪv] *adj* rimunerativo
Re•nais•sance [rɪ'neɪsəns] Rinascimento *m*
re•name [riː'neɪm] *v/t* ribattezzare; *file* rinominare
ren•der ['rendə(r)] *v/t service* rendere; ***render s.o. helpless*** rendere infermo qu
ren•der•ing ['rendərɪŋ] *of piece of music* interpretazione *f*
ren•dez-vous ['rɒndeɪvuː] (*meeting*) incontro *m*
re•new [rɪ'njuː] *v/t contract*, *licence* rinnovare; ***feel renewed*** sentirsi rinato
re•new•al [rɪ'njuːəl] *of contract etc* rinnovo *m*
re•nounce [rɪ'naʊns] *v/t title*, *rights* rinunciare a
ren•o•vate ['renəveɪt] *v/t* ristrutturare
ren•o•va•tion [renə'veɪʃn] ristrutturazione *f*
re•nown [rɪ'naʊn] fama *f*
re•nowned [rɪ'naʊnd] *adj* famoso
rent [rent] **1** *n* affitto *m*; ***for rent*** affittasi **2** *v/t flat* affittare; *car equipment*, noleggiare; (*rent out*) affittare
rent•al ['rentl] *for flat* affitto *m*; *for car* noleggio *m*; *for TV*, *phone* canone *m*
'rent•al a•gree•ment contratto *m* di noleggio
rent-'free *adv* gratis
re•o•pen [riː'əʊpn] *v/t & v/i* riaprire
re•or•gan•i•za•tion [riːɔːgənʌɪz'eɪʃn] riorganizzazione *f*
re•or•gan•ize [riː'ɔːgənʌɪz] *v/t* riorganizzare
rep [rep] COM rappresentante *m*/*f*
re•paint [riː'peɪnt] *v/t* ridipingere
re•pair [rɪ'peə(r)] **1** *v/t* riparare **2** *n*: ***in a good / bad state of repair*** in buono / cattivo stato; ***repairs*** riparazioni *fpl*
re'pair•man tecnico *m*
re•pa•tri•ate [riː'pætrɪeɪt] *v/t* rimpatriare
re•pa•tri•a•tion [riː'pætrɪ'eɪʃn] rimpatrio *m*
re•pay [riː'peɪ] *v/t* (*pret & pp* **-paid**) *money* restituire; *person* ripagare
re•pay•ment [riː'peɪmənt] pagamento *m*
re•peal [rɪ'piːl] *v/t law* abrogare
re•peat [rɪ'piːt] **1** *v/t* ripetere; ***am I repeating myself?*** l'ho già detto? **2** *n programme* replica *f*
re•peat 'busi•ness COM ulteriori ordini *mpl*
re•peat•ed [rɪ'piːtɪd] *adj* ripetuto
re•peat•ed•ly [rɪ'piːtɪdlɪ] *adv* ripetutamente
re•peat 'or•der COM ulteriore ordine *m*
re•pel [rɪ'pel] *v/t* (*pret & pp* **-led**) *invaders*, *attack* respingere; (*disgust*) ripugnare
re•pel•lent [rɪ'pelənt] **1** *n* (*insect repellent*) insettifugo *m* **2** *adj* ripugnante
re•pent [rɪ'pent] *v/i* pentirsi
re•per•cus•sions [riːpə'kʌʃnz] *npl* ripercussioni *fpl*
rep•er•toire ['repətwɑː(r)] repertorio *m*
rep•e•ti•tion [repɪ'tɪʃn] ripetizione *f*
re•pet•i•tive [rɪ'petɪtɪv] *adj* ripetitivo
re•place [rɪ'pleɪs] *v/t* (*put back*) mettere a posto; (*take the place of*) sostituire
re•place•ment [rɪ'pleɪsmənt] *person* sostituto *m*, -a *f*; *act* sostituzione *f*; ***this is the replacement for the old model*** questo è il modello che sostituisce il vecchio
re•place•ment 'part pezzo *m* di ricambio
re•play ['riːpleɪ] **1** *n recording* replay *m inv*; *match* spareggio *m* **2** *v/t match* rigiocare
re•plen•ish [rɪ'plenɪʃ] *v/t container* riempire; *supplies* rifornire
rep•li•ca ['replɪkə] copia *f*
re•ply [rɪ'plaɪ] **1** *n* risposta *f* **2** *v/t & v/i* (*pret & pp* **-ied**) rispondere
re•port [rɪ'pɔːt] **1** *n* (*account*) resoconto *m*; *by journalist* servizio *m*; EDU pagella *f* **2** *v/t facts* fare un servizio su; *to authorities* denunciare; ***report one's findings***

R

to s.o. riferire sulle proprie conclusioni a qu; ***report a person to the police*** denunciare qualcuno alla polizia; ***he is reported to be in London*** si dice che sia a Londra **3** *v/i of journalist* fare un reportage; (*present o.s.*) presentarsi
◆ **report to** *v/t in business* rendere conto a
re•port•er [rɪ'pɔːtə(r)] giornalista *m/f*
re•pos•sess [riːpə'zes] *v/t* COM riprendersi
rep•re•hen•si•ble [reprɪ'hensəbl] *adj* riprovevole
rep•re•sent [reprɪ'zent] *v/t* rappresentare
rep•re•sen•ta•tive [reprɪ'zentətɪv] **1** *n* rappresentante *m/f* **2** *adj* (*typical*) rappresentativo
re•press [rɪ'pres] *v/t* reprimere
re•pres•sion [rɪ'preʃn] POL repressione *f*
re•pres•sive [rɪ'presɪv] *adj* POL repressivo
re•prieve [rɪ'priːv] **1** *n* LAW sospensione *f* della pena capitale; *fig* proroga *f* **2** *v/t prisoner* sospendere l'esecuzione di
rep•ri•mand ['reprɪmɑːnd] *v/t* ammonire
re•print ['riːprɪnt] **1** *n* ristampa *f* **2** *v/t* ristampare
re•pri•sal [rɪ'praɪzl] rappresaglia *f*; ***take reprisals*** fare delle rappresaglie; ***in reprisal for*** per rappresaglia contro
re•proach [rɪ'prəʊʧ] **1** *n* rimprovero *m*; ***be beyond reproach*** essere irreprensibile **2** *v/t* rimproverare
re•proach•ful [rɪ'prəʊʧfʊl] *adj* di rimprovero
re•proach•ful•ly [rɪ'prəʊʧfʊlɪ] *adv* con aria di rimprovero
re•pro•duce [riːprə'djuːs] **1** *v/t* riprodurre **2** *v/i* riprodursi
re•pro•duc•tion [riːprə'dʌkʃn] riproduzione *f*
re•pro•duc•tive [rɪprə'dʌktɪv] *adj* riproduttivo
rep•tile ['reptaɪl] rettile *m*
re•pub•lic [rɪ'pʌblɪk] repubblica *f*
re•pub•li•can [rɪ'pʌblɪkn] **1** *n* repubblicano *m*, -a *f* **2** *adj* repubblicano
re•pu•di•ate [rɪ'pjuːdɪeɪt] *v/t* (*deny*) respingere
re•pul•sive [rɪ'pʌlsɪv] *adj* ripugnante
rep•u•ta•ble ['repjʊtəbl] *adj* rispettabile
rep•u•ta•tion [repjʊ'teɪʃn] reputazione *f*; ***have a good / bad reputation*** avere una buona / cattiva reputazione
re•put•ed [rep'jʊtəd] *adj*: ***be reputed to be*** avere la fama di essere
re•put•ed•ly [rep'jʊtədlɪ] *adv* a quanto si dice
re•quest [rɪ'kwest] **1** *n* richiesta *f*; ***on request*** su richiesta **2** *v/t* richiedere
re•quiem ['rekwɪəm] MUS requiem *m inv*
re•quire [rɪ'kwaɪə(r)] *v/t* (*need*) aver bisogno di; ***it requires great care*** richiede molta cura; ***as required by law*** come prescritto dalla legge; ***guests are required to …*** i signori clienti sono pregati di …
re•quired [rɪ'kwaɪəd] *adj* (*necessary*) necessario
re•quire•ment [rɪ'kwaɪəmənt] (*need*) esigenza *f*; (*condition*) requisito *m*
req•ui•si•tion [rekwɪ'zɪʃn] *v/t* requisire
re•route [riː'ruːt] *v/t aeroplane etc* deviare
re•run ['riːrʌn] **1** *n of programme* replica *f* **2** *v/t* (*pret* **-ran**, *pp* **-run**) *programme* replicare
re•sched•ule [riː'ʃedjuːl] *v/t* stabilire di nuovo
res•cue ['reskjuː] **1** *n* salvataggio *m*; ***come to s.o.'s rescue*** andare in aiuto a qu **2** *v/t* salvare
'res•cue par•ty squadra *f* di soccorso
re•search [rɪ'sɜːʧ] *n* ricerca *f*
◆ **research into** *v/t* fare ricerca su
re•search and de'vel•op•ment ricerca *f* e sviluppo *m*
re'search as•sist•ant assistente ricercatore *m*, -trice *f*
re•search•er [rɪ'sɜːʧə(r)] ricercatore *m*, -trice *f*
re'search proj•ect ricerca *f*
re•sem•blance [rɪ'zembləns] somiglianza *f*
re•sem•ble [rɪ'zembl] *v/t* (as)somigliare a
re•sent [rɪ'zent] *v/t* risentirsi per
re•sent•ful [rɪ'zentfʊl] *adj* pieno di risentimento
re•sent•ful•ly [rɪ'zentfʊlɪ] *adv* con risentimento
re•sent•ment [rɪ'zentmənt] risentimento *m*
res•er•va•tion [rezə'veɪʃn] *of room, table* prenotazione *f*; *mental, special area* riserva *f*; ***I have a reservation*** *in hotel, restaurant* ho prenotato
re•serve [rɪ'zɜːv] **1** *n* (*store*) riserva *f*; (*aloofness*) riserbo *m*; SP riserva *f*; ***reserves*** FIN riserve *fpl*; ***keep sth in reserve*** tenere qc di riserva **2** *v/t seat, table* prenotare; *judgment* riservarsi
re•served [rɪ'zɜːvd] *adj person, manner* riservato; *table, seat* prenotato
res•er•voir ['rezəvwɑː(r)] *for water* bacino *m* idrico
re•shuf•fle ['riːʃʌfl] **1** *n* POL rimpasto *m* **2** *v/t* POL rimpastare
re•side [rɪ'zaɪd] *v/i fml* risiedere
res•i•dence ['rezɪdəns] *fml: house etc* residenza *f*; (*stay*) permanenza *f*
'res•i•dence per•mit permesso *m* di resi-

denza

'res•i•dent ['rezɪdənt] **1** *n* residente *m/f* **2** *adj living in a building* residente sul posto

res•i•den•tial [rezɪ'denʃl] *adj district* residenziale

res•i•due ['rezɪdjuː] residuo *m*

re•sign [rɪ'zaɪn] **1** *v/t position* dimettersi da; ***resign o.s. to*** rassegnarsi a **2** *v/i from job* dimettersi

res•ig•na•tion [rezɪg'neɪʃn] *from job* dimissioni *fpl*; *mental* rassegnazione *f*

re•signed [re'zaɪnd] *adj* rassegnato; ***we have become resigned to the fact that …*** ci siamo rassegnati al fatto che …

re•sil•i•ent [rɪ'zɪlɪənt] *adj personality* che ha molte risorse; *material* resistente

res•in ['rezɪn] resina *f*

re•sist [rɪ'zɪst] **1** *v/t* resistere a **2** *v/i* resistere

re•sist•ance [rɪ'zɪstəns] resistenza *f*

re•sis•tant [rɪ'zɪstənt] *adj material* resistente; ***resistant to heat / rust*** resistente al calore / alla ruggine

re•sit ['riːsɪt] *v/t exam* ridare

res•o•lute ['rezəluːt] *adj* risoluto

res•o•lu•tion [rezə'luːʃn] (*decision*) risoluzione *f*; *made at New Year etc* proposito *m*; (*determination*) risolutezza *f*; *of problem* soluzione *f*; *of image* risoluzione *f*

re•solve [rɪ'zɒlv] *v/t problem, mystery* risolvere; ***resolve to do sth*** decidere di fare qc

re•sort [rɪ'zɔːt] *n place* località *f inv*; ***holiday resort*** luogo *m* di villeggiatura; ***ski resort*** stazione *f* sciistica; ***as a last resort*** come ultima risorsa

◆ **resort to** *v/t violence, threats* far ricorso a

◆ **re•sound with** [rɪ'zaʊnd] *v/t* risuonare di

re•sound•ing [rɪ'zaʊndɪŋ] *adj success, victory* clamoroso

re•source [rɪ'sɔːs] risorsa *f*; ***financial resources*** mezzi *mpl* economici; ***leave s.o. to his own resources*** lasciare qu in balia di se stesso

re•source•ful [rɪ'sɔːsfʊl] *adj* pieno di risorse

re•spect [rɪ'spekt] **1** *n* rispetto *m*; ***show respect to*** avere rispetto per; ***with respect to*** riguardo a; ***in this / that respect*** quanto a questo; ***in many respects*** sotto molti aspetti; ***pay one's last respects to s.o.*** rendere omaggio a qu **2** *v/t* rispettare

re•spect•a•bil•i•ty [rɪspektə'bɪlətɪ] rispettabilità *f inv*

re•spec•ta•ble [rɪ'spektəbl] *adj* rispettabile

re•spec•ta•bly [rɪ'spektəblɪ] *adv* rispettabilmente

re•spect•ful [rɪ'spektfʊl] *adj* rispettoso

re•spect•ful•ly [rɪ'spektflɪ] *adv* con rispetto

re•spec•tive [rɪ'spektɪv] *adj* rispettivo

re•spec•tive•ly [rɪ'spektɪvlɪ] *adv* rispettivamente

res•pi•ra•tion [respɪ'reɪʃn] respirazione *f*

res•pi•ra•tor [respɪ'reɪtə(r)] MED respiratore *m*

re•spite ['respaɪt] tregua *f*; ***without respite*** senza tregua

re•spond [rɪ'spɒnd] *v/i* rispondere

re•sponse [rɪ'spɒns] risposta *f*

re•spon•si•bil•i•ty [rɪspɒnsɪ'bɪlətɪ] responsabilità *f inv*; ***accept responsibility for*** assumersi la responsabilità di; ***a job with more responsibility*** un lavoro con più responsabilità

re•spon•si•ble [rɪ'spɒnsəbl] *adj* responsabile (***for*** di); *job, position* di responsabilità

re•spon•sive [rɪ'spɒnsɪv] *adj audience* caloroso; ***be responsive*** *of brakes* rispondere bene

rest¹ [rest] **1** *n* riposo *m*; ***set s.o.'s mind at rest*** tranquillizzare qu **2** *v/i* riposare; ***rest on …*** (*be based on*) basarsi su …; (*lean against*) poggiare su …; ***it all rests with him*** dipende tutto da lui **3** *v/t* (*lean, balance*) appoggiare

rest² [rest] *n*: ***the rest*** il resto *m*

res•tau•rant ['restrɒnt] ristorante *m*

'res•tau•rant car RAIL vagone *m* ristorante

'rest cure cura *f* del riposo

rest•ful ['restfʊl] *adj* riposante

'rest home casa *f* di riposo

rest•less ['restlɪs] *adj* irrequieto; ***have a restless night*** passare una notte agitata

rest•less•ly ['restlɪslɪ] *adv* nervosamente

res•to•ra•tion [restə'reɪʃn] restauro *m*

re•store [rɪ'stɔː(r)] *v/t building etc* restaurare; (*bring back*) restituire

re•strain [rɪ'streɪn] *v/t dog, troops* frenare; *emotions* reprimere; ***restrain o.s.*** trattenersi

re•straint [rɪ'streɪnt] (*self-control*) autocontrollo *m*

re•strict [rɪ'strɪkt] *v/t* limitare; ***I'll restrict myself to …*** mi limiterò a …

re•strict•ed [rɪ'strɪktɪd] *adj view* limitato

re•strict•ed 'ar•e•a MIL zona *f* militare

re•stric•tion [rɪ'strɪkʃn] restrizione *f*

'rest room *Am* gabinetto *m*

re•sult [rɪ'zʌlt] *n* risultato *m*; ***as a result***

of this in conseguenza a ciò
◆ **result from** *v/t* risultare da, derivare da
◆ **result in** *v/t* dare luogo a; ***this resulted in him feeling even worse*** questo ha fatto sì che stesse ancora peggio
re•sume [rɪ'zjuːm] *v/t & v/i* riprendere
ré•su•mé ['rezʊmeɪ] *Am* curriculum vitae *m inv*
re•sump•tion [rɪ'zʌmpʃn] ripresa *f*
re•sur•face [riː'sɜːfɪs] **1** *v/t roads* asfaltare **2** *v/i (reappear)* riaffiorare
Res•ur•rec•tion [rezə'rekʃn] REL resurrezione *f*
re•sus•ci•tate [rɪ'sʌsɪteɪt] *v/t* rianimare
re•sus•ci•ta•tion [rɪsʌsɪ'teɪʃn] rianimazione *f*
re•tail ['riːteɪl] **1** *adv* al dettaglio **2** *v/i*: ***retail at …*** essere in vendita a …
re•tail•er ['riːteɪlə(r)] dettagliante *m/f*
're•tail out•let punto *m* (di) vendita
're•tail price prezzo *m* al dettaglio
re•tain [rɪ'teɪn] *v/t* conservare
re•tain•er [rɪ'teɪnə(r)] FIN onorario *m*
re•tal•i•ate [rɪ'tælɪeɪt] *v/i* vendicarsi
re•tal•i•a•tion [rɪtælɪ'eɪʃn] rappresaglia *f*; ***in retaliation for*** per rappresaglia contro
re•tard•ed [rɪ'tɑːdɪd] *adj mentally* ritardato
rethink [riː'θɪŋk] *v/t (pret & pp **-thought**)* riconsiderare
re•ti•cence ['retɪsns] riservatezza *f*
re•ti•cent ['retɪsnt] *adj* riservato
re•tire [rɪ'taɪə(r)] *v/i from work* andare in pensione
re•tired [rɪ'taɪəd] *adj* in pensione
re•tire•ment [rɪ'taɪəmənt] pensione *f*; *act* pensionamento *m*
re'tire•ment age età *f inv* pensionabile
re•tir•ing [rɪ'taɪərɪŋ] *adj* riservato
re•tort [rɪ'tɔːt] **1** *n* replica *f* **2** *v/t* replicare
re•trace [rɪ'treɪs] *v/t*: ***retrace one's footsteps*** ritornare sui propri passi
re•tract [rɪ'trækt] *v/t claws* ritrarre; *undercarriage* far rientrare; *statement* ritrattare
re-train [riː'treɪn] *v/i* riqualificarsi
re•treat [rɪ'triːt] **1** *v/i* ritirarsi **2** *n* MIL ritirata *f*; *place* rifugio *m*
re•trieve [rɪ'triːv] *v/t* recuperare
re•triev•er [rɪ'triːvə(r)] *dog* cane *m* da riporto
ret•ro•ac•tive [retrəʊ'æktɪv] *adj law etc* retroattivo
ret•ro•ac•tive•ly [retrəʊ'æktɪvlɪ] *adv* retroattivamente
ret•ro•grade ['retrəgreɪd] *adj move, decision* retrogrado
ret•ro•spect ['retrəspekt] ***in retrospect*** ripensandoci
ret•ro•spec•tive [retrə'spektɪv] *n* retrospettiva *f*
re•turn [rɪ'tɜːn] **1** *n* ritorno *m*; *(giving back)* restituzione *f*; COMPUT (tasto *m*) invio *m*; *in tennis* risposta *f* al servizio; ***tax return*** dichiarazione *f* dei redditi; ***by return (of post)*** a stretto giro di posta; ***returns*** *(profit)* rendimento *m*; ***many happy returns (of the day)*** cento di questi giorni; ***in return for*** in cambio di **2** *v/t (give back)* restituire; *(put back)* rimettere; *favour, invitation* ricambiare **3** *v/i (go back, come back)* ritornare; *of symptoms, doubts etc* ricomparire
re•turn 'flight volo *m* di ritorno
re•turn 'jour•ney viaggio *m* di ritorno
re'turn match partita *f* (del girone) di ritorno
re'turn tick•et biglietto *m* (di) andata e ritorno
re•u•ni•fi•ca•tion [riːjuːnɪfɪ'keɪʃn] riunificazione *f*
re•u•nion [riː'juːnɪən] riunione *f*
re•u•nite [riːjuː'naɪt] *v/t* riunire
re•us•a•ble [riː'juːzəbl] *adj* riutilizzabile
re•use [riː'juːz] *v/t* riutilizzare
rev [rev] *n*: ***revs per minute*** giri al minuto
◆ **rev up** *v/t (pret & pp **-ved**) engine* far andare su di giri
re•val•u•a•tion [riːvæljʊ'eɪʃn] rivalutazione *f*
re•veal [rɪ'viːl] *v/t (make visible)* mostrare; *(make known)* rivelare
re•veal•ing [rɪ'viːlɪŋ] *adj remark* rivelatore; *dress* scollato
◆ **revel in** ['revl] *v/t (pret & pp **-led**, Am **-ed**)* godere di
rev•e•la•tion [revə'leɪʃn] rivelazione *f*
re•venge [rɪ'vendʒ] *n* vendetta *f*; ***take one's revenge*** vendicarsi; ***in revenge for*** per vendicarsi di
rev•e•nue ['revənjuː] reddito *m*
re•ver•be•rate [rɪ'vɜːbəreɪt] *v/i of sound* rimbombare
re•vere [rɪ'vɪə(r)] *v/t* riverire
rev•e•rence ['revərəns] rispetto *m*
Rev•e•rend ['revərənd] REL reverendo *m*
rev•e•rent ['revərənt] *adj* riverente
re•verse [rɪ'vɜːs] **1** *adj sequence* opposto; ***in reverse order*** in ordine inverso **2** *n (opposite)* contrario *m*; *(back)* rovescio *m*; MOT retromarcia *f* **3** *v/t sequence* invertire; ***reverse the car*** fare marcia indietro; ***reverse the charges*** TELEC telefonare a carico del destinatario **4** *v/i* MOT fare marcia indietro
revert [rɪ'vɜːt] *v/i*: ***revert to*** ritornare a
re•view [rɪ'vjuː] **1** *n of book, film* recensione *f*; *of troops* rivista *f*; *of situation etc*

revisione *f* **2** *v/t book, film* recensire; *troops* passare in rivista; *situation etc* riesaminare

re•view•er [rɪ'vjuːə(r)] *of book, film* critico *m*, -a *f*

re•vise [rɪ'vaɪz] **1** *v/t opinion, text* rivedere; EDU ripassare **2** *v/i* EDU ripassare

re•vi•sion [rɪ'vɪʒn] *of opinion, text* revisione *f*; *for exam* ripasso *m*

re•viv•al [rɪ'vaɪvl] *of custom, old style etc* revival *m inv*; *of patient* ripresa *f*

re•vive [rɪ'vaɪv] **1** *v/t custom, old style etc* riportare alla moda; *patient* rianimare **2** *v/i of business etc* riprendersi

re•voke [rɪ'vəʊk] *v/t licence* revocare

re•volt [rɪ'vɒlt] **1** *n* rivolta *f* **2** *v/i* ribellarsi

re•volt•ing [rɪ'vɒltɪŋ] *adj* (*disgusting*) schifoso

rev•o•lu•tion [revə'luːʃn] rivoluzione *f*

rev•o•lu•tion•ar•y [revə'luːʃn ərɪ] **1** *n* POL rivoluzionario *m*, -a *f* **2** *adj* rivoluzionario

rev•o•lu•tion•ize [revə'luːʃnaɪz] *v/t* rivoluzionare

re•volve [rɪ'vɒlv] *v/i* ruotare

re•volv•er [rɪ'vɒlvə(r)] revolver *m inv*

re•volv•ing 'door [rɪ'vɒlvɪŋ] porta *f* girevole

re•vue [rɪ'vjuː] THEA rivista *f*

re•vul•sion [rɪ'vʌlʃn] ribrezzo *m*

re•ward [rɪ'wɔːd] **1** *n financial* ricompensa *f*; *benefit derived* vantaggio *m* **2** *v/t financially* ricompensare

re•ward•ing [rɪ'wɔːdɪŋ] *adj experience* gratificante

re•wind [riː'wʌɪnd] *v/t* (*pret & pp* ***-wound***) *film, tape* riavvolgere

re•write [riː'rʌɪt] *v/t* (*pret* ***-wrote***, *pp* ***-written***) riscrivere

rhe•to•ric ['retərɪk] retorica *f*

rhe•to•ric•al 'ques•tion [rɪ'tɒrɪkl] domanda *f* retorica

rheu•ma•tism ['ruːmətɪzm] reumatismo *m*

rhi•no•ce•ros [raɪ'nɒsərəs] rinoceronte *m*

rhu•barb ['ruːbɑːb] rabarbaro *m*

rhyme [raɪm] **1** *n* rima *f* **2** *v/i* rimare; ***rhyme with*** fare rima con

rhythm ['rɪðm] ritmo *m*

rib [rɪb] ANAT costola *f*

rib•bon ['rɪbən] nastro *m*

rice [raɪs] riso *m*

rice 'pud•ding budino *m* di riso

rich [rɪʧ] **1** *adj* (*wealthy*) ricco; *food* pesante **2** *n*: ***the rich*** i ricchi *mpl*

rich•ly ['rɪʧlɪ] *adv deserved* pienamente

rick•et•y ['rɪkətɪ] *adj* traballante

ric•o•chet ['rɪkəʃeɪ] *v/i* rimbalzare

rid [rɪd]: ***get rid of*** sbarazzarsi di

rid•dance ['rɪdns] *n* F: ***good riddance!*** che liberazione!

rid•den ['rɪdn] *pp* → ***ride***

rid•dle ['rɪdl] **1** *n* indovinello *m* **2** *v/t*: ***be riddled with*** essere crivellato di

ride [raɪd] **1** *n on horse* cavalcata *f*; *in vehicle* giro *m*; (*journey*) viaggio *m*; ***do you want a ride into town?*** *Am* vuoi uno strappo in città? **2** *v/t* (*pret* ***rode***, *pp* ***ridden***): ***ride a horse*** andare a cavallo; ***ride a bike*** andare in bicicletta **3** *v/i* (*pret* ***rode***, *pp* ***ridden***) *on horse* andare a cavallo; *on bike* andare; *in vehicle* viaggiare; ***he rode home*** è andato a casa in bicicletta

rid•er ['raɪdə(r)] *on horse* cavallerizzo *m*, -a *f*; *on bike* ciclista *m/f*

ridge [rɪdʒ] *raised strip* sporgenza *f*; *of mountain* cresta *f*; *of roof* punta *f*

rid•i•cule ['rɪdɪkjuːl] **1** *n* ridicolo *m* **2** *v/t* ridicolizzare

ri•dic•u•lous [rɪ'dɪkjʊləs] *adj* ridicolo

ri•dic•u•lous•ly [rɪ'dɪkjʊləslɪ] *adv* incredibilmente

rid•ing ['raɪdɪŋ] *on horseback* equitazione *f*

ri•fle ['raɪfl] *n* fucile *m*

rift [rɪft] *in earth* crepa *f*; *in party etc* spaccatura *f*

rig [rɪg] **1** *n* (*oil rig*) piattaforma *f* petrolifera **2** *v/t* (*pret & pp* ***-ged***) *elections* manipolare

right [raɪt] **1** *adj* (*correct*) esatto; (*proper, just*) giusto; (*suitable*) adatto; *not left* destro; ***be right*** *of answer* essere esatto; *of person* avere ragione; *of clock* essere giusto; ***put things right*** sistemare le cose; → ***alright*** **2** *adv* (*directly*) proprio; (*correctly*) bene; (*completely*) completamente; *not left* a destra; ***right now*** (*immediately*) subito; (*at the moment*) adesso **3** *n civil, legal etc* diritto *m*; *not left* destra *f*; ***the right*** POL la destra; ***on the right*** a destra; ***turn to the right, take a right*** girare a destra; ***be in the right*** avere ragione; ***know right from wrong*** saper distinguere il bene dal male

right-'an•gle angolo *m* retto; ***at right-angles to …*** ad angolo retto con …

right•ful ['raɪtfʊl] *adj heir, owner etc* legittimo

'right•hand *adj* destro; ***on the righthand side*** a destra

right•hand 'drive MOT guida *f* a destra; *car* auto *f inv* con guida a destra

right•hand•ed [raɪt'hændɪd] *adj*: ***be righthanded*** usare la (mano) destra

right•hand 'man braccio *m* destro

right of 'way *in traffic* (diritto *m* di) prece-

R

denza *f*; *across land* diritto *m* di accesso
right 'wing *n* POL destra *f*; SP esterno *m* destro
right-'wing *adj* POL di destra
right-wing ex'trem•ism POL estremismo *m* di destra
right 'wing•er POL persona *f* di destra
rig•id ['rɪdʒɪd] *adj material, principles* rigido; *attitude* inflessibile
rig•or *Am* → ***rigour***
rig•or•ous ['rɪgərəs] *adj* rigoroso
rig•or•ous•ly ['rɪgərəslɪ] *adv check, examine* rigorosamente
rig•our ['rɪgə(r)] *of discipline* rigore *m*; ***the rigours of the winter*** i rigori dell'inverno
rile [raɪl] *v/t* F irritare
rim [rɪm] *of wheel* cerchione *m*; *of cup* orlo *m*; *of spectacles* montatura *f*
ring[1] [rɪŋ] (*circle*) cerchio *m*; *on finger* anello *m*; *in boxing* ring *m inv*, quadrato *m*; *at circus* pista *f*
ring[2] [rɪŋ] **1** *n of bell* trillo *m*; *of voice* suono *m*; ***give s.o. a ring*** TELEC dare un colpo di telefono a qu **2** *v/t* (*pret* ***rang***, *pp* ***rung***) *bell* suonare; TELEC chiamare **3** *v/i* (*pret* ***rang***, *pp* ***rung***) *of bell* suonare; TELEC chiamare; ***please ring for attention*** suonare il campanello
'ring•lead•er capobanda *m inv*
'ring-pull linguetta *f*
'ring road circonvallazione *f*
rink [rɪŋk] pista *f* di pattinaggio su ghiaccio
rinse [rɪns] **1** *n for hair colour* cachet *m inv* **2** *v/t* sciaquare
ri•ot ['raɪət] **1** *n* sommossa *f* **2** *v/i* causare disordini
ri•ot•er ['raɪətə(r)] dimostrante *m/f*
'riot police reparti *mpl* (di polizia) antisommossa
rip [rɪp] **1** *n in cloth etc* strappo *m* **2** *v/t* (*pret & pp* ***-ped***) *cloth etc* strappare; ***rip sth open*** aprire qc strappandolo
◆ **rip off** *v/t* F *customers* fregare F
◆ **rip up** *v/t letter, sheet* strappare
ripe [raɪp] *adj fruit* maturo
rip•en ['raɪpn] *v/i of fruit* maturare
ripe•ness ['raɪpnɪs] *of fruit* maturazione *f*
'rip-off *n* F fregatura *f* F
rip•ple ['rɪpl] *on water* increspatura *f*
rise [raɪz] **1** *v/i* (*pret* ***rose***, *pp* ***risen***) *from chair etc* alzarsi; *of sun* sorgere; *of price, temperature* aumentare; *of water level* salire **2** *n* aumento *m*; ***rise to power*** salita *f* al potere; ***give rise to*** dare origine a
ris•en ['rɪzn] *pp* → ***rise***
ris•er ['raɪzə(r)] *n*: ***be an early / be a late riser*** essere mattiniero / alzarsi sempre tardi
risk [rɪsk] **1** *n* rischio *m*; ***take a risk*** correre un rischio **2** *v/t* rischiare; ***let's risk it*** proviamo
risk•y ['rɪskɪ] *adj* rischioso
ri•sot•to [rɪs'ɒtəʊ] risotto *m*
ris•qué [rɪ'skeɪ] *adj* osé
rit•u•al ['rɪtjʊəl] **1** *n* rituale *m* **2** *adj* rituale
ri•val ['raɪvl] **1** *n in sport, love* rivale *m/f*; *in business* concorrente *m/f* **2** *v/t* competere con; ***I can't rival that*** non posso competere con quello
ri•val•ry ['raɪvlrɪ] rivalità *f inv*
riv•er ['rɪvə(r)] fiume *m*
'riv•er•bank sponda *f* del fiume
'riv•er•bed letto *m* del fiume
'riv•er•side 1 *adj* sul fiume **2** *n* riva *f* del fiume
riv•et ['rɪvɪt] **1** *n* ribattino *m* **2** *v/t* rivettare
riv•et•ing ['rɪvɪtɪŋ] *adj* avvincente
Riv•i•e•ra [rɪvɪ'eərə] *n*: ***the Italian Riviera*** la riviera (ligure)
road [rəʊd] strada *f*; ***it's just down the road*** è qui vicino
'road•block posto *m* di blocco
'road hog pirata *m* della strada
'road hold•ing *of vehicle* tenuta *f* di strada
'road map carta *f* automobilistica
road 'safe•ty sicurezza *f* sulle strade
'road•side: ***at the roadside*** sul ciglio della strada
'road•sign cartello *m* stradale
'road•way carreggiata *f*
'road works *npl* lavori *mpl* stradali
'road•wor•thy *adj* in buono stato di marcia
roam [rəʊm] *v/i* vagabondare
roar [rɔː(r)] **1** *n of engine* rombo *m*; *of lion* ruggito *m*; *of traffic* fragore *m* **2** *v/i of engine* rombare; *of lion* ruggire; *of person* gridare; ***roar with laughter*** ridere fragorosamente
roast [rəʊst] **1** *n beef etc* arrosto *m* **2** *v/t chicken, potatoes* arrostire; *coffee beans, peanuts* tostare **3** *v/i of food* arrostire; *in hot room, climate* scoppiare di caldo
roast 'beef arrosto *m* di manzo
'roast•ing tin [rəʊstɪŋ] teglia *f* per arrosti
roast 'pork arrosto *m* di maiale
rob [rɒb] *v/t* (*pret & pp* ***-bed***) *person, bank* rapinare; ***I've been robbed*** mi hanno rapinato
rob•ber ['rɒbə(r)] rapinatore *m*, -trice *f*
rob•ber•y ['rɒbərɪ] rapina *f*
robe [rəʊb] *of judge* toga *f*; *of priest* tonaca *f*; *Am* (*dressing gown*) vestaglia *f*
rob•in ['rɒbɪn] pettirosso *m*
ro•bot ['rəʊbɒt] robot *m inv*

ro•bust [rəʊ'bʌst] *adj* robusto
rock [rɒk] **1** *n* roccia *f*; MUS rock *m inv*; ***on the rocks*** *drink* con ghiaccio; *marriage* in crisi **2** *v/t baby* cullare; *cradle* far dondolare; (*surprise*) sconvolgere **3** *v/i on chair* dondolarsi; *of boat* dondolare
'**rock band** gruppo *m* rock
rock 'bot•tom: ***reach rock bottom*** toccare il fondo
'**rock-bot•tom** *adj prices* bassissimo
'**rock climb•er** rocciatore *m*, -trice *f*
'**rock climb•ing** roccia *f*
rock•et ['rɒkɪt] **1** *n* razzo *m* **2** *v/i of prices etc* salire alle stelle
rock•ing chair ['rɒkɪŋ] sedia *f* a dondolo
'**rock•ing horse** cavallo *m* a dondolo
rock 'n' roll [rɒkn'rəʊl] rock and roll *m inv*
'**rock star** rockstar *f inv*
rock•y ['rɒkɪ] *adj shore* roccioso; (*shaky*) instabile
rod [rɒd] sbarra *f*; *for fishing* canna *f*
rode [rəʊd] *pret* → ***ride***
ro•dent ['rəʊdnt] roditore *m*
rogue [rəʊg] briccone *m*, -a *f*
role [rəʊl] ruolo *m*
'**role mod•el** modello *m* di comportamento
roll [rəʊl] **1** *n of bread* panino *m*; *of film* rullino *m*; *of thunder* rombo *m*; (*list, register*) lista *f* **2** *v/i of ball etc* rotolare; *of boat* dondolare **3** *v/t*: ***roll sth into a ball*** appallottolare qc; ***roll sth along the ground*** far rotolare qc
◆ **roll over 1** *v/i* rigirarsi **2** *v/t person, object* girare; *loan, agreement* rinnovare
◆ **roll up 1** *v/t sleeves* arrotolare **2** *v/i* F (*arrive*) arrivare
'**roll call** appello *m*
roll•er ['rəʊlə(r)] *for hair* bigodino *m*
'**roll•er blade®** *n* roller blade *m inv*
'**roll•er blind** tenda *f* a rullo
roll•er coast•er ['rəʊləkəʊstə(r)] montagne *fpl* russe
'**roll•er skate** *n* pattino *m* a rotelle
roll•ing pin ['rəʊlɪŋ] matterello *m*
ROM [rɒm] *abbr* COMPUT (= ***read only memory***) ROM *f inv*
Ro•man ['rəʊmən] **1** *adj* romano **2** *n* Romano *m*, -a *f*
Ro•man 'Cath•o•lic 1 *n* REL cattolico *m*, -a *f* **2** *adj* cattolico
ro•mance [rə'mæns] (*affair*) storia *f* d'amore; *novel* romanzo *m* rosa; *film* film *m inv* d'amore
ro•man•tic [rəʊ'mæntɪk] *adj* romantico
ro•man•tic•al•ly [rəʊ'mæntɪklɪ] *adv* romanticamente; ***romantically involved with s.o.*** legato sentimentalmente a qu
Rome [rəʊm] Roma *f*
roof [ruːf] tetto *m*; ***have a roof over one's head*** avere un tetto sulla testa
'**roof rack** MOT portabagagli *m inv*
room [ruːm] stanza *f*; (*bedroom*) camera *f* (da letto); (*space*) posto *m*; ***there's no room for …*** non c'è posto per …
'**room mate** compagno *m*, -a *f* di stanza
'**room ser•vice** servizio *m* in camera
room 'tem•per•a•ture temperatura *f* ambiente
room•y ['ruːmɪ] *adj house, car etc* spazioso; *clothes* ampio
root [ruːt] *n* radice *f*; ***roots*** *of person* radici *fpl*
◆ **root for** *v/t* F fare il tifo per
◆ **root out** *v/t* (*get rid of*) eradicare; (*find*) scovare
rope [rəʊp] corda *f*, fune *f*; ***show s.o. the ropes*** F insegnare il mestiere a qu
◆ **rope off** *v/t* transennare
ro•sa•ry ['rəʊzərɪ] REL rosario *m*
rose[1] [rəʊz] BOT rosa *f*
rose[2] [rəʊz] *pret* → ***rise***
rose•ma•ry ['rəʊzmərɪ] rosmarino *m*
ros•trum ['rɒstrəm] podio *m*
ros•y ['rəʊzɪ] *adj* roseo
rot [rɒt] **1** *n* marciume *m* **2** *v/i* (*pret & pp **-ted***) marcire
ro•ta ['rəʊtə] turni *mpl*; *actual document* tabella *f* dei turni; ***on a rota basis*** a turno
ro•tate [rəʊ'teɪt] **1** *v/i of blades, earth* ruotare **2** *v/t* girare; *crops* avvicendare
ro•ta•tion [rəʊ'teɪʃn] *around the sun etc* rotazione *f*; ***in rotation*** a turno
rot•ten ['rɒtn] *adj food, wood etc* marcio; F (*very bad*) schifoso F; ***what rotten luck!*** che scalogna!; ***what a rotten thing to do!*** che carognata!
rough [rʌf] **1** *adj hands, skin, surface* ruvido; *ground* accidentato; (*coarse*) rozzo; (*violent*) violento; *crossing* movimentato; *seas* grosso; (*approximate*) approssimativo; ***rough draft*** abbozzo *m* **2** *adv*: ***sleep rough*** dormire all'addiaccio **3** *v/t*: ***rough it*** F vivere senza confort **4** *n in golf* erba *f* alta
◆ **rough up** *v/t* F malmenare
rough•age ['rʌfɪdʒ] *in food* fibre *fpl*
rough•ly ['rʌflɪ] *adv* (*approximately*) circa; (*harshly*) bruscamente; ***roughly speaking*** grosso modo
rou•lette [ruː'let] roulette *f inv*
round [raʊnd] **1** *adj* rotondo; ***in round figures*** in cifra tonda **2** *n of postman, doctor* giro *m*; *of toast* fetta *f*; *of drinks* giro *m*; *of competition* girone *m*; *in boxing match* round *m inv* **3** *v/t the corner* girare **4** *adv*

& prep → ***around***

◆ **round off** *v/t edges* smussare; *meeting, night out* chiudere

◆ **round up** *v/t figure* arrotondare; *suspects, criminals* radunare

round•a•bout ['raʊndəbaʊt] **1** *adj route, way of saying sth* indiretto **2** *n on road* rotatoria *f*

'**round-the-world** *adj* intorno al mondo

round trip '**tick•et** *Am* biglietto *m* (di) andata e ritorno

'**round-up** *of cattle* raduno *m*; *of suspects, criminals* retata *f*; *of news* riepilogo *m*

rouse [raʊz] *v/t from sleep* svegliare; *interest, emotions* risvegliare

rous•ing ['raʊzɪŋ] *adj speech, finale* entusiasmante

route [ruːt] *of car* itinerario *m*; *of plane, ship* rotta *f*; *of bus* percorso *m*

rou•tine [ruː'tiːn] **1** *adj* abituale **2** *n* routine *f*; ***as a matter of routine*** d'abitudine

row[1] [rəʊ] *n* (*line*) fila *f*; ***5 days in a row*** 5 giorni di fila

row[2] [rəʊ] *v/t & v/i boat* remare

row[3] [raʊ] *n* (*quarrel*) litigio *m*; (*noise*) baccano *m*

row•dy ['raʊdɪ] *adj* turbolento

row•ing boat ['rəʊɪŋ] barca *f* a remi

roy•al [rɔɪəl] *adj* reale

roy•al•ty ['rɔɪəltɪ] (*royal persons*) reali *mpl*; *on book, recording* royalty *f inv*

rub [rʌb] *v/t* (*pret & pp* ***-bed***) sfregare, strofinare

◆ **rub down** *v/t to clean* levigare

◆ **rub in** *v/t cream, ointment* far penetrare; ***don't rub it in!*** *fig* non rivoltare il coltello nella piaga!

◆ **rub off** **1** *v/t dirt* levare (strofinando) **2** *v/i*: ***it rubs off on you*** ti si comunica

◆ **rub out** *v/t with eraser* cancellare

rub•ber ['rʌbə(r)] **1** *n* gomma *f* **2** *adj* di gomma

rub•ber '**band** elastico *m*

rub•ber '**gloves** *npl* guanti *mpl* di gomma

rub•bish ['rʌbɪʃ] immondizia *f*; (*poor quality*) porcheria *f*; (*nonsense*) sciocchezza *f*; ***don't talk rubbish!*** non dire sciocchezze!

'**rub•bish bin** pattumiera *f*

rub•ble ['rʌbl] macerie *fpl*

ru•by ['ruːbɪ] *jewel* rubino *m*

ruck•sack ['rʌksæk] zaino *m*

rud•der ['rʌdə(r)] timone *m*

rud•dy ['rʌdɪ] *adj complexion* rubicondo

rude [ruːd] *adj person, behaviour* maleducato; *language* volgare; ***a rude word*** una parolaccia; ***it's rude to …*** è cattiva educazione …

rude•ly ['ruːdlɪ] *adv* (*impolitely*) scortesemente

rude•ness ['ruːdnɪs] maleducazione *f*

ru•di•men•ta•ry [ruːdɪ'mentərɪ] *adj* rudimentale

ru•di•ments ['ruːdɪmənts] *npl* rudimenti *mpl*

rue•ful ['ruːfʊl] *adj* rassegnato

rue•ful•ly ['ruːfəlɪ] *adv* con aria rassegnata

ruf•fi•an ['rʌfɪən] delinquente *m/f*

ruf•fle ['rʌfl] **1** *n* (*on dress*) gala *f* **2** *v/t hair* scompigliare; *person* turbare; ***get ruffled*** agitarsi

rug [rʌg] tappeto *m*; (*blanket*) coperta *f* (da viaggio)

rug•by ['rʌgbɪ] SP rugby *m inv*

rug•by '**league** rugby *m inv* a tredici

'**rug•by match** partita *f* di rugby

'**rug•by play•er** giocatore *m* di rugby

rug•by '**un•ion** rugby *m inv* a quindici

rug•ged ['rʌgɪd] *adj coastline* frastagliato; *face, features* marcato

ru•in ['ruːɪn] **1** *n* rovina *f*; ***ruins*** rovine; ***in ruins*** *city, building* in rovina; ***in ruins*** *plans, career* rovinato **2** *v/t* rovinare; ***be ruined*** *financially* essere rovinato

rule [ruːl] **1** *n of club, game* regola *f*; (*authority*) dominio *m*; *for measuring* metro *m* (a stecche); ***as a rule*** generalmente **2** *v/t country* governare; ***the judge ruled that …*** il giudice ha stabilito che … **3** *v/i of monarch* regnare

◆ **rule out** *v/t* escludere

rul•er ['ruːlə(r)] *for measuring* righello *m*; *of state* capo *m*

rul•ing ['ruːlɪŋ] **1** *n* decisione *f* **2** *adj party* di governo

rum [rʌm] *drink* rum *m inv*

rum•ble ['rʌmbl] *v/i of stomach* brontolare; *of thunder* rimbombare

◆ **rum•mage around** ['rʌmɪdʒ] *v/i* frugare

ru•mour ['ruːmə(r)] **1** *n* voce *f* **2** *v/t*: ***it is rumoured that …*** corre voce che …

rump [rʌmp] *of animal* groppa *f*

rum•ple ['rʌmpl] *v/t clothes, paper* spiegazzare

rump•'steak bistecca *f* di girello

run [rʌn] **1** *n on foot* corsa *f*; *distance* tragitto *m*; *in tights* sfilatura *f*; ***go for a run*** andare a correre; ***go for a run in the car*** andare a fare un giro in macchina; ***make a run for it*** scappare; ***a criminal on the run*** un evaso, un'evasa; ***in the short run / in the long run*** sulle prime / alla lunga; ***a run on the dollar*** una forte richiesta di dollari; ***it's had a three year run*** *of play* ha tenuto cartellone per tre anni **2** *v/i* (*pret* ***ran***, *pp* ***run***) *of person*, *animal* correre; *of river* scorrere; *of trains, buses* viaggiare; *of paint, makeup* sbavare; *of nose* colare; *of play* tenere il cartellone; *of software* girare; *of engine, machine* funzionare; ***don't leave the tap running*** non lasciare il rubinetto aperto; ***run for President*** *in election* candidarsi alla presidenza **3** *v/t* (*pret* ***ran***, *pp* ***run***) correre; (*take part in*: *race*) partecipare a; *business, hotel, project etc* gestire; *software* lanciare; *car* usare; *risk* correre; ***can I run you to the station?*** ti porto alla stazione?; ***he ran his eye down the page*** diede uno sguardo alla pagina

◆ **run across** *v/t* imbattersi in

◆ **run away** *v/i* scappare

◆ **run down 1** *v/t* (*knock down*) investire; (*criticize*) parlare male di; *stocks* ridurre **2** *v/i of battery* scaricarsi

◆ **run into** *v/t* (*meet*) imbattersi in; *difficulties* trovare

◆ **run off 1** *v/i* scappare **2** *v/t* (*print off*) stampare

◆ **run out** *v/i of contract, time* scadere; *of supplies* esaurirsi

◆ **run out of** *v/t patience* perdere; *supplies* rimanere senza; ***I ran out of petrol*** ho finito la benzina; ***we are running out of time*** il tempo sta per scadere

◆ **run over 1** *v/t* (*knock down*) investire; ***can we run over the details again?*** possiamo rivedere i particolari? **2** *v/i of water etc* traboccare

◆ **run through** *v/t rehearse, go over* rivedere

◆ **run up** *v/t debts, large bill* accumulare; *clothes* mettere insieme

run•a•way ['rʌnəweɪ] *n* ragazzo *m*, -a *f* scappato di casa

run-'down *adj person* debilitato; *part of town, building* fatiscente

rung[1] [rʌŋ] *of ladder* piolo *m*

rung[2] [rʌŋ] *pp* → ***ring***

run•ner ['rʌnə(r)] *athlete* velocista *m/f*

run•ner 'beans *npl* fagiolini *mpl*

run•ner-'up secondo *m*, -a *f* classificato (-a)

run•ning ['rʌnɪŋ] **1** *n* SP corsa *f*; *of business* gestione *f* **2** *adj*: ***for two days running*** per due giorni di seguito

run•ning 'wa•ter acqua *f* corrente

run•ny ['rʌnɪ] *adj substance* liquido; *nose* che cola

'run-up SP rincorsa *f*; ***in the run-up to*** nel periodo che precede …

'run•way pista *f*

rup•ture ['rʌptʃə(r)] **1** *n* rottura *f*; MED lacerazione *f*; (*hernia*) ernia *f* **2** *v/i of pipe etc* scoppiare

ru•ral ['rʊərəl] *adj* rurale

ruse [ruːz] stratagemma *m*

rush [rʌʃ] **1** *n* corsa *f*; ***do sth in a rush*** fare qc di corsa; ***be in a rush*** andare di fretta; ***what's the big rush?*** che fretta c'è? **2** *v/t person* mettere fretta *o* premura a; *meal* mangiare in fretta; ***rush s.o. to hospital / the airport*** portare qu di corsa all'ospedale / aeroporto **3** *v/i* affrettarsi

'rush hour ora *f* di punta

Rus•sia ['rʌʃə] Russia *f*

Rus•sian ['rʌʃən] **1** *adj* russo **2** *n* russo *m*, -a *f*; *language* russo *m*

rust [rʌst] **1** *n* ruggine *f* **2** *v/i* arrugginirsi

rus•tle ['rʌsl] **1** *n of silk, leaves* fruscio *m* **2** *v/i of silk, leaves* frusciare

'rust-proof *adj* a prova di ruggine

rust re•mov•er ['rʌstrɪmuːvə(r)] smacchiatore *m* per la ruggine

rust•y ['rʌstɪ] *adj also fig* arrugginito; ***I'm a little rusty*** sono un po' arrugginito

rut [rʌt] *in road* solco *m*; ***be in a rut*** *fig* essersi fossilizzato

ruth•less ['ruːθlɪs] *adj* spietato

ruth•less•ly *adv* spietatamente

ruth•less•ness ['ruːθlɪsnɪs] spietatezza *f*

rye [raɪ] segale *f*

'rye bread pane *m* di segale

S

sab•bat•i•cal [sə'bætɪkl] *n of academic* anno *m* sabbatico
sab•o•tage ['sæbətɑːʒ] **1** *n* sabotaggio *m* **2** *v/t* sabotare
sab•o•teur [sæbə'tɜː(r)] sabotatore *m*, -trice *f*
sac•cha•rin ['sækərɪn] *n* saccarina *f*
sa•chet ['sæʃeɪ] *of shampoo, cream etc* bustina *f*
sack [sæk] **1** *n bag* sacco *m*; ***get the sack*** F essere licenziato **2** *v/t* F licenziare
sa•cred ['seɪkrɪd] *adj* sacro
sac•ri•fice ['sækrɪfaɪs] **1** *n* sacrificio *m*; ***make sacrifices*** *fig* fare sacrifici **2** *v/t* sacrificare
sac•ri•lege ['sækrɪlɪdʒ] sacrilegio *m*
sad [sæd] *adj* triste; *state of affairs* deplorevole
sad•dle ['sædl] **1** *n* sella *f* **2** *v/t horse* sellare; ***saddle s.o. with sth*** *fig* affibbiare qc a qu
sa•dis•m ['seɪdɪzm] sadismo *m*
sa•dist ['seɪdɪst] sadista *m/f*
sa•dis•tic [sə'dɪstɪk] *adj* sadistico
sad•ly ['sædlɪ] *adv* tristemente; (*regrettably*) purtroppo
sad•ness ['sædnɪs] tristezza *f*
safe [seɪf] **1** *adj not dangerous* sicuro; *not in danger* al sicuro; *driver* prudente; ***is it safe to walk here?*** non è pericoloso camminare qui? **2** *n* cassaforte *f*
'**safe•guard 1** *n* protezione *f*, salvaguardia *f*; ***as a safeguard against*** per proteggersi contro **2** *v/t* proteggere
safe•ly ['seɪflɪ] *adv arrive, complete first test etc* senza problemi; *drive* prudentemente; *assume* tranquillamente
'**safe keep•ing**: ***give sth to s.o. for safe keeping*** dare qc in custodia a qu
safe•ty ['seɪftɪ] sicurezza *f*
'**safe•ty belt** cintura *f* di sicurezza
'**safe•ty-con•scious** *adj* attento ai problemi di sicurezza
safe•ty '**first** prudenza *f*
'**safe•ty pin** spilla *f* di sicurezza
sag [sæg] **1** *n in ceiling* incurvatura *f* **2** *v/i* (*pret & pp* ***-ged***) *of ceiling* incurvarsi; *of rope* allentarsi
sa•ga ['sɑːgə] saga *f*
sage [seɪdʒ] *n herb* salvia *f*
Sa•git•tar•i•us [sædʒɪ'teərɪəs] ASTR Sagittario *m*
said [sed] *pret & pp* → ***say***
sail [seɪl] **1** *n of boat* vela *f*; *trip* veleggiata *f*; ***go for a sail*** fare un giro in barca (a vela) **2** *v/t yacht* pilotare **3** *v/i* fare vela; (*depart*) salpare
'**sail•board 1** *n* windsurf *m inv* **2** *v/i* fare windsurf
'**sail•board•ing** windsurf *m inv*
sail•ing ['seɪlɪŋ] SP vela *f*
'**sail•ing boat** barca *f* a vela
'**sail•ing ship** veliero *m*
sail•or ['seɪlə(r)] marinaio *m*; ***be a bad / good sailor*** soffrire / non soffrire il mal di mare
saint [seɪnt] santo *m*, -a *f*
sake [seɪk] *n*: ***for my / your sake*** per il mio / il tuo bene; ***for the sake of*** per; ***for the sake of peace*** per amor di pace
sal•ad ['sæləd] insalata *f*
sal•ad '**dress•ing** condimento *m* per l'insalata
sal•a•ry ['sælərɪ] stipendio *m*
'**sal•a•ry scale** scala *f* salariale
sale [seɪl] vendita *f*; *at reduced prices* svendita *f*, saldi *mpl*; ***for sale*** *sign* in vendita; ***be on sale*** essere in vendita
sales [seɪlz] *npl department* reparto *m* vendite
'**sales as•sist•ant**, '**sales clerk** *Am in shop* commesso *m*, -a *f*
'**sales fig•ures** *npl* fatturato *m*
'**sales•man** venditore *m*
sales '**man•ag•er** direttore *m*, -trice *f* delle vendite
'**sales meet•ing** riunione *f* marketing e vendite
'**sales wom•an** venditrice *f*
sa•lient ['seɪlɪənt] *adj* saliente
sa•li•va [sə'laɪvə] saliva *f*
salm•on ['sæmən] (*pl* ***salmon***) salmone *m*
sa•loon [sə'luːn] MOT berlina *f*; *Am*: *bar* bar *m inv*
salt [sɒlt] **1** *n* sale *m* **2** *v/t food* salare
'**salt•cel•lar** saliera *f*
salt '**wa•ter** acqua *f* salata
'**salt-wa•ter fish** pesce *m* di mare
salt•y ['sɒltɪ] *adj* salato
sal•u•tar•y ['sæljʊtərɪ] *adj experience* salutare
sa•lute [sə'luːt] **1** *n* MIL saluto *m*; ***take the salute*** ricevere i saluti **2** *v/t & v/i* salutare
sal•vage ['sælvɪdʒ] *v/t from wreck* ricuperare
sal•va•tion [sæl'veɪʃn] salvezza *f*
Sal•va•tion '**Ar•my** Esercito *m* della Sal-

vezza
same [seɪm] **1** *adj* stesso **2** *pron* stesso; ***the same*** lo stesso, la stessa; ***Happy New Year – the same to you*** Buon anno! – Grazie e altrettanto!; ***he's not the same any more*** non è più lo stesso; ***all the same*** (*even so*) eppure; ***men are all the same*** gli uomini sono tutti uguali; ***it's all the same to me*** per me è uguale **3** *adv*: ***the same*** allo stesso modo; ***I still feel the same about that*** la penso sempre allo stesso modo
sam•ple ['sɑːmpl] **1** *n* campione *m* **2** *v/t food*, *product* provare
san•a•to•ri•um [sænə'tɔːrɪəm] casa *f* di cura
sanctimonious [sæŋktɪ'məʊnɪəs] *adj* moraleggiante
sanc•tion ['sæŋkʃn] **1** *n* (*approval*) approvazione *f*; (*penalty*) sanzione *f* **2** *v/t* (*approve*) sancire
sanc•ti•ty ['sæŋktətɪ] santità *f*
sanc•tu•a•ry ['sæŋktjʊərɪ] REL santuario *m*; *for wild animals* riserva *f*
sand [sænd] **1** *n* sabbia *f* **2** *v/t with sandpaper* smerigliare
san•dal ['sændl] sandalo *m*
'sand•bag sacchetto *m* di sabbia
'sand•blast *v/t* sabbiare
'sand dune duna *f*
sand•er ['sændə(r)] *tool* smerigliatrice *f*
'sand•pa•per **1** *n* carta *f* smerigliata **2** *v/t* smerigliare
'sand•stone arenaria *f*
sand•wich ['sænwɪdʒ] **1** *n* tramezzino *m* **2** *v/t*: ***be sandwiched between two …*** essere incastrato tra due …
sand•y ['sændɪ] *adj beach* sabbioso; *full of sand* pieno di sabbia; *hair* rossiccio
sane [seɪn] *adj* sano di mente
sang [sæŋ] *pret* → ***sing***
san•i•ta•ry ['sænɪtərɪ] *adj conditions* igienico; *installations* sanitario
'san•i•ta•ry tow•el assorbente *m* (igienico)
san•i•ta•tion [sænɪ'teɪʃn] (*sanitary installations*) impianti *mpl* igienici; (*removal of waste*) fognature *fpl*
san•i•ty ['sænətɪ] sanità *f inv* mentale
sank [sæŋk] *pret* → ***sink***
San•ta Claus ['sæntəklɔːz] Babbo *m* Natale
sap [sæp] **1** *n in tree* linfa *f* **2** *v/t* (*pret & pp* ***-ped***) *s.o.'s energy* indebolire
sap•phire ['sæfaɪə(r)] *n jewel* zaffiro *m*
sar•cas•m ['sɑːkæzm] sarcasmo *m*
sar•cas•tic [sɑː'kæstɪk] *adj* sarcastico
sar•cas•tic•al•ly [sɑː'kæstɪklɪ] *adv* sarcasticamente
sar•dine [sɑː'diːn] sardina *f*
Sar•din•i•a [sɑː'dɪnɪə] Sardegna *f*
Sar•din•i•an [sɑː'dɪnɪən] **1** *adj* sardo **2** *n* sardo *m*, -a *f*
sar•don•ic [sɑː'dɒnɪk] *adj* sardonico
sar•don•ic•al•ly [sɑː'dɒnɪklɪ] *adv* sardonicamente
sash [sæʃ] *on dress* fusciacca *f*; *on uniform* fascia *f*; *on window* vetro *m* scorrevole (di finestra a ghigliottina)
Sa•tan ['seɪtn] Satana *m*
satch•el ['sætʃl] *for schoolchild* cartella *f*
sat•el•lite ['sætəlaɪt] satellite *m*
'sat•el•lite dish antenna *f* parabolica
sat•el•lite T'V TV *f inv* satellitare
sat•in ['sætɪn] *adj* satin *m inv*
sat•ire ['sætaɪə(r)] satira *f*
sa•tir•i•cal [sə'tɪrɪkl] *adj* satirico
sat•i•rist ['sætərɪst] satirista *m*
sat•ir•ize ['sætəraɪz] *v/t* satireggiare
sat•is•fac•tion [sætɪs'fækʃn] soddisfazione *f*; ***I get satisfaction out of my job*** il lavoro mi dà molte soddisfazioni; ***is that to your satisfaction?*** è di suo gradimento?
sat•is•fac•to•ry [sætɪs'fæktərɪ] *adj* soddisfacente; *just good enough* sufficiente; ***this is not satisfactory*** non è sufficiente
satisfy ['sætɪsfaɪ] *v/t* (*pret & pp* ***-ied***) *customers*, *needs*, *curiosity* soddisfare; *requirement* rispondere a; ***satisfy s.o.'s hunger*** sfamare qu; ***I am satisfied*** *had enough to eat* sono sazio; ***I am satisfied that …*** (*convinced*) sono convinto che …; ***I hope you're satisfied!*** sei contento?
Sat•ur•day ['sætədeɪ] sabato *m*
sauce [sɔːs] salsa *f*, sugo *m*
'sauce•pan pentola *f*
sau•cer ['sɔːsə(r)] piattino *m*
sauc•y ['sɔːsɪ] *adj person*, *dress* provocante
Sa•u•di A•ra•bi•a [saʊdɪə'reɪbɪə] Arabia *f* Saudita
Sa•u•di A•ra•bi•an [saʊdɪə'reɪbɪən] **1** *adj* saudita **2** *n person* saudita *m/f*
sau•na ['sɔːnə] sauna *f*
saun•ter ['sɔːntə(r)] *v/i* passeggiare; ***he sauntered in at 10.30*** è arrivato tranquillamente alle 10.30
saus•age ['sɒsɪdʒ] salsiccia *f*
sav•age ['sævɪdʒ] **1** *adj animal* selvaggio; *attack*, *criticism* feroce **2** *n* selvaggio *m*, -a *f*
sav•age•ry ['sævɪdʒrɪ] ferocia *f*
save [seɪv] **1** *v/t* (*rescue*) salvare; *money*, *time*, *effort* risparmiare; (*collect*) raccogliere; COMPUT salvare; *goal* parare; ***you could save yourself a lot of effort***

potresti risparmiarti parecchi sforzi **2** *v/i* (*put money aside*) risparmiare; SP parare **3** *n* SP parata *f*
◆ **save up for** *v/t* risparmiare per
sav•er ['seɪvə(r)] *person* risparmiatore *m*, -trice *f*
savi•ng ['seɪvɪŋ] risparmio *m*
sav•ings ['seɪvɪŋz] *npl* risparmi *mpl*
'**sav•ings ac•count** libretto *m* di risparmio
sav•ings and 'loan *Am* → ***building society***
'**sav•ings bank** cassa *f* di risparmio
sa•vior *Am*, **sa•viour** ['seɪvjə(r)] REL salvatore *m*
sa•vor *etc Am* → ***savour*** *etc*
sa•vour ['seɪvə(r)] **1** *n* sapore *m* **2** *v/t* assaporare
sa•vour•y ['seɪvərɪ] *adj not sweet* salato (*non dolce*)
saw[1] [sɔː] **1** *n tool* sega *f* **2** *v/t* segare
saw[2] [sɔː] *pret* → ***see***
◆ **saw off** *v/t* segare via
'**saw•dust** segatura *f*
sax•o•phone ['sæksəfəʊn] sassofono *m*
say [seɪ] **1** *v/t* (*pret & pp* ***said***) dire; ***can I say something?*** posso dire una cosa?; ***that is to say*** sarebbe a dire; ***what do you say to that?*** cosa ne dici?; ***what does the note say?*** cosa dice il biglietto? **2** *n*: ***have one's say*** dire la propria; ***have a say in sth*** avere voce in capitolo in qc
say•ing ['seɪɪŋ] detto *m*
scab [skæb] *on skin* crosta *f*
scaf•fold•ing ['skæfəldɪŋ] *on building* impalcature *fpl*
scald [skɔːld] *v/t* scottare; ***scald o.s.*** scottarsi
scale[1] [skeɪl] *on fish* scaglia *f*
scale[2] [skeɪl] **1** *n of map*, MUS scala *f*; *on thermometer* scala *f* graduata; *of project* portata *f*; ***on a large scale*** su vasta scala; ***on a small scale*** su scala ridotta **2** *v/t cliffs etc* scalare
◆ **scale down** *v/t* ridurre
scale 'draw•ing disegno *m* in scala
scales [skeɪlz] *npl for weighing* bilancia *fsg*
scal•lop ['skɒləp] *n* capasanta *f*
scalp [skælp] *n* cuoio *m* capelluto
scal•pel ['skælpl] bisturi *m*
scam [skæm] F truffa *f*
scam•pi ['skæmpɪ] *gamberoni mpl in pastella fritti*
scan [skæn] **1** *v/t* (*pret & pp* ***-ned***) *horizon* scrutare; *page* scorrere; *foetus* fare l'ecografia di; *brain* fare la TAC di; COMPUT scannerizzare **2** *n* (*brain scan*) TAC *f inv*; *of foetus* ecografia *f*
◆ **scan in** *v/t* COMPUT scannerizzare
scan•dal ['skændl] scandalo *m*
scan•dal•ize ['skændəlaɪz] *v/t* scandalizzare
scan•dal•ous ['skændələs] *adj* scandaloso
Scan•di•na•vi•a [skændɪ'neɪvɪə] Scandinavia *f*
scan•ner ['skænə(r)] scanner *m inv*
scant [skænt] *adj* scarso
scant•i•ly ['skæntɪlɪ] *adv*: ***scantily clad*** succintamente vestito
scant•y ['skæntɪ] *adj clothes* succinto
scape•goat ['skeɪpgəʊt] capro *m* espiatorio
scar [skɑː(r)] **1** *n* cicatrice *f* **2** *v/t* (*pret & pp* ***-red***) *face* lasciare cicatrici su; *fig* segnare
scarce [skeəs] *adj in short supply* scarso; ***make o.s. scarce*** squagliarsela F
scarce•ly ['skeəslɪ] *adv* appena; ***there was scarcely anything left*** non rimaneva quasi più niente
scar•ci•ty ['skeəsɪtɪ] scarsità *f inv*
scare [skeə(r)] **1** *v/t* spaventare; ***be scared of*** avere paura di **2** *n* (*panic*, *alarm*) panico *m*; ***give s.o. a scare*** mettere paura a qu
◆ **scare away** *v/t* far scappare
'**scare•crow** spaventapasseri *m inv*
scare•mon•ger ['skeəmʌŋgə(r)] allarmista *m/f*
scarf [skɑːf] *around neck* sciarpa *f*; *over head* foulard *m inv*
scar•let ['skɑːlət] *adj* scarlatto
scar•let 'fe•ver scarlattina *f*
scar•y ['skeərɪ] *adj* che fa paura
scath•ing ['skeɪðɪŋ] *adj* caustico
scat•ter ['skætə(r)] **1** *v/t leaflets*, *seeds* spargere; *crowd* disperdere **2** *v/i of people* disperdersi
scat•ter•brained ['skætəbreɪnd] *adj* sventato
scat•tered ['skætəd] *adj family*, *villages* sparpagliato; ***scattered showers*** precipitazioni sparse
scat•ty ['skætɪ] *adj* sventato
scav•enge ['skævɪndʒ] *v/i* frugare tra i rifiuti
scav•eng•er ['skævɪndʒə(r)] *animal* animale *m* necrofago; (*person*) *persona f che fruga tra i rifiuti*
sce•na•ri•o [sɪ'nɑːrɪəʊ] scenario *m*
scene [siːn] scena *f*; (*argument*) scenata *f*; ***make a scene*** fare una scenata; ***scenes*** THEA scenografia *f*; ***jazz / rock scene*** il mondo del jazz / rock; ***behind the scenes*** dietro le quinte

sce•ne•ry ['si:nərɪ] paesaggio *m*; THEA scenario *m*
scent [sent] *n of roses* profumo *m*; *of animal* odore *m*
scep•tic ['skeptɪk] scettico *m*, -a *f*
scep•ti•cal ['skeptɪkl] *adj* scettico
scep•ti•cal•ly ['skeptɪklɪ] *adv* scetticamente
scep•ti•cism ['skeptɪsɪzm] scetticismo *m*
sched•ule ['ʃedju:l] **1** *n of events, work* programma *m*; *for trains* orario *m*; ***be on schedule*** *of work, of train etc* essere in orario; ***be behind schedule*** *of work, of train etc* essere in ritardo **2** *v/t put on schedule* programmare; ***it's scheduled for completion next month*** il completamento dei lavori è previsto per il mese prossimo
sched•uled 'flight ['ʃedju:ld] volo *m* di linea
scheme [ski:m] **1** *n* (*plan*) piano *m*; (*plot*) complotto *m* **2** *v/i* (*plot*) complottare, tramare
schem•ing ['ski:mɪŋ] *adj* intrigante
schiz•o•phre•ni•a [skɪtsə'fri:nɪə] schizofrenia *f*
schiz•o•phren•ic [skɪtsə'frenɪk] **1** *n* schizofrenico *m*, -a *f* **2** *adj* schizofrenico
schol•ar ['skɒlə(r)] studioso *m*, -a *f*
schol•ar•ly ['skɒlə(r)lɪ] *adj* dotto
schol•ar•ship ['skɒləʃɪp] (*scholarly work*) erudizione *f*; (*financial award*) borsa *f* di studio
school [sku:l] scuola *f*
'school bag (*satchel*) cartella *f*
'school•boy scolaro *m*
'school•children scolari *mpl*
'school days *npl* tempi *mpl* della scuola
'school•girl scolara *f*
'school•mas•ter maestro *m*
'school•mate compagno *m*, -a *f* di scuola
'school•mis•tress maestra *f*
'school•teach•er insegnante *m/f*
sci•at•i•ca [saɪ'ætɪkə] sciatica *f*
sci•ence ['saɪəns] scienza *f*
sci•ence 'fic•tion fantascienza *f*
sci•en•tif•ic [saɪən'tɪfɪk] *adj* scientifico
sci•en•tist ['saɪəntɪst] scienziato *m*, -a *f*
scis•sors ['sɪzəz] *npl* forbici *fpl*
scoff[1] [skɒf] *v/t food* sbafare
scoff[2] [skɒf] *v/i* (*mock*) canzonare
◆ **scoff at** *v/t* deridere
scold [skəʊld] *v/t* sgridare
scone [skɒn] *focaccina f o dolcetto m da mangiare con il tè*
scoop [sku:p] **1** *n for grain, flour* paletta *f*; *for ice cream* cucchiaio *m* dosatore; *of ice cream* pallina *f*; (*story*) scoop *m inv* **2** *v/t* (*pick up*) raccogliere
◆ **scoop up** *v/t* sollevare tra le braccia
scoot•er ['sku:tə(r)] *with motor* scooter *m inv*; *child's* monopattino *m*
scope [skəʊp] portata *f*; (*opportunity*) possibilità *f inv*
scorch [skɔ:tʃ] *v/t* bruciare
scorch•ing hot ['skɔ:tʃɪŋ] *adj* torrido
score [skɔ:(r)] **1** *n* SP punteggio *m*; (*written music*) spartito *m*; *of film etc* colonna *f* sonora; ***what's the score?*** SP a quanto sono / siamo?; ***have a score to settle with s.o.*** avere un conto in sospeso con qu; ***keep*** (***the***) ***score*** tenere il punteggio **2** *v/t goal, point* segnare; (*cut*) incidere **3** *v/i* segnare; (*keep the score*) tenere il punteggio
'score•board segnapunti *m inv*
scor•er ['skɔ:rə(r)] *of goal, point* marcatore *m*, -trice *f*; (*score-keeper*) segnapunti *m/f inv*
scorn [skɔ:n] **1** *n* disprezzo *m*; ***pour scorn on sth*** deridere qc **2** *v/t idea, suggestion* disprezzare
scorn•ful ['skɔ:nfʊl] *adj* sprezzante
scorn•ful•ly ['skɔ:nfʊlɪ] *adv* sprezzantemente
Scor•pi•o ['skɔ:pɪəʊ] ASTR Scorpione *m*
Scot [skɒt] scozzese *m/f*
Scotch [skɒtʃ] (*whisky*) scotch *m inv*
Scotch ˌtape® *Am* scotch® *m*
scot-'free *adv*: ***get off scot-free*** farla franca
Scot•land ['skɒtlənd] Scozia *f*
Scots•man ['skɒtsmən] scozzese *m*
Scots•wom•an ['skɒtswʊmən] scozzese *f*
Scot•tish ['skɒtɪʃ] *adj* scozzese
scoun•drel ['skaʊndrəl] birbante *m/f*
scour[1] ['skaʊə(r)] *v/t* (*search*) setacciare
scour[2] ['skaʊə(r)] *v/t pans* sfregare
scout [skaʊt] *n* (*boy scout*) boy-scout *m inv*
scowl [skaʊl] **1** *n* sguardo *m* torvo **2** *v/i* guardare storto
scram [skræm] *v/i* (*pret & **pp -med***) F filare F
scram•ble ['skræmbl] **1** *n* (*rush*) corsa *f* **2** *v/t message* rendere indecifrabile **3** *v/i climb* inerpicarsi; ***he scrambled to his feet*** si rialzò in fretta
scram•bled 'eggs ['skræmbld] *npl* uova *fpl* strapazzate
scrap [skræp] **1** *n metal* rottame *m*; (*fight*) zuffa *f*; (*little bit*) briciolo *m* **2** *v/t* (*pret & pp* **-ped**) *plan, project* abbandonare
'scrap•book album *m inv*
scrape [skreɪp] **1** *n on paintwork* graffio *m* **2** *v/t paintwork, one's arm etc* graffiare; *vegetables* raschiare; ***scrape a living*** sbarcare il lunario

S

◆ **scrape through** *v/i in exam* passare per il rotto della cuffia
'**scrap heap** cumulo *m* di rottami; ***good for the scrap heap*** da buttare via
scrap 'met•al rottami *mpl*
scrap 'pa•per carta *f* già usata
scrap•py ['skræpɪ] *adj work, writing* senza capo né coda
scratch [skrætʃ] **1** *n mark* graffio *m*; ***have a scratch*** *to stop itching* grattarsi; ***start from scratch*** ricominciare da zero; ***not up to scratch*** non all'altezza **2** *v/t* (*mark*) graffiare; *because of itch* grattare **3** *v/i of cat, nails* graffiare
scrawl [skrɔːl] **1** *n* scarabocchio *m* **2** *v/t* scarabocchiare
scraw•ny ['skrɔːnɪ] *adj* scheletrico
scream [skriːm] **1** *n* urlo *m*; ***screams of laughter*** risate *fpl* fragorose **2** *v/i* urlare
screech [skriːtʃ] **1** *n of tyres* stridio *m*; (*scream*) strillo *m* **2** *v/i of tyres* stridere; (*scream*) strillare
screen [skriːn] **1** *n in room, hospital* paravento *m*; *of smoke* cortina *f*; *cinema*, COMPUT, *of television* schermo *m*; ***on the screen*** *in film* sullo schermo; ***on (the) screen*** COMPUT su schermo **2** *v/t* (*protect, hide*) riparare; *film* proiettare; *for security reasons* vagliare
'**screen•play** sceneggiatura *f*
'**screen sav•er** COMPUT salvaschermo *m inv*
'**screen test** *for film* provino *m*
screw [skruː] **1** *n* vite *f* (metallica); V (*sex*) scopata *f* V **2** *v/t* V scopare V; F (*cheat*) fregare F; ***screw sth to sth*** avvitare qc a qc
◆ **screw up 1** *v/t eyes* strizzare; *piece of paper* appallottolare; F (*make a mess of*) mandare all'aria **2** *v/i* F (*make a bad mistake*) fare un casino F
'**screw•driv•er** cacciavite *m*
screwed 'up [skruːd'ʌp] *adj* F *psychologically* complessato
'**screw top** *on bottle* tappo *m* a vite
screw•y ['skruːɪ] *adj* F svitato
scrib•ble ['skrɪbl] **1** *n* scarabocchio *m* **2** *v/t & v/i* (*write quickly*) scarabocchiare
scrimp [skrɪmp] *v/i*: ***scrimp and scrape*** risparmiare fino all'ultimo soldo
script [skrɪpt] *for film, play* copione *m*; (*form of writing*) scrittura *f*
scrip•ture ['skrɪptʃə(r)]: ***the (Holy) Scriptures*** le Sacre Scritture *fpl*
'**script•writ•er** sceneggiatore *m*, -trice *f*
scroll [skrəʊl] *n* rotolo *m* di pergamena
◆ **scroll down** *v/i* COMPUT far scorrere il testo in avanti
◆ **scroll up** *v/i* COMPUT far scorrere il testo indietro
scrounge [skraʊndʒ] *v/t* scroccare
scroung•er ['skraʊndʒə(r)] scroccone *m*, -a *f*
scrub [skrʌb] *v/t* (*pret & pp* **-bed**) *floors, hands* sfregare (con spazzola)
scrub•bing brush ['skrʌbɪŋ] *for floor* spazzolone *m*
scruff•y ['skrʌfɪ] *adj* trasandato
scrum [skrʌm] *in rugby* mischia *f*
◆ **scrunch up** [skrʌntʃ] *v/t plastic cup etc* accartocciare
scru•ples ['skruːplz] *npl* scrupoli *mpl*; ***have no scruples about doing sth*** non avere scrupoli a fare qc
scru•pu•lous ['skruːpjʊləs] *adj* scrupoloso
scru•pu•lous•ly ['skruːpjʊləslɪ] *adv* (*meticulously*) scrupolosamente
scru•ti•nize ['skruːtɪnaɪz] *v/t text* esaminare attentamente; *face* scrutare
scru•ti•ny ['skruːtɪnɪ] attento esame *m*; ***come under scrutiny*** essere sottoposto ad attento esame
scu•ba div•ing ['skuːbə] immersione *f* subacquea
scuf•fle ['skʌfl] *n* tafferuglio *m*
sculp•tor ['skʌlptə(r)] scultore *m*, -trice *f*
sculp•ture ['skʌlptʃə(r)] scultura *f*
scum [skʌm] *on liquid* schiuma *f*; (*pej*: *people*) feccia *f*
sea [siː] mare *m*; ***by the sea*** al mare
'**sea•bed** fondale *m* marino
'**sea•bird** uccello *m* marino
sea•far•ing ['siːfeərɪŋ] *adj nation* marinaro
'**sea•food** frutti *mpl* di mare
'**sea•front** lungomare *m inv*
'**sea•go•ing** *adj vessel* d'alto mare
'**sea•gull** gabbiano *m*
seal[1] [siːl] *n animal* foca *f*
seal[2] [siːl] **1** *n on document* sigillo *m*; TECH chiusura *f* ermetica **2** *v/t container* chiudere ermeticamente
◆ **seal off** *v/t area* bloccare l'accesso a
'**sea lev•el**: ***above / below sea level*** sopra / sotto il livello del mare
seam [siːm] *n on garment* cucitura *f*; *of ore* filone *m*
'**sea•man** marinaio *m*
seam•stress ['siːmstrɪs] sarta *f*
'**sea•port** porto *m* marittimo
'**sea pow•er** *nation* potenza *f* marittima
search [sɜːtʃ] **1** *n for s.o./sth* ricerca *f*; *of person, building* perquisizione *f*; ***in search of*** alla ricerca di **2** *v/t person, building, baggage* perquisire; *area* perlustrare
◆ **search for** *v/t* cercare

search•ing ['sɜːʧɪŋ] *adj look* penetrante
'**search•light** riflettore *m*
'**search par•ty** squadra *f* di ricerca
'**search war•rant** mandato *m* di perquisizione
'**sea•shore** riva *f* (del mare)
'**sea•sick** *adj* con il mal di mare; ***be seasick*** avere il mal di mare; ***get seasick*** soffrire il mal di mare
'**sea•side** *n*: ***at the seaside*** al mare; ***go to the seaside*** andare al mare; ***seaside resort*** località *f* balneare
sea•son ['siːzn] *n* stagione *f*; ***in / out of season*** in / fuori stagione
sea•son•al ['siːznl] *adj* stagionale
sea•soned ['siːznd] *adj wood* stagionato; *traveller, campaigner etc* esperto
sea•son•ing ['siːznɪŋ] condimento *m*
'**sea•son tick•et** abbonamento *m*
seat [siːt] **1** *n* posto *m*; *of trousers* fondo *m*; POL seggio *m*; ***please take a seat*** si accomodi **2** *v/t* (*have seating for*) avere posti a sedere per; ***please remain seated*** state seduti, per favore
'**seat belt** cintura *f* di sicurezza
'**sea ur•chin** riccio *m* di mare
'**sea•weed** alga *f*
se•clud•ed [sɪ'kluːdɪd] *adj* appartato
se•clu•sion [sɪ'kluːʒn] isolamento *m*
sec•ond[1] ['sekənd] **1** *n of time* secondo *m*; ***just a second*** un attimo **2** *adj* secondo **3** *adv come in* secondo **4** *v/t motion* appoggiare
se•cond[2] [sɪ'kɒnd] *v/t*: ***be seconded to*** essere assegnato a
sec•ond•a•ry ['sekəndrɪ] *adj* secondario
sec•ond•a•ry ed•u'ca•tion istruzione *f* secondaria
se•cond 'best *adj* secondo (dopo il migliore)
sec•ond 'big•gest *adj* secondo in ordine di grandezza
sec•ond 'class *adj ticket* di seconda classe
sec•ond 'floor secondo piano *m*; *Am* terzo piano
sec•ond 'gear MOT seconda *f* (marcia)
'**sec•ond hand** *n on clock* lancetta *f* dei secondi
'**sec•ond-hand** *adj & adv* di seconda mano
sec•ond•ly ['sekəndlɪ] *adv* in secondo luogo
sec•ond-'rate *adj* di second'ordine
sec•ond 'thoughts: ***I've had second thoughts*** ci ho ripensato
se•cre•cy ['siːkrəsɪ] segretezza *f*
se•cret ['siːkrət] **1** *n* segreto *m*; ***do sth in secret*** fare qc in segreto **2** *adj* segreto
se•cret 'a•gent agente *m* segreto
sec•re•tar•i•al [sekrə'teərɪəl] *adj tasks, job* di segretaria
sec•re•tar•y ['sekrətərɪ] segretario *m*, -a *f*; POL ministro *m*
Sec•re•tar•y of 'State *in USA* Segretario *m* di Stato
se•crete [sɪ'kriːt] *v/t* (*give off*) secernere; (*hide away*) nascondere
se•cre•tion [sɪ'kriːʃn] secrezione *f*
se•cre•tive ['siːkrətɪv] *adj* riservato
se•cret•ly ['siːkrətlɪ] *adv* segretamente
se•cret po'lice polizia *f* segreta
se•cret 'ser•vice servizio *m* segreto
sect [sekt] setta *f*
sec•tion ['sekʃn] sezione *f*
sec•tor ['sektə(r)] settore *m*
sec•u•lar ['sekjʊlə(r)] *adj* laico
se•cure [sɪ'kjʊə(r)] **1** *adj shelf etc* saldo *feeling* sicuro; *job* stabile **2** *v/t shelf etc* assicurare; *s.o.'s help, finances* assicurarsi
se•cu•ri•ty [sɪ'kjʊərətɪ] *in job* sicurezza *f*; *in relationship* stabilità *f inv*; *for investment* garanzia *f*; *at airport etc* sicurezza *f*
se'cu•ri•ties mar•ket FIN mercato *m* dei titoli
se'cu•ri•ty a•lert stato *m* di allarme
se,cu•ri•ty check controllo *m* di sicurezza
se,cu•ri•ty-con•scious *adj* attento alla sicurezza
se,cu•ri•ty forces *npl police* forze *fpl* dell'ordine
se,cu•ri•ty forces *npl* forze *fpl* di sicurezza
se,cu•ri•ty guard guardia *f* giurata
se,cu•ri•ty risk minaccia *f* per la sicurezza
se•date [sɪ'deɪt] *v/t* somministrare sedativi a
se•da•tion [sɪ'deɪʃn]: ***be under sedation*** essere sotto l'effetto di sedativi
sed•a•tive ['sedətɪv] *n* sedativo *m*
sed•en•ta•ry ['sedəntərɪ] *adj job* sedentario
sed•i•ment ['sedɪmənt] sedimento *m*
se•duce [sɪ'djuːs] *v/t* sedurre
se•duc•tion [sɪ'dʌkʃn] seduzione *f*
se•duc•tive [sɪ'dʌktɪv] *adj smile, look* seducente; *offer* allettante
see [siː] *v/t* (*pret* ***saw***, *pp* ***seen***) vedere; (*understand*) capire; *romantically* uscire con; ***I see*** capisco; ***can I see the manager?*** vorrei vedere il direttore; ***you should see a doctor*** dovresti andare dal medico; ***see s.o. home*** accompagnare a casa qu; ***I'll see you to the door*** t'accompagno alla porta; ***see you!*** F ciao! F
◆ **see about** *v/t* (*look into*) provvedere a;

S

I'll see about it ci penso io
◆ **see off** *v/t at airport etc* salutare; (*chase away*) scacciare
◆ **see out** *v/t* : ***see s.o. out*** accompagnare qu alla porta
◆ **see to** *v/t*: ***see to sth*** occuparsi di qc; ***see to it that sth gets done*** assicurarsi che qc venga fatto
seed [siːd] *single* seme *m*; *collective* semi *mpl*; *in tennis* testa *f* di serie; ***go to seed*** *of person*, *district* ridursi male
seed•ling ['siːdlɪŋ] semenzale *m*
seed•y ['siːdɪ] *adj bar*, *district* squallido
see•ing (that) ['siːɪŋ] *conj* visto che
seek [siːk] *v/t & v/i* (*pret & pp* ***sought***) cercare
seem [siːm] *v/i* sembrare; ***it seems that ...*** sembra che ...
seem•ing•ly ['siːmɪŋlɪ] *adv* apparentemente
seen [siːn] *pp* → ***see***
seep [siːp] *v/i of liquid* filtrare
◆ **seep out** *v/i of liquid* filtrare
see•saw ['siːsɔː] *n* altalena *f* (a bilico)
seethe [siːð] *v/i fig* fremere di rabbia
'see-through *adj dress*, *material* trasparente
seg•ment ['segmənt] segmento *m*; *of orange* spicchio *m*
seg•mented [seg'məntɪd] *adj* frazionato
seg•re•gate ['segrɪgeɪt] *v/t* separare
seg•re•ga•tion [segrɪ'geɪʃn] segregazione *f*
seis•mol•o•gy [saɪz'mɒlədʒɪ] sismologia *f*
seize [siːz] *v/t s.o.*, *s.o.'s arm* afferrare; *power* prendere; *opportunity* cogliere; *of Customs*, *police etc* sequestrare
◆ **seize up** *v/i of engine* grippare
sei•zure ['siːʒə(r)] MED attacco *m*; *of drugs etc* sequestro *m*
sel•dom ['seldəm] *adv* raramente
se•lect [sɪ'lekt] **1** *v/t* selezionare **2** *adj* (*exclusive*) scelto
se•lec•tion [sɪ'lekʃn] scelta *f*; *that / those chosen* selezione *f*
se'lec•tion pro•cess procedimento *m* di selezione
se•lec•tive [sɪ'lektɪv] *adj* selettivo
self [self] (*pl* ***selves*** [selvz]) io *m*
self-ad•dressed 'en•ve•lope [selfə'drest] busta *f* col proprio nome e indirizzo
self-as,sur•ance sicurezza *f* di sé
self-assured [selfə'ʃʊəd] *adj* sicuro di sé
self-ca•ter•ing a,part•ment appartamento *m* indipendente con cucina
self-,cen•tered *Am*, **self-,cen•tred** [self'sentəd] *adj* egocentrico
self-,clean•ing *adj oven* autopulente
self-con,fessed [selfkən'fest] *adj* dichiarato
self-,con•fi•dence fiducia *f* in se stessi
self-,con•fi•dent *adj* sicuro di sé
self-,con•scious *adj* insicuro; *smile* imbarazzato; ***feel self-conscious*** sentirsi a disagio
self-,con•scious•ness disagio *m*
self-con•tained [selfkən'teɪnd] *adj flat* indipendente
self con,trol autocontrollo *m*
self-de,fence, **self-de,fense** *Am personal* legittima difesa *f*; *of state* autodifesa *f*
self-,dis•ci•pline autodisciplina *f*
self-,doubt dubbi *mpl* personali
self-em•ployed [selfɪm'plɔɪd] *adj* autonomo
self-e,steem autostima *f*
self-ex,pres•sion espressione *f* di sé
self-,ev•i•dent *adj* evidente
self-,gov•ern•ment autogoverno *m*
self-'in•terest interesse *m* personale
self•ish ['selfɪʃ] *adj* egoista
self•less ['selflɪs] *adj person* altruista; *attitude*, *dedication* altruistico
self-made 'man [self'meɪd] self-made man *m inv*
self-'pit•y autocommiserazione *f*
self-'por•trait autoritratto *m*
self-pos'sessed *adj* padrone di sé
self-re'li•ant *adj* indipendente
self-re'spect dignità *f inv*
self-'right•eous *adj pej* presuntuoso
self-'sat•is•fied *adj pej* soddisfatto di sé
self-'ser•vice *adj* self-service
self-ser•vice 'res•tau•rant self-service *m inv*
self-taught [self'tɔːt] *adj* autodidatta
sell [sel] (*pret & pp* ***sold***) **1** *v/t* vendere; ***you have to sell yourself*** devi saperti vendere **2** *v/i of products* vendere
◆ **sell out of** *v/t* esaurire; ***we are sold out of candles*** abbiamo esaurito le candele
◆ **sell up** *v/i* vendere
'sell-by date data *f* di scadenza; ***be past its sell-by date*** essere scaduto
sell•er ['selə(r)] venditore *m*, -trice *f*
sell•ing ['selɪŋ] *n* COM vendita *f*
'sell•ing point COM punto *m* forte (che fa vendere il prodotto)
Sel•lo•tape® ['seləteɪp] scotch® *m*
se•men ['siːmən] sperma *m*
se•mes•ter [sɪ'mestər] *Am* semestre *m*
sem•i ['semɪ] *n* → ***semidetached 'house***
'sem•i•cir•cle semicerchio *m*
sem•i'cir•cu•lar *adj* semicircolare
semi-'co•lon punto e virgola *m*
sem•i•con'duc•tor ELEC semiconduttore

S

m
sem•i•de•tached ('**house**) [semɪdɪ'tætʃt] villa *f* bifamiliare
semi'fi•nal semifinale *f*
sem•i•nar ['semɪnɑː(r)] seminario *m*
sem•i'skilled *adj* parzialmente qualificato
sen•ate ['senət] senato *m*
sen•a•tor ['senətə(r)] senatore *m*, -trice *f*
send [send] *v/t* (*pret & pp* ***sent***) mandare; ***send sth to s.o.*** mandare qc a qu; ***send s.o. to s.o.*** mandare qu da qu; ***send her my best wishes*** mandale i miei saluti
◆ **send back** *v/t* mandare indietro
◆ **send for** *v/t doctor, help* (mandare a) chiamare
◆ **send in** *v/t troops* inviare; *next interviewee* far entrare; *application form* spedire
◆ **send off** *v/t letter, fax etc* spedire; *footballer* espellere
◆ **send up** *v/t* (*mock*) prendere in giro
send•er ['sendə(r)] *of letter* mittente *m/f*
se•nile ['siːnaɪl] *adj pej* rimbambito
se•nil•i•ty [sɪ'nɪlətɪ] *pej* rimabambimento *m*
se•ni•or ['siːnɪə(r)] *adj* (*older*) più anziano; *in rank* di grado superiore; ***be senior to s.o.*** *in rank* essere di grado superiore rispetto a qu
se•ni•or 'cit•i•zen anziano *m*, -a *f*
se•ni•or•i•ty [siːnɪ'ɒrətɪ] *in job* anzianità *f inv*
sen•sa•tion [sen'seɪʃn] (*feeling*) sensazione *f*; (*surprise event*) scalpore *m*; ***be a sensation*** essere sensazionale
sen•sa•tion•al [sen'seɪʃnl] *adj* sensazionale
sense [sens] **1** *n* (*meaning*) significato *m*; (*purpose, point*) senso *m*; (*common sense*) buonsenso *m*; (*sight, smell etc*) senso *m*; (*feeling*) sensazione; ***in a sense*** in un certo senso; ***talk sense, man!*** ragiona!; ***come to one's senses*** tornare in sé; ***it doesn't make sense*** non ha senso; ***there's no sense in trying / waiting*** non ha senso provare / aspettare **2** *v/t* sentire
sense•less ['senslɪs] *adj* (*pointless*) assurdo
sen•si•ble ['sensəbl] *adj person, decision* assennato; *advice* sensato; *clothes, shoes* pratico
sen•si•bly ['sensəblɪ] *adv* assennatamente
sen•si•tive ['sensətɪv] *adj* sensibile
sen•si•tiv•i•ty [sensə'tɪvətɪ] sensibilità *f inv*
sen•sor ['sensə(r)] sensore *m*
sen•su•al ['sensjʊəl] *adj* sensuale
sen•su•al•i•ty [sensjʊ'ælətɪ] sensualità *f inv*
sen•su•ous ['sensjʊəs] *adj* sensuale
sent [sent] *pret & pp* → ***send***
sen•tence ['sentəns] **1** *n* GRAM frase *m*; LAW condanna *f* **2** *v/t* LAW condannare
sen•ti•ment ['sentɪmənt] (*sentimentality*) sentimentalismo *m*; (*opinion*) opinione *f*
sen•ti•ment•al [sentɪ'mentl] *adj* sentimentale
sen•ti•men•tali•ty [sentɪmen'tælətɪ] sentimentalismo *m*
sen•try ['sentrɪ] sentinella *f*
sep•a•rate ['sepərət] **1** *adj* separato **2** *v/t* ['sepəreɪt] separare; ***separate sth from sth*** separare qc da qc **3** *v/i of couple* separarsi
sep•a•rat•ed ['sepəreɪtɪd] *adj couple* separato
sep•a•rate•ly ['sepərətlɪ] *adv* separatamente
sep•a•ra•tion [sepə'reɪʃn] separazione *f*
Sep•tem•ber [sep'tembə(r)] settembre *m*
sep•tic ['septɪk] *adj* infetto; ***go septic*** *of wound* infettarsi
se•quel ['siːkwəl] seguito *m*
se•quence ['siːkwəns] sequenza *f*; ***in sequence*** di seguito; ***out of sequence*** fuori tempo; ***the sequence of events*** l'ordine dei fatti
se•rene [sɪ'riːn] *adj* sereno
ser•geant ['sɑːdʒənt] sergente *m*
se•ri•al ['sɪərɪəl] *n* serial *m inv*
se•ri•al•ize ['sɪərɪəlaɪz] *v/t novel on TV* trasmettere a puntate
'se•ri•al kill•er serial killer *m/f inv*
'se•ri•al num•ber *of product* numero *m* di serie
'se•ri•al port COMPUT porta *f* seriale
se•ries ['sɪəriːz] *nsg* serie *f inv*
se•ri•ous ['sɪərɪəs] *adj illness, situation, damage* grave; *person, company* serio; ***I'm serious*** dico sul serio; ***listen, this is serious*** ascolta, è una cosa seria; ***we'd better take a serious look at it*** dovremo considerarlo seriamente
se•ri•ous•ly ['sɪərɪəslɪ] *adv injured* gravemente; (*extremely*) estremamente; ***seriously though, ...*** scherzi a parte, ...; ***seriously?*** davvero?; ***take s.o. seriously*** prendere sul serio qu
se•ri•ous•ness ['sɪərɪəsnɪs] *of person* serietà *f inv*; *of situation, illness etc* gravità *f inv*
ser•mon ['sɜːmən] predica *f*
ser•vant ['sɜːvənt] domestico *m*, -a *f*
serve [sɜːv] **1** *n in tennis* servizio *m* **2** *v/t food, customer, one's country* servire; ***it serves you / him right*** ti / gli sta bene **3** *v/i give out food, in tennis* servire; *as*

politician etc prestare servizio
◆ **serve up** *v/t meal* servire
serv•er ['sɜːvə(r)] COMPUT server *m inv*
ser•vice ['sɜːvɪs] **1** *n to customers, community* servizio *m*; *for vehicle, machine* manutenzione *f*; *for vehicle* revisione *f*; *in tennis* servizio *m*; ***services*** servizi; ***the services*** MIL le forze armate **2** *v/t vehicle* revisionare; *machine* fare la manutenzione di
'**ser•vice ar•e•a** area *f* di servizio
'**ser•vice charge** *in restaurant, club* servizio *m*
'**ser•vice in•dus•try** settore *m* terziario
'**ser•vice•man** MIL militare *m*
'**ser•vice pro•vid•er** COMPUT fornitore *m* di servizi
'**ser•vice sec•tor** settore *m* terziario
'**ser•vice sta•tion** stazione *f* di servizio
ser•vi•ette [sɜːvɪ'et] tovagliolino *m*
ser•vile ['sɜːvaɪl] *adj pej* servile
serv•ing ['sɜːvɪŋ] *n of food* porzione *f*
ses•sion ['seʃn] *of parliament* sessione *f*; *with psychiatrist, consultant etc* seduta *f*
set [set] **1** *n of tools* set *m inv*; *of dishes, knives* servizio *m*; *of books* raccolta *f*; *group of people* cerchia *f*; MATH insieme *m*; (THEA: *scenery*) scenografia *f*; *where a film is made* set *m inv*; *in tennis* set *m inv*; ***television set*** televisore *m* **2** *v/t* (*pret & pp* ***set***) (*place*) mettere; *film, novel etc* ambientare; *date, time, limit* fissare; *mechanism* regolare; *alarm clock* mettere; *broken limb* ingessare; *jewel* montare; (*typeset*) comporre; ***set the table*** apparecchiare (la tavola); ***set a task for s.o.*** assegnare un compito a qu **3** *v/i* (*pret & pp* ***set***) *of sun* tramontare; *of glue* indurirsi **4** *adj views, ideas* rigido; (*ready*) pronto; ***be dead set on*** (***doing***) ***sth*** essere deciso a fare qc; ***be very set in one's ways*** essere abitudinario; ***set book / reading*** *in course* libro / lettura in programma; ***set meal*** menù *m inv* fisso
◆ **set apart** *v/t*: ***set sth apart from sth*** distinguere qc da qc
◆ **set aside** *v/t for future use* mettere da parte
◆ **set back** *v/t in plans etc* ritardare; ***it set me back £400*** F mi è costato 400 sterline
◆ **set off 1** *v/i on journey* partire **2** *v/t explosion* causare; *chain reaction, alarm* far scattare
◆ **set out 1** *v/i on journey* partire **2** *v/t ideas, proposal, goods* esporre; ***set out to do sth*** (*intend*) proporsi di fare qc
◆ **set to** *v/i start on a task* mettersi all'opera
◆ **set up 1** *v/t new company* fondare; *system* mettere in opera; *equipment, machine* piazzare; F (*frame*) incastrare F **2** *v/i in business* mettersi in affari
'**set•back** contrattempo *m*
set•tee [se'tiː] (*couch, sofa*) divano *m*
set•ting ['setɪŋ] *n of novel etc* ambientazione *f*; *of house* posizione *f*
set•tle ['setl] **1** *v/i of bird, dust, beer* posarsi; *of building* assestarsi; *to live* stabilirsi **2** *v/t dispute* comporre; *issue, uncertainty* risolvere; *s.o.'s debts, the bill* saldare; *nerves, stomach* calmare; ***that settles it!*** è deciso!
◆ **settle down** *v/i* (*stop being noisy*) calmarsi; (*stop wild living*) mettere la testa a posto; *in an area* stabilirsi
◆ **settle for** *v/t* (*take, accept*) accontentarsi di
◆ **settle up** *v/i* (*pay*) regolare i conti; *in hotel etc* pagare il conto
set•tled ['setld] *adj weather* stabile
set•tle•ment ['setlmənt] *of dispute* composizione *f*; (*payment*) pagamento *m*
set•tler ['setlə(r)] *in new country* colonizzatore *m*, -trice *f*
'**set-up** *n* (*structure*) organizzazione *f*; (*relationship*) relazione *f*; F (*frameup*) montatura *f*
sev•en ['sevn] sette
sev•en•teen [sevn'tiːn] diciassette
sev•en•teenth [sevn'tiːnθ] diciassettesimo, -a
sev•enth ['sevnθ] *n & adj* settimo, -a
sev•en•ti•eth ['sevntɪɪθ] *n & adj* settantesimo, -a
sev•en•ty ['sevntɪ] settanta
sev•er ['sevə(r)] *v/t arm, cable etc* recidere; *relations* troncare
sev•e•ral ['sevrl] **1** *adj* parecchi **2** *pron* parecchi *m*, -ie *f*
se•vere [sɪ'vɪə(r)] *adj illness* grave; *penalty, teacher, face* severo; *winter, weather* rigido
se•vere•ly [sɪ'vɪəlɪ] *adv punish* severamente; *speak, stare* duramente; *injured, disrupted* gravemente
se•ver•i•ty [sɪ'verətɪ] *of illness* gravità *f inv*; *of look etc* durezza *f*; *of penalty* severità *f inv*; *of winter* rigidità *f inv*
sew [səʊ] *v/t & v/i* (*pret* ***-ed***, *pp* ***sewn***) cucire
◆ **sew on** *v/t button* attaccare
sew•age ['suːɪdʒ] acque *fpl* di scolo
'**sew•age plant** impianto *m* per il riciclaggio delle acque di scolo
sew•er ['suːə(r)] fogna *f*
sew•ing ['səʊɪŋ] *n* cucito *m*
'**sew•ing ma•chine** macchina *f* da cucire
sex [seks] sesso *m*; ***have sex with*** avere

rapporti sessuali con
sex•ist ['seksɪst] **1** *adj* sessista **2** *n* sessista *m/f*
sex•u•al ['seksjʊəl] *adj* sessuale
sex•u•al as'sault violenza *f* sessuale
sex•u•al ha'rass•ment molestie *fpl* sessuali
sex•u•al 'in•ter•course rapporti *mpl* sessuali
sex•u•al•ity [seksjʊ'ælətɪ] sessualità *f inv*
sex•u•al•ly ['seksjʊlɪ] *adv* sessualmente
sex•u•al•ly trans•mit•ted dis'ease [seksjʊlɪtrænz'mɪtɪd] malattia *f* venerea
sex•y ['seksɪ] *adj* sexy *inv*
shab•bi•ly ['ʃæbɪlɪ] *adv dressed* in modo trasandato; *treat* in modo meschino
shab•bi•ness ['ʃæbɪnɪs] *of coat etc* trasandatezza *f*
shab•by ['ʃæbɪ] *adj coat etc* trasandato; *treatment* meschino
shack [ʃæk] baracca *f*
shade [ʃeɪd] **1** *n for lamp* paralume *m*; *of colour* tonalità *f inv*; ***in the shade*** all'ombra **2** *v/t from sun, light* riparare
shad•ow ['ʃædəʊ] *n* ombra *f*
shad•y ['ʃeɪdɪ] *adj spot* all'ombra; *character, dealings* losco
shaft [ʃɑːft] *of axle* albero *m*; *of mine* pozzo *m*
shag•gy ['ʃægɪ] *adj hair* arruffato; *dog* dal pelo arruffato
shake [ʃeɪk] **1** *n*: ***give sth a good shake*** dare una scrollata a qc **2** *v/t* (*pret* ***shook***, *pp* ***shaken***) scuotere; *emotionally* sconvolgere; ***shake hands*** stringersi la mano; ***shake hands with s.o.*** stringere la mano a qu **3** *v/i of hands, voice, building* tremare
shak•en ['ʃeɪkən] **1** *adj emotionally* scosso **2** *pp* → ***shake***
'shake-up rimpasto *m*
'shak•y ['ʃeɪkɪ] *adj table etc* traballante; *after illness, shock* debole; *grasp of sth, grammar etc* incerto; *voice, hand* tremante
shall [ʃæl] *v/aux* ◇ *future*: ***I shall do my best*** farò del mio meglio; ***I shan't see them*** non li vedrò
◇ *suggesting*: ***shall we go now?*** andiamo?
shal•low ['ʃæləʊ] *adj water* poco profondo; *person* superficiale
sham•bles ['ʃæmblz] *nsg* casino *m* F
shame [ʃeɪm] **1** *n* vergogna *f*; ***bring shame on ...*** disonorare ...; ***what a shame!*** che peccato!; ***shame on you!*** vergognati! **2** *v/t*: ***shame s.o. into doing sth*** indurre qu a fare qc per vergogna
shame•ful ['ʃeɪmfʊl] *adj* vergognoso
shame•ful•ly ['ʃeɪmfʊlɪ] *adv* vergognosamente
shame•less ['ʃeɪmlɪs] *adj* svergognato
sham•poo [ʃæm'puː] **1** *n* shampoo *m inv*; ***a shampoo and set*** shampoo e messa in piega **2** *v/t* fare lo shampoo a
shape [ʃeɪp] **1** *n* forma *f* **2** *v/t clay* dar forma a; *person's life, character* forgiare; *the future* determinare
shape•less ['ʃeɪplɪs] *adj dress etc* informe
shape•ly ['ʃeɪplɪ] *adv figure* ben fatto
share [ʃeə(r)] **1** *n* parte *f*; FIN azione *f*; ***do one's share of the work*** fare la propria parte del lavoro **2** *v/t* dividere; *s.o.'s feelings, opinions* condividere **3** *v/i* dividere; ***do you mind sharing with Patrick?*** ti dispiace dividere con Patrick?
◆ **share out** *v/t* spartire
'share•hold•er azionista *m/f*
shark [ʃɑːk] *fish* squalo *m*
sharp [ʃɑːp] **1** *adj knife* affilato; *mind, pain* acuto; *taste* aspro **2** *adv* MUS in diesis; ***at 3 o'clock sharp*** alle 3 precise
sharp•en ['ʃɑːpn] *v/t knife* affilare; *skills* raffinare
sharp 'prac•tice pratiche *fpl* poco oneste
shat [ʃæt] *pret & pp* → ***shit***
shat•ter ['ʃætə(r)] **1** *v/t glass* frantumare; *illusions* distruggere **2** *v/i of glass* frantumarsi
shat•tered ['ʃætəd] *adj* F (*exhausted*) esausto; (*very upset*) sconvolto
shat•ter•ing ['ʃætərɪŋ] *adj news, experience* sconvolgente; *effect* tremendo
shave [ʃeɪv] **1** *v/t* radere **2** *v/i* farsi la barba **3** *n*: ***have a shave*** farsi la barba; ***that was a close shave*** ce l'abbiamo fatta per un pelo
◆ **shave off** *v/t beard* tagliarsi; *from piece of wood* piallare
shav•en ['ʃeɪvn] *adj head* rasato
shav•er ['ʃeɪvə(r)] *electric* rasoio *m*
shav•ing brush ['ʃeɪvɪŋ] pennello *m* da barba
'shav•ing soap sapone *m* da barba
shawl [ʃɔːl] scialle *m*
she [ʃiː] *pron* lei; ***she has three children*** ha tre figli; ***you're funny, she's not*** tu sei spiritoso, lei no; ***there she is*** eccola
shears [ʃɪəz] *npl for gardening* cesoie *fpl*; *for sewing* forbici *fpl*
sheath [ʃiːθ] *n for knife* guaina *f*; *contraceptive* preservativo *m*
shed[1] [ʃed] *v/t* (*pret & pp* ***shed***) *blood* spargere; *tears* versare; *leaves* perdere; ***shed light on*** *fig* fare luce su
shed[2] [ʃed] *n* baracca *f*
sheep [ʃiːp] (*pl* ***sheep***) pecora *f*
'sheep•dog cane *m* pastore

S

sheep•ish ['ʃiːpɪʃ] *adj* imbarazzato
'**sheep•skin** *adj lining* di montone
sheer [ʃɪə(r)] *adj madness, luxury* puro; *drop, cliffs* ripido
sheet [ʃiːt] *for bed* lenzuolo *m*; *of paper* foglio *m*; *of metal, glass* lastra *f*
shelf [ʃelf] (*pl* ***shelves*** [ʃelvz]) mensola *f*; ***shelves*** scaffale *msg*, ripiani *mpl*
shelf•life *of product* durata *f* di conservazione
shell [ʃel] **1** *n of mussel etc* conchiglia *f*; *of egg* guscio *m*; *of tortoise* corazza *f*; MIL granata *f*; ***come out of one's shell*** *fig* uscire dal guscio **2** *v/t peas* sbucciare; MIL bombardare
'**shell•fire** bombardamento *m*; ***come under shellfire*** essere bombardato
'**shell•fish** crostacei *mpl*
shel•ter ['ʃeltə(r)] **1** *n* (*refuge*) riparo *m*; *construction* rifugio *m* **2** *v/i from rain, bombing etc* ripararsi **3** *v/t* (*protect*) proteggere
shel•tered ['ʃeltəd] *adj place* riparato; ***lead a sheltered life*** vivere nella bambagia
shelve [ʃelv] *v/t fig* accantonare
shep•herd ['ʃepəd] *n* pastore *m*
sher•ry ['ʃerɪ] sherry *m inv*
shield [ʃiːld] **1** *n* scudo *m*; *sports trophy* scudetto *m*; TECH schermo *m* di protezione *f* **2** *v/t* (*protect*) proteggere
shift [ʃɪft] **1** *n* (*change*) cambiamento *m*; *period of work* turno *m* **2** *v/t* (*move*) spostare; *stains etc* togliere **3** *v/i* (*move*) spostarsi; *of wind* cambiare direzione; ***that's shifting!*** F è un bolide!
'**shift key** COMPUT tasto *m* shift
'**shift work** turni *mpl*
'**shift work•er** turnista *m/f*
'**shift•y** ['ʃɪftɪ] *adj pej* losco
'**shift•y-look•ing** *adj pej* dall'aria losca
shilly-shally ['ʃɪlɪʃælɪ] *v/i* (*pret & pp* ***-ied***) F tentennare
shim•mer ['ʃɪmə(r)] *v/i* luccicare
shin [ʃɪn] *n* stinco *m*
shine [ʃaɪn] **1** *v/i* (*pret & pp* ***shone***) *of sun, shoes, metal* splendere; *fig*: *of student etc* brillare **2** *v/t* (*pret & pp* ***shone***) *torch etc* puntare **3** *n on shoes etc* lucentezza *f*
shin•gle ['ʃɪŋgl] *on beach* ciottoli *mpl*
shin•gles ['ʃɪŋglz] *nsg* MED fuoco *m* di Sant'Antonio
shin•y ['ʃaɪnɪ] *adj surface* lucido
ship [ʃɪp] **1** *n* nave *f* **2** *v/t* (*pret & pp* ***-ped***) (*send*) spedire; (*send by sea*) spedire via mare
ship•ment ['ʃɪpmənt] (*consignment*) carico *m*
'**ship•own•er** armatore *m*
ship•ping ['ʃɪpɪŋ] *n* (*sea traffic*) navigazione *f*; (*sending*) trasporto *m* (via mare)
'**ship•ping com•pa•ny** compagnia *f* di navigazione
'**shipshape** *adj* in perfetto ordine
'**ship•wreck** **1** *n* naufragio *m* **2** *v/t*: ***be shipwrecked*** naufragare
'**ship•yard** cantiere *m* navale
shirk [ʃɜːk] *v/t* scansare
shirk•er ['ʃɜːkə(r)] scansafatiche *m/f inv*
shirt [ʃɜːt] camicia *f*; ***in his shirt sleeves*** in maniche di camicia
shit [ʃɪt] **1** *n* P merda *f* P; *bad quality goods, work* stronzata *f* P **2** *v/i* (*pret & pp* ***shat***) cagare P **3** *int* merda P
shit•ty ['ʃɪtɪ] *adj* F di merda P
shiv•er ['ʃɪvə(r)] **1** *v/i* rabbrividire **2** *n* brivido *m*
shock [ʃɒk] **1** *n* shock *m inv*; ELEC scossa *f*; ***be in shock*** MED essere in stato di shock **2** *v/t* scioccare; ***be shocked by*** essere scioccato da
'**shock ab•sorb•er** MOT ammortizzatore *m*
shock•ing ['ʃɒkɪŋ] *adj behaviour, poverty* scandaloso; F *very bad* allucinante F
shock•ing•ly ['ʃɒkɪŋlɪ] *adv behave* scandalosamente; *bad, late, expensive* terribilmente
shod•dy ['ʃɒdɪ] *adj goods* scadente; *behaviour* meschino
shoe [ʃuː] scarpa *f*
'**shoe•horn** calzascarpe *m inv*
'**shoe-lace** laccio *m* di scarpa
'**shoe•mak•er**, '**shoe mender** calzolaio *m*
'**shoe-shop** negozio *m* di scarpe
'**shoe•string** *n*: ***do sth on a shoestring*** fare qc con pochi soldi
shone [ʃɒn] *pret & pp* → ***shine***
◆ **shoo away** [ʃuː] *v/t children, chicken* scacciare
shook [ʃʊk] *pret* → ***shake***
shoot [ʃuːt] **1** *n* BOT germoglio *m* **2** *v/t v/t* (*pret & pp* ***shot***) sparare; *film* girare; ***shoot s.o. in the leg*** colpire qu alla gamba; ***shoot s.o. for desertion*** fucilare qu per diserzione
◆ **shoot down** *v/t aeroplane* abbattere
◆ **shoot off** *v/i* (*rush off*) precipitarsi
◆ **shoot up** *v/i of prices* salire alle stelle; *of children* crescere molto; *of new suburbs, buildings etc* spuntare; F *of drug addict* farsi F
shoot•ing star ['ʃuːtɪŋ] stella *f* cadente
shop [ʃɒp] **1** *n* negozio *m*; ***talk shop*** parlare di lavoro **2** *v/i* (*pret & pp* ***-ped***) fare acquisti; ***go shopping*** andare a fare spese

S

'**shop as•sis•tant** commesso *m*, -a *f*
'**shop•keep•er** negoziante *m/f*
shop•lift•er ['ʃɒplɪftə(r)] taccheggiatore *m*, -trice *f*
shop•lift•ing ['ʃɒplɪftɪŋ] *n* taccheggio *m*
shop•per ['ʃɒpə(r)] *person* acquirente *m/f*
shop•ping ['ʃɒpɪŋ] *activity* fare spese; *items* spesa *f*; ***do one's shopping*** fare la spesa
'**shop•ping bag** borsa *f* per la spesa
'**shop•ping cen•ter** *Am*, '**shop•ping cen•tre** centro *m* commerciale
'**shop•ping list** lista *f* della spesa
'**shop•ping mall** centro *m* commerciale
shop '**stew•ard** rappresentante *m/f* sindacale
shop '**win•dow** vetrina *f*
shore [ʃɔː(r)] riva *f*; ***on shore*** *not at sea* a terra
short [ʃɔːt] **1** *adj in length, distance* corto; *in height* basso; *in time* breve; ***be short of*** essere a corto di **2** *adv*: ***cut a vacation / meeting short*** interrompere una vacanza / riunione; ***stop a person short*** interrompere una persona; ***go short of*** fare a meno di; ***in short*** in breve
short•age ['ʃɔːtɪdʒ] mancanza *f*
short '**cir•cuit** *n* corto *m* circuito
short•com•ing ['ʃɔːtkʌmɪŋ] difetto *m*
'**short cut** scorciatoia *f*
short•en ['ʃɔːtn] **1** *v/t* accorciare **2** *v/i* accorciarsi
'**short•fall** deficit *m inv*; *in hours etc* mancanza *f*
'**short•hand** *n* stenografia *f*
short-'handed *adj*: ***be short-handed*** essere a corto di personale
'**short•list** *n of candidates* rosa *f* dei candidati
short-lived ['ʃɔːtlɪvd] *adj* di breve durata
'**short•ly** ['ʃɔːtlɪ] *adv* (*soon*) tra breve; ***shortly before / after*** poco prima / dopo
short•ness ['ʃɔːtnɪs] *of visit* brevità *f inv*; *in height* bassa statura *f*
shorts [ʃɔːts] *npl* calzoncini *mpl*
short•sight•ed [ʃɔːt'saɪtɪd] *adj also fig* miope
short-sleeved ['ʃɔːtsliːvd] *adj* a maniche corte
short-staffed [ʃɔːt'stɑːft] *adj* a corto di personale
short '**sto•ry** racconto *m*
short-tem•pered [ʃɔːt'tempəd] *adj* irascibile
'**short-term** *adj* a breve termine
'**short time** *n*: ***be on short time*** *of workers* lavorare a orario ridotto
'**short wave** RAD onde *fpl* corte
shot [ʃɒt] **1** *n from gun* sparo *m*; (*photograph*) foto *f*; (*injection*) puntura *f*; ***be a good / poor shot*** essere un buon / pessimo tiratore; ***like a shot*** *accept*, *run off* come un razzo **2** *pret & pp* → **shoot**
'**shot•gun** fucile *m* da caccia
should [ʃʊd] *v/aux*: ***what should I do?*** cosa devo fare?; ***you shouldn't do that*** non dovresti farlo; ***that should be long enough*** dovrebbe essere lungo abbastanza; ***you should have heard him!*** avresti dovuto sentirlo!
shoul•der ['ʃəʊldə(r)] *n* ANAT spalla *f*
'**shoul•der bag** borsa *f* a tracolla
'**shoul•der blade** scapola *f*
'**shoul•der strap** spallina *f*
shout [ʃaʊt] **1** *n* grido *m*, urlo *m* **2** *v/t & v/i* gridare, urlare
◆ **shout at** *v/t* urlare a
shout•ing ['ʃaʊtɪŋ] *n* urla *fpl*
shove [ʃʌv] **1** *n* spinta *f* **2** *v/t & v/i* spingere
◆ **shove in** *v/i* passare davanti; ***he shoved in in front of me*** mi è passato davanti
◆ **shove off** *v/i* F (*go away*) levarsi di torno
shov•el ['ʃʌvl] **1** *n* pala *f* **2** *v/t* spalare
show [ʃəʊ] **1** *n* THEA, TV spettacolo *m*; (*display*) manifestazione *f*; ***on show*** *at exhibition* esposto; ***it's all done for show*** *pej* è tutta una scena **2** *v/t* (*pret* **-ed**, *pp* **shown**) *passport*, *ticket* mostrare; *interest*, *emotion* dimostrare; *at exhibition* esporre; *film* proiettare; ***show s.o. sth, show sth to s.o.*** mostrare qc a qu **3** *v/i* (*pret* **-ed**, *pp* **shown**) (*be visible*) vedersi; ***does it show?*** si vede?; ***what's showing at the cinema?*** cosa danno al cinema?
◆ **show around** *v/t* far visitare
◆ **show in** *v/t* far entrare
◆ **show off 1** *v/t skills* mettere in risalto **2** *v/i pej* mettersi in mostra
◆ **show up 1** *v/t s.o.'s shortcomings etc* far risaltare; ***don't show me up in public*** non farmi fare brutta figura **2** *v/i* F (*arrive, turn up*) farsi vedere F; (*be visible*) notarsi
'**show busi•ness** il mondo dello spettacolo
'**show•case** *n* vetrinetta *f*; *fig* vetrina *f*
'**show•down** regolamento *m* di conti
show•er ['ʃaʊə(r)] **1** *n of rain* acquazzone *m*; *to wash* doccia *f*; ***take a shower*** fare una doccia **2** *v/i* fare la doccia **3** *v/t*: ***shower s.o. with praise*** coprire qu di lodi
'**show•er cap** cuffia *f* da doccia
'**show•er cur•tain** tenda *f* della doccia
'**show•er•proof** *adj* impermeabile

show•jump•er ['ʃəʊdʒʌmpə(r)] cavaliere *m*, cavallerizza *f* di concorso ippico
'**show•jump•ing** concorso *m* ippico
'**show-off** *pej* esibizionista *m/f*
'**show•room** show-room *m inv*; ***in showroom condition*** mai usato
show•y ['ʃəʊɪ] *adj* appariscente
shrank [ʃræŋk] *pret* → ***shrink***
shred [ʃred] **1** *n of paper* strisciolina *f*; *of cloth* brandello *m*; *of evidence, etc* briciolo *m* **2** *v/t* (*pret & pp* ***-ded***) *paper* stracciare; *in cooking* sminuzzare
shred•der ['ʃredə(r)] *for documents* distruttore *m* di documenti
shrewd [ʃruːd] *adj person, businessman* scaltro; *investment* oculato
shrewd•ly ['ʃruːdlɪ] *adv* oculatamente
shrewd•ness ['ʃruːdnɪs] oculatezza *f*
shriek [ʃriːk] **1** *n* strillo *m* **2** *v/i* strillare
shrill [ʃrɪl] *adj* stridulo
shrimp [ʃrɪmp] gamberetto *m*
shrine [ʃraɪn] santuario *m*
shrink[1] [ʃrɪŋk] *v/i* (*pret* ***shrank***, *pp* ***shrunk***) *of material* restringersi; *level of support etc* diminuire
shrink[2] [ʃrɪŋk] *n* F (*psychiatrist*) strizzacervelli *m/f inv*
'**shrink-wrap** *v/t* cellofanare
'**shrink-wrap•ping** *process* cellofanatura *f*; *material* cellophane® *m inv*
shriv•el ['ʃrɪvl] *v/i* avvizzire
Shrove '**Tues•day** [ʃrəʊv] martedì *m* grasso
shrub [ʃrʌb] arbusto *m*
shrub•be•ry ['ʃrʌbərɪ] arboreto *m*
shrug [ʃrʌg] **1** *n* alzata *f* di spalle **2** *v/i* (*pret & pp* ***-ged***) alzare le spalle **3** *v/t* (*pret & pp* ***-ged***): ***shrug one's shoulders*** alzare le spalle
shrunk [ʃrʌŋk] *pp* → ***shrink***
shud•der ['ʃʌdə(r)] **1** *n of fear, disgust* brivido *m*; *of earth etc* tremore *m* **2** *v/i with fear, disgust* rabbrividire; *of earth, building* tremare; ***I shudder to think*** non oso immaginare
shuf•fle ['ʃʌfl] **1** *v/t cards* mescolare **2** *v/i in walking* strascicare i piedi; ***he shuffled into the bathroom*** è andato in bagno strascicando i piedi
shun [ʃʌn] *v/t* (*pret & pp* ***-ned***) evitare
shut [ʃʌt] (*pret & pp* ***shut***) **1** *v/t* chiudere **2** *v/i of door, box* chiudersi; *of shop, bank* chiudere; ***they were shut*** era chiuso
◆ **shut down** **1** *v/t business* chiudere; *computer* spegnere **2** *v/i of business* chiudere i battenti; *of computer* spegnersi
◆ **shut off** *v/t* chiudere
◆ **shut up** *v/i* F (*be quiet*) star zitto; ***shut up!*** zitto!

shut•ter ['ʃʌtə(r)] *on window* battente *m*; PHOT otturatore *m*
'**shut•ter speed** PHOT tempo *m* di apertura
shut•tle ['ʃʌtl] *v/i* fare la spola
'**shut•tle•bus** *at airport* bus *m inv* navetta
'**shut•tle•cock** SP volano *m*
'**shut•tle ser•vice** servizio *m* navetta
shy [ʃaɪ] *adj* timido
shy•ness ['ʃaɪnɪs] timidezza *f*
Si•a•mese '**twins** [saɪə'miːz] *npl* fratelli *mpl*/sorelle *fpl* siamesi
Si•cil•i•an [sɪ'sɪlɪən] **1** *adj* siciliano **2** *n* siciliano *m*, -a *f*
Sic•i•ly ['sɪsɪlɪ] Sicilia *f*
sick [sɪk] *adj* malato; *sense of humour* crudele; ***I feel sick*** *about to vomit* ho la nausea; ***I'm going to be sick*** *vomit* ho voglia di vomitare; ***be sick of*** (*fed up with*) essere stufo di
sick•en ['sɪkn] **1** *v/t* (*disgust*) disgustare **2** *v/i*: ***be sickening for sth*** covare qc
sick•en•ing ['sɪknɪŋ] *adj* disgustoso
'**sick leave** *n*: ***be on sick leave*** essere in (congedo per) malattia
sick•ly ['sɪklɪ] *adj person* delicato; *smell* stomachevole
sick•ness ['sɪknɪs] malattia *f*; (*vomiting*) nausea *f*
'**sick•ness ben•e•fit** *Br* indennità *f inv* di malattia
side [saɪd] *n of box, house* lato *m*; *of person, mountain* fianco *m*; *of page, record* facciata *f*; SP squadra *f*; ***take sides*** (*favour one side*) prendere posizione; ***take sides with*** parteggiare per; ***I'm on your side*** sono dalla tua (parte); ***side by side*** fianco a fianco; ***at the side of the road*** sul ciglio della strada; ***on the big / small side*** piuttosto grande / piccolo
◆ **side with** *v/t* prendere le parti di
'**side•board** credenza *f*
'**sideburns** *npl* basette *fpl*
'**side dish** contorno *m*
'**side ef•fect** effetto *m* collaterale
'**side•light** MOT luce *f* di posizione
'**side•line** **1** *n* attività *f inv* collaterale **2** *v/t*: ***feel sidelined*** sentirsi sminuito
'**side•step** *v/t* (*pret & pp* ***-ped***) scansare; *fig* schivare
'**side street** via *f* laterale
'**side•track** *v/t* distrarre; ***get sidetracked by*** essere distratto da
'**side•walk** *Am* marciapiede *m*
side•ways ['saɪdweɪz] *adv* di lato
siege [siːdʒ] assedio *m*; ***lay siege to*** assediare
sieve [sɪv] *n* setaccio *m*
sift [sɪft] *v/t* setacciare

◆ **sift through** *v/t details*, *data* passare al vaglio

sigh [saɪ] **1** *n* sospiro *m*; ***heave a sigh of relief*** tirare un respiro di sollievo **2** *v/i* sospirare

sight [saɪt] *n* vista *f*; ***sights*** *of city* luoghi *mpl* da visitare; ***catch sight of*** intravedere; ***know by sight*** conoscere di vista; ***be within sight of*** essere visibile da; ***out of sight*** non visibile; ***out of sight of*** fuori dalla vista di; ***what a sight you are!*** come sei conciato!; ***lose sight of*** *main objective etc* perdere di vista

sight•see•ing ['saɪtsiːɪŋ] *n* visita *f* turistica; ***I enjoy sightseeing*** mi piace visitare i posti; ***go sightseeing*** fare un giro turistico

'**sight•see•ing tour** giro *m* turistico

sight•seer ['saɪtsiːə(r)] turista *m/f*

sign [saɪn] **1** *n* (*indication*) segno *m*; (*road sign*) segnale *m*; *outside shop* insegna *f*; ***it's a sign of the times*** è tipico dei nostri giorni **2** *v/t & v/i document* firmare

◆ **sign in** *v/i* firmare il registro (all'arrivo)

◆ **sign up** *v/i* (*join the army*) arruolarsi

sig•nal ['sɪgnl] **1** *n* segnale *m*; ***be sending out the right / wrong signals*** *fig* lanciare il messaggio giusto / sbagliato **2** *v/i of driver* segnalare

sig•na•to•ry ['sɪgnətrɪ] *n* firmatario *m*, -a *f*

sig•na•ture ['sɪgnətʃə(r)] firma *f*

sig•na•ture '**tune** sigla *f* musicale

sig•net ring ['sɪgnɪtrɪŋ] anello *m* con sigillo

sig•nif•i•cance [sɪg'nɪfɪkəns] importanza *f*; (*meaning*) significato *m*

sig•nif•i•cant [sɪg'nɪfɪkənt] *adj event etc* significativo; (*quite large*) notevole

sig•nif•i•cant•ly [sɪg'nɪfɪkəntlɪ] *adv larger*, *more expensive* notevolmente

sig•ni•fy ['sɪgnɪfaɪ] *v/t* (*pret & pp* **-ied**) significare

'**sign lan•guage** linguaggio *m* dei segni

'**sign•post** cartello *m* stradale

S

si•lence ['saɪləns] **1** *n* silenzio *m*; ***in silence*** *work*, *march* in silenzio; ***silence!*** silenzio! **2** *v/t* mettere a tacere

si•lenc•er ['saɪlənsə(r)] *on gun* silenziatore *m*; *on car* marmitta *f*

si•lent ['saɪlənt] *adj* silenzioso; *film* muto; ***stay silent*** *not comment* tacere

sil•hou•ette [sɪluː'et] *n* sagoma *f*

sil•i•con ['sɪlɪkən] silicio *m*

sil•i•con '**chip** chip *m inv* al silicio

sil•i•cone ['sɪlɪkəʊn] silicone *m*

silk [sɪlk] **1** *n* seta *f* **2** *adj shirt etc* di seta

silk•y ['sɪlkɪ] *adj hair*, *texture* setoso

sil•li•ness ['sɪlɪnɪs] stupidità *f inv*

sil•ly ['sɪlɪ] *adj* stupido

si•lo ['saɪləʊ] silo *m*

sil•ver ['sɪlvə(r)] **1** *n metal* argento *m*; *silver objects* argenteria *f* **2** *adj ring* d'argento; *colour* argentato

sil•ver-plat•ed [sɪlvə'pleɪtɪd] *adj* placcato d'argento

'**sil•ver•ware** argenteria *f*

sil•ver '**wed•ding** nozze *fpl* d'argento

sim•i•lar ['sɪmɪlə(r)] *adj* simile

sim•i•lar•i•ty [sɪmɪ'lærətɪ] rassomiglianza *f*

sim•i•lar•ly ['sɪmɪləlɪ] *adv* allo stesso modo

sim•mer ['sɪmə(r)] *v/i in cooking* sobbollire; *with rage* ribollire

◆ **simmer down** *v/i* calmarsi

sim•ple ['sɪmpl] *adj method*, *life*, *dress* semplice; *person* sempliciotto

sim•ple-mind•ed [sɪmpl'maɪndɪd] *adj pej* sempliciotto

sim•pli•ci•ty [sɪm'plɪsətɪ] semplicità *f inv*

sim•pli•fy ['sɪmplɪfaɪ] *v/t* (*pret & pp* **-ied**) semplificare

sim•plis•tic [sɪm'plɪstɪk] *adj* semplicistico

sim•ply ['sɪmplɪ] *adv* (*absolutely*) assolutamente; *in a simple way* semplicemente; ***it is simply the best*** è assolutamente il migliore

sim•u•late ['sɪmjʊleɪt] *v/t* simulare

sim•ul•ta•ne•ous [sɪml'teɪnɪəs] *adj* simultaneo

sim•ul•ta•ne•ous•ly [sɪml'teɪnɪəslɪ] *adv* simultaneamente

sin [sɪn] **1** *n* peccato *m* **2** *v/i* (*pret & pp* **-ned**) peccare

since [sɪns] **1** *prep* da; ***since last week*** dalla scorsa settimana **2** *adv* da allora; ***I haven't seen him since*** non lo vedo da allora **3** *conj in expressions of time* da quando; (*seeing that*) visto che; ***since you left*** da quando sei andato via; ***ever since I have known her*** da quando la conosco; ***since you don't like it*** visto che non ti piace

sin•cere [sɪn'sɪə(r)] *adj* sincero

sin•cere•ly [sɪn'sɪəlɪ] *adv* con sincerità; *hope* sinceramente; ***Yours sincerely*** Distinti saluti

sin•cer•i•ty [sɪn'serətɪ] sincerità *f inv*

sin•ful ['sɪnfʊl] *adj* peccaminoso

sing [sɪŋ] *v/t & v/i* (*pret* **sang**, *pp* **sung**) cantare

singe [sɪndʒ] *v/t* bruciacchiare

sing•er ['sɪŋə(r)] cantante *m/f*

sin•gle ['sɪŋgl] **1** *adj* (*sole*) solo; (*not double*) singolo; *bed*, *sheet* a una piazza; (*not married*) single; *with reference to*

Europe unico; ***there wasn't a single ...*** non c'era nemmeno un ...; ***in single file*** in fila indiana **2** *n* MUS singolo *m*; (*single room*) (camera *f*) singola *f*; *ticket* biglietto *m* di sola andata; *person* single *m/f inv*; ***singles*** *in tennis* singolo
◆ **single out** *v/t* (*choose*) prescegliere; (*distinguish*) distinguere
sin•gle-breast•ed [sɪŋgl'brestɪd] *adj* a un petto
sin•gle-ˌhand•ed [sɪŋgl'hændɪd] *adj & adv* da solo
sin•gle-mind•ed [sɪŋgl'maɪndɪd] *adj* determinato
Sin•gle 'Mar•ket mercato *m* unico
sin•gle 'moth•er ragazza *f* madre
sin•gle 'pa•rent genitore *m* single
sin•gle pa•rent 'fam•i•ly famiglia *f* monoparentale
sin•gle 'room (camera *f*) singola *f*
sin•gu•lar ['sɪŋgjʊlə(r)] **1** *adj* GRAM singolare **2** *n* GRAM singolare *m*; ***in the singular*** al singolare
sin•is•ter ['sɪnɪstə(r)] *adj* sinistro
sink [sɪŋk] **1** *n* lavandino *m* **2** *v/i* (*pret* ***sank***, *pp* ***sunk***) *of ship* affondare; *of object* andare a fondo; *of sun* calare; *of interest rates, pressure etc* scendere; ***he sank onto the bed*** crollò sul letto **3** *v/t* (*pret* ***sank***, *pp* ***sunk***) *ship* (far) affondare; *funds* investire
◆ **sink in** *v/i of liquid* penetrare; ***it still hasn't really sunk in*** *of realization* ancora non mi rendo conto
sin•ner ['sɪnə(r)] peccatore *m*, -trice *f*
si•nus ['saɪnəs] seno *m* paranasale; ***my sinuses are blocked*** ho il naso bloccato
si•nus•i•tis [saɪnə'saɪtɪs] MED sinusite *f*
sip [sɪp] **1** *n* sorso *m* **2** *v/t* (*pret & pp* ***-ped***) sorseggiare
sir [sɜː(r)] signore *m*; ***Sir Charles*** Sir Charles
si•ren ['saɪrən] sirena *f*
sir•loin ['sɜːlɔɪn] controfiletto *m*
sis•ter ['sɪstə(r)] sorella *f*; *in hospital* (infermiera *f*) caposala *f*
'sis•ter-in-law (*pl* ***sisters-in-law***) cognata *f*
sit [sɪt] (*pret & pp* ***sat***) **1** *v/i* sedere; (*sit down*) sedersi; *for a portrait* posare; *of objects* stare; *of committee, assembly etc* riunirsi **2** *v/t exam* dare
◆ **sit down** *v/i* sedersi
◆ **sit up** *v/i in bed* mettersi a sedere; *straighten back* star seduto bene; *wait up at night* rimanere alzato
sit•com ['sɪtkɒm] sitcom *f inv*
site [saɪt] **1** *n* luogo *m* **2** *v/t new offices etc* situare
sit•ting ['sɪtɪŋ] *n of committee, court* sessione *f*; *for artist* seduta *f*; *for meals* turno *m*
'sit•ting room salotto *m*
sit•u•at•ed ['sɪtjʊeɪtɪd] *adj* situato; ***be situated*** trovarsi
sit•u•a•tion [sɪtjʊ'eɪʃn] situazione *f*; *of building etc* posizione *f*
six [sɪks] sei
six•teen [sɪks'tiːn] sedici
six•teenth [sɪks'tiːnθ] *n & adj* sedicesimo, -a
sixth [sɪksθ] *adj* sesto
six•ti•eth ['sɪkstɪɪθ] *n & adj* sessantesimo, -a
six•ty ['sɪkstɪ] sessanta
size [saɪz] dimensioni *fpl*; *of clothes* taglia *f*, misura *f*; *of shoes* numero *m*
◆ **size up** *v/t* valutare
size•a•ble ['saɪzəbl] *adj* considerevole
siz•zle ['sɪzl] *v/i* sfrigolare
skate [skeɪt] **1** *n* pattino *m* **2** *v/i* pattinare
skate•board ['skeɪtbɔːd] *n* skateboard *m inv*
skate•board•er ['skeɪtbɔːdə(r)] skateboarder *m/f inv*
skate•board•ing ['skeɪtbɔːdɪŋ] skateboard *m inv*
skat•er ['skeɪtə(r)] pattinatore *m*, -trice *f*
skat•ing ['skeɪtɪŋ] *n* pattinaggio *m*
'skat•ing rink pista *f* di pattinaggio
skel•e•ton ['skelɪtn] scheletro *m*
'skel•e•ton key passe-partout *m inv*
'skeptic *etc Am* → ***sceptic*** *etc*
sketch [sketʃ] **1** *n* abbozzo *m*; THEA sketch *m inv* **2** *v/t* abbozzare
'sketch•book album *m* da disegno
sketch•y ['sketʃɪ] *adj knowledge etc* lacunoso
skew•er ['skjʊə(r)] *n* spiedino *m*
ski [skiː] **1** *n* sci *m inv* **2** *v/i* sciare
'ski boots *npl* scarponi *mpl* da sci
skid [skɪd] **1** *n* sbandata *f* **2** *v/i* (*pret & pp* ***-ded***) sbandare
ski•er ['skiːə(r)] sciatore *m*, -trice *f*
ski•ing ['skiːɪŋ] sci *m inv*; ***go skiing*** andare a sciare
'ski in•struc•tor maestro *m*, -a *f* di sci
skil•ful ['skɪlfʊl] *adj* abile
skil•ful•ly ['skɪlflɪ] *adv* abilmente
'ski lift impianto *m* di risalita
skill [skɪl] (*ability*) abilità *f inv*; ***what skills do you have?*** quali capacità possiede?
skilled [skɪld] *adj* abile
skilled 'work•er operaio *m*, -a *f* specializzato, -a
skill•ful *etc Am* → ***skilful*** *etc*
skim [skɪm] *v/t* (*pret & pp* ***-med***) *surface*

S

sfiorare; *milk* scremare
◆ **skim off** *v/t the best* selezionare
◆ **skim through** *v/t text* scorrere
skimmed 'milk [skɪmd] latte *m* scremato
skimp•y ['skɪmpɪ] *adj account etc* scarso; *dress* succinto
skin [skɪn] **1** *n of person, animal* pelle *f*; *of fruit* buccia *f* **2** *v/t* (*pret & pp* ***-ned***) scoiare
'skin div•ing immersioni *fpl* subacquee
skin•flint ['skɪnflɪnt] F spilorcio *m* F
'skin graft innesto *m* epidermico
skin•ny ['skɪnɪ] *adj* magro
'skin-tight *adj* aderente
skip [skɪp] **1** *n little jump* salto *m* **2** *v/i* (*pret & pp* ***-ped***) saltellare; *with skipping rope* saltare **3** *v/t* (*pret & pp* ***-ped***) (*omit*) saltare
'ski pole racchetta *f* da sci
skip•per ['skɪpə(r)] NAUT skipper *m inv*; *of team* capitano *m*
skip•ping rope ['skɪpɪŋ] corda *f* (per saltare)
'ski re•sort stazione *f* sciistica
skirt [skɜːt] *n* gonna *f*
'ski run pista *f* da sci
'ski tow sciovia *f*
skit•tle ['skɪtl] birillo *m*
skit•tles ['skɪtlz] *nsg* (*game*) birilli *mpl*
skive [skaɪv] *v/i* F fare lo scansafatiche F
skull [skʌl] cranio *m*
sky [skaɪ] cielo *m*
'sky•light lucernario *m*
'sky•line profilo *m* (contro il cielo)
'sky•scrap•er ['skaɪskreɪpə(r)] grattacielo *m*
slab [slæb] *of stone* lastra *f*; *of cake etc* fetta *f*
slack [slæk] *adj rope* allentato; *person, work* negligente; *period* lento
slack•en ['slækn] *v/t rope* allentare; *pace* rallentare
◆ **slacken off** *v/i* rallentare
slacks [slæks] *npl* pantaloni *mpl* casual
◆ **slag off** [slæg] *v/t* P parlare male di
slain [sleɪn] *pp* → ***slay***
slam [slæm] *v/t & v/i* (*pret & pp* ***-med***) *door* sbattere
◆ **slam down** *v/t* sbattere
slan•der ['slɑːndə(r)] **1** *n* diffamazione *f* **2** *v/t* diffamare
slan•der•ous ['slɑːndərəs] *adj* diffamatorio
slang [slæŋ] slang *m inv*; *of a specific group* gergo *m*
slant [slɑːnt] **1** *v/i* pendere **2** *n* pendenza *f*; *given to a story* angolazione *f*
slant•ing ['slɑːntɪŋ] *adj roof* spiovente
slap [slæp] **1** *n blow* schiaffo *m* **2** *v/t* (*pret & pp* ***-ped***) schiaffeggiare
'slap•dash *adj work* frettoloso; *person* pressapochista
slap-up 'meal F pranzo *m* coi fiocchi
slash [slæʃ] **1** *n cut* taglio *m*; *in punctuation* barra *f* **2** *v/t skin, painting* squarciare; *prices, costs* abbattere; ***slash one's wrists*** tagliarsi le vene
slate [sleɪt] *n* ardesia *f*
slaugh•ter ['slɔːtə(r)] **1** *n of animals* macellazione *f*; *of people, troops* massacro *m* **2** *v/t animals* macellare; *people, troops* massacrare
'slaugh•ter•house *for animals* macello *m*
Slav [slɑːv] *adj* slavo
slave [sleɪv] *n* schiavo *m*, -a *f*
'slave-driv•er F negriero, -a *f* F
sla•ve•ry schiavitù *f inv*
slay [sleɪ] *v/t* (*pret* ***slew***, *pp* ***slain***) ammazzare
sleaze [sliːz] POL corruzione *f*
slea•zy ['sliːzɪ] *adj bar, characters* sordido
sled(ge) [sled, sledʒ] *n* slitta *f*
'sledge ham•mer mazza *f*
sleep [sliːp] **1** *n* sonno *m*; ***go to sleep*** addormentarsi; ***I need a good sleep*** ho bisogno di una bella dormita; ***I couldn't get to sleep*** non sono riuscito a dormire **2** *v/i* (*pret & pp* ***slept***) dormire
◆ **sleep in** *v/i* (*have a long lie*) dormire fino a tardi
◆ **sleep on** *v/t proposal, decision* dormire su; ***sleep on it*** dormirci su
◆ **sleep with** *v/t* (*have sex with*) andare a letto con
sleep•er ['sliːpə(r)] RAIL: *on track* traversina *f*; (*sleeping car*) vagone *m* letto; *train* treno *m* notturno; ***be a light / heavy sleeper*** avere il sonno leggero / pesante
sleep•i•ly ['sliːpɪlɪ] *adv* con aria assonnata
'sleep•ing bag ['sliːpɪŋ] sacco *m* a pelo
'sleep•ing car RAIL vagone *m* letto
'sleep•ing part•ner *Br* COM socio *m* inattivo
'sleep•ing pill sonnifero *m*
sleep•less ['sliːplɪs] *adj night* in bianco
'sleep walk•er sonnambulo *m*, -a *f*
'sleep walk•ing sonnambulismo *m*
sleep•y ['sliːpɪ] *adj child* assonnato; *town* addormentato; ***I'm sleepy*** ho sonno
sleet [sliːt] *n* nevischio *m*
sleeve [sliːv] *of jacket etc* manica *f*
sleeve•less ['sliːvlɪs] *adj* senza maniche
sleigh [sleɪ] *n* slitta *f*
sleight of 'hand [slaɪt] gioco *m* di prestigio
slen•der ['slendə(r)] *adj figure, arms* snello; *chance, income, margin* piccolo

slept [slept] *pret & pp* → ***sleep***
slew [sluː] *pret* → ***slay***
slice [slaɪs] **1** *n also fig* fetta *f* **2** *v/t loaf etc* affettare
sliced ˈ**bread** [slaɪst] pane *m* a cassetta; ***the greatest thing since sliced bread*** F il non plus ultra
slick [slɪk] **1** *adj performance* brillante; (*pej*: *cunning*) scaltro **2** *n of oil* chiazza *f* di petrolio
slid [slɪd] *pret & pp* → ***slide***
slide [slaɪd] **1** *n for kids* scivolo *m*; PHOT diapositiva *f*; *in hair* fermacapelli *m inv* **2** *v/i* (*pret & pp* ***slid***) scivolare; *of exchange rate etc* calare **3** *v/t* (*pret & pp* ***slid***) far scivolare
slid•ing door [slaɪdɪŋˈdɔː(r)] porta *f* scorrevole
slight [slaɪt] **1** *adj person*, *figure* gracile; (*small*) leggero; ***no, not in the slightest*** no, per nulla **2** *n* (*insult*) offesa *f*
slight•ly [ˈslaɪtlɪ] *adv* leggermente
slim [slɪm] **1** *adj* slanciato; *chance* scarso **2** *v/i* (*pret & pp* ***-med***) dimagrire; ***I'm slimming*** sono a dieta
slime [slaɪm] melma *f*
slim•y [ˈslaɪmɪ] *adj liquid* melmoso; *person* viscido
sling [slɪŋ] **1** *n for arm* fascia *f* a tracolla **2** *v/t* (*pret & pp* ***slung***) (*throw*) lanciare
slip [slɪp] **1** *n on ice etc* scivolata *f*; (*mistake*) errore *m*; ***a slip of paper*** un foglietto; ***a slip of the tongue*** un lapsus; ***give s.o. the slip*** seminare qu **2** *v/i* (*pret & pp* ***-ped***) *on ice etc* scivolare; *of quality etc* peggiorare; ***he slipped out of the room*** è sgattaiolato fuori dalla stanza **3** *v/t* (*pret & pp* ***-ped***) (*put*) far scivolare; ***he slipped it into his briefcase*** l'ha fatto scivolare nella valigetta; ***it slipped my mind*** mi è passato di mente
◆ **slip away** *v/i of time* passare; *of opportunity* andare sprecato; (*die quietly*) spirare
◆ **slip off** *v/t jacket etc* togliersi
◆ **slip on** *v/t jacket etc* infilarsi
◆ **slip out** *v/i* (*go out*) sgattaiolare
◆ **slip up** *v/i make mistake* sbagliarsi
slipped ˈ**disc** [slɪpt] ernia *f* del disco
slip•per [ˈslɪpə(r)] pantofola *f*
slip•pery [ˈslɪpərɪ] *adj* scivoloso
ˈ**slip road** rampa *f* di accesso
slip•shod [ˈslɪpʃɒd] *adj* trascurato
ˈ**slip-up** (*mistake*) errore *m*
slit [slɪt] **1** *n* (*tear*) strappo *m*; (*hole*) fessura *f*; *in skirt* spacco *m* **2** *v/t* (*pret & pp* ***slit***) *envelope*, *packet* aprire (tagliando); *throat* tagliare
slith•er [ˈslɪðə(r)] *v/i* strisciare
sliv•er [ˈslɪvə(r)] scheggia *f*
slob [slɒb] *pej* sudicione *m*, -a *f*
slob•ber [ˈslɒbə(r)] *v/i* sbavare
slog [slɒg] *n* faticata *f*
slo•gan [ˈsləʊgən] slogan *m inv*
slop [slɒp] *v/t* (*pret & pp* ***-ped***) rovesciare, versare
slope [sləʊp] **1** *n* pendenza *f*; *of mountain* pendio *m*; ***built on a slope*** costruito in pendio **2** *v/i* essere inclinato; ***the road slopes down to the sea*** la strada scende fino al mare
slop•py [ˈslɒpɪ] *adj work*, *editing* trascurato; *in dressing* sciatto; (*too sentimental*) sdolcinato
sloshed [slɒʃt] *adj* F (*drunk*) sbronzo F
slot [slɒt] **1** *n* fessura *f*; *in schedule* spazio *m*
◆ **slot in** (*pret & pp* ***-ted***) **1** *v/t* infilare **2** *v/i* infilarsi
ˈ**slot ma•chine** *for vending* distributore *m* automatico; *for gambling* slot-machine *f inv*
slouch [slaʊʧ] *v/i*: ***don't slouch!*** su con la schiena!
slov•en•ly [ˈslʌvnlɪ] *adj* sciatto
slow [sləʊ] *adj* lento; ***be slow*** *of clock* essere indietro
◆ **slow down** *v/t & v/i* rallentare
ˈ**slow•coach** *Br* F lumaca *f* F
ˈ**slow•down** *in production* rallentamento *m*
slow•ly [ˈsləʊlɪ] *adv* lentamente
slow ˈ**mo•tion** *n*: ***in slow motion*** al rallentatore
slow•ness [ˈsləʊnɪs] lentezza *f*
ˈ**slow•poke** *Am* F lumaca *f* F
slug [slʌg] *n animal* lumaca *f*
slug•gish [ˈslʌgɪʃ] *adj* lento
slum [slʌm] *n* slum *m inv*
slump [slʌmp] **1** *n in trade* crollo *m* **2** *v/i economically* crollare; (*collapse*: *of person*) accasciarsi
slung [slʌŋ] *pret & pp* → ***sling***
slur [slɜː(r)] **1** *n* calunnia *f* **2** *v/t* (*pret & pp* ***-red***) *words* biascicare
slurp [slɜːp] *v/t* bere rumorosamente
slurred [slɜːd] *adj speech* impappinato
slush [slʌʃ] fanghiglia *f*; (*pej*: *sentimental stuff*) smancerie *fpl*
ˈ**slush fund** fondi *mpl* neri
slush•y [ˈslʌʃɪ] *adj snow* ridotto in fanghiglia; *film*, *novel* sdolcinato
slut [slʌt] *pej* sgualdrina *f*
sly [slaɪ] *adj* scaltro; ***on the sly*** di nascosto
smack [smæk] **1** *n on the bottom* sculacciata *f*; *in the face* schiaffo *m* **2** *v/t child* picchiare; *bottom* sculacciare

small [smɔːl] **1** *adj* piccolo **2** *n*: ***the small of the back*** le reni
small 'change spiccioli *mpl*
small hours *npl*: ***the small hours*** le ore *fpl* piccole
small•pox ['smɔːlpɒks] vaiolo *m*
'small print parte *f* scritta in caratteri minuti
'small talk conversazione *f* di circostanza
smarm•y ['smɑːmɪ] *adj* F untuoso
smart [smɑːt] **1** *adj* (*elegant*) elegante; (*intelligent*) intelligente; *pace* svelto; ***get smart with*** fare il furbo con F **2** *v/i* (*hurt*) bruciare
smart al•ec(k) ['smɑːtælɪk] F sapientone *m* F
'smart ass P sapientone *m*
'smart card smart card *f inv*
◆ **smarten up** ['smɑːtn] *v/t* sistemare; ***smarten o.s. up*** mettersi in ghingheri
smart•ly ['smɑːtlɪ] *adv dressed* elegantemente
smash [smæʃ] **1** *n noise* fracasso *m*; (*car crash*) scontro *m*; *in tennis* schiacciata *f* **2** *v/t break* spaccare; *hit hard* sbattere; ***smash sth to pieces*** mandare in frantumi qc **3** *v/i break* frantumarsi; ***the driver smashed into …*** l'automobilista si è schiantato contro …
◆ **smash up** *v/t place* distruggere
smash 'hit F successone *m*
smash•ing ['smæʃɪŋ] *adj* F fantastico
smat•ter•ing ['smætərɪŋ] *of a language* infarinatura *f*
smear [smɪə(r)] **1** *n of ink etc* macchia *f*; MED striscio *m*; *on character* calunnia *f* **2** *v/t character* calunniare; ***smear mud over the wall*** imbrattare il muro di fango
'smear cam•paign campagna *f* diffamatoria
smell [smel] **1** *n* odore *m*; ***it has no smell*** non ha odore; ***sense of smell*** olfatto *m*, odorato *m* **2** *v/t* sentire odore di; *test by smelling* sentire **3** *v/i unpleasantly* puzzare; (*sniff*) odorare; ***what does it smell of?*** che odore ha?; ***you smell of beer*** puzzi di birra; ***it smells good*** ha un buon profumino
smell•y ['smelɪ] *adj* puzzolente; ***it's so smelly in here*** qui dentro c'è puzza
smile [smaɪl] **1** *n* sorriso *m* **2** *v/i* sorridere
◆ **smile at** *v/t* sorridere a
smirk [smɜːk] **1** *n* sorriso *m* compiaciuto **2** *v/i* sorridere con compiacimento
smog [smɒg] smog *m inv*
smoke [sməʊk] **1** *n* fumo *m*; ***have a smoke*** fumare **2** *v/t cigarettes etc* fumare; *bacon* affumicare **3** *v/i* fumare; ***I don't smoke*** non fumo
smok•er ['sməʊkə(r)] *person* fumatore *m*, -trice *f*
smok•ing ['sməʊkɪŋ] fumo *m*; ***no smoking*** vietato fumare
'smok•ing com•part•ment RAIL carrozza *m* fumatori
smok•y ['sməʊkɪ] *adj room, air* pieno di fumo
smol•der *Am* → ***smoulder***
smooth [smuːð] **1** *adj surface, skin, sea* liscio; *sea* calmo; *transition* senza problemi; *pej*: *person* mellifluo **2** *v/t hair* lisciare
◆ **smooth down** *v/t with sandpaper etc* levigare
◆ **smooth out** *v/t paper, cloth* lisciare
◆ **smooth over** *v/t*: ***smooth things over*** appianare le cose
smooth•ly ['smuːðlɪ] *adv without any problems* senza problemi
smoth•er ['smʌðə(r)] *v/t flames, person* soffocare; ***smother s.o. with kisses*** coprire qu di baci
smoul•der ['sməʊldə(r)] *v/i of fire* covare sotto la cenere; *fig*: *with anger, desire* consumarsi (***with*** di)
smudge [smʌdʒ] **1** *n* sbavatura *f* **2** *v/t* sbavare
smug [smʌg] *adj* compiaciuto
smug•gle ['smʌgl] *v/t* contrabbandare
smug•gler ['smʌglə(r)] contrabbandiere *m*, -a *f*
smug•gling ['smʌglɪŋ] contrabbando *m*
smug•ly ['smʌglɪ] *adv* con compiacimento
smut•ty ['smʌtɪ] *adj joke, sense of humour* sconcio
snack [snæk] *n* spuntino *m*
'snack bar snack bar *m inv*
snag [snæg] *n* (*problem*) problema *m*
snail [sneɪl] chiocciola *f*, *in cooking* lumaca *f*
snake [sneɪk] *n* serpente *m*
snap [snæp] **1** *n sound* botto *m*; PHOT foto *f* **2** *v/t* (*pret & pp* **-ped**) *break* spezzare; (*say sharply*) dire bruscamente **3** *v/i* (*pret & pp* **-ped**) *break* spezzarsi **4** *adj decision, judgement* immediato
◆ **snap up** *v/t bargains* accaparrarsi
snap•py ['snæpɪ] *adj person, mood* irritabile; F (*quick*) rapido; (*elegant*) elegante
'snap•shot istantanea *f*
snarl [snɑːl] **1** *n of dog* ringhio *m* **2** *v/i* ringhiare
snatch [snætʃ] **1** *v/t* afferrare; (*steal*) scippare; (*kidnap*) rapire **2** *v/i* strappare di mano
snaz•zy ['snæzɪ] *adj* F chic
sneak [sniːk] **1** *n* (*telltale*) spione *m*, -a *f* **2** *v/t* (*remove, steal*) rubare; ***sneak a glan-***

S

ce at dare una sbirciatina a **3** *v/i* (*tell tales*) fare la spia; ***sneak out of …*** sgattaoiolare fuori da …
sneak•ing ['sni:kɪŋ] *adj*: ***have a sneaking suspicion that …*** avere il vago sospetto che …
sneak•y ['sni:kɪ] *adj* F (*crafty*) scaltro
sneer [snɪə(r)] **1** *n* sogghigno *m* **2** *v/i* sogghignare
sneeze [sni:z] **1** *n* starnuto *m* **2** *v/i* starnutire
sniff [snɪf] **1** *v/i to clear nose* tirare su col naso; *of dog* fiutare **2** *v/t smell* annusare
snig•ger ['snɪgə(r)] **1** *n* risolino *m* **2** *v/i* ridacchiare
snip [snɪp] *n* F (*bargain*) affare *m*
snip•er ['snaɪpə(r)] cecchino *m*
sniv•el ['snɪvl] *v/i pej* frignare
snob [snɒb] snob *m/f inv*
snob•ber•y ['snɒbərɪ] snobismo *m*
snob•bish ['snɒbɪʃ] *adj* snob *inv*
snook•er ['snu:kə(r)] biliardo *m*
snoop [snu:p] *n* ficcanaso *m/f inv*
◆ **snoop around** *v/i* ficcanasare
snoot•y ['snu:tɪ] *adj* snob *inv*
snooze [snu:z] **1** *n* sonnellino *m*; ***have a snooze*** fare un sonnellino **2** *v/i* sonnecchiare
snore [snɔ:(r)] *v/i* russare
snor•ing ['snɔ:rɪŋ] *n* russare *m*
snor•kel ['snɔ:kl] *n* boccaglio *m*
snort [snɔ:t] *v/i* sbuffare
snout [snaʊt] *of pig* grugno *m*; *of dog* muso *m*
snow [snəʊ] **1** *n* neve *f* **2** *v/i* nevicare
◆ **snow under** *v/t*: ***be snowed under with …*** essere sommerso di …
'**snow•ball** palla *f* di neve
'**snow•bound** *adj* isolato dalla neve
'**snow chains** *npl* MOT catene *fpl* da neve
'**snow•drift** cumulo *m* di neve
'**snow•drop** bucaneve *m inv*
'**snow•flake** fiocco *m* di neve
'**snow•man** pupazzo *m* di neve
'**snow•storm** tormenta *f*
snow•y ['snəʊɪ] *adj weather* nevoso; *roofs*, *hills* innevato
snub [snʌb] **1** *n* affronto *m* **2** *v/t* (*pret & pp* ***-bed***) snobbare
snub-nosed ['snʌbnəʊzd] *adj* col naso all'insù
snug [snʌg] *adj* al calduccio; (*tight-fitting*) attillato
◆ **snuggle down** ['snʌgl] *v/i* accoccolarsi
◆ **snuggle up to** *v/t* rannicchiarsi accanto a
so [səʊ] **1** *adv* così; ***so hot / cold*** così caldo / freddo; ***not so much*** non così tanto; ***so much better / easier*** molto meglio / più facile; ***you shouldn't eat / drink so much*** non dovresti mangiare / bere così tanto; ***I miss you so*** mi manchi tanto; ***so am / do I*** anch'io; ***so is she / does she*** anche lei; ***and so on*** e così via **2** *pron*: ***I hope / think so*** spero / penso di sì; ***I don't think so*** non credo, credo di no; ***you didn't tell me – I did so*** non me l'hai detto - e invece sì; ***50 or so*** circa 50 **3** *conj* (*for that reason*) così; (*in order that*) così che; ***and so I missed the train*** e così ho perso il treno; ***so (that) I could come too*** così che potessi venire anch'io; ***so what?*** F e allora?
soak [səʊk] *v/t* (*steep*) mettere a bagno; *of water, rain* inzuppare
◆ **soak up** *v/t liquid* assorbire; ***soak up the sun*** crogiolarsi al sole
soaked [səʊkt] *adj* fradicio; ***be soaked to the skin*** essere bagnato fradicio
soak•ing (wet) ['səʊkɪŋ] *adj* bagnato fradicio
so-and-so ['səʊənsəʊ] F *unknown person* tal dei tali *m/f inv*; (*euph*: *annoying person*) impiastro *m*
soap [səʊp] *n for washing* sapone *m*
'**soap (op•e•ra)** soap (opera) *f inv*, telenovela *f*
soap•y ['səʊpɪ] *adj water* saponato
soar [sɔ:(r)] *v/i of rocket etc* innalzarsi; *of prices* aumentare vertiginosamente
sob [sɒb] **1** *n* singhiozzo *m* **2** *v/i* (*pret & pp* ***-bed***) singhiozzare
so•ber ['səʊbə(r)] *adj* (*not drunk*) sobrio; (*serious*) serio
◆ **sober up** *v/i* smaltire la sbornia
so-'called *adj* cosiddetto
soc•cer ['sɒkə(r)] calcio *m*
'**soc•cer hoo•li•gan** hooligan *m/f inv*
so•cia•ble ['səʊʃəbl] *adj* socievole
so•cial ['səʊʃl] *adj* sociale
so•cial 'dem•o•crat socialdemocratico *m*, -a *f*
so•cial•is•m ['səʊʃəlɪzm] socialismo *m*
so•cial•ist ['səʊʃəlɪst] **1** *adj* socialista **2** *n* socialista *m/f*
so•cial•ize ['səʊʃəlaɪz] *v/i* socializzare
'**soc•ial life** vita *f* sociale
so•cial 'sci•ence scienza *f* sociale
so•cial se'cu•ri•ty *Br* sussidio *m* della previdenza sociale
so•cial 'serv•i•ces *Br npl* servizi *mpl* sociali
'**so•cial work** assistenza *f* sociale
'**so•cial work•er** assistente *m/f* sociale
so•ci•e•ty [sə'saɪətɪ] società *f inv*; (*organization*) associazione *f*
so•ci•ol•o•gist [səʊsɪ'ɒlədʒɪst] sociologo *m*, -a *f*

S

so•ci•ol•o•gy [səʊsɪ'ɒlədʒɪ] sociologia *f*
sock[1] [sɒk] calzino *m*
sock[2] [sɒk] **1** *n* F (*punch*) pugno *m* **2** *v/t* F (*punch*) dare un pugno a
sock•et ['sɒkɪt] *for light bulb* portalampada *m inv*; *in wall* presa *f* (di corrente); *of eye* orbita *f*
so•da ['səʊdə] (*soda water*) seltz *m inv*
sod•den ['sɒdn] *adj* zuppo
so•fa ['səʊfə] divano *m*
'so•fa-bed divano *m* letto
soft [sɒft] *adj pillow* soffice; *chair, skin* morbido; *light, colour* tenue; *music* soft; *voice* sommesso; (*lenient*) indulgente; ***have a soft spot for*** avere un debole per
soft 'drink bibita *f* analcolica
'soft drug droga *f* leggera
soft•en ['sɒfn] **1** *v/t butter etc* ammorbidire; *position* attenuare; *impact, blow* attutire **2** *v/i of butter, ice-cream* ammorbidirsi
soft•ly ['sɒftlɪ] *adv speak* sommessamente
soft 'toy giocattolo *m* di pezza
soft•ware ['sɒftweə(r)] software *m inv*
sog•gy ['sɒgɪ] *adj* molle e pesante
soil [sɔɪl] **1** *n* (*earth*) terra *f* **2** *v/t* sporcare
so•lar 'en•er•gy ['səʊlə(r)] energia *f* solare
'so•lar pan•el pannello *m* solare
'solar system sistema *m* solare
sold [səʊld] *pret & pp* → ***sell***
sol•dier ['səʊldʒə(r)] soldato *m*
◆ **soldier on** *v/i* perseverare
sole[1] [səʊl] *n of foot* pianta *f* (del piede); *of shoe* suola *f*
sole[2] [səʊl] *adj* unico; (*exclusive*) esclusivo
sole[3] [səʊl] (*fish*) sogliola *f*
sole•ly ['səʊlɪ] *adv* solamente; ***be solely responsible*** essere il solo / la sola responsabile
sol•emn ['sɒləm] *adj* solenne
so•lem•ni•ty [sə'lemnətɪ] solennità *f inv*
sol•emn•ly ['sɒləmlɪ] *adv* solennemente
so•li•cit [sə'lɪsɪt] *v/i of prostitute* adescare
so•lic•i•tor [sə'lɪsɪtə(r)] avvocato *m*
sol•id ['sɒlɪd] *adj* (*hard*) solido; (*without holes*) compatto; *gold, silver* massiccio; (*sturdy*) robusto; *evidence* concreto; *support* forte; ***a solid hour*** un'ora intera
sol•i•dar•i•ty [sɒlɪ'dærətɪ] solidarietà *f inv*
so•lid•i•fy [sə'lɪdɪfaɪ] *v/i* (*pret & pp* ***-ied***) solidificarsi
sol•id•ly ['sɒlɪdlɪ] *adv built* solidamente; *in favour of sth* all'unanimità
so•lil•o•quy [sə'lɪləkwɪ] *on stage* monologo *m*
sol•i•taire ['sɒlɪteər] *Am: card game* solitario *m*
sol•i•ta•ry ['sɒlɪtərɪ] *adj life, activity* solitario; (*single*) solo
sol•i•ta•ry con'fine•ment isolamento *m*
sol•i•tude ['sɒlɪtjuːd] solitudine *f*
so•lo ['səʊləʊ] **1** *n* MUS assolo *m* **2** *adj performance* solista; *flight* in solitario
so•lo•ist ['səʊləʊɪst] solista *m/f*
sol•u•ble ['sɒljʊbl] *adj substance* solubile; *problem* risolvibile
so•lu•tion [sə'luːʃn] soluzione *f*
solve [sɒlv] *v/t* risolvere
sol•vent ['sɒlvənt] **1** *adj financially* solvibile **2** *n* solvente *m*
som•ber *Am*, **som•bre** ['sɒmbə(r)] *adj* (*dark*) scuro; (*serious*) tetro
some [sʌm] **1** *adj* (*unspecified amount*) un po' di, del; (*unspecified number*) qualche, dei *m*, delle *f*; ***would you like some water?*** vuoi un po' d'acqua *o* dell'acqua?; ***would you like some biscuits?*** vuoi dei biscotti *o* qualche biscotto?; ***some people say that ...*** alcuni dicono che ... **2** *pron* (*unspecified amount*) un po'; (*unspecified number*) alcuni *m*, -e *f*; ***would you like some?*** ne vuoi un po'?; ***give me some*** dammene un po'; ***some of the students*** alcuni studenti
some•bod•y ['sʌmbədɪ] *pron* qualcuno
'some•day *adv* un giorno
'some•how *adv* (*by one means or another*) in qualche modo; (*for some unknown reason*) per qualche motivo
'some•one *pron* → ***somebody***
som•er•sault ['sʌməsɔːlt] **1** *n* capriola *f* **2** *v/i* fare una capriola
'some•thing *pron* qualcosa; ***would you like something to drink / eat?*** vuoi (qualcosa) da mangiare / bere?; ***is something wrong?*** c'è qualcosa che non va?
'some•time *adv* (*one of these days*) uno di questi giorni; ***sometime last year*** l'anno scorso
'some•times ['sʌmtaɪmz] *adv* a volte
'some•what *adv* piuttosto
'some•where **1** *adv* da qualche parte **2** *pron* un posto; ***let's go somewhere quiet*** andiamo in un posto tranquillo
son [sʌn] figlio *m*
so•na•ta [sə'nɑːtə] MUS sonata *f*
song [sɒŋ] canzone *f*; *of birds* canto *m*
'song•bird uccello *m* canoro
'song•writ•er compositore *m*, -trice *f*
'son-in-law (*pl* ***sons-in-law***) genero *m*
son•net ['sɒnɪt] sonetto *m*
soon [suːn] *adv* presto; ***as soon as*** non appena; ***as soon as possible*** prima pos-

sibile; ***sooner or later*** presto o tardi; ***the sooner the better*** prima è, meglio è; ***how soon can you be ready?*** fra quanto sei pronto?
soot [sʊt] fuliggine *f*
soothe [suːð] *v/t* calmare
so•phis•ti•cat•ed [sə'fɪstɪkeɪtɪd] *adj* sofisticato
so•phis•ti•ca•tion [sə'fɪstɪkeɪʃn] *of person* raffinatezza *f*; *of machine* complessità *f inv*
sop•py ['sɒpɪ] *adj* F sdolcinato
so•pra•no [sə'prɑːnəʊ] *n* soprano *m/f*
sor•did ['sɔːdɪd] *adj affair, business* sordido
sore [sɔː(r)] **1** *adj* (*painful*) dolorante; ***is it sore?*** fa male? **2** *n* piaga *f*
sore 'throat mal *m* di gola
sor•row ['sɒrəʊ] *n* dispiacere *m*, dolore *m*
sor•ry ['sɒrɪ] *adj day, sight* triste; ***(I'm) sorry!*** *apologizing* scusa!; *polite form* scusi!; ***I'm sorry*** *regretting* mi dispiace; ***I won't be sorry to leave here*** non vedo l'ora di andarmene da qui; ***I feel sorry for her*** mi dispiace per lei
sort [sɔːt] **1** *n* tipo *m*; ***sort of …*** F un po' …; ***is it finished? – sort of*** F è terminato? - quasi **2** *v/t* separare; COMPUT ordinare
◆ **sort out** *v/t papers* mettere in ordine; *problem* risolvere; ***sort things out*** sistemare le cose
SOS [esəʊ'es] SOS *m inv*
so-'so *adv* F così così
sought [sɔːt] *pret & pp* → ***seek***
soul [səʊl] anima *f*; ***the poor soul*** il poverino, la poverina
sound[1] [saʊnd] **1** *adj* (*sensible*) valido; (*healthy*) sano; *sleep* profondo; *structure, walls* solido **2** *adv*: ***be sound asleep*** dormire profondamente
sound[2] [saʊnd] **1** *n* suono *m*; (*noise*) rumore *m* **2** *v/t* (*pronounce*) pronunciare; MED auscultare; ***sound one's horn*** suonare il clacson **3** *v/i*: ***that sounds interesting*** sembra interessante; ***that sounds like a good idea*** mi sembra un'ottima idea; ***she sounded unhappy*** dalla voce sembrava infelice
◆ **sound out** *v/t* F sondare l'opinione di
'sound bar•ri•er muro *m* del suono
'sound•bite slogan *m inv*
'sound ef•fects *npl* effetti *mpl* sonori
sound•ly ['saʊndlɪ] *adv sleep* profondamente; *beaten* duramente
'sound•proof *adj* insonorizzato
'sound•track colonna *f* sonora
soup [suːp] minestra *f*
'soup bowl scodella *f*
souped-up [suːpt'ʌp] *adj* F truccato F
'soup plate piatto *m* fondo
'soup spoon cucchiaio *m* da minestra
sour ['saʊə(r)] *adj apple, orange* aspro; *milk, expression, comment* acido
source [sɔːs] *n* fonte *f*; *of river* sorgente *f*
sour 'cream panna *f* acida
south [saʊθ] **1** *adj* meridionale, del sud **2** *n* sud *m*; ***to the south of*** a sud di **3** *adv* verso sud
South 'Af•ric•a Repubblica *f* Sudafricana
South 'Af•ri•can 1 *adj* sudafricano **2** *n* sudafricano *m*, -a *f*
South A'mer•i•ca Sudamerica *m*
South A'mer•i•can 1 *adj* sudamericano **2** *n* sudamericano *m*, -a *f*
south'east 1 *n* sud-est *m* **2** *adj* sud-orientale **3** *adv* verso sud-est; ***it's southeast of …*** è a sud-est di …
south'•east•ern *adj* sud-orientale
south•er•ly ['sʌðəlɪ] *adj* meridionale
south•ern ['sʌðən] *adj* del sud
south•ern•er ['sʌðənə(r)] abitante *m/f* del sud
south•ern•most ['sʌðənməʊst] *adj* più a sud
South 'Pole polo *m* sud
south•wards ['saʊθwədz] *adv* verso sud
south•'west 1 *n* sud-ovest *m* **2** *adj* sud-occidentale **3** *adv* verso sud-ovest; ***it's southwest of …*** è a sud-ovest di …
south'west•ern *adj* sud-occidentale
sou•ve•nir [suːvə'nɪə(r)] souvenir *m inv*
sove•reign ['sɒvrɪn] *adj state* sovrano
sove•reign•ty ['sɒvrɪntɪ] *of state* sovranità *f inv*
So•vi•et ['səʊvɪət] *adj* sovietico
So•vi•et 'U•nion Unione *f* Sovietica
sow[1] [saʊ] *n* (*female pig*) scrofa *f*
sow[2] [səʊ] *v/t seeds* seminare
sown [səʊn] *pp* → ***sow***[2]
soy•a bean ['sɔɪə] seme *m* di soia
soy(a) 'sauce salsa *f* di soia
spa [spɑː] località *f inv* termale
space [speɪs] *n* spazio *m*; *in car park* posto *m*
◆ **space out** *v/t* distanziare
'space-bar COMPUT barra *f* spaziatrice
'space•craft veicolo *m* spaziale
'space•ship astronave *f*
'space shut•tle shuttle *m inv*
'space sta•tion stazione *f* spaziale
'space•suit tuta *f* spaziale
spa•cious ['speɪʃəs] *adj* spazioso
spade [speɪd] *for digging* vanga *f*; ***spades*** *in card game* picche
'spade•work *fig* preparativi *mpl*
spa•ghet•ti [spə'getɪ] *nsg* spaghetti *mpl*
Spain [speɪn] Spagna *f*

span [spæn] *v/t* (*pret & pp* ***-ned***) coprire; *of bridge* attraversare
Span•iard ['spænjəd] spagnolo *m*, -a *f*
Span•ish ['spænɪʃ] **1** *adj* spagnolo **2** *n language* spagnolo *m*
spank [spæŋk] *v/t* sculacciare
spank•ing ['spæŋkɪŋ] sculaccione *m*
span•ner ['spænə(r)] *Br* chiave *f* inglese
spare [speə(r)] **1** *v/t* (*do without*) fare a meno di; ***can you spare £50?*** mi puoi prestare 50 sterline?; ***can you spare the time?*** hai tempo?; ***have money / time to spare*** avere soldi / tempo d'avanzo; ***there were 5 to spare*** (*left over, in excess*) ce n'erano 5 d'avanzo **2** *adj* in più **3** *n* ricambio *m*
spare 'part pezzo *m* di ricambio
spare 'ribs *npl* costine *fpl* di maiale
spare 'room stanza *f* degli ospiti
spare 'time tempo *m* libero
spare 'tire *Am*, **spare 'tyre** MOT ruota *f* di scorta
spar•ing ['speə(r)ɪŋ] *adj*: ***be sparing with*** andarci piano con F
spa•ring•ly ['speə(r)ɪŋlɪ] *adv* con moderazione
spark [spɑːk] *n* scintilla *f*
spark•ing plug ['spɑːkɪŋ] candela *f*
sparkle ['spɑːkl] *v/i* brillare
spark•ling 'wine ['spɑːklɪŋ] vino *m* frizzante
'spark plug candela *f*
spar•row ['spærəʊ] passero *m*
sparse [spɑːs] *adj vegetation* rado
sparse•ly ['spɑːslɪ] *adv*: ***sparsely populated*** scarsamente popolato
spar•tan ['spɑːtn] *adj* spartano
spas•mod•ic [spæz'mɒdɪk] *adj* irregolare
spat [spæt] *pret & pp* → ***spit***
spate [speɪt] *fig* ondata *f*
spa•tial ['speɪʃl] *adj* spaziale
spat•ter ['spætə(r)] *v/t mud, paint* schizzare
speak [spiːk] (*pret* ***spoke***, *pp* ***spoken***) **1** *v/i* parlare; ***we're not speaking*** (***to each other***) (*we've quarrelled*) non ci rivolgiamo la parola; ***speaking*** TELEC sono io **2** *v/t foreign language* parlare; *the truth* dire; ***speak one's mind*** dire quello che si pensa
◆ **speak for** *v/t* parlare a nome di
◆ **speak out** *v/i* prendere posizione; *say what you think* farsi sentire
◆ **speak up** *v/i* (*speak louder*) parlare ad alta voce
speak•er ['spiːkə(r)] oratore *m*, -trice *f*; *of sound system* cassa *f*
spear [spɪə(r)] lancia *f*
spear•mint ['spɪəmɪnt] menta *f*
spe•cial ['speʃl] *adj* speciale; (*particular*) particolare
spe•cial ef•fects *npl* effetti *mpl* speciali
spe•cial•ist ['speʃlɪst] specialista *m/f*
spe•cial•i•ty [speʃɪ'ælətɪ] specialità *f inv*
spe•cial•ize ['speʃəlaɪz] *v/i* specializzarsi; ***specialize in ...*** specializzarsi in; ***we specialize in ...*** siamo specializzati in ...
spe•cial•ly ['speʃlɪ] *adv* → ***especially***
spe•cial•ty ['speʃəltɪ] *Am* specialità *f inv*
spe•cies ['spiːʃiːz] *nsg* specie *f inv*
spe•cif•ic [spə'sɪfɪk] *adj* specifico
spe•cif•i•cal•ly [spə'sɪfɪklɪ] *adv* specificamente
spec•i•fi•ca•tions [spesɪfɪ'keɪʃnz] *npl of machine etc* caratteristiche *fpl* tecniche, specifiche *fpl*
spe•ci•fy ['spesɪfaɪ] *v/t* (*pret & pp* ***-ied***) specificare
spe•ci•men ['spesɪmən] campione *m*
speck [spek] *of dust, soot* granello *m*
specs [speks] *npl* F (*spectacles*) occhiali *mpl*
spec•ta•cle ['spektəkl] (*impressive sight*) spettacolo *m*; (***a pair of***) ***spectacles*** (un paio di) occhiali *mpl*
spec•tac•u•lar [spek'tækjʊlə(r)] *adj* spettacolare
spec•ta•tor [spek'teɪtə(r)] spettatore *m*, -trice *f*
spec'ta•tor sport sport *m inv* spettacolo
spec•trum ['spektrəm] *fig* gamma *f*
spec•u•late ['spekjʊleɪt] *v/i* fare congetture (***on*** su); FIN speculare
spec•u•la•tion [spekjʊ'leɪʃn] congetture *fpl*; FIN speculazione *f*
spec•u•la•tor ['spekjʊleɪtə(r)] FIN speculatore *m*, -trice *f*
sped [sped] *pret & pp* → ***speed***
speech [spiːtʃ] (*address*) discorso *m*; *in play* monologo *m*; (*ability to speak*) parola *f*; (*way of speaking*) linguaggio *m*; ***faculty / power of speech*** facoltà / uso della parola; ***her speech was slurred*** biascicava le parole
'speech de•fect difetto *m* del linguaggio
speech•less ['spiːtʃlɪs] *adj with shock, surprise* senza parole
'speech ther•a•pist logopedista *m/f*
speech 'ther•a•py logopedia *f*
'speech writ•er ghost writer *m inv*
speed [spiːd] **1** *n* velocità *f inv*; (*quickness*) rapidità *f inv*; ***at a speed of 150 mph*** a una velocità di 150 miglia orarie; ***reduce your speed*** rallentare **2** *v/i* (*pret & pp* ***sped***) (*go quickly*) andare a tutta velocità; (*drive too quickly*) superare il limite di velocità
◆ **speed by** *v/i* sfrecciare; *of days* volare

◆ **speed up** **1** *v/i* andare più veloce **2** *v/t* accelerare
'**speed•boat** motoscafo *m*
'**speed bump** dosso *m* di rallentamento
speed•i•ly ['spi:dɪlɪ] *adv* rapidamente
speed•ing ['spi:dɪŋ] *n when driving* eccesso *m* di velocità
'**speed•ing fine** multa *f* per eccesso di velocità
'**speed lim•it** *on roads* limite *m* di velocità
speed•om•e•ter [spi:'dɒmɪtə(r)] tachimetro *m*
'**speed trap** *sistema m con cui la polizia individua chi supera il limite di velocità*
speed•y ['spi:dɪ] *adj* rapido
spell[1] [spel] **1** *v/t*: ***how do you spell ...?*** come si scrive ...?; ***could you spell that please?*** me lo può dettare lettera per lettera? **2** *v/i* sapere come si scrivono le parole
spell[2] [spel] *n* (*period of time*) periodo *m*; (*turn*) turno *m*
'**spell•bound** *adj* incantato
'**spell•check** COMPUT controllo *m* ortografico; ***do a spellcheck on ...*** fare il controllo ortografico di ...
'**spell•check•er** COMPUT correttore *m* ortografico
spell•ing ['spelɪŋ] ortografia *f*
spend [spend] *v/t* (*pret & pp* ***spent***) *money* spendere; *time* passare
'**spend•thrift** *n pej* spendaccione *m*, -a *f*
spent [spent] *pret & pp* → ***spend***
sperm [spɜ:m] spermatozoo *m*; (*semen*) sperma *m*
'**sperm bank** banca *f* dello sperma
'**sperm count** numero *m* degli spermatozoi
sphere [sfɪə(r)] *also fig* sfera *f*; ***sphere of influence*** sfera d'influenza
spice [spaɪs] *n* (*seasoning*) spezia *f*
spic•y ['spaɪsɪ] *adj food* piccante
spi•der ['spaɪdə(r)] ragno *m*
'**spi•der's web** ragnatela *f*
spike [spaɪk] *n on railings* spunzone *m*; *on plant* spina *f*; *on animal* aculeo *m*; *on running shoes* chiodo *m*
spill [spɪl] **1** *v/t* versare **2** *v/i* versarsi **3** *n of oil etc* fuoriuscita *f*
spin[1] [spɪn] **1** *n* giro *m*; *on ball* effetto *m* **2** *v/t* (*pret & pp* ***spun***) far girare; *ball* imprimere l'effetto a **3** *v/i* (*pret & pp* ***spun***) *of wheel* girare; ***my head is spinning*** mi gira la testa
spin[2] [spɪn] *v/t* (*pret & pp* ***spun***) *wool, cotton* filare; *web* tessere
◆ **spin around** *v/i of person, car* girarsi
◆ **spin out** *v/t* F far durare
spin•ach ['spɪnɪdʒ] spinaci *mpl*
spin•al ['spaɪnl] *adj* spinale
spin•al 'col•umn colonna *f* vertebrale, spina *f* dorsale
spin•al 'cord midollo *m* spinale
'**spin doc•tor** F *persona f incaricata di far apparire un personaggio politico nella luce migliore*
'**spin-dry** *v/t* centrifugare
'**spin-dry•er** centrifuga *f*
spine [spaɪn] *of person, animal* spina *f* dorsale; *of book* dorso *m*; *on plant, hedgehog* spina *f*
spine•less ['spaɪnlɪs] *adj* (*cowardly*) smidollato
'**spin-off** applicazione *f* secondaria
spin•ster ['spɪnstə(r)] zitella *f*
spin•y ['spaɪnɪ] *adj* spinoso
spi•ral ['spaɪrəl] **1** *n* spirale *f* **2** *v/i* (*rise quickly*) salire vertiginosamente
spi•ral 'stair•case scala *f* a chiocciola
spire ['spaɪə(r)] spira *f*, guglia *f*
spir•it ['spɪrɪt] *n* spirito *m*; ***we did it in a spirit of cooperation*** abbiamo agito per spirito di collaborazione
spir•it•ed ['spɪrɪtɪd] *adj debate* animato; *defence* energico; *performance* brioso
'**spir•it lev•el** livella *f* a bolla d'aria
spir•its[1] ['spɪrɪts] *npl* (*alcohol*) superalcolici *mpl*
spirits[2] ['spɪrɪts] *npl* (*morale*) morale *msg*; ***be in good / poor spirits*** essere su / giù di morale
spir•i•tu•al ['spɪrɪtjʊəl] *adj* spirituale
spir•it•u•al•ism ['spɪrɪtjʊəlɪzm] spiritismo *m*
spir•it•u•al•ist ['spɪrɪtjʊəlɪst] *n* spiritista *m/f*
spit [spɪt] *v/i* (*pret & pp* ***spat***) *of person* sputare; ***it's spitting with rain*** pioviggina
◆ **spit out** *v/t food, liquid* sputare
spite [spaɪt] *n* dispetto *m*; ***in spite of*** malgrado
spite•ful ['spaɪtfʊl] *adj* dispettoso
spite•ful•ly ['spaɪtfəlɪ] *adv* dispettosamente
spit•ting 'im•age ['spɪtɪŋ]: ***be the spitting image of s.o.*** essere il ritratto sputato di qu
splash [splæʃ] **1** *n* (*noise*) tonfo *m*; (*small amount of liquid*) schizzo *m*; *of colour* macchia *f* **2** *v/t person* schizzare; *water, mud* spruzzare **3** *v/i* schizzare; *of waves* infrangersi
◆ **splash down** *v/i of spacecraft* ammarare
◆ **splash out** *v/i in spending* spendere un sacco di soldi (***on*** per)
'**splash•down** ammaraggio *m*

splen•did ['splendɪd] *adj* magnifico
splen•dor *Am*, **splen•dour** ['splendə(r)] magnificenza *f*
splint [splɪnt] *n* MED stecca *f*
splin•ter ['splɪntə(r)] **1** *n* scheggia *f* **2** *v/i* scheggiarsi
'**splin•ter group** gruppo *m* scissionista
split [splɪt] **1** *n in leather* strappo *m*; *in wood* crepa *f*; (*disagreement*) spaccatura *f*; (*division*, *share*) divisione *f* **2** *v/t* (*pret & pp* ***split***) *leather* strappare; *wood*, *logs* spaccare; (*cause disagreement in*) spaccare; (*divide*) dividere **3** *v/i* (*pret & pp* ***split***) *of leather* strapparsi; *of wood* spaccarsi; (*disagree*) spaccarsi
◆ **split up** *v/i of couple* separarsi
split per•son'al•i•ty PSYCH sdoppiamento *m* della personalità
split•ting ['splɪtɪŋ] *adj*: ***splitting headache*** feroce mal *m inv* di testa
splut•ter ['splʌtə(r)] *v/i* farfugliare
spoil [spɔɪl] *v/t child* viziare; *surprise*, *party* rovinare
'**spoil•sport** F guastafeste *m/f*
spoilt [spɔɪlt] *adj child* viziato; ***be spoilt for choice*** avere (solo) l'imbarazzo della scelta
spoke[1] [spəʊk] *of wheel* raggio *m*
spoke[2] [spəʊk] *pret* → ***speak***
spo•ken ['spəʊkən] *pp* → ***speak***
spokes•man ['spəʊksmən] portavoce *m*
spokes•per•son ['spəʊkspɜːsən] portavoce *m/f*
spokes•wom•an ['spəʊkswʊmən] portavoce *f*
sponge [spʌndʒ] *n* spugna *f*
◆ **sponge off / on** *v/t* F vivere alle spalle di
'**sponge cake** pan *m inv* di Spagna
spong•er ['spʌndʒə(r)] F scroccone *m*, -a *f*
spon•sor ['spɒnsə(r)] **1** *n for immigration* garante *m/f inv*; *for membership* socio *m*, -a *f* garante; *of TV programme*, *sports event*, *for fundraising* sponsor *m inv* **2** *v/t for immigration*, *membership* garantire per; *TV programme*, *sports event* sponsorizzare
spon•sor•ship ['spɒnsəʃɪp] sponsorizzazione *f*
spon•ta•ne•ous [spɒn'teɪnɪəs] *adj* spontaneo
spon•ta•ne•ous•ly [spɒn'teɪnɪəslɪ] *adv* spontaneamente
spook•y ['spuːkɪ] *adj* F sinistro
spool [spuːl] *n* bobina *f*
spoon [spuːn] *n* cucchiaio *m*
'**spoon•feed** *v/t* (*pret & pp* ***-fed***) *fig* scodellare la pappa a
spoon•ful ['spuːnfʊl] cucchiaio *f*
spo•rad•ic [spə'rædɪk] *adj* sporadico
sport [spɔːt] *n* sport *m inv*
sport•ing ['spɔːtɪŋ] *adj* sportivo; ***a sporting gesture*** un gesto sportivo
'**sports car** [spɔːts] auto *f inv* sportiva
'**sports cen•ter** *Am*, '**sports cen•tre** *indoor* palazzetto *m* dello sport
'**sports jack•et** giacca *f* sportiva
'**sports•man** sportivo *m*
'**sports med•i•cine** medicina *f* dello sport
'**sports news** *nsg* notizie *fpl* sportive
'**sports page** pagina *f* dello sport
'**sports•wear** abbigliamento *m* sportivo
'**sports•wom•an** sportiva *f*
sport•y ['spɔːtɪ] *adj* sportivo
spot[1] [spɒt] (*pimple*) brufolo *m*; *caused by measles etc* foruncolo *m*; *part of pattern* pois *m inv*; ***a spot of …*** (*a little*) un po' di …
spot[2] [spɒt] (*place*) posticino *m*; ***on the spot*** (*in the place in question*) sul posto; (*immediately*) immediatamente; ***put s.o. on the spot*** mettere in difficoltà qu
spot[3] [spɒt] *v/t* (*pret & pp* ***-ted***) (*notice*) notare; (*identify*) trovare
spot 'check *n* controllo *m* casuale
spot•less ['spɒtlɪs] *adj* pulitissimo
'**spot•light** *n* faretto *m*
spot•ted ['spɒtɪd] *adj fabric* a pois
spot•ty ['spɒtɪ] *adj with pimples* brufoloso
spouse [spaʊs] *fml* coniuge *m/f*
spout [spaʊt] **1** *n* beccuccio *m* **2** *v/i of liquid* sgorgare **3** *v/t* F: ***spout nonsense*** ciarlare
sprain [spreɪn] **1** *n* slogatura *f* **2** *v/t* slogarsi
sprang [spræŋ] *pret* → ***spring***
sprawl [sprɔːl] *v/i* stravaccarsi; *of city* estendersi; ***send s.o. sprawling*** *of punch* mandare qu a gambe all'aria
sprawl•ing ['sprɔːlɪŋ] *adj city*, *suburbs* tentacolare
spray [spreɪ] **1** *n of sea water*, *from fountain* spruzzi *mpl*; *for hair* lacca *f*; (*container*) spray *m inv* **2** *v/t* spruzzare; ***spray s.o./sth with sth*** spruzzare qu / qc di qc
'**spray•gun** pistola *f* a spruzzo
spread [spred] **1** *n of disease*, *religion etc* diffusione *f*; F *big meal* banchetto *m*; **2** *v/t* (*pret & pp* ***spread***) (*lay*) stendere; *butter*, *jam* spalmare; *news*, *rumour*, *disease* diffondere; *arms*, *legs* allargare **3** *v/i* (*pret & pp* ***spread***) diffondersi; *of butter* spalmarsi
'**spread•sheet** COMPUT spreadsheet *m inv*
spree [spriː] F: ***go*** (***out***) ***on a spree*** *having fun* andare a far baldoria; ***go on a***

shopping spree andare a fare spese folli
sprig [sprɪg] rametto *m*
spright•ly ['spraɪtlɪ] *adj* arzillo
spring[1] [sprɪŋ] *n season* primavera *f*
spring[2] [sprɪŋ] *n device* molla *f*
spring[3] [sprɪŋ] **1** *n* (*jump*) balzo *m*; (*stream*) sorgente *f* **2** *v/i* (*pret* ***sprang***, *pp* ***sprung***) scattare; ***spring from*** derivare da
'spring•board trampolino *m*
spring 'chick•en *hum*: ***she's no spring chicken*** non è più una ragazzina
spring-'clean•ing pulizie *fpl* di primavera
spring 'on•ion cipollotto *m*
'spring•time primavera *f*
spring•y ['sprɪŋɪ] *adj mattress*, *walk* molleggiato; *ground* morbido; *material* elastico
sprin•kle ['sprɪŋkl] *v/t* spruzzare; ***sprinkle sth with*** cospargere qc di
sprin•kler ['sprɪŋklə(r)] *for garden* irrigatore *m*; *in ceiling* sprinkler *m inv*
sprint [sprɪnt] **1** *n*: scatto *m*; ***the 100 metres sprint*** i cento metri piani **2** *v/i* fare uno scatto
sprint•er ['sprɪntə(r)] SP velocista *m/f*
sprout [spraʊt] **1** *v/i of seed* spuntare **2** *n* germoglio *m*; (***Brussels***) ***sprouts*** cavolini *mpl* di Bruxelles
spruce [spruːs] *adj* curato
sprung [sprʌŋ] *pp* → ***spring***
spun [spʌn] *pret & pp* → ***spin***
spry [spraɪ] *adj* arzillo
spud [spʌd] F patata *f*
spur [spɜː(r)] *n* sperone *m*; *fig* sprone *m*; ***on the spur of the moment*** su due piedi
◆ **spur on** *v/t* (*pret & pp* ***-red***) (*encourage*) spronare
spurt [spɜːt] **1** *n*: ***put on a spurt*** *in race* fare uno scatto; *in work* accelerare il ritmo **2** *v/i of liquid* sprizzare
sput•ter ['spʌtə(r)] *v/i of engine* scoppiettare
spy [spaɪ] **1** *n* spia *f* **2** *v/i* (*pret & pp* ***-ied***) fare la spia **3** *v/t* (*pret & pp* ***-ied***) F scorgere
◆ **spy on** *v/t* spiare
squab•ble ['skwɒbl] **1** *n* bisticcio *m* **2** *v/i* bisticciare
squal•id ['skwɒlɪd] *adj* squallido
squal•or ['skwɒlə(r)] squallore *m*
squan•der ['skwɒndə(r)] *v/t money* dilapidare
square [skweə(r)] **1** *adj in shape* quadrato; ***square mile*** miglio quadrato **2** *n shape* quadrato *m*; *in town* piazza *f*; *in board game* casella *f*; MATH quadrato *m*; ***we're back to square one*** siamo punto e a capo
◆ **square up** *v/i* (*settle up*) fare i conti
square 'root radice *f* quadrata
squash[1] [skwɒʃ] *n vegetable* zucca *f*
squash[2] [skwɒʃ] *n game* squash *m inv*
squash[3] [skwɒʃ] **1** *v/t* (*crush*) schiacciare **2** *n*: ***orange / lemon squash*** sciroppo *m* d'arancia / limone
squat [skwɒt] **1** *adj in shape* tozzo **2** *v/i* (*pret & pp* ***-ted***) (*sit*) accovacciarsi; *illegally* occupare abusivamente
squat•ter ['skwɒtə(r)] squatter *m inv*, occupante *m/f* abusivo, -a
squeak [skwiːk] **1** *n of mouse* squittio *m*; *of hinge* cigolio *m* **2** *v/i of mouse* squittire; *of hinge* cigolare; *of shoes* scricchiolare
squeak•y ['skwiːkɪ] *adj hinge* cigolante; *shoes* scricchiolante; *voice* stridulo
squeak•y clean *adj* F pulito
squeal [skwiːl] **1** *n of pain*, *laughter* strillo *m*; *of brakes* stridore *m* **2** *v/i* strillare; *of brakes* stridere
squeam•ish ['skwiːmɪʃ] *adj*: ***be squeamish*** avere lo stomaco delicato
squeeze [skwiːz] **1** *n of hand*, *shoulder* stretta *f*; ***a squeeze of lemon*** una spruzzata di limone **2** *v/t hand* stringere; *orange*, *lemon* spremere; *sponge* strizzare
◆ **squeeze in** **1** *v/i to a car etc* infilarsi **2** *v/t* infilare
◆ **squeeze up** *v/i to make space* stringersi
squid [skwɪd] calamaro *m*
squint [skwɪnt] *n* strabismo *m*
squirm [skwɜːm] *v/i* (*wriggle*) contorcersi; ***squirm*** (***with embarrassment***) morire di vergogna
squir•rel ['skwɪrəl] scoiattolo *m*
squirt [skwɜːt] **1** *v/t* spruzzare **2** *n* F *pej* microbo *m* F
St *abbr* (= ***saint***) S. (= santo *m*, santa *f*); (= ***street***) v. (= via *f*)
stab [stæb] **1** *n* F: ***have a stab at doing sth*** provare a fare qc **2** *v/t* (*pret & pp* ***-bed***) *person* accoltellare
sta•bil•i•ty [stə'bɪlətɪ] stabilità *f inv*
sta•bil•ize ['steɪbɪlaɪz] **1** *v/t prices*, *boat* stabilizzare **2** *v/i of prices etc* stabilizzarsi
sta•ble[1] ['steɪbl] *n building* stalla *f*; *establishment* scuderia *f*
sta•ble[2] ['steɪbl] *adj* stabile
stack [stæk] **1** *n* (*pile*) pila *f*; (*smokestack*) ciminiera *f*; ***stacks of*** F un sacco di F **2** *v/t* mettere in pila
sta•di•um ['steɪdɪəm] stadio *m*
staff [stɑːf] *npl* (*employees*) personale *msg*; (*teachers*) corpo *m* insegnante
'staff•room *in school* sala *f* professori
stag [stæg] cervo *m*
stage[1] [steɪdʒ] *in life*, *project etc* fase *f*; *of*

journey tappa *f*
stage² [steɪdʒ] **1** *n* THEA palcoscenico *m*; ***go on the stage*** *become actor* fare teatro **2** *v/t play* mettere in scena; *demonstration* organizzare
stage 'door ingresso *m* degli artisti
'stage fright attacco *m* di panico
'stage hand macchinista *m/f*
stag•ger ['stægə(r)] **1** *v/i* barcollare **2** *v/t* (*amaze*) sbalordire; *holidays, breaks etc* scaglionare
stag•ger•ing ['stægərɪŋ] *adj* sbalorditivo
stag•nant ['stægnənt] *adj also fig* stagnante
stag•nate [stæg'neɪt] *v/i of person, mind* vegetare
stag•na•tion [stæg'neɪʃn] ristagno *m*
'stag par•ty (festa *f* di) addio *m* al celibato
stain [steɪn] **1** *n* (*dirty mark*) macchia *f*; *for wood* mordente *m* **2** *v/t* (*dirty*) macchiare; *wood* dare il mordente a **3** *v/i of wine etc* macchiare; *of fabric* macchiarsi
stained-glass 'win•dow [steɪnd] vetrata *f* colorata
stain•less 'steel ['steɪnlɪs] **1** *n* acciaio *m* inossidabile **2** *adj* d'acciaio inossidabile
'stain re•mov•er smacchiatore *m*
stair [steə(r)] scalino *m*; ***the stairs*** le scale
'stair•case scala *f*
stake [steɪk] **1** *n of wood* paletto *m*; *when gambling* puntata *f*; (*investment*) partecipazione *f*; ***be at stake*** essere in gioco **2** *v/t tree* puntellare; *money* puntare
stale [steɪl] *adj bread* raffermo; *air* viziato; *fig*: *news* vecchio
'stale•mate *in chess* stallo *m*; *fig* punto *m* morto
stalk¹ [stɔːk] *n of fruit* picciolo *m*; *of plant* gambo *m*
stalk² [stɔːk] *v/t animal* seguire; *person* perseguitare (con telefonate, lettere ecc)
stalk•er ['stɔːkə(r)] *persona f che perseguita qualcun altro con telefonate, lettere ecc*
stall¹ [stɔːl] *n at market* bancarella *f*; *for cow, horse* box *m inv*
stall² [stɔːl] **1** *v/i of engine* spegnersi; *of vehicle* fermarsi; (*play for time*) temporeggiare **2** *v/t engine* far spegnere; *people* trattenere
stal•li•on ['stæljən] stallone *m*
stalls [stɔːlz] *npl* platea *f*
stal•wart ['stɔːlwət] *adj support, supporter* fedele
stam•i•na ['stæmɪnə] resistenza *f*
stam•mer ['stæmə(r)] **1** *n* balbuzie *f* **2** *v/i* balbettare
stamp¹ [stæmp] **1** *n for letter* francobollo *m*; (*date stamp etc*) timbro *m* **2** *v/t letter* affrancare; *document, passport* timbrare; ***stamped addressed envelope*** busta *f* affrancata per la risposta
stamp² [stæmp] *v/t*: ***stamp one's feet*** pestare i piedi
'stamp collec•ting filatelia *f*
'stamp col•lec•tion collezione *f* di francobolli
'stamp col•lec•tor collezionista *m/f* di francobolli
◆ **stamp out** *v/t* (*eradicate*) eliminare
stam•pede [stæm'piːd] **1** *n of cattle etc* fuga *f* precipitosa; *of people* fuggi-fuggi *m inv* **2** *v/i of cattle etc* fuggire precipitosamente; *of people* precipitarsi
stance [stɑːns] (*position*) presa *f* di posizione
stand [stænd] **1** *n at exhibition* stand *m inv*; (*witness stand*) banco *m* dei testimoni; (*support, base*) base *f*; ***take the stand*** LAW testimoniare **2** *v/i* (*pret & pp* ***stood***) (*be situated*: *of person*) stare; *of object, building* trovarsi; *as opposed to sit* stare in piedi; (*rise*) alzarsi in piedi; ***stand still*** stare fermo; ***where do you stand on the issue?*** qual è la tua posizione sulla questione? **3** *v/t* (*pret & pp* ***stood***) (*tolerate*) sopportare; (*put*) mettere; ***you don't stand a chance*** non hai alcuna probabilità; ***stand s.o. a drink*** offrire da bere a qu; ***stand one's ground*** non mollare, tenere duro
◆ **stand back** *v/i* farsi indietro
◆ **stand by 1** *v/i* (*not take action*) stare a guardare; (*be ready*) tenersi pronto **2** *v/t person* stare al fianco di; *decision* mantenere
◆ **stand down** *v/i* (*withdraw*) ritirarsi
◆ **stand for** *v/t* (*tolerate*) tollerare; (*mean*) significare; *freedom etc* rappresentare
◆ **stand in for** *v/t* sostituire
◆ **stand out** *v/i* spiccare; *of person, building* distinguersi
◆ **stand up 1** *v/i* alzarsi in piedi **2** *v/t* F *on date* dare buca a F
◆ **stand up for** *v/t* difendere
◆ **stand up to** *v/t* far fronte a
stan•dard ['stændəd] **1** *adj* (*usual*) comune; *model, size* standard *inv* **2** *n* (*level*) livello *m*; (*expectation*) aspettativa *f*; TECH standard *m inv*; ***moral standards*** principi *mpl*; ***be / not be up to standard*** essere / non essere di buona qualità
stan•dard•ize ['stændədaɪz] *v/t* standardizzare
'stan•dard lamp *Br* lampada *f* a stelo
stan•dard of 'li•ving tenore *m* di vita

S

'stand•by *ticket* biglietto *m* stand-by; ***on standby*** *at airport* in lista d'attesa; *of troops etc* pronto

'stand•by pas•sen•ger passeggero *m*, -a *f* in lista d'attesa

stand•ing ['stændɪŋ] *n in society etc* posizione *f*; (*repute*) reputazione *f*; ***a musician of some standing*** un musicista di una certa importanza; ***a friendship of long standing*** un'amicizia di lunga durata

stand•ing 'or•der FIN ordine *m* permanente

'stand•ing room posto *m* in piedi

stand•off•ish [stænd'ɒfɪʃ] *adj* scostante

'stand•point punto *m* di vista

'stand•still: ***be at a standstill*** essere fermo; ***bring to a standstill*** fermare

stank [stæŋk] *pret* → ***stink***

stan•za ['stænzə] *of poem* stanza *f*

sta•ple[1] ['steɪpl] *n* (*foodstuff*) alimento *m* base

sta•ple[2] ['steɪpl] **1** *n* (*fastener*) graffa *f* **2** *v/t* pinzare

sta•ple 'di•et alimentazione *f* base

'sta•ple gun pistola *f* sparachiodi

sta•pler ['steɪplə(r)] pinzatrice *f*

star [stɑː(r)] **1** *n in sky* stella *f*; *fig* star *f inv* **2** *v/t* (*pret & pp* ***-red***): ***a film starring Julia Roberts*** un film interpretato da Julia Roberts **3** *v/i* (*pret & pp* ***-red***): ***he starred in Psycho*** è il protagonista di Psycho

'star•board *adj* a tribordo

starch [stɑːʧ] *in foodstuff* amido *m*

stare [steə(r)] **1** *n* sguardo *m* fisso **2** *v/i* fissare; ***stare at*** fissare

'star•fish stella *f* di mare

stark [stɑːk] **1** *adj landscape* desolato; *colour scheme* austero; *reminder, contrast etc* brusco **2** *adv*: ***stark naked*** completamente nudo

star•ling ['stɑːlɪŋ] storno *m*

star•ry ['stɑːrɪ] *adj night* stellato

star•ry-eyed [stɑːrɪ'aɪd]] *adj person* idealista

start [stɑːt] **1** *n* (*beginning*) inizio *m*; ***make a start on sth*** iniziare qc; ***get off to a good / bad start*** *in marriage, career* cominciare bene / male; ***from the start*** dall'inizio; ***well, it's a start!*** è pur sempre un inizio! **2** *v/i* iniziare, cominciare; *of engine, car* partire; ***starting from tomorrow*** a partire da domani **3** *v/t* cominciare; *engine, car* mettere in moto; *business* mettere su; ***start to do sth, start doing sth*** cominciare a fare qc

start•er ['stɑːtə(r)] *part of meal* antipasto *m*; *of car* motorino *m* d'avviamento; *in race* starter *m inv*

'starting point punto *m* di partenza

'starting sal•a•ry stipendio *m* iniziale

start•le ['stɑːtl] *v/t* far trasalire

start•ling ['stɑːtlɪŋ] *adj* sorprendente

starv•a•tion [stɑː'veɪʃn] fame *f*

starve [stɑːv] *v/i* soffrire la fame; ***starve to death*** morire di fame; ***I'm starving*** F sto morendo di fame

state[1] [steɪt] **1** *n of car, house etc* stato *m*, condizione *f*; (*country*) stato *m*; ***the States*** gli Stati Uniti; ***be in a state*** essere agitato **2** *adj* di stato; *school* statale; *banquet etc* ufficiale

state[2] [steɪt] *v/t* dichiarare

'State De•part•ment *in USA* Ministero *m* degli Esteri

state•ment ['steɪtmənt] *to police* deposizione *f*; (*announcement*) dichiarazione *f*; (*bank statement*) estratto *m* conto

state of e'mer•gen•cy stato *m* d'emergenza

state-of-the-'art *adj* allo stato dell'arte

states•man ['steɪtsmən] statista *m*

state 'vis•it visita *f* ufficiale

stat•ic (e•lec'tric•i•ty) ['stætɪk] elettricità *f inv* statica

sta•tion ['steɪʃn] **1** *n* stazione *f* **2** *v/t guard etc* disporre; ***be stationed at*** *of soldier* essere di stanza in/a

sta•tion•a•ry ['steɪʃnərɪ] *adj* fermo

sta•tion•er's ['steɪʃənərz] cartoleria *f*

sta•tion•er•y ['steɪʃənərɪ] articoli *mpl* di cancelleria

sta•tion 'man•ag•er dirigente *m* della stazione ferroviaria

'sta•tion wag•on *Am* giardiniera *f*

sta•tis•ti•cal [stə'tɪstɪkl] *adj* statistico

sta•tis•ti•cal•ly [stə'tɪstɪklɪ] *adv* statisticamente

sta•tis•ti•cian [stætɪs'tɪʃn] esperto *m*, -a *f* di statistica

sta•tis•tics [stə'tɪstɪks] *nsg science* statistica *f*; *npl figures* statistiche *fpl*

stat•ue ['stætjuː] statua *f*

sta•tus ['steɪtəs] posizione *f*

'sta•tus bar COMPUT barra *f* di stato

'sta•tus sym•bol status symbol *m inv*

stat•ute ['stætjuːt] statuto *m*

staunch [stɔːnʧ] *adj* leale

stay [steɪ] **1** *n* soggiorno *m* **2** *v/i in a place* stare; *in a condition* restare; ***stay in a hotel*** stare in albergo; ***stay right there!*** non ti muovere!; ***stay put*** non muoversi

◆ **stay away** *v/i* stare alla larga

◆ **stay away from** *v/t* stare alla larga da

◆ **stay behind** *v/i* rimanere

◆ **stay up** *v/i* (*not go to bed*) rimanere alzato

S

stead•i•ly ['stedılı] *adv improve etc* costantemente; *look* fisso
stead•y ['stedı] **1** *adj voice, hands* fermo; *job, boyfriend* fisso; *beat* regolare; *improvement, decline, progress* costante **2** *adv*: ***be going steady*** fare coppia fissa; ***steady on!*** calma! **3** *v/t* (*pret & pp* **-ied**) *bookcase etc* rendere saldo; ***steady o.s.*** ritrovare l'equilibrio
steak [steık] bistecca *f*, carne *f* (di manzo)
steal [stiːl] (*pret* **stole**, *pp* **stolen**) **1** *v/t money etc* rubare **2** *v/i* (*be a thief*) rubare; ***steal in / out*** (*move quietly*) entrare / uscire furtivamente
stea / lth•y ['stelθı] *adj* furtivo
steam [stiːm] **1** *n* vapore *m* **2** *v/t food* cuocere al vapore
◆ **steam up** **1** *v/i of window* appannarsi **2** *v/t*: ***be steamed up*** F *angry* essere furibondo
steam•er ['stiːmə(r)] *for cooking* vaporiera *f*
'**steam i•ron** ferro *m* a vapore
steel [stiːl] **1** *n* acciaio *m* **2** *adj* d'acciaio
'**steel•work•er** operaio *m* di acciaieria
'**steel•works** acciaieria *f*
steep[1] [stiːp] *adj hill etc* ripido; F *prices* alto; ***that's a bit steep*** *expensive* è un po' caro
steep[2] [stiːp] *v/t* (*soak*) lasciare a bagno
stee•ple ['stiːpl] campanile *m*
'**stee•ple•chase** *in athletics* corsa *f* ad ostacoli
steep•ly ['stiːplı] *adv*: ***climb steeply*** *of path* salire ripidamente; *of prices* salire vertiginosamente
steer[1] [stıə(r)] *n animal* manzo *m*
steer[2] [stıə(r)] *v/t car, boat* manovrare; *person* guidare; *conversation* spostare
steer•ing ['stıərıŋ] *of motor vehicle* sterzo *m*
'**steer•ing wheel** volante *m*
stem[1] [stem] *n of plant, glass* stelo *m*; *of word* radice *f*
◆ **stem from** *v/t* derivare da
stem[2] [stem] *v/t* (*pret & pp* **-med**) (*block*) arginare
stench [stentʃ] puzzo *m*
sten•cil ['stensıl] **1** *n* stencil *m inv* **2** *v/t* (*pret & pp* **-led**, *Am* **-ed**) *pattern* disegnare con lo stencil
step [step] **1** *n* (*pace*) passo *m*; (*stair*) gradino *m*; (*measure*) provvedimento *m*; ***step by step*** poco a poco **2** *v/i* (*pret & pp* **-ped**) mettere il piede; ***step into / out of*** salire in / scendere da
◆ **step down** *v/i from post etc* dimettersi
◆ **step forward** *v/i also fig* farsi avanti
◆ **step up** *v/t* F (*increase*) aumentare
'**step•broth•er** fratellastro *m*
'**step•daugh•ter** figliastra *f*
'**step•fa•ther** patrigno *m*
'**step•lad•der** scala *f* a libretto
'**step•moth•er** matrigna *f*
step•ping stone ['stepıŋ] pietra *f* di un guado; *fig* trampolino *m* di lancio
'**step•sis•ter** sorellastra *f*
'**step•son** figliastro *m*
ster•e•o ['sterıəʊ] *n* (*sound system*) stereo *m inv*
ster•e•o•type ['sterıəʊtaıp] *n* stereotipo *m*
ster•ile ['steraıl] *adj* sterile
ster•il•ize ['sterəlaız] *v/t* sterilizzare
ster•ling ['stɜːlıŋ] *n* FIN sterlina *f*
stern[1] [stɜːn] *adj* severo
stern[2] [stɜːn] *n* NAUT poppa *f*
stern•ly ['stɜːnlı] *adv* severamente
ster•oids ['sterɔıdz] *npl* anabolizzanti *mpl*
steth•o•scope ['steθəskəʊp] fonendoscopio *m*
stew [stjuː] *n* spezzatino *m*
stew•ard ['stjuːəd] *n on plane, ship* steward *m inv*; *at demonstration, meeting* membro *m* del servizio d'ordine
stew•ard•ess [stjuːə'des] *on plane, ship* hostess *f inv*
stewed [stjuːd] *adj apples, plums* cotto
stick[1] [stık] *n wood* rametto *m*; (*walking stick*) bastone *m*; ***out in the sticks*** F a casa del diavolo F
stick[2] [stık] (*pret & pp* **stuck**) **1** *v/t with adhesive* attaccare; *needle, knife* conficcare; F (*put*) mettere **2** *v/i* (*jam*) bloccarsi; (*adhere*) attaccarsi
◆ **stick around** *v/i* F restare
◆ **stick by** *v/t* F: ***stick by s.o.*** rimanere al fianco di qu
◆ **stick out** *v/i* (*protrude*) sporgere; (*be noticeable*) spiccare
◆ **stick to** *v/t* F (*keep to*) attenersi a; F (*follow*) seguire
◆ **stick together** *v/i* F restare uniti
◆ **stick up** *v/t poster, leaflet* affiggere
◆ **stick up for** *v/t* F difendere
stick•er ['stıkə(r)] adesivo *m*
'**stick•ing plas•ter** cerotto *m*
'**stick-in-the-mud** F abitudinario *m*, -a *f*
stick•y ['stıkı] *adj hands, surface* appiccicoso; *label* adesivo
stiff [stıf] **1** *adj brush, cardboard, leather* rigido; *muscle, body* anchilosato; *mixture, paste* sodo; *in manner* freddo; *drink, competition* forte; *fine* salato **2** *adv*: ***be scared stiff*** F essere spaventato a morte F; ***be bored stiff*** F essere annoiato a morte F

S

stiff•en ['stɪfn] *v/i* irrigidirsi
◆ **stiffen up** *v/i of muscle* anchilosarsi
stiff•ly ['stɪflɪ] *adv* rigidamente; *fig* freddamente
stiff•ness ['stɪfnəs] *of muscles* indolenzimento *m*; *of material* rigidità *f*; *fig*: *of manner* freddezza *f*
sti•fle ['staɪfl] *v/t also fig* soffocare
sti•fling ['staɪflɪŋ] *adj* soffocante
stig•ma ['stɪgmə] vergogna *f*
sti•let•tos [stɪ'letəʊz] *npl* (*shoes*) scarpe *fpl* con tacco a spillo
still[1] [stɪl] **1** *adj* (*motionless*) immobile; *without wind* senza vento; *drink* non gas(s)ato; ***it was very still outside*** tutto era calmo fuori **2** *adv*: ***keep / stand still!*** stai fermo!
still[2] [stɪl] *adv* (*yet*) ancora; (*nevertheless*) comunque; ***she still hasn't finished*** non ha ancora finito; ***they are still my parents*** sono pur sempre i miei genitori; ***still more*** (*even more*) ancora più
'**still•born** *adj* nato morto
still 'life natura *f* morta
stilt•ed ['stɪltɪd] *adj* poco naturale
stilts [stɪlts] *npl* trampoli *mpl*
stim•u•lant ['stɪmjʊlənt] stimolante *m*
stim•u•late ['stɪmjʊleɪt] *v/t* stimolare
stim•u•lat•ing ['stɪmjʊleɪtɪŋ] *adj* stimolante
stim•u•la•tion [stɪmjʊ'leɪʃn] stimolazione *f*
stim•u•lus ['stɪmjʊləs] (*incentive*) stimolo *m*
sting [stɪŋ] **1** *n from bee* puntura *f*; *actual organ* pungiglione *m*; *from jellyfish* pizzico *m* **2** *v/t* (*pret & pp* **stung**) *of bee* pungere; *of jellyfish* pizzicare **3** *v/i* (*pret & pp* **stung**) *of eyes*, *scratch* bruciare
sting•ing ['stɪŋɪŋ] *adj remark*, *criticism* pungente
sting•y ['stɪndʒɪ] *adj* F tirchio F
stink [stɪŋk] **1** *n* (*bad smell*) puzza *f*; F (*fuss*) putiferio *m* F; ***kick up a stink*** F fare un casino F **2** *v/i* (*pret* **stank**, *pp* **stunk**) (*smell bad*) puzzare; F (*be very bad*) fare schifo F
stint [stɪnt] *n* periodo *m*; ***do a stint in the army*** arruolarsi nell'esercito per un periodo; ***do you want to do a stint now?*** vuoi darmi il cambio?
◆ **stint on** *v/t* F lesinare su
stip•u•late ['stɪpjʊleɪt] *v/t & v/i* stabilire
stip•u•la•tion [stɪpjʊ'leɪʃn] condizione *f*
stir [stɜː(r)] **1** *n*: ***give the soup a stir*** mescolare la minestra; ***cause a stir*** fare scalpore **2** *v/t* (*pret & pp* **-red**) mescolare **3** *v/i* (*pret & pp* **-red**) *of sleeping person* muoversi
◆ **stir up** *v/t* fomentare
'**stir-fry** *v/t* (*pret & pp* **-ied**) saltare (in padella)
stir•ring ['stɜːrɪŋ] *adj music*, *speech* commovente
stitch [stɪtʃ] **1** *n in sewing* punto *m*; *in knitting* maglia *f*; ***stitches*** MED punti *mpl* (di sutura); ***be in stitches*** *laughing* ridere a crepapelle; ***have a stitch*** avere una fitta al fianco **2** *v/t sew* cucire
◆ **stitch up** *v/t wound* suturare
stitch•ing ['stɪtʃɪŋ] (*stitches*) cucitura *f*
stock [stɒk] **1** *n* (*reserves*) provvista *f*; COM: *of store* stock *m inv*; *animals* bestiame *m*; FIN titoli *mpl*; *for soup etc* brodo *m*; ***in stock / out of stock*** disponibile / esaurito; ***take stock*** fare il punto **2** *v/t* COM vendere
◆ **stock up on** *v/t* fare provvista di
'**stock•brok•er** agente *m/f* di cambio
'**stock cube** dado *m* (da brodo)
'**stock ex•change** borsa *f* valori
stock•ing ['stɒkɪŋ] calza *f* (da donna)
stock•ist ['stɒkɪst] rivenditore *m*
'**stock mar•ket** mercato *m* azionario
stock•mar•ket 'crash crollo *m* del mercato azionario
'**stock•pile 1** *n of food*, *weapons* scorta *f* **2** *v/t* fare scorta di
'**stock•room** magazzino *m*
stock-'still *adv*: ***stand stock-still*** stare immobile
'**stock•tak•ing** inventario *m*
'**stock•y** ['stɒkɪ] *adj* tarchiato
stodg•y ['stɒdʒɪ] *adj food* pesante
sto•i•cal ['stəʊɪkl] *adj* stoico
sto•i•cism ['stəʊɪsɪzm] stoicismo *m*
stole [stəʊl] *pret* → ***steal***
stol•en ['stəʊlən] *pp* → ***steal***
stom•ach ['stʌmək] **1** *n* stomaco *m*; (*abdomen*) pancia *f* **2** *v/t* (*tolerate*) sopportare
'**stom•ach•ache** mal *m* di stomaco
stone [stəʊn] *n material* pietra *f*; (*pebble*) sasso *m*; (*precious stone*) pietra *f* preziosa; *in fruit* nocciolo *m*
stoned [stəʊnd] *adj* F *on drugs* fatto F
stone-'deaf *adj* sordo (come una campana)
'**stone•wall** *v/i* F menare il can per l'aia
ston•y ['stəʊnɪ] *adj ground*, *path* sassoso
stood [stʊd] *pret & pp* → ***stand***
stool [stuːl] *seat* sgabello *m*
stoop [stuːp] **1** *n*: ***walk with a stoop*** camminare con la schiena curva **2** *v/i* (*bend down*) chinarsi; (*have bent back*) essere curvo
stop [stɒp] **1** *n for train*, *bus* fermata *f*; ***come to a stop*** fermarsi; ***put a stop to*** met-

S

tere fine a **2** *v/t* (*pret & pp* **-ped**) (*put an end to*) mettere fine a; (*prevent*) fermare; (*cease*) smettere; *person*, *car*, *bus* fermare; ***it has stopped raining*** ha smesso di piovere; ***I stopped her from leaving*** le ho impedito di andar via; ***stop a cheque*** bloccare un assegno **3** *v/i* (*pret & pp* **-ped**) (*come to a halt*) fermarsi; *of rain*, *noise* smettere

◆ **stop by** *v/i* (*visit*) passare

◆ **stop off** *v/i* fermarsi, fare sosta; *at post office* passare a

◆ **stop over** *v/i* fare sosta

◆ **stop up** *v/t sink* intasare

'**stop•gap** *person* tappabuchi *m/f inv*; *thing* soluzione *f* temporanea

'**stop•o•ver** *n* sosta *f*; *in air travel* scalo *m* intermedio

stop•per ['stɒpə(r)] tappo *m*

'**stop sign** (segnale *m* di) stop *m inv*

'**stop•watch** cronometro *m*

stor•age ['stɔːrɪdʒ]: ***put sth in storage*** mettere qc in magazzino; ***not much space for storage*** poco spazio per riporre la roba

'**stor•age ca•pac•i•ty** COMPUT capacità *f* di memoria

'**stor•age space** spazio *m* per riporre la roba

store [stɔː(r)] **1** *n large shop* negozio *m*; (*stock*) riserva *f*; (*storehouse*) deposito *m* **2** *v/t* tenere; COMPUT memorizzare

'**store•room** magazzino *m*

sto•rey ['stɔːrɪ] piano *m*

stork [stɔːk] cicogna *f*

storm [stɔːm] *n* tempesta *f*

'**storm warn•ing** avviso *m* di tempesta

storm•y ['stɔːmɪ] *adj also fig* tempestoso

sto•ry[1] ['stɔːrɪ] (*tale*) racconto *m*; (*account*) storia *f*; (*newspaper article*) articolo *m*; F (*lie*) bugia *f*

sto•ry[2] ['stɔːrɪ] *Am* → ***storey***

stout [staʊt] *adj person* robusto; *defender* tenace

stove [stəʊv] *for cooking* cucina *f*; *for heating* stufa *f*

stow [stəʊ] *v/t* riporre

◆ **stow away** *v/i* imbarcarsi clandestinamente

'**stow•a•way** *n* passeggero *m*, -a *f* clandestino, -a

straggler ['stræglə(r)] persona *f* che rimane indietro

straight [streɪt] **1** *adj line* retto; *hair*, *whisky* liscio; *back*, *knees* dritto; (*honest*, *direct*) onesto; (*tidy*) in ordine; (*conservative*) convenzionale; (*not homosexual*) etero; ***keep a straight face*** non ridere **2** *adv* (*in a straight line*) dritto; (*directly*, *immediately*) dritto, direttamente; (*clearly*: *think*) con chiarezza; ***stand up straight!*** stai dritto!; ***look s.o. straight in the eye*** guardare qu dritto negli occhi; ***go straight*** F *of criminal* rigare dritto; ***give it to me straight*** F dimmi francamente; ***straight ahead*** avanti dritto; ***carry straight on*** proseguire dritto; ***straight away, straight off*** immediatamente; ***straight out*** *say sth* chiaro e tondo

straight•en ['streɪtn] *v/t* raddrizzare

◆ **straighten out 1** *v/t situation* sistemare; F *person* mettere in riga F **2** *v/i of road* tornare diritto

◆ **straighten up** *v/i* raddrizzarsi

straight'for•ward *adj* (*honest*, *direct*) franco; (*simple*) semplice

strain[1] [streɪn] **1** *n physical* sforzo *m*; *mental* tensione *f* **2** *v/t* (*injure*) affaticare; *fig*: *finances*, *budget* gravare su

strain[2] [streɪn] *v/t vegetables* scolare; *oil*, *fat etc* filtrare

strain[3] [streɪn] *n of virus* ceppo *m*

strained [streɪnd] *adj* teso

strain•er ['streɪnə(r)] *for vegetables etc* colino *m*

strait [streɪt] GEOG stretto *m*

strait•laced [streɪt'leɪst] *adj* puritano

strand[1] [strænd] *n of wool*, *thread* filo *m*; *of hair* ciocca *f*

strand[2] [strænd] *v/t* piantare in asso F; ***be stranded*** essere bloccato

strange [streɪndʒ] *adj* (*odd*, *curious*) strano; (*unknown*, *foreign*) sconosciuto

strange•ly ['streɪndʒlɪ] *adv* (*oddly*) stranamente; ***strangely enough*** strano ma vero

strang•er ['streɪndʒə(r)] *person you don't know* sconosciuto *m*, -a *f*; ***I'm a stranger here myself*** non sono di queste parti

stran•gle ['stræŋgl] *v/t person* strangolare

strap [stræp] *n of bag* tracolla *f*; *of bra*, *dress* bretellina *f*, spallina *f*; *of watch* cinturino *m*; *of shoe* listino *m*

◆ **strap in** *v/t* (*pret & pp* **-ped**) *with seatbelt* allacciare la cintura di sicurezza a

◆ **strap on** *v/t* allacciare

strap•less ['stræplɪs] *adj* senza spalline

stra•te•gic [strə'tiːdʒɪk] *adj* strategico

strat•e•gy ['strætədʒɪ] strategia *f*

straw[1] [strɔː] paglia *f*; ***that's the last straw!*** questa è la goccia che fa traboccare il vaso!

straw[2] [strɔː] *for drink* cannuccia *f*

straw•ber•ry ['strɔːbərɪ] fragola *f*

stray [streɪ] **1** *adj animal* randagio; *bullet* vagante **2** *n dog*, *cat* randagio *m* **3** *v/i of animal* smarrirsi; *of child* allontanarsi;

S

fig: *of eyes, thoughts* vagare
streak [striːk] *of dirt, paint* stria *f*; *fig*: *of nastiness etc* vena *f* **2** *v/i move quickly* sfrecciare **3** *v/t*: ***be streaked with*** essere striato di
streak•y ['striːkɪ] *adj* striato
stream [striːm] **1** *n* ruscello *m*; *fig*: *of people, complaints* fiume *m*; ***come on stream*** *of plant* entrare in attività; *of oil* arrivare **2** *v/i* riversarsi
stream•er ['striːmə(r)] stella *f* filante
'**stream•line** *v/t fig* snellire
'**stream•lined** *adj car, plane* aerodinamico; *fig*: *organization* snellito
street [striːt] strada *f*; *in address* via *f*
'**street•car** *Am* tram *m inv*
'**street•light** lampione *m*
'**street•light•ing** illuminazione *f* stradale
'**street value** *of drugs* valore *m* di mercato
'**street•walk•er** F passeggiatrice *f*
'**street•wise** *adj* scafato F
strength [streŋθ] *of person, wind, emotion, currency* forza *f*; (*strong point*) punto *m* forte
strength•en ['streŋθn] **1** *v/t* rinforzare **2** *v/i* consolidarsi
stren•u•ous ['strenjʊəs] *adj* faticoso
stren•u•ous•ly ['strenjʊəslɪ] *adv deny* recisamente
stress [stres] **1** *n* (*emphasis*) accento *m*; (*tension*) stress *m inv*; ***be under stress*** essere sotto pressione **2** *v/t syllable* accentare; *importance etc* sottolineare
stressed '**out** [strest] *adj* stressato
stress•ful ['stresfʊl] *adj* stressante
stretch [stretʃ] **1** *n of land, water* tratto *m*; ***at a stretch*** (*non-stop*) di fila **2** *adj fabric* elasticizzato **3** *v/t material* tendere; *small income* far bastare; ***stretch the rules*** F fare uno strappo (alla regola); ***he stretched out his hand*** allungò la mano; ***a job that stretches me*** un lavoro che mi impegna **4** *v/i to relax muscles* stirarsi; *to reach sth* allungarsi; (*spread*) estendersi; *of fabric*: *give* cedere; *of fabric*: *sag* allargarsi; ***stretch from X to Y*** (*extend*) estendersi da X a Y
stretch•er ['stretʃə(r)] barella *f*
strict [strɪkt] *adj person* severo; *instructions, rules* tassativo
strict•ly ['strɪktlɪ] *adv*: ***be brought up strictly*** ricevere un'educazione rigida; ***it is strictly forbidden*** è severamente proibito
strictness ['strɪktnəs] severità *f inv*
strid'den ['strɪdn] *pp* → ***stride***
stride [straɪd] **1** *n* falcata *f*; ***take sth in one's stride*** affrontare qc senza drammi; ***make great strides*** *fig* far passi da gigante **2** *v/i* (*pret* ***strode***, *pp* ***stridden***) procedere a grandi passi; ***he strode up to me*** avanzò verso di me
stri•dent ['straɪdnt] *adj* stridulo; *fig*: *demands* veemente
strike [straɪk] **1** *n of workers* sciopero *m*; *of oil* scoperta *f*; ***be on strike*** essere in sciopero; ***go on strike*** entrare in sciopero **2** *v/i* (*pret & pp* ***struck***) *of workers* scioperare; (*attack*) aggredire; *of disaster* colpire; *of clock* suonare **3** *v/t* (*pret & pp* ***struck***) (*hit*) colpire; *match* accendere (sfregando); *of idea, thought* venire in mente a; *oil* trovare; ***strike one's head against sth*** battere la testa contro qc; ***she struck me as being …*** mi ha dato l'impressione di essere …
◆ **strike out** *v/t* depennare
'**strike•break•er** crumiro *m*, -a *f*
strik•er ['straɪkə(r)] *person on strike* scioperante *m/f*; *in football* bomber *m inv*, cannoniere *m*, punta *f*
strik•ing ['straɪkɪŋ] *adj* (*marked*) marcato; (*eye-catching*) impressionante; (*attractive*) attraente; *colour* forte
string [strɪŋ] *n* (*cord*) spago *m*; *of violin, tennis racket* corda *f*; ***the strings*** MUS gli archi; ***pull strings*** esercitare la propria influenza; ***a string of*** (*series*) una serie di
◆ **string along 1** *v/i* (*pret & pp* ***strung***) F: ***do you mind if I string along?*** posso venire anch'io? **2** *v/t* (*pret & pp* ***strung***) F: ***string s.o. along*** menare qu per il naso
◆ **string up** *v/t* F impiccare
stringed '**in•stru•ment** [strɪŋd] strumento *m* ad arco
strin•gent ['strɪndʒnt] *adj* rigoroso
'**string play•er** suonatore *m*, -trice *f* di strumento ad arco
strip [strɪp] **1** *n* striscia *f*; (*comic strip*) fumetto *m*; *of soccer player* divisa *f* **2** *v/t* (*pret & pp* ***-ped***) (*remove*) staccare; *bed* disfare; (*undress*) spogliare; ***strip s.o. of sth*** spogliare qu di qc **3** *v/i* (*pret & pp* ***-ped***) (*undress*) spogliarsi; *of stripper* fare lo spogliarello
'**strip club** locale *m* di spogliarelli
stripe [straɪp] striscia *f*; *indicating rank* gallone *m*
striped [straɪpt] *adj* a strisce
'**strip joint** F → ***strip club***
strip•per ['strɪpə(r)] spogliarellista *f*; ***male stripper*** spogliarellista *m*
'**strip show** spogliarello *m*
strip'tease spogliarello *m*
strive [straɪv] *v/i* (*pret* ***strove***, *pp* ***striven***): ***strive to do sth*** sforzarsi di fare qc; ***strive for sth*** lottare per (ottenere) qc

S

striv•en ['strɪvn] *pp* → ***strive***
strobe (light) [strəʊb] luce *f* stroboscopica
strode [strəʊd] *pret* → ***stride***
stroke [strəʊk] **1** *n* MED ictus *m inv*; *when painting* pennellata *f*; *in swimming* bracciata *f*; *style of swimming* stile *m* di nuoto; ***stroke of luck*** colpo di fortuna; ***she never does a stroke*** (***of work***) non fa mai un bel niente **2** *v/t* accarezzare
stroll [strəʊl] **1** *n* passeggiata *f*; ***go for a stroll*** fare una passeggiata **2** *v/i* fare due passi; ***she strolled back to the office*** tornò in ufficio in tutta calma
strong [strɒŋ] *adj person*, *wind*, *drink*, *currency* forte; *structure* resistente; *candidate* valido; *taste*, *smell* intenso; *views*, *beliefs* fermo; *arguments* convincente; *objections* energico; ***strong support*** largo consenso
'**strong•hold** *fig* roccaforte *f*
strong•ly ['strɒŋlɪ] *adv believe*, *object* fermamente; *built* solidamente; ***feel strongly about sth*** avere molto a cuore qc
strong-mind•ed [strɒŋ'maɪndɪd] *adj* risoluto
'**strong point** (punto *m*) forte *m*
'**strong•room** camera *f* blindata
strong-'willed [strɒŋ'wɪld] *adj* deciso
strove [strəʊv] *pret* → ***strive***
struck [strʌk] *pret & pp* → ***strike***
struc•tur•al ['strʌktʃərl] *adj* strutturale
struc•ture ['strʌktʃə(r)] **1** *n something built* costruzione *f*; *of novel*, *society etc* struttura *f* **2** *v/t* strutturare
strug•gle ['strʌgl] **1** *n* (*fight*) colluttazione *f*; *fig* lotta *f*; (*hard time*) fatica *f* **2** *v/i with a person* lottare; (*have a hard time*) faticare; ***struggle to do sth*** faticare a fare qc
strum [strʌm] *v/t* (*pret & pp* ***-med***) strimpellare
strung [strʌŋ] *pret & pp* → ***string***
strut [strʌt] *v/i* (*pret & pp* ***-ted***) camminare impettito
stub [stʌb] **1** *n of cigarette* mozzicone *m*; *of cheque*, *ticket* matrice *f* **2** *v/t* (*pret & pp* ***-bed***): ***stub one's toe*** urtare il dito del piede
◆ **stub out** *v/t* spegnere
stub•ble ['stʌbl] *on man's face* barba *f* ispida
stub•born ['stʌbən] *adj person* testardo; *defence*, *refusal*, *denial* ostinato
stub•by ['stʌbɪ] *adj* tozzo
stuck [stʌk] **1** *pret & pp* → ***stick*** **2** *adj* F: ***be stuck on s.o.*** essere cotto di qu F
stuck-'up *adj* F presuntuoso
stu•dent ['stju:dnt] studente *m*, -essa *f*
stu•dent 'nurse infermiere *m*, -a *f* tirocinante
stu•dent 'teach•er insegnante *m/f* tirocinante
stu•di•o ['stju:dɪəʊ] studio *m*; (*recording studio*) sala *f* di registrazione
stu•di•ous ['stju:dɪəs] *adj* studioso
stud•y ['stʌdɪ] **1** *n* studio *m* **2** *v/t & v/i* (*pret & pp* ***-ied***) studiare
stuff [stʌf] **1** *n* roba *f* **2** *v/t turkey* farcire; ***stuff sth into sth*** ficcare qc in qc
stuff•ing ['stʌfɪŋ] *for turkey* farcia *f*; *in chair*, *teddy bear* imbottitura *f*
stuff•y ['stʌfɪ] *adj room* mal ventilato; *person* inquadrato
stum•ble ['stʌmbl] *v/i* inciampare
◆ **stumble across** *v/t* trovare per caso
◆ **stumble over** *v/t* inciampare in; *words* incespicare in
stum•bling-block ['stʌmblɪŋ] *fig* scoglio *m*
stump [stʌmp] **1** *n of tree* ceppo *m* **2** *v/t of question*, *questioner* sconcertare
◆ **stump up** *v/t* F sganciare F
stun [stʌn] *v/t* (*pret & pp* ***-ned***) *of blow* stordire; *of news* sbalordire
stung [stʌŋ] *pret & pp* → ***sting***
stunk [stʌŋk] *pp* → ***stink***
stun•ning ['stʌnɪŋ] *adj* (*amazing*) sbalorditivo; (*very beautiful*) splendido
stunt [stʌnt] *n for publicity* trovata *f* pubblicitaria; *in film* acrobazia *f*
'**stunt•man** *in film* cascatore *m*
stu•pe•fy ['stju:pɪfaɪ] *v/t* (*pret & pp* ***-ied***) sbalordire
stu•pen•dous [stju:'pendəs] *adj* (*marvellous*) fantastico; *mistake* enorme
stu•pid ['stju:pɪd] *adj* stupido
stu•pid•i•ty [stju:'pɪdətɪ] stupidità *f inv*
stu•por ['stju:pə(r)] stordimento *m*; ***in a drunken stupor*** stordito dall'alcool
stur•dy ['stɜ:dɪ] *adj* robusto
stut•ter ['stʌtə(r)] *v/i* balbettare
sty [staɪ] *for pig* porcile *m*
style [staɪl] *n* stile *m*; (*fashion*) moda *f*; (*fashionable elegance*) classe *f*; (*hairstyle*) pettinatura *f*; ***go out of style*** passare di moda
styl•ish ['staɪlɪʃ] *adj* elegante
styl•ist ['staɪlɪst] (*hair stylist*) parrucchiere *m*, -a *f*
sub•com•mit•tee ['sʌbkəmɪtɪ] sottocommissione *f*
sub•con•scious [sʌb'kɒnʃəs] *adj* subconscio; ***the subconscious*** (***mind***) il subconscio
sub•con•scious•ly [sʌb'kɒnʃəslɪ] *adv* inconsciamente
sub•con•tract [sʌbkən'trakt] *v/t* subap-

paltare
sub•con•trac•tor [sʌbkən'træktə(r)] subappaltatore *m*, -trice *f*
sub•di•vide [sʌbdɪ'vaɪd] *v/t* suddividere
sub•due [səb'dju:] *v/t* sottomettere
sub•dued [səb'dju:d] *adj person, voice* pacato; *light, colour* soffuso
sub•head•ing ['sʌbhedɪŋ] sottotitolo *m*
sub•hu•man [sʌb'hju:mən] *adj* subumano
sub•ject ['sʌbdʒɪkt] **1** *n of monarch* suddito *m*, -a *f*; (*topic*) argomento *m*; EDU materia *f*; GRAM soggetto *m*; ***change the subject*** cambiare argomento **2** *adj*: ***be subject to*** essere soggetto a; ***subject to availability*** nei limiti della disponibilità **3** *v/t* [səb'dʒekt] sottoporre; ***be subjected to criticism*** essere criticato
sub•jec•tive [səb'dʒektɪv] *adj* soggettivo
sub•junc•tive [səb'dʒʌŋktɪv] GRAM congiuntivo *m*
sub•let ['sʌblet] *v/t* (*pret & pp* ***-let***) subaffittare
sub•ma'chine gun mitra *m*
sub•ma•rine ['sʌbməri:n] sottomarino *m*, sommergibile *m*
sub•merge [səb'mɜ:dʒ] **1** *v/t* sommergere **2** *v/i of submarine* immergersi
sub•mis•sion [səb'mɪʃn] (*surrender*) sottomissione *f*; *request to committee etc* richiesta *f*
sub•mis•sive [səb'mɪsɪv] *adj* sottomesso
sub•mit [səb'mɪt] (*pret & pp* ***-ted***) **1** *v/t plan, proposal* presentare **2** *v/i* sottomettersi
sub•or•di•nate [sə'bɔ:dɪnət] **1** *adj employee, position* subalterno **2** *n* subalterno *m*, -a *f*
sub•poe•na [sə'pi:nə] **1** *n* citazione *f* **2** *v/t person* citare in giudizio
◆ **subscribe to** [səb'skraɪb] *v/t magazine etc* abbonarsi a; *theory* condividere
sub•scrib•er [səb'skraɪbə(r)] *to magazine* abbonato *m*, -a *f*
sub•scrip•tion [səb'skrɪpʃn] abbonamento *m*
sub•se•quent ['sʌbsɪkwənt] *adj* successivo
sub•se•quent•ly ['sʌbsɪkwəntlɪ] *adv* successivamente
sub•side [səb'saɪd] *v/i of waters, winds* calare; *of building* sprofondare; *of fears, panic* calmarsi
sub•sid•i•a•ry [səb'sɪdɪərɪ] *n* filiale *f*
sub•si•dize ['sʌbsɪdaɪz] *v/t* sovvenzionare
sub•si•dy ['sʌbsɪdɪ] sovvenzione *f*
◆ **subsist on** *v/t* vivere di
sub•sis•tence farm•ing [səb'sɪstəns] agricoltura *f* di sussistenza
sub'sis•tence lev•el livello *m* minimo di vita
sub•stance ['sʌbstəns] (*matter*) sostanza *f*
sub•stan•dard [sʌb'stændəd] *adj* scadente
sub•stan•tial [səb'stænʃl] *adj* considerevole; *meal* sostanzioso
sub•stan•tial•ly [səb'stænʃlɪ] *adv* (*considerably*) considerevolmente; (*in essence*) sostanzialmente
sub•stan•ti•ate [səb'stænʃɪeɪt] *v/t* comprovare
sub•stan•tive [səb'stæntɪv] *adj* sostanziale
sub•sti•tute ['sʌbstɪtju:t] **1** *n for person* sostituto *m*, -a *f*; *for commodity* alternativa *f*; SP riserva *f* **2** *v/t*: ***substitute X for Y*** sostituire Y con X **3** *v/i*: ***substitute for s.o.*** sostituire qu
sub•sti•tu•tion [sʌbsũtɪ'tju:ʃn] (*act*) sostituzione *f*; ***make a substitution*** SP fare una sostituzione
sub•ti•tle ['sʌbtaɪtl] *n* sottotitolo *m*
sub•tle ['sʌtl] *adj hint, difference* sottile; *flavour* delicato
sub•tract [səb'trækt] *v/t number* sottrarre
sub•urb ['sʌbɜ:b] sobborgo *m*; ***the suburbs*** la periferia
sub•ur•ban [sə'bɜ:bən] *adj* di periferia
sub•ur•bi•a [sə'bɜ:bɪə] periferia *f*
sub•ver•sive [səb'vɜ:sɪv] **1** *adj* sovversivo **2** *n* sovversivo *m*, -a *f*
sub•way ['sʌbweɪ] *Br* (*passageway*) sottopassaggio *m*; *Am* metropolitana *f*
sub'ze•ro *adj*: ***subzero temperatures*** temperature sottozero
suc•ceed [sək'si:d] **1** *v/i* (*be successful*) avere successo; *to throne* succedere; ***succeed in doing sth*** riuscire a fare qc **2** *v/t* (*come after*) succedere a
suc•ceed•ing [sək'si:dɪŋ] *adj* successivo
suc•cess [sək'ses] successo *m*; ***be a success*** avere successo
suc•cess•ful [sək'sesfʊl] *adj person* affermato; *marriage, party* riuscito; ***be successful*** riuscire; ***he's very successful*** è arrivato
suc•cess•ful•ly [sək'sesflɪ] *adv* con successo; ***we successfully completed ...*** siamo riusciti a portare a termine ...
suc•ces•sion [sək'seʃn] (*sequence*) sfilza *f*; *to the throne* successione *f*; ***in succession*** di seguito
suc•ces•sive [sək'sesɪv] *adj* successivo; ***three successive days*** tre giorni di seguito
suc•ces•sor [sək'sesə(r)] successore *m*

S

suc•cinct [sək'sɪŋkt] *adj* succinto
suc•cu•lent ['ʃʌkjʊlənt] succulento
suc•cumb [sə'kʌm] *v/i* (*give in*) cedere; ***succumb to temptation*** cedere alla tentazione
such [sʌʧ] **1** *adj* (*of that kind*) del genere; ***such a*** (*so much of a*) un / una tale; ***such as*** come; ***such people*** gente del genere; ***he made such a fuss*** ha fatto una tale scenata; ***there is no such word as …*** la parola … non esiste **2** *adv* così; ***such nice people*** gente così simpatica; ***as such*** (*in that capacity*) in quanto tale; ***as such*** (*in itself*) di per sé
suck [sʌk] **1** *v/t lollipop etc* succhiare; ***suck one's thumb*** succhiarsi il dito **2** *v/i*: ***it sucks*** P (*is awful*) fa schifo P
◆ **suck up** *v/t* assorbire; *dust* aspirare
◆ **suck up to** *v/t* F leccare i piedi a F
suck•er ['sʌkə(r)] F *person* pollo F
suc•tion ['sʌkʃn] aspirazione *f*
sud•den ['sʌdn] *adj* improvviso; ***all of a sudden*** all'improvviso
sud•den•ly ['sʌdnlɪ] *adv* improvvisamente
suds [sʌdz] *npl* (*soap suds*) schiuma *fsg*
sue [suː] **1** *v/t* fare causa a **2** *v/i* fare causa
suede [sweɪd] *n* pelle *f* scamosciata
suf•fer ['sʌfə(r)] **1** *v/i* (*be in great pain*) soffrire; (*deteriorate*) risentirne; ***be suffering from*** avere; ***suffer from*** soffrire di **2** *v/t loss*, *setback* subire
suf•fer•ing ['sʌfərɪŋ] *n* sofferenza *f*
suf•fi•cient [sə'fɪʃnt] *adj* sufficiente
suf•fi•cient•ly [sə'fɪʃntlɪ] *adv* abbastanza
suf•fo•cate ['sʌfəkeɪt] *v/t & v/i* soffocare
suf•fo•ca•tion [sʌfə'keɪʃn] soffocamento *m*
sug•ar ['ʃʊgə(r)] **1** *n* zucchero *m* **2** *v/t* zuccherare
'**sug•ar bowl** zuccheriera *f*
sug•gest [sə'dʒest] *v/t* proporre, suggerire; ***I suggest that we stop now*** propongo di fermarci ora
sug•ges•tion [sə'dʒesʧən] *n* proposta *f*, suggerimento *m*
su•i•cide ['suːɪsaɪd] *n* suicidio *m*; ***commit suicide*** suicidarsi
'**su•i•cide pact** *n* patto *m* suicida
suit [suːt] **1** *n for man* vestito *m*, completo *m*; *for woman* tailleur *m inv*; *in cards* seme *m* **2** *v/t of clothes*, *colour* stare bene a; ***suit yourself!*** F fai come ti pare!; ***be suited for sth*** essere fatto per qc
sui•ta•ble ['suːtəbl] *adj* adatto
sui•ta•bly ['suːtəblɪ] *adv* adeguatamente
'**suit•case** valigia *f*
suite [swiːt] *of rooms* suite *f inv*; *of furniture* divano *m* e poltrone *fpl* coordinati; MUS suite *f inv*
sul•fur *etc Am* → ***sulphur*** *etc*
sulk [sʌlk] *v/i* fare il broncio
sulk•y ['sʌlkɪ] *adj* imbronciato
sul•len ['sʌlən] *adj* crucciato
sul•phur ['sʌlfə(r)] zolfo *m*
sul•phur•ic acid [sʌl'fjuːrɪk] acido *m* solforico
sul•try ['sʌltrɪ] *adj climate* afoso; *sexually* sensuale
sum [sʌm] somma *f*; *in arithmetic* addizione *f*; ***a large sum of money*** una forte somma di denaro; ***that's the sum total of his efforts*** quello è tutto quello che ha fatto
◆ **sum up** (*pret & pp* **-med**) **1** *v/t* (*summarize*) riassumere; (*assess*) valutare **2** *v/i* LAW riepilogare
sum•mar•ize ['sʌməraɪz] *v/t* riassumere
sum•ma•ry ['sʌmərɪ] *n* riassunto *m*
sum•mer ['sʌmə(r)] estate *f*
sum•mit ['sʌmɪt] *of mountain* vetta *f*; POL summit *m inv*
'**sum•mit meet•ing** → ***summit***
sum•mon ['sʌmən] *v/t* convocare
◆ **summon up** *v/t strength* raccogliere
sum•mons ['sʌmənz] *nsg* LAW citazione *f*
sump [sʌmp] *for oil* coppa *f* dell'olio
sun [sʌn] sole *m*; ***in the sun*** al sole; ***out of the sun*** all'ombra; ***he has had too much sun*** ha preso troppo sole
'**sun•bathe** *v/i* prendere il sole
'**sun•bed** lettino *m* solare
'**sun•block** protezione *f* solare totale
'**sun•burn** scottatura *f*
'**sun•burnt** *adj* scottato
Sun•day ['sʌndeɪ] domenica *f*
'**sun•dial** meridiana *f*
sun•dries ['sʌndrɪz] *npl* varie *fpl*
sung [sʌŋ] *pp* → ***sing***
'**sun•glass•es** *npl* occhiali *mpl* da sole
sunk [sʌŋk] *pp* → ***sink***
sunk•en ['sʌnkn] *adj cheeks* incavato
sun•ny ['sʌnɪ] *adj day* di sole; *spot* soleggiato; *disposition* allegro; ***it's sunny*** c'è il sole
'**sun•rise** alba *f*
'**sun•set** tramonto *m*
'**sun•shade** ombrellone *m*
'**sun•shine** (luce *f* del) sole *m*
'**sun•stroke** colpo *m* di sole
'**sun•tan** abbronzatura *f*; ***get a suntan*** abbronzarsi
su•per ['suːpə(r)] *adj* F fantastico
su•perb [sʊ'pɜːb] *adj* magnifico
su•per•fi•cial [suːpə'fɪʃl] *adj* superficiale
su•per•flu•ous [sʊ'pɜːflʊəs] *adj* superfluo
su•per'hu•man *adj efforts* sovrumano

su•per•in•tend•ent [suːpərɪn'tendənt] *of police* commissario *m*
su•pe•ri•or [suː'pɪərɪə(r)] **1** *adj* (*better*) superiore **2** *n in organization, society* superiore *m*
su•per•la•tive [suː'pɜːlətɪv] **1** *adj* (*superb*) eccellente **2** *n* GRAM superlativo *m*
'**su•per•mar•ket** supermarket *m inv*, supermercato *m*
su•per'nat•u•ral **1** *adj powers* soprannaturale **2** *n*: ***the supernatural*** il soprannaturale
'**su•per•pow•er** POL superpotenza *f*
su•per•son•ic [suːpə'sɒnɪk] *adj flight, aircraft* supersonico
su•per•sti•tion [suːpə'stɪʃn] *n* superstizione *f*
su•per•sti•tious [suːpə'stɪʃəs] *adj person* superstizioso
su•per•vise ['suːpəvaɪz] *v/t* supervisionare
su•per•vi•sor ['suːpəvaɪzə(r)] *at work* supervisore *m*
sup•per ['sʌpə(r)] cena *f*
sup•ple ['sʌpl] *adj person, limbs* snodato; *material* flessibile
sup•ple•ment ['sʌplɪmənt] supplemento *m*
sup•pli•er [sə'plaɪə(r)] *n* COM fornitore *m*
sup•ply [sə'plaɪ] **1** *n* fornitura *f*; ***supply and demand*** domanda e offerta; ***supplies*** rifornimenti **2** *v/t* (*pret & pp* ***-ied***) *goods* fornire; ***supply s.o. with sth*** fornire qc a qu; ***be supplied with*** *fitted with etc* essere dotato di
sup•port [sə'pɔːt] **1** *n for structure* supporto *m*; (*backing*) sostegno *m* **2** *v/t building, structure* sostenere; *financially* mantenere; (*back*) sostenere; *football team* fare il tifo per
sup•port•er [sə'pɔːtə(r)] sostenitore *m*, -trice *f*; *of football team etc* tifoso *m*, -a *f*
sup•port•ive [sə'pɔːtɪv] *adj*: ***be supportive towards s.o.*** dare il proprio appoggio a qu
sup•pose [sə'pəʊz] *v/t* (*imagine*) supporre; ***I suppose so*** suppongo di sì; ***it is supposed to …*** (*is meant to*) dovrebbe …; (*is said to*) dicono che …; ***you are not supposed to …*** (*not allowed to*) non dovresti …
sup•pos•ed•ly [sə'pəʊzɪdlɪ] *adv* presumibilmente
sup•pos•i•to•ry [sə'pɒzɪtrɪ] MED supposta *f*
sup•press [sə'pres] *v/t rebellion etc* reprimere
sup•pres•sion [sə'preʃn] repressione *f*
su•prem•a•cy [suː'preməsɪ] supremazia *f*
su•preme [suː'priːm] *adj* supremo
sur•charge ['sɜːtʃɑːdʒ] *for travel* sovrapprezzo *m*; *for mail* soprattassa *f*
sure [ʃʊə(r)] **1** *adj* sicuro; ***I'm sure*** sono sicuro; ***be sure about sth*** essere sicuro di qc; ***make sure that …*** assicurarsi che … **2** *adv* certamente; ***sure enough*** infatti; ***sure!*** F certo!
sure•ly ['ʃʊəlɪ] *adv* certamente; (*gladly*) volentieri; ***surely that's not right!*** non può essere!; ***oh, surely you've heard of him*** non puoi non conoscerlo
sur•e•ty ['ʃʊərətɪ] *for loan* cauzione *f*
surf ['sɜːf] **1** *n on sea* spuma *f* **2** *v/t the Net* navigare
sur•face ['sɜːfɪs] **1** *n of table, object,water* superficie *f*; ***on the surface*** *fig* superficialmente, in apparenza **2** *v/i of swimmer, submarine* risalire in superficie, riemergere; (*appear*) farsi vivo
'**sur•face mail** posta *f* ordinaria
'**surf•board** tavola *f* da surf
surf•er ['sɜːfə(r)] *on sea* surfista *m/f*
surf•ing ['sɜːfɪŋ] surf *m inv*; ***go surfing*** fare surf
surge [sɜːdʒ] *n in electric current* sovratensione *f* transitoria; *in demand* impennata *f*; *of interest, financial growth etc* aumento *m*
◆ **surge forward** *v/i of crowd* buttarsi avanti
sur•geon ['sɜːdʒən] chirurgo *m*
sur•ge•ry ['sɜːdʒərɪ] intervento *m* chirurgico; *Br: place of work* ambulatorio *m*; ***undergo surgery*** sottoporsi a un intervento chirurgico; ***surgery hours*** orario *m* d'ambulatorio
sur•gi•cal ['sɜːdʒɪkl] *adj* chirurgico
sur•gi•cal•ly ['sɜːdʒɪklɪ] *adv* chirurgicamente
sur•ly ['sɜːlɪ] *adj* scontroso
sur•mount [sə'maʊnt] *v/t difficulties* sormontare
sur•name ['sɜːneɪm] cognome *m*
sur•pass [sə'pɑːs] *v/t* superare
sur•plus ['sɜːpləs] **1** *n* surplus *m inv* **2** *adj* eccedente
sur•prise [sə'praɪz] **1** *n* sorpresa *f*; ***it'll come as no surprise to hear that …*** non ti sorprenderà sapere che … **2** *v/t* sorprendere; ***be surprised*** essere sorpreso; ***look surprised*** avere l'aria sorpresa
sur•pris•ing [sə'praɪzɪŋ] *adj* sorprendente
sur•pris•ing•ly [sə'praɪzɪŋlɪ] *adv* sorprendentemente
sur•ren•der [sə'rendə(r)] **1** *v/i of army* arrendersi **2** *v/t weapons etc* consegnare **3** *n*

S

resa *f*
sur•ro•gate 'moth•er ['sʌrəgət] madre *f* biologica
sur•round [sə'raʊnd] **1** *v/t* circondare; ***be surrounded by ...*** essere circondato da ... **2** *n of picture etc* bordo *m*
sur•round•ing [sə'raʊndɪŋ] *adj* circostante
sur•round•ings [sə'raʊndɪŋz] *npl of village etc* dintorni *mpl*; *fig* ambiente *m*
sur•vey ['sɜːveɪ] **1** *n of modern literature etc* quadro *m* generale; *of building* perizia *f*; *poll* indagine *f* **2** *v/t* [sə'veɪ] (*look at*) osservare; *building* periziare
sur•vey•or [sə'veɪə(r)] perito *m*
sur•viv•al [sə'vaɪvl] sopravvivenza *f*
sur•vive [sə'vaɪv] **1** *v/i* sopravvivere; ***how are you? – I'm surviving*** come stai? - si tira avanti; ***his two surviving daughters*** le due figlie ancora in vita **2** *v/t* sopravvivere a
sur•vi•vor [sə'vaɪvə(r)] superstite *m/f*; ***he's a survivor*** *fig* se la cava sempre
sus•cep•ti•ble [sə'septəbl] *adj emotionally* impressionabile; ***be susceptible to the cold / heat*** soffrire il freddo / caldo
sus•pect ['sʌspekt] **1** *n* indiziato *m*, -a *f* **2** *v/t* [sə'spekt] *person* sospettare; (*suppose*) supporre
sus•pected [sə'spektɪd] *adj murderer* presunto; *cause, heart attack etc* sospetto
sus•pend [sə'spend] *v/t* (*hang*) sospendere; *from office, duties* sospendere
sus•pend•ers [sə'spendəz] *npl* giarrettiere *fpl*; *Am* (*braces*) bretelle *fpl*
sus•pense [sə'spens] suspense *f inv*
sus•pen•sion [sə'spenʃn] sospensione *f*
sus'pen•sion bridge ponte *m* sospeso
sus•pi•cion [sə'spɪʃn] sospetto *m*
sus•pi•cious [sə'spɪʃəs] *adj causing suspicion* sospetto; *feeling suspicion* sospettoso; ***be suspicious of*** sospettare di
sus•tain [sə'steɪn] *v/t* sostenere
sus•tain•able [sə'steɪnəbl] *adj* sostenibile
swab [swɒb] tampone *m*
swag•ger ['swægə(r)] *n* andatura *f* spavalda
swal•low[1] ['swɒləʊ] **1** *v/t liquid, food* inghiottire **2** *v/i* inghiottire
swal•low[2] ['swɒləʊ] *n bird* rondine *f*
swam [swæm] *pret* → ***swim***
swamp [swɒmp] **1** *n* palude *f* **2** *v/t*: ***be swampped with*** essere sommerso da
swamp•y ['swɒmpɪ] *adj ground* paludoso
swan [swɒn] cigno *m*
swap [swɒp] (*pret & pp* **-ped**) **1** *v/t*: ***swap sth for sth*** scambiare qc con qc **2** *v/i* fare scambio
swarm [swɔːm] **1** *n of bees* sciame *m* **2** *v/i*: ***the town was swarming with ...*** la città brulicava di ...
swar•thy ['swɔːðɪ] *adj face, complexion* scuro
swat [swɒt] *v/t* (*pret & pp* **-ted**) *insect, fly* schiacciare
sway [sweɪ] **1** *n* (*influence, power*) influenza *f* **2** *v/i* barcollare
swear [sweə(r)] (*pret* ***swore***, *pp* ***sworn***) **1** *v/i* (*use swearword*) imprecare; ***swear at s.o.*** dire parolacce a qu **2** *v/t* (*promise*) giurare; LAW, *on oath* giurare
◆ **swear in** *v/t*: ***the witness was sworn in*** il testimone ha prestato giuramento
'swear•word parolaccia *f*
sweat [swet] **1** *n* sudore *m*; ***covered in sweat*** tutto sudato **2** *v/i* sudare
'sweat band fascia *f* asciugasudore
sweat•er ['swetə(r)] maglione *m*
'sweat•shirt felpa *f*
sweat•y ['swetɪ] *adj hands* sudato; *smell* di sudore
Swede [swiːd] svedese *m/f*
Swe•den ['swiːdn] Svezia *f*
Swe•dish ['swiːdɪʃ] **1** *adj* svedese **2** *n* svedese *m*
sweep [swiːp] **1** *v/t* (*pret & pp* ***swept***) *floor, leaves* spazzare **2** *n* (*long curve*) curva *f*
◆ **sweep up** *v/t mess, crumbs* spazzare via
sweep•ing ['swiːpɪŋ] *adj changes* radicale; ***a sweeping statement*** una generalizzazione
sweet [swiːt] **1** *adj taste, tea* dolce; F (*kind*) gentile; F (*cute*) carino **2** *n* caramella *f*; (*dessert*) dolce *m*
sweet and 'sour *adj* agrodolce
'sweet•corn mais *m inv*
sweet•en ['swiːtn] *v/t drink, food* zuccherare
sweet•en•er ['swiːtnə(r)] *for drink* dolcificante *m*
'sweet•heart innamorato *m*, -a *f*
swell [swel] **1** *v/i of wound, limb* gonfiarsi **2** *n of the sea* mare *m* lungo
swell•ing ['swelɪŋ] *n* MED gonfiore *m*
swel•ter•ing ['sweltərɪŋ] *adj heat, day* afoso, soffocante
swept [swept] *pret & pp* → ***sweep***
swerve [swɜːv] *v/i of driver, car* sterzare (bruscamente)
swift [swɪft] *adj* rapido
swim [swɪm] **1** *v/i* (*pret* ***swam***, *pp* ***swum***) nuotare; ***go swimming*** andare a nuotare; ***my head is swimming*** mi gira la testa **2** *n* nuotata *f*; ***go for a swim*** andare a nuotare
swim•mer ['swɪmə(r)] nuotatore *m*, -trice *f*

swim•ming ['swɪmɪŋ] nuoto *m*
'**swim•ming baths** *npl* piscina *f* pubblica
'**swim•ming cos•tume** costume *m* da bagno
'**swim•ming pool** piscina *f*
swin•dle ['swɪndl] **1** *n* truffa *f* **2** *v/t* truffare; ***swindle s.o. out of sth*** estorcere qc a qu (con l'inganno)
swine [swaɪn] F *person* mascalzone *m*
swing [swɪŋ] **1** *n of pendulum etc* oscillazione *f*; *for child* altalena *f*; ***a swing to the left*** una svolta verso la sinistra **2** *v/t* (*pret & pp* ***swung***) far dondolare; ***swing one's hips*** ancheggiare **3** *v/i* (*pret & pp* ***swung***) dondolare; (*turn*) girare; *of public opinion etc* indirizzarsi
swing-'door porta *f* a vento
Swiss [swɪs] **1** *adj* svizzero **2** *n person* svizzero *m*, -a *f*; ***the Swiss*** gli svizzeri
switch [swɪʧ] **1** *n for light* interruttore *m*; (*change*) cambiamento *m* **2** *v/t* (*change*) cambiare **3** *v/i* (*change*) cambiare; ***switch to*** passare a
◆ **switch off** *v/t* spegnere
◆ **switch on** *v/t* accendere
'**switch•board** centralino *m*
'**switch•o•ver** *to new system* passaggio *m*
Swit•zer•land ['swɪtsələnd] Svizzera *f*
swiv•el ['swɪvl] *v/i* (*pret & pp* ***-led***, *Am* ***-ed***) *of chair, monitor* girarsi
swol•len ['swəʊlən] *adj* gonfio
swoop [swu:p] *v/i of bird* scendere in picchiata
◆ **swoop down on** *v/t prey* scendere in picchiata su
◆ **swoop on** *v/t of police etc* piombare su
sword [sɔ:d] spada *f*
swore [swɔ:(r)] *pret* → ***swear***
sworn [swɔ:n] *pp* → ***swear***
swum [swʌm] *pp* → ***swim***
swung [swʌŋ] *pret & pp* → ***swing***
syc•a•more ['sɪkəmɔ:] sicomoro *m*
syl•la•ble ['sɪləbl] sillaba *f*
syl•la•bus ['sɪləbəs] programma *m*
sym•bol ['sɪmbəl] simbolo *m*
sym•bol•ic [sɪm'bɒlɪk] *adj* simbolico
sym•bol•ism ['sɪmbəlɪzm] simbolismo *m*
sym•bol•ist ['sɪmbəlɪst] simbolista *m/f*
sym•bol•ize ['sɪmbəlaɪz] *v/t* simboleggiare
sym•met•ri•c(al) [sɪ'metrɪkl] *adj* simmetrico
sym•me•try ['sɪmətrɪ] simmetria *f*
sym•pa•thet•ic [sɪmpə'θetɪk] *adj* (*showing pity*) compassionevole; (*understanding*) comprensivo; ***be sympathetic towards an idea*** simpatizzare per un'idea
◆ **sympathize with** ['sɪmpəθaɪz] *v/t person, views* capire
sym•pa•thiz•er ['sɪmpəθaɪzə(r)] *n* POL simpatizzante *m/f*
sym•pa•thy ['sɪmpəθɪ] *n* (*pity*) compassione *f*; (*understanding*) comprensione *f*; ***don't expect any sympathy from me!*** non venire a lamentarti da me!
sym•pho•ny ['sɪmfənɪ] sinfonia *f*
'**sym•pho•ny or•ches•tra** orchestra *f* sinfonica
symp•tom ['sɪmptəm] *also fig* sintomo *m*
symp•to•mat•ic [sɪmptə'mætɪk] *adj*: ***be symptomatic of*** *fig* essere sintomatico di
syn•chro•nize ['sɪŋkrənaɪz] *v/t* sincronizzare
syn•o•nym ['sɪnənɪm] sinonimo *m*
sy•non•y•mous [sɪ'nɒnɪməs] *adj* sinonimo; ***be synonymous with*** *fig* essere sinonimo di
syn•tax ['sɪntæks] sintassi *f inv*
syn•the•siz•er ['sɪnθəsaɪzə(r)] MUS sintetizzatore *m*
syn•thet•ic [sɪn'θetɪk] *adj* sintetico
syph•i•lis ['sɪfɪlɪs] sifilide *f*
Syr•i•a ['sɪrɪə] Siria *f*
Syr•i•an ['sɪrɪən] **1** *adj* siriano **2** *n* siriano *m*, -a *f*
sy•ringe [sɪ'rɪndʒ] *n* siringa *f*
syr•up ['sɪrəp] sciroppo *m*
sys•tem ['sɪstəm] (*method*) metodo *m*, sistema *m*; (*orderliness*) ordine *m*; (*computer*) sistema *m*; ***the braking system*** il sistema di frenata; ***the digestive system*** l'apparato digerente
sys•te•mat•ic [sɪstə'mætɪk] *adj approach, person* sistematico
sys•tem•at•i•cal•ly [sɪstə'mætɪklɪ] *adv* sistematicamente
sys•tems 'an•a•lyst ['sɪstəmz] COMPUT analista *m/f* di sistemi

T

tab [tæb] *n for pulling* linguetta *f*; *in text* tabulazione *f*
ta•ble ['teɪbl] *n* tavolo *m*; *of figures* tabella *f*, tavola *f*; ***sit at the table*** sedersi a tavola
'**ta•ble•cloth** tovaglia *f*
'**table lamp** lampada *f* da tavolo
table of 'con•tents indice *m*
'**ta•ble•spoon** cucchiaio *m* da tavola
ta•blet ['tæblɪt] MED compressa *f*
'**ta•ble ten•nis** ping pong *m*
tab•loid ['tæblɔɪd] *n newspaper* quotidiano *m* formato tabloid; *pej* quotidiano *m* scandalistico
ta•boo [tə'buː] *adj* tabù *m inv*
ta•cit ['tæsɪt] *adj* tacito
ta•ci•turn ['tæsɪtɜːn] *adj* taciturno
tack [tæk] **1** *n* (*nail*) chiodino *m* **2** *v/t* (*sew*) imbastire **3** *v/i of yacht* virare di bordo
tack•le ['tækl] **1** *n* (*equipment*) attrezzatura *f*; SP: *in rugby* placcaggio *m*; *in football*, *hockey* contrasto *m* **2** *v/t in rugby* placcare; *in football*, *hockey* contrastare; *problem*, *intruder* affrontare
tack•y ['tækɪ] *adj paint* fresco; *glue* appiccicoso; F (*cheap*, *poor quality*) di cattivo gusto
tact [tækt] tatto *m*
tact•ful ['tæktfʊl] *adj* pieno di tatto
tact•ful•ly ['tæktflɪ] *adv* con grande tatto
tac•tic•al ['tæktɪkl] *adj* tattico
tac•tics ['tæktɪks] *npl* tattica *f*
tact•less ['tæktlɪs] *adj* privo di tatto
tad•pole ['tædpəʊl] girino *m*
tag [tæg] (*label*) etichetta *f*
◆ **tag along** *v/i* (*pret & pp* **-ged**) accodarsi
tail [teɪl] *n* coda *f*
'**tail•back** coda *f*
'**tail coat** frac *m inv*
'**tail light** luce *f* posteriore
tai•lor ['teɪlə(r)] sarto *m*, -a *f*
tai•lor-made [teɪlə'meɪd] *adj suit*, *solution* (fatto) su misura
'**tail•wind** vento *m* in coda
taint•ed ['teɪntɪd] *adj* contaminato
Tai•wan [taɪ'wɑːn] Taiwan *f*
Tai•wan•ese [taɪwə'niːz] **1** *adj* taiwanese **2** *n* taiwanese *m/f*; *dialect* taiwanese *m*
take [teɪk] *v/t* (*pret* **took**, *pp* **taken**) prendere; (*transport*) portare; (*accompany*) accompagnare; (*accept*: *money*, *gift*) accettare; *maths*, *French*, *photograph*, *exam*, *shower*, *stroll* fare; (*endure*) sopportare; (*require*) richiedere; ***how long does it take?*** quanto ci vuole?; ***I'll take it*** *when shopping* lo prendo
◆ **take after** *v/t* aver preso da
◆ **take apart** *v/t* (*dismantle*) smontare; F (*criticize*, *beat*) fare a pezzi F
◆ **take away** *v/t pain* far sparire; (*remove*: *object*) togliere; MATH sottrarre; ***take sth away from s.o.*** togliere qc a qu; ***to take away*** *food* da asporto
◆ **take back** *v/t* (*return*: *object*) riportare; (*receive back*) riprendere; *person* riaccompagnare; (*accept back*: *husband etc*) rimettersi insieme a; ***I take back what I said*** ritiro quello che ho detto; ***that takes me back*** *of music*, *thought etc* mi riporta al passato
◆ **take down** *v/t from shelf* tirare giù; *scaffolding* smontare; *trousers* allungare; (*write down*) annotare
◆ **take in** *v/t* (*take indoors*) portare dentro; (*give accommodation*) ospitare; (*make narrower*) stringere; (*deceive*) imbrogliare; (*include*) includere
◆ **take off 1** *v/t clothes*, *10%* togliere; (*mimic*) imitare; ***can you take a bit off here?*** *to barber* può spuntare un po' qui?; ***take a day / week off*** prendere un giorno / una settimana di ferie **2** *v/i of aeroplane* decollare; (*become popular*) far presa
◆ **take on** *v/t job* intraprendere; *staff* assumere
◆ **take out** *v/t from bag*, *pocket* tirare fuori; *stain*, *appendix*, *tooth*, *word* togliere; *money from bank* prelevare; *to dinner etc* portar fuori; *insurance policy* stipulare, fare; ***take it out on s.o.*** prendersela con qu
◆ **take over 1** *v/t company etc* assumere il controllo di; ***tourists take over the town*** i turisti invadono la città **2** *v/i of new management etc* assumere il controllo; (*do sth in s.o.'s place*) dare il cambio
◆ **take to** *v/t* (*like*) prendere in simpatia; (*form habit of*) prendere l'abitudine di; ***take to drink*** darsi all'alcol; ***he immediately took to the idea*** la nuova idea gli è piaciuta subito
◆ **take up** *v/t carpet etc* togliere; (*carry up*) portare sopra; (*shorten*: *dress etc*) accorciare; *judo*, *Spanish*, *new job* incominciare; *offer* accettare; *space*, *time* occupare; ***I'll take you up on your offer*** accetto la tua offerta

ˈ**take•away** *meal* piatto *m* da asporto; (*restaurant*) *ristorante m che prepara piatti da asporto*
ˈ**take-home pay** stipendio *m* in busta
ˈ**take•off** *of aeroplane* decollo *m*; (*impersonation*) imitazione *f*
ˈ**take•o•ver** COM rilevamento *m*
ˈ**take•o•ver bid** offerta *f* pubblica di acquisto, OPA *f*
tak•en [ˈteɪkən] *pp* → ***take***
ta•kings [ˈteɪkɪŋz] *npl* incassi *mpl*
tal•cum pow•der [ˈtælkəmpaʊdə(r)] talco *m*
tale [teɪl] storia *f*
tal•ent [ˈtælənt] talento *m*
tal•ent•ed [ˈtæləntɪd] *adj* pieno di talento; ***he's not very talented*** non ha molto talento
ˈ**tal•ent scout** talent scout *m/f inv*
talk [tɔːk] **1** *v/i* parlare; ***can I talk to …?*** posso parlare con …?; ***I'll talk to him about it*** gliene parlo **2** *v/t English etc* parlare; *business, politics* parlare di; ***talk s.o. into doing sth*** convincere qu a fare qc; ***talk s.o. out of doing sth*** dissuadere qu dal fare qc **3** *n* (*conversation*) conversazione *f*; (*lecture*) conferenza *f*; ***talks*** (*negotiations*) trattative *fpl*, negoziati *mpl*; ***he's all talk*** *pej* è tutto chiacchiere
◆ **talk back** *v/i* ribattere
◆ **talk down to** *v/t* trattare dall'alto in basso
◆ **talk over** *v/t* discutere di
talk•a•tive [ˈtɔːkətɪv] *adj* loquace
talk•ing-to [ˈtɔːkɪŋtuː] sgridata *f*
ˈ**talk show** talk show *m inv*
tall [tɔːl] *adj* alto
tall ˈ**or•der** bella impresa *f*
tall ˈ**sto•ry** baggianata *f*
tal•ly [ˈtælɪ] **1** *n* conto *m* **2** *v/i* (*pret & pp* ***-ied***) quadrare
◆ **tally with** *v/t* quadrare con
tame [teɪm] *adj animal* addomesticato; *joke etc* blando
◆ **tamper with** [ˈtæmpə(r)] *v/t* manomettere
tam•pon [ˈtæmpɒn] tampone *m*
tan [tæn] **1** *n from sun* abbronzatura *f*; *colour* marrone *m* rossiccio **2** *v/i* (*pret & pp* ***-ned***) *in sun* abbronzarsi **3** *v/t* (*pret & pp* ***-ned***) *leather* conciare
tan•dem [ˈtændəm] *bike* tandem *m inv*
tan•gent [ˈtændʒənt] MATH tangente *f*
tan•ge•rine [tændʒəˈriːn] tangerino *m*
tan•gi•ble [ˈtændʒɪbl] *adj* tangibile
tan•gle [ˈtæŋgl] *n* nodo *m*
◆ **tangle up**: ***get tangled up*** *of string etc* aggrovigliarsi
tan•go [ˈtæŋgəʊ] *n* tango *m*
tank [tæŋk] recipiente *m*; MOT serbatoio *m*; MIL carro *m* armato; *for skin diver* bombola *f* (d'ossigeno)
tank•er [ˈtæŋkə(r)] *ship* nave *f* cisterna; *truck* autocisterna *f*
tan•ned [tænd] *adj* abbronzato
Tan•noy® [ˈtænɔɪ] altoparlante *m*
tan•ta•liz•ing [ˈtæntəlaɪzɪŋ] *adj* allettante; *smell* stuzzicante
tan•ta•mount [ˈtæntəmaʊnt] *adj*: ***be tantamount to*** essere equivalente a
tan•trum [ˈtæntrəm] capricci *mpl*; ***throw a tantrum*** fare (i) capricci
tap [tæp] **1** *n* rubinetto *m* **2** *v/t* (*pret & pp* ***-ped***) (*hit*) dare un colpetto a; *phone* mettere sotto controllo; ***he was tapping his fingers on the table*** tamburellava con le dita sul tavolo
◆ **tap into** *v/t resources* attingere a
ˈ**tap dance** *n* tip tap *m*
tape [teɪp] **1** *n magnetic* nastro *m* magnetico; *recorded* cassetta *f*; (*sticky*) nastro *m* adesivo; ***on tape*** registrato **2** *v/t conversation etc* registrare; ***tape sth to sth*** attaccare qc a qc col nastro adesivo
ˈ**tape deck** registratore *m*
ˈ**tape drive** COMPUT unità *f inv* di backup a nastro
ˈ**tape meas•ure** metro *m* a nastro
tap•er [ˈteɪpə(r)] *v/i* assottigliarsi
◆ **taper off** *v/i of production* calare gradualmente; *of figures* decrescere
ˈ**tape re•cor•der** registratore *m* a cassette
ˈ**tape re•cor•ding** registrazione *f* su cassetta
ta•pes•try [ˈtæpɪstrɪ] arazzo *m*
tape•worm [ˈteɪpwɜːm] verme *m* solitario
tar [tɑː(r)] *n* catrame *m*
tar•get [ˈtɑːgɪt] **1** *n in shooting* bersaglio *m*; *for sales, production* obiettivo *m* **2** *v/t market* rivolgersi a
tar•get ˈ**au•di•ence** target *m inv* di pubblico
ˈ**tar•get date** data *f* fissata
tar•get ˈ**fig•ure** target *m inv*
ˈ**tar•get group** COM gruppo *m* target
ˈ**tar•get language** lingua *f* d'arrivo
ˈ**tar•get mar•ket** mercato *m* target
tar•iff [ˈtærɪf] (*price*) tariffa *f*; (*tax*) tassa *f*
tar•mac [ˈtɑːmæk] *at airport* pista *f*
tar•nish [ˈtɑːnɪʃ] *v/t metal* ossidare; *reputation* macchiare
tar•pau•lin [tɑːˈpɔːlɪn] tela *f* cerata
tart[1] [tɑːt] *n* torta *f*
tart[2] [tɑːt] *n* F (*prostitute*) sgualdrina *f*; *pej*: *woman* stronza *f*
tar•tan [ˈtɑːtn] tartan *m*
task [tɑːsk] compito *m*
ˈ**task force** task force *f inv*

tas•sel ['tæsl] nappa *f*
taste [teɪst] **1** *n* gusto *m*; ***he has no taste*** non ha nessun gusto **2** *v/t food* assaggiare; (*experience*: *freedom etc*) provare; ***I can't taste anything*** non sento nessun sapore **3** *v/i*: ***it tastes like …*** ha sapore di …; ***it tastes very nice*** è molto buono
'**taste buds** *npl* papille *fpl* gustative
taste•ful ['teɪstfʊl] *adj* di gusto
taste•ful•ly ['teɪstfəlɪ] *adv* con gusto
taste•less ['teɪstlɪs] *adj food* insapore; *remark*, *person* privo di gusto
tast•ing ['teɪstɪŋ] *of wine* degustazione *f*
tast•y ['teɪstɪ] *adj* gustoso
tat•tered ['tætəd] *adj clothes*, *book* malridotto
tat•ters ['tætəz]: ***in tatters*** *of clothes* a brandelli; *of reputation*, *career* a pezzi
tat•too [tə'tuː] *n* tatuaggio *m*
tat•ty ['tætɪ] *adj* malandato
taught [tɔːt] *pret & pp* → ***teach***
taunt [tɔːnt] **1** *n* scherno *m* **2** *v/t* schernire
Taur•us ['tɔːrəs] ASTR Toro *m*
taut [tɔːt] *adj* teso
taw•dry ['tɔːdrɪ] *adj* pacchiano
tax [tæks] **1** *n* tassa *f*; ***before / after tax*** al lordo / al netto di imposte **2** *v/t* tassare
tax•a•ble 'in•come reddito *m* imponibile
ta•x•ation [tæk'seɪʃn] tassazione *f*
'**tax avoid•ance** elusione *f* fiscale
'**tax brack•et** fascia *f* di reddito
'**tax code** codice *m* fiscale
'**tax de•duct•i•ble** *adj* deducibile dalle imposte
'**tax disc** *for car* bollo *m* (di circolazione)
'**tax eva•sion** evasione *f* fiscale
'**tax free** *adj* esentasse *inv*
tax•i ['tæksɪ] taxi *m inv*
'**tax•i dri•ver** tassista *m*/*f*
tax•ing ['tæksɪŋ] *adj* estenuante
'**tax in•spect•or** ispettore *m*, -trice *f* fiscale
'**tax•i rank, tax•i stand** stazione *f* dei taxi
'**tax•man** fisco *m*
'**tax •pay•er** contribuente *m*/*f*
'**tax re•turn** *form* dichiarazione *f* dei redditi
'**tax year** anno *m* fiscale
TB [tiː'biː] *abbr* (= ***tuberculosis***) tbc *f* (= tubercolosi *f*)
tea [tiː] *drink* tè *m inv*; *meal* cena *f*
tea•bag ['tiːbæg] bustina *f* di tè
teach [tiːtʃ] (*pret & pp* ***taught***) **1** *v/t subject* insegnare; *person* insegnare a; ***teach s.o. to do sth*** insegnare a qu a fare qc **2** *v/i* insegnare
tea•cher ['tiːtʃə(r)] insegnante *m*/*f*
tea•cher 'train•ing tirocinio *m* per insegnanti
tea•ching ['tiːtʃɪŋ] *profession* insegnamento *m*
'**tea•ching aid** sussidio *m* didattico
'**tea cloth** strofinaccio *m* da cucina
'**tea•cup** tazza *f* da tè
'**tea drink•er** bevitore *m*, -trice *f* di tè
teak [tiːk] tek *m*
'**tea leaf** foglia *f* di tè
team [tiːm] *in sport* squadra *f*; *at work* équipe *f inv*
'**team mate** compagno *m*, -a *f* di squadra
team 'spirit spirito *m* d'équipe
'**team•work** lavoro *m* d'équipe
tea•pot ['tiːpɒt] teiera *f*
tear[1] [teə(r)] **1** *n in cloth etc* strappo *m* **2** *v/t* (*pret* ***tore***, *pp* ***torn***) *paper*, *cloth* strappare; ***be torn between two alternatives*** essere combattuto tra due alternative **3** *v/i* (*pret* ***tore***, *pp* ***torn***) (*run fast*, *drive fast*) sfrecciare
◆ **tear down** *v/t poster* strappare; *building* buttar giù
◆ **tear out** *v/t* strappare
◆ **tear up** *v/t paper* distruggere; *agreement* rompere
tear[2] [tɪə(r)] *n in eye* lacrima *f*; ***burst into tears*** scoppiare a piangere; ***be in tears*** essere in lacrime
tear•drop ['tɪədrɒp] lacrima *f*
tear•ful ['tɪəfʊl] *adj person* in lacrime; *look*, *voice* piangente
'**tear gas** gas *m inv* lacrimogeno
'**tea•room** sala *f* da tè
tease [tiːz] *v/t person* prendere in giro; *animal* stuzzicare
'**tea serv•ice**, '**tea set** servizio *m* da tè
'**tea•spoon** cucchiaino *m* da caffè
'**tea strain•er** colino *m* da tè
teat [tiːt] capezzolo *m*; *made of rubber* tettarella *f*
'**tea to•wel** strofinaccio *m* da cucina
tech•ni•cal ['teknɪkl] *adj* tecnico
tech•ni•cal•i•ty [teknɪ'kælətɪ] (*technical nature*) tecnicismo *m*; LAW vizio *m* di procedura; ***that's just a technicality*** è solo un dettaglio
tech•ni•cal•ly ['teknɪklɪ] *adv* tecnicamente
tech•ni•cian [tek'nɪʃn] tecnico *m*
tech•nique [tek'niːk] tecnica *f*
tech•no•log•i•cal [teknə'lɒdʒɪkl] *adj* tecnologico
tech•no•lo•gy [tek'nɒlədʒɪ] tecnologia *f*
tech•no•phob•i•a [teknə'fəʊbɪə] tecnofobia *f*
ted•dy bear ['tedɪbeə(r)] orsacchiotto *m*
te•di•ous ['tiːdɪəs] *adj* noioso
tee [tiː] *n in golf* tee *m inv*
teem [tiːm] *v/i* pullulare; ***be teeming with***

rain piovere a dirotto; ***be teeming with tourists / ants*** pullulare di turisti / formiche
teen•age ['ti:neɪdʒ] *adj problems* degli adolescenti; *gangs* di ragazzi; ***teenage boy / girl*** ragazzo *m*/ragazza *f* adolescente; ***teenage fashions*** moda giovane
teen•ag•er ['ti:neɪdʒə(r)] adolescente *m/f*
teens [ti:nz] *npl* adolescenza *f*; ***be in one's teens*** essere adolescente; ***reach one's teens*** entrare nell'adolescenza
tee•ny ['ti:nɪ] *adj* F piccolissimo
teeth [ti:θ] *pl* → ***tooth***
teethe [ti:ð] *v/i* mettere i denti
'**teething problems** *npl* difficoltà *fpl* iniziali
tee•to•tal [ti:'təʊtl] *adj person* astemio; *party* senza alcolici
tee•to•tal•ler [ti:'təʊtlə(r)] astemio *m*, -a *f*
tel•e•com•mu•ni•ca•tions [telɪkəmju:nɪ'keɪʃnz] telecomunicazioni *fpl*
tel•e•gram ['telɪgræm] telegramma *m*
tel•e•graph pole ['telɪgrɑ:fpəʊl] palo *m* del telegrafo
tel•e•path•ic [telɪ'pæθɪk] *adj* telepatico; ***you must be telepathic!*** devi avere poteri telepatici!
te•lep•a•thy [tɪ'lepəθɪ] telepatia *f*
tel•e•phone ['telɪfəʊn] **1** *n* telefono *m*; ***be on the telephone*** *be speaking* essere al telefono; *possess a phone* avere il telefono **2** *v/t person* telefonare a **3** *v/i* telefonare
'**tel•e•phone bill** bolletta *f* del telefono
'**tel•e•phone book** guida *f* telefonica
'**tel•e•phone booth** cabina *f* telefonica
'**tel•e•phone box** cabina *f* telefonica
'**tel•e•phone call** telefonata *f*
'**tel•e•phone con•ver•sa•tion** conversazione *f* telefonica
'**tel•e•phone di•rec•to•ry** elenco *m* telefonico
'**tel•e•phone ex•change** centralino *m* telefonico
'**tel•e•phone mes•sage** messaggio *m* telefonico
'**tel•e•phone num•ber** numero *m* telefonico
tel•e•pho•to lens [telɪfəʊtəʊ'lenz] teleobiettivo *m*
tel•e•sales ['telɪseɪlz] vendita *f* telefonica
tel•e•scope ['telɪskəʊp] telescopio *m*
tel•e•scop•ic lens [telɪskɒpɪk'lenz] lente *f* telescopica
tel•e•thon ['telɪθɒn] telethon *m inv*
tel•e•vise ['telɪvaɪz] *v/t* trasmettere in televisione
tel•e•vi•sion ['telɪvɪʒn] televisione *f*; *set* televisione *f*, televisore *m*; ***on television*** alla televisione; ***watch television*** guardare la televisione
'**tel•e•vi•sion au•di•ence** pubblico *m* televisivo
'**tel•e•vi•sion li•cence** canone *m* (televisivo)
'**tel•e•vision pro•gramme** programma *m* televisivo
'**tel•e•vision set** televisore *m*
'**tel•e•vision stu•di•o** studio *m* televisivo
tell [tel] (*pret & pp* ***told***) **1** *v/t* dire; *story* raccontare; ***tell s.o. sth*** dire qc a qu; ***don't tell Mum*** non dirlo alla mamma; ***tell s.o. to do sth*** dire a qu di fare qc; ***I've been told that …*** mi hanno detto che …; ***it's hard to tell*** è difficile a dirsi; ***you never can tell*** non si può mai dire; ***tell X from Y*** distinguere X da Y; ***I can't tell the difference between …*** non vedo nessuna differenza tra …; ***you're telling me!*** F a chi lo dici! F **2** *v/i* (*have effect*) farsi sentire; ***the heat is telling on him*** il caldo si fa sentire su di lui; ***time will tell*** il tempo lo dirà
◆ **tell off** *v/t* rimproverare
tell•er ['telə(r)] *in bank* cassiere *m*, -a *f*
tell•ing ['telɪŋ] *adj argument* efficace; ***a telling sign*** un segnale chiaro
tell•ing '**off** rimprovero *m*; ***give s.o. a telling off*** rimproverare qu
tell•tale ['telteɪl] **1** *adj signs* rivelatore **2** *n* spione *m*, spiona *f*
tel•ly ['telɪ] F tele *f*
temp [temp] **1** *n employee* impiegato *m*, -a interinale **2** *v/i* fare lavori interinali
tem•per ['tempə(r)] (*bad temper*): ***have a terrible temper*** essere irascibile; ***be in a temper*** essere arrabbiato; ***keep one's temper*** mantenere la calma; ***lose one's temper*** perdere le staffe
tem•pe•ra•ment ['temprəmənt] temperamento *m*
tem•pe•ra•men•tal [temprə'mentl] *adj* (*moody*) lunatico; *machine* imprevedibile
tem•pe•rate ['tempərət] *adj* temperato
tem•pe•ra•ture ['temprətʃə(r)] temperatura *f*; (*fever*) febbre *f*; ***have a temperature*** avere la febbre; ***take s.o.'s temperature*** prendere la temperatura a qu
tem•ple[1] ['templ] REL tempio *m*
tem•ple[2] ['templ] ANAT tempia *f*
tem•po ['tempəʊ] ritmo *m*; MUS tempo *m*
tem•po•rar•i•ly [tempə'reərɪlɪ] *adv* temporaneamente
tem•po•ra•ry ['tempərərɪ] *adj* temporaneo, provvisorio
tempt [tempt] *v/t* tentare
temp•ta•tion [temp'teɪʃn] tentazione *f*

tempt•ing ['temptɪŋ] *adj* allettante; *meal* appetitoso
ten [ten] dieci
te•na•cious [tɪ'neɪʃəs] *adj* tenace
te•nac•i•ty [tɪ'næsɪtɪ] tenacità *f*
ten•ant ['tenənt] inquilino *m*, -a *f*, locatario *m*, -a *f fml*; *in office* affittuario *m*, -a *f*
tend[1] [tend] *v/t* (*look after*) prendersi cura di
tend[2] [tend]: ***tend to do sth*** tendere a fare qc, avere la tendenza a fare qc; ***tend towards sth*** avere una tendenza verso qc
ten•den•cy ['tendənsɪ] tendenza *f*
ten•der[1] ['tendə(r)] *adj* (*sore*) sensibile; (*affectionate*) tenero; *steak* tenero
ten•der[2] ['tendə(r)] *n* COM offerta *f* ufficiale
ten•der•ness ['tendənɪs] (*soreness*) sensibilità *f*; *of kiss*, *steak* tenerezza *f*
ten•don ['tendən] tendine *m*
ten•nis ['tenɪs] tennis *m*
'**ten•nis ball** palla *f* da tennis
'**ten•nis court** campo *m* da tennis
'**ten•nis pla•yer** tennista *m/f*
'**ten•nis rack•et** racchetta *f* da tennis
ten•or ['tenə(r)] MUS tenore *m*
tense[1] [tens] *n* GRAM tempo *m*
tense[2] [tens] *adj voice*, *person* teso; *moment*, *atmosphere* carico di tensione
◆ **tense up** *v/i of muscles* contrarre; *of person* irrigidirsi
ten•sion ['tenʃn] tensione *f*
tent [tent] tenda *f*
ten•ta•cle ['tentəkl] tentacolo *m*
ten•ta•tive ['tentətɪv] *adj* esitante
ten•ter•hooks ['tentəhʊks]: ***be on tenterhooks*** essere sulle spine
tenth [tenθ] *n & adj* decimo, -a
tep•id ['tepɪd] *adj water*, *reaction* tiepido
term [tɜːm] periodo *m*; *of office* durata *f* in carica; EDU: *of three months* trimestre *m*; *of two months* bimestre *m*; (*condition*, *word*) termine *m*; ***be on good / bad terms with s.o.*** essere in buoni / cattivi rapporti con qu; ***in the long / short term*** a lungo / breve termine; ***come to terms with sth*** venire a patti con qc
ter•mi•nal ['tɜːmɪnl] **1** *n at airport*, *for containers*, COMPUT terminale *m*; *for buses* capolinea *m inv*; ELEC morsetto *m* **2** *adj illness* in fase terminale
ter•mi•nal•ly ['tɜːmɪnəlɪ] *adv*: ***terminally ill*** malato (in fase) terminale
ter•mi•nate ['tɜːmɪneɪt] **1** *v/t contract*, *pregnancy* interrompere **2** *v/i* terminare
ter•mi•na•tion [tɜːmɪ'neɪʃn] *of contract*, *pregnancy* interruzione *f*
ter•mi•nol•o•gy [tɜːmɪ'nɒlədʒɪ] terminologia *f*
ter•mi•nus ['tɜːmɪnəs] *for buses* capolinea *m inv*; *for trains* stazione *f* di testa
ter•race ['terəs] *of houses* fila *f* di case a schiera; *on hillside*, *at hotel* terrazza *f*
ter•raced house [terəst'haʊs] casa *f* a schiera
ter•ra cot•ta [terə'kɒtə] *adj* di terracotta
ter•rain [tə'reɪn] terreno *m*
ter•res•tri•al [tə'restrɪəl] **1** *n* terrestre *m/f* **2** *adj television* di terra
ter•ri•ble ['terəbl] *adj* terribile
ter•ri•bly ['terəblɪ] *adv play* malissimo; (*very*) molto
ter•rif•ic [tə'rɪfɪk] *adj* eccezionale; ***terrific!*** bene!
ter•rif•i•cal•ly [tə'rɪfɪklɪ] *adv* (*very*) eccezionalmente
ter•ri•fy ['terɪfaɪ] *v/t* (*pret & pp* ***-ied***) terrificare; ***be terrified*** essere terrificato
ter•ri•fy•ing ['terɪfaɪɪŋ] *adj* terrificante
ter•ri•to•ri•al [terɪ'tɔːrɪəl] *adj* territoriale
ter•ri•to•ri•al '**wa•ters** *npl* acque *fpl* territoriali
ter•ri•to•ry ['terɪtərɪ] *also fig* territorio *m*
ter•ror ['terə(r)] terrore *m*
ter•ror•is•m ['terərɪzm] terrorismo *m*
ter•ror•ist ['terərɪst] terrorista *m/f*
'**ter•ror•ist at•tack** attentato *m* terroristico
'**ter•ror•ist or•gan•i•za•tion** organizzazione *f* terroristica
ter•ror•ize ['terəraɪz] *v/t* terrorizzare
terse [tɜːs] *adj* brusco
test [test] **1** *n* prova *f*, test *m inv*; *for driving*, *medical* esame *m*; ***blood test*** analisi *f inv* del sangue **2** *v/t soup*, *bathwater* provare; *machine*, *theory* testare; *person*, *friendship* mettere alla prova; ***test the water*** *fig* tastare il terreno
tes•ta•ment ['testəmənt] testimonianza *f* (***to*** di); ***Old / New Testament*** REL Vecchio / Nuovo Testamento
'**test-drive**: ***go for a test-drive*** fare un giro di prova
tes•ti•cle ['testɪkl] testicolo *m*
tes•ti•fy ['testɪfaɪ] *v/i* (*pret & pp* ***-ied***) LAW testimoniare
tes•ti•mo•ni•al [testɪ'məʊnɪəl] referenze *fpl* scritte
tes•ti•mo•ny ['testɪmənɪ] LAW testimonianza *f*
'**test tube** provetta *f*
'**test tube ba•by** bambino *m*, -a *f* (concepito, -a) in provetta
tes•ty ['testɪ] *adj* suscettibile
te•ta•nus ['tetənəs] tetano *m*
teth•er ['teðə(r)] **1** *v/t horse* legare **2** *n*: ***be at the end of one's tether*** essere allo stremo

T

text [tekst] testo *m*
'**text•book** libro *m* di testo
tex•tile ['tekstaɪl] tessuto *m*
tex•ture ['tekstʃə(r)] consistenza *f*
Thai [taɪ] **1** *adj* tailandese **2** *n person* tailandese *m/f*; *language* tailandese *m*
Thai•land ['taɪlænd] Tailandia *f*
than [ðæn] *adv*: ***older / faster than me*** più vecchio / veloce di me; ***she's more French than Italian*** è più francese che italiana
thank [θæŋk] *v/t* ringraziare; ***thank you*** grazie; ***no thank you*** no, grazie
thank•ful ['θæŋkfʊl] *adj* riconoscente
thank•ful•ly ['θæŋkfʊlɪ] *adv* con riconoscenza; (*luckily*) fortunatamente
thank•less ['θæŋklɪs] *adj* ingrato
thanks [θæŋks] *npl* ringraziamenti *mpl*; ***thanks!*** grazie!; ***thanks to*** grazie a
that [ðæt] **1** *adj* quel; *with masculine nouns before s+consonant, gn, ps and z* quello; ***that one*** quello **2** *pron* quello *m*, -a *f*; ***what is that?*** cos'è?; ***who is that?*** chi è?; ***that's mine*** è mio; ***that's tea*** quello è tè; ***that's very kind*** è molto gentile **3** *relative pron* che; ***the person / car that you saw*** la persona / macchina che hai visto; ***the day that he was born*** il giorno in cui è nato **4** *adv* (*so*) così; ***that big / expensive*** così grande / caro **5** *conj* che; ***I think that …*** credo che …
thaw [θɔː] *v/i of snow* sciogliersi; *of frozen food* scongelare
the [ðə] il *m*, la *f*; i *mpl*, le *fpl*; *with masculine nouns before s+consonant, gn, ps and z* lo *m*, gli *mpl*; *before vowel* l' *m/f*, gli *mpl*; ***to the bathroom*** al bagno; ***the sooner the better*** prima è, meglio è
the•a•ter *Am* → ***theatre***
the•a•tre ['θɪətə(r)] teatro *m*
'**the•a•tre crit•ic** critico *m* teatrale
the•a•tre•go•er ['θɪətəgəʊə(r)] frequentatore *m*, -trice *f* di teatro
the•at•ri•cal [θɪ'ætrɪkl] *also fig* teatrale
theft [θeft] furto *m*
their [ðeə(r)] *adj* il loro *m*, la loro *f*; i loro *mpl*, le loro *fpl*; (*his or her*) il suo *m*, la sua *f*, i suoi *mpl*, le sue *fpl*; ***their daughter / son*** la loro figlia / il loro figlio
theirs [ðeəz] *pron* il loro *m*, la loro *f*; i loro *mpl*, le loro *fpl*; ***it was an idea of theirs*** è stata una loro idea
them [ðem] *pron direct object* li *m*, le *f*; *referring to things* essi *m*, esse *f*; *indirect object* loro, gli; *after preposition* loro; *referring to things* essi *m*, esse *f*; (*him or her*) lo *m*, la *f*; ***I know them*** li / le conosco; ***I sold it to them*** gliel'ho venduto, l'ho venduto a loro
theme [θiːm] tema *m*
'**theme park** parco *m* a tema
'**theme song** canzone *f* principale
them•selves [ðem'selvz] *pron reflexive* si; *emphatic* loro stessi *mpl*, loro stesse *fpl*; *after prep* se stessi / se stesse; ***they themselves*** loro stessi / stesse; ***they enjoyed themselves*** si sono divertiti; ***they only think about themselves*** pensano solo a se stessi / stesse; ***by themselves*** (*alone*) da soli *mpl*, da sole *fpl*
then [ðen] *adv* (*at that time*) allora; (*after that*) poi; (*deducing*) allora; ***by then*** allora
the•o•lo•gian [θɪə'ləʊdʒɪən] teologo *m*, -a *f*
the•ol•o•gy [θɪ'ɒlədʒɪ] teologia *f*
the•o•ret•i•cal [θɪə'retɪkl] *adj* teorico
the•o•ret•i•cal•ly [θɪə'retɪklɪ] *adv* teoricamente
the•o•ry ['θɪərɪ] teoria *f*; ***in theory*** in teoria
ther•a•peu•tic [θerə'pjuːtɪk] *adj* terapeutico
ther•a•pist ['θerəpɪst] terapista *m/f*, terapeuta *m/f*
ther•a•py ['θerəpɪ] terapia *f*
there [ðeə(r)] *adv* lì, là; ***over there*** là; ***down there*** laggiù; ***there is …*** c'è; ***there are …*** ci sono; ***is there …?*** c'è …?; ***are there …?*** ci sono …?; ***isn't there?*** non c'è …?; ***aren't there?*** non ci sono …?; ***there you are*** *giving sth* ecco qui; *finding sth* ecco; *completing sth* ecco fatto; ***there and back*** andata e ritorno; ***there he is!*** eccolo!; ***there, there!*** *comforting* su, dai!
there•a•bouts [ðeərə'baʊts] *adv* giù di lì
there•fore [ðeəfɔː(r)] *adv* quindi, pertanto
ther•mom•e•ter [θə'mɒmɪtə(r)] termometro *m*
ther•mos flask ['θɜːməsflɑːsk] termos *m inv*
ther•mo•stat ['θɜːməstæt] termostato *m*
these [ðiːz] **1** *adj* questi **2** *pron* questi *m*, -e *f*
the•sis ['θiːsɪs] (*pl* ***theses*** ['θiːsiːz]) tesi *f inv*
they [ðeɪ] *pron* ◇ loro; ***they're going to the theatre*** vanno a teatro; ***they're going to the theatre, we're not*** loro vanno a teatro, noi no; ***there they are*** eccoli *mpl*, eccole *fpl*
◇ ***if anyone looks at this, they will see that …*** se qualcuno lo guarda, vedrà che …; ***they say that …*** si dice che …; ***they are going to change the law*** cambieranno la legge
thick [θɪk] *adj* spesso; *hair* folto; *fog, fo-*

rest fitto; *liquid* denso; F (*stupid*) ottuso
thick•en ['θɪkən] *v/t sauce* ispessire
thick•set ['θɪkset] *adj* tarchiato
thick•skinned ['θɪkskɪnd] *adj fig* insensibile
thief [θiːf] (*pl* ***thieves*** [θiːvz]) ladro *m*, -a *f*
thigh [θaɪ] coscia *f*
thim•ble ['θɪmbl] ditale *m*
thin [θɪn] *adj* sottile; *person* magro; *hair* rado; *liquid* fluido
thing [θɪŋ] cosa *f*; ***things*** (*belongings*) cose *fpl*; ***how are things?*** come vanno le cose?; ***it's a good thing you told me*** è un bene che tu me l'abbia detto; ***what a thing to do / say!*** che razza di cosa da fare / dire!
thing•um•a•jig ['θɪŋʌmədʒɪg] F coso *m*, cosa *f* F
think [θɪŋk] *v/i* (*pret & pp* ***thought***) pensare; ***I think so*** penso *o* credo di sì; ***I don't think so*** non credo; ***I think so too*** lo penso anch'io; ***what do you think?*** cosa ne pensi?; ***what do you think of it?*** cosa ne pensi?; ***I can't think of anything more*** non mi viene in mente nient'altro; ***think hard!*** pensaci bene!; ***I'm thinking about emigrating*** sto pensando di emigrare
◆ **think over** *v/t* riflettere su
◆ **think through** *v/t* analizzare a fondo
◆ **think up** *v/t plan* escogitare
'**think tank** comitato *m* di esperti
thin-skinned [θɪn'skɪnd] *adj fig* sensibile
third [θɜːd] *n & adj* terzo, -a
third•ly ['θɜːdlɪ] *adv* in terzo luogo
'**third-par•ty** terzi *mpl*
third-par•ty in'sur•ance assicurazione *f* sulla responsabilità civile
third 'per•son GRAM terza persona *f*
'**third-rate** *adj* scadente
Third 'World Terzo Mondo *m*
thirst [θɜːst] sete *f*
thirsty ['θɜːstɪ] *adj* assetato; ***be thirsty*** avere sete
thir•teen [θɜː'tiːn] tredici
thir•teenth [θɜː'tiːnθ] *n & adj* tredicesimo, -a
thir•ti•eth ['θɜːtɪɪθ] *n & adj* trentesimo, -a
thir•ty ['θɜːtɪ] trenta
this [ðɪs] **1** *adj* questo; ***this one*** questo (qui) **2** *pron* questo *m*, -a *f*; ***this is easy*** è facile; ***this is …*** *introducing s.o.* questo / questa è …; TELEC sono … **3** *adv*: ***this big / high*** grande / alto così
thorn [θɔːn] spina *f*
thorn•y ['θɔːnɪ] *adj also fig* spinoso
thor•ough ['θʌrə] *adj search, knowledge* approfondito; *person* scrupoloso
thor•ough•bred ['θʌrəbred] *horse* purosangue *inv*
thor•ough•ly ['θʌrəlɪ] *adv clean, search for* accuratamente; *know, understand* perfettamente; *agree, spoil* completamente; ***thoroughly stupid*** stupidissimo
those [ðəuz] **1** *adj* quelli; *with masculine nouns before s+consonant, gn, ps and z* quegli **2** *pron* quelli *m*, -e *f*; *with masculine nouns before s+consonant, gn, ps and z* quegli
though [ðəu] **1** *conj* (*although*) benché; ***though it might fail*** benché possa non riuscire; ***say it as though you meant it*** dillo come se lo sentissi davvero; ***it looks as though …*** sembra che … **2** *adv* però; ***it's not finished though*** non è finito, però
thought [θɔːt] **1** *n* pensiero *m* **2** *pret & pp* → ***think***
thought•ful ['θɔːtfʊl] *adj* pensieroso; *reply* meditato; (*considerate*) gentile
thought•ful•ly [əθɔːtflɪ] *adv* (*pensively*) con aria pensierosa; (*considerately*) gentilmente
thought•less ['θɔːtlɪs] *adj* sconsiderato
thought•less•ly ['θɔːtlɪslɪ] *adv* in modo sconsiderato
thou•sand ['θaʊznd] mille; ***a thousand pounds*** mille sterline; ***thousands of*** migliaia di
thou•sandth ['θaʊzndθ] *n & adj* millesimo, -a
thrash [θræʃ] *v/t* picchiare; SP battere
◆ **thrash about** *v/i with arms etc* sferrare colpi in aria
◆ **thrash out** *v/t solution* mettere a punto
thrash•ing ['θræʃɪŋ] botte *fpl*; SP batosta *f*
thread [θred] **1** *n* filo *m*; *of screw* filettatura *f* **2** *v/t needle* infilare il filo in; *beads* infilare
thread•bare ['θredbeə(r)] *adj* liso
threat [θret] minaccia *f*
threat•en ['θretn] *v/t* minacciare
threat•en•ing ['θretnɪŋ] *adj* minaccioso; ***threatening letter*** lettera *f* minatoria
three [θriː] tre
three 'quart•ers tre quarti *mpl*
thresh [θreʃ] *v/t corn* trebbiare
thresh•old ['θreʃhəʊld] *of house, new era* soglia *f*; ***on the threshold of*** sulla soglia di
threw [θruː] *pret* → ***throw***
thrift [θrɪft] parsimonia *f*
thrift•y ['θrɪftɪ] *adj* parsimonioso
thrill [θrɪl] **1** *n* emozione *f*; *physical feeling* brivido *m* **2** *v/t*: ***be thrilled*** essere emozionato
thrill•er ['θrɪlə(r)] giallo *m*
thrill•ing ['θrɪlɪŋ] *adj* emozionante

thrive [θraɪv] *v/i of plant* crescere rigoglioso; *of business, economy* prosperare
throat [θrəʊt] gola *f*; ***have a sore throat*** avere mal di gola
ˈ**throat loz•enge** pastiglia *f* per la gola
throb [θrɒb] *v/i* (*pret & pp* **-bed**) pulsare; *of heart* battere; *of music* rimbombare
throb•bing [ˈθrɒbɪŋ] pulsazione *f*; *of heart* battito *m*; *of music* rimbombo *m*
throne [θrəʊn] trono *m*
throng [θrɒŋ] *n* calca *f*
throt•tle [ˈθrɒtl] **1** *n on motorbike* manetta *f* di accelerazione; *on boat* leva *f* di accelerazione **2** *v/t* (*strangle*) strozzare
◆ **throttle back** *v/i* decelerare
through [θruː] **1** *prep* (*across*) attraverso; (*during*) durante; (*by means of*) tramite; ***go through the city*** attraversare la città; ***through the winter / summer*** per tutto l'inverno / tutta l'estate; ***arranged through him*** organizzato tramite lui **2** *adv*: ***wet through*** completamente bagnato; ***watch a film through*** guardare un film fino alla fine **3** *adj*: ***be through*** *of couple* essersi lasciati; *have arrived*: *of news etc* essere arrivato; ***you're through*** TELEC è in linea; ***I'm through with …*** (*finished with*) ho finito con …; ***I'm through with him*** ho chiuso con lui
ˈ**through flight** volo *m* diretto
through•out [θruːˈaʊt] **1** *prep*: ***throughout the night*** per tutta la notte **2** *adv* (*in all parts*) completamente
ˈ**through train** treno *m* diretto
throw [θrəʊ] **1** *v/t* (*pret* **threw**, *pp* **thrown**) lanciare; *into bin etc* gettare; *of horse* disarcionare; (*disconcert*) sconcertare; *party* dare **2** *n* lancio *m*
◆ **throw away** *v/t* buttare via, gettare
◆ **throw off** *v/t jacket etc* togliersi in fretta; *cold etc* liberarsi di
◆ **throw on** *v/t clothes* mettersi in fretta
◆ **throw out** *v/t old things* buttare via; *from bar, house etc* buttare fuori; *plan* scartare
◆ **throw up 1** *v/t ball* lanciare; ***throw up one's hands*** alzare le mani al cielo **2** *v/i* (*vomit*) vomitare
ˈ**throw-a•way** *adj remark* buttato lì; (*disposable*) usa e getta *inv*
ˈ**throw-in** SP rimessa *f*
thrown [θrəʊn] *pp* → **throw**
thrush [θrʌʃ] *bird* tordo *m*
thrust [θrʌst] *v/t* (*pret & pp* **thrust**) (*push hard*) spingere; *knife* conficcare; ***thrust sth into s.o.'s hands*** ficcare qc in mano a qu; ***thrust one's way through the crowd*** farsi largo tra la folla
thud [θʌd] *n* tonfo *m*
thug [θʌg] *hooligan* teppista *m*; *tough guy* bullo *m*
thumb [θʌm] **1** *n* pollice *m* **2** *v/t*: ***thumb a lift*** fare l'autostop
thump [θʌmp] **1** *n blow* pugno *m*; *noise* colpo *m* **2** *v/t person* dare un pugno a; ***thump one's fist on the table*** dare un pugno sul tavolo **3** *v/i of heart* palpitare; ***thump on the door*** battere alla porta
thun•der [ˈθʌndə(r)] *n* tuono *m*
thun•der•ous [ˈθʌndərəs] *adj applause* fragoroso
thun•der•storm [ˈθʌndəstɔːm] temporale *m*
ˈ**thun•der•struck** *adj* allibito
thun•der•y [ˈθʌndərɪ] *adj weather* temporalesco
Thurs•day [ˈθɜːzdeɪ] giovedì *m inv*
thus [ðʌs] *adv* (*in this way*) così
thwart [θwɔːt] *v/t person, plans* ostacolare
thyme [taɪm] timo *m*
thy•roid gland [ˈθaɪrɔɪdglænd] tiroide *f*
Ti•ber [ˈtaɪbə(r)] Tevere *m*
tick [tɪk] **1** *n of clock* ticchettio *m*; *in text* segno *m* **2** *v/i of clock* ticchettare **3** *v/t with a tick* segnare
◆ **tick off** *v/t* rimproverare; *item in a list* segnare
tick•et [ˈtɪkɪt] biglietto *m*; *in cloakroom* scontrino *m*
ˈ**ti•cket col•lec•tor** bigliettaio *m*, -a *f*
ˈ**ti•cket in•spec•tor** controllore *m*
ˈ**ti•cket ma•chine** distributore *m* di biglietti
ˈ**ti•cket of•fice** biglietteria *f*
tick•ing [ˈtɪkɪŋ] *noise* ticchettio *m*
tick•le [ˈtɪkl] **1** *v/t person* fare il solletico a **2** *v/i of material* dare prurito; *of person* fare il solletico
tickl•ish [ˈtɪklɪʃ] *adj*: ***be ticklish*** soffrire il solletico
ti•dal wave [ˈtaɪdlweɪv] onda *f* di marea
tide [taɪd] marea *f*; ***high tide*** alta marea; ***low tide*** bassa marea; ***the tide is in / out*** c'è l'alta / la bassa marea
◆ **tide over** *v/t* togliere d'impiccio
ti•di•ness [ˈtaɪdɪnɪs] ordine *m*
ti•dy [ˈtaɪdɪ] *adj* ordinato
◆ **tidy away** *v/t* (*pret & pp* **-ied**) mettere a posto
◆ **tidy up 1** *v/t room, shelves* mettere in ordine; ***tidy o.s. up*** darsi una sistemata **2** *v/i* mettere in ordine
tie [taɪ] **1** *n* (*necktie*) cravatta *f*; (SP: *even result*) pareggio *m*; ***he doesn't have any ties*** non ha legami **2** *v/t knot, hands* legare; ***tie a knot*** fare un nodo; ***tie two ropes together*** annodare due corde **3** *v/i* SP

T

pareggiare

◆ **tie down** *v/t with rope* legare; (*restrict*) vincolare

◆ **tie up** *v/t person, laces, hair* legare; *boat* ormeggiare; ***I'm tied up tomorrow*** sono impegnato domani

tier [tɪə(r)] *of hierarchy* livello *m*; *in stadium* anello *m*

ti•ger ['taɪgə(r)] tigre *f*

tight [taɪt] **1** *adj clothes* stretto; *security* rigido; *rope* teso; *hard to move* bloccato; *not leaving much time* giusto; *schedule* serrato; F (*drunk*) sbronzo F **2** *adv*: ***hold s.o./sth tight*** tenere qu / qc stretto; ***shut sth tight*** chiudere bene qc

tight•en ['taɪtn] *v/t screw* serrare; *belt* stringere; *rope* tendere; *control, security* intensificare

◆ **tighten up** *v/i in discipline, security* intensificare il controllo

tight-fist•ed [taɪt'fɪstɪd] *adj* taccagno

tight•ly ['taɪtlɪ] *adv* → ***tight*** *adv*

tight•rope ['taɪtrəʊp] fune *f* (per funamboli)

tights [taɪts] *npl* collant *mpl*

tile [taɪl] *on floor* mattonella *f*; *on wall* piastrella *f*; *on roof* tegola *f*

till[1] [tɪl] *prep & conj* → ***until***

till[2] [tɪl] *n* (*cash register*) cassa *f*

till[3] [tɪl] *v/t soil* arare

tilt [tɪlt] **1** *v/t* inclinare **2** *v/i* inclinarsi

tim•ber ['tɪmbə(r)] legname *m*

time [taɪm] tempo *m*; *by the clock* ora *f*; (*occasion*) volta *f*; ***time is up*** il tempo è scaduto; ***for the time being*** al momento; ***have a good time*** divertirsi; ***have a good time!*** divertiti!; ***what's the time?, what time is it?*** che ora è?, che ore sono?; ***by the time you finish*** quando avrai finito; ***the first time*** la prima volta; ***four times*** quattro volte; ***time and again*** ripetutamente; ***all the time*** per tutto il tempo; ***I've been here for some time*** sono qui da un po'; ***take your time*** fai con calma; ***for a time*** per un po' (di tempo); ***at any time*** in qualsiasi momento; (***and***) ***about time!*** era ora!; ***two / three at a time*** due / tre alla volta; ***at the same time*** *speak, reply etc* contemporaneamente; (*however*) nel contempo; ***in time*** in tempo; (*eventually*) col tempo; ***on time*** in orario; ***in no time*** in un attimo

'**time bomb** bomba *f* a orologeria

'**time clock** *in factory* bollatrice *f*

'**time-con•sum•ing** *adj* lungo

'**time dif•fer•ence** fuso *m* orario

'**time-lag** scarto *m* di tempo

'**time lim•it** limite *m* temporale

time•ly ['taɪmlɪ] *adj* tempestivo

tim•er ['taɪmə(r)] cronometro *m*; *person* cronometrista *m/f*; *on oven* timer *m inv*

'**time•sav•ing** *n* risparmio *m* di tempo

'**time•scale** *of project* cronologia *f*

'**time share** *Br* (*house, apartment*) multiproprietà *f inv*

'**time switch** interruttore *m* a tempo

'**time•ta•ble** orario *m*

'**time•warp** trasposizione *f* temporale

'**time zone** zona *f* di fuso orario

tim•id ['tɪmɪd] *adj* timido

tim•id•ly ['tɪmɪdlɪ] *adv* timidamente

tim•ing ['taɪmɪŋ] (*choosing a time*) tempismo *m*; ***that's good timing!*** che tempismo!

tin [tɪn] *metal* stagno *m*; *container* barattolo *m*

tin•foil ['tɪnfɔɪl] carta *f* stagnola

tinge [tɪndʒ] *n of colour, sadness* sfumatura *f*

tin•gle ['tɪŋgl] *v/i* pizzicare

◆ **tinker with** ['tɪŋkə(r)] *v/t* armeggiare con

tin•kle ['tɪŋkl] *n of bell* tintinnio *m*

tinned [tɪnd] *adj* in scatola

'**tin o•pen•er** apriscatole *m inv*

tin•sel ['tɪnsl] fili *mpl* d'argento

tint [tɪnt] **1** *n of colour* sfumatura *f*; *in hair* riflessante *m* **2** *v/t hair* fare dei riflessi a

tint•ed ['tɪntɪd] *glasses* fumé *inv*

ti•ny ['taɪnɪ] *adj* piccolissimo

tip[1] [tɪp] *n of stick, finger* punta *f*; *of cigarette* filtro *m*

tip[2] [tɪp] **1** *n* (*piece of advice*) consiglio *m*; *money* mancia *f* **2** *v/t* (*pret & pp* ***-ped***) *waiter etc* dare la mancia a

◆ **tip off** *v/t* fare una soffiata a

◆ **tip over** *v/t jug, liquid* rovesciare; ***he tipped water all over me*** mi ha rovesciato dell'acqua addosso

'**tip-off** soffiata *f*

tipped [tɪpt] *adj cigarettes* col filtro

Tipp-Ex® *n* bianchetto *m*

tip•sy ['tɪpsɪ] *adj* alticcio

tip•toe ['tɪptəʊ]: ***on tiptoe*** sulla punta dei piedi

tire[1] ['taɪə(r)] **1** *v/t* stancare **2** *v/i* stancarsi; ***he never tires of it*** non se ne stanca mai

tire[2] ['taɪə(r)] *Am n* → ***tyre***

tired ['taɪəd] *adj* stanco; ***be tired of s.o./sth*** essere stanco di qu / qc

tired•ness ['taɪədnɪs] stanchezza *f*

tire•less ['taɪəlɪs] *adj* instancabile

tire•some ['taɪəsəm] *adj* (*annoying*) fastidioso

tir•ing ['taɪrɪŋ] *adj* stancante

Ti•rol → ***Tyrol***

tis•sue ['tɪʃuː] ANAT tessuto *m*; (*handkerchief*) fazzolettino *m* (di carta)

'tis•sue pa•per carta *f* velina
tit[1] [tɪt] *bird* cincia *f*
tit[2] [tɪt]: ***tit for tat*** pan per focaccia
tit[3] [tɪt] V (*breast*) tetta *f* V
ti•tle ['taɪtl] titolo *m*; LAW diritto *m*
'ti•tle•hold•er SP detentore *m*, -trice *f* del titolo
'ti•tle role *in play, film* ruolo *m* principale
tit•ter ['tɪtə(r)] *v/i* ridacchiare
to [tuː], *unstressed* [tə] **1** *prep* a; ***to Italy*** in Italia; ***to Rome*** a Roma; ***let's go to my place*** andiamo a casa mia; ***walk to the station*** andare a piedi alla stazione; ***to the north / south of …*** a nord / sud di …; ***give sth to s.o.*** dare qc a qu; ***from Monday to Wednesday*** da lunedì a mercoledì; ***from 10 to 15 people*** tra 10 e 15 persone; ***count to 20*** contare fino a venti; ***it's 5 to 11*** sono le undici meno cinque **2** *with verbs*: ***to speak, to see*** parlare, vedere; ***learn to drive*** imparare a guidare; ***nice to eat*** buono da mangiare; ***too heavy to carry*** troppo pesante da trasportare; ***to be honest …*** per essere franco …; ***to learn Italian*** *in order to* per imparare l'italiano **3** *adv*: ***to and fro*** avanti e indietro
toad [təʊd] rospo *m*
toad•stool ['təʊdstuːl] fungo *m* velenoso
toast [təʊst] **1** *n* pane *m* tostato; (*drinking*) brindisi *m inv*; ***propose a toast to s.o.*** fare un brindisi in onore di qu **2** *v/t bread* tostare; *drinking* fare un brindisi a
to•bac•co [tə'bækəʊ] tabacco *m*
to•bac•co•nist [tə'bækənɪst] tabaccaio *m*
to•bog•gan [tə'bɒgən] *n* toboga *m inv*
to•day [tə'deɪ] oggi
tod•dle ['tɒdl] *v/i of child* gattonare
tod•dler ['tɒdlə(r)] bambino *m*, -a *f* ai primi passi
to-do [tə'duː] F casino *m* F
toe [təʊ] **1** *n* dito *m* del piede; *of shoes, socks* punta *f*; ***big toe*** alluce *m* **2** *v/t*: ***toe the line*** attenersi alle direttive
toe•nail ['təʊneɪl] unghia *f* del piede
tof•fee ['tɒfɪ] caramella *f* al mou
to•geth•er [tə'geðə(r)] *adv* insieme
toil [tɔɪl] *n* duro lavoro *m*
toi•let ['tɔɪlɪt] gabinetto *m*; *place* bagno *m*, gabinetto *m*; ***go to the toilet*** andare in bagno
'toil•et pa•per carta *f* igienica
toil•et•ries ['tɔɪlɪtrɪz] *npl* prodotti *mpl* da toilette
'toi•let roll rotolo *m* di carta igienica
to•ken ['təʊkən] (*sign*) pegno *m*; *for gambling* gettone *m*; (*gift token*) buono *m*
told [təʊld] *pret & pp* → ***tell***
tol•e•ra•ble ['tɒlərəbl] *adj pain etc* tollerabile; (*quite good*) accettabile
tol•e•rance ['tɒlərəns] tolleranza *f*
tol•e•rant ['tɒlərənt] *adj* tollerante
tol•e•rate ['tɒləreɪt] *v/t noise, person* tollerare; ***I won't tolerate it!*** non intendo tollerarlo!
toll[1] [təʊl] *v/i of bell* suonare
toll[2] [təʊl] *n* (*deaths*) bilancio *m* delle vittime
toll[3] [təʊl] *n for bridge, road* pedaggio *m*
'toll booth casello *m*
'toll road strada *f* a pedaggio
to•ma•to [tə'mɑːtəʊ] pomodoro *m*
to•ma•to 'ketch•up ketchup *m inv*
to•ma•to 'sauce *for pasta etc* salsa *f* o sugo *m* di pomodoro; (*ketchup*) ketchup *m inv*
tomb [tuːm] tomba *f*
tom•boy ['tɒmbɔɪ] maschiaccio *m*
tomb•stone ['tuːmstəʊn] lapide *f*
tom•cat ['tɒmkæt] gatto *m* (maschio)
to•mor•row [tə'mɒrəʊ] domani; ***the day after tomorrow*** dopodomani; ***tomorrow morning*** domattina, domani mattina
ton [tʌn] tonnellata *f*
tone [təʊn] *of colour, musical instrument* tonalità *f inv*; *of conversation etc* tono *m*; *of neighbourhood* livello *m* sociale; ***tone of voice*** tono di voce
◆ **tone down** *v/t demands, criticism* moderare il tono di
ton•er ['təʊnə(r)] toner *m inv*
tongs [tɒŋz] *npl* pinze *fpl*; *for hair* ferro *m* arricciacapelli
tongue [tʌŋ] *n* lingua *f*
ton•ic ['tɒnɪk] MED ricostituente *m*
'ton•ic (wa•ter) acqua *f* tonica
to•night [tə'naɪt] stanotte; (*this evening*) stasera
ton•sil ['tɒnsl] tonsilla *f*
ton•sil•li•tis [tɒnsə'laɪtɪs] tonsillite *f*
too [tuː] *adv* (*also*) anche; (*excessively*) troppo; ***me too*** anch'io; ***too big / hot*** troppo grande / caldo; ***too much rice*** troppo riso; ***too many mistakes*** troppi errori; ***eat too much*** mangiare troppo
took [tʊk] *pret* → ***take***
tool [tuːl] attrezzo *m*; *fig* strumento *m*
toot [tuːt] *v/t* F suonare
tooth [tuːθ] (*pl* **teeth** [tiːθ]) dente *m*
'tooth•ache mal *m* di denti
'tooth•brush spazzolino *m* da denti
tooth•less ['tuːθlɪs] sdentato
'tooth•paste dentifricio *m*
'tooth•pick stuzzicadenti *m inv*
top [tɒp] **1** *n of mountain, tree* cima *f*; *of wall, screen* parte *f* alta; *of page, list, street* inizio *m*; (*lid*: *of bottle etc, pen*) tappo *m*;

of the class, *league* testa *f*; (*clothing*) maglia *f*; (MOT: *gear*) marcia *f* più alta; ***on top of*** in cima a; ***at the top of*** *list*, *tree*, *mountain* in cima a; *league* in testa a; *page*, *street* all'inizio di; ***get to the top*** *of company etc* arrivare in cima; ***get to the top*** *of mountain* arrivare alla vetta; ***be over the top*** (*exaggerated*) essere esagerato **2** *adj branches* più alto; *floor* ultimo; *management* di alto livello; *official* di alto rango; *player* migliore; *speed*, *note* massimo **3** *v/t* (*pret & pp* ***-ped***): ***topped with cream*** ricoperto di crema

◆ **top up** *v/t glass* riempire; ***top up the tank*** fare il pieno

top 'hat tuba *f*

top•ic ['tɒpɪk] argomento *m*

top•ic•al ['tɒpɪkl] *adj* attuale

top•less ['tɒplɪs] *adj* topless *inv*

top•most ['tɒpməʊst] *adj branches*, *floor* più alto

top•ping ['tɒpɪŋ] *on pizza* guarnizione *f*

top•ple ['tɒpl] **1** *v/i* crollare **2** *v/t government* far cadere

top 'se•cret *adj* top secret *inv*

top•sy-tur•vy [tɒpsɪ'tɜːvɪ] *adj* sottosopra *inv*

torch [tɔːtʃ] *Br* pila *f*; *with flame* torcia *f*

tore [tɔː(r)] *pret* → ***tear***

tor•ment ['tɔːment] **1** *n* tormento *m* **2** *v/t* [tɔː'ment] *person*, *animal* tormentare; ***tormented by doubt*** tormentato dal dubbio

torn [tɔːn] *pp* → ***tear***

tor•na•do [tɔː'neɪdəʊ] tornado *m*

tor•pe•do [tɔː'piːdəʊ] **1** *n* siluro *m* **2** *v/t* silurare; *fig* far saltare

tor•rent ['tɒrənt] torrente *m*; *of lava* fiume *m*; *of abuse*, *words* valanga *f*

tor•ren•tial [tə'renʃl] *adj rain* torrenziale

tor•toise ['tɔːtəs] tartaruga *f*

tor•ture ['tɔːtʃə(r)] **1** *n* tortura *f* **2** *v/t* torturare

toss [tɒs] **1** *v/t ball* lanciare; *rider* disarcionare; *salad* mescolare; ***toss a coin*** fare testa o croce **2** *v/i*: ***toss and turn*** rigirarsi

to•tal ['təʊtl] **1** *n* totale *m* **2** *adj amount*, *disaster* totale; *stranger* perfetto

to•tal•i•tar•i•an [təʊtælɪ'teərɪən] *adj* totalitario

to•tal•ly ['təʊtəlɪ] *adv* totalmente, completamente

tot•ter ['tɒtə(r)] *v/i of person* barcollare

touch [tʌtʃ] **1** *n* tocco *m*; *sense* tatto *m*; *small detail* tocco *m*; *in rugby* touche *f*; ***he felt a touch on his shoulder*** si è sentito toccare sulla spalla; ***lose one's touch*** perdere la mano; ***kick the ball into touch*** calciare la palla fuoricampo; ***lose touch with s.o.*** perdere i contatti con qu; ***keep in touch with s.o.*** rimanere in contatto con qu; ***we kept in touch*** siamo rimasti in contatto; ***be out of touch*** *with news* non essere al corrente; *with people* non avere contatti; ***a touch of*** *little bit* un po' di ... **2** *v/t* toccare; *emotionally* commuovere **3** *v/i* toccare; *of two lines etc* toccarsi

◆ **touch down** *v/i of aeroplane* atterrare; SP fare meta

◆ **touch on** *v/t* (*mention*) accennare a

◆ **touch up** *v/t photo* ritoccare; *sexually* palpeggiare

touch-and-'go: ***it was touch-and-go*** la situazione era critica

touch•down ['tʌtʃdaʊn] *of aeroplane* atterraggio *m*

touch•ing ['tʌtʃɪŋ] *adj* commovente

touch•line ['tʌtʃlaɪn] SP linea *f* laterale

'touch screen schermo *m* tattile

touch•y ['tʌtʃɪ] *adj person* suscettibile

tough [tʌf] *adj person* forte; *question*, *exam*, *meat*, *punishment* duro; *material* resistente

◆ **toughen up** ['tʌfn] *v/t person* rendere più forte

'tough guy F duro *m* F

tour [tʊə(r)] **1** *n* visita *f* **2** *v/t area* fare il giro di

'tour guide guida *f* turistica

tour•i•sm ['tʊərɪzm] turismo *m*

tour•i•st ['tʊərɪst] turista *m/f*

'tour•ist at•trac•tion attrazione *f* turistica

'tour•ist in•dus•try industria *f* del turismo

'tour•ist (in•for•'ma•tion) of•fice azienda *f* (autonoma) di soggiorno

'tour•ist sea•son stagione *f* turistica

tour•na•ment ['tʊənəmənt] torneo *m*

'tour op•er•a•tor operatore *m* turistico

tous•led ['taʊzld] *adj hair* scompigliato

tout [taʊt] *n* bagarino *m*

tow [təʊ] **1** *v/t car*, *boat* rimorchiare **2** *n*: ***give s.o. a tow*** rimorchiare qu

◆ **tow away** *v/t car* portare via col carro attrezzi

to•wards [tə'wɔːdz] *prep* verso; ***rude towards*** maleducato nei confronti di; ***work towards*** (***achieving***) ***sth*** lavorare per (raggiungere) qc

tow•el ['taʊəl] asciugamano *m*

tow•er ['taʊə(r)] torre *f*

◆ **tower over** *v/t* sovrastare

'tow•er block condominio *m* a torre

town [taʊn] città *f inv*; *opposed to city* cittadina *f*

town 'cen•tre centro *m*

town 'coun•cil consiglio *m* comunale

town 'coun•cil•lor consigliere *m*, -a *f* comunale
town 'hall municipio *m*
'tow•rope cavo *m* da rimorchio
tox•ic ['tɒksɪk] *adj* tossico
tox•ic 'waste scorie *fpl* tossiche
tox•in ['tɒksɪn] BIO tossina *f*
toy [tɔɪ] giocattolo *m*
◆ **toy with** *v/t object* giocherellare con; *idea* accarezzare
'toy shop negozio *m* di giocattoli
trace [treɪs] **1** *n of substance* traccia *f* **2** *v/t (find)* rintracciare; *(follow: footsteps)* seguire; *(draw)* tracciare
track [træk] *n (path)* sentiero *m*; *on race course* pista *f*; *(race course)* circuito *m*; RAIL binario *m*; *on record, CD* brano *m*; ***keep track of sth*** tenersi al passo con qc; *keep record of* registrare
◆ **track down** *v/t* rintracciare
'track•suit tuta *f* (da ginnastica)
trac•tor ['træktə(r)] trattore *m*
trade [treɪd] **1** *n (commerce)* commercio *m*; *(profession, craft)* mestiere *m* **2** *v/i (do business)* essere in attività; ***trade in sth*** commerciare in qc **3** *v/t (exchange)* scambiare; ***trade sth for sth*** scambiare qc con qc
◆ **trade in** *v/t when buying* dare in permuta
'trade fair fiera *f* campionaria
'trade•mark marchio *m* registrato
trad•er ['treɪdə(r)] commerciante *m/f*
trade 'se•cret segreto *m* industriale
trades•man ['treɪdzmən] *plumber etc* operaio *m*; *milkman etc* fornitore *m*
trade(s) 'u•nion sindacato *m*
tra•di•tion [trə'dɪʃn] tradizione *f*
tra•di•tion•al [trə'dɪʃnl] *adj* tradizionale
tra•di•tion•al•ly [trə'dɪʃnlɪ] *adv* tradizionalmente
traf•fic ['træfɪk] *n on roads, in drugs* traffico *m*; *at airport* traffico *m* aereo
◆ **traffic in** *v/t (pret & pp* ***-ked****) drugs* trafficare
'traf•fic cop F vigile *m* (urbano)
'traf•fic is•land isola *f* salvagente
'traf•fic jam ingorgo *m*
'traf•fic lights *npl* semaforo *m*
'traf•fic po•lice polizia *f* stradale
'traf•fic sign segnale *m* stradale
'traf•fic war•den ausiliario *m* (del traffico)
tra•ge•dy ['trædʒədɪ] tragedia *f*
tra•gic ['trædʒɪk] *adj* tragico
trail [treɪl] **1** *n (path)* sentiero *m*; *of person, animal* tracce *fpl*; *of blood* scia *f* **2** *v/t (follow)* seguire; *(drag)* trascinare; *caravan etc* trainare **3** *v/i (lag behind)* trascinarsi; ***they're trailing 3-1*** stanno perdendo 3 a 1
trail•er ['treɪlə(r)] *pulled by vehicle* rimorchio *m*; *of film* trailer *m inv*; *Am (caravan)* roulotte *f inv*
train[1] [treɪn] *n* treno *m*; ***go by train*** andare in treno
train[2] [treɪn] **1** *v/t team, athlete* allenare; *employee* formare; *dog* addestrare **2** *v/i of team, athlete* allenarsi; *of teacher etc* fare il tirocinio
train•ee [treɪ'ni:] apprendista *m/f*
train•er ['treɪnə(r)] SP allenatore *m*, -trice *f*; *of dog* addestratore *m*, -trice *f*
train•ers ['treɪnəz] *npl shoes* scarpe *fpl* da ginnastica
train•ing [treɪnɪŋ] *of new staff* formazione *f*; SP allenamento *m*; ***be in training*** SP allenarsi; ***be out of training*** SP essere fuori allenamento
'train•ing course corso *m* di formazione
'train•ing scheme programma *m* di formazione
'train sta•tion stazione *f* ferroviaria
trait [treɪt] tratto *m*
trai•tor ['treɪtə(r)] traditore *m*, -trice *f*
tram [træm] tram *m inv*
tramp [træmp] **1** *n (vagabond)* barbone *m*, -a *f* **2** *v/i* camminare con passo pesante
tram•ple ['træmpl] *v/t*: ***be trampled to death*** morire travolto; ***be trampled underfoot*** essere calpestato
◆ **trample on** *v/t person, object* calpestare
tram•po•line ['træmpəli:n] trampolino *m*
trance [trɑ:ns] trance *f inv*; ***go into a trance*** cadere in trance
tran•quil ['træŋkwɪl] *adj* tranquillo
tran•quil•li•ty [træŋ'kwɪlətɪ] tranquillità *f*
tran•quil•liz•er ['træŋkwɪlaɪzə(r)] tranquillante *m*
trans•act [træn'zækt] *v/t deal, business* trattare
trans•ac•tion [træn'zækʃn] transazione *f*
trans•at•lan•tic [trænzət'læntɪk] *adj* transatlantico
tran•scen•den•tal [trænsen'dentl] *adj* trascendentale
tran•script ['trænskrɪpt] trascrizione *f*
trans•fer [træns'fɜ:(r)] **1** *v/t (pret & pp* ***-red****)* trasferire; LAW cedere **2** *v/i (pret & pp* ***-red****)* cambiare **3** *n* ['trænsfɜ:(r)] trasferimento *m*; LAW cessione *f*; *of money* bonifico *m* bancario
trans•fer•a•ble [træns'fɜ:rəbl] *adj ticket* trasferibile
'trans•fer fee *for football player* prezzo *m* d'acquisto
trans•form [træns'fɔ:m] *v/t* trasformare
trans•form•a•tion [trænsfə'meɪʃn] trasformazione *f*

trans•form•er [træns'fɔːmə(r)] ELEC trasformatore *m*
trans•fu•sion [træns'fjuːʒn] trasfusione *f*
tran•sis•tor [træn'zɪstə(r)] transistor *m inv*; *radio* radiolina *f*
tran•sit ['trænzɪt]: ***in transit*** *of goods, passengers* in transito
tran•si•tion [træn'sɪʒn] transizione *f*
tran•si•tion•al [træn'sɪʒnl] *adj* di transizione
'**tran•sit lounge** *at airport* sala *f* passeggeri in transito
'**trans•it pas•sen•ger** passeggero *m*, -a *f* in transito
trans•late [træns'leɪt] *v/t* tradurre
trans•la•tion [træns'leɪʃn] traduzione *f*
trans•la•tor [træns'leɪtə(r)] traduttore *m*, -trice *f*
trans•mis•sion [trænz'mɪʃn] trasmissione *f*
trans•mit [trænz'mɪt] *v/t* (*pret & pp* ***-ted***) *news, programme, disease* trasmettere
trans•mit•ter [trænz'mɪtə(r)] *for radio, TV* trasmettitore *m*
trans•par•en•cy [træns'pærənsɪ] PHOT diapositiva *f*
trans•par•ent [træns'pærənt] *adj* trasparente
trans•plant [træns'plɑːnt] **1** *v/t* MED trapiantare **2** *n* ['trænsplɑːnt] MED trapianto *m*
trans•port [træn'spɔːt] **1** *v/t goods, people* trasportare **2** *n* ['trænspɔːt] *of goods, people* trasporto *m*; *means of transport* mezzo *m* di trasporto; ***public transport*** i trasporti pubblici
trans•por•ta•tion [trænspɔː'teɪʃn] *of goods, people* trasporto *m*; ***means of transportation*** mezzo *m* di trasporto
trans•ves•tite [træns'vestaɪt] travestito *m*
trap [træp] **1** *n* trappola *f*; *question* tranello *m*; ***set a trap for s.o.*** tendere una trappola a qu **2** *v/t* (*pret & pp* ***-ped***) *animal* intrappolare; *person* incastrare; ***be trapped*** *by enemy, flames, landslide etc* essere intrappolato
trap•door ['træpdɔː(r)] botola *f*
tra•peze [trə'piːz] trapezio *m*
trap•pings ['træpɪŋz] *npl of power* segni *mpl* esteriori
trash [træʃ] (*garbage*) spazzatura *f*; *poor product* robaccia *f*; *despicable person* fetente *m/f*
trash•y [træʃɪ] *adj goods, novel* scadente
trau•mat•ic [trɔː'mætɪk] *adj* traumatico
trau•ma•tize ['trɔːmətaɪz] *v/t* traumatizzare
trav•el ['trævl] **1** *n* viaggiare *m*; ***travels*** viaggi *mpl* **2** *v/i* (*pret & pp* ***-led***, *Am* ***-ed***) viaggiare; ***I travel to work by train*** vado a lavorare in treno **3** *v/t* (*pret & pp* ***-led***, *Am* ***-ed***) *miles* percorrere
'**trav•el a•gen•cy** agenzia *f* di viaggio
'**trav•el a•gent** agente *m/f* di viaggio
'**trav•el bag** borsa *f* da viaggio
'**trav•el ex•penses** *npl* spese *fpl* di viaggio
'**trav•el in•sur•ance** assicurazione *f* di viaggio
trav•el•er *Am*, **trav•ell•er** ['trævələ(r)] viaggiatore *m*, -trice *f*
'**trav•el•er's check** *Am*, '**trav•ell•er's cheque** traveller's cheque *m inv*
'**trav•el pro•gram** *Am*, '**trav•el programme** *on TV etc* programma *m* di viaggi
trawl•er ['trɔːlə(r)] peschereccio *m*
tray [treɪ] *for food, photocopier* vassoio *m*; *to go in oven* teglia *f*
treach•er•ous ['tretʃərəs] *adj* traditore, infido
treach•er•y ['tretʃərɪ] tradimento *m*
tread [tred] **1** *n* passo *m*; *of staircase* gradino *m*; *of tyre* battistrada *m inv* **2** *v/i* (*pret* ***trod***, *pp* ***trodden***) camminare
◆ **tread on** *v/t s.o.'s foot* pestare
trea•son ['triːzn] tradimento *m*
trea•sure ['treʒə(r)] **1** *n also person* tesoro *m* **2** *v/t gift etc* custodire gelosamente
trea•sur•er ['treʒərə(r)] tesoriere *m*, -a *f*
treat [triːt] **1** *n* trattamento *m* speciale; ***it was a real treat*** è stato magnifico; ***I have a treat for you*** ho una sorpresa per te; ***it's my treat*** (*I'm paying*) offro io **2** *v/t* trattare; *illness* curare; ***treat s.o. to sth*** offrire qc a qu
treat•ment ['triːtmənt] trattamento *m*; *of illness* cura *f*
treat•y ['triːtɪ] trattato *m*
tre•ble[1] ['trebl] *n* MUS: *boy's voice* voce *f* bianca; *register* alti *mpl*
tre•ble[2] ['trebl] **1** *adv*: ***treble the price*** il triplo del prezzo **2** *v/i* triplicarsi
tree [triː] albero *m*
trem•ble ['trembl] *v/i* tremare
tre•men•dous [trɪ'mendəs] *adj* (*very good*) fantastico; (*enormous*) enorme
tre•men•dous•ly [trɪ'mendəslɪ] *adv* (*very*) incredibilmente; (*a lot*) moltissimo
trem•or ['tremə(r)] *of earth* scossa *f*
trench [trentʃ] trincea *f*
trend [trend] tendenza *f*
trend•y ['trendɪ] *adj* alla moda
tres•pass ['trespəs] *v/i* invadere una proprietà privata; ***no trespassing*** divieto d'accesso
◆ **trespass on** *v/t s.o.'s land, privacy* invadere; *s.o.'s rights, time* abusare di
tres•pass•er ['trespəsə(r)] intruso *m*, -a *f*

T

tri•al ['traɪəl] LAW processo *m*; *of equipment* prova *f*; ***on trial*** LAW sotto processo; ***stand trial for sth*** essere processato per qc; ***have sth on trial*** *equipment* avere qc in prova
tri•al 'pe•ri•od periodo *m* di prova
tri•an•gle ['traɪæŋgl] triangolo *m*
tri•an•gu•lar [traɪ'æŋgjʊlə(r)] *adj* triangolare
tribe [traɪb] tribù *f inv*
tri•bu•nal [traɪ'bju:nl] tribunale *m*
tri•bu•ta•ry ['trɪbjʊtərɪ] *of river* affluente *m*
trick [trɪk] **1** *n to deceive* stratagemma *m*; (*knack*) trucco *m*; ***a trick of the light*** un effetto di luce; ***play a trick on s.o.*** fare uno scherzo a qu **2** *v/t* ingannare; ***trick s.o. into doing sth*** convincere qu con l'inganno a fare qc
trick•e•ry ['trɪkərɪ] truffa *f*
trick•le ['trɪkl] **1** *n* filo *m*; ***a trickle of replies*** poche risposte sporadiche **2** *v/i* gocciolare
trick•ster ['trɪkstə(r)] truffatore *m*, -trice *f*
trick•y ['trɪkɪ] *adj* (*difficult*) complicato
tri•cy•cle ['traɪsɪkl] triciclo *m*
tri•fle ['traɪfl] *n* (*triviality*) inezia *f*; *pudding* zuppa *f* inglese
tri•fling ['traɪflɪŋ] *adj* insignificante
trig•ger ['trɪgə(r)] *n on gun* grilletto *m*; *on camcorder* pulsante *m* (di accensione)
◆ **trigger off** *v/t* scatenare
trim [trɪm] **1** *adj* (*neat*) ordinato; *figure* snello **2** *v/t* (*pret & pp* ***-med***) *hair, hedge* spuntare; *budget, costs* tagliare; (*decorate: dress*) ornare **3** *n* (*light cut*) spuntata *f*; ***in good trim*** in buone condizioni
trim•ming ['trɪmɪŋ] *on clothes* ornamento *m*; ***with all the trimmings*** con tutti gli annessi e connessi
trin•ket ['trɪŋkɪt] ninnolo *m*
tri•o ['tri:əʊ] MUS trio *m*
trip [trɪp] **1** *n* (*journey*) viaggio *m*, gita *f* **2** *v/i* (*pret & pp* ***-ped***) (*stumble*) inciampare (***over*** in) **3** *v/t* (*pret & pp* ***-ped***) (*make fall*) fare inciampare
◆ **trip up 1** *v/t* (*make fall*) fare inciampare; *cause to make a mistake* confondere **2** *v/i* (*stumble*) inciampare; (*make a mistake*) sbagliarsi
tripe [traɪp] trippa *f*
trip•le ['trɪpl] → ***treble***[2]
trip•lets ['trɪplɪts] *npl* tre gemelli *mpl*
tri•pod ['traɪpɒd] PHOT treppiedi *m inv*
trite [traɪt] *adj* trito
tri•umph ['traɪʌmf] *n* trionfo *m*
triv•i•al ['trɪvɪəl] *adj* banale
triv•i•al•i•ty [trɪvɪ'ælətɪ] banalità *f inv*
trod [trɒd] *pret* → ***tread***
trod•den ['trɒdn] *pp* → ***tread***
trol•ley ['trɒlɪ] *in supermarket, at airport* carrello *m*
trom•bone [trɒm'bəʊn] trombone *m*
troops [tru:ps] *npl* truppe *fpl*
tro•phy ['trəʊfɪ] trofeo *m*
tro•pic ['trɒpɪk] tropico *m*
trop•i•cal ['trɒpɪkl] *adj* tropicale
trop•ics ['trɒpɪks] *npl* tropici *mpl*
trot [trɒt] *v/i* (*pret & pp* ***-ted***) trottare
trou•ble ['trʌbl] **1** *n* (*difficulties*) problemi *mpl*; (*inconvenience*) fastidio *m*; (*disturbance*) disordini *mpl*; ***go to a lot of trouble to do sth*** darsi molto da fare per fare qc; ***no trouble!*** nessun problema!; ***the trouble with you is …*** il tuo problema è …; ***get into trouble*** mettersi nei guai **2** *v/t* (*worry*) preoccupare; (*bother, disturb*) disturbare; *of back, liver etc* dare dei fastidi a
'trou•ble-free senza problemi
'trou•ble•mak•er attaccabrighe *m/f inv*
'trou•ble•shoot•er (*mediator*) mediatore *m*, trice *f*
'trou•ble•shoot•ing mediazione *f*; *in software manual* ricerca *f* problemi e soluzioni
trou•ble•some ['trʌblsəm] *adj* fastidioso
trou•sers ['traʊzəz] *npl* pantaloni *mpl*; ***a pair of trousers*** un paio di pantaloni
'trou•ser suit tailleur *m inv* pantaloni
trout [traʊt] (*pl* ***trout***) trota *f*
tru•ant ['tru:ənt]: ***play truant*** marinare la scuola
truce [tru:s] tregua *f*
truck [trʌk] (*lorry*) camion *m inv*
trudge [trʌdʒ] **1** *v/i* arrancare; ***trudge around the shops*** trascinarsi per i negozi **2** *n* camminata *f* stancante
true [tru:] *adj* vero; ***come true*** *of hopes, dream* realizzarsi
trul•y ['tru:lɪ] *adv* davvero; ***Yours truly*** distinti saluti
trum•pet ['trʌmpɪt] tromba *f*
trum•pet•er ['trʌmpɪtə(r)] trombettiere *f*
trun•cheon ['trʌntʃn] manganello *m*
trunk [trʌŋk] *of tree, body* tronco *m*; *of elephant* proboscide *f*; (*large case*) baule *m*; *Am* MOT bagagliaio *m inv*
trunks [trʌŋks] *npl for swimming* calzoncini *mpl* da bagno
trust [trʌst] **1** *n* fiducia *f*; FIN fondo *m* fiduciario; COM trust *m inv* **2** *v/t* fidarsi di; ***I trust you*** mi fido di te
trusted ['trʌstɪd] *adj* fidato
trust•ee [trʌs'ti:] amministratore *m*, -trice *f* fiduciario, -a
trust•ful, trust•ing ['trʌstfʊl, 'trʌstɪŋ] *adj*

fiducioso
trust•wor•thy ['trʌstwɜːðɪ] *adj* affidabile
truth [truːθ] verità *f inv*
truth•ful ['truːθfʊl] *adj account* veritiero; *person* sincero
try [traɪ] **1** *v/t* (*pret & pp* ***-ied***) provare; LAW processare; ***try to do sth*** provare a fare qc, cercare di fare qc **2** *v/i* (*pret & pp* ***-ied***) provare, tentare; ***you must try harder*** devi provare con più impegno **3** *n* tentativo *m*; *in rugby* meta *f*; ***can I have a try?*** *of food* posso assaggiare?; *at doing sth* posso fare un tentativo?
◆ **try on** *clothes* provare
◆ **try out** *new machine*, *method* provare
try•ing ['traɪɪŋ] *adj* (*annoying*) difficile
T-shirt ['tiːʃɜːt] maglietta *f*
tub [tʌb] (*bath*) vasca *f* da bagno; *of liquid* tinozza *f*; *for yoghurt*, *icecream* barattolo *m*
tub•by ['tʌbɪ] *adj* tozzo
tube [tjuːb] (*pipe*) tubo *m*; (*underground railway*) metropolitana *f*; *of toothpaste*, *ointment* tubetto *m*
tube•less ['tjuːblɪs] *adj tyre* senza camera d'aria
tu•ber•cu•lo•sis [tjuːbɜːkjʊ'ləʊsɪs] tubercolosi *f*
tuck [tʌk] **1** *n in dress* pince *f inv* **2** *v/t*: ***tuck sth into sth*** infilare qc in qc
◆ **tuck away** *v/t* (*put away*) mettere via; (*eat quickly*) sbafare; ***be tucked away*** *of house*, *village* essere nascosto
◆ **tuck in 1** *v/t children* rimboccare le coperte a; *sheets* rimboccare **2** *v/i* (*eat*) mangiare; (*start eating*) incominciare a mangiare
◆ **tuck up** *v/t sleeves etc* rimboccarsi; ***tuck s.o. up in bed*** rimboccare le coperte a qu
Tues•day ['tjuːzdeɪ] martedì *m inv*
tuft [tʌft] ciuffo *m*
tug [tʌg] **1** *n* (*pull*) tirata *f*; NAUT rimorchiatore *m*; ***I felt a tug at my sleeve*** mi sono sentito tirare la manica **2** *v/t* (*pret & pp* ***-ged***) (*pull*) tirare
tu•i•tion [tjuː'ɪsn] lezioni *fpl*
tu•lip ['tjuːlɪp] tulipano *m*
tum•ble ['tʌmbl] *v/i* ruzzolare; *of wall*, *prices* crollare
tum•ble•down ['tʌmbldaʊn] *adj* in rovina, fatiscente
tum•ble-dry•er ['tʌmbldraɪə(r)] asciugatrice *f*
tum•bler ['tʌmblə(r)] *for drinker* bicchiere *m* (senza stelo); *in circus* acrobata *m/f*
tum•my ['tʌmɪ] F pancia *f*
'**tum•my ache** mal *m* di pancia
tu•mour ['tjuːmə(r)] tumore *m*
tu•mult ['tjuːmʌlt] tumulto *m*
tu•mul•tu•ous [tjuː'mʌltjʊəs] *adj* tumultuoso
tu•na ['tjuːnə] tonno *m*; ***tuna salad*** insalata *f* di tonno
tune [tjuːn] **1** *n* motivo *m*; ***in tune*** *instrument* accordato; *person* intonato; ***out of tune*** *instrument* scordato; *person* stonato **2** *v/t instrument* accordare; *engine* mettere a punto
◆ **tune in** *v/i of radio*, *TV* sintonizzarsi
◆ **tune in to** *v/t radio*, *TV* sintonizzarsi su
◆ **tune up 1** *v/i of orchestra*, *players* accordare gli strumenti **2** *v/t engine* mettere a punto
tune•ful ['tjuːnfʊl] *adj* melodioso
tun•er ['tjuːnə(r)] (*hi-fi*) sintonizzatore *m*, tuner *m inv*
tune-up ['tjuːnʌp] *of engine* messa *f* a punto
tu•nic ['tjuːnɪk] tunica *f*; *protective* grembiule *m*; *of uniform* giacca *f*
tun•nel ['tʌnl] *n* galleria *f*, tunnel *m inv*
tur•bine ['tɜːbaɪn] turbina *f*
tur•bu•lence ['tɜːbjʊləns] *in air travel* turbolenza *f*
tur•bu•lent ['tɜːbjʊlənt] *adj* turbolento
turf [tɜːf] tappeto *m* erboso; (*piece*) zolla *f*
Tu•rin [tjʊ'rɪn] Torino *f*
Turk [tɜːk] turco *m*, -a *f*
Tur•key ['tɜːkɪ] Turchia *f*
tur•key ['tɜːkɪ] tacchino *m*
Turk•ish ['tɜːkɪʃ] **1** *adj* turco **2** *n language* turco *m*
tur•moil ['tɜːmɔɪl] agitazione *f*
turn [tɜːn] **1** *n* (*rotation*) giro *m*; *in road* curva *f*; *in variety show* numero *m*; ***take turns in doing sth*** fare a turno a fare qc; ***it's my turn*** è il mio turno, tocca a me; ***it's not your turn yet*** non è ancora il tuo turno; ***take a turn at the wheel*** prendere il volante per un po'; ***do s.o. a good turn*** fare un favore a qu **2** *v/t wheel*, *corner* girare; ***turn one's back on s.o.*** girare le spalle a qu **3** *v/i of driver*, *car*, *wheel* girare; (*become*) diventare; ***turn right / left here*** gira a destra / sinistra qui; ***it has turned sour / cold*** è diventato acido / freddo; ***he has turned 40*** ha compiuto 40 anni
◆ **turn around 1** *v/t object* girare; *company* dare una svolta positiva a; (COM: *deal with*) eseguire; *order* evadere **2** *v/i of person* girarsi; *of driver* girare
◆ **turn away 1** *v/t* (*send away*) mandare via **2** *v/i* (*walk away*) andare via; (*look away*) girarsi dall'altra parte
◆ **turn back 1** *v/t edges*, *sheets* ripiegare **2**

v/i of walkers etc tornare indietro; *in course of action* tirarsi indietro

◆ **turn down** *v/t offer, invitation* rifiutare; *volume, TV, heating* abbassare; *edge, collar* ripiegare

◆ **turn in 1** *v/i* (*go to bed*) andare a letto **2** *v/t to police* denunciare

◆ **turn off 1** *v/t radio, TV, heater, engine* spegnere; *tap* chiudere; F (*sexually*) far passare la voglia a **2** *v/i of car, driver* svoltare

◆ **turn on 1** *v/t radio, TV, heater, engine* accendere; *tap* aprire; F (*sexually*) eccitare **2** *v/i of machine* accendersi

◆ **turn out 1** *v/t lights* spegnere **2** *v/i*: ***as it turned out*** come è emerso; ***it turned out well*** è andata bene

◆ **turn over 1** *v/i in bed* girarsi; *of vehicle* capottare **2** *v/t object, page* girare; FIN fatturare

◆ **turn up 1** *v/t collar, volume, heating* alzare **2** *v/i* (*arrive*) arrivare

turn•ing ['tɜːnɪŋ] svolta *f*

'**turn•ing point** svolta *f* decisiva

tur•nip ['tɜːnɪp] rapa *f*

'**turn•out** *of people* affluenza *f*

'**turn•o•ver** FIN fatturato *m*; *of staff* ricambio *m*

'**turn•stile** cancelletto *m* girevole

'**turn•ta•ble** *of record player* piatto *m*

'**turn-up** (*on trousers*) risvolto *m*

tur•quoise ['tɜːkwɔɪz] *adj* turchese

tur•ret ['tʌrɪt] *of castle, tank* torretta *f*

tur•tle ['tɜːtl] tartaruga *f* marina

tur•tle•neck '**sweater** maglia *f* a lupetto

Tus•can•y ['tʌskənɪ] Toscana *f*

tusk [tʌsk] zanna *f*

tu•tor ['tjuːtə(r)] EDU *insegnante universitario che segue un piccolo gruppo di studenti*; (***private***) ***tutor*** insegnante *m/f* privato, -a

tu•to•ri•al [tjuː'tɔːrɪəl] *n at university* incontro *m* con il tutor

tu•xe•do [tʌk'siːdəʊ] *Am* smoking *m inv*

TV [tiː'viː] tv *f inv*; ***on TV*** alla tv

T'V din•ner piatto *m* pronto

T,V guide guida *f* dei programmi tv

T,V pro•gramme programma *m* televisivo

twang [twæŋ] **1** *n in voice* suono *m* nasale **2** *v/t guitar string* vibrare

tweez•ers ['twiːzəz] *npl* pinzette *fpl*

twelfth [twelfθ] *n & adj* dodicesimo, -a

twelve [twelv] dodici

twen•ti•eth ['twentɪɪθ] *n & adj* ventesimo, -a

twen•ty ['twentɪ] venti

twice [twaɪs] *adv* due volte; ***twice as much*** il doppio; ***twice as fast*** veloce due volte tanto

twid•dle ['twɪdl] *v/t* girare; ***twiddle one's thumbs*** girarsi i pollici

twig [twɪg] *n* ramoscello *m*

twi•light ['twaɪlaɪt] crepuscolo *m*

twin [twɪn] gemello *m*

'**twin beds** *npl* due lettini *mpl*

twinge [twɪndʒ] *of pain* fitta *f*

twin•kle ['twɪŋkl] *v/i of stars, eyes* scintillare

twin '**room** camera *f* a due letti

'**twin town** città *f inv* gemellata

twirl [twɜːl] **1** *v/t* fare roteare **2** *n of cream etc* ricciolo *m*

twist [twɪst] **1** *v/t* attorcigliare; ***twist one's ankle*** prendere una storta **2** *v/i of road* snodarsi; *of river* serpeggiare **3** *n in rope* attorcigliata *f*; *in road* curva *f*; *in plot, story* svolta *f*

twist•y ['twɪstɪ] *adj road* contorto

twit [twɪt] F scemo *m*, -a *f*

twitch [twɪʧ] **1** *n nervous* spasmo *m* **2** *v/i* (*jerk*) contrarsi

twit•ter ['twɪtə(r)] *v/i* cinguettare

two [tuː] due; ***the two of them*** loro due

'**two-faced** *adj* falso

'**two-piece** (*woman's suit*) tailleur *m inv*

'**two-stroke** *adj engine* a due tempi

two-way '**traf•fic** traffico *m* nei due sensi di marcia

ty•coon [taɪ'kuːn] magnate *m*

type [taɪp] **1** *n* (*sort*) tipo *m*; ***what type of ...?*** che tipo di ...? **2** *v/t & v/i* (*use a keyboard*) battere (a macchina)

type•writ•er ['taɪpraɪtə(r)] macchina *f* da scrivere

ty•phoid ['taɪfɔɪd] febbre *f* tifoide

ty•phoon [taɪ'fuːn] tifone *m*

ty•phus ['taɪfəs] tifo *m*

typ•i•cal ['tɪpɪkl] *adj* tipico; ***that's typical of you / him!*** tipico!

typ•i•cal•ly ['tɪpɪklɪ] *adv*: ***typically American*** tipicamente americano; ***he would typically arrive late*** arriva sempre tardi

typ•ist ['taɪpɪst] dattilografo *m*, -a *f*

ty•ran•ni•cal [tɪ'rænɪkl] *adj* tirannico

ty•ran•nize [tɪ'rənaɪz] *v/t* tiranneggiare

ty•ran•ny ['tɪrənɪ] tirannia *f*

ty•rant ['taɪrənt] tiranno *m*, -a *f*

tyre ['taɪə(r)] gomma *f*, pneumatico *m*

Ty•rol [tɪ'rɒl] Tirolo *m*

Ty•ro•le•an [tɪrə'liːən] *adj* tirolese

Tyr•rhe•ni•an Sea [taɪ'riːnɪən] mar *m* Tirreno

U

ug•ly ['ʌglɪ] *adj* brutto

UK [juː'keɪ] *abbr* (= ***United Kingdom***) Regno *m* Unito

ul•cer ['ʌlsə(r)] ulcera *f*

ul•ti•mate ['ʌltɪmət] *adj* (*best*, *definitive*) definitivo; (*final*) ultimo; (*basic*) fondamentale

ul•ti•mate•ly ['ʌltɪmətlɪ] *adv* (*in the end*) in definitiva

ul•ti•ma•tum [ʌltɪ'meɪtəm] ultimatum *m inv*

ul•tra•sound ['ʌltrəsaʊnd] MED ecografia *f*

ul•travi•o•let [ʌltrə'vaɪələt] *adj* ultravioletto

um•bil•i•cal cord [ʌm'bɪlɪkl] cordone *m* ombelicale

um•brel•la [ʌm'brelə] ombrello *m*

um•pire ['ʌmpaɪə(r)] *n* arbitro *m*

ump•teen [ʌmp'tiːn] *adj* F ennesimo

UN [juː'en] *abbr* (= ***United Nations***) ONU *f inv* (= Organizzazione *f* delle Nazioni Unite)

un•a•ble [ʌn'eɪbl] *adj*: ***be unable to do sth*** *not know how to* non saper fare qc; *not be in a position to* non poter fare qc

un•ac•cept•a•ble [ʌnək'septəbl] *adj* inaccettabile; ***it is unacceptable that …*** è inaccettabile che …

un•ac•count•a•ble [ʌnə'kaʊntəbl] *adj* inspiegabile

un•ac•cus•tomed [ʌnə'kʌstəmd] *adj*: ***be unaccustomed to sth*** non essere abituato a qc

un•a•dul•ter•at•ed [ʌnə'dʌltəreɪtɪd] *adj* (*fig*: *absolute*) puro; *activities* anti-americano

u•nan•i•mous [juː'nænɪməs] *adj verdict* unanime; ***be unanimous on*** essere unanimi su

u•nan•i•mous•ly [juː'nænɪməslɪ] *adv vote*, *decide* all'unanimità

un•ap•proach•a•ble [ʌnə'prəʊʧəbl] *adj person* inavvicinabile

un•armed [ʌn'ɑːmd] *adj person* disarmato; ***unarmed combat*** combattimento senz'armi

un•as•sum•ing [ʌnə'sjʊːmɪŋ] *adj* senza pretese

un•at•tached [ʌnə'tæʧt] *adj without a partner* libero

un•at•tend•ed [ʌnə'tendɪd] *adj* incustodito; ***leave sth unattended*** lasciare qc incustodito

un•au•thor•ized [ʌn'ɔːθəraɪzd] *adj* non autorizzato

un•a•void•a•ble [ʌnə'vɔɪdəbl] *adj* inevitabile

un•a•void•a•bly [ʌnə'vɔɪdəblɪ] *adv* inevitabilmente; ***be unavoidably detained*** essere trattenuto per cause di forza maggiore

un•a•ware [ʌnə'weə(r)] *adj*: ***be unaware of*** non rendersi conto di

un•a•wares [ʌnə'weəz] *adv*: ***catch s.o. unawares*** prendere qu alla sprovvista

un•bal•anced [ʌn'bælənst] *adj* non equilibrato; PSYCH squilibrato

un•bear•a•ble [ʌn'beərəbl] *adj* insopportabile

un•beat•a•ble [ʌn'biːtəbl] *adj team*, *quality* imbattibile

un•beat•en [ʌn'biːtn] *adj team* imbattuto

un•be•lie•va•ble [ʌnbɪ'liːvəbl] *adj* incredibile

un•bi•as(s)ed [ʌn'baɪəst] *adj* imparziale

un•block [ʌn'blɒk] *v/t pipe* sbloccare

un•born [ʌn'bɔːn] *adj* non ancora nato

un•break•a•ble [ʌn'breɪkəbl] *adj plates* infrangibile; *world record* imbattibile

un•but•ton [ʌn'bʌtn] *v/t* sbottonare

un•called-for [ʌn'kɔːldfɔː(r)] *adj* ingiustificato

un•can•ny [ʌn'kænɪ] *adj resemblance*, *skill* sorprendente; (*worrying*: *feeling*) inquietante

un•ceas•ing [ʌn'siːsɪŋ] *adj* incessante

un•cer•tain [ʌn'sɜːtn] *adj future*, *weather* incerto; *origins* dubbio; ***what will happen? – it's uncertain*** cosa succederà? – non si sa; ***be uncertain about sth*** non essere certo su qc

un•cer•tain•ty [ʌn'sɜːtntɪ] *of the future* incertezza *f*; ***there is still uncertainty about …*** ci sono ancora dubbi su …

un•checked [ʌn'ʧekt] *adj*: ***let sth go unchecked*** non controllare qc

un•cle ['ʌŋkl] zio *m*

un•com•for•ta•ble [ʌn'kʌmftəbl] *adj* scomodo; ***feel uncomfortable about sth*** sentirsi a disagio per qc; ***I feel uncomfortable with him*** mi sento a disagio con lui

un•com•mon [ʌn'kɒmən] *adj* raro; ***it's not uncommon*** non è raro

un•com•pro•mis•ing [ʌn'kɒmprəmaɪzɪŋ] *adj* fermo; *in a negative way* intransigente

un•con•cerned [ʌnkən'sɜːnd] *adj* indifferente; ***be unconcerned about s.o./sth*** non darsi pensiero di qu / qc
un•con•di•tion•al [ʌnkən'dɪʃnl] *adj* incondizionato
un•con•scious [ʌn'kɒnʃəs] *adj* MED svenuto; PSYCH inconscio; ***knock s.o. unconscious*** stordire qu con un colpo; ***be unconscious of sth*** (*not aware*) non rendersi conto di qc
un•con•trol•la•ble [ʌnkən'trəʊləbl] *adj anger, desire, children* incontrollabile
un•con•ven•tion•al [ʌnkən'venʃnl] *adj* poco convenzionale
un•co•op•er•a•tive [ʌnkəʊ'ɒprətɪv] *adj* poco cooperativo
un•cork [ʌn'kɔːk] *v/t bottle* stappare
un•cov•er [ʌn'kʌvə(r)] *v/t* scoprire
un•dam•aged [ʌn'dæmɪdʒd] *adj* intatto
un•daunt•ed [ʌn'dɔːntɪd] *adj*: ***carry on undaunted*** continuare imperterrito
un•de•cid•ed [ʌndɪ'saɪdɪd] *adj question* irrisolto; ***be undecided about sth*** essere indeciso su qc
un•de•ni•a•ble [ʌndɪ'naɪəbl] *adj* innegabile
un•de•ni•a•bly [ʌndɪ'naɪəblɪ] *adv* innegabilmente
un•der ['ʌndə(r)] **1** *prep* (*beneath*) sotto; (*less than*) meno di; ***it is under review / investigation*** viene rivisto / indagato; ***it is under construction*** è in costruzione **2** *adv* (*anaesthetized*) sotto anestesia
un•der'age *adj*: ***underage drinking*** alcolismo *m* minorile
'**un•der•arm** *adv throw* sottinsù
'**un•der•car•riage** carrello *m* d'atterraggio
'**un•der•cov•er** *adj agent* segreto
un•der'cut *v/t* (*pret & pp* ***-cut***) COM vendere a minor prezzo di
'**un•der•dog**: ***they were the underdogs*** dovevano perdere
un•der'done *adj meat* al sangue; *not cooked enough* non cotto abbastanza
un•der'es•ti•mate *v/t person, skills, task* sottovalutare
un•der•ex'posed *adj* PHOT sottoesposto
un•der'fed *adj* malnutrito
un•der'go *v/t* (*pret* ***-went***, *pp* ***-gone***) *surgery, treatment* sottoporsi a; *experiences* vivere; ***undergo refurbishment*** venire ristrutturato
un•der'grad•u•ate studente *m*, -essa *f* universitario, -a
'**un•der•ground 1** *adj passages etc* sotterraneo; POL: *resistance, newspaper etc* clandestino **2** *adv work* sottoterra; ***go underground*** POL entrare in clandestinità **3** *n* RAIL metropolitana *f*
'**un•der•growth** sottobosco *m*
un•der'hand *adj* (*devious*) subdolo
un•der'lie *v/t* (*pret* ***-lay***, *pp* ***-lain***) (*form basis of*) essere alla base di
un•der'line *v/t text* sottolineare
un•der'ly•ing *adj causes, problems* di fondo
un•der'mine *v/t s.o.'s position* minare
un•der•neath [ʌndə'niːθ] *prep adv* sotto **2** *adv* sotto
'**un•der•pants** *npl* mutande *fpl* da uomo
'**un•der•pass** *for pedestrians* sottopassaggio *m*
un•der•priv•i•leged [ʌndə'prɪvɪlɪdʒd] *adj* svantaggiato
un•der'rate *v/t* sottovalutare
'**un•der•shirt** *Am* canottiera *f*
un•der•sized [ʌndə'saɪzd] *adj* troppo piccolo
'**un•der•skirt** sottogonna *f*
un•der•staffed [ʌndə'stɑːft] *adj* a corto di personale
un•der•stand [ʌndə'stænd] (*pret & pp* ***-stood***) **1** *v/t* capire; ***I understand that you …*** mi risulta che tu …; ***they are understood to be in Canada*** pare che siano in Canada **2** *v/i* capire
un•der•stand•able [ʌndə'stændəbl] *adj* comprensibile
un•der•stand•ably [ʌndə'stændəblɪ] *adv* comprensibilmente
un•der•stand•ing [ʌndə'stændɪŋ] **1** *adj person* comprensivo **2** *n of problem, situation* comprensione *f*; (*agreement*) intesa *f*; ***on the understanding that we agree a price*** a patto che ci troviamo d'accordo sul prezzo
'**un•der•state•ment** understatement *m inv*
un•der'take *v/t* (*pret* ***-took***, *pp* ***-taken***) *task* intraprendere; ***undertake to do sth*** impegnarsi a fare qc
'**un•der•tak•er** impresario *m* di pompe funebri
'**un•der•tak•ing** (*enterprise*) impresa *f*; (*promise*) promessa *f*
un•der'val•ue *v/t* sottovalutare
'**un•der•wear** biancheria *f* intima
un•der'weight *adj* sottopeso
'**un•de•rworld** *criminal* malavita *f inv*; *in mythology* inferi *mpl*
un•der'write *v/t* (*pret* ***-wrote***, *pp* ***-written***) FIN sottoscrivere
un•de•served [ʌndɪ'zɜːvd] *adj* immeritato
un•de•sir•a•ble [ʌndɪ'zaɪərəbl] *adj features, changes* indesiderato; *person* poco

raccomandabile; ***undesirable element*** *person* persona indesiderabile
un•dis•put•ed [ʌndɪ'spjuːtɪd] *adj champion, leader* indiscusso
un•do [ʌn'duː] *v/t* (*pret* ***-did***, *pp* ***-done***) *parcel, wrapping* disfare; *shirt* sbottonare; *shoes, shoelaces* slacciare; *s.o. else's work* annullare, sciupare
un•doubt•ed•ly [ʌn'daʊtɪdlɪ] *adv* indubbiamente
un•dreamt-of [ʌn'dremtɒv] *adj riches* impensato
un•dress [ʌn'dres] **1** *v/t* spogliare; ***get undressed*** spogliarsi **2** *v/i* spogliarsi
un•due [ʌn'djuː] *adj* (*excessive*) eccessivo
un•du•ly [ʌn'djuːlɪ] *adv punished, blamed* ingiustamente; (*excessively*) eccessivamente
un•earth [ʌn'ɜːθ] *v/t ancient remains* portare alla luce; (*fig: find*) scovare
un•earth•ly [ʌn'ɜːθlɪ] *adv*: ***at this unearthly hour*** a quest'ora (impossibile)
un•eas•y [ʌn'iːzɪ] *adj relationship, peace* precario; ***feel uneasy about*** non sentirsela di
un•eat•a•ble [ʌn'iːtəbl] *adj* immangiabile
un•e•co•nom•ic [ʌniːkə'nɒmɪk] *adj* poco redditizio
un•ed•u•cat•ed [ʌn'edjʊkeɪtɪd] *adj* senza istruzione
un•em•ployed [ʌnɪm'plɔɪd] *adj* disoccupato; ***the unemployed*** i disoccupati
un•em•ploy•ment [ʌnɪm'plɔɪmənt] disoccupazione *f*; ***unemployment benefit*** sussidio *m* di disoccupazione
un•end•ing [ʌn'endɪŋ] *adj* interminabile
un•e•qual [ʌn'iːkwəl] *adj* disuguale; ***be unequal to the task*** non essere all'altezza del compito
un•er•ring [ʌn'erɪŋ] *adj judgement, instinct* infallibile
un•e•ven [ʌn'iːvn] *adj quality* irregolare; *ground* accidentato
un•e•ven•ly [ʌn'iːvnlɪ] *adv distributed, applied* in modo irregolare; ***unevenly matched*** *of two contestants* mal assortiti
un•e•vent•ful [ʌnɪ'ventfʊl] *adj day, journey* tranquillo
un•ex•pec•ted [ʌnɪk'spektɪd] *adj* inatteso
un•ex•pec•ted•ly [ʌnɪk'spektɪdlɪ] *adv* inaspettatamente
un•fair [ʌn'feə(r)] *adj* ingiusto
un•faith•ful [ʌn'feɪθfʊl] *adj husband, wife* infedele; ***be unfaithful to s.o.*** essere infedele a qu
un•fa•mil•i•ar [ʌnfə'mɪljə(r)] *adj* sconosciuto; ***be unfamiliar with sth*** non conoscere qc
un•fas•ten [ʌn'fɑːsn] *v/t belt* slacciare
un•fa•vo•ra•ble *Am*, **un•fa•vou•ra•ble** [ʌn'feɪvərəbl] *adj report, review* negativo; *weather conditions* sfavorevole
un•feel•ing [ʌn'fiːlɪŋ] *adj person* insensibile
un•fin•ished [ʌn'fɪnɪʃt] *adj job, letter, building* non terminato; *business* in sospeso; ***leave sth unfinished*** non terminare qc
un•fit [ʌn'fɪt] *adj physically* fuori forma; ***be unfit to ...*** *morally* non essere degno di ...; ***unfit to eat / drink*** non commestibile / non potabile
un•flap•pa•ble [ʌn'flæpəbl] *adj* F calmo, imperturbabile
un•fold [ʌn'fəʊld] **1** *v/t sheets, letter* spiegare; *one's arms* aprire **2** *v/i of story etc* svolgersi; *of view* spiegarsi
un•fore•seen [ʌnfɔː'siːn] *adj* imprevisto
un•for•get•ta•ble [ʌnfə'getəbl] *adj* indimenticabile
un•for•giv•a•ble [ʌnfə'gɪvəbl] *adj* imperdonabile; ***that was unforgivable (of you)*** è una mancanza imperdonabile
un•for•tu•nate [ʌn'fɔːtʃənət] *adj people* sfortunato; *event, choice of words* infelice; ***that's unfortunate for you*** è spiacevole per lei
un•for•tu•nate•ly [ʌn'fɔːtʃənətlɪ] *adv* sfortunatamente
un•found•ed [ʌn'faʊndɪd] *adj* infondato
un•friend•ly [ʌn'frendlɪ] *adj* poco amichevole; *software* di non facile uso
un•fur•nished [ʌn'fɜːnɪʃt] *adj* non ammobiliato
un•god•ly [ʌn'gɒdlɪ] *adj*: ***at this ungodly hour*** ad un'ora impossibile
un•grate•ful [ʌn'greɪtfʊl] *adj* ingrato
un•hap•pi•ness [ʌn'hæpɪnɪs] infelicità *f inv*
un•hap•py [ʌn'hæpɪ] *adj* infelice; *customers etc* non soddisfatto; ***be unhappy with the service / an explanation*** non essere soddisfatto del servizio / della giustificazione
un•harmed [ʌn'hɑːmd] *adj* illeso
un•health•y [ʌn'helθɪ] *adj person* malaticcio; *conditions* malsano; *food, atmosphere* poco sano; *economy* traballante; *balance sheet* in passivo
un•heard-of [ʌn'hɜːdɒv] *adj* inaudito
un'hoped-for *adj* insperato
un•hurt [ʌn'hɜːt] *adj* illeso
un•hy•gi•en•ic [ʌnhaɪ'dʒiːnɪk] *adj* non igienico
u•ni•fi•ca•tion [juːnɪfɪ'keɪʃn] unificazione *f*
u•ni•form ['juːnɪfɔːm] **1** *n of school pupil, air hostess* divisa *f*; *of soldier* divisa *f*, uni-

forme *f* **2** *adj* uniforme
u•ni•fy ['juːnɪfaɪ] *v/t* (*pret & pp* **-ied**) unificare
u•ni•lat•e•ral [juːnɪ'lætrəl] *adj* unilaterale
un•i•ma•gi•na•ble [ʌnɪ'mædʒɪnəbl] *adj* inimmaginabile
un•i•ma•gi•na•tive [ʌnɪ'mædʒɪnətɪv] *adj* senza fantasia
un•im•por•tant [ʌnɪm'pɔːtənt] *adj* senza importanza
un•in•hab•i•ta•ble [ʌnɪn'hæbɪtəbl] *adj* inabitabile
un•in•hab•it•ed [ʌnɪn'hæbɪtɪd] *adj building* disabitato; *region* deserto
un•in•jured [ʌn'ɪndʒəd] *adj* incolume
un•in•tel•li•gi•ble [ʌnɪn'telɪdʒəbl] *adj* incomprensibile
un•in•ten•tion•al [ʌnɪn'tenʃnl] *adj* involontario
un•in•ten•tion•al•ly [ʌnɪn'tenʃnlɪ] *adv* involontariamente
un•in•te•rest•ing [ʌn'ɪntrəstɪŋ] *adj* poco interessante
un•in•ter•rupt•ed [ʌnɪntə'rʌptɪd] *adj sleep, work* ininterrotto
u•nion ['juːnɪən] POL unione *f*; (*trade union*) sindacato *m*
u•nique [juː'niːk] *adj* (*also very good*) unico; ***with his own unique humour / style*** con quel senso dell'umorismo / quello stile tutto suo
u•nit ['juːnɪt] *of measurement* unità *f inv*; (*section: of machine, structure*) elemento *m*; (*part with separate function*) unità *f inv*; (*department*) reparto *m*; MIL unità *f inv*; ***we must work together as a unit*** dobbiamo lavorare insieme come squadra
u•nit 'cost COM costo *m* unitario
u•nite [juː'naɪt] **1** *v/t* unire **2** *v/i* unirsi
u•nit•ed [juː'naɪtɪd] *adj* unito
U•nit•ed 'King•dom Regno *m* Unito
U•nit•ed 'Na•tions Nazioni *fpl* Unite
U•nit•ed 'States (of A'mer•i•ca) Stati *mpl* Uniti (d'America)
u•ni•ty ['juːnətɪ] unità *f inv*
u•ni•ver•sal [juːnɪ'vɜːsl] *adj* universale
u•ni•ver•sal•ly [juːnɪ'vɜːsəlɪ] *adv* universalmente
u•ni•verse ['juːnɪvɜːs] universo *m*
u•ni•ver•si•ty [juːnɪ'vɜːsətɪ] **1** *n* università *f inv*; ***he is at university*** fa l'università **2** *adj* universitario
un•just [ʌn'dʒʌst] *adj* ingiusto
un•kempt [ʌn'kempt] *adj hair* scarmigliato; *appearance* trasandato
un•kind [ʌn'kaɪnd] *adj* cattivo
un•known [ʌn'nəʊn] **1** *adj* sconosciuto **2** *n*: ***a journey into the unknown*** un viaggio nell'ignoto
un•lead•ed [ʌn'ledɪd] *adj* senza piombo
un•less [ən'les] *conj* a meno che; ***unless he pays us tomorrow*** a meno che non ci paghi domani; ***unless I am mistaken*** se non mi sbaglio
un•like [ʌn'laɪk] *prep* diverso da; ***it's unlike him to drink so much*** non è da lui bere così tanto; ***the photograph was completely unlike her*** la foto non le somigliava per niente; ***unlike Tom, I ...*** a differenza di Tom, io ...
un•like•ly [ʌn'laɪklɪ] *adj* improbabile; ***he is unlikely to win*** è improbabile che vinca; ***it is unlikely that ...*** è improbabile che ...
un•lim•it•ed [ʌn'lɪmɪtɪd] *adj* illimitato
un•load [ʌn'ləʊd] *v/t lorry, goods* scaricare
un•lock [ʌn'lɒk] *v/t* aprire (con la chiave)
un•luck•i•ly [ʌn'lʌkɪlɪ] *adv* sfortunatamente
un•luck•y [ʌn'lʌkɪ] *adj day, choice, person* sfortunato; ***that was so unlucky for you!*** che sfortuna hai avuto!
un•made-up [ʌnmeɪd'ʌp] *adj face* acqua e sapone
un•manned [ʌn'mænd] *adj spacecraft* senza equipaggio
un•mar•ried [ʌn'mærɪd] *adj* non sposato
un•mis•ta•ka•ble [ʌnmɪ'steɪkəbl] *adj* inconfondibile
un•moved [ʌn'muːvd] *adj*: ***be unmoved*** *emotionally* non essere commosso
un•mu•si•cal [ʌn'mjuːzɪkl] *adj person* non portato per la musica; *sounds* disarmonico
un•nat•u•ral [ʌn'nætʃrəl] *adj* non normale; ***it's not unnatural to be annoyed*** è naturale essere seccati
un•ne•ces•sa•ry [ʌn'nesəsrɪ] *adj* non necessario; *comment, violence* gratuito
un•nerv•ing [ʌn'nɜːvɪŋ] *adj* inquietante
un•no•ticed [ʌn'nəʊtɪst] *adj* inosservato; ***it went unnoticed*** passare inosservato
un•ob•tain•a•ble [ʌnəb'teɪnəbl] *adj goods* introvabile; TELEC non ottenibile
un•ob•tru•sive [ʌnəb'truːsɪv] *adj* discreto
un•oc•cu•pied [ʌn'ɒkjʊpaɪd] *adj building, house* vuoto; *post* vacante; *room* libero; ***he doesn't like being unoccupied*** *person* non gli piace stare senza far niente
un•of•fi•cial [ʌnə'fɪʃl] *adj world record, leader* non ufficiale; *announcement* ufficioso
un•of•fi•cial•ly [ʌnə'fɪʃlɪ] *adv* non ufficialmente

un•pack [ʌn'pæk] **1** *v/t* disfare **2** *v/i* disfare le valige
un•paid [ʌn'peɪd] *adj work* non retribuito
un•pleas•ant [ʌn'pleznt] *adj person, thing to say* antipatico; *smell, taste* sgradevole; ***he was very unpleasant to her*** si è comportato malissimo con lei
un•plug [ʌn'plʌg] *v/t* (*pret & pp* ***-ged***) *TV, computer* staccare (la spina di)
un•pop•u•lar [ʌn'pɒpjʊlə(r)] *adj person* mal visto; *decision* impopolare; ***an unpopular teacher with the students*** un insegnante che non ha la simpatia degli studenti
un•pre•ce•den•ted [ʌn'presɪdentɪd] *adj* senza precedenti; ***it was unprecedented for a woman to be …*** è senza precedenti che una donna sia …
un•pre•dict•a•ble [ʌnprɪ'dɪktəbl] *adj person, weather* imprevedibile
un•pre•ten•tious [ʌnprɪ'tenʃəs] *adj person, style, hotel* senza pretese
un•prin•ci•pled [ʌn'prɪnsɪpld] *adj* senza scrupoli
un•pro•duc•tive [ʌnprə'dʌktɪv] *adj meeting, discussion* sterile; *soil* improduttivo
un•pro•fes•sion•al [ʌnprə'feʃnl] *adj person, workmanship* poco professionale; ***it is unprofessional not to …*** è mancanza di professionalità non …; ***unprofessional behaviour*** *of doctor etc* scorrettezza *f* professionale
un•prof•i•ta•ble [ʌn'prɒfɪtəbl] *adj* non redditizio
un•pro•nounce•a•ble [ʌnprə'naʊnsəbl] *adj* impronunciabile
un•pro•tect•ed [ʌnprə'tektɪd] *adj borders* indifeso; *machine* non riparato; ***unprotected sex*** sesso non protetto
un•pro•voked [ʌnprə'vəʊkt] *adj attack* non provocato
un•qual•i•fied [ʌn'kwɒlɪfaɪd] *adj worker, instructor* non qualificato; *doctor, teacher* non abilitato
un•ques•tio•na•bly [ʌn'kwestʃnəblɪ] *adv* (*without doubt*) indiscutibilmente
un•ques•tion•ing [ʌn'kwestʃnɪŋ] *adj attitude, loyalty* assoluto
un•rav•el [ʌn'rævl] *v/t* (*pret & pp* ***-led***, *Am* ***-ed***) *string* dipanare; *knitting* disfare; *mystery, complexities* risolvere
un•rea•da•ble [ʌn'riːdəbl] *adj book* illeggibile
un•re•al [ʌn'rɪəl] *adj creature* irreale; *impression* inverosimile; ***this is unreal!*** F incredibile!
un•rea•lis•tic [ʌnrɪə'lɪstɪk] *adj person* poco realista; *expectations* poco realistico
un•rea•so•na•ble [ʌn'riːznəbl] *adj person* irragionevole; *demand, expectation* eccessivo
un•re•lat•ed [ʌnrɪ'leɪtɪd] *adj issues* senza (alcuna) attinenza; *people* non imparentato
un•re•lent•ing [ʌnrɪ'lentɪŋ] *adj* incessante
un•rel•i•a•ble [ʌnrɪ'laɪəbl] *adj* poco affidabile
un•rest [ʌn'rest] agitazione *f*
un•re•strained [ʌnrɪ'streɪnd] *adj emotions* incontrollato, sfrenato
un•road•wor•thy [ʌn'rəʊdwɜːðɪ] *adj* non sicuro
un•roll [ʌn'rəʊl] *v/t carpet, scroll* srotolare
un•ru•ly [ʌn'ruːlɪ] *adj* indisciplinato
un•safe [ʌn'seɪf] *adj bridge, vehicle, wiring, district* pericoloso; ***unsafe to drink / eat*** non potabile / non commestibile; ***it is unsafe to …*** è rischioso …
un•san•i•tar•y [ʌn'sænɪtrɪ] *adj conditions, drains* antigienico
un•sat•is•fac•to•ry [ʌnsætɪs'fæktrɪ] *adj* poco soddisfacente
un•sa•vou•ry [ʌn'seɪvrɪ] *adj person, reputation,* poco raccomandabile; *district* brutto
un•scathed [ʌn'skeɪðd] *adj* (*not injured*) incolume; (*not damaged*) intatto
un•screw [ʌn'skruː] *v/t* svitare
un•scru•pu•lous [ʌn'skruːpjələs] *adj* senza scrupoli
un•self•ish [ʌn'selfɪʃ] *adj person* altruista; *act, gesture, behaviour* altruistico
un•set•tled [ʌn'setld] *adj issue* irrisolto; *weather, stock market* instabile; *lifestyle* irrequieto; *bills* non pagato
un•shav•en [ʌn'ʃeɪvn] *adj* non rasato
un•sight•ly [ʌn'saɪtlɪ] *adj* brutto
un•skilled [ʌn'skɪld] *adj* non specializzato
un•so•cia•ble [ʌn'səʊʃəbl] *adj* poco socievole
un•so•phis•ti•cat•ed [ʌnsə'fɪstɪkeɪtɪd] *adj person, beliefs* semplice; *equipment* rudimentale
un•sta•ble [ʌn'steɪbl] *adj person* squilibrato; *structure, area, economy* instabile
un•stead•y [ʌn'stedɪ] *adj ladder* malsicuro; ***be unsteady on one's feet*** non reggersi bene sulle gambe
unstint•ing [ʌn'stɪntɪŋ] *adj support* incondizionato; *generosity* illimitato; *praise* senza riserve; ***be unstinting in one's efforts*** prodigarsi negli sforzi
un•stuck [ʌn'stʌk] *adj*: ***come unstuck*** *of notice etc* staccarsi; F *of plan etc* fallire
un•suc•cess•ful [ʌnsək'sesfʊl] *adj writer etc* di scarso successo; *candidate, party*

sconfitto; *attempt* fallito; ***he tried but was unsuccessful*** ha provato ma non ha avuto fortuna
un•suc•cess•ful•ly [ʌnsək'sesflɪ] *adv try, apply* senza successo
un•suit•a•ble [ʌn'suːtəbl] *adj partner, clothing* inadatto; *thing to say, language* inappropriato; ***be unsuitable for*** non essere adatto per; ***they're unsuitable for each other*** non sono fatti l'uno per l'altra
un•sus•pect•ing [ʌnsəs'pektɪŋ] *adj* ignaro
un•swerv•ing [ʌn'swɜːvɪŋ] *adj loyalty, devotion* incrollabile
un•think•a•ble [ʌn'θɪŋkəbl] *adj* impensabile
un•ti•dy [ʌn'taɪdɪ] *adj room, desk, hair* in disordine
un•tie [ʌn'taɪ] *v/t knot* disfare; *laces* slacciare; *prisoner* slegare
un•til [ən'tɪl] **1** *prep* fino a; ***I can wait until tomorrow*** posso aspettare fino a domani; ***from Monday until Friday*** da lunedì a venerdì; ***not until Friday*** non prima di venerdì; ***it won't be finished until July*** non sarà finito prima di luglio **2** *conj* finché (non); ***can you wait until I'm ready?*** puoi aspettare che sia pronta?; ***they won't do anything until you say so*** non faranno niente finché non glielo dici tu
un•time•ly [ʌn'taɪmlɪ] *adj death* prematuro
un•tir•ing [ʌn'taɪrɪŋ] *adj efforts* instancabile
un•told [ʌn'təʊld] *adj riches* incalcolabile; *suffering* indescrivibile; *story* inedito
un•trans•lat•a•ble [ʌntræns'leɪtəbl] *adj* intraducibile
un•true [ʌn'truː] *adj* falso
un•used[1] [ʌn'juːzd] *adj goods* mai usato
un•used[2] [ʌn'juːst] *adj*: ***be unused to sth*** non essere abituato a qc; ***be unused to doing sth*** non essere abituato a fare qc
un•u•su•al [ʌn'juːʒʊəl] *adj* insolito; ***it's unusual for them not to write*** non è da loro non scrivere
un•u•su•al•ly [ʌn'juːʒʊəlɪ] *adv* insolitamente
un•veil [ʌn'veɪl] *v/t memorial, statue etc* scoprire
un•well [ʌn'wel] *adj*: ***be / feel unwell*** stare / sentirsi male
un•will•ing [ʌn'wɪlɪŋ] *adj*: ***be unwilling to do sth*** non essere disposto a fare qc
un•will•ing•ly [ʌn'wɪlɪŋlɪ] *adv* malvolentieri
un•wind [ʌn'waɪnd] (*pret & pp* ***-wound***) **1** *v/t tape* svolgere **2** *v/i of tape* svolgersi; *of story* dipanarsi; F (*relax*) rilassarsi
un•wise [ʌn'waɪz] *adj* avventato, imprudente
un•wrap [ʌn'ræp] *v/t* (*pret & pp* ***-ped***) *gift* aprire, scartare
un•writ•ten [ʌn'rɪtn] *adj law, rule* tacito
un•zip [ʌn'zɪp] *v/t* (*pret & pp* ***-ped***) *dress etc* aprire (la chiusura lampo di); COMPUT espandere
up [ʌp] **1** *adv*: ***up in the sky / up on the roof*** in alto nel cielo / sul tetto; ***up here / there*** quassù / lassù; ***be up*** (*out of bed*) essere in piedi; *of sun* essere sorto; (*be built*) essere costruito; *of shelves* essere montato; *of prices, temperature* essere aumentato; (*have expired*) essere scaduto; ***the road is up*** ci sono lavori in corso; ***what's up?*** F che c'è?; ***up to the year 1989*** fino al 1989; ***he came up to me*** mi si è avvicinato; ***what are you up to these days?*** cosa fai di bello?; ***what are those kids up to?*** cosa stanno combinando i bambini?; ***be up to something*** (***bad***) stare architettando qualcosa; ***I don't feel up to it*** non me la sento; ***it's up to you*** dipende da te; ***it is up to them to solve it*** *their duty* sta a loro risolverlo; ***be up and about*** *after illness* essersi ristabilito **2** *prep*: ***further up the mountain*** più in alto sulla montagna; ***he climbed up the tree*** si è arrampicato sull'albero; ***they ran up the street*** corsero per strada; ***the water goes up this pipe*** l'acqua sale su per questo tubo; ***we travelled up to Milan*** siamo arrivati fino a Milano **3** *n*: ***ups and downs*** alti e bassi *mpl*
'up•bring•ing educazione *f*
'up•com•ing *adj* (*forthcoming*) prossimo
up'date **1** *v/t file, records* aggiornare; ***update s.o. on sth*** mettere qu al corrente di qc **2** *n* (**'update**) *of files, records* aggiornamento *m*; *software version* upgrade *m inv*; ***can you give me an update on the situation?*** può darmi gli ultimi aggiornamenti sulla situazione?
up'grade *v/t computers, equipment etc* aggiornare; *memory* potenziare, aumentare; (*replace with new versions*); *passenger* promuovere a una classe superiore; *product* migliorare; ***I upgraded the monitor*** ho comprato un monitor migliore; ***we could upgrade you to a bigger room*** possiamo offrirle una camera più grande
up•heav•al [ʌp'hiːvl] *emotional* sconvolgimento *m*; *physical* scombussolamento *m*; *political, social* sconvolgimento *m*

U

up•hill [ʌp'hɪl] **1** *adv*: ***go / walk uphill*** salire **2** *adj* ['ʌphɪl] *climb* in salita; *struggle* arduo
up'hold *v/t* (*pret & pp* ***-held***) *traditions, rights* sostenere; (*vindicate*) confermare
up•hol•ster•y [ʌp'həʊlstərɪ] *coverings of chairs* tappezzeria *f*; *padding of chairs* imbottitura *f*
'up•keep *of old buildings, parks etc* manutenzione *f*
'up•load *v/t* COMPUT caricare
up'mar•ket *adj restaurant, hotel* elegante; *product* di qualità
upon [ə'pɒn] *prep* → ***on***
up•per ['ʌpə(r)] *adj part of sth* superiore; *deck, rooms* di sopra; ***the earth's upper atmosphere*** la parte più alta dell'atmosfera terrestre; ***the upper Thames*** l'alto Tamigi
up•per 'class *adj accent* aristocratico; *family* dell'alta borghesia
up•per 'clas•ses *npl* alta borghesia *f*
'up•right 1 *adj citizen* onesto **2** *adv sit* (ben) dritto
'up•right (pi'an•o) pianoforte *m* verticale
'up•ris•ing insurrezione *f*
'up•roar *loud noise* trambusto *m*; (*protest*) protesta *f*
up'set 1 *v/t* (*pret & pp* ***-set***) *drink, glass* rovesciare; (*make sad*) fare stare male; (*distress*) sconvolgere; (*annoy*) seccare **2** *adj* (*sad*) triste; (*distressed*) sconvolto; (*annoyed*) seccato; ***be / get upset*** prendersela (***about*** per); ***get upset about sth*** prendersela per qc; ***have an upset stomach*** avere l'intestino in disordine
up'set•ting *adj*: ***it's so upsetting(for me)*** mi fa stare male, mi turba
'up•shot (*result, outcome*) risultato *m*
'up•side vantaggio *m*
up•side 'down *adv* capovolto; ***turn sth upside down*** capovolgere qc
up'stairs 1 *adv* di sopra **2** *adj room* al piano di sopra
'up•start *novellino m che si comporta in modo arrogante*
up'stream *adv* a monte; ***follow the river upstream*** risalire la corrente
'up•take: ***be quick on the uptake*** capire le cose al volo; ***be slow on the uptake*** essere lento nel capire
up'tight *adj* F (*nervous*) nervoso; (*inhibited*) inibito
up-to-'date *adj information* aggiornato; *fashions* più attuale
'up turn *in economy* ripresa *f*
up•wards ['ʌpwədz] *adv fly, move* in su; ***upwards of 10,000*** oltre 10.000
u•ra•ni•um [jʊ'reɪnɪəm] uranio *m*

U

ur•ban ['ɜːbən] *adj areas, population* urbano; *redevelopment* urbanistico
ur•ban•i•za•tion [ɜːbənaɪ'zeɪʃn] urbanizzazione *f*
ur•chin ['ɜːʧɪn] monello *m*, -a *f*
urge [ɜːdʒ] **1** *n* (forte) desiderio *m* **2** *v/t*: ***urge s.o. to do sth*** raccomandare (caldamente) a qu di fare qc
◆ **urge on** *v/t* (*encourage*) incitare
ur•gen•cy ['ɜːdʒənsɪ] urgenza *f*; ***the urgency of the situation*** la gravità della situazione
ur•gent ['ɜːdʒənt] *adj job, letter* urgente; ***be in urgent need of sth*** avere bisogno urgente di qc; ***is it urgent?*** è urgente?
u•ri•nate ['jʊərɪneɪt] *v/i* orinare
u•rine ['jʊərɪn] urina *f*
urn [ɜːn] urna *f*
us [ʌs] *pron direct & indirect object* ci; *when two pronouns are used* ce; *after prep* noi; ***they know us*** ci conoscono; ***don't leave us*** non ci lasciare, non lasciarci; ***she gave us the keys*** ci ha dato le chiavi; ***she gave them to us*** ce le ha date; ***that's for us*** quello è per noi; ***who's that? – it's us*** chi è? – siamo noi
US [juː'es] *abbr* (= ***United States***) USA *mpl*
USA [juːes'eɪ] *abbr* (= ***United States of America***) USA *mpl*
us•a•ble ['juːzəbl] *adj* utilizzabile
us•age ['juːzɪdʒ] *linguistic* uso *m*
use [juːz] **1** *v/t tool, skills, knowledge* usare, utilizzare; *word, s.o.'s car* usare; *a lot of petrol* consumare; *pej*: *person* usare; ***I could use a drink*** F berrei volentieri qualcosa **2** *n* [juːs] uso *m*; ***be of great use to s.o.*** essere di grande aiuto a qu; ***be of no use to s.o.*** non essere d'aiuto a qu; ***is that of any use?*** ti è d'aiuto?; ***it's no use*** non c'è verso; ***it's no use trying / waiting*** non serve a niente provare / aspettare
◆ **use up** *v/t* finire
used[1] [juːzd] *adj car etc* usato
used[2] [juːst] *adj*: ***be used to s.o./sth*** essere abituato a qu / qc; ***get used to s.o./sth*** abituarsi a qu / qc; ***be used to doing sth*** essere abituato a fare qc; ***get used to doing sth*** abituarsi a fare qc
used[3] [juːst]: ***I used to know him*** lo conoscevo; ***I used to like him*** un tempo mi piaceva; ***I don't work there now, but I used to*** ora non più, ma una volta lavoravo lì
use•ful ['juːsfʊl] *adj information, gadget* utile; *person* di grande aiuto
use•ful•ness ['juːsfʊlnɪs] utilità *f inv*

use•less ['juːslɪs] *adj information, advice* inutile; F *person* incapace; *machine, computer* inservibile; ***feel useless*** sentirsi inutile; ***it's useless trying*** *there isn't any point* non serve a niente provare
us•er ['juːzə(r)] *of product* utente *m/f*
us•er'friend•ly *adj software, device* di facile uso
ush•er ['ʌʃə(r)] *n* (*at wedding*) *persona f che accompagna gli invitati ai loro posti*; *in a cinema* maschera *f*
◆ **usher in** *v/t new era* inaugurare
ush•er•ette [ʌʃə'ret] maschera *f*
u•su•al ['juːʒʊəl] *adj* solito; ***it's not usual for this to happen*** non succede quasi mai; ***as usual*** come al solito; ***the usual, please*** il solito, per favore
u•su•al•ly ['juːʒʊəlɪ] *adv* di solito
u•ten•sil [juː'tensl] utensile *m*
u•te•rus ['juːtərəs] utero *m*
u•til•i•ty [juː'tɪlətɪ] (*usefulness*) utilità *f inv*; ***public utilities*** servizi pubblici
u•til•ize ['juːtɪlaɪz] *v/t* utilizzare
ut•most ['ʌtməʊst] **1** *adj* massimo **2** *n*: ***do one's utmost*** fare (tutto) il possibile
ut•ter ['ʌtə(r)] **1** *adj* totale **2** *v/t sound* emettere; *word* proferire
ut•ter•ly ['ʌtəlɪ] *adv* totalmente
U-turn ['juːtɜːn] inversione *f* a U; *fig*: *in policy* dietro-front *m inv*

U

V

va•can•cy ['veɪkənsɪ] *at work* posto *m* vacante; *in hotel* camera *f* libera; ***vacancy for a driver*** *as advert* autista cercasi; ***do you have any vacancies?*** avete bisogno di personale?; ***"no vacancies"*** "completo"
va•cant ['veɪkənt] *adj building* vuoto; *room* libero; *position* vacante; *look*, *expression* assente
va•cant•ly ['veɪkəntlɪ] *adv* con sguardo assente
va•cate [veɪ'keɪt] *v/t room* lasciar libero
va•ca•tion [veɪ'keɪʃn] *Am* vacanza *f*; ***be on vacation*** essere in vacanza
vac•cin•ate ['væksɪneɪt] *v/t* vaccinare; ***be vaccinated against …*** essere vaccinato contro …
vac•cin•a•tion [væksɪ'neɪʃn] vaccinazione *f*
vac•cine ['væksiːn] vaccino *m*
vac•u•um ['vækjʊəm] **1** *n also fig* vuoto *m* **2** *v/t floors* passare l'aspirapolvere su
'**vac•u•um clean•er** aspirapolvere *m inv*
'**vac•u•um flask** termos *m inv*
vac•u•um-'packed *adj* sottovuoto
vag•a•bond ['vægəbɒnd] *n* vagabondo *m*, -a *f*
va•gi•na [və'dʒaɪnə] vagina *f*
va•gi•nal ['vædʒɪnl] *adj* vaginale
va•grant ['veɪgrənt] *n* vagabondo *m*, -a *f*
vague [veɪg] *adj* vago; ***I'm still vague about it*** non ho ancora le idee chiare al riguardo
vague•ly ['veɪglɪ] *adv* vagamente
vain [veɪn] **1** *adj person* vanitoso; *hope* vano **2** *n*: ***in vain*** invano; ***their efforts were in vain*** i loro sforzi sono stati inutili
val•en•tine ['væləntaɪn] (*card*) *biglietto m per San Valentino*; ***Valentine's Day*** San Valentino
val•et ['væleɪ] **1** *n person* cameriere *m* personale **2** *v/t* ['vælət]: ***have one's car valeted*** far lavare la macchina dentro e fuori
'**val•et ser•vice** *for clothes* servizio *m* di lavanderia; *for cars* servizio *m* completo di lavaggio
val•iant ['vælɪənt] *adj* valoroso
val•iant•ly ['vælɪəntlɪ] *adv* valorosamente
val•id ['vælɪd] *adj* valido
val•i•date ['vælɪdeɪt] *v/t with official stamp* convalidare; *s.o.'s alibi* confermare
va•lid•i•ty [və'lɪdətɪ] *of reason*, *argument* validità *f inv*
val•ley ['vælɪ] valle *f*
val•u•a•ble ['væljʊəbl] **1** *adj* prezioso **2** *n*: ***valuables*** oggetti *mpl* di valore
val•u•a•tion [væljʊ'eɪʃn] valutazione *f*; ***at his valuation*** secondo la sua valutazione
val•ue ['væljuː] **1** *n* valore *m*; ***be good value*** essere conveniente; ***get value for money*** fare un affare; ***rise / fall in value*** aumentare / perdere di valore **2** *v/t s.o.'s friendship*, *one's freedom* tenere a; ***I value your advice*** ci tengo alla tua opinione; ***have an object valued*** far valutare un oggetto
'**val•ue-ad•ded tax** imposta *f* sul valore aggiunto
valve [vælv] valvola *f*
van [væn] furgone *m*
van•dal ['vændl] vandalo *m*
van•dal•is•m ['vændəlɪzm] vandalismo *m*
van•dal•ize ['vændəlaɪz] *v/t* vandalizzare
van•guard ['vængɑːd] *n* avanguardia *f*; ***be in the vanguard of*** essere all'avanguardia di
va•nil•la [və'nɪlə] **1** *n* vaniglia *f* **2** *adj ice cream* alla vaniglia; *flavour* di vaniglia
van•ish ['vænɪʃ] *v/i* sparire
van•i•ty ['vænətɪ] *of person* vanità *f inv*
'**van•i•ty case** beauty-case *m inv*
van•tage point ['vɑːntɪdʒ] *on hill etc* punto *m* d'osservazione
va•por *Am* → ***vapour***
va•por•ize ['veɪpəraɪz] *v/t* vaporizzare
va•pour ['veɪpə(r)] vapore *m*
'**va•pour trail** *of aeroplane* scia *f*
var•i•a•ble ['veərɪəbl] **1** *adj* variabile **2** *n* MATH, COMPUT variabile *f*
var•i•ant ['veərɪənt] *n* variante *f*
var•i•a•tion [veərɪ'eɪʃn] variazione *f*
var•i•cose 'vein ['værɪkəʊs] vena *f* varicosa
var•ied ['veərɪd] *adj range*, *diet* vario; *life* movimentato
va•ri•e•ty [və'raɪətɪ] varietà *f inv*; (*type*) tipo *m*; THEA varietà *f inv*; ***a variety of things to do*** varie cose da fare
var•i•ous ['veərɪəs] *adj* (*several*) vario; (*different*) diverso
var•nish ['vɑːnɪʃ] **1** *n for wood* vernice *f*; (*nail varnish*) smalto *m* **2** *v/t wood* verniciare; *nails* smaltare
var•y ['veərɪ] *v/t & v/i* (*pret & pp* **-ied**) variare
vase [vɑːz] vaso *m*

vas•ec•to•my [və'sektəmɪ] vasectomia *f*
vast [vɑːst] *adj desert, knowledge* vasto; *improvement* immenso
vast•ly ['vɑːstlɪ] *adv* immensamente
VAT [viːeɪ'tiː, væt] *abbr* (= ***value added tax***) IVA *f* (=imposta *f* sul valore aggiunto)
Vat•i•can ['vætɪkən]: ***the Vatican*** il Vaticano
vau•de•ville ['vɔːdvɪl] *Am* varietà *f inv*
vault[1] [vɒlt] *n in roof* volta *f*; *cellar* cantina *f*; ***vaults*** *of bank* caveau *m inv*
vault[2] [vɒlt] **1** *n* SP volteggio *m* **2** *v/t* saltare
VCR [viːsiː'ɑː(r)] *abbr* (= ***video cassette recorder***) videoregistratore *m*
veal [viːl] (carne *f* di) vitello *m*
veer [vɪə(r)] *v/i of car* sterzare; *of wind, party* cambiare direzione
veg [vedʒ] F verdure *fpl*
ve•gan ['viːgn] **1** *n* vegetaliano *m*, -a *f* **2** *adj* vegetaliano
vege•ta•ble ['vedʒtəbl] verdura *f*
ve•ge•tar•i•an [vedʒɪ'teərɪən] **1** *n* vegetariano *m*, -a *f* **2** *adj* vegetariano
ve•ge•tar•i•an•ism [vedʒɪ'teərɪənɪzm] vegetarianismo *m*
veg•e•ta•tion [vedʒɪ'teɪʃn] vegetazione *f*
ve•he•mence ['viːəməns] veemenza *f*
ve•he•ment ['viːəmənt] *adj* veemente
ve•he•ment•ly ['viːəməntlɪ] *adv* veementemente
ve•hi•cle ['viːɪkl] veicolo *m*; *for information etc* mezzo *m*
veil [veɪl] **1** *n* velo *m* **2** *v/t* velare
vein [veɪn] ANAT vena *f*; ***in this vein*** *fig* su questo tono
Vel•cro® ['velkrəʊ] velcro *m*
ve•loc•i•ty [vɪ'lɒsətɪ] velocità *f inv*
vel•vet ['velvɪt] *n* velluto *m*
vel•vet•y ['velvɪtɪ] *adj* vellutato
ven•det•ta [ven'detə] vendetta *f*
vend•ing ma•chine ['vendɪŋ] distributore *m* automatico
vend•or ['vendə(r)] LAW venditore *m*, -trice *f*
ve•neer [və'nɪə(r)] *on wood* impiallacciatura *f*; *of politeness etc* parvenza *f*
ven•e•ra•ble ['venərəbl] *adj* venerabile
ven•e•rate ['venəreɪt] *v/t* venerare
ven•e•ra•tion [venə'reɪʃn] venerazione *f*
ve•ne•re•al dis•ease [vɪ'nɪərɪəl] malattia *f* venerea
Ve•ne•tian [və'niːʃn] **1** *adj* veneziano **2** *n* veneziano *m*, -a *f*
ve•ne•tian 'blind veneziana *f*
ven•geance ['vendʒəns] vendetta *f*; ***with a vengeance*** a più non posso
Ven•ice ['venɪs] Venezia *f*
ven•i•son ['venɪsn] (carne *f* di) cervo *m*
ven•om ['venəm] *also fig* veleno *m*
ven•om•ous ['venəməs] *also fig* velenoso
vent [vent] *n for air* presa *f* d'aria; ***give vent to*** *feelings, emotions* dare sfogo a
ven•ti•late ['ventɪleɪt] *v/t room, building* ventilare
ven•ti•la•tion [ventɪ'leɪʃn] ventilazione *f*
ven•ti'la•tion shaft condotto *m* di aerazione
ven•ti•la•tor ['ventɪleɪtə(r)] ventilatore *m*; MED respiratore *m*
ven•tril•o•quist [ven'trɪləkwɪst] ventriloquo *m*, -a *f*
ven•ture ['ventʃə(r)] **1** *n* impresa *f* **2** *v/i* avventurarsi
ven•ue ['venjuː] *for meeting, concert etc* luogo *m*
ve•ran•da [və'rændə] veranda *f*
verb [vɜːb] verbo *m*
verb•al ['vɜːbl] verbale
verb•al•ly ['vɜːbəlɪ] verbalmente
ver•ba•tim [vɜː'beɪtɪm] *adv* parola per parola
ver•dict ['vɜːdɪkt] LAW verdetto *m*; (*opinion, judgment*) giudizio *m*; ***a verdict of guilty / not guilty*** un verdetto di colpevolezza / non colpevolezza
verge [vɜːdʒ] *n of road* bordo *m*; ***be on the verge of …*** *ruin, collapse* essere sull'orlo di …; ***on the verge of tears*** sul punto di piangere
◆ **verge on** *v/t* rasentare
ver•i•fi•ca•tion [verɪfɪ'keɪʃn] verifica *f*
ver•i•fy ['verɪfaɪ] *v/t* (*pret & pp* ***-ied***) verificare
ver•mi•cel•li [vɜːmɪ'tʃelɪ] *nsg* vermicelli *mpl*
ver•min ['vɜːmɪn] animali *mpl* nocivi
ver•mouth ['vɜːməθ] vermut *m inv*
ver•nac•u•lar [və'nækjʊlə(r)] *n* vernacolo *m*
ver•sa•tile ['vɜːsətaɪl] *adj* versatile
ver•sa•til•i•ty [vɜːsə'tɪlətɪ] versatilità *f inv*
verse [vɜːs] *poetry* poesia *f*; *part of poem, song* strofa *f*
versed [vɜːst] *adj*: ***be well versed in a subject*** essere versato in una materia
ver•sion ['vɜːʃn] versione *f*
ver•sus ['vɜːsəs] *prep* SP, LAW contro
ver•te•bra ['vɜːtɪbrə] vertebra *f*
ver•te•brate ['vɜːtɪbreɪt] *n* vertebrato *m*
ver•ti•cal ['vɜːtɪkl] *adj* verticale
ver•ti•go ['vɜːtɪgəʊ] vertigini *fpl*
ver•y ['verɪ] **1** *adv* molto; ***was it cold? – not very*** faceva freddo? – non molto; ***very fast / easy*** molto veloce / semplice, velocissimo / semplicissimo; ***the very***

best il meglio **2** *adj*: ***at that very moment*** in quel preciso momento; ***that's the very thing I need*** è proprio quello che mi serve; ***the very thought*** il solo pensiero; ***right at the very top / bottom*** proprio in cima / in fondo
ves•sel ['vesl] NAUT natante *m*
vest [vest] canottiera *f*; *Am* (*waistcoat*) gilè *m inv*
ves•tige ['vestɪdʒ] vestigio *m* (*pl* vestigia *f*); ***not a vestige of truth*** neanche un'ombra di verità
vet[1] [vet] *n* (*veterinary surgeon*) veterinario *m*, -a *f*
vet[2] [vet] *v/t* (*pret & pp* **-ted**) *applicants etc* passare al vaglio
vet•e•ran ['vetərən] **1** *n* veterano *m*, -a *f*; MIL reduce *m/f* **2** *adj* veterano
vet•e•ri•na•ry 'sur•geon ['vetərɪnərɪ] veterinario *m*, -a *f*
ve•to ['viːtəʊ] **1** *n* veto *m* **2** *v/t* mettere il veto a
vex [veks] *v/t* (*concern*, *worry*) preoccupare
vexed [vekst] *adj* (*worried*) preoccupato; ***the vexed question of ...*** la questione controversa di ...
vi•a ['vaɪə] *prep* attraverso
vi•a•ble ['vaɪəbl] *adj life form*, *company* in grado di sopravvivere; *alternative*, *plan* fattibile
vi•brate [vaɪ'breɪt] *v/i* vibrare
vi•bra•tion [vaɪ'breɪʃn] vibrazione *f*
vic•ar ['vɪkə(r)] parroco *m* anglicano
vic•ar•age ['vɪkərɪdʒ] casa *f* del parroco
vice[1] [vaɪs] *for holding* morsa *f*
vice[2] [vaɪs] vizio *m*
vice 'pres•i•dent vice-presidente *m*
'vice squad buoncostume *f*
vi•ce ver•sa [vaɪs'vɜːsə] *adv* viceversa
vi•cin•i•ty [vɪ'sɪnətɪ] *n*: ***in the vicinity of ...*** *the church etc* nelle vicinanze di ...; *£500 etc* approssimativamente ...
vi•cious ['vɪʃəs] *adj dog* feroce; *attack*, *criticism* brutale
vi•cious 'cir•cle circolo *m* vizioso
vi•cious•ly ['vɪʃəslɪ] *adv* brutalmente
vic•tim ['vɪktɪm] vittima *f*
vic•tim•ize ['vɪktɪmaɪz] *v/t* perseguitare
vic•tor ['vɪktə(r)] vincitore *m*, -trice *f*
vic•to•ri•ous [vɪk'tɔːrɪəs] *adj army* vittorioso; *team* vincente
vic•to•ry ['vɪktərɪ] vittoria *f*; ***win a victory over ...*** riportare una vittoria su ...
vid•e•o ['vɪdɪəʊ] **1** *n* video *m inv*; *tape* videocassetta *f*; (*VCR*) videoregistratore *m* **2** *v/t* registrare
'vid•e•o cam•e•ra videocamera *f*
'vide•o cas•sette videocassetta *f*
'vid•e•o con•fer•ence TELEC videoconferenza *f*
'vid•e•o game videogame *m inv*
'vid•e•o•phone videotelefono *m*
'vid•e•o re•cord•er videoregistratore *m*
'vid•e•o re•cord•ing videoregistrazione *f*
'vid•e•o•tape videocassetta *f*
'vid•e•o•tape li•bra•ry videoteca *f*
vie [vaɪ] *v/i* competere
Vi•et•nam [vɪet'næm] Vietnam *m*
Vi•et•nam•ese [vɪetnə'miːz] **1** *adj* vietnamita *m/f* **2** *n* vietnamita *m/f*; *language* vietnamita *m*
view [vjuː] **1** *n* veduta *f*; *of situation* parere *m*; ***in view of*** considerato; ***be on view*** *of paintings* essere esposto; ***with a view to*** con l'intenzione di **2** *v/t events*, *situation* vedere; *TV programme* guardare; *house for sale* vedere **3** *v/i* (*watch TV*) guardare la TV
view•er ['vjuːə(r)] *TV* telespettatore *m*, -trice *f*
'view•find•er PHOT mirino *m*
'view•point punto *m* di vista
vig•or *Am* → ***vigour***
vig•or•ous ['vɪgərəs] *adj* vigoroso
vig•or•ous•ly ['vɪgərəslɪ] *adv* vigorosamente
vig•our ['vɪgə(r)] vigore *m*
vile [vaɪl] *adj* disgustoso
vil•la ['vɪlə] villa *f*
vil•lage ['vɪlɪdʒ] paese *m*
vil•lag•er ['vɪlɪdʒə(r)] abitante *m/f* (del paese)
vil•lain ['vɪlən] cattivo *m*, -a *f*; F *criminal* delinquente *m/f*
vin•di•cate ['vɪndɪkeɪt] *v/t show to be correct* confermare; *show to be innocent* scagionare; ***I feel vindicated by the report*** il resoconto mi dà ragione
vin•dic•tive [vɪn'dɪktɪv] *adj* vendicativo
vin•dic•tive•ly [vɪn'dɪktɪvlɪ] *adv* vendicativamente
vine [vaɪn] (*grapevine*) vite *f*; *climber* rampicante *m*
vin•e•gar ['vɪnɪgə(r)] aceto *m*
vine•yard ['vɪnjɑːd] vigneto *m*
vin•tage ['vɪntɪdʒ] **1** *n of wine* annata *f* **2** *adj* (*classic*) d'annata
vi•o•la [vɪ'əʊlə] MUS viola *f*
vi•o•late ['vaɪəleɪt] *v/t* violare
vi•o•la•tion [vaɪə'leɪʃn] violazione *f*
vi•o•lence ['vaɪələns] violenza *f*; ***outbreaks of violence*** episodi di violenza
vi•o•lent ['vaɪələnt] *adj* violento; ***have a violent temper*** avere un carattere violento
vi•o•lent•ly ['vaɪələntlɪ] *adv* violentemente; ***fall violently in love*** innamorarsi

follemente
vi•o•let ['vaɪələt] *n colour* viola *m*; *plant* viola *f*
vi•o•lin [vaɪə'lɪn] violino *m*
vi•o•lin•ist [vaɪə'lɪnɪst] violinista *m/f*
VIP [viːaɪ'piː] *abbr* (= ***very important person***) VIP *m/f*
vi•per ['vaɪpə(r)] *snake* vipera *f*
vi•ral ['vaɪrəl] *adj infection* virale
vir•gin ['vɜːdʒɪn] vergine *m/f*
vir•gin•i•ty [vɜː'dʒɪnətɪ] verginità *f inv*; ***lose one's virginity*** perdere la verginità
Vir•go ['vɜːgəʊ] ASTR Vergine *f*
vir•ile ['vɪraɪl] *adj* virile
vi•ril•i•ty [vɪ'rɪlətɪ] virilità *f inv*
vir•tu•al ['vɜːtjʊəl] *adj* effettivo; COMPUT virtuale
vir•tu•al•ly ['vɜːtjʊəlɪ] *adv* (*almost*) praticamente
vir•tu•al re'al•i•ty realtà *f* virtuale
vir•tue ['vɜːtjuː] virtù *f inv*; ***in virtue of*** in virtù di
vir•tu•o•so [vɜːtʊ'əʊzəʊ] MUS virtuoso *m*, -a *f*
vir•tu•ous ['vɜːtjʊəs] *adj* virtuoso
vir•u•lent ['vɪrʊlənt] *adj disease* virulento; *fig*: *attack*, *hatred* feroce
vi•rus ['vaɪərəs] MED, COMPUT virus *m inv*
vi•sa ['viːzə] visto *m*
vise [vaɪz] *Am* → ***vice***[1]
vis•i•bil•i•ty [vɪzə'bɪlətɪ] visibilità *f inv*
vis•i•ble ['vɪzəbl] *adj object*, *difference* visibile; *anger* evidente; ***not visible to the naked eye*** invisible ad occhio nudo
vis•i•bly ['vɪzəblɪ] *adv different* visibilmente; ***he was visibly moved*** era visibilmente emozionato
vi•sion ['vɪʒn] (*eyesight*) vista *f*; REL *etc* visione *f*
vis•it ['vɪzɪt] **1** *n* visita *f*; ***pay a visit to the doctor / dentist*** andare dal medico / dentista; ***pay s.o. a visit*** fare una visita a qu **2** *v/t person* andare a trovare; *place*, *country*, *city* visitare; *doctor*, *dentist* andare da
vis•it•ing card ['vɪzɪtɪŋ] biglietto *m* da visita
'vis•it•ing hours *npl at hospital* orario *m* delle visite
vis•it•or ['vɪzɪtə(r)] (*guest*) ospite *m*; *to museum etc* visitatore *m*, -trice *f*; (*tourist*) turista *m/f*
vi•sor ['vaɪzə(r)] visiera *f*
vis•u•al ['vɪzjʊəl] *adj organs*, *memory* visivo; *arts* figurativo
vis•u•al 'aid sussidio *m* visivo
vis•u•al dis'play u•nit videoterminale *m*
vis•u•al•ize ['vɪzjʊəlaɪz] *v/t* immaginare; (*foresee*) prevedere
vis•u•al•ly im'paired ['vɪzjʊəlɪ] *adj* videoleso
vi•tal ['vaɪtl] *adj* (*essential*) essenziale; ***it is vital that …*** è essenziale che …
vi•tal•i•ty [vaɪ'tælətɪ] *of person*, *city etc* vitalità *f inv*
vi•tal•ly ['vaɪtəlɪ] *adv*: ***vitally important*** di vitale importanza
vi•tal 'or•gans *npl* organi *mpl* vitali
vi•tal sta'tis•tics *npl of woman* misure *fpl*
vit•a•min ['vɪtəmɪn] vitamina *f*
'vit•a•min pill (confetto *m* di) vitamina *f*
vit•ri•ol•ic [vɪtrɪ'ɒlɪk] *adj* caustico
vi•va•cious [vɪ'veɪʃəs] *adj* vivace
vi•vac•i•ty [vɪ'væsətɪ] vivacità *f inv*
viv•id ['vɪvɪd] *adj* vivido
viv•id•ly ['vɪvɪdlɪ] in modo vivido
V-neck ['viːnek] maglione *m* con scollo a V
vo•cab•u•la•ry [və'kæbjʊlərɪ] vocabolario *m*; *list of words* glossario *m*
vo•cal ['vəʊkl] *adj to do with the voice* vocale; *expressing opinions* eloquente; ***become vocal*** cominciare a farsi sentire
'vo•cal cords *npl* corde *fpl* vocali
'vo•cal group MUS gruppo *m* vocale
vo•cal•ist ['vəʊkəlɪst] MUS cantante *m/f*
vo•ca•tion [və'keɪʃn] (*calling*) vocazione *f* (***for*** a); (*profession*) professione *f*
vo•ca•tion•al [və'keɪʃnl] *adj guidance* professionale
vod•ka ['vɒdkə] vodka *f inv*
vogue [vəʊg] *n* moda *f*; ***be in vogue*** essere in voga
voice [vɔɪs] **1** *n* voce *f* **2** *v/t opinions* esprimere
'voice mail segreteria *f* telefonica
void [vɔɪd] **1** *n* vuoto *m* **2** *adj*: ***void of*** privo di
vol•a•tile ['vɒlətaɪl] *adj personality*, *moods* volubile
vol•ca•no [vɒl'keɪnəʊ] vulcano *m*
vol•ley ['vɒlɪ] *n of shots* raffica *f*; *in tennis* volée *f inv*
'vol•ley•ball pallavolo *f*
volt [vəʊlt] volt *m inv*
volt•age ['vəʊltɪdʒ] voltaggio *m*; ***high voltage*** alta tensione *f*
vol•ume ['vɒljuːm] volume *m*
vol•ume con'trol volume *m*
vol•un•tar•i•ly [vɒlən'teərɪlɪ] spontaneamente
vol•un•ta•ry ['vɒləntərɪ] *adj helper* volontario; ***voluntary work*** volontariato
vol•un•teer [vɒlən'tɪə(r)] **1** *n* volontario *m*, -a *f* **2** *v/i* offrirsi volontario
vo•lup•tu•ous [və'lʌptjʊəs] *adj woman*, *figure* giunonico
vom•it ['vɒmɪt] **1** *n* vomito *m* **2** *v/i* vomi-

V

tare
◆ **vomit up** *v/t* vomitare
vo•ra•cious [vəˈreɪʃəs] *adj appetite* vorace
vo•ra•cious•ly [vəˈreɪʃəslɪ] *eat* voracemente; *fig*: *read* avidamente
vote [vəʊt] **1** *n* voto *m*; *right to vote* diritto *m* di voto **2** *v/i* POL votare; ***vote for / against s.o./sth*** votare a favore di / contro qu / qc **3** *v/t*: ***they voted him President*** l'hanno eletto presidente; ***I vote we stay behind*** propongo di rimanere
◆ **vote in** *v/t new member* eleggere
◆ **vote on** *v/t issue* mettere ai voti
◆ **vote out** *v/t of office* respingere
vot•er [ˈvəʊtə(r)] POL elettore *m*, -trice *f*
vot•ing [ˈvəʊtɪŋ] POL votazione *f*
ˈ**vot•ing booth** cabina *f* elettorale
◆ **vouch for** [vaʊʧ] *v/t truth of sth* garantire; *person* garantire per
vouch•er [ˈvaʊʧə(r)] buono *m*
vow [vaʊ] **1** *n* voto *m* **2** *v/t*: ***vow to do sth*** giurare di fare qc
vow•el [vaʊl] vocale *f*
voy•age [ˈvɔɪɪdz] *n by sea, in space* viaggio *m*
V-sign [ˈviːsaɪn] *for victory* segno *m* di vittoria; ***give s.o. the V-sign*** *mandare qu a quel paese*
vul•gar [ˈvʌlgə(r)] *adj person, language* volgare
vul•ne•ra•ble [ˈvʌlnərəbl] *adj* vulnerabile
vul•ture [ˈvʌlʧə(r)] avvoltoio *m*

V

W

wad [wɒd] *n of cotton wool* batuffolo *m*; *of paper* fascio *m*; *of banknotes* mazzetta *f*
wad•dle ['wɒdl] *v/i* camminare ondeggiando
wade [weɪd] *v/i* guadare
◆ **wade through** *v/t*: ***I've still got this lot to wade through*** devo ancora leggermi tutto questo
wa•fer ['weɪfə(r)] *biscuit* cialda *f*; REL ostia *f*
'**wa•fer-thin** *adj* sottilissimo
waf•fle[1] ['wɒfl] *n* (*to eat*) *tipo m di cialda*
waf•fle[2] ['wɒfl] *v/i* parlare a vuoto
wag [wæg] (*pret & pp* **-ged**) **1** *v/t finger* scuotere; ***the dog wagged its tail*** il cane scodinzolò **2** *v/i*: ***the dog's tail was wagging*** il cane scodinzolava
wage[1] [weɪdʒ] *v/t*: ***wage war against*** *also fig* fare la guerra a
wage[2] [weɪdʒ] *n* paga *f*; ***wages*** paga *f*
'**wage earn•er** salariato *m*, -a *f*
'**wage freeze** blocco *m* dei salari
'**wage ne•go•ti•a•tions** *npl* rivendicazioni *fpl* salariali
'**wage pack•et** *fig* busta *f* paga
wag•gle ['wægl] *v/t ears, loose screw, tooth etc* far muovere; ***waggle one's hips*** ancheggiare
wag•gon *Am*, **wag•on** ['wægən] RAIL carro *m* merci; ***be on the waggon*** F non bere alcolici
wail [weɪl] **1** *n of person* gemito *m*; *of baby* vagito *m*; *of siren* ululato *m* **2** *v/i of person* gemere; *of baby* vagire; *of siren* ululare
waist [weɪst] vita *f*
'**waist•coat** gilè *m inv*
'**waist•line** vita *f*
wait [weɪt] **1** *n* attesa *f* **2** *v/i* aspettare; ***we'll wait until he's ready*** aspetteremo che sia pronto; ***I can't wait to ...*** non vedo l'ora di ... **3** *v/t meal* ritardare
◆ **wait for** *v/t* aspettare; ***wait for me!*** aspettami!
◆ **wait on** *v/t* (*serve*) servire
◆ **wait up** *v/i* restare alzato ad aspettare
wait•er ['weɪtə(r)] cameriere *m*; ***waiter!*** cameriere!
wait•ing ['weɪtɪŋ] *n* attesa *f*; ***no waiting sign*** divieto *m* di sosta
'**wait•ing list** lista *f* d'attesa
'**wait•ing room** sala *f* d'attesa
wait•ress ['weɪtrɪs] cameriera *f*
waive [weɪv] *v/t* (*renoune*) rinunciare a; (*dispense with*) fare al meno di, lasciar perdere
wake[1] [weɪk] (*pret* **woke**, *pp* **woken**) **1** *v/i*: ***wake (up)*** svegliarsi **2** *v/t* svegliare
wake[2] [weɪk] *n of ship* scia *f*; ***in the wake of*** *fig* a seguito di; ***follow in the wake of*** seguire le tracce di
'**wake-up call** sveglia *f* (telefonica)
Wales [weɪlz] Galles *m*
walk [wɔːk] **1** *n* camminata *f*; ***it's a long walk to the office*** è una bella camminata fino all'ufficio; ***it's a short walk to the office*** l'ufficio è a due passi; ***go for a walk*** fare due passi **2** *v/i* camminare; *as opposed to taking the car, bus etc* andare a piedi; (*hike*) passeggiare; ***learn to walk*** imparare a camminare; ***we walked for hours*** abbiamo camminato per ore; ***she walked over to the window*** andò alla finestra **3** *v/t dog* portare fuori; ***I'll walk you home*** ti accompagno a casa; ***walk the streets*** (*walk around*) girare in lungo e in largo
◆ **walk out** *v/i of husband etc, from theatre* andarsene; (*go on strike*) scendere in sciopero
◆ **walk out on** *v/t spouse, family* abbandonare
'**walk•a•bout** bagno *m* di folla; ***go walkabout*** F *of monarch, politician* fare un bagno di folla
walk•er ['wɔːkə(r)] (*hiker*) escursionista *m/f*; *for baby* girello *m*; *for old person* deambulatore *m*; ***be a slow / fast walker*** avere il passo lento / spedito
walk•ie-'talk•ie [wɔːkɪ'tɔːkɪ] walkie-talkie *m inv*
walk•ing ['wɔːkɪŋ] *n as opposed to driving* camminare *m*; (*hiking*) escursionismo *m*; ***it's within walking distance*** ci si arriva a piedi
'**walk•ing stick** bastone *m* da passeggio
'**walk•ing tour** escursionismo *m*
'**Walk•man**® walkman *m inv*
'**walk•out** *strike* sciopero *m* selvaggio
'**walk•over** (*easy win*) vittoria *f* facile
wall [wɔːl] *external* muro *m*; *internal* parete *f*; *fig*: *of silence etc* muro *m*; ***go to the wall*** *of company* andare in rovina; ***walls*** *of a city* mura *fpl*; ***drive s.o. up the wall*** F far diventare matto qu
wal•let ['wɒlɪt] portafoglio *m*
wal•lop ['wɒləp] **1** *n* F *blow* colpo *m* **2** *v/t* F

colpire; *opponent* stracciare F
'**wall•pa•per 1** *n* tappezzeria *f*, carta *f* da parati **2** *v/t* tappezzare
wall-to-'wall *adj*: ***wall-to-wall carpet*** moquette *f*
wal•nut ['wɔːlnʌt] noce *f*
waltz [wɔ́ːlts] *n* valzer *m inv*
wan [wɒn] *adj face* pallido
wand•er ['wɒndə(r)] *v/i* (*roam*) gironzolare; (*stray*) allontanarsi; ***my attention began to wander*** mi sono distratto
◆ **wander around** *v/i* girare
wane [weɪn] *v/i of interest, enthusiasm* calare
wan•gle ['wæŋgl] *v/t* F rimediare F
want [wɒnt] **1** *n*: ***for want of*** per mancanza di **2** *v/t* volere; (*need*) avere bisogno di; ***want to do sth*** volere fare qc; ***I want to stay here*** voglio stare qui; ***do you want to come too? – no, I don't want to*** vuoi venire anche tu? - no, grazie; ***you can have whatever you want*** puoi avere tutto ciò che vuoi; ***it's not what I wanted*** non è quello che volevo; ***she wants you to go back*** vuole che torni indietro; ***he wants a haircut*** dovrebbe tagliarsi i capelli **3** *v/i*: ***want for nothing*** non mancare di niente
'**want ad** annuncio *m* economico
want•ed ['wɒntɪd] *adj by police* ricercato
want•ing ['wɒntɪŋ] *adj*: ***be wanting in*** mancare di
wan•ton ['wɒntən] *adj cruelty, neglect* gratuito
war [wɔː(r)] *n* guerra *f*; *fig* lotta *f*; ***be at war*** essere in guerra
war•ble ['wɔːbl] *v/i of bird* gorgheggiare
ward [wɔːd] *n in hospital* corsia *f*; *child* minore *m* sotto tutela
◆ **ward off** *v/t blow* parare; *attacker* respingere; *cold* combattere
war•den ['wɔːdn] (*traffic warden*) vigile *m* urbano; *of hostel* direttore *m*, -trice *f*; *of nature reserve* guardiano *m*, -a *f*; *Am*: *of prison* agente *m/f* di custodia
ward•er ['wɔːdə(r)] agente *m/f* di custodia
'**ward•robe** *for clothes* armadio *m*; *clothes* guardaroba *m*
ware•house ['weəhaʊs] magazzino *m*
'**war•fare** guerra *f*
'**war•head** testata *f*
war•i•ly ['weərɪlɪ] *adv* con aria guardinga
warm [wɔːm] **1** *adj* caldo; *welcome, smile* caloroso; ***it's warm*** *of weather* fa caldo; ***it's warm in here*** qui c'è caldo; ***are you warm enough?*** ti fa freddo? **2** *v/t*: → ***warm up***
◆ **warm up 1** *v/t* scaldare **2** *v/i* scaldarsi; *of athlete etc* fare riscaldamento
warm•heart•ed ['wɔːmhɒːtɪd] *adj* cordiale
warm•ly ['wɔːmlɪ] *adv dressed* con abiti pesanti; *welcome, smile* calorosamente
warmth [wɔːmθ] calore *m*; *of welcome, smile* calorosità *f inv*
'**warm-up** SP riscaldamento *m*
warn [wɔːn] *v/t* avvertire
warn•ing ['wɔːnɪŋ] *n* avvertimento *m*; ***without warning*** senza preavviso
warp [wɔːp] **1** *v/t wood* deformare; *character* segnare **2** *v/i of wood* deformarsi
warped [wɔːpt] *adj fig* contorto
'**war•plane** aereo *m* militare
war•rant ['wɒrənt] **1** *n* mandato *m* **2** *v/t* (*deserve, call for*) giustificare
war•ran•ty ['wɒrəntɪ] (*guarantee*) garanzia *f*; ***be under warranty*** essere in garanzia
war•ri•or ['wɒrɪə(r)] guerriero *m*, -a *f*
'**war•ship** nave *f* da guerra
wart [wɔːt] verruca *f*
'**war•time** tempo *m* di guerra
war•y ['weərɪ] *adj* guardingo; ***be wary of*** diffidare di
was [wɒz] *pret* → **be**
wash [wɒʃ] **1** *n*: ***have a wash*** darsi una lavata; ***that skirt needs a wash*** quella gonna va lavata **2** *v/t* lavare; ***wash one's hands / hair*** lavarsi le mani/i capelli **3** *v/i* lavarsi
◆ **wash up** *v/i Br* (*wash the dishes*) lavare i piatti
wash•a•ble ['wɒʃəbl] *adj* lavabile
'**wash•ba•sin**, '**wash•bowl** lavandino *m*
washed out [wɒʃt'aʊt] *adj* sfinito
wash•er ['wɒʃə(r)] *for tap etc* guarnizione *f*; → ***washing machine***
wash•ing ['wɒʃɪŋ] *washed clothes* bucato *m*; *clothes to be washed* biancheria *f* da lavare; ***do the washing*** fare il bucato
'**wash•ing ma•chine** lavatrice *f*
'**wash•ing pow•der** detersivo *m* per bucato
wash•ing-'up: ***do the washing-up*** lavare i piatti
wash•ing-'up liq•uid detersivo *m* per i piatti
wasp [wɒsp] vespa *f*
waste [weɪst] **1** *n* spreco *m*; *from industrial process* rifiuti *mpl*; ***it's a waste of time / money*** è tempo sprecato / sono soldi sprecati **2** *adj material* di scarto **3** *v/t* sprecare
◆ **waste away** *v/i* deperire
'**waste dis•pos•al (unit)** tritarifiuti *m inv*
waste•ful ['weɪstfʊl] *adj person* sprecone; *methods, processes* dispendioso
'**waste•land** distesa *f* desolata

wast•ˌpa•per cartaccia *f*
waste•pa•per ˈbas•ket cestino *m* della cartaccia
ˈ**waste prod•uct** scorie *fpl* industriali
watch [wɒtʃ] **1** *n timepiece* orologio *m*; MIL guardia *f*; ***keep watch*** stare all'erta **2** *v/t film, TV* guardare; (*spy on*) sorvegliare; (*look after*) tenere d'occhio **3** *v/i* guardare
◆ **watch for** *v/t* aspettare
◆ **watch out** *v/i* fare attenzione; ***watch out!*** attento!
◆ **watch out for** *v/t* fare attenzione a
ˈ**watch•dog** *fig* comitato *m* di controllo
watch•ful [ˈwɒtʃfʊl] *adj* vigile
ˈ**watch•mak•er** orologiaio *m*, -a *f*
wa•ter [ˈwɔːtə(r)] **1** *n* acqua *f*; ***waters*** NAUT acque (territoriali) **2** *v/t plant* annaffiare **3** *v/i of eyes* lacrimare; ***my mouth is watering*** ho l'acquolina in bocca
◆ **water down** *v/t drink* diluire
ˈ**water can•non** idrante *m*
ˈ**wa•ter•col•or** *Am*, ˈ**wa•ter•col•our** *n* acquerello *m*
ˈ**wa•ter•cress** crescione *m*
watered ˈdown [ˈwɔːtəd] *adj fig* edulcorato
ˈ**wa•ter•fall** cascata *f*
wa•ter•ing can [ˈwɔːtərɪŋ] annaffiatoio *m*
ˈ**wa•ter•ing hole** *hum* bar *m inv*
ˈ**wa•ter lev•el** livello *m* delle acque
ˈ**wa•ter lil•y** ninfea *f*
wa•ter•logged [ˈwɔːtəlɒgd] *adj* allagato
ˈ**wa•ter main** conduttura *f* dell'acqua
ˈ**wa•ter mark** filigrana *f*
ˈ**wa•ter mel•on** anguria *f*, cocomero *m*
ˈ**wa•ter pol•lu•tion** inquinamento *m* dell'acqua
ˈ**wa•ter•proof** *adj* impermeabile
ˈ**wa•ter•shed** *fig* svolta *f*; TV*ora f dopo la quale sono ammessi programmi per un pubblico adulto*
ˈ**wa•ter•side** *n*: ***at the waterside*** sulla riva
ˈ**wa•ter•ski•ing** sci *m inv* nautico
ˈ**wa•ter•tight** *adj compartment* stagno; *fig* inattaccabile
ˈ**wa•ter•way** corso *m* d'acqua navigabile
ˈ**wa•ter•wings** *npl* braccioli *mpl*
ˈ**wa•ter•works**: ***turn on the waterworks*** F piangere
wa•ter•y [ˈwɔːtərɪ] *adj* acquoso
watt [wɒt] watt *m inv*
wave[1] [weɪv] *n in sea* onda *f*
wave[2] [weɪv] **1** *n of hand* saluto *m* (con la mano) **2** *v/i with hand* salutare (con la mano); ***wave to s.o.*** salutare qu (con la mano) **3** *v/t flag etc* sventolare
ˈ**wave•length** RAD lunghezza *f* d'onda; ***be on the same wavelength*** *fig* essere sulla stessa lunghezza d'onda
wa•ver [ˈweɪvə(r)] *v/i* vacillare
wav•y [ˈweɪvɪ] *adj hair, line* ondulato
wax [wæks] *n for floor, furniture* cera *f*; *in ear* cerume *m*
way [weɪ] **1** *n* (*method, manner*) modo *m*; (*manner*) maniera *f*; (*route*) strada *f*; ***this way*** (*like this*) così; (*in this direction*) da questa parte; ***by the way*** (*incidentally*) a proposito; ***by way of*** (*via*) passando per; (*in the form of*) come; ***in a way*** (*in certain respects*) in un certo senso; ***be under way*** essere in corso; ***give way*** MOT dare la precedenza; (*collapse*) crollare; ***X has given way to Y*** (*been replaced by*) Y ha preso il posto di X; ***have one's (own) way*** averla vinta; ***OK, we'll do it your way*** OK, faremo come dici tu; ***lead the way*** *also fig* fare strada; ***lose one's way*** smarrirsi; ***be in the way*** (*be an obstruction*) essere d'intralcio; ***it's on the way to the station*** è sulla strada della stazione; ***I was on my way to the station*** stavo andando alla stazione; ***no way!*** neanche per sogno!; ***there's no way he can do it*** è impossibile che ce la faccia **2** *adv* F (*much*); ***it's way too soon to decide*** è veramente troppo presto per decidere; ***they are way behind with their work*** sono molto indietro con il lavoro
way ˈin entrata *f*
way of ˈlife stile *m* di vita
way ˈout *n* uscita *f*; *fig*: *from situation* via *f* d'uscita
we [wiː] *pron* noi; ***we're the best*** siamo i migliori; ***they're going, but we're not*** loro vanno, noi no
weak [wiːk] *adj physically, morally* debole; *tea, coffee* leggero
weak•en [ˈwiːkn] **1** *v/t* indebolire **2** *v/i* indebolirsi
weak•ling [ˈwiːklɪŋ] *morally* smidollato *m*, -a *f*; *physically* mingherlino *m*, -a *f*
weak•ness [ˈwiːknɪs] debolezza *f*; ***have a weakness for sth*** (*liking*) avere un debole per qc
wealth [welθ] ricchezza *f*; ***a wealth of*** una grande abbondanza di
wealth•y [ˈwelθɪ] *adj* ricco
weap•on [ˈwepən] arma *f*
wear [weə(r)] **1** *n*: ***wear (and tear)*** usura *f*; ***clothes for everyday wear*** vestiti per tutti i giorni; ***clothes for evening wear*** abiti da sera **2** *v/t* (*pret* **wore**, *pp* **worn**) (*have on*) indossare; (*damage*) logorare **3** *v/i* (*pret* **wore**, *pp* **worn**) (*wear out*) logorarsi; (*last*) durare
◆ **wear away 1** *v/i* consumarsi **2** *v/t* con-

sumare
◆ **wear down** *v/t resistance* fiaccare
◆ **wear off** *v/i of effect, feeling* svanire
◆ **wear out 1** *v/t* (*tire*) estenuare; *shoes* consumare **2** *v/i of shoes, carpet* consumarsi
wea•ri•ly ['wɪərɪlɪ] *adv* stancamente
wear•ing ['weərɪŋ] *adj* (*tiring*) stancante
wear•y ['wɪərɪ] *adj* stanco
weath•er ['weðə(r)] **1** *n* tempo *m*; ***be feeling under the weather*** sentirsi poco bene **2** *v/t crisis* superare
'**weath•er-beat•en** *adj* segnato
'**weath•er fore•cast** previsioni *fpl* del tempo
'**weath•er•man** meteorologo *m*
weave [wiːv] **1** *v/t* (*pret* ***wove***, *pp* ***woven***) *cloth* tessere; *basket* intrecciare **2** *v/i* (*move*) zigzagare
web [web] *of spider* ragnatela *f*; ***the Web*** COMPUT il web *m inv*, la Rete *f inv*
webbed '**feet** piedi *mpl* palmati
'**web page** pagina *f* web
'**web site** sito *m* web
wed•ding ['wedɪŋ] matrimonio *m*
'**wed•ding an•ni•ver•sa•ry** anniversario *m* di matrimonio
'**wed•ding cake** torta *f* nuziale
'**wed•ding day** giorno *m* del matrimonio
'**wed•ding dress** abito *m or* vestito *m* da sposa
'**wed•ding ring** fede *f*
wedge [wedʒ] **1** *n to hold sth in place* zeppa *f*; *of cheese etc* fetta *f* **2** *v/t*: ***wedge open*** tenere aperto
Wed•nes•day ['wenzdeɪ] mercoledì *m inv*
wee [wiː] *adj* F piccolo; ***a wee bit*** un pochino
weed [wiːd] **1** *n* erbaccia *f* **2** *v/t* diserbare
◆ **weed out** *v/t* (*remove*) eliminare
'**weed-kill•er** diserbante *m*
weed•y ['wiːdɪ] *adj* F mingherlino
week [wiːk] settimana *f*; ***a week tomorrow*** una settimana a domani
'**week•day** giorno *m* feriale
week'end fine *m* settimana, weekend *m inv*; ***at*** *or Am* ***on the weekend*** durante il fine settimana
week•ly ['wiːklɪ] **1** *adj* settimanale **2** *n magazine* settimanale *m* **3** *adv* settimanalmente
weep [wiːp] *v/i* (*pret & pp* ***wept***) piangere
weep•y ['wiːpɪ] *adj*: ***be weepy*** essere piagnucoloso
wee-wee 1 *n* F pipì *f inv* F; ***do a wee-wee*** fare la pipì **2** *v/i* F fare la pipì
weigh [weɪ] *v/t & v/i* pesare
◆ **weigh down** *v/t*: ***be weighed down with*** *with bags* curvarsi sotto il peso di; *with worries* essere oppresso da
◆ **weigh on** *v/t* preoccupare
◆ **weigh up** *v/t* (*assess*) valutare
weight [weɪt] *of person, object* peso *m*; ***put on / lose weight*** ingrassare / dimagrire
◆ **weight down** *v/t* fermare con pesi
weight•less•ness ['weɪtləsnəs] assenza *f* di peso
'**weight•lift•er** pesista *m/f*
'**weight•lift•ing** sollevamento *m* pesi
weight•y ['weɪtɪ] *adj fig: important* importante
weir [wɪə(r)] chiusa *f*
weird [wɪəd] *adj* strano
weird•ly ['wɪədlɪ] *adv* stranamente
weird•o ['wɪədəʊ] *n* F pazzoide *m/f*
wel•come ['welkəm] **1** *adj* benvenuto; ***make s.o. welcome*** accogliere bene qu; ***it makes a welcome change*** è un gradito cambiamento; ***you're welcome!*** prego!; ***you're welcome to try some*** serviti pure **2** *n also fig* accoglienza *f*; *fig: to news, proposal* accoglienza *f* **3** *v/t guests etc* accogliere; *fig: decision etc* rallegrarsi di; ***she welcomes a challenge*** apprezza le sfide
weld [weld] *v/t* saldare
weld•er ['weldə(r)] saldatore *m*, -trice *f*
wel•fare ['welfeə(r)] bene *m inv*
wel•fare '**state** stato *m* sociale
'**wel•fare work** assistenza *f* sociale
'**wel•fare work•er** assistente *m/f* sociale
well[1] [wel] *n for water, oil* pozzo *m*
well[2] [wel] **1** *adv* bene; ***well done!*** bravo!; ***as well*** (*too*) anche; ***as well as*** *in addition to* oltre a; ***it's just as well you told me*** hai fatto bene a dirmelo; ***very well*** *acknowledging an order* benissimo; *when you don't agree with sth but are doing it anyway* va bene; ***well, well!*** *surprise* bene, bene!; ***well …*** *uncertainty, thinking* beh … **2** *adj*: ***be well*** stare bene; ***feel well*** sentirsi bene; ***get well soon!*** guarisci presto!
well-'bal•anced *adj person, meal* equilibrato; *meal, diet* equilibrato
well-be,haved *adj* educato
well-,be•ing benessere *m*
well-,built *adj* ben fatto; *euph* (*fat*) robusto
well-,done *adj meat* ben cotto
well-,dressed *adj* ben vestito
well-,earned *adj* meritato
well-,heeled *adj* F danaroso
wel•lies ['welɪz] *npl* F → ***wellingtons***
well-in'formed *adj* ben informato
wel•ling•tons ['welɪŋtənz] *npl* stivali *mpl* di gomma

well-ˈknown *adj* famoso
well-ˌmade *adj* ben fatto
well-ˌman•nered *adj* ben educato
well-ˌmean•ing *adj* spinto da buone intenzioni
well-ˌoff *adj* benestante
well-ˌpaid *adj* ben pagato
well-ˌread *adj* colto
well-ˌtimed *adj* tempestivo
well-to-ˌdo *adj* abbiente
well-ˌworn *adj* liso
Welsh [welʃ] **1** *adj* gallese **2** *n language* gallese *m*; ***the Welsh*** i gallesi
went [went] *pret* → ***go***
wept [wept] *pret & pp* → ***weep***
were [wɜː(r)] *pret pl* → ***be***
west [west] **1** *n* ovest *m*, occidente *m*; ***the West*** POL l'Occidente; *western part of a country* parte *f* occidentale del paese **2** *adj* occidentale **3** *adv* verso ovest; ***west of*** a ovest di
west•er•ly [ˈwestəlɪ] *adj* occidentale; ***in a westerly direction*** verso ovest
west•ern [ˈwestən] **1** *adj* occidentale; ***Western*** occidentale **2** *n* (*film*) western *m inv*
West•ern•er [ˈwestənə(r)] occidentale *m/f*
west•ern•ized [ˈwestənaɪzd] *adj* occidentalizzato
west•ward [ˈwestwəd] *adv* verso ovest
wet [wet] *adj* bagnato; (*rainy*) piovoso; ***wet paint*** *as sign* vernice fresca; ***be wet through*** essere fradicio
wet ˈblan•ket F guastafeste *m/f inv*
ˈwet suit *for diving* muta *f*
whack [wæk] **1** *n* F (*blow*) colpo *m*; F (*share*) parte *f* **2** *v/t* F colpire
whacked [wækt] *adj* F stanco morto
whack•ing [ˈwækɪŋ] *adj* F enorme
whale [weɪl] balena *f*
whal•ing [ˈweɪlɪŋ] caccia *f* alla balena
wharf [wɔːf] *n* banchina *f*
what [wɒt] **1** *pron* (che) cosa; ***what is that?*** (che) cos'è?; ***what is it?*** (*what do you want*) (che) cosa c'è?; ***what?*** cosa?; *astonishment* (che) cosa?; ***it's not what I meant*** non è ciò che volevo dire; ***what about some dinner?*** e se mangiassimo qualcosa?; ***what about heading home?*** e se ce ne andassimo a casa?; ***what is the date today?*** quanti ne abbiamo oggi?; ***what for?*** (*why*) perché?; ***so what?*** e allora? **2** *adj* che *inv*, quale; ***what colour is the car?*** di che colore è la macchina?; ***what university are you at?*** in quale università studi? **3** *adv*: ***what a brilliant idea!*** che bella idea!
what•ev•er [wɒtˈevə(r)] **1** *pron*: ***I'll do whatever you want*** farò (tutto) quello che vuoi; ***whatever I do, it'll be a problem*** qualsiasi cosa faccia, ci saranno problemi; ***whatever the season*** *regardless of* in qualunque stagione; ***whatever people say*** qualunque cosa dica la gente; ***whatever gave you that idea?*** cosa mai te lo ha fatto pensare? **2** *adj* qualunque; ***you have no reason whatever to worry*** non hai nessun motivo di preoccuparti
wheat [wiːt] grano *m*, frumento *m*
whee•dle [ˈwiːdl] *v/t* F: ***wheedle sth out of s.o.*** ottenere qc da qu con lusinghe
wheel [wiːl] **1** *n* ruota *f*; (*steering wheel*) volante *m* **2** *v/t bicycle* spingere **3** *v/i of birds* roteare
◆ **wheel around** *v/i* voltarsi
ˈwheel•bar•row carriola *f*
ˈwheel•chair sedia *f* a rotelle
ˈwheel clamp ceppo *m* bloccaruote
wheeze [wiːz] *v/i* ansimare
when [wen] *adv conj* quando **2** *conj* quando; ***when I was a child*** quand'ero bambino
when•ev•er [wenˈevə(r)] *adv* (*each time*) ogni volta che; *regardless of when* in qualunque momento
where [weə(r)] **1** *adv* dove **2** *conj* dove; ***this is where I used to live*** io abitavo qui
where•a•bouts [weərəˈbaʊts] **1** *adv* dove **2** *npl*: ***know s.o.'s whereabouts*** sapere dove si trova qu
where•as [weərˈæz] mentre
wher•ev•er [weərˈevə(r)] **1** *conj* dovunque; ***wherever you go*** dovunque tu vada **2** *adv* dove; ***wherever can he be?*** dove sarà mai?
whet [wet] *v/t v/t* (*pret & pp* ***-ted***) *appetite* stuzzicare
wheth•er [ˈweðə(r)] *pron* se
which [wɪtʃ] **1** *adj* quale; ***which one is yours?*** qual è il tuo? **2** *pron interrogative* quale; *relative* che; ***on / in which*** su / in cui; ***take one, it doesn't matter which*** prendine uno, non importa quale
which•ev•er [wɪtʃˈevə(r)] **1** *adj* qualunque **2** *pron* quello che *m*, quella che *f*; ***whichever of the methods*** qualunque metodo
whiff [wɪf] *unpleasant* zaffata *f*; ***catch a whiff of*** sentire
while [waɪl] **1** *conj* mentre; (*although*) benché **2** *n*: ***a long while ago*** molto tempo fa; ***wait a long while*** aspettare molto *o* lungo; ***for a while*** per un po'; ***in a while*** fra poco; ***I'll wait a while longer*** aspetto un altro po'

◆ **while away** *v/t* passare
whim [wɪm] capriccio *m*
whim•per ['wɪmpə(r)] **1** *n of person, baby* gemito *m*; *of animal* mugolio *m* **2** *v/i of person, baby* gemere; *of animal* mugolare
whine [waɪn] *v/i of dog* guaire; F (*complain*) piagnucolare
whip [wɪp] **1** *n* frusta *f* **2** *v/t* (*pret & pp* **-ped**) (*beat*) sbattere; *cream* montare; F (*defeat*) stracciare F
◆ **whip out** *v/t* F tirar fuori (fulmineamente)
◆ **whip up** *v/t* (*arouse*) sobillare; F *meal* improvvisare
whipped cream [wɪpt] panna *f* montata
whip•ping ['wɪpɪŋ] (*beating*) bastonata *f*; F (*defeat*) batosta *f*
'**whip•ping cream** panna *f* da montare
'**whip•round** F colletta *f*; ***have a whip-round*** fare una colletta
whirl [wɜːl] **1** *n*: ***my mind is in a whirl*** mi gira la testa **2** *v/i of blades etc* roteare; *of leaves* volteggiare; *of person* girarsi
'**whirl•pool** *in river* mulinello *m*; *for relaxation* vasca *f* per idromassaggio
whirr [wɜː(r)] *v/i* ronzare
whisk [wɪsk] **1** *n* frusta *f*; *mechanical* frullino *m* **2** *v/t eggs* frullare
◆ **whisk away** *v/t* togliere in fretta
whis•kers ['wɪskəz] *npl of man* basette *fpl*; *of animal* baffi *mpl*
whis•ky whisky *m inv*
whis•per ['wɪspə(r)] **1** *n* bisbiglio *m*; (*rumour*) voce *f* **2** *v/t & v/i* bisbigliare
whis•tle ['wɪsl] **1** *n sound* fischio *m*; *device* fischietto *m* **2** *v/i* fischiare **3** *v/t* fischiettare
whis•tle-blow•er ['wɪslbləʊə(r)] F *persona f che denuncia irregolarità all'interno della propria azienda*
white [waɪt] **1** *n colour* bianco *m*; *of egg* albume *m*, bianco *m* F; *person* bianco *m*, -a *f* **2** *adj* bianco; *person* bianco; ***go white*** sbiancare (in viso)
white 'Christ•mas natale *m* con la neve
white 'cof•fee *Br* caffè *m inv* con latte *o* panna
white-col•lar 'work•er impiegato *m*, -a *f*
'**White House** Casa *f* Bianca
white 'lie bugia *f* innocente
white 'meat carne *f* bianca
'**white•wash 1** *n* calce *f*; *fig* copertura *f* **2** *v/t* imbiancare (con calce)
white 'wine vino *m* bianco
Whit•sun ['wɪtsn] Pentecoste *f*
whit•tle ['wɪtl] *v/t wood* intagliare
◆ **whittle down** *v/t* ridurre
whiz(z) [wɪz] *n*: ***be a whiz at*** F essere un genio in
◆ **whizz by, whizz past** *v/i of time, car* sfrecciare
'**whizz•kid** F mago *m*, -a *f* F
who [huː] *pron interrogative* chi; *relative* che; ***the man who I was talking to*** l'uomo con cui parlavo; ***I don't know who to believe*** non so a chi credere
who•dun(n)•it [huː'dʌnɪt] giallo *m*
who•ev•er [huː'evə(r)] *pron* chiunque; (*interrogative*) chi mai; ***whoever can that be?*** chi sarà mai?
whole [həʊl] **1** *adj*: ***the whole town*** tutta la città; ***two whole hours / days*** ben due ore / giorni; ***a whole chicken*** un pollo intero; ***he drank / ate the whole lot*** ha bevuto / mangiato tutto; ***it's a whole lot easier / better*** è molto più facile / meglio **2** *n* tutto *m*; ***the whole of the United States*** tutti gli Stati Uniti; ***on the whole*** nel complesso
whole-heart•ed [həʊl'hɑːtɪd] *adj* senza riserve
whole-heart•ed•ly [həʊl'hɑːtɪdlɪ] *adv* senza riserve
whole•meal 'bread pane *m* integrale
'**whole•sale 1** *adj* all'ingrosso; *fig* in massa **2** *adv* all'ingrosso
whole•sal•er ['həʊlseɪlə(r)] grossista *m/f*
whole•some ['həʊlsəm] *adj* sano
whol•ly ['həʊlɪ] *adv* completamente
whol•ly owned 'sub•sid•i•ar•y consociata *f* interamente controllata
whom [huːm] *pron fml* chi; ***to / for whom*** a cui
whoop•ing cough ['huːpɪŋ] pertosse *f*
whop•ping ['wɒpɪŋ] *adj* F enorme
whore [hɔː(r)] *n* puttana *f*
whose [huːz] **1** *pron interrogative* di chi; *relative* il / la cui; ***whose is this?*** di chi è questo?; ***a man whose wife ...*** un uomo la cui moglie ...; ***a country whose economy is booming*** un paese dall'economia fiorente **2** *adj* di chi; ***whose bike is that?*** di chi è quella bici?; ***whose car are we taking?*** che macchina prendiamo?
why [waɪ] *adv* perché; ***that's why*** ecco perché; ***why not?*** perché no?; ***the reason why he left*** il motivo per cui se ne è andato
wick•ed ['wɪkɪd] *adj* (*evil*) malvagio; (*mischievous*) malizioso
wick•er ['wɪkə(r)] *adj* di vimini
wick•er 'chair poltrona *f* di vimini
wick•et ['wɪkɪt] porta *f*
wide [waɪd] *adj* largo; *experience* vasto; *range* ampio; ***be 12 metres wide*** essere largo 12 metri

wide a'wake *adj* sveglio
wide•ly ['waɪdlɪ] *adv used, known* largamente; ***it is widely believed that …*** è una credenza diffusa che …
wid•en ['waɪdn] **1** *v/t* allargare **2** *v/i* allargarsi
wide-'o•pen *adj* spalancato
wide-ˌrang•ing *adj* di largo respiro
'wide•spread *adj* diffuso
wid•ow ['wɪdəʊ] *n* vedova *f*
wid•ow•er ['wɪdəʊə(r)] vedovo *m*
width [wɪdθ] larghezza *f*; *of fabric* altezza *f*
wield [wiːld] *v/t weapon* brandire; *power* esercitare
wife [waɪf] (*pl* ***wives*** [waɪvz]) moglie *f*
wig [wɪg] parrucca *f*
wig•gle ['wɪgl] *v/t loose screw etc* muovere; ***wiggle one's hips*** ancheggiare
wild [waɪld] **1** *adj animal, flowers* selvatico; *teenager, party* scatenato; (*crazy: scheme*) folle; *applause* fragoroso; ***be wild about …*** (*keen on*) andare pazzo per …; ***go wild*** impazzire; (*become angry*) andare su tutte le furie; ***run wild*** *of children* scatenarsi; *of plants* crescere senza controllo **2** *n*: ***the wilds*** le zone sperdute
wil•der•ness ['wɪldənɪs] *empty place* deserto *m*; *fig*: *garden etc* giungla *f*
'wild•fire: ***spread like wildfire*** allargarsi a macchia d'olio
wildˌgoose chase ricerca *f* inutile
'wild•life fauna *f*; ***wildlife programme*** programma *m* sulla natura
wild•ly ['waɪldlɪ] *adv* F terribilmente
wil•ful ['wɪlfʊl] *adj person* ostinato; *action* intenzionale
will[1] [wɪl] *n* LAW testamento *m*
will[2] [wɪl] *n* (*willpower*) volontà *f inv*
will[3] [wɪl] *v/aux*: ***I will let you know tomorrow*** ti farò sapere entro domani; ***will you be there?*** ci sarai?; ***I won't be back*** non tornerò; ***you will call me, won't you?*** mi chiamerai, vero?; ***I'll pay for this – no you won't*** questo lo pago io - no, lascia stare; ***the car won't start*** la macchina non parte; ***will you tell her that …?*** dille che …; ***will you have some more tea?*** vuoi dell'altro tè?; ***will you stop that!*** smettila!
will•ful *Am* → ***wilful***
will•ing ['wɪlɪŋ] *adj* disponibile; ***are you willing to pay more?*** sei disposto a pagare di più?; ***he was not willing to accept*** no ha voluto accettare
will•ing•ly ['wɪlɪŋlɪ] *adv* volentieri
will•ing•ness ['wɪlɪŋnɪs] disponibilità *f inv*
wil•low ['wɪləʊ] salice *m*
'will•pow•er forza *f* di volontà
wil•ly-nil•ly [wɪlɪ'nɪlɪ] *adv* (*at random*) a casaccio
wilt [wɪlt] *v/i of plant* appassire
wi•ly ['waɪlɪ] *adj* astuto
wimp [wɪmp] F pappamolle *m/f*
win [wɪn] **1** *n* vittoria *f* **2** *v/t & v/i* (*pret & pp* ***won***) vincere
◆ **win back** *v/t* riconquistare
wince [wɪns] *v/i* fare una smorfia
wind[1] [wɪnd] **1** *n* vento *m*; (*flatulence*) aria *f*; ***get wind of …*** venire a sapere … **2** *v/t* ***wind s.o.*** togliere il fiato a qu
wind[2] [waɪnd] (*pret & pp* ***wound***) **1** *v/i of path, stream* snodarsi; *of plant* avvolgersi **2** *v/t* avvolgere
◆ **wind down 1** *v/i*: ***the party began to wind down*** la gente cominciò ad andar via dalla festa **2** *v/t car window* abbassare; *business* chiudere gradualmente
◆ **wind up 1** *v/t clock* caricare; *car window* tirar su; *speech, presentation* concludere; *business, affairs, company* chiudere **2** *v/i*: ***wind up in hospital*** finire in ospedale
'wind-bag F trombone *m*
'wind•fall *fig* colpo *m* di fortuna
wind•ing ['waɪndɪŋ] *adj* tortuoso
'wind in•stru•ment strumento *m* a fiato
'wind•mill mulino *m*
win•dow ['wɪndəʊ] *of house* finestra *f*; *of shop* vetrina *f*; *of car, train* finestrino *m*; COMPUT finestra *f*; ***in the window*** *of shop* in vetrina
'win•dow box fioriera *f*
'win•dow clean•er lavavetri *m/f inv*
'win•dow•pane vetro *m* (della finestra)
'win•dow seat *on plane, train* posto *m* di finestrino
'win•dow-shop *v/i* (*pret & pp* ***-ped***): ***go window-shopping*** guardare le vetrine
win•dow•sill ['wɪndəʊsɪl]
'wind•screen parabrezza *m inv*
'wind•screen wip•er tergicristallo *m*
'wind•shield *Am* parabrezza *m inv*
'wind•surf•er *person* windsurfista *m/f*; *board* windsurf *m inv*
'wind•surf•ing windsurf *m inv*
'wind•y ['wɪndɪ] *adj weather, day* ventoso; ***it's getting windy*** si sta alzando il vento
wine [waɪn] vino *m*
'wine bar enoteca *f*, bar *m inv*
'wine cel•lar cantina *f*
'wine glass bicchiere *m* da vino
'wine list lista *f* dei vini
'wine mak•er viticoltore *m*, -trice *f*
'wine mer•chant *company* azienda *f* vinicola; *individual* vinaio *m*, -a *f*

wing [wɪŋ] *n also* SP ala *f*
'wing•span apertura *f* alare
wink [wɪŋk] **1** *n* occhiolino *m*; ***I didn't sleep a wink*** F non ho chiuso occhio **2** *v/i of person* strizzare gli occhi; ***wink at s.o.*** fare l'occhiolino a qu
win•ner ['wɪnə(r)] vincitore *m*, -trice *f*
win•ning ['wɪnɪŋ] *adj* vincente
'win•ning post traguardo *m*
win•nings ['wɪnɪŋz] *npl* vincita *fsg*
win•ter ['wɪntə(r)] *n* inverno *m*
win•ter 'sports *npl* sport *m inv* invernali
win•try ['wɪntrɪ] *adj* invernale
wipe [waɪp] *v/t* (*dry*) asciugare; (*clean*) pulire; *tape* cancellare
◆ **wipe out** *v/t* (*kill*, *destroy*) distruggere; *debt* estinguere
wip•er ['waɪpə(r)] → ***windscreen wiper***
wire ['waɪə(r)] **1** *adj* metallico **2** *n* fil *m* di ferro; ELEC filo *m* elettrico
wire•less ['waɪələs] radio *f inv*
wire 'net•ting rete *f* metallica
wir•ing ['waɪərɪŋ] *n* ELEC impianto *m* elettrico
wir•y ['waɪərɪ] *adj person* dal fisico asciutto
wis•dom ['wɪzdəm] saggezza *f*
'wis•dom tooth dente *m* del giudizio
wise [waɪz] *adj* saggio
'wise•crack *n* F spiritosaggine *f*
'wise guy *pej* spiritoso *m*
wise•ly ['waɪzlɪ] *adv act* saggiamente
wish [wɪʃ] **1** *n* desiderio *m*; ***make a wish*** esprimere un desiderio; ***against his family's wishes*** contro il volere della famiglia; ***best wishes*** *for birthday etc* tanti auguri; *as greetings* cordiali saluti **2** *v/t* volere; ***I wish that he'd stop*** vorrei che la smettesse; ***wish s.o. well*** fare tanti auguri a qu; ***I wished him good luck*** gli ho augurato buona fortuna **3** *v/i*: ***wish for*** desiderare
'wish•bone forcella *f* (di pollo)
wish•ful 'think•ing ['wɪʃfʊl] illusione *f*
wish•y-wash•y ['wɪʃɪwɒʃɪ] *adj person* insulso; *colour* slavato
wisp [wɪsp] *of hair* ciocca *f*; *of smoke* filo *m*
wist•ful ['wɪstfʊl] *adj* malinconico
wist•ful•ly ['wɪstfəlɪ] *adv* malinconicamente
wit [wɪt] (*humour*) spirito *m*; *person* persona *f* di spirito; ***be at one's wits' end*** non sapere più che fare; ***keep one's wits about one*** non perdere la testa; ***be scared out of one's wits*** essere spaventato a morte
witch [wɪtʃ] strega *f*
'witch•hunt *fig* caccia *f* alle streghe
with [wɪð] *prep* con; (*proximity*) con; (*agency*) con; (*cause*) di; (*possession*) con; ***shiver with fear*** tremare di paura; ***a girl with blue eyes*** una ragazza dagli *o* con gli occhi azzurri; ***with a smile/a wave*** con un sorriso / un gesto della mano; ***are you with me?*** (*do you understand*) mi segui?; ***with no money*** senza soldi
withdraw [wɪð'drɔː] (*pret* **-drew**, *pp* **-drawn**) **1** *v/t complaint*, *application*, *troops* ritirare; *money from bank* prelevare; *troops* ritirare **2** *v/i* ritirarsi; ritirarsi
with•draw•al [wɪð'drɔːəl] *of complaint*, *application*, *troops* ritiro *m*; *of money* prelievo *m*; *of troops* ritiro *m*; *from drugs* crisi *f inv* di astinenza
with'draw•al symp•toms *npl* sindrome *f* da astinenza
with•drawn [wɪð'drɔːn] *adj person* chiuso
with•er ['wɪðə(r)] *v/i* seccare
with'hold *v/t* (*pret & pp* **-held**) *information* nascondere; *consent* rifiutare; *payment* trattenere
with'in *prep* (*inside*) dentro; *in expressions of time* nel giro di, entro; *in expressions of distance* a meno di; ***is it within walking distance?*** ci si arriva a piedi?; ***we kept within the budget*** abbiamo rispettato il budget; ***it is not within my power*** non rientra nelle mie competenze; ***within reach*** a portata di mano
with'out *prep* senza; ***without you/him*** senza (di) te / lui; ***without looking/asking*** senza guardare / chiedere; ***without his seeing*** senza che lo vedesse
with'stand *v/t* (*pret & pp* **-stood**) resistere a
wit•ness ['wɪtnɪs] **1** *n* testimone *m/f* **2** *v/t accident*, *crime* essere testimone di; *signature* attestare l'autenticità di
'wit•ness box banco *m* dei testimoni
wit•ti•cis•m ['wɪtɪsɪzm] arguzia *f*
wit•ty ['wɪtɪ] *adj* arguto
wob•ble ['wɒbl] *v/i of person* vacillare; *of object* traballare
wob•bly ['wɒblɪ] *adj person* vacillante; *object* traballante; *voice*, *hand* tremante
wok [wɒk] wok *m inv*
woke [wəʊk] *pret* → ***wake***
wok•en ['wəʊkn] *pp* → ***wake***
wolf [wʊlf] **1** *n* (*pl* **wolves** [wʊlvz]) *animal* lupo *m*; (*fig*: *womanizer*) donnaiolo *m* **2** *v/t*: **wolf (down)** divorare
'wolf whis•tle *n* fischio *m*
'wolf-whis•tle *v/i*: ***wolf-whistle at s.o.*** fischiare dietro a qu
wom•an ['wʊmən] (*pl* **women** ['wɪmɪn])

donna *f*
wom•an 'doc•tor dottoressa *f*
wom•an 'driv•er autista *f*
wom•an•iz•er ['wʊmənaɪzə(r)] donnaiolo *m*
wom•an 'priest donna *f* sacerdote
womb [wuːm] utero *m*
wom•en [wɪmɪn] *pl* → ***woman***
women's lib [wɪmɪnz'lɪb] movimento *m* di liberazione della donna
women's lib•ber [wɪmɪnz'lɪbə(r)] femminista *f*
won [wʌn] *pret & pp* → ***win***
won•der ['wʌndə(r)] **1** *n (amazement)* stupore *m*, meraviglia *f*; *of science etc* meraviglia *f*; ***no wonder!*** non mi stupisce!; ***it's a wonder that …*** è incredibile che … **2** *v/i* pensare **3** *v/t* domandarsi; ***I wonder if you could help*** mi chiedevo se potessi aiutarmi
won•der•ful ['wʌndəfʊl] *adj* stupendo
won•der•ful•ly ['wʌndəflɪ] *adv (extremely)* estremamente
won't [wəʊnt] = ***will not***
wood [wʊd] legno *m*; *for fire* legna *f*; *(forest)* bosco *m*
wood•ed ['wʊdɪd] *adj* boscoso
wood•en ['wʊdn] *adj made of wood* di legno
wood•peck•er ['wʊdpekə(r)] picchio *m*
'wood•wind MUS fiati *mpl*
'wood•work *parts made of wood* strutture *fpl* in legno; *activity* lavorazione *f* del legno
wool [wʊl] lana *f*
wool•en *Am*, **wool•len** ['wʊlən] **1** *adj* di lana **2** *n* indumento *m* di lana
word [wɜːd] **1** *n* parola *f*; *(news)* notizie *fpl*; *(promise)* parola *f*; ***is there any word from …?*** ci sono notizie da …?; ***you have my word*** hai la mia parola; ***have words*** *(argue)* litigare; ***have a word with s.o.*** parlare con qu **2** *v/t article, letter* formulare
word•ing ['wɜːdɪŋ] formulazione *f*
word 'pro•cess•ing trattamento *m* testi
word 'pro•ces•sor *software* word processor *m inv*
wore [wɔː (r)] *pret* → ***wear***
work [wɜːk] **1** *n* lavoro *m*; ***out of work*** disoccupato; ***be at work*** essere al lavoro; ***I go to work by bus*** vado a lavorare in autobus **2** *v/i of person* lavorare; *study* studiare; *of machine*, *(succeed)* funzionare; ***I used to work with him*** lavoravamo insieme; ***how does it work?*** *of device* come funziona? **3** *v/t employee* far lavorare; *machine* far funzionare
◆ **work off** *v/t bad mood, anger* sfogare; *flab* smaltire
◆ **work out 1** *v/t problem* capire; *solution* trovare **2** *v/i at gym* fare ginnastica; *of relationship etc* funzionare
◆ **work out to** *v/t (add up to)* ammontare a
◆ **work up** *v/t*: ***work up enthusiasm*** entusiasmarsi; ***I worked up an appetite*** mi è venuto appetito; ***get worked up*** *(get angry)* infuriarsi; *(get nervous)* agitarsi
work•a•ble ['wɜːkəbl] *adj solution* realizzabile
work•a•hol•ic [wɜːkə'hɒlɪk] *n* F stacanovista *m/f*
work•er ['wɜːkə(r)] lavoratore *m*, -trice *f*; ***she's a good worker*** lavora bene
'work•day *hours of work* giornata *f* lavorativa; *not a holiday* giorno *m* feriale
'work•force forza *f* lavoro
work•ing ['wɜːkɪŋ] *adj day, week* lavorativo; *clothes* da lavoro; *lunch* di lavoro; ***in working order*** funzionante
'work•ing class classe *f* operaia
'work•ing-class *adj* operaio
'work•ing con•di•tions *npl* condizioni *fpl* di lavoro
work•ing 'day → ***workday***
'work•ing hours *npl* orario *m* di lavoro
work•ing 'knowledge conoscenza *f* di base
work•ing 'moth•er madre *f* che lavora
'work•load carico *m* di lavoro
'work•man operaio *m*
'work•man•like *adj* professionale
'work•man•ship fattura *f*
work of 'art opera *f* d'arte
'work•out allenamento *m*
'work per•mit permesso *m* di lavoro
'work•shop laboratorio *m*; *for mechanic* officina *f*; *(seminar)* workshop *m inv*
'work sta•tion work station *f inv*
'work•top piano *m* di lavoro
work-to-'rule sciopero *m* bianco
world [wɜːld] mondo *m*; ***the world of computers / the theatre*** il mondo dei computer / del teatro; ***out of this world*** F fantastico
World 'Cup mondiali *mpl* (di calcio)
world•ly ['wɜːldlɪ] *adj goods* materiale; *not spiritual* terreno; *power* temporale; *person* mondano
world-'class *adj* di livello internazionale
world-'fa•mous *adj* di fama mondiale
world 'pow•er potenza *f* mondiale
world 're•cord record *m inv* mondiale
world 'war guerra *f* mondiale
'world•wide 1 *adj* mondiale **2** *adv* a livello mondiale

worm [wɜːm] *n* verme *m*
worn [wɔːn] *pp* → ***wear***
worn-'out *adj shoes, carpet, part* logoro; *person* esausto, sfinito
wor•ried ['wʌrɪd] *adj* preoccupato
wor•ried•ly ['wʌrɪdlɪ] *adv* con aria preoccupata
wor•ry ['wʌrɪ] **1** *n* preoccupazione *f* **2** *v/t* (*pret & pp* **-ied**) preoccupare; (*upset*) turbare **3** *v/i* (*pret & pp* **-ied**) proccuparsi; ***it will be alright, don't worry!*** andrà tutto bene, non preoccuparti!
wor•ry•ing ['wʌrɪɪŋ] *adj* preoccupante
worse [wɜːs] **1** *adj* peggiore; ***things will get worse*** le cose peggioreranno **2** *adv* peggio
wors•en ['wɜːsn] *v/i* peggiorare
wor•ship ['wɜːʃɪp] **1** *n* culto *m* **2** *v/t* (*pret & pp* **-ped**) venerare; *fig* adorare
worst [wɜːst] **1** *adj* peggiore **2** *adv* peggio **3** *n*: ***the worst*** il peggio; ***if the worst comes to the worst*** nel peggiore dei casi
worst-case scen'a•ri•o: ***the worst-case scenario*** la peggiore delle ipotesi
worth [wɜːθ] **1** *adj*: ***be worth*** valere; ***it's worth reading / seeing*** vale la pena leggerlo / vederlo; ***be worth it*** valerne la pena **2** *n* valore *m*; ***£20 worth of petrol*** 20 sterline di benzina
worth•less ['wɜːθlɪs] *adj object* senza valore; *person* inetto
worth'while *adj cause* lodevole; ***be worthwhile*** (*beneficial, useful*) essere utile; (*worth the effort, worth doing*) valere la pena
worth•y ['wɜːðɪ] *adj* degno; *cause* lodevole; ***be worthy of*** (*deserve*) meritare
would [wʊd] *v/aux*: ***I would help if I could*** ti aiuterei se potessi; ***I said that I would go*** ho detto che sarei andato; ***I told him I would not leave unless …*** gli ho detto che non me ne sarei andato se non …; ***would you like to go to the cinema?*** vuoi andare al cinema?; ***would you mind if I smoked?*** la disturba se fumo?; ***would you tell her that …?*** le dica che …; ***would you close the door?*** le dispiace chiudere la porta?; ***I would have told you but …*** te l'avrei detto ma …; ***I would not have been so angry if …*** non mi sarei arrabbiato tanto se …
wound[1] [wuːnd] **1** *n* ferita *f* **2** *v/t also with remark* ferire; *with remark* ferire
wound[2] [waʊnd] *pret & pp* → ***wind***[2]
wove [wəʊv] *pret* → ***weave***
wov•en ['wəʊvn] *pp* → ***weave***
wow [waʊ] *int* wow
wrap [ræp] *v/t* (*pret & pp* **-ped**) *parcel, gift* incartare; (*wind, cover*) avvolgere
◆ **wrap up** *v/i against the cold* coprirsi bene
wrap•per ['ræpə(r)] incarto *m*
wrap•ping ['ræpɪŋ] involucro *m*
'wrap•ping pa•per carta *f* da regalo
wreath [riːθ] corona *f*; *for funeral* corona *f* funebre
wreck [rek] **1** *n of ship* relitto *m*; *of car* carcassa *f*; ***be a nervous wreck*** sentirsi un rottame **2** *v/t ship* far naufragare; *car* demolire; *plans, career, marriage* distruggere
wreck•age ['rekɪdʒ] *of car, plane* rottami *mpl*; *of marriage, career* brandelli *mpl*
wrench [rentʃ] **1** *n tool* chiave *f* inglese; *injury* slogatura *f* **2** *v/t injure* slogarsi; (*pull*) strappare
wres•tle ['resl] *v/i* fare la lotta
◆ **wrestle with** *v/t problems* lottare con
wres•tler ['reslə(r)] lottatore *m*, -trice *f*
wrest•ling ['reslɪŋ] lotta *f* libera
'wres•tling match incontro *m* di lotta libera
wrig•gle ['rɪgl] *v/i* (*squirm*) dimenarsi; *along the ground* strisciare
◆ **wriggle out of** *v/t* sottrarsi a
◆ **wring out** *v/t* (*pret & pp* **wrung**) *cloth* strizzare
wrin•kle ['rɪŋkl] **1** *n in skin* ruga *f*; *in clothes* grinza *f* **2** *v/t clothes* stropicciare **3** *v/i of clothes* stropicciarsi
wrist [rɪst] polso *m*
'wrist watch orologio *m* da polso
write [raɪt] (*pret* **wrote**, *pp* **written**) **1** *v/t* scrivere; *cheque* fare **2** *v/i* scrivere; *of author* scrivere; (*send a letter*) scrivere
◆ **write down** *v/t* annotare, scrivere
◆ **write off** *v/t debt* cancellare; *car* distruggere
writ•er ['raɪtə(r)] autore *m*, -trice *f*; *professional* scrittore *m*, -trice *f*
'write-up F recensione *f*
writhe [raɪð] *v/i* contorcersi
writ•ing ['raɪtɪŋ] *as career* scrivere *m*; (*hand-writing*) scrittura *f*; (*words*) scritta *f*; (*script*) scritto *m*; ***in writing*** per iscritto
'writ•ing pa•per carta *f* da lettere
writ•ten ['rɪtn] *pp* → ***write***
wrong [rɒŋ] **1** *adj* sbagliato; ***be wrong*** *of person* sbagliare; *of answer* essere errato; *morally* essere ingiusto; ***it's wrong to steal*** non si deve rubare; ***what's wrong?*** cosa c'è?; ***there is something wrong with the car*** la macchina ha qualcosa che non va **2** *adv* in modo sbagliato; ***go wrong*** *of person* sbagliare; *of marria-*

ge, plan etc andar male **3** *n immoral action* torto *m*; *immorality* male *m*; ***be in the wrong*** avere torto

wrong•ful ['rɒŋfʊl] *adj* illegale

wrong•ly ['rɒŋlɪ] *adv* erroneamente

wrong 'num•ber numero *m* sbagliato

wrote [rəʊt] *pret* → ***write***

wrought 'i•ron [rɔːt] ferro *m* battuto

wrung [rʌŋ] *pret & pp* → ***wring***

wry [raɪ] *adj* beffardo

X, Y

xen•o•pho•bi•a [zenəʊ'fəʊbɪə] xenofobia *f*
X-ray ['eksreɪ] **1** *n* raggio *m* X; *picture* radiografia *f*; ***have an X-ray*** farsi fare una radiografia **2** *v/t* radiografare
xy•lo•phone [zaɪlə'fəʊn] xilofono *m*
yacht [jɒt] *for pleasure* yacht *m inv*; *for racing* imbarcazione *f* da diporto
yacht•ing ['jɒtɪŋ] navigazione *f* da diporto
yachts•man ['jɒtsmən] diportista *m*
Yank [jæŋk] *n* F yankee *m inv*
yank [jæŋk] *v/t* dare uno strattone a
yap [jæp] *v/i* (*pret & pp* ***-ped***) *of small dog* abbaiare; F *talk a lot* chiacchierare
yard[1] [jɑːd] *of prison, institution etc* cortile *m*; *for storage* deposito *m* all'aperto
yard[2] [jɑːd] *measurement* iarda *f*
'yard•stick *fig* metro *m*
yarn [jɑːn] *n* (*thread*) filato *m*; F *story* racconto *m*
yawn [jɔːn] **1** *n* sbadiglio *m* **2** *v/i* sbadigliare
year [jɪə(r)] anno *m*; ***I've known here for years*** la conosco da (tanti) anni; ***it will last for years*** durerà anni; ***we were in the same year*** *at school* frequentavamo lo stesso anno; ***be six years old*** avere sei anni
year•ly ['jɪəlɪ] **1** *adj* annuale **2** *adv* annualmente; ***twice yearly*** due volte (al)l'anno
yearn [jɜːn] *v/i*: ***yearn to do sth*** struggersi dal desiderio di fare qc
◆ **yearn for** *v/t* desiderare ardentemente
yearn•ing ['jɜːnɪŋ] *n* desiderio *m* struggente
yeast [jiːst] lievito *m*
yell [jel] **1** *n* urlo *m* **2** *v/t & v/i* urlare
yel•low ['jeləʊ] **1** *n* giallo *m* **2** *adj* giallo
yel•low 'pag•es® *npl* pagine *fpl* gialle
yelp [jelp] **1** *n* guaito *m* **2** *v/i* guaire
yen [jen] FIN yen *m inv*
yes [jes] *int* sì; ***say yes*** dire di sì
'yes•man *pej* yes man *m inv*
yes•ter•day ['jestədeɪ] **1** *adv* ieri; ***the day before yesterday*** l'altro ieri **2** *n* ieri *m inv*
yet [jet] **1** *adv* finora; ***the fastest yet*** il più veloce finora; ***as yet*** *up to now* per ora; ***it is as yet undecided*** rimane ancora da decidere; ***have you finished yet?*** (non) hai (ancora) finito?; ***he hasn't arrived yet*** non è ancora arrivato; ***is he here yet? – not yet*** è arrivato? - non ancora; ***yet bigger / longer*** ancora più grande / lungo **2** *conj* eppure; ***yet I'm not sure*** eppure non sono sicuro
yield [jiːld] **1** *n from fields etc* raccolto *m*; *from investment* rendita *f* **2** *v/t fruit, harvest* dare, produrre; *interest* fruttare **3** *v/i* (*give way*) cedere
yob [jɒb] P teppista *m/f*
yo•ga ['jəʊgə] yoga *m*
yog•hurt ['jɒgət] yogurt *m inv*
yolk [jəʊk] tuorlo *m*
you [juː] *pron* ◇ *subject*: *familiar singular* tu; *familiar polite plural* voi; *polite singular* lei; ***do you know him?*** lo conosci / conosce / conoscete?; ***you go, I'll stay*** tu vai / lei vada / voi andate, io resto
◇ *direct object*: *familiar singular* ti; *familiar polite plural* vi; *polite singular* la; ***he knows you*** ti / vi / la conosce
◇ *indirect object*: *familiar singular* ti; *when two pronouns are used* te; *familiar polite plural* vi; *when two pronouns are used* ve; *polite singular* le; ***did he talk to you?*** ti / vi / le ha parlato?; ***I need to talk to you*** devo parlarti / parlarvi / parlarle; ***I told you*** te / ve l'ho detto, glielo ho detto
◇ *after prep familiar singular* te; *familiar polite plural* voi; *polite singular* lei; ***this is for you*** questo è per te / voi / lei
◇ *impersonal*: ***you never know*** non si sa mai; ***you have to pay*** si deve pagare; ***fruit is good for you*** la frutta fa bene
young [jʌŋ] *adj* giovane
young•ster ['jʌŋstə(r)] ragazzo *m*, -a *f*
your [jɔː(r)] *adj familiar singular* il tuo *m*, la tua *f*, i tuoi *mpl*, le tue *fpl*; *polite singular* il suo *m*, la sua *f*, i suoi *mpl*, le sue *fpl*; *familiar & polite plural* il vostro *m*, la vostra *f*, i vostri *mpl*, le vostre *fpl*; ***your brother*** tuo / suo / vostro fratello
yours [jɔːz] *pron familiar singular* il tuo *m*, la tua *f*, i tuoi *mpl*, le tue *fpl*; *polite singular* il suo *m*, la sua *f*, i suoi *mpl*, le sue *fpl*; *familiar & polite plural* il vostro *m*, la vostra *f*, i vostri *mpl*, le vostre *fpl*; ***a friend of yours*** un tuo / suo / vostro amico; ***yours ...*** *at end of letter* saluti ...; ***yours sincerely*** distinti saluti
your'self *pron reflexive* ti; *reflexive polite* si; *emphatic* tu stesso *m*, tu stessa *f*; *emphatic polite* lei stesso *m*, lei stessa *f*; ***did you hurt yourself?*** ti sei / si è fatto male?; ***you said so yourself*** l'hai detto

tu stesso/l'ha detto lei stesso; ***keep it for yourself*** tienilo per te / lo tenga per sé; ***by yourself*** da solo

your'selves *pron reflexive* vi; *emphatic* voi stessi *mpl*, voi stesse *fpl*; ***did you hurt yourselves?*** vi siete fatti male?; ***can you do it yourselves?*** potete farlo da voi?; ***by yourselves*** da soli *mpl*, da sole *fpl*

youth [juːθ] *n age* gioventù *f*; (*young man*) ragazzo *m*; (*young people*) giovani *mpl*

'youth club circolo *m* giovanile

youth•ful ['juːθfʊl] *adj* giovanile; *ideas* giovane; *idealism* di gioventù

'youth hos•tel ostello *m* della gioventù

Yu•go•sla•vi•a [juːgə'slɑːvɪə] Jugoslavia *f*

Yu•go•sla•vi•an [juːgə'slɑːvɪən] **1** *adj* jugoslavo **2** *n* jugoslavo *m*, -a *f*

yup•pie ['jʌpɪ] F yuppie *m/f inv*

Z

zap [zæp] *v/t* (*pret & pp* ***-ped***) F COMPUT (*delete*) cancellare; (*kill*) annientare; (*hit*) colpire; (*send*) mandare

◆ **zap along** *v/i* F *move fast* sfrecciare

zapped [zæpt] *adj* F (*exhausted*) stanchissimo

zap•per ['zæpə(r)] *for changing TV channels* telecomando *m*

zap•py ['zæpɪ] *adj* F *car, pace* veloce; (*lively, energetic*) brioso

zeal [ziːl] zelo *m*

ze•bra ['zebrə] zebra *f*

ze•bra 'cross•ing *Br* strisce *fpl* pedonali

ze•ro ['zɪərəʊ] zero *m*; ***10 below zero*** 10 (gradi) sotto zero

ze•ro 'growth crescita *f* zero

◆ **zero in on** *v/t* (*identify*) identificare

zest [zest] (*enthusiasm*) gusto *m*; (*peel*) scorza *f*

zig•zag ['zɪgzæg] **1** *n* zigzag *m inv* **2** *v/i* (*pret & pp* ***-ged***) zigzagare

zilch [zɪltʃ] F un bel niente

zinc [zɪŋk] zinco *m*

zip [zɪp] (cerniera *f*) lampo *f*

◆ **zip up** *v/t* (*pret & pp* ***-ped***) *dress, jacket* allacciare; COMPUT zippare, comprimere

'zip code *Am* codice *m* di avviamento postale

zo•di•ac ['zəʊdɪæk] ASTR zodiaco *m*; ***signs of the zodiac*** segni *mpl* zodiacali

zom•bie ['zɒmbɪ] F (*idiot*) cretino *m*, -a *f*; ***feel like a zombie*** *exhausted* sentirsi uno zombie

zone [zəʊn] zona *f*

zonked [zɒŋkt] *adj* P (*exhausted*) stanco morto

zoo [zuː] zoo *m inv*

zo•o•log•i•cal [zuːə'lɒdʒɪkl] *adj* zoologico

zo•ol•o•gist [zuː'ɒlədʒɪst] zoologo *m*, -a *f*

zo•ol•o•gy [zuː'ɒlədʒɪ] zoologia *f*

zoom [zuːm] *v/i* F *move fast* sfrecciare

◆ **zoom in on** *v/t* PHOT zumare su

zoom 'lens zoom *m inv*

zuc•chi•ni [zuː'kiːnɪ] *Am* zucchino *m*

APPENDIX

Italian Verb Conjugations

You can find the conjugation pattern of an Italian verb by looking up the infinitive form in the dictionary. The numbers and letters given there after the infinitive refer to the conjugation patterns listed below.

The tables (**1a, 2a, 3a, 4a**) show the full conjugations. The verb stem is given in ordinary type and the endings in *italics*. Compound tenses are given at **1a**. The three main conjugations (-are, -ere, -ire) are divided into four sets so as to illustrate the two different stress patterns of the second conjugation. Variations in form, stress pattern and vowel length are then shown for each of these four sets.

An underscore shows the stressed vowel in each conjugated form.

First Conjugation

1a mandare. The stem remains the same with regard to both spelling and pronunciation.

I. Simple Tenses

indicativo				condizionale
pr	*imperf*	*p.r.*	*fut*	
mand*o*	mand*avo*	mand*ai*	mand*erò*	mand*erei*
mand*i*	mand*avi*	mand*asti*	mand*erai*	mand*eresti*
mand*a*	mand*ava*	mand*ò*	mand*erà*	mand*erebbe*
mand*iamo*	mand*avamo*	mand*ammo*	mand*eremo*	mand*eremmo*
mand*ate*	mand*avate*	mand*aste*	mand*erete*	mand*ereste*
mand*ano*	mand*avano*	mand*arono*	mand*eranno*	mand*erebbero*

congiuntivo		imperativo
pr	imperf	
mand*i*	mand*assi*	—
mand*i*	mand*assi*	mand*a*
mand*i*	mand*asse*	mand*i*
mand*iamo*	mand*assimo*	mand*iamo*
mand*iate*	mand*aste*	mand*ate*
mand*ino*	mand*assero*	mand*ino*

Participio presente: mand*ante* *Participio passato*: mand*ato*
Gerundio presente: mand*ando*

II. Compound Tenses

1. Active voice

(Formed by placing *avere* before the verb form *participio passato*)

Infinito

passato: *aver* mandato

Gerundio

passato: *avendo* mandato

Indicativo

passato pross: *ho* mandato
trapassato prossimo: *avevo* mandato
futuro anteriore: *avrò* mandato

Condizionale

passato: *avrei* mandato

Congiuntivo

passato: *abbia* mandato
trapassato: *avessi* mandato

2. Passive voice

(Formed by placing *avere* before the verb form *participio passato*)

Infinito

presente: *essere* mandato, *-a*, *-i*, *-e*
passato: *essere stato* (*stata*, *stati*, *state*) mandato, *-a*, *-i*, *-e*

Gerundio

presente: *essendo* mandato,*-a*,*-i*,*-e*
passato: *essendo stato* (*stata*, *stati*, *state*) mandato, *-a*, *-i*, *-e*

Indicativo

presente: *sono* mandato, *-a*
imperf : *ero mandato*, *-a*
passato remoto: *fui* mandato, *-a*
passato prossimo: *sono stato* (*stata*) *mandato*, *-a*
trap. prossimo: *ero stato* (*stata*) mandato, *-a*
fut semplice: *sarò* mandato, *-a*
fut anteriore: *sarò stato* (*stata*) mandato, *-a*

Condizionale

presente: *sarei* mandato, *-a*
passato: *sarei stato* (*stata*) *mandato*, *-a*

Congiuntivo

presente: *sia* mandato, *-a*
imperf : *fossi* mandato, *-a*
passato: *sia stato* (*stata*) mandato, *-a*
trapassato: *fossi stato* (*stata*) mandato, *-a*

Imperativo

sii mandato, *-a*

This pattern applies to the compound tenses of all verbs

pr ind	*p.r.*	*fut*	*pr congiunt*	*imper*

1b celare. The stressed, closed *-e* in the stem becomes an open *e*.

celo	celai	celerò	celi	—
celiamo	celammo	celeremo	celiamo	celiamo
celano	celarono	celeranno	celino	celino
		pp: celato		

1c lodare. The stressed, closed *-o* in the stem becomes an open *o*.

lodo	lodai	loderò	lodi	—
lodiamo	lodammo	loderemo	lodiamo	lodiamo
lodano	lodarono	loderanno	lodino	lodino
		pp: lodato		

pr ind	*p.r.*	*fut*	*pr congiunt*	*imper*

1d cercare. The final consonant in the verb stem, -*c*, becomes *ch* before *i* and *e*.

cerco	cercai	cercherò	cerchi	—
cerchiamo	cercammo	cercheremo	cerchiamo	cerchiamo
cercano	cercarono	cercheranno	cerchino	cerchino
		pp: cercato		

1e pagare. The final consonant in the verb stem, -*g*, becomes *gh* bevor *i* and *e*.

pago	pagai	pagherò	paghi	—
paghiamo	pagammo	pagheremo	paghiamo	paghiamo
pagano	pagarono	pagheranno	paghino	paghino
		pp: pagato		

1f baciare. The *i* is dropped if it is followed immediately by a second *i* or an *e*.

bacio	baciai	bacerò	baci	—
baciamo	baciammo	baceremo	baciamo	baciamo
baciano	baciarono	baceranno	bacino	bacino
		pp: baciato		

1g pigliare. The *i* is dropped if it is followed immediately by a second *i*.

piglio	pigliai	piglierò	pigli	—
pigliamo	piagliammo	piglieremo	pigliamo	pigliamo
pigliano	pigliarono	piglieranno	piglino	piglino
		pp: pigliato		

1h inviare. Verb forms in which the *i* is stressed retain the *i* even if it is followed by another *i*.

invio	inviai	invierò	invii	—
inviamo	inviammo	invieremo	inviamo	inviamo
inviano	inviarono	invieranno	inviino	inviino
		pp: inviato		

1i annoiare. Verbs ending in *-iare* with an unstressed *i* and a preceding vowel, drop the *i* which would be added.

annoio	annoiai	annoierò	annoi	—
annoiamo	annoiammo	annoieremo	annoiamo	annoiamo
annoiano	annoiarono	annoieranno	annoino	annoino
		pp: annoiato		

pr ind	*p.r.*	*fut*	*pr congiunt*	*imper*

1k studiare. Verbs ending in *-iare* with an unstressed *i* and a preceding consonant, usually drop the *i* which would be added, even when the *i* in the verb stem is stressed: i.e. *tu studi*. Verbs ending in *-liare* always have *-lii*, eg *esiliare*, *esilii*.

studio	studiai	studierò	studi	—
studiamo	studiammo	studieremo	studiamo	studiamo
studiano	studiarono	studieranno	studino	studino
		pp: studiato		

1l abitare. In the verb forms in which the stem is stressed, the stress comes on the first syllable.

abito	abitai	abiterò	abiti	—
abitiamo	abitammo	abiteremo	abitiamo	abitiamo
abitano	abitarono	abiteranno	abitino	abitino
		pp: abitato		

1m collaborare. In the verb forms in which the stem is stressed, the stress comes on the second syllable.

collaboro	collaborai	collaborerò	collabori	—
collaboriamo	collaborammo	collaboreremo	collaboriamo	collaboriamo
collaborano	collaborarono	collaboreranno	collaborino	collaborino
		pp: collaborato		

1n aggomitolare. In the verb forms in which the stem is stressed, the stress comes on the third or fourth syllable.

aggomitolo	-mitolai	-mitolerò	-mitoli	—
-mitoliamo	-mitolammo	-mitoleremo	-mitoliamo	-mitoliamo
-mitolano	-mitolarono	-mitoleranno	-mitolino	-mitolino
		pp: aggomitolato		

1o giocare. The stressed *-o* in the stem can be extended to *-uo*, but this is rarer.

gi(u)oco	giocai	giocherò	gi(u)ochi	—
giochiamo	giocammo	giocheremo	giochiamo	giochiamo
gi(u)ocano	giocarono	giocheranno	gi(u)ochino	gi(u)ochino
		pp: giocato		

1p andare. Two stems: *and-* and *vad-*. In *fut* and *cond* the *e* at the start of the ending is dropped.

pr ind	*p.r.*	*fut*	*pr congiunt*	*imper*
vado	andai	andrò	vada	—
vai	andasti	andrai	vada	va, va', vai,
va	andò	andrà	vada	vada
andiamo	andammo	andremo	andiamo	andiamo
andate	andaste	andrete	andiate	andate
vanno	andarono	andranno	vadano	vadano
		pp: andato		

1q stare. Verb stem *sta*; *p.r.* (*stetti* etc); *imperf del congiunt* (*stessi* etc) as in the 2nd Conjugation; in *fut* and *cond e* becomes *a*.

pr ind	*p.r.*	*fut*	*pr congiunt*	*imper*
sto	stetti	starò	stia	—
stai	stesti	starai	stia	sta', stai
sta	stette	starà	stia	stia
stiamo	stemmo	staremo	stiamo	stiamo
state	steste	starete	stiate	state
stanno	stettero	staranno	stiano	stiano
		pp: stato		

1r dare. Verb stem *da*; *imperf del congiunt dessi* etc; in the *p.r.* alternative forms *detti*, *dette*, *dettero*.

pr ind	*p.r.*	*fut*	*pr congiunt*	*imper*
do	diedi, detti	darò	dia	—
dai	desti	darai	dia	da', dai
dà	diede, dette	darà	dia	dia
diamo	demmo	daremo	diamo	diamo
date	deste	darete	diate	date
danno	diedero, dettero	daranno	diano	diano
		pp: dato		

Second Conjugation – First Pattern

2a temere. The stem remains the same with regard to both spelling and pronunciation.

I. Simple Tenses

indicativo				condizionale
pr	*imperf*	*p.r.*		
tem*o*	tem*evo*	tem*ei*, tem*etti*	tem*erò*	tem*erei*
tem*o*	tem*evo*	tem*ei*, tem*etti*	tem*erò*	tem*erei*
tem*i*	tem*evi*	tem*esti*	tem*erai*	tem*eresti*
tem*e*	tem*eva*	tem*ette*	tem*erà*	tem*erebbe*
tem*iamo*	tem*evamo*	tem*emmo*	tem*eremo*	tem*eremmo*
tem*ete*	tem*evate*	tem*este*	tem*erete*	tem*ereste*
tem*ono*	tem*evano*	tem*ettero*, tem*erono*	tem*eranno*	tem*erebbero*

congiuntivo		imperativo
pr	imperf	
tem*a*	tem*essi*	—
tem*a*	tem*essi*	tem*i*
tem*a*	tem*esse*	tem*a*
tem*iamo*	tem*essimo*	tem*iamo*
tem*iate*	tem*este*	tem*ete*
tem*ano*	tem*essero*	tem*ano*

Participio presente: tem*ente* *Participio passato*: tem*uto*

Gerundio presente: tem*endo*

II. Compound Tenses

Auxiliary verb *essere* or *avere*, followed by *participio passato* (see 1a).

pr ind	*p.r.*	*fut*	*pr congiunt*	*imper*

2b avere. In *fut* and *cond* the final *e* in the ending is omitted.

ho	ebbi	avrò	abbia	—
hai	avesti	avrai	abbia	abbi
ha	ebbe	avrà	abbia	abbia
abbiamo	avemmo	avremo	abbiamo	abbiamo
avete	aveste	avrete	abbiate	abbiate
hanno	ebbero	avranno	abbiano	abbiano
		pp: avuto		

pr ind	*p.r.*	*fut*	*pr congiunt*	*imper*

2c cadere. In *fut* and *cond* the final *e* in the ending is omitted.

cado	caddi	cadrò	cada	—
cadiamo	caddemmo	cadremo	cadiamo	cadiamo
cadono	caddero	cadranno	cadano	cadano
		pp: caduto		

2d calere. Used almost exclusively in 3rd person singular; now obsolete.

cale	calse	—	caglia	—
		pp: caluto		

2e dolere. In *pr*, *g* is added between the verb stem and the ending *o* or *a*. In *fut* and *cond* *l* becomes *r* and the final *e* of the ending is dropped.

dolgo	dolsi	dorrò	dolga	—
duole	dolse	dorrà	dolga	dolga
dogliamo	dolemmo	dorremo	dogliamo	dogliamo
dolgono	dolsero	dorranno	dolgano	dolgano
		pp: doluto		

2f dovere. In the forms with the emphasis on the stem vowel, *o* becomes *e*. Omission of *e* in *fut* and *cond*.

devo	dovetti	dovrò	debba, deva	—
devi	dovesti	dovrai	debba, deva	devi
deve	dovette	dovrà	debba, deva	debba, deva
dobbiamo	dovemmo	dovremo	dobbiamo	dobbiamo
dovete	doveste	dovrete	dobbiate	dovete
devono	dovettero	dovranno	debbano, devano	debbano, devano
		pp: dovuto		

2g lucere. Used only in 3rd person singular and plural of *pr dell'ind* (luce, lucono), *imperf* (luceva, lucevano), *fut* (lucerà, luceranno), *pr del congiunt* (luca, lucano), and *imperf del congiunt* (lucesse, lucessero). Also *p pr* lucente, *ger* lucendo.

2h parere. In *fut* and *cond* the final *e* in the ending is omitted.

paio	parvi	parrò	paia	—
pa(r)iamo	paremmo	parremo	pa(r)iamo	—
paiono	parvero	parranno	paiano	—
		pp: parso		

2i persuadere.

persuado	persuasi	persuaderò	persuada	—
persuadiamo	persuademmo	persuaderemo	persuadiamo	persuadiamo
persuadono	persuasero	persuaderanno	persuadano	persuadano
		pp: persuaso		

pr ind	*p.r.*	*fut*	*pr congiunt*	*imper*

2k piacere.

pr ind	*p.r.*	*fut*	*pr congiunt*	*imper*
piaccio	piacqui	piacerò	piaccia	–
piacciamo	piacemmo	piaceremo	piacciamo	piacciamo
piacciono	piacquero	piaceranno	piacciano	piacciano
		pp: piaciuto		

2l potere. In *fut* and *cond* the final *e* in the ending is omitted.

pr ind	*p.r.*	*fut*	*pr congiunt*	*imper*
posso	potei	potrò	possa	–
puoi	potesti	potrai	possa	–
può	poté	potrà	possa	–
possiamo	potemmo	potremo	possiamo	–
potete	poteste	potrete	possiate	–
possono	poterono	potranno	possano	–
		pp: potuto		

2m rimanere. In *pr g* is added between stem and ending *o* or *a*; *p.r.* ending in *-si* and *pp* ending in *-sto* drop the *-n* from the stem; in *fut* and *cond n* becomes *r*.

pr ind	*p.r.*	*fut*	*pr congiunt*	*imper*
rimango	rimasi	rimarrò	rimanga	–
rimaniamo	rimanemmo	rimarremo	rimaniamo	rimaniamo
rimangono	rimasero	rimarranno	rimangano	rimangano
		pp: rimasto		

2n sapere. In *fut* and *cond* the *e* is dropped; 2nd person plural of *imperf* formed from *congiunt*.

pr ind	*p.r.*	*fut*	*pr congiunt*	*imper*
so	seppi	saprò	sappia	–
sai	sapesti	saprai	sappia	sappi
sa	seppe	saprà	sappia	sappia
sappiamo	sapemmo	sapremo	sappiamo	sappiamo
sapete	sapeste	saprete	sappiate	sappiate
sanno	seppero	sapranno	sappiano	sappiano
		p pr: sapiente *pp*: saputo		

2o sedere. The *e* in the stem becomes *ie* in forms with the emphasis on the stem vowel; in *pr* alternative forms with *segg…*

pr ind	*p.r.*	*fut*	*pr congiunt*	*imper*
siedo, seggo	sedei	sederò	sieda, segga	–
sediamo	sedemmo	sederemo	sediamo	sediamo
siedono, seggono	sederono	sederanno	siedano, seggano	siedano, seggano
		pp: seduto		

pr ind	*p.r.*	*fut*	*pr congiunt*	*imper*

2p solere. Only used in *pr*, *p.r.*, *ger* and *pp*. In *pr dell'ind* (except 2nd person singular: *suoli*) and *congiunt* it follows the pattern of *volere*.

soglio	solei	–	soglia	–
sogliamo	–	–	sogliamo	–
sogliono	–	–	sogliano	–
	ger: solendo		*pp*: solito	

2q tenere. Addition of *g* between stem and ending *o* or *a*. In *fut* and *cond n* becomes *r*.

tengo	tenni	terrò	tenga	–
tieni	tenesti	terrai	tenga	tieni
teniamo	tenemmo	terremo	teniamo	teniamo
tengono	tennero	terranno	tengano	tengano
		pp: tenuto		

2r valere. Addition of *g* between stem and ending *o* or *a*. In *fut* and *cond n* becomes *r*.

valgo	valsi	varrò	valga	–
valiamo	valemmo	varremo	valiamo	valiamo
valgono	valsero	varranno	valgano	valgano
		pp: valso		

2s vedere. In *fut* and *cond* the final *e* in the ending is omitted.

vedo	vidi	vedrò	veda	–
vediamo	vedemmo	vedremo	vediamo	vediamo
vedono	videro	vedranno	vedano	vedano
		pp: visto		

2t volere. In *fut* and *cond l* becomes *r* and the final *e* of the ending is omitted; 2nd person plural of *imper* from the *congiunt.*

voglio	volli	vorrò	voglia	–
vuoi	volesti	vorrai	voglia	vogli
vuole	volle	vorrà	voglia	voglia
vogliamo	volemmo	vorremo	vogliamo	vogliamo
volete	voleste	vorrete	vogliate	vogliate
vogliono	vollero	vorranno	vogliano	vogliano
		pp: voluto		

Second Conjugation – Second Pattern

3a vendere. The stem remains the same with regard to both spelling and pronunciation.

I. Simple Tenses

indicativo				condizionale
pr	*imperf*	*p.r.*		
vend*o*	vend*evo*	vend*etti*, vend*ei*	vend*erò*	vend*erei*
vend*i*	vend*evi*	vend*esti*	vend*erai*	vend*eresti*
vend*e*	vend*eva*	vend*ette*	vend*erà*	vend*erebbe*
vend*iamo*	vend*evamo*	vend*emmo*	vend*eremo*	vend*eremmo*
vend*ete*	vend*evate*	vend*este*	vend*erete*	vend*ereste*
vend*ono*	vend*evano*	vend*ettero*, vend*erono*	vend*eranno*	vend*erebbero*

congiuntivo		imperativo
pr	imperf	
vend*a*	vend*essi*	—
vend*a*	vend*essi*	vend*i*
vend*a*	vend*esse*	vend*a*
vend*iamo*	vend*essimo*	vend*iamo*
vend*iate*	vend*este*	vend*ete*
vend*ano*	vend*essero*	vend*ano*

Participio presente: vend*ente* *Participio passato*: vend*uto**

Gerundio presente: vend*endo*

**Participio passato* of *spandere* is *spanto*.

II. Compound Tenses

Auxiliary verb *essere* or *avere*, followed by *participio passato* (see 1a).

pr ind	*p.r.*	*fut*	*pr congiunt*	*imper*
3b chiudere.				
chiudo	chiusi	chiuderò	chiuda	—
chiudiamo	chiudemmo	chiuderemo	chiudiamo	chiudiamo
chiudono	chiusero	chiuderanno	chiudano	chiudano
		pp: chiuso		

pr ind	*p.r.*	*fut*	*pr congiunt*	*imper*
3c prendere.				
prendo	presi	prenderò	prenda	–
prendiamo	prendemmo	prenderemo	prendiamo	prendiamo
prendono	presero	prenderanno	prendano	prendano
		pp: preso		
3d fingere. The *pp* of *stringere* is *stretto.*				
fingo	finsi	fingerò	finga	–
fingiamo	fingemmo	fingeremo	fingiamo	fingiamo
fingono	finsero	fingeranno	fingano	fingano
		pp: finto		
3e addurre. Shorter form of *adducere.*				
adduco	addussi	addurrò	adduca	–
adduci	adducesti	addurrai	adduca	adduci
adduce	addusse	addurrà	adduca	adduca
adduciamo	adducemmo	addurremo	adduciamo	adduciamo
adducete	adduceste	addurrete	adduciate	adduciate
adducono	addussero	addurranno	adducano	adducano
		pp: addotto		
3f assistere. In *p.r.* alternative forms end in *-etti.*				
assisto	assistei	assisterò	assista	–
assistiamo	assistemmo	assisteremo	assistiamo	assistiamo
assistono	assisterono	assisteranno	assistano	assistano
		pp: assistito		
3g assolvere.				
assolvo	assolsi, -vetti	assolverò	assolva	–
assolviamo	assolvemmo	assolveremo	assolviamo	assolviamo
assolvono	assolsero, assolvettero	assolveranno	assolvano	assolvano
		pp: assolto		
3h assumere.				
assumo	assunsi	assumerò	assuma	–
assumiamo	assumemmo	assumeremo	assumiamo	assumiamo
assumono	assunsero	assumeranno	assumano	assumano
		pp: assunto		

3i bere. Conjugated according to the pattern of *bevere*. In *fut* and *cond* *v* becomes *r* and the *e* of the ending is dropped.

pr ind	*p.r.*	*fut*	*pr congiunt*	*imper*
bevo	bevvi, bevetti	berrò	beva	—
bevi	bevesti	berrai	beva	bevi
beve	bevve, bevette	berrà	beva	beva
beviamo	bevemmo	berremo	beviamo	beviamo
bevete	beveste	berrete	beviate	bevete
bevono	bevvero, bevettero	berranno	bevano	bevano
		pp: bevuto		

3k chiedere.

pr ind	*p.r.*	*fut*	*pr congiunt*	*imper*
chiedo	chiesi	chiederò	chieda	—
chiediamo	chiedemmo	chiederemo	chiediamo	chiediamo
chiedono	chiesero	chiederanno	chiedano	chiedano
		pp: chiesto		

3l concedere.

pr ind	*p.r.*	*fut*	*pr congiunt*	*imper*
concedo	concessi, concedetti	concederò	conceda	—
concediamo	concedemmo	concederemo	concediamo	concediamo
concedono	concessero, concedettero	concederanno	concedano	concedano
		pp: concesso		

3m connettere.

pr ind	*p.r.*	*fut*	*pr congiunt*	*imper*
connetto	connessi, connettei	connetterò	connetta	—
connettiamo	connettemmo	connetteremo	connettiamo	connettiamo
connettono	connessero, connetterono	connetteranno	connettano	connettano
		pp: connesso		

3n conoscere.

pr ind	*p.r.*	*fut*	*pr congiunt*	*imper*
conosco	conobbi	conoscerò	conosca	—
conosciamo	conoscemmo	conosceremo	conosciamo	conosciamo
conoscono	conobbero	conosceranno	conoscano	conoscano
		pp: conosciuto		

3o correre.

pr ind	*p.r.*	*fut*	*pr congiunt*	*imper*
corro	corsi	correrò	corra	—
corriamo	corremmo	correremo	corriamo	corriamo
corrono	corsero	correranno	corrano	corrano
		pp: corso		

pr ind	*p.r.*	*fut*	*pr congiunt*	*imper*

3p cuocere. In unstressed syllables *uo* becomes *o*. *Imperf cocevo* or *cocessi*.

pr ind	*p.r.*	*fut*	*pr congiunt*	*imper*
cuocio	cossi	cuocerò	cuocia	—
cociamo	cocemmo	cuoceremo	cociamo	cociamo
cuociono	cossero	cuoceranno	cuociano	cuociano
		pp: cotto		

3q decidere.

pr ind	*p.r.*	*fut*	*pr congiunt*	*imper*
decido	decisi	deciderò	decida	—
decidiamo	decidemmo	decideremo	decidiamo	decidiamo
decidono	decisero	decideranno	decidano	decidano
		pp: deciso		

3r deprimere.

pr ind	*p.r.*	*fut*	*pr congiunt*	*imper*
deprimo	depressi	deprimerò	deprima	—
deprimiamo	deprimemmo	deprimeremo	deprimiamo	deprimiamo
deprimono	depressero	deprimeranno	deprimano	deprimano
		pp: depresso		

3s devolvere.

pr ind	*p.r.*	*fut*	*pr congiunt*	*imper*
devolvo	devolvei, devolvetti	devolverò	devolva	—
devolviamo	devolvemmo	devolveremo	devolviamo	devolviamo
devolvono	devolverono, devolvettero	devolveranno	devolvano	devolvano
		pp: devoluto, devolto		

3t dire.

pr ind	*p.r.*	*fut*	*pr congiunt*	*imper*
dico	dissi	dirò	dica	—
dici	dicesti	dirai	dica	
dice	disse	dirà	dica	
diciamo	dicemmo	diremo	diciamo	diciamo
dite	diceste	direte	diciate	dite
dicono	dissero	diranno	dicano	dicano
		pp: detto		

3u dirigere.

pr ind	*p.r.*	*fut*	*pr congiunt*	*imper*
dirigo	diressi	dirigerò	diriga	—
dirigiamo	dirigemmo	dirigeremo	dirigiamo	dirigiamo
dirigono	diressero	dirigeranno	dirigano	dirigano
		pp: diretto		

pr ind	*p.r.*	*fut*	*pr congiunt*	*imper*

3v discutere.

discuto	discussi	discuterò	discuta	–
discutiamo	discutemmo	discuteremo	discutiamo	discutiamo
discutono	discussero	discuteranno	discutano	discutano
		pp: discusso		

3w esigere.

esigo	esigei, esigetti	esigerò	esiga	–
esigiamo	esigemmo	esigeremo	esigiamo	esigiamo
esigono	esigerono, esigettero	esigeranno	esigano	esigano
		pp: esatto		

3x esimere. Has no *pp*, and the *p.r. esimei* is rarely used. Instead the corresponding forms of *esentare* are used. Otherwise regular, following the pattern of *vendere* 3a.

3y espellere.

espello	espulsi	espellerò	espella	–
espelliamo	espellemmo	espelleremo	espelliamo	espelliamo
espellono	espulsero	espelleranno	espellano	espellano
		pp: espulso		

3z essere. Completely irregular. *Imperf dell'ind*: ero, eri, era, eravamo, eravate, erano; *imperf del congiunt*: fossi, fossi, fosse, fossimo, foste, fossero.

sono	fui	sarò	sia	–
sei	fosti	sarai	sia	sii
è	fu	sarà	sia	sia
siamo	fummo	saremo	siamo	siamo
siete	foste	sarete	siate	siate
sono	furono	saranno	siano	siano
		pp: stato		

3aa fare. Shorter form of *facere*. *Imperf* regular, following the pattern of *facere*: *facevo* etc

faccio	feci	farò	faccia	–
fai	facesti	farai	faccia	fa', fai
fa	fece	farà	faccia	faccia
facciamo	facemmo	faremo	facciamo	facciamo
fate	faceste	farete	facciate	fate
fanno	fecero	faranno	facciano	facciano
		pp: fatto		

pr ind	*p.r.*	*fut*	*pr congiunt*	*imper*
3bb fondere.				
fondo	fusi	fonderò	fonda	—
fondiamo	fondemmo	fonderemo	fondiamo	fondiamo
fondono	fusero	fonderanno	fondano	fondano
		pp: fuso		
3cc leggere.				
leggo	lessi	leggerò	legga	—
leggiamo	leggemmo	leggeremo	leggiamo	leggiamo
leggono	lessero	leggeranno	leggano	leggano
		pp: letto		
3dd mescere.				
mesco	mescei	mescerò	mesca	—
mesciamo	mescemmo	mesceremo	mesciamo	mesciamo
mescono	mescerono	mesceranno	mescano	mescano
		pp: mesciuto		
3ee mettere.				
metto	misi	metterò	metta	—
mettiamo	mettemmo	metteremo	mettiamo	mettiamo
mettono	misero	metteranno	mettano	mettano
		pp: messo		
3ff muovere. In unstressed syllables *uo* becomes *o*.				
muovo	mossi	muoverò	muova	—
muoviamo	movemmo	muoveremo	muoviamo	muoviamo
muovono	mossero	muoveranno	muovano	muovano
		pp: mosso		
3gg nascere.				
nasco	nacqui	nascerò	nasca	—
nasciamo	nascemmo	nasceremo	nasciamo	nasciamo
nascono	nacquero	nasceranno	nascano	nascano
		pp: nato		
3hh nascondere.				
nascondo	nascosi	nasconderò	nasca	—
nascondiamo	nascondemmo	nasconderemo	nascondiamo	nascondiamo
nascondono	nascosero	nasconderanno	nascondano	nascondano
		pp: nascosto		

3ii nuocere. In unstressed syllables *uo* becomes *o*.

pr ind	*p.r.*	*fut*	*pr congiunt*	*imper*
nuoccio	nocqui	nuocerò	nuoccia	—
nociamo	nocemmo	nuoceremo	nociamo	nuociamo
nuocciono	nocquero	nuoceranno	nuocciano	nuocciano
		pp: nociuto		

3kk piovere. Used only in the 3rd person singular and plural, in the two participial forms and in the *ger*; *pr ind* piove, piovono; *p.r.* piovve, piovvero; *fut* pioverà, pioveranno; *pr congiunt* piova, piovano; *pp* piovuto.

3ll porre. When followed by an *r* in *fut* and *cond n* becomes *r*.

pr ind	*p.r.*	*fut*	*pr congiunt*	*imper*
pongo	posi	porrò	ponga	—
poni	ponesti	porrai	ponga	poni
pone	pose	porrà	ponga	ponga
poniamo	ponemmo	porremo	poniamo	poniamo
ponete	poneste	porrete	poniate	ponete
pongono	posero	porranno	pongano	pongano
		pp: posto		

3mm prefiggere

pr ind	*p.r.*	*fut*	*pr congiunt*	*imper*
prefiggo	prefissi	prefiggerò	prefigga	—
prefiggiamo	prefiggemmo	prefiggeremo	prefiggiamo	prefiggiamo
prefiggono	prefissero	prefiggeranno	prefiggano	prefiggano
		pp: prefisso		

3nn recere. Addition of *i* between stem and endings *o*, *a*, *u*.

pr ind	*p.r.*	*fut*	*pr congiunt*	*imper*
recio	recetti	recerò	recia	—
reciamo	recemmo	receremo	reciamo	reciamo
reciono	recettero	receranno	reciano	reciano
		pp: reciuto		

3oo redigere.

pr ind	*p.r.*	*fut*	*pr congiunt*	*imper*
redigo	redassi	redigerò	rediga	—
redigiamo	redigemmo	redigeremo	redigiamo	redigiamo
redigono	redassero	redigeranno	redigano	redigano
		pp: redatto		

3pp redimere.

pr ind	*p.r.*	*fut*	*pr congiunt*	*imper*
redimo	redensi	redimerò	redima	—
redimiamo	redimemmo	redimeremo	redimiamo	redimiamo
redimono	redensero	redimeranno	redimano	redimano
		pp: redento		

pr ind | *p.r.* | *fut* | *pr congiunt* | *imper*

3qq riflettere. In *p.r.* and in *pp* in the sense of "think about" forms usually end in *-ei* and *-uto*; in the sense of "reflect back" usually *-ssi*, *-sso*.

pr ind	p.r.	fut	pr congiunt	imper
rifletto	riflettei, riflessi	rifletterò	rifletta	—
riflettiamo	riflettemmo	rifletteremo	riflettiamo	riflettiamo
riflettono	rifletterono, riflessero	rifletteranno	riflettano	riflettano
		pp: riflettuto, riflesso		

3rr rompere.

pr ind	p.r.	fut	pr congiunt	imper
rompo	ruppi	romperò	rompa	—
rompiamo	rompemmo	romperemo	rompiamo	rompiamo
rompono	ruppero	romperanno	rompano	rompano
		pp: rotto		

3ss scegliere. The stem ending *gli* becomes *lg* before endings *o* and *a*.

pr ind	p.r.	fut	pr congiunt	imper
scelgo	scelsi	sceglierò	scelga	—
scegli	scegliesti	sceglierai	scelga	scegli
sceglie	scelse	sceglierà	scelga	scelga
scegliamo	scegliemmo	sceglieremo	scegliamo	scegliamo
scegliete	sceglieste	sceglierete	scegliate	scegliete
scelgono	scelsero	sceglieranno	scelgano	scelgano
		pp: scelto		

3tt scrivere.

pr ind	p.r.	fut	pr congiunt	imper
scrivo	scrissi	scriverò	scriva	—
scriviamo	scrivemmo	scriveremo	scriviamo	scriviamo
scrivono	scrissero	scriveranno	scrivano	scrivano
		pp: scritto		

3uu spargere.

pr ind	p.r.	fut	pr congiunt	imper
spargo	sparsi	spargerò	sparga	—
spargiamo	spargemmo	spargeremo	spargiamo	spargiamo
spargono	sparsero	spargeranno	spargano	spargano
		pp: sparso		

3vv spegnere. The stem sound *gn* becomes *ng* before the endings *o* and *a*.

pr ind	p.r.	fut	pr congiunt	imper
spengo	spensi	spegnerò	spenga	—
spegni	spegnesti	spegnerai	spenga	spegni
spegne	spense	spegnerà	spenga	spenga
spegniamo	spegnemmo	spegneremo	spegniamo	spegniamo
spegnete	spegneste	spegnerete	spegniate	spegnete
spengono	spensero	spegneranno	spengano	spengano
		pp: spento		

pr ind	*p.r.*	*fut*	*pr congiunt*	*imper*

3ww svellere.

svello	svelsi	svellerò	svella	—
svelliamo	svellemmo	svelleremo	svelliamo	svelliamo
svellono	svelsero	svelleranno	svellano	svellano
		pp: svelto		

3xx trarre.

traggo	trassi	trarrò	tragga	—
trai	traesti	trarrai	tragga	trai
trae	trasse	trarrà	tragga	tragga
traiamo	traemmo	trarremo	traiamo	traiamo
traete	traeste	trarrete	traiate	traete
traggono	trassero	trarranno	traggano	traggano
		pp: tratto		

3yy vigere. Common only in the following forms: 3rd person singular and plural of *ind pr*, *imperf* and *fut*; *cond*; *congiunt imperf* and *p pr Ind pr*: vige, vigono; *imperf*: vigeva, vigevano; *fut*: vigerà, vigeranno. *Congiunt imperf*: vigesse, vigessero. *Cond*: vigerebbe, vigerebbero. *P pr*: vigente.

3zz vivere.

vivo	vissi	vivrò	viva	—
viviamo	vivemmo	vivremo	viviamo	viviamo
vivono	vissero	vivranno	vivano	vivano
		pp: vissuto		

Third Conjugation

4a partire. The stem remains the same with regard to both spelling and pronunciation.

I. Simple Tenses

indicativo				condizionale
pr	*imperf*	*p.r.*		
parto*	partivo	partii	partirò	partirei
parti	partivi	partisti	partirai	partiresti
parte	partiva	partì	partirà	partirebbe
partiamo	partivamo	partimmo	partiremo	partiremmo
partite	partivate	partiste	partirete	partireste
partono*	partivano	partirono	partiranno	partirebbero

congiuntivo		imperativo
pr	imperf	
parta*	partissi	—
parta*	partissi	parti
parta*	partisse	parta*
partiamo	partissimo	partiamo
partiate	partiste	partite
partano*	partissero	partano*

Participio presente: partente *Participio passato*: partito
Gerundio presente: partendo

* In *cucire* and *sdrucire* an *i* is added before *a* and *o*: *cucio*, *sdruciono* etc

II. Compound Tenses

Auxiliary verb *essere* or *avere*, followed by *participio passato* (see 1a).

pr ind	*p.r.*	*fut*	*pr congiunt*	*imper*

4b sentire. The stressed, closed *-e* of stem ending becomes an open *-e*.

sento	sentii	sentirò	senta	—
sentiamo	sentimmo	sentiremo	sentiamo	sentiamo
sentono	sentirono	sentiranno	sentano	sentano
		pp: sentito		

pr ind	*p.r.*	*fut*	*pr congiunt*	*imper*

4c dormire. The stressed, closed *-o* of stem ending becomes an open *-o*.

dormo	dormii	dormirò	dorma	—
dormiamo	dormimmo	dormiremo	dormiamo	dormiamo
dormono	dormirono	dormiranno	dormano	dormano
		pp: dormito		

4d finire. In the 1st, 2nd and 3rd person singular and 3rd person plural of *pr* (*ind* and *congiunt*) and *imper*, *isc* is added between stem and ending.

finisco	finii	finirò	finisca	—
finisci	finisti	finirai	finisca	finisci
finisce	finì	finirà	finisca	finisca
finiamo	finimmo	finiremo	finiamo	finiamo
finite	finiste	finirete	finiate	finite
finiscono	finirono	finiranno	finiscano	finiscano
		pp: finito		

4e apparire.

appaio, apparisco	apparvi, apparsi, apparii	apparirò	appaia apparisca	—
appariamo	apparimmo	appariremo	appariamo	appariamo
appaiono, appariscono	apparvero, apparsero, apparirono	appariranno	appaiano, appariscano	appaiano, appariscano
		pp: apparso		

4f aprire.

apro	apersi, aprii	aprirò	apra	—
apriamo	aprimmo	apriremo	apriamo	apriamo
aprono	apersero, aprirono	apriranno	aprano	aprano
		pp: aperto		

4g compire. In most forms of the *pr ind*, *pr congiunt* and *imperf*, *compire* is conjugated according to the pattern of *compiere*. An *i* is therefore added between the stem and the ending except in forms whose ending begins with an *i*.

compio	compii	compirò	compia	—
compiamo	compimmo	compiremo	compiamo	compiamo
compiono	compirono	compiranno	compiano	compiano
	pp: compito, compiuto; *p pr*: compiente; *ger*: compiendo			

pr ind	*p.r.*	*fut*	*pr congiunt*	*imper*

4h gire. Defective verb. Apart from the forms listed below, is used only in the *imperf* (*ind* and *congiunt*) and in the *cond*. This verb is now obsolete.

pr ind	*p.r.*	*fut*	*pr congiunt*	*imper*
—	—	girò	—	—
—	gisti	girai	—	—
—	gì	girà	—	—
—	gimmo	giremo	—	—
gite	giste	girete	—	gite
—	girono	giranno	—	—
		pp: gito		

4i ire. Defective verb. This verb is now obsolete. It was used only in *imperf dell'ind* (*ivo* etc) and in the following forms and persons:

pr ind	*p.r.*	*fut*	*pr congiunt*	*imper*
—	*2nd pers sg* isti	—	—	—
—	—	*1st pers pl* iremo	—	—
2nd pers pl ite	—	*2nd pers pl* irete	—	*2nd pers pl* ite
—	*3rd pers sg* irono	*3rd pers pl* iranno	—	—
		pp: ito		

4k morire.

pr ind	*p.r.*	*fut*	*pr congiunt*	*imper*
muoio	morii	mor(i)rò	muoia	—
moriamo	morimmo	mor(i)remo	moriamo	moriamo
muoiono	morirono	mor(i)ranno	muoiano	muoiano
		pp: morto		

4l olire. Defective verb. Used only in *imperf dell'ind* 3rd person singular (*oliva*) and 3rd person plural (*olivano*) and in *p pr* (*olente*). This verb is now obsolete.

4m salire. *Pr* as 4a, adding a *g* before *o* and *a*.

pr ind	*p.r.*	*fut*	*pr congiunt*	*imper*
salgo	salii	salirò	salga	—
saliamo	salimmo	saliremo	saliamo	saliamo
salgono	salirono	saliranno	salgano	salgano
		pp: salito		

4n udire. *Pr* as 4a, with *u* becoming *o* in the forms in which the stem is stressed.

pr ind	*p.r.*	*fut*	*pr congiunt*	*imper*
odo	udii	ud(i)rò	oda	—
udiamo	udimmo	ud(i)remo	udiamo	udiamo
odono	udirono	ud(i)ranno	odano	odano
		pp: udito		

pr ind	*p.r.*	*fut*	*pr congiunt*	*imper*

4o uscire.

esco	uscii	uscirò	esca	—
esci	uscisti	uscirai	esca	esci
esce	uscì	uscirà	esca	esca
usciamo	uscimmo	usciremo	usciamo	usciamo
uscite	usciste	uscirete	usciate	uscite
escono	uscirono	usciranno	escano	escano
		pp: uscito		

4p venire.

vengo	venni	verrò	venga	—
vieni	venisti	verrai	venga	vieni
viene	venne	verrà	venga	venga
veniamo	venimmo	verremo	veniamo	veniamo
venite	veniste	verrete	veniate	venite
vengono	vennero	verranno	vengano	vengano
		pp: venuto		

Numbers – Numerali

Cardinal Numbers – I numeri cardinali

0 *zero* zero
1 *one* uno
2 *two* due
3 *three* tre
4 *four* quattro
5 *five* cinque
6 *six* sei
7 *seven* sette
8 *eight* otto
9 *nine* nove
10 *ten* dieci
11 *eleven* undici
12 *twelve* dodici
13 *thirteen* tredici
14 *fourteen* quattordici
15 *fifteen* quindici
16 *sixteen* sedici
17 *seventeen* diciassette
18 *eighteen* diciotto
19 *nineteen* diciannove
20 *twenty* venti
21 *twenty-one* ventuno
22 *twenty-two* ventidue
23 *twenty-three* ventitrè
28 *twenty-eight* ventotto
29 *twenty-nine* ventinove
30 *thirty* trenta
40 *forty* quaranta
50 *fifty* cinquanta
60 *sixty* sessanta
70 *seventy* settanta
80 *eighty* ottanta
90 *ninety* novanta
100 *one/a hundred* cento
101 *one/a hundred and one* centouno
102 *one/a hundred and two* centodue
200 *two hundred* duecento
201 *two hundred and one* duecento uno
300 *three hundred* trecento
400 *four hundred* quattrocento
500 *five hundred* cinquecento
600 *six hundred* seicento
700 *seven hundred* settecento
800 *eight hundred* ottocento
900 *nine hundred* novecento
1,000 *one/a thousand* mille
1,001 *one/a thousand and one* milleuno/ mille e uno
2,000 *two thousand* duemila
3,000 *three thousand* tremila
4,000 *four thousand* quattromila
5,000 *five thousand* cinquemila

10,000 *ten thousand* diecimila
100,000 *one/a hundred thousand* centomila
1,000,000 *one/a million* un milione
2,000,000 *two million* due milioni
1,000,000,000 *one/a billion* un miliardo

Notes:

i) In Italian numbers a comma is used for decimals:
1,25 **one point two five** uno virgola venticinque

ii) A full stop is used where, in English, we would use a comma:
1.000.000 = 1,000,000

Italian can also write numbers like this using a space instead of a comma:
1 000 000 = 1,000,000

Ordinal numbers – I numeri ordinali

1st	*first*	**1°**	il primo, la prima
2nd	*second*	**2°**	secondo
3rd	*third*	**3°**	terzo
4th	*fourth*	**4°**	quarto
5th	*fifth*	**5°**	quinto
6th	*sixth*	**6°**	sesto
7th	*seventh*	**7°**	settimo
8th	*eighth*	**8°**	ottavo
9th	*ninth*	**9°**	nono
10th	*tenth*	**10°**	decimo
11th	*eleventh*	**11°**	undicesimo
12th	*twelfth*	**12°**	dodicesimo
13th	*thirteenth*	**13°**	tredicesimo
14th	*fourteenth*	**14°**	quattordicesimo
15th	*fifteenth*	**15°**	quindicesimo
16th	*sixteenth*	**16°**	sedicesimo
17th	*seventeenth*	**17°**	diciassettesimo
18th	*eighteenth*	**18°**	diciottesimo
19th	*nineteenth*	**19°**	diciannovesimo
20th	*twentieth*	**20°**	ventesimo
21st	*twenty-first*	**21°**	ventunesimo
22nd	*twenty-second*	**22°**	ventiduesimo
30th	*thirtieth*	**30°**	trentesimo
40th	*fortieth*	**40°**	quarantesimo
50th	*fiftieth*	**50°**	cinquantesimo
60th	*sixtieth*	**60°**	sessantesimo
70th	*seventieth*	**70°**	settantesimo
80th	*eightieth*	**80°**	ottantesimo
90th	*ninetieth*	**90°**	novantesimo
100th	*hundredth*	**100°**	centesimo
101st	*hundred and first*	**101°**	centunesimo
103rd	*hundred and third*	**103°**	centotreesimo
200th	*two hundredth*	**200°**	duecentesimo
1000th	*thousandth*	**1000°**	millesimo
1001st	*thousand and first*	**1001°**	millesimo primo
2000th	*two thousandth*	**2000°**	duemillesimo
1000000th	*millionth*	**1000000°**	milionesimo

Note:

Italian ordinal numbers are ordinary adjectives and consequently must agree:

her 13th granddaughter la sua tredicesima nipote

Fractions – Frazioni

1/2	*one half, a half*	un mezzo
1/3	*one third, a third*	un terzo
2/3	*two thirds*	due terzi
1/4	*one quarter, a quarter*	un quarto
3/4	*three quarters*	tre quarti
1/5	*one fifth, a fifth*	un quinto
1/10	*one tenth, a tenth*	un decimo
1 1/2	*one and a half*	uno e mezzo
2 3/4	*two and three quarters*	due e tre quarti
1/100	*one hundredth, a hundredth*	un centesimo
1/1000	*one thousandth, a thousandth*	un millesimo

Approximate numbers – Valori approssimativi

a couple	un paio
about ten	una decina
about twenty	una ventina
about eighty	un'ottantina
about a hundred	un centinaio
hundreds (of people)	centinaia (di persone)
about a thousand	un migliaio
thousands	migliaia

A
B
C
D
E
F
G
H
I
J
K
L
M
N
O
P
Q
R
S
T
U
V
W
XY
Z

Headword in **blue**

im•pact ['ɪmpækt] *n of meteorite, vehicle* urto *m*; *of new manager etc* impatto *m*; (*effect*) effetto *m*

International Phonetic Alphabet

in•sult ['ɪnsʌlt] **1** *n* insulto *m* **2** *v/t* [ɪn'sʌlt] insultare

Translation in normal characters with gender shown in *italics*

cou•ri•er ['kʊrɪə(r)] (*messenger*) corriere *m*; *with tourist party* accompagnatore *m* turistico, accompagnatrice *f* turistica

Hyphenation points

con•sum•er 'con•fi•dence fiducia *f* dei consumatori

con'sum•er goods *npl* beni *mpl* di consumo

Stress shown in headwords

'mouth•wa•ter•ing *adj* che fa venire l'acquolina

Examples and phrases in ***bold italics***

i•deal•ly [aɪ'dɪəlɪ] *adv*: ***the hotel is ideally situated*** l'albergo si trova in una posizione ideale; ***ideally, we would do it like this*** l'ideale sarebbe farlo così

Indicating words in *italics*

montaggio *m* (*pl* -ggi) TECH assembly; *di film* editing

definire ⟨4d⟩ define; (*risolvere*) settle

imbalsamare ⟨1a⟩ embalm; *animale* stuff

land•ing ['lændɪŋ] *n of aeroplane* atterraggio *m*; *top of staircase* pianerottolo *m*